The SAGE
Handbook *of*
Qualitative Methods
in Health Research

The SAGE
Handbook *of*
Qualitative Methods
in Health Research

Edited by
Ivy Bourgeault,
Robert Dingwall,
and Raymond De Vries

Los Angeles | London | New Delhi
Singapore | Washington DC

Introduction and Editorial Arrangement © Ivy Bourgeault, Robert Dingwall and Raymond De Vries

Chapter 1 © Stefan Timmermans 2010
Chapter 2 © Arthur W. Frank, Michael K. Corman,
 Jessica A. Gish and Paul Lawton 2010
Chapter 3 © Johanne Collin 2010
Chapter 4 © Carol A. Caronna 2010
Chapter 5 © Sirpa Wrede 2010
Chapter 6 © Gareth Williams and Eva Elliott 2010
Chapter 7 © Mita Giacomini 2010
Chapter 8 © Rebecca Prentice 2010
Chapter 9 © Dorothy Pawluch and
 Elena Neiterman 2010
Chapter 10 © Helen Malson 2010
Chapter 11 © Timothy Halkowski and
 Virginia Teas Gill 2010
Chapter 12 © Carol L. McWilliam 2010
Chapter 13 © Karen Staniland 2010
Chapter 14 © Claire Hooker 2010
Chapter 15 © Jenny Popay and
 Sara Mallinson 2010
Chapter 16 © Susan E. Kelly 2010
Chapter 17 © Rosaline S. Barbour 2010
Chapter 18 © Davina Allen 2010
Chapter 19 © Ruth Parry 2010

Chapter 20 © Srikant Sarangi 2010
Chapter 21 © Lindsay Prior 2010
Chapter 22 © Louise Potvin, Sherri L. Bisset
 and Leah Walz 2010
Chapter 23 © Isobel MacPherson and Linda McKie 2010
Chapter 24 © Elizabeth Ettorre 2010
Chapter 25 © Marie L. Campbell 2010
Chapter 26 © Susan E. Bell 2010
Chapter 27 © Clive Seale and Jonathan
 Charteris-Black 2010
Chapter 28 © Kath M. Melia 2010
Chapter 29 © Alicia O'Cathain 2010
Chapter 30 © Laura Stark and Adam Hedgecoe 2010
Chapter 31 © Julia Abelson 2010
Chapter 32 © Carine Vassy and Richard Keller 2010
Chapter 33 © Kerreen Reiger and
 Pranee Liamputtong 2010
Chapter 34 © Tiago Moreira and Tim Rapley 2010
Chapter 35 © Dave Holmes, Patrick O'Byrne
 and Denise Gastaldo 2010
Chapter 36 © Ilina Singh and Sinéad Keenan 2010
Chapter 37 © Ruth Pinder 2010
Chapter 38 © Phil Brown 2010

First published 2010
Reprinted 2011

SAGE Publications Ltd
1 Oliver's Yard
55 City Road
London EC1Y 1SP

SAGE Publications Inc.
2455 Teller Road
Thousand Oaks, California 91320

SAGE Publications India Pvt Ltd
B 1/I 1 Mohan Cooperative Industrial Area
Mathura Road
New Delhi 110 044

SAGE Publications Asia-Pacific Pte Ltd
33 Pekin Street #02-01
Far East Square
Singapore 048763

Library of Congress Control Number: 2009942537

British Library Cataloguing in Publication data

A catalogue record for this book is available from the British Library

ISBN 978-1-84787-292-0

Typeset by Glyph International
Printed by MPG Books Group, Bodmin, Cornwall
Printed on paper from sustainable resources

Contents

List of Tables, Figures and Boxes

Tables

Figures

Boxes

Qualitative Research Review and Synthesis

Systematic reviews have increasingly replaced the traditional literature reviews used to produce overviews of current knowledge in a particular field. Until relatively recently, however, the idea of synthesizing findings from multiple qualitative studies was not taken seriously. It is only during the last decade that the contribution which qualitative research can make to the evidence base in all areas of policy and practice, and for lay people, has been acknowledged. Researchers now agree that reviews of qualitative research can and should be more systematic than they have been in the past.

We discuss: how systematic reviews of qualitative research findings can inform the evidence base for decision making by policy makers, professionals and lay people; the general characteristics of the process of systematic review and synthesis as applied to qualitative research; four examples of approaches to systematic review appropriate for use with qualitative evidence; and how potential reviewers might select an approach.

KEY WORDS: *evidence base, qualitative research, systematic review, evidence synthesis, literature reviews, realist synthesis, meta-ethnography, narrative synthesis.*

List of Contributors

Julia Abelson, PhD, is a Professor in the Department of Clinical Epidemiology and Biostatistics, and Director of the Centre for Health Economics and Policy Analysis (CHEPA) at McMaster University. Dr. Abelson's research focuses on the role of public values in health policy making. She has led numerous projects involving the design, implementation and evaluation of public deliberation processes to inform various policy making and advisory bodies such as regional health authorities, health planning councils and provincial health technology advisory committees. She publishes regularly in journals such as *Social Science and Medicine* and *Health Policy* and has been awarded consecutive grants from the Canadian Institutes of Health Research (CIHR) since 2001. She has held an Ontario Ministry of Health and Long-Term Care Career Scientist award and a CIHR New Investigator award and was an Associate of the Commonwealth Fund's Harkness Fellowship program in Health Care Policy in 2005–06. Through her research, education and service activities, Dr. Abelson works closely with decision makers at provincial, regional and local government levels in Canada.

Davina Allen is Professor in the School of Nursing and Midwifery Studies, Cardiff University. She is a sociologist and a registered nurse, and has brought together social sciences expertise and clinical knowledge in a number of ethnographic studies of different aspects of the social organization of healthcare work. She is the author of *The Changing Shape of Nursing Practice* (Allen, 2001), *The Social Organization of Healthcare Work* (with Alison Pilnick) (Allen and Pilnick, 2006), *Nursing and the Division of Labour in Health* (with David Hughes) (Allen and Hughes, 2002) and *The Reality of Nursing Research* (with Patricia Lyne) (Allen and Lyne, 2006).

Rosaline (Rose) Barbour has a particular interest in rigour in qualitative research and has published widely on this issue. She is Professor of Health and Social Care in the School of Nursing and Midwifery at the University of Dundee in Scotland (UK). A medical sociologist, her research career has covered a wide variety of topics located at the intersection of the clinical and the social, for example, HIV/AIDS; reproductive health and fertility; psychological health; and obesity. Reflecting her conviction that qualitative research is a craft skill, Rose has developed an innovative series of 'hands-on' qualitative methods workshops. These have given rise to a number of books, including *Developing Focus Group Research: Politics, Theory and Practice* (co-edited with Jenny Kitzinger, Sage, 1999);

Introducing Qualitative Research: A Student Guide to the Craft of Doing Qualitative Research (Sage, 2008) and *Doing Focus Groups* (Sage, 2008).

Susan E. Bell is Professor of Sociology and the A. Myrick Freeman Professor of Social Sciences in the Department of Sociology and Anthropology, Bowdoin College, Brunswick, Maine, USA. Her many scholarly publications investigate the experience of illness, women's health, narrative, and visual and performative representations of the politics of cancer, medicine, and women's bodies. She is the author of *DES Daughters: Embodied Knowledge and the Transformation of Women's Health Politics* (Temple University Press, 2009). She is a member of the editorial board of *health*, and an editorial advisor for *Sociology of Health & Illness*.

Sherri L. Bisset, PhD, defended her thesis in Public Health in 2008 (health promotion option). Her thesis presents the implementation of a nutrition education program in the school setting using the sociology of translation as a theoretical framework to understand how the nutrition interventionists negotiate their own health promotion goals with education actors. She is continuing her research training as a Canadian Institute of Health Research post-doctoral fellow in the department of Psycho-education at the Université of Montréal, where she is learning about the health potential of the school and how this setting associates with health promotion goals.

Phil Brown is Professor of Sociology and Environmental Studies at Brown University, where he leads the Contested Illnesses Research Group and directs the Community Outreach Core of Brown's Superfund Research Program and the community outreach and translation core of Brown's Children's Environmental Health Center. He is the author of *No Safe Place: Toxic Waste, Leukaemia, and Community Action*, and *Toxic Exposures: Contested Illnesses and the Environmental Health Movement*, and co-editor of *Illness and the Environment: A Reader in Contested Medicine* and *Social Movements in Health*. His current research includes connections between breast cancer activism and environmental justice, biomonitoring and household exposure to chemicals and particulate matter, nanoscientists' views of social and ethical impacts, and health social movements.

Ivy Bourgeault, PhD, is a Professor in the Faculty of Health Sciences at the University of Ottawa. She holds the Canadian Institutes of Health Research Chair in Health Human Resource Policy, which is jointly funded by the federal ministry of Health Canada. She is also the Scientific Director of the Population Health Improvement Research Network (PHIRN) and the Ontario Health Human Resources Research Network (OHHRRN) funded by the Ontario Ministry of Health and Long-term Care. She held a Canada Research Chair in Comparative Health Labour Policy in her previous position at McMaster University. She has

been a consultant to various provincial Ministries of Health in Canada, to Health
Canada and to the World Health Organization.

Marie L. Campbell, PhD (Ontario Institute for Studies in Education, University
of Toronto), is a sociologist and Professor Emeritus at the University of Victoria.
Her scholarly interests include social organization of professional knowledge;
institutional ethnography; research on policy and practice in human service/
public sector organizations. Her most recent book is *Managing to Nurse: Inside
Canada's Health Care Reform*, co-authored with Janet Rankin (University of
Toronto Press, 2006).

Carol A. Caronna is an associate professor in the Department of Sociology,
Anthropology, and Criminal Justice at Towson University in Maryland, USA.
Her areas of research include the interrelationship of health care organizations
and institutional environments, particularly the impact of federal policy on
organizational identity, and the provision of reproductive health services by
religious hospitals. She has published articles in the *Journal of Health and
Social Behavior*, *Social Science & Medicine*, and *Research in the Sociology
of Organizations*, and is a co-author of *Institutional Change and Healthcare
Organizations: From Professional Dominance to Managed Care* (Chicago, 2000).

Jonathan Charteris-Black is Professor of Linguistics at the University of West
of England. He has research interests in metaphor; critical metaphor analysis; persuasive communication; cognitive linguistics; and corpus-based research. He is
author of *Politicians and Rhetoric: The Persuasive Power of Metaphor* (Palgrave-
MacMillan, 2005), *The Communication of Leadership: The Design of Leadership
Style* (Routledge, 2007) and *Gender and the Language of Illness* (Palgrave 2010).

Johanne Collin is a sociologist and historian, and professor in the Medication
and Population Health Sector at the Faculty of Pharmacy of the University of
Montreal, Canada. Her doctoral thesis (*Changement d'ordonnance*, Edition Boreal,
1995) examined the history of pharmacy in Canada and the transformation of the
profession within the rapid development of the multinational pharmaceutical
industry in the 20th century. She completed a postdoctoral fellowship at IRESCO
(Paris) and at McGill University. Her research concerns clinical practices and
professional dynamics; medication use in recent cultural history of the human body;
antidepressants and new sociality. Since its inception six years ago, she has headed
a research group on medication as social object (see www.meos.qc.ca). She is currently conducting research on the ways in which knowledge about medications is
disseminated via the mass media and the Internet. She received the Eliot Freidson
Outstanding Publication Award (as a co-author) in medical sociology in 2001.

Michael K. Corman is a Doctoral student in the Department of Sociology at the
University of Calgary, Alberta, Canada and a part-time faculty member in the

Department of Sociology and Anthropology at Mount Royal University, Alberta, Canada. His research and teaching interests include the sociology of health and illness, aging, institutional ethnography, caregiving, autism spectrum disorders, and health care work. His current research project focuses on exploring how new technologies of knowledge and governance organize health care relations in the arena of emergency medical services.

Raymond De Vries, PhD, is Professor in the Bioethics Program, the Department of Obstetrics and Gynaecology, and the Department of Medical Education at the Medical School, University of Michigan, USA. He received his MA and PhD in sociology from the University of California, Davis. Before moving to the University of Michigan he taught at Gordon College, Westmont College, and St. Olaf College. He is the author of *A Pleasing Birth: Midwifery and Maternity Care in the Netherlands* (Temple University Press, 2005) and co-editor of *The View from Here: Bioethics and the Social Sciences* (Blackwell, 2007). He is at work on a critical social history of bioethics, and is studying the regulation of science, international research ethics, the difficulties of informed consent, bioethics and the problem of suffering, and the social, ethical, and policy issues associated with non-medically indicated surgical birth.

Robert Dingwall is a freelance consultant in research, organizations and policy. He was formerly a professor and Director of the Institute for Science and Society at the University of Nottingham, UK, until being made redundant in 2010. He received a PhD in medical sociology from the University of Aberdeen in 1974 and worked at the Centre for Socio-Legal Studies at the University of Oxford, before moving to Nottingham in 1990. From 1997 until 2009, he led the development of a research and graduate centre for the study of the social, legal cultural and ethical implications of science and technology. He has written widely on issues in medical sociology, the sociology of law and the sociology of science and technology, with particular interests in work, occupations and interaction in these sites. He is currently working on studies of public health early warning systems, particularly in relation to pandemics, and on the implications of developments in research governance for the social sciences and humanities. He recently edited a four-volume collection of selected classics in medical sociology, *Qualitative Health Research* (Sage, 2008).

Eva Elliott is a UK Research Council Academic Fellow in Social and Economic Change at the Cardiff Institute of Society and Health, in the School of Social Sciences at Cardiff University. She is also the project manager of the Wales Health Impact Assessment Support Unit. She has 16 years experience of public health research and evaluation from a critical social sciences perspective. Her methodological expertise is in qualitative approaches, which have usually been deployed within a multi-method and multi-disciplinary research context. More recently she has developed an active interest in the role of regeneration, in the context of a global neo-liberal economy, in addressing the consequences of health inequality.

Elizabeth Ettorre is Professor of Sociology at the University of Liverpool. She has carried out research on women and substance use; reproduction; genetics; mental health; sexuality and the body; and auto/ethnography and autobiography. She has worked on a number of European Union funded research projects in the area of genetics, prenatal screening and bioethics of rare diseases. She has published a number of books and her most recent ones include: *Revisioning Women and Drug Use: Gender, Power and the Body* (Palgrave Macmillan, 2007); *Making Lesbians Visible in the Substance Use Field* (Haworth Press Inc, 2005); and *Reproductive Genetics, Gender and the Body* (Routledge, 2002).

Arthur W. Frank is professor of sociology at the University of Calgary, Alberta, Canada. He is the author of *At the Will of the Body: Reflections on Illness* (First Mariner Books, 1991), *The Wounded Storyteller: Body, Illness, and Ethics* (University of Chicago Press, 1995), *The Renewal of Generosity: Illness, Medicine, and How to Live* (University of Chicago Press, 2004), and *Letting Stories Breathe: A Socio-Narratology* (2010). His most recent visiting professorship was at the Dalla Lana School of Public Health, University of Toronto (2008–2009). He is on the editorial boards of numerous journals, and is a contributing editor to *Literature and Medicine*. In 2008 he was awarded the annual medal in bioethics from The Royal Society of Canada.

Mita Giacomini is a Professor in Clinical Epidemiology and Biostatistics at McMaster University, and a member of the Centre for Health Economics and Policy Analysis. She holds graduate degrees in health services and policy analysis, history of medicine and public health. Her publications have addressed topics including health policy ethics, political reasoning in health technology assessment, health resource allocation, values in evaluation and policy-making, interdisciplinarity, and the clinical uses of qualitative evidence. Current research projects focus on health policy ethics, argumentation and evidence in health technology coverage decisions, values and ethics in Canadian health policy, and life support technologies in intensive care. Mita has provided consultation and service to local, provincial, national and international health agencies in related areas, and is currently a member of the Ontario Health Technology Assessment Committee. Mita teaches in the areas of philosophy of science and health policy.

Denise Gastaldo is Associate Professor at the Bloomberg Faculty of Nursing and Associate Director of the Centre for Critical Qualitative Health Research, University of Toronto. For the last 20 years, she has been working internationally on qualitative health methodologies, with a particular focus on community-based and participatory approaches. Her work includes international research projects, interdisciplinary post-graduate education, and continued education for health care professionals and community peer researchers. One of her most significant contributions to the field has been the publication of two co-edited volumes (with F. Mercado and C. Calderon), which compiled contributions from 17 Ibero-American countries to qualitative health research.

Virginia Teas Gill is Associate Professor of Sociology in the Department of Sociology and Anthropology at Illinois State University. In her research, she uses conversation analysis to study social interaction in medical settings, especially processes of persuasion and resistance in regard to diagnosing illness, labeling, and requesting medical interventions. Professor Gill has examined physician-patient interaction in a variety of primary care settings, as well as clinician-parent interaction in a clinic for childhood developmental disabilities. She is co-editor (with Alison Pilnick and Jon Hindmarsh) of *Communication in Healthcare Settings: Policy, Participation and New Technologies* (Wiley-Blackwell).

Jessica A. Gish is a PhD candidate in sociology at the University of Calgary. She is interested in new ways of theorizing age and the aging body. Her current research studies how health care professionals treat age as an object of practice within the cosmetic enhancement industry, and how that industry's technologies bring age into being in specific ways. Her research connects the recent proliferation in repairable age technologies (i.e. anti-aging products and procedures) to what it means to age well or 'successfully' in contemporary society.

Timothy Halkowski, PhD, is a professor in the Division of Communication at the University of Wisconsin – Stevens Point. Professor Halkowski's research has focused on interactional uses of the concept of 'role' (1990), ways in which answers to questions are interactionally generated (1992), the interactional accomplishment of coherent aphasic discourse (1999), and how patients convey themselves to be reliable and reasonable reporters of their physical symptoms (2006). Currently he is researching how the quantification of tobacco and alcohol use is managed in doctor-patient discourse. Professor Halkowski also regularly serves as a grant reviewer for the National Institute of Health.

Adam Hedgecoe is Professor of the Social Sciences and Associate Director of Cesagen, the ESRC Centre for Economic and Social Aspects of Genomics, at Cardiff University. He has researched the social impact of genetic testing and has recently completed a four-country ethnographic study of research ethics committees in the EU.

Dave Holmes is Professor and Vice-Dean (Academic) at the University of Ottawa's Faculty of Health Sciences. He is also University of Ottawa Research Chair in Forensic Nursing (2009–2014). To date, Holmes has received funding, as principal investigator, from CIHR and SSHRC, to conduct his research program (risk management) in the fields of Public Health and Forensic Nursing.

Most of his work, comments, essays, analyses and research are based on the poststructuralist works of Deleuze and Guattari and Michel Foucault. His works have been published in top-tier journals in nursing, criminology, sociology and medicine. He was appointed as Honorary Visiting Professor in Australia, the United States and the United Kingdom.

Claire Hooker, PhD, is an historian of science and medicine and a qualitative research scholar in health and medicine. Having completed a PhD in the history of science, Claire has gone on to work in three different faculties on issues to do with understanding and communicating science and medicine; feminism and science and medicine; social understandings of and responses to health risks; health promotion; and public health ethics. Claire continues to like both the methodological formality of qualitative research and the literary explorations of history. The author of one monograph (*Irresistible Forces: Women in Australian Science*, MUP, 2005), two edited books, lots of book chapters and several journal articles, Claire is now Director of the Medical Humanities program at Sydney University.

Richard Keller is Associate Professor of Medical History and Bioethics, the History of Science, and Population Health Sciences at the University of Wisconsin-Madison, and is a research affiliate at the the Institut de Recherche sur les Enjeux Sociaux (CNRS-INSERM-EHESS, Université de Paris-Nord). He is the author of *Colonial Madness: Psychiatry in French North Africa* (Chicago: University of Chicago Press, 2007). He is currently engaged in a historical and ethnographic study of the deadly heat wave of 2003 in Paris. His articles have appeared in the *Journal of Social History*, *Bulletin of the History of Medicine*, *Historical Geography* and *Mouvements*.

Susan E. Kelly is a Senior Research Fellow at Egenis, University of Exeter, UK. She received her PhD from the University of California, San Francisco, where she trained in medical sociology and qualitative research methods. She began conducting research on genetics, medical technologies and families while a post-doctoral research fellow at the Stanford Center for Biomedical Ethics, and continued research and teaching in sociology and public health at the University of Louisville and University of Southampton. She currently researches social responses to and implications of genetic technologies in health care settings. She has published qualitative research findings in journals including *The American Journal of Public Health*, *Sociology of Health & Illness*, *Contemporary Ethnography* and *Social Science & Medicine*, as well as numerous book chapters, and is currently writing a book entitled *Parenting in the Genetic Age*.

Sinead Keenan is a Research Assistant in the BIOS Centre at the London School of Economics. She holds a Masters Degree in Social Psychology from the LSE.

Paul Lawton is a PhD candidate in sociology at the University of Calgary, Canada and an instructor at the University of Lethbridge. His current projects and research interests are related to digital culture and healthcare and include the use of ICT by patients and health-care professionals, as well as an overall interest in Actor-Network Theory.

Pranee Liamputtong is a medical anthropologist and holds a Personal Chair in Public Health at the School of Public Health, La Trobe University, Australia. Her main interests are related to women's reproductive and sexual health. She has undertaken many research projects with immigrant women in Australia and women in Asia. Pranee has published a large number of papers and books in these areas. Her most recent book is *The Journey of Becoming a Mother Amongst Thai Women in Northern Thailand* (Lexington Books, 2007). Pranee teaches qualitative methods and has published several method books, including *Researching the Vulnerable: A Guide to Sensitive Research Methods* (Sage, 2007); *Doing Cross-Cultural Research: Ethical and Methodological Issues* (Springer Science, 2008); *Qualitative Research Methods* (Oxford University Press, 2009); and *Performing Qualitative Cross-cultural Research* (Cambridge University Press, 2010).

Isobel MacPherson runs her own business Community Health Research and Evaluation and was previously a Senior Research Fellow, Glasgow Caledonian University. Her interests lie in health and social services innovation. Over 20 years of research Isobel has worked on numerous projects funded by research councils and governments. Isobel has taught the design and use of qualitative research methods and data analysis to medical and nursing undergraduate and postgraduate students as well as health and social service professionals.

Sara Mallinson is a senior lecturer in social science in the Division of Health Research, Lancaster University. She is an applied health researcher with experience of working in different disciplinary contexts including geography, public health, health services research, and sociology. Her areas of research interest include lay accounts of health and illness; popular memory, local history, and public health policy implementation; diverse evidence synthesis; and knowledge mobilization. She teaches qualitative research methods and qualitative evidence synthesis courses for post-graduate and professional development programmes, and is Associate Director of the NIHR Research Design Service for the North West.

Helen Malson is a Reader in Social Psychology in the Centre for Appearance Research at the University of the West of England, Bristol. Her research focuses on feminist post-structuralist analyses of girls' and women's 'eating disordered' subjectivities and practices and, more recently, she has been exploring service users' and service providers' accounts about treatment for 'eating disorders'.

Her publications include *The Thin Woman: Feminism, Post-Structuralism And The Social Psychology Of Anorexia Nervosa* (Routledge, 1998) and an edited collection (with Maree Burns), *Critical Feminist Approaches to Eating Dis/ Orders* (Psychology Press, 2009).

Linda McKie is Professor of Sociology at Glasgow Caledonian University, Associate Director of the Centre for Research on Families and Relationships, and Visiting Senior Fellow at Hanken School of Economics, Helsinki. Prior to taking up her post in Glasgow she was Senior Lecturer in the Sociology of Health and Illness, Department of General Practice and Primary Care, University of Aberdeen. Her current research interests are in organizations, work and care. The most recent co-authored book is Interdependency and Care over the Lifecourse (Routledge 2010). She is also a trustee for Evaluation Support Scotland and the Institute of Rural Health.

Carol L. McWilliam, MScN, EdD, is Professor, Faculty of Health Sciences, University of Western Ontario, London, Canada. Carol has focused her research on health promotion, especially aiming to refine health care practice and policy to achieve greater independence and health as a resource for every day living amongst older people. Her phenomenological studies have uncovered the disempowering relational approaches of health and social service professionals, informed a clinical practice model of empowering partnering, and evolved social interaction knowledge translation theory and practice. The insights and understandings arising from this work have been applied to refine health services delivery, particularly in the home care sector.

Kath M. Melia graduated from the Department of Social and Preventive Medicine, University of Manchester, in 1973 and moved to Edinburgh to work in intensive care. She joined the Nursing Research Unit (University of Edinburgh) as a Research Associate working on a study of ward organization and during that time completed a doctorate on the occupational socialisation of nurses. Kath was appointed to the Chair of Nursing Studies in 1996 after 20 years at the University of Edinburgh as a researcher, lecturer and senior lecturer. She served as Head of the Department of Nursing Studies (1992–1998) and as Head of a Planning Unit in the Faculty Group of Law and Social Science (1992–2001). She was the first Head of the new School of Health in Social Science (2003–2007). Kath is a member of the University Research Ethics Committee and Convener of the University Student Survey Ethics Committee. Outside of the University she contributes to Scottish Government Health Department NHS policy development through consultations and working conferences.

Tiago Moreira is a Senior Lecturer in Sociology at Durham University, UK. His research is concerned with the production and political mediation of health care standards, the changing role of science and technology in the ageing domain and the involvement of patient organizations in research. Recent publications include papers on changes in the knowledge practices, techno-economic configurations and political evaluations of the issue of cognitive aging in contemporary societies (*Journal of Aging Studies*, 22(4); *Social Studies of Science*, 39(4)).

Elena Neiterman is a PhD candidate in the Department of Sociology at McMaster University, Hamilton Ontario, Canada. Her dissertation deals with the social construction of pregnancy. Her broader research interests fall in the areas of sociology of health and health care; sociology of gender; women's studies; pregnancy and motherhood.

Patrick O'Byrne is Assistant Professor in the School of Nursing, Faculty of Health Sciences, at the University of Ottawa, Canada. His field of research and clinical practice is public health, particularly in relation to sexually transmitted infections and HIV. As part of this, Patrick has been involved in various Canadian Institute of Health Research and federally funded projects involving marginalised populations, such as men who have sex with men (gay, bisexual, queer men), teens, and the homeless.

Alicia O'Cathain is professor of Health Services Research at the School of Health and Related Research, University of Sheffield, UK. She has worked in health services research for over 20 years with interests in measuring patients' views of services, evaluating new services, and combining qualitative and quantitative methods in research studies. She has completed a fellowship funded by the Medical Research Council to study mixed methods research. She is an associate editor of the *Journal of Mixed Methods Research*.

Ruth Parry is a Senior Research Fellow in the School of Nursing, Midwifery and Physiotherapy at the University of Nottingham, UK. Ruth practised as a physiotherapist for several years before moving into academic healthcare research. Her PhD and postdoctoral studies entailed sociological studies of physiotherapy communication. Her abiding interest is in building knowledge useful to healthcare practitioners in reflecting on and developing practice with regards interacting with service-users. Current work includes video-based conversation analytic work on how reasons for treatment are communicated, and on how practitioners and healthcare recipients interact about and with the body. Past work has included analysis of goal-setting during rehabilitation treatment sessions, and examination of the communication challenges and skills entailed in dealing with patients' physical limitations. In addition, she has conducted research on the effectiveness and practice of communication training for healthcare professionals and trainees. She also teaches qualitative research methods.

Dorothy Pawluch is an Associate Professor and Chair of the Department of Sociology at McMaster University, Hamilton, Canada. She has written and taught on social constructionist theory, deviance and social problems, professions and health. Her book, *The New Paediatrics: A Profession in Transition* uses a constructionist approach to analyze how paediatricians redefined their professional role to take in the behavioural problems of children, thus contributing to the medicalisation of childhood deviance. She has also co-edited *Doing Ethnography: Studying Everyday Life*.

Ruth Pinder now semi-retired, she holds a Senior Research Fellowship at City University, UK, and still teaches ethnography at the Open University. She has also developed special study modules on human rights and mental health for medical students at University College London. She has researched and written extensively on chronic illness and disability, ageing and medical education, including a major collaborative study on Balint groups in medicine, published by the Royal College of General Practitioners. Her most recent work is on health and the environment in community forestry, and the wider role of ethnography within policy research.

Jennie Popay is a Professor of Sociology and Public Health, Institute for Health Research, University of Lancaster, UK. She has worked as a sociologist in social policy and public health in academia, the voluntary sector, and the NHS. Her research interests include the social determinants of health and health equity; the sociology of knowledge with a particular focus on lay expertise/knowledge; the evaluation of complex social interventions; community engagement/empowerment; and methods for the synthesis of diverse evidence and knowledge exchange. Most recently, she has been working with the WHO Commission on the Social Determinants of Health, co-ordinating a global knowledge network reviewing evidence on action to promote health equity by addressing social exclusion, and is currently working with the Marmot review of health inequalities policy in England. She was the founding convenor of the Cochrane Qualitative Research Methods Group and the Campbell Process Implementation Methods Group, and has completed several mixed methods evidence reviews focusing on community engagement in health development, the uptake and maintenance of domestic smoke alarms, and people's experience of diagnosis and treatment for TB. She is a member of the UK Medical Research Council's Research Methodology Panel, the NICE Research Advisory Group, and a Governor of the BUPA Medical Research Foundation; she has served on the boards of voluntary organizations and held several public appointments, including to the UK Commission for Health Improvement and the English Commission for Patient and Public Involvement in Health.

Louise Potvin, PhD, is currently Professor, Department of Social and Preventive Medicine, Université de Montreal and Scientific Director of the Centre Léa-Roback sur les inégalités sociales de Santé de Montréal. She holds the CHSRF/CIHR Chair on Community Approaches and Health Inequalities. Her main research interests are the evaluation of community health promotion programs and how local environments contribute to population health. She is a Fellow of the Canadian Academy of Health Sciences.

Rebecca Prentice is a Lecturer in Social Anthropology at the University of Sussex and a Research Fellow at the Brighton and Sussex Medical School. Her research focuses on the everyday politics of work, craft, skill, and injury in two ethnographic contexts: the garment industry in Trinidad and medical schools in the UK. Her work has been published in *Anthropology of Work Review* and *Research in Economic Anthropology*.

Lindsay Prior is a Professor of Sociology at Queens University, Belfast, and a Principal Investigator in the Northern Ireland Centre of Excellence for Public Health. In the past, he has acted as Principal Investigator for major UK awards from the Wellcome Trust (Biomedical Ethics Programme), the ESRC (Innovative Health Technologies Programme), the Joseph Rowntree Foundation, and various National Heath Service R&D Offices. The research work associated with these grants has covered a wide range of health-related topics and interests, including a focus on the application of qualitative research methods to health service research. He is currently editing a four volume work on the use of documents in social research.

Tim Rapley is a Staff Scientist at the Institute of Health and Society, Newcastle University, UK. His research focuses on the coordination of work, knowledge, interaction and technology in the context of health and social care and the theory and practice of qualitative research.

Kerreen Reiger teaches sociology in the School of Social Sciences at La Trobe University, Australia and is also a Visiting Professor in the Nursing and Midwifery Research Unit at Queen's University Belfast, UK. Her books *The Disenchantment of the Home: Modernizing the Australian Family, 1880–1940* (Oxford University Press, Melbourne, 1985) and *Our Bodies Our Babies: the Forgotten Women's Movement* (Melbourne University Press, 2001) examine historical struggles over Australian maternity care and the medicalisation of childbirth. Her recent work focuses on midwifery professionalisation and inter-professional relationships between midwives and doctors. As a founder of the advocacy organization the Maternity Coalition, Kerreen is also working on issues of public participation in maternity policy.

Srikant Sarangi is Professor of Language and Communication and Director of the Health Communication Research Centre at Cardiff University. He is also Professor in Language and Communication at Norwegian University of Science and Technology (NTNU), Trondheim (Norway) and Honorary Professor, Faculty of Humanities, Aalborg University (Denmark). His research interests are in applied linguistics and institutional/professional discourse studies (e.g., healthcare, social work, bureaucracy, education). He has held several project grants (Funding bodies include The Wellcome Trust, The Leverhulme Trust, ESRC) to study various aspects of health communication, e.g., genetic counselling, Quality of Life in HIV/AIDS and Telemedicine. The other areas of healthcare research include communication in primary care, palliative care, with particular reference to assessment of consulting and communication skills. He is author and editor of ten books, guest-editor of five journal special issues and has published over one hundred fifty journal articles and book chapters. He is the editor of Text & Talk as well as the founding editor of Communication & Medicine and with (C. N. Candlin) of *Journal of Applied Linguistics and Professional Practice* and three book series[es].

Clive Seale is Professor of Medical Sociology at Queen Mary University of London. He has research interests in communication in medical settings, mass media and health, internet and health, end-of-life-care and social research methods. He is author of *The Quality of Qualitative Research* (Sage, 1999) and has written and edited *Researching Society and Culture* (Sage, 2004) and *Social Research Methods: A Reader* (Routledge, 2004).

Ilina Singh is Reader in Bioethics and Society at the London School of Economics and Political Science. Her research explores the interface of neuroscience and society, with particular attention to implications of neuroscientific developments, practices and technologies for children and families. She is currently writing a book on children's experiences with ADHD and stimulant medications tentatively titled: *Distracted:Childhood, ethics, stimulants and ADHD*. Other research interests include the use of biomarkers in psychiatry; fMRI research into anorexia nervosa; and global mental health and neuroethics.

Karen Staniland is Senior Lecturer in the School of Nursing, Faculty of Health and Social Care, University of Salford, UK. Her PhD is in sociology and she is a registered nurse. Karen is involved with the promotion of work-based and e-learning in nursing and with health media technology. Her research interests lie in sociological ethnographic studies of healthcare work which seek to improve the quality of care at the bedside. She is the co-editor of two books *Clinical Skills: the Essence of Caring* (Iggulden; Macdonald and Staniland, 2009) and *The Nurse Mentor and Reviewer update Book* (Murray; Rosen and Staniland, 2010).

Laura Stark is Assistant Professor at Wesleyan University in the Department of Sociology and Program of Science in Society. She works on morality, medicine, and the modern state. She is currently completing a book, *Behind Closed Doors*, that re-examines the history and present-day practices of Institutional Review Boards in the United States.

Stefan Timmermans, PhD, is professor of sociology at UCLA. He is the author of *Sudden Death and the Myth of CPR* (Temple University Press, 1999) and *Postmortem: How Medical Examiners Explain Suspicious Deaths* (University of Chicago Press, 2006).

Carine Vassy is a senior lecturer in Sociology at the Université de Paris-Nord, France, and a researcher at the Institut de Recherche Interdisciplinaire sur les Enjeux Sociaux (CNRS-INSERM-EHESS, Université de Paris-Nord). She is also a research associate at the Institute for Science and Society, University of Nottingham, UK. Her research interests are sociology of health; health policies; sociology of organizations; and methodology of cross-national comparisons. Her current research focuses on genetic and reproductive technologies, with a study of antenatal screening programmes in England and France. She has published in *Sociology of Health and Illness*, *Social Science and Medicine* and *Revue Française de Sociologie*.

Leah Walz, PhD, is a medical anthropologist by training and is currently a CIHR/CHSRF post-doctoral fellow within the department of social and preventive medicine at the Université de Montréal, Canada. Her research interests include discourses of motherhood, the determinants of infant health, the history of public health, the social construction of health problems, and the development, implementation, and evaluation of health programs. Her current project involves ethnographic fieldwork within a infant health promotion program for vulnerable families in Montreal and focuses on the discourses and practices of front-line health and social service workers.

Gareth Williams has been a Professor of Sociology in the School of Social Sciences at Cardiff University since 1999. He is Co-Director of the Regeneration Institute (a joint initiative with the School of City and Regional Planning), Associate Director of the Cardiff Institute of Society Health and Ethics, and Director of the Wales Health Impact Assessment Support Unit. He has published widely in academic and professional journals and has written and edited a number of books, including *Community Health and Wellbeing: Action Research on Health Inequalities* (Policy Press, 2007).

Sirpa Wrede is a sociologist and Research Coordinator at the Centre for Research on Ethnic Relations and Nationalism, CEREN, in the Swedish School of Social Science at the University of Helsinki. She specialises in comparative as well as nationally-based research in the fields of maternity care and midwifery as well as health care occupations and professions. She is co-editor of *Birth by Design* (Routledge, 2001) and lead editor of *Care Work in Crisis: Reclaiming the Nordic Ethos of Care* (Studentlitteratur, 2008). Her current research focuses on the ethnic diversification of health and social care occupations.

Introduction

Ivy Lynn Bourgeault, Robert Dingwall
and Raymond De Vries

The contribution that qualitative evidence can make in informing decision makers about the use of interventions is becoming increasingly recognized. Qualitative research involves the collection, analysis and interpretation of data that are not easily reduced to numbers. ... It plays a crucial role in shaping the decisions of bodies, like NICE [National Institute for Clinical Excellence], when advising on the use of interventions for whole health care systems such as the NHS [National Health Service] (Sir Michael Rawlins, Harveian Oration to the Royal College of Physicians, 2008, p. 32).

We are social scientists who work among clinical researchers, clinicians, and bench scientists in health care settings. We find it exhilarating to lend the insights of social and behavioural science to those who provide care to the injured and ill, and to those who find themselves struggling to regain their health. Our work can be both fascinating and challenging. Not only do we face the difficulty that besets all social science – the sheer difficulty of studying humans in all their variety – we must also overcome attitudes of some medical researchers towards social science. We have lost count of the times we have been told, 'Oh, you are not a real doctor, you are *just* a PhD'. A common response to this challenge to the credibility of social-science-based research in health and health care is to mimic the research methods of clinical or bench science by devising 'objective measures' and developing sophisticated mathematical models to predict behaviour. These methods, based on data typically collected at a distance from the settings where caregiving is done – social surveys, experiments, demographic or epidemiological studies – have improved our understanding of individuals, groups, organizations, and societies, but they have been less successful in explaining how we organize our social relationships, communicate with each other, and make sense of the situations in which we find ourselves. As Deutscher (1973) noted more than thirty years ago, what we say is not always what we do. Surveys give us a fine account of what we *say*, but as health researchers have become more interested in what we *do*, and *why*, they have turned to qualitative methods.

Over the past two decades, health professionals, managers, and policy makers have come to acknowledge that progress in health care requires a rich understanding of 'what we do'. As a result, qualitative methods are now recognized as essential tools for improving the management, planning, and provision of health care and health services. Monographs and articles using qualitative methods have begun to appear in great numbers, not just in those places traditionally known for publishing such research, but also in mainstream medical journals and university presses that once rejected work of this kind as unscientific and anecdotal (Borreani et al., 2004; Kuper et al., 2008; Pope and Mays, 2006). Indeed, qualitative health research has led to, and supported, important innovations, including patient-centred care and evidence-based decision making (Grypdonck, 2006; Sandelowski, 2004).

This wave of interest has generated research of varying quality. Social scientists know all too well that it is not unusual for people with little or no training to assume that social research is easy to do. At one level, this is true: qualitative research rests on ordinary human skills like watching events happen, asking questions about them, and reading relevant documents. We normally use these skills in fairly loose and untutored ways. Survey designers are familiar with the results in the form of poorly designed questionnaires with items that are confusing, time-consuming, and will never produce analyzable data. Qualitative research is no different. Having read a well-written monograph or article, a health professional may say, 'This looks easy enough, I'll do my own little study!' On the basis of three unstructured interviews and 12 hours of observation, our novice 'ethnographer' writes a report that is predictably sloppy, unsystematic, and incapable of transferring insights to other settings. Such studies – and some do see the light of publication – diminish respect for the rigour and value of good qualitative research. This Handbook is our response to this situation. Qualitative research is an essential tool for anyone charged with delivering and improving health care, but its value can only be realized if it is done well.

Many disciplines have contributed to the phenomenal growth of qualitative health research. Reflecting this, our Handbook includes contributions from researchers in several fields including sociology, anthropology, psychology, linguistics/communication studies, health policy, health services research, history, and bioethics. Some contributors have a professional background in health care and have gained recognition for their contribution to the social sciences. Others are social scientists who are acknowledged to be particularly effective translators of their basic disciplines for policy, planning, or practice in health care.

The essays of these researchers, collected here, form an authoritative resource for those who are called upon to commission, conduct, or use qualitative health research. In this book, we bring together, in one place, examples of the applications of qualitative research in specific health care settings, clearly written introductions to the fundamentals of the method, and careful descriptions of innovations in its theory and practice. It will be a valuable addition to the libraries of students and practitioners in the health professions and health sciences who wish to use qualitative approaches, qualitative social scientists interested in applying their disciplines to the field of health care, and those trained in quantitative methods – including applied social scientists, epidemiologists, health providers, health educators, and programme managers – who wish better to understand what qualitative research might offer them. Users of this book will become better users and consumers of research because they will understand not only *how* to do qualitative research, but also *when* and *why* to do it.

This Handbook does not assume that its readers are complete novices in qualitative social research. It is intended to complement more generic introductions like David Silverman's *Doing Qualitative Research* or Uwe Flick's *An Introduction to Qualitative Research,* or a more specialist text like Green and Thorogood's *Qualitative Methods for Health Research.* Readers, whether students or experienced professionals, will be prompted to reflect on how the qualitative approaches in various social sciences can be used to probe more deeply into a variety of questions in the field of health and health care. In this respect, it supplements existing texts by placing discipline-specific introductions in a wider context that will help readers recognize the heterogeneity of qualitative research and make choices about method that suit the problems they are investigating. These choices range from the well-established methods of interviewing and field research to recent innovations in the form of autoethnography and visual studies. Importantly, readers are also offered insight into the historical development and theoretical underpinnings of qualitative research. This is important for two reasons. First, it will remind readers that, simply because a method is new in its application to health research, it does not mean that it is a new method lacking a solid foundation of experience in use, technical development, and intellectual refinement. Second, knowledge of how theory operates allows the findings of specific local studies to be linked to wider frameworks that often stretch well beyond health care, making specific findings transferable as resources for planners, managers, or practitioners who may be quite remote in time and/or space from the original study.

THE DRIVE FOR QUALITATIVE HEALTH RESEARCH

As they have come to recognize the complex nature of contemporary health, illness, and health care, many practitioners, managers, and policy makers have turned to qualitative health research for help in informing and guiding their work. They have seen that important practical questions about health behaviour, organizations, policy, and practice cannot appropriately be addressed with the quantitative techniques that they have relied on in the past. As Pope and Mays (1995) note in the opening paper of a series dedicated to qualitative health research in the *British Medical Journal*:

> Medical advances, increasing specialization, rising patient expectations, and the sheer size and diversity of health service provision mean that today's health professionals work in an increasingly complex arena. The wide range of research questions generated by this complexity has encouraged the search for new ways of conducting research. ... Although the more qualitative approaches found in certain of the social sciences may seem alien alongside the experimental, quantitative methods used in clinical and biomedical research, they should be an essential component of health services research (p. 42).

In the decade and a half since this was written, health care has become even more complex, reinforcing the case for the use of a broad range of methods that includes qualitative.

A much cited phrase from the Pope and Mays (1995) article is its title claims that qualitative health research is important for '*Reaching the parts other methods cannot reach*' – that is, questions not amenable to measurement (see also Pope and Mays, 2006). This has often been elaborated to characterize the aims of qualitative research as seeking answers to questions about the '*what*', '*how*', or '*why*' of a phenomenon, rather than questions about '*how many*', '*how much*', or '*how often*' (Green and Thorogood, 2004). Put another way, qualitative health research offers 'an emphasis on the qualities of entities and on processes and meaning that are not experimentally examined or measured in terms of quantity, amount, intensity and frequency' (Denzin and Lincoln, 2000, p. 8). Qualitative health research focuses on how social processes and practices in health care are *created* and what *meaning* they have for people within specific contexts (Lempp and Kingsley, 2007). It also identifies the perceptions, experiences, and behaviour of both users and providers of care that are helpful in addressing issues related to implementing system change to improve quality (Tripp-Reimer and Doebbelin, 2004). One of sociology's classic findings is that people act on the basis of their definitions of situations – what the situation means to them – rather than on the basis of the 'objective reality' of the situation (see Thomas, 1923; Thomas and Thomas, 1928: 572). Given this, 'rational' reforms – that is, reforms based on objective measures – cannot help but be limited in their ability to influence the behaviour of the providers and users of health care.

Qualitative health research helps close the gap between objective and subjective reality by examining: behaviours, attitudes, and perceptions influencing health outcomes; patient experiences of health and illness, and the social institutions that frame these; the experiences of both professional and non-professional health care workers, from initial socialization to the provision of care in organizational environments; the development, execution, and evaluation of interventions, programmes, and clinical trials; and the wider understanding of the policy, social, and legal contexts of care (Grypdonck, 2006; Hutchinson, 2001; Morse, 2007; Murphy et al., 1998; Pope et al., 2002; Ulin et al., 2004). Qualitative health research has particular value in providing descriptions of mundane or taken-for-granted aspects of familiar settings, aspects that have a significant influence on patients and providers but that often remain unnoticed (Murphy et al., 1998). As Murphy and Dingwall (2003) observe, qualitative health research may not necessarily provide definitive answers to policy or management questions so much as it helps formulate new questions and specify the implications of possible answers. It can inform managerial or professional judgement and effective improvisation in specific response to novel or unexpected problems, rather than generating algorithms that provide 'average' responses to well-known challenges. Qualitative research supports creative managerial and professional practice.

It should be clear that qualitative health research is not an unfortunate necessity, that is, a method to be called upon only when quantitative approaches are impractical. Qualitative and quantitative methods are complementary and mutually reinforcing (Munhall and Boyd, 1993). Many have noted how qualitative methods are useful at the outset of research to help clarify research questions, generate grounded hypotheses (Murphy et al., 1998), develop sensitive quantitative instruments (Imle and Atwood, 1988) helpful in interpreting, qualifying, or illuminating the findings of quantitative research, and in 'validating' quantitative research or providing a different perspective on the same phenomena (Pope and Mays, 2006). Qualitative health research is also inherently flexible in design, facilitating discovery and further investigation of unexpected findings (Ulin et al., 2004). Qualitative research can also be important in the effective dissemination or translation of quantitative evidence because of the way in which it helps make findings relevant to patients and care providers by linking it to their experiences and social and organizational environments (Pope et al., 2002).

Some methodologists adopt a more polarized position, pointing out that qualitative and quantitative research are derived from fundamentally different paradigms. According to their argument, qualitative health research is based on philosophical assumptions of idealism and constructionism, which are incommensurable with the realism and positivism of quantitative approaches. Many, however, find this argument misleading, noting that the dichotomizing of qualitative and quantitative health research misrepresents the variability within each category (cf. Murphy et al., 1998). This position, by extension, implies that the choice of method is best made on the basis of the purposes and circumstances of research (Hammersley, 1992; Silverman, 1993). A brief examination of the history of qualitative research methods illuminates this point.

A BRIEF HISTORY OF QUALITATIVE RESEARCH[1]

Although qualitative methods may seem novel to many working in the health field, they are long-established in the social sciences. As a result, they should not

---

[1] This is summarized from a more detailed and highly recommended chapter in Murphy et al., 1998.

necessarily be treated as controversial merely because they are different from the dominant approaches in early twenty-first-century health research. Qualitative research has roots that predate modern scientific thought, though most link it with the renaissance development of the philosophical scepticism that formed the basis of modern social sciences. Critical thinkers like Hume, Kant, and Leibniz examined the relationship between experience, reason, and method. They argued that although experience provides the *content* of our knowledge, reason was necessary to provide the *form* or *structure* – giving theory and data equal status. Towards the end of the nineteenth century, this perspective explicitly informed the methodological practices within the developing social sciences. One of the founders of sociology, Max Weber, for example, argued that 'if the goal of scientific inquiry is to produce a disinterested statement about the condition of a world which, if not exactly observer-independent, has a substantial degree of autonomy and conditioning of the possibilities of observation, then any appropriately *disciplined* procedure can be used' (cited in Murphy et al., 1998, p. 30; emphasis added). Weber argued further that experience and intuition can only be part of a scientific enterprise if they are transformed into concepts and subjected to appropriate verification procedures so as to discover regularities or general principles.

The major impetus for the development and use of qualitative methods in the twentieth century came primarily from two sources: British social anthropology and the American 'Chicago School' of sociology. Within the field of social anthropology, Malinowski had a particularly strong influence on the modern method of participant observation in the distinction that he made in the three principles of research: scientific values, living among the people being studied, and applying special techniques for collecting, ordering, and presenting evidence. Although some inflate the importance of the University of Chicago in the development of qualitative methods by claiming (incorrectly) that participant observation was invented there, the Chicago School did make important theoretical and methodological contributions to the field of qualitative research, with a number of particularly influential studies in the health field being produced by its graduates after the Second World War. These include *Boys in White* by Becker et al. (1961); Erving Goffman's *Asylums* (1961); Julius Roth's *Timetables* (1963); and Fred Davis's *Passage Through Crisis* (1963). In the United Kingdom, the tradition of qualitative health research was disseminated particularly through researchers associated with the Medical Research Council's Medical Sociology Unit at the University of Aberdeen, including Sally Macintyre's *Single and Pregnant* (1976), P.M. Strong's *The Ceremonial Order of the Clinic* (1979), Jim McIntosh's *Communication and Awareness in a Cancer Ward* (1979), Robert Dingwall et al.'s *The Protection of Children* (1983), and Michael Bloor et al.'s *One Foot in Eden* (1988).

As a result of its varied lineage, qualitative research cannot be considered a unified category. A range of different theoretical and epistemological starting points have resulted in a wide variety of topics and approaches. These are highlighted in this Handbook. Moreover, as Kuper et al. (2008) recently commented, 'Different qualitative methodologies are useful for asking different sorts of questions. Thus, just as randomized controlled trials, meta-analyses, and case-control studies are designed for answering different types of research questions, different kinds of qualitative research are useful in studying a variety of problems' (p. 404). In keeping with this diversity, different qualitative methods also need to be evaluated in different ways.

PERSISTENT MISUNDERSTANDINGS

Many misunderstandings of qualitative methods exist (and persist) within the health research community. Despite the proliferation of qualitative studies, health care professionals, managers, and policy decision makers remain uncertain about their credibility. These often reveal a lack of familiarity with social scientific approaches and a reluctance to accept their usefulness (Kuper et al., 2008; Pope and Mays, 2006). A recent empirical study of biomedical researchers in Canada is illuminating in this regard (Albert et al., 2008). Although some were receptive to qualitative and other social scientific work, the vast majority were either ambivalent or unreceptive. Those who were most receptive had worked collaboratively with social scientists, participated in the development of social science research projects, or evaluated such projects as a member of an interdisciplinary peer review committee. Borreani et al. (2004) similarly found that health researchers in oncology and palliative care 'show a complete awareness of the specificity of this kind of research, while others are still largely influenced by the quantitative paradigm prevailing in the medical field' (p. 2). We hope that this Handbook puts an end to these unfounded concerns with the rigour of good qualitative health research.

THE QUALITY OF QUALITATIVE HEALTH RESEARCH

Quality in qualitative research is a mystery to many health services researchers (Dingwall et al., 1998, p. 167).

While those of us who do qualitative health research welcome our growing acceptance, we cannot ignore those who continue to be sceptical about our approach (Green and Thorogood, 2004, p. 25). Their scepticism is particularly salient in an era defined by evidence-based health care, an approach that has been dominated by quantitative methods (Grypdonck, 2006; Jack, 2006; Long and Godfrey, 2004). Many criticisms of qualitative health research come from sources with a narrow view of objectivity and generalizability and an allegiance to 'evidence hierarchies' that tend to exclude or demote qualitative health research (Dixon-Woods et al., 2001; Giacomini, 2001; Sandelowski, 2004).

The notion of simple 'evidence hierarchies' has been increasingly questioned within the evidence-based movement itself. In his 2008 Harveian Oration, from which this Introduction's epigraph is taken, Sir Michael Rawlins, Chair of the UK National Institute for Health and Clinical Excellence, an organization that is a leading player in the evidence-based movement, directly criticizes the notion:

> Hierarchies attempt to replace judgement with an oversimplistic, pseudo-quantitative, assessment of the quality of the available evidence. Decision makers have to incorporate judgements as part of the appraisal of evidence in reaching their conclusions. Such judgements relate to the extent to which each component of the evidence base is 'fit for purpose' (Rawlins, 2008, p. 34).

In spite of Rawlins' comments, there have been attempts to quantify qualitative health research in order to make it better suited to the evidence-based model of analysis. Perhaps the best example is that of Daley et al. (2007) who offer a four-level hierarchy of qualitative evidence-for-practice. Long and Godfrey (2004) argue that this is made possible by an explicit focus on the systematization of qualitative health data collection and analysis (cf. Miles and Huberman, 1994). Indeed, as Borreani et al. (2004) show, concern with the rigour and credibility of qualitative health research has led to the development of a number of quality checklists (cf. Walsh, 2006). Do these efforts to 'legitimize' qualitative health research in the eyes of quantitative researchers diminish the approach? Many researchers think they do. Murphy and Dingwall (2003) point out that the proliferation of typologies reflects their limited usefulness, a point also made by Rawlins (2008, p. 34). Others are calling for an 'end to criteriology' (Schwandt, 1996) because it tends to privilege positivist methodological traditions, stifling the interpretive and creative aspects of qualitative health research (Dixon-Woods et al., 2007).

We agree with Boutilier et al. (2001) that we should not be using a ruler to measure a sphere. At the same time, we remain concerned by statements that 'there is no "right" way of doing qualitative research' (Dew, 2007, p. 436). Assessments of the quality of qualitative health research are needed. This will involve more explicit recognition of the intellectual and theoretical roots of qualitative methodologies in the social sciences in the face of the empiricist pull of much health research towards 'practical' work driven by users' goals. In practice, user goals will be more effectively achieved by qualitative research that acknowledges its roots, and uses these as the bases for evaluation, than by studies that rely purely on technique. We can collect endless stories from patients, but they only become meaningful through a critical process of analysis that draws on, and contributes to, theories about health, illness, and medical care. As Reeves et al. (2008) argued in a more recent series on qualitative health research in the *BMJ*:

> Theories provide complex and comprehensive conceptual understandings of things that cannot be pinned down: how societies work, how organizations operate, why people interact in certain ways. Theories give researchers different 'lenses' through which to look at complicated problems and social issues, focusing their attention on different aspects of the data and providing a framework within which to conduct their analysis. ... The use of theory

makes it possible for researchers to understand, and to translate for policy makers and health care providers, the processes that occur beneath the visible surface and so to develop knowledge of underlying (generating) principles. Importantly, theory can help people move beyond individual insights gained from their professional lives to a situation where they can understand the wider significance and applicability of these phenomena (p. 631).

Although theoretical perspectives are not necessarily *applied* in qualitative health research, they do provide important starting points for *scrutiny* and for the generation of new theoretical insights (Charmaz, 2004). It is particularly important to recognize, therefore, the relevance of theoretical perspective to the proper execution of qualitative health research. Dixon-Woods et al. (2007) describe this well:

An interview-based study conducted within a grounded theory framework may therefore have very different characteristics from an interview-based study conducted within a discourse analysis framework, and this clearly needs to be reflected in the framework for appraising a study. The key task then lies in defining what the expectations should be for a particular study design within a particular theoretical field (p. 223).

In addition to these concerns with the theoretical positioning of qualitative health research, there are also worries about 'less-than-strenuous efforts to be accurate' (Charmaz, 2004, p. 986). Accuracy, according to Charmaz (2004), means 'excavating the implicit meanings in our participants' statements and actions. It means that we take a measured stance about the data we select to show. It means choosing excerpts and anecdotes that *represent* larger issues, not just choosing the juiciest stories. ... Accuracy means collecting sufficient data that we have as full a range of observations of the phenomenon as possible' (p. 986). Charmaz challenges us to avoid the mechanical use of qualitative methods, to open ourselves up to the experience of research, to gather sufficient data to make our study credible, to pay attention to language, and to be sure to look beneath the surface to uncover important contextual features of the phenomenon being studied. Confidence in the validity of qualitative health research findings is also increased when researchers have spent an extended period of time in the setting, when explicit procedures for data collection are used, when researchers have spent time searching for disconfirming data, and where they are sensitive to the ways in which they may have shaped the data (Murphy et al., 1998). All of these must, of course, be balanced by resource and other constraints; it is easy to become precious about the duration of fieldwork and fail to recognize that important and useful results can be achieved in a rapid ethnography by experienced researchers (Millen, 2000, http://portal.acm.org/citation.cfm?id=347763).

While the question of how (and indeed whether) qualitative research should be evaluated is highly contested, qualitative health researchers must pay attention to their reception in the larger research and health care communities (Murphy et al., 1998). We believe, with others (e.g., Pope and Mays, 2000), that quality in qualitative research can be assessed with the same broad concepts of *validity* and *relevance* used for quantitative research. Indeed, as Pope and Mays (2006) argue, if qualitative health research is to be taken seriously, it will need to ensure that its trustworthiness can be assessed and expressed in criteria that quantitative researchers understand and use. We acknowledge, however, that these will need to be operationalized in different ways to take into account the distinctive nature of qualitative research. The development of criteria for assessing the quality of qualitative health research will allow us to better challenge the quality of quantitative research, through demonstrating the ways in which the quantification of behaviour misrepresents what is really going on in health care settings. As Murphy and Dingwall (2003) conclude, 'The hallmarks of high-quality qualitative research are to be found in the same commitment to rigour, clarity, and systematicity, which are the hallmarks of all good science' (p. 13).

OVERVIEW OF HANDBOOK

Newcomers to research often assume that they will find an orderly terrain, with clear instructions about where to go and what to do. In fact, of course, all science proceeds by way of conflict, challenge, and disagreement as methods, ideas, and findings are picked over and tested for their robustness. A scientific field in which there is total agreement is a field that has ceased to be scientific and been replaced by inherited dogma. Hence, the reader should not expect to find that this collection presents a single point of view about anything, that contributors necessarily agree with each other, or even that the editors personally subscribe to every idea presented here. At most, it is unified by a consensus that qualitative health research matters, or should matter, for those engaged in policy, planning, management, or clinical practice. All of these tasks can be performed more effectively, more equitably, more humanely, and, even, more efficiently, when those engaged in them appreciate what qualitative evidence has to offer in informing their professional judgement. Our collection encompasses the diversity of the field, demonstrating the different things that qualitative research can offer and exemplifying the debates that go on within it about how precisely to understand ideas like reliability and validity, and to operationalize these in research practice.

Key topics

The Handbook opens with a section of case studies of the ways in which qualitative methods have contributed to specific fields relevant to policy and practice in health care. These chapters illustrate the diversity of qualitative methods and highlight their different contributions. They allow readers to explore what qualitative research can offer to health policy and practice before becoming immersed in more detailed arguments about theoretical underpinnings and choices of method. This practical background helps establish the relevance of these more abstract debates. By taking a substantive topic, each chapter shows how different qualitative methods can be used and how their cumulative contributions lead to helpful ways of understanding common issues. The chapters also exemplify the kinds of choices about research design and analysis that must be made (discussed more fully in Section D). The rich qualitative literature on institutionalized dying and the medical management of end-of-life is explored by Stefan Timmermans. Arthur Frank and colleagues take up the important topic of the interactions between health professionals/healers and patients where they examine new mediators of these interactions. Professions and their work are addressed by Johanne Collin, who demonstrates how qualitative research has advanced our understanding of current issues affecting health professions. Carol Caronna then addresses the application of qualitative methods to the study of health organizations, revealing their complex and multi-layered nature. This is followed by Sirpa Wrede's discussion of the contributions of qualitative health research to the comparative study of health policy. The final chapter in this section, by Gareth Williams and Eva Elliot, shows the value of thinking qualitatively when exploring social inequities in health.

Having established the potential utility of qualitative methods for the practitioner, manager, planner, or policymaker, Section B looks more closely at the different foundational assumptions and theoretical traditions that inform their application in health research. The authors still quote extensively from empirical studies adopting particular theoretical positions, but here they focus on the underlying *ideas* rather than the substantive findings or the research practices. The section begins with Mita Giacomini's discussion of why theory matters in qualitative health research. She concentrates on the philosophical bases of qualitative methodologies, characterizing the various forms of theory generated by different traditions and the ways these might be understood by readers and users. Rebecca Prentice explores the theoretical contributions from anthropology and the centrality of fieldwork to theory-making. The important topic of grounded theory is addressed by Dorothy Pawluch and Elena Neiterman. They describe its main features and locate it in relation to its sources, principally in the theoretical tradition of Symbolic Interactionism. The revival of qualitative research methods in contemporary psychology is reviewed by Helen Malson. Tim Halkowski and Virginia Gill examine the conversation analytic perspective and its roots in ethnomethodology. Carol McWilliam looks at phenomenology, another interpretive, humanistic theoretical tradition. Her chapter includes discussion of the socio-historical evolution and continuing challenges presented by this approach. The revival of institutionalism and institutionalist theoretical perspectives in the study of health care organizations is discussed by Karen Staniland, highlighting the contributions of both 'old' and 'new' approaches. In this section's final chapter, Claire Hooker presents the theoretical issues foundational to historical qualitative health research, through a discussion of the emergence of tobacco control.

The solid understanding provided in Section B of the theoretical traditions from which various qualitative methods originated prepares the way for chapters describing specific techniques for the collection of qualitative data in Section C. This section focuses on how people collect data and what they then do with it.

These chapters are not just compilations of 'tips and tricks'; each author examines the kinds of evidence generated by the method and the ways in which it can contribute to the overall analysis of particular research questions. Jennie Popay and Sara Mallinson describe the value of systematic reviews of qualitative research findings for decision making by policy makers, professionals, and lay people. Using four specific examples, they set out the general characteristics of the process of systematic review and synthesis as applied to qualitative research. Qualitative interviewing techniques and styles are described by Susan Kelly. She distinguishes this kind of interviewing from standardized interviews, and considers the kinds of research questions to which the various techniques are best suited. Rosalind Barbour writes about the challenges and potential of focus groups for qualitative health research. She reviews appropriate and inappropriate uses of the method and enumerates the advantages and disadvantages of this approach. Next, Davina Allen discusses the fieldwork and participation observation, and the methodological choices involved in designing research that uses these methods. Growing recognition of the complexity of human communication in health care is the backdrop for Ruth Parry's description of video-based conversation analysis. She describes the increasingly sophisticated ways to identify and understand what people do and why, in ways that carefully attend to the contribution of nonvocal and vocal conduct. Srikant Sarangi offers a practically relevant – albeit critical and reflexive – introduction to the methodological tradition known as discourse analysis, including a description of its application to health care settings. The analysis of documents, which are becoming increasingly rife in health care, is taken up by Lindsay Prior. He outlines some of the markedly different ways in which documents can be used in qualitative health research. In her chapter on participatory action research, Louise Potvin challenges researchers to be guided by a relevant theory of action when studying health interventions. Linda McKie and Isobel MacPherson describe the collection and analysis of qualitative data for the purposes of health care programme evaluation. Elizabeth Ettore uses her own life experience and research to introduce the method of autoethnography and to describe the way it has been used to make sense of personal illness journeys. The ethnographic tradition of institutional ethnography is addressed by Marie Campbell. Susan Bell draws on visual sociology to demonstrate how visual methods can be used to answer questions about health policy and practice. Clive Seale and Jonathan Charteris-Black conclude this section by describing keyword analysis, a new tool in qualitative health research that exploits the availability of massive quantities of health-related text and the processing power of modern personal computers.

Section D covers a more generic set of issues related to the strategic place of qualitative research in health care. Kath Melia offers an in-depth discussion of how to recognize quality in qualitative research. The mixing of methods – both with quantitative health research and within qualitative studies – has become popular in recent years. Alicia O'Cathain looks at 'mixed methods', their wide appeal and some limitations. A practical guide to the ethical challenges of qualitative health research is provided by Laura Stark and Adam Hedgecoe. Julia Abelson discusses 'deliberative methods', an increasingly popular approach for eliciting public values and priorities to inform policy decisions. Carine Vassy and Richard Keller close this section with an examination of teamwork in cross-national qualitative health research.

The book concludes similar to the way it began, with examples of qualitative research being used in health care settings. Kerreen Reiger and Pranee Liamputtong discuss the intersections of personal and political issues in their chapter on researching reproduction. Tim Rapley and Tiago Moreira describe how qualitative health research has been used to better understand the way in which technologies interact with work, ideas, and identities in health care contexts. David Holmes and colleagues direct our attention to what they learned about conducting qualitative research into radical sexual expression. Ilina Singh and Sinead Keenan challenge some of the assumptions about the perils and promises of qualitative health research with children, focusing in particular on the potential ethical risks around children's competence, capacity, and consent. Ruth Pinder offers a thoughtful discussion of the dilemmas of advocacy in disability research framed in terms of a paradox of giving. Phil Brown identifies the contributions of qualitative health research to environmental health research and activism. The range of issues presented in these chapters is wide enough to allow students and teachers to find a reasonable parallel for any particular project they envisage. The chapters in this section also return to the issues about the design and practice of qualitative research introduced in earlier parts of the Handbook.

This Handbook includes both critical studies *of* health from various social science perspectives and critical studies *for* health from within particular health and health services research disciplines. It is our hope that this book can become a tool to improve the quality of qualitative research in health, and, through this, to enhancing the delivery of health care in ways that use resources *efficiently*, deliver care *effectively*, distribute access *equitably*, and treat staff and patients *humanely*.

ACKNOWLEDGEMENTS

Pulling together a volume of this magnitude is clearly a group effort. We would first like to extend our thanks to Patrick Brindle and others at Sage who initiated the development of this Handbook and provided helpful advice and support. Patrick and his staff offered the perfect mix of patience and encouragement that allowed us to complete this manuscript in spite of various health crises and long-distance household and office moves. Our colleague Elizabeth Murphy made a great contribution to the conception of the Handbook and helped us identify many of the fine scholars who became our authors.

We are, of course, also indebted to the authors whose work appears here. We thank them for their detailed and reflective contributions to this volume, for their open and respectful approach to the suggestions from the editors and reviewers, and for their patience with the necessary back-and-forth of editing and revising.

We are also deeply grateful for the time and commitment of the members of our international advisory board. Their collective wisdom and deep knowledge of the theory and practice of qualitative research is responsible for all that is good in this Handbook. Their thoughtful and constructive reviews were delivered with grace. In alphabetical order, these members are: Ellen Annandale, Cecilia Benoit, Charles Bosk, Kathy Charmaz, Peter Conrad, Kathryn Church, Peter Davis, Jonathan Gabe, Leah Gilbert, John Grady, David Hughes, Nelya Koteyko, Ellen Kuhlmann, Valerie Leiter, Anssi Peräkylä, Alison Pilnick, Jonathan Potter, Jane Sandall, Jane Seymour, Fred Stevens, and Evan Willis.

Support for our work came from Sage Publications, from the Canada Research Chair in Comparative Health Labour Policy at McMaster University, and from the University of Ottawa.

Since she is not the least in the list of those to whom we are indebted, we mention last our most able assistant Amanda Hammill. With her adept, timely, and patient administrative support, she kept us all on task. Without her efforts, this book would still be just an idea in the editors' heads.

REFERENCES

Albert, M., Laberge, S., Hodges, B.D., Regehr, G., and Lingard, L. (2008) 'Biomedical Scientists' Perception of the Social Sciences in Health Research', *Social Science and Medicine*, 66(12): 2520–31.

Becker, H.S., Geer, B., Hughes, E.C., and Strauss, A.L. (1961) *Boys in White*. New York: Transaction Books.

Bloor M., McKeganey, N. and Fonkert, D. (1988) *One Foot in Eden: a Sociological Study of the Range of Therapeutic Community Practice*. London: Routledge.

Borreani, C., Miccinesi, G., Brunelli, C., and Lina, M. (2004) 'An Increasing Number of Qualitative Research Papers in Oncology and Palliative Care: Does It Mean a Thorough Development of the Methodology of Research?' *Health and Quality of Life Outcomes*, 2:7, available at: http://www.hqlo.com/content/2/1/7

Boutilier, M.A., Rajkumar, E., Poland, B.D., Tobin, S., and Badgley, R.F. (2001) 'Community Action Success in Public Health: Are We Using a Ruler to Measure a Sphere?' *Canadian Journal of Public Health*, 92(2): 90–4.

Charmaz, K. (2004) 'Premises, Principles, and Practices in Qualitative Research: Revisiting the Foundations', *Qualitative Health Research*, 14(7): 976–93.

Daly, J., Willis, K., Small, R., Green, J., Welch, N., Kealy, M., and Hughes, E. (2007) 'A hierarchy of evidence for assessing qualitative health research', *Journal of Clinical Epidemiology*, 60: 43–9.

Davis, F. (1963) *Passage Through Crisis: Polio Victims and Their Families*. Indianapolis: Bobbs-Merrill.

Denzin, N. and Lincoln, Y. (2000) *Handbook of Qualitative Research*. London: Sage.

Deutscher, I. (1973) *What We Say/What We Do: Sentiments & Acts*. Glenview, IL: Scott, Foresman and Co.

Dew, K. (2007) 'A Health Researcher's Guide to Qualitative Methodologies', *Australian and New Zealand Journal of Public Health*, 31(5): 433–37.

Dingwall, R., Eekelaar, J., and Murray, T. (1983) *The Protection of Children: State Intervention and Family Life*. London: B. Blackwell.

Dingwall, R., Murphy, E., Watson, P., Greatbatch, D., and Parker, S. (1998) 'Catching Goldfish: Quality in Qualitative Research. *Journal of Health Services Research and Policy*, 3: 167–72.

Dixon-Woods, M., Fitzpatrick, R., and Roberts, K. (2001) 'Including Qualitative Research in Systematic Reviews: Problems and Opportunities', *Journal of Evaluation in Clinical Practice*, 7: 125–33.

Dixon-Woods, M., Booth, A., and Sutton, A.J. (2007) 'Synthesizing Qualitative Research: A Review of Published Reports', *Qualitative Research*, 7: 375–422.

Giacomini, M.K. (2001) 'The Rocky Road: Qualitative Research as Evidence', *Evidence-Based Medicine*, 6: 4–6.

Goffman, E. (1961) *Asylums*. Harmondsworth: Penguin.

Green, J. and Thorogood, N. (2004) *Qualitative Methods for Health Research*. London: Sage.

Grypdonck, M.H.F. (2006) 'Qualitative Health Research in the Era of Evidence-Based Practice', *Qualitative Health Research*, 16: 1371–85.

Hammersley, M. (1992) *What's Wrong with Ethnography?* London: Routledge.

Holman, H.R. (1993) 'Qualitative Inquiry in Medical Research', *Journal of Clinical Epidemiology*, 46: 29–36.

Hutchinson, S.A. (2001) 'The Development of Qualitative Health Research: Taking Stock', *Qualitative Health Research*, 11(4): 505–21.

Imle, M.A. and Atwood, J.R. (1988) 'Retaining Qualitative Validity While Gaining Quantitative Reliability and Validity', *Advances in Nursing Science*, 11(1): 61–75.

Jack, S.M. (2006) 'Utility of Qualitative Research Findings in Evidence-Based Public Health Practice', *Public Health Nursing*, 23(3): 277–83.

Kuper, A., Reeves, S., and Levinson, W. (2008) 'An Introduction to Reading and Appraising Qualitative Research', *BMJ*, 2008:337:404–409 (published 7 August 2008).

Lempp, H. and Kingsley, G. (2007) 'Qualitative Assessments', *Best Practice and Research Clinical Rheumatology*, 21(5): 857–69.

Long, Andrew F. and Godfrey, Mary (2004) 'An Evaluation Tool to Assess the Quality of Qualitative Research Studies', *International Journal of Social Research Methodology*, 7(2): 181–96.

Macintyre, S. (1977) *Single and Pregnant*, London: Croom Helm.

McIntosh, J. (1977) *Communication and Awareness in a Cancer Ward*. London: Croom Helm.

Miles, M.B. and Huberman, A.M. (1994) *Qualitative Data Analysis*. Thousand Oaks, CA: Sage.

Morse, J.M. (2007) 'What is the Domain of Qualitative Health Research?' *Qualitative Health Research*, 17(6):715–7.

Murphy, E. and Dingwall, R. (2003) *Qualitative Methods and Health Policy Research*. NJ: Aldine.

Murphy, E., Dingwall, R., Greatbatch, D., Parker, S., and Watson, P. (1998) 'Qualitative Research Methods in Health Technology Assessment: A Review of the Literature', *Health Technology Assessment*, 2(16).

Munhall, P.L. and Boyd, C.O. (1993) *Nursing Research: A Qualitative Perspective*, 2nd edition. New York: National League for Nursing Press.

Pope, C. and Mays, N. (1995) 'Qualitative Research: Reaching the Parts Other Methods Cannot Reach: An Introduction to Qualitative Methods in Health and Health Services Research', *BMJ*, Jul.1: 311: 42–45.

Pope, C. and Mays, N. (2000) 'Qualitative Research in Health Care: Assessing Quality in Qualitative Research', *BMJ*, Jan 1: 320(7226): 50–2.

Pope, C. and Mays, N. (2006) *Qualitative Research in Health Care*. Oxford: Wiley-Blackwell.

Pope, C., van Royen, P., and Baker, R. (2002) 'Qualitative Methods in Research on Healthcare Quality', *Quality and Safety in Health Care*, 11: 148–52.

Rawlins, M. (2008) Harveian Oration to the Royal College of Physicians available at: http://www.rcplondon.ac.uk/pubs/contents/304df931-2ddc-4a54-894e-e0cdb03e84a5.pdf

Reeves, S., Albert, M., Kuper, A., and Hodges, B.D. (2008) 'Why Use Theories in Qualitative Research?', *BMJ*, 2008; 337:631–634 (published 7 August 2008).

Roth, J.A. (1963) *Timetables: Structuring the Passage of Time in Hospital Treatment and Other Careers*, Indianapolis: Bobbs-Merrill Company, Inc.

Sandelowski, M. (2004) 'Using Qualitative Research', *Qualitative Health Research*, 14(10): 1366–86.

Schwandt, T.A. (1996) 'Farewell to Criteriology', *Qualitative Inquiry*, 2: 58–72.

Silverman, D. (1993) *Interpreting Qualitative Data – Methods for Analysing Talk, Text, and Interaction*. London: Sage.

Strong, P.M. (1979) *The Ceremonial Order of the Clinic: Parents, Doctors, and Medical Bureaucracies*, London: Routledge & Kegan Paul Books.

Thomas, W.I. (1923) *The Unadjusted Girl*. Boston: Little, Brown, and Co.

Thomas, W.I. and Thomas, D.S. (1928) *The Child in America: Behavior Problems and Programs*. New York: Knopf.

Tripp-Reimer, T. and Doebbelin, B. (2004) 'Qualitative Perspectives in Translational Research', *Worldviews in Evidence-Based Nursing'*, Third Quarter (Suppl.): S65–SS72.

Ulin, P.R., Robinson, E.T., and Tolley, E.E. (2004) *Qualitative Methods in Public Health: A Field Guide for Applied Research*. CA: Wiley.

Contributions of Qualitative Research

There's More to Dying than Death: Qualitative Research on the End-of-Life

Stefan Timmermans[1]

Since human death is often regarded as one of the most individual and biological events, the broad field of death and dying forms a counterintuitive – and therefore attractive – case to establish the intellectual legitimacy of social science generally and qualitative health research in particular. Emile Durkheim (1979) argued that every society produces its own suicide rate dependent on how people are integrated and regulated to establish that the seemingly isolated fact of taking one's life has deep societal origins that could be discovered. More recently, several scholars have tested the obduracy of their theories with society's attitudes towards death and dying in times of war and peace.

Qualitative research also aspired to acquire formal legitimacy through an ambitious study of death and dying. In 1958, researchers declared the study of death and dying neglected and barren, but this situation changed in the early 1960s when Anselm Strauss and Barney Glaser (1970) conducted a study of interactions between dying patients and health care providers in six San Francisco Bay area hospitals. The study was groundbreaking for substantive and methodological reasons. Especially, the notion of awareness contexts captured the zeitgeist that institutionalized dying led to widespread alienation and isolation. At a time where patients received euphemisms, embellishments, or lies about the severity or exact

[1] I thank Ivy Bourgeault and a helpful reviewer for comments on a previous version of this chapter.

nature of their diagnosis and prognosis, Glaser and Strauss (1965) documented that terminally ill patients often went to great lengths to figure out their status to be confronted by a wall of silence of health care providers and complicit family members. Their analysis, along with Kübler-Ross (1969) influential writings on the five stages of grief, galvanized a social movement aimed at humanizing contemporary dying that took the form of various hospice and palliative care initiatives. Besides crystallizing late modern unease with the medicalization of the dying process, the books *Awareness of Dying*, *Time for Dying*, and the case-study *Anguish* foreshadowed the emergence of the influential labelling theory, produced a collection of concepts that became part of the intellectual canon, prompted change in how terminal patients were informed about the prognosis of their disease, and constituted a prime example of the application of a systematic qualitative methodology.

In conjunction with their study of dying in hospitals, Strauss and Glaser wrote a methodological manifesto that articulated the principles of grounded theory as a general approach to conducting qualitative research in a period where quantitative research took centre stage, much theorizing was not grounded in empirical research, and some qualitative research lacked clearly defined standards. They proposed that sociologists build theory from the ground up through systematic conceptualization and constant comparisons with similar and distinct research areas. Theories grounded in substantive areas could then lead, through further abstraction, to formal theories of social life. In the heydays of Parsonian and Mertonian functionalist theorizing, the boom in social survey research, and C. Wright Mill's empirically weak writings, the book became a research standard; in the traditional sense of a powerful rallying point for an alternative social science.

Thus, also for qualitative research the area of death and dying formed a dare: if Strauss and Glaser could refine qualitative methodology in what looked at first sight a hostile domain, then they had proven the method's merits beyond doubt. Once launched in the area of death and dying, grounded theory became established as a generic qualitative research methodology with an especially strong presence in health research (see Bryant and Charmaz, 2007). At the same time, a full range of qualitative methods from discourse analysis, historical research, focus group research, in-depth interviewing, and especially ethnography dominated the study of death and dying for the next decades.

In the remainder of this chapter, I will review the rich qualitative studies of institutionalized dying since Strauss and Glaser, focusing on the medical staff's management of lingering, slow dying trajectories and on the much smaller literature of managing unexpected death and explaining suspicious and violent death. I will also sketch a research agenda that explores the forms of contemporary death and dying that are rarely qualitatively investigated, in part because of the focus on studying institutions, expected deaths, and using qualitative methods. First, I will explain why death and dying forms such a good match with qualitative research methods. I argue that this has less to do with Strauss and Glaser's foray in this field than with the broader cultural consensus about what is wrong with contemporary dying.

THE FIT BETWEEN QUALITATIVE RESEARCH AND DEATH AND DYING

Did Strauss and Glaser (1970) initiate a decade – long research tradition of study-ing death qualitatively or were they also products of their time? Strauss and Glaser's prolific endeavours constitute the most explicit linkage between qualita-tive methods and the field of death and dying and they are often regarded as founders of this field. Yet, while they were doing their study, other social scien-tists also employed qualitative methods to study dying in hospitals and the topic was on the mind of many others in ways that made qualitative methods a good fit. Strauss and Glaser may thus have reflected the spirits of the times rather than initiated the research of decades to come. Indeed, the original merger of qualita-tive research and the topic of death and dying may be less a consequence of the pioneering study of Strauss and Glaser than the result of what can be called a broad post-Second World War humanist focus of the death and dying scholarship.

Influential philosophers, psychoanalyst, historians, and social scientists have argued that mortality forms the ultimate limit in modern societies, because it constitutes the defeat of reason, since reason cannot conceive of the reality of death and conquer mortality. Elias (1985) summarizes, 'it is not actually death, but the knowledge of death, that creates problems for human beings'. Mortality awareness conjures an existential ambivalence in individual and social life gen-erating defence mechanisms. In premodern Europe, Aries (1977) situated a 'tamed death' as cultural coping mechanism; death was tame in the European Middle Ages not because of domestication but because it 'was never wild before'. Death simply *was*, it could be bewailed or regretted but not manipulated. In this fatalistic perspective, the 'dance macabre' gripped rich and poor, young and old alike; religious authorities explained death as a predetermined egalitarian part of cruel human fate. In the wake of the philosophy of Enlightenment with its emphasis on mastery of nature and contingency, life expectancy might have increased but mortality remained ultimately indifferent to instrumental human efforts. A medical, legal, and – later – therapeutic ethos gradually replaced religion as moral authority. In the realm of death and dying medicine prevailed.

While questioning the inevitability of death, modernity added anguish to it: security of small victories over some acute, devastating diseases enhanced inse-curity in light of the ultimate demise. One much publicized reaction in modern societies to this frontier of reason is *seclusion and professional management*: hide death in institutions, disavowing its existence through spatial and social segregation under supervision of medically trained experts. Secondly, while mor-tality itself cannot be avoided, individual *causes of death* can be *determined*, and then manipulated and postponed. Bauman (1992) characterizes this frantic search for pertinent causes while losing sight of the ultimate futility of the endeavour as the 'analytical deconstruction' of mortality in which 'fighting the causes of dying turns into the meaning of life'. Mortality was deconstructed in autopsies to be tabulated in public health instruments such as the International Classification of Disease, which in turn form the basis of epidemiological health policies.

The result of those twin modern death brokering strategies is simultaneously a professionalization of the dying process and an 'excessive preoccupation with the risk of death' in daily life leading to a society organized around risk.

The broad consensus in intellectual circles that modernity gave rise to a frantic search to postpone death and ignore the dying formed a good fit for qualitative research explorations. Health scientists became interested in how exactly death was managed in institutions and what alternatives were possible. The research agenda of much of the past four decades was to retrieve the experience of death and dying and taking care of the terminally ill in hospitals and nursing homes. When hospices materialized, health scientists studied how these new institutions fulfilled their missions to break the mould of institutionalized dying. These experiences were not only difficult to capture in surveys but also the notion of standardized research instruments went against the grain of the broader focus on retrieving socially contextualized experiences. In addition, the concentration of the dying and their caregivers in institutions made observations and in-depth interviews logistically feasible. Consequently, death and dying is a rare research area in medicine where qualitative studies are well established.

QUALITATIVE STUDIES OF DEATH AND DYING

In Western societies, about 75 percent of people die in institutions, mainly hospitals and nursing homes. The proportion of people dying in the United States from chronic illnesses in acute care hospitals has been declining between 1989 and 2001 from 62.3 percent to 49.5 percent. Over that same period, the percentage of deaths in nursing homes increased from 19.2 percent to 23.2 percent, and the percentage of people dying at a place they considered home increased from 15.9 percent to 23.4 percent.[1] People who die suddenly may paradoxically also die in hospitals, even if they collapse in public places or at home: when bystanders or relatives alert emergency services patients will be transported to emergency departments where the death will be verified and certified. Deaths thus are centralized in institutions for diverse reasons.

Concentrating their research efforts in these places where deaths occur, social and health scientists have been struck by how health professionals work towards ideals of culturally appropriate dying but often fall short of achieving humanistic deaths. In an earlier review of the literature on which the following section is based, I distinguished several of the iterations of culturally appropriate deaths: death without dying, natural deaths, resuscitated deaths, and good deaths.[2]

The deaths without dying occur when patients have been kept in, what Strauss and Glaser called 'closed awareness'. Patients remain uninformed about the seriousness of their diagnosis and prognosis. This situation is less common in the United States as it was in the sixties, but it still occurs regularly in countries with a more paternalistic medical profession such as Italy, Belgium, or Israel. In the United States, 'bad news' is now routinely communicated to terminal patients, giving rise to the opposite situation of 'truth dumping', where a clinician informs patients and relatives of the worst-case scenario but offers little follow-up on how this information has been processed. Patients are more likely to be kept in the dark of their pending death if they die from non-oncological conditions. If such a patient dies, the staff may not be surprised, but relatives may be shocked. This death still corresponds to the ideal of slipping away in one's sleep. Anspach and Kaufman have documented that these deaths may occur for organizational reasons, because a consensus among health care providers is only necessary to withdraw or withhold care; as long as at least one key member of the medical team wants to continue with therapy, the treatment paradigm will prevail. Health care providers may also be reluctant to breach a terminal prognosis, because they fear creating a self-fulfilling prophecy.

In her recent study of dying in hospitals using ethnographic methods, anthropologist Sharon Kaufman (2005) noted that 'what is natural is negotiable'. She and others have found that 'natural deaths' are tightly scripted and organized in hospital settings, especially intensive care units where between 15 and 35 percent of hospital deaths occur. The staff actively harnesses drugs and medical technologies to mimic a gradually declining 'natural' dying trajectory by a piecemeal withdrawal of therapies. Because most patients are comatose in intensive care units and admittance signifies life-threatening conditions, there is little emphasis on the patients' death acceptance. Still, assent of relatives to withdraw and withhold care is crucial in US intensive care units where relatives have legally supported proxy decision making powers and the actual time and manner of death is often determined in difficult ethics conferences between clinicians and relatives. The staff's 'orchestration' of the death as an inevitable transitory process with a measured balance of action and nonaction involves matching their interventions with the expectations of relatives, including actively shaping those expectations when relatives are 'unrealistic', showering them with technical information, presenting ready-made decisions, relieving guilt feelings, and 'psychologizing' them when they resist staff. Staff also invites relatives to be present at the moment of active dying, quietly say their goodbyes, and keep physical contact. In addition, the staff's decisions to withdraw care are measured in such a way that they obliterate the impression that the staff 'killed' the patient but that the death was preordained by the terminal disease, lowering the possibility of litigation.

The specific meaning of sudden unexpected deaths is now offered by resuscitation techniques, turning a sudden death into a stretched standardized dying process, leading to the paradoxical situation of the resuscitated death. In light of the remarkably low survival rates of resuscitative efforts inside and outside hospitals, several social observers have noted that resuscitation procedures soften the abruptness of sudden death. With relatives waiting in separate counselling rooms, physicians 'stage' information, gradually informing relatives about the worsening situation, occasionally even stretching the reviving effort to facilitate informing relatives or running 'slow codes' to give the impression that life-saving efforts took place even if the staff did not believe in them. In some hospitals, relatives are invited to attend the tail end of the reviving effort and say their good-byes. The emphasis on restoring ventilation and circulation during resuscitative efforts frames the sudden death as a cardiac failure, offering a readymade 'cause' of death. Because resuscitative efforts ultimately aim to save lives, the ideal of the resuscitated death reassures relatives and clinicians that the death was pain-less, unpreventable, and quick with everything medically possible done. Research also shows that advance directives are not always able to stop the resuscitative momentum, particularly when clinicians see an opportunity for successful treat-ment. Relatives seem to have residual impact when care providers have determined that too much uncertainty prevents a clear medical course of action.

The hospice and palliative care movement reacted to the alienating image of technology mediated hospital deaths. Critics of modern dying remained divided whether the site of dying, the technologies surrounding death, or a combination of both were the fundamental cause of dehumanization. Hospice care and palliative care advocates did not necessarily renounce institutional settings or technolo-gies, but they aimed to develop a care setting focused on holistic terminal care, including the spiritual, religious and social needs of the dying. Many social observers have noted that during the past decades hospice has lost its alternative, holistic edge with institutionalization while hospice workers have 'routinized' the good death into 'a socially approved form of dying and death with powerfully prescribed and normalized behaviors and choices'. Hospice care has been insti-tutionalized around the highly specific 'ideology' of the 'good' death. The good death involves aggressive symptom management, and attention to the religious, social, psychological needs of the dying and their loved ones to achieve the nor-mative goal of accepting impending death. As such, the good death constitutes a historical continuation of the *Ars Moriendi* that links the devastation of the Black Death in the Middle Ages to the mass casualties of the Civil War period into the present.

As with the ideal of the natural death, staffs negotiate the 'good' death through active management of both the physical condition of the patient and the actions and expectations of the dying and their relatives. Hospice workers aggressively treat thirst, bed sores, constipation, and pain – even if the pain management with morphine might depress breathing (the 'double effect') – in order to keep the dying patient comfortable, but draw the line at curative interventions, including prescribing antibiotics for infections. While some critics have charged that pain management has overshadowed the psychodynamic and religious acceptance of death, relatives and the dying patient still have to 'assent' to the ideology of hos-pice care aimed at a particular kind of good death. Thus, for example, while hospice workers might take pride in facilitating the smoking habit of a dying patient, relatives are instructed not to call an ambulance in a crisis and possibly negating the cost savings of hospice care. Even the sequence of saying goodbyes is optimized in hospice care. When the stage of active dying or 'death watch' occurs, the hospice worker takes the relatives in to say their goodbyes, and leaves the dying person with a close 'confidant'. With such tight management of expectations and dying trajectories, patients might request to die but hospice care workers, largely for religious reasons, oppose hastening death. Instead, hospice workers offer comfort care as the alternative to assisted suicide. Yet some patients might not respond to such care.

Contemporary institutional death management involves attending to the physiological aspects of dying with medical technologies in order to preserve life, to allow dying to occur uninterruptedly, or to hasten death but without being held accountable for the actual death. Most qualitative research has reiterated how medical personnel do not simply take their clues from relatives but manage the expectations of relatives and patients in an attempt to align them with a medically acceptable notion of dying, even if this involves not informing relatives to avoid giving up 'hope'. Dying ideals depend on the anticipation of the death, the length of dying, the disease process, available resources, and to a limited extent on the activism of relatives. The contemporary normative ideals fuelling the actions of medical experts are aimed at rendering dying meaningful for an intimate social network of relatives and care providers without disturbing institutional routines.

Social and health scientists have detailed how the staff often fails to obtain an ideal death. Among the barriers are staff-related factors such as opposing opinions among clinicians, diagnostic and prognostic uncertainty and ambivalence, staff shortages, staff apathy, diverse staff cultures, and medical errors. Other barriers include patients refusing to die, wanting to die, or dying too quickly, relatives abandoning the dying or refusing to let go, and divided families or relatives intending to speed up dying. Finally, researchers noted budget cuts, failing technologies, apparently divine interventions, lack of resources, and other unforeseen contingencies. The deaths that clearly deviate from the ideals might provoke anger, embarrassment, expense, suspicions of medical error and iatrogenics, and possible litigation if the relatives feel wronged. If relatives disengage, the staff might get away with an approximation of acceptable deaths.

EXPLAINING DEATH AND IMMORTALITY

Besides institutionalized dying, the other emphasis in modern societies is the push to explain death in order to avoid premature death and extend the life-course. Here, among the domains of action of interest to qualitative social and health scientists are deducing causes of death through autopsies, organ and tissue transplantation, and, outside the strict medical field, immortality in cell line development.

The number of autopsies, once the hard-fought hallmark of scientific medicine for centuries, has been steadily waning. Autopsies used to be the defining socialization moment in medical education, but they have been gradually replaced by virtual autopsies and other computer-aided teaching tools. In hospitals, autopsies used to be the final arbiter of clinical acumen but asking for the 'post' has declined due to the surge of imaging technologies, reluctance of relatives to assent to autopsies, cost consciousness due to the rise of managed care, fear of litigation if therapeutic mistakes are discovered, new instruments of quality control, changes in the medical curriculum, and shifts in the discipline of pathology. The death knell came in 1971 when the Joint Commission on the Accreditation of Hospitals eliminated autopsy requirement for hospital accreditation. An autopsy rate of 41 percent in 1961 had declined from 5 percent to 10 percent by the mid-1990s. The main place where the autopsy thrives is in forensic medicine where pathologists conduct a postmortem investigation to identify the deceased and determine the cause and manner of death, including homicide and suicide.

Social and health scientists have been suspicious of forensic death investigators' determination of suicide arguing that official suicide statistics tell us more about the way officials construct official statistics than about the phenomenon of suicide. Alternatively, epidemiologists have tried to determine whether official statistics undercount the official suicide rate, agreeing that while underreporting may occur, these statistics are sufficiently approximate for social analysis. Yet, how do forensic investigators relying on autopsies decide that a suicide took place when confronted with a dead body? This issue is complicated by the fact that Western society's understanding of suicide depends on the intent of the deceased to take his or her own life and verbalization of intent disappears at the moment of death. Viewing this occupational dilemma, I conducted an ethnographic study of death classification in a medical examiners' office observing forensic pathologists at work. I concluded that deaths are classified as suicide when they form a tight fit with forensic investigative criteria. Evidence of a suicide only qualifies as such because medical examiners have the legal mandate and the medical skills to retrieve and interpret it. Medical examiners exchange information within an organizational network of key allies in law enforcement to exclude other causes of death and bolster their determinations. Medical examiners have few incentives to boost suicide rates: a suicide is never a default option but needs to be positively proven according to professionally relevant criteria. Trauma to the body inconsistent with suicide or potential lethal, natural disease will be taken seriously as alternative explanations. As a group, medical examiners tend to privilege similar sets of information and investigative procedures, but because of the tremendous variation in organizational networks and occupational resources, variation in death classification is inevitable. The question of suicide underreporting is thus impossible to settle: different professional groups working in a different sociopolitical and organizational environment may draw the boundaries of suicide differently. As long as an external postmortem suicide standard is lacking, the problem of variation between and within geographic jurisdictions will likely continue.

Organ transplantation has traditionally been associated with the redefinition of death. As Giacomini (1997) and Lock (1995) have shown using historical documentary analysis, the notion of brain death – in which a patient's brain has ceased to function but heartbeat and respiration continue with the support of medical technologies – was introduced to allow organ and tissue transplantation to take place after the development of the ventilator. This conceptual–technological development allowed people previously considered alive to be declared dead. Cross-cultural ethnographic research shows that the implementation of brain death varies. At one end of the continuum, brain death has been routinely accepted in North America where altruistic organ donation dovetails on long-standing traditions of charity. Still, even in North America among both medical specialists and the general public, doubts remain about how dead brain death really is. At the other end of the acceptance continuum is Japan where Lock (1995) relied on ethnographic methods to document a protracted public debate over brain death and where the practice is considered a bioethical issue of major contention. Concern persists in Japan about the vulnerability of organ donors. Even after the practice of brain death received legal status in 1997, a person can only be declared brain dead when they have provided written consent to organ donation and a close relative has co-signed an advance directive. The reluctance to embrace brain death results from scandals in heart transplantation, mistrust of medical specialties, greater focus on family consensus, well-established norms of reciprocal gift-giving, and religious objections. Other countries, such as Mexico, may lack the infrastructure of technologies, personnel, and other resources on which the definition of brain death depends.

Over the last decades, various developments of 'anti-aging' medicine, stem cells, cloning, and genetic technologies have forcefully brought the chimera of immortality back to the forefront. Similar to the once culturally cutting edge transplantation technologies, these new biomedical technologies promise a continued physical presence via biological tissues and genetic materials. Much of this remains still hyperbolic and actual instances of animal and people 'immortality' remain iconographic (e.g., Dolly, the cloned sheep). Still, under the public radar screen in hundreds of laboratories, immortality of the tissue kind may already been achieved. Hannah Landecker (2007) notes that the first widely used human cell line, HeLa, has been present in laboratories since 1951. A researcher took the cells during a biopsy from Henrietta Lacks, a young African American woman, who sought help for intermenstrual bleeding but died eight months after the biopsy with a malignant cervical tumour. Her cells, however, continued growing and dividing, unperturbed by their artificial environment outside the body in laboratories. Research scientists designated the cells as 'immortal'. By reviewing the historical representations of the cells and their body of origin, Landecker shows how the 'human interest' story reflects ambivalence to cell biology as harbinger of immortality.

CONCLUSION

With never-ending existential dilemmas and an unabated sense that modern death falls short of ideals, the way we die remains a rewarding research topic for qualitative health researchers. An interpretive orientation that reveals how organizational, technological, and broader sociopolitical factors influence dying in various institutionalized settings from either a patient's or a care provider's setting remains a topic that plays to the strengths of qualitative researchers. There is always room for a study of how artificial ventilators or feeding tubes not only save lives but also tend to continuously generate bioethical dilemmas. Research, following the footsteps of Anspach (1993) or Chambliss (1996), will be able to show that the recurrent bioethical quandaries are to some extent dependent on organizational arrangements and only scratch the surface of problematized issues. Bioethical dilemmas are not inherent to feeding tubes or ventilators but these technologies as part of institutionalized hospital practices generate fodder for bioethicists, especially when aging patients with dementia receive feeding tubes.

The strong existential dimension of contemporary dying is both an opportunity for built in drama but it is also somewhat of a limitation in the sense that a study about dying has difficulty being about anything but death. Is it possible to conduct a study of death and dying that addresses the broader political context? Eric Klinenberg's study of the 1995 Chicago heat wave, in spite of well-documented shortcomings, may have achieved such a cross-over. In essence, Klinenberg aims to explain mortality in an urban environment, but he does not produce a study of death: the heat wave victims become a rallying point to examine the workings of city government's crisis management, the role of the media in holding politicians accountable and reporting decisions, the colliding agendas of various neighbourhood stakeholders, and the crumbling of a social welfare infrastructure. Studies about lethal natural disasters caused by tsunamis, earthquakes, or volcano eruptions or research on terrorism, homicide, suicide, or even HIV-AIDS are rarely shelved with the death and dying literature but provide interesting entrance points for a more political and broad sociological perspective of contemporary dying.

Similarly, we can imagine studies in hospices that besides the well-trodden theme of how these settings live up to their promises to humanize the dying experience, address broader political, economical, and sociological themes. Hospice and palliative care, for example, lends itself to approaches sensitive to a professional perspective that examines turf wars as well as the struggle for legitimacy within medical hierarchies and between medicine and the broader general public. The critical observations of hospice's normalization of the good death can then be viewed as a professional challenge for hospice workers.

Another theme that has received less attention in the study of death and dying is the role of money and finances and governmental regulations. Reading the social scientific literature on death and dying, one easily receives the impression that financial resources are nothing but necessary evils that may be mentioned in passing but rarely are explored for how they circumscribe the possibilities of death and dying. This contrasts strongly with the broader writing on the health care field where finances are deeply implicated in access problems, therapeutic choices, and practice variation. In addition, researchers have documented how finances soar at the end of life, even for the indigent. Yet, social scientists have paid little attention to how, for example, Medicare payment schedules and regulations affect the kinds of care provided at the end of life.

Death and dying in developing countries tends to emphasize reduction of excess mortality rather than the dying experience. Still, there are some notable exceptions. For example, Nancy Scheper-Hughes' (1992) provocative study of infant mortality in Brazil questions taken-for-granted assumptions about mother–child attachment and brings the differential values of human lives at death into perspective. Others have examined cross-cultural differences in terminal illness and death. Here, again, opportunities abound to explore both the dying experience and its political economy.

Finally, the time may be ripe for a comprehensive study of death and dying in the twenty-first century that examines not only where and how people die but also how death avoidance and the aspiration of immortality motivates and organizes other areas of life. Such a study should cover the institutionalized locales where the majority of people die as well as the culturally salient deaths such as homicides and war fatalities. Throughout the literature of death and dying runs a major theme of *ars moriendi*. With the medicalization of death and dying, this good way of dying has been challenged. Yet, the institutionalization of death and dying has been going on for more than a century in Western countries and we may want to examine how changes in technologies, medical practices, and organizations keep affecting how people die now.

NOTES

1 Brown atlas of dying, http://www.chcr.brown.edu/dying/usastatistics.htm, accessed January 3, 2008.

2 I also distinguished 'dignified death' as interpreted by the assisted dying movement but because little qualitative research has been done on these deaths, I will skip this here. See Timmermans (2005) for more information.

REFERENCES

Anspach, Renee (1993) *Deciding Who Lives: Fateful Choices in the Intensive Care Nursery*. Berkeley, CA: University of California Press.

Aries, Philippe (1977) *The Hour of Our Death*. London: Allen Lane.

Armstrong, David (1986) 'The invention of infant mortality', *Sociology of Health and Illness*, 8(3): 211–32.

Atkinson, Maxwell, J. (1978) *Discovering Suicide: Studies in the Social Organization of Sudden Death*. London and Bastingstoke: The Macmillan Press Ltd.

Baszanger, Isabelle (2000) 'Entre traitement de la dernière chance et palliatif pur: les frontières invisibles des innovations thérapeutiques', *Sciences Sociales et Santé*, 18(2): 67–94.

Bauman, Zygmunt (1992) *Mortality, Immortality and Other Life Strategies*. Palo Alto, CA: Stanford University Press.

Beck, Ulrich (1992) *Risk Society: Towards a New Modernity*. London, Newbury Park, CA: Sage.

Bennett, Elizabeth, S. (1999) 'Soft Truth: Ethics and Cancer in Northeast Thailand', *Anthropology and Medicine*, 6(3): 395–404.

Bosk, Charles (1979) *Forgive and Remember: Managing Medical Failure*. Chicago: University of Chicago Press.

Bowker, Geoffrey and S. Leigh Star (1999) *Sorting Things Out*. Cambridge: MIT Press.

Bradshaw, Ann (1996) 'The Spiritual Dimension of Hospice: The Secularization of an Ideal', *Social Science and Medicine*, 43(3): 409–19.

Bryant, Antony and Charmaz Kathy (2007) *The Sage Handbook of Grounded Theory*. London: Sage.

Chambliss, Daniel, F. (1996) *Beyond Caring: Hospitals, Nurses, and the Social Organization of Ethics*. Chicago: University of Chicago Press.

Charmaz, Kathy (2006) *Constructing Grounded Theory: A Practical Guide through Qualitative Analysis*. Thousand Oaks: Sage.

Christakis, Nicholas, A. (1999) *Death Foretold: Prophecy and Prognosis in Medical Care*. Chicago: University of Chicago Press.

Clarke, Adele (2005) *Situational Analysis: Grounded Theory after the Postmodern Turn*. Thousand Oaks: Sage.

Crowley-Matoka, Megan and Margaret M. Lock (2006) 'Organ Transplantation in a Globalised World', *Mortality*, 11(2): 166–81.

De Beauvoir, Simone (1965) *A Very Easy Death*. New York: Pantheon Books.

Douglas, Jack (1967) *The Social Meanings of Suicide*. Princeton, NJ: Princeton University Press.

Durkheim, Emile (1979[1897]) *Suicide: A Study in Sociology*. Translated by George and John A. Spaulding Simpson. New York: Free Press.

Elias, Norbert (1985) *The Loneliness of the Dying*. Oxford: Basil Blackwell Inc.

Exley, Catherine (2004) 'Review Article: The Sociology of Dying, Death and Bereavement', *Sociology of Health and Illness*, 26(1): 110–22.

Fadiman, Anne (1997) *The Spirit Catches You and You Fall Down*. New York: The Noonday Press.

Faunce, W.A. and R.L. Fulton (1958) 'The Sociology of Death: A Neglected Area of Research?', *Social Forces*, 36: 205–09.

Faust, Drew Gilpin (2008) *This Republic of Suffering: Death and the American Civil War*. New York: Knopf.

Feifel, Herman (1959) *The Meaning of Death*. New York: McGraw-Hill.

Field, David, David Clark, J. Corner, and Davis C. (eds) (2001) *Researching Palliative Care*. Buckingham, UK: Open University Press.

Field, David and Nicky James (1993) 'Where and How People Die'. In *The Future for Palliative Care: Issues of Policy and Practice*, edited by David Clark, 6–29. Buckingham, UK: Open University Press.

Field, J. Marilyn and Christine K. Cassel (eds) (1997) *Approaching Death: Improving Care at the End of Life*. Washington, DC: National Academy Press.

Finkler, Kaja (2005) 'Family, Kinship, Memory and Temporality in the Age of New Genetics', *Social Science and Medicine*, 61: 1059–71.

Franklin, Sarah (2007) *Dolly Mixtures: The Remaking of Genealogy*. Durham, NC: Duke University Press.

Freud, Sigmund (1918) *Reflections on War and Death*. New York: Moffat, Yard.

Giacomini, Mita (1997) 'A Change of Heart and a Change of Mind? Technology and the Redefinition of Death in 1968', *Social Science and Medicine*, 44(10): 1465–82.

Glaser, Barney G. and Anselm L. Strauss (1965) *Awareness of Dying*. Chicago: Aldine Publishing Company.

—— (1967) *The Discovery of Grounded Theory*. New York: Aldine Publishing Company.

—— (1968) *Time for Dying*. Chicago: Aldine Publishing Company.

Glasner, Peter (2005) 'Banking on Immortality? Exploring the Stem Cell Supply Chain from Embryo to Therapeutic Application', *Current Sociology*, 53(2): 355–66.

Gordon, Deborah R. (1990) 'Embodying Illness, Embodying Cancer', *Culture, Medicine, and Psychiatry*, 14: 275–97.

Gorer, Geoffrey (1965) *Death, Grief, and Mourning*. Garden City, NY: Doubleday.

Hafferty, Frederic (1991) *Into the Valley: Death and the Socialization of Medical Students*. New Haven, CT: Yale University Press.

Hamilton, M. and Reid, H. (1990) *A Hospice Handbook: A New Way to Care for the Dying*. Grand Rapids, MI: William B. Eerdmans.

Hart, Bethne, Peter Sainsbury, and Stephanie Short (1998) 'Whose Dying? A Sociological Critique of the "Good Death"', *Mortality*, 3(1): 65–77.

Harvey, Janet (1997) 'The Technological Regulation of Death: With Reference to the Technological Regulation of Birth', *Sociology*, 31(4): 719.

Hasson, Jack and Herbert Schneiderman (1995) 'Autopsy Training Programs to Right a Wrong', *Archives of Pathology and Laboratory Medicine*, 119: 289–91.

Heidegger, Martin (1996[1927]) *Being and Time*. Translated by Joan Stambaugh. Albany, NY: SUNY Press.

Heimer, Carol A. and Lisa R. Staffen (1998) *For the Sake of the Children: The Social Organization of Responsibility in the Hospital and the Home*. Chicago: University of Chicago Press.

Illich, Ivan (1974) 'The Political Uses of Natural Death'. In *Death inside Out*, edited by Peter Steinfels and Robert M. Veatch, 25–43. New York: Harper and Row.

Inwood, M.J. (1989) *Hegel: Selections*. Edited by Paul Edwards, *The Great Philosophers*. New York: Macmillan Publishing Company.

Jung, Carl (1959) 'The Soul and Death'. In *The Meaning of Death*, edited by Herman Feifel, 3–16. New York: McGraw-Hill.

Kaufman, Sharon R. (2002) 'Life Support: Locating Person and Soul', Paper presented at the AAA Annual Conference, New Orleans.

—— (2005) *And a Time to Die: How American Hospitals Shape the End of Life*. New York: Scribner.

Kellehaer, A. (1990) *Dying of Cancer: The Final Year of Life*. Melbourne: Harwood Academic Press.

Kelner, Merrijoy J. and Ivy L. Bourgeault (1993) 'Patient Control over Dying: Responses of Health Care Professionals', *Social Science and Medicine*, 36(6): 757–65.

Klinenberg, Eric (2002) *Heat Wave: A Social Autopsy of Disaster in Chicago*. Chicago: University of Chicago Press.

Kubler-Ross, Elizabeth (1969) *On Death and Dying*. New York: Macmillan Press.

Landecker, Hannay (2007) *Culturing Life: How Cells Became Technologies*. Cambridge, UK: Harvard University Press.

Lawton, Julia (1998) 'Contemporary Hospice Care: The Sequestration of the Unbounded Body and "Dirty Dying"', *Sociology of Health and Illness*, 20(2): 121–43.

Leich, Jennifer (2000) 'Preventing Hospitalization: Home Hospice Nurses, Caregivers, and Shifting Notions of a Good Death', *Research in the Sociology of Health Care*, 18: 207–28.

Lock, Margaret (1995) 'Contesting the Natural in Japan: Moral Dilemmas and Technologies of Dying', *Culture, Medicine, and Psychiatry*, 19(1): 1–38.

—— (2000) 'On Dying Twice: Culture, Technology, and the Determination of Death'. In *Living and Working with the New Medical Technologies*, edited by Margaret Lock, Alan Young, and Alberto Cambrosio, 233–63. Cambridge, UK: Cambridge University Press.

—— (2002) *Twice Dead: Organ Transplants and the Reinvention of Death*. Berkeley and Los Angeles, CA: University of California Press.

Logue, Barbara, J. (1994) 'When Hospice Fails: The Limits of Palliative Care', *Omega*, 29(4): 291–301.

Marcuse, Herbert (1959) 'The Ideology of Death', In *The Meaning of Death*, edited by Herman Feifel, 64–78. New York: McGraw-Hill Book Company.

Maynard, Douglas W. (2003) *Bad News, Good News: Conversational Order in Everyday Talk and Clinical Settings*. Chicago: University of Chicago Press.

McNamara, Beverley, Charles Waddell, and Margaret Colvin (1994) 'The Institutionalization of the Good Death', *Social Science and Medicine*, 39(11): 1501–08.

Mesler, Mark A. and Pameal, J. Miller (2000) 'Hospice and Assisted Suicide: The Structure and Process of an Inherent Dilemma', *Death Studies*, 24: 135–55.

Muller, Jessica (1982) 'Shades of Blue: The Negotiation of Limited Codes by Medical Residents', *Social Science and Medicine,* 1992(34): 8.

Munley, A. (1983) *The Hospice Alternative: A New Context for Death and Dying.* New York: Basic Books.

Mykytyn, Courtney Everts (2006) 'Anti-Aging Medicine: A Patient/Practitioner Movement to Redefine Aging', *Social Science and Medicine,* 62: 643–55.

Parker-Oliver, Debra (1999–2000) 'The Social Construction of The "Dying Role" and the Hospice Drama', *Omega,* 40(4): 493–512.

Pescosolido, Bernice A. and Robert Mendelsohn (1986) 'Social Causation or Social Construction of Suicide? An Investigation into the Social Organization of Official Rates', *American Sociological Review,* 51: 80–101.

Phillips, David P. and Todd E. Ruth (1993) 'Adequacy of Official Suicide Statistics for Scientific Research and Public Policy', *Suicide and Life-Threatening Behavior,* 23(4): 307–19.

Prentice, Rachel (2005) 'The Anatomy of a Surgical Stimulation: The Mutual Articulation of Bodies in and Through the Machine', *Social Studies of Science,* 35(6): 837–66.

Rier, David (2000) 'The Missing Voice of the Critically Ill: A Medical Sociologist's Fist-Person Account', *Sociology of Health and Illness,* 22(1): 68–93.

Rose, Nicolas (1989) *Governing the Soul.* London: Free Association Books.

Rosenthal, G.E., Kaboli, P.J., Barnett, M.J. and Sirio C.A. (2002) 'Age and the Risk of in-Hospital Death: Insights from a Multihospital Study of Intensive Care Patients', *Journal of the American Geriatrics Society,* 50(7): 1205–12.

Sartre, Jean-Paul (1966) *Being and Nothingness: A Phenomenological Essay on Ontology.* New York: Pocket Books.

Saunders, Cicely (1978) (ed.) *The Management of Terminal Disease.* London: Arnold.

Scheper-Hughes, Nancy (1992) *Death Without Weeping.* Berkeley, CA: University of California Press.

Scitovsky, Anne A. (1984) 'The High Cost of Dying: What Do the Data Show?', *The Milbank Quarterly,* 62(4): 591–608.

Seale, Clive (1991) 'A Comparison of Hospice and Conventional Care', *Social Science and Medicine,* 32(2): 147–52.

—— (2000) 'Changing Patterns of Death and Dying', *Social Science and Medicine,* 51(6): 917–30.

Seymour, Jane (2001) *Critical Moments: Death and Dying in Intensive Care.* Buckingham, UK: Open University Press.

Siebold, C. (1992) *The Hospice Movement: Easing Death's Pain.* New York: Twayne.

Strauss, Anselm L. and Barney G. Glaser (1970) *Anguish.* San Francisco: Sociology Press.

Sudnow, David (1967) *Passing On: The Social Organization of Dying.* Englewood Cliffs, NJ: Prentice-Hall, Inc.

Teno, J., Lynn, J., Wenger, N., Phillips, R.S., Murphy, D.P., Jr. Connors, A.F., Desbiens, N., Fulkerson, W., Bellamy, P. and Knaus, W.A. (1997) 'Advance Directives for Seriously Ill Hospitalized Patients: Effectiveness with the Patient Self-Determination Act and the Support Intervention. Support Investigators. Study to Understand Prognoses and Preferences for Outcomes and Risks of Treatment', *Journal of the American Geriatrics Society,* 45(4): 500–07.

Tercier, J. (2002) 'The Lips of the Dead and the "Kiss of Life": The Contemporary Deathbed and the Aesthetic of CPR', *Journal of Historical Sociology,* 15(3): 283–327.

Timmermans, Stefan (1993) 'The Paradox of Nursing Terminal Patients in a General Belgian Hospital'. *Omega,* 27(4): 281–93.

—— (1999) *Sudden Death and the Myth of CPR.* Philadelphia, PA: Temple University Press.

—— (2005) 'Suicide Determination and the Professional Authority of Medical Examiners', *American Sociological Review,* 70(2): 311–33.

—— (2005) 'Death Brokering: Constructing Culturally Appropriate Deaths', *Sociology of Health and Illness,* 27(7): 993–1013.

Tolstoy, Leo (1960) *The Death of Ivan Illych.* New York: Penguin.

Tsai, E. (2002) 'Should Family Members Be Present During Cardiopulmonary Resuscitation?', *New England Journal of Medicine,* 346(March 28): 1019–21.
Twycross, R.G. (1982) 'Ethical and Clinical Aspects of Pain Treatment in Cancer Patients', *Acta Anaesthesiology Scandinavia*, 26(Suppl. 74): 83–90.
Vovelle, Michel (1983) *La Mort Et L'occident: De 1300 a Nos Jours.* Paris: Gallimard.
Zola, Irving, K. (1972) 'Studying the Decision to See a Doctor'. In *Advances in Psychosomatic Medicine*, edited by Z. Lipowski, 216–36. Basel: Karger.
Zussman, Robert (1992) *Intensive Care.* Chicago: University of Chicago Press.

2

Healer–Patient Interaction: New Mediations in Clinical Relationships

Arthur W. Frank, Michael K. Corman,
Jessica A. Gish and Paul Lawton[1]

INTRODUCTION

This chapter is about how interactions between patients and healers have become increasingly mediated by forces – seen or unseen, recognized or unknown – that have become presences in consulting and treatment rooms. We begin by providing a historical look into patient–healer interactions to set the scene for changes in how persons become patients, and how patients relate to healers in recent years. Next, we address the capacity of different qualitative methods for exposing the challenges and opportunities brought on by these new mediations or presences in the patient–healer interaction. The utility of three qualitative methods – Institutional Ethnography, traditional ethnography, and Actor-Network Theory – is demonstrated by showing how these methods allow recognition and analysis of mediating forces in healer–patient interactions.

A strong point of qualitative research is its ability to make known what becomes taken-for-granted or familiar in patient–healer interactions. Qualitative methods make explicit the interpretive frameworks used in patient–healer inter-actions. By investigating people in their everyday actions – by talking with people about what they do or observing people doing things or the different technologies they use – the organization of knowledge implicit in these actions can be problematized and explicated. In doing so, qualitative researchers reveal important differences in what counts for healers and patients in clinical interactions. Thorough observation and analysis helps recognize complexities and the differential effects of multiple mediations in patient–healer interactions.

FROM PROFESSIONS TO MEDIATIONS

Study of healer–patient interactions goes back at least to the 1930s, when Harvard physician and teacher of sociology L.J. Henderson described interactions between physicians and patients as processes of mutual feedback, in which each is constantly affecting the behaviour of the other. Henderson's pioneering observations were taken up, but also redirected, by Talcott Parsons, who has as great a claim as anyone to being the founder of medical sociology. Because Parsons' theoretical interest was in how the professions reflected the distinctive potential of modernity, he focused on physicians as the epitome and paradigm of professional work.

Parsons understood interactions between physicians and patients to be mediated by normative role expectations that are shared throughout a society. The success of an interaction depends on the degree to which each participant has internalized appropriate role expectations. On the patient side, the 'sick role' balances legitimated withdrawal from normal work obligations against the expectation of becoming a patient: seeking and complying with medical diagnosis and treatment. On the physician side, role expectations included evaluating patients according to universal criteria (e.g., professionally standardized diagnoses), taking a specific interest in medical issues rather than a diffuse interest in the person's whole life, and remaining emotionally detached. These qualities allowed patients to reveal themselves, both physically and emotionally, without embarrassment.

Parsons (1951) understood medicine as a practice of *social control*: physicians legitimate but also must regulate their patients' withdrawal from normal role obligations during periods of illness. Physicians have a dual responsibility, both to the welfare of individual patients and to society's interest in restoring patients to productive health. In Parsons' view, trust and social control are able to coexist, because patients can reliably trust professionals' social control as being in patients' best interest. Parsons revised his ideas throughout his long career (see Parsons, 1978; Frank, 1991), but the presuppositions of his writing remain remarkably consistent.

The most influential studies of the 1970–80s perpetuated Parsonian interests in professions, medicine as a form of control, and the importance of trust, although observations of specific clinical practices often contradicted Parsons. Already in the 1950s, Erving Goffman (1961) undercut the claim to medicine's professional distinctiveness by emphasizing comparisons between medicine and other 'tinkering trades'. Eliot Freidson (1970) emphasized how physicians' livelihood depends on referral networks; their orientations to patients' interests are mixed with an orientation to the interests of their medical colleagues who refer those patients to them. Moreover, Freidson directed attention to patients' lay referral networks that exist outside the medical system; patients, he observed, are also examining doctors and consulting with each other.

Elliot Mishler (1984) analyzed transcriptions of physician–patient talk to demonstrate the radical differences between what he called the *lifeworld* of patients and the voice of medicine. What counts for Mishler are not shared role expectations, which Parsons looks for and thus finds, but interaction as a meeting of discrepant attitudes towards sickness and treatment. Howard Waitzkin (1991), also using discourse analysis of taped clinical sessions, reverses Parsons' attitude towards the social control functions of medicine. The control that is a functional necessity for Parsons becomes an imposition for Waitzkin, who demonstrates how physicians impose values on their patients. Waitzkin is especially insightful about the processes by which people are taught how to be the patients that medicine wants them to be, so that medicine can proceed with its agenda. Following Marxist philosopher Louis Althusser, Waitzkin (1991) writes how the person who enters the medical office is *interpellated* into the role of patient – the person is called to act like and to think of him or herself as a patient, with all the qualifications of that identity. Thus, physician–patient interaction begins with interactions between patients and receptionists; the old Parsonian professional boundaries are shown to be inadequate conceptualizations of interaction processes.

Especially significant for this chapter is Irving Zola's 1973 article, 'Pathways to the doctor – from person to patient' (Zola, 1989). Zola's interest was in how physicians select who will be designated as legitimately ill and treatable, from among the multitude of potential patients. Citing research showing that after medical examinations of a significant sample of 'supposedly healthy people', 'there was scarcely an individual who did not possess some symptom, some clinical entity worthy of treatment', Zola is led to 'rather uncomfortable sense in which we may to some degree be sick every day of our lives' (1989: 224). In an age of multiple risk factors, this 'uncomfortable sense' has become more pervasive for more people, most of the time.

Zola makes at least two assumptions that mark the distance between the time of his research and the present, and that lead to the concerns of this chapter. First, Zola (1989: 236) assumes that physicians decide who will 'become a case'. Physicians are the sole mediators of how, from among 'the many eligible, so few are chosen'. Complementary to that, he assumes a dichotomy between patient and non-patient. Today, neither assumption is clear-cut. In many aspects of medical practice, especially tertiary care in hospitals, what seems to have changed is not the reality of medical selection, but rather the increasingly impersonal basis of those selections in an age of textually mediated, evidence-based standards of diagnosis and treatment. Qualitative observation of clinical sessions shows that Parsonian universalism – judging the present case according to universal standards of judgment – has reached a level that would probably trouble Parsons, because it bypasses the professionalism of individual practitioners and thus undermines trust in the professional relationship.

Nevertheless, the contemporary scene is hardly monolithic. Contradicting this impersonally mediated selection processes are consumer-driven, fee-for-service medical practices, illustrated by cosmetic surgery, which represents the leading edge of healing work in which patient–consumers self-select. Healers retain residual rights to refuse to treat, but the power of selection has clearly shifted: today, many are eligible, and the few are self-selected.

Zola's 'few are chosen' assumption – his apparent dichotomy between patients and non-patients – is further complicated by health work that proliferates possibilities of being a patient outside of direct medical supervision. Today, medical legitimation of patienthood is not always required. Any person, even if not the diagnosed patient of some particular physician, can continue to seek diagnostic information, join groups of fellow-sufferers, and search treatment possibilities. The Internet extends, and makes affordable, consumer-driven medicine, allowing people themselves to decide how far to follow pathways of self-diagnosis, decisions about optimal treatment, and, as online pharmaceutical sales increase, even self-medication (with attendant risks, both in obtaining the drugs and in ingesting them). Crucially, people have limited control over the design of any particular pathway they follow, but they have greater choice among multiple predesigned and readily accessible pathways.

This chapter demonstrates the utility of qualitative methods in tracking changes in how persons become patients, and how patients relate to healers. By *mediations*, we look beyond internalized norms, asking instead: *What external, material forces affect how healers and patients interact? What mediates who healer and patient feel themselves able be, in relation to each other?* Our emphasis is anticipated by Anselm Strauss and colleagues' (1985) interest in the *work* that people do, the scope of research interest expanding to include multiple medical workers, patients, and families. We consider interaction in healing settings the variety of which strains old boundaries of what counts as medical. Boundary strains are very much our concern. In the twenty-first century, healer–patient interactions both reflect and negotiate boundaries that all parties are somewhat unsure of, just as everyone is unsure what other seen or unseen presences are in the room, affecting what happens.

We begin with the external mediators that healers and patients are most readily aware of: written texts through which administrative, managerial interests impose themselves on clinical interactions at moments that include diagnosis, treatment, and reimbursements. This section demonstrates the particular capacity of Institutional Ethnography as a qualitative method to study how interactions are affected by the proliferation of texts that prescribe what can happen between healers and patients, and specify the categories and formats in which the interaction must be reported. Second, we consider cosmetic surgery as exemplifying the consumer-driven medicine of enhancement: medicine that seeks to improve bodies rather than simply restoring them (Parens, 1998). Our third external mediator is the proliferating collection known as information and communication technology (ICT). ICT has brought a new actor – the computer – into patient–healer interactions, and it is changing the distribution of expertise and the quality of healer–patient asymmetry. The method known as Actor Network Theory (ANT) is effective for research on how ICT mediates healer–patient interactions, especially in the creation of what are called expert patients.

We make no claims that these three forms of mediation are new, although we do claim each has crossed a threshold at which its effects have become qualitatively different in significance (Frank, 2005). Nor do we claim that these three forms are the only new mediations changing how healers and patients interact; other mediators certainly exist and may be more significant. We do claim that qualitative methods are not only effective but also actually necessary to study these new mediations, though again there are more contemporary methodological innovations than this chapter can possibly review. We present what are three case studies of new mediations in healer–patient interaction, as indicators of the changing nature of clinical work.

TEXTUAL MEDIATORS IN CLINICAL INTERACTIONS

Institutional ethnography problematizes the everyday world by focusing on the often invisible complex of text-mediated and regulated relations – technologies of knowledge and governance – that organize and coordinate people's everyday doings (Smith, 1987; 2005; for a more detailed description of institutional ethnography, refer to Campbell's chapter in this volume). For instance, in health care settings, healers and patients do not interact as two people responding only to each other; each activates and is activated by a diversity of texts. Medical records track specific information, including history of previous illnesses, blood pressure and chemistry, heart rate, and medications administered. Forms fulfil administrative purposes including billing, and they signify completion of a required task or procedure. Referrals are texts that allow patients to access specialized treatments, services, and supports. Some of these texts are clearly visible to both patient and healer, other texts are visible to one but invisible to the other, and some texts may be virtually invisible to both.

Texts are integral to healthcare's shift towards practices based on principles of evidence-based medicine (Mykhalovskiy and Weir, 2004) and other forms of new managerialism that privilege specific ways of knowing and doing (Campbell, 2001; Rankin, 2001; Rankin and Campbell, 2006). As one example, consider the sequence of events between a child suspected of having autism spectrum disorder (hereafter simply 'autism'), a proxy patient (the mother of the child), and healers (including a psychologist, paediatrician, social worker, speech–language pathologist, and perhaps others). A mother seeks help, motivated by concerns about her child's development – 'things just weren't right'. Referrals are written by institutionally appropriate healers based on a suspicion of autism. A sequence of referrals eventually allows the mother and child to officially enter into the assessment stage of the diagnostic process of autism. She calls the assessment centre, an appointment is made, and a specialized, multi-disciplinary diagnostic team is assembled to assess the child and the mother's experiences in an attempt to determine if the child fits the diagnosis of autism. This process can take weeks, months, or even years.

The sequence of what happens is organized by specific texts that claim authority as 'evidence-based' and prescribe procedural standards (Timmermans and Berg, 2003); one such local example is *Standards and Guidelines* (British Columbia Ministry of Health Planning, 2003). Such guidelines specify how, during the assessment stage of the diagnostic process, a specifically accredited psychologist conducts a 'standardized, structured caregiver interview'. Interaction begins when the psychologist picks up the *Autism Diagnostic Interview-Revised* (ADI-R). This text determines what questions are asked, what count as answers, and how to assign scores, leading to a diagnostic outcome. The ADI-R, described as the 'gold standard' in autism diagnoses (Reaven et al., 2008), is designed to identify what another, more generalized text, the *Diagnostic and Statistical Manual of Mental Disorders, Fourth Edition* (American Psychiatric Association, 1994), has already specified as the key signs of autism.

These texts, and others like them, are activated by people; once activated, texts 'occur' in the course of the work of patients and healers, thereby mediating interactions (Smith, 1990; 2006). The mediating work of texts opens up the autism diagnosis scene, described earlier, making it more than a face-to-face interaction between persons who are co-present. Examples from studies of hospital nursing and nursing-home care clarify the mediating work of texts highlighting the capacity of institutional ethnography and the tools of interviewing, observation and textual analysis to make visible these ruling relations and how they work.

Textual mediators in hospital nursing

Janet Rankin and Marie Campbell's (2006) research on how health-reform practices affect nurses' work explores what they call technologies of management and governance in hospital settings. These technologies include: *tracking systems* that record admissions, discharges, and transfers of patients (ADT); *clinical pathways* that specify what happens on which days, culminating in discharge; and *alternative levels of care* designations that attempt to determine 'appropriate' levels of care for patients and where they are to be located in hospitals (acute care vs. recovery beds). For example, Rankin and Campbell demonstrate the power of a clinical pathway by describing the experience of a nurse, Trudy. After some days off, Trudy returns to work and is supposed to discharge an elderly patient recovering from surgery into the care of his wife (proxy patient). Despite expressing concerns about discharging this patient – 'I think his wife is going to have her hands full' (2006: 65) – Trudy's interaction with her patient and proxy patient is mediated by the textual presence of a clinical pathway that dictates 'on day seven, he is to be discharged' (2006: 66).

In addition to mediating interactions, texts mediate what is known and what counts as knowable. Knowing is no longer based on first-hand knowledge, but rather on 'knowing in text-mediated ways' (Campbell and Gregor, 2002: 36), transforming what is experienced into 'virtual' or textual realities (Campbell and Gregor, 2002). This social organization of knowledge mediates healers' 'views and responses to patient care' (Rankin and Campbell, 2006: 20). Rankin and Campbell (2006: 20–21) explain this in the context of nursing:

> Nurses who activate the text-mediated processes that categorize patients learn to treat people as instances of the categories, absorbing as their own the perspective of restructuring with its valuing of 'efficiency'. ... Nurses' *consciousness is restructured* as they become agents of the restructuring technologies. (emphases added)

Returning to Trudy, the clinical pathway transforms her concerns about discharging her patient to his wife, because Trudy has to 'mediate the care of her patient through the requirements of the clinical pathway' (2006: 72). Texts connect what healers and patients know to broader administrative and managerial regimes, determining what does and does not get acted upon and how action proceeds.

Texts, actions and reporting

Timothy Diamond's *Making Gray Gold* (1992) demonstrates how texts mediate the interactional work between nursing assistants and residents in long-term care facilities. Diamond's (1992: 1) interest in the social organization of nursing homes began during his 'leisurely weekend mornings' at a coffee shop; he overheard nursing assistants talk and began to speak with them about their work during their break from the nursing homes in which they worked. These initial conversations constituted for him what institutional ethnographers call the *problematic* (see Smith, 2005); they activated his interest in nursing home life, specifically how everyday happenings in nursing homes were organized. In order to explore and explicate his problematic, Diamond sought training as a nursing assistant and obtained employment as an assistant in various nursing homes through which he observed, talked to (DeVault and McCoy, 2002), and reflected upon his work with residents and staff. Of interest here is how Diamond's ethnographic work helped him to investigate the mediating work of texts in patient–healer interactions.

For example, Diamond discusses a variety of patient–healer interactions, including nursing assistants waking up residents or giving them baths, toileting residents, leading exercise groups for residents, and preparing residents to be seen by visitors. His insider knowledge as a worker in the nursing home allows him to recognize how these patient–healer interactions are organized by specific texts, including schedules that standardize weekly routines and charts that direct assistants when to take a resident's blood pressure and other vitals.

Diamond describes a sequence of interactions mediated by a Board of Health Directive at one of the facilities where he worked as an assistant. 'Restraint and Position sheets' in the charts had to 'be completed and signed every two hours of the twenty-four hour day' (Diamond, 1992: 88). These sheets determined when bedridden residents received 'the crucial gesture of turning them to one of three rotating positions so as to make at least a formal attempt at circumventing bed-sores' (1992: 88). For residents who were not bedridden, nursing assistants had to record that they were 'up with restraints. "Up" meant out of bed, but the only real up was there on the records; in actual practice it meant down, that is, secured into the chair. In writing this into the records down became up …' (1992: 88). The interactions between nursing assistants and residents reflected links between chart entries and more generalized ideas of 'quality of care'. The nursing facility and other governing agencies authorize not only specific knowledge, but also how this knowledge is made observable and recordable: what is recorded as being done displaces and subsumes what actually happened. The texts that effect this displacement thus form 'the contours of the job, both in doing the prescribed work and in certifying that it had been done' (Diamond, 1992: 160).

Material interaction becomes virtual reality

Healer–patient interactions are increasing mediated by texts, whether these are evidence-based standards and guidelines, technologies of management and governance that have transformed nursing work, or standardized schedules and charts that mediate the work of nursing home assistants and residents. Immediate, specific, face-to-face knowledge and judgment is displaced by textual authority exercised from a distance, and this displacement is troubling to institutional ethnographers. Institutional ethnography directs attention to exploring and explicating how text-based mediations affect interactions between healers and patients in any healthcare setting.

IMAGES AS MEDIATORS OF DESIRE AND PRACTICE

Cosmetic surgery is not a new form of medicine (Davis, 2003), but its contemporary expansion exemplifies how consumer desire for new medical products and provider desire for increased revenues (Sullivan, 2001) mutually reinforce each other. Cosmetic surgery practice introduces new mediators and problems of mediation into the healer–patient interaction. We first consider two-dimensional images, then a diagnostic category from the Diagnostic and Statistical Manual of Mental Disorders (DSM), and finally the debate over how women are positioned as users of cosmetic surgery. As elsewhere in this chapter, the mediations discussed here are by no means exhaustive but reflect how qualitative research reveals significant aspects of a clinical practice that is changing expectations for healer–patient interactions.

Patients' desire

In traditional medicine, the patient is animated by bodily breakdown. In cosmetic enhancements, the patient is animated by desire; but what animates this desire? Virginia Blum (2003) exemplifies scholars who focus on patients' motivation for treatment. For Blum, cosmetic surgery is linked to celebrity culture. The new mediator is the *two-dimensional* image that directs and enables patients and surgeons to look for beauty, or at least normality, in surfaces. Blum draws upon multiple qualitative research materials: interviews with patients and plastic surgeons, observations of actual surgeries, and popular culture texts, especially films, to understand how patients and healers work differently with the quality of two-dimensionality.

Patients' desire for surgical intervention – their sense of themselves as appropriate patients – begins in popular culture: movies, television, novels, websites, and magazines. Star culture, as materialized in two-dimensional images, creates 'as-if' beauty personalities. On Blum's account (2003: 101), patients who desire surgery have 'engaged in the cultural goal of becoming photographable'.[2] For all that is new about the transmission of images, Blum's argument returns to Parsons' emphasis on the internalization of cultural standards, those standards instigating a motivation to interact within prescribed parameters.

Two-dimensional images affect surgeons differently as they go about their work. From the perspective of patients, surgery may be about personal or physical transformation, but the surgeon is attempting the 'realignment of what constitutes the surface' (Blum, 2003: 71). The use of television screens and digital imaging during surgery allows the body to be turned inside out through projection onto the screen. Two-dimensional images, found both on screens and in surgeons' freehand sketches, make possible surgical alteration. Blum (2003: 93) writes of patients: 'in the end we are all reduced to photographs, and the surgeon is our superphotographer who will correct all our worst angles, capture in the right light the most fleeting glimpse of our perfection'. Alternatively, in enhancement medicine, the healer is a craftsperson who realizes a version of the patient's desire.

Diagnostic categories

However, are all patients' desires *healthy*? That question becomes another mediator in interactions between enhancement healers and their patients. Victoria Pitts-Taylor (2007) shows, through interviews and content analysis of popular, medical, legal and specialty texts, how both surgeons and patients must negotiate the boundary between cosmetic wellness and psychic pathology. This boundary has no other external referent, but one crucial mediator is the diagnostic category of Body Dysmorphic Disorder (BDD), which both reflects and intensifies public perception that cosmetic surgery can become an addiction. Pitts-Taylor describes how surgeons' relations with patients are affected not only by television reality programs like *Extreme Makeover* – on which viewers send personal stories and those selected receive extensive medical and dental surgeries, making before and after appearances on the program – but more directly by public legal conflicts over responsibility for surgical addiction. 'Whatever the reality, the term [BDD] has become a readily available code for any surgery or patient considered crazy or disturbing' (Pitts-Taylor, 2007: 112).

To understand how cosmetic surgery addiction matters to surgeons and patients, Pitts-Taylor interviews patients, surgeons, and psychiatrists, and she analyzes materials produced by professional associations and legal documents. Predictably, surgeons want patients who will be happy with the results of surgery in spite of scaring, one undesirable side effect of surgery. Unhappy patients have the potential of leading to malpractice suits. One example is the case of Dr. Hugo, who performed multiple surgeries over the course of several years on Lynn G., who sued him for performing surgery on someone with BDD. The case of *Lynn vs. Hugo* was settled before trial, but the court's willingness to hear the case affects surgeons' awareness of their responsibility to identify patients with BDD and refuse treatment. Yet, if BDD puts surgeons at legal risk, the diagnostic category also works to their benefit, because it provides surgeons with a justification for refusing to treat patients they perceive as potentially difficult to satisfy.

Diagnostic categories bring in their wake screening tools that have the potential to help surgeons identify patients with BDD, but such tools remain limited in application. One surgeon explains:

> These patients sitting in my waiting room, I've got what they want. They're not going to answer these questions. They want to have surgery. They're not going to admit they think about their nose twelve hours a day (Pitts-Taylor, 2007: 118).

Thus, the DSM category mediates the surgeon–patient interaction twice over: it not only marks those who are difficult patients for physicians, but also teaches patients how surgeons want them to be. Patients know that they must appear to be good surgical candidates if surgery is to happen.

Agency in an age of consumer-driven medicine

In medical treatments for illness or trauma, the patient's motivation is self-evidently to repair the body. Cosmetic surgery complicates the question of motive, and with it the issue of agency: what kind of *agents* are such patients? Davis (1995), in what remains the most extensive interview study that focuses exclusively on cosmetic-surgery patients, argued that women are active, self-aware, strategic users of surgeons' services. Bordo (2003), anticipating Blum's (2003) arguments discussed in the foregoing section, agrees that women describe surgical decisions in a language of agency, but these women's sense of value and potential action has already been crucially limited by pervasive standards of beauty that have been internalized. Each makes a valid point in this argument that has roots in theological debates about free will and Marxist ideas of false consciousness, but motivational analysis reaches an impasse. Researchers tend to find confirmation of their prior theoretical positions.

Suzanne Fraser (2003) moves beyond this impasse by examining cosmetic surgery *discourse*: her focus is the limits of what it is possible to say at a particular cultural moment about cosmetic surgery. Instead of assessing women's motives for having surgery, Fraser emphasizes culturally available rhetorics of motives, examining popular culture and professional texts rather than interviewing patients or healers, whose accounts could only reproduce the discourse that these texts make available. The potential of discourse analysis is its ability to discover how concepts like agency are 'constructed in culture' (Fraser, 2003: 112). Fraser analyzes four domains of writing about cosmetic surgery – women's magazines, feminist literature, medical material, and regulatory documents – showing how different forms of writing produce preferred readings. Predictably, women's magazines present a wider range of options about women's agency than do medical and feminist writing.

Medicine may credit women as able to assess the risks of surgery and be in control of their destiny, but surgeons still control access to surgical procedures and information about procedures. Women's autonomy is ultimately tied to the judgment of the surgeon and 'rearticulated within the supposedly reasonable limits set by the surgeon' (Fraser, 2003: 193). For example, surgery can be denied if a woman is found to be having surgery to satisfy her husband. One surgeon writes in medical journal, as reported by Fraser:

> [C]areful review of those who did not respond positively revealed that the surgery was carried out to please someone else, and the operation failed to satisfy the other party (Fraser, 2003: 141).

Blum (2003), Pitts-Taylor (2007), and Fraser (2003) each incorporate a variety of methods (interviews, discourse analysis, observation) and sources (magazines, novels, films, legal documents). As the mediators of clinical interactions become increasingly diverse, qualitative methods need to be equally diverse, to understand how the patient–healer interaction is mediated. As healer–patient interactions are increasingly affected by the perspectives and doings of people who are neither health care professionals nor patients – whether these are administrators, lawyers and courts, or producers of popular culture – only the broadest range of methods can observe and report on these mediations.

THE COMPUTER AS THIRD PARTY IN INTERACTIONS

Information and communications technology (ICT) has become a crucial mediator in patient–healer interactions, with unlimited scope for expanded influence; qualitative research has only recently started looking into the consequences of this mediation. For patients, ICT use includes direct consultation with healing professionals, online searches for symptoms and treatments, participation in support groups, and consumption, including ordering prescription drugs. For healers, ICT makes possible quick reference to up-to-date medication lists, the use of electronic patient records and associated notes, electronic decision support, and access to state of the art research materials (Burstin, 2000). For both healers and patients, ICT use mediates interaction by allowing access to *more*: more information and more support.

ICT becomes increasingly present in consulting rooms because of the growing implementation of electronic health records (EHR). Ventres et al. make the strong claim that EHR becomes 'much like a third party to a conversation, which has its own separate identity in the encounter … both physicians and patients project their perceptions onto this identity' (2006: 130). Blumenthal and Glaser argue that doctors who use EHR have 'the information they need to make good decisions at the exact time and place they need it, and computerized decision support will ensure that they use that information to make and implement correct decisions' (2007: 2528). Reports from doctors using EHR and other forms of ICT in their practice support this claim (Burstin, 2000; Gans et al., 2005), as do patients whose doctors have switched to electronic records (Lee et al., 2005).

Bringing ICT into the patient–healer interaction is, however, not without costs to the quality of interaction. Using ethnographic methods, Ventres et al. (2006) found that doctors using EHR worried about computer systems 'pulling' them away from the interaction, and 'interfering' with developing a relationship with some patients. This interference can occur in subtle but consequential forms, such as a physician walking straight to the computer monitor after briefly greeting a patient. Most physicians share these concerns, but the potential benefits of computer usage, such as avoiding missed diagnoses and unnecessary tests, outweigh worries about an electronic third party entering into healer–patient interaction.

ICT also makes possible new forms and intensity of patient *health work* that takes place outside of interactions with healers, but later affects those interactions. Health work includes the extensive mental, emotional, and physical activities undertaken by people in their day-to-day efforts to look after themselves and to sustain their health (Mykhalovskiy and McCoy, 2002). Optimistic commentators claim the use of ICT in health work can be entirely positive and empowering for patients willing to engage these resources, as they are able to gain, maintain, and display familiarity with an extensive body of medical and experiential knowledge (Mead et al., 2003). The management and implementation of information and advice gathered using ICT, coupled with the ability to become technically proficient and discriminating users of this information, enable patients to display a new level of competence in living with illness and making self-care and treatment decisions (Ziebland et al., 2004).

Although healers rely upon patients maintaining a certain amount of knowledge and self-care, they become troubled by patients who gain too much expertise as a result of thorough health work. These so-called 'expert patients' present unique and complex challenges to the medical profession (Hardey, 2001; Kaplan and

Brennan, 2001; Fox et al., 2005). Expertise is especially important for patients who live with chronic illnesses like diabetes, and who have become 'implicated as responsible for their illness through discourses of individualism' (Wellard, 1998: 54). Given the time required to manage chronic illness, physicians need chronically ill patients to gain sufficient expertise to self-manage their illness day-to-day. They encourage patients to engage resources including ICT, even when many patients do not want to do the work involved in gaining the technical competence required in becoming an expert (Henwood et al., 2003).

Yet, self-reliance can upset compliance. Patients who engage ICT resources often gain, or believe they gain, more expertise than the health care providers who care for them. As a consequence, some medical professionals see the move towards the 'expert patient' as a threat, 'representing a loss of power within the consultation, in which a patient grasping printouts from the Internet entails a time-consuming negotiation of illness management' (Fox et al., 2005: 1308). Ethnographic work on Internet users suggest that a patient accessing information and support online does not necessarily result in a better healer–patient interaction, because patients who bring in information found online create situations leading to 'hostility, irritation, and a less satisfactory level of care' (Broom, 2005: 335). Far from being an unmitigated good, 'the Internet forms the site of a new struggle over expertise in health that will transform the relationship between health professionals and their clients' (Hardey, 1999: 820).

Despite these conflicts, the march of technology seems inexorable, and research must expand the list of actors that have demonstrable effects on health-care. Here we reach a fine line in how different theory/methods presented in this chapter direct research. In the foregoing sections, we saw how texts mediate healer–patient interactions; these texts were understood as activated by human actors. Institutional ethnography affords a privilege to human consciousness. Texts mediate interaction, but texts are second-class, or second-order, actors that require human activation. By contrast, ANT directs researchers not only to take account of the *non-human actors* in interaction, but also to afford these actors equal status with human actors. The presiding image is no longer a two-person interaction mediated by various other objects and effects, but rather a multi-actor network, in which any of the actors is made possible by other actors. Understanding patient–healer interaction begins by tracing how the ever growing numbers of heterogeneous materials (e.g., computers and printouts) and social practices (between patients and healers) enact *this* reality. All of the parties in the consulting room play their part, not just the human actors.

ANT is a theory/method that 'describes the enactment of materially and discursively heterogeneous relations that produce and reshuffle all kinds of actors including objects, subjects, human beings, machines, animals, 'nature', ideas, organizations, inequalities, scale and sizes, and geographical arrangements' (Law, 2007: 2). Within these clinical encounters, researchers can therefore account for an increasing multiplicity of actors (the computer running the EHR software, the stack of printouts, and advice gathered online, etc.), which hold a relatively new and still-controversial status. Researchers can also recognize and explore controversial new enactments of the clinical encounter such as when patients see their physician being 'pulled away' by the call of the screen, or when physicians feel forced to negotiate the stack of printouts brought in by their expert patients.

ANT is also well prepared to study the controversies generated by increasing ICT use; the present controversy, which may be displaced in the next several years, is the appropriate balance between necessity and threat that expert patients represent for healers. The study of controversies reveals opposing versions of reality, enabling understanding of why some versions become 'true' while others fade into obscurity (Garrety, 1997). An ANT study follows how actors *themselves* first generate and then stabilize controversies and uncertainties. The researcher seeks to gauge the numbers and natures of new actors, and how these old and new actors come together in assemblages to build formats and standards that become increasingly invisible, as they become non-controversial (Latour, 2005: 249). Movement towards stabilization of controversy is illustrated on the healer side of the interaction by professional attempts to accept and incorporate the initially contested use of ICT. For example, online sites such as *The Medscape Journal of Medicine* feature regular articles advising physicians on how to manage email with patients (Gaster et al., 2003; Patt et al., 2003; Brooks and Menachemi, 2006), and how to advise patients' on-line searches (Cotten and Gupta, 2004; Shaw and Baker, 2004). Such online sites/articles help to stabilize, and thus to make true, a reality in which ICT is part of the patient–healer interaction, and in turn present new opportunities for qualitative research.

Among the consequences of recognizing the non-human actors who enter into healer–patient interactions, research will inevitably contribute to the increasing *deauratization* of medicine; physicians will lose the mystique that exclusive access to knowledge once gave them. Patients' access to health information, once mediated by a small group of physician colleagues, is now mediated by multiple sources, sometimes including patients themselves. Many patients, on at least some days, find increased abilities to access information and share experiences with other patients to be empowering. For those patients on other days, and for some patients on any day, becoming an expert patient is a burden they are unwilling or unable to assume. Healers will have to deal with expert patients bringing in outside, and variously verified information, and these dealings can be both a promise of more collaborative relationships and a threat of endless contests over treatment availability and appropriateness. Using theory/methods like ANT, researchers have the ability to provide enriched description that account for *all* of the actors at work in clinical encounters, human and non-human.

MEDIATIONS AND MIRAGES

Healer–patient interactions have always been mediated, but we argue that the mediators are becoming increasingly intrusive and determinative. What happens *during* interaction is substantially affected by what happens *outside* interaction. Qualitative methods are well suited for turning observations into narratives and revealing the complexity and quality of these new mediations.

The mediators we have described are significant, but they are neither the only ones nor the most significant ones. Perhaps our most consequential omission has been financial mediators, which lurk behind all three of our cases. Hedgecoe's (2007) title expresses this mediation well: 'It's the money that matters: the financial context of ethical decision-making in modern biomedicine'. It is the money that leads to attempted clinical micro-management at a distance through standardized texts; it is the money that drives cosmetic surgery, whether that is paid for the procedure or anticipated as the asset of an improved body; and it is the money that drives ICT, although different participants anticipate different payoffs, and how money is made becomes increasingly complex. If one aspect of the contemporary scene makes the assumptions of mid-twentieth-century medical sociology seem wholly outdated, that would be money: not simply the amount of money (health costs as a proportion of some measure of total expenditures), but also the multiple sources of payoff for an increasing multitude of financially interested parties. Each source of payoff becomes a mediator in healer–patient interactions.

We conclude on two issues: so-called shared decision-making between healers and patients, and what philosopher Hans-Georg Gadamer (1996) called 'the enigma of health'. For it is this enigma – health as combination of desire, illusion, science, and possibility – that is the core of healer–patient interaction. Qualitative methods have traditionally shown a capacity to bring philosophical insights like Gadamer's into the scope of empirical research, enriching the capacity of researchers to see all that can be seen.

How treatment decisions are shared between healers and patients has been a topic of voluminous research investigation and commentary since the model proposed by Szasz and Hollander (1956). Our three studies of new mediations in clinical interactions suggest that decision-making might be better thought of as *distributed* rather than *shared*. Shared implies a dyadic process of communication, in which options are explored, expertise is invoked, preferences and values are mutually acknowledged, and finally a decision is reached. All this happens, certainly. Yet, what happens depends on multiple other mediators, including but hardly limited to the ones explored in this chapter. The distribution metaphor is spatial, implicating multiple sites, as opposed to the normative and communicative metaphor of sharing. For sharing to occur, as a normative goal that we affirm, healers and patients must work through, and across, multiple distributions.

The idea of distributed decision-making best captures how our mediators effect differences between what affects the respective actions of healers and patients. To return to our examples: a mother knows her child's development is 'not quite right', even if the child 'fails' to meet prescribed diagnostic criteria, but these criteria determine the healer's assessment. Cosmetic surgeons and their patients are each affected by two-dimensional images, but each is guided by different images – one an image of desire, the other an image of technical feasibility – and their respective assessments of results may differ according to these images. Moreover, in an age of ICT, both healers and patients have their own, different sources of what they understand as expert information and peer advice.

Qualitative methods have the capacity to open up new problematics of practice, and our three studies of contemporary medicine, taken together, suggest the increasing complexity of what people expect of *health* and healing. A classic work in the foundation of bioethics was Jay Katz's (2002) *The Silent World of Doctor and Patient*, originally published in 1984. To borrow Katz's trope, in a medical milieu of increasingly pervasive mediators, investigators can predict an inverse relationship between the number of voices competing for recognition and authority in healthcare interactions, and the quality of dialogue – the communicative mutual recognition that exceeds interaction (Frank, 2004) – between patients and healers. Patients and healers can be predicted to face increasing difficulty knowing and making sense of which voices affect each other. Or, to adapt Mishler's (1984) trope, in order to make sense of differences between the voices *of* medicine (now diverse healers) and of the lifeworld, researchers must attend to the different voices heard by healers and by patients, and how each is compelled differently by those respective voices.

The proliferation of health information and medical services complicates achieving common understandings of *health*, which may well be the most overloaded word in the modern lexicon, as multiple interests appropriate it. Qualitative methods are necessary when dealing with overloaded words that mean different things to different people, and *health* now has very different meanings. We return to the conclusion offered in 1973 by Irving Zola, in the article discussed earlier in this chapter. Zola (1989: 236) writes: 'the cure for all men's ills seems right over the next hill. Yet … this vision is only a mirage and the sooner we realize it the better'. The mediators described in this chapter all create mirages – whether of a cure or of an external locus of certainty and accountability – that seem tangibly objective, attainable, and even necessary. Are we – both potential patients and increasingly diffuse participants in the work of healing – even further from realizing the truth of which Zola reminds us? This question, bridging social science, policy, the philosophy, and ethics, is so nuanced that only qualitative methods can begin to unpack it. Yet, that unpacking has crucially practical implications for what patients expect to receive and what healers expect to provide.

NOTES

1 All authors contributed to revision of the final manuscript, but primary authorial responsibility was: Frank for the introduction and conclusion, as well as being the primary editor; Corman for texts and institutional ethnography; Gish for cosmetic surgery and images; and Lawton for information and communication technology and Actor Network Theory. Corman wishes to thank Janet Rankin for her comments on his section.

2 For an alternative account of patients' motivation, see Davis, 1995.

REFERENCES

American Psychiatric Association (1994) *Diagnostic and Statistical Manual of Mental Disorder*, 4th Edition. Washington, DC: American Psychiatric Association.

Blum, V. L. (2003) *Flesh Wounds: The Culture of Cosmetic Surgery*. Berkeley, CA: University of California Press.

Blumenthal, D. and Glaser, J.P. (2007) 'Information Technology Comes to Medicine', *New England Journal of Medicine*, 356(24): 2527–34.

Bordo, S. (2003 [1993]) *Unbearable Weight. Feminism, Western Culture, and the Body*. Berkeley, CA: University of California Press.

British Columbia Ministry of Health Planning (2003) *Standards and Guidelines for the Assessment and Diagnosis of Young Children with Autism Spectrum Disorder in British Columbia*. Available at: http://www.healthservices.gov.bc.ca/cpa/publications/asd_standards_0318.pdf, accessed April, 2008.

Brooks, R.G. and Menachemi, N. (2006) 'Physicians' Use of Email with Patients: Factors Influencing Electronic Communication and Adherence to Best Practices', *Journal of Medical Internet Research*, 8(1): 2–2.

Broom, A. (2005) 'Virtually Healthy: The Impact of Internet Use on Disease Experience and the Doctor–Patient Relationship', *Qualitative Health Research*, 15(3): 325–45.

Burstin, H. (2000) 'Traversing the Digital Divide: On Doctoring With and Without Computers', *Health Affairs*, 19(6): 245–49.

Campbell, M. (2001) 'Textual Accounts, Ruling Action: The Intersection of Power and Knowledge in the Routine Conduct of Community Nursing Work', *Studies in Cultures, Organizations and Societies*, 7: 231–50.

Campbell, M. and Gregor, F. (2002) *Mapping Social Relations – A Primer in Doing Institutional Ethnography*. Toronto: Garamond Press.

Corman, K.M. (2007) 'Panning for Gold – An Institutional Ethnography of Health Relations in the Process of Diagnosing Autism in British Columbia'. Paper presented at *the Society for Study of Social Problems*. New York.

Cotten, S.R. and Gupta, S.S. (2004) 'Characteristics of Online and Offline Health Information Seekers and Factors that Discriminate Between Them', *Social Science and Medicine*, 59(9): 1795–806.

Davis, K. (1995) *Reshaping the Female Body: The Dilemma of Cosmetic Surgery*. New York and London: Routledge.

Davis, K. (2003) *Dubious Equalities and Embodied Differences: Cultural Studies on Cosmetic Surgery*. Lanham, MD: Rowman & Littlefield.

DeVault, M. and McCoy, L. (2002) 'Institutional Ethnography: Using Interviews to Investigate Ruling Relations', pp. 751–76 in *Handbook of Interview Research: Context and Method*, edited by J. Gubrium and J. Holstein. Thousand Oaks, CA: Sage.

Diamond, T. (1992) *Making Gray Gold: Narratives of Nursing Home Care*. Chicago, IL: The University of Chicago Press.

Fox, N.J., Ward, K.J., and O'Rourke, A.J. (2005) 'The "Expert Patient": Empowerment or Medical Dominance? The Case of Weight Loss, Pharmaceutical Drugs and the Internet', *Social Science and Medicine*, 60(6): 1299–309.

Frank, A.W. (1991) 'From Sick Role to Health Role: Deconstructing Parsons'. In Roland Robertson and Bryan S. Turner (eds) *Talcott Parsons: Theorist of Modernity*. London: Sage.

Frank, A.W. (2004) *The Renewal of Generosity: Illness, Medicine, and How to Live*. Chicago, IL: University of Chicago Press.

Frank, A.W. (2005) 'The Perfect Storm of Enhancement', *Hastings Center Report*, 35(1): 46–7.

Fraser, S. (2003) *Cosmetic Surgery, Gender and Culture*. New York: Palgrave MacMillan.

Freidson, E. (1970) *Profession of Medicine: A Study of the Sociology of Applied Knowledge*. Chicago: University of Chicago Press.

Gadamer, H-G. (1996) *The Enigma of Health*. Stanford: Stanford University Press.

Gans, D., Kralewski, J., Hammons, T., and Dowd, B. (2005) 'Medical Groups' Adoption of Electronic Health Records and Information Systems', *Health Affairs*, 24(5): 1323–33.

Garrety, K. (1997) 'Social Worlds, Actor-Networks and Controversy: The Case of Cholesterol, Dietary Fat and Heart Disease', *Social Studies of Science*, 27(5): 727–73.

Gaster, B., Knight, C.L., DeWitt, D.E., Sheffield, J.V.L., Assefi, N.P., and Buchwald, D. (2003) 'Physicians' Use of and Attitudes Toward Electronic Mail for Patient Communication', *Journal of General Internal Medicine*, 18(5): 385–89.

Goffman, E. (1961) *Asylums: Essays on the Social Situation of Mental Patients and Other Inmates*. Garden City: Doubleday Anchor.

Hardey, M. (1999) 'Doctor in the House: The Internet as a Source of Lay Health Knowledge and the Challenge to Expertise', *Sociology of Health and Illness*, 21(6): 820–35.

Hardey, M. (2001) '"E-Health": The Internet and the Transformation of Patients into Consumers and Producers of Health Knowledge', *Information, Communication and Society*, 4(3): 388–405.

Hedgecoe, A.M. (2007) 'It's the Money that Matters: The Financial Context of Ethical Decision-Making in Modern Biomedicine'. In Raymond De Vries, Leigh Turner, Kristina Orfali, and Charles L. Bosk (eds) *The View from Here: Bioethics and the Social Sciences* (pp. 101–16). London: Blackwell.

Henwood, F., Wyatt, S., Hart, A., and Smith, J. (2003) '"Ignorance is Bliss Sometimes": Constraints on the Emergence of the "Informed Patient" in the Changing Landscapes of Health Information', *Sociology of Health and Illness*, 25(6): 589–607.

Kaplan, B. and Brennan, P.F. (2001) 'Consumer Informatics Supporting Patients as Co-producers of Quality', *Journal of the American Medical Informatics Association*, 8(4): 309–16.

Katz, J. (2002) *The Silent World of Doctor and Patient*. Baltimore, MD: Johns Hopkins University Press.

Latour, B. (2005) *Reassembling the Social: An Introduction to Actor-Network Theory*. New York: Oxford University Press.

Law, J. (2007) 'Actor-Network Theory and Material Semiotics', Version of 25th April 2007, available at: http://www.heterogeneities.net/publications/Law-ANTandMaterialSemiotics.pdf.

Lee, J., Cain, C., Young, S., Chockley, N., and Burstin, H. (2005) 'The Adoption Gap: Health Information Technology in Small Physician Practices', Health Affairs, 24(5): 1364–66.

Mead, N., Varnam, R., Rogers, A. and Roland, M. (2003) 'What Predicts Patients Interest in the Internet as a Health Resource in Primary Care in England?', *Journal of Health Services Research and Policy*, 8: 33–9.

Mishler, E. (1984) *The Discourse of Medicine: Dialectics of Medical Interviews*. Norwood: Ablex Publishing Corporation.

Mykhalovskiy, E. and McCoy, L. (2002) 'Troubling Ruling Discourses of Health: Using Institutional Ethnography in Community-Based Research', Critical Public Health, 12(1): 17–37.

Mykhalovskiy, E. and Weir, L. (2004) 'The Problem of Evidence-Based Medicine: Directions for Social Science', *Social Science and Medicine*, 59(5): 1059–69.

Parens, E. (ed.) (1998) *Enhancing Human Traits*. Washington, DC: Georgetown University Press.

Parsons, T. (1951) *The Social System*. Glencoe: Free Press.

—— (1964) 'Some Theoretical Considerations Bearing on the Field of Medical Sociology'. In Parsons, *Social Structure and Personality* (pp. 325–58). Glencoe: Free Press.

—— (1978) 'The Sick Role and the Role of the Physician Reconsidered'. In Parsons, *Action Theory and the Human Condition*. New York: Free Press.

Pitts-Taylor, V. (2007) *Surgery Junkies: Wellness and Pathology in Cosmetic Culture*. New Jersey: Rutgers University Press.

Rankin, M.J. (2001) 'Texts in Action: How Nurses are Doing the Fiscal Work of Health Care Reform', *Studies in Cultures, Organizations and Societies*, 7(2): 25–267.

Rankin, M.J. and Campbell, L.M. (2006) *Managing to Nurse: Inside Canada's Health Care Reform*. Canada: University of Toronto Press.

Reaven, A.J., Hepburn, L.S. and Ross, G.R. (2008) 'Use of the ADOS and AD-R in Children with Psychosis: Importance of Clinical Judgement', *Clinical Child Psychology and Psychiatry*, 13(1): 81–94.

Shaw, J. and Baker M. (2004) '"Expert Patient" – Dream or Nightmare? The Concept of a Well Informed Patient is Welcome, but a New Name is Needed', *British Medical Journal*, 328(27): 723–24.

Smith, D. (1987) *The Everyday World as Problematic: A Feminist Sociology*. Toronto: University of Toronto Press.

—— (1990) *Texts, Facts, and Femininity: Exploring the Relations of Ruling*. London: Routledge.

—— (1999) *Writing the Social: Critique, Theory, and Investigations*. Toronto: University of Toronto Press.

—— (2005) *Institutional Ethnography: A Sociology for People*. Toronto: AltaMira Press.

—— (2006) 'Incorporating Texts into Ethnographic Practices'. In Dorothy E. Smith (ed.) *Institutional Ethnography as Practice* (pp. 65–88). Maryland, USA: Rowman & Littlefield Publishers, Inc.

Strauss, A., Fagerhuagh, S., Suczek, B., and Wiener, C. (1985) *The Social Organization of Medical Work*. Chicago: University of Chicago Press.

Sullivan, D.A. (2001) *Cosmetic Surgery: The Cutting Edge of Commercial Medicine in America*. New Brunswick, NJ: Rutgers University Press.

Szasz, T. and Hollander, M. (1956) 'A Contribution to the Philosophy of Medicine', *Archives of Internal Medicine*, 97: 585–92.

Thorne, S., Paterson B., and Russell, C. (2003) 'The Structure of Everyday Self-care Decision Making in Chronic Illness', *Qualitative Health Research*, 13(10): 1337–52.

Timmermans, S. and Berg, M. (2003) *The Gold Standard: The Challenges of Evidence-Based Medicine and Standardization in Health Care*. Philadelphia: Temple University Press.

Ventres, W., Kooienga, S., Vuckovic, N., Marlin, R., Nygren, P., and Stewart, V. (2006) 'Physicians, Patients, and the Electronic Health Record: An Ethnographic Analysis', *Annals of Family Medicine*, 4(2): 124–31.

Waitzkin, H. (1991) *The Politics of Medical Encounters: How Patients and Doctors Deal with Social Problems*. New Haven, CT: Yale University Press.

Wellard, S. (1998) 'Constructions of Chronic Illness', *International Journal of Nursing Studies*, 35(1–2): 49–55.

Ziebland, S., Chapple, A., Dumelow, E., Evans, J., Prinjha, S., and Rozmovits, L. (2004) 'How the Internet Affects Patients' Experience of Cancer: A Qualitative Study', *British Medical Journal*, 328(7439): 564–67.

Zola, I.K. (1989) 'Pathways to the Doctor: From Person to Patient'. In Phil Brown (ed.) *Perspectives in Medical Sociology* (pp. 223–38). Prospect Heights, IL: Waveland Press.

3

Qualitative Contributions to the Study of Health Professions and their Work

Johanne Collin

About three decades ago, many Western countries initiated major health care reforms in response to rising costs, leading to a rationalization of professional work. The most concrete expressions of this process was the introduction of best practice criteria inspired by the private sector, efforts to standardize clinical practice through guidelines and evidence-based medicine (EBM) and the reorganization of professional work around interdisciplinary teams. There is a need, in the context of these transformations, to understand how health professionals respond and adapt to organizational and policy reforms. Indeed, as Caronna describes in Chapter 4 of the volume, responses to organizational changes, which vary according to professional groups and their work units, can have a profound impact on health reform initiatives. It is thus important to identify and analyze resistance to change and tensions that arise between different professional subcultures and the organizations in which they work. It is also important to grasp how, and to what extent, different professionals translate and integrate the principles of EBM into practice. Are they perceived as a threat to professional autonomy? How are professional identities transformed in an organizational context in which teamwork and inter-professional practice play an increasingly central role? What is the impact of the rapid feminization of the health care field and of male dominated professions such as medicine? Finally, what types of training and modes of teaching are needed to prepare the health professions for these new types of practices?

Because they enable researchers to identify the values and views of different actors in the system, qualitative studies provide a highly valuable perspective on such questions and a real understanding of how reforms are received by professionals and implemented on the ground. The aim of this chapter is therefore to describe the contribution of qualitative methods (focus groups, semistructured interviews, key informant interviews, document analysis, and participant observation) to the study of professions in the field of health care. By linking the key debates within different theoretical traditions and current issues in the study of health professions, I will demonstrate how qualitative research has advanced our knowledge of these debates, and therefore, show the relevance of qualitative methods for exploring the key themes in contemporary reflections on the health professions. As an introduction to these debates, let us first turn to a brief overview of the major theoretical perspectives in the study of professions.

PROFESSIONS IN PROCESS: AN INTRODUCTION

The late nineteenth century was a time of rapid industrialization and urbanization. During this period, North American cities underwent tremendous change. As industrialization was accelerating, thousands of people moved into the cities, seeking jobs in new industries. Population grew quickly, giving rise to significant shifts in community organization and forms of social interaction. The founding fathers of sociology, namely, Emile Durkheim, Max Weber, and Karl Marx, began to reflect on the emergence of modern professions within this process.[1] From the first decades of the twentieth century, the field of health care was becoming increasingly complex, particularly as a result of the emergence of new specialties and health-related occupations. The liberal ideology of professionalism was gaining in popularity in society as a whole and was being mobilised by a growing number of occupational groups claiming professional status.

Inspired by the work of Durkheim, it was in this context that the functionalist or trait perspective developed in the 1930s. It aimed to identify the principal traits of professions that distinguish them from the bulk of common occupations. Functionalist studies primarily focused on medicine and law. They postulated that physicians and lawyers acquired a professional status, because their professions were radically different from other occupations and were fulfilling essential functions in society (Carr-Saunders and Wilson, 1933). Moreover, from the Parsonian perspective, professions were animated by an ideal of service combining moral and economic dimensions (Parsons, 1951).

The functionalist perspective on professions was later questioned by the symbolic interactionists of the 1950s and 60s. Qualitative methods enabled interactionists to explore the every day reality of the professions and to highlight similarities and convergences between these and less prestigious occupations. According to Hughes (1970), the essential difference between recognized professions and other occupations is that professions have succeeded in obtaining a privileged status. This led to a turning point in the sociology of occupations from which the focus was now on trying to understand in what contexts and under what conditions occupations come to be recognized as professions. Scholars of the professions thus turned, during the 1970s, towards the study of professionalization as a historical and political process and towards the sociopolitical implications of the rise of professionalism as an ideology. The neo-Weberian perspective represents a major contribution to this topic in that professionalization is enabled through strategies of social closure and legal recognition of their autonomy (Parkin, 1971). This approach explores the particular role of the state in attributing professional privileges, and the territorial struggles between professions through the notion of *professional projects* (Larson, 1977; Witz, 1992).

During the same period, there developed a no less fundamental questioning of the concept of autonomy and professional power and the conditions under which the latter is acquired and maintained by professional groups (Freidson, 1970). For Freidson, the concept of autonomy has several dimensions. On one hand, it refers to the autonomy enjoyed by a professional group (as an organized corporate body); on the other hand, it denotes the autonomy granted to individual professionals in their work, particularly the freedom to exercise their clinical judgment. In addition, the autonomy of a profession can exist relatively independently at one or several levels (economic, political, and clinical). Finally, a profession acquires autonomy, but can also lose it during the course of its evolution. Indeed, as we will see later, autonomy is not a neutral criterion for the achievement of professional status; it is a very complex notion that is closely linked to governance and regulation (Blättel-Mink and Kuhlmann, 2003).

Thus, by the end of the 1970s, trends towards increasing rationalization, managerialism, and technological determinism raised questions about the autonomy of professionals practicing within large bureaucratic organizations (Derber, 1982). Neo-Marxist scholars raised then the issue of the decline in professional status of a variety of professions, medicine in particular. Advocates of this thesis predicted transformations in hospital management and the implantation, in administrative posts, of a *management stratum* that would be insensitive to professionalism and wholly focused on the pursuit of the aim of rationalizing work (McKinlay and Arches, 1985). In this context, would the ever-increasingly extensive and specialized nature of professional knowledge protect professions from losing autonomy and control over their work? How should professional training adapt to those transformations? And finally, what would be the impact of the rapid feminization of previously dominant and predominantly male professions such as medicine on the organization of work and professional status in health care (Davies, 1996; Riska, 2001)?

Many of the themes addressed by recent qualitative studies in the field of health[2] draw on the concepts and perspectives just summarized. In the following sections, I will address five major issues currently being debated in the study of health professions: (1) socialization and professional training; (2) governance, managerialism, and professionalism; (3) uncertainty, evidence-based practice, and clinical autonomy; (4) professionalization and professional projects; (5) feminization and asymmetrical integration. I will illustrate each of these topics with specific examples of contributions made by qualitative methods to the study of health care professionals.

PROFESSIONAL SOCIALIZATION AND PROFESSIONAL TRAINING

The issue of socialization is a salient theme in both the functionalist and interactionist literature (Merton et al., 1957; Becker, 1961). It refers to the social processes through which students learn to become members of a profession. Thus conceptualized, the study of socialization requires an examination of the relationship between the formal transmission of knowledge (pedagogy) and informal modes of influence that play a role in the education of professionals. Interaction between the formal and informal acquisition of codified knowledge and of technical skills, as well as the internalization of norms, values, and modes of professional conduct, also figure in the process of socialization.

The first important study on that topic was based on a typically functionalist quantitative approach. In *The Student Physician*, Merton et al. (1957) examined the socialization of medical students and argued that they do not assimilate only formal knowledge over the course of their extensive training. The students also integrate the norms and values conveyed by their teachers. Functionalist and interactionist perspectives confront each other on the issue of socialization. In *Boys in White* (Becker, 1961), a qualitative study published around the same time as Merton's study, medical students are described as particularly active in challenging their teachers' values. Students in Becker's study are rather distant from their professors. They pursue their diplomas by orienting their efforts towards obtaining results with a sense of pragmatism, and even of cynicism, which contrasts with the docility implied by the functionalist analysis. Both studies agreed on the fact that, at one point in their training, students come to perceive the outside world and society through the prism of the values and norms that dominate their profession.

From then on, qualitative methods have been fruitfully mobilised to engage in a close examination of a range of phenomena associated with socialization. Several contemporary studies adopting qualitative methodologies have also explored the identities and values of different types of professionals who have been called upon to work together, as we will see in the next sections of the chapter.

The questions pertaining to socialization raised by the studies in the 1950s certainly remain relevant (Nieuwhof et al., 2005). Yet, recent studies are less centrally concerned with these than they are with modes of learning, and the development, maintenance and assessment of professional competence. Indeed, the notion of competence, which is one of the cornerstones of current university program reforms, is of particular concern to the health professions. Professionalism, which may be defined as the adoption of professional behaviour, has been identified as one of the forms of competence that is applicable across different health professions; it has therefore attracted particular attention (van de Camp et al., 2004; Wagner et al., 2007). The use of focus groups among students and professors contributes to this issue by showing that learning activities requiring critical analysis are particularly effective in instilling a sense of professionalism among students (Ginsburg et al., 2003). Other studies, using a similar methodology, find that both role models and early clinical contacts play an important part in the process of developing professionalism (Goldie et al., 2007).

This new emphasis on teaching know-how and skills rather than focusing only on theoretical knowledge, also calls for a reflection on the interplay of theory and practice, and on how connections are made between the acquisition of scientific knowledge and its practical application through internships. Which modalities of teaching are the most effective in enabling future professionals to develop and integrate requisite forms of competence into their professional practice? What is the value of practice-based learning in this respect (Kane, 2007) and what can we learn from problem-based learning (Williams and Beattie, 2008). Qualitative methods are particularly suited to such evaluations because their techniques – interviews, observation and documentary analysis – can be applied in longitudinal studies of the learning process over several months, even years. Over the last decade, the creation of communities of practice involving students, residents, and clinicians has attracted the attention of researchers (Wilson and Pirrie, 1999). The idea behind this project is to encourage both students and practicing professionals to think of contexts of practice as sites of continual learning; sites which stimulate 'learners' active engagement with their educational experiences' (Wilson and Pirrie, 1999: 212).

Finally, experiences of transition from university to practice environments have also prompted several longitudinal qualitative studies among medical residents and other health professionals (Park et al., 2005; Bahn, 2007). They come to the same conclusion: that it is extremely important to create bridges between the academic world and clinical settings in order to ease the transition into practice for newly graduated professionals.

Further research is needed to identify modes of teaching able to integrate the assimilation of codified knowledge and its application. Qualitative methods, which have proven useful both for exploring new avenues and for evaluating ongoing experiments and pilot projects, are thus essential research tools in this respect (Kennedy and Lingard, 2006).

GOVERNANCE, MANAGERIALISM AND PROFESSIONALISM

The impact of managerial governance and structural reorganization of work in the health care sector has also been an important issue. The notion of governance is about 'how institutions relate to actors' and more precisely, 'how formal and informal rules or norms relate to the preferences and actions of actors'

(Burau, 2005: 115). Governance is a multilevel phenomenon. Authors identify a *macro-level* of institutional regulation, which includes government ministries, public policies, and insurance funds; a *meso-level*, which gives attention to organizations and professional associations; and a *micro-level*, which focuses on the internal boundaries within a profession or within the professional work itself. In this context, managerial governance represents a new model of governing through performance within the entire service sector, which is distinct from hierarchical governance. It seeks to 'make professions more accountable to the interests of the citizens and their services more transparent, manageable, and cost effective' (Kuhlmann and Bourgeault, 2008: 9). Consequently, as stated by Kuhlmann and Bourgeault, 'the role of professions and their self-regulatory capacity is subject to re-negotiation ...' (2008: 9). Moreover, the emergence of a new management stratum leads to a reconfiguration of the relationship between managerialism and professionalism and a redefinition of autonomy as a professional attribute.

In this respect, qualitative methods have proven particularly valuable in determining how professionals respond to changing work environments and to transformations in the resources available to them. By providing insiders' perspectives on the profound transformations currently affecting health care, research involving different groups of professionals (GPs [Lewis et al., 2003], nurses [Cooke, 2006], midwives [Pollard, 2003]) has elucidated various dimensions of the concept of professional autonomy. For example, according to a study based on four focus groups attended by 25 GPs in Melbourne, professional autonomy is essentially defined as the freedom to decide what is best for one's patients, that is autonomy of clinical judgment. From the perspective of these GPs, threats to this autonomy arise from financial constraints, from the increasing burden imposed by bureaucratic rationalities, and from pressure exerted by increasingly demanding patients (Lewis et al., 2003). As for nurses, a qualitative study of three cases carried out in health care trusts in Northern England and involving in depth interviews with nurses, managers and trade union representatives revealed that, despite the celebratory rhetoric of professional empowerment that surrounds them, nurses are entrusted with a growing amount of responsibility while also subjected to increasingly rigid controls over their work (Cooke, 2006).

While managerialism tends to be associated, in these studies, with a threat to professional autonomy and thus as potentially undermining the very essence of professionalism, another set of studies nonetheless proposes a more complex and nuanced view of this phenomenon. An example is Germov's (2005) study of the introduction of best practice managerial strategies in the Australian public health sector. Drawing on a neo-Weberian conceptual framework, the author analyzed the attitudes and actions of various health professionals in response to managerialism. Using a qualitative case-study protocol in the context of a government-funded independent evaluation of a BPHS program (Best Practice in the Health Sector), the aim of which was 'to develop organizational strategies to improve quality, productivity and cost-effectiveness in health-care delivery' (p. 742), Germov interviewed 71 public sector health professionals (mainly nurses and allied health professionals, doctors, and managers) and collected data from project documentation (project reports and minutes of meetings).

As a result, he developed the notion of *hyper-rationality*, an ideal-type drawing on the four Weberian types of rationality: formal, practical, substantive, and theoretical rationality. In the context of Germov's study, these rationalities correspond to logics of thought and action. Formal rationality is associated with performance measurement, work protocols, and contracts associated with a management philosophy. Practical rationality designates actions motivated by self-interest, such as professional projects and teamwork that aim to promote the status of a professional group within the organizations in which they work. Substantive rationality refers to the actions inspired by a belief in certain values (for example, pay equity). Finally, theoretical rationality is associated with the use of theoretical concepts to explain and justify the meaning of actions that are undertaken.

Although teamwork and work protocols are tools used to implement a new managerial strategy, the various professionals interviewed in Germov's study do not perceive this standardization as a threat to their autonomy or as a set of norms that places constraints on their professional work. How is this apparent contradiction resolved? In fact, Germov's cases reveal that professionals themselves often take the initiative of introducing new modes of standardization and teamwork inspired by the philosophy of *best practice*. Thus, best practice managerialism is not imposed from the outside but initiated from within by professionals themselves, who actively shape its form and content in order to adapt it to their practice. The motives that give rise to the programs or initiatives instigated by professionals are often opportunistic – and thus inspired by a practical rationality. Indeed, the aim is to generate projects that will allow them to secure a particular source of financing and/or will provide an opportunity to demonstrate the efficacy of their service or health care unit (for example, a department of pharmacy). According to Germov, the self-imposed work standardization can then be seen as a way of using the managerial prescriptions to achieve their own professional goals. The study concludes that 'given the complex and indeterminate nature of professional work, hyper-rationalization is only possible with the active participation of health professionals themselves (Germov, 2005: 752). This is very similar to what Coburn et al. (1997) argue in regards to clinical versus contextual autonomy in their study of the medical profession in Ontario; that is, that the medical profession was willing to concede control of its work context as represented by medical fees to government but wanted to maintain control of its clinical autonomy through clinical practice guidelines (as we shall see in the following section).

The highly flexible and complex nature of professionalism is also a theme explored in Kuhlmann's (2006a) article about doubt and trust in an era of managerialism. Her analysis is drawn from a qualitative study on the modernization of ambulatory care in Germany (2006b). The data was collected among separate patient and physician (GP and specialist) focus groups. Like Germov, the author argued that managerial strategies of standardization of professional work are not simply imposed from the outside. Rather, they are mobilised and redefined by professionals themselves as a means of grounding their relations with colleagues, as well as with patients/users, in concrete and visible markers of quality and competence. Following Evetts (2003), the author asks: Is the introduction of complex systems of control and accountability replacing trust in expertise and professional competence? Or does it instead represent a new means of increasing trust in professionals? In fact, the results of her qualitative study show that trust remains central in health care systems. New technologies for building trust, however, are profoundly influenced by an increase in the circulation of knowledge and the greater availability of specialized information for laypeople. As a result, trust is no longer automatic; it requires proof in the form of specified indicators. This serves to consolidate the relation between patient and professional, but also functions 'as a moral exoneration for the physicians and an instrument for risk management in decision making' (Kuhlmann, 2006a: 613).

Thus, qualitative studies provide critical in-depth analyses of transformations taking place in the professional division of labour in hospitals and elsewhere. By moving beyond the seemingly obvious, such as stating the loss of autonomy or status of professions, these studies put forth a more nuanced perspective on these transformations. Qualitative studies are able to reveal a picture in which professionals themselves participate actively; as agents who are not simply subjected to the dictates of an omnipotent managerial stratum, but who also act – by engaging in negotiations and redefinitions of professionalism – in ways that reorient these transformations.

EVIDENCE-BASED PRACTICE, UNCERTAINTY AND CLINICAL AUTONOMY

A third major theme that lends itself to the use of qualitative methods is the clinical autonomy in the health professions. As defined previously by Freidson (1970), it would correspond to the autonomy granted to professionals in their work and to the freedom to exercise their clinical judgment. Since the introduction of evidence-based medicine in the training and practice of health professionals, it has been seen as a threat to clinical autonomy by some of the professionals.

The movement of evidence-based medicine began to emerge in the 1970s in medicine. By the 1990s, it was diffused beyond a strictly medical framework into the practice of other health professions, and became referred to more broadly as evidence-based practice (EBP). The central vehicle of this new epistemology is the *practice guideline*. Guidelines can be defined as systematically developed recommendations designed to assist the clinician and the patient in decision making with respect to the most appropriate course of action in a given clinical situation. The goal of EBP is the objectification of therapeutic decision making through the quantification of clinical data. Health care decisions are to be based on a statistically significant number of cases that have been grouped according to precise scientific criteria; these are determined by a consensus between experts, rather than being generated by the subjective dimension of clinical experience that is unique to each professional. EBP is also oriented towards the goal of standardizing professional work. Quantification and standardization are thus presented as guarantees of a scientifically grounded practice by professionals who claim to possess an expertise that is both unique and essential to society.

Emerging at a time when professions, and especially the medical profession, became the target of a significant critique (in the early 1970s), EBP appears to have been developed as a strategy for supporting professional claims. Yet, while guidelines may respond to a need to maintain professional status, they also, at the same time, threaten another crucial dimension of medical professionalism: clinical autonomy (Armstrong, 2002; Pope, 2003). It seems, therefore, important to ask: How are guidelines elaborated and integrated into clinical practice within different professions? How is the movement of EBP perceived and interpreted by professionals, and how do they adapt to it in practice? Given that the development of guidelines is part of a social reorganization of knowledge in the health care sector, how does this reorganization take place? (French, 2005). Qualitative studies offer the means of addressing these fundamental issues.

Several studies have thus focused on the perception of EBP among professionals, mainly doctors (Armstrong, 2002) but also other professionals (French, 2005). Based on various methods of data collection (focus groups, individual interviews), these studies point out ways in which professionals resist the constraining norms that are constitutive of EBP. Generally, one of the main criticisms directed by professionals against EBP and guidelines is that these infringe upon the professional autonomy of clinical judgment. Experience and clinical skills are seen to be undermined by the movement. Many professionals also perceive a fundamental gap between population evidence and individual patient cases (Kovarsky and Curran, 2007).

For example, one study highlights this issue in an analysis of attitudes among GPs towards the prescription of psychotropic medication (Damestoy et al., 1999). Based on in-depth interviews with GPs, the study reveals that doctors who work among a mostly elderly clientele are often reluctant to act on the basis of well-known, and abundantly documented risks associated with the use of psychotropic medication in this population. Instead, they do not hesitate to represcribe psychotropic medication over a long period, thus going against the therapeutic indications for these products. They base this decision on their experience and clinical judgment, combined with the knowledge they have of their patients; they deem these to be the only reliable guides to treatment. From their perspective, basing a medical decision solely on EBP does not take the patients' perspectives into account and results in a neglect of their narratives, as illustrated by the case of psychotropic medication for elderly individuals. Therefore, professionals emphasize the difficulties involved in translating the concept of 'evidence' into daily practice.

Finally, EBP does not necessarily reduce clinical uncertainty; instead, it seems to promote it in different ways.

The theme of uncertainty first arose from the functionalist school. In a study published in 1959, Renée Fox demonstrated that students are trained to tolerate and manage the forms of uncertainty associated with the medical field. According to Fox, students are exposed to three types of uncertainty: (1) Uncertainty stemming from gaps in their knowledge; (2) Uncertainty created by the limits of medical knowledge per se; (3) Uncertainty resulting from the difficulty of distinguishing the first from the second. Contemporary debates about health professionals have given rise to a renewed interest in these issues. Indeed, after reflecting on the notion of uncertainty among medical students, Fox (2000) revisited the concept in light of recent transformations in the field of health and medical practice. She notes that the development of preventive and predictive medicine generates new types of uncertainty – both clinical and ethical – among professionals as well as their patients.

Epistemological uncertainty, which is generated by the tension between evidence provided by epidemiological studies and the information unique to the case and profile of each patient, has been explored by Griffiths et al. (2006). Using a qualitative approach based on interviews with doctors and women diagnosed with breast cancer, the authors show that screening tests (mammography) evoke anxiety and life disruptions for these women. The incidence of false positive and false negative results, and their impact on patients' health, thus fuels this new type of uncertainty, which is further amplified by ethical dilemmas.

Qualitative studies also make it possible to determine whether, in the context of this 'culture of safety', how guidelines are actually followed by different professional groups, and how varying attitudes towards guidelines might affect inter-professional relations. On the basis of participant observation and semi-structured interviews among doctors in various specialties (surgery, anaesthesia, etc.) and nurses, McDonald et al. (2005), for instance, found that doctors have a tendency to reject written rules in favour of implicit norms of acceptable behaviour for the medical profession. The attitude of nurses, however, was found to be quite different. They tend to adhere to guidelines, because they identify them with professionalism, and are thus critical of doctors who do not conform to them. Another study addressing the tendency to report incidents occurring in the course of practice argues along the same lines (Kingston et al., 2004). The professional culture of nursing, described by the authors as 'a culture which provided directives, protocols and the notion of security' (Kingston et al., 2004: 36), seems to provide more incentive to report incidents than the professional culture of medicine. The latter appears to be less inclined towards transparency and more reticent to follow directives when these are imposed from outside. Conflicting definitions of professional conduct seem to be operating here. These studies emphasize the importance of striving to decode implicit rules of professional conduct in order to better grasp how these norms are produced and legitimized within each profession.

In sum, the standardization of practices as promoted by EBP can be seen as a response to a double professional imperative: first, to reassert the value of clinical practice by providing it with new scientific foundations, and second, to maintain autonomy in the face of managerial rules and norms of practice imposed by a bureaucracy that is playing an increasingly important role in hospitals and health care systems. On the one hand, EBP reinforces the collective autonomy of each profession, but, on the other, it weakens the individual autonomy of professionals. The quantification of clinical evidence is perceived as hinging on a double denial: that of the specificity of the patient, and that of their own clinical experience. The issue of clinical autonomy, EBP and uncertainty is therefore a fairly complex one requiring qualitative methods to decipher, beyond the objective factors, the norms and values that are challenged in clinical practice by the transformations in health care systems.

PROFESSIONALIZATION/PROFESSIONAL PROJECTS

Professionalization is also an issue addressed in recent debates on governance. It calls attention to the role of welfare states in the regulation of professional projects and of what is defined as 'public interest' on a macro-level. Earlier studies of professionalization were largely based on cases drawn from the medical profession and, to a lesser extent, from legal and other traditional liberal professions. After the 1970s, and notably with the work of Witz (1992), the focus broadened to include other professions, particularly female professions, which are numerous in the field of health. Witz thus elaborated a broader model of female professional projects that was better suited to the study of professionalization, particularly for understanding the double-faceted domination faced by female professions – gender and medical dominance. According to her perspective, social closure mechanisms mobilised by occupational groups striving for a professional status take a 'gendered form' (Witz, 1992: 46). Witz's historical study (1992) of health care professions in Britain reveals that the success or failure of the attempts to professionalize does not only differ between 'male' and 'female' professional projects; Witz is also able to demonstrate that *legalistic tactics*, have historically been more successful than *credentialist tactics* when they were applied by female players in the professions (Bourgeault, 2006). In other words, female occupational groups who have gained the support of the state for their professional project have usually been successful in obtaining a professional status.

The case of midwives is particularly illustrative of the ways in which qualitative approaches can contribute to the analysis of these themes. Several studies, for example, have used an approach of documentary analysis in some cases combined with key informant interviews to highlight the long and nonlinear trajectory of the profession over time. From one society to another, there has been considerable variation in maternity care systems. Whereas, in Europe, midwives never ceased to exist as a professional group, the profession has been marginalized and excluded from the North American division of labour in the field of health since the end of the nineteenth century. It only re-emerged as an official profession in the last two decades of the twentieth century (Collin et al., 2000; Bourgeault et al., 2004). This trajectory provides an excellent illustration of medical dominance as a process in which medical control progressively subordinates other health occupations by restricting their work to peripheral tasks. In Canada, midwives began to lose their power in the nineteenth century as doctors appropriated the market of urban wealthy clientele for themselves. The medical profession also succeeded in placing legal restrictions on midwives' jurisdiction of practice. Midwives were forbidden recourse to instruments and medications during labour and delivery under threat of prosecution for illegal practice of medicine. This process of social closure of the field of obstetrics was completed by the gradual restriction of midwives' access to practical training.

It was only in the late twentieth century that midwifery re-emerged as a profession, promoted as an alternative to the medicalization of birth for women in the context of converging movements for women's rights and for the humanization of care. By developing a professional project, the group would obtain the legal recognition of their profession (Collin et al., 2000; Bourgeault, 2006). The route by which midwifery practice is reprofessionalized varies between different societies, largely due to the influence of the nature of the state and its interests in shaping maternity care (Benoit et al., 2005). For example, in the context of welfare states, midwifery care is often recognized in part, because it is seen as a low-tech and therefore low-cost measure. Still, qualitative studies of the professionalization of the group have also revealed cases in which professional boundaries have been successfully contested. Indeed, the reintroduction of midwives into the health division of labour entails a demarcation of their practice jurisdiction that encroaches on that of other professions occupying the field of obstetrics (obstetricians and GPs) as well as the profession of nursing (working in perinatal care) (Doray et al., 2004).

Thus, the professionalization of midwifery does not stem from the emergence of a new area of knowledge or technology. Instead, qualitative research has revealed the development of a professional culture that positions itself as a counterweight to medical culture in the field of perinatal care. Furthermore, the success of this female professional project is clearly embedded in governmental strategies of legitimization and regulation.

FEMINIZATION AS ASYMMETRICAL INCLUSION

The multiplication and relative 'success' of female professional projects in the health care field can be seen as part of a larger process of the feminization of the health care professions. Feminization of male dominated professions also requires that it be considered a major issue in itself and calls for more complex interpretations than those put forward until recently. In fact, during the last four decades, there has been a great increase in the number of women entering male dominated health professions (medicine, dentistry, pharmacy, etc.) across countries, and this tendency is expected to grow. Thus, as stated by Kuhlmann and Bourgeault:

> In this situation, essentialist approaches on gender face a revival, not only in professional and media discourse but also in research. They appear in an optimistic version if gender is reduced to numbers (or sex category), and women are expected to bring change to the content and organization of professional work – or men to upgrade predominantly female professional groups. ... They also appear as the 'ghost of feminization' that has nurtured a fear of deprofessionalization since the nineteenth century debates on the access of women to the professions (2008: 6).

Yet, feminization, in neither triumph nor defeat, calls for a more analytical stance in terms of its interpretation. In this regard, if we acknowledge that quantitative studies reveal the extent to which feminization occurs, and at what levels (in terms of education, subspecialties, etc.), it follows that qualitative methods would allow us to add more depth to the study of this phenomenon. In fact, qualitative studies have been extremely useful in helping elucidate the dynamics of the process of feminization. Through observation, interviews with professionals (both men and women), and document analysis, these studies show that the inclusion of women in male dominated professions has not been a linear process reflecting a balance in gender ratio throughout all areas of specialization and work (Riska, 2001). On the contrary, there is a rapid feminization in certain areas, while in others there are still very few women. A persistent gendering of professional work and identity is therefore a major trend in all male dominated professions. Feminization can thus be considered a synonym for asymmetrical inclusion (Riska, 2001; Denekens, 2002). This takes place through a double process of stratification and segmentation of the professional group. Stratification implies that men often continue to occupy positions of authority and prestige, even within feminized segments. Segmentation refers to the formation of feminine segments (the specialty of paediatrics, for example) that are often less prestigious and less well paid than other male dominated groups within the profession. Interviews with professionals in these disciplines have provided information about women and men's career choices and trajectories, allowing us to better understand how gender dynamics are reproduced within these professions.

The theory most frequently cited in explaining the unequal representation of men and women within the professions is that of *gender socialization*. According to this theory, women have different aspirations than that of men when entering a profession – aspirations that are shaped by gender-related preferences. Career choices are seen as a mere reflection of so-called sex roles in society. In this perspective, it is argued that women, because of their socialization, often lack the characteristics needed for achievement within male dominated professions. Nevertheless, more nuanced studies have shown that female skills or female labour characteristics may lead to the development of new professional identities that are no longer subject to the devaluation of the profession or of women as such.

For example, a study of dentistry in Germany has revealed that 'the reference to specific "female" competencies that may better serve the "public interest" than those of their male counterparts do not necessarily end up as being disadvantageous or subordinating to women in the professions' (Kulhmann and Bourgeault, 2008: 4).

Studies of the feminization of pharmacy in Canada provide further illustration of this point (Muzzin et al., 1994; Collin, 1995). One qualitative study, based on interviews and document analysis, explored the changing nature of pharmacy practice in Québec after the Second World War (Collin, 1995). In this study, the author argued that the rise of the pharmaceutical industry produced changes in drug manufacturing that plunged the profession into a serious identity crisis. As a result, during the 1960s, pharmacists had to redefine their role and the purpose of their work within the health field, especially because the concentration of commercial capital was forcing many small pharmacy owners out of business. From this followed an expansion of the workforce within the profession. From owners of their own pharmacies, pharmacists gradually became employees, with women filling these positions in greater numbers. The rapid increase in the number of women entering the profession resulted in a radical change in the demographic profile of pharmacy practice. It also forced (or resulted in) a redefinition of the pharmacist's role, a role that was geared more towards pharmaceutical care and counselling than focused exclusively on its traditional business base. Indeed, a revalorization of the profession required coming to terms with the tension between professionalism and commercialism that has always characterized pharmacy. With the status of salaried professional, pharmacists could now claim their professionalism without the risk of being seen as in conflict of interest. They were no longer owners of the pharmacies in which they worked and therefore did not benefit from the profits generated by the sale of drugs. Thus, in the context of the 1960s, rapid feminization of the profession allowed pharmacists to take on this new role, and contributed to producing a professionalization response to commercialization.

CONCLUSION

Current debate on professions and work in the health field has greatly benefited from the proliferation of qualitative studies over the past few years. Through focus groups, semistructured interviews, document analysis, and participant observation, these studies have helped to identify the values and perceptions of various actors. They have also served to analyze how health professionals have dealt with profound changes in their work. When applied to the health sector, qualitative methods thus become effective instruments for evaluating policies, reforms, and programs.

From the outset, and before the rise of specialization in medicine, researchers have questioned what distinguishes professions from other occupations. They soon focused on the process of professionalization and sought to understand the mechanisms by which certain occupations are recognized as professions. If certain forms of governance that threatened the autonomy of established professions such as medicine, or halted the professionalization of related occupations, qualitative studies have shown that the reality was much more complex. These studies have uncovered the existence of female professional projects distinct from those of male dominated professions. They have also demonstrated that the government had a more leveraging than braking role in the professionalization of these occupations, since female professional projects are often clearly embedded in governmental strategies of legitimization and regulation.

Qualitative approaches have also shown the resistance to change and tensions that arise between different subcultures and the professional organizations in which they work. In particular, they have highlighted the resistance to EBP of certain occupations. While doctors and other professionals may resist, to varying degrees, what they perceive as pressure to standardize their practice, they nevertheless do not reject the managerialist strategies they face in everyday life. Qualitative studies have shown, to the contrary, how professionals themselves reappropriate these strategies in order to strengthen their position within the system. The complex nature of professionalism is thus underscored by qualitative studies.

Feminization also appears to be a much more complex phenomenon than that revealed by conventional statistical analysis. Contrary to longstanding beliefs, the influx of women into a profession can bring positive, even beneficial changes in identity, and can lead to a reprofessionalization of the field.

Finally, in light of this multitude of structural changes, we are faced with the question as to the socialization of future professionals. What emerges is the challenge to find forms of training that are most likely to prepare health professionals to continually adapt to changes that have shaken the health sector over the past three decades. On this issue, which is so important for the future of health professions, qualitative methods once again prove themselves to be an effective means for grasping the complexity of the phenomenon.

NOTES

1 While Durkheim and Weber wrote specifically about the phenomenon of professions, Marx did not directly address this topic. However, his work on the transformation of modes of production inspired several authors who examined the issue professionalization in the 1970s.

2 The material presented in this part of the chapter is based on a search of the principal databases in sociology (Sociofile, Sociological Abstracts, Social Science Index) and the social sciences of health and nursing (Current Content, Cindhal) using the keywords 'health', 'profession', and 'qualitative', in order to grasp the more salient current issues/reflections/questions.

REFERENCES

Armstrong, D. (2002) 'Clinical Autonomy, Individual and Collective: The Problem of Changing Doctors' Behaviour', *Social Science and Medicine*, 55(10): 1771–7.

Bahn, D. (2007) 'Orientation of Nurses Towards Formal and Informal Learning: Motives and Perceptions', *Nurse Education Today*, 27(7): 723–30.

Becker, H.S. (1961) *Boys in White: Student Culture in Medical School.* Chicago: University of Chicago Press.

Benoit, C., Wrede, S., Bourgeault, I., Sandall, J., De Vries, R., and van Teijlingen, E.R. (2005) 'Understanding the Social Organization of Maternity Care Systems: Midwifery as a Touchstone', *Sociology of Health and Illness*, 27(6): 722–37.

Blättel-Mink, B. and E. Kuhlmann (2003) 'Health Professions, Gender and Society: Introduction and Outlook', *International Journal of Sociology and Social Policy*, 23(4/5): 1–21.

Bourgeault, I.L. (2000) 'Delivering the 'New' Canadian Midwifery: The Impact on Midwifery of Integration into the Ontario Health Care System', *Sociology of Health & Illness*, 22(2): 172–96.

Bourgeault, I.L., (2006) *Push: The Struggle to Integrate Midwifery in Ontario.* McGill-Queen's University Press: Kingston/Montreal.

Bourgeault, I.L., Benoit, C., and Davies-Floyd, R. (2004) *Reconceiving Midwifery.* Kingston/Montreal: McGill University Press.

Burau, V. (2005) 'Comparing Professions Through Actor-Centred Governance: Community Nursing in Britain and Germany', *Sociology of Health and Illness*, 27(1): 114–37.

Carr-Saunders, A.M. and P.A. Wilson (1933) *The Professions.* Oxford: Clarendon Press.

Coburn, D., Rappolt, S., and Bourgeault, I. (1997) 'Decline vs. Retention of Medical Power Through Restratification: An Examination of the Ontario Case', *Sociology of Health and Illness*, 19(1): 1–22.

Collin, J. (1995) *Changement d'ordonnance. Feminisation et transformation de la profession pharmaceutique au Québec, 1940–1980.* Montreal: Boréal.

Collin, J., Blais, R., White, D., Demers, A., and Desbiens, F. (2000) 'Integration of Midwives into the Quebec Health Care System', *Canadian Journal of Public Health*, *Revue Canadienne* de Sante Publique. 91(1): I16–20.

Cooke, H. (2006) 'Seagull Management and the Control of Nursing Work', *Work Employment and Society,* 20(2): 223–43.

Damestoy, N., Collin, J., and Lalande, R. (1999) 'Prescribing Psychotropic Medication for Elderly Patients: Some Physicians' Perspectives', *Canadian Medical Association Journal*, 161(2): 143–5.

Davies, C. (1996) 'The Sociology of Professions and the Profession of Gender', *Sociology*, 30(4): 661–78.

Denekens, J.P.M. (2002) 'The Impact of Feminisation on General Practice', *Acta Clinica Belgica*, 57(1): 5–10.

Derber, C. (1982) *Professionals as Workers: Mental Labor in Advanced Capitalism.* Boston, MA: G.K. Hall.

Doray, P., Collin, J., and Aubin-Horth, S. (2004) 'The State and the Emergence of Professional Groups', *Canadian Journal of Sociology/Cahiers Canadiens de Sociologie*, 29(1): 83–110.

Evetts, J. (2003) 'The Sociological Analysis of Professionalism: Occupational Change in the Modern World', *International Sociology*, 18 (2): 395–415.

Fox, R.C. (1959) *Experiment Perilous: Physicians and Patients Facing Unknown.* Glencoe, IL: Free Press.

Fox, R.C. (2000) 'Medical Uncertainty Revisited'. In G.L. Albrecht, R. Fitzpatrick, and S.C. Scrimshaw (eds.), *Handbook of Social Studies in Health and Medicine*, 545–54; London; Thousand Oaks, CA: Sage.

Freidson, E. (1970) *Profession of Medicine: A Study of the Sociology of Applied Knowledge.* New York, Dodd: Mead.

French, B. (2005) 'Evidence-Based Practice and the Management of Risk in Nursing', *Health, Risk and Society*, 7(2): 177–92.

Germov, J. (2005) 'Managerialism in the Australian Public Health Sector: Towards the Hyper-Rationalisation of Professional Bureaucracies', *Sociology of Health and Illness*, 27(6): 738–58.

Ginsburg, S., Regehr, G., and Lingard, L. (2003) 'The Disavowed Curriculum – Understanding Students' Reasoning in Professionally Challenging Situations', *Journal of General Internal Medicine*, 18(12): 1015–22.

Goldie, J., Dowie, A., Cotton, P., and Morrison, J. (2007) 'Teaching Professionalism in the Early Years of a Medical Curriculum: A Qualitative Study', *Medical Education*, 41(6): 610–7.

Griffiths, F., Green, E., and Bendelow, G. (2006) 'Health Professionals, Their Medical Interventions and Uncertainty: A Study Focusing on Women at Midlife', *Social Science and Medicine*, 62(5): 1078–90.

Hughes, E.C. (1970) 'The Humble and the Proud: The Comparative Study of Occupations', *Sociological Quarterly*, 11(2): 147–56.

Kane, G.M. (2007) 'Step-by-Step: A Model for Practice-Based Learning', *Journal of Continuing Education in the Health Professions*, 27(4): 220–6.

Kennedy, T.J.T. and Lingard, L.A. (2006) 'Making Sense of Grounded Theory in Medical Education', *Medical Education*, 40(2): 101–8.

Kingston, M.J., Evans, S.M., Smith, B.J., and Berry, J.G. (2004) 'Attitudes of Doctors and Nurses Towards Incident Reporting: A Qualitative Analysis', *Medical Journal of Australia*, 181(1): 36–9.

Kovarsky, D. and Curran, M. (2007) 'A Missing Voice in the Discourse of Evidence-Based Practice', *Topics in Language Disorders*, 27(1): 50–61.

Kuhlmann, E. (2006a) 'Traces of Doubt and Sources of Trust: Health Professions in an Uncertain Society', *Current Sociology*, 54(4): 607–20.

Kuhlmann, E. (2006b) *Modernising Health Care: Reinventing Professions, the State and the Public.* Bristol: The Polity Press.

Kuhlmann, E. and Bourgeault, I.L. (2008) 'Introduction to Reinventing Gender and the Professions: New Governance, Equality and Diversity', *Equal Opportunities International*, Special Issue 27(2): 5–18.

Larson, M.S. (1977). *The Rise of Professionalism: A Sociological Analysis.* Berkeley, CA: University of California Press.

Lewis, J.M., Marjoribanks, T., and Pirotta, M. (2003) 'Changing Professions – General Practitioner's Perceptions of Autonomy on the Frontline', *Journal of Sociology*, 39(1): 44–61.

McDonald, R., Waring, J., Harrison, S., Walshe, K., and Boaden, R. (2005) 'Rules and Guidelines in Clinical Practice: A Qualitative Study in Operating Theatres of Doctors' and Nurses' Views', *Quality and Safety in Health Care*, 14(4): 290–94.

McKinlay, J.B. and Arches, J. (1985), 'Towards the Proletarization of Physicians', *International Journal of Health Services*, 15(2): 161–95.

Merton, R.K., Reader, G.G., and Kendall, P.L. (1957) *The Student–Physician.* Cambridge, MA: Harvard University Press.

Muzzin, L., Brown, G.P., and Hornosty, R.W. (1994) 'Consequences of Feminization of a Profession: The Case of Canadian Pharmacy', *Women and Health*, 21(2–3): 39–56.

Nieuwhof, M.G.H., Rademakers, J., Kuyvenhoven, M.M., Soethout, M.B.M., and Ten Cate, T.J. (2005) 'Students' Conceptions of the Medical Profession: An Interview Study', *Medical Teacher*, 27(8): 709–14.

Park, E.R., Betancourt, J.R., Kim, M.K., Maina, A.W., Blumenthal, D., and Weissman, J.S. (2005) 'Mixed Messages: Residents' Experiences Learning Cross-Cultural Care', *Academic Medicine*, 80(9): 874–80.

Parkin, F. (1971) *Class Inequality and Political Order: Social Stratification in Capitalist and Communist Societies.* London: MacGibbon and Kee; New York: Praeger.

Parsons, T. (1951) *The Social System.* Glencoe, IL: Free Press.

Pollard, K. (2003) 'Searching for Autonomy', *Midwifery*, 19(2): 113–24.

Pope, C. (2003) 'Resisting Evidence: The Study of Evidence-Based Medicine as a Contemporary Social Movement', *Health*, 7(3): 267–82.

Riska, E. (2001) 'Towards Gender Balance: But Will Women Physicians Have an Impact on Medicine?', *Social Science and Medicine*, 52(2001): 179–87.

Van de Camp, K., Vernooij-Dassen, M., Grol, R., and Bottema, B. (2004) 'How to Conceptualize Professionalism: A Qualitative Study', *Medical Teacher*, 26(8): 696–702.

Wagner, P., Hendrich, J., Moseley, G., and Hudson, V. (2007) 'Defining Medical Professionalism: A Qualitative Study', *Medical Education*, 41(3): 288–94.

Williams, S.M. and Beattie H.J. (2008) 'Problem-Based Learning in the Clinical Setting – A Systematic Review', *Nurse Education Today*, 28(2): 146–54.

Wilson, V. and Pirrie, A. (1999) 'Developing Professional Competence: Lessons from the Emergency Room', *Studies in Higher Education*, 24(2): 211–24.

Witz, A. (1992) *Professions and Patriarchy*. London; New York: Routledge.

4

Why Use Qualitative Methods to Study Health Care Organizations? Insights from Multi-Level Case Studies

Carol A. Caronna

In the last few decades, health care organizations in industrialized nations have faced numerous challenges and changes. These include the rapid development of new medical technologies and treatment protocols; widespread efforts to improve patient safety; a growing interest in alternative and complementary medicine; and the increased impact of managerialism and market forces on organizational structure and strategy. Understanding the process of how these changes have taken place, their outcomes and consequences, and their influence on our future health care is of fundamental importance to social and health scientists and policy makers alike.

The potential difficulty of studying these issues lies in their complexity and multilayered nature: they involve professional practices and identities; patients' experiences and rights; health care organizations' structures and cultures; and the broader societal values and belief systems. Exploring and understanding these issues requires research methodologies that not only are able to analyze process and change but also allow for diverse and possibly contradictory perspectives. Qualitative methods, such as organizational ethnographies and case studies, are best suited to address these complexities. They can capture 'the unfolding of social processes' (Van Maanen, 1979: 520; see also Hoff and Witt, 2000) and uncover the processes of and barriers to change (Ragin, 1999). They provide 'rich descriptions of complex phenomena ... to illuminat[e] the experience and interpretation of events by actors with widely differing stakes and roles' (Sofaer, 1999: 1101; see also Bradley et al., 2007; Hoff and Witt, 2000), and also play an important role in theoretical elaboration and theory development (Eisenhardt, 1989; Vaughan, 1992; 1996; Bradley et al., 2007).

Each of these different applications of qualitative methods allows researchers to improve our understanding of health care organizations in ways that conventional quantitative methods cannot. For example, in Barley's (1986) classic organizational ethnography, the introduction of Computed Tomography (CT) scanners into the observed radiology departments affected the existing status hierarchies and caused radiologists and technicians to renegotiate their professional relations. As adjustments to change unfolded, the same technology had a differential impact on social process and hierarchies in the two departments, but the eventual outcome of each adjustment period was similar. In a quantitative study focused on outcomes, the CT scanner's impact on the departments might be interpreted as direct and obvious. The value of Barley's qualitative research was the insight that these processes were complex, varied, and not entirely predictable.

The use of qualitative methods also is crucial for understanding the complicated nature of organizational change, including the subtle and sometimes latent causes of failed initiatives. McDonald and colleagues' (2006) study of 'safety culture', for example, demonstrated the intricate and nuanced ways practitioners' day-to-day enactment of their professional identities prevented their compliance with formal safety rules. In a different study, Lewin and Green (2009) found that the culture of tuberculosis (TB) clinics in South Africa included conflicting rituals that constructed practitioners as both the patients' equals and their superiors. This contradiction was an important factor contributing to the clinic's difficulty implementing the World Health Organization's TB treatment protocol. Likewise, Coulter and colleagues (2008) used qualitative methods to uncover the reasons an integrative medical centre in the United States collapsed.

One of the challenges of using qualitative methods is incorporating and moving between multiple levels of analysis: micro (individual), meso (organizational), and macro (environmental). To some extent, all qualitative studies of organizations incorporate more than one level; for example, an investigation of individual behaviour within an organizational context is both a micro and a meso study. Most research, however, focuses on one level more than others do (Bourgeault and Mulvale, 2006), with common themes across studies. At the micro (individual) level, prevalent topics of research include practitioner behaviour (e.g., McDonald et al., 2006; Lewin and Green, 2009), patient–practitioner relations (e.g., Lewin and Green, 2009); and the interactions between different types of health care providers (e.g., Barley, 1986; Shuval et al., 2002). At the meso (organizational) level of analysis, typical studies concern organizational structure, strategy, culture, and change, such as the effects of managerialist practices on health care organizations (Martin et al., 2003; Sheaff et al., 2003; Germov, 2005); the creation of mergers and joint ventures (e.g., Kitchener, 2002; Lake et al., 2003); and effective organizational change (e.g., Buchanan et al., 2007). At the macro (environmental) level, researchers examine changes in health policy, regulatory structures, professional norms, and broad meaning systems (Scott et al., 2000; Reay and Hinings, 2005).

To move forward in our understanding of health care organizations requires multilevel data collection and analysis (Bourgeault and Mulvale, 2006; see also Klein and Kozlowski, 2000). Indeed, there is an expectation that a 'case study concentrates on experiential knowledge of the case and pays close attention to the influence of its social, political, and other contexts' (Stake, 2005: 444; see also Caronna et al., 2009). There exists little methodological guidance for systematically linking together case study data from multiple levels of analysis. This lack of guidance may be due, in part, to the tendency of qualitative researches (possibly because of conditions set by reviewers and editors) to describe in general instead of specific terms their methodological strategies and techniques (Hoff and Witt, 2000).

The goal of this chapter is to provide elaborated, specific descriptions of multilevel qualitative analysis as well as demonstrate how qualitative methods can be used to improve our understanding of health care organizations. First, I briefly review different types of qualitative methods that can be used to study health care organizations. Then I provide examples from my own research (conducted in collaboration with others or by myself) to demonstrate a number of different, specific multilevel case study methodologies I have used to study health care organizations. The methods I describe include theoretical sampling, meso/macro cross-case comparisons, micro/meso cross-case comparisons, and coding strategies for analyzing organizational-level documents using macro frameworks. At the end of the chapter, I summarize the key findings from these examples and other studies to illustrate the types of insights that can be gained from qualitative multilevel case study research.

ETHNOGRAPHIES AND CASE STUDIES: TYPES OF QUALITATIVE METHODS

A number of different qualitative methods can be used to study health care organizations, such as organizational ethnography and the case study. These methods are tied together by a belief that researchers:

> … know little about what a given piece of observed behavior means until they have developed a description of the context in which the behavior takes place and attempted to see that behavior from the position of its originator. That such contextual understandings and empathetic objectives are unlikely to be achieved without direct, firsthand, and more or less intimate knowledge of a research setting is a most practical assumption that underlies and guides most qualitative study (Van Maanen, 1979: 520).

Organizational ethnography involves in-depth, long-term observation and/or participant observation (see other chapters in this Handbook). Researchers take field notes during or following observation periods, and these field notes generally constitute the bulk of the researchers' data. Ethnographers also may interview subjects and collect and analyze documents to supplement their data. In Barley's (1986) study, over the length of a year, he observed approximately 400 individual examinations in the two hospital radiology departments. McDonald and colleagues' (2006) study of a teaching hospital's safety culture involved two years of observation and participant observation in the operating department, as well as formal interviews and documentary evidence. Lewin and Green (2009) also spent two years studying seven South African TB clinics, collecting data by observation, participant observation, and interviews.

A range of nonethnographic qualitative research falls into the category of the case study (Ragin and Becker, 1992; Ragin, 1999; Yin, 1999; Denzin and Lincoln, 2005; Stake, 2005). A case study is 'an empirical inquiry that: investigates a contemporary phenomenon within its real-life context; when the boundaries between phenomenon and context are not clearly evident; and in which multiple sources of evidence are used' (Yin, 1989: 23). The data collected for a case study generally include interviews, documents, and observation (Devers, 1999), but a case study 'typically does not involve continuous immersion in a setting or group' (Sofaer, 1999: 1110). The number of interviews conducted can range widely. In his study of the merger of two academic medical centres, Kitchener (2002) interviewed eleven informants; in their study of physician–hospital organizations, Lake and colleagues (2003) interviewed 895 senior executives in twelve metropolitan areas of the United States. The types of documents collected for case studies include annual reports (Arndt and Bigelow, 2000), minutes of meetings and project reports (Germov, 2005), organization charts and maps (Sheaff et al., 2003); association journals (Reay and Hinings, 2005); local newspaper articles (Reay and Hinings, 2005) and press reports (Kitchener, 2002); legislative debate transcripts (Reay and Hinings, 2005), and national policy documents (Sheaff et al., 2003). Observations conducted for case studies are shorter-term than those of ethnographies, and often are observations of specifically planned events instead of day-to-day routines; example include site visits (Germov, 2005), group meetings and deliberations (Martin et al., 2003), and one-day workshops (Coulter et al., 2008).

Cases are chosen for uniqueness, typicality, or comparative purposes (Ragin, 1999) or for their role in a historically situated process (Czarniawska, 1997). For example, Buchanan and colleagues (2007) investigated changes in prostate cancer treatment at an acute care hospital in England. This hospital was chosen to study as a 'deviant case' or 'positive outlier' because its treatment protocols changed without explicit direction from senior managers and practitioners (Buchanan et al., 2007: 1070). Kitchener's (2002) examination of academic health centre mergers in the United States focused on the case of Stanford University and the University of California, San Francisco, because of their unique position to illustrate 'the adoption of one managerial innovation (merger) in a highly institutionalized and professional field' (Kitchener, 2002: 394). Shuval and colleagues (2002) selected the four Jewish-sponsored hospitals in Jerusalem for their study of alternative and biomedical practitioner relations, eliminating hospitals in Moslem and Christian sectors of Jerusalem in order to hold relatively constant the organizational context.

The analysis of ethnographic and case study data generally follows the techniques of constant comparison and grounded theory (Glaser and Strauss, 1967; Miles and Huberman, 1994; for examples, see Lewin and Green, 2009; McDonald et al., 2006; Arndt and Bigelow, 2000). Field notes, interview transcripts, and documents are coded for keywords and themes in a series of inductive and iterative rounds (for coding techniques, see Ayres et al., 2003; Corbin and Strauss, 2008; for empirical uses of specific coding techniques, see Lewin and Green, 2009; Martin et al., 2003; for specific descriptions of coding decisions, see Reay and Hinings, 2005; Arndt and Bigelow, 2000; Barley, 1986). Some researchers use software programs, such as Atlas.ti (Muhr, 1997), to aid in coding and analysis (for examples, see Lake et al., 2003; McDonald et al., 2006; Coulter et al., 2008). To address issues of reliability and validity, researchers use a variety of tools, including interrater agreement (Arndt and Bigelow, 2000), negative evidence testing (Kitchener, 2002), and member checking (Kitchener, 2002; Martin et al., 2003; Coulter et al., 2008).

WHICH ORGANIZATIONS TO STUDY? THEORETICAL SAMPLING TECHNIQUES AND RATIONALES

My first example of multilevel case study methodology is the use of case studies in *Institutional Change and Healthcare Organizations: From Professional Dominance to Managed Care* (Scott et al., 2000). In this book, my coauthors and I presented four case studies of health care organizations in the San Francisco Bay Area: Stanford Hospital and Medical Center, Kaiser Permanente (Northern California Region), the Palo Alto Medical Clinic, and San Jose Hospital. These four cases were embedded in the much broader study of changes in the institutional environment of the health care field since the Second World War and in five specific organizational populations: hospitals, health maintenance organizations (HMOs), multihospital and/or health care systems, home health agencies, and end-stage renal disease treatment centres. Our data for these five populations were mostly quantitative. We developed quantitative indicators of change at the level of the organizational field: 'those organizations that, in the aggregate, constitute a recognized area of institutional life: key suppliers, resource and product consumers, regulatory agencies, and other organizations that produce similar services or products' (DiMaggio and Powell, 1983: 148). We originally intended to use the case studies simply as side stories: complementary, qualitative illustrations of the broader changes found using quantitative methods. The case studies, however, became important data sources in their own right. They demonstrated the ways organizations do not simply react to their environments, but influence and in part create the organizational field.

When we set out to choose the particular organizations to serve as our cases, we used the technique of theoretical sampling (Glaser and Strauss, 1967). Often during theoretical sampling 'it makes sense to choose cases such as extreme situations and polar types in which the process of interest is "transparently observable"' (Eisenhardt, 1989: 537). We decided to examine two major players in our local environment of Palo Alto, California: the Palo Alto Medical Clinic and Stanford Medical Center. The Palo Alto Medical Clinic, founded in 1931, represented an example of an innovative multispecialty medical group. The Clinic was not representative of any of our five focal populations (although in 1992 it became affiliated with a health care system) but represented a prototypical group practice of physicians. The founders of the Clinic were involved in helping to create national health policies, such as Medicare and Medicaid, and thus the Clinic represented a health care organization that intentionally influenced the health care field in which it was embedded.

Our local tertiary hospital and medical school at Stanford University, founded in the early 1900s, served as an example of a traditional academic medical centre. From studying this organization, we were able to see the effects of federal research funding on a local organization, as well as examine the effects of various legislative policies and field-level trends on the unique needs of tertiary medicine. Of the two academic medical centres in the San Francisco Bay Area (Stanford in Palo Alto and the University of California, San Francisco), we chose Stanford because of our local access to its archives and because of its ties to the Palo Alto Medical Clinic.

Our third case, the Kaiser Permanente Medical Care Program of Northern California, encompassed all of our populations. As a large health care system, Kaiser Permanente owned its own hospitals, end-stage renal disease treatment centres, and home health services. In addition, it represented a precursor health maintenance organization, as it had operated as a prepaid group practice since it opened to the public in 1945. With the case of Kaiser Permanente, we gained insight into the events that led to the development of HMOs at a national level in the 1970s, as well as the experiences of an organization considered deviant by organized medicine in the 1940s and 1950s.

With three prominent organizations as cases, we intentionally chose a 'typical' hospital as our fourth case study. Because each of our three cases was at times a player on the national scene, we wanted to examine an organization that reacted more to the field than enacted the field. To us, this hospital would represent a 'carrier' of widespread beliefs and values rather than an organization that helped create them. In order to select this hospital from many possible cases, we identified six potential hospitals in the Bay Area that had previously provided us with access to their historical data, and then narrowed our choice of one hospital by our interest in multihospital systems and our desire to match the fourth case with the secular, nonprofit characteristics of the other three. This process of elimination left us with San Jose (Good Samaritan) Hospital, which was founded before the Second World War as an investor owned hospital but converted to non-profit status a few years before our study period began. Like most hospitals, it remained independent until it faced competitive pressures in the 1980s. In 1986, it was acquired by a local health care system, then nine years later the system was sold to Columbia/HCA, at the time the nation's largest for-profit health care system. At the close of our data collection period in the mid-1990s, rumours circulated that Columbia/HCA would close San Jose (Good Samaritan) Hospital. This case gave us much insight into the way a typical community hospital weathered over time a number of field-level changes.

SAME POLICY, DIFFERENT REACTIONS: DEVELOPING FRAMEWORKS FOR MESO/MACRO CROSS-CASE COMPARISONS

After we had finished theoretically sampling our four cases, we had to determine how to keep our data collection efforts organized and systematic. One of our first steps was to define key concepts and generate a list of topics to guide our reading of archival materials. Here we used our unfolding knowledge of the health care field, identifying the main trends that were driving our determination of institutional eras: the era of professional dominance (1945–65), characterized by the dominance of professional bodies, such as the American Medical Association, and an emphasis on quality; the era of federal involvement (1966–82), characterized by a concern for equity in health care services and the federal government's involvement in funding and regulating health care services; and the era of managerial control and market mechanisms (1983–95), characterized by federal deregulation, a reliance on market forces, the rise of large investor owned corporations in the field, and an emphasis on efficiency. To capture these eras and their changes over time, we developed a set of questions and terms for each researcher to look for throughout all years of the case study covering the specific areas of:

- Professional norms and affiliations: What is the role of physicians in the organization? What are the case's affiliations with accreditation agencies and professional associations?
- Government regulation: Which pieces of state and federal legislation are mentioned in the case history? Which government programs and agencies are mentioned? When and why?
- Market: What is the case's conception of its competitors, clients, and network affiliations? Is there evidence of external growth such as mergers, acquisitions, or vertical and horizontal integration?
- Internal growth strategies: Are there expansions in building, staff, and/or patient-base over time?
- Organizational identity: How does the organization portray itself over time?
- Governance structures: What is the ownership status of the organization (for-profit, not-for-profit)? Who is on the board and how does the board change over time?
- Leadership: Who are the administrators/executives? How do these positions change over time?
- Technology: What kinds of technology are mentioned? When does the organization acquire equipment and other new technologies?

These questions helped us generate ideas about what to look for in the data, so we had some focus as we read through archival materials. By examining indicators of professional dominance, federal involvement, and market mechanisms throughout the study period, we were also able to examine the ways each of these three areas were important even when they were not defining the 'era' within the field. These findings, such as a case's concerns with market share during the era of professional dominance, prevented us from having an overly rigid sense of the transition between eras in the field.

The framework we developed for data collection also allowed us to create consistency across the four cases, which led to effective cross-case comparisons. One of our most effective strategies was to select key national events in the health care field and compare how the four cases responded to the events (or helped create the events). First, we would choose an event to study, such as the Hill-Burton Act of 1946 that provided federal funding for hospital expansion from 1947–71. Next, independently we wrote memos describing each case's experiences with the event. Once we had generated each memo, we created a chart comparing our summaries of each memo for each case.

From our study of the Hill-Burton Act, we found that each case had a different reaction to the federal funding. Our 'typical' community hospital, San Jose Hospital, got a grant from the Hill-Burton program in 1950 for $426,000, which it used to expand the hospital building and invest in technological improvements. The Stanford Medical Center expanded in the 1950s, but did not apply for federal funding. Instead, it used loans, bonds, gifts, and financial support from the city of Palo Alto in order to build a medical centre in 1956 and hospital in 1959. The Palo Alto Medical Clinic did not have a hospital and tentative plans to build one in this period never came to fruition. Kaiser Permanente, who had used internal funds and bank loans to build hospitals and facilities, also did not apply for Hill-Burton funding. Kaiser Permanente's leaders realized that the American Medical Association (AMA) would block any attempt by Kaiser Permanente to secure federal funding, because of the AMA's opposition to prepaid group practices. Also, because the Kaiser Foundation hospitals were restricted to members, they diverged from the 'voluntary' hospitals supported by the Hill-Burton program. In addition, Henry Kaiser believed that the government should provide loans for hospital construction but not funding, and lobbied against federal subsidies for hospital construction.

We used the same strategy of cross-case comparison to examine the four cases' reactions to the creation of Medicare and Medicaid in 1965 and to the imposition of federal health planning and cost containment in the 1970s. Medicare, a health insurance and financing program for the elderly, was generally considered a 'cash cow' because it reimbursed health practitioners on a fee-for-service basis. This program became an important source of revenue for the Palo Alto Medical Clinic and San Jose Hospital. By contrast, the Stanford Medical Center criticized the program for its one-size-fits-all model, claiming it failed to provide enough reimbursement for tertiary care. In Kaiser Permanente's case, its members were already insured by Kaiser and thus did not need federal health insurance.

Because the reimbursement mechanism was fee-for-service, Kaiser Permanente argued that the federal program ignored the needs of prepaid group practices. For Kaiser Permanente, Medicare had symbolic meaning that was only loosely related to the needs of individual patients.

Examining these four cases studies helped us see the effects of government programs at the organizational level. From our quantitative data alone, we would not have seen the diversity of reactions of health care organizations to the Hill Burton program, and might have overlooked ways hospitals expanded during this period without soliciting federal funding. In addition, we would not have learned of the ways different types of health care organizations perceived Medicare. We would not have uncovered the controversies surrounding the seemingly benign hospital-building program, or the ways some prominent organizations criticized Medicare in the hope of enacting institutional change. Our use of qualitative case studies greatly improved our understanding of these events and the experiences of each health care organization as it reacted to and helped enact changes in the US health care field.

DIFFERENCES IN PHYSICIAN AUTONOMY AND BUREAUCRATIC CONTROL: STRATEGIES FOR MICRO/MESO CROSS-CASE COMPARISONS

Another example of multilevel approaches to case study methodology comes from a project on the nature of bureaucratic control in eight US integrated health care systems and its effects on physician autonomy (Kitchener et al., 2005). The eight systems are examples of American organizations that own (or contract with) and integrate specific health plans, providers, and suppliers in an attempt to decrease costs and increase quality of care (Shortell et al., 2000). One of the goals of the project was to explore the extent of control of the systems' lay managers over the contracted or employed physicians. A second goal was to assess the utility of applying to health organizations three models of professional control already established in the literature: *custodial control* (Ackroyd et al., 1989), in which physicians in bureaucratic organizations have a high degree of autonomy over their work; *conjoint control* (Scott, 1982), in which physicians and lay managers share some varying responsibility for the system's administrative and organizational issues; and *heteronomous control* (Scott, 1965), in which managers and the bureaucratic controls they set in place regulate professional action. In order to operationalize these different models, we developed a set of dimensions and measurements common to each model and predicted how each dimension would vary across the three types of bureaucratic control. These dimensions and measurements were:

- Physician autonomy over terms of work, measured by control over physician credentialing.
- Physician autonomy over content of work, measured by the use of standardized medical records and clinical software.

- Physician remuneration, measured by the control physicians and/or managers had over physician salary and incentives, as well as the percentage of affiliated physicians employed by the system.
- Quality assurance, measured by physician versus management responsibility for quality assurance leadership.
- Physician–organization integration, measured by participation of physicians on system boards of directors, physician participation in system administration, and physician participation in strategy.

The eight health care systems we examined varied in their degree of centralization (Bazzoli et al., 1999) and size (number of hospitals), total assets, religious affiliation, and geographical region. Our individual-level data consisted of transcripts of telephone interviews with four to five executives and physician leaders at each of the eight systems. We also collected secondary and internal documents pertaining to the organizational structure of, the strategic plans of, and nature of physician control within each system.

Using these data, the way we determined the types of control of a system was to compare each system with the ideal typical (predicted) dimensions of each control type. For example, if in a system physicians controlled physician credentialing, that would indicate a conjoint or custodial model, but not a heteronomous model. As we conducted our analysis, we found we had to decide how to categorize systems that shared characteristics with each model of professional control. For example, one system shared six characteristics with the conjoint ideal type and three each with the custodial and heteronomous ideal types. We ended up coding this system as conjoint, because 'conjoint' had the most matches. For seven of the eight systems, this method of assigning the majority type as the control type was applied. For the one system that shared equal numbers of characteristics with each mode of control, we relied on interview data about physicians' high level of participation in strategic planning to assign a mode (conjoint). Strategic planning stood out among the indicators as clearly communicating the integration of physicians into the executive order of a system. From these indicators, we were able to determine that four of our eight systems had conjoint modes of control, three of the eight had heteronomous modes of control, and one had a custodial mode of control.

Our use of qualitative methods revealed the limitations of applying these three abstract models of professional control to the eight systems specifically, as well as health care organizations generally. Our in-depth qualitative analysis uncovered complexities and complications quantitative methods would have overlooked. We found that our focal systems displayed the characteristics of at least two and sometimes all three of the ideal types. From a theoretical point of view, the mixing of heteronomous and conjoint or custodial control within one organization seems unlikely, if not counterproductive. We assumed there would be more consistency in the cultures and practices of these systems, but found each system was, if not a contested terrain, at least a bit murky. Certainly, the way we operationalized the dimensions of each ideal type and the types of measurements we used may have driven our findings, but our findings were consistent with the work of others who have evaluated other models of bureaucratic control (e.g., Sheaff et al., 2003; Germov, 2005). Our qualitative case studies more clearly illuminated the nature of professional control in integrated health care systems. They undermined simplistic assumptions that managerialist practices automatically reduce physician autonomy, as well as demonstrated the great diversity of manager–physician relations within the set of eight systems. In addition, our study illustrated the need to develop more accurate theoretical models of professional practice within bureaucracies.

CODING ORGANIZATIONAL IDENTITY OVER TIME: UNCOVERING USEFUL KEY WORDS AND THEMES

A final example of multilevel case study methodology comes from my dissertation (Caronna, 2000), an in-depth study of Kaiser Permanente that built off of the case studies and field-level framing in Scott et al. (2000). The goal of the study was to examine the role Kaiser Permanente played in influencing changes in the field and how it interpreted and presented itself in changing eras. Although one cannot generalize from a single case, an examination of Kaiser Permanente's experiences over time could lead to improved theories of how health organizations react to radical and incremental change in policies, field-level governance, and broad-based beliefs and values; how health organizations help enact these changes, either intentionally or unintentionally; and how long-established organizations reacted to the importation of managerial logics and market mechanisms into the health care field.

The data I collected came from many sources, including Kaiser Permanente annual reports; oral histories of Kaiser Permanente founders and leaders; archival collections of memos and personal papers; interviews conducted by myself and others; histories of Kaiser Permanente in books and magazines; and three biographies of Henry J. Kaiser. I tried to assemble a wide variety of data, but stopped collecting when I felt new sources confirmed what I already knew. I also asked a few current leaders of the organization to recommend sources, and found that each person recommended similar articles and books. Therefore, I believe I reached a point of saturation in my data collection.

To examine how Kaiser Permanente interpreted and presented itself in changing eras, I adopted the concept *organizational identity*: the central, enduring, and characteristics of an organization (Dutton and Dukerich, 1991; Whetten and Godfrey, 1998). It turned out that this was fairly easy to operationalize, because Kaiser Permanente had a set of seven characteristics its leaders called its principles, its 'genetic code' (Smillie, 1991) and the 'Kaiser formula' (Somers, 1971). These principles, which remained constant throughout the study period, were: prepayment for services; physician group practice; integrated medical facilities; comprehensive, preventive medical care; voluntary enrolment with a choice of at least two physicians; physician responsibility for medical care and medical decision making; and operation of the health plan and hospitals as nonprofit corporations.

When Kaiser Permanente opened to the public in 1945, some of these principles led to considerable opposition and persecution from medical societies. In particular, prepayment and group practice contrasted with the dominant model of fee-for-service reimbursement and solo practice. As the health care field changed in the 1960s and 1970s, Kaiser Permanente emerged as a model for a new type of medical organization (the health maintenance organization), and was praised on the national scene by federal administrators. As managerialist beliefs and market mechanisms overtook the health care field in the 1980s and 1990s, Kaiser Permanente faced increasing competition and worked to maintain and project its distinctive edge.

One of the coding techniques I developed helped me analyze Kaiser Permanente's annual reports and the opening letter in each report written by the president or chief executive officer (CEO). The annual reports were particularly helpful for assessing changes over time in the presentation of Kaiser Permanente's identity, because the reports explicitly listed program principles and structures in various years. My strategy for analyzing the annual reports included both inductive and deductive phases. In my first round of coding, I read each CEO letter and looked for words and phrases used to describe Kaiser Permanente and the US health care field in general. I generated a list of key words through this process, such as 'affordable', 'comprehensive', 'efficient', 'incongruent', 'leader', 'pioneer', and 'quality'.

In the second round, I counted the number of times each key word appeared in each CEO letter and recorded the frequencies of each key word for all years. In the third round, I counted the number of sentences and words in each CEO letter and labelled each sentence as one of four types ('identity', 'progress', 'environment', and 'other'). In the fourth round, I identified the frequency of key words according to their sentence types in order to sort out words about the health care field from words referring specifically to Kaiser Permanente (a word would have to be in an 'identity' or 'progress' sentence to count). In the fifth round, I checked for key words year-by-year, keyword-by-keyword to catch any I missed and updated my frequencies accordingly.

After completing this coding procedure, I used the data to focus on several aspects of Kaiser Permanente's identity and presentation of its identity over time. First, I looked at the presentation of Kaiser Permanente's seven principles. I found that each of the core principles was mentioned fairly regularly and consistently until the early 1980s, when HMOs and other forms of managed care organizations developed and began to dominate the market. At this point, the CEO letters began to downplay certain principles that demonstrated the organization's congruence with other organizations in the field, and instead emphasized principles that distinguished Kaiser Permanente from other providers. For example, because of the growth of managed care organizations in the United States, being a prepaid group practice was no longer distinctive. In addition, the growth of multihospital and integrated health care systems lessened the distinctiveness of Kaiser's own integrated facilities. Nevertheless, its nonprofit status became a salient principle as investor-owned health organizations increased in numbers, especially in the managed care industry. Kaiser Permanente also emphasized their principle that physicians, not lay managers, controlled all decisions about medical care. In this competitive arena, the CEO letters selectively discussed aspects of Kaiser Permanente's identity in attempts at self-definition and justification in order to reinforce its status as a unique health care organization.

In addition to examining the principles discussed in CEO letters, I coded the letters for statements about conformity and distinctiveness in order to investigate how Kaiser Permanente presented its identity as its legitimacy in the health care field improved over time. I looked at the 'identity' and 'progress' sentences in each CEO letter to see if any contained statements comparing Kaiser Permanente to other organizations in the field or discussed Kaiser Permanente's congruence with the field. After the mid-1970s, as it became more legitimate and less distinctive, I found that there were more attempts to distinguish Kaiser Permanente from other organizations and HMOs than expressions of its similarity to the field. The CEO letters showed an almost perfect shift in the mid-1970s from claiming conformity to constructing distinctiveness. Although compared to its environment, Kaiser Permanente was at its most unusual in the 1940s and 1950s, CEOs did not discuss its unique qualities until it had gained legitimacy and the HMO population had grown.

These various coding techniques helped me create a more systematic analysis of my case study data than I would have had if I had relied on my own readings of the annual reports. By creating multiround coding strategies, I was able to catch key words and phrases I had overlooked on the first read-through, and I was able to better examine and understand the nuances of the data by doing multiple rounds. Although qualitative data analysis computer software existed at this time, I chose to conduct my analyses by hand. A computer could have picked up key word frequencies more quickly than I could, and with fewer mistakes, but I didn't think a computer could handle the subtlety of coding a sentence as 'distinctive', 'conforming', or 'legitimate' without a clear deductive strategy. Since this analysis required a degree of induction, I chose to take the more arduous route of coding by hand. In the end, these analyses of the annual reports were invaluable for supporting my overall findings gleaned from simply reading histories, oral history transcripts, and other materials, but also pointed out more complex ways Kaiser Permanente's history unfolded over time than I would have picked up from less systematic attention to the data.

CONCLUSION: INSIGHTS FROM MULTILEVEL CASE STUDIES

As these examples demonstrate, the qualitative case study methods my colleagues and I used helped us develop in-depth and nuanced understandings of changes in the US health care field and the impact of these changes on health organizations and practitioners. The comparison of four San Francisco Bay Area health organizations demonstrates the use of qualitative methods to provide rich description as well as theoretical elaboration. Here, our use of a 'typical' case to contrast with more unique organizations helped us verify the standard stories told about federal policies and programs – that Medicare was a 'cash cow', for example, or that community hospitals benefited from the Hill-Burton hospital construction funds. We also found it useful to contrast the reactions of our unique organizations to San Jose Hospital's, as well as note when the unique organizations shared the typical hospital's response. The relationship across eras between Kaiser Permanente and the health care field was an important indicator of the field's flexibility in its norms and expectations. Overall, our qualitative data allowed us to capture the range and complexity of health organizations' experiences in different historical eras, as well as the ways each organization contributed to and helped create the health care field. Our quantitative data and analyses, by design, simply could not provide us with this type of understanding. Thus, our use of case studies greatly enriched our project's findings and conclusions.

The Kitchener et al. (2005) study discussed in the foregoing section is one of a number of studies of the role of physicians in health bureaucracies. The use of qualitative case studies to explore this topic has revealed the limitations of our abstract models of bureaucracy. In this study, we found that definitions of conjoint, custodial, and heteronomous control were too simple to capture the complexity of our focal integrated health care systems. Most of the systems we studied shared characteristics with more than one model. Sheaff et al. (2003) similarly found the model of 'soft bureaucracy' only partially applicable to English Primary Care Groups and Primary Care Trusts, in which sophisticated management strategies were adopted but physicians diluted them through scepticism and passivity. Germov's (2005) study of hyper-rationalization in the Australian public health sector found that rationality existed in varying degrees; different types of rationality were not necessarily integrated into a hyper-rational whole; and the presence of irrationalities undermined the explanatory power of the hyper-rationalization model. These nuanced and complex findings, which would be difficult to address in a quantitative study, reveal the need for health care organizations researchers to develop more accurate theoretical models of bureaucracy and control. In addition, the studies illuminate the degree to which professional dominance and autonomy survives in an era of managerialism and market forces.

With the rapid and radical changes occurring in many nations' health care organizations, the use of qualitative methods enhances researchers' ability to better understand the history and nature of these changes and refine the theories we will use to guide future research. Qualitative studies that incorporate data from multiple levels of analysis, and that employ well-designed and systematic sampling and coding procedures, are a necessary means to fully understand the complexities of today's health care organizations, and ultimately, improve our systems of health and health care.

REFERENCES

Ackroyd, Stephen, Hughes, John A., and Soothill, Keith (1989) 'Public Sector Services and Their Management', *Journal of Management Studies*, 26(6): 603–19.

Arndt, Margarete and Bigelow, Barbara (2000) 'Presenting Structural Innovation in an Institutional Environment: Hospitals' Use of Impression Management', *Administrative Science Quarterly*, 45(2000): 494–522.

Ayres, Lioness, Kavanaugh, Karen, and Knafl, Kathleen A. (2003) 'Within-Case and Across-Case Approaches to Qualitative Data Analysis', *Qualitative Health Research*, 13(6): 871–83.

Barley, Stephen R. (1986) 'Technology as Occasion for Structuring: Evidence from Observations of CT Scanners and the Social Order of Radiology Departments', *Administrative Science Quarterly*, 31(1986): 78–108.

Bazzoli, Gloria J., Shortell, Stephen M., Dubbs, Nicole, Chan, Cheeling, and Krovolac, Peter (1999) 'A Taxonomy of Health Networks and Systems: Bringing Order Out of Chaos', *Health Services Research*, 33(6): 1683–717.

Bourgeault, Ivy Lynn and Mulvale, Gillian (2006) 'Collaborative Health Care Teams in Canada and the USA: Confronting the Structural Embeddedness of Medical Dominance', *Health Sociology Review*, 15(5): 481–95.

Bradley, Elizabeth H., Curry, Leslie A., and Devers, Kelly J. (2007) 'Qualitative Data Analysis for Health Services Research: Developing Taxonomy, Themes, and Theory', *Health Services Research*, 42(4): 1758–72.

Buchanan, David A., Addicott, Rachael, Fitzgerald, Louise, Ferlie, Ewan, and Baeza, Juan I. (2007) 'Nobody in Charge: Distributed Change Agency in Healthcare', *Human Relations*, 60(7): 1065–90.

Caronna, Carol A. (2000) 'Organizational Identity in Changing Contexts: The Case of Kaiser Permanente and the U.S. Health Care Field'. PhD dissertation, Stanford University.

Caronna, Carol A., Pollack, Seth S., and Scott, W. Richard (2009) 'Organizations, Populations, and Fields: Investigating Organizational Heterogeneity Through a Multilevel Case Study Design'. In Brayden G. King, Teppo Felin, and David A. Whetten (eds), *Research in the Sociology of Organizations (Volume 26): Studying Differences between Organizations: Comparative Approaches to Organizational Research,* 249–70. London: Emerald Group Publishing Limited.

Corbin, Juliet and Strauss, Anselm (2008) *Basics of Qualitative Research: Techniques and Procedures of Developing Grounded Theory* (3rd Edition). Thousand Oaks, CA: Sage.

Coulter, Ian, Hilton, Lara, Ryan, Gery, Ellison, Marcia and Rhodes, Hilary (2008) 'Trials and Tribulations on the Road to Implementing Integrative Medicine in a Hospital Setting', *Health Sociology Review*, 17(4): 368–83.

Czarniawska, Barbara (1997) *Narrating the Organization: Dramas of Institutional Identity.* Chicago: University of Chicago Press.

Denzin, Norman K. and Lincoln, Yvonna S. (eds) (2005) *The Sage Handbook of Qualitative Research* (3rd Edition). Thousand Oaks, CA: Sage.

Devers, Kelly J. (1999) 'How Will We Know "Good" Qualitative Research When We See It? Beginning the Dialogue in Health Services Research', *Health Services Research*, 34(5 Part II): 1153–88.

DiMaggio, Paul J. and Powell, Walter W. (1983) 'The Iron Cage Revisited: Institutional Isomorphism and Collective Rationality in Organizational Fields', *American Sociological Review*, 48: 147–60.

Dutton, Jane E. and Dukerich, Janet M. (1991) 'Keeping an Eye on the Mirror: The Role of Image and Identity in Organizational Adaptation', *Academy of Management Journal*, 34: 517–54.

Eisenhardt, Kathleen M. (1989) 'Building Theories from Case Study Research', *Academy of Management Review*, 14(4): 532–50.

Germov, John (2005) 'Managerialism in the Australian Public Health Sector: Towards the Hyper-Rationalisation of Professional Bureaucracies', *Sociology of Health and Illness*, 27(6): 738–58.

Glaser, Barney and Strauss, Anselm (1967) *The Discovery of Grounded Theory: Strategies of Qualitative Research.* London: Wiedenfeld and Nicholson.

Hoff, Timothy J. and Witt, Lori C. (2000) 'Exploring the Use of Qualitative Methods in Published Health Services and Management Research', *Medical Care Research and Review*, 57(2): 139–60.

Kitchener, Martin (2002) 'Mobilizing the Logic of Managerialism in Professional Fields: The Case of Academic Health Centre Mergers', *Organization Studies*, 23(3): 391–420.

Kitchener, Martin, Caronna, Carol A., and Shortell, Stephen M. (2005) 'From the Doctor's Workshop to the Iron Cage? Evolving Modes of Physician Control in U.S. Health Systems', *Social Science and Medicine*, 60: 1311–22.

Klein, Katherine and Kozlowski, Steve W.J. (eds) (2000) *Multilevel Theory, Research, and Methods in Organizations*. San Francisco, CA: Jossey-Bass.

Lake, Timothy, Devers, Kelly, Brewster, Linda, and Casalino, Lawrence (2003) 'Something Old, Something New: Recent Developments in Hospital–Physician Relationships', *Health Services Research*, 38(1, Part II): 471–88.

Lewin, Simon and Green, Judith (2009) 'Ritual and the Organization of Primary Care Clinics in Cape Town, South Africa', *Social Science and Medicine*, 68(2009): 1464–71.

Martin, Douglas, Shulman, Ken, Santiago-Sorrell, Patricia and Singer, Peter (2003) 'Priority-Setting and Hospital Strategic Planning: A Qualitative Case Study', *Journal of Health Services Research and Policy*, 8(4): 197–201.

McDonald, Ruth, Waring, Justin and Harrison, Stephen (2006) 'Rules, Safety and the Narrativisation of Identity: A Hospital Operating Theatre Case Study', *Sociology of Health and Illness*, 28(2): 178–202.

Miles, Matthew. B. and Huberman, A. Michael (1994) *Qualitative Data Analysis* (2nd Edition). Thousand Oaks, CA: Sage.

Muhr, Thomas (1997) *ATLAS.ti: The Knowledge Workbench.* Berlin: Scientific Software Development.

Ragin, Charles C. (1999) 'The Distinctiveness of Case-Oriented Research', *Health Services Research*, 34(5, Part II): 1137–51.

Ragin, Charles C. and Becker, Howard S. (eds) (1992) *What is a Case? Exploring the Foundations of Social Inquiry.* New York: Cambridge University Press.

Reay, Trish and Hinings, C.R. (Bob) (2005) 'The Recomposition of an Organizational Field: Health Care in Alberta', *Organization Studies,* 26(3): 351–84.

Scott, W. Richard (1965) 'Reaction to Supervision in a Heteronomous Professional Organization', *Administrative Science Quarterly,* 10: 65–81.

Scott, W. Richard (1982) 'Managing Professional Work: Three Models of Control for Health Organizations', *Health Services Research*, 17(3): 213–40.

Scott, W. Richard, Ruef, Martin, Mendel, Peter J., and Caronna, Carol A. (2000) *Institutional Change and Healthcare Organizations: From Professional Dominance to Managed Care.* Chicago: University of Chicago Press.

Sheaff, R., Rogers, A., Pickard, S., Marshall, M., Campbell, S., Sibbald, B., Halliwell, S., and Roland, M. (2003) 'A Subtle Governance: "Soft" Medical Leadership in English Primary Care', *Sociology of Health and Illness*, 25(5): 408–28.

Shortell, Stephen M., Gillies, Robin R., Anderson, David A., Erickson, Karen Morgan, and Mitchell, John B. (2000) *Remaking Health Care in America: The Evolution of Organized Delivery Systems* (2nd Edition). San Francisco: Jossey-Bass.

Shuval, Judith T., Mizrachi, Nissim, and Smetannikov, Emma (2002) 'Entering the Well-Guarded Fortress: Alternative Practitioners in Hospital Settings', *Social Science and Medicine,* 55(2002): 1745–55.

Smillie, John G. (1991) *Can Physicians Manage the Quality and Costs of Care?: The Story of The Permanente Medical Group.* New York: Mc-Graw Hill.

Sofaer, Shoshanna (1999) 'Qualitative Methods: What Are They and Why Use Them?', *Health Services Research,* 34(5, Part II): 1101–18.

Somers, Anne R. (1971) *Health Care in Transition: Directions for the Future.* Chicago: Hospital Research and Education Trust.

Stake, Robert E. (2005) 'Qualitative Case Studies'. In Norman K. Denzin and Yvonna S. Lincoln (eds), *The Sage Handbook of Qualitative Research,* 443–66. Thousand Oaks, CA: Sage.

Van Maanen, John (1979) 'Reclaiming Qualitative Methods for Organizational Research: A Preface', *Administrative Science Quarterly*, 24(4): 520–6.

Vaughan, Diane (1992) 'Theory Elaboration: The Heuristics of Case Analysis'. In Charles C. Ragin and Howard S. Becker (eds) *What is a Case?: Exploring the Foundations of Social Inquiry*, 172–202. New York: Cambridge University Press.

Vaughan, Diane (1996) *The Challenger Launch Decision: Risky Technology, Culture, and Deviance at NASA*. Chicago: University of Chicago Press.

Whetten, David A. and Godfrey, Paul C. Godfrey (eds) (1998) *Identity in Organizations: Building Theory through Conversations*. Thousand Oaks, CA: Sage.

Yin, Robert K. (1989) *Case Study Research: Design and Methods* (Revised edition). Newbury Park, CA: Sage.

Yin, Robert K. (1999) 'Enhancing the Quality of Case Studies in Health Services Research', *Health Services Research*, 34(5, Part II): 1209–24.

5

How Country Matters: Studying Health Policy in a Comparative Perspective

Sirpa Wrede

INTRODUCTION

The aim of this chapter is to offer an introduction to the use of qualitative methods in comparative health policy. The argument is that when the cases designed for comparative health policy research are composed in a reflexive way, qualitative research provides the most promising means to forward an in-depth, context-sensitive understanding of health policy and of country as a macro-social frame for the social and cultural organization of health care systems.

The use of qualitative methods has been commonplace in health policy analysis from the outset (Mechanic, 1975), and, considering the complexity of the subject of research, this is hardly surprising. Policy making is a complex process politically as well as socially, involving multiple actors and arenas employing diverse material as well as symbolic resources. Qualitative methods offer the means to tackle this complexity of policy making.

Recent literature has, however, critiqued the lack of methodological clarity in comparative health care policy, calling for greater reflexivity in the use of qualitative methods and particularly, in the use of the case study methods (Walt et al., 2008, p. 312). In policy analysis, the identification of a 'case' is a process where the researcher typically actively selects to examine some instances of the policy process and excludes others, in an effort to be able to identify a meaningful configuration of events, actors and processes. When examining only one case, however, there is a risk that the analysis remains descriptive, without the means to identify more general dynamics of policymaking (Clark et al., 2002). For researchers interested in explanation and generalization, comparison offers a means to systematize qualitative analysis. To compare is to classify with the aim to explain, and unlike description, comparison therefore presupposes analytical frameworks that surpass the specific case so that the cases to be compared can be interrogated in relation to each other, allowing the search for both similar and different dynamics (Bradshaw and Wallace, 1991). Comparison, however, is a method that needs to be used reflexively. Comparative health policy, to be discussed in this chapter, provides a good example of both the potential and the challenges of comparative qualitative research. Even though comparisons within countries as well as within and between regions and organizations are of interest for policy analysis, the term comparative health policy traditionally refers to comparisons across countries, states or nations. This definition is in the starting point for this chapter that considers how and why country matters in comparative research on health care policy.

In the following, I first discuss qualitative research on health policy, identifying the rationale for the reflexive comparative approach suggested in this chapter. The subsequent sections focus first on qualitative case studies as the key methodological approach and the principles for how cases are developed. The next section discusses the use of qualitative methods in comparative health policy, presenting first documentary approaches, involving use of materials that have been created by other actors independent from research. Then ethnographic approaches and interviewing are discussed. After the presentation of the key methods, the remainder of the chapter considers key analytical concerns in research design in qualitative comparative studies. The conclusion summarizes the rationale for the main argument of the chapter.

HEALTH POLICY RESEARCH AND THE RENAISSANCE OF QUALITATIVE METHODS

Health policy scholars often emphasize the analytical framework they use at the expense of specifying the methodological design of their research. The neglect to discuss research methods may be associated with the impact of the positivist tradition in social science that favours quantitative research designs. Positivist research tends to use qualitative methods out of necessity, rather than by choice, as the aim is to find universal, culture-free explanations. Approached from this perspective, qualitative data appears 'idiosyncratic' and unavoidably 'descriptive of particular locations and periods of time' (Mechanic, 1975, p. 43), thus falling short when compared with the ideal data that would allow for quantitative analysis.

In the same vein, the assumptions underpinning the analytical frameworks employed may also serve as an explanation of the absence of reflexivity concerning the use of research methods. Early health policy scholars, working in a tradition that assumed universal social laws, commonly took for granted that Western health care systems were following a shared path towards modernization. This *convergence hypothesis* maintained that Western industrialized countries were separate societies evolving towards 'increased uniformity of social structures' (Field, 1989, p. 13). The country as a context for health care delivery systems accounted for particularistic variation, but not in ways interesting to research. The analysis of health policy compared instead the assumed outcomes of health care delivery systems with the aim to compare their effectiveness in advancing medical progress. Sociology, health administration and health economics emerged as distinct approaches to the comparative study of health care delivery systems, reflecting attention to society, organizations, and economics respectively, all organized within the country context (Mechanic, 1975). In this vein, much of policy analysis is concentrated on developing tools for the evaluation of policy options. A recent textbook offers an example of the approach, with its focus on themes such as resource allocation, priority setting, or regulation of professionals (Blank and Burau, 2007). The policy development perspective defines the study of health policy as analysis of 'those courses of action taken *by governments* that deal with the financing, provision or governance of health services' (Blank and Burau, 2007, p. 2, emphasis added). Even though qualitative methods are commonly used, their role in research design tends not to be given attention, as the emphasis is on developing typologies that capture the various generalizable models of policy making (see Blank and Burau, 2007).

Another strand in the literature on comparative research is rooted in critical and social constructivist perspectives in the study of health policy. Here a broader understanding of the topic is adopted. Scholars who work with the more open-ended approaches emphasize the view of health policy as a contested area of politics rather than an ultimately strategic process, primarily mastered by the government (Walt, 1994). In this vein, health care policy is viewed as enmeshed in economics, ideologies and culture (Green and Thorogood, 1998) and health policy is most fruitfully conceptualized as processes occurring at multiple levels that can be analytically separated. A leading proponent of this approach, Walt (1994), argues that she recognizes eclectically the relevance of multiple theoretical approaches to capture the complexity of the 'process and power' in health care policy. In addition to the international and national level, she emphasizes the face-to-face level of 'the actual processes of policy and the actors involved at every stage' (Walt, 1994, p. 6). This is in line with how comparative social scientists in many areas of research have since the late 1980s promoted the more reflexive use of qualitative methods, underlining the need to take the complexity of data into account in comparative analysis (Øyen, 1990). Reflecting the renaissance of qualitative methods, such scholarship on comparative health care policy approaches policy from a social constructivist position, treating policy as inevitably shaped by its social context (e.g., Lee et al., 2002; Freeman, 2006; Gilson and Raphaely, 2008).

The social–constructivist view of health care policy recognizes that 'policy' can itself be defined in many different ways. From this perspective, the 'making' of policy may involve a complex set of actors not limited to the government or the organizations internal to the health system (Walt et al., 2008, p. 310). In this vein, Buse et al. (2005, p. 6, emphasis added) suggest that it is useful to think of health care policy as embracing 'courses of *action* (*and inaction*) that affect the set of institutions, organizations, services and funding arrangements of the health system'. The multilevel understanding of health care policy helps to explore the sociocultural embeddedness of health care policy, that is, the way that national health policies and structures reflect deeply rooted values and norms which differ between societies. Saltman's (1997) analysis of the explanatory power of the convergence thesis versus that of the embeddedness thesis of divergence suggests, however, that it is not fruitful to treat sociocultural embeddedness as the new grand theory for comparative research on health policy. Rather, in his view, comparative research should take as a starting point a complex interplay of partners between and within countries, dependent upon economic, cultural, historical and geographical as well as political elements. This means that while some aspects of health systems between two countries may be converging, at the same time other aspects may be diverging. In Saltman's view, therefore most suitable to capture such complexity is the notion of a *convergence/divergence mix* (Saltman, 1997, p. 452). This position is in line with current developments in national health policies that are increasingly influenced and even displaced by global decisions as well as domestic actions. Qualitative methods, and particularly comparative case studies, are well suited precisely for capturing such complexity (Bradshaw and Wallace, 1991).

CASE STUDIES ORIENTED TOWARDS INTERNATIONAL COMPARISON

Even though it is common to refer to qualitative comparative research on health care policy as case study research or case-oriented research, no unified, self-conscious methodological approach of conducting case study research oriented towards international comparison exists. Rather, there are several, more or less integrated research traditions that build on the use of historical and qualitative methods that became termed the 'case-oriented tradition' *post-hoc*, to separate them from a quantitative variable-oriented approach (Ragin, 1987, p. ix). In the 1980s, the topic of comparative methodology emerged as a theoretical concern parallel to the renaissance of qualitative methods, inspiring the more reflexive use of qualitative case studies in comparative research (Bradshaw and Wallace, 1991). To be sure, one strand in comparative literature has engaged with the complexity of case study data by developing an approach that builds on Boolean algebra (Ragin, 1987). This 'small-N research' has, however, been shaped by its close association with statistical analyses (see Caramani, 2009).

A methodologically reflexive use of qualitative methods in case-based research entails the comparison of relatively few cases that are carefully chosen for well-specified theoretical and/or substantive reasons (Bradshaw and Wallace, 1991, p. 156). The qualitative case-oriented method to comparison involves a comprehensive and detailed approach that typically combines several qualitative methods (Lian, 2008; see, for example, Chapter 4 by Caronna in this volume). Case research has become advocated particularly as the method of choice when the emphasis is on theorizing, but the arguments for reflexivity are both analytical and practical. Case study research as such is a time and resource intensive process, and comparative case studies introduce further challenges, involving relatively expensive work across multiple languages and cultures (Walt et al., 2008, p. 313). A thoughtful approach to qualitative methods thus both saves time and money, and secures a higher quality of research. The following sections discuss common challenges, considering the different methods that can be used in case-oriented research.

ASKING COMPARATIVE QUESTIONS ABOUT POLICY: CONSTRUCTING THE 'CASE'

All kinds of comparative social research face the shared challenge of defining the object of comparison in a consistent way, when shared definitions of basic terms are missing. Health policy terms tend to carry with them the histories of specific policy programs in particular countries, and particular conceptions of, for instance, service organization or health problems are naturalized in that terminology. This is not unique to comparative health care policy: all areas of comparative studies struggle with problem of translating complex concepts between languages and societies (Clark et al., 2002, p. 277). A political term such as 'liberalism' may have very different meanings in different political traditions. Similarly, the organization of political institutions, such as the state, varies greatly and particularly the state has very different powers in health policy in different countries. The consistency of the terms used in different languages becomes an even more complicated matter in a historical perspective and when the terms refer to ideas that are influential in political processes (Dutton, 2007, pp. 24–26). The analysis of such terms therefore becomes one of the tasks that researchers have to engage with in order to be able to define the phenomenon under study. It is important to note that even such shared folk concepts as doctor, nurse or patient mean different things in different contexts (Mechanic and Rochefort, 1996). Organizational roles in health care are complex products of long-term developments in health policy and therefore, in the words of an early scholar, everywhere situated in 'a defining and delimiting institutional matrix' (Davies, 1979, p. 515). She recommends a study of that matrix rather than the variation in occupational roles as a more promising avenue to achieve context-sensitive understanding.

Davies's study is an example of how a shared language does not guarantee the consistency of terminology. The Anglo-American context and the Commonwealth are examples of wider sociocultural spheres where a shared language as well as numerous historical links can facilitate research, but also pose a challenge. By choosing cases with cultural affinity, the researchers hope to avoid the problems of translation and construct their cases with greater precision. With reference to J.S. Mill's method of difference, such strategy in case selection is often referred to as the choice of 'most similar' cases, another possible strategy being a focus on 'most different' cases (Ragin, 1987, pp. 44–49). Assumed cultural affinity and a long tradition of comparisons between certain countries may, however, become blinders that are not present in fresher comparisons. Furthermore, from a social constructivist perspective, a case is never representative of a category of cases but unique. Accordingly, each case needs to be considered in its own terms, rather than assuming that a shared term signifies shared culture. Thus, the issues of translation in a comparative research project are never merely technical, rather translation lies at heart of the development of robust concepts that 'travel' between contexts (Wrede et al., 2006). This means that the analysis of terminology is a key avenue to an understanding about institutional matrices, cultural ideas, political traditions, policy concerns et cetera. Therefore, a shared language does not remove the challenges related to language in the construction of concepts.

Compared with the complex variation of the ways similar ideas are formulated in different health policy contexts, physiological phenomena like pregnancy, birth, or death appear to provide conceptual stability in the area of health care around which research concepts can be built. While such phenomena offer fruitful foci for comparative analyses, these seemingly definite notions need to be approached with caution. Even when the physiological processes in themselves may be very similar, the social and cultural meanings of these phenomena vary (De Vries et al., 2001). This is not an argument against comparative analysis. Rather it is a methodological concern to be accounted for (Clark et al., 2002). One means of analyzing such variation is by examining the complex processes of classification that organize social phenomena (Bowker and Star, 1999).

Taking into consideration the challenges involved in conceptualizing the object of comparisons, it becomes evident that the construction of cases to examine involves the active hand of the researcher who chooses how to define and delimit the phenomenon under study, the level of abstraction on which the phenomenon is identified and the context against which it is considered. With the various configurations of health care policy processes worldwide, what is defined as macro, meso or micro level is unavoidably a matter of empirical consideration, not one of employing fixed previously existing definitions. Thus, cases are to be perceived as *interpretive constructs* rather than objective facts to be identified in an empirical context (Carmel, 1999).

Policy scholarship offers numerous frameworks to employ for a systematic discussion of policy making processes (Blank and Burau, 2007; Walt et al., 2008). Rather than looking for the ultimate frameworks, a reflexive approach to the construction of cases recognizes both the research interests that drove their development and the intellectual and political context the frameworks were developed in. Issues in health policy are political everywhere, but the history of *how* an issue has been politicised varies between policy contexts. Readymade frameworks are particularly problematic when the comparative study involves countries that previously have rarely been included in comparative studies. A grounded approach involves mapping of policy systems and actors as well as tracing of policy processes. The collection of materials in health policy analysis often takes places through a snowball method of combining different approaches to map the complex scene where the phenomenon under study takes place, in order to be able to delimit the core case to be subjected to more detailed study.

Shiffman's (2007) study of the comparative level of political priority given to maternal mortality in five low-income countries provides an example of a study that builds on pre-existing wider case studies to be able to carry out a more focused analysis. Based on a secondary analysis of five single-country case studies by the same author, the study employs a process-tracing methodology, involving multiple sources of data about agenda setting on maternal mortality in the countries under consideration. In a similar vein, Lian (2008) compared primary health care reforms of the 1990s to examine claims on convergence. The researcher constructed his cases following a predefined list of organizational dimensions that was used as a tool for selecting data and organizing analysis. Aiming to achieve depth rather than breadth in his analysis of 'similarities and differences in patterns of structural change' Lian (2008, p. 30) like Shiffman used a combination of different qualitative methods, including documentary analysis and fieldwork, to build his cases. In this vein, the combination of several different methods often found in case research form an asset for the 'tracing of policy processes' and identification of 'patterns of change' in organizational structures. Diversity of data also allows the triangulation of the types of bias or, more aptly put, perspective in data. Policy data is always situated somehow in relation to the process examined. The rhetoric in political talk and texts is a particular consideration to be accounted for in the analysis, especially when tracing policy processes. Not surprisingly, scholars struggle to avoid confusing 'words with actions' (Lian, 2008, p. 30). At the same time, it is evident that the expressions of political culture may be particularly interesting to capture in a comparative study.

Health policy analysts are further constrained by the way they themselves are viewed or 'situated' as researchers, most markedly, whether they are viewed (by themselves or others) as insiders or outsiders (Walt et al., 2008, p. 314). Such limiting conditions shape the research, but the researcher can also actively try to influence the conditions of positionality, within certain limits. In comparative research, while it is not possible to become native of some other country context, it is possible to increase familiarity of that context with numerous strategies, and researchers can also choose to collaborate in teams that involve both insiders and outsiders. Reflexivity of the role of health policy research for the policy processes examined is also of importance.

A recent reformulation of case study methods advocates qualitative approaches precisely for their particular potential to grasp the rich ambiguity of politics and planning in a modern democracy. In his critique of the 'misunderstandings concerning case-study research', Flyvbjerg (2006) argues that the case study in itself is a result. In his view, the story should be told 'in its diversity', allowing it to unfold from the many-sided, complex and sometimes conflicting stories told by the actors in the case (Flyvbjerg, 2006, p. 238). Echoing Walt's (1994) eclectic approach, Flyvbjerg (2006) explicitly warns against linking the 'telling of the story' to the theories of any one academic specialty. In this vein, and supporting both the notion of convergence/divergence mix and the related aim of capturing the story in its diversity, Lian (2008, p. 38) concludes on the basis of his comparison of primary health care reforms in three countries that each country has its own unique story and even while influenced by global ideas, the present developments represent a continuation of that story.

METHODS OF CREATING DATA FOR CASE STUDIES

The following focuses in greater detail on how researchers gather or, from a social constructivist perspective more aptly, create data on their health policy cases.

Documentary methods

Documentary methods involve the use of already *existing materials*. Documents are bound to a specific point in time and therefore they can be used to examine, for instance, how a specific actor argued in a specific stage of a policy process. The data content in documents is fixed and therefore the researcher is limited to formulating research questions that the available documents can respond to. Accordingly, it is common for researchers to combine documentary materials with other means of acquiring data, such as interviewing. For some studies the fact that documents are not influenced by the researcher may, however, be a particular advantage, when the researcher is interested in, for instance, spontaneous expressions of policy rhetoric. The researcher may also want to map debates and examine exchanges between policy actors et cetera.

Even though the data exists independently from research and the researcher does not shape the individual documents, documentary research does involve the active role of the researcher who chooses which documents to include in the study, often from a great number of possible materials. These particular conditions do not, however, exclude the multiple uses of documents if such conditions are taken into consideration (Prior, 2003).

Documentary research also requires language expertise as well as in-depth knowledge of the society under scrutiny (Dutton, 2007, p. 2). A researcher working alone is often constrained in his or her work by the shortage of context-specific expertise (Wrede et al., 2006). Close collaboration between scholars may help to overcome this challenge. Altenstetter and Björkman (1981), for instance, broadened the scope of their separate case studies, using an analytic strategy that differs from those implemented in the earlier studies. Instead of focusing on the detailed level, Altenstetter and Björkman (1981) applied a documentary approach to comparatively map the health planning institutions in the five countries included in their respective studies. They adopted a broad time frame to capture the processes they were contrasting and comparing across countries. Their secondary analysis of their work allowed Altenstetter and Björkman to triangulate data, methods and investigator.

Documentary research is a basic source of data for health care policy study in general and comparative analysis in particular. When discussing their study on the role of multinational health care companies, Waitzkin and his colleagues (2005; Jasso-Aguilar et al., 2004), for instance, reviewed a wide range of professional and business publications as well as policy documents from multiple different sources and used a selection of these texts as their primary data. One key aim was to allow the identification of the central actors or stakeholders, map their ties with each other as well as the arenas where they act and the strategies they use. The mapping of key actors served the planning of interviews that complemented the documentary research. A second key aim achieved with the analysis of documents was to map the historical unfolding of the phenomenon under study. Both aims presuppose the collection of documents for a long research period, in this example 25 years (Waitzkin et al., 2005). van Herk and his colleagues (2001) whose comparative study of the politics of medical audit in the United Kingdom and the Netherlands covered a 30-year period also chose a long research period but focused in the final analysis on the early stages of the process in question, arguing that through this focus they were able to observe the gradual appearance of new stakeholders.

While policy documents are commonly used to map policy processes and contexts and to identify and trace policy actors and stake holders, social constructivist approaches that consider the role of language, rhetorical argument and stories in framing policy debate remain rare in the study of health care policy (Gilson and Raphaely, 2008, p. 303). A few examples of the potential of such analyses of policy discourse or policy rhetoric, however, do exist. Working in this vein, Freeman (2006, p. 66) holds that documents and reports are principal vehicles of health policymaking, the analysis of which allows an examination of the belief systems of governments with focus on how normative ideas such as equity are converted into health policy. Arguing for the importance of taking account of cross-national learning, Freeman's (2006) study focused on the travel of ideas as well as 'translation processes' between different cultural contexts, providing an example of how this type of approach can be developed into an international comparison across countries in a way that avoids treating countries as isolated cases. Freeman employs the concept of 'document architecture' to examine the production and organizations of documents as well as the ways documents are located in relationships with other documents.

The documentary materials used in health care policy research are usually textual documents. Documentary analysis as a methodological approach can, however, study any cultural product, such as architectural designs, a building or an object (Prior, 2003). Health care policy could thus be examined comparatively by comparing hospital design or other examples of material culture. The field of Science and Technology Studies suggests novel research strategies pointing in such new directions. For instance, Bowker and Star (1999) present a historical analysis of the formation of the international classification of diseases (ICD), a transnational standardization devise with a complex history of 'tangled and crisscrossing classification schemes' (Bowker and Star, p. 21). In a similar vein, Timmermans and Berg (2003, p. 22) examine how universal medical standards are made, revealing situated knowledge, blurred agency and emergent politics through which 'the world of medicine is "remade and molded" through standardization'. Berg (2004) provides numerous examples of how documentary research can be used in country-framed comparative case studies to trace historical processes as well as identify key actors in different contexts. Such analyses reveal how seemingly universal standards are the outcome of interactions between top-down design and bottom-up adoption.

Ethnographic approaches

Though health policy research is seldom based only on ethnographic research, there are examples of both early qualitative studies of health policy and more recent work that in the manner of ethnographic research identifies fields and sites to be examined and includes observation. This means that research links the process of health policy making with practices in concrete social milieus and actors that the researcher can observe and study. For instance, Björkman (1985, p. 401) describes his in-depth studies of health policymaking in three countries as 'based on thirty months of field work in Sweden, Britain and the United States (…). The materials are derived from extensive interviews with personnel in the health sector – both governmental and private – as well as from participant-observation in health agencies'. Björkman (1985) did not, however, limit himself to field methods rather his research also included substantial investigation of government documents and budgets.

In a similar fashion, many other researchers have combined observation in research fields to other methods. Shiffman (2007), for instance, used interviews and observation in combination with documentary research to consider the different interpretations of the events and circumstances offered by the different forms of data. Many scholars refer to ethnographic field work as a method of getting first-hand knowledge about society and culture (Lian, 2008). De Vries (2004) has demonstrated how a researcher who is an outsider to a country can find insights about its culture not only in the formal field work undertaken but in all aspects of living in a country. In-depth ethnographies framed by country tend to be limited to a handful of cases, and due to the character of the method, collaborative approaches are challenging.

Recent alternatives to framing the case in field work through country have potential to enrich comparative health policy research. In the emerging literature, research design aims at grasping the different dimensions of 'global cultural flows' with studies that involve field work in multiple sites (Clarke, 2005, p. 165). A recent research project that focuses on 'emerging infections in the global city' offers an example of what could be characterized as complex comparison. Working in this vein, researchers who follow a network approach bring insights from ethnographic field work as well as from other forms of qualitative research from different locations to a shared framework that assumes flows and 'traffic' between the networked 'global cities' (Ali and Keil, 2008). A similar turn to emphasizing connections and interrelatedness across national boundaries has occurred in the field of health geography that links health, culture and place (Gesler and Kearns, 2002). When examining the meanings of place, field work can be employed as a key research strategy. Comparative health care policy that instead of a country treats a global city, or indeed 'global ruralities', as its 'spatial unit of analysis' is able to construct new, more focused comparative cases. Such research typically flexibly combines field work with other qualitative and even quantitative methods (e.g., Rodwin, 2008).

Interviewing

Interviewing can be conducted as a part of an ethnographic study or separately. Policy researchers commonly use interviewing to explore policy processes and related action, and to systematize information about policy making and about the views of specific policy actors vis-à-vis the issues in question. This type of interview is often identified as a key informant or *expert interview* (Flick, 2009). The analysis of expert interviews typically proceeds on a meso or macro level.

Waitzkin and his colleagues (2005; Jasso-Aguilar et al., 2004) describe a multicountry study examining how multinational corporations in the area of health care have expanded their influence from the United States to Latin America. The interviewing of experts was conducted for a particular purpose, to investigate specific practices of health care delivery (Jasso-Aguilar et al., 2004, p. 138). The researchers used a semistructured interview protocol with close-ended and open-ended items, a strategy that allows consistency in a situation where the conditions for organizing interviews vary. This type of interview protocol also guides the interviewee to respond to the questions with reference to his or her expertise, rather than with reference to his or her personal experience (Flick, 2009, p. 167).

The choice of respondents on the basis of their specific insights about the topic examined presupposes relatively systematic prior knowledge about the context to be studied so that researchers can identify suitable interviewees (e.g., van Herk et al., 2001). Close consideration of the strategy for selecting informants is particularly important, when the interviews are used to acquire documentary data where the factual content of the data is important. The materials need to be treated critically, as any respondent is limited by a partial perspective, and it is the responsibility of the researcher to make sure that the pool of interviewees includes the perspectives identified as relevant for the study.

In drawing upon expert interview data, it is important to take into consideration that the interviews often provide *post-hoc accounts,* where the respondents are able to take into consideration the end result of the process. Particularly in such situations, expert interviews are best combined with documentary data. When both post-hoc and data produced during the process are available, the researcher has possibilities to examine how the interpretations of different dimensions of the policy process vary and differ, depending on the contextual aspects framing the ways actors think. Furthermore, as experts in the field, the interviewees commonly have a view about the role of the researcher and their interpretation of this role may impact how they view their own roles as respondents and experts (Walt et al., 2008).

When expert interviews are conducted in different countries terminology may vary greatly, reflecting the various traditions of organizing health care (e.g., Dent, 2003, pp. viii–xiv). Documentary research conducted prior to interviews serves as a method of identifying key 'vocabularies' and 'dialectal uses' of the shared policy terms. Furthermore, when research interviews are conducted in multiple languages, interviewing, as well as transcribing, coding and analyzing the materials, is particularly demanding. Translation to one shared language is expensive, and may introduce new problems when some data is translated and other not, for instance. The presence of several languages in the materials may limit the choice of analytical strategies, particularly those focused on language. An advisable strategy supported by both practical and analytical concerns is to conduct qualitative analysis of interviews on the original materials and only translate quotations to be used in the reporting to another language. Sometimes researchers choose to use the original words in their reporting, explaining their meaning, to emphasize the different conceptualization of the phenomenon considered (e.g., De Vries, 2004).

It is helpful to identify expert interviews as distinct from *experiential interviews.* Experiential interviews focus on the individual experiences of the respondent. This type of interviews is less commonly used in the comparative study of health policy. They typically serve the micro level of analysis, but may be combined with analysis conducted on other levels. The work of Bourgeault and her colleagues (2001) on everyday experiences of implicit rationing provides a rare example of such a study. While the researchers analyzed the *micro experiences* of health care providers, they perceived such analysis also as means of accessing the meso context of managerial strategies.

The interview strategies used in expert interviews and in experiential interviews differ. When semi-structured interviewing is common in expert interviews, experiential interviews typically follow a more loose structure, as researchers aim at obtaining in-depth, experiential accounts, for instance by focusing on episodes rather than themes (Flick, 2009, pp. 185–186). For example, in order to secure data where the respondents rather than the researchers formulated the issue Bourgeault and her colleagues (2001, pp. 636–637) conducted conversational interviews, posing loose questions and requesting the respondents to discuss their experiences and the issue of rationing that was the topic of the study emerged from these discussions. In the analysis, the researchers organized the accounts of the interviewees around the main claims of managed care. Even though the focus in the data collection was on the micro level, the researchers' use of strategic sampling allowed them to create robust data. They selected interviewees from different types of workplaces and with different work roles, to secure materials with a variety of experiences of the phenomenon under study.

Focus groups rather than individual interviews can be used both with experts and with other types of respondents, but in all kinds of research, this strategy differs from individual interviews as the element of group dynamics needs to be taken into account. For comparative health policy research, the method may offer a means of acquiring rich data in a rapid way, allowing the exploration of a new field or diversity of views among the participants. Focus groups do, however, pose both practical and analytical demands on the researcher (see Chapter 17 by Barbour in this volume).

ACHIEVING SENSITIVITY TO CONTEXT

Perhaps most importantly, sensitivity to context in comparative health care policy research means accounting for the institutional arrangements that structure health care policy. Countries have divergent paths (Lian, 2008). In this vein, Immergut (1990) provides an example of how to compare the lobbying efforts of national medical associations in relation to one specific type of policy initiative, government efforts to enact national health insurance. She examines three cases providing examples of different institutional paths. Immergut (1990, pp. 395–398) conceptualizes institutional context by envisioning the health care system as a political system with sets of interconnected arenas involving mechanisms that allow a core of political representatives to veto legislative proposals. She further examines the rules of representation within each context in order to 'predict where such "veto points" are likely to arise' (p. 396). The framework allows Immergut to pursue the analysis of her country cases paying attention to the necessarily particularistic explanations to why specific veto points occur and how they influence the particular developments in the different countries.

Currently, health care systems all over the world are undergoing rapid and profound transformations in ways that not only fundamentally reorder relations between the different actors but redefine the basic logics of health care delivery and reframe policy making. The new developments cannot be captured by approaches that take the country as an unquestioned context or 'frame' for health care policy (Lee et al., 2002). While the country-context and governmental policies remain important for comparative health care policy, globalization as well the complex constellations of nonstate actors need also to be taken into consideration. Attention is turning to 'complex cross-border, inter-organizational and network relationships, with policies influenced by global decisions as well as by domestic actions', meaning that 'while government and its hierarchical institutions remain important, all policy analysis must also take into account a range of open-ended, more ad hoc arrangements which increasingly affect decision making' (Walt et al., 2008, p. 309).

Recent internationally framed scholarship on health care policy is beginning to tackle the emerging 'crossborder' influences on health care policy. Often qualitative case-based methods are used. Cartwright's (2000) case study of tele-medicine traces with diverse documents how primarily US-based corporations develop new technologies that transgress national boundaries. These technologies, in turn, transform the construction of social space as well as social identities, as the corporations target profitable regions globally. By tracing the making of new, networked 'geographies of care' Cartwright (2000) demonstrates how tele-medicine is made into a technique of globalizing populations that are ordered hierarchically by the inherent centre–periphery relations on which the idea of telemedicine builds. Cartwright traces her documentary materials from diverse sources, but qualitative documentary data can also be collected in more focused way. Ranson and his colleagues (2002) examine the public health implications of multilateral trade agreements that standardize policy arrangements across countries. Their documentary analysis centre on how supranational agencies apply the trade agreements to concrete disputes. Their focused analyses are combined with more general mapping of the roles that the different supranational agencies play allowing them to examine the broader implications of how institutional developments in the global trade environment restructure and reorder health care policy.

A similar agent-centred starting point for the construction of the case for documentary research can also be used in combination with other qualitative methods such as discourse analysis. Freeman (1998) examines how supranational agencies set ideas in motion, identifying the Organization for Economic Cooperation and Development (OECD) as a major player in the politics of health care reform in Europe. Atkinson (2002), in turn, used ethnographic fieldwork in combination with a quantitative survey to examine the implications of the World Development Report of 1993 in the context of a low-income country. In a similar vein, but with an entirely qualitative research strategy, Mills (2006), in her analysis of the maternal health policy developments in Mexico, combined traditional ethno-graphic methods of observation and interviews with analysis of documents. Her ethnography of policy making and implementation provides a rich understanding of the local context, but she also manages to reveal how the implementation of the United Nation's Millennium Development Goals (MDGs) displaces the authority of the national state. Together, these studies provide examples of how qualitative case-based research can study the impact of the global flows of resources and ideas as well as the role of global policy networks.

TRACING POLICY TRANSFERS AND TRAVEL OF IDEAS

It has already been suggested that treating countries as isolated cases and separate societies may miss the interconnected character of many social developments. It is this interconnectedness that lies underneath the dynamics of the convergence/divergence mix in a country. Interconnectedness is not unique for present developments that commonly are linked to economic, political and cultural globalization. Comparative health policy history is rare, but the few examples demonstrate the interplay of 'common ideals, divergent nations' (Dutton, 2007). Dutton's comparison of the development of health care financing and organization in France and the United States provides also an example of how reflexively chosen shared notions and critical turning-points can offer a starting-point for contrasting the divergent ways the history has unfolded in two distinct but not unrelated sociocultural settings.

Historical analyses, including the analyses of technological and scientific developments in health care (Bowker and Star, 1999) demonstrate that voluntary and involuntary policy transfers and travel of ideas are not unique to the present time, even though the constitution and roles of the agents that drive policy across borders have changed. In the same vein, globalization is not a unitary engine of social change, but a short word for numerous trends. As a result of the new transnational features in policy processes, the number of actors and arenas increase in number and reconfigure. The policy environment is becoming populated by complex cross-border, inter-organizational and network relationships (Walt et al., 2008, p. 309). Qualitative case-based methods are well suited to capture these complexities and when reflexively designed, comparison across cases is possible at the same time as the interconnectedness of cases is recognized. Recent scholarship argues that the study of the rise of new health policy actors and processes and the changes in the content of health policy requires new, network-oriented research approaches (Lee et al., 2002). In a slightly different vein, Timmermans and Berg (2003), through their study that identifies a 'standardization movement in health care', offer an analysis of the role of science and technology in the convergence of medical practice. The authors show that this movement has global implications but divergent local adaptations. Their empirical case examples are taken primarily from two countries, the United States and the Netherlands, but without employing an explicit comparative research design. Instead, the researchers apply different research techniques and combine several case studies to trace the travel of the different ideas that they link to their broader discussion of the 'dynamic, emergent politics of standardization'. Similarly, efforts to map the impact of economic globalization on health policy lead researchers to trace the stakeholders of transnational policy processes (Waitzkin et al., 2005).

The scholarship that draws attention to the different networks that shape health care and health care policy is related to a wider theoretical perspective of the rise of *network society* in a globalizing world. The network society is underpinned by the worldwide spread of ideas, made increasingly easy and rapid by new communication technologies (Lee et al., 2002, pp. 13–15). The view of network society does not, however, profess a convergence approach as the network approach is commonly rooted in the recent theoretical turn in social theory to complexity (e.g., Ali and Keil, 2008). The network approaches share with the most recent developments in case study research the aim of rejecting simplification as a necessary research strategy. Instead, scholars seek to accommodate an analysis of more complex objects of study.

CONCLUSION

As policy processes are changing everywhere, health policy scholars tackle a much larger array of policy actors than was the case when health care policies were less multidimensional. Health policy processes are increasingly complex and new arenas emerge. Traditional comparative health care policy relied on the country as a self-evident way to frame cases, even when the meaning of this macro-social frame was not necessarily analyzed. Now, when alternative 'spatial units' as well as networks offer alternative ways to frame comparative health research, researchers are considering more closely how the country matters for health care policy. Thoughtful approaches to conceptualizing the country context demonstrate that the country still *does* matter, as the world continues to be spatially ordered as countries with different political cultures. Case studies of specific health policy processes need to take into account the divergent historical paths of different countries and their relevance for future developments, parallel to that of the emergent global connections. For many, the solution is to turn to qualitative case-based methods that offer, as shown in the foregoing section, many imaginative approaches to capture the complexity of health care policy and examine it comparatively. At the very basic level, the demand for methodological reflexivity means that researchers in the field of comparative health policy need to identify their research design and the way they use qualitative methods more clearly than often is the case at present. Future research benefits from approaches that employ the 'cross-fertilization' potential of the available interdisciplinary scholarship that is increasingly collaborative and international in its outlook.

REFERENCES

Ali, Harris S. and Keil, Roger (eds) (2008) *Networked Disease: Emerging Infections in the Global City*. Malden, MA: Wiley-Blackwell.

Altenstetter, Christa and Björkman, James W. (1981) 'Planning and Implementation: A Comparative Perspective on Health Policy', *International Political Science Review*, 2(1): 11–42.

Atkinson, Sarah (2002) 'Political Cultures, Health Systems and Health Policy', *Social Science and Medicine*, 55(1): 113–24.

Berg, Marc (ed.) (2004) *Health Information Management: Integrating Information Technology in Health Care Work*. London: Routledge.

Björkman, James W. (1985) 'Who Governs the Health Sector? Comparative European and American Experiences with Representation, Participation, and Decentralization', *Comparative Politics*, 17(4): 399–420.

Blank, Robert H. and Burau, Viola (2007) *Comparative Health Policy* (Revised and updated 2nd Edition). Houndsmills: Palgrave Macmillan (1st Edition, 2004).

Bourgeault, Ivy Lynn, Armstrong, Pat, Armstrong, Hugh, Choiniere, Jacqueline, Lexchin, Joel, Mykhalovskiy, Eric, Peters, Suzanne, and White, Jerry (2001) 'The Everyday Experiences of Implicit Rationing: Comparing the Voices of Nurses in California and British Columbia', *Sociology of Health and Illness*, 23(5): 633–53.

Bowker, Geoffrey and Star, Susan Leigh (1999) *Sorting Things Out: Classification and Its Consequences*. Cambridge, MA: The MIT Press.

Bradshaw, York and Wallace, Michael (1991) 'Informing Generality and Explaining Uniqueness: The Place of Case Studies in Comparative Research', *International Journal of Comparative Sociology*, 32(1–2): 154–71.

Buse, Kent, Mays, Nicholas and Walt, Gill (2005) *Making Health Policy*. Milton Keynes: Open University Press.

Caramani, Daniele (2009) *Introduction to the Comparative Method with Boolean Algebra (Quantitative Applications in the Social Sciences)*. Thousand Oaks, CA: Sage.

Carmel, Emma (1999) 'Concepts, Context and Discourse in a Comparative Case Study', *International Journal of Social Research Methodology*, 2(2): 141–50.

Cartwright, Lisa (2000) 'Reach Out and Heal Someone: Telemedicine and the Globalization of Health Care', *Health*, 3: 347–77.

Clark, Gordon L., Tracey, Paul, and Smith, Helen Lawton (2002) 'Rethinking Comparative Studies: An Agent-Centred Perspective', *Global Networks*, 2(4): 263–84.

Clarke, Adele (2005) *Situational Analysis: Grounded Theory after the Postmodern Turn*. Thousand Oaks, CA: Sage.

Davies, Celia (1979) 'Comparative Occupational Roles in Health Care', *Social Science and Medicine*, 13A: 515–21.

Dent, Mike (2003) *Remodelling Hospitals and Health Professions in Europe – Medicine, Nursing and the State*. London: Palgrave/Macmillan.

De Vries, Raymond (2004) *A Pleasing Birth: Midwives and Maternity Care in the Netherlands*. Philadelphia, PA: Temple University Press.

De Vries, Raymond, Benoit, Cecilia, van Teijlingen, Edwin, and Wrede, Sirpa (eds) (2001) *Birth by Design: Pregnancy, Maternity Care, and Midwifery in North America and Europe*. New York: London.

Dutton, Paul V. (2007) *Differential Diagnosis: A Comparative History of Health Care Problems and Solutions in the United States and France*. Ithaca, NY: Cornell University Press.

Field, Mark (1989) 'Introduction'. In Mark Field (ed.), *Success and Crisis in National Health Systems: A Comparative Approach*. New York: Routledge, pp. 1–22.

Flick, Uwe (2009) *An Introduction to Qualitative Research* (4th Edition). London: Sage.

Flyvbjergh, Bent (2006) 'Five Misunderstandings about Case-Study Research', *Qualitative Inquiry*, 12(2): 219–45.

Freeman, Richard (1998) 'Competition in Context: The Politics of Health Care Reform in Europe', *International Journal for Quality in Health Care*, 10(5): 395–401.

Freeman, Richard (2006) 'The Work the Document Does: Research, Policy, and Equity in Health', *Journal of Health Politics, Policy and Law*, 31(1): 51–70.

Gesler, Wilbert M. and Kearns, Robin A. (2002) *Culture/Place/Health*. London: Routledge.

Gilson, Lucy and Raphaely, Nika (2008) 'The Terrain of Health Policy Analysis in Low and Middle Income Countries: A Review of Published Literature 1994–2007', *Health Policy and Planning*, 23: 294–307.

Green, Judith and Thorogood, Nicki (1998) *Analysing Health Policy: A Sociological Approach*. London: Longman.

Immergut, Ellen (1990) 'Institutions, Veto Points, and Policy Results: A Comparative Analysis of Health Care', *Journal of Public Policy*, 10(4): 391–416.

Jasso-Aguilar, Rebeca, Waitzkin, Howard, and Landwehr, Angela (2004) 'Multinational Corporations and Health Care in the United States and Latin America: Strategies, Actions and Effects', *Journal of Health and Social Behavior*, 45: 136–57.

Lee, Kelley, Buse, Kent, and Fustukian, Suzanne (2002) 'An Introduction to Global Health Policy'. In Kelley Lee, Kent Buse and Suzanne Fustukian (eds), *Health Policy in a Globalising World* (pp. 3–17). Cambridge: Cambridge University Press.

Lian, Olaug S. (2008) 'Global Challenges, Global Solutions? A Cross-National Comparison of Primary Health Care in Britain, Norway and the Czech Republic', *Health Sociology Review*, 17(1): 27–40.

Mechanic, David (1975) 'The Comparative Study of Health Care Delivery Systems', *Annual Review of Sociology*, 1: 43–65.

Mechanic, David and Rochefort, David A. (1996) 'Comparative Medical Systems', *Annual Review of Sociology*, 22: 239–70.

Mills, Lisa (2006) 'Maternal Health Policy and the Politics of Scale in Mexico', *Social Politics*, 13(4): 487–521.

Øyen, Elsa (1990) 'The Imperfection of Comparisons'. In Elsa Øyen (ed.) *Comparative Methodology: Theory and Practice in International Social Research* (pp. 1–18). London: Sage and International Sociological Association.

Prior, Lindsay (2003) *Using Documents in Social Research*. London: Sage.

Ragin, Charles C. (1987) *The Comparative Method: Moving Beyond Qualitative and Quantitative Strategies*. Berkeley, CA: University of California Press.

Ranson, Kent M., Beaglehole, Robert, Correa, Carlos M., Mirza, Zafar, Buse, Kent, and Drager, Nick (2002) 'The Public Health Implications of Multilateral Trade Agreements'. In Kelley Lee, Kent Buse, and Suzanne Fustukian (eds), *Health Policy in a Globalising World* (pp. 18–40). Cambridge: Cambridge University Press.

Rodwin, Victor G. (2008) 'Health and Disease in Global Cities: A Neglected Dimension of National Health Policy'. In S. Harris Ali and Roger Keil (eds), *Networked Disease: Emerging Infections in the Global City* (pp. 27–48). Malden, MA: Wiley-Blackwell.

Saltman, Richard B. (1997) 'Convergence versus Social Embeddedness: Debating the Future Directions of Health Care Systems', *European Journal of Public Health*, 7(4): 449–53.

Shiffman, Jeremy (2007) 'Generating Political Priority for Maternal Mortality Reduction in 5 Developing Countries', *American Journal of Public Health*, 97(5): 796–803.

Timmermans, Stefan and Berg, Marc (2003) *The Gold Standard: The Challenge of Evidence-Based Medicine and Standardization in Health Care*. Philadelphia, PA: Temple University Press.

Waitzkin, Howard, Jasso-Aguilar, Rebeca, Landwehr, Angela, and Mountain, Carolyn (2005) 'Global Trade, Public Health, and Health Services: Stakeholders' Construction of Key Issues', *Social Science and Medicine*, 61: 893–906.

Walt, Gill (1994) *Health Policy: An Introduction to Process and Power*. London and New Jersey: Zed Books.

Walt, Gill, Shiffman, Jeremy, Schneider, Helen, Murray, Susan F., Brugha Ruairi, and Gilson, Lucy (2008) '"Doing" Health Policy Analysis: Methodological and Conceptual Reflections and Challenges', *Health Policy and Planning*, 23: 308–17.

Wrede, Sirpa, Benoit, Cecilia, Bourgeault, Ivy Lynn, van Teijlingen, Edwin R., Sandall Jane, and De Vries Raymond G. (2006) 'Decentred Comparative Research: Context Sensitive Analysis of Maternal Health Care', *Social Science and Medicine*, 63: 2986–97.

van Herk, R., Klazinga, N.S., Schepers, R.M.J., and Casparie, A.F. (2001) 'Medical Audit: Threat of Opportunity for the Medical Profession: A Comparative Study of Medical Audit among Medical Specialists in General Hospitals in the Netherlands and England, 1970–1999', *Social Science and Medicine*, 53: 1721–32.

6

Exploring Social Inequalities in Health: the Importance of Thinking Qualitatively

Gareth Williams and Eva Elliott

INTRODUCTION

The debate on the characteristics and extent of health inequalities has been dominated by epidemiology and public health. Epidemiology is ordinarily understood as the study of factors affecting the health and illness of populations; and this concern with whole populations means that it is, *ipso facto*, a highly statistical discipline: enumeration and measurement is the core of it. It would be wrong to think of epidemiology as simply a collection of statistical tools to describe the associations between exposures or risk factors and rates of illness or death. Its underlying purpose is to provide a deeper understanding of causal relationships by developing and testing theories.

The contribution of more qualitative styles of investigation to Victorian public health and social reform movements is often forgotten. In her introduction to an edition of the work of the Victorian journalist and social reformer, Henry Mayhew, Eileen Yeo contrasts Mayhew with the better-known Charles Booth. Both men attempted to map the extent of poverty, its causes and effects, in nineteenth-century London. However: 'In his use of qualitative evidence and in his sensitivity to sub-cultures among the poor, Mayhew far surpassed both Booth and Rowntree'[1] (Yeo, 1973); producing, from direct and sympathetic personal observation, vivid and detailed descriptions of the slop-workers and needlewomen, the tailors, the boot and shoe-makers, the toy-makers and many others among the labouring poor of old London town. In his methodological synthesis Mayhew was undoubtedly ahead of his time, albeit carrying many of the ideological prejudices of it.

Similarly, Friedrich Engels, tramping the streets of Manchester and other towns and cities in search of the 'conditions of the working class in England', went beyond the facts and figures of working hours and wages to get inside the experience of working class life during an epoch of European revolutions:

> That a class which lives under the conditions already sketched and is so ill-provided with the most necessary means of subsistence cannot be healthy, and can reach no advanced age, is self-evident ... They are given damp dwellings ... They are supplied bad, tattered, or rotten clothing, adulterated and indigestible food. They are exposed to the most exciting changes of mental condition, the most violent vibrations between hope and fear ...They are deprived of all enjoyments except that of sexual indulgence and drunkenness, are worked every day to the point of complete exhaustion of their mental and physical energies, and are thus constantly spurred on to the maddest excess in the only two enjoyments at their command ... How is it possible, under such conditions, for the lower class to be healthy and long lived? What else can be expected than an excessive mortality, an unbroken series of epidemics, a progressive deterioration in the physique of the working population? (Engels, 1982 [1892]:129).

The terrain of epidemiological investigation and public health practice in developed societies has shifted markedly since the end of the nineteenth century: from controlling the incidence of and mortality from infectious diseases, through mapping the multiple and interacting causes and consequences of chronic diseases, to identifying risk factors for future diseases. We would argue that many of the public health problems we face today, problems of 'unhealthy' behaviours, chronic or limiting long-term illness and unhappiness and damaged 'well-being', and in particular questions about their unequal distribution and what is to be done about them, require more than ever the direct investigation by the researcher of the social contexts in which the problems arise. We would suggest that if the underlying purpose of epidemiology is indeed one of understanding causal relationships and testing theories, then it cannot do without the insights qualitative thinking provides.

NARRATIVES OF INEQUALITIES

In spite of overall improvements in health, the unequal distribution of ill health is a continuing and growing feature (Dorling et al., 2007). On a global scale, a girl born in Japan or Sweden can expect to live more than 80 years, and remain in reasonably good health for most of her life. At the other extreme, in several African countries, a girl born today can expect to live less than 45 years, with many of these years being lived in chronic ill health. Within a single country, such as the United Kingdom, the differences are equally stark: in Scotland, a boy born in the suburb of Calton, east of Glasgow city centre, can expect to live 28 years less than one born in Lenzie a few miles away in East Dunbartonshire – a lower life expectancy than that in many parts of India (WHO Commission on Social Determinants of Health, 2008).

The debate about health inequalities has quite properly taken place in relation to statistical evidence, focussing on the size, proportion and distribution of health inequalities. Much of the literature on health inequalities has struggled to move beyond a 'social factors' approach that mimics epidemiology and brackets out any broader reflection on either social structures or the meanings that people give to the situations of inequality they experience. A constructive dialogue is now emerging between social epidemiology and more interpretative forms of social science. The developments arising out of this dialogue emphasize the gains to be made from exploring lay perceptions of, and narratives about, health inequalities (Popay et al., 1998) in order to help explain why individuals and groups behave the way they do in relation to wider social structures – to link agency and structure through a detailed examination of contexts. We argue that this approach complements epidemiological research on health inequalities by illuminating 'the hidden injuries of class' rooted in history and social conditions (Sennett and Cobb, 1973). What people know is not simply data for epidemiological or social scientific extraction. It co-constitutes the world as it is, and helps social and health scientists to understand how structures determine health and well being through where people live and what they do.

'Narrative analysis' is characteristically associated with micro-level, often inward experiences; a vehicle for phenomenological exploration. There has also been an understanding that people's accounts or stories can be used to deepen our understanding of the constitution and impact of social structure or macro-context (Lawton, 2003; Pierret, 2003); including age (Pound et al., 1998), socioeconomic position (d'Houtard and Field, 1984), gender (Bendelow, 1993) and ethnicity (Anderson et al., 1989). Recently, social scientists have looked at the recursive relationships, to use the jargon, between people's 'knowledgeable narratives' (Williams, 2000) and the places or locales in which they live. Much of this work can be said to take its starting point from the philosophical principle that there is 'no place without self and no self without place' (Casey, 2001: 684), even where the relationship between self and place is characterized by mobility or, as in the experience of homelessness, social exclusion (Gowman, 2000).

These narratives have been collected through standard methods of in-depth unstructured and semistructured interviews, in which people talk about their lives at length in response to an interviewer's questions or comments. The narrative analysis depends not on the reproduction of lengthy verbatim quotation – though it can take this form – but upon the identification of key meaning-points, or 'matters of significance' (Taylor, 1985), in the 'emplotted story' being told (Somers, 1994). Narrative analysis may therefore be performed upon small fragments of data. In one study in inner city Salford in the north west of England undertaken in the mid-1990s, for example, we looked at people's perceptions and understandings of 'health risks' (Williams et al., 1995). The interviews ranged across personal and social realities in an attempt to explore where the risks fall:

> I think the biggest health risk is mentally … 'cause it's a lot of pressure and there's nothing really for you to do … you're sort of segregated all the time.

In this powerful statement, a middle-aged man is thinking about the position in which he finds himself and the forces that shape his experience of ill health. He resists the pressure to see everything as either his fault, or the fault of someone else, and begins to develop a broader structural analysis. Within this fragment of a story, he identifies the ways in which the world weighs upon him, drawing us into an understanding of what in our work–stress culture is an almost counter-intuitive argument that the pressures which may lead to mental ill health are produced by the absence rather than the excess of activity. The startling use of 'segregated' also invites pause for thought. Here is a white man living in an eco-nomically highly developed 'free society', close to the heart of one of Britain's major cities, using a word more commonly associated with apartheid South Africa, or the American deep South at the time of the civil rights movement.

How can this narrative fragment help us? It cannot be described as a story, but what the respondent says provides a point of entry into his relationship to the social contexts in which lives, and his understanding of the ways in which social structure shapes this. We could talk about his socioeconomic circumstances in more objective detail: the amount that he gets in benefits, the kind of housing he lives in, the accessibility of shops and public services, the quality of his friend-ships; all of which would be very important. Within this small fragment of the long interview, we are able to see 'first order' lay concepts being used to generate an understanding that could not be delivered by 'social facts' alone. It tells us some-thing about the social organization of everyday life in an inner-city locality. It begins to describe some of the effects of this on personal experience, and it offers certain concepts – pressure, segregation – with which we can better understand the way in which the determinants of health and inequalities in health play out in the relation-ship between this man and the place in which he lives.

The fragment tells us something about the life of this one man. Nevertheless, we would not want to stop at that point. It also offers us a window onto certain aspects of the society in which he lives. He is offering an interpretation of the multivariate economic, social and cultural factors affecting him within the com-pressed or condensed form of his own life. It is precisely because the story is personal that it is able to offer a broader interpretation that draws structure, con-text, behaviour and ill health into a single frame. It provides a way of thickening our understanding of the thin descriptions and explanations provided by more quantitative methods (Geertz, 1973). In this way, fragments of the narratives people develop for making sense of the trouble they are in can be highly political. Another respondent from the same study told us:

> Smoking and drinking and drug taking, I put it down to one thing ... until money is spent on these areas ... there doesn't seem to be much point in trying to stop people smoking and what else. As long as the environment is going down the pan, the people will go down with it.

Knowledgeable narratives illustrate the need to contextualize risk factors – smoking, diet, alcohol and lack of exercise – by reference to the wider material and envi-ronmental conditions in which the risks are embedded. The respondents in this study understood the behavioural risk factors that made ill-health more likely and for which they were, in a limited sense, responsible, but they were also aware that the risks they faced were part of social conditions that they could do little to change. For these working class residents of a declining inner city, the 'way of life' – in this case, unemployment, poor housing, low income, stressful and some-times violent lives – provided a context for 'making sense' of smoking, drinking and drug-taking and other 'behaviours'. These narrative fragments, elements of stories, are complex bodies of contextualized rationality that are central to our understanding of social structure and its impact (Good, 1994).

In these quotations from research interviews, words and phrases like 'segre-gated all the time', 'the people will go down with it' carry a heavy semantic load that it is difficult to unpack with any certainty or finality. There are many differ-ent interpretations that could be made of what these people are saying, interpretations that they themselves might contest. The point is that their stories *are* interpretative. They are not merely descriptions waiting for social scientists to interpret them, and they invite us to acknowledge the ability of people to turn routine, taken-for-granted knowledge into discourse or narrative, and the need to find ways of interpreting the relationship between structure, context and experi-ence through a reading of people's own stories. These accounts lack finality, awaiting other interpretations.

NARRATIVES: PERSONAL, PUBLIC AND 'META'

Narratives provide a link between experience and social structure, and in doing so they provide some understanding of what to do in difficult situations. The narratives we have just explored are 'ontological narratives' which are used to define who we are and provide the basis for knowing what to do (Somers, 1994). It is through these that apparently disconnected sets of events are turned into meaningful episodes, as seen in the examples quoted from research interviews. Narratives such as these are often revealed in situations in which difficulties or crises threaten to overwhelm, situations of 'biographical disruption' (Bury, 1982); and they carry a sense of urgency, a feeling that something must be done. Much of the work on biographical disruption, and narrative reconstruction (Williams, 1984), has been developed in relation to personal crises, such as the onset of chronic illness and impairment, and have explored the crisis from the point of view of the individual at the centre of it. The data from which we have quoted above are about personal experiences of more 'structural' problems but are fundamentally ontological in character.

We can see, however, even in these very personal accounts, connections to more public and 'meta' narratives about changes taking place in society. Public narratives are often articulated by the mass media that transcend the individual but resonate with his or her everyday experiences of life: illness, families, work, leisure or other institutional formations. They often provide the legitimating context for ontological narratives. Meta narratives are 'master' narratives of progress, decline and crisis, which transcend the immediate context and are often used politically to construct a particular ideological position (Somers, 1994). We can illustrate these narrative forms more explicitly in relation to a study of the experiences of a major crisis in local employment are seen by people whose employment was not itself directly affected.

Following a major strategic review in February 2001, a multinational steel company announced that they were going to restructure their enterprise and activities in Wales with the projected loss of thousands of jobs. As part of the research, we interviewed a small number of people working in the towns and villages which provided labour for the steelworks: health professionals, church ministers, welfare officers and other 'key informants', asking them about what they thought was going to happen in the area (Fairbrother and Morgan, 2001). In addition to the effects of the direct loss of jobs on individuals and their families, many people with deep ties to the area are only too well aware that the direct loss of jobs in steel is only part of the story. Not only do individual workers feel the harshness of layoffs the community as a whole is undermined by these events.

One health visitor working in the area said:

> People talk not only about the effect on individuals; it's the effect on the [area] – everybody, regardless of whether they are employed by [the steel company] or not. I think that there is a huge concern […] that in an area that appeared to be going downhill anyway this is the final nail in the coffin.

The area in question was already one of the most deprived, with amongst the lowest levels of earnings in Britain, a large percentage of the population with no qualifications, and high levels of long-term ill health. Moreover, with low car ownership and limited access to public transport the prospects of finding work elsewhere were limited.

Many respondents talked about the way in which the running down of the steel works, as well as the mines, affected the way in which local people would interact with each other. Solidarity extended beyond the work into the 'social capital' of the local community. An educational welfare officer told us:

> The changes in the area over the past thirty years have been tremendous. It had a feeling all of its own thirty years ago, a very strong community of miners and steelworkers […] and now that's gone.

A district nurse who had always worked in the area spoke in similar terms, drawing attention to the impact of these changes on structures of feeling:

> That sort of comradeship has all gone. You knew who you could trust and everyone would help you, but that is disappearing, that sort of feeling is disappearing.

The nature of the work defined the kind of relationships that emerged: the communities, the politics and the aesthetics. The sights, sounds and smells associated with the steelworks imprinted themselves on the social and physical character of the surrounding towns. Whereas in the previous discussion respondents were talking of their personal experiences of processes of decline, in these extracts we see people talking about the likely impact on others of a specific change in the economic environment in the localities surrounding the steelworks, once the major employer in the area. The methodological point here is that in these excerpts we can see how qualitative data that allow people to narrate their experiences provide an understanding of an economic process that again thickens the statistical analysis of jobs and job replacement. We are given a sense of the interconnection between personal narratives and a social history that is particular to these people, but also illustrative of something more general. The litany of loss and change (see Marris, 1974) connects the ontological narration to public narratives of identity, work and family life, and to meta-narratives of decline into something that sounds like a dystopian vision of 'the end of history' (Fukyama, 1992). The culture or 'structures of feeling' of a whole place and period, as the post-war Welsh intellectual Raymond Williams referred to them (Williams, 1965; Smith, 2008), social worlds of hardship but also of 'comradeship', 'community' and 'trust', have been broken down and the 'resources of hope' (Williams, 1989) have been depleted.

In a field dominated by neo-positivism, it is all too easy for such interpretivist contributions to be regarded as, at best, an interesting diversion. In fact, in most standard discussions of health inequalities, they are simply ignored (Siegrist and Marmot, 2006), although in more recent reports we can see a creative synthesis of statistical evidence and qualitative case studies beginning to emerge (WHO Commission on the Social Determinants of Health, 2008). What we would want to argue here is that analyses of these sorts of narratives is much more important than the somewhat supercilious perspective of many neo-positivists would lead us to believe. Narrative analysis of qualitative data is important for a number of reasons: first, it provides us with a 'thick description' which unpacks the meaning and social context that, in epidemiological research, remains firmly shut up and uninterpreted in a black box (Frohlich et al., 2001; Williams, 2003); secondly, it reminds us of the existence of considerable 'lay knowledge' embedded in lifeworlds (Williams and Popay, 2001); thirdly, it allows us to explore the connections of personal lives to history and social structure in a way that is simply left out in positivist accounts; and finally, it suggests something about the possibilities for action in situations in which people may seem pressed down by the 'weight of the world' (Bourdieu et al, 1999). In the next section we explore how qualitative research can act as the catalyst for bringing 'lay knowledge' into a deliberative setting in order to inform political decisions about social change.

USING STORIES IN ACTION

In a recent important discussion of the purposes of the social sciences, Burawoy (2005) has called for a more engaged *'public sociology'*. Whilst the boundaries between different forms of sociology are contested, they offer a useful, heuristic device to facilitate reflection on what social scientists actually do and the methods they use to do it. This is important not just for sociology, but for all those working at the complex interfaces of research, policy and practice across social and health sciences. In some recent commissioned work, we have undertaken for the Welsh Assembly Government,[2] we have used qualitative methods to develop a form of public sociology in a context that is more usually associated with quantitative methods.

In the light of the widening health inequalities across the United Kingdom, and indeed Europe (Mackenbach and Bakker, 2002) and elsewhere (WHO Commission on the Social Determinants of Health, 2008) to which we have referred, governments have increasingly come to recognize that reducing health inequalities requires action across policy sectors (Wanless, 2004). In the United Kingdom, the 1997 Independent Inquiry into Inequalities chaired by Sir Donald Acheson had already helped to refocus health policy towards the social and economic determinants of health, urging action on these as a means of reducing health inequalities. One 'tool' that many of these documents urge policy and key decision makers to use is health impact assessment (HIA) which is defined as:

> ... a combination of procedures, methods and tools by which a policy, programme or project may be judged as to its potential effects on the health of a population, and the distribution of those effects within the population (European Centre for Health Policy, 1999: 4).

It is characteristically a process used by decision makers to generate information, expert opinion and data to inform policy development and communicate risks and opportunities generally as to possible *future* effects on health, however narrowly or broadly defined. Although qualitative methods are not always used in health impact assessments, we have used it to bring both lay and professional 'ways of knowing' (Brown, 1992) into a discourse about particular places and the possible consequences of decisions. The methods used here are often traditional ones of interviews and focus groups but could also incorporate visual data, such as photographs, observation and mobile technologies, such as walk-led interviews, where a respondent walks and talks an interviewer around a neighbourhood, and participatory mapping. These primary data, together with published evidence of different kinds, can be brought into a deliberative environment in which the formal data are exposed to discussion and debate from different standpoints. Let us illustrate this with two examples of health impact assessments.

Loss and change

The first example comes from a former coal-mining village in South Wales. The social and economic life of the village had been affected in much the same way as many other villages in the area, by the slow process of de-industrialization, with poor educational attainment, high economic inactivity and long-term ill health. Most of the housing in the estate in which residents lived was owned by the local authority and had a mixture of traditional post-war housing and a more problematic 1970s infill development. These houses were considered unattractive and were of poor quality with problems of damp, mould and the consequences of bad design. Many of these houses were empty and a target for vandalism. The housing estate was a priority for action, but it was felt by the local authority cabinet minister for social services and housing that any decisions had to consider the consequences on the health of residents.

As the researchers commissioned to do the HIA, we decided that in order to make sense of the lived environment and the village's future possibilities, we had to talk to people living and working in the area as well as 'see' and 'feel' what it was like. As well as conducting one-to-one interviews, we also undertook group interviews with school children, young teenagers, primary health care workers and an older people's social group. The researchers also took time to walk the territory and take field-notes of more casual encounters and observations. Walking with a husband and wife on the estate, they revealed what they felt symbolized their own sense of having been neglected by the public authorities. Previous housing demolition had left empty spaces of land which were not transformed into places of recreation or to enhance its visual aesthetics but were used to dump rubbish or 'needles'. They complained that the mess was seldom cleared and that it was not surprising that local people did not bother to tend to their own properties if the local authority themselves did not bother to look after the village.

The important point here is that the interviews revealed insights into the condition of local housing in a way that would have been impossible to unveil without qualitative methods of inquiry. They drew out, for example, the highly interconnected and complex connections between, for instance housing conditions, personal autonomy, domestic routine and health problems. One female resident talked about the way in which 'thin walls' failed to block out to noise of gangs of boys outside as well as the sounds of neighbours. With regard to gangs of youth she said:

> In the end there was so much noise … gangs of boys would be here all hours, you couldn't get any quiet. The TV had to be on so loud because you couldn't hear it. As you can see my TV is about four foot from my settee and it would have to be up full, otherwise you couldn't hear it. [My daughter] couldn't go to sleep in her bedroom. Because of the noise up the front of the house she had to sleep with me all the time which was affecting my health as well because of my bad back and I wasn't getting a good night's sleep.

We were expected to explore a range of different views and standpoints. Interviews with local health workers also indicated that they were sensitive to the social contexts in which people lived and the impact that particular housing decisions may have. In this particular village, attachment to both the immediate and extended family was said to be particularly strong. Similar to many ex-mining villages, it is a place that is characterized by its industrial past and the strong extended family networks that it produced. While the coal mines disappeared a long time ago, the extended family has endured providing informal social support and care. It was felt that it was because of this attachment to family that many people, including those who lived in some of the poorest housing conditions, were reluctant to move. Residents and local health workers expressed some concern if housing plans disrupted these important social ties.

> I don't want to move from this village, especially because I've got involved in the community. My family live in this village, my family have always lived in this village. … I mean they are care-providers for my child and I've only ever used one babysitter in her entire life. You know, it is family first (local resident).
>
> There are still a lot of extended families in the village and I think that's very important for young mothers who are single parents to have their family around. And I think that it's important that people are kept in their community. I don't think it is going to benefit the community if people are moved out or particularly benefit the families themselves. The children say 'Oh I'm so-and-so's cousin and so-and-so's cousin', and there's quite a lot of family and I think a lot of them get a lot of support from that (local health worker).

The same understanding of the specific contexts where people live and how this may inform decisions were found in other reflections on the 'determinants of health' in the area. For instance, the way in which the 1970s housing had been designed was felt to be inadequate in a number of ways. They spoke about the lack of natural light in some rooms, the social problems associated with having garages under some of the houses, the lack of privacy in having bedrooms that abutted the pavement and the disadvantages of having dark stairwells in the context of housing change and policy where you may not know all your neighbours any more.

> … you come up the dark stairways for a start which, when you go down in the night anyone could be hiding underneath and you wouldn't know until you got there (local resident).
>
> He [an older resident] wouldn't dare leave his front door. He cannot leave his door open. It's dark and not lit up round there and there's no one to call if he is in trouble. He's got no one to call on (local health worker).

In contrast to the quotes reflecting on the strength of family ties, the foregoing quotes highlight that this is a village in transition. The bonds of support are there for extended families and in relation to childcare, but the village is shrinking along with the local labour market. Empty houses are offered to 'outsiders' needing a home and mistrust is felt on the dark doorsteps which are 'hidden' from the wider neighbourhood.

The methods used in this health impact assessment allowed two distinct but connected things to happen. Firstly, alongside the research literature, they provide contextual data on the way in which the social determinants of health were experienced and illuminated how these could be altered given different housing scenarios. Secondly, these insights were used within a process that was directed towards change or action. Discussions about the data were held within four steering group meetings, held at the village community centre, throughout the HIA. This steering group included senior local authority housing officers, primary health care representatives, a Welsh Assembly Government officer, elected members, voluntary sector representatives and local residents. The report was submitted to the local cabinet and provided the evidence base for the final decision. This was to demolish the properties of concern, in a process which did not require residents to move, and build a smaller number of new houses which took the individual and collective needs of residents into account.

Through the unlikely vehicle of a policy-driven health impact assessment, we developed qualitative social research as a way of exploring a range of points of view in a situation of uncertainty and then as a mechanism to facilitate social change. The methodology helped to support the development of a form of 'civic intelligence' which we have defined as:

> ... the combination of lay knowledge, scientific evidence and professional judgement, grounded in the contexts in which people live, and directed towards decisions and action (Elliott and Williams, 2005).

We developed the methodology to ensure a 'balanced' approach to data collection, recognizing that 'the community' did not represent one voice or one narrative, that the 'evidence' on the effects of particular actions may conflict with resident's views, and that data indicating what action could or should be taken may not fit with what the Local Authority was prepared to do. The role of the researchers was complex, having to display some kind of 'value neutrality' and impartiality, while also supporting and quietly advocating the legitimacy and validity of qualitative methods which are not typically used within an HIA process.

Community protest

Protests by local citizens against perceived exposure to environmental hazards have recently been of interest to social scientists (see Chapter 38 by Brown in this volume). These have included mobilisations around the impact of landfill waste sites, open cast mines and contaminated water on illnesses or diseases such as asthma, breast cancer, leukaemia and congenital birth defects (see Brown, 2007; Crouch and Kroll-Smith, 2000; Moffatt and Pless-Mulloli, 2003; Williams and Popay, 2006). Brown (2007) highlights how public protest has had an important historic role in identifying emerging disease clusters, as well as in challenging the role, methods and values of science itself. He argues for the development of a 'critical epidemiology', rooted in an analysis of social structure, social inequalities and social justice, which makes use of qualitative methods to explore the perspectives of lay people inside and outside of social movements.

In a later HIA, the research entered the territory of risk assessment in a much more charged and contested scenario. In this case, it was a group of residents who approached the researchers about conducting a health impact assessment of a proposed extension to an opencast mine, again in South Wales. The researchers in this HIA provided skills on data collection, analysis and synthesis to assist residents who wanted to undertake an HIA. The residents felt that they had been let down by the two local authorities involved and that the impact on the health of people living in close proximity to the proposed site and their views on this had not been taken into account. They did not trust the planning authorities to turn down the application from the company involved.

The researchers in this case supported the collection of qualitative and quantitative data, on behalf of the residents, but in a context where the residents were keen to see a particular outcome, and the private company applying for planning was unwilling to 'permit' what they considered to be 'prejudices' of the vocal few to form the basis of scientific evidence. The researcher was therefore in territory where the methods used would be scrutinized by interest groups who were in open hostility. The HIA had to fulfil the dual requirements of including diverse forms of lay, professional and scientific data and the production of a report that would have 'credibility' with the officials who would ultimately decide whether the report provided evidence that was robust enough to inform decisions on the future of the proposed extension.

In terms of data collection, studies on the available evidence of the impact on opencast mining on air quality were supplemented by focus group data on a variety of environmental, social and economic determinants. Focus groups were chosen for two reasons. Firstly, because they can be useful when there are power differentials between participants and decision makers and where groups may have had limited power and influence (Morgan and Krueger, 1993). Secondly, focus group methods can be a way of demonstrating that a range of groups or stakeholders have been accessed, ensuring the widest possible range of 'standpoints'.

With advice from the researcher, participants were recruited by residents using a variety of methods to ensure they reflected a range of local interests. The aim was to recruit six to eight people for each focus group but final numbers ranged between four and ten. The residents and researchers agreed the make-up of the groups which were a mix of community members (FG1), residents living in an area near the existing opencast site (FG2), older people (FG3), those involved with outdoor pursuits (FG4), local business representatives (FG5) and younger parents (FG6). In total, 38 people participated, 23 women and 15 men, with ages ranging from 18 to over 75 years. They were facilitated by one of the researchers using a topic guide generated through discussions between the residents and the researcher. The majority of data used in the report reflected topics, concerns and views which were repeated by other individuals and/or in other focus groups and verbatim quotes were used for illustrative purposes.

As in the previous HIA, the qualitative methods provided very different kinds of insight into the lived experience of determinants than the research evidence on potential impact could provide. Indeed qualitative methods provided data which challenged what are often very narrow views about what human health is. For instance one resident, whose house looked over the current site, said:

> Sit looking over it every day of your life. Unless you actually live with one of these things, you couldn't *imagine* [original emphasis] the sort of feeling it gives you – the level of depression … 'black void' actually mirrors the way you feel (FG2).

The sense of hopelessness, powerlessness and despair were reflected in other groups:

> At the moment I walk up the road and have a look at the pit to see how big it's getting – how deep it's getting – and getting more and more depressed all the time. Because you are just looking at this big huge hole …'cause you are thinking to yourself: 'that's coming a bit closer, that's moving down' (FG5, shopkeeper).

> When I heard [about the proposed extension] I thought 'they can't do this to us again, they just can't'. I just felt completely and hopelessly in despair. I just couldn't go through all that again [campaigning] (FG1).

The focus groups allowed access to views and perspectives on health that challenged the very terms in which health is considered in more traditional consultation processes. Statements of risk to human health usually refer to minimal thresholds, but as far as the residents who were interviewed were concerned a minimal threshold of what could be tolerated in terms of the disruption to everyday life that opencast mining brings had been breeched a long time ago. What these methods do is to put at the centre of any assessment the emotions and values that different stakeholders inevitably hold in relation to any decision making process. These are not irrelevant to health as it is experienced but form the essence of what health might mean to people living under conditions which are felt to be oppressive.

As with the first HIA, the report was submitted to the decision making body in the local authority and, in this case, may have contributed to the decision not to permit the application. Furthermore, the report and a subsequent HIA of a similar application in another part of South Wales brought the concerns of people confronted by the prospect of an opencast mine in their locality into the public and political domain. In a document outlining the agenda of the coalition government in Wales referred to opencast mining stating:

> We will introduce compulsory Health Impact Assessments for open cast coal applications, together with buffer zones, and with an emphasis on planners and developers working closely with local communities (Welsh Assembly Government, 2007).

Whilst it would be naïve to suppose there is a direct link between the use of qualitative methods and the foregoing statement, these methods did place the private concerns of people likely to be affected by opencast mining directly into the public sphere in a way that engaged decision makers intellectually and emotionally.

CONCLUSIONS

In this chapter, we have explored the use of qualitative methods in terrain usually associated with quantitative methods: social inequalities in health and the use of health impact assessment to inform policy developments. Although the traditions of epidemiology include approaches that we would understand today as qualitative social science, the knowledge base developed by public health through a better understanding of the relationships between bacteria, disease and mortality has caused the importance of the study of both social structure and social context to decline. What had been intimately connected to issues of social reform increasingly became a more reductive, laboratory-based search for better explanations for the behaviour of germs. In recent years, there has been growing recognition that even the more sophisticated and elegant epidemiological studies of health inequalities fail fully to encapsulate the structural and meaningful dimensions of the issue. Indeed, the more sophisticated and elegant the epidemiology becomes the more it loses contact with the rough and ready realities which shape people's lives and experiences.

As societies have gone through what Wilkinson (1994) refers to as the 'epidemiological transition', the focus of epidemiology has shifted from a primary concern with infectious diseases to an interest in the problems of chronic disease and social and behavioural risk factors for chronic disease. While intense work on the biology and genomics of diseases like heart disease and cancer continues, it is recognized that understanding these diseases and their distribution requires an exploration of the quality of the relationships between the distribution of illness, the behaviour of individuals and social groups, the experiences of class and place and the meanings that people attribute to them.

Part of the response to these health problems will certainly require the reconnection of epidemiology and public health with political economy. The case is made all the more powerful when it is recognized that unless engagement in health improvement becomes part of wider social programmes, the health services in the United Kingdom and elsewhere, already the main items of domestic public expenditure, will become unsustainable (Wanless, 2004). This is a macro-issue, involving the exploration of large-scale economic and political change. What we have explored in this chapter is the importance of seeing health in its social context: a context which includes the 'fabric' of every day life, the resources and assets, the 'resilience' (Bartley and Head, 2007) which people can access or not, the qualities of the 'social suffering' they experience, and the ways in which they make sense of the often difficult situations in which they find themselves. It is, if you like, the social structure, the State and globalization as people experience them on a daily basis (Burawoy et al., 2000). The examples that we have used from two HIAs in which we have been involved also illustrate the use of qualitative methods in both exploring community-based narratives of health and then using those data to inform debates over public policy and to reconnect peoples everyday experiences to wider issues of political economy.

We do not pretend to any kind of methodological innovation, but simply a modest attempt to reconnect qualitative ways of thinking to an area of intellectual life that has been dominated by increasingly quantified and complex epidemiology. It is clearly the case, given the continuing and widening inequalities between people at the bottom of economically advanced societies and those at the top, between different socioeconomic groups across the whole of the social gradient, and between people living in different kinds of places, that forms of interpretive understanding are required to make theoretical sense of the epidemiological picture. We have explored different attempts to use qualitative methods to do this, and have argued that using these methods provides unique insight into the structural forces at work in people's daily lives and, in some circumstances, provides a way of connecting the 'lay knowledge' that people derive from the social contexts of their everyday lives to more traditional forms of knowledge and expertise in order to inform policy and political action.

NOTES

1 Seebohm Rowntree was the other great poverty campaigner who did his research in York, in the north of England.

2 Welsh Assembly Government was formed in 1999 as part of the UK Labour Government's commitment to a process of devolution of powers to assemblies or parliaments in Wales, Northern Ireland and Scotland.

REFERENCES

Anderson, J.M., Effert, H., and Lai, M. (1989) 'Ideology in the Clinical Context: Chronic Illness, Ethnicity and the Discourse on Normalization', *Sociology of Health and Illness*, 11: 253–78.

Bartley, M. and Head, J. (2007) 'Resilience and Change: The Relationship of Work to Health'. In A. Scriven and S. Garman (eds) *Public Health: Social Context and Action.* Maidenhead: Open University Press: MaGraw-Hill.

Bendelow, G. (1993) 'Pain Perceptions, Emotions and Gender'. *Sociology of Health and Illness*, 15: 273–94.

Bourdieu, P. et al. (1999) *The Weight of the World: Social Suffering in Contemporary Society.* Cambridge: Polity.

Brown, P. (1992) 'Popular Epidemiology and Toxic Waste Contamination: Lay and Professional Ways of Knowing', *Journal of Health and Social Behaviour*, 33: 267–81.

Brown, P. (2007) *Toxic Exposure: Contested Illnesses and the Environmental Health Movement.* New York: Columbia University Press.

Burawoy, M. (2005) '2004 American Sociological Association Presidential Address: For Public Sociology', *The British Journal of Sociology,* 56: 259–94.

Burawoy, M., Blum, J.A., George, S., Gille, Z., Gowan, T., Haney, L., Klawiter, M., Lopez, S.H., Ó Riain, S., and Thayer, M. (eds) (2000) *Global Ethnography.* Berkeley: University of California Press.

Bury, M. (1982) 'Chronic Illness as Biographical Disruption', *Sociology of Health and Illness*, 4: 167–82.

Casey, E.S. (2001) 'Between Geography and Philosophy: What Does It Mean to Be in the Place-World?', *Annals of the Association of American Geographers*, 91: 683–93.

Commission on Social Determinants of Health (2008) *Closing the Gap in a Generation: Health Equity Through Action on the Social Determinants of Health* (Chair: Sir Michael Marmot). Geneva: World Health Organization.

Crouch, S.R. and Kroll-Smith, S. (2000) 'Environmental Movements and Expert Knowledge: Evidence for a New Populism'. In S. Kroll-Smith, P. Brown, and V.J. Gunter. (eds) *Illness and the Environment: A Reader in Contested Medicine.* New York: New York University Press.

d'Houtard and Field (1984) 'The Image of Health: Variations in Perceptions by Social Class in a French Population', *Sociology of Health and Illness*, 6: 30–60.

Dorling, D., Shaw, M., and Davey Smith, G. (2007) 'Inequalities in Mortality Rates under New Labour'. In E. Dowler and N. Spencer (eds) *Challenging Health Inequalities*. Bristol: the Policy Press.

Elliott, E. and Williams, G.H. (2005) 'Developing New Forms of "Civic Intelligence" through Health Impact Assessment'. Paper presented at Social Policy Association Annual Conference, University of Bath.

Engels, F. (1982 [1892]) *The Conditions of the Working Class in England in 1844*. London: Panther.

European Centre for Health Policy (1999) *Health Impact Assessment: Main Concepts and Suggested Approach (Gothenburg Consensus)*. Brussels: European Centre for Health Policy.

Fairbrother, P.D, Morgan, K.J. (eds) (2001) *Steel Communities Study*. Regeneration Institute, Cardiff University, Wales.

Frohlich, K.L., Corin, E., and Potvin, L. (2001) 'A Theoretical Proposal for the Relationship Between Context and Disease', *Sociology of Health and Illness*, 23: 776–97.

Fukyama, F. (1992) *The End of History and the Last Man*. New York: Free Press.

Geertz, C. (1973) *The Interpretation of Cultures*. New York: Basic Books.

Good, B. (1994) *Medicine, Rationality and Experience: An Anthropological Perspective*. Cambridge University Press.

Gowman, T. (2000) 'Excavating "Globalization" from Street Level: Homeless Men Recycle Their Pasts'. In M. Burawoy, J.A. Blum, S. George, Z. Gille, T. Gowman, L. Haney, M Klawiter, S.H. Lopez, S. Ó Riain, and M Thayer (eds) *Global Ethnography*. Berkeley: University of California Press.

Lawton, J. (2003) 'Lay Experiences of Health and Illness: State of Knowledge and Perspectives for Research', *Sociology of Health and Illness*, 25: 23–40.

Mackenbach, J. and Bakker, M. (2002) *Reducing Inequalities in Health: A European Perspective*. London: Routledge.

Marris, P. (1974) *Loss and Change*. London: Routledge and Kegan Paul.

Moffatt, S. and Pless-Mulloli, T. (2003) '"It Wasn't the Plague We Expected." Parents' Perceptions of the Health and Environmental Impact of Opencast Coal Mining', *Social Science and Medicine,* 57(3): 437–51.

Morgan, D.L. and Krueger, R.A. (1993) 'When to Use Focus Groups and Why'. In D.L. Morgan (ed.) *Successful Focus Groups*. London: Sage.

Pierret, J. (2003) 'The Illness Experience: State of Knowledge and Perspectives for Research', *Sociology of Health and Illness*, 25: 4–22.

Popay, J., Williams, G., Thomas, C., and Gatrell, A.C. (1998) 'Theorising Inequalities in Health: The Place of Lay Knowledge'. In M. Bartley, D. Blane, and G. Davey Smith (eds) *The Sociology of Health Inequalities*. Oxford: Blackwell.

Pound, P., Gompertz, P., and Ebrahim, S. (1998) 'Illness in the Context of Older Age: The Case of Stroke', *Sociology of Health and Illness*, 20: 489–506.

Sennett, R. and Cobb, J. (1973) *The Hidden Injuries of Class*. New York: Vintage Books.

Siegrist, J. and Marmot, M. (eds) (2006) *Social Inequalities in Health: New Evidence and Implications*. Oxford University Press.

Smith, D. (2008) *Raymond Williams: a Warrior's Tale*. Cardigan, Wales: Parthian.

Somers, M. (1994) 'The Narrative Constitution of Identity: A Relational and Network Approach', *Theory and Society*, 23: 605–49.

Taylor, C. (1985) *Human Agency and Language: Philosophical Papers, Volume 1*. Cambridge University Press.

Wanless, D. (2004) *Securing Good Health for the Whole Population: Final Report* ('Wanless Report'). London: HM Treasury.

Welsh Assembly Government (2007) *One Wales: A Progressive Agenda for the Government of Wales – An Agreement Between the Labour and Plaid Cymru Groups in the National Assembly*, Cardiff: Welsh Assembly Government. Available at: http://news.bbc.co.uk/1/shared/bsp/hi/pdfs/27_06_07_onewales.pdf

Wilkinson, R. (1994) 'The Epidemiological Transition: From Material Scarcity to Social Disadvantage', *Daedalus*, 123: 61–77.

Williams, G.H. (1984) 'The Genesis of Chronic Illness: Narrative Reconstruction', *Sociology of Health and Illness*, 6: 175–200.

Williams, G.H. (2000) 'Knowledgeable Narratives', *Anthropology and Medicine*, 7: 135–40.
Williams, G.H. (2003) 'The Determinants of Health: Structure, Context and Agency', *Sociology of Health and Illness*, 25: 131–54.
Williams, G.H., Popay, J., and Bissell, P. (1995) 'Public Health Risks in the Material World: Barriers to Social Movements in Health'. In Gabe J. (ed.) *Medicine, Health and Risk*. Oxford: Blackwell.
Williams, G.H. and Popay, J. (2001) 'Lay Health Knowledge and the Concept of the Lifeworld'. In G. Scambler (ed.) *Habermas, Critical Theory and Health*. London: Routledge.
Williams, G.H. and Popay, J. (2006) 'Lay Knowledge and the Privilege of Experience'. In D. Kelleher, J. Gabe, G. Williams (eds) *Challenging Medicine*. London: Routledge (2nd Edition).
Williams, R. (1965) *The Long Revolution*. Harmondsworth: Penguin.
Williams, R. (1989) *Resources of Hope: Culture, Democracy, Socialism*. London: Verso.
Yeo, E. (1973) 'Mayhew as a Social Investigator'. In E.P. Thompson and E. Yeo (eds) *The Unknown Mayhew: Selections from the Morning Chronicle, 1849–1850*. Harmondsworth: Penguin.

Theory

7

Theory Matters in Qualitative Health Research

Mita Giacomini

INTRODUCTION

This chapter reviews some basic theoretical features of qualitative health research traditions – both their fundamental theoretical commitments and their characteristic findings. More detailed overviews of the epistemological roots of the various qualitative traditions appear elsewhere (e.g., Creswell, 2007; Guba and Lincoln, 2005; Lincoln and Guba, 2000; Ponterotto, 2005; Willis et al., 2007). While it is helpful to understand the philosophical bases of qualitative methodologies, it is equally important to consider the forms of theory *generated* by different qualitative research traditions – and how others may read, understand, and use these. The increasingly collaborative, interdisciplinary, and user-oriented world of health research creates challenges for understanding the directions in which qualitative work can aim, and for keeping one's own work located and oriented.

Twenty years ago, a chapter on theory in qualitative health research methodology might have been devoted to defending the legitimacy of qualitative methodologies within their own frame of reference. It would have also highlighted the limitations of natural science paradigms for understanding questions of social meaning, action, and culture in health. Many qualitative researchers have been motivated by the imperative to question authoritative biomedical knowledge as a social construct and to recast objectivist science as a culture (Schwandt, 2000; Wright and Treacher, 1982). Themes in these 'science wars' – such as the question of whether quantitative or qualitative methods yield better truths, or whether social scientists have any business studying biomedical science as a social phenomenon – dominated reflections on theoretical matters for many years. This conflict has now faded as qualitative research approaches have become more fully developed, respected, taught, institutionalized, funded, published, read, and used throughout the health research and practice communities. Biomedical culture itself evolves. Many qualitative researchers work in biomedical settings, and health researchers increasingly receive training in both qualitative and quantitative methodologies. In health research, it has become imperative to identify which methodologies best suit which questions of policy and practice, to appraise research practices and results, and to understand how different methodologies relate to each other in collaborative work.

Theories brought into, and theories produced by, a specific qualitative research project link that project to wider bodies of knowledge. In qualitative health research, a project often relates not only to social science or humanities disciplines, but also to interdisciplinary or professional knowledge (Figure 7.1). Different academic fields have generated distinctive research approaches. Conventional qualitative methodologies have formed within social science and humanities disciplines such as sociology, anthropology, psychology, literature, and philosophy, as well as the clinical discipline of nursing. Yet, many qualitative researchers now train outside these disciplines, often in multi or inter disciplinary research communities less oriented to the academic pedigrees of methodologies. Many researchers also draw upon specific, substantive theories to formulate their research questions, guide analysis, and fashion their findings. The works of specific philosophers of knowledge and society guide many qualitative analysis frameworks. For example, researchers approach questions of empowerment

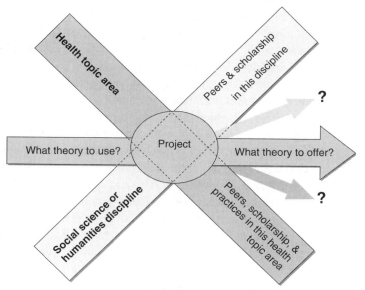

Figure 7.1   Allegiances and tensions for theory in qualitative health research

quite differently depending on whether they use a lens of Marxist political econ-omy, Foucauldian archaeology or genealogy (Foucault, 1972, 1979), or Freirian pedagogical dialectics (Freire, 1970).

The theory that a qualitative project produces – the findings – can contribute to various bodies of knowledge. This creates tensions for qualitative health researchers, as different audiences for qualitative work have different expecta-tions for how results must relate to prevailing ideas. Interdisciplinary and applied researchers typically feel less compelled to relate their work to legacies of disci-plinary theory, while disciplinary researchers find neglect of existing work unsophisticated, if not irresponsible. Researchers outside disciplinary bounds may struggle to determine whether they have developed a genuinely new insight, or unwittingly and inexpertly reinvented the established knowledge of an unfa-miliar field (Nissani, 1997). Many qualitative health researchers publish in inter disciplinary journals, and must make their findings meaningful to readers who share no common base of theory, although they share a concern with a topical health problem. Readers outside a discipline tend to dismiss disciplinary terms and ideas as jargon, and disciplinary researchers may sacrifice some theoretical richness and context to make their findings more accessible.

Almost all health researchers must contend with the biomedical disciplines in some way. Traditionally, qualitative researchers have tended to work in ideologi-cal opposition to the biomedical model of health and illness, with research designed to escape, critique, or undermine it. Particularly challenging has been the treatment of biomedical knowledge itself as a social construct (Lock and Gordon, 1988; Wright and Treacher, 1982). Social scientists have studied bio-medical science extensively, and have reinterpreted much ostensibly objective, value-free biomedical knowledge as laden with values and fashioned from social ideas. Yet, many qualitative researchers now emerge from the biomedical disci-plines themselves, or work in close collaboration with biomedical colleagues. Clinical journals publish more qualitative work, targeting these reports at clinical readers and users. Biomedical peer reviewers require qualitative researchers to make sense to biomedical audiences, and speak in terms they can understand (an uncomfortable demand for qualitative projects that challenge biomedical fram-ings of health and research). The biomedical worldview itself changes. Biomedical professions have become more self-reflective and academically interested in the questions of meaning and social organization that have been the traditional prov-ince of the social sciences and humanities. Many patrons – those who invite, commission, fund, and publish qualitative research projects – want to see that research makes a difference, especially to improve health. The imperative for research to have implications and usefulness carries a whiff of instrumentality associated more with the causal theories of biomedicine than the descriptive, inter-pretive or critical theories of contemporary social sciences and the humanities.

Paradoxically, beyond the philosophical fray, research gets done, and innova-tive methodologies seem to flourish despite fundamental questions about their possibly contradictory premises. An emerging critical appraisal industry now struggles to identify markers of credibility and value for the growing volume and variety of qualitative findings. Legitimate expectations about what qualitative research can tell us, and critiques of whether it has done so well, shift with the theoretical stances of both researchers and readers.

THEORY

The term 'theory' may mean many things. The word has Greek roots meaning to look at, or to contemplate. Here, in its broadest sense, it indicates *a system of ideas*. Empirical researchers use systems of ideas – theories – to generate information, make sense of it, and transform it into usable knowledge. Qualitative research also generates theory – new systems of ideas that revise prior beliefs and change practices. Theories enter qualitative research as the assumptions that underpin expectations, methods, and analyses; they exit research in the form of findings and suggested implications.

Theories may take numerous forms in the social and biomedical health sciences. A partial list of some common types offers a sense of the diversity. *Normative* theories include value systems and ideologies, and inform judgments about desirable ways of being, goals to achieve, or ways of getting things done. *Descriptive theories* represent phenomena abstractly (e.g., a Julian calendar date, a diagram of an eyeball). Users of a descriptive theory must share a common understanding of the symbols used for representation (e.g., date notation conventions, arrows, and terms), yet, these symbolic systems also evolve. *Interpretive theories* describe and translate systems of meanings, whether symbolic meaning (*semiotic* interpretation) or textual meaning (*hermeneutic* interpretation). People may use *classification schemes, typologies*, and *conceptual frameworks* either descriptively or interpretively to organize phenomena. Constructs such as *variables* in quantitative health research, or *categories* in qualitative research, typify phenomena. Labels, definitions, and other types of terminology serve similar purposes in research. In the social sciences, *grand theories* provide wide ranging, generalized characterizations or explanations of social phenomena and often have rather deductive, philosophically based origins. *Middle-range* theories, in contrast, address more local and contextualized phenomena. Researchers may employ *metaphors*, and other literary tropes (irony, analogy, synecdoche, etc.) either interpretively or heuristically to organize and convey ideas. *Causal theories* explain the origins of current phenomena, or predict future ones. Causal explanations may presume underlying deterministic laws (as in epidemiology), or a more idiosyncratic, path-dependent unfolding of events and sequelae (as in history). *Accounts* of all kinds, including *narratives*, serve as theories when presenting the context of research findings. *Storytelling*, probably the oldest form of teaching, offers selective vicarious experiences and lessons to others.

Our most fundamental theories address the essential nature of things. *Ontologies* are beliefs about the basic entities that make up reality. In research, ontology dictates the essential phenomena we can expect to find and thus may seek (e.g., natural laws and social rules), as well as that which we will never find, so need not look for (e.g., magical powers). A basic ontological question in health research asks whether to consider the phenomena of research as comprised of our ideas about things (*idealism*) or of the things in themselves, unmediated by ideas (*realism*). An important dimension of ontology includes beliefs about the nature of *values*, and how they operate in relation to other phenomena. For example, researchers take a variety of positions on whether one can separate values from facts, and whether there exist universal human values or relative values only.

At the next layer of fundamental theory, *epistemologies* suggest how researchers can empirically access phenomena (given the ontological assumptions about what phenomena are). Both ontologies and epistemologies represent deep philosophical commitments; researchers cannot revise them through empirical investigation. Upon these philosophical foundations, researchers build the *methodologies* that guide empirical research. Methodologies offer frameworks of logically related means and ends to guide empirical research design, while *methods* more commonly refer to specific research procedures and techniques to implement the methodology.

Figure 7.2 presents one way of organizing health research methodologies. It maps 'neighbourhoods' of methodological traditions, as defined by underlying ontological and epistemological assumptions. Each health research methodology occupies a characteristic neighbourhood, although qualitative approaches often overlap or migrate across the terrain. This figure serves for orientation throughout this chapter, using the conventions of 'north', 'south', 'east', and 'west' to indicate ontological and epistemological inclinations of various methodological traditions (i.e., references to 'east' and 'west' do not indicate Eastern or Western ideas in the geopolitical sense). All such overviews of qualitative methodologies include a warning about superficiality, as does this. Each methodological tradition forms a world of its own, with a rich legacy of scholars, texts, evolving methods, and motivating ideologies. To those deeply involved in any specific tradition, apparently minor distinctions made here may point to profound philosophical disagreements about the nature of experience, reality, meaning, moral commitments, and things themselves. Figure 7.2 offers a sense of how each methodological tradition relates to neighbouring traditions in principle, by differences in basic assumptions and aims. In practice, however, one often encounters grey zones between traditions as well as crises of orientation within and across them.

Figure 7.2 maps three philosophical (fundamental and theoretical) features that help to locate and characterize research methodologies: ontology, epistemology, and the presumed role of values in relation to facts. First, *ontological* beliefs concern the essential phenomena researchers can expect to find empirically – their ideas about 'that which there is' (Blackburn, 1996, p. 320). Before seeking anything, one must have a prior notion of what could be found empirically – and

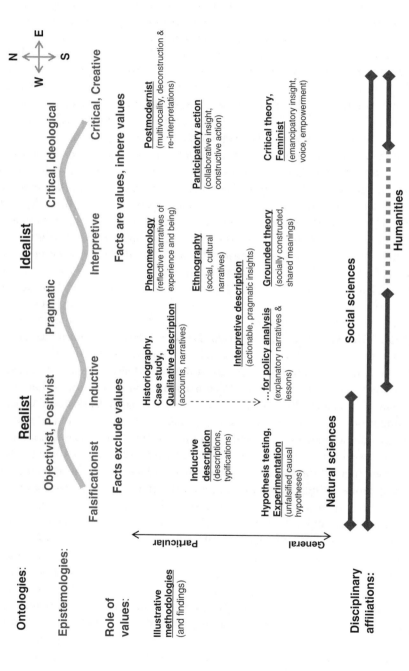

Figure 7.2   Health research traditions, by ontological & epistemological neighbourhood

what could not. Health research traditions range from realist to idealist (Figure 7.2). The ontology of *realism* holds that the world (social or natural) possesses qualities both independent of our ideas and empirically accessible to us as such. This leads to faith that, with the right methodology, one's data would correspond directly to these things without bias created by one's perspective, values, and so forth. *Idealism,* by contrast, holds that we have direct access only to our ideas and subjective experiences, and no empirical access to the world beyond, except through these ideas. It follows that when researchers study the world they necessarily examine only their mental constructs of it. Data do not correspond directly with reality; they are researchers' representations. This holds whether researchers study mental constructs themselves (e.g., cognition in the field of psychology), social constructs (e.g., culture in the field of anthropology) or the natural world (e.g., gravity in the field of physics).

Second, *epistemological* beliefs concern how phenomena come to be known. Epistemologies (how we must find out) flow necessarily from ontological beliefs (what we want to find out about). *Positivist* epistemology, flowing from realist ontology, pursues empirical facts that correspond directly to reality, undistorted by the observer's expectations or ideas. *Logical positivism*, a distinctive form of positivism, refers to the goal of proving facts through objective observation and logically rigorous inductive inference. *Induction* infers general conclusions (e.g., laws, descriptive categories) from particular phenomena (i.e., data observations). Inductive inference involves repeated empirical observations of similar phenomena, to make conclusions about their shared nature. Unfortunately, inductive arguments suffer from inherent logical fallibility. To observe that something is 'so' again and again does not allow one to infer with absolute certainty a law that it will be 'so' in all cases, and at all times not yet observed. For this reason, logical positivism fails as a guarantor of certain truth (for a straightforward interdisciplinary introduction to the philosophy of inference, see Chalmers, 1999). Although induction fails to ensure certainty through logic, researchers across the spectrum of research methodologies use inductive inference to describe and classify phenomena of interest. Researchers use such data not with certainty, but with a provisional confidence, which allows both the development of new knowledge and its later revision (Hammersley, 2009).

Some researchers in health and social sciences use the term positivism more loosely to refer roughly to *determinism* – the expectation of mechanistic causal laws and variables. These laws, when discovered empirically, could render phenomena explainable, predictable, and technologically controllable. Epistemological *objectivism* follows from deterministic ontology. It counts only objectively observable phenomena – those that may be seen in the same way by any similarly equipped observer – as legitimate empirical facts. Quantifiably measurable variables appeal to objectivist researchers. For this reason, many refer informally to research that rests on this set of assumptions – realism, objectivism, determinism – as *quantitative methodology.* However, quantifiable data are neither sufficient nor necessary to pursue objectivity, and may be employed in qualitative research traditions with very different epistemological commitments. Likewise, the term *qualitative methodology* refers informally to more idealist approaches (described in the following section), despite the fact that researchers can also approach qualitative data in positivist, deterministic, and objectivist ways.

More philosophically viable than logical positivism has been an indirect form of positivism – sometimes captured under the rubric of *post-positivism*, but more commonly termed *falsificationism* or *hypothetico-deductive methodology* in health research. This epistemology establishes theories as true by rigorously testing yet failing to falsify them. Falsification relies on logically sound deductive logic, thus sidestepping the logical flaws of induction and logical positivism. It is more logically sound to fail to show a hypothesis (or its antithesis, the null hypothesis) to be untrue, than to establish its positive truth. This falsificationist logic forms the basis for hypothesis testing and inferential statistics widely practiced in quantitative health research. Even so, falsificationist methodologies do not successfully establish logically indisputable, objective facts for several reasons. The premises necessary to conduct an empirical test, or to argue that a test has failed to support a specific hypothesis, still must rely on inductively gained, thus logically fallible, knowledge. Establishing merely that a hypothesis is 'not untrue' does not suffice to build new knowledge – one must take the logically fallible, if reasonable, leap of embracing the unfalsified hypothesis 'as if it were true'. Falsification applies to testable hypotheses only, but many theories in social and natural sciences cannot be expressed as empirically testable hypotheses. Finally, scientific progress requires discrimination between hypotheses worth testing, hypothesis adequately tested, and hypotheses either not testable or not worth the bother of testing. Falsification itself cannot generate these crucial judgments (again, for an excellent introductory overview, see Chalmers, 1999).

Pragmatic epistemology occupies a middle ground between realist and idealist ontology. It presumes that phenomena do operate independently of our ideas, but also grants that we must apprehend these phenomena through our ideas. The state of current knowledge delimits the capacity of our understanding, and the problems that motivate the research determine the scope of discovery possible. The value of findings depends not on their representation of either a real or ideal world (such representation being philosophically untenable), but on their ability to justify new beliefs within the context of prevailing beliefs (Avis, 2003). The term 'pragmatic' suggests that practical problems (not methodological or theoretical imperatives) determine how phenomena interest researchers. It also implies that researchers can approach a problem in many credible ways, with different methodologies, albeit with somewhat different results. A pragmatic epistemological orientation also obliges the researcher to fashion findings in recognition that they could be used, and to present findings in accessible and actionable terms (Thorne, 2008).

Interpretive epistemology arises directly from idealist ontology. It understands our world foremost as a world of ideas, whether about ourselves, society, or nature. In the social sciences, an interpretive orientation fits well with the study of social phenomena such as symbolic systems, discourse, and socially shared meanings. Researchers themselves are an integral part of these social worlds. They can neither stand apart to take an objective view, nor refrain from affecting that which they study. The symbolic languages that researchers know, or are able to learn, mediate their findings. Different perspectives lead to diverse meaningful interpretations of social phenomena. The principle of *constructivism* holds that people mentally construct, rather than receive, their ideas of the world. Qualitative researchers, in turn, have access to little more than their own constructs of others' constructs. Different constructivist theorists make different assumptions about how this knowledge construction works (Phillips, 1995). Some constructivist philosophies deny any role for an external reality, others hold a soft form of realism that nature 'instructs' while people construct. Some hold that people construct knowledge actively and wilfully, others unconsciously and passively. Some researchers (notably, radical constructivists and some phenomenologists) consider construction of a private cognitive process, while others (most notably, social constructionists in sociology) look to more public, collective processes of developing shared meanings. A thoroughgoing idealist ontology would place 'reality' into quotation marks: any account of reality is merely one claim among multitudes possible. Because interpretivist researchers recognize the relative, not absolute, truth of their own constructs, they will typically offer findings as contextualized and open to further interpretations.

At the far 'eastern' end of the epistemological spectrum on Figure 7.2 lie *critical* and *ideological* epistemologies. These share the idealist ontological assumptions of most qualitative epistemologies, but go beyond interpretation to construct new knowledge ideologically or creatively. Critical and ideological researchers assume that hegemonic interests have constructed the prevailing accounts of reality. Researchers must not continue to privilege these as the best accounts but, rather, investigate them for the social, political, or economic agendas they may serve. Any depiction of 'the way things are' invites interpretation, challenge, or reinterpretation according to alternative, and often marginalized, views. Research traditions vary in how they choose and articulate these views. Approaches range from apathetic, seeing all views as equal and relative, to activist, relating projects explicitly to moral or political causes. Often, critical and ideological epistemologies strive for findings that will have the effect of levelling power relations.

The third defining feature of research methodologies depicted on Figure 7.2 concerns ideas about the nature of *values* in relation to facts, and the proper role of values in research. As traditions move from 'west' to 'east' in Figure 7.2, they make characteristic assumptions about values. Traditions in the 'western' realist and positivist neighbourhoods view facts and values as made of different, ontologically irreconcilable stuff. Facts concern questions of what 'is', and lie within the remit of empirical research. Values, in contrast, concern questions of what 'ought' to be. For such normative questions, nonempirical, ethical or philosophical analysis is more appropriate than empirical inquiry into the nature of things. At this 'western' end of Figure 7.2, researchers must guard against their own values possibly biasing their observations or compromising their scientific objectivity. This entails methodologies that include strategies to prevent investigators from manipulating results toward favoured conclusions (e.g., blinding, randomization, etc.). The resulting research findings should be value-neutral. When such researchers study 'values' per se, they typically describe or measure them objectively (e.g., to survey public values), but refrain from presenting the findings as right or good (e.g., to conclude that these public values should guide action). Doing the latter would commit Hume's 'naturalistic fallacy', which holds that one cannot deduce the good from the true (or an 'ought' from an 'is'). It is possible and acceptable, however, for readers and users of the finished research to employ the findings in the service of their own values, for example, to bolster a policy argument with ostensibly unbiased, scientific evidence.

At the other, 'eastern' end of Figure 7.2, through the idealist, interpretive, and critical epistemological neighbourhoods, an entirely opposing philosophy holds that values are inherent in all facts – whether researchers want them there or not. First, values motivate researchers to ask certain research questions (and not others), so values drive the research enterprise. Consequently, it is neither coincidental nor value-neutral when the resulting findings serve certain moral or political imperatives better than other ones. Researchers who work with ideas-as-facts (idealists) cannot step outside their personal, social, or cultural perspective to view those ideas objectively. To do so entails leaving the web of ideas that allow them to recognize and understand the facts in the first place. Values, as ideas, form an integral part of this web. Finally, semantics deeply entangle values with fact, because language mediates the expression of facts. The words that describe research findings carry ethical valence, whether explicitly or implicitly. Importantly, implied or understood values may not match those intended by the researcher, author, dictionary, or other authority – rather, the meanings of words and statements accrue through use, and change with changing contexts (Root, 1993). Idealist researchers – including those in most qualitative research traditions – expect to find values infused through all phenomena including research questions, methodologies, and findings. Explicit concern for these values, their representation, and their use consequently pervades qualitative approaches.

METHODOLOGICAL TRADITIONS

We can locate more specific research methodologies, and characterize important theoretical qualities of their findings, by identifying their ontological and epistemological 'neighbourhoods' in Figure 7.2. Building lightly on this geographic metaphor, this map also helps in understanding the theoretical affinities and tensions created by the dynamics and collaborations of qualitative health research. Figure 7.2 organizes methodologies primarily by the three key features described earlier (ontology, epistemology, and assumptions about the role of values), which describe the lie of general methodologies across the 'west–east' realist–idealist axis of Figure 7.2. The figure further distinguishes methodologies on a 'north–south' axis by their scope of intended inference. Those represented in the more 'northerly' neighbourhoods of Figure 7.2 tend to offer more *particularist* findings. These findings pertain quite closely to the settings, participants, and authors involved with the given study. They often offer detailed descriptions or narratives, and tend to resist much abstraction or generalization. The findings of methodologies in the 'southerly' half of Figure 7.2 have more *generalist* ambitions. They offer more abstracted, conceptual findings, or suggest lessons applicable to other situations. Both types of findings entail theorizing, but offer different levels of theory. Figure 7.2 as a whole distinguishes readily between methodologies in distant neighbourhoods. However, the lines between abutting neighbourhoods often blur in principle as well as practice, so lines do not appear on Figure 7.2, and rigid dividing lines should not be inferred.

Our tour of specific research traditions begins in the 'southwest' corner of Figure 7.2. In this realist ontological neighbourhood, researchers seek an objective understanding of reality. The researcher hopes to experience true reality as directly as possible, unbiased by expectations or previous knowledge. As discussed earlier, researchers cannot inductively prove facts through direct experience and observation. The philosopher Karl Popper promoted the more logically sound *deductive* argument for establishing empirical truth (Popper, 1993). In deduction, particulars (data) are inferred from principles (theory). Data may not directly prove a theory, as induction would have it. However, the absence of data necessarily predicted by a theory will disconfirm that theory. Such deductive, *falsificationist* reasoning provides the central justification for truth claims in health research methodologies that use hypothesis tests and inferential statistics. Typical methods include observational modelling, summative program evaluation, and controlled experimentation. In the philosophy of science, falsificationism has been proposed to demarcate scientific research from nonscientific research (Popper, 1993). This would restrict the legitimate domain of science to falsifiable hypotheses, and characterize as unscientific any theory not amenable to testing. However, while falsificationism serves some widely admired philosophical ideals in health research, it does not fully describe the realm of empirical investigation, nor does it fully capture what even hypothesis-testing health researchers actually do. Even devoted falsificationists rely on unfalsifiable theory when, as a fundamental example, they make any ontological assumption (such as realism), or resort to induction for tasks such as identifying and describing the variables they will use in hypothesis tests.

Inductive descriptive methodologies span the realist, objectivist, and the pragmatist neighbourhoods of Figure 7.2. At a basic level, all empirical description relies on inductive inference. Researchers use induction whenever they classify data into more abstract terms – for example, when coding in qualitative research or assigning observations to the attributes of categorical variables in quantitative research. Inductive description is so deeply necessary to learning, and apprehending any new phenomena, that all researchers rely on it in some way.

In biomedicine, for example, schematizing and labelling anatomical structures is an inductive, descriptive act. Inductive practices may be central or peripheral to the aims of a research project. In *qualitative description,* they are central. Qualitative description has been characterized as a research methodology of its own, defined as descriptive accounts written in 'everyday terms' and involving eclectic methods (Sandelowski, 2000). As an example, Dobbins et al. (2007) conducted interviews with public health decision makers about their preferred formats for receiving research information. The investigators took participants' stated preferences at face value, and summarized them in participants' own terms – terms which converged comfortably and meaningfully with the researchers' perspective. Researchers in this neighbourhood deemphasize interpretation and abstract theorizing. For example, this study did not ask questions such as whether 'evidence' might mean different things to different people, or what influences in the social milieu might account for such differences.

Historiography, case study, and related methods also rely heavily on inductive description to construct narratives of past events, or accounts of specific cases. Researchers gather descriptive data pragmatically – to determine who's who, what happened when, what institutional relationships can be identified, and so forth, as the scaffolding for their analysis. *Narrative inquiry* seeks the stories behind peoples' actions and social contexts (Clandinin and Connelly, 2000). Studies leaning 'westward' on Figure 7.2 may resemble a highly methodical form of investigative journalism. As approaches lean 'eastward', interpretation plays a more significant role. Researchers, for example, must read between the lines of organizational documents, reconcile information and perspectives of informants, and identify broad dynamics or themes that informants may not articulate well individually. An example is Wright et al.'s recent history of the idea of physician 'brain drain' (Wright et al., 2008), which takes as given statistical records of physician training and migration patterns. The researchers use this background of reasonably objective facts to investigate stakeholders' strategic use and meaning of the 'brain drain' concept to frame policy and popular responses to migration. Findings often serve as exemplars, cautionary tales, or vicarious experience; readers, in turn, use these to theorize about other situations. Yin notes that case accounts do not generalize to populations of like cases, but rather 'to theory' (Yin, 2003).

Findings from historical and case study research can inform thinking about novel situations. Qualitative *policy analysis* appears 'southward' on Figure 7.2 for its efforts to produce general lessons for policy. Methodologically, qualitative policy analysis takes many forms, including case study and historical study, as well as more 'easterly' interpretive methods such as interpretation of documents, ethnography grounded theory, and critical theory (Orsini and Smith, 2007; Sadovnik, 2006; Shore and Wright, 1997). Health policy literature includes a substantial number of case and historical accounts of how policy is made, its nature, and its impacts. An example is Mayes and Horowitz' explanatory narrative of the emergence of the psychiatric disease classification system, the

DSM-III, and its political, professional, and institutional repercussions for US mental health clinicians (Mayes and Horwitz, 2005).

Moving 'eastward' in Figure 7.2, we find *interpretive description* – a pragmatic, practice-informing methodology developed within the clinical field of nursing (Thorne, 2008; Thorne et al., 1997). This problem-driven methodology strategically applies a variety of interpretive techniques from the social sciences (grounded theory, ethnography, and phenomenology, discussed in the following section.) to generate clinically useful, applicable knowledge. Thorne et al., for example, use interpretive descriptive inquiry to develop a clear list of helpful vs. unhelpful clinician communication tactics and features of communication competence, for use in the context of caring for persons with multiple sclerosis (Thorne et al., 2004).

Ethnographic and *naturalistic* research traditions are quintessentially interpretive. These have evolved from the fieldwork-based anthropology of culture, but other disciplines (e.g., sociology and political science) have adapted them as well. Ethnographers seek an intimate interpretive understanding of a particular culture, a life, a people, or a social setting. The methodology typically involves prolonged engagement in the setting, most often through fieldwork. The resulting ethnographic findings take the form of a narrative account. Such accounts may assume biographical, autobiographical, or hybrid formats to include both the researchers' and research participants' unfolding process of understanding each other's worlds. Findings often invite the reader into a vicarious experience of the research process as well as the culture studied. Researchers may highlight selected metaphors or images within the culture's symbolic system to aid translation between the social world studied and that of the researcher or the research's intended audience. Beyond this, however, findings remain particularistic and most researchers in this tradition resist too much conceptual abstraction. As Clifford Geertz eloquently cautioned in his classic treatise on 'thick description':

> Only short flights of ratiocination tend to be effective in anthropology; longer ones tend to drift off into logical dreams, academic bemusements with formal symmetry. The whole point of a semiotic approach to culture is ... to aid us in gaining access to the conceptual world in which our subjects live so that we can, in some extended sense of the term, converse with them (Geertz, 1973, p. 24).

Since Geertz wrote these words, the field of ethnography has evolved through critical and ideological influences to view the research subject as an equal to the researcher. The methodology now emphasizes a more inter-subjective approach to the 'conversation', regarding research participants as collaborators or coauthors in the resulting story (e.g., Denzin, 1997). The many newer variants of ethnography span the 'west–east' span of qualitative traditions in Figure 7.2. As an example, ethnographies of 'contaminated communities' have created new explanatory narratives for contamination and its impacts (Brown, 2003). Research participants, researchers, and readers alike draw upon these ethnographic narratives to animate their arguments for action to improve polluted conditions.

Phenomenological methodologies originated from the disciplines of philosophy and psychology. They focus on individuals' experiences and sense making, often posing research questions in terms of the experience of 'being' in relation to a given role, event, or condition. Researchers strive to understand how individuals create and sustain the subjective, personal meanings they use to make sense of their experiences and who they are in context (Van Manen, 1990). Researchers regard participants as people immersed in their own epistemological projects, in relation to their own ontological worlds. Phenomenological analyses favour the particular over the general, and delve into individuals' interior thoughts. Phenomenologists typically impose little prior theory about the ways of knowing that they might find in participants. Different methodological variants make characteristically different assumptions about the subjectivity vs. objectivity of phenomenological research findings (Cohen and Omery, 1994; Ray, 1994). In the method as originally inspired by Husserlian philosophy (e.g., Schutz, 1962), researchers practice *epoche*, or *bracketing* – a conscious distancing of their own inner lives and sense making from those of the persons studied, to gain a more authentic view. This nudges the method 'westward' in Figure 7.2, as researchers strive for a form of objectivity. Other phenomenological approaches reject both the desirability and possibility of such distancing, and occupy more 'eastward' positions on Figure 7.2. *Hermeneutic phenomenology* emphasizes intersubjective interpretation, focused on understanding 'lived experiences' of individuals (Cohen et al., 2000). To understand another's experience, one must nevertheless draw upon one's own subjective, phenomenological knowledge (Lindseth and Norberg, 2004; Streubert and Carpenter, 1995). In this more interpretive tradition, participants and researchers jointly create phenomenological accounts. The findings of phenomenological research typically include few and selective detailed case narratives, derived from intensive dialogue and reflection between the researcher and study participants. Researchers recognize that social conventions affect individuals' ways of knowing, yet do not expect social constructs per se to sufficiently characterize or explain them. Researchers may highlight patterns across accounts of individuals, but the discovery of common themes is not always a central aim of phenomenological investigation. As an example, Beltran et al. (2008) investigate phenomenologically how clinicians who work with extreme trauma victims 'typify' the mental sequelae of trauma. They use the findings to identify clinical features and reasoning that are crucial to clinical understanding, yet are poorly captured by current diagnostics schemas. The findings suggest more meaningful diagnostic criteria for a trauma syndrome. Another illustrative phenomenological study investigates of nurses' relationship with critical care technologies, focusing on the feelings evoked by the technology (e.g., safety, control, being informed, and being technically competent), and how technology mediates the nurses' own knowledge of the patient (Alasad, 2002).

Grounded theory methodologies also focus on the interpretation of meaning. However, in contrast to phenomenology's focus on individuals' inner sense-making, grounded theory characterizes the systems of meanings occurring within groups and constructed through social interactions. Glaser's seminal formulation of the method for sociology (Glaser and Strauss, 1967) draws upon symbolic interactionism theory (Blumer, 1969), which allows researchers to regard social meanings as entities in their own right, created through social interactions. Because symbolic systems regulate social behaviour, understanding these may serve powerful descriptive, explanatory, or predictive analytic purposes. As systems of ideas, social symbolic meanings are themselves types of theories, grounded theory characterizes these commonplace theories used at the ground of social interaction. Analysis involves the fragmentation and reassembly of data into thematic categories, and the categories into an increasingly coherent conceptual framework that spans the individuals studied and captures a broader social system of ideas. The resulting 'grounded theory' serves as an abstracted, stylized version of the commonplace theories that prevail in the social world studied. If more particularist methodologies leave readers a vicarious feeling of having walked through someone else's world, grounded theory gives readers more of a feeling that they carry someone else's social rulebook. Grounded theory researchers differ somewhat by their tendency to treat social meanings as objectively real entities versus subjectively relative ideas. Dissent on this fundamental issue has generated important variants of the method. Grounded theory's concern with symbolic interaction entails the analysis of symbolic systems (semiotics), which ought to locate the methodology squarely within the idealist, interpretivist neighbourhood. Yet, some suggest that Glaser's original formulation of grounded theory implies a kind of objectivism by aiming, and claiming, to 'discover' social phenomena external to the researcher (Charmaz, 2000; Thomas and James, 2006). More recent reformulations (Charmaz, 2006; Strauss and Corbin, 1990) shift grounded theory methodologies progressively 'eastward' on Figure 7.2. More interpretive approaches to grounded theory share much in common with naturalistic and ethnographic traditions, in practice as well as results (Stern, 1994). A grounded theory study in Germany, for example, investigated how young adults conceived by IVF (*in vitro* fertilization) view the meaning of their *in vitro* conception (Siegel et al., 2008). The investigators identify an overriding theme that children view IVF as a positive demonstration of being intensely wanted by their parents. This empirically grounded theory contradicts other, principle-driven, ethical theories in the early years of IVF that warned that the technology would dehumanize or alienate parent–child relationships.

Postmodernism is a sweeping philosophical movement, and not in itself a research methodology. However, postmodernist ontological ideas generate distinctive epistemological challenges and methodological approaches in research. Postmodernist philosophical, aesthetic and stylistic features prevail in many qualitative methodologies – most palpably in idealistic, critical and creative methodological traditions (see, e.g., Vidich and Lyman, 2000). Postmodern researchers strive to identify, critique, and defuse metanarratives. Metanarratives are the sweeping explanatory or moral stories a society takes as given (e.g., humanism, rationality, major religions, and ontological ideas). Communities use metanarratives pervasively to make sense of all things, as well as to judge and control them (see Rolfe (Rolfe, 2001) and Rosenau (Rosenau, 1992b) for introductions to the postmodern perspective). The postmodern researcher investigates social life in the context of this deep critique, and deconstructs found narratives into all manner of possible meanings, alternative readings, and implications. Researchers thus create, as much as empirically encounter, the phenomena with which they work. Postmodern researchers question any form of authority, including the researcher's own authority, and that of research altogether. Central phenomena in any project include reflexivity (the effect of research on the things studied) and the investigator's role. Research is foremost the researcher's doing, and findings, the researcher's experience. Project reports often have strong overtones of personal quest, reflection, or introspection. Rosenau (Rosenau, 1992a) characterizes two genres of postmodern analysis, sceptical and affirmative, that may flow from postmodernism's ontological premises. For the sceptical postmodernist, there is nothing 'out there' to find empirically, and nothing decisive to understand from a shared viewpoint. Researchers respond with epistemological nihilism (if nothing is to be found, why bother looking?) and ideological apathy (how could one endorse any knowledge as scientifically or morally worth pursuing?). In contrast, affirmative postmodernists take the limitless possibilities of uncertain ontological foundations as a license for creativity. They celebrate diversity, and seize the projects they prefer with unapologetic passion. In practice, postmodern-styled researchers pursue a vast variety of research strategies (Rosenau, 1992a). The term 'postmodern' (and its philosophical tenets, without the label) has been associated in various ways with qualitative methodologies across the 'west–east' span of Figure 7.2 (Travers, 2006). Postmodernism lacks traction only in the far 'western' traditions that hold a strongly realist ontology, as the postmodern researcher rejects claims of rational objectivity.

Postmodern researchers tend to present their findings as problematic, without apology for their being so. Findings may resist generalization or even internal validation. Researchers may offer their reports as exploratory and impressionistic, noncommittal and inconclusive. They may also be playful, creative, or transparently fictional. Some researchers express findings through alternative and artistic media, to leave much interpretation up to audiences. This practice raises the methodological issue of whether qualitative researchers require skills at artistic expression (Travers, 2006), and whether researchers have left the realm of social science research when creating art or literature (Hammersley, 1999). Many postmodern-styled findings use abstruse language that tends to alienate those unschooled in the tradition. This slippery language emerges in part from the nihilist's acute sensitivity to the idea that to name a thing is to form it – and thus to exert unwarranted power or control over it. An example of a postmodern-styled qualitative investigation is Learmonth's study of UK National Health Service chief executives' discourse (Learmonth, 2001). The study shows how imagery depicting the executive role draws on ancient hero mythology. This implied heroism pervades accounts of executives' work and subtly serves their interests. A caveat accompanies these intriguing findings: 'Of course, by spot-lighting the heroic, other things are put in the shade – any reading is partial and misleading because all non-trivial texts are capable of nearly endless rereadings. This paper therefore makes no claim to have exhausted the transcripts' meanings or to be intrinsically superior to other possible "findings"' (Learmonth, 2001, pp. 432–433).

The *participatory action* research tradition involves active collaboration between the formally trained qualitative researcher and the people involved in the setting of the research. Participatory action research is particularistic, as researchers undertake these projects on behalf of the interests of specific com-munities, in the service of their self-defined interests. The research problem and questions must originate from the setting, and participants play a major role in data collection and analysis. Characteristic principles of this approach include the situation of the researcher as an active participant within the setting studied, attention to process of participating, learning through experience and reflection, and an action orientation to better the situation (Koch and Kralik, 2006). Some variants of participatory action methodologies consciously follow a social reform agenda (e.g., social justice), sometimes informed by values drawn from beyond the setting. Such commitments draw the methodology closer in philosophy to feminist and critical theory approaches (discussed in the following section), yet, other participatory action researchers consider empowerment best achieved according to participants' own values and terms and resist allegiance to broader ideological agendas (Koch and Kralik, 2006). In principle, a participatory action study might employ any research methodology. Researchers typically favour qualitative approaches for their nuanced attention to participants' perspectives and power relations, and the usefulness of qualitative findings for redressing power imbalances (Minkler and Wallerstein, 2003). Participatory action studies by def-inition produce action-oriented findings, intended to bring about positive change for those in the study setting. Researchers often aim their reports at audiences outside academia, towards those who can use the information to improve condi-tions of study participants. Because findings must map closely onto the particular setting and its problems, researchers do not consider abstract theorizing or gen-eralization desirable in themselves, beyond their uses for local arguments and action (Kemmis and McTaggart, 2000). As a result, findings may be more highly valued by those studied than by the researcher's academic community. For this reason, investigators may find themselves writing different versions of their find-ings for these different audiences. For example, a community-based participatory action study addressed the Russian émigré experience in San Francisco cancer clinics (Dohan and Levintova, 2007). The research identifies conflicts between the clinical imperative of fully informed consent to treatment, and Russian cul-tural taboos against telling people they have cancer. The researchers published their study for peers in a clinical journal, but also used the findings to develop more culturally sensitive patient education materials and processes in the study setting.

Critical theory qualitative research traditions are distinctive for bringing well-developed social or political theories to empirical work. These frame the research question, guide the analysis, and make sense of findings. Critical theorists view socially constructed realities as the products of power relations. Power is distributed unequally, to the detriment of the powerless. Consequently, many of the social phenomena researchers will encounter in a qualitative study are constructs that serve the powerful and oppress the weak. The empirical quest, then, is not so much to discover as to uncover constructs that oppress. Figure 7.2 depicts the critical theory tradition in the 'eastern', idealist region of Figure 7.2, as it searches for signs of power dynamics in discourse. This requires both interpretive epistemology, to interpret these signs, and critical epistemology, to look beyond their immediate meanings to their implications for power relations. The critical theory tradition is difficult to place on a two-dimensional map such as Figure 7.2, because it paradoxically invokes some realist assumptions. Foremost, researchers presume the real existence of power and power relations, as well as their own ability to identify these in ways valid and compelling to others. Some critical theory traditions (e.g., those emerging from Marxist political economy) examine the distribution of material resources and the materially real consequences of symbolic commitments. Ideologically, an ethic of social justice motivates most critical theory methodologies: 'Inquiry that aspires to the name "critical" must be connected to an attempt to confront the injustice of a particular society or public sphere within the society' (Kincheloe and McLaren, 2005, p. 305). Frameworks for diagnosing, understanding, and remedying injustice vary across critical researchers and research programs. Indeed, the ability to identify and empirically investigate societal pathologies rests on moral convictions which themselves invite ethical critique (Honneth, 2007). In particular, critical theory researchers face the dilemma of how to justify the moral stance of their own analysis when it differs from the values they encounter in the study setting, and must question whether such a critique 'just replace[s] the values of one ruling class with that of another that wants to rule' (Forst, 1996, p. 146). Ideological commitments often draw critical theorists to question the very activity of empirical research altogether, and research's role in sustaining power relations (Kincheloe and McLaren, 2005). As with participatory action research, critical theory research could employ a variety of empirical methods, qualitative or quantitative, in the pragmatic service of critique. Researchers must consider their methodological choices carefully for their ideological implications (Morrow and Brown, 1994). They will favour qualitative approaches to give voice to those who have been silenced, to render visible the condition of those whose interests have been erased from view, and to create emancipatory visions of how conditions might improve under an alternative form of discourse. It is a challenge for readers examining the findings of a critical theory analysis to decide whether researchers really have authentically represented the interests of oppressed people, and served their interests through the research process and findings. An example of an ethnographic study in the critical theory tradition is Warin et al.'s (2008) study of how women embody gender and class identities through largeness. The investigators applied Bourdieu's theory of 'habitus' to frame the research question and guide the analysis. They identify the relative irrelevance – if not repugnance – of medical and health promotion concepts such as obesity and Body Mass Index (BMI) for capturing the meaning of body size.

Feminist philosophies have influenced methodologies across the range of research approaches; there is no discrete *feminist methodology* per se. Hallmarks of the feminist qualitative research community include a spectrum of methods and perennial dialogue over principles and approaches (Oleson, 2000, 2005). The location of a feminist qualitative research tradition in Figure 7.2 should not confine it to one place, but rather highlight the interpretive, critical, and creative epistemological approaches that characterize such work. Feminist ideology has an ambivalent relationship to realist vs. idealist ontologies and their entailed epistemologies. On the one hand, claims that research findings are real in an objective sense improves their use in arguments for real and material responses; on the other hand, gender is a social construct, with meanings and implications change best understood interpretively (Ramazanoglu and Holland, 2002). Feminist research identifies with certain characteristic topics, particularly concerning gender, otherness, and power. Work on these and related concepts guides research questions as well as analysis. In health research, for example, researchers problematize seemingly basic concepts such as health, healing, and medicine (Clarke and Olesen, 1999). The concept of gender itself embraces: '... sexuality and reproduction; sexual difference, embodiment, the social constitution of male, female, intersexual, other; masculinity and femininity; ideas, discourses, practices, subjectivities and social relationships' (Ramazanoglu and Holland, 2002, p. 5). Concerns with the situated perspectives of research participants, the investigator, and envisioned readers, pervade feminist projects (Reinharz and Davidman, 1992). To present research findings, feminist methodologists have pioneered alternative media, including for example alternative graphic and textual formats, plays, poetry, performances, storytelling, and more, in addition to conventional academic venues (Oleson, 2000). Such modes target audiences beyond the academic elite, and aim to involve and touch them on an emotional and moral, as well as intellectual, level. Through their findings, feminist qualitative researchers often strive to raise consciousness and inspire action in their audiences. Anderson et al., for example, apply a standpoint perspective to analyze how the 'discourse of efficiency' in health care reform standardizes services and fails to understand or meet the needs of groups perceived as Other (Anderson et al., 2007). The authors demonstrate how providers stylize and attribute 'culture' to those they characterize as outsiders (particularly immigrants), while the ubiquitous culture of biomedical institutions – particularly its commitment to scientific efficiency – remains unrecognized and unquestioned. The authors argue that accessible health care requires attention to the organizational cultures of health care, and an end to externalizing culture as an attribute of other social groups.

This brief tour of qualitative research traditions has touched on the ontological places one may start from, and the epistemological and methodological routes one may take from various starting points (see Figure 7.2). This framework also helps to characterize the distinctive kinds of theoretical findings that are rooted in particular ontological and epistemological starting points. The underlying philosophical foundations of the different methodologies – that is, the range of possible assumptions about reality and the imperatives they create for knowing – are relatively stable. What shifts a great deal, however, is the overlying architecture of research work – the specific methodologies, techniques, schools, and labels that health researchers build upon these foundations. A satellite view of qualitative health research today might look more like a wild frontier than this tidy map. One would see crowds in some places, emptiness in others. Various methodologists would have flags staked all over the map of Figure 7.2. Other methodologists would furiously move these flags elsewhere, or paint them over with different labels. Some areas burgeon with happy collaborations, even over vast distances, and others with icy standoffs, even at close quarters. Researchers on a given project may weave in and out of many locales – sometimes well aware of their route, sometimes lost. A great deal of hopping, connecting, and bridge-building renders the lines between neighbourhoods increasingly blurry (Guba and Lincoln, 2005). Some researchers relish the opportunity to collaborate with others in deeply opposing traditions, as this 'boundary work' clarifies the contours and value of their own approach (Clandinin and Connelly, 2000). The resulting and ever-growing 'bricolage' of patch-worked qualitative approaches (Denzin and Lincoln, 2000) offers opportunities for both innovation and disorientation. Hammersley offers boat building as a metaphor superior to bricolage (Hammersley, 1999): research programs, like ships, require working parts that fit together with each other and a good sense of both origin and destination. This metaphor allows for the existence of many 'ships' headed in many directions, but cautions against interchanging their parts carelessly. This image does not imply one ideal design, but calls for coherence within designs.

Some qualitative health research seems unanchored to ontological and epistemological premises. Especially in clinical journals, published qualitative studies commonly describe hybrid methodologies that are difficult to characterize epistemologically, or qualitative methods attributed to no particular tradition at all. 'Generic' approaches appeal to some health researchers who relate less well to the academic agendas behind more 'branded' approaches, and want to design studies closely around practical problems (Cooper and Endacott, 2007). Some argue that strict allegiance to discipline-rooted, named methods impedes the innovation needed to do useful, practice-relevant research (Avis, 2003; Cooper and Endacott, 2007; Thorne, 2008). A review of empirical research publication patterns in nursing finds that 37 percent of studies published in nursing journals use qualitative methods, but 41 percent of these studies do not specify a methodological tradition (Mantzoukas, 2009). Other reviews find that qualitative reports some-times declare adherence to one tradition, while describing methods or findings more characteristic of another (Cohen and Omery, 1994; Giacomini et al., 2009). Some researchers publish qualitative studies without offering much in the way of findings at all, but instead, partially finished analyses or unanalyzed data (Sandelowski and Barroso, 2002).

'Mixed methods' are popular among health researchers from different discipli-nary backgrounds with interests in common problems. Mixed-methods projects focus on problems, generate relevant questions, and only then employ whatever empirical methodologies can address the questions. Often the development of a compelling research design itself requires smaller empirical projects – possibly from different traditions – to explore phenomena, develop variables or tools, and so forth. 'Mixing' may occur in the design, analysis, or interpretation phase of collaborations between qualitative and quantitative traditions (Creswell and Plano Clark, 2007). Researchers justify multiple methods on the grounds of pragmatism, the epistemological middle ground in Figure 7.2. Nevertheless, in a mixed methods study, researchers often do not so much meet on the same episte-mological ground as jump from one neighbourhood to another, asking different questions and using answers in one tradition to inform knowledge and frame questions in another. As researchers pass questions and answers back and forth, subjective, values-infused ideas may become reified as objects (when moving 'westward' on Figure 7.2), while real, value-free facts about objects become prob-lematized as value-laden ideas (when moving 'eastward'). Redrawing such ontological lines remains controversial within the qualitative research community. In practice, mixed-methods research teams vary widely in how they employ and relate their various methods; epistemological cross-purposes sometimes generate dysfunctional projects (O'Cathain et al., 2008). Questions about the legitimacy of mixing methods point to the much broader issues of what 'users' can – or should – do with qualitative research questions and findings.

THEORY MATTERS

Theory matters in two basic ways in qualitative health research. First, the theory researchers bring to the research enterprise – their ontological and epistemological stances – influences their choice of methodologies and gives characteristic shapes to their findings. Second, qualitative research *findings* themselves are theoretical con-structs: systems of ideas for understanding. After publication, research-generated theory takes on a life of its own. This life of qualitative research findings matters increasingly for health policy and practice. Health research becomes ever more interdisciplinary and collaborative, and the readers of research ever more diverse in backgrounds, and action-oriented in aims. Many qualitative researchers today find themselves working and writing in application-oriented policy or clinical settings that influence how theoretical findings take form. Interdisciplinary collaborations, adapted and mixed methodologies proliferate – often in efforts to improve the pragmatic relevance of qualitative work. In this dynamic context, qualitative researchers need to keep their theoretical bearings, and recognize when tugging interests pull them away from the commitments that justify their chosen methodologies. Without an orientation to theory and its myriad forms in health and social science fields, researchers risk incoherence. With attention to theory, however, traditional methodologies generate richer findings, and innovative methodologies may flourish to yield fruitful results.

The inferential warrant of each research methodology rests on basic ontological and epistemological beliefs. These allow researchers to chart their course into and through their research projects. They also suggest legitimate and illegitimate uses for findings as claims supporting knowledge or action. Health research traditions vary by the kinds of phenomena upon which they primarily focus (e.g., natural or social), how they problematize phenomena (e.g., as real, objective facts or as subjective ideas), and the types of phenomena considered problematic (e.g., physical matter or social power). Researchers involved in 'mixed methods' projects, collaborating outside their usual methodology or developing novel methods, must keep track of their epistemological bearings. Colleagues who have opposing epistemological aims (i.e., residing in distant neighbourhoods of Figure 7.2) could not collaborate fruitfully on the same question, because their assumptions about the world do not allow them to seek, or to find, the same essential sorts of things. For example, 'obesity' has been widely defined as a quantitatively measurable variable by biomedical researchers. Viewed in that tradition, it is an objective, measurable phenomenon having no intrinsic values content. For large women (through the qualitative researchers who relate their experiences) the matter takes on entirely different meaning: they reject the label 'obese' for its stigma (Warin et al., 2008). Preferred characterizations (e.g., 'chubby' and 'cuddly') entail richer meanings shaped by the relation of women's bodies to their social roles and context (Warin et al., 2008). The biomedical construct of obesity thus acts not only as a biomedical measure, but also as a social value judgment and a facet of personal identity. The agenda to measure and pathologize body size forms part of women's social milieu and lived experiences. Thus, the researchers who measure BMI, and the researchers who interpret embodiment experience, work in ontologically and epistemologically different worlds. Their findings will not speak of the same things. It is possible, however, for these researchers to speak to, and learn, from each other – if they understand each others' epistemological stances.

The ontological positions that define the epistemological neighbourhoods in Figure 7.2 do not move: fundamental philosophical principles keep these neighbourhoods from piling together into one happy high-rise. Extreme realist vs. idealist convictions are particularly irreconcilable (Smith and Heshusius, 1986). The legacy of the 'science wars' in academic politics has left many qualitative researchers reluctant to consolidate or adapt methods, for fear of compromising their hard-won epistemological legitimacy and identities (Onwuegbuzie, 2002).

However, ensuring epistemological integrity is no straightforward matter in the complex, interdisciplinary, and highly applied environments of health research. The problem cannot be solved by keeping qualitative and quantitative researchers safely at arms-length, or requiring researchers rigidly to follow canonical methodologies. Neither extreme of the ontological and epistemological spectrum of Figure 7.2 ensures empirical certainty. Each faces philosophical paradoxes that prevent them from making infallible claims. All researchers make some compromises in their work – for example, realists must rely on conceptually mediated induction to classify phenomena; idealists must presume some degree of consensus about reality to frame the conditions of their work and to communicate their findings. Many researchers now train in more than one methodological tradition, and approach their methodologies as tools rather than as thoroughgoing doctrines. Calls to adopt and adapt multiple approaches, especially to answer complex, relevant questions of applied health research (Hammersley, 2009; Thorne, 2008) increasingly replace longstanding cautions against muddying methodologies (Baker et al., 1992; Smith and Heshusius, 1986). Some suggest that researchers abandon allegiances to epistemological premises such as realism or idealism altogether and subscribe solely to pragmatism to justify their methodologies (Avis, 2003). Researchers need not declare a personal faith in realism or idealism: 'Given that [knowledge] 'discovery' and 'construction' are metaphors, we do not have to choose one or the other, and we would be foolish to do so' (Hammersley, 2009, p. 20); it is possible to ask different questions and seek different kinds of answers within a common topic. Even so, it remains important to discern when empirical methods or claims slide away from the deeper epistemological arguments that justify them (Morse, 2005).

Conditions in the practice of health research prevent the showdowns entailed by extreme philosophical differences, particularly those between objective realism and interpretive idealism. Deep conflict only arises over a *given* phenomenon: to disagree hopelessly about the nature of things, researchers must address the same things. However, one cannot make both a subjectivist, interpretive truth claim and a positivist, objectivist truth claim about exactly the same thing. In research practice, researchers tend to make different kinds of claims about different phenomena. We distinguish methodologies by the specific types of phenomena they take for granted as real, versus those they treat as ideation to be understood interpretively. On a given project, a practicing researcher inevitably develops a portfolio of the stances represented in Figure 7.2. Which ontological and epistemological assumptions to make, when, and how, depend on the aims of the project, the information at hand, and terms of reference afforded by the current state of knowledge. The process of treating some phenomena as more or less objectively describable (typically, as conditions), while problematizing other phenomena as relative and available for interpretation, has been termed *ontological gerrymandering* in sociology (Woolgar and Pawluch, 1985). In the growing practice of mixed methods projects that involve both qualitative and quantitative approaches, qualitative researchers have markedly different levels of tolerance for easing their commitments to idealism (Creswell and Plano Clark, 2007), for example, when quantitative aims reify qualitative findings as variables, or experimental design problems dictate the interpretive research questions to ask. Such gerry-mandering in the interest of problem-solving works as long as collaborators sustain reasonable consensus on the nature of 'the' problem. Collaboration (or method-mixing) can lose common ground when, for example, a critical or interpretivist researcher problematizes 'the problem' itself for investigation.

Theory matters not only for justifying and shaping research methodologies, but also for creating meaning and implications from research findings. When qualitative researchers develop their findings, they formulate theories intended for others to learn, know, and use. The philosopher of science, Philip Kitcher (2001) has analogized research to mapping a part of the world. A *perfectly* com-prehensive representation, if possible, would simply match the uncharted terrain itself, and would accomplish no helpful analysis. Drawing a map always requires some degree of abstraction and interpretation of the terrain studied. This holds true for objectivist as well as interpretivist methodologies. Health research meth-odologies differ in terms of the problem areas considered to need mapping, the particular phenomena considered worth highlighting, and the representation of phenomena according to the imagined requirements of those who might use the maps.

'Health' research entails a pragmatic agenda: health is at stake. Much of the value and impact of qualitative health research findings depends upon how researchers imagine that health stakeholders will understand, interpret, and use research findings. Some uses of the kinds of theories produced by qualitative research may include, for example: challenging the fundamental assumptions within which health policy and health care agendas are framed; understanding the social, cultural, or personal contexts of health and disease; investigating how conditions come to be defined as health problems; and envisioning or designing clinical, program, or policy interventions. There are, as well, many evaluative applications of qualitative research that range from discerning valued goals, to formative accounts exploring complex causal dynamics, to reconceptu-alizing variables in the service of more meaningful quantitative hypothesis testing.

Once published, research findings have lives of their own. As Bruno Latour has noted, research findings exist as statements, or sentences – and 'By itself a given sentence is neither a fact nor a fiction; *it is made so by others, later on*' (Latour, 1987, p. 25, emphasis mine). When a qualitative account leaves the hand of its author, it joins prevailing knowledge, as well as ideological, technological, policy, and practice agendas. It takes new forms, and becomes part of new rhetorical arguments. The imagined and actual users of research, the researcher, and the participants all contribute to the meaning and impact of qualitative research findings. To the extent qualitative research has generalizability, this is created by its readers rather than warranted by its investigators or its design (Willis et al., 2007). Different readers will, quite naturally, take different lessons from the same piece of work. The theories offered by qualitative research are compact but elastic. Research audiences take qualitative findings and stretch them into many useful forms – yet, not just 'any' form – to serve the purposes of other ideas and other projects. In the current context of health practice and policy communities, this second life may sometimes take a more instrumental interpretation than qualitative researchers typically intend. It is beyond the scope of this chapter to prescribe a resolution to this important epistemological tension. Over time, qualitative health researchers will increasingly face the question of how the potential and possible uses of their research should affect the research and writing process.

What business do others have with the theories produced by qualitative health researchers? Some trends in health research are noteworthy. Foremost, the 'evidence-based decision making' movement in clinical care, and the ensuing 'knowledge translation and exchange' movement in health policy, strive to put research findings into the hands of potential users. For example, the Cochrane Collaboration Qualitative Methods Research Group considers how qualitative evidence can aid the synthesis of clinical effectiveness evidence (Dixon-Woods et al., 2001). Here, qualitative research serves a relatively narrow instrumental purpose. It seems important to find ways that qualitative research might more systematically help *shape* clinical instruments and evaluation goals themselves. There remains much relevant but unread qualitative health research that could offer insights for clinicians, administrators, and policy makers. Currently, there exists no clearinghouse analogous to the Cochrane Collaboration for making qualitative research widely accessible to those who might apply its insights to their own conceptual work, enlightenment, question framing, and the like. Much qualitative methodological and empirical literature appears in published books, which remain less electronically accessible to interdisciplinary or lay audiences. High-impact, high-visibility health journals currently carry very little of the qualitative research available.

The historical aversion of evidence-oriented decision makers to theorizing poses a second challenge to the appreciation and use of qualitative research findings in health. Early advocates of evidence-based medicine (EBM) strove to reorient clinicians away from authority-based arguments, and redirect them towards experimental trial results to determine the value of clinical practices (Haynes, 2002). EBM rhetoric has built a false dichotomy between theory and evidence, as argument from authority has become characterized as 'theory', and the randomized controlled clinical trial has become the paradigm for 'evidence'. Both caricatures have cost EBM in terms of scientific sophistication and credibility (Giacomini, 2009). Recently, EBM leaders have tempered their stance regarding evidence, accepting now that clinicians and policy makers require a wide variety of methodologies to answer a wide variety of questions (Haynes, 2002). Their scepticism about theorizing has softened less. Users of research in health contexts need to understand better the role of theory in the generation, understanding, and practical use of evidence.

Qualitative research information poses an interesting challenge to the evidence-based ethos prevailing in health. Researchers clearly derive qualitative findings empirically – thus, qualitative findings stand as evidence. However, these findings are also conceptual and theoretical in nature, and strive neither for objectivity or certainty. What should evidence-oriented decision makers do, then, to 'use' qualitative research results? Leaders in health policy now advocate broadening systematic reviews beyond the Cochrane-style instrumental focus on 'what works' to support questions about mechanisms, relationships, and meanings (Lavis et al., 2006:1). Systematic review methods, as currently practiced, aim to reduce large bodies of research literature and findings to simpler messages for lay and applied audiences. They do not capture well qualitative social theories or particu-laristic narratives. It remains to be seen how the information-processing engines of the knowledge translation movement will cope with the voluminous, often relativistic, sometimes ideological, and always-interpretive information produced by qualitative health researchers.

Theory matters, too, in assessing the information value of qualitative research findings. As qualitative evidence receives wider attention and respect in health fields, there looms the issue of critical appraisal of individual studies – especially by non-expert 'users'. Many readers wish to learn in accessible, interdisciplinary terms how to recognize valuable, well-done qualitative research. The biomedical literature has published numerous novices' guides to reading and appraising qualitative research reports (Elder and Miller, 1995; Giacomini and Cook, 2000b, 2000a; Inui and Frankel, 1991; Kitto et al., 2008; Kuper et al., 2008; Mays and Pope, 2000; Tong et al., 2007; Walsh and Downe, 2006); many reframe similar messages for different audiences. Early formulations of criteria for appraising qualitative research often borrowed or attempted to translate language from quantitative, objectivist traditions, referring to rigour, validity, reliability, and so forth (Kirk and Miller, 1986; Sandelowski, 1986). These discipline-bridging terms eventually gave way to forms of critique more in keeping with idealist commitments (Sandelowski, 2006a). Even so, we still find efforts to map the aims of qualitative research onto quasi-quantitative criteria in disciplines where realist, objectivist research traditions dominate, e.g., quality improvement (Collingridge and Gantt, 2008). Other treatises focus less on dilemmas faced by the novice reader and more on the need for expert discrimination between the proper aims and achievements of different qualitative traditions. Some reject the generic appraisal criteria now popular in biomedical journals, because they gloss over the differences among traditions and the important aims that distinguish one qualitative methodology from another (Sale, 2008). For the same reason, qualita-tive researchers in one tradition may lack the expertise to criticize work done in another.

At an extreme position, some authors deny the possibility of critical appraisal of qualitative research, given the underlying ontology of idealism that prohibits access to an objective reality (Denzin, 1997; Eakin and Mykhalovskiy, 2003). From this viewpoint, research itself is a social construct relative to the perspective of the knower (Schwandt, 1996). All qualitative studies reckon with the philosophical impossibility of authentically representing other peoples' social or personal worlds; synthesizing multiple qualitative studies compounds the problem (Sandelowski, 2006b). Naturally, qualitative researchers also resist having their work appraised on the basis of epistemological assumptions rejected within their own paradigms; for this reason, most qualitative researchers reject constructs such as validity, reliability, and so forth despite their appeal as hooks for quantitative researchers to begin to grasp qualitative appraisal. Even so, some call for qualitative researchers to admit the soft realism involved in their projects and claims, and to reconsider criteria for appraising fallible (as opposed to certain) truths (Hammersley, 2009). All qualitative research appraisals face the impediment that published reports lack descriptions of the myriad interpretive manoeuvres on which empirical credibility rests (Eakin and Mykhalovskiy, 2003). It is unclear, however, what disclosures (short of an extensive audit) would allow for adequate appraisal.

Critical appraisal guides to date have focused on the front-end of proper methodological procedure, and relations between methods and findings. Less attention has been given to the back-end problem of understanding the capacities, uses, and limits of the qualitative findings in the hands of others – especially those outside the research setting and academia. We need to understand how the aims, content, and style of qualitative approaches affect the subsequent lives of research findings, and the value of qualitative contributions to knowledge in multidisciplinary, interdisciplinary, or even a-disciplinary health contexts. These challenges mark interesting frontiers for both the evidence-based decision making movement and qualitative health research communities.

Theory matters in health research – it dictates methods, shapes findings, and in turn is reshaped by the knowledge produced. Matters concerning the ontological and epistemological genesis of qualitative research findings have preoccupied qualitative researchers in recent decades. In coming years, this matter should not distract from the rather different, and increasingly important, matter of examining the nature of the theories that qualitative findings can offer, and the theories they accrue in our increasingly interdisciplinary and applied health research communities.

REFERENCES

Alasad, J. (2002) 'Managing Technology in the Intensive Care Unit: The Nurses' Experience', *International Journal of Nursing Studies*, 39: 407–13.

Anderson, J.M., Tang, S., and Blue, C. (2007) 'Health Care Reform and the Paradox of Efficiency: "Writing in" Culture', *International Journal of Health Services*, 37(2): 291–320.

Avis, M. (2003) 'Do We Need Methodological Theory to Do Qualitative Research?', *Qualitative Health Research*, 13(7): 995–1104.

Baker, C., Wuest, J., and Stern, P.N. (1992) 'Method Slurring: The Grounded Theory/Phenomenology Example', *Journal of Advanced Nursing*, 17: 1355–60.

Beltran, R.O., Llewellyn, G.M., and Silove, D. (2008) 'Clinicians' Understanding of International Statistical Classification of Diseases and Related Health Problems, 10th Revision Diagnostic Criteria: F62.0 Enduring Personality Change after Catastrophic Experience', *Comprehensive Psychiatry*, 49: 593–602.

Blackburn, S. (1996) *The Oxford Dictionary of Philosophy.* New York.

Blumer, H. (1969) *Symbolic Interactionism: Perspective and Method.* Englewood Cliffs, NJ: Prentice-Hall Inc.

Brown, P. (2003) 'Qualitative Methods in Environmental Health Research', *Environmental Health Perspectives,* 111(14): 1789–98.

Chalmers, A.F. (1999) *What Is This Thing Called Science?* (3rd Edition). Indianapolis, IN: Hackett Publishing Company, Inc.

Charmaz, K. (2000) 'Grounded Theory: Objectivist and Constructivist Methods'. In N.K. Denzin and Y.S. Lincoln (eds) *Handbook of Qualitative Research* (2nd Edition) (pp. 509–36). Thousand Oaks, CA: Sage.

Charmaz, K. (2006) *Constructing Grounded Theory: A Practical Guide Through Qualitative Analysis.* Los Angeles: Sage.

Clandinin, D.J. and Connelly, F.M. (2000) *Narrative Inquiry: Experience and Story in Qualitative Research.* San Francisco, CA: Jossey-Bass.

Clarke, A.P. and Olesen, V.L. (1999) *Revisioning Women, Health and Healing: Feminist, Cultural, and Technoscience Perspectives.* New York: Routledge.

Cohen, M.Z. and Omery, A. (1994) 'Schools of Phenomenology: Implications for Research'. In J.M. Morse (ed.) *Critical Issues in Qualitative Research Methods* (pp. 136–57), Thousand Oaks, CA: Sage.

Cohen, M.Z., Kahn, D.L., and Steeves, R.H. (2000) *Hermeneutic Phenomenological Research: A Practical Guide for Nurse Researchers.* Thousand Oaks, CA: Sage.

Collingridge, D.S. and Gantt, E.E. (2008) 'The Quality of Qualitative Research', *American Journal of Medical Quality,* 23: 389–95.

Cooper, S. and Endacott, R. (2007) 'Generic Qualitative Research: A Design for Qualitative Research in Emergency Care?', *Emergency Medical Journal,* 24: 816–9.

Creswell, J.W. (2007) 'Philosophical, Paradigm, and Interpretive Frameworks', *Qualitative Inquiry and Research Design: Choosing Among Five Approaches* (pp. 15–34). Thousand Oaks, CA: Sage.

Creswell, J.W. and Plano Clark, V.L. (2007) *Designing and Conducting Mixed Methods Research.* Thousand Oaks, CA: Sage.

Denzin, N.K. (1997) *Interpretive Ethnography: Ethnographic Practices for the 21st Century.* Thousand Oaks, CA: Sage.

Denzin, N.K. and Lincoln, Y.S. (2000) 'Introduction: The Discipline and Practice of Qualitative Research'. In N.K. Denzin and Y.S. Lincoln (eds) *Handbook of Qualitative Research* (2nd Edition). Thousand Oaks, CA: Sage.

Dixon-Woods, M., Fitzpatrick, R., and Roberts, K. (2001) 'Including Qualitative Research in Systematic Reviews: Opportunities and Problems', *Journal of Evaluation in Clinical Practice,* 7(2): 125–33.

Dobbins, M., Jack, S., Thomas, H., and Kothari, A. (2007) 'Public Health Decision-Makers' Informational Needs and Preferences for Receiving Research Evidence', *Worldviews on Evidence Based Nursing,* 4(3): 156–63.

Dohan, D. and Levintova, M. (2007) 'Barriers Beyond Words: Cancer, Culture, and Translation in a Community of Russian Speakers', *Journal of General Internal Medicine,* 22(Suppl 2): 300–05.

Eakin, J.M. and Mykhalovskiy (2003) 'Reframing the Evaluation of Qualitative Health Research: Reflections on Review of Appraisal Guidelines in Health Sciences', *Journal of Evaluation in Clinical Practice,* 9(2): 187–94.

Elder, N.C. and Miller, W.L. (1995) 'Reading and Evaluating Qualitative Research Studies', *Journal of Family Practice,* 41: 279–85.

Forst, R. (1996) 'Social Science, Discourse Ethics, and Justice'. In D.M. Rasmussen (ed.) *Handbook of Critical Theory* (pp. 138–62). Cambridge, MA: Blackwell Publishers.

Foucault, M. (1972) *The Archaeology of Knowledge.* London: Tavistock Publications.

Foucault, M. (1979) *Discipline and Punish: The Birth of the Prison.* New York: Vintage Books.

Freire, P. (1970) *Pedagogy of the Oppressed.* New York: Herder and Herder.

Geertz, C. (1973) 'Thick Description: Toward an Interpretive Theory of Culture', *The Interpretation of Cultures* (pp. 3–30). New York: Basic Books.

Giacomini, M. (2009) 'Theory Based Medicine and the Role of Evidence: Why the Emperor Needs New Clothes, Again', *Perspectives in Biology and Medicine*, 52(2): 234–51.

Giacomini, M.K. and Cook, D.J. (2000a) 'A User's Guide to Qualitative Research in Health Care: Part II. What Are the Results and How Do They Help Me Care for My Patients?', *JAMA*, 284(4): 478–82.

Giacomini, M.K. and Cook, D.J. (2000b) 'A User's Guide to Qualitative Research in Health Care: Part I. Are the Results of the Study Valid?', *JAMA*, 284(3): 357–62.

Giacomini, M., Cook, D., and DeJean, D. (2009) 'Life Support Decision Making in Critical Care: Identifying and Appraising the Qualitative Research Evidence', *Critical Care Medicine*, 37(4): 1475–82.

Glaser, B. and Strauss, A.L. (1967) *Discovery of Grounded Theory*. New York: Aldine de Gruyter.

Guba, E.G. and Lincoln, Y.S. (2005) 'Paradigmatic Controversies, Contradictions, and Emerging Confluences'. In N.K. Denzin and Y.S. Lincoln (eds) *The Sage Handbook of Qualitative Research* (pp. 191–215). Thousand Oaks, CA: Sage.

Hammersley, M. (1999) 'Not Bricolage but Boatbuilding: Exploring Two Metaphors for Thinking about Ethnography', *Journal of Contemporary Ethnography*, 28(5): 574–85.

Hammersley, M. (2009) 'Challenging Relativism: The Problem of Assessment Criteria', *Qualitative Inquiry*, 15(1): 3–29.

Haynes, R. (2002) 'What Kind of Evidence is It that Evidence-Based Medicine Advocates Want Health Care Providers and Consumers to Pay Attention to?', *BMC Health Services Research*, 2(3). Available at: http://www.biomedcentral.com/1472-6963/1472/1473

Honneth, A. (2007) 'Pathologies of the Social: The Past and Present of Social Philosophy', *Disrespect: The Normative Foundations of Critical Theory* (pp. 3–48). Cambridge, MA: Polity Press.

Inui, T.S. and Frankel, R.M. (1991) 'Evaluating the Quality of Qualitative Research: A Proposal Pro Tem', *Journal of General Internal Medicine*, 6: 485–6.

Kemmis, S. and McTaggart, R. (2000) 'Participatory Action Research'. In N.K. Denzin and Y.S. Lincoln (eds) *Handbook of Qualitative Research* (2nd Edition) (pp. 567–606). Thousand Oaks, CA: Sage.

Kincheloe, J.L. and McLaren, P. (2005) 'Rethinking Critical Theory and Qualitative Research', *The Sage Handbook of Qualitative Research* (3rd Edition) (pp. 303–42). Thousand Oaks, CA: Sage.

Kirk, J. and Miller, M.L. (1986) *Reliability and Validity in Qualitative Research*. London: Sage.

Kitcher, P. (2001) 'Mapping reality', *Science, Truth, and Democracy* (pp. 55–62). Oxford: Oxford University Press.

Kitto, S.C., Chesters, J., and Grbich, C. (2008) 'Quality in Qualitative Research: Criteria for Authors and Assessors in the Submission and Assessment of Qualitative Research Articles for the Medical Journal of Australia', *Medical Journal of Australia*, 188: 243–6.

Koch, T. and Kralik, D. (2006) *Participatory Action Research in Health Care*. Malden, MA: Blackwell Publishers.

Kuper, A., Lingard, L., and Levinson, W. (2008) 'Critically Appraising Qualitative Research', *British Medical Journal*, 337: 687–9.

Latour, B. (1987) 'Literature', *Science in Action: How to Follow Scientists and Engineers Through Society* (pp. 21–62). Cambridge, MA: Harvard University Press.

Lavis, J., Davies, H., and Gruen, R. (2006;1) 'Working Within and Beyond the Cochrane Collaboration to Make Systematic Reviews More Useful to Healthcare Managers and Policy Makers', *Healthcare Policy*, 2: 21–33.

Learmonth, M. (2001) 'NHS Trust Chief Executives as Heroes?', *Health Care Analysis*, 9: 417–36.

Lincoln, Y.S. and Guba, E.G. (2000) 'Paradigmatic Controversies, Contradictions, and Emerging Confluences'. In N.K. Denzin and Y.S. Lincoln (eds) *Handbook of Qualitative Research* (2nd Edition) (pp. 163–88). Thousand Oaks, CA: Sage.

Lindseth, A. and Norberg, A. (2004) 'A Phenomenological Hermeneutical Method for Researching Lived Experience', *Scandinavian Journal of Caring Sciences*, 18: 145–53.

Lock, M.M. and Gordon, D.R. (1988) *Biomedicine Examined*. Boston, MA: Kluwer Academic Publishers.

Mantzoukas, S. (2009) 'The Research Evidence Published in High Impact Nursing Journals Between 2000 and 2006: A Quantitative Content Analysis', *International Journal of Nursing Studies* [Epub ahead of print].

Mays, N. and Pope, C. (2000) 'Qualitative Research in Health Care: Assessing Quality in Qualitative Research', *British Medical Journal*, 320: 50–2.

Mayes, R. and Horwitz, A.V. (2005) 'DSM-III and the Revolution in the Classification of Mental Illness', *Journal of the History of the Behavioral Sciences*, 41(3): 249–67.

Minkler, M. and Wallerstein, N. (2003) *Community Based Participatory Research for Health*. San Francisco, CA: Jossey-Bass.

Morrow, R.A. and Brown, D.D. (1994) *Critical Theory and Methodology*. Thousand Oaks, CA: Sage.

Morse, J.M. (2005) 'Qualitative Research Is Not a Modification of Quantitative Research', *Qualitative Health Research*, 15: 1003–05.

Nissani, M. (1997) 'Ten Cheers for Interdisciplinarity: The Case for Interdisciplinary Knowledge and Research', *Social Science Journal*, 34(2): 201–16.

O'Cathain, A., Murphy, E., and Nicholl, J. (2008) 'Multidisciplinary, Interdisciplinary, or Dysfunctional? Team Working in Mixed-Methods Research', *Qualitative Health Research*, 18(11): 1574–85.

Oleson, V.L. (2000) 'Feminisms and Qualitative Research at and into the Millennium'. In N.K. Denzin, and Y.S. Lincoln (eds) *Handbook of Qualitative Research, 2nd Edition* (pp. 215–56). Thousand Oaks, CA: Sage.

Oleson, V.L. (2005) 'Early Millenial Feminist Qualitative Research: Challenges and Contours', *The Sage Handbook of Qualitative Research* (pp. 235–78). Thousand Oaks, CA: Sage.

Onwuegbuzie, A.J. (2002) 'Why Can't We All Get Along? Towards a Framework for Unifying Research Paradigms', *Education*, 122(3): 518–30.

Orsini, M. and Smith, M. (2007) *Critical Policy Studies*. Vancouver: UBC Press.

Phillips, D.C. (1995) 'The Good, the Bad and the Ugly: The Many Faces of Constructivism', *Educational Researcher*, 24(7): 5–12.

Ponterotto, J.G. (2005) 'Qualitative Research in Counseling Psychology: A Primer on Research Paradigms and Philosophy of Science', *Journal of Counseling Psychology*, 52(2): 126–36.

Popper, K.R. (1993) 'Science: Conjectures and Refutations', *Foundations of the Philosophy of Science: Recent Developments* (pp. 341–60). New York: Paragon House.

Ramazanoglu, C. and Holland, J. (2002) *Feminist Methodology: Challenges and Choices*. Thousand Oaks, CA: Sage.

Ray, M. (1994) 'The Richness of Phenomenology: Philosophic, Theoretic, and Methodologic Concerns'. In J.M. Morse (ed.) *Critical Issues in Qualitative Research Methods* (pp. 117–33). Thousand Oaks, CA: Sage.

Reinharz, S. and Davidman, L. (1992) *Feminist Methods in Social Research*. New York: Oxford University Press.

Rolfe, G. (2001) 'Postmodernism for Healthcare Workers in 13 Easy Steps', *Nurse Education Today*, 21(1): 38–47.

Root, M. (1993) 'The Fact-Value Distinction', *Philosophy of Social Science: The Methods, Ideals, and Politics of Social Inquiry* (pp. 205–28). Cambridge, MA: Blackwell.

Rosenau, P.M. (1992a) 'Into the Fray: Crisis, Continuity and Diversity', *Postmodernism and the Social Sciences: Insights, Inroad, and Intrusions* (pp. 3–24). Princeton, NJ: Princeton University.

Rosenau, P.M. (1992b) *Postmodernism and the Social Sciences: Insights, Inroad, and Intrusions* Princeton, NJ: Princeton University.

Sadovnik, A.R. (2006) 'Qualitative Research and Public Policy'. In F. Fischer, G. Miller, and M.S. Sidney (eds) *Handbook of Public Policy Analysis* (pp. 417–27). Boca Raton, FL: CRC Press.

Sale, J.E.M. (2008) 'How to Assess Rigour ... or Not in Qualitative Papers', *Journal of Evaluation in Clinical Practice*, 14: 912–3.

Sandelowski, M. (1986) 'The Problem of Rigor in Qualitative Research', *Advances in Nursing Science*, 8(3): 27–37.

Sandelowski, M. (2000) 'Whatever Happened to Qualitative Description?', *Research in Nursing and Health*, 23: 334–40.

Sandelowski, M. and Barroso, J. (2002) 'Finding the Findings in Qualitative Studies', *Journal of Nursing Scholarship*, 34(3): 213–9.

Sandelowski, M. (2006a) 'In Response to: de Witt L. and Ploeg J. (2006) Critical Appraisal of Rigor in Interpretive Phenomenological Nursing Research', *Journal of Advanced Nursing*, 55(2): 215–29, 55(5): 643–5.

Sandelowski, M. (2006b) '"Meta-Jeopardy": The Crisis of Representation in Qualitative Metasynthesis', *Nursing Outlook*, 54: 10–6.

Schutz, A. (1962) *The Problem of Social Reality*. The Hague: Marinus Nijhoff.

Schwandt, T.A. (1996) 'Farewell to Criteriology', *Qualitative Inquiry*, 2: 58–72.

Schwandt, T.A. (2000) 'Three Epistemological Stances for Qualitative Inquiry: Interpretivism, Hermeneutics, and Social Constructionism'. In N.K. Denzin and Y.S. Lincoln (eds) *Handbook of Qualitative Research* (2nd Edition) (pp. 189–214). Thousand Oaks, CA: Sage.

Shore, C. and Wright, S. (1997) 'Policy: A New Field of Anthropology', *Anthropology of Policy: Critical Perspectives on Governance and Power*, (pp. 3–42). London: Routledge.

Siegel, S., Dittrich, R., and Vollmann, J. (2008) 'Ethical Opinions and Personal Attitudes of Young Adults Conceived by in Vitro Fertilisation', *Journal of Medical Ethics*, 34: 236–40.

Smith, J.K. and Heshusius, L. (1986) 'Closing Down the Conversation: The End of the Qualitative–Quantitative Debate Among Educational Inquirers', *Educational Researcher*, 15: 4–12.

Stern, P.N. (1994) 'Eroding Grounded Theory'. In J.M. Morse (ed.) *Critical Issues in Qualitative Research Methods* (pp. 212–23). Thousand Oaks, CA: Sage.

Strauss, A. and Corbin, J. (1990) *Basics of Qualitative Research: Grounded Theory Procedures and Techniques*. London: Sage.

Streubert, K. and Carpenter, D. (1995) *Qualitative Research in Nursing: Advancing the Humanistic Imperative*. Philadelphia: Lippincott.

Thomas, G. and James, D. (2006) 'Re-inventing Grounded Theory: Some Questions about Theory, Ground and Discovery', *British Educational Research Journal*, 32(6): 767–95.

Thorne, S. (2008) *Interpretive Description*. Walnut Creek, CA: Left Coast Press, Inc.

Thorne, S., Kirkham, S.R., and MacDonaled-Emes, J. (1997) 'Interpretive Description: A Noncategorical Qualitative Alternative for Developing Nursing Knowledge', *Research in Nursing and Health*, 20: 169–77.

Thorne, S., Con, A., McGuinness, L., McPherson, G., and Harris, S.R. (2004) 'Health Care Communication Issues in Multiple Sclerosis: An Interpretive Description', *Qualitative Health Research*, 14: 5–22.

Tong, A., Sainsbury, P., and Craig, J. (2007) 'Consolidated Criteria for Reporting Qualitative Research (COREQ): A 32-Item Checklist for Interviews and Focus Groups', *International Journal for Quality in Health Care*, 19(6): 349–57.

Travers, M. (2006) 'Postmodernism and Qualitative Research', *Qualitative Research*, 6(2): 267–73.

Van Manen, M. (1990) *Researching Lived Experience: Human Science for an Action Sensitive Pedagogy*. Albany, NY: State University of New York Press.

Vidich, A. and Lyman, S. (2000) 'Qualitative Methods: Their History in Sociology and Anthropology'. In N.K. Denzin and Y.S. Lincoln (eds) *Handbook of Qualitative Research* (2nd Edition) (pp. 37–84). Thousand Oaks, CA: Sage.

Walsh, D. and Downe, S. (2006) 'Appraising the Quality of Qualitative Research', *Midwifery*, 22: 108–19.

Warin, M., Turner, K., Moore, V., and Davies, M. (2008) 'Bodies, Mothers and Identities: Rethinking Obesity and the BMI', *Sociology of Health and Illness*, 30(1): 97–111.

Willis, J.W., Jost, M., and Nilakanta, R. (2007) *Foundations of Qualitative Research: Interpretive and Critical Approaches*. Thousand Oaks, CA: Sage.

Woolgar, S. and Pawluch, D. (1985) 'Ontological Gerrymandering: The Anatomy of Social Problems Explanations', *Social Problems*, 32(3): 214–27.

Wright, P. and Treacher, A. (1982) *The Problem of Medical Knowledge: Examining the Social Construction of Medicine.* Edinburgh, UK: Edinburgh University Press.

Wright, D., Flis, N., and Gupta, M. (2008) 'The "Brain Drain" of Physicians: Historical Antecedents to an Ethical Debate, c. 1960–79'. *Philosophy, Ethics, and Humanities in Medicine,* 3(24).

Yin, R.K. (2003) *Case Study Research: Design and Methods* (3rd Edition). Thousand Oaks, CA: Sage.

8

Ethnographic Approaches to Health and Development Research: the Contributions of Anthropology

Rebecca Prentice

INTRODUCTION

Perhaps more than any other social science discipline, anthropology has defined itself through its relationship to qualitative methods. Anthropology emerged as a professional academic discipline in the late nineteenth century, concerned with the comparative study of non-European societies. By the early twentieth century, 'ethnographic' fieldwork was established as the principal form of anthropological research, with anthropologists living *among* the communities they studied for extended periods, conducting interviews in the native language, and participating in everyday activities alongside their research participants ('informants'). This form of research provided anthropologists with a rich, detailed view of local institutions and practices, while at the same time generating an empathic understanding of diverse cultural values, beliefs, and ways of life (Eriksen, 2001:24–39).

Commentators have suggested that it is the practice of ethnographic fieldwork, rather than a subject matter or theoretical position that fundamentally unites anthropology as a discipline (Berger, 1993:174; Howell, 1990:4). Although the very concept of 'the field' has come under increased scrutiny in recent years (Coleman and Collins, 2006; Gupta and Ferguson, 1997; Marcus, 1995), these discussions have done little to attenuate the symbolic and institutional power of fieldwork in defining disciplinary norms and identities. Fieldwork has been called the *sine qua non*, 'the only (or the most important) characteristic of social anthropology, separating it from the other social science disciplines, and having done it is the primary badge of membership in the guild' (Ellen, 1984:64–5).

Through ethnographic field research, anthropologists cultivate a distinctive way of seeing and interpreting social life. As researchers, anthropologists are oriented towards understanding local phenomena on their own terms – also called an 'emic' view. Through long-term immersion in a foreign setting, an anthropologist attempts to step outside his or her habitual way of seeing the world in order to consider what life looks and feels like to the people under study. Anthropologists then generate theory (an 'etic', or external point of view) by interpreting the meanings and functions of particular social practices and comparing them to other examples produced by anthropologists working elsewhere (Eriksen, 2001:35).

Although initially concerned with recording and interpreting the diverse customs, social structures, and beliefs of non-European societies, anthropology today is equally applied to Western contexts and to contemporary questions of political, cultural, and social change. Nowadays 'the field' can be a surgical theatre (Katz, 1998), a multinational corporation (Rajak, 2009), or a high-energy physics laboratory (Traweek, 1992). What remains constant in anthropological research is a commitment to 'naturalistic' study – examining human activity in the ordinary situations in which it takes place, and analyzing this activity through comparison with examples gathered elsewhere (Sobo, 2009:35). When applied to the study of health, illness, and medical institutions, anthropology has emphasized the role of culture in shaping illness experiences, therapeutic practices, and the distribution of disease, while at the same time examining social hierarchies, power dynamics, and the socioeconomic context, giving a 'holistic, systems-oriented, comparative perspective' (Sobo, 2009:34).

This chapter explores anthropology's theoretical underpinnings and the unique perspectives generated by anthropological field research, with emphasis on their value for research on health and the related field of development studies. I draw upon four diverse case studies (on African witchcraft, HIV/AIDS prevention in Nepal, peasant–state relations in Costa Rica, and multi-drug-resistant tuberculosis in Haiti) to illuminate four principles of anthropological research: the centrality of fieldwork to theory-making, an emphasis on meaning and classification, the negotiated nature of reality, and the importance of context. In so doing, my aim is to elucidate the methods and analytical approaches that anthropology brings to the qualitative study of health, illness, and medicine.

A familiarity with anthropology (its history, methods, and theories) will help policy makers, medical professionals, and health managers navigate, interpret, appraise, and make use of anthropological studies on topics of interest to them. At the same time, qualitative health researchers working in other disciplines may find it useful to experiment with anthropological approaches through integrating them into their own research. By selectively adapting and adopting anthropological methods and concepts in carrying out their own studies, researchers may discover fresh ways of investigating existing problems and topics.

ANTHROPOLOGY IN/OF MEDICINE

The application of anthropology's fieldwork method to issues of health, illness, and medicine is broadly referred to as 'medical anthropology'. Medical anthropology is a diverse subfield that includes research on the experience and distribution of illness; healing practices and beliefs; the construction of medical knowledge, science, and rationality; comparative epistemologies and treatments of disease; political economies of health; illness narratives and identity construction; and medical institutions and professional practices (Pool and Geissler, 2005; van der Geest and Rienks, 1998).

Medical anthropology emerged after the Second World War as the comparative, cross-cultural study of medical systems, with particular emphasis on practical issues of public health and hygiene (Foster and Anderson, 1998:3). In recent decades, medical anthropology has also developed a critical perspective, concerned with the ways in which medical knowledge (particularly biomedical knowledge) is constructed, legitimated, and put into practice (Good, 1994:5). According to Robert Pool and Wenzel Geissler, medical anthropology thus appears in two guises: anthropology *in* medicine and anthropology *of* medicine (Pool and Geissler, 2005:31–32). Both entail the study of health and illness, but from different perspectives and different kinds of disciplinary and institutional commitments.

'Anthropology *in* medicine' refers to anthropologists using the theories and methods of the discipline to confront biomedically defined health problems, usually working collaboratively on multidisciplinary research teams (Pool and Geissler, 2005:31). 'Anthropology *of* medicine', in contrast, examines health and illness as cultural phenomena, privileging scholarly debate over policy relevance. A crucial aspect of the anthropology of medicine is analyzing medicine as a complex assemblage of knowledge, power relations, formal institutions, and everyday practices. While anthropologists in medicine are more likely to be employed in a medical institution or NGO (non-governmental organization), anthropologists of medicine usually pursue their careers in the university setting.

The distinction between 'anthropology *in*' and 'anthropology *of*' – loosely designating a commitment to practical application in the first instance, and a commitment to theory making in the second – can be attributed to the sociologist Robert Straus (1957), who originally used it to categorize different types of medical sociologists (Foster and Anderson, 1998). This neat dichotomy has also been used to describe development anthropology: anthropologists in development tend to work in an applied capacity, while anthropologists of development are generally found in academia. The implicit suggestion in this categorization is that anthropologists *of* medicine or development are somehow less compromised, more independent observers of the processes at hand (Grillo and Stirrat, 1997).

However, anthropologists *in* versus anthropologists *of* are convenient fictions, over-simplifying their practitioners' complex involvement in institutions and practices of both 'medicine' and 'development', neither of which are monolithic. Medical anthropologists frequently traverse disciplinary boundaries, may be employed both as university researchers and as temporary consultants, are often dedicated to making both substantive and theoretical contributions to the field, and usually possess a dual commitment to a 'critical' view of medicine and one that wishes to see universal access to basic health services (cf. Farmer, 2004 and following section). Although Byron Good notes that 'the duality of the anthropologist's role as critic and participant has provided an ironic cast to that commitment' (Good, 1994:27), most anthropologists agree that these dual roles are a source of unique insight. We now turn to some of the basic principles of anthropological research, beginning with the importance of fieldwork.

THE CENTRALITY OF FIELDWORK TO THEORY MAKING

The most common form of anthropological research is ethnographic fieldwork, defined by Sherry Ortner as an attempt 'to understand another life world using the self – as much of it as possible – as the instrument of knowing' (Ortner, 1995:173). Ethnography requires the researcher to participate in the daily lives of the people under study, 'watching what happens, listening to what is said, [and] asking questions' (Hammersley and Atkinson, 1995:1). These techniques are generally glossed as 'participant observation', the practice of taking part in everyday activities while observing and recording impressions, ideas, and the words of informants.

Bronislaw Malinowski, one of the pioneers of British anthropology, is often credited with establishing modern anthropological fieldwork. A Polish national, Malinowski was interned in Australia during the outbreak of the First World War. After his release, being unable to return to Europe, he took the opportunity to travel to the Trobriand Islands (Melanesia), where between 1915 and 1918 he undertook extended ethnographic field research (Hendry, 2008:10; See also Young, 2004). Malinowski became a fervent proponent of living among one's research subjects, and staying in the field for sufficient time until the anthropologist's presence was no longer regarded as a curiosity by locals (Malinowski, 1972[1922]:7).

The aim of ethnographic fieldwork, according to Malinowski, is to cultivate the 'native's point of view' by building up an empirical account of the local context in three stages. First, the ethnographer is tasked with establishing and recording the social structures, rules, and institutions of a given society – the frameworks within which people act. Second, the ethnographer observes and participates in the daily lives of local people in order to grasp the 'imponderabilia of actual life' – meaning how people go about their everyday lives within the structures, roles, and expectations of society. Third, and perhaps most challengingly, the ethnographer must try to ascertain how native informants interpret, understand, and represent their own lives. Taken together this provides the native's point of view: 'his relation to life, to realize *his* vision of *his* world' (1972:24–25).

The meaning and emphasis of anthropological fieldwork has changed over time as competing disciplinary interests and debates have come to the fore (Sluka and Robben, 2007:6–10). While in Malinowski's era, fieldworkers were concerned with the scientific accuracy and exhaustiveness of field data, recent years have seen a move towards 'reflexive anthropology [which] turns the fieldworker's ongoing negotiation of his or her professional role into an object of study, analyzes the power relations involved, and questions the nature of participant observation' (2007:9). Particularly since the 1970s and 1980s, when critics both within and outside the discipline challenged anthropology's colonial entanglements and its authority to represent the exotic 'Other', contemporary anthropologists have become concerned with ethical and power-related dimensions of their research, demonstrating an increased political consciousness and self-critique (Barrett, 1996).

Ethnography is a notoriously time-consuming and indirect form of research (Eriksen, 2001:27). Anthropologists usually conduct field research in the local language over an extended period: doctoral research generally includes at least a year of fieldwork. It is through this long-term field experience that a novice researcher develops an anthropological 'disposition' (Bourdieu, 2000 in Malkki, 2007:163), and comes to understand that ethnography is not simply a method or set of research techniques, but also a way of seeing and knowing the world (Gay Y Blasco and Wardle, 2007).

The contribution that long-term participant observation can make to a critical understanding of health and illness is well evidenced in early twentieth-century anthropology, such as E.E. Evans-Pritchard's seminal work, *Witchcraft, Oracles and Magic Among the Azande* (1976[1937]). Evans-Pritchard's ethnography is credited with establishing the foundations of medical anthropology, because it provided a sympathetic window onto alternative epistemologies of illness causation. This work was based on ethnographic fieldwork with the Azande – a people living in territory comprising parts of present-day Sudan, Central African Republic, and Democratic Republic of the Congo – for twenty months between 1926 and 1930 (1976:251).

E.E. Evans-Pritchard's detailed study of Azande life revealed that witchcraft beliefs contained a sophisticated internal logic. Arguing against a prevailing contemporary view (presented most famously by Lucien Lévy-Bruhl) that the 'primitive' mindset could neither distinguish the natural from the supernatural nor see its own logical contradictions; Evans-Pritchard discovered witchcraft to be a thoroughly 'rational' system of belief, with clear conceptions of causality and blame. Witchcraft, he wrote, 'provides [the Azande] with a natural philosophy by which the relations between men and unfortunate events are explained and a ready and stereotyped means of reacting to such events' (1976:18).

The Azande used witchcraft to explain misfortune. The most famous example is that of a granary whose roof collapses, injuring a group of people taking shelter beneath it. Evans-Pritchard describes the 'natural' cause of the granary's collapse as termites eating through its supports. However, Zande notions of causality require another element to explain why the roof collapsed when it did. Explains Evans-Pritchard:

> To our minds the only relationship between these two independently caused facts is their coincidence in time and space. We have no explanation of why the two chains of causation intersected at a certain time and in a certain place, for there is no interdependence between them. Zande philosophy can provide the missing link (Evans-Pritchard, 1976:23).

The link, of course, is that 'witchcraft' caused the granary to collapse – most likely in the form of a nearby witch's enmity directed towards the people sheltering under it. Witchcraft beliefs thus contain a theory of causation and explanation for *why* things happen. Natural and supernatural activities are inextricably related, and always carry a moral and social value. When a Zande person becomes ill, a witchdoctor is employed to assess *whose* witchcraft has caused the sickness. The witch–culprit, once identified, is approached and asked to relent without having to admit guilt; the accused then makes a show of goodwill by blowing on a chicken wing to cool the witchcraft substance supposedly residing in his belly.

Evans-Pritchard's ethnography provides an exemplary illustration of the distinction between 'emic' (insider) and 'etic' (outsider) understandings of phenomena. The etic view is that of the anthropologist, who is a foreign visitor and curious observer. The emic view is that of the Azande themselves – the view that Evans-Pritchard sought to attain through participant observation. Evans-Pritchard recognized that Zande witchcraft had to be understood on its own terms, because it relied upon different logics than those to which he was accustomed. He famously posed the question:

> Is Zande thought so different from ours that we can only describe their speech and actions without comprehending them, or is it essentially like our own though expressed in an idiom to which we are unaccustomed? (Evans-Pritchard, 1976:4).

Evans-Pritchard's nuanced and sympathetic understanding of Zande witchcraft influenced anthropological approaches to health beliefs for years to come. His ability to penetrate an alternate mode of knowledge challenged his readers to question the seeming naturalness of their habitual ways of thinking.

Although Evans-Pritchard insisted on the importance of 'rigorous training in general theory' (1976:240) before heading to the field, he asserted that it was *long-term fieldwork* – including intensive participant observation – that made possible his rich insights into Zande life. Evans-Pritchard lived in a village alongside his informants: 'I had a hut and byre like theirs; I went hunting with them with spear and bow and arrow; I learnt to make pots; I consulted oracles; and so forth' (Evans-Pritchard, 1976:243). He did not pretend that these activities made him a Zande man, or that he would ever see things entirely from a Zande point of view. Nevertheless, Evans-Pritchard believed that participating in daily life facilitated a complex and sensitive understanding of Zande cultural practices and beliefs. This is reflected in Evans-Pritchard's experience with oracles. While undertaking fieldwork, Evans-Pritchard had to submit himself to local rules and prohibitions, such as consulting oracles before the beginning of each trip or hunting expedition. In spite of himself, by doing these things everyday, Evans-Pritchard came to perceive – in a situated, provisional, and experiential way – the 'reality' of witchcraft:

> In my own culture … I rejected, and reject, Zande notions of witchcraft. In their culture, in the set of ideas I then lived in, I accepted them; in a kind of way I believed them. … If one must act as though one believed, one ends in believing, or half-believing as one acts (Evans-Pritchard, 1976:244).

Anthropology engenders a radical way of seeing the world, treating with seriousness alternate modes of perception, rationality, and causality. In *Witchcraft, Oracles, and Magic among the Azande,* Evans-Pritchard successfully translated and interpreted indigenous beliefs for his mid-century European audience. Long-term, sensitive, open-minded fieldwork was central to this endeavour. Although fieldwork alone is not sufficient to provide insight into cultural values, norms, and lifeways, it is an indispensable part of theory making, for it constitutes the world of experience from which the anthropologist makes interpretations.

AN EMPHASIS ON MEANING AND CLASSIFICATION

If ethnographic fieldwork is indispensable for generating insight into cross-cultural views of disease aetiology and modes of healing, it also facilitates another dimension of anthropological practice: thinking critically about local categories. Anthropologists have shown the cross-cultural variability of disease classifications – different societies recognize different diseases, symptoms, and diagnoses, and have therefore developed different therapeutic responses. *Susto,* for example, is a condition of soul loss recognized in Latin America (Rubel, 1964; Rubel et al., 1984; Bolton, 1981). The symptoms of *susto* are sleeplessness, listlessness, and distraction, but *susto* does not directly correspond to any equivalent biomedical category. This means that there is a problem of translation between two kinds of classifications: folk and biomedical. However, this is not to say that folk illness categories are cultural, unempirical, and imprecise, while biomedical categories are scientific, empirical, and exact. Instead, anthropologists recognize that medical categories of *all* kinds do not simply index the natural world, but are instead richly cultural:

> [T]he language of medicine is hardly a simple mirror of the empirical world. It is a rich *cultural language*, linked to a highly specialized version of reality and system of social relations, and

when employed in medical care, it joins deep moral concerns with its more obvious technical functions (Good, 1994:5).

According to Helen Lambert and Christopher McKevitt, anthropologists are particularly attentive to classifications and meanings:

> This interest probably derives from anthropology's development as a discipline associated with the ethnographic study of 'other' cultures, in which the nature and boundaries of apparently basic categories – such as family, religion, and medicine – could not be presumed but required empirical investigation. Thus an anthropological approach, rather than taking phenomenon x or y as a given and investigating views of or beliefs about it, also investigates the form and contents of the thing (x or y) itself (Lambert and McKevitt, 2002:212).

Anthropology's emphasis on classification and the cultural variability of meaning is apparent in its research practices. During fieldwork, anthropologists are primed to ask questions not only *using* key categories but also *about* them. Therefore, anthropologists working on health-related issues understand that biomedical and public health categories are neither neutral nor absolute, but should themselves be considered dimensions of the object of study. Stacy Leigh Pigg and Linnet Pike exemplify this approach in their research on HIV/AIDS and STD prevention in Nepal (Pigg, 2001; Pigg and Pike, 2001). The late 1990s saw foreign donors and the national government funding campaigns to educate Nepalis about the transmission and prevention of HIV/AIDS and STDs, despite the fact that national incidence and prevalence were extremely low. These educational programmes were therefore tasked with making concepts like AIDS meaningful to Nepali publics 'through a process that transmutes medical and epidemiological facts into social knowledge' (Pigg and Pike, 2001:177).

The HIV/AIDS and STD-related health education programmes included informational posters and pamphlets and small group education sessions in urban and village settings. Pigg and Pike investigated how different communities were responding to these programmes by observing and participating in educational interventions, analyzing the relevant health promotion materials being distributed, and interviewing a wide-ranging group of local actors – including health educators, public health officials, villagers, and sex workers.

Pigg and Pike discovered that HIV/AIDS and STD prevention campaigns were assumed by their sponsors to be morally neutral, because they were based on 'biomedically derived conceptualizations of sexuality and health' (2001:195). However, Nepali participants believed that discussions of sexuality cannot and should not be decontextualized from ideas of family and morality. In proposing that they could, health promoters were in fact importing Western ideas of appropriate sexuality and appropriate talk to the Nepali context. Frank discussion of sexual knowledge in the group educational sessions proved to be problematic. Not only did these discussions cause embarrassment in a social milieu where brandishing sexual knowledge indicates a lack of chastity, but also because the description of 'risk' ensconced in biomedical bodies and sexual activities did not resonate with the local categories relating to love, family, morality, and reproduction (Pigg, 2001).

As in many health-promotion programmes (Launiala, 2009) the local health educators used 'Knowledge, Attitudes, Beliefs, and Practices' (KABP) surveys to assess Nepalis' understandings of HIV/AIDS and to evaluate the 'success' of targeted educational programmes (Pigg and Pike, 2001:178, 183). Because of their nuanced attention to the cultural politics of public health categories, Pigg and Pike perceived the KABP surveys to be an inadequate analytical framework for understanding the impact of HIV/AIDS and STD prevention in Nepal. They discovered that, while public health officials saw the 'knowledge, attitudes, beliefs, and practices' of Nepali people as obstacles to HIV prevention (to be overcome with further education), officials failed to recognize that their health promotions campaigns were likewise enmeshed in their *own* situated 'knowledge, attitudes, beliefs, and practices'. HIV/AIDS educators, far from being the neutral agents of a neutral public health message, drew upon moral frameworks and social distinctions to educate about 'respectable' and 'transgressive' forms of sex. Ostensibly promoting a medicalized and socially decontextualized view of sexual activity, 'most NGO leaders, outreach workers, and government officials place AIDS prevention within an implicit socio-moral framework' (2001:182).

Pigg and Pike show that public health categories are always shaped by social relations and moral discourses. Recognizing this social fact requires not looking *through* the KABP categories (by using the categories as a conceptual framework) but instead looking *at* the categories and their meaning, function, and effects. For Pigg and Pike, this meant instead of approaching informants to assess their 'knowledge', 'attitudes', 'beliefs', and 'practices' in relation to HIV/AIDS risk, looking at the constitution and socio–moral operation of those categories both within and through public health interventions. This endeavour led them to conclude that:

> … in the process of publicising facts about HIV/AIDS and STDs [health educators] also convey messages that structure and limit understandings of personal risk and social responsibility (Pigg and Pike, 2001:177).

Ethnographic approaches to health research help us move beyond simply asking about 'knowledge', 'attitudes', 'beliefs', and 'practices' of health education recipients, urging us to look instead at the constitution of these very categories. Anthropologists of medicine rarely take biomedical concepts and meanings for granted, instead choosing to make the construction and circulation of medical knowledge itself part of the study. What is revealed is how these categories are the product of *politics* of medicine and culture; they are best treated not as an analytic framework, but instead as products of social action and therefore contestation.

THE NEGOTIATED NATURE OF REALITY

As Stacy Leigh Pigg and Linnet Pike's work suggests, anthropologists do not conduct research by 'testing' informants with a prescribed and narrow set of questions.

Instead, they work inductively – an iterative process of observing, participating, conducting formal and informal interviews, formulating interpretations, and reflecting on the emerging analysis. The kind of knowledge generated through these means – ethnographic knowledge – is neither 'scientific truth' nor personal experience. Instead, as Michael Agar tells us, 'ethnography is neither 'subjective' nor 'objective'. It is interpretive, mediating two worlds through a third' (Agar, 1982:783).

One of the key features of ethnographic fieldwork is that data collection and analysis are not separated from one another in any strict sense (de Vries, 1992). The construction of Agar's 'third' world requires participation from both the anthropologist and his or her informants. Although both do not participate on equal terms – with equal authority and authorship – they are both crucial participants in contributing to the script.

Pieter de Vries's work on peasant–state relations in Costa Rica reveals a concern with the provisional and even improvisational nature of ethnographic knowledge (de Vries, 1992). He conducted fieldwork on an integrated rural development programme funded by USAID in Costa Rica's Atlantic zone. De Vries's research was initially based in a local land development institute, but he branched out from the institution to cultivate informants from a range of sectors, including peasant farmers, front-line outreach workers, shop keepers, and local leaders and officials. As he moved (both physically and methodologically) through various sites to interview and spend time with these informants, his analysis emerged through recognition of a 'negotiated' reality (1992:69). De Vries questioned the authorship of his emerging analysis, and who had the right to contribute:

> In rejecting a quasi-positivistic stance that claims to attain an understanding that is in some ways superior or detached from those of my informants, the issue arises of whether the actors entering my ethnography are simply protagonists of a script I am merely recording, or whether they are themselves scriptwriters like me? And if I hold to the latter view, as I do, then what is the difference in the scripts? My answer to this is that I draw upon their scripts for a narrative I am writing for a different audience, in a different language and genre. And to that end I have to enrol them in my ethnographic project, while letting them simultaneously enrol me in theirs (de Vries, 1992:65).

De Vries draws attention to the notion that informants are never simply fonts of information about their own lives and experiences, to be recorded, transcribed, and interpreted by the ethnographer. Instead, through the process of detailed field research and repeated communication over long periods, informants and researchers become coproducers of ethnographic knowledge. Recognition of this process forces us into the (sometimes uncomfortable) stance that social reality is always provisional – never stable, never fixed. De Vries contends that these social products, and their meaning, become realized in specific *places*.

Although any discussion of anthropological methods must note the discipline's transformation in recent years – from a discipline firmly enmeshed within colonial relationships that sought to understand non-Western worlds through the personage of the lone fieldworker, to an increasing concern with the politics and ethics of research (Barrett, 1996:3; Marcus and Fischer, 1986) – many of the 'new' insights that emerged from the 'crisis of representation' have clear predecessors in the anthropological record. On the issue of ethnographic truth, Bronislaw Malinowski, like Pieter de Vries fifty years later, recognized that ethnographic knowledge is constructed in the field, rather than being a set of 'facts' waiting to be discovered:

> While making his observations, the fieldworker must constantly construct: he must place isolated data in relation to one another and study the manner in which they integrate. To put it paradoxically, one could say that 'facts' do not exist in sociological any more than in physical reality; that is, they do not dwell in the spatial and temporal continuum open to the untutored eye. The principles of social organization, of legal constitution, of economics and religion have to be constructed by the observer out of the multitude of manifestations of varying significance and relevance (Malinowski, 1935:317 in Malkki, 2007:171).

For anthropologists, qualitative methods are not used to 'uncover' or 'reveal' social realities, but instead to constitute social realities anew through communication and analysis. Ethnographic knowledge is therefore interpretive, emerging from social interaction and negotiation. Pieter de Vries's account resonates with Liisa Malkki's description of fieldwork as 'not a matter of the gradual accumulation of "data" into a stable structure, but of moments of puzzlement and sudden realization' (Malkki, 2007:175).

In reflecting upon methods, Pieter de Vries tells us that by recognizing the 'theoretical ladenness of methodological choices as well as their situational character, we can achieve an understanding of social research that goes beyond a mere discussion of technicalities and skills. Only then are we able to grapple with the epistemological issues pertaining to the nature of sociological understanding itself' (de Vries, 1992:47).

THE IMPORTANCE OF CONTEXT

Although anthropology is conventionally associated with the study of small-scale societies through microlevel participation and one-on-one interviews, contemporary anthropological writings demonstrate a concern with the broad-scale influences of history, politics, and economic change on social life. Whereas previous generations of anthropologists concerned themselves with 'holism' – the conceit that a community (a 'culture') can and should be understood in its entirety, taking in kinship, politics, economics, and ecology – today's practitioners are more concerned with *situating* their studies within complex processes of the market economy, history, and political change (Ortner, 1995:174). Holism, then, has been recast as contextualization – the notion that 'any culture has to be understood not only in its local manifestations, but in relation to the wider global context in which it occurs' (Sluka and Robben, 2007:4–5).

Anthropological contextualization has two aspects to it. According to Paloma Gay Y Blasco and Huon Wardle, in the first instance contextualization is simply concerned with appreciating 'people in context' (Gay Y Blasco and Wardle, 2007:4). Human behaviour is always shaped by social expectations and institutions, relationships of power and meaning, and landscapes of economy and ecology. Anthropologists suggest that many aspects of cultural practice can only be understood in relation to their social milieu. Therefore, culture must not be studied in isolation but rather in relation to broader values and expectations. The ethnographer's task is to distinguish significant details of social life from the contextual settings in which they are embedded, interpreting each in relation to the other. In this way, anthropologists are able to differentiate between expected social roles and an individual's agency to act otherwise.

Secondly, anthropological contextualization is concerned with the relationship between local ways of life and 'a larger social order', including the capitalist world system (Marcus, 1995:95). Anthropologists attempt to understand how macrostructural processes shape experiences at a local level of analysis. Such structural processes might include the global market economy, mass media, political upheaval and war, climate change and environmental disasters, and political institutions and processes. In medical anthropology, this kind of contextualization has often taken the form of tracing and interpreting the geographic, socioeconomic, and gendered dimensions of the distribution and progression of disease. Doing so means acknowledging that diseases (as well as the institutions and practitioners who work to counteract them) are always imbricated within wider structures, and are intensely affected by them.

Paul Farmer's research on multi-drug-resistant tuberculosis (MDR TB) is an example of a deeply contextualized view. An anthropologist and a physician, Farmer draws on two decades of ethnographic research and clinical practice in Haiti to argue that infectious disease is patterned by socioeconomic inequalities (Farmer, 1997; Farmer, 2004). Although rates of tuberculosis declined throughout the twentieth century, they have experienced a profound resurgence since the 1980s, particularly in poor countries and impoverished areas of developed countries (Farmer, 1997:347). Despite being eminently treatable, TB persists. Moreover, recent years have seen the emergence of drug-resistant strains of tuberculosis (TB that does not respond to two of the first-line treatments), particularly within already-vulnerable populations (1997:348).

Farmer asks: 'By what mechanisms, precisely, do large-scale and impersonal forces come to be embodied as individual pathology? As epidemic disease?' (Farmer, 1997:349) Although the existence of tuberculosis' social component has long been recognized, Farmer says that social scientists (including many anthropologists) have focused too narrowly on cultural dimensions of risk, such as a lack of patient compliance with treatment regimens. He argues that this misplaced focus on 'culture' wrongly diagnoses the cause of MDR TB, and blames the poor by exaggerating their agency as patients.

To illustrate his point, Farmer traces the story of Robert David, a young man who visited Farmer's clinic in Haiti's central plateau in 1993 (Farmer, 1997). After seven years of erratic treatment for tuberculosis (frequently disrupted by poverty, lack of available medicines, political disturbances, and lack of adequate transportation), Robert David presented with MDR TB. Although considerable attempts were made to save his life, he died from tuberculosis in 1995. Farmer reveals the supposedly 'biological' journey of MDR TB to be actually social and political.

It was not Robert David's 'cultural beliefs' or lack of formal education that caused him to develop – and die from – MDR TB. Instead, the cause was his poverty, the lack of transportation and health infrastructure in Haiti, and the ongoing political turmoil and violence that disrupted every treatment regimen that Robert David began. As Farmer writes: 'Any thorough understanding of the modern epidemics of AIDS and tuberculosis in Haiti or elsewhere in the postcolonial world requires a thorough knowledge of history and political economy' (2004:305). Farmer argues that health researchers must attend to the social, economic, and political processes that generate vulnerability in certain populations and not others. Rather than focusing on the individual actor as 'non-compliant' with a TB treatment regimen, anthropologists must examine the lived conditions of economic and political inequality and their relationship to health. Haitians are vulnerable to MDR TB because of the structural inequalities inherent in a world system that limits and withholds medical treatment. The emergence of MDR TB is therefore an effect of political economy, rather than patients' failed 'compliance' to treatment regimens.

This kind of contextualization is important to anthropological research; ironically, it is a component of anthropology with which many outside the discipline are unfamiliar. In my own work on a multidisciplinary team of researchers evaluating HIV/AIDS prevention programmes in California (2000–2002), I was often struck by my colleague's expectation that I would provide information on the 'cultural factors' influencing HIV/AIDS risk within minority communities, which they imagined might include female circumcision or blood sacrifices. My continual insistence that poverty, racism, and access to health services were the most important dimensions of risk was accepted, although not interpreted as an 'anthropological' contribution.

Contextualization can be difficult to achieve. Anthropologists, for the most part, continue to conduct face-to-face ethnographic research in single sites (see Marcus, 1995, Coleman and von Hellermann, 2009). Contextualization is therefore pursued by working in historical archives, consulting secondary sources, and integrating the scholarship of macrotheorists with ethnographic portraits of local life. By 'juxtaposing multiple levels and styles of analysis' (Marcus, 1989:11) an anthropologist might combine historical, structural, and narrative analysis to explore the same phenomenon from multiple angles.

The challenge of contextualization is drawing theoretical conclusions between microlevel data gathered through face-to-face participant observation and macrolevel data drawn from a range of primary and secondary sources. Paul Farmer attempts to theorize these connections with his concept of 'structural violence', through which he traces several centuries of slavery, economic exploitation, impoverishment, and political violence in Haiti, and shows their causal relationship to the intimate struggles of patients battling infectious diseases (Farmer, 2004). If attempts to synthesize the macro and the micro within a single theoretical frame seem strained at times, it may be because the conventional tools of anthropological research were not developed for the task, and that new, innovative approaches are required.

Anthropologists strive to depict cultures, people, and practices not in isolation, but as embedded within broader social, political, and economic processes. Although different anthropologists will choose to emphasize different aspects of these, the foundational idea behind this principle is that we cannot understand social action separate from wider contexts.

CONCLUSIONS

Anthropologists have long worked on health issues, making substantial contributions to knowledge of the cultural dimensions of diseases, diagnoses, healing regimens, and the social and institutional settings in which they occur. Yet, according to Helen Lambert and Christopher McKevitt, despite anthropology's relevance to the field, discussions of qualitative health research methods too often dismiss or ignore the discipline's theoretical and methodological contributions (Lambert and McKevitt, 2002). By focusing on both the fieldwork method and the conceptual underpinnings of anthropological knowledge, this chapter has drawn attention to the distinctive contributions that anthropology makes to the study of health, illness, and medicine.

Anthropology is a discipline rooted in the study of small-scale societies through in-depth, long-term, ethnographic fieldwork. Although this history has shaped the discipline in its contemporary form, its traditional fieldwork methods have been revised and modified in order to address a diverse array of topics and locations. Anthropological research can provide unique insight into topics of interest to health policymakers, managers, and practitioners. My hope is that through this chapter, members of these groups will become more familiar with anthropological concepts, theories, and methods, and will feel comfortable navigating, evaluating, and using anthropological scholarship on issues that interest them.

Qualitative health researchers may find that using anthropologically informed research methods provides new insights into the topics on which they work. I have proposed four main (but certainly not exclusive) principles of anthropological research that may serve as a starting point. First, that ethnographic fieldwork is central to theory making. Although anthropologists traditionally spend an extended amount of time (often a year or more) undertaking fieldwork, qualitative health researchers may recognize the value of shorter and more contained fieldwork projects. The emphasis must be on researching human activity in the natural setting in which it occurs; the analytic power of ethnographic research derives from a commitment to cultivating the 'native's point of view' (Malinowski, 1972) through immersive participant observation.

Second, I have argued that anthropological research pays particular attention to classifications and meanings. Because they are primed to think critically about local categories, anthropologists can bring a fresh, critical perspective to health-related topics by focusing on the very terms of discussion. By questioning how problems are posed, anthropologists can sometimes help reconfigure the boundaries of the problems themselves (Lambert and McKevitt, 2002).

Third, anthropology recognizes the negotiated nature of social reality, and therefore of ethnographic knowledge itself. Anthropologists understand research to be a profoundly social undertaking, in which empirical 'facts' are not simply waiting to be discovered, but rather emerge from the research process. Finally, anthropologists insist that context is key to understanding social and cultural phenomena. All ethnographic findings must be situated not only within the immediate social and institutional contexts in which they occur, but also within the more broad-scale systems of political economy – which, admittedly, are difficult to grasp using the conventional tools of anthropological research. A valuable aim, then, is fostering deeper and more satisfying interdisciplinary collaborations that can spur new research approaches, by synthesizing the contributions of multiple disciplines.

REFERENCES

Agar, Michael (1982) 'Toward an Ethnographic Language', *American Anthropologist*, 84(4): 779–95.

Barrett, Stanley R. (1996) *Anthropology: A Student's Guide to Theory and Method.* Toronto: University of Toronto Press.

Berger, Roger (1993) 'From Text to (Field)Work and Back Again: Theorizing a Post(Modern) Ethnography', *Anthropological Quarterly*, 66(4): 174–86.

Bolton, Ralph (1981) 'Susto, Hostility, and Hypoglycemia', *Ethnology*, 20(4): 261–76.

Coleman, Simon and Peter Collins (2006) 'Introduction: "Being … Where?": Performing Fields on Shifting Grounds'. In Simon Coleman and Peter Collins (eds) *Locating the Field: Space, Place and Context in Anthropology* (pp. 1–21). Oxford: Berg.

Coleman, Simon and Pauline von Hellermann (eds) (2009) *Multi-Sited Ethnography: Problems and Possibilities in the Translocation of Research Methods.* London: Routledge.

de Vries, Pieter (1992) 'A Research Journey: On Actors, Concepts and the Text'. In Norman Long and Ann Long (eds) *Battlefields of Knowledge: The Interlocking of Theory and Practice in Social Research and Development* (pp. 47–84). London: Routledge.

Ellen, R.F. (1984) *Ethnographic Research: A Guide to General Conduct.* London: Academic Press.

Eriksen, Thomas Hylland (2001) *Small Places, Large Issues: An Introduction to Social and Cultural Anthropology.* London: Pluto.

Evans-Pritchard, E.E. (1976[1937]) *Witchcraft, Oracles and Magic among the Azande.* Oxford: Clarendon Press.

Farmer, Paul (1997) 'Social Scientists and the New Tuberculosis', *Social Science and Medicine*, 44(3): 347–58.

Farmer, Paul (2004) 'An Anthropology of Structural Violence', *Current Anthropology*, 45(3): 305–25.

Foster, George M. and Barbara G. Anderson (1998[1978]) 'The New Field of Medical Anthropology'. In Sjaak van der Geest and Adri Rienks (eds) *The Art of Medical Anthropology: Readings* (pp. 3–9). Amsterdam: Het Spinhuis.

Gay y Blasco, Paloma and Huon Wardle (2007) *How to Read Ethnography*. London: Routledge.

Good, Byron J. (1994) *Medicine, Rationality, and Experience: An Anthropological Perspective*. Cambridge: Cambridge University Press.

Grillo, Ralph and Roderick Stirrat (eds) (1997) *Discourses of Development: Anthropological Perspectives*. New York: Berg.

Gupta, Akhil and James Ferguson (1997) 'Discipline and Practice: "The Field" as Site, Method, and Location in Anthropology'. In James Ferguson and Akhil Gupta (eds) *Anthropological Locations: Boundaries and Grounds of a Field Science* (pp. 1–46). Berkeley: University of California Press.

Hammersley, Martyn and Paul Atkinson (1995) *Ethnography: Principles in Practice*. London: Routledge.

Hendry, Joy (2008) *An Introduction to Social Anthropology: Sharing Our Worlds*. Basingstoke: Palgrave Macmillan.

Howell, Nancy (1990) *Surviving Fieldwork: A Report of the Advisory Panel on Health and Safety in Fieldwork*. Washington, DC: American Anthropological Association.

Katz, Pearl (1998) *The Scalpel's Edge: The Culture of Surgeons*. Boston: Allyn and Bacon.

Lambert, Helen and Christopher McKevitt (2002) 'Anthropology in Health Research: From Qualitative Methods to Multidisciplinarity', *British Medical Journal*, 325(7357): 210–13.

Launiala, Annika (2009) 'How Much Can a KAP Survey Tell Us About People's Knowledge, Attitudes and Practices? Some Observations from Medical Anthropology Research on Malaria in Pregnancy in Malawi', *Anthropology Matters*, 11(1): 1–13.

Malinowski, Bronislaw (1972[1922]) *Argonauts of the Western Pacific*. London: Routledge and Kegan Paul.

Malkki, Liisa H. (2007) 'Tradition and Improvisation in Ethnographic Field Research'. In Allaine Cerwonka and Liisa H. Malkki (eds) *Improvising Theory: Process and Temporality in Ethnographic Fieldwork* (pp. 162–87). Chicago: University of Chicago Press.

Marcus, George E. (1989) 'Imagining the Whole: Ethnography's Contemporary Efforts to Situate Itself', *Critique of Anthropology*, 9(3): 7–30.

Marcus, George E. (1995) 'Ethnography in/of the World System: The Emergence of Multi-Sited Ethnography', *Annual Review of Anthropology*, 24: 95–117.

Marcus, George E. and Michael Fischer (1986) *Anthropology as Cultural Critique: An Experimental Moment in the Human Sciences*. Chicago: University of Chicago Press.

Ortner, Sherry B. (1995) 'Resistance and the Problem of Ethnographic Refusal', *Comparative Studies in Society and History*, 37(1): 173–93.

Pigg, Stacy Leigh (2001) 'Languages of Sex and AIDS in Nepal: Notes on the Social Production of Commensurability', *Cultural Anthropology*, 16(4): 481–541.

Pigg, Stacy Leigh and Linnet Pike (2001) 'Knowledge, Attitudes, Beliefs, and Practices: The Social Shadow of AIDS and STD Prevention in Nepal', *South Asia*, 24(1): 177–95.

Pool, Robert and Wenzel Geissler (2005) *Medical Anthropology*. Maidenhead: Open University Press.

Rajak, Dinah (2009) 'I Am the Conscience of the Company: Responsibility and the Gift in a Transnational Mining Corporation'. In Katherine E. Browne and B. Lynne Milgram (eds) *Economics and Morality: Anthropological Approaches* (pp. 211–31). Lanham, MD: Altamira Press.

Rubel, Arthur (1964) 'The Epidemiology of a Folk Illness: Susto in Hispanic America', *Ethnology*, 3(3): 268–83.

Rubel, Arthur J., Carl W. O'Nell, and Rolando Collado-Ardon (1984) *Susto, A Folk Illness*. Berkeley: University of California Press.

Sluka, Jeffrey A. and Antonius C.G.M. Robben (2007) 'Fieldwork in Cultural Anthropology: An Introduction'. In Antonius C.G.M. Robben and Jeffrey A. Sluka (eds) *Ethnographic Fieldwork: An Anthropological Reader* (pp. 1–28). Oxford: Blackwell.

Sobo, Elisa J. (2009) *Culture and Meaning in Health Services Research: A Practical Field Guide*. Walnut Creek, CA: Left Coast Press.

Straus, Robert (1957) 'The Nature and Status of Medical Sociology', *American Sociological Review*, 22: 200–4.

Traweek, Sharon (1992) *Beamtimes and Lifetimes: The World of High Energy Physicists.* Cambridge, MA: Harvard University Press.

van der Geest, Sjaak and Adri Rienks (eds) (1998) *The Art of Medical Anthropology: Readings.* Amsterdam: Het Spinhuis.

Young, Michael W. (2004). *Malinowski: Odyssey of an Anthropologist, 1884–1920.* London and New Haven: Yale University Press.

9

What is Grounded Theory and Where Does it Come From?

Dorothy Pawluch and
Elena Neiterman

INTRODUCTION

Grounded theory had its origins as a concept in the publication in 1967 of Barney Glaser and Anselm Strauss' book *The Discovery of Grounded Theory*. In that book Glaser and Strauss, both sociologists, set out to describe an approach to social research and the generation of theory that was at odds with the dominant paradigm at the time. Claiming that too much of sociology had become an exercise in merely verifying theories logically deduced from *a priori* assumptions, Glaser and Strauss sought to lay out an approach to the generation of theory that was firmly grounded in data. Grounded theory, as they defined it, was theory that rose directly out of observation of the social world and that was grounded in the experience of social actors.

Over the 40 odd years since the publication of the book both the idea of grounded theory and the practice of a grounded theory approach have become extremely popular in sociology and beyond. The approach has found particular appeal in health research among those with interests in the social and experiential aspects of health, illness and the body. One might even argue that the concept of grounded theory has become one of sociology's most successful methodological exports. Over that same time, however, there has been growing confusion, or at least disagreement, over precisely what constitutes grounded theory and how to produce it. Contributing to that confusion was a divergence of views that developed in the late 1980s between the book's coauthors. We return to the debate between them and the various permutations of the grounded theory approach later in our chapter. Our primary objective as a start is to look back to the emergence of the approach and to situate it within the theoretical tradition that most analysts agree played a pivotal role in inspiring its development. The emergence of the grounded theory approach was strongly influenced by a set of ideas about the nature of social reality and ways of studying it that is linked to the interpretive tradition in sociology, and more particularly with symbolic interactionism, a perspective that emphasizes meanings and interactions as key to understanding human behaviour. We begin by laying out the basic elements of symbolic interactionism and some of the related perspectives that fall under the interpretive umbrella. We then turn our attention to the grounded theory approach, considering the connections between the approach and the interpretive tradition. In the final section of our paper, we look at the directions that the grounded theory approach has taken since the publication of Glaser and Strauss' seminal book.

THE INTERPRETIVE TRADITION

Symbolic interactionism

The origins of symbolic interactionism are typically traced back to the ideas of George Herbert Mead, a social philosopher who taught at the University of Chicago from 1894 until his death in 1931. (For a theoretical genealogy that traces many of the central concepts of symbolic interactionism back much further to the writing of the ancient Greeks, see Prus, 2003.) Building on the insights of the pragmatist philosophers like Charles Pierce, William James and John Dewey and drawing on the work of sociologists like Charles Horton Cooley and W.I. Thomas, Mead argued that as human beings, we are different from other organisms in the sense that we do not react mechanically or in a reflex-like way to stimuli in our environment. Instead, Mead saw us as active agents, creatively constructing meanings and interpreting stimuli using significant symbols (language and gestures). Mead also saw human beings as distinct in our ability to take the role of others. The cooperation that characterizes our interactions is not physiologically or instinctively driven; it results from our ability to put ourselves in the position of the other, to anticipate the perspectives of the other and to align our actions with those of others. For Mead, our ability to attach meaning and role-take is what makes a sense of self possible. Self depends on our being able to step outside of ourselves into the position of others (particular, significant or generalized), treating ourselves as an object and giving meaning to ourselves.

While the foundational premises of symbolic interactionism are rooted in Mead, it was Herbert Blumer, a student of Mead, who actually gave symbolic interactionism its name, presented the perspective in terms that made it accessible to sociologists, considered its implications in terms of how it could be translated into empirical studies and became one of its most ardent champions through the 1950s. Blumer took Meadian notions about the relationship between the individual and society, and fashioned them into three often cited basic premises: (1) Human beings act towards things (objects, situations, people and themselves) on the basis of the meanings that these things have for them. (2) The meaning of things arises out of interaction. (3) The meanings of things are handled and modified through a process of interpretation that individuals engage in as they deal with the things they encounter.

Blumer's formulation retains Mead's emphasis on agency, that is, our capacity to make decisions about whom we are what we do. From a symbolic interactionist perspective, social structures do not act on individuals in a deterministic way. Individuals create these structures through their interactions, enacting and re-enacting them anew, and sometimes changing them, in their encounters. Social class, divisions of labour and patriarchy are constituted in and through communication and interaction. To suggest otherwise, is to reify these structures – to give them an independent existence as constraints on human action. Similarly, power is not something tangible that resides in the hands of particular individuals or groups; power plays itself out in interactions and in whose definitions of the situation prevail over others. Symbolic interactionists adhere to a processual understanding of power (Dennis and Martin, 2005; Prus, 1999). Power is as power does. Criticisms that symbolic interactionism is a microsociological approach with an astructural bias and an inability to deal with power relations are rooted in a failure to fully appreciate the perspective and the position of its adherents on these issues (see Lyman and Vidich (1988) for a collection of Blumer's writings on such issues as race prejudice, desegregation, labour management relations, industrialization and an analysis of these writings as the foundations of a political sociology.)

Following through on this basic understanding of what social activity is all about and the primacy of interaction, Blumer wrote extensively about how such activity should be studied. What he had to say about appropriate methodological approaches is worth considering closely because Blumer's views align in many ways with Glaser and Strauss' objectives in *The Discovery of Grounded Theory*. According to Blumer, symbolic interactionism encompassed not only a set of assumptions about how the social world works but also a particular methodological stance that was consistent with those assumptions. If the empirical social world is fundamentally about the interpretive work and meaning-making of social actors, in order to understand it, one needs to get close to it. If "society" consists of individuals interacting, defining situations and fitting their lines of action together, it becomes critical to take the actors' perspective, and to grasp the meanings that they construct and that provide the context for their actions:

> It is my conviction that an empirical science necessarily has to respect the nature of the empirical world that is its object of study. In my judgment symbolic interactionism shows that respect for the nature of human group life and conduct. But that respect necessitates, in turn, the development of a methodological perspective congruent with the nature of the empirical world under study (Blumer, 1969: vii).

Blumer was critical of social research based on a positivist, deductive model, where researchers begin by specifying a problem in their area of interest, use existing knowledge to deduce or derive a set of hypotheses that they then test against data (usually quantitative) in order to arrive at a conclusion about social reality. 'Instead of going to the empirical social world in the first and last instances', he complained, 'resort is made instead to *a priori* theoretical schemes, to sets of unverified concepts, and to canonized protocols of research procedure. These come to be the governing agents in dealing with the empirical social world, forcing research to serve their character and bending the empirical world to their premises' (1969: 33). Blumer was impatient with what he called 'the almost slavish adherence to what passes as the proper protocol of research inquiry' (Blumer, 1969: 33) and with the 'innumerable instances of scholars designing and pursuing elegant schemes of research into areas of social with which they have little if any familiarity'.

Blumer called for an inductive (rather than deductive) approach to research. Drawing on Charles Horton Cooley's concept of sympathetic introspection, he recommended a more naturalistic approach, a direct examination of the empirical social world. 'Very simply put', he insisted, 'the only way to get [the assurance that genuine empirical social science requires] is to go directly to the empirical social world – to see through meticulous examination of it whether one's premises or root images of it, one's questions and problems posed for it, the data one chooses out of it, the concepts through which one sees and analyzes it, and the interpretations one applies to it are actually borne out' (Blumer, 1969: 32).

How does one get close to the empirical social world and dig deeply into it? Blumer urged firsthand and deep acquaintance with the sphere of life under study. He advised researchers to become intimately familiar with the groups they were studying and to continuously test and modify the images they were forming.

> This is not a simple matter of just approaching a given area and looking at it. It is a tough job requiring a high order of careful and honest probing, creative yet disciplined imagination, resourcefulness and flexibility in study, pondering over what one is finding, and a constant readiness to test and recast one's views and images of the area (Blumer, 1969: 40).

Another student of Mead – Everett Hughes – also deserves attention. Hughes' contributions to the development of symbolic interactionism are often overlooked, perhaps because he did not identify himself as a symbolic interactionist. Nor did he contribute theoretical or conceptual statements to the development of the perspective. In his empirical writings, however, Hughes demonstrated the possibilities of an interactionist approach and through his courses at the University of Chicago convinced graduate students of the value of fieldwork in uncovering social processes. In this sense, Hughes served as a significant bridge between the founders and more contemporary practitioners of the perspective (Stryker and Vryan, 2006: 17–18). His interests were broad, covering everything from nurses' work and physician education to social movements in Nazi Germany and transitions in French Canadian society. Wherever he cast his sociological eye, Hughes had an abiding interest in the fundamental processes that played themselves out in social situations. 'It is important and fascinating to find out', he once wrote, 'what things do and do not repeat themselves in human history' (Hughes, 1984: 411). The task for sociologists, he believed, was to understand those things that repeat. Elsewhere Hughes (1984: xix) wrote: 'One of my assumptions is that if one quite clearly sees something happen once, it is almost certain to have happened again and again'. Much of Hughes' work was about uncovering these fundamental social processes. He is described as having a 'peculiar double vision, which sees the specific and the general almost at once' (Becker et al., 1968: x). His writings are rich in conceptual insights about human behaviour. Concerning occupational processes alone, Hughes made observations about 'good people doing dirty work', the self-destroying feature of occupational roles (the hazards of losing faith in what one does for a living) and using his well-known invitation to compare priests and prostitutes, the secrets about clients that service workers are often required to keep (Holstrom, 1984: 474).

Variant perspectives

Blumer and Hughes were not the only sociologists inspired by Mead and others interested in the symbol-using, meaning-making capacities and selves of social actors. There were others who took core ideas about the centrality of meaning and developed them in different directions, producing variants of the interpretive approach. Precisely how many variations there are on the central interpretive theme, which approaches count as variants, the cross-influences and similarities and differences among them have all been subjects of much discussion over the years. Without getting into the finer points of those debates, it is worth mentioning some of the main variants or 'offshoots' (Meltzer et al., 1975).

Erving Goffman (1959; 1961; 1963) developed the dramaturgical approach, which conceives of social life as a form of theatre, where individuals strive to manage the impressions they make on others. Harold Garfinkel (1967) moved beyond the concern with the meanings that guide individuals' actions to look more specifically at how individuals *construct* these meanings and engage in what he calls practical reasoning. Phenomenology (Schutz, 1967) and the social constructionist approach (Berger and Luckmann, 1966) consider how social actors construct shared visions and beliefs about their 'realities'. Existential sociology (Kotarba and Fontana, 1984) highlights the role of embodiment and feelings in how human agency is exercised. Exchange theory (Homans, 1958) draws on economic thinking and rational choice theory in focusing on the cost-benefit analyses individuals engage in as they make decisions about their behaviours, interactions and relationships. The Iowa School of symbolic interactionism (contrasted with Blumer's Chicago School), developed by Manfred Kuhn and continued by Carl Couch and his students (1975; 1986), is known for its efforts to operationalize Mead's concepts, especially the notion of the self.

With the development of theory over recent decades and the appearance of new frameworks, yet other variants have emerged. In a survey of symbolic inter-actionism 'in the post-Blumerian age', Gary Alan Fine (1990) lists the following variants – structural, dramaturgical, phenomenological, semiotic, behaviourist, postmodern, Simmelian, Marxist, Weberian and feminist – suggesting that sym-bolic interactionism has become 'intellectually promiscuous' (Fine, 1993: 69). The proliferating list of variants raises questions for some about the extent to which symbolic interactionism has become too fractured a perspective to still be considered coherent, (Prus, 1996; Sandstrom and Fine, 2003). Maines (2001: xiv), on the other hand, takes a more positive view, arguing that the wide adop-tion and integration of symbolic interactionist premises into a broad range of theories is evidence of a healthy diversity within the interpretive tradition and a sign that a great number of social scientists are dealing with interactionist ideas in a serious way.

THE DISCOVERY OF GROUNDED THEORY

Whether one sees the current widespread use of symbolic interactionist ideas as evidence of the perspective's ultimate triumph or demise as a distinctive way of understanding social reality (Fine, 1993), these more recent developments do not reflect the state of affairs in the late 1960s when *The Discovery of Grounded Theory* was first published. Glaser and Strauss wrote their book at a time when symbolic interactionism enjoyed less acceptance and where there was great scepticism about the inductive approach and qualitative methods that most inter-actionists preferred – ethnographic or field research, with as total an immersion in the social worlds of those they were studying as researchers could manage, participant observation and in-depth, naturalistic interviewing. In comparison with the sophisticated deductive models, formulae and calculations of quantita-tive sociologists, qualitative approaches to data gathering and analysis were seen as loose, unsystematic, impressionistic and unscientific. Those who used these approaches saw themselves as 'an embattled minority railing against mainstream quantitative excesses and "positivism"' (Lofland, 1995: 34). The challenge for those who worked in this tradition was to rationalize and explain what they were doing. In writing *The Discovery of Grounded Theory*, Glaser and Strauss took on that challenge.

Anselm Strauss had trained during the 1950s at the University of Chicago where he had studied with Herbert Blumer, Everett Hughes and others who laid down the foundations of symbolic interactionism. Barney Glaser, on the other hand, was trained at the Columbia University, home of Talcott Parsons and Robert Merton – two of sociology's pre-eminent structuralist theorists. Glaser's mentor at Columbia, Paul Lazarsfeld, was a sociologist noted for his pioneering contri-butions to the development of quantitative techniques such as survey analysis, focus groups and panel studies. Through his association with Strauss, Glaser came to appreciate an inductive approach as a valid way to generate knowledge about the interactions that constitute the social, but as a result of his training he brought to the table a concern for clarity and precision with respect to how to conduct research. Charmaz (2006) points out that up to that point the techniques of qualitative interactionist research were passed on largely as an oral tradition and that symbolic interactionists learned primarily by watching and doing. Together, Glaser and Strauss sought to legitimize induction as an approach to the generation of sociological theory and to begin the process of specifying exactly how to put the approach into practice in a systematic and rigorous way.

The Discovery of Grounded Theory began with a critique of what Glaser and Strauss called the 'embarrassing gap between theory and empirical research' (1967: vii). Most departments of sociology, they insisted (1967: 10), had become 'mere repositories of 'great man' theories', with an elite group engaging in speculative or armchair theorizing about social structures while the rest – the empiricists who conducted social research – devoted themselves to trying to verify these theories. Echoing Blumer, Glaser and Strauss questioned the usefulness of the prevailing logicodeductive approach whereby *a priori* assumptions and hypotheses derived deductively from grand theories were tested. In place of this top-down approach, the primary thrust of which was theory verification, they proposed a bottom-up approach centred on theory generation. 'We believe', they wrote in the book's first sentences, 'that the discovery of theory from data – which we call *grounded theory* – is a major task confronting sociology today, for, as we shall try to show, such a theory fits empirical situation, and is understandable to sociologists and layman alike. Most important, it works – provides us with relevant predictions, explanations, interpretations and applications' (Glaser and Strauss, 1967: 1; emphasis in the original).

Beyond making the case for an empirically grounded inductive approach, Glaser and Strauss laid down the essential steps to follow in generating grounded theory. In doing so they used as an extended example their own work on death and dying, especially *Awareness of Dying* (Glaser and Strauss, 1965), a study of dying hospital patients and the extent to which interactions with such patients were influenced by who knew what about their impending deaths. The main strategy for generating grounded theory, they proposed, was constant comparative analysis. They envisioned theorizing not as a series of sequential steps where data is first collected and then coded, analyzed and interpreted, but as a synchronous process where analysis begins as soon as one has a bit of data to think about and where data collection and analysis are continually intermeshed. They pictured researchers moving back and forth constantly between the observations they make of the empirical situations they are studying and their analyses of those observations. They emphasized the need for 'theoretical sampling', which involves taking one's initial analysis of the data and ideas about what might be happening in a given situation and deciding what next step to take, who next to speak to, what group to next look at, what additional data to collect as one moves towards developing the emerging theory. This comparative process continues until one reaches the point of 'saturation', where new data confirm or reinforce the emergent theory without really adding new insights or ideas.

The building blocks of any grounded theory, for Glaser and Strauss, were the conceptual categories that emerge from analyzing the data, the properties of those categories and propositions about how categories are related. Using their data on nursing care for dying patients, they provided as an example of a conceptual category the notion of social loss – the nurses' view of the degree of loss that the death of a patient represents to his/her family and others. Nurses see the loss of some patients as higher than the loss of others (property). Their calculation of the magnitude of the loss influences both their attitudes and behaviours, including the quality of care they provide (hypothesis).

In an argument clearly suggestive of Hughes' influence, Glaser and Strauss challenged sociologists to use these building blocks to move from substantive theories (specific to the particular situations studied) to formal theories that had broader applicability. Understandings grounded in research in areas such as health, work, organizations and education, they felt, could lead to higher levels of abstraction in theorizing. Comparing a social process in one area of life to another creates the basis for saying something more general and less context-specific about such processes. Going back to the case of social loss, for example, comparing the calculation of social loss in one area of health work (nurses among dying patients) to another area of health work (emergency room physicians) can potentially lead to statements about the relationship between social loss and health care provision, or moving to a higher level of abstraction, between the social value of individuals and the quality of services provided by experts in any of a number of different fields, or moving higher still, about the impact of one's social value on one's interactions with others.

While the grounded theory approach is often viewed today as synonymous with qualitative research, Glaser and Strauss were explicit in arguing that they saw a place for both qualitative and quantitative data in generating theory (as did Blumer; see Maines 2001: 7) 'There is no fundamental clash', they wrote (1967: 17), 'between the purposes and capacities of qualitative and quantitative methods or data'. In many instances, they suggested, both forms of data can be useful and necessary. Nor did they subscribe to the view of the relationship between qualitative and quantitative data that underlies how grounded qualitative studies are often framed today, as 'exploratory' or 'preliminary' studies that require quantitative verification. Glaser and Strauss argued that qualitative and quantitative data supplement *each other*, can mutually verify *each other*, and most importantly, when compared, can *each* lead to the generation of new theory.

The grounded theory approach that Glaser and Strauss described also allowed for theory testing either through more extensive fieldwork or through experiments or survey methods, to raise the level of rigour, credibility and generalizability of one's theory. The decision as to how further testing should proceed, however, should be driven always by an appreciation for what methods are best suited to the research situation and not by researchers' ideological commitments 'with associated career contingencies' (Glaser and Strauss, 1967: 233).

That said, Glaser and Strauss appreciated the particular value of qualitative data in generating theory, pointing out that 'qualitative research is often the most "adequate" and "efficient" way to obtain the type of information required and to contend with the difficulties of an empirical situation' (Glaser and Strauss, 1967: 18). While some accounts of the approach's emergence stress the centrality of ethnographic field notes and participant observation as sources of data (Timmermans and Tavory, 2007), Glaser and Strauss in fact promoted the use of a wide range of qualitative data – letters, biographies, autobiographies, diaries, memoirs, speeches, novels, annual reports, instruction manuals, deeds, jokes, photographs, city plans etc. – providing an insightful assessment of why sociologists have traditionally tended to stay away from such materials. The libraries within which these types of materials are often found were described (1967: 165) as an 'amazingly rich' resource for sociological theorizing.

In the years since the publication of *The Discovery of Grounded Theory*, the approach that Glaser and Strauss described has generated both proponents and critics. While there are many points of disagreement, on one point there is consensus: Considered in the context of the time when it was written and the prevailing orthodoxies about sociological theories and methods, the book was a major contributor to the acceptance of inductive approaches to social research, legitimating qualitative inquiry but also the interpretive traditions behind such inquiry.

SUBSEQUENT DEVELOPMENTS

The Discovery of Grounded Theory encouraged and guided generations of sociologists, many of them in the sociology of health. There are few areas of inquiry within the health area – the illness experience, disability, medicalization, the body, mental illness, death and dying, health care workers, medical organizations – that have not benefited from the distinctive contributions that these studies have made (Charmaz and Oleson, 1997; 2003).

The grounded theory approach has been embraced particularly in nursing research (Benoliel, 1996; Wuest, 2007). According to Mills et al. (2006: 25), between the 1960s and 2006, more than 3,650 journal articles in nursing have been published on either the grounded theory approach itself or the outcome of studies that have explicitly acknowledged using the approach. This number does not take into account the countless journal papers where the grounded theory approach may not be mentioned explicitly but is recognizable nevertheless in the description of analytical methods or terminology used. Nor does it take into account the countless edited volumes and collections of papers the approach has generated.

The special appeal of the approach in nursing research may be explained in part by the health-related focus of much of the grounded theory Glaser and

Strauss generated as well as by the fact that Glaser and Strauss made their institutional home for many years in the School of Nursing at the University of California, San Francisco (UCSF) where they trained several generations of nurse researchers. (For an account of how Strauss became involved in teaching in the newly created doctoral program in nursing at the UCSF in the 1960s, recruiting Barney Glaser, Fred Davis (1964; 1966), Leonard Schatzman (1991; Schatzman and Bucher, 1964; Schatzman and Strauss, 1966) and Virginia Oleson, see Stern and Covan, 2001.)

With the increasing popularity of qualitative methods more generally, the grounded theory approach has generated a massive number of studies internationally (for some examples, see Adamson, 2001; Baarnhielm and Ekblad, 2000; DeSouza and Ciclitira, 2005, Ekstrom et al., 2005; Huyard, 2008; Klyma et al., 2008; Lonardi, 2007; Plakas et al., 2009; and across disciplines including education (Babchuk, 2004), psychology (Henwood and Pidgeon, 2003), social work (Gilgun, 2001), management (Locke, 2001), marketing research (Goulding, 2002), accounting (Gurd, 2008) and information systems (Bryant, 2002; Urquhart, 2003). Indeed, it has been claimed that the grounded theory approach has become the most cited qualitative approach globally (Clarke, 2007).

Through these years the approach has been elaborated, extended and adapted so that there is now great variability in what researchers mean when they say that they are following a grounded approach, with some studies using the term 'grounded' in only the loosest sense and exhibiting little if any understanding of the approach as Glaser and Strauss described it (Titscher et al., 2000: 74). Glaser and Strauss themselves are responsible for some of the variance. Strauss (1987), both on his own and in collaboration with Juliet Corbin (1990; 1994; 1998) and Glaser (1978; 1992; 1998; 1999; 2001) continued to write about and refine their visions of precisely how to analyze data in the pursuit of grounded theory. While the differences in their separate contributions were seen initially in terms of emphases and style, by the late 1980s, it was clear that the Glaser and Strauss were not thinking about the approach in the same way and perhaps never had. Descriptions of the grounded theory approach are now often qualified as either 'traditional/classic' (Glaser) or 'evolved' (Strauss and Corbin), 'Glaserian' or 'Straussian' (Stern, 1994: 212).

At the risk of exaggerating the points of contention between them and minimizing the substantial common ground, the main issues appear to be where to start, how to proceed and how to characterize what one ends up with. Glaser stresses that theory building starts only and always with data. The research problem, he insists, emerges from data. The only legitimate questions to ask in relation to data, he argues (1978: 57), are: 'What is happening here?' and 'What are these data a study of?' The freer of preconceptions and questions the researcher, the greater the likelihood that the story in the data will emerge. In the view of Strauss and Corbin, on the other hand, researchers bring insights and experiences to their consideration of the data as well as research questions they may be seeking to answer or existing (grounded) theories they seek to extend or test.

Moreover, while Strauss and Corbin have moved towards an understanding of the approach as a way of rendering theory from *qualitative* data, Glaser has insistently maintained that 'all is data'.

Glaser highlights emergence through the analytical part of the research process as well. He insists on the need for flexibility and creativity, guided by the basic principle of the constant comparative method. Despite his own more careful specification of steps, he insists on 'keeping it simple'. Strauss and Corbin, on the other hand, have produced a highly complex and technical system of operations and procedures for each step in the analytical process – coding, memo-writing, theoretical sampling, sorting, diagramming and writing. Each of these steps is broken down as well so that coding encompasses open, axial and selective coding. Theoretical sampling encompasses open, relational, variational and discriminate sampling. A variety of analytical aids (e.g., the flip-flop technique, making close-in and far-out comparisons and the 'waving the red flag' technique) are offered as is a coding paradigm (examining context, conditions and consequences) and a 'conditional matrix'. (For an example of ongoing efforts to elaborate the operational aspects of the grounded theory approach, see Wasserman et al., 2009.) Stern (1994: 220) and Kearney (2007) suggest that this densely codified and formulaic rendition of the approach was a function of Strauss and Corbin continuing to work within the academy where they were subject to pressures to specify in ever finer detail precisely what one does with one's data to generate grounded theory, while Glaser, who left UCSF and university teaching to found his own press in 1970, was free to think about the grounded theory approach in more general terms.

According to Glaser, in compromising on the principle of starting without *a priori* assumptions or questions, Strauss and Corbin have moved the grounded theory approach back from theory generation to theory verification. Moreover, the complicated array of techniques they have developed intrude on, rather than facilitate, discovery of what is in the data. In the end, he suggests, Strauss and Corbin 'force' the data in a variety of ways. In fact, Glaser (1992) has referred to the debate between them as the *emergence* versus *forcing* debate. In Glaser's view, these forms of forcing do not produce grounded theory at all, but something he calls 'full conceptual description'. (For more detailed discussions of the differences between Glaser, and Strauss and Corbin, see Charmaz, 2008; Duchscher and Morgan, 2004; Kelle, 2005; Walker and Myrick, 2006.)

There is also the issue of whether the grounded theory approach is necessarily tied to symbolic interactionism (Milliken and Schreiber, 2001). Few would disagree that the approach was originally developed to 'harness the logic and rigour of quantitative methods to the rich, interpretive insights of the symbolic interactionist tradition' (Dey, 1999: 25) or that there continue to be 'strong compatibilities' and a 'good fit' between them (Bryant and Charmaz, 2007: 21). However, for Strauss, the grounded theory approach rests inextricably on symbolic interactionist assumptions and offers what Clarke (2005) has called an inseparable theory/methods package. 'Grounded theory', Strauss and Corbin (1990: 104;

emphasis in the original) wrote, 'is an *action/interactional oriented method of theory building*'. Glaser (2005), on the other hand, has taken the position that grounded theory can be done outside of the theoretical framework of symbolic interactionism and should be thought of more as simply a theory-generating data analysis technique.

RECENT DEBATES

The grounded theory approach has been dismissed, predictably, as 'adhocery' (Goldthorpe, 2000: 89) by those who subscribe to variable-centred empirical studies that apply the logic of deduction and testing, and as 'theoretical simple-mindedness' (Wacquant, 2002: 1524) by those qualitative researchers who want to start with theory rather than deriving it from data (see Mjoset, 2005 for one response to these criticisms). Burawoy (1998; 2000), for example, argues that analysts who start with no theory are reinventing the wheel; he advocates instead starting with 'a favourite theory' (in his case Marxist theory) and seeking 'not confirmations but refutations that inspire us to deepen that theory. Instead of discovering grounded theory we elaborate existing theory' (Burawoy, 1998: 16). Taking the grounded theory approach to task for not contextualizing local experiences within macrostructures, Buroway has developed the extended case method which involves working in multiple sites, extending observations over time and space to reveal broader social, political, global and economic forces play out in people's choices and in their lives. Wacquant (2002: 1523; emphasis in the original) tells qualitative researchers to integrate theories at '*at every step in the construction of the [research] object* rather than to pretend to discover theory "grounded" in the field, import it wholesale postbellum, or to borrow it ready-made in the form of clichés from policy debates'.

In the hands of those who promote critical, structural and theory-driven field-work, research is not so much about grasping the meanings and microexperiences of social actors, as it is about uncovering the workings of power and structural inequalities (Gellert and Shefner, 2009). Every story is a story of power – whether social actors understand their realities in these terms or not. Interactions are only and always about reifying structures of power or resisting them, and for the analyst an opportunity to 'see structure happen' (Lichterman, 2002). As Timmermans and Tavory (2007: 500) point out with respect to Buraway's argument: 'Taken to its logical conclusion, the extended case researcher does not need to bother with research since empirical verification is subservient to the veracity of a theory long ago established by Marx and elaborated by Gramsci'.

A more serious 'in-house' challenge to the original formulation of the grounded theory approach has been issued by proponents of the approach like Kathy Charmaz (2006; Bryant and Charmaz, 2007) and Adele Clarke (2005). Charmaz and Clarke have drawn attention to the objectivist assumptions in the grounded theory approach as it was originally formulated. By this, they mean that the approach assumes a single external, knowable reality separate from those who observe it. Further, it positions the researcher as the dispassionate, neutral, all-knowing observer of that reality. Reflecting the growing interest in postmodernist thinking in the social sciences and elsewhere, Charmaz and Clarke argue that *all* knowledge is situated knowledge. Just as social actors interpret and make sense of what is 'real', so too do the researchers who study them. What are those who use a grounded theory approach doing, then, when they present their findings? What do those findings represent?

On the basis of these criticisms, both Charmaz and Clarke have argued that rather than throwing the grounded theory approach out, a reconceptualization is in order. As Bryant (2003) has put it, the approach is ultimately too valuable a method to leave to the objectivists. Charmaz (2006) has made a case for a con-structivist grounded theory approach that recognizes the interpretive work of the researcher in generating grounded theory and where the product of a grounded theory analysis is understood 'as a social construction of the social constructions found and explicated in the data' (Charmaz, 1990: 1165). According to Charmaz, any theory that comes out of applying a grounded theory approach '*depends* on the researcher's view; it does not and cannot stand outside of it' (2006: 130; emphasis in the original). Constructivist grounded theorists take a reflexive stance towards what they are doing when they engage in their studies and what they are producing. Context for constructivists – their own as well as that of the social actors they are studying – matters. As a logical extension, Charmaz argues (2006: 130):

> ... the constructivist approach means learning how, when and to what extent the studied experience is embedded in larger and often hidden, positions, networks, situations, and relationships. Subsequently, differences and distinctions between people become visible as well as the hierarchies of power, communication, and opportunity that maintain and per-petuate such difference and distinctions. A constructivist approach means being alert to conditions under which such differences and distinctions arise and are maintained.

Similarly, Adele Clarke (2003: 553) has sought to 'resituate grounded theory ... around the postmodern turn' by shifting the analytical attention from the social (meaning-making) processes that were at the heart of the original formulation of the grounded theory approach to a situation-centred, social worlds/arenas/nego-tiations framework. In an approach that has become known as situational analysis, '*the situation per se becomes the ultimate unit of analysis*' (Clarke, 2005: xxii; emphasis in the original). Objects of study are conceived in terms situational maps (which identify or bound the situation of inquiry one is curious about), social worlds/arenas maps (which lay out all of the actors and nonhuman ele-ments within that situation) and positional maps (which lay out the major positions taken and not taken vis-à-vis particular axes of difference, concern and controversy around issues in the situation of inquiry). Clarke's situational analysis allows researchers to go beyond the (meaning-making) actions of social actors – 'the knowing subject' – to the contexts (situations and discourses) within which they are embedded and which account for their constructions or under-standings of the world. In situational analysis, there is an explicitly political agenda behind taking a grounded theory approach. According to Clarke, without understanding why social actors think and act as they do, 'we will continue to be paralyzed in terms of constructing ways to share the planet that work effectively toward greater social justice and more democratic participation' (Clarke, 2005: xx).

Whether these more recent versions of the grounded theory approach deal satisfactorily with the complicated ontological and epistemological issues with which social theorists are currently grappling is open for debate. Acknowledgments of their situatedness notwithstanding, in their substantive work both Charmaz (1991) on experiences of chronic illness and Clarke (1998) on reproductive tech-nologies, purport to have grasped, albeit in a less definitive, more tenuous way 'what is going on out there'. Where and what is the 'there' if not an external and knowable reality? For both Charmaz and Clarke, it is possible to come more or less close to the 'true' perspectives of the social actors they are studying; hence the need for the finely grained analyses, their detailed and carefully prescribed conceptual and methodological guidelines are intended to produce. Nevertheless, how is it possible to ascertain how close or how far one has come without presup-posing some objective way of grasping the other's perspective? They veer even further away from the symbolic interactionist premises they both espouse and closer to the objectivist stance they eschew in suggesting that it is possible to grasp not only *what* definitions of the situation influence the behaviours of social actors, but also *why* they come to hold these definitions (i.e., their embeddedness in situations, discourses, hierarchies of power, communication and opportunity). Some might hear this argument as old wine (structure determines behaviour) in new postmodernist bottles. Nevertheless, in formulating versions of the grounded theory approach that speak to, and in the language of, those who subscribe to at least some forms of postmodernist, constructionist, feminist and critical theory, Charmaz and Clarke may indeed be extending the relevance of the grounded theory approach for a broader community of scholars.

CONCLUSION

What is grounded theory? We started with a brief definition which, while accu-rate on the broadest level, did not capture the nuances and complexities required for an adequate answer. We trust that the remainder of our paper has provided a fuller picture. As Charmaz (2007: 2) has pointed out: 'Now what grounded theory is, which and whose innovations and revisions are acceptable, and which version should hold sway are contested issues'. It has become impossible to think of the approach as unitary.

It is also impossible to miss the many ironies surrounding the grounded theory approach. Two sociologists came together, despite their disparate theo-retical and methodological training, and produced a book that marked a critical tipping point in the discipline's development, only to part ways – apparently acrimoniously.

They embarked on a project to demystify and explicate the process of inductively producing theory that captures the lived experience of social actors. Yet, each elaborated on their initial statement to produce formulations that many readers find inaccessible and arcane, and that many symbolic interactionists do not recognize as what they do when they analyze and produce generalizations from their data. One commentator describes the evolution of the grounded theory approach has having moved 'from the sublime to the meticulous' (Kearney, 2007). And to the extent that this observation applies more to one of the two authors than the other, it is ironic that it is Glaser, with his quantitative training and concern for 'rigour', who advocates for a more emergent and creative use of the approach, while Strauss, the more naturalistically trained of the two, is connected with the more rigorously regimented version.

As the approach has evolved, its goal to generate theory has increasingly given way to discussions about procedures, and the more elaborate the procedures have become, the more they seem to get in the way of theory generation. 'The technical tail', as Melia (1996) has put it, 'is beginning to wag the theoretical dog'. This has led to alternative ways of thinking about how grounded theories might be generated. For example, Schatzman (1991), a colleague of Glaser and Strauss at the University of California, proposes that researchers take a dimensional analysis approach, a more 'natural' analytical process focused on the symbolic interactionist axiom of starting always with the meanings in the interactions one is studying (Robrecht, 1995: 172). Similarly, Lofland's (1995) analytic ethnography approach is driven by 'a spirit of unfettered or naturalistic inquiry'. The perceived need in the 1960s for a clear specification of methods has ultimately led back to calls for more intuitive engagement with one's data.

There is irony also in the fact that a methodological approach that arose out of, and was so intimately connected with, symbolic interactionism and the interpretive tradition more generally has become unhinged from that tradition, which has itself undergone transformations that make it less distinguishable as a unitary theoretical perspective. The grounded theory approach is now viewed as serviceable by researchers of various theoretical predilections, and where it is used as a data analysis technique only, by some not particularly interested in theory at all.

Finally, there is the observation that an approach that emerged out of a critique of positivist and objectivist understandings of social reality has itself been subject to criticisms that it is reliant on a view of the social world (or at least the processes that constitute it) as external, immutable and objectively knowable. Out of these criticisms have come yet newer versions that may well propel the approach into the next chapter in its history.

In spite of the ironies and the constantly shifting ground when it comes to grounded theory, one indisputable fact remains. The ground continues to bear fruit. Sociologists, and now many others, are still talking about, debating and using grounded theory approaches, however they understand them. The essential idea behind grounded theory – the notion of trying to understand human experience by becoming intimately familiar with those we are studying – also persists and continues to inspire researchers in health and in so many other areas of study.

REFERENCES

Adamson, Joy (2001) 'Awareness and Understanding of Dementia in African/Caribbean and South Asian Families', *Health and Social Care in the Community*, 9(6): 391–6.

Baarnhielm, Sofie and Solvig Ekblad (2000) 'Turkish Migrant Women Encountering Health Care in Stockholm: A Qualitative Study of Somatization and Illness Meaning', *Culture, Medicine and Psychiatry*, 24(4): 431–52.

Babchuck, Wayne A. (2004) 'Glaser or Strauss? Grounded Theory and Adult Education'. In R.L. Gabriel (ed.) *Search for Shared Meanings* (pp. 89–100). Los Baños, Philippines: Lumos Publishing House.

Becker, Howard S., Blanche Geer, David Riesman, and R.S. Weiss (eds) (1968) *Institutions and the Person: Papers Presented to Everett C. Hughes.* Chicago, IL: Aldine.

Benoliel, Jeanne Quint (1996) 'Grounded Theory and Nursing Knowledge', *Qualitative Health Research*, 6(3): 406–28.

Berger, Peter and Thomas Luckmann (1966) *The Social Construction of Reality: A Treatise in the Sociology of Knowledge.* Garden City, NY: Anchor.

Blumer, Herbert (1969) *Symbolic Interactionism: Perspective and Method.* Englewood Cliffs, NJ: Prentice-Hall, Inc.

Bryant, Antony (2002) 'Re-grounding Grounded Theory', *Journal of Information Technology Theory and Application*, 4(1): 25–42.

Bryant, Antony and Kathy Charmaz (2007) *Handbook of Grounded Theory.* Thousand Oaks, CA: Sage.

Burawoy, Michael (1998) 'The Extended Case Method', *Sociological Theory*, 16: 4–13.

Burawoy, Michael (2000) 'Introduction: Reaching for the Global'. In M. Burawoy, Joseph A. Blum, Sheba George, Zsuzsa Gille, Teresa Gowan, Lynne Haney, Maren Klawiter, Steven H. Lopez, Sean O'Riain, and Millie Thayer (eds) *Global Ethnography: Forces, Connections and Imaginations in a Postmodern World* (pp. 1–40). Berkeley, CA: University of California Press.

Charmaz, Kathy (1990) 'Discovering Chronic Illness: Using Grounded Theory', *Social Science and Medicine*, 30: 1161–72.

Charmaz, Kathy (1991) *Good Days, Bad Days: The Self in Chronic Illness and Time.* New Brunswick, NJ: Rutgers University Press.

Charmaz, Kathy (2006) *Constructing Grounded Theory: A Practical Guide Through Qualitative Analysis.* Los Angeles, CA: Sage.

Charmaz, Kathy (2007) 'Grounded Theory'. In George Ritzer (ed.) *Blackwell Encyclopedia of Sociology.* Blackwell Publishing. Blackwell Reference Online (29 January 2009). Available from: http://www.sociologyencyclopedia.com

Charmaz, Kathy (2008) 'Grounded Theory as an Emergent Method'. In S.N. Hesse-Biber and Patricia Leavy (eds), *Handbook of Emergent Methods.* NY: Guilford Press.

Charmaz, Kathy and Virginia Olesen (1997) 'Ethnographic Research in Medical Sociology: Its Foci and Distinctive Contributions', *Sociological Methods and Research*, 25(4): 452–94.

Charmaz, Kathy and Virginia Olesen (2003) 'Medical Institutions'. In Larry T. Reynolds and Nancy J. Herman-Kinney (eds) *Handbook of Symbolic Interactionism* (pp. 637–56). Walnut Creek, CA: Altamira Press.

Clarke, Adele (1998) *Disciplining Reproduction: Modernity, American Life Sciences and the Problem of Sex.* Berkeley, CA: University of California Press.

Clarke, Adele (2003) 'Situational Analysis: Grounded Theory Mapping After the Postmodern Turn', *Symbolic Interaction*, 26(4): 553–76.

Clarke, Adele (2005) *Situational Analysis: Grounded Theory after the Postmodern Turn.* Thousand Oaks, CA: Sage.

Clarke, Adele (2007) 'Strauss, Anselm L. (1916–1996)'. In George Ritzer (ed.) *Blackwell Encyclopedia of Sociology.* Blackwell Publishing. Blackwell Reference Online (21 January 2009). Available from: http://www.sociologyencyclopedia.com

Couch, Carl (1975) 'Obdurate Features of Group Life'. In *Constructing Social Life: Readings in Behavioral Sociology from the Iowa School* (pp. 237–54). Champagne, IL: Stipes.

Couch, Carl, Stanley L. Saxton and Michael A. Katovich. (1986) *The Iowa School.* Greenwich, Conn: JAI Press.

Davis, Fred (1963) *Passage Through Crisis: Polio Victims and Their Families.* Indianapolis, MN: Bobbs-Merill.

Davis, Fred (1964) 'Deviance Disavowal: The Management of Strained Interaction by the Visibly Handicapped'. In Howard S. Becker (ed.) *The Other Side: Perspectives on Deviance* (pp. 119–37). Glencoe, IL: Free Press.

Davis, Fred (1966) *The Nursing Profession: Five Sociological Essays.* NY: John Wiley and Sons.

Dennis, Alex and Peter J. Martin (2005) 'Symbolic Interactionism and the Concept of Power', *British Journal of Sociology,* 56(2): 191–213.

DeSouza, Paula and Karen E. Ciclitira (2005) 'Men and Dieting: A Qualitative Analysis', *Journal of Health Psychology,* 10(6): 793–804.

Dey, Ian (1999) *Grounding Grounded Theory: Guidelines for Qualitative Inquiry.* San Diego: Academic Press.

Duchscher, Judy E. and Debra Morgan (2004) 'Grounded Theory: Reflections on the Emergence vs. Forcing Debate', *Journal of Advanced Nursing,* 48(6): 605–12.

Ekstrom, Helene, Johanna Esseveld, and Briggita Hovelius (2005) 'Keeping My Ways of Being: Middle-Aged Women Dealing with the Passage Through Menopause', *Grounded Theory Review,* 5(1): 21–53.

Fine, Gary Alan (1990) 'Symbolic Interaction in the Post-Blumerian Age'. In George Ritzer (ed.) *Frontiers of Social Theory* (pp. 117–57). New York: Columbia University Press.

Fine, Gary Alan (1993) 'The Sad Demise, Mysterious Disappearance, and Glorious Triumph of Symbolic Interactionism', *Annual Review of Sociology,* 19: 61–87.

Garfinkel, Harold (1967) *Studies in Ethnomethodology.* Englewood Cliffs, NJ: Prentice-Hall.

Gellert, Paul K. and Jon Shefner (2009) 'People, Place and Time: How Structural Fieldwork Helps World-Systems Analysis', *Journal of World Systems Research,* 15(2): 193–218.

Gilgun, Jane R. (2001) 'Grounded Theory, Other Inductive Methods and Social Work'. In B. Thyer (ed.) *Handbook of Social Work Research* (pp. 345–64). Thousand Oaks, CA: Sage.

Glaser, Barney G. (1978) *Theoretical Sensitivity: Advances in the Methodology of Grounded Theory.* Mill Valley, CA: Sociology Press.

Glaser, Barney G. (1992) *Basics of Grounded Theory Analysis: Emergence vs. Forcing.* Mill Valley, CA: Sociology Press.

Glaser, Barney G. (1998) *Doing Grounded Theory: Issues and Discussions.* Mill Valley, CA: Sociology Press.

Glaser, Barney G. (1999) 'The Future of Grounded Theory', *Qualitative Health Research,* 9(6): 836–45.

Glaser, Barney G. (2001) *The Grounded Theory Perspective: Conceptualization Contrasted with Description.* Mill Valley, CA: Sociology Press.

Glaser, Barney G. (2005) 'The Impact of Symbolic Interaction on GT'. In *The Grounded Theory Perspective III.* Mill Valley, CA: Sociology Press.

Glaser, Barney G. and Anselm L. Strauss (1965) *Awareness of Dying.* Chicago: Aldine.

Glaser, Barney G. and Anselm L. Strauss (1967) *The Discovery of Grounded Theory: Strategies for Qualitative Research.* New York: Aldine.

Goffman, Erving (1959) *The Presentation of Self in Everyday Life.* Garden City, NY: Doubleday Anchor Books.

Goffman, Erving (1961) *Asylums.* New York: Doubleday Anchor.

Goffman, Erving (1963) *Stigma.* Englewood Cliffs, NJ: Prentice Hall.

Goldthorpe, John H. (2000) *On Sociology*. Oxford: Oxford University Press.

Goulding, Christina (2002) *Grounded Theory: A Practical Guide for Management, Business and Market Researchers*. London: Sage.

Gurd, B. (2008) 'Remaining Consistent with Method? An Analysis of Grounded Theory Research in Accounting', *Qualitative Research in Accounting and Management*, 5(2): 122–38.

Henwood, Karen and Nick Pidgeon (2003) 'Grounded Theory in Psychological Research'. In P.M. Camic, J.E. Rhodes, and L. Yardely (eds) *Qualitative Research in Psychology: Expanding Perspectives in Methodology and Design* (pp. 131–155). Washington, DC: American Psychological Association.

Holstrom, Lynda Lytle (1984) 'Everett Cherrington Hughes: A Tribute to a Pioneer in the Study of Work and Occupations', *Work and Occupations*, 11: 471–81.

Homans, George C. (1958) 'Social Behavior as Exchange', *American Journal of Sociology*, 63: 597–606.

Hughes, Everett C. (1984) *The Sociological Eye: Selected Papers on Work, Self and the Study of Society*. New Brunswick, NJ: Transaction.

Huyard, Caroline (2008) 'Exploring One's Own Human Condition: Adults Affected by Cystic Fibrosis', *Qualitative Health Research*, 18(4): 535–44.

Kearney, Margaret H. (2007) 'From the Sublime to the Meticulous: The Continuing Evolution of Grounded Formal Theory'. In Antony Bryant and Kathy Charmaz (eds) *Handbook of Grounded Theory* (127–64). Thousand Oaks, CA: Sage.

Kelle, Udo (2005) 'Emergence vs. Forcing of Empirical Data?: A Crucial Problem of "Grounded Theory" Reconsidered', *Forum: Qualitative Social Research*, 6(2): Art 27. Available at: http://www.qualitative-research.net/index.php/fqs/article/viewArticle/467/1000 (accessed 26 April 2010).

Kotarba, Joseph A. and Andrea Fontana (eds.) (1984) *The Existential Self in Society*. Chicago: University of Chicago Press.

Kylma, Jari, Katri Vehvilainen-Jukunen, and Juhani Lahdevirta (2008) 'Hope, Despair and Hopelessness in Living with HIV/AIDS: A Grounded Theory Study', *Journal of Advanced Nursing*, 33(6): 764–75.

Lichterman, Paul (2002) 'Seeing Structure Happen: Theory-Driven Participant Observation'. In Bert Klandermans and Suzanne Staggenborg (eds) *Methods of Social Movement Research* (pp. 24–38). Minneapolis, MN: University of Minnesota Press.

Locke, K. (2001) *Grounded Theory in Management Research*. London: Sage.

Lofland, John (1995) 'Analytic Ethnography: Features, Failing and Futures', *Journal of Contemporary Ethnography*, 24(1): 30–67.

Lonardi, Cristina (2007) 'The Passing Dilemma in Socially Invisible Diseases: Narratives on chronic Headache', *Social Science and Medicine*, 65(8): 1619–29.

Lyman, Stanford M. and Arthur J. Vidich (1988) *Social Order and Public Policy: An Analysis and Interpretation of the Work of Herbert Blumer*. Fayetteville, AR: University of Arkansas Press.

Maines, David R. (2001) *The Faultline of Consciousness: A View of Interactionism in Sociology*. New York: Aldine de Gruyter.

Melia, Kath M. (1996) 'Rediscovering Glaser', *Qualitative Health Research*, 6(3): 368–78.

Meltzer, Bernard, John W. Petras, and Larry T. Reynolds (1975) *Symbolic Interactionism: Genesis, Varieties and Criticism*. London: Routledge and Kegan Paul.

Milliken, P. Jane and Rita Sara Schreiber (2001) 'Can You "Do" Grounded Theory Without Symbolic Interactionism?'. In Rita Sara Schreiber and Phyllis Noerager (eds) *Using Grounded Theory in Nursing* (pp. 177–90). New York: Springer Publishing Co.

Mills, Jane, Ann Bonner, and Karen Francis (2006) 'The Development of Constructivist Grounded Theory', *International Journal of Qualitative Methods,* 5(1): 25–35.

Mjoset, Lars (2005) 'Can Grounded Theory Solve the Problems of its Critics', *Sosiologisk Tidsskrift*, 13: 379–408.

Plakas, Sotirios, Bob Cant, and Ann Taket (2009) 'The Experiences of Families of Critically Ill Patients in Greece: A Social Constructionist Grounded Theory Study', *Intensive Critical Care Nursing*, 25(1): 10–20.

Prus, Robert (1996) *Symbolic Interaction and Ethnographic Research: Intersubjectivity and the Study of Human Lived Experience*. Albany, NY: State University of New York Press.

Prus, Robert (1999) *Beyond the Power Mystique: Power as Intersubjective Accomplishment*. Albany, NY: Suny Press.

Prus, Robert (2003) 'Ancient Forerunners'. In Larry T. Reynolds and Nancy J. Herman-Kinney (eds) *Handbook of Symbolic Interactionism* (pp. 19–38). Walnut Creek, CA: Altamira Press.

Robrecht, Linda C. (1995) 'Grounded Theory: Evolving Methods', *Qualitative Health Research*, 5(2): 169–77.

Sandstrom, Kent L. and Gary Alan Fine (2003) 'Triumphs, Emerging Voices and the Future'. In Larry T. Reynolds and Nancy J. Herman-Kinney (eds) *Handbook of Symbolic Interactionism* (pp. 1041–57). Walnut Creek, CA: Altamira Press.

Schatzman, Leonard (1991) 'Dimensional Analysis: Notes on an Alternative Approach to the Grounding of Theory in Qualitative Research'. In David R. Maines (ed.) *Social Organization and Social Process: Essays in Honor of Anselm Strauss* (pp. 303–14). NY: Aldine de Gruyter.

Schatzman, Leonard and Rue Bucher (1964) 'Negotiating a Division of Labor Among Professions in the State Mental Hospital', *Psychiatry*, 27: 266–7.

Schatzman, Leonard and Anselm Strauss (1966) 'A Sociology of Psychiatry: A Perspective and Some Organizing Foci', *Social Problems*, 14(1): 3–16.

Schutz, Alfred (1967) *The Phenomenology of the Social World*. Evanston, IL: Northwestern University Press.

Stern, Phyllis Noerager (1994) 'Eroding Grounded Theory'. In Janice M. Morse (ed.) *Critical Issues in Qualitative Research Methods* (pp. 210–23). London: Sage.

Stern, Phyllis Noerager and Eleanor Krassen Covan (2001) 'Early Grounded Theory: Its Processes and Products'. In Rita Sara Schreiber and Phyllis Noerager Stern (eds) *Using Grounded Theory in Nursing* (pp. 17–34). NY: Springer Publishing Co.

Strauss, Anselm L. (1987) *Qualitative Analysis for Social Scientists*. Cambridge: Cambridge University Press.

Strauss, Anselm L. and Juliet M. Corbin (1990) *Basics of Qualitative Research*. Newbury Park, CA: Sage.

Strauss, Anselm L. and Juliet M. Corbin (1994) 'Grounded Theory Methodology – An Overview'. In Norman K. Denzin and Yvonne S. Lincoln (eds) *Handbook of Qualitative Research*. Thousand Oaks, CA: Sage.

Strauss, Anselm L. and Juliet M. Corbin (1998) *Basics of Qualitative Research* (2nd Edition). Thousand Oaks, CA: Sage.

Stryker, Sheldon and Kevin D. Vryan (2006) 'The Symbolic Interactionist Frame'. In John D. DeLamater (ed.) *Handbook of Social Psychology* (pp. 3–28). New York: Springer.

Sun, Fan-Ko, Ann Long, Xuan-Yi Huang, and Hui-Man Huang (2008) 'Family Care of Taiwanese Patients Who Had Attempted Suicide: A Grounded Theory Study', *Journal of Advanced Nursing*, 62(1): 53–61.

Timmermans, Stefan and Iddo Tavory (2007) 'Advancing Ethnographic Research through Grounded Theory Practice'. In Antony Bryant and Kathy Charmaz (eds) *Handbook of Grounded Theory* (pp. 493–512). Thousand Oaks, CA: Sage.

Titscher, Stefan, Michael Meyer, Ruth Wodak, and Eva Vetter (2000) *Methods of Text and Discourse Analysis*. Thousand Oaks, CA: Sage.

Urquhart, Cathy (2003) 'Re-grounding Grounded Theory or Reinforcing Old Prejudices? A Brief Response to Bryant', *Journal of Information Technology Theory and Application*, 4: 43–54.

Wacquant, Loic (2002) 'Scrutinizing the Street: Poverty, Morality, and the Pitfalls of Urban Ethnography', *American Journal of Sociology*, 107(6): 1468–1532.

Walker, Diane and Florence Myrick (2006) 'Grounded Theory: An Exploration of Process and Procedure', *Qualitative Health Research*, 16(4): 547–59.

Wasserman, Jason Adam, Jeffrey Michael Clair, and Kenneth L. Wilson (2009) 'Problematics of Grounded Theory: Innovations for Developing an Increasingly Rigorous Qualitative Method?', *Qualitative Research*, 9(3): 355–81.

Wuest, Judith (2007) 'Grounded Theory: The Method'. In Patricia L. Munhall (ed.) *Nursing Research: A Qualitative Perspective* (4th Edition). Sudbury, MA: Jones and Barlett.

10

Qualitative Methods from Psychology

Helen Malson

There are times in life when the question of knowing if one can think differently than one thinks, and perceive differently than one sees, is absolutely necessary if one is to go on looking and reflecting at all (Foucault, 1992: 8).

Science, since people must do it, is a socially embedded activity (Gould, 1996: 53).

INTRODUCTION

This chapter discusses the revival of qualitative research methods in contemporary psychology, exploring some of the ways in which these methods contribute to health research. While psychology's quantitative methods have much to offer, its qualitative methods open up new possibilities for health researchers to think *differently* about a topic, problem or issue; to formulate different kinds of research questions, generate different kinds of data and produce very different analyses.

Qualitative psychology's research methods are varied. Broadly speaking, however, they provide ways of collecting or generating *rich* (usually textual) data about objects, identities, experiences or events and for producing *in-depth* analyses of these. For health researchers concerned with, for example, understanding the experience of living with a particular diagnosis; patients' or health providers' perspectives on a particular health care intervention; the ways in which, say, new reproductive technologies re-configure women's experiences of pregnancy and childbirth or infertility, or the sociopolitical dimensions and experiential implications of 'healthism', qualitative methods will be vital. To give one brief example: whilst quantitative research is useful when, for instance, comparing outcomes for mothers who delivered babies 'naturally' with those undergoing caesarean sections, qualitative approaches enable exploration of women's *experiences* of 'natural' and caesarean births (interpretative phenomenological analysis [IPA]and grounded theory) and the meanings around 'natural' and caesarean births (discourse analysis). Similarly, they enable analysis of various stakeholders' perspectives (e.g., mothers, midwives and obstetricians) on decisions about managing the birth (IPA, grounded theory and discourse analysis) and how one perspective may become privileged over others in that process (discursive psychology [DP] and discourse analysis).

Psychology's qualitative research methods thus have much to offer health researchers. In discussing them, I will outline some of the key methodological and epistemological debates which have mobilised this revival in qualitative research in psychology. I will then map out some of the principal features and methodological diversity to be found here and illustrate some of the ways in which qualitative psychological methods can be usefully deployed in health research. Before embarking on this discussion, however, a comment on the fact that the current strength of qualitative approaches within psychology can be termed a 'revival' seems in order.

CONTEXTUALIZING THE REVIVAL OF QUALITATIVE PSYCHOLOGY

However much they have sometimes been marginalized, qualitative methods have never been entirely absent from psychology. Case studies, for example, have always been central to psychoanalysis and clinical psychology. Recent psychology has nevertheless been characterized by a drive to scientistic quantification (Stainton Rogers et al., 1995), claiming foundations in evolutionary science and experimental methods (Richards, 1996) and zealously guarding its disciplinary borders against the potential incursions of 'less scientific' neighbours in the social sciences and humanities through insisting on a particular (post-)positivist position. If, as Stainton Rogers et al. (1995) suggested, mainstream psychology was engaged in 'methodolatry', worshiping a particular method, it was – and to a degree still is – methodolatry of a remarkably monotheistic kind.

When, in the late 1980s, I enrolled as a PhD student in psychology, having recently completed an interdisciplinary degree in human sciences, I was woefully naïve of psychology's disciplinary isolationism and disdain for qualitative methods. Psychology at Sussex University, where I began my doctoral research, was less hidebound by disciplinary strictures than at many universities, and I was lucky to receive considerable intellectual support for my less-than-orthodox research. Nevertheless, I was surprised at how, as a discipline, psychology appeared so methodologically and theoretically constrained. I had had no idea that so many psychologists were uninterested in, for example, how psychoanalytic theory was used by feminist literary theorists; how structuralist linguistics or Nietzsche's work was relevant to understanding truth; or how the concept of 'persons' was configured so differently across different disciplines. I had no idea that my feminist and psychoanalytically informed qualitative research would so often be viewed as peculiar; that such incredulity could be elicited by the mere fact that I planned to interview women about 'anorexia' and write about their words with my words; that nowhere was I going to turn 'anorexia' or girls' and women's experiences into numbers. It was not that I viewed (or view) numbers as inherently less useful than words. Clearly, for some questions – the proportion of girls and women amongst those diagnosed as anorexic, for example – statistical analyses are indispensable. But I found psychology's pursuit of a 'scientific' status through a veneration of quantification and a suspicion of qualitative research immensely puzzling in its seeming disregard for the complexities of human experience.

As others (e.g., Kitzinger, 1987) have noted, mainstream psychology has, since the 1930s, been dominated by a hypothetico-deductive methodology characterized by the idealization of experimentation, quantification and statistical analysis. Underpinned by a positivist epistemology, mainstream psychology held that reality was objectively knowable, that true knowledge must be grounded in observation (Harré and Secord, 1972) and that objectivity was guaranteed by rigorous adherence to particular research procedures which could verify (or falsify) the logical propositions of hypotheses (Bechtel, 1988). As Harré and Secord (1972: 33) argued:

> By reducing complex concepts to logical functions of simple concepts, related to unambiguous experimental operations, science, it was thought, could build upon a solid foundation of indisputable facts.

Despite numerous radical critiques, from both within and outside psychology (e.g., Harré and Secord, 1972; Gergen, 1973; Wilkinson, 1986; Jordanova, 1989), such characterizations of 'proper' research still dominated the landscape in the 1980s. While critiques of positivism proposed by, for example, Popper, Kuhn, Quine, Lakatos and Feyerabend clearly impacted upon mainstream psychology's epistemological stance, resulting in post-positivist perspectives (Bechtel, 1988; Outhwaite, 1987), the effects of more radical critiques were less immediate but considerably more far-reaching.

THE MOBILISING DEBATES

These more radical critiques of mainstream psychological research played a central role in the revival of qualitative methods. Qualitative approaches and the debates which mobilised them (see Henwood and Pidgeon, 1992) can be read as moves against and away from – rather than as incrementally building upon – the orthodoxies and disciplinary isolationism of mainstream psychology – so that, as Gergen (1996) noted, '[f]or some the emerging writings seemed anti-science, anti-psychological, and even nihilistic'.

Critiques from 'new paradigm' psychology

Many of these critiques came from 'new paradigm' psychologists like Harré (1979), Shotter (1975, 1984) and Gergen (1973) who argued that psychology's attempts to emulate (a particular view of) the natural sciences were fundamentally misguided (see also Parker and Shotter, 1990). Gergen (1973: 10–11), for example, challenged the scientific pursuit of universal psychological truths by pointing to the historical variability of human experience, practice and thought, and the historically contingent and value-laden nature of psychological inquiry itself, arguing that:

> Social psychology is primarily an historical inquiry. Unlike the natural sciences, it deals with facts that are largely nonrepeatable and which fluctuate markedly over time. … Knowledge cannot accumulate in the usual scientific sense because such knowledge does not generally transcend its historical boundaries. … as socialized human beings, we harbour numerous values about the nature of social relations. It is a rare social psychologist whose values do not influence the subject of his research, his methods of observation, or the terms of description. In generating knowledge about social interaction, we also communicate our personal values.

Gergen thus asserted the inevitable complexity, context-specificity and value-laden nature of people *and* of any knowledge to be gained of them. Harré and Secord (1972: 28) similarly argued against the established belief in 'procedural truth' – the idea that objectively true knowledge could be guaranteed by correctly following a particular method – pointing to the inadequacy of assuming that behaviours observed in psychology laboratories replicated those in everyday social contexts or that findings could be considered, as they so often were, to be universally applicable. Positivisitic quantitative approaches, they argued, failed to take account of the meanings of people's behaviours and experiences or of the contexts within which people live, act and make sense of their worlds. A more person-centred and context-sensitive approach was required (Harré and Secord, 1972; see also Parker, 1989; Parker and Shotter, 1990).

Critiques from feminist psychologies

At much the same time, feminists, both within and outside psychology, were also engaged in rigorous disciplinary critiques and in developing new theories, research agendas and methodologies. These were intended to counter the gender inequalities promulgated by established scientific and social scientific knowledge – including that produced by psychological research – and to better address the lived experiences of women. Broverman et al.'s (1970) now-classic study, showing how clinicians' conceptualizations of mental health and illness were gendered such that masculinity, but not femininity, coincided with health, represents one of many studies in the liberal feminist project of remaking quantitative psychological research. Many feminists argued, however, that the quest for scientific objectivity was more fundamentally flawed: it was not sufficient to revise the research questions whilst leaving the epistemological and methodological framework intact. As Stanley and Wise (1983: 3) put it: 'if you take women seriously, if you make women's experience the central feature of what you're doing, then you *can't* leave the rest undisturbed'.

One way in which the sciences and social sciences were viewed as masculinist rather than value-free was via a critique of the gendered assumptions entailed in empiricist epistemology (Fee, 1981). Feminist historians of science (e.g., Jordanova, 1989) showed how 'man' was systematically associated with culture, rationality and science and 'woman' with nature, superstition/intuition and emotion. In this context the agents of science are thus assumed, however implicitly, to be (at least ideally) male or masculine (Harding, 1987). Hence 'woman' was – and arguably still is – more easily imagined as the object rather than the agent of scientific research (see also Fee, 1981; Bleier, 1984). The androcentric patriarchalism of traditional (objectivist and quantitative) social scientific research was also exemplified by its 'male as norm' principle (Griffin, 1986). This was so blatant (see e.g., Condor, 1991) that feminist critics dubbed mainstream research as 'the academic male-stream' (Siltanen and Stanworth, 1984) and 'men's studies' (Spender, 1980). These arguments went beyond the well-rehearsed, and generally accepted, criticism of psychology's over-reliance on participant pools of (historically, though not currently) predominantly (white, middle class) male undergraduates. They encompassed critiques of how many aspects of women's lives were excluded from 'legitimate' research (Harding, 1987) and of how women (when not thereby rendered invisible) were represented as inferior deviations from a masculine norm (Jordanova, 1989; Condor, 1991). As numerous feminist critics argued, scientific research, including psychological research, played a considerable part in naturalizing, and 'justifying' gender inequalities by producing seemingly 'objective' truths that women were, for example, less intelligent than men (see Sayers, 1982, 1990; Bleier, 1984), less able at maths (see Walkerdine, 1988) and visual–spatial tasks (see Maccoby and Jacklin, 1974), exhibited less developed moral reasoning (see Gilligan, 1982) and were more prone to mental illness (see Ussher, 1991).

In short, an allegedly value-free science tended either to ignore gender or to produce knowledge of women as inferior to men (Jordanova, 1989; Harding, 1987). This was often achieved by exaggerating the magnitude of differences between women and men, minimizing the similarities, and giving a masculinist spin to the meanings of any differences found (Maccoby and Jacklin, 1974). More importantly though, in terms of how feminist critiques mobilised a revival in qualitative methods, were the arguments that researching gender in terms of measurable differences was fundamentally inadequate, because it obscured the diversity within the categories of 'women' and 'men' and failed to engage with aspects of gender such as identity and experience (e.g., Phoenix et al., 1991; Stanley and Wise, 1983).

These critiques thus entailed much more than a demand for better sampling and/or an inclusion of 'women's issues' in 'legitimate' research agendas. They profoundly challenged the idea that psychological research was, or could be, an apolitical endeavour producing objective truths. They demonstrated how 'patriarchal' gender ideologies were inextricably implicated in both the premises and processes of psychological research, and in the effects of the knowledge it generated. While liberal feminists sought to rectify this 'gender-bias' *within* the established methodological framework, many feminists developed new approaches that would be better suited to feminist-informed research (Stanley and Wise, 1983; Harding, 1987; Griffin and Phoenix, 1994; Wilkinson, 1986; 1996; Kitzinger, 1987). Many of these are now mainstays of contemporary qualitative research in psychology and represent a significant element of psychology's contribution to qualitative health research.

The focus on women's experience – including women's experiences of health, illness and health-care services – and the championing of interviewing as a key method of data collection, resulted in a growing body of qualitative research into, for example, female sexuality (Choi and Nicolson, 1994), menstruation (Ussher, 1989; Swann, 1997), motherhood, infertility, reproductive health (Phoenix et al., 1991; Weaver, 2000; Nicolson and Ussher, 1992), abortion (Boyle, 1997) and mental health (Ussher, 1991; Stoppard, 1997). What is significant here is not only the knowledge produced about women's experiences of health and health-care, and the gender-power relations embedded therein, but also the ways in which this research shifts how health-related issues can be approached and research questions formulated. It replaces a mainstream health psychology focus on identifying and measuring the psychological determinants and effects of health and illness and the attitudes, beliefs and cognitions associated with particular health–behaviours, with a focus on how aspects of health and health-care are experienced and on the ways in which such experiences are produced by, and expressive of, cultural representations of gender and gender–power relations.

The critical impetus

The contributions of new paradigm and feminist psychologists in critiquing 'scientific' psychology and developing new research approaches clearly differed in various ways. They also converged, however, perhaps most significantly in their insistence on the value-laden and culture-specific nature of social scientific research and the necessity of attending to the meanings and cultural locatedness of the experiences and practices being investigated. As such, many of those involved in these debates were also part of 'the discursive turn' (Parker and Shotter, 1990; Parker, 1989) that emerged in psychology during the 1980s and 1990s. This 'turn' drew heavily from feminist (Burman, 1990; Gavey, 1989) and new paradigm (Gergen, 1996) psychologies, while also taking ideas and methods from other disciplines including ethnomethodology (Garfinkel, 1967; Stanley and Wise, 1983), feminist and poststructuralist scholarship (Wilkinson, 1996; Weedon, 1997; Foucault, 1972; 1977), Wittgenstein (1953; see Potter, 1996), Speech Act Theory (Austin, 1962), Marxism (Smith, 1990; see Spears, 1997), dialogics (Bakhtin, 1981; see Maybin, 2001; Saukko, 2009) and psychoanalytic theory (Lacan, 1977/92; see Hollway, 1989;

Malson, 1998; Eckermann, 2009). Given these sources, the critical qualitative research resulting from the discursive turn is inevitably diverse. Broadly speaking, however, it is premised on the argument that viewing knowledge as 'true or false by virtue of the way the world is, cannot fruitfully be used to characterize a defensible realism' (Harré, 1992: 153). That is, critical qualitative research shares a postmodern rejection of scientist notions of apolitical objectivity and insists on the inescapable contingency and partiality of truths (Kvale, 1992) because 'facts are theory-laden; theories are value-laden; values are story-laden' (Haraway, 1984: 79) and because, therefore, 'by choosing a certain method we are opting for a particular picture of humans. It is not a question of accuracy but a question of values' (Tseelon, 1991: 313).

Critical approaches are also premised on a retheorization of language, now understood not as a transparent medium through which to convey already-existing meanings but as a culturally-located, social practice in which 'versions of reality' (Potter and Wetherell, 1987) – objects, events, identities, experiences and so forth – are actively brought into being, asserted, negotiated and contested. From this perspective, meaning does not already exist out in the world, or wait inside people's heads, to be discovered and more or less accurately conveyed. It is, rather, understood as created *within* language. Discourse (primarily talk and text but potentially any signifying practice) involves 'the more active labour of *making things mean*' (Hall, 1982: 64). An instance of discourse articulates one possible version of things – but there are always other possible versions (Potter and Wetherell, 1987) and asserting one version rather than another has effects. It articulates, maintains or opposes particular power-relations or 'regimes of truth' (Foucault, 1977).

Crucially, especially for psychology, this retheorization of language as discourse has not only entailed a 'deconstruction' of the 'grand narrative' of Science. It also disrupts other modernist 'grand narratives' including that of the unitary, psychologized, Cartesian individual with whom psychology was – and remains – so particularly familiar (Henriques et al., 1984; Hall, 1996; Rose, 1996). 'The discursive turn' thus required a new view of psychology's subject matter, moving the focus away from internal landscapes of individual traits, attitudes, beliefs, cognitive schemas and so forth (now understood as discursively constituted, reified fictions) and towards an exploration of the discursive work done in talk and text and of the ways in which subjectivities and experiences are constituted within and regulated by, discourse (Burman and Parker, 1993; Henriques et al., 1984; Potter and Wetherell, 1987).

'The discursive turn' entailed both new epistemologies that acknowledged the culturally-contingent, value-laden nature of research and knowledge, and new research methods that attended to the meanings and cultural specificity of human experiences and practices and to the argumentative and constructive (rather than simply transparent) nature of language itself. With the exception of Q-methodology (see e.g., Kitzinger, 1987; Stainton Rogers et al., 1995), the research methods developed in this context, which now constitute a substantial presence and a significant dynamic in the contemporary revival of qualitative research in psychology, were qualitative (see e.g., Lyons and Coyle, 2007; Willig, 2001).

EPISTEMOLOGIES AND METHODOLOGIES IN QUALITATIVE PSYCHOLOGY

As Jonathan Smith (2008: 1) recently noted, 'we are witnessing an explosion in qualitative psychology. This is a significant shift in a discipline which has hitherto emphasized the importance of quantitative methodology'. My inevitably partial overview of the qualitative revival clearly foregrounds critical and feminist psychologies. It is important to note though that this rapidly expanding body of research includes a range of different epistemological positions as well as different methods. There are empiricist as well as critical qualitative researchers and those who take up a variety of stances 'in-between' (see e.g., Willig, 2001; Smith, 2008; Lyons and Coyle, 2007). While qualitative researchers in psychology share, in general, a broadly defined concern with exploring experiences and/or meanings and a concomitant antipathy to – or at least recognition of the limitations of – the reductionism entailed in empiricist quantification, they also differ markedly in the kinds of research questions they ask, in their methods of data collection or generation, their methods of analysis and in their epistemological assumptions.

Qualitative methods as adjuncts to quantitative methods

At the empiricist end of this spectrum are those researchers who incorporate qualitative data within predominantly quantitative and hypothetico-deductive research designs (Willig, 2001). Interviews might be conducted to identify salient issues about a relatively unresearched topic and then used to inform the design of a new questionnaire. Alternatively, as with some health research projects assessing the needs of a particular patient population (e.g., Clark et al., 1995), participants' verbal or written responses to open-ended questions might be used to supplement statistical analysis of questionnaire data with illustrative quotes, shedding additional light on how, for example, a particular illness can be experienced as distressing or why a particular service is found helpful or wanting. In this kind of qualitative research, participants' accounts are taken as largely straightforward and transparent expressions of beliefs, attitudes and experiences. The research is conducted within an entirely empiricist framework.

Interpretative phenomenological analysis (IPA) and grounded theory: Qualitative methods as a route to experience

Participants' responses to interview questions are treated in a similar way by researchers using qualitative approaches such as IPA and some forms of Grounded

Theory research, although, in both, the analysis of rich or 'thick' (Geertz, 1973, cited in Smith, 2008) accounts of participants' experiences is the aim of the research, rather than being an 'add-on' to quantitative analysis. IPA, for example, using a phenomenological framework, is concerned with exploring participants' *actual* experiences (Smith and Eatough, 2007), assuming that experiences are captured by participants' accounts (Willig, 2001). While it is acknowledged that researchers' views are implicated in the process of analysing participants' accounts (Smith and Eatough, 2007), the approach is premised on the assumption that analysis can elucidate the 'essential qualities' of an experience (Willig, 2001). Hence, although analysis is understood to be inflected by the analyst's perspective, the relationship between an experience and an account of that experience is viewed as relatively unproblematic.

Grounded Theory research also entails a qualitative analysis of interviews with participants although its analytic procedures differ from those of IPA, and it seeks to generate new theory in addition to elucidating particular experiences (Willig, 2001; Charmaz, 2008). Where IPA is specifically suited to health research projects aiming to explore a particular kind of illness experience (e.g., Osborne and Smith, 1998) or the experience (whether service users' or providers') of a particular health-care intervention (e.g., Jarman et al., 1997), Grounded Theory research has a broader remit of exploring contextualized social processes *and/or* experiences (Willig, 2001). It can address a range of research questions from those about, for example, women's experiences of dropping out from treatment for anorexia (Eivors et al., 2003) to questions about, say, the role of community mental health nurses in caring for a particular patient group (Huang et al., 2008). In its original form (Glaser and Strauss, 1967), while clearly concerned with analysing meaning, Grounded Theory takes a largely unreconstructed empiricist stance, aiming to *discover* theory in data and viewing the process of analysis as one in which categories of meaning *emerge* from accounts (Willig, 2001). The relationship between reality and representation is assumed to be largely transparent and the analyst's work in *interpreting* participants' accounts is essentially occluded. In its more recent constructionist form (e.g., Eivors et al., 2003), however, Grounded Theory retheorizes and problematizes those relationships so that categories of meaning are no longer understood as discovered but, rather, as constructed.

Discourse-oriented research methods in psychology

In its latter incarnation, then, Grounded Theory research can be positioned alongside a range of other critical research methodologies[1] which arguably predominate in contemporary qualitative research in psychology. These encompass a heterogeneity of approaches, styles and (sometimes vociferously argued) epistemological positions including social constructionism, poststructuralism, critical feminisms, postmodernism, critical realism and critical relativism (see Ibáñez and Íñiguez, 1997). While the distinctions between these stances are important, 'what needs to be recognized here', as Stainton Rogers and Stainton Rogers's (1997: 69) assert:

> ... is that the argument [about epistemology] *within* critical social psychology is a different one than that between critical social psychologists and the mainstream ... The case Parker [as a critical realist] is making against what he calls 'relativism' arises from his view that the purpose of criticality is a political one – challenging the complacency of liberal humanism by bringing injustice and oppression into visibility (and thus to our attention). ... The 'critical realist' rejection of a criticality which admits no foundation is therefore not a call to naïve materialism but a foreboding over relativism as a 'slippery slope' (ibid: 69–70).

For qualitative psychologists taking a critical realist stance, there are things which 'exist and act independently of our descriptions, but we can only know them under particular descriptions' (Bhaskar, 1978: 250). The world is understood as comprising both the discursive and the extra-discursive – or at least the discursive and the extra-textual since discursive representation is understood as intimately entwined with discursive practice and the 'regimes of truth' by which we live.

> The relations between the 'real material' object and the practices of its production are complex: there is never a moment of 'reality' which is comprehensible or possible outside of a framework of discursive practices which render it possible and transformable (Walkerdine, 1984: 163).

For those taking a critical relativist stance there is much the same understanding of (any) knowledge as always culturally contingent and contestable, but the ontological assumptions of critical realism are bracketed off. Jonathan Potter (1996: 6–7), for example, outlines this position as ...

> ... not trying to resolve classic philosophic disputes between, say, advocates of realism and anti-realism. And I am certainly not trying to answer ontological questions about what sorts of things exist. The focus is on the way people construct descriptions as factual, and how others undermine those constructions. This does not require an answer to the philosophical question of what factuality is.

Critical relativism is then 'not a position in which 'everything goes' but in which "nothing goes"' (Stainton Rogers and Stainton Rogers, 1997: 71).

In short, there are (arguably) important, if sometimes subtle, differences between critical realist and critical relativist stances. For qualitative health researchers these differences require consideration since each stance enables or precludes assumptions about the ontological status of, say, a particular bodily state or surgical procedure and provide a meta-theoretical framework which shapes how the relationships between data, analysis and 'reality' can be theorized. Moreover, these different frameworks also translate, as outlined below, into quite different 'styles' of doing discourse analysis, with critical relativists tending to discursive psychology (DP) and critical realists tending more often to Foucauldian and feminist forms of discourse analysis. While both varieties[2] of critical research reject the 'naïve realism' of empiricist research and focus on analyses of how *multiple* realities are discursively constituted and/or negotiated, critical realist research assumes a material reality whose discursive representation is always culturally contingent and whose very existence may be understood as constituted in and by discourse. Critical relativist research, on the other hand, is concerned with how a reality is represented *as reality*, and with the discursive work achieved in talk and texts, but is generally unconcerned with theorizing relationship(s) between 'reality' and discourse.

Discursive psychology

Thus, a DP approach to discourse analysis, drawing on rhetorical ideas (e.g., Billig et al., 1988) and contemporary conversation analysis (see Potter and Hepburn 2005a), is primarily concerned with the argumentative nature of discourse (Edwards and Potter, 1992; Potter, 1996). As such DP is concerned with analysing not just interview data but also more 'naturally' occurring text (indeed these are often preferred [Potter and Hepburn, 2005b]) including audio-recorded conversations and consultations, website interactions, historical and contemporary academic and clinical documents, policy documents, newspaper, magazine and TV scripts. Because of its emphasis on the situated action-orientation of talk, this methodology, as Potter and Hepburn (2005a) suggest, can be particularly useful for health researchers interested in analysing interactions between, for example, service users and providers. Taking their analysis of a caller's crying on a child protection helpline as an example, they illustrate how such analysis can 'explicate the organization of interaction' (ibid.: 343) in a particular setting and can thus contribute to the training of those working in these settings. Similarly Antaki (1999), analysing the transcripts of quality of life assessments for people with learning disabilities, elucidated how interviewers frequently rephrased questions in ways which may have been 'sensitive' to interviewees' cognitive impairments but which nevertheless thereby 'lowered the bar' to potentially inflate the quality of life scores.

In everyday settings DP has also been used in health-related ways to, for example, elucidate how the nature of food is negotiated and contested and how hunger and satiety function rhetorically in family mealtime conversation (Wiggins et al., 2001). The 'actual' niceness (or otherwise) of the meal or the fullness (or otherwise) of a participant's stomach are of no concern here. Rather, the emphasis is on how the 'realities' of meals and bodily states are worked up in interactions to produce specific effects such as justifying or challenging a particular mealtime behaviour. This kind of discourse analytic work is thus particularly suited to health research aiming, for example, to explore interactions between particular client groups and service providers or to explicate how a particular truth claim about health or health behaviours can be made to appear credible or spurious (e.g., Hepburn, 2005; Hepburn and Wiggins, 2005). The rhetoric of the current 'obesity epidemic' (see Markula et al., 2008; Aphromore and Gingras, 2008; Gard, 2009) is one rather prominent contemporary candidate for such analysis in health research.

Foucauldian and feminist discourse analysis

Foucauldian and critical feminist approaches to discourse analysis in psychology have also contributed hugely to qualitative health research (see Murray, 1999; Yardley, 1997; Ussher, 1997, 2000) and much of the aforementioned feminist research could be included here. While these kinds of discourse analytic studies are frequently interview-based, like DP, they also analyze media, academic, institutionally produced and other kinds of texts (see e.g., Burman and Parker, 1993; Malson and Burns, 2009 for examples) and are increasingly applied to visual material too (e.g., Frith and Harcourt, 2007; Marshall and Woollett, 2000; Gillies et al., 2005). But, whereas DP analyses are concerned with the rhetorical aspects of discourse, and tend to focus on interactions within texts, Foucauldian and critical feminist discourse analyses are concerned with elucidating how identities, bodies, experiences and so forth are discursively constituted and with locating these constructions in relation to cultural 'ideologies', regimes of truth and power-relations within which that power/knowledge is constituted (Foucault, 1977, 1980; Weedon, 1997; Henriques et al., 1984).

Thus, for example, much of my own and others' critical feminist research on 'eating disorders' has been concerned with exploring the discursive production and regulation of girls' and women's 'anorexic' (Bordo, 1993; Hepworth, 1999; Malson, 1998; Eckermann, 1994, 2009) and 'bulimic' (Burns, 2004, 2009) subjectivities and practices; with 'deconstructing' the diagnostic categories of 'anorexia' and 'bulimia'; and, more recently, with exploring the discursive production and regulation of treatment experiences and practices (Gremillion 2003; Malson and Ryan, 2008; Malson et al., 2004; Moulding, 2009). This research includes analyses of popular media and advertising texts (Bordo, 1993; Probyn, 1987), historical and contemporary academic and clinical texts (Hepworth, 1999; Malson, 1998; Saukko, 2009), pro-anorexia/bulimia websites (Day and Keys, 2009) as well as interview material (Malson, 1998, 2004; Eckermann, 1994; Burns, 2004; Gremillion, 2003) to explore how normative cultural 'ideals' of gender, bodies and body-management are rearticulated (and resisted) in 'anorexic' and 'bulimic' experiences and practices.

Much of this research has been based on interviews with girls and women diagnosed as 'eating disordered' and has explored the meanings of, for example, fatness, thinness, emaciation, self-starvation, binging and purging embedded within participants' accounts. Being critical, such analyses have not been concerned with seeking allegedly typical causes or anorexic/bulimic psychological characteristics (such as 'dysfunctional' beliefs or cognitive 'biases'), as might be the case with more mainstream health psychology approaches. Nor is it concerned with identifying an 'essential', 'anorexic' or 'bulimic' experience, as would be the case with IPA.

Instead, these analyses explicate the *multiple*, and sometimes contradictory, ways in which 'anorexia', 'bulimia', thinness, self-starvation and so forth are discursively constructed and the ways in which 'anorexia' and 'bulimia' can thus be understood as constituted *within*, not outside, the normative values of contemporary Western(ized) cultures (Malson and Burns, 2009). Taking a critical feminist approach, these analyses produce knowledges of 'anorexia' and 'bulimia', not as objectively existing clinical entities to be understood in terms of linear causation and individual psycho-pathology but as heterogeneous collectivities of subjectivities and practices that often rearticulate culturally dominant values.

Amongst those cultural values there is, obviously, the ubiquitous contemporary cultural prescription of feminine beauty as thinness, (e.g., Bordo, 1993, 2009; Malson, 1998). Crucially, though, critical feminist analyses go beyond this, elucidating other ways in which cultural ideals are implicated in 'eating disordered' experiences (Bordo, 1993; Malson, 1998; Burns, 2004, 2009, Gremillion, 2002). They illustrate how 'anorexia' and 'bulimia' are constituted as expressing, for example, the Cartesian ideal of bodily control (Bordo, 1993; Malson and Ussher, 1996), cultural ideologies of individualism (Brumberg, 1988; Saukko, 2009), tensions entailed in inhabiting the antithetical identities of self-controlled worker and self-indulgent consumer (Bordo, 1993; Turner, 1992), a search for selfhood and, conversely, for sainthood (Eckermann, 1994, 2009), cultural values and dilemmas of postmodernity (Probyn, 1987; Malson, 1999, 2009), and, more recently, both conformity and resistance to current 'healthist' orthodoxies of 'healthy' weight management as well as pursuit of unhealthy/damaging practices of body-management (Burns and Gavey, 2004, 2008).

In short, critical feminist discourse analytic research into 'eating disorders' has illustrated myriad ways in which the discursive contexts of contemporary cultures can be seen to produce and mobilise girls' and women's 'eating disordered' subjectivities, experiences and practices. In contrast with some other socially oriented research approaches (see Blood, 2005 for further discussion of these issues in relation to research on body image), they avoid an over-simplified and 'belittling stereotype' of 'eating disorders' as 'a transitory, self-inflicted problem developed by young women lost in their world of fashion and calorie restricting' (Katzman and Lee, 1997: 389). They produce knowledge of 'anorexia' and 'bulimia' as *multiply* constituted, illustrating both their cultural locatedness and their complex and shifting heterogeneity. As an example of critical qualitative health research, critical feminist research into 'eating disorders' illustrates the profound shift that qualitative research from psychology can make to the field of health research by unsettling commonplace distinctions between the normal/ healthy and the deviant/unhealthy; by mapping out some of the diversity to be found within a particular category of health or illness; and in explicating the politics of gender and other power-relations entailed in the discursive production and regulation of health-related subjectivities, experiences and practices.

CONCLUSIONS

This chapter has explored some of the epistemological, methodological and political debates and developments involved in the revival of qualitative methods in psychology and shown their utility in health research. This utility might be summarized as, first, opening for investigation the richness and complexities of health-related experiences, objects and practices; second, insistence on the interrogation of health-related issues as socio-historically specific and culturally located; and, third, foregrounding the significance of the (various) epistemological assumptions that underpin and shape any research and, hence, any health-related knowledge. While my discussion of contemporary qualitative research in psychology has focused on discourse analytic research, I do not intend to suggest that this represents the culmination of these methodological developments. The continuing debates over, for example, preferred methods of data collection (e.g., Potter and Hepburn, 2005), the relationships between experience and discourse (Malson, 2007), the development of visual analyses (e.g., Frith and Harcourt, 2007) and of methodologies that might better address the embodied nature of subjectivities (Gillies et al., 2004, 2005; Burns, 2009) all indicate the dynamic nature of this field and its potential to contribute in new ways to qualitative health research.

NOTES

1 Within psychology critical methodologies include genealogical analysis, narrative analysis, conversation analysis, critical memory work and some forms of action research. However, discourse analytic research is, by far, the most common and is frequently used in the analysis stage of 'other' approaches (e.g., critical memory work and action research). For the sake of brevity my discussion here is limited to discourse analytic research within can be distinguished Foucauldian and feminist discourse analysis, rhetoric analysis and discursive psychology. See Willig (2001), Smith (2008) and Lyons and Coyle (2007) for details of other critical methodologies in psychology.

2 Whilst this characterization of critical qualitative psychology as comprising two styles of discourse analysis concurs broadly with that of others (e.g., Willig, 2001, 2008), it is important to note that it is entirely contestable both because some analyses combine aspects of both styles and because some critical researchers might identify with neither as they are outlined here.

REFERENCES

Antaki, C. (1999) 'Interviewing Persons with a Learning Disability: How Setting Lower Standards May Inflate Well-Being Scores', *Qualitative Health Psychology*, 9(4): 437–54.
Aphromore, L. and Gingras, J. (2008) 'Sustaining Imbalance'. In Riley, S., Burns, M., Frith, H., Wiggins, S., and Markula, P. (eds) *Critical Bodies: Representations, Practices and Identities of Weight and Body Management*. Basingstoke: Palgrave.
Austin, J.L. (1962) *How to Do Things with Words*. Oxford: Clarendon Press.
Bakhtin, M. (1981) 'Discourse in the Novel'. In M. Holquist (ed.) *The Dialogic Imagination*. Austin: University of Texas Press.
Bechtel, W. (1988) *Philosophy of Science: An Overview of Cognitive Science*. Hillsdale, NJ: Erlbaum.
Bhaskar, R. (1978) *A Realist Theory of Science* (2nd edition). Brighton: Harvester.
Billig, M. Condor, S., Edwards, D., and Gane, M. (eds) (1988) *Ideological Dilemmas a Social Psychology of Everyday Thinking*. London: Sage.
Bleier, R. (1984) *Science and Gender: A Critique of Biology and Its Theories on Women*. New York: Pergamon Press.

Blood, S. (2005) *Body Work*. London: Routledge.

Bordo, S. (1993) *Unbearable Weight*. Berkley, CA: University of California Press.

Bordo, S. (2009) 'Not Just "A White Girl's Thing": The Changing Face of Food and Body Image Problems'. In H. Malson and M. Burns (eds) *Critical Feminist Approaches to Eating Dis/Orders*. London: Routledge.

Boyle, M. (1997) *Re-Thinking Abortion Psychology, Gender, Power and the Law*. London: Routledge.

Broverman, I.K., Broverman, D.M., Clarkson, F.E., Rosenkrantz, P.S., and Vogel, S.R. (1970) 'Sex Role Stereotypes and Clinical Judgements of Mental Health', *Journal of Consulting and Clinical Psychology*, 34 (1): 1–7.

Brumberg, J.J. (1988) *Fasting Girls: The Emergence of Anorexia Nervosa as a Modern Disease*. Harvard, MA: Harvard University Press.

Burman, E. (1990) 'Differing with Deconstruction: A Feminist Critique'. In Parker, I. and Shotter, J. (eds) (1990) *Deconstructing Social Psychology*. London: Routledge.

Burman, E. and Parker, I. (eds) (1993) *Discourse Analytic Research: Repertoires and Readings of Texts in Action*. London: Routledge.

Burns, M. (2004) 'Eating Like an Ox: Femininity and Dualistic Constructions of Bulimia and Anorexia', *Feminism and Psychology*, 4(2): 269–95.

Burns, M., Riley, S., Burns, M., Frith, H., Wiggins, S., and Markula, P. (eds) (2008) *Critical Bodies: Representations, Practices and Identities of Weight and Body Management*. Basingstoke: Palgrave.

Burns, M. (2009) 'Bodies as (Im)Material? Bulimia and Body Image Discourse'. In H. Malson and M. Burns (eds) *Critical Feminist Approaches to Eating Dis/Orders*. London: Routledge.

Burns, M. and Gavey, N. (2004) 'Healthy Weight at What Cost? Bulimia and a Discourse of Weight Control', *Journal of Health Psychology*, 9(4): 549–65.

Burns, M. and Gavey, N. (2008) 'Dis/Orders of Weight Control: Bulimic and/or "Health Weight" Practices'. In Riley, S., Burns, M., Frith, H., Wiggins, S., and Markula, P. (eds) *Critical Bodies: Representations, Practices and Identities of Weight and Body Management*. Basingstoke: Palgrave.

Charmaz, K. (2008) 'Grounded Theory'. In Smith, J. (ed.) (2008) *Qualitative Psychology: A Practical Guide to Research Methods* (pp. 81–110). London: Sage.

Choi, P.Y.L. and Nicolson, P. (1994) *Female Sexuality Psychology, Biology and Social Context*. Brighton: Harvester Press.

Clark, D., Heslop, J., Malson, H., and Craig, B. (1995) *As Much Help as Possible: Assessing Palliative Care Needs in Southern Derbyshire*. Report for Southern Derbyshire Health Authority.

Condor S, (1991) 'Sexism in Psychological Research: A Brief Note', *Feminism and Psychology, Oct 1991*; 1: 430–34.

Day, K. and Keys, T. (2009) 'Anorexia/Bulimia as Resistance and Conformity in Pro-Ana and Pro-Mia Virtual Conversations'. In H. Malson and M. Burns (eds) *Critical Feminist Approaches to Eating Dis/Orders*. London: Routledge.

Eckermann, E. (1994) 'Self-Starvation and Binge-Purging: Embodied Selfhood/Sainthood', *Australian Cultural History*, 13: 82–99.

Eckermann, L. (2009) 'Eating Orders/Disorders: Beyond Risk, Governmentality and the Normalizing Gaze'. In H. Malson and M. Burns (eds) *Critical Feminist Approaches to Eating Dis/Orders*. London: Routledge.

Edwards, D. and Potter, J. (1992) *Discursive Psychology*. London: Sage.

Eivors, A., Button, E., Warner, S., and Turner, K. (2003) 'Understanding the Experience of Drop Out from Treatment for Anorexia', *European Eating Disorders Review*, 11: 90–107.

Fee, E. (1981) 'Is Feminism a Threat to Scientific Objectivity?', *International Journal of Women's Studies*, 4: 378–92.

Foucault, M. (1972) *The Archaeology of Knowledge*. New York: Pantheon Books.

Foucault, M. (1977) *Discipline and Punish: The Birth of the Prison*. Hammondsworth: Penguin.

Foucault, M. (1992) *The Uses of Pleasure: The History of Sexuality, Volume 2*. London: Penguin.

Frith, H. and Harcourt, D. (2007) 'Using Photographs to Capture Women's Experiences of Chemotherapy: Reflecting on the Method', *Qualitative Health Research*, 17(10): 1340–50.

Gard, M. (2009) 'Understanding Obesity by Understanding Desire'. In H. Malson and M. Burns (eds) *Critical Feminist Approaches to Eating Dis/Orders.* London: Routledge.

Garfinkel, H. (1967) *Studies in Ethnomethodology.* New York: Prentice Hall.

Gavey, N. (1989) 'Feminist Post-Structuralism and Discourse Analysis: Contributions to Feminist Psychology', *Psychology of Women Quarterly,* 13: 459–75.

Gergen, K. (1973) 'Social Psychology as History', *Journal of Personality and Social Psychology,* 26: 309–20.

Gergen, K. (1996) 'Social Psychology as Social Construction: The Emerging Vision'. In C. McGarty and A. Haslam (eds) *The Message of Social Psychology: Perspectives on Mind in Society.* Oxford: Blackwell, http://www.swarthmore.edu/SocSci/kgergen1/web/page.phtml?id=manu1 (accessed on September 5, 2008).

Gillies, V., Harden, A., Johnson, K., Reavey, P., Strange, V., and Willig, C. (2004) 'Women's Collective Constructions of Embodied Practices through Memory Work: Cartesian Dualism in Memories of Sweating and Pain', *British Journal of Social Psychology,* 43: 99–112.

Gillies, V., Harden, A., Johnson, K., Reavey, P., Strange, V., and Willig, C. (2005) 'Painting Pictures of Embodied Experience: The Use of Nonverbal Data Production for the Study of Embodiment', *Qualitative Research in Psychology,* 2: 1–13.

Gilligan, C. (1982) *In a Different Voice: Psychological Theory and Women's Development.* Cambridge, MA: Harvard UP.

Glaser, B.G. and Strauss, A.L. (1967) *The Discovery of Grounded Theory.* Chicago: Aldine.

Gould, S.J. (1996) *The Mismeasure of Man.* New York: Norton.

Gremillion, H. (2002) 'In Fitness and in Health: Crafting Bodies in the Treatment of Anorexia Nervosa', *Signs,* 27(2): 381–596.

Gremillion, H. (2003) *Feeding Anorexia: Gender and Power at a Treatment Center.* Durham: Duke University Press.

Griffin, C. (1986) 'Qualitative Methods and Female Experience: Young Women form School to the Job Market'. In S. Wilkinson (ed.) (1986) *Feminist Social Psychology.* Milton Keynes: Open University.

Griffin, C. and Phoenix, A. (1994) 'The Relationship Between Qualitative and Quantitative Research, Lessons from Feminist Psychology', *Journal of community and applied social psychology,* 4: 277–98.

Hall, S. (1982) 'The Rediscovery of "Ideaology": Returning to the Repressed in Media Studies'. In M. Gurevitch, T. Bennett, J. Curran, and J. Woollacott (eds) *Culture, Society and the Media.* London: Methuen.

Hall, S. (1996) 'Who Needs Identity?'. In S. Hall and P. du Gay (eds) *Questions of Cultural Identity.* London: Sage.

Haraway, D. (1984) 'Primatology is Politics by Other Means'. In R. Bleier (ed.) *Feminist Approaches to Science* (pp. 77–118). London: Pergamon.

Harding, S. (1987) 'Is There a Feminist Methodology?'. In S. Harding (ed.) (1987) *Feminism and Methodology: Social Science Issues* (pp. 1–14). Milton Keynes: Open University Press.

Harré, R. (1979) *Social Being: A Theory for Social Psychology.* Oxford: Blackwell.

Harré, R. (1992) 'What Is Real in Psychology: A Plea for Persons', *Theory and Psychology,* 2(2): 153–58.

Harré, R. and Secord, P. (1972) *The Explanation of Social Behaviour.* Oxford: Blackwell.

Henriques, J., Hollway, W., Urwin, C., Venn, C., and Walkerdine, V. (1984) *Changing the Subject: Psychology, Social Regulation and Subjectivity.* London: Methuen.

Henwood, K. and Pidgeon, N. (1992) 'Qualitative Research and Psychological Theorising', *British Journal of Psychology,* 83: 97–111.

Hepburn, A. (2005) ' "You're Not Taking Me Seriously": Ethics and Asymmetry in Calls to a Child Protection Helpline', *Journal of Constructivist Psychology,* 18: 255–76.

Hepburn, A. and Wiggins, S. (2005) 'Size Matters: Constructing Accountable Bodies in NSPCC Helpline and Family Mealtime Talk', *Discourse and Society,* 16: 625–47.

Hepworth, J. (1999) *The Social Construction of Anorexia Nervosa.* London: Sage.

Hollway, W. (1989) *Subjectivity and Method in Psychology, Gender, Meaning and Science.* London: Sage.

Ibáñez, T. and Íñiguez, L. (eds) (1997) *Critical Social Psychology*. London: Sage.

Jarman, M., Smith, J.A., and Walsh, S. (1997) 'The Psychological Battle for Control: A Qualitative Study of Healthcare Professionals' Understandings of Treatment of Anorexia Nervosa', *Journal of Community and Applied Social Psychology*, 7: 137–52.

Jordanova, L. (1989) *Sexual Visions: Images of Gender in Science and Medicine Between the Eighteenth and Twentieth Centuries*. London: Harvester Wheatsheaf.

Katzman, M.A. and Lee, S. (1997) 'Beyond Body Image: The Integration of Feminist and Transcultural Theories in the Understanding of Self Starvation', *International Journal of Eating Disorders*, 22(4): 385–94.

Kitzinger, C. (1987) *The Social Construction of Lesbianism*. London: Sage.

Kvale, S. (ed.) (1992) *Psychology and Postmodernism*. London: Sage.

Lacan, J. (1977/92) *Ecrits: A Selection (trans. A Sheridan)* (pp. 146–78). London: Routledge.

Lyons, E. and Coyle, A. (eds) (2007) *Analysing Qualitative Data in Psychology*. London: Sage.

Maccoby, E.E. and Jacklin, J.W. (1974) *The Psychology of Sex Difference*. Palo Alto, CA: Stanford University Press.

Malson, H. (1998) *The Thin Woman: Feminism, Post-structuralism and the Social Psychology of Anorexia Nervosa*. London: Routledge.

Malson, H. (1999) 'Women Under Erasure: Anorexic Bodies in Postmodern Context', *Journal of Community and Applied Social Psychology*, 9: 137–53.

Malson, H. (2007) *Self Starvation and Persuasion: Interviewing Women about Experiences of Treatment for 'Eating Disorders'*. Invited Presentation at Showcasing Qualitative Psychology, 7 December 2006, BPS, London.

Malson, H. (2008) 'Deconstructing Body Weight and Weight Management'. In Riley, S., Burns, M., Frith, H., Wiggins, S., and Markula, P. (eds) *Critical Bodies: Representations, Practices and Identities of Weight and Body Management*. Basingstoke: Palgrave.

Malson, H. (2009) 'Appearing to Disappear: Postmodern Femininities and Self-starved Subjectivities'. In H. Malson and M. Burns (eds) (2009) *Critical Feminist Approaches To Eating Dis/Orders*, London: Routledge.

Malson, H. and Burns, M. (eds) (2009) *Critical Feminist Approaches To Eating Dis/Orders*. Routledge: London.

Malson, H. and Ryan, V. (2008) 'Tracing the Matrix of Gender: A Feminist Post-Structuralist Analysis of the Feminine in Hospital-Based Treatment for Eating Disorders', *Feminism and Psychology*, 18(1): 112–32.

Malson, H. and Ussher, J.M. (1996) 'Body Poly-Texts: Discourses Of The Anorexic Body', *Journal of Community and Applied Social Psychology*, 6: 267–80.

Malson, H., Finn, D.M., Treasure, J., Clarke, S., and Anderson, G. (2004) 'Constructing "The Eating Disordered Patient": A Discourse Analysis of Accounts of Treatment Experiences', *Journal of Community and Applied Social Psychology*, 14(6): 473–89.

Markula, P., Burns, M., and Riley, S. (2008) 'Introducing Critical Bodies: Representations, Identities and Practices of Weight and Body Management'. In Riley, S., Burns, M., Frith, H. Wiggins, S., and Markula, P. (eds) *Critical Bodies: Representations, Practices and Identities of Weight and Body Management*. Basingstoke: Palgrave.

Marshall, H. and Woollett A (2000) 'Changing Youth: An Exploration of Visual and Textual Cultural Identification'. In C. Squire (ed.) *Culture in Psychology* (pp. 118–32). London: Routledge.

Maybin, J. (2001) 'Language Struggle and Voice: The Bakhtin/Volosinov Writings'. In M. Wetherell, S. Taylor, and S.J. Yates (eds) *Discourse Theory and Practice: A Reader*. London: Sage.

Moulding, N. (2009) 'The Anorexic as Femme Fatale: Reproducing Gender through the Father/Psychiatrist–Daughter/Patient Relationship'. In H. Malson and M. Burns (eds) *Critical Feminist Approaches to Eating Dis/Orders*. London: Routledge.

Murray, M. (1999) *Qualitative Health Psychology: Theories and Methods*. London: Sage.

Nicolson, P. and Ussher, J. (eds) (1992) *The Psychology of Women's Health and Health Care*. London: Macmillan.

Osborne, M. and Smith, J. (1998) 'The Personal Experience of Chronic Benign Lower Back Pain: An Interpretative Phenomenological Analysis', *British Journal of Health Psychology*, 3: 65–83.
Outhwaite, W. (1987) *New Philosophies of Social Science: Realism, Hermeneutics and Critical Theory.* London: Macmillan.
Parker, I. (1989) *The Crisis in Modern Social Psychology and How to End It.* London: Routledge.
Parker, I. and Shotter, J. (eds) (1990) *Deconstructing Social Psychology.* London: Routledge.
Phoenix, A., Woollett, A. and Lloyd, E. (1991) *Motherhood Meanings, Practices and Ideologies.* London: Sage.
Potter, J. (1996) *Representing Reality: Discourse Rhetoric and Social Construction.* London: Sage.
Potter, J. and Hepburn, A. (2005a) 'Qualitative Interviews in Psychology: Problems and Possibilities', *Qualitative Research in Psychology*, 2: 38–55.
Potter, J. and Hepburn, A. (2005b) 'Discursive Psychology as a Qualitative Approach for Analysing Interaction in Medical Settings', *Medical Education*, 39: 338–44.
Potter, J. and Wetherell, M. (1987) *Discourse and Social Psychology.* London: Sage.
Probyn, E. (1987) 'The Anorexic Body'. In A. Kroker and M. Kroker (eds) *Panic Sex in America.* New York: St Martins Press.
Richards, G. (1996) *Putting Psychology in Its Place: An Introduction from a Critical Historical Perspective.* Routledge, London.
Rose, N. (1996) *Inventing Our Selves: Psychology, Power, and Personhood.* Cambridge University Press.
Saukko, P. (2009) 'Critical Discussion of Normativity in Discourses of Eating Disorders'. In H. Malson and M. Burns (eds) *Critical Feminist Approaches to Eating Dis/Orders.* London: Routledge.
Sayers, J. (1982) *Biological Politics: Feminist and Anti-Feminist Perspectives.* London: Tavistock.
Sayers, J. (1990) 'Psychoanalytic Feminism: Deconstructing Power in Theory and Therapy'. In I. Parker and J. Shotter (eds.) *Deconstructing Social Psychology* (pp. 196–207). London: Routledge.
Shotter, J. (1975) *Images of Man in Psychological Research.* London: Methuen.
Shotter, J. (1984) *Accountability and Selfhood.* Oxford: Blackwell.
Siltanen, J. and Stanworth, M. (eds) (1984) *Women and the Public Sphere: A Critique of Sociology and Politics.* London: Hutchinson.
Smith, D.E. (1990) *Texts, Facts and Femininity.* London: Routledge.
Smith, J. (ed.) (2008) *Qualitative Psychology: A Practical Guide to Research Methods.* London: Sage.
Smith, J. and Eatough, V. (2007) 'Interpretative Phenomenological Analysis'. In Lyons E. and Coyle, A. (eds) (2007) *Analysing Qualitative Data in Psychology* (pp. 32–50). London: Sage.
Spears, R. (1997) 'Introduction'. In T. Ibáñez and L. Íñiguez, 1997 (eds) (1997) *Critical Social Psychology.* London: Sage.
Spender, D. (1980) *Man Made Language.* London: Routledge.
Stainton Rogers, R. and Stainton Rogers, W. (1997) 'Going Critical?'. In T. Ibáñez and L. Íñiguez, 1997 (eds) (1997) *Critical Social Psychology* (pp. 42–54). London: Sage.
Stainton Rogers, R., Stenner, P., Gleeson, K., and Stainton Rogers, W. (1995) *Social Psychology: A Critical Agenda.* Cambridge: Polity Press.
Stanley, L. and Wise, S. (1983) *Breaking Out: Feminist Consciousness and Feminist Research.* London: Routledge.
Stoppard, J. (1997) 'Women's Bodies, Women's Lives and Depression: Towards a Reconciliation of Material and Discursive Accounts'. In J. Ussher (ed.), *Body Talk: the Material and Discursive Regulation of Sexuality, Madness and Reproduction* (pp.10–32). London: Routledge.
Swann, C. (1997) 'Reading the Bleeding Body: Discourses of Premenstrual Syndrome'. In J. Ussher (ed.) *Body Talk: the Material and Discursive Regulation of Sexuality, Madness and Reproduction* (pp. 176–98). London: Routledge.
Tseelon, E. (1991) 'The Method Is the Message: On the Meaning of Methods as Ideologies', *Theory and Psychology*, 1(3): 299–316.
Turner, B.S. (1992) *Regulating Bodies: Essays in Medical Sociology.* London: Routledge.
Ussher, J.M. (1989) *The Psychology of the Female Body.* London: Routledge.

Ussher, J.M. (1991) *Women's Madness: Misogyny or Mental Illness?* Hemel Hempstead: Harvester Wheatsheaf.

Ussher, J.M. (1997) *Body Talk: the Material and Discursive Regulation of Sexuality, Madness and Reproduction.* London: Routledge.

Ussher J.M. (ed.) (2000) *Women's Health: Contemporary International Perspectives.* Leicester: British Psychological Society.

Walkerdine, V. (1984) 'Developmental Psychology and the Child-Centred Pedagogy'. In Henriques, J., Hollway, W., Urwin, C., Venn, C., and Walkerdine, V. (1984) *Changing the Subject: Psychology, Social Regulation and Subjectivity.* London: Methuen.

Walkerdine, V. (1988) *The Mastery of Reason.* London: Routledge.

Weaver, J. (2000) in J.M. Ussher (ed.) *Women's Health: Contemporary International Perspectives.* Leicester: British Psychological Society.

Weedon, C. (1997) *Feminist Practice and Poststructuralist Theory.* Oxford: Blackwell.

Wiggins, S., Potter, J., and Wildsmith, A. (2001) 'Eating Your Words: Discursive Psychology and the Reconstruction of Eating Practices', *Journal of Health Psychology*, 6(1): 5–15.

Wilkinson, S. (ed.) (1986) *Feminist Social Psychology.* Milton Keynes: Open University Press.

Wilkinson, S. (ed.) (1996) *Feminist Social Psychologies.* Milton Keynes: Open University Press.

Willig, C. (2001) *Introducing Qualitative Research in Psychology: Adventures in Theory and Method.* Milton Keynes: Open University Press.

Wittgenstein, L. (1953) *Philosophical Investigations.* Oxford: Blackwell.

Yardley, L. (1997) *Material Discourses of Health and Illness.* London: Routledge.

11

Conversation Analysis and Ethnomethodology: the Centrality of Interaction

Timothy Halkowski and
Virginia Teas Gill

INTRODUCTION

The conversation analytic perspective focuses on the moment-by-moment production of human social life. Conversation analysis (CA) affords a unique and powerful view of the ways in which people's vocal and nonvocal actions interlock in a temporal weave to generate organized patterns of interaction (Garfinkel, 1984[1967]; Sacks, 1992; Heritage, 1984; Maynard and Clayman, 1991). It allows us to see the deep and fine-grained organization of health care interactions, an organization that becomes part of the experiences of patients and health care providers.

This unique view is a function of the questions conversation analysts ask about health care interactions (as well as CA's theoretical assumptions). In this chapter, we discuss these distinctive questions and focus on two core aspects of the CA perspective: its emphasis on the social and the temporal nature of human interaction. We also discuss examples of CA research on health care interactions, giving special attention to the ways that 'practical epistemics' shape the opportunities for patients and health care providers to demonstrate their knowledge and experience to each other (Whalen and Zimmerman, 1990). Our aim is to show when and how CA can be useful to researchers who are interested in interaction in medical settings, doctor – patient consultations.

THE FUNDAMENTAL TEMPORALITY AND SOCIALITY OF INTERACTION

Conversation analysts who study medical interaction are interested in *what* goes on in these interactions and *how* this is achieved. Recognizing that talk-in-interaction is the means through which people achieve a wide range of social actions and activities, conversation analysts ask how participants in interaction organize their behaviour to accomplish actions and activities in the consultation.[1] What are the specific patterns of vocal and nonvocal behaviour through which health problems emerge in the consultation and are diagnosed, patients' and providers' roles are manifested, sustained, shifted and altered, and medical settings are accomplished? These questions lead conversation analysts to investigate and document the achievement of 'social facts' in the medical consultation – specifically, the practices participants use to produce (and show understanding of) what is going on in the interaction – as it unfolds over time, collaboratively and contingently.

Reflecting CA's roots in ethnomethodology (Garfinkel, 1967), conversation analytic studies of medical (and other) interactions focus on members' practices for achieving understanding with one another in the real-time flow of interaction. The researcher does not aim to uncover underlying meanings or intentions in talk: a conversation analyst relocates the 'problem' of understanding in interaction to its original domain – as a practical matter for the participants themselves to resolve, on a moment by moment basis, in every interaction. Schegloff and Sacks (1973) offered this rationale for approaching the 'understanding question' as a participant's issue:

> We have proceeded under the assumption (an assumption borne out by our research) that in so far as the materials we worked with exhibited orderliness, they did so not only to us, indeed not in the first place for us, but for the co-participants who had produced them. If the materials (records of natural conversation) were orderly, they were so because they had been methodically produced by members of the society for one another, and it was a feature of the conversations we treated as data that they were produced so as to allow the display by the co-participants to each other of their orderliness, and to allow the participants to display to each other their analysis, appreciation and use of the orderliness (1973:290).

Here, a comparison with another tradition of research on medical interaction may be useful. In studies of medical interaction based on Interaction Process Analysis (e.g., Roter and Larson, 2002), researchers record interactions and then code participants' speech into content-based categories that correspond to the thoughts speakers are conveying with their utterances, and whether they signify task-oriented or socioemotional exchanges (e.g., Roter and Larson, 2002).[2] Understanding what participants meant and what actions they were doing is regarded as a researcher's task, to be approached by listening for cues in the content of their talk, such as speakers' tone of voice or intonation.[3] Once the participants' utterances are categorized, the analyst can then determine, via quantitative analysis, whether there are patterns in the interactions that correspond to variables such as the participants' demographic characteristics (e.g., gender; Hall et al., 1994), or outcomes such as patients' satisfaction with their medical encounters (Roter and Hall, 1992). Researchers using this approach are fundamentally concerned with those correlations and how information about them could be used to improve medical practice.

Conversation analysts approach the 'understanding question' differently, seeking evidence in the talk or other actions for how the participants orient to and understand each other. The rationale for this approach is that human interaction irremediably occurs in sequences of turns, over time.[4] Every action in an interaction cannot help but follow some other action, and occur in its 'shadow' as it were. Likewise, each action cannot help but cast an interactional shadow on what is to follow. This inescapable temporality of interaction creates the conditions within which actions will be understood and within which each successive action will therefore be undertaken.[5] Therefore, the positioning of utterances in the stream of conversation is a crucial *social resource* participants employ to make their utterances recognizable and to determine what actions co-participants are doing.[6] As Schegloff (2007:8) explains, it is a resource for the analyst as well:

> ... we start from an observation about how some bit of talk was done, and ask: What could someone be doing by talking in this way? What does that bit of talk appear designed to do? What is the action that it is a practice for? We try to ground our answer to this sort of question by showing that it is *that* action which *co-participants in the interaction* took to be what was getting done, as revealed in/by the response they make to it.

When a patient responds to a doctor's utterance, he or she displays an understanding of it as an action (Sacks et al., 1974). The doctor then has to react to the 'public' sense of the initial utterance (Schegloff, 1992), and may confirm (or correct) that initial understanding (Schegloff and Sacks, 1973). The patient's reaction is therefore partially constitutive of what the original utterance comes to mean and do (cf. Mills, 1940). At an even more fine-grained level, recipients' reactions can affect speakers' utterances even as they are being produced (Reddy, 1979; Goodwin, 1979, 1980, 1981; Maynard and Perakyla, 2003). For example, a person (in the midst of hearing a speaker's utterance) might react in ways that cause the speaker to reshape, edit or delete parts of what he or she said or was demonstrably heading toward saying.

Certainly, when we speak with each other, the particular words we use shape the type of action we are thereby doing. But the *positioning* of an utterance and the recipient's reception of it also matters deeply for what it will come to mean and do in an interaction (Schegloff, 1993: 121). For example, consider the following from a clinic visit:

Example 1

(Gill and Maynard, 2006: 121–2)

```
[16:1032]

1   Dr:  You mention some easy bruising? An bleeding?
         Fatigue?
2   Pt:  Yea::h. I- an the- an: that you know: has been
         (.) most recently
```

```
3          that I have the fatigue. But I guess: you know:
           you're just
4          not supposed ta (2.5) keephh (0.5) burning the
           candle at
5          both ends all the ti(h)me(h)(h)[(h)
6   Dr:                                      [.hh Ah:: well-?
7   Pt:    .HHH
8   Dr:    We'll (0.7) look inta tha[t.=See if there's]
9   Pt:                             [Y' know::]
10         (.)
11  Dr:    might be any underlying cau[ses for fatigue.]
```

The patient's remark in lines 3–5, 'But I guess: you know: you're just not supposed ta (2.5) keephh (0.5) burning the candle at both ends all the ti(h)me(h)(h)(h)' gains its potential sense as *an explanation* by virtue of its placement immediately after she confirms (in lines 2–3) that she has been experiencing fatigue (Gill and Maynard, 2006). She invites the physician to hear the remark in context; to ask '*why that now?*' and to interpret what she might mean by speaking those words at just this point (Schegloff and Sacks, 1973: 299). By subsequently proposing to look for 'underlying causes for fatigue', the doctor shows the patient (and thereby us) his sense that she was suggesting a reason for the fatigue and inviting him to look deeper into the matter.

Therefore, a CA researcher would ask how the participants (in the moment-by-moment unfolding of the interaction) make themselves understood and understand each other. This leads to new and powerful ways of analyzing medical encounters. For example, consider patients' 'requests' in health care interactions (for screening tests, or particular treatments). A lexical, semantic, grammatical or other content-based coding system might catch some actual instances of patients' requests. But by attending to the ways that patients place turns of talk in particular locations over the course of the conversation, and to how doctors orient to them, one can capture some of the subtle but pervasive ways that patients effectively make requests and the subtle ways doctors may grant, resist or deny them (Gill et al., 2001; Gill, 2005).

By focusing attention on *both* the speaker and the hearer in an interaction, CA shows how deeply attentive and responsive recipients are to each other on a moment-by-moment basis (Jefferson, 1973; Sacks et al., 1974; Sacks, 1992; Schegloff, 1982; Goodwin, 1979, 1981). When we recognize this, we can note how participants build their talk (and nonvocal aspects of interaction) for their recipients, how they tailor their contributions to recipients' reactions (Goodwin, 1979), and thus how meaning emerges and activities are accomplished over time in interaction.

The privileging of the participants' displayed orientations to each others' actions in CA also precludes the lamination of theoretical assumptions onto the interaction, such as assumptions that all interactions are sites of class domination and that participants will adhere to social/institutional roles. Researchers who work within the tradition of Critical Discourse Analysis focus on the way interaction is shaped by 'macro' social arrangements. Doctors' and patients' socialization within their culture(s), the roles, ideologies, attitudes, values, and bodies of knowledge they have learned and internalized, and their institutional prerogatives (such as power and authority) are thought to affect 'micro' level interactions.[7] This follows Weber's (1949) insight that subjective meanings influence behaviour, and incorporates Parsonian (1951) theories on the impact of norms, values, and social roles in particular on human behaviour. For example, Fisher (1983) and Todd, (1983), having observed that doctors tend to support the status quo and patients often accept medical definitions (even when they are not in their best interests), argue that doctors' and patients' socialization has provided them with these orientations. They contend that 'the medical event becomes much more understandable when relations among abstract worldviews, more concrete structural and organizational contingencies, and medical discourse are considered' (Fisher and Todd, 1983: 7).

The fact that researchers in the Critical Discourse Analysis tradition draw upon theory to make sense of interaction is a function of their research interests: fundamentally, they seek to understand *why* participants in medical interactions behave the way they do. In a CA study, to draw upon theory to interpret why participants behave as they do would displace and preclude the work of discovering *what* they do and *how* it is done. Because of this orientation, the CA approach is a powerful means of understanding the very generation of social arrangements that Critical Discourse Analysts use as explanatory resources: asymmetric social relationships, rights and obligations, power, and authority (Wetherell, 1998, Schegloff, 1997).

Consider the following extract from an interaction between a primary care physician and patient. Some researchers might seek to explain the participants' behaviour, by considering how their actions are influenced by factors such as their respective beliefs, understandings, and knowledge, which were themselves products of their gender role socialization (the doctor and patient are both female), their institutional statuses (patient, doctor), and so forth. In contrast, when employing CA, one's focus shifts from explaining why to understanding *what* and *how*. The analyst focuses on documenting how speakers organize their utterances and embodied actions (such as gestures, gaze, and posture) so that recipients will understand (1) what speakers are doing and (2) why they (recipients) are being invited, compelled, allowed (etc.) to do in return. Therefore, the specific focus is on the endogenous organization of the interaction itself, especially the fundamental social resources – such as the positioning of utterances in the stream of conversation over time – that the participants use to make their actions recognizable and understandable to each other.

Prior to the exchange the patient reported having dry skin on her face. The doctor examined her and suggested it could be due to 'sun damage'. The patient countered, reporting that she did not get very much sun exposure, and speculated whether it could be related to working in front of a computer or to 'age'.

Claiming not to know what she was looking at, the doctor offered to refer the patient to a dermatologist and after some ensuing talk about dermatological procedures, the doctor turned towards her desk and began writing in the patient's chart. It is at this moment that the patient raises the matter of the relationship between dry skin and hormones (lines 1–4). We will focus on just a few key features of the practice she uses to raise the explanation and what ensues, to illustrate what the CA approach can yield.

Example 2

(Gill and Maynard, 2006:129)

```
(12) [9:539]

1  Pt:  The only thing I was wondering if dere
        is .hhhhh you kno:w
2       ah::n (2.0) ((doctor turns from desk to look
        at patient))
3       hormone deficiencies or something like this
        that it (0.6)
4       (>°you know°<) that dries your skin out too.
5       (0.5)
6  Dr:  °Mm°
7       (0.5)
8  Dr:  Tch .hhh ah:m
9       (0.8)
10 Pt:  Or no[t too much
11 Dr:  [tch There are some hormone problems like thyroid
12      p[roblems]=
13 Pt:  [°Mm hm°] ((nodding))
14 Dr:  =which can do tha:t. Um we've never found that
        (.) on you
15      before.
```

While the non-fluent nature and general discontinuity of the patient's turn at lines 1–4 might seem to indicate that she is unsure of herself or hesitant about what she is saying, (and perhaps intimidated by the doctor's authority), upon closer inspection, one can see that the patient designs her turn in a way that invites the doctor to attend to her. The doctor is facing the desk, writing in the patient's chart. The patient begins her utterance by proposing that she has a question to ask: 'The only thing I was wondering if dere is', and at the precise location where she could be expected to produce the topic of her inquiry, she delays the continuation of the turn by taking a long inbreath, saying 'you kno:w ah::n', and pausing for two seconds. The doctor abandons her writing and turns to face the patient. Thus, features of the patient's turn that might seem to be evidence that she is following the traditional (i.e., submissive) patient role, can be understood in terms of what they accomplish as actions: they attract the doctor's attention away from writing and on to the patient (Goodwin, 1980, 1981).

Having obtained the doctor's attention, the patient continues with her turn. As a whole, the turn is a speculation about the relationship between hormone problems and dry skin: the patient asks whether hormone deficiencies exist that dry 'your' skin. By structuring it this way, the patient offers the doctor an opportunity to respond to it as a generic (i.e., hypothetical) question and tell her whether dry skin can ever be related to hormones. However, by placing the speculation within an environment where they have been considering possible causes for the skin problem, the patient provides for it to be heard as a candidate explanation for *her own* skin condition. She thus gives the doctor an alternative option: to respond to it as a nongeneric question and to address the issue of whether *she* has hormone problems that could be causing the dry skin. Using this practice, the patient cautiously invites the doctor to explore a potential explanation for the skin problem (Gill and Maynard, 2006).

At a point where it would be relevant for the doctor to respond to the patient's speculation, there are a number of features (such as silences) that serve to delay the production of a response (lines 5–9). The patient demonstrably treats the delay as a harbinger of *disagreement*. Evidence for this claim can be found on line 10, where the patient modifies her speculation with 'or not too much', a move that may make it possible for the doctor to produce an agreement (Pomerantz, 1984a; Sacks, 1987). Here we see the crucial role of temporality in interaction as well as the impact of recipients' responses on speakers' in-course actions; participants themselves treat the timing of recipients' responses (e.g., whether they occur immediately or not) as a resource for gauging their likely reactions, and they may backtrack on a stance, shore up a claim, and in other ways modify the actions they were in the midst of doing and thus change the response implications for the recipient even as he or she is in the midst of responding (Pomerantz, 1984a, 1984b).

In partial overlap with the patient's modification, the doctor initially responds to the patient's speculation as if it were a generic question about the possibility that hormone deficiencies could cause dry skin. She confirms that it is possible, citing an example of a hormone problem that could cause dry skin ('There are some hormone problems like thyroid problems which can do tha:t'.). However, the next component of the doctor's turn treats the patient's speculation as nongeneric. She responds as if the patient had implied that she might have hormone deficiencies herself, and that they could be causing the skin problem: 'Um we've never found that (.) on you before'. Note that the doctor never officially asserts that hormone problems *are not* causing the patient's dry skin. Rather, by 'citing the evidence' (Maynard, 2004) that previous lab tests have not revealed hormone problems, she invites the patient to hear it as an unlikely possibility in her case.

By giving detailed attention to the particulars of the talk and other behaviour in this interaction, we see how the patient exhibits agency in directing the doctor's attention to a potential cause for her skin problem, and how the doctor manages to cast it as unlikely without dismissing it entirely. By focusing on the endogenous organization of such interactions we can begin to see how the 'social fact' of a medical diagnosis emerges from the moment-by-moment actions of the doctor and the patient. In the next section, we discuss how attending to the participants' orientation to each other's epistemic rights and responsibilities provides a fine-grained understanding of asymmetry and 'authority' in health care encounters.

THE SOCIAL EPISTEMICS OF KNOWLEDGE, EXPERIENCE AND SENSATIONS

By attending to the particulars of the talk and other behaviour, CA reveals how patients and doctors interactionally manage central issues in health care (Beach, 2005; Boyd, 1998; Greatbatch et al., 1995; Haakana, 2001). In and through these discussions they also manage who has what rights to make what sorts of medical assertions. Given CA's emphasis on participants' activities and how they are jointly produced, it might seem surprising that conversation analysts would investigate topics such as knowledge asymmetries in medical encounters. The surprise would be justified if CA researchers treated knowledge as an external factor that affected interaction, as in numerous studies of asymmetry in medicine (e.g., Tannen and Wallat, 1986; Paget, 1983; Cicourel, 1983). Drew (1991) notes that in these studies:

> ... the analytical dimensions associated with asymmetry of knowledge in institutional settings appear to be that by virtue of exogenous factors, participants do not share access to the same body of knowledge; and because that knowledge is consequential for some decision or outcome, this works to the disadvantage of the one who does not have access to it. And the communicative effects of such asymmetries are detected by the analyst locating instances of the participants' mutual incomprehension, even though they may have been unaware at the time of such breakdowns (Drew, 1991:25).

However, the CA approach treats knowledge itself as a social phenomenon. As Drew explains, conversation analysts examine how participants *orient to* what they 'know' in interaction with one another. This reveals the social (i.e., *interactional*) genesis and management of knowledge and knowledge asymmetries:

> Where ... one is put at some disadvantage by the other, that is achieved interactionally. Furthermore, the ways in which knowledge asymmetries are consequential for conversational interaction arise from speakers' orientations to such asymmetry. Thus we are looking for ways in which asymmetries of knowledge are demonstrably relevant to the participants in the design of their talk (Drew, 1991:26).

When using this approach, the analyst focuses on the orientations towards knowledge that the participants display to one another (rather than on their 'cognitive states'). Participants' public displays of knowledge (and the *grounds* for their knowledge) are consequential for their interactions with one another, and these are not equivalent to the type and amount of knowledge they 'actually' have (cf. Wittgenstein, 1953, 1958).

In addressing the question, 'what is causing the patient's illness?' during the medical visit, participants display an orientation to a set of rights and obligations in regard to knowledge. Conversation analysts have investigated how patients and physicians orient to the boundaries of their respective 'legitimate' realms of knowledge regarding their bodies and medicine (Drew, 1991; Gill, 1998, 2005; Gill et al., 2001; Gill and Maynard, 2006; Maynard, 1991; Pomerantz et al., 2007).

For instance, consider Maynard's analysis of the perspective display series in clinical interactions. A physician, about to give parents bad news regarding the cognitive testing of their child, starts by asking them, 'What do you see as – as his difficulty?' (Maynard, 1991: 468). As Maynard points out, this move by the doctor operates as a 'perspective display invitation', and gets the parents to offer an assessment of their child to which the doctor can respond, and in responding, tailor the specific delivery of diagnostic news. Note that this method of 'setting up' the delivery of diagnostic news allows the news delivery to incorporate aspects of the parents' view, knowledge and experience. The doctor's professional epistemic authority is not simply asserted over the parents' knowledge and experience, but, as much as possible, is tailored to it (Maynard 2003). Thus one way professional epistemic authority is asserted and sustained is to fold into it (as much as possible) lay experience and expertise. This relationship between professional and lay bases of knowledge regarding health and illness is more refined and subtle than theory would predict, and can only be elucidated via detailed analysis of the participants' own displayed orientations during actual health care interactions.

Similarly, conversation analysts have investigated how patients (or their surrogates, such as parents of children) orient to boundaries regarding their rights to ask for medical services, and to disagree with professional medical advice (Costello and Roberts, 2001; Gill, 1998; Heath, 1992; Stivers, 2005a, 2005b, 2006, 2007). For example, in an analysis of how parents sometimes resist doctors' treatment recommendations, Stivers (2005b) shows that the predominant methods of parental resistance are quite subtle and indirect, e.g., withholding acceptance of the doctor's advice (2005b). Through this indirect mode of resistance, parents simultaneously pay deference to the professional authority and expertise of the doctor, while exerting their own authority, (as parents), implicitly to pass judgment on the acceptability of the advice.

Returning to Example 2, note that when the patient invites the doctor to explore a candidate explanation for the skin problem (lines 1–4), she treats the potential causal link between hormone deficiencies and dry skin (as well as the actual causal link between hormone deficiencies and *her* dry skin) as things the doctor has both the right and the obligation to know about. The doctor also orients to this right and obligation. However, there is another side to the practice the patient employs, which is part of the unique texture of doctor–patient interaction made visible by CA. When patients make such inferences (rather than forthright claims) about what causes their illnesses, they can safely direct their doctors' attention towards diagnostic possibilities, and simultaneously exhibit attention to the logic of medical inquiry (Gill, 1998). It is CA's focus on sequences of action – attention not only to the actions utterances themselves do, but also to what responses they call for or permit in return, and how these responses figure in the very constitution of actions *as, recognizably, particular actions* – that permits such findings.

Another outcome of CA investigations into asymmetries of knowledge is the finding that they are not always tipped 'in favour' of the doctor. Both doctors and patients treat the latter as having the right and the obligation to know about their personal health experiences – how they feel, where pains and other sensations are located, when they began, and the like, a realm that doctors can only access via their questions (Boyd and Heritage, 2006; Drew, 1991; Gill, 1998; Halkowski, 2008; Heritage and Robinson, 2006; Gill et al., 2010). Through patients' reports of their symptoms (Halkowski, 2006; Heritage and Robinson, 2006), doctors' questions and patients' responses (Boyd and Heritage, 2006; Halkowski, 2008) and other interactional practices, participants display and draw upon patients' license to make particular assertions and observations about their own bodies.

However, the 'license' patients have to own and report their bodily experiences is still itself subject to social (i.e., interactional) management, and patients do extensive work to show that they are responsible and appropriate experiencers of their bodily sensations (Hilbert, 1984). For instance, when patients narrate to their doctor the discovery of new symptoms, they regularly do so in a manner that casts the symptoms' discovery as 'unmotivated', 'accidental', or 'out-of-the-blue', while simultaneously conveying the sense that they were appropriately monitoring their own health (Halkowski, 2006: 110–111). Through these two aspects of patients' narratives of new symptom discovery, they display themselves to the doctor as 'reasonable patients' (neither excessively attentive nor inattentive to bodily sensations). This analysis of patients' new symptoms reports thus helps to reveal the interactional bases for a 'social epistemics of sensation' (Halkowski, 2006:110).

The interactional practices through which these rights and obligations to knowledge, experience, and sensation are managed are the very practices that serve partially to constitute our sense of institutional identities such as 'doctor' and 'patient'. This is part of the interactive work through which these identities emerge or come into view (Hilbert, 1981, 1992; Halkowski, 1990; Zimmerman and Boden, 1991). These interactional practices are also, then, partially constitutive of the institutional setting: 'a clinic', 'a hospital', etc. (Drew and Heritage, 1992). A primary focus on people's activities in interaction, including their precise temporal details, gives us a deeper view into the social constitution of things we might otherwise theoretically reify or essentialize (Pollner, 1979, 1987; Maynard and Wilson, 1980).[8]

The foregoing examples of CA research on health care interactions demonstrate some of the characteristics of the approach which make it especially useful to those who wish to address policy, management, and professional practice questions in health care. CA focuses on the actual, moment-by-moment pro-duction (by providers, patients, family members, and others) of health care interactions. This focus on people's actual interactive practices and behaviours allows the researcher to make discoveries that might not be anticipated (or demanded) by theory, ideology, or even common sense. Thus, the sorts of research questions for which a conversation analytic approach is best suited are those that have at their centre a concern with how some actions or sequences of actions *actu-ally unfold* in health care interaction. For example, CA provides a means to discover how health care policy is being implemented in practice, during interac-tions between medical professionals (Boyd, 1998) and between clinicians and patients or their parents (Pilnick and Coleman, 2003; Butler et al., 2010). It can uncover the dynamics involved in negotiations surrounding sensitive issues such as HIV status (Kinnel and Maynard, 1996), difficult diagnostic news (Lutfey and Maynard, 1998), genetic abnormalities (Pilnick, 2002), lack of physical compe-tence (Parry, 2004), and the management of chronic illness (Lutfey, 2004).

Nevertheless, some of the most profound studies started with no particular practical or programmatic question in mind. Instead, they started with the moti-vation to investigate how some aspect of health care interaction occurs, thus holding back from any commonsense presumption that we know what parts of health care interactions are deep, interesting and important. These presumptions short circuit analysis, and can prevent us from making discoveries that change our understanding of health care processes. They can also prevent us from learn-ing how the participants address interactional problems. Indeed, before some CA studies of health care were initiated, there was no sense or hunch that a particular solution to a problem was nesting in some quiet corner of these interactions. These participant-generated solutions can be deeply instructive for health care providers and those who are involved in physician education and training, as well as patients and their advocates.

For instance, the series of studies of clinicians' descriptions of what they are seeing, hearing, or feeling during physical examinations started from no particu-lar *practical* problem or question, but simply from an interest in what sorts of talk and action physicians engaged in the midst of physical exams (Heritage and Stivers, 1999; Stivers, 2005a, 2005b, 2006, 2007). With that focus, the research-ers uncovered what turned out to be a rather powerful tool for the very important practical problem of how to lessen the number of unwarranted prescriptions of antibiotics (see Stivers, 2007).

CONCLUSION

In this chapter, we have focused on two foundational aspects of conversation analysis, and have shown how they inform CA research on doctor-patient encounters. First, for interaction to be deeply understood, we must give sharp attention to its irremediably temporal character – the fact that every action occurs in the flow of time, following some actions and preceding others. That actions occur in temporal sequences fundamentally shapes the character of each and every act. The second foundational aspect we have focused on emerges from the first: every action in human interaction is profoundly social. As Volosinov puts it:

> The stylistic shaping of an utterance is shaping of a social kind, and the very verbal stream of utterances, which is what the reality of language actually amounts to, is a social stream. Each drop of that stream is social, and the entire dynamics of its generation is social (Volosinov, 1973: 93–94).

Interaction is more than a conduit for information and more than a mirror upon which larger social dynamics are reflected. If one uses a conversation analytic approach, each action in the interaction becomes a potential phenomenon for detailed analysis. By *exploring* these phenomena we can illuminate social processes in health care that might otherwise go unnoticed. Such a perspective is vital if we want to analytically recover how each (always contingent) aspect of health care interaction is generated, maintained, and changed. By attending closely to features of the interaction itself – investigating the social practices the participants use to achieve their actions and activities – we can gain a much deeper appreciation of health care delivery.

NOTES

1 This insight was pioneered by a number of scholars, most prominently Mills 1940, Wittgenstein 1953, 1958, Austin 1962, and Sacks 1992.

2 'Interaction process analysis' is a method of coding interaction originally developed by Bales (1950) to code behaviour in small groups and later adapted to the study of doctor–patient interaction (see Heritage and Maynard, 2006).

3 For an example of the types of behaviors coded by researchers using the Roter system, see: www.acgme.org/outcome/downloads/IandC_9.pdf.

4 A fascination with temporality has possessed philosophers for ages, and a few scholars of interaction and communication have been equally possessed by it, puzzling over its implications. See Augustine's *Confessions* (Book 11, Chapt 27). Cf. W. Ong, 1967, 1969, 1982.

5 Stanley Fish persuasively argued that readers make sense of texts in a similar fashion. In the midst of reading, the reader makes a provisional sense – a sense that the very next sentence, clause or word might adjust, alter or completely undercut (Fish, 1997[1967]: 23, 30–34).

6 The insight that participants in conversation make and derive meaning from the positioning of utterances was crucial to the work that Sacks, Schegloff, and Jefferson did in their initial investigations into the organization of human interaction (Sacks, 1992; Schegloff, 1968; Jefferson, 1973). As Rawls put it:

> … The ordering features of talk – the placement of utterances – is a huge and essential tool that people use to render their 'thoughts' in a mutually intelligible form. And they never manage this without having the sequential back and forth character of interaction change what they mean. That is, what they will have meant in the end, even to themselves, will be what emerges from a collaborative sequential production, not what they thought they meant before the sequential series was produced (Rawls, 2005: 175).

7 Heritage and Maynard (2006) call this tradition 'microanalysis', and note that it was also inspired by the Chicago School of ethnography and pioneering studies of professionalization within

medicine (e.g., Freidson, 1970); it includes the work of researchers such as Fisher, (1984), Mishler (1984), Todd (1989), and Waitzkin (1991). By contrast with this work, for review articles on CA studies of medical interaction, see Heritage and Maynard (2006b), Maynard and Heritage (2005), Pilnick, Hindmarsh and Gill (2009), and Halkowski (forthcoming).

8 CA takes a unique 'field' perspective towards interaction, rather than a perspective that would privilege the 'objects' in the interactional field (McDermott and Baugh, 1992; Halkowski 1992, 1999). This is the logical outgrowth of Goffman's (1967: 3) statement of the need to make interaction *itself* our analytic focus: 'not, then, men and their moments. Rather, moments and their men'.

REFERENCES

Atkinson, J.M. and J. Heritage (1984) *Structures of Social Action: Studies in Conversation Analysis*. Cambridge: Cambridge University Press.

Augustine of Hippo (2006) *Confessions* (trans. Garry Wills). New York: Penguin Classics.

Austin, J.L. (1962) *How to Do Things with Words: The William James Lectures Delivered at Harvard University in 1955*. Oxford: Clarendon.

Bales, R.F. (1950) *Interaction Process Analysis: A Method for the Study of Small Groups*. Reading, MA: Addison-Wesley.

Beach, Wayne A. (2005) 'Disclosing and Responding to Cancer "Fears" During Oncology Interviews', *Social Science and Medicine*, 60: 893–910.

Boyd, Elizabeth (1998) 'Bureaucratic Authority in the "Company of Equals": the Interactional Management of Medical Peer Review', *American Sociological Review*, 62(2): 200–24.

Boyd, Elizabeth and J. Heritage (2006) 'Taking the History: Questioning During Comprehensive History Taking'. In John Heritage, Douglas W. Maynard, (eds) *Communication in Medical Care: Interaction between Primary Care Physicians and Patients* (pp. 151–84). Cambridge: Cambridge University Press.

Butler, Carly, Susan Danby, Michael Emmison and Karen Thorpe (2010) 'Managing Medical Advice-Seeking in Calls to a Child Health Line'. In Alison Pilnick, Jon Hindmarsh, and Virginia Teas Gill (eds) *Communication in Healthcare Settings: Policy, Participation and New Technologies* (pp. 31–47). Blackwell Publishers.

Cicourel, A. (1983) 'Language and the Structure of Belief in Medical Communication'. In S. Fisher and A. Todd (eds) *The Social Organization of Doctor–Patient Communication*. Washington, DC: Center for Applied Linguistics.

Costello, B. and F. Roberts (2001) 'Medical Recommendations as Joint Social Practice', *Health Communication*, 13(3; July 2001): 241–60.

Drew, P. (1991) 'Asymmetries of Knowledge in Conversational Interactions'. In I. Markova and K. Foppa (eds) *Asymmetries in Dialogue*. Hemel Hempstead: Harvester Wheatsheaf.

Drew, P and J. Heritage (eds) (1992) *Talk at Work: Interaction in Institutional Settings*. Cambridge: Cambridge University Press.

Fish, Stanley (1997[1967]) *Surprised by Sin: The Reader in Paradise Lost*. Cambridge, MA: Harvard University Press.

Fisher, Sue (1984) 'Doctor–Patient Communication: A Social and Micro-Political Performance', *Sociology of Health and Illness*, 6: 1–27.

Fisher, Sue and Alexandra Dundas Todd (1983) 'Introduction: Communication and Social Context – Toward Broader Definitions'. In S. Fisher and A. Todd (eds) *The Social Organization of Doctor–Patient Communication* (pp. 3–17). Washington, DC: Center for Applied Linguistics.

Friedson, E. (1970) Profession of Medicine: A Study of the Sociology of Applied Knowledge. NY: Dodd, Mead and Company.

Garfinkel, Harold (1984[1967]) *Studies in Ethnomethodology*. London: Polity Press.

Gill, V. (1998) 'Doing Attributions in Medical Interaction: Patients' Explanations for Illness and Doctors' Responses', *Social Psychology Quarterly*, 61(4; Dec 1998): 342–60.

Gill, V. (2005) 'Patient "Demand" for Medical Interventions: Exerting Pressure for an Offer in a Primary Care Clinic Visit', *Research on Language and Social Interaction*, 38(4; Jan 2005): 451–79.

Gill, Virginia, T. Halkowski and F. Roberts (2001) 'Accomplishing a Request Without Making One: A Single Case Analysis of a Primary Care Visit', *Text*, 21 (1/2; 2001): 55–81.

Gill, Virginia Teas and Douglas W. Maynard (1995) 'On "Labelling" in Actual Interaction: Delivering and Receiving Diagnoses of Developmental Disabilities', *Social Problems*, 42: 11–13.

Gill, Virginia and D. Maynard (2006) 'Explaining Illness: Patients' Proposals and Physicians' Responses'. In John Heritage, Douglas W. Maynard, (eds) *Communication in Medical Care: Interaction Between Primary Care Physicians and Patients* (pp. 115–50). Cambridge: Cambridge University Press.

Gill, V. T., A. Pomerantz, and P. Denvir (2010) 'Preemptive resistance: Patients' participation in diagnostic sense-making activities'. *Sociology of Health and Illness*, 32(1): 1–20(20).

Goffman, E. (1967) *Interaction Ritual: Essays in Face to Face Behavior. Chicago: Aldine.*

Goodwin, C. (1979) 'The Interactive Construction of a Sentence in Natural Conversation'. In G. Psathas (ed.) *Everyday Language: Studies in Ethnomethodology* (pp. 97–121). New York: Irvington.

Goodwin, C. (1980) 'Restarts, Pauses, and the Achievement of Mutual Gaze at Turn-Beginning', *Sociological Inquiry*, 50(3–4): 272–302 (special double issue on language and social interaction, edited by Don Zimmerman and Candace West).

Goodwin, C. (1981) *Conversational Organization: Interaction Between Speakers and Hearers.* New York: Academic Press.

Greatbatch, David, Christian Heath, Peter Campion, and Paul Luff (1995) 'How Do Desk-top Computers Affect the Doctor–Patient Interaction?', *Family Practice*, 12/1: 32–6.

Haakana, Markku (2001) 'Laughter as a Patient's Resource: Dealing with Delicate Aspects of Medical Interaction', *Text*, 21: 187–219.

Halkowski, T. (1990) '"Role" as an Interactional Device', *Social Problems*, 1990, 37(4): 564–77.

Halkowski, T. (1992) 'Hearing Talk: Generating Answers and Accomplishing Facts', *Perspectives on Social Problems*, Vol. 4 (pp. 25–45). Stamford, CT: JAI Press.

Halkowski, T. (1999) 'Achieved Coherence in Aphasic Narrative', *Perspectives on Social Problems*, Vol. 11 (pp. 261–76). Stamford, CT: JAI Press.

Halkowski, T. (2006) 'Realizing the Illness: Patients' Narratives of Symptom Discovery'. In J. Heritage and D. Maynard (eds) *Communication in Medical Care: Interaction Between Primary Care Physicians and Patients* (pp. 86–114). Cambridge: Cambridge University Press.

Halkowski, T. (2008) 'Approximation Elicitors and Accountability in Pursuit of Amounts'. Presented at the Annual Meeting of the National Communication Association, November 21, 2008, San Diego, CA.

Halkowski, T. (forthcoming) 'Medical Discourse', in Continuum Companion to Discourse Analysis, Ken Hyland and Brian Paltridge (eds)., London: Continuum International Publishing Group Ltd.

Hall, Judith, Irish, Julie, Roter, Debra, Ehrlich, Carol, and Miller, Lucy (1994) 'Gender in Medical Encounters: An Analysis of Physician and Patient Communication in a Primary Care Setting', *Health Psychology*, 13(5): 384–92.

Heath, C. (1992) 'The Delivery and Reception of Diagnosis in the General-Practice Consultation'. In Drew, P. and Heritage, J. (eds) *Talk at Work: Interaction in Institutional Settings.* Cambridge: Cambridge University Press.

Heritage, J. (1984) *Garfinkel and Ethnomethodology.* Cambridge, UK: Cambridge University Press.

Heritage, John and Douglas Maynard (2006) *Communication in Medical Care: Interaction Between Primary Care Physicians and Patients.* Cambridge: Cambridge University Press.

Heritage, J. and J. Robinson (2006) 'Accounting for the Visit: Giving Reasons for Seeking Medical Care'. In J.Heritage and D.Maynard (eds.) *Communication in Medical Care: Interactions between Primary Care Physicians and Patients* (pp. 48–85). Cambridge: Cambridge University Press.

Heritage, J. and Tanya Stivers (1999) 'Online Commentary in Acute Medical Visits: A Method of Shaping Patient Expectations', *Social Science and Medicine*, 49: 1501–17.

Hilbert, Richard (1981) 'Toward an Improved Understanding of "Role"', *Theory and Society*, 10(2): 207–26.

Hilbert, Richard (1984) 'The Acultural Dimensions of Chronic Pain: Flawed Reality Construction and the Problem of Meaning', *Social Problems*, 31(4; Apr, 1984): 365–78.

Hilbert, Richard (1992) *The Classical Roots of Ethnomethodology*. Chapel Hill, NC: University of North Carolina Press.

Jefferson, Gail (1973) 'A Case of Precision Timing in Ordinary Conversation: Overlapped Tag-Positioned Address Terms in Closing Sequences', *Semiotica*, 9: 47–96.

Kinnell, Anne Marie, and Douglas W. Maynard (1996) 'The Delivery and Receipt of Safer Sex Advice in Pre-test Counseling Sessions for HIV and AIDS', *Journal of Contemporary Ethnography*, 35: 405–37.

Lutfey, Karen (2004) 'On Assessment, Objectivity, and Interaction: The Case of Compliance with Medical Treatment Regimens', *Social Psychology Quarterly*, 67(4): 343–68.

Lutfey, Karen and Douglas W. Maynard (1998) 'Bad News in Oncology: How Physician and Patient Talk about Death and Dying without Using those Words', *Social Psychology Quarterly*, 61(4): 321–41.

Maynard, Douglas W. (1991) 'Interaction and Asymmetry in Clinical Discourse'. *American Journal of Sociology*, 97(2): 448–95.

Maynard, Douglas W. (2003) *Bad News, Good News: Conversational Order in Everyday Talk and Clinical Settings*. Chicago: University of Chicago Press.

Maynard, Douglas W. (2004) 'On Predicating a Diagnosis as an Attribute of a Person', *Discourse Studies*, 6: 53–76.

Maynard, D. and S. Clayman (1991) 'The Diversity of Ethnomethodology', *Annual Review of Sociology*, 17 (Aug 1991): 385–418.

Maynard, D. and A. Perakyla (2003) 'Language and Social Interaction'. In J. Delamater (ed.) the *Handbook of Social Psychology*. New York: Kluwer Academic/Plenum Publishers.

Maynard, Douglas, W. and Thomas P. Wilson (1980) 'On the Reification of Social Structure', *Current Perspectives in Social Theory*, 1: 287–322.

McDermott, R.P. and John Baugh (1992) 'A Review of "Erving Goffman: Exploring the Interaction Order"'. In Paul Drew and Anthony Wootton (eds) *Language*, 68(4; Dec 1992): 833–6.

Mills, C.W. (1940) 'Situated Actions and Vocabularies of Motive', *American Sociological Review*, 5(6; Dec 1940): 904–13.

Mishler, E. (1984) *The Discourse of Medicine: Dialectics of Medical Interviews*. NY: Ablex Publishing Corporation.

Ong, W. (1967) *The Presence of the Word: Some Prolegomena for Cultural and Religious History*. New Haven, CT: Yale University Press.

Ong, W. (1969) 'World as View and World as Event', *American Anthropologist*, 71(4; Aug 1969): 634–47.

Ong, W. (1982) *Orality and Literacy: The Technologizing of the Word*. London: Muthuen and Co., Ltd.

Paget, M. (1983) 'On the Work of Talk: Studies in Misunderstanding'. In Sue Fisher, Alexandra, and Dundas Todd (eds) *The Social Organization of Doctor–Patient Communication* (pp. 55–74). Washington, DC: Center for Applied Linguistics.

Parry, Ruth (2004) 'The Interactional Management of Patients' Physical Incompetence: A Conversation Analytic Study of Physiotherapy Interactions', *Sociology of Health and Illness*, 26(7): 976–1007.

Parsons, T. (1951) *The Social System*. New York: Free Press.

Peräkylä, A. (2004) 'Two Traditions of Interaction Research', *British Journal of Social Psychology*, 43: 1–20.

Pilnick, Alison (2002) 'There Are No Rights and Wrongs in These Situations: Identifying Interactional Difficulties in Genetic Counseling', *Sociology of Health and Illness*, 24(1): 66–88.

Pilnick, Alison and Tim Coleman (2003) '"I'll Give Up Smoking When You Get Me Better". Patients' Resistance to Attempts to Topicalize Smoking in GP Consultations', *Social Science and Medicine*, 57: 135–45.

Pollner, M. (1979) 'Explicative Transaction: Making and Managing Meaning in Traffic Court'. In Psathas, G. (ed.) *Everyday Language: Studies in Ethnomethodology* (pp. 229–55). New York: Irvington.

Pollner, M. (1987) *Mundane Reason: Reality in Everyday and Sociological Discourse.* Cambridge: Cambridge University Press.

Pomerantz, A. (1984a) 'Pursuing a Response'. In M. Atkinson and J. Heritage (eds.) *Structures of Social Action: Studies in Conversation Analysis* (pp. 152–63). Cambridge: Cambridge University Press.

Pomerantz, A. (1984b) 'Agreeing and Disagreeing with Assessments: Some Features of Preferred/ Dispreferred Turn Shapes'. In Atkinson, J.M. and J. Heritage (eds) *Structures of Social Action: Studies in Conversation Analysis* (pp. 57–101). Cambridge: Cambridge University Press.

Pomerantz, Anita, V.T. Gill, and P. Denvir (2007) 'When Patients Present Serious Health Conditions as Unlikely: Managing Potentially Conflicting Issues and Constraints'. In Alexa, Hepburn, and Sally Wiggins (eds) *Discursive Research in Practice: New Approaches to Psychology and Interaction* (pp. 127–46). Cambridge: Cambridge University Press.

Rawls, A. (2005) 'Garfinkel's Conception of Time', *Time and Society*, 14(2/3): 163–90.

Reddy, Michael, J. (1979/1993) 'The Conduit Metaphor: A Case of Frame Conflict in Our Language about Language'. In Andrew Ortony (ed.) *Metaphor and Thought* (2nd Edition) (pp. 164–201). Cambridge: Cambridge University Press, 1993.

Roter, Debra and Hall, Judith (1992) *Doctors Talking with Patients/Patients Talking with Doctors: Improving Communication in Medical Visits.* Westpost, CT: Auburn House.

Roter, Debra and Larson, Susan (2002) 'The Roter Interaction Analysis System: Utility and Flexibility for Analysis of Medical Interactions', *Patient Education and Counseling*, 42: 2443–51.

Sacks, H. (1987) 'On the Preferences for Agreement and Contiguity in Sequences in Conversation'. In Button, G. and J.R.E. Lee (eds) *Talk and Social Organization* (pp. 54–69). Clevedon: Multilingual Matters.

Sacks, H. (1992) *Lectures on Conversation*, Vols. 1 and 2. Oxford: Blackwell Publishers.

Sacks, H., E. Schegloff, and G. Jefferson (1974) 'A Simplest Systematics for the Organization of Turn-Taking for Conversation', *Language*, 50(4; Part 1; Dec 1974): 696–735.

Schegloff, E.A. (1968) 'Sequencing in Conversational Openings', *American Anthropologist*, 70: 1075–95.

Schegloff, E.A. (1982) 'Discourse as an Interactional Achievement: Some Uses of "Uh Huh" and Other Things that Come Between Sentences'. In D. Tannen (ed.) *Analyzing Discourse: Text and Talk* (pp. 71–93) (Georgetown University Roundtable on Languages and Linguistics). Washington, DC: Georgetown University Press.

Schegloff, E.A. (1992) 'Repair After Next Turn: The Last Structurally Provided Defense of Intersubjectivity in Conversation', *American Journal of Sociology*, 97(5; Mar 1992): 1295–345.

Schegloff, E.A. (1993) 'Reflections on Quantification in the Study of Conversation', *Research on Language and Social Interaction*, 26: 99–128.

Schegloff, E.A. (1997) 'Whose Text? Whose Context?', *Discourse and Society*, 8(2): 165–87.

Schegloff, E.A. (2007) *Sequence Organization in Interaction: A Primer in Conversation Analysis, Vol. 1.* Cambridge: Cambridge University Press.

Schegloff, E. and H. Sacks (1973) 'Opening Up Closings', *Semiotica*, VIII, 4 (1973): 289–327.

Stivers, T. (1998) 'Prediagnostic Commentary in Veterinarian–Client Interaction', *Research on Language and Social Interaction*, 31(2): 241–77.

Stivers, T. (2005a) 'Non-Antibiotic Treatment Recommendations: Delivery Formats and Implications for Parent Resistance', *Social Science and Medicine*, 60: 949–64.

Stivers, T. (2005b) 'Parent Resistance to Physicians' Treatment Recommendations: One Resource for Initiating a Negotiation of the Treatment Decision', *Health Communication*, 18(1): 41–74.

Stivers, T. (2006) 'Treatment Decisions: Negotiations between Doctors and Patients in Acute Care Encounters'. In John Heritage and Douglas W. Maynard (eds) *Communication in Medical Care: Interaction between Primary Care Physicians and Patients* (pp. 279–312). Cambridge: Cambridge University Press.

Stivers, T. (2007) *Prescribing under Pressure: Parent–Physician Conversations and Antibiotics.* New York, NY: Oxford University Press.

Tannen, D. and Wallat, C. (1986) 'Medical Professionals and Parents: A Linguistic Analysis of Communication Across Contexts', *Language in Society*, 15(3): 295–311.

Todd, Alexandra Dundas (1989) *Intimate Adversaries: Cultural Conflict Between Doctors and Women Patients*. Philadelphia, PA: University of Pennsylvania Press.

Volosinov, V.N. (1973) *Marxism and the Philosophy of Language*. Cambridge, MA: Harvard University Press.

Waitzkin, H. (1991) *The Politics of Medical Encounters: How Patients and Doctors Deal with Social Problems*. New Haven, CT: Yale University Press.

Weber, Max (1949) *The Methodology of the Social Sciences* (trans. E. Shils and H. Finch). New York: Free Press.

Wetherell, M. (1998) 'Positioning and Interpretative Repertoires: Conversation Analysis and Post-Structuralism in Dialogue', *Discourse and Society*, 9(3): 387–412.

Whalen, M. and Zimmerman, D. (1990) 'Describing Trouble: Practical Epistemology in Citizen Calls to the Police', *Language in Society*, 19(4; Dec 1990): 465–92.

Wilson, T. (1970) 'Conceptions of Interaction and Forms of Sociological Explanation', *American Sociological Review*, 35(4; Aug 1970): 697–710.

Wilson, Thomas P. and Zimmerman, D.H. (1986) 'The Structure of Silence Between Turns in Two-Party Conversation', *Discourse Processes*, 9: 375–90.

Wittgenstein, L. (1953) *Philosophical Investigations*. Oxford: Blackwell Publishing.

Wittgenstein, L. (1958) *The Blue and Brown Books: Preliminary Studies for the 'Philosophical Investigations'*. Oxford: Blackwell Publishers.

Zimmerman, D. and Boden, D. (1991) 'Structure-in-Action: An Introduction'. In Boden, D. and Zimmerman, D. (eds) *Talk and Social Structure: Studies in Ethnomethodology and Conversation Analysis* (pp. 4–21). Cambridge: Polity Press.

Zimmerman, D. and Pollner, M. (1970) 'The Everyday World as Phenomenon'. In Jack Douglas (ed.) *Understanding Everyday Life* (pp. 80–103). Chicago: Aldine.

Zimmerman, D. and Weider, L. (1970) 'Ethnomethodology and the Problem of Order'. In Jack Douglas (ed.) *Understanding Everyday Life* (pp. 285–95). Chicago: Aldine.

12

Phenomenology

Carol L. McWilliam

INTRODUCTION

Health, health care and health services delivery are subjective phenomena that are understood, enacted and experienced by human beings. Objective measurement and analysis of these phenomena can inform rational decisions about maximizing health as a social good. However, greater understanding of the complex, multidimensional nature of humanity, human consciousness, subjectivity, intentionality and actions is essential if we are to optimize the quality of health care, health services delivery and, ultimately, the health of individuals, communities and society at large. Phenomenology offers a way for researchers to address these humanistic aims.

At its simplest, phenomenology is the search for meaning or understanding of a phenomenon, that is, anything that appears or presents itself, as one experiences it (Hammond et al., 1991). This approach shifts our focus from things and nature to human beings and their lived worlds and from explaining to clarifying (Giorgi, 2005). Phenomenology allows researchers to gain insights that inform practice strategies and enhance practitioners' understanding of, and sensitivity to, those they serve. For example, the research question, 'What is the meaning of health for those living with chronic illness?' might suggest novel health promotion strategies. Questions like 'What is the nature of caring?' might lead practitioners towards more humanistic health care. Questions like 'What is clients' experience of health services provided by multiple disciplines?' might inform health services delivery, in this instance, enhancing interdisciplinary communication, coordination and collaboration. Questions like 'What is clients' experience of informed consent?' might lead to refinements in policies and procedures, in this instance, guiding the ethical conduct of research. Overall, phenomenology has the potential to promote human development, enhance professional practice, advance the theoretical and practice foundations of disciplines, and inform programmes, services and policies in ways that promote positive change.

Of all the methodologies for qualitative health research, however, phenomenology may be the most confusing (Tymieniecka, 2002a). A review of the literature quickly leaves neophytes asking whether phenomenology is 'social' or 'philosophical' research? Is phenomenology a method or an overarching paradigm for qualitative research? Given that description requires interpretation, and interpretation, description, can phenomenology clearly be categorized as 'descriptive' or 'interpretive?'

The answer to such theory-related questions is simple enough: 'It depends!' Although this answer may not sound helpful, it is genuine. It reflects the phenomenologist's understanding that 'social inquiry is a distinctive praxis, a kind of activity (like teaching) that in the doing transforms the very theory and aims that guide it' (Schwandt, 2000: 190). This chapter presents the theoretical basis and socio-historical evolution of phenomenology. The account is brief and readers seeking a more detailed picture should consult the compendium: *Phenomenology World-Wide: Foundations – Expanding Dynamics – Life Engagements: A Guide for Research and Study* (Tymieniecka, 2002b). Nevertheless, this overview illuminates the construction of the methodological and theoretical agendas of phenomenology and their contribution to current research on health, health care and health service delivery.

THE SOCIO-HISTORICAL CONSTRUCTION OF PHENOMENOLOGICAL APPROACHES

Phenomenological research is generally categorized as transcendental/descriptive; interpretive/hermeneutic/existential; or social. Four philosophers, Husserl, Heidegger, Sartre and Merleau-Ponty, and subsequently, several 'schools', have played a major role in the first two types. The third, social phenomenology, largely rests on the work of a social scientist, Alfred Schutz.

Transcendental/descriptive phenomenology advances human understanding by revealing the nature and organized structure of phenomena. Edmund Husserl (1859–1938), a German philosopher, is commonly portrayed as its founder. Traditionally, science has followed the sixteenth-century French philosopher, Descartes, by emphasizing the differences between mind and body, or consciousness and matter. Husserl dismissed this as 'naïve objectivism' and proposed instead a science-grounded description of ordinary conscious experience devoid of presuppositions. In this view, reality is constituted by our subjective conscious experience of the outer world, not objective facts (Hammond et al., 1991).

The methods of transcendental/descriptive phenomenology are prescribed. The researcher must consciously 'cogitate', suspending, withholding or 'bracketing out' pre-conceptions and setting aside questions of reference, a process called 'epoche' (Balaban, 2002). Two stages of disciplined meditation follow. The first is 'eidetic reduction' which moves from particular facts to general essences, and the second is 'phenomenological reduction' proper, where the phenomenon is brought directly into view undistorted by preconceptions (Bello, 2002; Giorgi and Giorgi, 2003). Through this process, the researcher mentally transcends the specifics of the phenomenon being investigated creating an in-depth description that captures its essence.

Interpretive, *hermeneutic* or *existential* phenomenology was developed in the mid 1900s (Hammond et al., 1991). Husserl's German student, Martin Heidegger (1889–1976), and two French philosophers, Jean Paul Sartre (1905–1985) and Maurice Merleau-Ponty (1908–1961), extended this methodological approach from questions of epistemology, how we know something, to questions of ontology – the nature of existence.

Unlike transcendental phenomenologists, existential phenomenologists do not consider that we can suspend our preconceptions. Rather, they believe that even the researcher's presence shapes the lived experience that is being investigated (Leonard, 1999; Golomb, 2002; Raynova, 2002). Phenomenological understanding is necessarily intersubjective. It arises from the everyday life world where practices and meanings shared between humans become intermingled and merged (Darbyshire et al., 1999).

There are variations in methodology within the interpretive/hermeneutic/existential approach, attributable to differences between the philosophers who contributed to its evolution. Heidegger and Sartre approached phenomenology through a focus on ontology, where humans and the objects of their perceptions were inextricably intertwined. Heidegger saw our existence as an inseparable relationship between Human and World, encapsulated in his term *Dasein,* or *Being-in-the-World*, through which we determine what we will accept as truth, often without being consciously aware that we are doing so (1996[1927]). 'Being' is an experience that takes place in a historical and spatial context (Mackey, 2004), a world that is dynamic and constantly changing (Heidegger, 1962).

Sartre (1943) distinguished between 'being-in-itself', or being as the everyday process of simple existence, and 'being-for-itself', or existing with conscious awareness of, and attention to, one's being. In contrast to Heidegger, Sartre maintained that human action is freely chosen at each moment, rather than constrained by history, so that, through the exercise of will and commitment, we determine our own experience.

Merleau-Ponty, a third existentialist, blended the ontological focus shared by Heidegger and Sartre with Husserl's epistemological orientation (Bourgeois, 2002; Thomas, 2005). He concentrated on theoretical issues related to developmental psychology (Carman and Hansen, 2005), drawing empirical data and theoretical insights regarding the scientific treatment of behaviours from the biological and social sciences. While intersubjectivity, aesthetic experience and pursuit of understanding all formed part of Merleau-Ponty's framework, he believed that these realms of experience are naturally situated within the experiencing person's network of relations (Thomas, 2005). The aim of phenomenology is to access first-hand understanding of human behaviour through perception (Merleau-Ponty, 1962).

Thus, Merleau-Ponty moved beyond Husserl's objective subjectivism to intersubjectivism and historicity, intentionally extending the methodology to the historical and social sciences (O'Neill, 1970). He saw people's paths as intersecting and engaging of one another (Thomas, 2005). This orientation made Merleau-Ponty's approach more directly relevant to what has come to be known as social phenomenology (Bourgeois, 2002; Carman and Hansen, 2005).

Over time, *schools of phenomenology* developed from these various foundations. After the Second World War, the *Dutch or Utrecht School* made an original contribution to the evolution of phenomenology (Levering and van Manen, 2002). Members of this school included an assortment of 'phenomenologically-oriented' psychologists, educators, pedagogues, paediatricians, sociologists, criminologists, jurists, psychiatrists and other physicians, who devoted their efforts to the clarification of the relations between phenomenology and the sciences, particularly human sciences, including religion (G. Van der Leeuw), language (H.J. Po), psychology, pedagogy and psychopathology (See Kockelmans (1987) for examples.). The school's leading representative, F.J. Buytendijk (1887–1974), began his studies in medicine, but subsequently conducted research in physiology and psychology (Mazzu, 2002). The Utrecht School aimed to achieve scientific explication of the intentional structures of human being as situated existence. They adopted humanism and personalism as key concepts and often used poetry and literature to illustrate key points about the pre-reflective sphere of the lifeworld (Levering and van Manen, 2002). Their approach used both description and interpretation to capture human behaviour in relation to its natural and cultural world (Levering and van Manen, 2002; Mazzu, 2002).

Duquesne University in Pittsburgh welcomed European phenomenologists immigrating after the Second World War. The *Duquesne School* adapted Husserl's approach into a North American version of descriptive phenomenology which focussed on capturing fundamental knowledge of the structural essence of phenomena through description.

Phenomenological sociology emerged in the North American context from the work of Alfred Schutz (1899–1959), who had studied law and the social sciences in Vienna. His foundational work, *Der Sinnhafte Aufbau der Sozialen Welt,* was published in 1932 (Wagner, 1970).[1] Schutz was influenced by Max Weber's (1864–1920) causal analyses of empirical socio-historical phenomena, which, while not phenomenological, had introduced an interpretive approach to sociological research (Backhaus, 2002). Following emigration to the United States after the Second World War, Schutz further solidified Weber's synthesis of sociology and phenomenology, developing the concepts of subjectively meaningful action, observational and motivational understanding and subjective and objective inter-pretation, all premised on Weber's conception of subjective meaning and human conduct as social in nature (Wagner, 1970). Schutz also addressed Husserl's failure to confront the problem of intersubjectivity, attributing this to a lack of grounding in the social sciences (Schutz, 1962).

This *social phenomenology* integrated Merleau-Ponty's (1960) essay *The Philosopher and Sociology*, Cicourel's (1964) critique of quantitative methodol-ogy in *Method and Measurement in Sociology*, and Stephan Strasser's (1963) *Phenomenology and the Human Sciences: A Contribution to a New Scientific Ideal* (Backhaus, 2002), as well as the quasi-phenomenological works of early American sociologists, particularly Charles Cooley, William Thomas and George Herbert Mead (Backhaus, 2002). In this version, phenomenology might be better understood as a paradigm than a methodology.

Nevertheless, social phenomenology also evolved as a methodology. Schutz saw subjective meaning as socially constructed, with thought and action as inter-subjective, integral parts of human existence, behaviour, symbols, signs, social groups, institutions and legal and economic systems, all embedded in history, time and space (Janowitz, 1970). The foundational research question therefore was 'What does this social world mean for the observed actor within this world and what did he mean by his acting within it?' (p. 269). Its aim was to overcome the naïve acceptance of the social world and its idealizations and formalizations as readymade and meaningful beyond all question.

The methods of social phenomenology focus on the general principles accord-ing to which the individual organizes his experiences in daily life and the subjective elements of action, from his own point of view. Interpretive analysis begins with identifying the first-level constructs involved in common sense, everyday experience of the intersubjective world (Janowitz, 1970). These may be organized into second level, objective, ideal-typical constructs, the interpreta-tions that a distanced, disinterested observer would make of the 'subjective meaning of the actions of human beings from which the social reality originates' (p. 275). The findings take the form of a non-generalizable, 'typical construction' (p. 314). Thus, like transcendental / descriptive phenomenology, social phenom-enology combines a belief in the objective execution of methods with subjective, interpretive analysis – neither a pure reflection of the positivist nor of the subjec-tivist paradigm.

CURRENT APPROACHES TO PHENOMENOLOGY

Phenomenology has been transformed beyond its original philosophical, and, subsequently, social science disciplinary roots. Although its influence persists in pedagogy and education, the Utrecht School is said to have dissolved when Buytendijk assumed emeritus status in 1957, in the face of the increasing influ-ence of behaviourism in North America, Marxist critical theory in Germany and post-structuralism in France (Levering and van Manen, 2002). However, while there is considerable diversity among European phenomenologists (Sweeney, 2002), 'traditional' phenomenology focused on constructing understanding of pre-reflective experience has persisted (Caelli, 2000).

In North America, developments continue to be inspired by the Utrecht School. More recent work reflects greater sensitivity to the subjective and intersubjective roots of meaning, and the complexity of relations among language, experience, the cultural and gendered context of meaning and the textual dimensions of phenomenological writing and reflection. The work of Max van Manen in Canada, (for example, *Modalities of Body Experience in Illness and Health*, 1998) continues to typify this School. In addition, a range of other perspectives have emerged, combining with and borrowing from other traditions, often only loosely associated with phenomenology's European roots (Sweeney and Carroll, 2002).

Amongst health disciplines in North America, phenomenology has mostly been considered to be either 'descriptive' or 'interpretive/hermeneutic' (Lopez and Willis, 2004; Mackey, 2004) and implemented and/or reported without significant consideration of its philosophical basis. Consequently, it is common to find ambiguity about the purpose, structure and findings of phenomenological work (Lopez and Willis, 2004). Work labelled as Heideggerian, hermeneutic or interpretive (Benner, 1994; Diekelmann, 1992) focuses on interpreting hidden meanings contained within lived experience, to better understand human everydayness (Darbyshire et al., 1999). While these scholars (Benner, 1994; Darbyshire, Diekelmann and Diekelmann, 1999) approach phenomenology as an interpretive methodology focused on the exploration of subjective and/or intersubjective experience, others (Schwandt, 2000) conceptualize phenomenology as an interpretive research paradigm.

'Social phenomenology' is said to have no well-defined group of scholars and no established tradition (Backhaus, 2002). Yet, researchers still include 'social phenomenology' among their current methodologies. One recent author (Aho, 1998) characterizes it as 'how ... the things of the world [are] ordinarily experienced, how ... they [are] thought, felt, recalled and seen by the average person', emphasizing 'social' to indicate that, '... although ... occasionally allud[ing] to the ethical, epistemological and ontological issues raised by phenomenology' (p. 3), there is no intent to address these philosophical issues in any complete way. The aim is simply to represent personal experiences and other primary documents as typical socially constituted patterns (Aho, 1998).

Rather than adopting a specific methodology, several renowned North American sociologists have taken up elements of phenomenological research. The work of Erving Goffman has been described as indirectly influenced by phenomenology and that of Harold Garfinkel, as quite directly influenced (Backhaus, 2002). Ethnomethodology is reported to have been greatly influenced by Garfinkel's engagement with the work of Husserl and professional dialogues with Schutz (Backhaus, 2002) and Aron Gurwitsch, another émigré phenomenologist (Dingwall, personal communication).

Beyond Europe and North America, another recent perspective, from a group of philosophers, political scientists, anthropologists and ethnologists linking Norway, Sweden, Croatia, Australia and New Zealand, also reveals the methodological creativity of researchers. This group has addressed the practical connections between philosophical traditions and contemporary cultural analysis. In this re-presentation, phenomenology focuses on the relationships of people, things and places just as they are experienced and created, thus enabling us to see culture as something that is constructed through 'use' in everyday activities (Frykman and Gilje, 2003, p. 48).

While a comprehensive overview of the socio-historical evolution of postmodernism and post-structuralism is beyond the scope of this chapter, these paradigms have also been identified as 'new phenomenologies of politics, agency and culture' (Doyle, 2001). Amongst researchers in the health disciplines, this specialized application of the interpretive tradition in phenomenology is labelled critical hermeneutics, an approach founded on the assumption that any act of interpretation is influenced by socially accepted ways of viewing reality (Thompson, 1990). These forms of social phenomenology are grounded through the work of Hegel, Derrida and others back to Husserl, Heidegger (Schurmann, 1990; Vahabzadeh, 2003), and, in particular, Sartre (Raynova, 2002) and Merleau-Ponty (Doyle, 2001). 'Phenomenological themes, including the materiality of speech, the decentered nature of the subject, the retroactive quality of being in time, and the visible as a phenomenon we inhabit' (Doyle, 2001, p. xxxii) are said to be attributes of these more recent constructions.

Present-day research on health issues reflects the diversity of methodological and theoretical agendas contained within the phenomenological tradition. Nevertheless, these studies do share certain commonalities.

DYNAMIC CONTRIBUTIONS: THE VALUE OF ARTISTIC EXPRESSION IN HEALTH RESEARCH

It is extraordinary that phenomenological research survives in investigations of health, health care and health services delivery today. In a predominantly capitalistic world, health, health care and health services delivery have been increasingly commodified and objectified (Gallagher, 1988; Pellegrino, 2008). Health has come to be understood not only as the absence of disease, and a state of complete mental, physical and social well being, but also as a 'resource' (WHO, 1986); health care, as a biomedical commodity to be doled out in measured quantities to treat disease, with due attention to cost constraints; and health services delivery, as an exercise in providing that commodity within parameters 'benchmarked' to system-driven, standardized outcomes – service access rates; morbidity and mortality rates; adverse incident rates. Thus, while they are very real human phenomena, 'health', 'health care' and 'health services delivery' readily escape critical reflection. In the rapidly changing, information-overloaded context of their daily enactment and experience, from a societal, system and professional service lens, 'health', 'health care' and 'health services delivery' simply 'are what they are'. At the individual level, the same observations about meaning and experience hold true, unless and until, that is, first-hand experience of issues with health, health care and/or health service delivery give cause for reflection.

Nevertheless, such a context also creates a powerful motive for undertaking phenomenological research. Phenomenologists have risen to this challenge, adopting and adapting the socially constructed methodological and theoretical agendas discussed in this chapter. In doing so, these researchers have made major contributions, advancing understanding and discussion of the human condition.

Descriptive phenomenology continues to offer timeless appreciations of health and illness. For example, in work to 'develop a phenomenology of illness', Svenaeus (2000, p. 3) draws on Heidegger's existential theory and Freud's psychological theory, applying a transcendental, Husserlian approach to explicate the existential essence of illness as 'unhomelikeness'. While recognizing the 'danger of a total medicalization of life' (p. 11), Svenaeus illuminates the implications for human understanding and care, opening possible paths for health care beyond biological investigation and treatment. Equally powerfully, building from the work of Husserl, Schutz, Sartre and Merleau-Ponty, Toombs (1993) presents a rigorous social phenomenological account of the meaning of illness, its experience and lived-throughness from the perspectives of patient and physician.

In nursing, several scholars (for example, Mitchell et al., 2005; Aquino-Russell, 2006), have undertaken descriptive phenomenology, inspired by the work of Rosemarie Parse, a leading nursing theorist. Their approach reflects rigorous attention to highly descriptive data subjected to prescribed epistemological analysis–synthesis strategies, creating overarching objectively subjective interpretations or general essences of experiences of health as human becoming. Such findings afford nurses, and indeed all health disciplines, the opportunity to consider and apply a more holistic health-oriented understanding in their practice, one with the potential to broaden 'health' beyond the biomedical model and to deepen 'care' to encompass humanistic elements that are too often missing.

Interpretive/hermeneutic phenomenology grounded in the work of Martin Heidegger (Benner, 1994; Dickinson et al., 2006; Ironside et al., 2003) and Merleau-Ponty (Thomas and Pollio, 2002) also makes an impressive contribution. Many researchers use this methodology to engage research participants in a reflexive, circular process of critical reflection that often elicits creative linkages of empirical, experiential, intuitive and theoretical knowledge invaluable to the development of quality health care. For example, Dickinson et al. (2006) draw on the work of Heidegger (1996[1927]), Arendt (1998[1958]) and Buber (2002) to illuminate the experience of families of children with chronic illness, exposing families' experience of being suddenly thrown into a complex web of health practitioner relationships over which they have little control. Thomas and Pollio (2002) use existential phenomenology to evoke nurses' moral imperative of humanistic caring through rigorous and richly nuanced phenomenological inter-pretations of patients' experiences of illness and illness care.

The findings of these, and other, works deepen our understanding of the expe-rience of health/illness (Ironside et al., 2003; Thomas and Pollio, 2002), health care (Benner, 1994; Thomas and Pollio, 2002) and health services delivery (Dickinson et al., 2006; McWilliam and Ward-Griffin, 2006). However, the research process, in and of itself also contributes to health care. Participants invariably find themselves enlightened by their engagement in reflexive critical reflection and co-creation of understanding related to health, health care or health services delivery. This can be observed directly in Ironside et al.'s (2003) use of narrative pedagogy to co-create new understandings of experiencing chronic illness. In this study, people with chronic illness served as both participants and co-researchers, exploring the meaning of living with chronic illness with nursing students. As participants, these individuals experienced new understand-ings of the possibilities contained within living with their chronic illnesses. As co-researchers, they became teachers of practical wisdom rather than research sub-jects or exemplars, affording nursing students unforgettable practice-enhancing lessons.

Combinations of the epistemological leanings of Husserl's *transcendental phenomenology* and the *ontological orientation* of the existential philosophers also continue to make significant contributions. For example, in *Modalities of Body Experience in Illness and Health*, van Manen (1998) presents an evocative experiential description of the bathing of a hospitalized patient, from both the perspective of the nurse and that of the ill individual, transcending the ontologi-cal experience of each with his own meditation on the bodily experience of the person who is ill or injured. To achieve this aim, van Manen builds on other literature about the phenomenology of the body, creating an intensification of meaning that cannot go unconsidered by nurse-readers who subsequently undertake similar tasks.

Two studies that might be classified as *social phenomenology*, one from the United Kingdom and one from North America, exemplify the value of this phe-nomenological tradition. Both emphasize exploratory sociological research methods, rather than their philosophical underpinnings. In contrast to interpre-tive/hermeneutic phenomenology, but in line with transcendental or descriptive phenomenology, the findings are presented objectively as general essences that capture the description of human experience. In *The Phenomenology of Death, Embodiment and Organ Transplantation*, Haddow (2005) uses Schutz's arguments about the intersubjectivity of thought and action in an investigation of the meaning of personal identity, what is lost at death in relation to the body, the self and relationships with others. She describes four configurations of death, embodiment and organ transplantation that make decisions by potential donors unpredictable. Understanding the lack of clear differentiation between the biological and social meanings of death, and between death and existence can help those working in health care to support donation decisions. Hansen and Hansen (2006) also draw on Schutz (1970) to capture the essence of parents' experience of living with the realities of stimulant medications being used to treat their children's attention deficit hyperactivity disorders. Describing this experience as 'a flux of dilemmas' (p. 1272), enacted as 'a complex balancing act' (p. 1280), Hanson and Hanson convey the intersubjectivity of both thought and action, again potentially guiding supportive care.

This *eclecticism* suggests the value of artistic expression of phenomenological methodologies to inform practice. For example, Stoltz, Willman and Uden (2006) report the meaning of support to family carers of senior relatives in the home setting and Stoltz, Lindholm, Uden and Willman (2006) report the meaning to palliative care nurses of being supportive of family caregivers. These researchers describe a 'phenomenological hermeneutic method inspired by the philosophy of Ricoeur (1976) ... developed and ... further developing at the University of Tromso, Norway, and Umea University, Sweden' (Stoltz et al., 2006, p. 596). Their approach includes the use of narrative as a method for data collection, and an interpretive analysis strategy comprised of recurring phases of 'naïve reading, structural analyses and comprehensive understanding'. The structural analyses are described as the 'explanation of the text'; the comprehensive understanding as the 'interpreted whole' (Stoltz et al., 2006, p. 164). Davidson (2000) explores the nature of agoraphobic sufferers' fears of social spaces by applying the work of Merleau-Ponty to interpretive case study analysis, arguing that 'Merleau-Ponty presents a philosophical problematic that provides a framework for understanding the nuanced vocabulary capable of expressing the existential trauma and spatially mediated experience of the agoraphobic' (p. 655).

Overall, the literature on health, health care and health services delivery provides evidence that this creativity in phenomenological health research is both multi-disciplinary and global in scope (Eggenberger and Nelms, 2007; Nordgren and Asp, 2007; Schmid, 2004). This begs the question – in the name of scholarly work, is there, or should there be, a limit to artistic expression?

KEY 'SILENCES' AND ISSUES

The legitimacy of artistry in the conduct of research continues to challenge phenomenological scholars. Researchers must consciously confront several fundamental issues. The first is the issue of how to re-present the nature and process of phenomenology. The second, more 'silent', issue arises in conjunction with the voice used to re-present phenomenological work in published form. The third constitutes the ultimate academic challenge: Where should scholars with pressing research questions about health, health care and health services delivery take the art of phenomenology?

The *re-presentation of the nature and process of phenomenology* is a persistent issue. Much has been said about the theoretical and methodological misrepresentation of phenomenology (see Caelli, 2000; Crotty, 1996; Paley 1997, 1998, 2005).

Paley (1997) maintains that this misrepresentation includes inadequate attention to both the philosophical roots of phenomenology and the application of methods that bear little resemblance to the eidetic reduction of Husserl. Alternative methods, including those of Colaizzi (1978), Giorgi (1970) and van Manen (1990) are categorized as those of qualitative sociology in general. Paley argues that 'description of meaning' cannot be understood as 'a description of something which 'patterns the specific experience uniquely' and, at the same time, as a description that is "essential to the experience, no matter which specific individual has that experience"' (p. 192).

Such criticisms of false labelling and mixed methods have been directed largely at nurse researchers, whose education has been much more likely to include social sciences than philosophy. Darbyshire et al. (1999) have countered this criticism, arguing that it is premised on a narrow existentialist, misguided and poorly informed view of Heidegger's work. Barkway (2001) argues that the validity of seeking subjective understanding of the experience of the phenomenon, not the phenomenon *per se*, legitimizes a 'new phenomenology' (p. 195). Rapport and Wainwright (2006) suggest that debate regarding the differentiation of transcendental and interpretive phenomenology should be replaced by recognition of the evolution of phenomenology as a research paradigm encompassing the similarities of both perspectives, namely, the understanding of the nature of knowledge and the way in which phenomenologists pursue that knowledge.

Is this a sound resolution of the issue? Most would agree that all variations of phenomenology, by their very nature, and in contrast to scientific research, rely mainly on inductive thinking. Inductive thinking is a creative act, an art form rather than a technique. This conclusion invites further critical reflection. Several questions come to mind. If *doing* phenomenological research is preponderantly a creative act/ art, can its execution be pre-scribed? If it cannot be pre-scribed, will the execution of phenomenology not be unique to the researcher(s) undertaking it? If the researcher's subjectivity is either transcendentally or inter-subjectively a part of the findings arising from phenomenological research, is the researcher not also subjectively engaged in the process of uncovering these findings?

If 'social inquiry is [indeed] a distinctive praxis, a kind of activity (like teaching) that in the doing transforms the very theory and aims that guide it' (Schwandt, 2000, p. 190), and if a fundamental assumption of doing that research is that human beings are unique individuals, each with a unique social–historical–cultural context, one can only expect there will be as many different re-presentations of phenomenology as there are researchers. Layers of human diversity add further complexity to this conclusion. In applying phenomenology, each researcher does so with both a personal and a disciplinary lens, filtering and perceiving knowledge, beliefs and assumptions accordingly. Moreover, in keeping with current understandings of knowledge as something that is co-created and constantly evolving in the context of time, space and disciplinary culture (Ellerman et al., 2001; Yorks, 2005), researchers work with co-investigators and participants. In any such collaboration, inevitably both the conceptualization and the execution of phenomenology also are altered.

Surely, of all qualitative research approaches, phenomenology, so definitely subjective in both process and outcome, invites and indeed, requires, respect for this creativity. Admittedly, any disciplined undertaking of research that changes or evolves its theoretical and/or methodological underpinnings rightfully involves 'conscious deliberate decisions and a clear rationale' (Morse, 1996, p. 468). Even creative acts, to be understood and valued, need explication. Thus, researchers undertaking phenomenology might make more of a contribution through greater effort to explicate the details of what they have elected to do, and why. Laying out the philosophical and methodological foundations on which the work is built is essential to critique of its coherence. Identifying, examining and challenging pre-understandings, presuppositions, fore-structures, preconceptions and prejudices are equally important. However, these are simply the techniques that optimize the creative work that constitutes the re-presentation of phenomenology.

Re-presenting phenomenological work in the literature is a secondary but related, longstanding issue. Scholars of the Chicago School of Sociology are attributed with a legacy of evocative writing in the first-person (Gilgun, 2005). From a theoretical perspective, the reflection of one's own voice in re-presenting phenomenological research quite appropriately addresses the researcher's agency (Harwood, 2006) in transcendental phenomenological research, and its more recent re-incarnation, 'social phenomenology'. Intersubjective interpretive research theoretically invites the use of 'we', as participants' experiences and contributions inform the research question, shape the sampling, data collection, and methods, and co-construct the findings and discussion (Gilgun, 2005). Thus, many scholars who do phenomenology maintain that phenomenological studies should be written in the first person, and often equate the use of 'I' to the 'signature' of their work.

Papers reporting phenomenological investigation often do not reflect this stance, however. Generally speaking, practices related to the use of pronouns vary considerably (Harwood, 2006). Of the fifteen papers cited as examples in this chapter, only two (Haddow, 2005; Svenaeus, 2000), one classified as social phenomenology and the other as transcendental phenomenology, have been published in the first person. Two additional papers (Ironside et al., 2003; Stoltz et al., 2006), more interpretive in nature, have been published largely in the third person, but include the use of 'we' in reporting the methods followed, referring to the collaboration amongst research team members, rather than that with participants. Thus, of the current re-presentations of phenomenology in the health field selected for this chapter, 80 percent have been published in the third person, despite the commonly accepted 'rule'.

In part, these circumstances may reflect the diversity of approaches to phenomenology. Additionally, the hegemony of the Western scientific paradigm and the valuing of objectivity both generally and in the context of the health 'sciences' undoubtedly influence scholars wanting to re-present phenomenology as legitimately scholarly work. Nevertheless, these same scholars undoubtedly are equally aware that publishing phenomenology in the third person brings their academic integrity into question. Anonymous third-person voices have been chastised as 'the God trick' (Haraway, 1988) and more specific to qualitative research, as a form of appropriation of the voices of study participants (Hooks, 1990). Even *The Publication Manual of the American Psychological Association* (American Psychological Association, 2001) states that clarity requires the use of the first person, specifically to indicate participation in one's own investigation. This latter purpose is particularly germane in re-presenting phenomenological research.

Nevertheless, if the art form of phenomenology is to be honoured, this issue also perhaps merits more cautious critical reflection. Scholars' stances in writing are shaped not only by epistemological, methodological and disciplinary leanings, and the larger scientific context in which they work (Harwood, 2006), but also by their personal experiential and tacit knowledge and way of being in the world (Harwood, 2006; Hyland, 2005; Widdowson, 2000). On the one hand, the use of 'I' may be motivated by a declaration of agency (Harwood, 2006), ownership (Hyland, 2001a; MacDonald, 1992), clarity (Harwood, 2006) and a desire to take the reader with oneself (Harwood, 2006; Hyland, 2001b) and 'we' may be used to construct intimacy and involvement with the audience/reader (Harwood, 2005). On the other hand, the use of 'I' and 'we' may intentionally or unintentionally establish the author(s) as the authority, and the audience/reader as the novice in need of enlightenment or direction (Gragson and Selzer, 1990), convey egocentricity and/or disregard for the many others pursuing or having knowledge in the field (Harwood, 2006), and unwittingly undermine the significance of the messages contained within the text (Harwood, 2006).

Writing practices and the use of pronouns are not static or immutable (Atkinson, 2001; Canagarajah, 2002; Ivanic, 1998). Due respect for the creativity of doing phenomenology may also give cause to pause and reflect. Drawing on the analogy of art, one might well ask: If *I/we* have undertaken the task of re-presenting *my/our* work, is that voice not apparent both within and between the lines of the text? Is it the artist's signature (that is, the use of 'I/we') on a painting that makes the work what it is? Does the act of signing one's painting change the re-presentation that the artist intends? Does signature contribute to the authenticity of the work, or is it merely a symbol of authenticity? Does signature change another's appreciation of the art that is portrayed? Does the artist's signature add value beyond its role in commodification (Gallagher, 1988; Pellegrino, 2008) of the work of art? The answers to these questions, which undoubtedly may vary amongst scholars, may not be important. However, asking the questions may help scholars to draw their own conclusions, and to act intentionally and self-directedly, in presenting and defending any re-presentation of phenomenology.

The *challenge of creating the future of phenomenology* will undoubtedly be addressed in part as scholars find answers to these issues. Nevertheless, other considerations also demand attention. Not the least of these is conceptualizing and creating the identity of phenomenological researchers themselves.

Undoubtedly, sociologists may most comfortably re-present phenomenology as social phenomenology, while philosophers may excel in more existential re-presentations. Health professionals may well continue to adopt and adapt both theory and methods of other disciplines in undertaking phenomenological investigation. In the increasingly interdisciplinary, and evolving *transdisciplinary* world of health care, however, there may be merit in focusing across this diversity of lenses, building upon the shared commitment to explore and capture subjective human experience.

Human nature and experience is complex and multidimensional. Human inquiry therefore stands to be advanced by holistically exploring the philosophical, social, psychological, emotional, physical and spiritual dimensions that are inextricably intertwined components. In the current context, health, health care and health services delivery are socially constructed and re-presented in ways that often are all but devoid of subjective human elements. Much of the current 'phenomenological' research in health, health care and health services delivery allows us to 'see' new things intellectually, but does not speak loudly to our 'non-cognitive sensibilities' (van Manen, 1997, p. 345). Hence, Paley (1997; 2005), Crotty (1996) and others may be justifiably incensed, not by our failure to *do* phenomenological research, but by our failure to convey in our written and spoken reports that which we have done.

Albeit with a distinctively Husserlian lens, van Manen (1997) illuminates the characteristics that he believes need to be reflected in qualitative health research texts labelled 'phenomenology': lived-throughness; evocation; intensification; tone and epiphany. Perhaps most importantly, much of the published health research bearing the label of 'phenomenology' does not create an 'epiphany'. That is, these texts do not 'bring about a transformative effect so that [their] deeper meaning makes an edifying appeal to the self of the reader … [being] so strong or striking … [that they] stir us at the core of our being' (p. 357).

Herein lies a challenge. Not only is the field of health, health care and health services delivery firmly entrenched in objective science, but also as the socio-historical evolution of phenomenology portrays, social phenomenologists have never claimed any intent beyond explanation. Phenomenologists from a diversity of other disciplines have also limited their re-presentations to explanation. To complicate matters further, no one, van Manen included, has openly recognized that it is not just the researchers who construct their readers' experiences of their findings, but the 'end users', too, all embedded in this current socio-cultural context. Thus, a more pressing question confronting phenomenology scholars eager to build the field's future may be: How do we speak to an audience for health, health care and health services delivery in ways that create 'feeling understanding'? Perhaps in the context of this Western scientific world, phenomenological researchers need to direct their attention beyond the current focus on theory and method to a focus on creating shared meaning and understanding with due respect and regard for all of its human components.

CONCLUSION: SKETCHING THE POSSIBILITIES FOR TOMORROW'S PHENOMENOLOGISTS

As a theoretical foundation and methodological approach for human inquiry, phenomenology is, at one and the same time, both social science and philosophy, overarching research paradigm and research methodology, description and interpretation. As this chapter has shown, the socio-historical construction of phenomenological approaches to qualitative research has evolved over time and context, creating a current state of the art that reflects diversity, authenticity and importantly, valuable contributions. Thus, phenomenological research holds exciting possibilities for researchers choosing to undertake more creative scholarly work in this field.

Clarification of meaning through careful, considered execution of the art of phenomenology holds the potential to create a deeper understanding of the possibilities of how human beings feel, experience and act in this world, in given circumstances, and in relation to one another. Such understanding often exposes discrepancies between actual lived experience and what that experience is thought to be. At an individual level, critical consideration, and the understanding of unique dimensions of human existence derived from this, holds the potential of human development. At a more global level, understanding holds the potential to inform constructive change in ways that improve the world (Giorgi, 2005).

Given commonly held and enacted understandings, health, health care and health services delivery, now perhaps as never before, demand scholarly phenomenological investigation. This is not to deny the importance of scientific research in this field. It is simply to ensure that the human component inherent in all health, health care and health services delivery is retained, addressed and forever evolving.

NOTE

1 Translated as 'The Phenomenology of the Social World' by George Walsh and Frederick Lehnert. London: Heinemann Educational, 1967.

REFERENCES

Aho, J.A. (1998) The Things of the World: A Social Phenomenology. Westport, CT: Praeger.
American Psychological Association (ed.) (2001) Publications Manual of the American Psychological Association (5th Edition). Washington, DC: Author.
Aquino-Russell, C.E. (2006) 'A Phenomenological Study: The Lived Experience of Persons Having a Different Sense of Hearing', Nursing Science Quarterly, 19(4): 339–48.
Arendt, H. (1998[1958]) The Human Condition (2nd Edition). Chicago, Il: University of Chicago Press.

Atkinson, D. (2001) 'Scientific Discourse Across History: A Combined Multi-Dimensional/Rhetorical Analysis of the *Philosophical Transactions of the Royal Society of London*'. In S. Conrad and D. Biber (eds) *Variation in English: Multi-Dimensional Studies* (pp. 45–65). Harlow, UK: Longman.

Backhaus, G. (2002) 'Phenomenological Sociology'. In Anna-Teresa Tymieniecka (ed.) *Phenomenology World-Wide: Foundations – Expanding Dynamics – Life Engagements: A Guide for Research and Study* (pp. 562–8). Boston: Kluwer Academic Publishers.

Balaban, O. (2002) 'Epoche: Meaning, Objective and Existence in Husserl's Phenomenology'. In Anna-Teresa T. (ed.) *Phenomenology World-Wide: Foundations – Expanding Dynamics – Life Engagements: A Guide for Research and Study* (pp. 103–13). Boston: Kluwer Academic Publishers.

Barkway, P. (2001) '"Michael Crotty and Nursing Phenomenology" Criticism or Critique?', *Nursing Inquiry*, 8(3): 191–5.

Bello, A.A. (2002) 'The Generative Principles of Phenomenology, Their Genesis, Development and Early Expansion'. In Anna-Teresa Tymieniecka (ed.) *Phenomenology World-Wide: Foundations – Expanding Dynamics – Life Engagements: A Guide for Research and Study* (pp. 29–60). Boston: Kluwer Academic Publishers.

Benner, P. (1994) 'The Tradition and Skill of Interpretive Phenomenology in Studying Health, Illness and Caring Practices'. In Patricia Benner (ed.) *Interpretive Phenomenology: Embodiment, Caring and Ethics in Health and Illness* (pp. 99–128). Thousand Oaks, CA: Sage.

Bourgeois, P. (2002) 'Maurice Merleau-Ponty, Philosophy as Phenomenology'. In Anna-Teresa Tymieniecka (ed.) *Phenomenology World-Wide: Foundations – Expanding Dynamics – Life Engagements: A Guide for Research and Study* (pp. 342–83). Boston: Kluwer Academic Publishers.

Buber, M. (2002) *Between Man and Man*. (trans. R. Gregor-Smith). London: Routledge Classics.

Caelli, K. (2000) 'The Changing Face of Phenomenological Research: Traditional and American Phenomenology in Nursing', *Qualitative Health Research* (pp. 366–77). Thousand Oaks, CA: Sage.

Canagarajah, A.S. (2002) *Critical Academic Writing and Multilingual Students*. Ann Arbor: University of Michigan Press.

Carman, T. and Hansen, Mark, B.N. (2005) 'Introduction'. In Carman, T. and Hansen, Mark B.N. (eds) *The Cambridge Companion to Merleau-Ponty* (pp. 1–25). Cambridge, UK: Cambridge University Press.

Cicourel, A.V. (1964) *Method and Measurement in Sociology*. London, UK: The Free Press of Glencoe.

Colaizzi, P.F. (1978) 'Psychological Research as the Phenomenologist Views It'. In R. Valle and M. King (eds) *Existential Phenomenological Alternatives for Psychology*, (pp. 48–71). Oxford, UK: Oxford University Press.

Crotty, M. (1996) *Phenomenology and Nursing Research*. Melbourne, Australia: Churchill Livingstone.

Darbyshire, P., Diekelmann, J., and Diekelmann, N. (1999) 'Reading Heidegger and Interpretive Phenomenology: A Response to the Work of Michael Crotty', *Nursing Inquiry*, 6: 17–25.

Davidson, (2000) 'A Phenomenology of Fear: Merleau-Ponty and Agoraphobic Life-Worlds', *Sociology of Health and Illness*, 22(5): 640–60.

Dickinson, A., Smythe, E., and Spence, D. (2006) 'Within the Web: The Family–Practitioner Relationship in the Context of Chronic Childhood Illness', *Journal of Child Health Care*, 10(4): 309–25.

Diekelmann, N. (1992) 'Learning-as-Testing. A Heideggerian Hermeneutical Analysis of the Lived Experience of Students and Teachers in Nursing', *Advances in Nursing Science*, 14(3): 72–83.

Doyle, L. (ed.) (2001) *Bodies of Resistance: New Phenomenologies of Politics, Agency and Culture*. Evanston, IL: Northwestern University Press.

Ellerman, D., Denning, S., and Hanna, N. (2001) 'Active Learning and Development Assistance', *Journal of Knowledge Management*, 5(2): 171–9.

Eggenberger, S.K., and Nelms, T.P. (2007) 'Being Family: The Family Experience When an Adult Member is Hospitalized with a Critical Illness', *Journal of Clinical Nursing*, 16: 1618–28.

Frykman, J. and Gilje, N. (2003) 'Being There: An Introduction'. In Frykman, Jonas and Gilje, Nils (eds) *Being There: New Perspectives on Phenomenology and the Analysis of Culture* (pp. 7–52). Lund, Sweden: Nordic Academic Press.

Gallagher, E.B. (1988) 'Modernization and Medical Care', *Sociological Perspectives*, 31(1): 59–87.

Gilgun, J. (2005) '"Grab" and Good Science: Writing Up the Results of Qualitative Research', *Qualitative Health Research*, 15(2): 256–62.

Giorgi, A. (2005) 'The Phenomenological Movement and Research in the Human Sciences', *Nursing Science Quarterly*, 18(1): 75–82.

Giorgi, A. (1970) *Psychology as a Human Science: A Phenomenologically Based Approach.* New York: Harper and Row.

Giorgi, A. and Giorgi, B. (2003) 'The Descriptive Phenomenological Psychological Method'. In P.M. Camic, J.E. Rhodes, and L. Yardley (eds) *Qualitative Research in Psychology: Expanding Perspectives in Methodology and Design* (pp. 243–73). Washington, DC: American Psychological Association.

Golomb, J. (2002) 'Sartre's Early Phenomenology of Authenticity in Relation to Husserl'. In Anna-Teresa Tymieniecka (ed.) *Phenomenology World-Wide: Foundations – Expanding Dynamics – Life Engagements: A Guide for Research and Study* (pp. 335–41). Boston: Kluwer Academic Publishers.

Gragson, G. and Selzer, J. (1990) 'Fictionalizing the Readers of Scholarly Articles in Biology', *Written Communication*, 7(1): 25–58.

Haddow, G. (2005) 'The Phenomenology of Death, Embodiment and Organ Transplantation', *Sociology of Health and Illness*, 27(1): 92–113.

Hammond, M., Howarth, J. and Keat, R. (1991) *Understanding Phenomenology.* Oxford, UK: Basil Blackwell.

Hansen, D.L. and Hansen, E.H. (2006) 'Caught in a Balancing Act: Parents' Dilemmas Regarding Their ADHD Child's Treatment with Stimulant Medication', *Qualitative Health Research*, 16(9): 1267–85.

Haraway, D. (1988) Situated Knowledge. *Feminist Studies*, 14: 575–99.

Harwood, N. (2005) '"We Do Not Seem to Have a Theory ... The Theory I Present Here Attempts to Fill This Gap": Inclusive and Exclusive Pronouns in Academic Writing', *Applied Linguistics*, 26(3): 343–75.

Harwood, N. (2006) '(In)appropriate Personal Pronoun Use in Political Science: A Qualitative Study and a Proposed Heuristic for Future Research', *Written Communication*, 23(4): 424–50.

Heidegger, M. (1962) *Being and Time* (trans) Maquarrie, J. and Robinson, E. Oxford, UK: Basil Blackwell.

Heidegger, M. (1996[1927]) *Sein und Seit [Being and Time]* (trans. J Stambaugh). Albany, NY: State University of New York Press.

Hooks, B. (1990) *Yearning: Race, Gender, and Cultural Politics.* Boston: South End.

Hyland, K. (2001a) 'Humble Servants of the Discipline? Self-Mention in Research Articles', *English for Specific Purposes*, 20: 207–26.

Hyland, K. (2001b) 'Bringing in the Reader: Addressee Features in Academic Articles', *Written Communication*, 18(4): 549–74.

Hyland, K. (2005) 'Stance and Engagement: A Model of Interaction in Academic Discourse', *Discourse Studies*, 7(2): 173–92.

Ironside, P. M., Scheckel, Martha, Wessels, Constance, Bailey, Mary, Powers, Sharon, and Seeley, Deana (2003) 'Experiencing Chronic Illness: Co-Creating New Understandings', *Qualitative Health Research*, 13(2): 171–83.

Ivanic, R. (1998) *Writing and Identity: The Discoursal Construction of Identity in Academic Writing.* Amsterdam: John Benjamins.

Janowitz, M. (ed.) (1970) *Alfred Schultz on Phenomenology and Social Relations: Selected Writings.* Chicago: the University of Chicago Press.

Kockelmans, J. (1987) *Phenomenological Psychology. The Dutch School.* Dordrexht: Kluwer (Phaenomenologica 103).

Leonard, V.W. (1999) 'A Heideggerian Phenomenological Perspective on the Concept of the Person'. In E.C. Polifroni and M. Welch (eds) *Perspectives on Philosophy of Science in Nursing: An Historical and Contemporary Anthology* (pp. 315–27). Philadelphia, PA: Lippincott.

Levering, B. and van Manen, M. (2002) 'Phenomenological Anthropology in the Netherlands and Flanders'. In Anna-Teresa Tymieniecka (ed.) *Phenomenology World-Wide: Foundations – Expanding Dynamics – Life Engagements: A Guide for Research and Study* (pp. 274–85). Boston: Kluwer Academic Publishers.

Lopez, K.A. and Willis, D.G. (2004) 'Descriptive versus Interpretive Phenomenology: Their Contributions to Nursing Knowledge', *Qualitative Health Research*, 14(5): 726–35.

MacDonald, S.P. (1992) 'A Method for Analyzing Sentence-Level Differences in Disciplinary Knowledge Making', *Written Communication*, 9(4): 533–69.

Mackey, S. (2004) 'Phenomenological Nursing Research: Methodological Insights Derived from Heidegger's Interpretive Phenomenology', *International Journal of Nursing Studies*, 42: 179–86.

Mazzu, A. (2002) 'The Development of Phenomenology in Belgium and the Netherlands'. In Anna-Teresa Tymieniecka (ed.) *Phenomenology World-Wide: Foundations – Expanding Dynamics – Life Engagements: A Guide for Research and Study* (pp. 265–73). Boston: Kluwer Academic Publishers.

McWilliam, C.L. and Ward-Griffin, C. (2006) 'Implementing Organizational Change in Health and Social Services', *Journal of Organizational Change Management*, 19(2): 119–35.

Merleau-Ponty, M. (1960) 'The Philosopher and Sociology'. In *Signs* (trans. Richard C. McCleary). Evanston, IL: Northwestern University Press.

Merleau-Ponty, M. (1962) *Phenomenology of Perception* (p. 57; trans. Colin Smith). London: Routledge and Kegan Paul; New York: Humanities Press.

Mitchell, G.J., Pilkington, F.B., Jonas-Simpson, C., Aiken, F., Carson, M.G., Fisher, A., and Lyno, P. (2005) 'Exploring the Lived Experience of Waiting for Persons in Long-Term Care', *Nursing Science Quarterly*, 18(2): 163–70.

Morse, J. (1996) 'What Is a Method?', *Qualitative Health Research*, 6(4): 468.

Nordgren, L. and Asp, Margareta (2007) 'Living with a Moderate-Severe Chronic Health Failure as a Middle-Aged Person', *Qualitative Health Research*, 17(1): 4–13.

O'Neill, J. (1970) *Perception, Expression and History: the Social Phenomenology of Maurice Merleau-Ponty.* Evanston, IL: Northwestern University Press.

Paley, J. (1997) 'Husserl, Phenomenology and Nursing', *Journal of Advanced Nursing*, 26(1): 187–93.

Paley, J. (1998) 'Misinterpretive Phenomenology: Heidegger, Ontology and Nursing Research', *Journal of Advanced Nursing*, 27(4): 817–24.

Paley, J. (2005) 'Phenomenology as Rhetoric', *Nursing Inquiry*, 12(2): 106–16.

Pellegrino, E.D. (2008) 'The Commodification of Medical and Health Care: The Moral Consequences of a Paradigm Shift from a Professional to a Market Ethic'. In H. Tristram Englehardt, Jr. and Fabrice Jotterand (eds) *The Philosophy of Medicine Reborn: A Pellegrino Reader/Edmund D. Pelegrino* (pp. 101–26). Notre Dame, UK: University of Notre Dame Press.

Rapport, F. and Wainwright, P. (2006) 'Phenomenology as a Paradigm of Movement', *Nursing Inquiry*, 13(3): 228–36.

Raynova, Y.B. (2002) 'Jean-Paul Sartre, A Profound Revision of Husserlian Phenomenology'. In Anna-Teresa Tymieniecka (ed.) *Phenomenology World-Wide: Foundations – Expanding Dynamics – Life Engagements: A Guide for Research and Study* (pp. 103–13). Boston: Kluwer Academic Publishers.

Ricoeur, P. (1976) *Interpretation Theory: Discourse and the Surplus of Meaning.* Fort Worth, TX: Texas Christian University Press.

Sartre, J. (1943) *L'etre et le neant: Essai d'ontologie phenomenologique.* Paris: Gallimard. *Being and Nothingness: A Phenomenological Essay on Ontology.* Translated with an introduction by Hazel E. Barnes, University of Colorado. New York: Washington Square Press, 1956.

Schmid, T. (2004) 'Meanings of Creativity Within Occupational Therapy Practice', *Australian Occupational Therapy Journal*, 51: 80–8.

Schurmann, R. (1990) *Heidegger on Being and Acting: From Principles to Anarchy* (trans. Christine-Marie Gros). Bloomington, MN: Indiana University Press, 1990, 1.

Schutz, A. (1962) 'Concept and Theory Formation in the Social Sciences'. In Maurice Natanson (ed.) *Collected Papers I: The Problem of Social Reality*. The Hague: M. Nijhoff.

Schutz, A. (1970) *On phenomenology and social relations*. Chicago: University of Chicago Press.

Schwandt, T.A. (2000) 'Three Epistemological Stances for Qualitative Inquiry: Interpretivism, Hermeneutics and Social Constructionism'. In Denzin, N. and Lincoln, Y. (eds) *Handbook of Qualitative Research* (2nd Edition). Thousand Oaks, CA: Sage.

Stoltz, P., Lindholm, M., Uden, G., and Willman, A. (2006) 'The Meaning of Being Supportive for Family Caregivers as Narrated by Registered Nurses Working in Palliative Homecare', *Nursing Science Quarterly*, 19(2): 163–73.

Stoltz, P., Willman, A., and Uden, G. (2006) 'The Meaning of Support as Narrated by Family Carers Who Care for a Senior Relative at Home', *Qualitative Health Research*, 16(5): 594–610.

Strasser, S. (1963) *Phenomenology and the Human Sciences: A Contribution to a New Scientific Ideal*. Pittsburgh, PA: Duquesne University Press.

Svenaeus, F. (2000) 'Das Unheimliche – Towards a Phenomenology of Illness', *Medicine, Health Care and Philosophy*, 3: 3–16.

Sweeney, R. (2002) 'Phenomenology in North America and "Continental" Philosophy'. In Anna-Teresa T. (ed.) *Phenomenology World-Wide: Foundations – Expanding Dynamics – Life Engagements: A Guide for Research and Study* (pp. 286–92). Boston: Kluwer Academic Publishers.

Sweeney, R. and Carroll, J. (2002) 'Paul Ricoeur on Language, Ethics, and Philosophical Anthropology'. In Anna-Teresa Tymieniecka (ed.) *Phenomenology World-Wide: Foundations – Expanding Dynamics – Life Engagements: A Guide for Research and Study* (pp. 641–4). Boston: Kluwer Academic Publishers.

Thomas, S. (2005) 'Through the Lens of Merleau-Ponty: Advancing the Phenomenological Approach to Nursing Research', *Nursing Philosophy*, 6: 63–76.

Thomas, S.P. and Pollio, H.R. (2002) *Listening to Patients: A Phenomenological Approach to Nursing Research and Practice*. New York: Springer.

Thompson, J.L. (1990) 'Hermeneutic Inquiry'. In L.E. Moody (ed.) *Advancing Nursing Science through Research* (pp. 223–80) Newbury Park, CA: Sage.

Toombs, S.K. (1993) *The Meaning of Illness: A Phenomenological Account of the Different Perspectives of Physician and Patient*. Boston: Kluwer Academic Publishers.

Tymieniecka, A. (2002a) 'Introduction: Phenomenology as the Inspirational Force of Our Times'. In Anna-Teresa Tymieniecka (ed.) *Phenomenology World-Wide: Foundations – Expanding Dynamics – Life Engagements: A Guide for Research and Study* (pp. 1–10). Boston: Kluwer Academic Publishers.

Tymieniecka, A. (ed.) (2002b) *Phenomenology World-Wide: Foundations – Expanding Dynamics – Life Engagements: A Guide for Research and Study*. Boston: Kluwer Academic Publishers.

Vahabzadeh, P. (2003) *Articulated Experiences: Toward a Radical Phenomenology of Contemporary Social Movements*. Albany, NY: State University of New York Press.

Van Manen, M. (1990) *Researching the Lived Experience: Human Science as an Action Sensitive Pedagogy*. London, ON: The Althouse Press.

Van Manen, M. (1997) 'From Meaning to Method', *Qualitative Health Research*, 7(3): 345–69.

Van Manen, M. (1998) 'Modalities of Body Experience in Illness and Health', *Qualitative Health Research*, 8(1): 7–24.

Van Manen, M. and Levering, B. (1996) *Childhood's Secrets: Intimacy, Privacy and the Self Reconsidered*. New York: Teachers College Press.

Wagner, H.R. (1970) 'Introduction: The Phenomenological Approach to Sociology'. In Janowitz, Morris (ed.) *Alfred Schultz On Phenomenology and Social Relations: Selected Writings* (pp. 1–50). Chicago: the University of Chicago Press.

Widdowson, H.G. (2000) 'On the Limitations of Linguistics Applied', *Applied Linguistics*, 27(1): 3–25.
World Health Organization Regional Office for Europe (1986) 'Health Promotion: A Discussion Document on the Concept and Principles, ICP/HSR602', *Health Promotion*. Geneva: World Health Organization, 1: 73–6.
Yorks, L. (2005) 'Adult Learning and the Generation of New Knowledge and Meaning: Creating Liberating Spaces for Fostering Adult Learning Through Practitioner-Based Collaborative Action Inquiry', *Teachers' College Record*, 107(6): 1217–44.

13

Studying Organizations: the Revival of Institutionalism

Karen Staniland

Most health care in modern societies is carried out within or through organizations. Although hospitals may not be quite as central as they were as recently as the 1970s, primary and community health care are taking increasingly organized forms. The single-handed primary care physician of the 1950s has given way to the member of a group practice or the employee of a managed care organization, forming part of a complex set of professionals, paraprofessionals, health care assistants and managers who deal collectively with patients, government or private purchasers and suppliers. There is a considerable industry in quantitative research that measures inputs to, and outputs from, health care organizations and seeks to correlate them in terms of their relative efficiency, effectiveness and equity. However, these relationships are just that, correlations, and, as such, have limited value in guiding the actions of professionals or managers in designing and developing processes to achieve organizational goals. They also tend to be weak in dealing with aspects of organizational behaviour that are not readily susceptible to numerical measurement, particularly the humanity or civility with which care is delivered. When we come to examine the practice of health care, then, we cannot neglect its organizational contexts and we can only learn about important aspects of these through qualitative methods.

The most important contemporary approach to organizational research in health care is known as *new institutionalism*. This chapter will introduce this approach and discuss how it has been used in qualitative health research, through some examples from case studies in England. It begins by outlining the history of institutional approaches and the reasons why they have revived in recent years and been used so productively in studies of health care organizations.

BACKGROUND

The term 'institution' has particular associations in health care, where it is often linked to the large-scale, poor quality residential facilities that were historically provided for those who were poor and sick, those who had mental health problems and those who had learning disabilities. These negative images are reflected in the idea of 'institutionalization', where a patient or resident has become psychologically dependent on their care environment and unable to function effectively outside this. In the social sciences, however, it has a more neutral sense. An 'institution' may take the physical form of a building where particular people perform particular activities. However, the focus is on the activities rather than on the building. Institutions are the structural components of a society, through which its main activities are organized in a regular and repeated manner, for example, the church, the law, the government or the family. They are the rules or principles of collaboration that make it possible for people to cooperate in stable, consistent and predictable ways to achieve their various goals. These rules may be formal (as in written regulations, policies or procedures) or informal (as in cultural norms and mutual expectations). The study of these rules, and the activities that relate to them, is known as 'institutionalism'.

INSTITUTIONALISM

People have long studied the ways in which institutions structure societies. You could argue that *The Republic*, written around 380 BCE by the Greek philosopher, Plato, is the foundation of all subsequent work. In this text, Plato examines the institutions of contemporary government in Greek city states, and the ways that they interact, to determine how they could be redesigned in ways that would increase justice and welfare. Within the modern social sciences, however, institutionalism originated in three fields in the late 1800s and early 1900s with studies in the context of what we would now call economics, political science and sociology. It may be described as an approach that examines institutions in order to construct sequences of economic, political and social behaviour and transformation across time. This approach has generated a vast research literature, examining the way that institutions function, prescribing managerial structures and reviewing the behaviour of groups and individuals in organizational settings.

Within sociology, institutionalism is based on the concept of an institution as a social framework that influences human behaviour. Institutions are embedded in social, political and cultural contexts that influence both their general character and their interactions with one another. In contrast to rational choice approaches, institutionalism does not assume that decision makers are either wholly rational or entirely self-interested: decision makers operate within a context of partial information where choices are constrained by culture and history as much as by economic efficiency. Rational choice approaches were first developed by economists, and later exported to political science and sociology, to explain the emergence and functioning of political institutions. They include such theories as public choice, principal-agent or market theories, all of which emphasize the pursuit of rational self-interest in individual decision making. However, these approaches did not locate these decisions in their context so they tend to be seen as a contrast to, rather than a variant of, institutional theory (Garson, 2008). Rational choice institutionalists focus more on the 'rules of the political game … the important question is not so much what institutions are but what they represent, an equilibrium' (Lecours, 2005:6). Rational choice models view institutions as governance or rule systems that represent the results of individuals seeking to promote or guard their interests.

OLD INSTITUTIONALISM

Fifty years ago, organizations were depicted as tightly bounded entities that were wholly separate from any surrounding environment, as 'rational systems' or social machines for the efficient transformation of material inputs into material outputs (Scott, 1987). 'Old institutionalism' studies concentrated on efforts to discover the most efficient 'structures' of command and control for the achievement of the organization's goals. It was recognized that workers could subvert this rational project for the efficient structuring of their behaviour but this could be addressed by removing ambiguity from work design and introducing incentives and controls to shape the workforce into mature and sober workers. This generation identified institutions with formal 'structures' that generated self-contained systems of norms and values consistent with their economic goals (Lecours, 2005).

The analysis of institutions was strongly influenced by Max Weber (1864–1920), a German political economist and sociologist, considered one of the founders of the modern study of sociology and public administration. One of Weber's central interests was the exploration of the role of organizations in the economic life of modern societies, particularly through the emergence of the form known as 'bureaucracy' (Weber, 1946). His contribution is still central to the contemporary study of organizations. He examined the ways in which institutions such as bureaucracy had come to dominate political, social and economic life as a result of cultural shifts in the basis of power and control. He described three main principles – charismatic, traditional and rational–legal – as the possible bases for turning power and control into the legitimate exercise of authority (Scott, 2001). The charismatic principle supplied legitimacy from the presence of an inspirational, often spiritual, leader, the traditional from the legacy of custom and practice that influenced all members of a social group, and the rational–legal from the group's compliance with an impersonal body of rules, ideally derived from the rational actions of a democratic government or legislature. This concern for legitimacy has been Weber's abiding legacy to institutionalism. How do these bases of authority generate particular kinds of institutional forms? For example, how did the charismatic basis of the authority of Christ or the Prophet Mohammed come to be transformed into the powerful bureaucracy of the Catholic Church on the one hand and into the loose and often conflicting networks that characterize Islam, on the other? Weberian ideas about bureaucracy, which were strongly influenced by his observations of the Prussian state that dominated Germany during his lifetime, used to have a strong influence on thinking about public sector organizations. Government intentions, expressed in laws and regulations, would be implemented by managers in an impartial and disinterested fashion to supply a planned service to citizens through frontline or 'street-level' staff: if public sector 'management structures and processes, channels of communication and clarity of communication are 'right' effective action will be assured' (Barrett and Fudge, 1981:9).

Another important influence on old institutionalism studies was John Commons (1862–1945), an institutional economist. Institutional economics dominated in the United States until the 1920s when it was displaced by the neoclassical approaches that are almost universally adopted today. Unlike contemporary economics, Commons and his followers saw economics as a discipline that began from direct observations of economic life and then tried to build theories to explain them. Neoclassical economics tends to start from a set of assumptions about individually rational behaviour under ideal conditions, to develop models of the consequences, adjusting these to produce what is judged to be an optimum outcome and then seeking to propose ways of remaking the real world so that it approximates more closely to this ideal. If you start from the real world, however, as Commons (1910; 1934) did, you necessarily become more interested in collective actions and the ways in which these give effect to, or constrain, individual choices. You may also have a more diverse view of desirable outcomes: while Commons was certainly interested in the efficient use of scarce resources, which is the core problem for all economists, he took a much broader view of efficiency than would many contemporary economists. For him, wealth distribution stood alongside wealth maximization as legitimate concerns for the economist, and he made significant contributions to the expansion of workers' protections under law in order to promote this.

A third important figure was Everett Hughes (1897–1983), an American sociologist who drew on both Weber and Commons in developing an ecological approach to the study of institutions that formed the theoretical frame of reference for numerous studies of class, status, political power, industrialization, work and occupations. Hughes (1956; 1962; 1971) took up Commons' idea of organizations as 'going concerns', sites of collective action, and linked this to ecological thinking about the ways in which socioeconomic systems offered niches for potential colonization that, in turn, shaped the going concerns that could compete to occupy them. Institutions were not self-sufficient and autonomous, but existed in relation to one another and to a wider cultural field in the way that Weber (1946; 1968) had described.

By the 1960s, however, institutionalist approaches were in decline in the face of rationalist theories of economic and social organization. Commons' work had been marginalized within economics since the late 1920s, although Weber's thinking continued to be influential in some areas of sociology. The work of Hughes and his students was respected within sociology, but not considered as a pathway to follow so much as an anachronism left over from an earlier age. The project of remaking all social sciences after the model of economics seemed irresistible. Apart from research in sociology, interest in 'old institutionalism' largely died out during the early 1950s. However, in 1976, James March, Professor of Political Science and Sociology Emeritus at Stanford University, and Johan Olsen, a Professor of Political Science at the University of Oslo (March and Olsen, 1976), published a major restatement of institutionalist arguments that reasserted the value of conceptualizing organizations in terms of norms, values and interrelated rules and routines.

March and Olsen regarded institutions as 'expressing norms of interrelated roles and routines that define appropriate actions in terms of relations between roles and situations' (1989:21). Rules are sets of expected behaviours, sustained by trust that institutions impose on their members. Rules may be either formal or informal: while formal rules might be changed, informal rules are difficult to change. In sum, March and Olsen presented a more holistic view of action within organizations, seeing this not just as an aggregate of atomized individual choices but as profoundly influenced by the informal and symbolic dimensions of culture. Institutional cultures are as powerful a source of sanctions as rational management in making some courses of action available to members of an organization and blocking others. The possibilities for action are simultaneously a source of opportunity and control: members can do *these* things, but not *those* things. At the same time, they always have an element of indeterminacy – they must be recognized by members, interpreted by them and applied by them in a highly contingent organizational environment.

Where the 'old institutionalism' was thought to be descriptive, a-theoretical and narrow-minded, this 'new institutionalism' embedded organizations with their societal context as a source of variability and began to develop a base of theoretically founded generalizations from comparative investigations of different organizations operating within the same social field, or of similar organizations operating within different social fields (Lecours, 2005).

NEW INSTITUTIONALISM

A series of articles by March and Olsen (1976; 1984; 1989) defined the revolution against the methodological individualism, behaviourism and formal rationality that had marked their immediate predecessors. The movement that came to be known as 'new institutionalism' developed through a series of contributions, including Meyer and Rowan (1977), Zucker (1977), DiMaggio and Powell (1983), Tolbert and Zucker (1983), Meyer and Scott (1983), and Powell and DiMaggio (1991). It was a collective reaction against rational choice accounts of political and organizational behaviour that saw this as an aggregate of individual responses to economic and technological stimuli that had, themselves, no social origin or context (Powell and DiMaggio, 1991).These authors sought different answers to questions about how social choices are shaped, mediated and channelled. Although previous organizational researchers had recognized that organizations possessed both formal (governed by rationality) and informal (governed by culture) dimensions, they had tended to treat the latter as pathological, an obstruction to efficiency and effectiveness. New institutionalism transcended these distinctions, insisting that rationality was itself a cultural form, the product of a particular and contingent historical moment, and was not to be given precedence over the other sociocultural elements in the relations between members of an organization, and between those members and the environment in which the organization operate.

For the old political institutionalists, institutions were material structures, comprising constitutions, cabinets etc. 'Institutions referred to the state or more exactly to 'Government' (Lecours, 2005:6). New institutionalists, however, do not define institutions in material terms, as action that is coordinated by its location or technology. They focus instead on the way actions are coordinated by shared references to beliefs, values or cognitive scripts (Scott, 2001). These ideas contribute to a 'mythic' self-description, which members create as they form organizations, or learn, as they join, which defines the organization's goals, structures and boundaries in cultural and normative terms (Dingwall and Strong, 1997). Sociological institutionalists see organizations as cognitive frameworks rather than as the formal structures on organization charts, which are merely one representation of the organization among many that are possible. Institutions are constructed by the actions of their members with reference to these shared frameworks of ideas, which can be used both to design and develop actions – and to make sense of the actions of other members or of outsiders. Although change may be provoked by economic or technological developments, these are always filtered through the organization's culture and the ways in which it is used by members (Lecours, 2005).

In particular, the new institutionalists suggested that Weber had overemphasized the competitive market place as the major environmental driver for organizational change (DiMaggio and Powell, 1983). Powell and DiMaggio (1991) preferred to read Weber in a way that stressed his analysis of legitimacy that the main goal of organizations was to act in ways that would be regarded as legitimate by key actors in their environments and would, as a result, win them resources from those actors. Those resources might be economic, or they might be essentially symbolic, but capable of being translated into economic or political support if the organization came under challenge. When forced to choose, organizations select options that preserve and enhance their legitimacy.

The most important way to achieve legitimacy was to adopt cultural forms that either copied those of the most successful organizations operating in the same field or that reflected the models preferred by the most powerful actors in the environment. The result was an 'iron cage' of 'institutional isomorphism'. This involves three mechanisms: *coercive*, where external audiences compel conformity, often through law or regulation; *mimetic*, where uncertainty leads the organization to adopt the practices of their most successful competitor, however 'success' is defined; and normative, often where a strong professional interest that cuts across specific organizations drives the adoption of particular values and beliefs by all of them (Powell and DiMaggio, 1991:67). Legitimacy always has a 'ceremonial' dimension – it is not enough just to respond to isomorphic pressures, an organization must be *seen* to have responded (Meyer and Rowan, 1977). However, ceremonial action can remain divorced from an organization's day-to-day activities and working practices. Compliance would often obstruct these, although the *appearance* of compliance may be crucial to external legitimacy and the flow of resources from the environment to the organization.

Powell and DiMaggio (1991) originally argued that the new institutionalism was more concerned with 'persistence' rather than change and that 'the legitimacy imperative' acts as a source of 'inertia'. As a result, new institutionalism emphasizes the homogeneity of organizations and the stability of institutional components (Powell and DiMaggio, 1991:13/14). However, Oliver (1991:165) proposes that new institutional theory can explain 'not only homogeneity and isomorphism in organizations but also heterogeneity and variability'. He links this with resource-based theory to suggest that where institutional pressures exert strong influences, competitive advantage might be gained through heterogeneity in resources and capability. If all organizations wholly succumbed to isomorphism, no one would have any competitive edge. Managers must have some degree of freedom that allows them to manage their adaptation to environmental pressures in order to gain such an advantage.

Citing work by Edelman (1992); Dobbin and Sutton (1998) and Edelman et al. (1999), Powell (2007:4) acknowledges their findings that organizational fields are 'fragmented, contained multiple institutional influences and were thus subject to ambiguous requirements'. He also recognized that organizations 'helped construct the law and created the regulations that shaped 'best' practice' (Powell 2007:5). The heterogeneity of response to isomorphic pressures should renew concern with the role of agency in institutionalization. This should be seen as a political process, reflecting the relative power of different agents. This is apparent in the changes and increases in rules, normative systems and cognitive beliefs which 'eroded the sovereignty' of physicians and changed organizational fields as described by Scott et al. (2000). Powell accepts that it was a limitation of the original work to assume that ideas and practices 'diffuse seamlessly' and acknowledges the importance of political opportunity and cultural frames in shaping diffusion so that 'social movements are critical to the acceptance of ideas'. Further analysis of the 'forces that account for institutional heterogeneity and homogeneity' would 'bode well for the robustness of institutional analysis' (Powell, 2007:8).

New institutionalism, then, provides an alternative to economic analyses, offering explanations as to how institutions, although created in different ways, end up having similar structures and how these institutions might shape, and be shaped by, the behaviour of their members. It focuses on the 'cultural basis of all organizational structures and action' and views 'organizational boundaries as open and fluid so that the cultural foundation of action was not contained within the organization but reflected the organization's interactions with its environment' (Dingwall and Strangleman, 2005:248).

NEW INSTITUTIONALISM AND HEALTH CARE STUDIES

New institutionalist approaches have influenced a number of studies of health care organizations. Scott et al. (2000) examined the transformations that had occurred in the medical care systems in the San Francisco Bay area since 1945. Conducted during the 1990s, a period described as one of great turbulence in US health care, Scott et al. describe the changes in the Bay Area health care organizations and their responses to external forces, particularly in the adoption of new organizational forms. Scott et al. showed how these changes related to three institutional eras: professional dominance (before 1965), federal involvement (1966 to 1982), and market forces (1983 to 1999). The authors describe each era in detail, relating changes both to sociodemographic trends in the Bay Area and to shifts in regulatory systems and policy environments at local, state and national levels.

There has also been increasing interest in applying this approach to studies of the English National Health Service (NHS) which has undergone extensive and rapid change in its environment and organization over the last thirty-five years. One example is the way that 'in the space of four years the NHS went from a situation where there were no hospital Trusts to one in which almost every provider had converted to the Trust format' (Pollitt et al., 1998:98–99). In the NHS, coercive isomorphic pressures derive from the state's requirement that NHS Trusts conform to certain processes, policies and protocols, in order to be viewed as legitimate. Arguably, however, these changes are largely ceremonial. While they shape organizations in similar ways, they lead to a focus on outputs that are unrelated to the real work of the organization. This is more influenced by normative isomorphic pressures from the process of professionalization (Powell and DiMaggio, 1991). Organizations are also influenced by the differences that result from the varied training and philosophical approaches that underpin the health professions. These generate a set of cognitive bases that, on the one hand, unify professions and, on the other, contribute to conflict between them. Professionalism creates a countervailing system of legitimacy that links workers across the different organizations that hire them. Currie and Suhomlinova (2006:1), for example, 'highlighted the influence of regulatory normative and cultural–cognitive aspects of institutions operating in the health field on the boundaries that impede knowledge sharing'. Managers, orienting to coercive pressures from the state, did not always recognize the cultural and political dimensions of knowledge sharing, oriented to within the normative frameworks of professionals, so that 'knowledge sharing across [professional] boundaries will be difficult to realize'. As Dingwall (2009) notes, the result has been a state initiative to undermine professional authority, in the name of quality and safety, in order to weaken the normative influences that check the state's coercive interventions. My own work (Staniland, 2008) investigated the implementation of clinical governance, (a quality initiative) into one English NHS hospital Trust and showed, however, that external legitimacy, in response to state coercion, could be achieved, to the benefit of the organization, without any evident improvement in the quality of care received by patients.

AN INSTITUTIONALIST ANALYSIS OF CLINICAL GOVERNANCE

Clinical governance was introduced into the NHS as the organizational response to a perceived decline in clinical standards, service provision and delivery, reinforced by media coverage of major clinical failures (Harvey, 1998; Scally and Donaldson, 1998; Swage, 2000). However, there is considerable dissent about its meaning, substance and essential nature, which were not clearly articulated by the 'official' definition as 'a framework through which NHS organizations are accountable for continuously improving the quality of their services and safeguarding high standards of care by creating an environment in which excellence in clinical care will flourish' (DH, 1998:33; See Staniland, 2008). However, it is generally accepted that it requires organizations to carry out a number of component activities such as standard setting, in the form of protocols and policies; risk management; audits; adverse incident recording; and training, reflection and professional development, in the form of a 'Learning Organization'. In this sense, clinical governance can be seen as a coercive pressure that NHS Trusts must respond to in order to sustain their legitimacy with the state. If they are successful, certain rewards follow; if they are not, there may be sanctions, particularly on the Chief Executive Officer.

The NHS Trust studied was broadly typical of any large university teaching hospital in England. Wards were grouped into directorates and departments actively engaged in teaching and research. The Trust employs over 4,200 staff and trains approximately 300 medical students. Three hundred student nurses and therapists are accommodated on practice placements in any one year. On a day-to-day basis, the Trust is able to handle 1,000 outpatients and may treat up to 250 patients in the Accident & Emergency Department. There are in-patient facilities for over 900 patients and the day surgery unit can treat over 70 patients on a day case basis.

The study adopted an ethnographic methodology. Data were obtained over a two-and-a-half-year period by the documentary analysis of paperwork related to the implementation of clinical governance, such as public and official minutes of meetings, policies and procedures; observation of clinical governance meetings and semistructured interviews with nurses and stakeholders involved in clinical governance implementation within the Trust; and day-to-day observation of ward activity. During my fieldwork, I attended corporate Trust level clinical governance meetings and analysed their decisions. I tracked and asked about intranet information resources available for hospital staff, conducted staff interviews and observed everyday practice on Elderly Care and Neurosciences wards. Hammersley and Atkinson's (1995) classification of official, formal and informal documents was utilized. Official documents included public records, official data and statistics. Formal documents were those circulated to committee members within the Trust (such as annual reviews, reports, protocols, strategies and action plans). Informal documentation was my own field notes and recordings taken during meetings and periods of observation. These were analysed using established conventions for qualitative data (Bryman and Burgess, 1994).

If documents were considered at a superficial level, they appeared to be an appropriate account of what had taken place at the meetings. However, when the progress of agenda items from the official minutes was tracked and compared with my own observations of the same meetings, I found that important issues identified for action simply did not appear in the documentation again. There were many discrepancies between the official documentary records and what was actually done and observed and, from the summary of events, it was apparent that information given to committee members varied. The attendance of key personnel at meetings was erratic, with some members never appearing. Approval of protocols and policies, (a main function of the committee), appeared at times to be just a paper exercise (ten protocols being endorsed in nine minutes on one occasion), and many inconsistencies were found in these documents. More importantly, the dissemination, implementation and embedding of protocols in working practice was obscure. On this basis, the main corporate clinical governance committee was considered to be an essentially 'ceremonial' body.

From a new institutionalist perspective, however, the fact that it was ceremonial did not mean that it was ineffective or irrelevant, merely that its role needed to be correctly understood. This committee successfully met the 'coercive' requirement of central government that such a committee must be set up if the institution were to be recognized as legitimate by its main funders and most powerful stakeholders. The committee was not actually required to show that it had improved the quality of care but to show that it had conducted appropriate business in an appropriate way, as evidence by the documents that it created. As Murphy and Dingwall (2003:66) suggest, documents 'provide valuable evidence about what people and organizations would like to be thought to be doing' rather necessarily about what they have actually done. In Garfinkel's (1967) terminology, the committee's records are 'contractual' rather than 'actuarial': they are not literal accounts of what happened but evidence that the appropriate personnel went about their business in a competent way.

Other meetings, involving lower levels of Trust management in relation to clinical governance, were also observed. These meetings were supposed to disseminate the clinical governance process within the Trust. My observations identified the difficulties experienced by staff in trying to make sense of the Trust's corporate intentions. The internal governance systems created by the Trust were fraught with problems that were not being addressed at higher levels. The information on protocols and policies placed on the hospital intranet, for example, was unusable as a tool to inform practice, because few staff had access to IT and the organization's search tools were poor. Nevertheless, complaints made to higher-level management about system weaknesses failed to initiate any change. Again, this underlined the information's success in its ceremonial function, it was posted on the intranet and its availability could be audited, although there was no expectation that anyone would actually make use of it. No one needs to refer to this information in order to carry out their job, but the organization could demonstrate that the work must have an evidence base, because, if it was carried out within the organization, it must necessarily comply with the protocols. Should the Trust's legitimacy be questioned by its stakeholders, they could be shown the body of information posted on the intranet. Should everyday practice be shown to be noncompliant, management would be buffered from the consequences, because the policies had been stated, even if they had not been accessed.

I conducted semistructured interviews with thirteen nurses of various grades from Assistant Director of Nursing Services to recently qualified Staff Nurses, and fifteen semistructured interviews with senior members of other professional groups who had some responsibility for clinical governance within the Trust. From these, I generated a number of theoretical categories including 'Somebody Else's Job' and 'Real Work'.

It quickly became clear that there was no consensus on what 'clinical governance' meant within this group. The interpretation varied with the grade of the informant. Nurses involved in higher-level management gave 'ceremonial' examples of how the clinical governance implementation systems worked:

> Clinical governance is a framework within, which the Government have brought in to embed quality into everyday practice. It has seven pillars and those seven pillars provide a framework, to enhance care and quality (Matron).

Staff at the bedside, however, found it difficult to describe or identify any change that they could clearly relate to clinical governance, apart from the requirement to complete the increased amount of documentation that the systems generated:

> I don't know, it sounds as if I am whingeing, but it is time constraints, staffing levels, although the Trust will say, have remained consistent, they haven't, trained staff have been reduced and reduced and reduced, replaced by people like assistant practitioners, who are not trained nurses at the end of the day. So that puts more and more pressure on qualified

nurses, paperwork has quadrupled, the number of meetings that are mandatory has gone through the roof and it all adds to time constraints that previously were not there (Ward Manager).

We're busy on the ward, the shifts busy, it comes to the end of the day you think do I want to go to a meeting or do I want to go home and it's bad you choose you want to go home I mean … We were told the X-ray dept, once, I remember them saying we've got protected time this morning so we're not doing any, (work) and I remember thinking well, if they can get it, but we're never going to get protected time because who's going to be left on the ward if that happened? (Senior Bedside Nurse).

While senior professionals in medicine and nursing could give well-articulated accounts of clinical governance, it was much less clear whose responsibility it was to implement. Professionals saw it as a management tool to improve quality, and managers saw it as a framework for professionals to improve their own practice. A senior management member of the Trust responded to my question about designation of roles and responsibilities stating:

It is not my responsibility. It's nobody's responsibility that is the problem.

Everyone thought it was 'Somebody Else's Job'. This played out particularly strongly at lower levels. In my interviews with nurses, they recurrently complained about the lack of communication with managers, with the result that managers did not appreciate what happened at ward level and the problems that existed. I wanted to establish how managers identified their role in relation to the ward areas they managed and asked if they spent any time visiting the wards:

No I haven't, because nursing isn't my field, so mine is the overall picture of the organization, really about the systems, and getting the systems right for the Board. … I haven't no (GM 4).

The majority of managers interviewed clearly felt that they could manage their directorates without actually visiting the areas that they were responsible for managing and relied on communicating at meetings that nurses did not attend. This lack of contact reinforced the communication problems that the ward sisters had highlighted. It was extremely hard to identify any individual who took corporate responsibility when things went wrong. Again, it is important to stress that, from an institutionalist perspective, this is not necessarily pathological. The existence of the clinical governance system satisfied key external stakeholders but the lack of implementation avoided internal conflict between managers and professionals, while buffering each group from the potential implications of errors or failures. By defining implementation as 'somebody else's job', it became 'nobody's job', so that nobody could be held accountable for any adverse consequences.

Finally, I investigated whether nurses and other stakeholders at the point of care thought that clinical governance had achieved its ostensible objective of improving the quality of patient care, my original interest in conducting this study. As clinical governance had clearly increased the amount of paperwork at ward level, I was particularly interested in the auditing systems of clinical governance, and if staff could see any result linked to the improvement of care as a result of these. What this yielded, however, was a contrast between ceremonial work and 'Real Work'. Real work was the practical, everyday care of patients. Ceremonial work disappeared into some vague ether, where other departments might, or might not; make some use of it to sanction frontline staff:

> We are aware that when we deliver the care it's audited, our documentation's audited, our care plans audited. We have audits like infection control so everything's looked at and we know that where we, what we're good at and to continue doing and where we're perhaps falling behind on something that we're not doing that we can learn from (Junior Ward Sister).

Compliance with the ceremonial order was, however, very burdensome, involving much collation of documentation driven by unfriendly IT systems that failed to integrate and return this in any form usable at lower levels.

> In respect of the paperwork around clinical governance I would say that possibly half of my time is spent providing either evidence, auditing, or responding to clinical governance issues. … With the adverse incident reporting again, it's not the actual paperwork it's the system on the computer that doesn't make it particularly easy. But my web master file is absolutely full of it and there is no way of identifying, either on the system, of which, say like. If one of the gatekeepers (Clinical Governance Facilitator) phoned me up and said, I needed some information off one of the adverse incidents she got, it's number 504, there is no way on the system you could find that without going through every single one and there must be thousands, because you've got the original report, my response, the manager's form back then you've got an incident accept, so the file is enormous and there is no way you can link any of them together (Ward Manager).

Time spent on this was not available for either direct care delivery or for addressing management issues. We should not necessarily take at face value the professional consensus in my interviews that the integrated approach of clinical governance had brought about little or no identifiable improvement in the quality of bedside care. Interviews with professionals often generate accounts that are designed to project their claims to autonomy and their resistance to managerialist interventions like clinical governance.

On the other hand, these comments were entirely consistent with my own participant observation data from the wards where I found that actual practise showed little evidence of change attributable to clinical governance and that frontline staff had little awareness of the Trust's formal goals. Where they did, they found them to be ambiguous and unrealistic on a day-to-day basis, which resulted in a lack of commitment. In the specific area of clinical governance, there was little evidence of active knowledge management or organizational learning. Fundamentally, there was no interest in 'trying to understand and conceptualize the nature of knowledge that is contained within the organization' (Easterby-Smith and Lyles, 2003:3). However, as I have stressed, this does not necessarily mean that the systems had failed. They had to be understood in different terms, where they were highly successful in delivering external legitimacy.

Ultimately, legitimacy was more important than improving quality or effectiveness. During my fieldwork, the Trust obtained a recognition status from its insurer for its structures and systems and recognition that led to a significant reduction in insurance premiums. The Trust's documentation was considered to be among the best of any hospital in the region, which brought financial benefits that could be invested in service improvement. The value of the new institutionalist perspective lay in the way it helped me to understand that the clinical governance system could still be important, successful and valuable to the Trust despite the complete absence of any evidence that it was contributing to its ostensible goal of improving everyday clinical practice. Although much of this badly needed improving, from a professional perspective, the legitimacy gained for the organization by its ability to create the appearance of compliance with the coercive expectations of its main stakeholder created a space in which such change could, in theory, occur. The problem was that the preoccupation of line management with this ceremonial system inhibited any engagement with the practice of frontline care delivery that could actually bring about improvement.

If a hospital demonstrates conspicuous, but ceremonial, compliance with the expectations of its stakeholders everyone is happy, and it becomes legitimate. However, we need to understand this only affects its ceremonial order, rather than its workplace culture, delivery of bedside care, patient experience and recognition of patients. Legitimacy is the precondition of organizational success rather than its consequence. Clinical governance in the hospital I studied is not a failure. Its lack of impact is an unintended consequence of an attempt to introduce reforms based on an inadequate understanding of how organizations work. Successful reform would demand both a better-informed approach to organizational change *and* the management of stakeholder expectations to have this approach accepted as legitimate.

CONCLUSION

The last forty years have seen a general revival of institutional theories in both political and social science. This chapter has explored these perspectives by outlining old and new institutionalism approaches and discussing their implications for social science and health care. While it is evident organizational studies of the NHS have not been prominent in recent years, and that the study of the hospital as a social organization has declined globally, this chapter has given examples of studies that have utilized institutional theories as useful frameworks. As Davies (2003) has argued, health care organizations are very different from the hospitals studied by medical sociologists forty years ago and more research is needed on their contemporary forms and practices.

New institutionalism theory offers a coherent framework to understand why organizations adopt procedures and practices which appear to promote uniformity and standardization. However, they can also reveal some of the complexities – and local difficulties – of such processes in a health care setting.

REFERENCES

Barrett, S. and Fudge, C. (eds) (1981) *Policy and Action: Essays on the Implementation of Public Policy.* London: Methuen.

Bryman, A. and Burgess, R. (1994) *Analysing Qualitative Data.* London: Routledge: Taylor and Francis.

Commons, J. (ed.) (1910) *A Documentary History of American Industrial Society.* Vols. 1–10. Cleveland, Ohio: The Arthur H. Clark Co.

Commons, J. (1934) *Institutional Economics.* New York: Macmillan.

Currie, G. and Suhomlinova, O. (2006) 'The Impact of Institutional Forces upon Knowledge Sharing in the UK NHS: The Triumph of Professional Power and the Inconsistency of Policy', *Public Administration*, 84(1): 1–30.

Davies, C. (2003) 'Some of Our Concepts Are Missing: Reflections on the Absence of a Sociology of Organizations in Sociology of Health and Illness', *Sociology of Health and Illness*, 25(Silver Anniversary Issue): 172–90.

Department of Health (1998) *A First Class Service: Quality in the New NHS.* Leeds: Department of Health.

DiMaggio, P. and Powell, W. (1983) 'The Iron Cage Revisited Institutional Isomorphism and Collective Rationality in Organizational Fields', *American Sociological Review*, 48: 147–60.

Dingwall, R. (2009) 'The Inevitability of Professions'. In Currie, G., Ford, J. Harding, N., and Learmonth, M. (eds) *Public Services Management* (pp. 71–85). London: Routledge 2009.

Dingwall, R. and Strangleman, T. (2005) 'Organizational Culture'. In E. Ferlie, L.E. Lynn and C. Pollitt (eds) *Oxford Handbook of Public Management* (pp. 468–90). New York: Oxford University Press.

Dingwall, R. and Strong, P.M. (1997) 'The Interactional Study of Organizations: A Critique and Reformulation'. In G. Miller and R. Dingwall (eds) *Context and Method in Qualitative Research* (pp. 139–55), Original Article in *Urban Life special issue*, (1985) 14: 205–31.

Dobbin, F. and Sutton, J. (1998) 'The Strength of a Weak State: The Employment Rights Revolution and the Rise of Human Resources Management Divisions', *American Journal of Sociology*, 104: 441–76 cited by Powell, W. (2007) *The New Institutionalism* in Garson, D. (2008) *Institutional Theory*. Available at: http://faculty.chass.ncsu.edu/garson/PA765/institutionalism.htm [accessed 22 May 2009].

Easterby-Smith, M. and Lyles, M.A. (eds) (2003) *The Blackwell Handbook of Organizational Learning and Knowledge Management.* Oxford: Blackwell Publishing Ltd.

Edelman, L. (1992) 'Legal Ambiguity and Symbolic Structures: Organization Mediation of Civil Rights', *American Journal of Sociology*, 95: 1401–40 cited by Powell, W. (2007) *The New Institutionalism: to appear in The International Encyclopaedia of Organization Studies*, Sage. Available at: http://www.stanford.edu/group/song/papers/NewInstitutionalism.pdf [accessed 22 May 2009].

Edelman, L., Uggen, C., and Erlanger, H. (1999) 'The Endogeneity of Legal Regulation', *American Journal of Sociology*, 105: 406–54 cited by Powell, W. (2007) *The New Institutionalism: to appear in* The International Encyclopaedia of Organization Studies, Sage. Available at: http://www.stanford.edu/group/song/papers/NewInstitutionalism.pdf [accessed 22 May 2009].

Garfinkel, H. (1967) *Studies in Ethnomethodology.* Englewood Cliffs, NJ: Prentice-Hall.

Garson, D. (2008) *Institutional Theory. Available at:* http://faculty.chass.ncsu.edu/garson/PA765/institutionalism.htm [accessed 22 May 2009].

Hammersley, M. and Atkinson, P. (1995) *Ethnography, Principles in Practice.* London: Routledge.

Harvey, G. (1998) 'Improving Patient Care: Getting to Grips with Clinical Governance', *RCN Magazine*, Autumn 8–9.

Hughes, E. (1956) 'The "Gleichschaltung" of the German Statistical Yearbook: A Case in Professional Neutrality', *The American Statistician,* 9 (Dec 1955): 8–11.

Hughes, E. (1962) *Good People and Dirty Work* article published in Social Problems, Vol. 10, Summer, 1962.

Hughes, E. (1971) *The Sociological Eye. Selected Papers.* New York: Aldine.

Lecours, A. (2005) *New Institutionalism Theory and Analysis.* University of Toronto Press.

March, J. and Olsen, J. (1976) *Ambiguity and Choice in Organizations.* Universitetsforlaget, Bergen.

March, J.G. and Olsen, J.P. (1984) 'The New Institutionalism: Organizational Factors in Political Life', *American Political Science Review*, 78: 734–49.

March, J.G. and Olsen, J.P. (1989) *Rediscovering Institutions: The Organizational Basis of Politics*. New York: The Free Press.

Meyer, J.W. and Rowan, B. (1977) 'Institutionalized Organizations: Formal Structure as Myth and Ceremony', *American Journal of Sociology*, 83(2): 41–4.

Meyer, J. and Scott, W. (1983) (eds) *Organizational Environments: Ritual and Rationality.* Beverly Hills: Sage.

Murphy, E. and Dingwall, R. (2003) *Qualitative Methods and Health Care Policy Research.* New York: Aldine de Gruyter.

Oliver, C. (1991) 'Strategic Responses to Institutional Processes', *Academy of Management Review*, 16(1): 145–79.

Pollitt, C., Birchall, J., and Putman, K. (1998) *Decentralising Public Service Management.* Macmillan Press Ltd.

Powell, W. (2007) *The New Institutionalism: to appear in The International Encyclopaedia of Organization Studies*, Sage. Available at: http://www.stanford.edu/group/song/papers/NewInstitutionalism.pdf [accessed 22 May 2009].

Powell, W. and DiMaggio, P. (1991) *The New Institutionalism in Organizational Analysis.* Chicago: The University of Chicago Press.

Scally, G. and Donaldson, L. (1998) 'Clinical Governance and the Drive for Quality improvement in the New NHS in England', *British Medical Journal*, 317: 61–5.

Scott, W.R. (1987) *Organizations: Rational, Natural and Open Systems* (2nd Edition). Englewood Cliffs, NJ: Prentice Hall.

Scott, W.R. (2001) *Institutions and Organizations* (2nd Edition). Thousand Oaks, CA: Sage.

Scott, W.R., Ruef, M., Mendel, P.J., and Caronna, C. (2000) *Institutional Change and Healthcare Organization: From Professional Dominance to Managed Care.* Chicago: The University of Chicago Press.

Staniland, K. (2008) *Clinical Governance and Nursing – a Sociological Analysis* (unpublished PhD Thesis). England: University of Salford.

Swage, T. (2000) C*linical Governance in Health Care Practice.* London: Butterworth Heinemann.

Tolbert, P. and Zucker, L. (1983) 'Institutional Sources of Change in the Formal Structure of Organizations: The Diffusion of Civil Service Reform, 1880–1935', *Administrative Science Quarterly*, 28: 22–39.

Weber, M. (1946) (1924 in German) *The Theory of Social and Economic Greanization*, edited by A.H. Henderson and T. Parsons. Glencoe, IL: Free Press.

Weber, M. (1968) 'Economy and Society: An Outline of Interpretive Sociology (First published in 1922)'. In G. Roth and C. Wittich (eds) New York: Bedminister Press vol 1–3, cited by Ruef, M. and Scott, R. (1998) 'A Multidimensional Model of Organizational Legitimacy: Hospital Survival in Changing Institutional Environments', *Administrative Science Quarterly*, 43(4): 877–904.

Zucker, L.G. (1977) 'The Role of Institutionalization in Cultural Persistence', *American Sociological Review*, 42: 726–43.

14

History and Social Change in Health and Medicine

Claire Hooker

In general, qualitative research – in health or otherwise – has not paid much attention to history. And why should it? While most qualitative scholars, particularly the more constructivist among us, would naturally acknowledge that the people and societies they study are different to those that preceded them, this mostly has little or no influence in practice on research design or conduct. History is interesting, yes, but in most cases must seem either too arcane, or too removed, to inform health research.

There are, however, occasions where history may seem to have some instrumental value for health research: to learn about the efficacy and impacts of interventions in the past; to avoid past mistakes or reinventing the wheel; to be more influential advocates. For example, health researchers may be interested in social histories of Prohibition-era United States in order to think about the feasibility of drug bans. Similarly, studies using oral history interviews with politicians and other stakeholders involved in tobacco control legislation were conducted to delineate the set of social conditions and processes that resulted in legislative change, in order to identify any generalizable features that might allow advocates to achieve further tobacco control more quickly and efficiently in the future, or at least to predict and produce conditions conducive to accomplishing further control (Bryan-Jones and Chapman, 2006; Hooker and Chapman, 2006). These studies have empirically verified the utility of Kingdon's model of policy change (Hooker and Chapman, 2006; Jacobson et al., 1997; Studlar, 2002) and underscored the key role of 'policy entrepreneurs' and 'windows of opportunity' in getting tobacco control onto the policy (and eventually, legislative) agenda.

These sorts of studies are certainly compelling and often useful. What they do *not* do, however, is capture the unique qualities of people's action and experience in a specific time and place, nor situate or understand these things in relation to wider social influences. There are different, good, reasons for qualitative researchers to be interested in history: for its capacity to enhance sensitivity to social context and its unique critical perspectives on health and medicine. The approaches and perspectives of history – the development of what I refer to as an 'historian's nose' – can lead scholars to ask important new analytic questions, challenging their assumptions and goals, and leading to much deeper or more novel analyses. For example, an analysis, from a cultural history perspective, of those same oral history interviews relating to tobacco control, looked totally different. It identified a broader discourse on 'drugs' that delineated social and moral concerns about consumer society, including its capacity for social alienation and political and commercial manipulation, that influenced (and was influenced by) talk and policy about tobacco (Hooker and Chapman, 2007). This was not only interesting, but also had instrumental advantages as well, since it means that an advocate may well be more successful if they are sensitive to the broader discourses and concerns that frame social and political debate for a specific group of people at a specific time in history. (It also produced a critical theory approach to tobacco control itself, which was very important but also rather discomfiting for tobacco control advocates. I say more about this in the following section.)

History is a form of qualitative research, and historians and qualitative researchers do similar things – interviews, document analysis – and have similar sets of concerns – such as how to access and understand minority voices, or how to conceptualize someone's experience of illness. Nonetheless, in practice I have found that many historians have never even heard of qualitative research and that qualitative researchers rarely understand their topic in historical terms. Further, what each group means by 'methodology' is often quite divergent: the emphasis on procedure and process in qualitative research in particular is very foreign to imaginative and theoretical historical methods. Naturally, the results also diverge: which is why 'qualitative research' is likely to yield the instrumentalist model of policy change and 'history' the exploration of discourse on drugs I indicated earlier.

In this chapter, I will review different approaches to the history of health and medicine and briefly comment on their implications for qualitative research in health. Historians and qualitative researchers confront many of the same puzzles about the relationship between theory, method and knowledge, and converge in their engagement with issues of power and representation, in their questions about what to count as evidence, and in their speculations about how to go about understanding it. I will therefore muse on the relationship between theory and method in history as we go.

ORIENTATION: WHAT IS DISTINCTIVE ABOUT HISTORY?

As we know, qualitative research has its roots in the social sciences, principally anthropology and sociology, and in the philosophical traditions within these (e.g., pragmatism and phenomenology). History has developed as a separate, distinct discipline alongside the social sciences. The distinctions between them are a matter of degree, not of kind: there is, and has always been, considerable cross-fertilization. Both are characterized by the same tensions – between aesthetics and formal reasoning, between humanistic descriptive exploration of people's experiences and identifying the processes and consequences of social systems, between attention to the general and theoretical and to the empirical and particular (Giddens, 2006) – that will be very familiar to qualitative health researchers.

So what is distinctive about history? In general – and throughout this discussion, the reader should bear in mind that overlap is considerable and counter-examples not uncommon – firstly, history is interested in tracking social *change*, and also *continuities* that have amazingly endured across social change. It is unsurprising that qualitative research has been largely uninterested in change over time, since it originated in forms of sociological inquiry, like symbolic interactionism, that were focused on the immediacies of social activity.

Secondly, historians have been somewhat more interested in the specific and particular, in delineating what is *unique* to each episode (Goldthorpe, 1991; Thompson, 1994). Historians are not the only ones interested in social change: there is an entire field of sociological research, 'historical sociology', devoted precisely (though not solely!) to the question of how and why societies alter (Smith, 1992) (see also new trends in 'world history', e.g., Curthoys and Lake, 2006). To a (small!) degree 'historical sociology' still remains different to 'history', because they are interested in different kinds of social change at different times and for different reasons (San Pedro Lopez, 2004). A primary focus for historical sociologists from Weber to Parsons to Giddens has been identifying 'big picture' theories of what social processes have driven large-scale social and political changes, such as the rise of democracies or the occurrence of dictatorship or the creation of the working class. (Let us remember that Marx's was a deeply historical theory. In his view, it was the dialectical relation between labour and capital that was the 'engine' of history and the motor for social change.)

Nevertheless, the very aspect of a social theory that makes it compelling, namely its ability to identify common processes and the *generalizable* features of events and relationships, are precisely what hinders its ability to be very meaningful about a local context. Historians like to use these theories to understand the past, but they like even more to add detail and complexity to them. Many qualitative researchers will sympathize with the tension between developing 'theory', that is identifying causal relationships and social processes from a set of similar situations, and weaving together theory-based insights into a coherent explanation of the occurrence and character of a unique situation. This tension also exists *within* both qualitative research (think phenomenology and portraiture versus grounded theory) and history itself.

The most obvious difference between the practice of scholarly history and that of qualitative research is in their different approaches to the relationship between theory and method. Qualitative research has developed several formal methods to guide the processes of data collection, analysis and writing in each of the different traditions of qualitative research (Creswell, 2007). By contrast, it is virtually unheard of that any historian would have a formal plan for data collection or analysis. The practice of coding data is in itself already a far more self-conscious process than anything I ever encountered in history, let alone strategies like member checking or constant comparison. By and large, you just follow your nose, and at some level, I think most of us really value the emergent qualities of this loose approach.

Yet, historians often mentally invent for themselves exactly the sorts of practices that qualitative researchers have named, discussed and formalized. We/they mentally make note of 'themes' and concepts; we/they identify discourses, explore social categories and describe relationships. Like qualitative researchers, historians tend to iteratively (abductively) move between primary sources and 'secondary' or published theoretical material, using the latter to illuminate the subjects of the former, and then returning to the primary sources to reconsider and gather more material. Therefore, slowly, analysis develops which may or may not include the explicit development of new theory.

Historians are very conscious that writing is a central act of analysis (Berger et al., 2003; Burke, 2001; Curthoys and Docker, 2006; Rusen, 2005). History is much more deeply entrenched in literary traditions than qualitative inquiry, which conforms more to the genre of scientific writing. While historians naturally privilege their own accounts and retain claims on truth telling and the accuracy and appropriateness of their interpretations (as we shall see in the following section), they have also always been conscious, in a way most qualitative researchers are *not*, that their work is literary, that its persuasiveness inheres as much in its style and in the way the story is put together as in its empirical bases (Clendinnen, 1999; Curthoys and Docker, 2006). The conventions of published history do not lie in the format of aims, methods, results and conclusions. Historical writing is often without organizational subheadings; its genre is the literary essay, in which the reader is led along a path of argued interpretation with the writer acting as narrator, tour guide and fabricator.

As an increasing number of scholars begin to work in both history *and* qualitative research, historians may become more deliberate in their process-methods and qualitative researchers more sophisticated in their approach to context. Adele Clarke is an outstanding example of a scholar who works in both traditions, and whose practice can incorporate both the literary, imaginative and rhetorical *and* the formal, methodical and empirical at relevant points in her work. It is perhaps not surprising that a scholar who was impelled to move from qualitative research to history (and then to continue with both) was working on health and medical issues (especially reproduction) from a feminist perspective, which, as I show in the following section, often tends to beg historical questions (Clarke, 1998). Clarke's theory-method package – situational analysis – deliberately includes time, change and history as important components of analysis (Clarke, 2005).

But for now, the relationship between theory and method for the historian, then, is not predominantly located in the research process itself. It is a more subtle matter, involving conceptually locating historical practice in the ideological aims and approach of one's history writing.

HISTORIOGRAPHY AND THE USES OF HISTORY

To explore the theoretical foundations and methodologies of history, or any other discipline for that matter, we must first understand why it was written. The uses of history range from the heavily ideological and utilitarian (and this is often the *primary* way in which public health encounters history) to the domains of pleasure, entertainment and curiosity. However, mostly they converge on what cultural ('postmodern') historian Hayden White described as 'some idea of what a good society might be'. 'Any science of society', according to White, 'should be' – I would say, always is – 'launched in the service of some conception of social justice, equity, freedom, and progress' (White, 1973). This was as true for historians in the past as the present, but their versions of what might make society 'better' were often very different from our own.

Empiricist / 'Whig' history

Should not history be the incontrovertible record of the past? Leopold von Ranke (1795–1886), the nineteenth-century German founding father of the modern scholarly field of history (Krieger, 1977; Rusen, 1990), is traditionally regarded as the chief exponent of this view. For Ranke, history ought to be as objective and reliable as chemistry or botany (which were just coming into being at that time: science was new then, too, the word 'scientist' not even invented until the 1830s [Fisch, 1991]). History should be 'just the facts', an account drawn from close examination of 'all the documents' (by which he meant political records, diaries, letters and newspaper articles), with the historian as an external, neutral observer whose job was to neither 'judge the past' nor 'instruct one's contemporaries about the future', but merely to 'show how it actually was'. In other words, for historians today Ranke represents the *empiricist* approach to history (Gilbert, 1990; Huisman and Warner, 2004; Iggers and Powell, 1990).

This form of history exercises considerable attraction to scholars in public health. For many public health researchers, history is often primarily considered simply as a *source of data* used simply to generate a *record* of the past, very much in the Rankean mould. This is the case for most histories of individual hospitals or medical schools, which aim simply to record events and people.

Similarly, many practitioner-authored works, in the traditions of antiquarian research (Griffiths, 1996), are largely chronological lists of the experiences and accomplishments of their counterparts in the past. Empiricist history is also of interest to health researchers whose historical research is conducted in order to *develop and test theories* about, for example, the habits of infectious diseases or the effectiveness of public health interventions. One of the most famous examples of this sort of history is the debate about whether decline in mortality in Western nations over the past century and a half (or so) can be attributed to public health interventions such as immunization, or if have arisen almost entirely as a result of increasing nutrition and fertility (Colgrove, 2002; Huisman and Warner, 2004; McKeown and Record, 1962; Szreter, 1988, 2002). Historical data of this kind is often of particular interest to researchers interested in the social determinants of health.

But of course, there is no such thing as an objective just-the-facts record of the past. The historian must choose what documents and events to select and discard; s/he must then make the selections meaningful and interesting by weaving them together in a story. In health and medicine, an often dominating story was that of 'the conquest of epidemic disease' (Winslow, 1980 [1943]). Frequently written by physicians and health officers, these histories detailed the progress of medical science from primitive times to the present, from Hippocrates and Galen to Pasteur and Koch (Cunningham, 1996; Latour, 1988; Parish, 1968). Practitioner–authors who had worked for government departments of public health wrote a similar story about the development of public health itself, from the heroic quarantine measures applied to control plague in medieval Europe to the sanitary measures advocated, in the days before germ theory, by men like Edwin Chadwick (architect of a raft of sanitary reforms like nightsoil disposal, building codes of housing and the regulation of refuse and industry), John Snow (who identified a water pump as the source of an outbreak of cholera, and hence cholera as waterborne), August Semmelweis (who insisted on physicians washing their hands between patients as a means of preventing puerperal fever and lowering maternal mortality), and Joseph Lister (who generated *antiseptic* and *aseptic* conditions for surgery) (Newsholme, 1927; Rosen, 1993 [1958]; Lewis, 2003; D. Porter, 1999b).

Although purporting to simply record the series of events that led up to present day conditions, these sorts of histories in fact serve several functions – and the awareness of these multiple functions has led historians to a critique of empiricist history. What seems merely factual is in fact, as I have said, a powerful *story*, one told (like any good story) to produce a particular set of effects on its audience. The sort of story I have described in the preceding section does several things. Firstly, it assumes a trajectory: it superimposes a beginning, middle and end onto the past, and in so doing generates a sense that history is moving towards a particular place, that it is *teleological*. This sense has strong imaginative power and has been common in narratives in the West since the Industrial Revolution (which was, and often still is, represented in terms of 'achievement', 'progress' and 'accomplishment'). Progress narratives were and are in everything from evolutionary biology – evolution as 'progress' from single celled critters to that pinnacle of alleged superiority, *homo sapiens* – to political nationalism (Beer, 1983; Jardine, 2003).

However, they are not true. The history of health and medicine does not show a linear increase of enlightenment and progress. Scientists did not just accumulate increasingly accurate evidence and concepts, nor did health bureaucrats keep making better, more informed decisions (as public health advocates ought to know from bitter experience, if nothing else!). Nor did health officials always make decisions for the 'right' reasons: sanitation proceeded on the basis of miasmatic theory, which today we consider 'wrong', and could even have been *hindered* by germ theory, which today we consider 'right' (Cunningham and Williams, 1992; Worboys, 2000). (Evolution doesn't 'progress' either, and I refer the lay reader to Stephen Jay Gould's books, especially *Wonderful Life,* for a stunning understanding of this and of how concepts of natural and human history get troublesomely intertwined (Gould, 1990). The most famous critique of progress narratives can be found in Thomas Kuhn's paradigmatic analysis of paradigm change (Kuhn, 1996).)

Secondly, this story serves mostly unstated social and ideological purposes: to celebrate and legitimate government-based, institutionalized, scientific health and medicine. The story is a story of *triumph*, a quality that validates the public health enterprise and shields it from critique. It is a good story, too, full of familiar and compelling plot devices: men of vision and courage (= hero), like Louis Pasteur, fight to overcome the forces of evil (= disease), struggling along the way to convince the prejudiced and the ignorant (= opponent), such as doctors who thought disease was caused by unpleasant odours associated with the socially devalued (the poor and the non-White). These plot devices lend the story moral weight. It serves to *commemorate*, and by corollary to reaffirm, the authority of the 'great men' who built and controlled the public health enterprise. It generates *originary moments* by commemorating what science values: the claim of discovery. So many histories of health and medicine are written to celebrate 'the first' clinical trial, the first discoverer of vaccination, and so forth (Parish, 1968). It also serves to establish a *tradition* in remembering and valuing the past, and, by anchoring us to that past, to construct our collective (Western) identity as rational, scientific and forward-thinking (Huisman and Warner, 2004; D. Porter, 1999a).

This kind of teleological history is termed 'Whig history' (after a genre of late eighteenth and early nineteenth-century histories that viewed history as the path towards the apex of human political development, British parliamentary, constitutional monarchy [Jardine, 2003]). It has long been subject to critique by those who recognize what the story leaves out. For example, this story about public health only includes particular actors – 'great men' who made significant discoveries or who, as doctors or as statesmen, had enormous influence on their social sphere, as is if it were individuals, rather than social changes or shifts in practice, that affect history (Reverby and Rosner, 1979). This makes the many other actors that took part in past events invisible, which is why women and non-White folk get left out of so many histories (Scott, 1996). In other words, empiricist/Whig history fails to acknowledge that theoretical perspectives inform the selection, interpretation and representation of 'facts'.

(The reader will have noticed that I've just done some Whig history myself by positioning Ranke as a 'founding father' of his field, as if it were 'fathers' who 'found' things and as if there was no real history written before him. Scholarly historians often reject histories written by earlier generations and those written by nonprofessional historians, like doctors. So by beginning my story, per tradition, with Ranke as history-to-be-rejected, I make the rejection of empiricist history normative and validate my approach to history as correct (Huisman and Warner, 2004). Yet, like most historians and qualitative researchers, I too ground my research in primary sources; I try to put aside my own preconceived ideas in order to 'listen' to those sources; and therefore, while I acknowledge that history is always interpretive, I like to insist on the realness of my histories.)

The other problem with empiricist history is that its claims of objectivity are very often only a thin disguise for deeply ideological purposes. This explains my discomfort with my public health colleagues' use of history to support their advocacy for tobacco control. Theirs is a largely triumphalist narrative of progress towards ever-increasing tobacco control, accomplished through heroic advocacy in the face of pitched battles with corporate interests (Cunningham, 1996; Glantz and Balbach, 2000). Their approach has been empiricist: mining millions of tobacco industry documents – letters, reports, marketing materials, notes of meetings – for any quotations that demonstrate how tobacco companies have deceived the public and manipulated and corrupted government practice for profit (Chapman et al., 2003; Byrne, and Carter, 2003; Glantz and Balbach, 2000). I was and am politically deeply committed to tobacco control, but I was and am simultaneously deeply uncomfortable with this kind of history: one claiming objectivity, but pursuing a preset intellectual and moral agenda; one that excludes material *not* related to the project of shaming the tobacco industry; one that sidelines discussions of the ideas, representations, language and values that frame its own politics or those of the actors of the past. Other histories of tobacco are both possible and, *pace* advocates, even desirable, as I shall show in the following section.

Social history

The strongest critical thrust against Whiggish history came from what was, in the 1970s, termed 'the "new" social history' (in fact it had many antecedents). Emerging from the feminist, civil rights and other liberationist movements of the 1960s and 1970s, and with foundations in what was by then a half century of Marxist/left wing social critique and historical writing, these histories were driven by the ideological and political agendas of the day. Firstly, they intended to bring actors other than 'great men' into historical view, and secondly, they were written to validate the experiences and capacities of these social groups.

In the arena of health and medicine, the manifesto for the new social history was laid out in the introduction to an edited collection produced by Susan Reverby and David Rosner while they were graduate students, generating a still-expanding universe of new insights and new research (Reverby and Rosner, 1979). The search for the history of various minority groups led to an enormous expansion of topics that could be studied: for instance by examining the history of nursing as well as of surgery, or exploring institutions, such as hospitals and asylums, founded by and for these groups. A major challenge for 'history from below' was that of accessing the voices and experiences of these groups, since the poor and excluded were often illiterate, leaving few records behind them (Fissell, 1991; Joyce, 1991). Reverby and Rosner were especially interested in acknowledging the agency of non-White populations, so that public health and medicine did not appear simply as things that happened *to* minority populations – a way 'to teach them how to live' (Sears, 1992) – but were altered and incorporated into their own practices, or rejected (Reverby and Rosner, 2004). A recent, elegant example of social history is Margaret Humphrey's history of malaria in the United States, which includes the reflections and views of the impoverished black communities that were mostly affected (Humphreys, 2001).

Researching the socially disadvantaged rapidly led historians to examine the power relations in which their subjects were enmeshed. For example, social historians examined how nineteenth-century welfare (substantively including medical care) was distributed to the 'deserving' but withheld from the 'undeserving' poor, and how these categories were defined and redefined over time (Fissell, 1991). Similarly, feminist historians traced the exclusion of midwifery by the processes of professionalization in (mostly masculine) medicine, and the subsequent 'medicalization' of women's reproductive bodies (English and Ehrenreich, 1978; Feldberg et al., 2003; Clarke, 1998) – though of course (as I discuss in the next section) it turns out that this was a very *middle class* 'feminist' view: getting *access* to 'medicalized' case such as caesareans was and remains much more important to women from low socioeconomic locations.

Public health interventions were suddenly revealed, not as benign or even well intentioned, but as the exercise of often punitive social power. For example, historians revealed biomedicine's primary role in the construction of deviant sexuality and in the policing and literal incarceration (in so-called 'lock hospitals' or on islands) of women defined as immoral, diseased or disorderly (Bashford, 2004, 2006; Lewis, 1998; D. Porter, 1999a; Spongberg, 1997; Strange and Bashford, 2003). Perhaps the most tragic end of this spectrum is the history of 'social hygiene' (eugenics), which was a fundamental component of public health policy in all Western nations in the period between the First and Second World Wars. Social historians explored the institutionalization and/or forced sterilization of people defined as 'unfit', including those medically classified as mentally retarded and large numbers of indigenous peoples, and of course, the coercive euthanasia policies of the national socialists (Kevles, 1985; D. Porter, 1999a; Proctor, 1988). Reverby herself produced several works on women's history (Reverby, 1987;

Reverby and Helly, 1992) and then explored the vexed social and ethical issues that arose from the revelation that the US Public Health Service had deliberately withheld diagnoses and treatment in order to study 'the natural progression of syphilis' over the course of 40 years in a town of poor black sharecroppers without their knowledge or consent (Reverby, 2000).

While it was largely focused on reading wider social relations 'in' to the contexts of health and medicine, social historians did not forget to study the reverse – the influence of disease (and disease control measures, not to mention changes in agricultural practice, lifestyle and consumption,) on society itself. Present day 'ecological' histories are important in returning historical focus to macro and geographical social changes, such as patterns of human migration (Anderson, 2004; Crosby, 1986). Some of the most important have charted the devastating impacts of disease on former European colonies and the long-lasting implications for indigenous populations (Anderson, 2004; Diamond, 1997). But, as eminent social historians Charles Rosenberg commented about the three devastating epidemics of cholera in early nineteenth-century America (which provided the stimulus and context for initiating considerable public health reform), each epidemic occurs in unique social circumstances and hence may be understood differently and generate quite different social responses (Rosenberg, 1962).

Many diseases can, and have, been seen as primary shapers of society in similar ways – leprosy and the identification and exclusion of the stigmatized (Bashford and Hooker, 2001; Strange and Bashford, 2003); syphilis and the rearrangement of social and sexual mores (Quetel, 1990; Brandt, 1985); smallpox and the development of vaccination (Bashford, 2004; Farmer, 1993) – and so forth, up to and including SARS (shadowed by avian influenza) with its capacity to influence the reorganization of global health governance and its reidentification of Asian peoples (but also travellers) as the reservoir of danger in the modern world (Bashford, 2006; Fidler, 2004). (The historical eye here also reveals the extent to which attention to the 'new and re-emerging' infectious diseases, far from altering practices, actually re-inscribe many of colonial-era ideologies of medicine and public health (King, 2002).)

My own micro study of tobacco control legislation in Australia was grounded in social history. Social historians have documented the vastly different forms and practices of smoking in the past, from the peace pipes of the 'New World' to the rise of the cigarette in the context of mass production and marketing and the reorganization of the working day in industrialized nations (Goodman, 1993). They tracked the social significances of smoking from the daring postures of the flappers to various poses of power, authority and reflection (Brandt, 2007). One historical sociologist identified smoking practices as extensions of the 'civilizing' process in the history of manners (Hughes, 2003). Unsurprisingly, a prime focus of their attention has been to the ways in which smoking was practiced and controlled, particularly in across the increasingly adversarial political environment of the late twentieth century (Tyrrell, 1999; Walker, 1984). Histories of control practices and campaigns are of course forms of social history (Chapman, 1992; Jacobson et al., 1997; Studlar, 2002; Troyer and Markle, 1983).

Social history has left historians with a twin legacy: it encouraged health advocacy and activism on the one hand, but generated critiques of public health endeavours on the other. Many qualitative health researchers would relate to this dilemma; think, for example, of indigenous health, where public health interventions are so urgently needed, and where so many public health interventions have had such destructive effects in the past.

History can help qualitative health researchers to think critically about their own projects, while remaining committed to the values and ideals that inspired them in the first place. History offers the perspective afforded by distance: once the immediate exigencies of politics and personalities are gone, it is often easier to be critical of how health issues in the past have been framed and acted upon. It is easier, now, to see how otherwise admirable and certainly well intentioned public health workers framed indigenous women as poor mothers and removed their children, with disastrous consequences; easier to see prostitutes as vulnerable women in need of support, not as moral monsters in need of control; easier to identify and analyze the different kinds of bodily ideals that have framed public health endeavours, and so question, not merely our own physical ideals, but the entire project of self-discipline with the objective of achieving what public health and medicine deem to be an appropriate body. In time, perhaps, if and when tobacco companies become less threatening opponents, it might be more possible to see tobacco control as enmeshed in marketing and other processes of persuasion, not simply as scientific and moral righteousness. This critical stance is sharpened and honed by attention, not just to experience and outcomes, but also to meanings.

Cultural history

The 'add minority group and stir' (Noddings, 2001) approach of social history inevitably raises questions about knowledge and meaning. Start wondering about how women were active in Victorian era public health, when all the officials were men, and one soon realizes the answer to this depends on how women were seen (which turns out to be often in terms of 'purity', as the agents of bodily, domestic and behavioural and moral 'hygiene', and 'pollution', as agents of physical and moral contamination [Bashford, 1998]). Ask further about how gendered binaries – mind/body, hard/soft, public/private (Reverby and Helly, 1992) – colour our worldview, and you start seeing categories like 'woman' and 'man' not as starting places for writing history (as in, 'where were all the women?'), but as *themselves* historical (Scott, 1986) ('what did they mean by "woman"?'). As Mary Fissell put in, she suddenly saw all the 'social facts' she had so painstakingly garnered about early nineteenth-century working 'families' from parish records as *cultural constructions*. What she was witnessing was the construction (and reconstruction) of the very idea of 'the family': families were not (just) facts, they were *artefacts* of systems of cultural attitudes and social power (Fissell, 2004).

The focus on meaning (which also comes under the umbrella term 'postmodernism') has been, and continues to be, an enormously and productive area of research in the history of health and medicine. For example, the HIV/AIDS (human immunodeficiency virus/acquired immune deficiency syndrome) epidemic has been treated as an 'epidemic of signification' that has had profound implications as to who was identified as 'at risk' or as 'sick' and how they were governed and 'treated' (both by medicine and by other people in their society) (Treichler, 1999; Sontag, 1991). (For the purposes of comparison, a 'social history' approach might have stopped with identifying the experience of discriminatory treatment for homosexuals, prostitutes and IV (intravenous) drug users.)

New theoretical approaches to the history of health and medicine have been derived from these insights. For example, Charles Rosenberg, the author of some of the most canonical works in the social history of medicine, proposed that we understand 'disease as 'frame': 'pictures' derived variously from social preoccupations, cultural beliefs and biomedicine, whose creation and implications for various social actors can be historically traced (Huisman and Warner, 2004; Rosenberg and Golden, 1992). As qualitative researchers know well, a 'frame' offers us a particular view of a picture: it sharpens some aspects of an issue and obscures others (Goffman, 1974). Actor network theory, whose methodology effectively required scholars to trace the 'histories' of ideas and technologies (pasteurization was an early, famous example (Latour, 1988)), was developed to overcome formerly assumed, and now increasingly untenable, distinctions, such as that between structure and agency and between 'nature' and 'society'.

This 'cultural turn' is of course familiar to qualitative health researchers under the guise of 'critical theory'. As is the case for qualitative health researchers, the work of Michel Foucault – itself deeply historical – has been much utilized in the cultural history of health and medicine (Dean, 1994; Huisman and Warner, 2004). His interest in 'discourse', in how systems of power/knowledge are generated and what sorts of effects they have in constructing identity and subjectivity, sharpened critiques of gender and race in medicine (Anderson, 2002; Bashford, 2004). His insistence that bodies were and are not simply biological entities, but that 'the body' itself also *has a history*, directed attention to the importance of health and medicine in constituting bodies marked with gender, race, class and sexuality (Gilman, 1985, 1998; Huisman and Warner, 2004; Jordanova, 1989). And his concepts of biopolitics and governmentality allowed historians to newly explore how public health operated as a means of government, from the level of self-government – the populace trained in all sorts of practices to micromanage their bodies, from hand washing and nose blowing to calorie-control – to the patrolling of national borders and the identification and exclusion of potentially dangerous 'Others' (Bashford, 2004, 2006; D. Porter, 1999a).

The 'cultural turn' has drawn from, and added to, research that questioned the nature and the limits to the validity of scientific evidence (for examples on the contraceptive pill see (Marks, 2001; Martin, 1987)), including that gold standard of public health, epidemiology (Lupton and Petersen, 1996; Latour, 1988; Cunningham and Williams, 1992). Historians of ideas traced how apparently factual, well-established scientific concepts, like germ theory, had complicated histories that were shaped by social structures (such as the professionalization of medicine [R. Porter, 1999]) and cultural values (including concepts of purity and pollution as well as of objectivity, an attribute that has a reasonably recent history [Bashford, 1998]) as well as by metaphors (of 'seed' and 'soil' [Worboys, 2000]), narratives (of growth, fertility, invasion [Martin, 1994]) and technical practices (laboratories, microscopes and cultures [Cunningham and Williams, 1992]).

Questioning evidence about health may be discomfiting for some in public health, and make cultural history look at best tangential, and at worst, absurd. For example, historians trained to examine the 'social construction of science' are currently curious about how particular forms of epidemiology became constructed as a widely understood and acceptable evidence base for the early studies that linked cigarette smoking with lung cancer and heart disease (Berridge, 1998, 2003b). This sort of history can seem nonsensical to tobacco control advocates, because it seems to be self-evident ('of course we needed epidemiology to identify this problem!'), or it can be viewed as an anathema to those who have fought bitterly to establish that the negative health outcomes of tobacco smoking are *real* in the face of industry denial and malfeasance. But for the many qualitative health researchers who grapple with concepts of 'evidence' in their own research practice or in complicated health issues, cultural histories may provide useful insights into the many factors that influence what is regarded as true or authoritative and what is not.

I was trained in history-since-the-cultural-turn, and that explains why, when reading debates about tobacco control, I wanted to go hunting for the many meanings loaded words like 'drug' and 'addict' were bearing. I certainly was not going to treat these terms as self-evidence biological entities. Instead, I wanted to trace the social circumstances that produced these meanings, among them, perhaps, a shift to a sort of high-corporatization of politics, circumstances in which the politics of 'drugs' could fit neoliberal discourses that posited autonomous individual choice as the key determinant of health, and on the other could be mobilised to critique the corruptions and predations of hyper-consumer society-capitalism (Berridge, 1990, 2003a; Boon, 2002; Courtwright, 2001; Davenport-Hines, 2002; Goodman, 1995; Hooker and Chapman, 2007; Knipe, 1995; Porter and Teich, 1995). In a more sophisticated approach, Jordan Goodman saw the history of tobacco through the lens of 'cultures of dependence' (Goodman, 1993), which were at once conceptual, physical, economic and cultural, and which were located in the very real structures of colonialism and industrialization (and see his subsequent interest in the cultural history of 'drugs' [Goodman, 1995]).

In the end, scholars in both history and qualitative research are often similarly concerned with the consequences of health and health practices for experience and identity. I therefore conclude this essay by thinking a little further about these issues.

MAKING THINGS STRANGE: INVESTIGATING EXPERIENCE AND IDENTITY

How to understand and represent those many 'Others' who lack social power has been, and remains, a challenge for both historians and qualitative health researchers.

A primary response to this problem was and is to try to have those Others speak for themselves as much as possible. For historians, this means looking for letters, diaries, speeches, photographs, interview notes, reports of conversations, drawings and material objects that might allow them to draw directly from these other peoples' experiences. Where it is possible to undertake this, oral history is a favoured approach by both historians and qualitative researchers alike. However, as qualitative researchers are only too aware, oral histories do not present reliable evidence. Interviewees are constantly *reconstructing* both their memories of their experiences and the significance of those memories throughout the interview process, in narratives that dynamically (re)create their sense of identity (Phillips, 2004). These days we even know something of the biological basis of the constant reprocessing and resourcing of memory.

Nevertheless, it is not just the partiality of memory that is worrisome. As feminist historian Joan Scott points out, and as I discussed in the preceding section, uncritically accepting the evidence of experience avoids analysing how the social categories with which the 'experience' is associated are *themselves* historical. 'The evidence of experience then becomes evidence for the fact of difference, rather than a way of exploring how difference is established, how it operates, how and in what ways it constitutes subjects who see and act in the world' (Scott, 1991). That is, researching black experience only serves to emphasize difference. In a foundational paper, Richard Dyer argued instead that we should 'make whiteness strange' (Dyer, 1997) – to see instead how white culture has become so well established as a norm that it has become invisible, and hence how 'coloured' identities are defined through their differences to white. History can help us to make our own assumptions and approaches 'strange'.

Let us take for example the adolescent – a group whose health practices are often regarded as of enormous importance. Interventions with adolescents are often seen as crucial in terms of generating lifelong protective health habits, especially for diet, physical activity and drug use. We could, and many do, research adolescent experience, most usefully by asking adolescents themselves. But if we look historically, we can see that the category 'adolescent' is itself only a recent arrival, a product of the interlocking systems of medical knowledge and social power in the mid twentieth century (Prescott, 1998; Johnson, 1993).

This kind of questioning can be disquieting, because it questions concepts, categories and narratives that are attached to political goals that research in health supports. Scott's paper, for example, critiques a triumphalist narrative of empowerment – an autobiographical account of a gay man whose experience of entering a bathhouse for the first time, in the 1970s, tells of the ways homosexual desire was so irrepressible that it evaded social control and became visible. Scott's alternate reading of this account shows how identity, political power and consciousness were coconstituted, rather than their being some prediscursive unmediated 'experience' of a gay identity (Scott, 1991). In plainer language, you do not just 'feel' something anymore than you just smoke (Hughes, 2003): 'experience' is always learned, mediated and interpreted in a social context.

In fact, a great deal of historical attention has been recently devoted to the extraordinary importance of public health in the fabrication of identity (personal and collective) and of many social categories themselves. At the most basic level of analysis, biomedicine works by defining the boundary between 'normal' and 'pathological', producing new sets of identities in consequence (Gilman, 1985). Historians influenced by Foucault's explorations of forms of discipline and regulation and their production of different categories of bodies have suggested that public health acts *spatially* to 'fabricate' forms of modern identity (Foucault, 1973, 1977, 1978). David Armstrong applied Mary Douglas' observations about the boundary rituals that separated the polluted from the pure to different hygiene regimes to argue that the spaces thus created became constitutive of modern forms of identity (Armstrong, 1983, 1993). Later scholars applied the varying forms of disciplinary and regulatory power Foucault identified in relation to crime to the government and care of personal and national bodies. Viewed from this angle, public health looks like a series of modes of surveillance and governance, from the most direct and impositional – Foucault's residual 'power of the sword', expressed in forcible quarantine, involuntary confinement, or the exclusion of unwanted Others by health checks at immigration – to those that are more subtle and pervasive, such as through clinics and screening programs (Bashford, 2004; Rosenberg, 1989). Identity may also be *produced* by epidemiology and discourses of risk, with new categories of identity being generated, experienced, accepted and sometimes contested and resisted by categories that are derived from population-based data (Lupton and Petersen, 1996; Bashford and Hooker, 2001; Hooker and Bashford, 2002).

The importance of tracing discourses of power/knowledge in biomedicine – while imperfectly but stubbornly respecting the separate integrity of local voices – may be most vivid in the case of the history of 'tropical' – now 'postcolonial' – health and medicine (Anderson, 2004). Mainstream histories of health and medicine largely have had, and continue to have, a focus limited to Europe and North America. The first histories of tropical medicine, for example, charted the geographical spread and impact of various 'new world' diseases (Ackerknecht, 1965; Crosby, 1972), recorded white achievements in understanding, controlling and treating them, and celebrated heroic 'great doctor' (European) characters who fought extraordinary battles against little known diseases alone and unaided in jungle settings (Wilson, 1942; Anderson, 1996). This has not only normalized Europe as the standard against which other histories can be compared (leading to questions such as 'how far behind is public health in Africa?' or to expectations that health and medicine in non-Western nations will 'develop' in the same pattern and stages), but has obscured the imperial/ colonial context in which health and medicine themselves developed and the degree to which public health and medicine are inherently imperial projects.

Critiques of colonialism led to historical interest in the experiences and lives of the colonized, and this gave the history of health and medicine prominence, since the study of disease and treatment gave them access to personal and social life in the colonies and revealed much of the functioning of the colonial state (Macleod and Lewis, 1988; Manderson, 1996). Historians offered critical insights into how health and medicine were central in generating concepts and categories of race and citizenship, and how government practices of health were mechanisms by which White identities could be realized and validated while non-White bodies could be marked, segregated, disciplined and retrained for citizenship in the colonial world (Anderson, 2006). In later works, the extent to which Western models of health and medicine actually became hegemonic in colonial settings have been questioned, and some of the ways that local identities and practices could remain resistant to the colonial state's attempts to reform them have been identified (Anderson, 1995; Arnold, 1993).

As is the case for qualitative research in health, these studies inevitably raise questions about the relationship between researchers, who are socially privileged in many ways, and their subjects (Chakrabarty, 1992; Stoler, 2006). As Warwick Anderson pointed out, a truly postcolonial history might actually seek to treat the history of their subject in the developed and developing worlds in the same frame, looking at the links and movements of metaphors, people, money, techniques and practice between different sites (Anderson, 2004). But while in this instance, historians might remain highly sensitive to the construction of whiteness as well as of other racial identities (Anderson, 2002) (not to mention the colonial relation of medicine to the body itself), it would take a radical alteration of the entire genre of scholastic history to actually engage the voices and experiences of the colonized Others.

CONCLUDING COMMENT: THE LONG VIEW AND THE LOCAL – KEEPING AN EYE ON SOCIAL CHANGE

If you are a poor immigrant being directed to hospital-based childbirth in a Western nation – or an Italian grandmother with a heart attack overhearing doctors wonder if it is worth treating you because of your weight – or an Asian-looking person in a Western city during an outbreak of avian influenza – or the mother of a First Nation child being examined in a clinic staffed by White health care workers – you might well feel that history often matters to health and medicine.

There is something about holding the long view of history that lends itself to a mentally reflective pose. It is hard to commit full and unqualified belief in scientific knowledge when one has observed how equally deeply held supposed 'facts' have been superseded time and again – and this is true for those of us who simultaneously accept the uniquely powerful purchase science has on reality. It is even harder to place an unqualified and passionate faith in public health intervention, when the historical eye has revealed time and again that well-intentioned actions can also be methods for imposing hegemony, for generating social stigma and for reconstructing highly negative forms of self-identity.

Even while historians can and do pay attention to the nitty-gritty of everyday life, historical methods tend to understand and represent these anecdotes and details in relation to the wider social arrangements and cultural discourses that constitute them and are shaped by them in turn. Historical writing tracks – and a lot of qualitative research does not – at least the before, and not infrequently comments on the 'after', of their subject. Historians can keep an eye on both social change – new policies in health, new public concerns, changes in the framing of diseases – but also the continuities – ongoing power structures, methods of governance. Often health issues that seem novel today turn out to express long-standing cultural anxieties or attitudes, as in the relationship between genetics today and eugenics of yesteryear. Alternatively, changes in health policy, practice and especially promotion may actually appear superficial when the effects of the deep continuities of economics and social structure are considered.

History can be instrumentally useful. It can provide a critique of current practices and thinking, as when feminists referred to the history of noninterventionist, midwife supported forms of active labour when protesting against medicalized childbirth – or, as now, when histories of the regulated and unregulated body can remind us to keep our critical distance from the discourses and policies surrounding the 'obesity epidemic' (Gard and Wright, 2005). It can provide comparable and sample events from which to draw expectations about events of concern today (is the swine flu epidemic of 2009 like or unlike that of 1976? [Neustadt, 1983]), or demonstrate the limitations and consequences of particular ways of thinking. Much of the approach of critical theory and of recent sociology has emerged from considering social change.

Qualitative researchers should use this chapter to clarify for themselves *how* history may be useful to their research and to be explicit about that use in undertaking historical research. Is it simply to get data in support of their cause, or is it to understand some dimension of how that cause came to exist? Qualitative researchers should be equally self-conscious about the sorts of questions they ask of their primary sources. Accepting the particularities of each case, while simultaneously analysing the set of changing social and cultural circumstances in which the case is embedded, even while pursuing an instrumentalist project, may help identify significant new features or significant limitations to one's work.

And possibly one may then also succumb to enchantments, to the power and wonder of human stories as they emerge from the past.

REFERENCES

Ackerknecht, E. (1965) *History and Geography of the Most Important Diseases.* New York: Hafner.

Anderson, W. (1995) 'Excremental Colonialism: Public Health and the Poetics of Pollution', *Critical Inquiry*, 21: 640–69.

Anderson, W. (1996) 'Immunities of Empire: Race, Disease and the New Tropical Medicine, 1900–1940', *British History of Medicine*, 70: 94–118.

Anderson, W. (2002) *The Cultivation of Whiteness: Science, Health and Racial Destiny in Australia.* Melbourne: Melbourne University Press.

Anderson, W. (2004) 'Postcolonial Histories of Medicine'. In F. Huisman and J.H. Warner (eds) *Locating Medical History* (pp. 285–308). Baltimore, MD: The Johns Hopkins University Press.

Anderson, W. (2006) *Colonial Pathologies: American Tropical Medicine, Race, and Hygiene in the Philippines.* Durham, NC: Duke University Press.

Armstrong, D. (1983) *Political Anatomy of the Body: Medical Knowledge in Britain in the Twentieth Century.* Cambridge: Cambridge University Press.

Armstrong, D. (1993) 'Public Health Spaces and the Fabrication of Identity', *Sociology*, 27: 393–410.

Arnold, D. (1993) *Colonizing the Body: State Medicine and Epidemic Disease in Nineteenth-Century India.* Berkeley, CA: University of California Pres.

Bashford, A. (1998) *Purity and Pollution: Gender, Embodiment and Victorian Medicine.* London: MacMillan.

Bashford, A. (2004) *Imperial Hygiene: A Critical History of Colonialism, Nationalism and Public Health.* London: Palgrave MacMillan.

Bashford, A. (ed.) (2006) *Medicine at the Border: Disease, Globalization and Security, 1850 to the Present.* London: Palgrave MacMillan.

Bashford, A. and Hooker, C. (eds) (2001) *Contagion: Historical and Cultural Studies.* London: Routledge.

Beer, G. (1983) *Darwin's Plots: Evolutionary Narrative in Darwin, George Eliot, and Nineteenth-Century Fiction.* London: Routledge and Kegan Paul.

Berger, S., Feldner, H., and Passmore, K. (eds) (2003) *Writing History: Theory and Practice.* Oxford: Oxford University Press.

Berridge, V. (1990) *Drugs Research and Policy in Britain: A Review of the 1980s.* Avebury: Gower Pub. Co.

Berridge, V. (1998) 'Science and Policy: The Case of Postwar British Smoking Policy'. In S. Lock, L.A. Reynolds, and E.M. Tansey (eds) *Ashes to Ashes: The History of Smoking and Health.* Amsterdam: Rodopi, 46: 143–71

Berridge, V. (2003a) 'History and Twentieth-Century Drug Policy: Telling True Stories?', *Medical History*, 47(4): 518–24.

Berridge, V. (2003b) 'Postwar Smoking Policy in Britain and the Redefinition of Public Health', *Twentieth Century British History*, 14(1): 61–82.

Boon, M. (2002) *The Road of Excess: A History of Writers on Drugs.* Cambridge, MA: Harvard University Press.

Brandt, A. (1985) *No Magic Bullet: A Social History of Venereal Disease in the United States Since 1880.* Oxford: Oxford University Press.

Brandt, A. (2007) *The Cigarette Century: The Rise, Fall, and Deadly Persistence of the Product that Defined America.* New York: Basic Books.

Bryan-Jones, K. and Chapman, S. (2006) 'Political Dynamics Promoting the Incremental Regulation of Secondhand Smoke: A Case Study of New South Wales, Australia', *BMC Public Health*, 6: 192.

Burke, P. (ed.) (2001) *New Perspectives on Historical Writing*. University Park, PA.: Pennsylvania State University Press.

Chakrabarty, D. (1992) 'Postcoloniality and the Artifice of History: Who Speaks for "Indian" Pasts?', *Representations*, 37: 1–26.

Chapman, S. (1992) 'Anatomy of a Campaign: The Attempt to Defeat the NSW Tobacco Advertising Prohibition Bill 1991', *Tobacco Control*, 1: 50–6.

Chapman, S., Byrne, F., and Carter, S.M. (2003) 'Australia is One of the Darkest Markets in the World: The Global Importance of Australian Tobacco Control', *Tobacco Control*, 12(Suppl 3): 1–3.

Clarke, A. (1998) *Disciplining Reproduction: Modernity, American Life Sciences, and 'the Problems of Sex'*. Berkeley, CA: University of California Press.

Clarke, A. (2005) *Situational Analysis: Grounded Theory after the Postmodern Turn*. Thousand Oaks, CA: Sage.

Clendinnen, I. (1999) *True Stories*. Sydney: ABC Books for the Australian Broadcasting Corporation.

Colgrove, J. (2002) 'The McKeown Thesis: A Historical Controversy and Its Enduring Influence', *American Journal of Public Health*, 92(5): 725–9.

Courtwright, D. (2001) *Forces of Habit: Drugs and the Making of the Modern World*. Cambridge, MA: Harvard University Press.

Creswell, J. (2007) *Qualitative Inquiry and Research Design: Choosing Among Five Approaches* (2nd Edition). Thousand Oaks, CA: Sage.

Crosby, A. (1972) *The Columbian Exchange: Biological and Cultural Consequences of 1492*. Westport, CT: Greenwood Press.

Crosby, A. (1986) *Ecological Imperialism: The Biological Expansion of Europe, 900–1900*. Cambridge: Cambridge University Press.

Cunningham, A. and Williams, P. (eds) (1992) *The Laboratory Revolution in Medicine*. Cambridge: Cambridge University Press.

Cunningham, R. (1996) *Smoke and Mirrors: The Canadian Tobacco War*. Ottawa: International Development Research Centre.

Curthoys, A. and Docker, J. (eds) (2006) *Is History Fiction?* Sydney: University of New South Wales Press.

Curthoys, A. and Lake, M. (eds) (2006) *Connected Worlds: History in Trans-national Perspective*. Canberra: ANU Press.

Davenport-Hines, R.P.T. (2002) *The Pursuit of Oblivion: A Global History of Narcotics*. New York: Norton.

Dean, M. (1994) *Critical and Effective Histories: Foucault's Methods and Historical Sociology*. London, New York: Routledge.

Diamond, J. (1997) *Guns, Germs, and Steel: The Fates of Human Societies*. New York: W.W. Norton and Co.

Dyer, R. (1997) *White*. London: Routledge.

English, D. and Ehrenreich, B. (1978) *For Her Own Good: 150 Years of the Experts' Advice to Women*. New York: Anchor.

Farmer, P. (1993) *AIDS and Accusation: Haiti and the Geography of Blame*. San Francisco: University of California Press.

Feldberg, G., Ladd-Taylor, M., Li, A., and McPherson, K. (eds) (2003) *Women, Health and Nation: Canada and the United States since 1945*. Toronto: McGill-Queens University Press.

Fidler, D. (2004) *SARS: Governance and the Globalization of Disease*. Houndmills, UK: Palgrave Macmillan.

Fisch, M. (1991) *William Whewell: A Composite Portrait*. Oxford: Clarendon Press.

Fissell, M. (1991) *Patients, Power, and the Poor in Eighteenth-Century Bristol*. Cambridge: Cambridge University Press.

Fissell, M. (2004) 'Making Meaning from the Margins: The New Cultural History of Medicine'. In F. Huisman and J.H. Warner (eds) *Locating Medical History*. Baltimore, MD: The Johns Hopkins University Press.

Foucault, M. (1973) *The Birth of the Clinic: An Archaeology of Medical Perception.* London: Routledge.

Foucault, M. (1977) *Discipline and Punish: The Birth of the Prison.* New York: Pantheon Books.

Foucault, M. (1978) *The History of Sexuality.* New York: Pantheon Books.

Gard, M. and Wright, J. (2005) *The Obesity Epidemic: Science, Morality and Ideology.* New York: Routledge.

Giddens, A. (2006) *In Defence of Sociology: Essays, Interpretations, and Rejoinders.* Cambridge: Polity Press.

Gilbert, F. (1990) *History: Politics or Culture? Reflections on Ranke and Burchardt.* Princeton: Princeton University Press.

Gilman, S. (1985) *Difference and Pathology: Stereotypes of Sexuality, Race, and Madness.* Ithaca, NY: Cornell University Press.

Gilman, S. (1998) *Creating Beauty to Cure the Soul: Race and Psychology in the Shaping of Aesthetic Surgery.* Durham, NC: Duke University Press.

Glantz, S. and Balbach, E.D. (2000) *Tobacco War.* Berkeley, CA: University of California Press.

Goffman, E. (1974) *Frame Analysis: An Essay on the Organization of Experience.* London: Harper and Row.

Goldthorpe, J. (1991) 'The Uses of History in Sociology: Reflections on Some Recent Tendencies', *British Journal of Sociology*, 42(2): 211–30.

Goodman, J. (1993) *Tobacco in History: The Cultures of Dependence.* London: Routledge.

Goodman, J. (1995) *Consuming Habits: Drugs in History and Anthropology.* New York: Routledge.

Gould, S.J. (1990) *Wonderful Life: The Burgess Shale and the Nature of History.* London: Hutchinson Radius.

Griffiths, T. (1996) *Hunters and Collectors: The Antiquarian Imagination in Australia.* Cambridge: Cambridge University Press.

Hooker, C. and Bashford, A. (2002) 'Diphtheria and Australian Public Health: Bacteriology and Its Complex Applications, c. 1890–1930', *Medical History*, 46(1): 41–64.

Hooker, C. and Chapman, S. (2006) 'Structural Elements in Achieving Legislative Tobacco Control in NSW, 1955–95: Political Reflections and Implications', *Australian and New Zealand Journal of Public Health*, 10–5.

Hooker, C. and Chapman, S. (2007) 'Our Youth Must Be Protected from Drug Abuse: Talking Tobacco in the NSW Parliament 1950–2003', *Health and History*, 9(1): 106–28.

Hughes, J. (2003) *Learning to Smoke: Tobacco Use in the West.* Chicago: University of Chicago Press.

Huisman, F. and Warner, J.H. (eds) (2004) *Locating Medical History: The Stories and Their Meanings.* Baltimore, MD: The Johns Hopkins University Press.

Humphreys, M. (2001) *Malaria: Poverty, Race and Public Health in the United States.* Baltimore, MD: Johns Hopkins University Press.

Iggers, G. and Powell, J.M. (eds) (1990) *Leopold von Ranke and the Shaping of the Historical Discipline.* Syracuse, NY: Syracuse University Press.

Jacobson, P., Wasserman, J., and Anderson, J.R. (1997) 'Historical Overview of Tobacco Legislation and Regulation', *Journal of Social Issues*, 53(1): 75–95.

Jardine, N. (2003) 'Whigs and Stories: Herbert Butterfield and the Historiography of Science', *History of Science*, 41: 125–40.

Johnson, L. (1993) *The Modern Girl: Girlhood and Growing up.* Philadelphia, PA: Open University Press.

Jordanova, L. (1989) *Sexual Visions: Images of Gender in Science and Medicine Between the Eighteenth and Twentieth Centuries.* London: Harvester Wheatsheaf.

Joyce, P. (1991) *Visions of the People: Industrial England and the Question of Class, 1848–1914.* Cambridge: Cambridge University Press.

Kevles, D. (1985) *In the Name of Eugenics: Genetics and the Uses of Human Heredity.* New York: Knopf.

King, N. (2002) 'Security, Disease, Commerce: Ideologies of Postcolonial Public Health', *Social Studies of Science*, 32(5–6): 763–89.

Knipe, E. (1995) *Culture, Society, and Drugs: The Social Science Approach to Drug Use.* Prospect Heights, IL: Waveland Press.

Krieger, L. (1977) *Ranke: The Meaning of History.* Chicago: University of Chicago Press.

Kuhn, T. (1996) *The Structure of Scientific Revolutions.* Chicago: University of Chicago Press.

Latour, B. (1988) *The Pasteurization of France.* Boston, MA: Harvard University Press.

Lewis, M. (1998) *Thorns on the Rose: The History of Sexually Transmitted Diseases in Australia in International Perspective.* Canberra: Australian Govt. Pub. Service.

Lewis, M. (2003) *The People's Health.* Westport, CT: Praeger.

Lupton, D. and Petersen, A. (1996) *The New Public Health: Health and Self in the Age of Risk.* Sydney: Allen and Unwin.

Macleod, R. and Lewis, M. (eds) (1988) *Disease, Medicine, and Empire: Perspectives on Western Medicine and the Experience of European Expansion.* London: Routledge.

Manderson, L. (1996) *Sickness and the State: Health and Illness in Colonial Malaya, 1870–1940.* Cambridge: Cambridge University Press.

Marks, L. (2001) *Sexual Chemistry: A History of the Contraceptive Pill.* New Haven, CT: Yale University Press.

Martin, E. (1987) *The Woman in the Body: A Cultural Analysis of Reproduction.* Boston, MA: Beacon Press.

Martin, E. (1994) *Flexible Bodies: Tracking Immunity in American Culture from the Days of Polio to the Age of AIDS.* Boston, MA: Beacon Press.

McKeown, T. and Record, R.G. (1962) 'Reasons for the Decline in Mortality in England and Wales During the Nineteenth Century', *Population Studies*, 19: 94–122.

Neustadt, R. (1983) *The Epidemic that Never Was: Policy-making and the Swine Flu Scare.* New York: Vintage Books.

Newsholme, A. (1927) *Evolution of Preventive Medicine.* London: Bailliere, Tindall and Cox.

Noddings, N. (2001) 'The Care Tradition: Beyond "Add Women and Stir"', *Theory Into Practice*, 40(1): 29–34.

Parish, H.J. (1968) *Victory with Vaccines: The Story of Immunization.* Edinburgh: E. and S. Livingstone.

Phillips, K. (ed.) (2004) *Framing Public Memory.* Tuscaloosa, AL: University of Alabama Press.

Porter, D. (1999a) *Health, Civilization and the State: A History of Public Health from Ancient to Modern Times.* London: Routledge.

Porter, D. (1999b) *Health, Civilization, and the State: A History of Public Health from Ancient to Modern Times.* London: Routledge.

Porter, R. (1999) *The Greatest Benefit to Mankind: A Medical History of Humanity from Antiquity to the Present.* London: Fontana.

Porter, R. and Teich, M. (eds) (1995) *Drugs and Narcotics in History.* Cambridge: Cambridge University Press.

Prescott, H. (1998) *A Doctor of Their Own: The History of Adolescent Medicine.* Boston, MA: Harvard University Press.

Proctor, R. (1988) *Racial Hygiene: Medicine under the Nazis.* Boston, MA: Harvard University Press.

Quetel, C. (1990) *History of Syphilis.* London: Polity Press.

Reverby, S. (1987) *Ordered to Care: The Dilemma of American Nursing, 1850–1945.* Cambridge: Cambridge University Press.

Reverby, S. (ed.) (2000) *Tuskegee's Truths: Rethinking the Tuskegee Syphilis Study.* Chapel Hill, NC: University of North Carolina Press.

Reverby, S. and Helly, D. (eds) (1992) *Gendered Domains: Rethinking Public and Private in Women's History: Essays from the Seventh Berkshire Conference on the History of Women.* Ithaca, NY: Cornell University Press.

Reverby, S. and Rosner, D. (2004) 'Beyond the Great Doctors' Revisited'. In F. Huisman and J.H. Warner (eds) *Locating Medical History.* Baltimore, MD: The Johns Hopkins University Press.

Reverby, S. and Rosner, D. (eds) (1979) *Health Care in America: Essays in Social History.* Philadelphia, PA: Temple University Press.

Rosen, G. (1993 [1958]) *A History of Public Health.* Baltimore, MD: Johns Hopkins University Press.

Rosenberg, C. (1962) *The Cholera Years, the United States in 1832, 1849, and 1866.* Chicago: University of Chicago Press.

Rosenberg, C. (1989) *Caring for the Working Man: The Rise and Fall of the Dispensary: An Anthology of Sources.* New York: Garland Publications.

Rosenberg, C. and Golden, J. (eds) (1992) *Framing Disease: Studies in Cultural History.* New Brunswick, NJ: Rutgers University Press.

Rusen, J. (1990) 'Rhetoric and Aesthetics of History: Leopold von Ranke', *History and Theory*, 29(2): 190–204.

Rusen, J. (2005) *History: Narration, Interpretation, Orientation.* New York: Berghahn Books.

San Pedro Lopez, P.S.P. (2004) 'Social History or Historical Sociology: The Debate in the North American Academy in the Postwar Period, 1945–1970', *Sociologica*, 19(55): 13–47.

Scott, J. (1986) 'Gender: A Useful Category of Historical Analysis', *American Historical Review*, 91(5); 1053–75.

Scott, J. (1991) 'The Evidence of Experience', *Critical Inquiry*, 17(4): 773–97.

Scott, J. (ed.) (1996) *Feminism and History.* Oxford: Oxford University Press.

Sears, A. (1992) 'To Teach Them How to Live: The Politics of Public Health from Tuberculosis to AIDS', *Journal of Historical Sociology*, 5(1): 61–83.

Smith, D. (1992) *The Rise of Historical Sociology.* Philadelphia, PA: Temple University Press.

Sontag, S. (1991) *Illness as Metaphor and AIDS and its Metaphors.* London: Penguin.

Spongberg, M. (1997) *Feminising Venereal Disease: Constructing the Body of the Prostitute in Nineteenth Century British Medical Discourse.* London: MacMillan.

Stoler, A.L. (ed.) (2006) *Haunted By Empire: Geographies of Intimacy in North American History.* Durham, NC: Duke University Press.

Strange, C. and Bashford, A. (eds) (2003) *Isolation: Places and Practices of Exclusion.* London: Routledge.

Studlar, D.T. (2002) *Tobacco Control: Comparative Politics in the United States and Canada.* Ontario: Broadview Press.

Szreter, S. (1988) 'The Importance of Social Intervention in Britain's Mortality Decline c. 1850–1914: A Reinterpretation of the Role of Public Health', *Social History of Medicine*, 1: 1–38.

Szreter, S. (2002) 'Rethinking McKeown: The Relationship Between Public Health and Social Change', *American Journal of Public Health*, 92(5): 722–5.

Thompson, E.P. (1994) *Making History: Writings on History and Culture.* New York: New Press.

Treichler, P. (1999) *How to Have Theory in an Epidemic: Cultural Chronicles of AIDS.* Durham, NC: Duke University Press.

Troyer, R.J. and Markle, G.E. (1983) *Cigarettes, the Battle over Smoking.* New Brunswick, NJ: Rutgers University Press.

Tyrrell, I. (1999) *Deadly Enemies: Tobacco and Its Opponents in Australia.* Sydney: University of New South Wales Press.

Walker, R. (1984) *Under Fire: A History of Tobacco Smoking in Australia.* Melbourne: Melbourne University Press.

White, H. (1973) *Metahistory: The Historical Imagination in Nineteenth-Century Europe.* Baltimore, MD: Johns Hopkins University Press.

Wilson, C. (1942) *Ambassadors in White: The Story of American Tropical Medicine.* New York: Henry Hold.

Winslow, C.E.A. (1980 [1943]) *The Conquest of Epidemic Disease: A Chapter in the History of Ideas.* Madison, WI: University of Wisconsin Press.

Worboys, M. (2000) *Spreading Germs: Disease Theories and Medical Practice in Britain, 1865–1900.* Cambridge: Cambridge University Press.

Collecting and Analyzing Data

15

Qualitative Research Review and Synthesis

Jennie Popay and Sara Mallinson

INTRODUCTION

Policy makers, service providers and laypeople often seek information from research (what academics call evidence) to help them make decisions about health care. The type of research evidence they are looking for will vary depending on the issues at stake and the questions asked. For example, questions about the effectiveness of interventions in health, social care and education are best answered by findings from high-quality experimental studies, particularly randomized controlled trials (RCTs). In contrast, for questions about the experience of services, findings from qualitative studies will be the best source of information/evidence. Importantly, however, combining the results of multiple studies using systematic review methodologies will produce more reliable evidence than findings from a single study.

The development of robust systematic methods for the review and synthesis of findings from multiple research studies with the aim of informing policy and professional practice has a long history (Oakley, 2000). Over the past few decades, and particularly in health research, systematic reviews increasingly have replaced the traditional literature reviews used in many disciplines to produce overviews of current knowledge in a particular field, to inform the development of new research and on occasion to inform policy and practice (See for example, Petticrew and Roberts, 2006; Pope et al., 2006). Most of this methodological work has focused on the systematic review and synthesis of numerical evidence on the outcomes of interventions/services, although one formal approach to the synthesis of findings from multiple qualitative studies – meta-ethnography – was first published more than two decades ago by the American social scientists Noblit and Hare (1988). However, until recently, the idea of synthesizing findings from multiple qualitative studies was not taken seriously.

Resistance to systematic review of qualitative studies can be linked to two factors. Historically, the possibility that findings from qualitative research could have policy and practice relevance was not widely accepted and as a result, few literature reviews of qualitative research were supported by funding bodies. Additionally, the idea that systematic syntheses (as opposed to descriptive summaries) of findings from multiple qualitative studies was both methodologically possible and scientifically justifiable was hotly contested. However, in the past decade things have changed dramatically. The number of published papers reporting methodological research and substantive systematic reviews of qualitative research has increased rapidly (see for example, Estabrooks et al., 1994; Jensen and Allen, 1996; Britten et al., 2002; Arai et al., 2005; Dixon-Woods et al., 2006a, 2006b; Popay, 2006; Roen et al., 2006; Noyes and Popay, 2007). The Cochrane Collaboration now has a Qualitative Research Methods Group and the Collaboration's 2008 Handbook has a section on the review and synthesis of qualitative research (Noyes et al., 2008). It is now widely accepted that qualitative research has an important contribution to make to the evidence base for all areas of policy and practice and for laypeople (Murphy et al., 1998; Dixon-Woods and Fitzpatrick, 2001; Mays et al., 2005). Researchers now agree that reviews of qualitative research can and should be more systematic than they have been in the past.

It is important to acknowledge that debates about the legitimacy of synthesizing findings from multiple qualitative studies continue and that many methodological challenges remain. In the context of these debates an increasing number of qualitative researchers are adopting a pragmatic position noting for instance that while 'concerns about theory, method and in particular, the issue of context are important they should not prevent us attempting to build a cumulative knowledge base' (Pope et al., 2007:873). In this spirit of pragmatism, systematic, rigorous and transparent methods for the review and synthesis of findings from multiple qualitative studies have been developing apace. Several detailed overviews of these approaches have been published including practical examples of their use and discussions of associated methodological challenges (e.g., Patterson et al., 2001; Dixon-Woods et al, 2004; Pope et al., 2007). Importantly, these writers highlight the dearth of evaluative data on the relative merits and limitations of different approaches.

In this chapter, we: (1) identify the potential contribution systematic reviews of qualitative research findings can make to the evidence base for decision-making by policy makers, professionals and laypeople; (2) describe the general characteristics of the process of systematic review and synthesis as applied to qualitative research and how it differs from systematic reviews of effectiveness evidence; and (3) discuss four examples of approaches to systematic review appropriate for use with qualitative evidence offering guidance on how potential reviewers might best decide which approach to use.

THE CONTRIBUTION OF QUALITATIVE RESEARCH SYNTHESIS

The value of qualitative research to policy and practice is frequently presented in one of two general ways. The first emphasizes the *enhancement* role of qualitative research as adding value to the findings of quantitative research. The second emphasizes the *different* and unique contribution qualitative research makes to knowledge about the social world: why people behave the way they do, the relationship between social structure and individual/collective agency, between policies and practices, understanding and action, experiences and values.

Qualitative research reviews can help extend quantitative reviews of effectiveness by helping to formulate appropriate questions to be asked and identifying relevant outcome measures. They can also help in the interpretation of the results of quantitative reviews by offering insight into why actions/interventions are or are not effective in certain situations and/or with particular groups. Alternatively, systematic reviews of qualitative research can answer questions that are different from questions of effectiveness. By illuminating the needs of particular population groups, systematic reviews of qualitative research can point to new types of actions/interventions to meet these needs and highlight barriers and/or enablers to the implementation of interventions that have been shown to be effective in 'real life'. As examples discussed later illustrate, a single systematic review of qualitative research findings may both enhance the relevance of effectiveness of reviews and answer unanticipated, but critical questions.

THE PROCESS OF QUALITATIVE EVIDENCE REVIEW AND SYNTHESIS

At its simplest – and regardless of the question being addressed or the type of evidence included – the process of systematic review involves the juxtaposition of findings from multiple studies with some analysis of similarities and/or differences of findings across studies. More sophisticated approaches, such as statistical meta-analysis and meta-ethnography for example, involve attempts to 'combine' findings from multiple studies (through processes of integration or interpretation) with the aim of producing new knowledge.

At one level, all systematic reviews include the same basic elements shown in Figure 15.1. Within an effectiveness review, these elements form a linear staged process regulated by strict rules to ensure that potential for bias is, as far as possible, removed. For example, in an effectiveness review, the protocol acts as a 'rule–book' for the conduct of the review with reviewers. For the review to be registered with an organization such as the Cochrane or Campbell Collaboration, reviewers are required to submit the protocol to peer review and, once finalized,

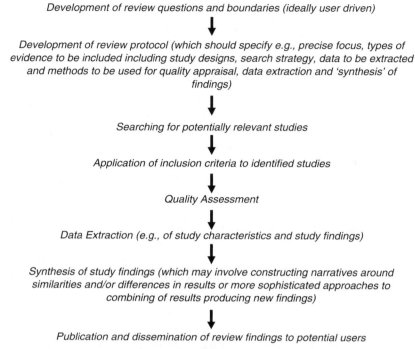

Development of review questions and boundaries (ideally user driven)

↓

Development of review protocol (which should specify e.g., precise focus, types of evidence to be included including study designs, search strategy, data to be extracted and methods to be used for quality appraisal, data extraction and 'synthesis' of findings)

↓

Searching for potentially relevant studies

↓

Application of inclusion criteria to identified studies

↓

Quality Assessment

↓

Data Extraction (e.g., of study characteristics and study findings)

↓

Synthesis of study findings (which may involve constructing narratives around similarities and/or differences in results or more sophisticated approaches to combining of results producing new findings)

↓

Publication and dissemination of review findings to potential users

Figure 15.1   Generic elements of the systematic review process

to adhere to the processes and methods it describes. The published protocol is also a way of ensuring that the review process is transparent from the beginning and can act as an audit tool at the end.

Once the parameters of the review are set – for example, agreeing on the precise questions and the population groups and outcomes that are to be the focus – they should not be changed. In order to limit publication bias favouring positive results, searches should be as comprehensive as possible within resource constraints, with reviewers attempting to identify all relevant studies, published and unpublished. The process of excluding certain study designs and studies with methodological flaws also serves to reduce bias.

Although these basic elements can be identified in most systematic reviews of qualitative studies, the nature of the processes involved are profoundly different. Perhaps most importantly, regardless of the specific approach adopted, the defining characteristic of systematic reviews of qualitative research is that they involve iterative rather than linear processes. This is powerfully illustrated in Figure 15.2 taken from the book on systematic review of qualitative and quantitative evidence by Pope et al. (2007: 22).

It is good practice to produce a protocol for a qualitative systematic review, keeping in mind that this operates as an enabling framework guiding the review

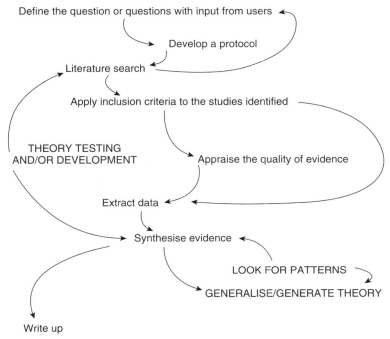

Figure 15.2   The interactive nature of review and synthesis of qualitative evidence

rather than a straitjacket. All reviews should focus on questions that are specified as clearly as possible before the review begins with active input from potential users of the review. However, in systematic reviews of qualitative findings, the question may be revised as the review proceeds. The 'currency' of synthesis in qualitative research reviews is the *concepts* that emerge from the analytical process, not variables chosen prior to data collection and defined in numerical terms. Therefore, whilst it is possible to identify outcomes of interest in the protocol for a quantitative effectiveness review, it is not possible to identify in advance of a systematic review of qualitative research what the concepts of interest will be. These will be identified as the review proceeds through the literature search, data extraction and synthesis. At any point, reviewers may decide to revise the question(s) being addressed or the criteria for including studies in the review.

Identifying potentially relevant studies is also an interactive process. These may be identified through a comprehensive search but they may also be identified through a sampling strategy which could be random and/or purposeful. As data extraction and synthesis proceeds, reviewers may go back to the literature to purposefully identify studies to fill gaps or to search for 'deviant cases'. Most qualitative research reviews involve an appraisal of study quality but this aspect of the review process is perhaps the most contentious. Important questions are still to be resolved such as: when is study quality appraisal best done; what is the nature of the appraisal process, and how are the product(s) of appraisal most appropriately used? The technical appraisal of quality is not necessarily the same as an appraisal of the relevance and worth of a study to the review (Popay and Williams, 1998). It is also vital to recognize that questions about 'truth claims' are very different in the context of qualitative research reviews. The application of appraisal processes and standards of evidence as rigid checklists informing an 'in/out' decision has been argued to be inappropriate for qualitative research review (Popay et al., 1998; Dixon-Wood and Fitzpatrick, 2001). Even qualitative studies of generally mediocre or poor methodological quality may generate useful findings for a qualitative evidence review (Pawson, 2006a).

Given these unresolved issues, it is not surprising that there is no consensus over the role of study quality appraisal in systematic reviews of qualitative research. As a result, if methodological quality is assessed, it is typically not a criterion for deciding whether a study is to be included or excluded but rather is taken into account as part of a process of exploration and interpretation in the synthesis process (Spencer et al., 2003). Reviewers may, for example, accord studies different weights in a synthesis depending on the fit between the study design and the review question and/or a study's methodological quality.

Figure 15.2 also highlights the pivotal role of theory in the systematic review of findings of qualitative research. Petticrew and Egan (2006) have argued that there is a general neglect of the potential for systematic reviews to both test and develop theory. This neglect is particularly significant in qualitative evidence review. In an important sense, the quality of a synthesis of qualitative evidence will be determined by the visibility of the theoretical perspectives informing the review and the extent to which the synthesis process has involved theory testing and generation. At its simplest, the product of a qualitative research synthesis will be the juxtaposition of concepts/themes extracted from included studies. This is typically embedded in a discussion of similarities and differences and the analysis may also include a count of the most and/or least common themes. In the qualitative research community, there is rightly anxiety about such 'atheoretical' analyses and the potential for 'thin' thematic description to replace 'thick', theoretically connected and enriched analysis.

A recent systematic review of qualitative research on parents' decision-making about childhood vaccination provides an example of the limitations of thematic syntheses that fail to develop the potential of theory (Mills et al., 2005). The product of this review was a simple listing of recurring themes in qualitative research on parents' perspectives on vaccination. The list highlights how parents feel about vaccination but fails to add to our understanding of 'why' they feel and/or behave the way they do. Good quality qualitative research not only describes the meanings that people attach to their experience of the social world, it can also reveal the purpose these meanings serve. For example, primary qualitative research on the experience of chronic illness moves beyond descriptions of people's accounts of their experience of their illness to argue that through these narratives, people reconstruct a sense of worth in a social context in which illness has moral overtones (Williams, 1984). From this perspective, Mills and his colleagues (2005) have produced an initial descriptive synthesis of qualitative research on parents' views on vaccination, but the ultimate aim of a synthesis of qualitative research should be to move these useful but limited lists onto a higher conceptual level that has more explanatory purchase (Popay, 2005; Pawson and Bellamy, 2006). It is also through the development of explanatory theory that the product of systematic reviews of qualitative research can be generalized beyond the contexts of the studies included in the review. Our discussion of four specific approaches to the review and synthesis of findings from multiple qualitative studies provides some examples of what theoretically enriched 'explanatory' syntheses look like.

FOUR EXEMPLAR APPROACHES TO QUALITATIVE EVIDENCE REVIEW AND SYNTHESIS

In this short chapter, we cannot review all of the approaches to qualitative evidence review described in published literature. Instead, we have chosen four approaches to illustrate the richness and diversity of this rapidly evolving methodological field. The approaches considered are: literature review, a highly flexible, typically uncodified strategy; realistic synthesis, a theory-driven loosely codified approach; meta-ethnography, a formal codified approach specifically focused on qualitative research review; and narrative synthesis, a more eclectic formalized approach. All four approaches can produce more or less theoretically informed syntheses but this is the *express* purpose of both realist synthesis and meta-ethnography. Only meta-ethnography is restricted to use with qualitative research: all the others can accommodate diverse evidence types: quantitative and qualitative, research and non-research.

Literature reviews

Literature reviews have recently been referred to as narrative reviews (Dixon-Woods et al., 2004; Pawson and Bellamy, 2006), but here we reserve the word *narrative* to describe a more formalized approach to synthesis (see later). Literature reviews usually seek to summarize and interpret evidence on a particular topic/question and can include qualitative and/or quantitative research- and non-research-based evidence (for example, from official enquiries or routine data sources such as the census). They can address a wide range of questions from summarizing knowledge about the nature and causes of a particular 'problem', through reflections on what should be done about such problems, to what is known about the impact and acceptability of existing responses. They have also been used to develop and test theories and explanations.

What have been termed 'first-generation' literature reviews (Pope et al., 2007) paid little attention to methodological quality or to searching systematically for relevant studies. Instead, authors typically selected studies to develop their argument with no consideration of the issue of bias and a lack of transparency. Not surprising the trustworthiness of first-generation literature reviews has been questioned. However, a recent analysis of a first-generation literature review on antisocial behaviour (Pope et al., 2007: pp. 4–6) suggests that the analytical processes involved may be more systematic and sophisticated than is often acknowledged and that these reviews can make a significant contribution to new theory/knowledge.

In their book length review of the research literature on factors associated with antisocial behaviour in children and young people, for example, Rutter and colleagues (1998) analyzed a wide range of primarily quantitative studies, although the lack of transparency makes it difficult to say precisely how many studies were included in their synthesis. While their approach to synthesis was not made explicit, it reflects elements of the process of systematic review of qualitative research discussed earlier, even though the studies they included were primarily quantitative. For instance, although they do not discuss how studies were selected for inclusion, the approach they use is sampling for relevance rather than a systematic, exhaustive search. Similarly, although they do not explicitly consider methodological quality, they offer an implicit hierarchy of evidence with longitudinal survey research presented as the gold standard. In selecting studies for their review, the authors appear to be aiming to provide a context for, and substance to, a story they are developing. The authorial voice establishes a tone of authority and trustworthiness drawing the reader through complex material, painting a clear and coherent picture of the literature and eventually telling a 'convincing story'. As the review proceeds, conceptual frameworks and hypotheses are developed iteratively and these in turn shape the review and analysis. Their review identifies what they, as expert–authors, judge to be key studies, key findings, key contradictions, and key gaps.

Notably, the reviewers use methods that resonate strongly with aspects of meta-ethnography (Noblit and Hare, 1988), considering as they do whether each source of evidence 'fits' with their emerging story. For example, their description of 'theorising what … processes and meanings are reflected in statistical findings' (p. 182) is quite similar to the 'line of argument' approach in meta-ethnography. In the final chapter, the reviewers note that they are going to draw on different strands to develop an overarching argument describing the process as a 'translation', echoing the notion of 'reciprocal translation' elaborated in meta-ethnography. In this way, they develop what could be termed a 'third order construct' – 'school ethos' – and consider how process measures they have identified 'operate' in the context of a 'school ethos'.

More recently, a *second-generation literature review* has developed. These reviews adopt elements of a systematic review process, using explicit approaches to search for and select studies to include, and giving due consideration to methodological quality. Some second-generation literature reviews explicitly aim to move beyond a thin description or summary of key findings from a body of research to produce higher-order syntheses resulting in the production of new knowledge and/or theory. As with narrative synthesis (described later) the methods used to do this are eclectic.

Literature reviews are very flexible. A wide range of different kinds of evidence, both research and non-research can be included. Most do not follow standardized procedures, but they are becoming more transparent and, as the review by Rutter and colleagues illustrates, even first generation reviews can be conceptually and analytically sophisticated. Additionally, as Pawson and Bellamy (2006) have argued, it would be wrong to assume that a lack of standardized methods inevitably means that there is no logic to the methods used in literature reviews. Of course, flexibility can also be problematic. Idiosyncratic or selective approaches to study selection introduce the potential for bias and hence for unreliable conclusions to be drawn. Lack of transparency in the review process makes it difficult for users to form a judgement about the trustworthiness of the results. Shadish and colleagues (1991) argue that literature reviews can produce generalizable results if they ensure 'proximal similarity': by limiting the number and type of study to include and programme characteristics to explore. However, Pawson (2006b) argues that this approach can introduce other types of biases by excluding evidence from studies or about some characteristics of programmes that may make a significant, but unknown and unknowable (because they are excluded from the review) contribution to programme impacts.

Realist synthesis

This approach, developed by Ray Pawson (2006b), an English sociologist, is focused on answering questions about the impact of action/policy. However, that is where the similarities between systematic reviews of effectiveness and realist synthesis end, for realistic synthesis is a highly iterative, theory-driven process. It aims to build explanations for the impact of interventions or programmes sharing similar underlying theories about why they would be expected to work for particular groups in particular contexts.

Realistic synthesis begins by asking, what is it about a program that works? And the answer is given in terms of a programme theory or 'mechanism'. Data extraction involves a search of a broad body of 'evidence' (including but not restricted to research evidence) to test whether the mechanism works and in what context. In other words, the aim is to answer the questions 'what works, for whom, in what circumstances?'

Realist synthesis adopts the principle of 'falsification': if careful analysis uncovers an exception to a rule or an instance when a theory does not 'fit' then the existing explanatory framework or theory has to be adapted (Popper, 1959). If an analysis in realist synthesis reveals that a programme works in certain ways for certain people, the reviewer develops an explanation or theory for why this happens. This explanation is then applied to a second programme underpinned by the same theory, and if it performs as predicted, the theory is supported and/or expanded. However, if there are mixed results, the theory has to be revised to take account of – or explain – these differences. Time and other resources determine the number of comparisons undertaken.

There are very few examples of this approach to synthesis. All of the published examples have involved Ray Pawson. An early example (Pawson, 2002) focused on programmes underpinned by the theory that *'naming and shaming'* people would deter them from certain behaviours. Megan's Law in the United States was used to test this programme theory, a law that required the publication of the names and addresses of sex offenders released from prison as a means of stopping them from reoffending. This synthesis suggests that Megan's Law did not succeed in deterring people from reoffending indicating that if future interventions are to be successful the *'naming and shaming'* programme theory will need to be amended. Pawson argues that realist synthesis adds rigour and structure to traditional literature reviews while retaining the ability of the best scholarly reviews to present highly detailed and reasoned arguments about the mechanisms of programme success or failure. However, the generalizability of this approach has yet to be demonstrated.

Meta-ethnography

This approach to qualitative research synthesis was developed by George Noblit and Dwight Hare (1988), two American social scientists who used it to evaluate the impact of school desegregation policies introduced in the United States in the 1960s. The term 'meta-ethnography' implies it can only be used with ethnographic studies but published meta-ethnographic reviews have demonstrated that the approach can accommodate qualitative studies with a range of different theoretical and methodological approaches.

Meta-ethnography consists of seven iterative steps (Pope et al., 2007: pp. 80–83) that may repeat and/or overlap during the synthesis process.

1 Identifying an area of interest that is 'worthy of the synthesis effort' (Noblit and Hare 1988: p. 27).
2 Purposive rather than comprehensive searching for and selection of relevant studies.
3 Repeated reading of included studies to identify key concepts and interpretations or explanations – the 'raw data' for the synthesis.
4 Exploring relationships between individual studies by compiling a list of key concepts and explanatory schema, and considering how these are connected.
5 Translating studies into one another by considering whether a concept identified in one study can be mapped onto another and/or identifying any conceptual differences between studies.
6 Synthesizing the translations by identifying concepts from step 5 which transcend individual studies and hence can be used to produce new interpretation or conceptual development.
7 Expressing the final product of the synthesis, normally in written form, but Noblit and Hare also note that other forms (video, artistic) are possible depending on purpose and audience.

One of the most frequently cited examples of meta-ethnography is Pound et al.'s (2005) review of 37 papers reporting qualitative research on patients' views on the medicine they take. They introduced two further steps to Noblit and Hare's process for meta-ethnography. In order to manage the reading and translation of included studies they organized the papers into seven medicine groups. They undertook a process of translation within each group separately, looking at whether concept's from one study could be mapped onto those in another study within the group and/or identifying any conceptual differences between studies. They then undertook the same process of translation across the medicine groups and synthesized translations across all these groups. Their review proposed a new concept of active and/or passive 'resistance' as a way of understanding patients' responses to prescribed medicines. This new concept captured the wide range of strategies employed in relation to medicine taking (or not) reported in the original 37 studies.

This same team of reviewers has published other meta-ethnographic reviews (see for example, Britten et al., 2002; Campbell et al., 2003). They highlight continuing problems associated with study quality appraisal and problems with searching caused by the limited indexing of qualitative research in electronic databases. They also argue that the approach requires a high level of expertise in qualitative methods. The validity of the product of meta-ethnography can be explored by sending the synthesis results for comment to researchers involved in the original studies (much like respondent validation in primary qualitative research). Doyle (2003) and Britten et al. (2002) report doing this. However, as with primary research, this practice can be problematic since social phenomena are always open to multiple interpretations and a challenge to the reviewers' interpretation does not automatically invalidate it.

Narrative synthesis

The fourth and final approach to the review and synthesis of qualitative research findings to be considered here is *narrative synthesis* (NS). Guidance on the conduct of NS was produced in 2005 by a team at the universities of Lancaster, York, City and Glasgow funded by the UK Economic and Social Research Council (Popay et al., 2005). According to this guidance, a narrative synthesis approach can be used with both qualitative and quantitative data. It is a flexible and eclectic approach that can be used in three situations: before undertaking a statistical meta-analysis; instead of a statistical meta-analysis (because the experimental or quasi-experimental studies included are not sufficiently similar to allow for this); and where the review questions dictate the inclusion of a wide range of different research designs, producing qualitative and/or quantitative findings, and/or non-research evidence, for which no other specialist approach to synthesis is appropriate. The guidance provides advice on the conduct of narrative synthesis and describes specific tools and techniques that can be used in the review process.

Dixon-Wood and colleagues (2004) argue that different types of evidence synthesis can be located along a continuum from quantitative approaches, which involve the pooling of findings from multiple studies (e.g., meta-analysis), to qualitative approaches, which involve an interpretative approach (e.g., meta-ethnography). Narrative synthesis lies between these two extremes. The key purpose of a process of narrative synthesis is the organization, description, exploration and interpretation of the study findings and the attempt to find explanations for, and/or 'moderators' of, these findings. Narrative synthesis always involves the juxtaposition of findings from included studies but where the evidence allows, it can move beyond this to include some element of integration and/or interpretation.

The emphasis of the NS guidance produced by Popay and colleagues (2005) is the synthesis process. Not covered in this guidance document are ways of defining the review question, developing a protocol, searching and appraising studies, and applying inclusion criteria. Figure 15.3 is taken from a test of the NS guidance which consisted of a partial synthesis of evidence on barriers and/or enablers to the effective implementation of domestic smoke alarms (Arai et al., 2007). The test involved three of the four main elements of narrative synthesis, which, like the other approaches to qualitative synthesis is iterative.

One element of a narrative synthesis *not* undertaken for the smoke alarm review was theory building. The NS guidance recommends that reviewers should identify or develop a relevant theoretical framework at an early point in their review. This will inform decisions about the review question and the types of studies to include and will contribute to the interpretation of findings from the studies selected. The smoke alarm review begins with the second element of a narrative synthesis: developing a preliminary synthesis. This involves the extraction of relevant data from included studies in order to produce an initial description of patterns found in the studies. At this stage, reviewers may return to search for additional studies or refine the review question. Exploration of relationships within and between studies is the next element of the NS. In the smoke alarm review, this step leads to the production of a final synthesis which is then tested for robustness – the fourth element of the process. Robustness is a complicated concept that is dependent upon the methodological quality of the included studies, reviewers' judgments about the relevance of study findings for the review question, and the trustworthiness of the synthesis product. As already noted, there will be no single 'true' interpretative synthesis of the findings from multiple qualitative studies so the 'trustworthiness' of the synthesis is dependent in large part on the transparency with which the review is conducted and the believability of the 'story' constructed from the data. Figure 15.3 also lists the analytical tools and techniques, described in the NS guidance, which are potentially useful during a synthesis process. The authors highlight those that were judged to be appropriate for use for the smoke alarm review.

Below, we provide two examples of the use of two specific tools and techniques during the smoke alarm review. The first is a brief narrative description of one of the included study which was used in the development of the preliminary synthesis.

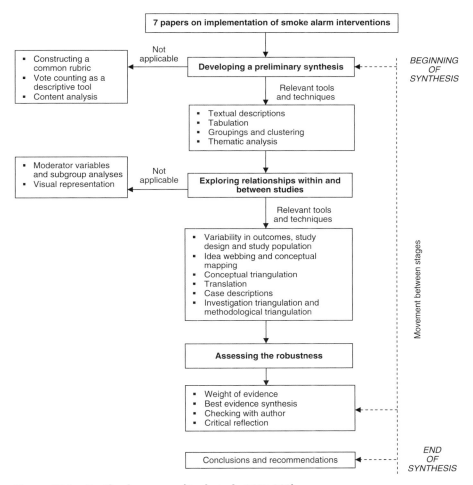

Figure 15.3   Synthesis process (Arai et al., 2007:369)

EXAMPLE 1: NARRATIVE DESCRIPTION

Young et al. (1999) and Camit (2002) report on the effectiveness and implementation of a smoke alarm promotion campaign in New South Wales, Australia, oriented to the needs of Arabic, Chinese and Vietnamese communities. Qualitative data were collected in focus groups and interviews. Survey data were also collected. Their main observations in relation to implementation are that, among the target community, there was a lack of awareness of the need for smoke alarms. Living in rented property where the landlord was thought to be unsympathetic to the need for a smoke alarm also created barriers to the installation of smoke alarms (Arai et al., 2007:370).

Figure 15.4, also from the smoke alarm implementation review, is an example of *ideas webbing* used in the exploration of relationships across study concepts.

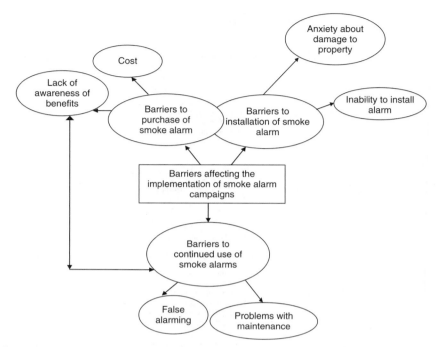

Figure 15.4   Ideas webbing from review of barriers/enablers to smoke alarm implementation (Arai et al., 2007)

On the basis of this work and the results of other analyses, the reviewers suggested that three concepts seemed to offer themselves for translation across studies: the level of landlords' commitment to installation and maintenance; residents' perception of the risk of fire compared with other risks; and residents' level of trust in the intervention. The reviewers conclude that these three concepts may start to characterize the elements necessary for a successful implementation of domestic smoke alarms and inform the development of future intervention to promote their use.

Narrative synthesis can be used to address a wide range of review questions using diverse evidence – research and non-research. The NS guidance (Popay et al., 2005) presents a formal process to deal with potential biases particularly those which may be introduced when an established methodology such as meta-ethnography is not being used. The NS guidance also describes a variety of analytical tools and techniques which may be used in the synthesis process and as a framework for making choices about which tools and techniques to use with which data. Hence, following the NS guidance should increase the transparency, reliability, and generalizablity of the review synthesis. At this point, however, only papers reporting on exploratory use of the NS guidance have been published (Arai et al., 2007; Rodgers et al., 2009). No fully worked-through examples of narrative synthesis based on the guidance are available.

CONCLUDING COMMENTS

In this chapter, we argued that there is now widespread recognition of the contribution qualitative research can make to the evidence base for policy and practice decision-making in many fields. Qualitative research can also help laypeople make decisions as service users or as they seek help for problems. As with other forms of research, an assessment of knowledge and understanding across a body of relevant qualitative studies is likely to be more trustworthy and generalizable than the findings of a single study. This is especially true when a robust and transparent process of synthesis is used to produce new knowledge by combining findings from multiple studies.

Historically, the possibility of synthesizing findings from several qualitative research studies has been vigorously debated. These debates continue, but over the past decade, an increasing body of work describing ways of conducting such a synthesis has been published. Today, people wishing to undertake systematic reviews and syntheses of qualitative research evidence have a number of approaches to choose from. It is unlikely that there will ever be a consensus around a 'gold standard' approach. For example, the Cochrane Qualitative Research Methods Group has not recommended any single method (Noyes et al., 2008). Instead, it is likely that the choice of approach will always have to be made on the basis of a careful consideration of a number of factors including the resources available, the type and scope of the review, the size, quality and diversity of available evidence, and the expertise of the team.

There is growing consensus on the need for the inclusion of researchers with experience of qualitative research on teams doing systematic reviews. In their exposition of meta-ethnography, Noblit and Hare (1988) emphasize that this kind of review requires previous experience in qualitative methods. Like primary qualitative research, qualitative evidence review involves an inductive, iterative and emergent process. The initial review question or area of interest may be adapted or redirected as the review proceeds, and there are numerous judgements along the way which the novice is likely to find difficult if not impossible to make.

As in primary qualitative research, reflexivity is crucial to the conduct of qualitative evidence synthesis. Reviewers must acknowledge and make explicit the ways in which their values, theoretical perspectives and readings of the studies may influence the synthesis. The product of a qualitative evidence synthesis is one possible interpretation of what are already interpretations of interpretations. Like quantitative evidence reviews, the process of synthesizing qualitative studies will inevitably involve a qualitative judgment process, a point well-illustrated in a recent narrative synthesis of effectiveness data done by Rodgers et al. (2009).

Perhaps one of the most important methodological challenges is how 'high-quality' systematic reviews of qualitative research are to be recognized. A key issue here is the role of theory in the production of the synthesis. A qualitative evidence synthesis should be more than a thematic analysis – generalizable explanations of social phenomena are the ultimate prize. But only by building and testing theory in the process of review and synthesis will the qualitative research community achieve this.

REFERENCES

Arai, L., Popay, J., Roen, K., and Roberts, H. (2005) 'It Might Work in Oklahoma but Will it Work in Oakhampton? What Does the Effectiveness Literature on Domestic Smoke Detectors Tell Us about Context and Implementation?' *Injury Prevention*, 11: 148–51.

Arai, L., Britten, N., Popay, J., Roberts, H., Petticrew, M., Rodgers, M., and Sowden, A. (2007) 'Testing Methodological Developments in the Conduct of Narrative Synthesis: A Demonstration Review of Research on the Implementation of Smoke Alarm Interventions', *Evidence & Policy*, 3(3): 361–83.

Britten, N., Campbell, R., Pope, C., Donovan, J., Morgan, M., and Pill, R. (2002) 'Using Meta Ethnography to Synthesise Qualitative Research: A Worked Example', *Journal of Health Services Research and Policy*, 7(4): 209–15.

Camit, M. (2002) 'Smoke Alarms Wake You Up if There's a Fire: A Smoke Campaign Targeting Arabic, Chinese and Vietnamese Communities in New South Wales', *Social Marketing Quarterly*, 8(1): 52–4.

Campbell, R., Pound, P., Pope, C., Britten, N., Pill, R., Morgan, M., and Donovan, J. (2003) 'Evaluating Meta-Ethnography: A Synthesis of Qualitative Research on Lay Experiences of Diabetes and Diabetes Care', *Social Science and Medicine*, 56: 671–84.

Dixon-Woods, M. and Fitzpatrick, R. (2001) 'Qualitative Research in Systematic Reviews has Established a Place for Itself', In *British Medical Journal*, 765: 765–60.

Dixon-Woods, M., Agarwal, S., Young, B., Jones, D., and Sutton, A. (2004) *Integrative Approaches to Qualitative and Quantitative Evidence*. London: Health Development Agency.

Dixon Woods, M., Bonas, S., Booth, A., Jones, D.R., Miller, T., Sutton, A.J., Shaw, R.L., Smith, J.A., and Young, B. (2006a) 'How Can Systematic Reviews Incorporate Qualitative Research? A Critical Perspective', *Qualitative Research*, 6(1): 27–44.

Dixon-Woods, M., Cavers, D., Agarwal, S., Annandale, E., Arthur, A., Harvey, J., Hsu, R., Katbamna, S., Olsen, R., Smith, L.K., Riley, R., and Sutton, A. (2006b) 'Conducting Critical Interpretive Synthesis of the Literature on Access to Healthcare by Vulnerable Groups'. *BMC Research Methodology*, 6: 35. Doi; 10.1086/1471-2288-6-35.

Doyle, L. (2003) 'Synthesis Through Meta-Ethnography: Paradoxes, Enhancement and Possibilities', *Qualitative Research*, 3(3): 321–44.

Estabrooks, C.A. Field, P.A., and Morse, J.M. (1994) 'Aggregating Qualitative Findings: An Approach to Theory Development', *Qualitative Health Research*, 4: 503–11.

Jensen, L.A. and Allen, M.N. (1996) 'Meta-Synthesis of Qualitative Findings', *Qualitative Health Research*, 6: 553–60.

Mays, N., Pope, C., and Popay, J. (2005) 'Systematically Reviewing Qualitative and Quantitative Evidence to Inform Management and Policy-Making in the Health Field', *Journal of Health Services Research & Policy*, 10(1): 1–15.

Mills, E., Alejandro, R., Jadad, C.R., and Kumanan, W. (2005) 'Systematic Review of Qualitative Studies Exploring Parental Beliefs and Attitudes Towards Childhood Vaccination Identifies Common Barriers to Vaccination', *Journal of Clinical Epidemiology*, 58(11): 1081–88.

Murphy, E., Dingwall, R., Greatback, D., Parker, S., and Watson, P. (1998) 'Qualitative Research Methods in Health Technology Assessment: A Review of the Literature', *Health Technology Assessment*, 2(16).

Noblit, G. and Hare, R. (1988) *Meta-Ethnography: Synthesising Qualitative Studies.* Newbury Park, CA: Sage.

Noyes, J. and Popay, J. (2007) 'Directly Observed Therapy and Tuberculosis: How Can a Systematic Review of Qualitative Research Contribute to Improving Services? A Qualitative Meta-Synthesis', *Journal of Advanced Nursing*, 57(3): 227–43.

Noyes, J., Popay, J., Pearson, A., Hanes, K., and Booth, A. (2008) 'Qualitative Research and Cochrane Reviews'. In Higgins, J.P.T. and Green, S. (eds) *Cochrane Handbook for Systematic Reviews of Interventions.* The Cochrane Handbook Version 5.0.1. Chapter 20. Available at: www.cochrane.handbook.org

Oakley, A. (2000) *Experiments in Knowing: Gender and Method in the Social Sciences.* Cambridge, UK: Polity Press.

Pawson, R. (2002) 'Does Megan's Law Work? A Theory Driven Systematic Review'. ESRC UK Centre for Evidence Based Policy and Practice, Working Paper 8, Queen Mary College, University of London, UK.

Pawson, R. (2006b) *Evidence Based Policy: A Realist Perspective.* London: Sage.

Pawson, R. and Bellamy, J. (2006) 'Realist Synthesis: An Explanatory Focus for Systematic Reviews'. In Popay, J (ed) *Moving Beyond Effectiveness: Methodological Issues in the Synthesis of Diverse Sources of Evidence* (pp. 83–93). London: National Institute for Health and Clinical Excellence.

Petticrew, M. and Egan, M. (2006) 'Relevance, Rigour and Systematic Reviews'. In Popay, J. (2006, ed.) *Moving Beyond Effectiveness: Methodological Issues in the Synthesis of Diverse Sources of Evidence* (pp. 7–8). London: National Institute for Health and Clinical Excellence.

Petticrew, M. and Roberts, H. (2006) *Systematic Reviews in the Social Sciences: a Practical Guide.* Oxford: Blackwell.

Popay, J. (2005) 'Moving Beyond Floccinaucinihilipilification: Enhancing the Utility of Systematic Reviews', *Journal of Clinical Epidemiology*, 58(11): 1079–80.

Popay, J. (2006) (ed.) *Moving Beyond Effectiveness: Methodological Issues in the Synthesis of Diverse Sources of Evidence.* London: National Institute for Health and Clinical Excellence.

Popay, J. and Williams, G. (1998) 'Qualitative Research and Evidence Based Healthcare', *Journal Royal Social Med,* 91(Suppl 35).

Popay, J., Rogers, A., and Williams, G. (1998) 'Rationale and Standards for the Systematic Review of Qualitative Literature in Health Services Research', *Qualitative Health Research*, 8(3): 341–51.

Popay, J., Roberts, H., Sowden, A., Petticrew, M., Arai, L., and Rodgers, M. (2005) *Guidance on the Conduct of Narrative Synthesis in Systematic Reviews.* Version 2. Lancaster, UK: Lancaster University.

Pope, C., Mays, N., and Popay, J. (2006) 'Informing Policy Making and Management in Healthcare: The Place for Synthesis', *Health Care Policy*, 1(2): 43–8.

Pope, C., Mays, N., and Popay, J. (2007) *Synthesising Qualitative and Quantitative Health Evidence: A Guide to Methods.* Maidenhead, Berks: Open University Press.

Popper, K. (1959) *The Logic of Scientific Discovery.* London: Hutchinson.

Pound, P., Britten, N., Morgan, M., Yardley, L., Pope, C., Daker-White, G., and Campbell, R. (2005) 'Resisting Medicines: A Synthesis of Qualitative Studies of Medicine Taking', *Social Science and Medicine,* 61: 133–55.

Roen, K., Arai, L., Roberts, H., and Popay, J. (2006) 'Extending Systematic Reviews to Include Evidence on Implementation: Methodological Work on a Review of Community-Based Initiatives to Prevent Injuries', *Social Science and Medicine*, 63: 1060–71.

Rodgers, M., Petticrew, M., Sowden, A., Arai, L., Britten, N., Popay, J., and Roberts, H. (2009) 'Testing the Guidance on the Conduct of Narrative Synthesis in Systematic Reviews: Effectiveness of Interventions to Promote Smoke Alarm Ownership and Function', *Evaluation*, 15(1): 49–74.

Rutter, M., Maughan, B., Mortimore, P., and Ouston, J. (1998) *Anti-Social Behaviour by Young People*. Cambridge: Cambridge University Press.

Shadish, W., Cook, T., and Leviton, L. (1991) *Foundations of Program Evaluation*. Newbury Park: Sage.

Spencer, L., Ritchie, J., Lewis, J., and Dillon, L. (2003) *Quality in Qualitative Evaluation: A Framework for Assessing Research Evidence*. London: Government Chief Social Researcher's Office, Prime Minister's Strategy Unit, Cabinet Office.

Williams, G.H. (1984) 'The Genesis of Chronic Illness: Narrative Reconstruction', *Sociology of Health Illness*, 6: 175–200.

Young, M., Camit, M., Mihajlovic, M. (1999) 'A Smoke Alarm Campaign in Arabic, Chinese and Vietnamese Communities', *New South Wales Public Health Bulletin*, 10: 133–5.

16

Qualitative Interviewing Techniques and Styles

Susan E. Kelly

INTRODUCTION

The qualitative interview is gaining in popularity among health researchers, as they have come to realize that in-depth understanding of the behaviours of care-givers and clients is critical for improving care and informing health policy. In this chapter, I explain how to do qualitative interviewing, drawing on years of experience using and teaching the method in medical school and other health-related settings. My main goals are to describe what qualitative interview techniques entail, discuss the types of considerations and concerns that set them apart from standardized interviews, and consider the kinds of research questions to which the various techniques are best suited. This chapter will assist the novice researcher in deciding whether qualitative interviews are the appropriate approach for a particular research topic and setting. My introduction will also provide a guide to the mechanics of qualitative interviewing techniques, including strategies for sampling, considering ethics review, constructing an interview guide, and recording and transcribing qualitative interviews.

The term 'qualitative interviews' refers to interview techniques that provide qualitative (textually rich) data. A qualitative interview is unlike a structured or standardized interview, where the goal is to generate data amenable to quantitative analysis.[1] The relationship between 'qualitative' and standardized interviews is best conceptualized as a continuum along which the 'researcher seeks [greater or lesser] control over the content and structure of the encounter' (Murphy and Dingwall, 2003: 77) or one in which control over the data is structured more or less tightly (Green and Thorogood, 2004: 80). Informal interviews in an ethnographic field setting and 'natural conversation' are at one end of the continuum and standardized interviews at the opposite end. Standardized interviews are highly structured in terms of question wording, order, and response categories (most questions being 'fixed choice') and are conducted in as standardized a manner as possible, with the researcher conducting the interview acting as a 'neutral' instrument. (This is often more an ideal than reality, and managing 'interviewer effects' an important element of standardized interview strategies.) Qualitative interviews, on the other hand, explicitly involve the interviewer and respondent in interaction, as interaction partners. The data produced in qualitative interviews is understood explicitly to be the product of such interaction, with the attention to reflexivity and subjectivity that this involves. Thus data produced through qualitative interviews is not only 'thick' (Geertz, 1973: Ch. 1) and textual (rather than discrete and quantifiable), but it is also an interactive accomplishment in which respondents are collaborators in the research process (Mishler, 1988). While this entanglement may appear messy when compared with the 'hard facts' produced by standardized techniques, it is the core strength of qualitative interviews, and it is precisely the reflexivity of qualitative interviews and their basis in shared human competencies of communication that make them particularly valuable tools in research on human behaviour.

As such, qualitative interviews are appropriate to research questions regarding the meaning of events or phenomena to research participants. A primary consideration of good interviewing strategy and technique is the need to balance the desire to uncover and probe the meanings and perspectives of respondents with the need to accomplish a researcher's objectives (or those of her sponsor). Qualitative interviews are often presented as appropriate to exploratory research questions, whether used in a standalone or mixed method approach; however, the deeper exploration of meaning qualitative interviewing techniques provide may be used to better understand a range of phenomena relevant to health research.

Qualitative interview techniques, therefore, must address and incorporate both rigour *and* subjectivity in the scientific process. Exactly how (and whether) qualitative research should be evaluated, and how 'rigour' is achieved, are contentious issues within the qualitative research community, tracing as they do familiar tensions between 'positivism' and interpretivism in social science (cf. Smith, 1984). However, increasing interest in, and ability to publish, qualitative interviews in health research, along with the rise of interdisciplinary research and evidence-based practice, makes it important to consider criteria against which the quality of qualitative interview research might be judged (by peers, editors, and funders). The methodological literature contains numerous attempts to develop such criteria, suggesting a range of 'good research' conventions and considerations the researcher will want to explore when designing, carrying out and reporting research using qualitative interview techniques. Primary among these are the importance of the topic, its contribution to knowledge, and the relevance of the evidence developed to address it (Hammersley, 1992). At a more procedural level, transparency of research activities is key to rigorous research, including clear descriptions of sampling strategy, data collection and analysis, consideration of the relationship of researcher(s) to participants, and systematic data collection and record-keeping (Blaxter, 2000). Specific sampling strategies can enhance the validity of interview findings and analytic interpretations, such as searching for contradictory evidence (Glaser and Strauss, 1967; Murphy and Dingwall, 2003). Combining different methods (e.g., observational and interview), checking findings with research participants (i.e., member checking), and being self-critical about biases with which we approach a field are further strategies for promoting rigour and quality in qualitative interview research. These procedures support criteria of *authenticity, criticality* and *integrity* against which qualitative research may be judged. In addition to these criteria of quality are those of *explicitness, vividness, creativity, thoroughness, congruence* and *sensitivity*, all of which are important when data are reported as textual accounts through which the experiences, views and voices of respondents are represented (Whittemore et al., 2001).

In qualitative interviewing, the researcher is explicitly seeking to gain access to the knowledge, experience and perspectives of research subjects, *rather than organizing the beliefs, experience and perspectives of research subjects into preset categories.* This stands in contrast to the standardized interview which generally reflects how the researcher (or research community) structures the world. It is reasonable to say that qualitative interviews are most useful when we are concerned about gaining insight into the worlds of others. That is, qualitative interviews are used when the researcher wishes to gain an understanding of how participants view, experience, or conceptualize an aspect of social life. Following from the well-known proposition in sociology regarding the power of definitions held by social actors for understanding human behaviour (Thomas, 1923), Merton and Kendall (1946: 545) argue that in the qualitative interview '(s)ubjects' definition of the situation should find full and specific expression'. In health research, this may entail researchers suspending their own clinical knowledge and judgement in order to elicit the everyday knowledge, experience and judgement of the person being interviewed. Health care-related research often involves the juxtaposition of 'expert' and 'lay' perspectives, although these concepts can be thought of as reversed such that the person being interviewed is understood to be the 'expert' with regard to their experience and understanding.

There are important limitations to what can be known through qualitative interviews, particularly concerning 'external realities' to which respondents do not have first hand access or accurate recall (e.g., the objective number of tests offered, the internal states of others or events to which the respondent was not present). Qualitative interviews provide insight into meaning *in context*, rather than stable inner states. Qualitative interview techniques may reflect assumptions about what Holloway and Jefferson (2000: 3) term the 'transparent self problem' and the 'transparent account problem' (see also Hammersley and Atkinson, 2007: Ch. 5). In essence, these reflect the assumption that what a respondent says in an interview context gives the researcher a direct window into their lives, thoughts and meanings. Rather, the researcher strives to be reflexive – self-critical – regarding how respondents' accounts and representations of selves and experiences are shaped by the interview as a social interaction, by the respondent's own biases, ideologies or mood, or by the context in which the interview takes place. These limitations are important considerations when designing and carrying out qualitative interview research.

The most common form of qualitative interview is the semistructured interview, in which the researcher works from a more or less determined list of question areas and probes. Narrative interviews are 'conversations' in which the aim of the researcher is to guide the interview subject through their own story of an event, process or life trajectory. Group interviews such as focus groups are discussions with the interviewer acting as moderator, guiding the group through topics of interest. All types of qualitative interviews are a form of social interaction, and as such require consideration of a range of interpersonal factors and communication skills. These skills include the ability to make a respondent feel comfortable and safe in disclosing, the ability to communicate clearly, the ability to listen attentively, the ability to direct or intervene in a narrative stream with insight and tact, and the ability to engage with the respondent while maintaining distance (neutrality). The researcher's skills in all of these areas face somewhat different challenges across the techniques discussed in the following section. Because qualitative interviews are sometimes usefully triangulated with other techniques of eliciting information, I will also present some aspects of multitechnique interviews in health research.

GENERAL CONCERNS IN QUALITATIVE INTERVIEWING IN HEALTH RESEARCH

A. Concepts and language

Language is fundamental to qualitative interview techniques, both theoretically and practically. Language constitutes both the method used to produce data *and* the data itself in qualitative interviews (Green and Thorogood, 2004). Again, we can look to the standardized interview for contrast. Standardized interview techniques use language as a tool to elicit 'facts' about a phenomenon or behaviour, with the language problem of the researcher being to use language sufficiently precisely to elicit the appropriate response. While standardized interview techniques recognize ambiguities and cultural differences in language use, these are methodological problems to be overcome, rather than understood to be data in themselves. This approach to language as a medium for representing the facts of a situation is reflected in the use of preset response categories. These in turn reflect the specific concepts and understandings of the situation held by the researcher.

In contrast, qualitative interview techniques are employed to seek access to concepts, cultural understandings and classifications of the world in the accounts of interview respondents. How do our respondents structure their worlds conceptually? How do they categorize and prioritize events and phenomena in their lives? The data produced through qualitative interview techniques is intended to reflect the conceptual frameworks of the study population. Therefore, attention to the language used by respondents is integral to qualitative interviews.

Qualitative interview techniques also require sensitivity to the *contexts* of language use. As researchers, we share some aspects of social and cultural understanding with respondents, but are likely also to understand the world through the concepts and meanings specific to the scientific communities to which we belong. In the use of qualitative interview techniques in health research, the distinctions between 'expert' and 'lay' understandings of concepts and language can be of considerable importance, not merely in the choice of words, but also how language is used to express opinions, assert authority and disclose.

An example from my research experience illustrates how qualitative interview techniques can be used to explore the conceptual territory of respondents. Our research focussed on a clinical question: why do women who experience symptoms of incontinence not seek medical treatment? We conducted a series of focus group discussions with a diverse set of respondents, in which we sought to understand the symptoms women experienced, how these symptoms affected or were accommodated in their daily lives, and how they conceptualized the causes and appropriate responses to their symptoms. It was important, therefore, to examine the language women used when talking about symptoms, encounters with health professionals, and self-perceptions. We found these women placed symptoms of incontinence in conceptual frameworks that were quite different from those used by specialists. They did not conceptualize incontinence as a 'medical' or 'health' condition, but rather as a natural consequence of childbirth or aging, or a condition they had caused themselves. We found that women used highly normative language when describing how they and others dealt with symptoms, and what behaviours they believed may have caused them. Furthermore, we discovered that the conceptual framework used by these women was strongly influenced by a national advertisement for incontinence products, which classified symptoms as appropriately responded to with home care and without disclosure.

Qualitative interview techniques allow the use of language, as well as its intrinsic content, to become part of the analysis. For example, in a study in which I interviewed parents about their experiences with childhood genetic conditions, I found parents to seldom use general concepts or language such as 'disabled' or 'disability' but rather to speak of their child's specific symptoms and diagnosis. This was one way in which parents' strong sense of the individuality of their child was conveyed through language. The term 'disabled' was used nearly exclusively in the context of discussions of disability rights, work, culture, or specific legislation. Similarly, Kathy Charmaz, in her study of how people experience chronic illness, demonstrates the importance of attending to the words respondents use and *do not use* to describe their experiences. Respondents described experiences of suffering without using the word 'suffering'; 'Talking about events that indicate past suffering is one thing; identifying self as continually suffering is quite another. The language of suffering may remain implicit; people may tell of pain and talk about problems but limit their view to specific events and situations' (Charmaz, 1999: 366).

Language presents practical concerns as well. Most researchers record interviews and produce a written transcript that becomes the data to be analyzed, along with observation notes and any other form of data collected. When transcribing an interview the researcher must make a number of decisions about how language is represented. (See Oliver et al., 2005 for a good discussion of transcription as representation, and the nature and consequences of transcription decisions.) The many variations of transcription technique fall between the poles of 'naturalism' in which every speech act – including pauses, stutters, laughter, etc. – is captured in as much detail as possible and 'denaturalism' in which grammar is corrected and utterances are smoothed out to read as much like standard text as possible. Decisions about transcription styles should be based on the nature of the research question and the extent to which language and representation are central to the analytic techniques employed. It is important to think through how textual data will be analyzed and used. Will direct quotations be used in reports? Is analyzing long chunks of narrative important? Will text be entered into a computer software system for analysis?

Some uses of qualitative interview data such as conversation analysis – analysis of how talk is used by participants in social interaction – require specific and quite detailed notation conventions. (West, 1984, offers a classic example of conversation analysis examining discussions between physicians and women patients.) In all forms of qualitative interviewing, cultural uses of language are important for conveying meaning and context. For example, in the study with parents discussed earlier, I used a naturalistic approach to transcription that captured hesitancies, uncertainties and cultural uses of language, all of which became important in later narrative analysis where large sections of text were analyzed for narrative structure and use of language. Maintaining individual voices was an important part of credibility of the data, as similarities of experience were conveyed in very different language styles by different respondents. I used a different transcription style in a focus group study I and colleagues conducted with parents regarding their children's dental care (Kelly et al., 2005). In this study, the transcriptions were not verbatim but followed the general flow of conversation. In analysis, transcriptions were supplemented by detailed observation notes and videotapes of each meeting. In the end, this arrangement proved to be less than ideal: we were able to connect speech acts to specific speakers, to identify quotes, and to examine the social setting and interaction dynamics of the group, but the specifics of speech acts were cumbersome to capture and we were hindered by assumptions made by the transcriptionists concerning what speech was important.

A later set of focus groups in this study, conducted with Spanish speaking participants, further complicated the issues of transcription and representation. As English speakers, we faced the question of whether to translate transcripts for analysis, or to leave analysis to a Spanish-speaking researcher, a process that would violate our validity check mechanisms that required multiple researchers to participate in analysis. We ultimately decided to use verbatim Spanish transcripts of the focus groups and to translate them to English for analysis by English speaking researchers. We faced an additional complication in this study, because our moderators were not natives of the same Spanish speaking part of the world as our respondents. (Gunaratnam, 2003, presents a useful discussion about the potential reification of ethnic and racial categories through methodological practices such as 'ethnic matching'.)

In general, then, qualitative interviews should be understood as discursive practices which are constituted by the use of language in everyday practice and as 'methodology'.

Qualitative interview techniques require attention to the role language plays in the objectives and design of the study, the way language is represented as data, the analysis processes to be used, and the cultural and language competencies of the researchers and participants.

A.1 A note on recording qualitative interviews

I and other researchers strongly advise that interviews be audio-recorded, with the consent of respondents. A good quality recording is the best record of an interview, and reconstructing an interview from notes is notoriously subject to interviewer-recall bias, even when undertaken immediately. Concurrent note taking is also very useful, as it provides an alternative record and memory trigger should parts of the recording prove unintelligible. Audio recording also facilitates the interview by eliminating the interruption of constant note taking and allowing normal conventions of social interaction such as eye contact between interviewer and respondent.

The importance of the recording requires that precautions be taken to ensure that the equipment is working properly, that electrical supplies or extra batteries are on hand when necessary, and that the recording device is positioned properly in a setting in which there is low noise interference. Recording technologies are evolving rapidly to digital formats which facilitate transcription, and it is advisable to investigate equipment options early in the project design. For group interviews, it is advisable to use several recorders placed strategically to record all voices; group interviews may be video recorded to provide a visual record of who is speaking, body language, etc. Video recording of individual interviews is generally a specific technique used for specific purposes (such as capturing body language). Video recoding must be used with caution, as it raises ethical problems of the identifiability of respondents.

A good transcript facilitates the practice of multiple researchers separately analyzing the data within agreed analytic conventions, a practice that enhances the validity of interpretation. Text is required for some types of analysis, including use of computer software for qualitative data analysis. Not all uses of qualitative interview techniques require transcription. Particularly when dealing with large amounts of narrative data some researchers prefer to listen to the audio or visual record and take notes. Recordings can in some circumstances be partially transcribed to provide illustrative verbatim quotes, for example. However, it is important to recognize that these are decisions about analysis and interpretation and should be undertaken by the researcher, not the transcriptionist!

B. Power and context

The relationship between interviewer and respondent in the qualitative research interview is often characterized by a power imbalance as the interviewer has the authority to frame the interview and ask the questions. Further, power relationships such as those involving gender, race/ethnicity, class and education are an important aspect of all qualitative interview research. Questions of power, context and representation have been debated extensively in qualitative research literatures, particularly reflecting feminist, postmodern, and postcolonialist accounts. Rather than recapitulate those debates, I have here a more limited concern with general considerations of power and context faced when using qualitative interview techniques in health research. There are three levels I wish to explore: the power relations that structure the research setting, the power relations of the interview encounter and the negotiation of power within the interview itself.

In health-related research, the health care provider/patient relationship is a significant power relationship. When doing qualitative interviews, the researcher must attend to relationships between patients and specific health care providers, as well as relationships with health care institutions and organizations. Further, research in health care settings may involve respondents who are receiving treatment for stigmatizing conditions. The potential vulnerability and marginality of patients and research subjects requires considerable attention to issues of power and context (see e.g., Liamputtong, 2007).

Interviewing within health care settings raises questions of power not least, because participants, if they are patients, may be concerned about ongoing access to treatment and advice, and may participate in interviews with a sense that important relationships or access may be jeopardized if they do not. In addition, interviewers, whether they are health care workers or not, are likely to be perceived as 'experts' in a context already structured by professional/lay distinctions. This unequal relationship may affect the willingness of respondents to disclose information that can be perceived as deviant (e.g., not following a prescribed medical regimen) or discrediting (e.g., engaging in risky health-related behaviour). Respondents may feel constrained in providing critical views of health care providers or medical practice. Qualitative interviews are a more intimate form of data collection than standardized interviews and often involve the revelation of private information. They can be perceived as more intrusive and can take a considerable amount of a respondent's time. These are all considerations when thinking through the ethics of a qualitative interview project as well as the nature of the data produced.

Selecting appropriate sites in which to conduct interviews may seem a simple design problem, but it is fraught with issues of power and authority (see e.g., Elwood and Martin, 2007). Taking the power structures of specific research settings seriously may become part of the qualitative interviewing strategy, driven by the kinds of information sought. For example, in a study of family understandings of Huntington's disease risk, Cox and McKellin (1999) conducted interviews within family homes rather than clinic settings. This was done to separate interview participants from the power and meanings associated with the clinic setting, as particular aspects and understandings of risk and disease may be 'cued' by the clinic contexts. To study meanings within families, interviews were located in family settings.

I followed a similar strategy in my narrative interview study with parents. I sought to ground the interviews in parents' everyday lives and to minimize association of the research with established relationships with health care professionals. I allowed respondents to select a setting in which they were comfortable, which in most cases was the family home. I also discovered that the kinds of interruptions that are likely to occur within a home setting can provide useful background information to the interview. For example, I was able to observe children's behaviour, parental interactions, the setup of therapeutic equipment within home environments and, in many cases, the therapy sessions themselves, all of which provided important contextual information that would not have been visible in other settings.

Power and context are also important considerations when qualitative interviews are conducted in institutional or organizational contexts, particularly when research involves crossing hierarchical lines of authority. For example, research conducted within a nursing home on how goals of care discussions were understood and handled by various staff required sensitivity to lines of authority within the institution (Furman et al., 2006). Because qualitative interviews are both interpersonal and potentially revealing, researchers must be sensitive in all aspects of the research design (recruitment, location of interviews, visibility of participation and data reporting).

B.1 A note on ethics and accessing potential respondents

In most places, qualitative interview-based research proposals, like other forms of research using human subjects, must be submitted to a research ethics committee for review. Requirements and standards vary internationally and by location. However, research ethics committees expect the researcher to recognize and respond to problems raised by unequal power relationships and the vulnerability of subjects. This is particularly the case when respondents are psychologically, socially or legally vulnerable.

Gaining informed consent from respondents is the central element of research ethics, although the specific approaches and wording required by research ethics committees vary locally and practice continues to change. The principle of informed consent requires prospective research subjects to be given full and accessible information about the research in which they have been asked to take part, including information about potential risks or benefits to them. It further requires that subjects are fully able to decline to participate in the research and to withdraw should they wish to do so.

Qualitative interview techniques raise particular issues with regard to these requirements. Given the more open, emergent, and iterative nature of qualitative interviews, fully informing a potential respondent about the research can prove difficult. Research ethics committees often require inclusion of the interview guide for their review, and yet, these guides may change 'in the field' over the course of a project. Risks of participating in qualitative interviews are often difficult to perceive. They include emotional distress such as from reliving painful events, unintended disclosure of personal information and disclosure of information – such as abuse – to which a legal requirement to act is attached. Accessing respondents may itself pose risks and care should be taken that approaching potential respondents avoid identifying them (to themselves or others) with a stigmatized group, condition or behaviour, and does not jeopardize any treatment, service or relationship they enjoy. Written informed consent may not be appropriate with certain populations. Qualitative interviews usually involve the establishment of interpersonal rapport between interviewer and respondent. In such situations, respondents may find withdrawing from a project difficult. A self-critical attitude towards the generally unequal power relationship that exists between interviewer and respondent should always be taken by the researcher, with requirements of informed consent in mind and practice. A growing literature on formal and informal ethics requirements and qualitative research exists (Richards and Schwartz, 2002; Van Den Hoonard, 2002; Crow et al., 2006).

C. Phenomenology, discourse analysis and grounded theory

The many approaches to qualitative interviews in health research generally fall into three broad methodological areas: phenomenology, discourse analysis and grounded theory. The goals of the inquiry and the intended products of the study guide the choice of which approach should be used. Phenomenological approaches are appropriate when our interest is to study how people make meaning of their lived experience. Discourse analysis is appropriate when our primary interest is in the use of language in the accomplishment of aspects of social life (including personal, clinical and political arenas). This type of analysis is often used when the researcher is interested in the ways in which social interactions are governed by relationships of power (see Waitzkin, 1991; Ten Have, 1999; West, 1984). Grounded theory approaches are appropriate when the goal of inquiry is to develop explanatory theories of social processes studied in context. Examples of grounded theory approaches in health research are numerous (see Morse et al., 2008).

C.1 A note on sampling and sample size

Sampling strategies in qualitative interview research do not follow the precepts of probabilistic sampling, but rather employ a range of 'naturalistic' techniques. These include convenience sampling, judgement or purposeful sampling and theoretical sampling. Convenience sampling seeks to access respondents with characteristics of interest from easily located groups among a population. Convenience sampling may be the appropriate approach when initiating a new area of research or exploring a new population. Methods of convenience sampling include recruitment from a general population via a public or centralized location or recruiting through notices or flyers. Respondents recruited in this fashion are likely to vary from a general population in a number of ways, including their interest in the topic, limiting generalizability. Judgement or purposeful sampling is used to select respondents that are most likely to yield appropriate and useful information. The researcher may use a set of eligibility criteria to define the research population and select cases from this population through a number of strategies, including maximum variation sampling, deviant or outlier sampling, negative case sampling, critical case sampling, key informant sampling or snowball sampling.

Theoretical sampling is suited to the iterative nature of some qualitative research designs. Theoretical sampling is driven by emerging interpretations of data and is organized around the goal of achieving 'theoretical saturation' where additional cases yield no new information or insights. This approach is associated with the grounded theory method of building theory from observations (Glaser and Strauss, 1967).

Unlike standardized interview research, determination of sample size in qualitative interview research does not strive for statistical adequacy but rather ties adequacy to the interview technique, the quality of the information collected, the population from which samples are drawn and the intended uses of data. There is no agreement among researchers as to the adequate number of subjects to fully explore a topic, but this is not to say that numbers are not important to ensuring an adequate sample (Sandelowski, 1995). Generally speaking, the researcher must justify her sample size on the basis of achieving informational redundancy or theoretical saturation, balanced against the amount of information generated and the analytic tasks it poses. In a study in which in-depth semistructured interviews are used to examine experiences and perspectives within a defined population group (e.g., a community of intravenous drug users) a sample of 6–10 may be adequate. Should the researcher discover important themes and differences within this population, the sample size may be expanded to achieve redundancy regarding these new data. A research design employing deep case analysis, using an in-depth narrative interview technique, may be limited to a small number of cases. The quality criteria discussed at the beginning of this chapter provide a useful guide for judging the appropriate sample size for qualitative interview research.

VARIETIES OF QUALITATIVE INTERVIEW TECHNIQUE

A. Semistructured interviews

Semistructured interviews retain the flexibility of qualitative research while permitting a greater degree of standardization than naturalistic, or 'field', interviews. They are thus appropriate in research situations in which the researcher intends to focus on specific research interests rather than to examine an individual's experiences more holistically (e.g., 'thick' examinations of a culture; for example, Katz's 1999 study of the culture of surgeons). They generally include a set of topic areas to be explored in some depth, and allow new questions to emerge as relevant avenues of information are suggested. Generally, this type of interview seeks open-ended responses; the extent to which a semistructured interview is formally structured depends upon the nature of the research question and the overall research strategy. Less structured interviews are appropriate to exploratory studies, where little previous work has been done. More structured interviews are appropriate when examining manifestations of a local phenomenon, where a considerable body of literature exists or when a researcher is comparing across a range of cases. A formally structured guide may consist of open-ended questions, probes and follow-up questions in which the order of questions and the wording are relatively standardized. However, even in this format, a skilled interviewer will allow the sequence of topics to follow the flow of the particular encounter.

When dealing with a very large number of cases, a structured interview will be easier to analyze. For example, I conducted eighty interviews in the study of parents discussed earlier; in order to make sense of such a large amount of qualitative data, the interview guide contained several highly structured portions and a standard sequence of questions within topic areas.

The tension between flexibility and focus is one of the strengths of semistructured interviews, and managing this tension is an important skill. The semistructured interview also is characterized by tension between 'normal' skills of interpersonal interaction – attention, active listening, reflecting, tact – and the professional skills of the researcher – guidance, focusing, tracking, progression.

Put another way, the semistructured interview requires the interviewer to maintain normal interactional involvement (Goffman, 1963) while managing the quality of information – data – produced. An important, and practical, example is the recording of interview data. Discrete management of recording equipment and limited concurrent note taking are important to achieving and maintaining appropriate attentiveness and rapport within the interview. For this reason, good research and data management practice includes attention to 'backstage' as well as 'front-stage' work (Goffman, 1959). Pre-prepared data collection packages, backup recording equipment, prelabelled data storage devices (e.g., cassettes or disks), are all important to effective interview conduct and good quality data.

Probes and follow-up questions are important aspects of semistructured interviews. They are important in terms of guiding the interview towards fuller explication of topics of interest, and ensuring that specific dimensions of a question area are explored in all interviews. The use of probes and follow-up questions, while important, necessarily involves negotiating a line between too much guidance of an interview and fully covering the research ground intended.

The length of the interview guide depends on the extent to which it is structured, how much time is available per interview and how much prior information has gone into developing the interview. In my experience, an interview guide with 10 to 15 topics areas can take from 1–3 hours to administer, depending on the nature of the conversation and how many probes or follow-up questions are considered necessary. A related concern in semistructured interviews is whether the topic area(s) have been covered in sufficient depth and include a broad enough scope of what is relevant. Conducting and analyzing a handful of pilot interviews, and including a summary question such as 'Is there anything else you would like to say about the topics we've discussed?', is a useful approach to gauging the sufficiency of topic coverage.

A.1 A note on constructing interview guides

An important first step to constructing an interview guide is to develop a list of topics to be covered. This means drawing from available knowledge, research interests and research objectives to identify the types and areas of information that should be included in an interview. Selected topic areas should be arranged in a sequence that is conversationally 'logical' and follows the general rule of moving from the general to the specific. Specific interview questions can then be designed within the topic areas.

Opening questions are an opportunity to introduce the research topic, establish rapport and some common ground, and engage respondents with relatively easy and nonthreatening questions. There are a range of techniques for designing useful research questions. For example, a useful temporal lead into a subject may begin, 'Tell me about when you first learned about your diagnosis…'. Other forms of question ask respondents to make associations between words, concepts or experiences, to agree or disagree with a position attributed to others ('Some say that… would you agree?') or to rank or prioritize ('What aspect of your experience with this service is most important to you?'). Questions should elicit open responses, address one concept at a time and be free of jargon. They should avoid leading the respondent to a position or answer and not reflect biases or prejudices of the researcher.

Knowing when and how to probe for more information or clarification is an important part of interviewing skill. Learning how to do this effectively is a matter of experience. Probing questions are most effectively part of 'active listening' – rather than anticipating the next question or topic, the interviewer listens and considers whether the information provided by the respondent is clear, relevant and explores the dimensions of meaning in which the researcher is interested. On the other hand, the interviewer should avoid too tightly controlling or leading the interview. Probes are a method of encouraging elaboration. Probing questions should not be an opportunity for the interviewer to insert themselves into the interview, make judgements or give advice. Probing questions may include, 'Can you tell me more about that?' or 'What did you mean by …?'

Probes are a part of the 'performance' of eliciting information in the depth and clarity desired. Follow-up questions are intended to provide more information about the main topics of the interview. While specific follow-up questions depend on the context of the particular interview, common follow-up questions can be identified in advance and included in the interview guide. Important follow-up questions, concerning emerging themes and concepts, for example, may be added to the interview guide as research progresses.

Narrative interview techniques require the researcher to 'construct' a narrative from responses to an extended semistructured interview format. In this case, the narrative structure is provided by the interviewer rather than the subject telling and shaping his or her story. This method directs analytic attention to content rather than form of the narrative, or how and why events are 'storied'. More typically, narrative interviews are guided – that is, conducted with a topic guide rather than preset questions, and begin with an opening 'invitation' to elicit first, the respondent's understanding of a concept or phenomenon (e.g., 'what do you understand 'health' to mean?) and followed by the elicitation of a first event or experience ('tell me about the first time you felt concerned about your health'). Narratives encompass 'long sections of talk' (Riessman, 2004), and are often developed over the course of multiple, repeat interviews. Narrative analysis typically treats extended speech accounts within interviews as analytic units, attending to sequence, language, contexts, threads, counter narratives, contradictions and consequences, rather than breaking accounts into thematic categories as in grounded theory and its variants.

Pilot testing is an important step in developing an interview guide, although this may be difficult to accomplish when respondents are difficult to access or are limited in number. The purpose of pilot testing is to determine how well the interview guide elicits information that fits with the research objectives, is effective in establishing rapport, uses appropriate and sensitive language, allows a conversational flow, allows comparison across interviews, provides space for respondents to reflect on and present experiences through their own eyes, and does not lead respondents to a uniform set of answers.

I find it useful to leave space on the interview guide for taking notes during the interview and recording demographic or other standard information as appropriate and to include a few instructions to the interviewer (e.g., 'check the recorder').

B. *Narrative interviews*

With roots in phenomenology (Ricouer, 1984), narrative interviewing techniques have gained a strong foothold in the social sciences and are now widely applied in health research. Narratives have increasingly been viewed within the social sciences as means through which actors construct and deploy identity, particularly in instances of biographical disruption (Becker, 1999; Bury, 2001). Narratives create and sustain the fabric of everyday life, and 'feature prominently in the repair and restoring of meaning' when this fabric is threatened or disrupted (Bury, 2001: 264). As such, they have fruitfully been deployed to in studies of the experience of chronic illness or other potentially disruptive experiences that involve coping, negotiation and adjustment. As Hydén (1997:49) notes: 'patients' narratives give voice to suffering in a way that lies outside the domain of the biomedical voice' (cf. Becker, 1999).

Narrative interviews draw upon the social psychological insight that humans organize understandings of experience as stories, using culturally available proto-narrative schemes (Polkinghorne, 1988). As such, narratives should be understood as 'contextualized and socially shared forms of knowledge' (Flick, 1997: 3) that tell us something about context and culture as well as individual experience. For example, the stories I collected from parents revealed something about their experiences *and* the broader experiences of parenting, caring for an ill child, and negotiating genetic diagnoses and treatment regimes.

Narrative constructions of experience are not only temporal in the sense of having a beginning, middle and end (I refer to a Western sense of temporal narrative), but they are also temporal in their production, meaning and validity – individuals rework their stories of experience and events over time, incorporating new knowledge and experience, tinkering with representations of self and others, and importantly, strengthening the coherence of narratives and situating them within salient cultural narratives of moral action. In the development of a coherent story line, actors construct and maintain a morally comprehensible self (Riessman, 1990), creating accounts of what Presser (2004: 86) terms 'trajectories of the moral self'. Presser further points to the situationally contingent construction of narratives of the moral self in the interactive context of the research interview. The narratives constructed in interviews may also be organized thematically and episodically (Flick, 1997).

Narrative interviews elicit a story: the interviewer guides the conversation through discussion of the individual's experience as it has unfolded over time. While all 'stories' we tell ourselves and others about our experiences are 'constructed', the narrative interview explicitly involves the elicitation of a story of *unfolding by the interviewer*. It is important, particularly analytically, to be attentive to how and why a particular story was constructed, whether there are inconsistencies or gaps, and whether we might identify counter narratives? What is taken for granted in the construction?

My interviews with parents of children with genetic conditions followed a narrative approach; they were designed to elicit individual stories by guiding parents through a common temporal trajectory of experiences with pregnancy, birth, infancy, diagnosis, treatment, parenting and projections into the future (e.g., Kelly, 2005). I was particularly interested in eliciting narratives of self and parenting, and to this end, I was attentive to both the narrative forms respondents followed and to the different strands of stories they developed throughout the interview. Specifically, the structure of the interviews moved from relatively standardized guiding questions to a format with open spaces and guiding prompts in which the stories could be further developed and reflected upon.

The narrative approach uses attentive listening and provides space for key events, counter-narratives and contradictions to emerge. Counter narratives and contradictions give evidence of 'breaks' with conventional or culturally appropriate responses to experience and events, a disruption of linearity: a particularly important aspect of narratives of parenting, self and childhood impairment. For example, parents identified coping with the emergence into adolescence of children with severe impairments as a common important 'event', one that is particularly destabilizing and challenging for parents' narratives of 'good parenting'. Counter-narratives frequently emerged regarding this period. In a particularly long interview, a young woman who was currently a single parent to four children, the oldest of whom required constant physical care, interrupted a description of her approach to parenting with the information that she was in the process of gradually transferring the fulltime care of her daughter from the family to an institution. This disclosure revisited her previous descriptions of herself as the 'perfect mother' of a disabled child, in which she revealed internal conflicts concerning this identity, both for herself and for social representation (Kelly, 2005). Another important narrative form that emerged in these interviews was anagnoresis – the moment in a narrative in which the protagonist recognizes the true nature of herself or another. In parents' narratives, this device was often deployed to explain coming to terms with a child's diagnosis or impairment (Kelly, 2005).

While recognizing the contributions of what he terms the 'narrative turn', Atkinson has criticized the representation by some users of the narrative interview technique as offering privileged access to 'private' experience of the interior self of those being interviewed (Atkinson, 1997). In spite of this critical take, Atkinson admits that narrative interviews in health research offer an important advantage, because experiences of illness, healing and health care work are often conveyed within the social worlds of family, friendship networks and clinics *as narratives*. Within the clinic, for example, there is a 'general exchange of narratives' through formal and informal interactions. At their best, narrative interviews take advantage of rhetorical forms of storytelling – particularly as constructing stories of self and identity – in which actors are frequently engaged in social life. That is, narrative interviews engage 'conventional acts of narrating' through which social actors construct memory, biography and experience (Atkinson, 1997: 327).

C. Notes on mixed interviewing techniques

While qualitative interview techniques traditionally involve eliciting information by asking questions, other ways of stimulating responses that maintain the qualitative nature of the interview can be employed. These include the use of vignettes, or stories about an individual or situation, to which the interview participant is asked to respond (see for example Hughes, 1998). Vignettes may be provided as text – for example, on a card – or orally. The response can then be guided by the use of probes. Vignettes have the advantage of distancing the content of the interview from the interview participant, something that proves useful when studying normatively sensitive behaviour such as criminal behaviour or risky sex. This technique does not necessarily require a hypothetical response (what would the respondent do in a similar situation) but can allow exploration of normative structures and conceptual categories. Visual stimuli such as photographs or pictures can be used to similar purpose (see for example Clark-IbáÑez, 2004 and Epstein et al., 2006).

CONCLUSION

In this chapter, I have provided brief discussions of the primary qualitative interview techniques, drawing out themes that I have found important in my research in health-related settings and research questions. Each of these techniques is the subject of large literatures in which theoretical and practical debates continue, taking somewhat different forms across specific disciplines. For each of these techniques, a range of variants, developed for specific purposes (e.g., Flick, 1997) has emerged. Qualitative interview techniques have sustained critical attention from feminist, postmodern and postcolonialist approaches, and my discussion reflects the general impact of these critiques on how qualitative interviews are understood.

NOTE

1 It should be noted, however, that qualitative and standardized interview techniques can fruitfully be combined to meet some research objectives.

REFERENCES

Atkinson, Paul (1997) 'Narrative Turn or Blind Alley?' *Qualitative Health Research,* 7(3): 325–44.

Baker, C. and Stern, P.N. (1992) 'Finding Meaning in Chronic Illness as the Key to Self-Care', *Canadian Journal of Nursing Research,* 25(2): 23–36.

Barbour, Rosaline S. and Kitzinger, Jenny (eds) (1999) *Developing Focus Group Research: Politics, Theory and Practice.* London: Sage.

Becker, Gay (1999) *Disrupted Lives: How People Create Meaning in a Chaotic World.* Berkeley, CA: University of California Press.

Blaxter, M. (2000) 'Criteria for Qualitative Research', *Medical Sociology News,* 26: 34–7.

Bloor, M., Frankland, J., Thomas, M., and Robson, K. (2001) *Focus Groups in Social Research.* London: Sage.

Bury, Michael. (2001) 'Illness Narratives: Fact or Fiction?', *Sociology of Health and Illness,* 23(2): 263–85.

Carey, Martha Ann and Smith, Mickey W. (1994) 'Capturing the Group Effect in Focus Groups: A Special Concern in Analysis', *Qualitative Health Research,* 4: 123–7.

Charmaz, Kathy (1999) 'Stories of Suffering: Subjective Tales and Research Narratives', *Qualitative Health Research,* 9(3): 362–82.

Clark-Ibáñez, Marisol (2004) 'Framing the Social World with Photo-Elicitation Interviews', *American Behavioral Scientist,* 47(12): 1507–27.

Cox, Susan M. and McKellin, William (1999) 'There's This Thing in Our Family': Predictive Testing and the Construction of Risk for Huntington's Disease'. In Conrad, P. and Gabe, J. (eds) *Sociological Perspectives on the New Genetics.* Oxford: Blackwell Publishers.

Crow, Graham, Wiles, Rose, Heath, Sue, and Charles, Vikki (2006) 'Research Ethics and Data Quality: The Implications of Informed Consent', *International Journal of Research Methodology,* 9(2): 83–95.

Epstein, Iris, Stevens, Bonnie, McKeever, Patricia, and Baruchel, Sylvain (2006) 'Photo Elicitation Interview (PEI): Using Photos to Elicit Children's Perspectives', *International Journal of Qualitative Methods,* 5(3), Article 1. Retrieved from http://www.ualberta.ca/~iiqm/backissues/5_2/html/epstein.htm

Flick, Uwe (1997) 'The Episodic Interview: Small Scale Narratives as Approach to Relevant Experience', LSE Methodology Institute Discussion Papers – Qualitative Series.

Furman, Catherine, Kelly, Susan.E, Mowery, R.L., and Miles, Tony, P. (2006) 'Eliciting Goals of Care in an Academic Nursing Home', *Journal of the American Medical Directors Association,* 7(8): 473–9.

Geertz, Clifford (1973) *The Interpretation of Culture.* New York: Basic Books.

Glaser, Barney and Strauss, Anselm (1967) *The Discovery of Grounded Theory: Strategies for Qualitative Research.* New Jersey: Aldine Transaction.

Goffman, Erving (1959) *The Presentation of Self in Everyday Life.* New York: Doubleday.

Grbich, C. (1999) *Qualitative Research in Health.* London: Sage.

Green, Judith and Thorogood, Nicki (2004) *Qualitative Methods for Health Research.* London: Sage.

Gunaratnam, Yasmin (2003) *Researching Race and Ethnicity: Methods, Knowledge and Power.* London: Sage.

Hammersley, Martyn (1992) *What's Wrong with Ethnography?* London: Routledge.

Hammersley, Martyn and Atkinson, Paul (2007) *Ethnography: Principles in Practice* (3rd Edition). London: Routledge.

Hydén, L-C (Lars-Christer) (1997) 'Illness and narrative', *Sociology of Health and Illness,* 19(1): 48–69.

Holloway, Wendy and Jefferson, Tony (2000) *Doing Qualitative Research Differently: Free Association, Narrative and the Interview Method.* London: Sage.

Hughes, Rhidian (1998) 'Considering the Vignette Technique and Its Application to a Study of Drug Injecting and HIV Risk and Safer Behaviour', *Sociology of Health and Illness,* 20(3): 381–400.

Katz, Pearl (1999) *The Scalpel's Edge: The Culture of Surgeons.* Boston: Allyn and Bacon.

Kelly, S.E. (2005) '"A Different Light": Examining Impairment Through Parent Narratives of Childhood Disability', *Journal of Contemporary Ethnography,* 43(2): 180–205.

Kelly, S.E., Marshall, P.A., Koenig, B.A., Sanders, L.M., and Raffin, T.A. (1997) 'Understanding the Practice of Ethics Consultation: Results of an Ethnographic Multi-Site Study', *Journal of Clinical Ethics*, 8(2): 136–49.

Kelly, S.E., Binkley, C.J., Neace, W.P., and Gale, B.S. (2005) 'Barriers to Parental Care Seeking Behavior for Children's Oral Health Among Low Income Parents', *American Journal of Public Health*, 95: 1345–51.

Kidd, Pamela S. and Parshall, Mark B. (2000) 'Getting the Focus and the Group: Enhancing Analytic Rigor in Focus Group Research', *Qualitative Health Research* 19: 293–308.

Kitzinger, Jennifer (1994) 'The Methodology of Focus Groups: The Importance of Interaction Between Research Participants', *Sociology of Health and Illness*, 16: 103–21.

Kitzinger, Celia, and Hannah Frith (1999) 'Just Say No? The Use of Conversation Analysis in Developing a Feminist Perspective on Sexual Refusal', *Discourse and Society*, 10(3): 293–316.

Krueger, Richard A. and Casey, Mary Anne (2008) *Focus Groups: A Practical Guide for Applied Research, Fourth Edition*. London; Thousand Oaks, CA: Sage.

Liamputtong, Pranee (2007) *Researching the Vulnerable*. London: Sage.

Merton, Robert K. and Kendall, P.L. (1946) 'The Focused Interview', *American Journal of Sociology*, 51: 541–57.

Mishler, Elliot (1984) *The Discourse of Medicine: Dialectics of Medical Interviews*. Norwood NJ: Ablex.

Mishler, Elliot (1988) *Research Interviewing: Context and Narrative*. Cambridge Mass: Harvard University Press.

Morse, Janice M., Phyllis Noerager Stern, Juliet M. Corbin, Kathy C. Charmaz, Barbara Bowers, and Adele E. Clarke (2008) *Developing Grounded Theory: The Second Generation*. California: Left Coast Press.

Murphy, Elizabeth and Dingwall, Robert (2003) *Qualitative Methods and Health Policy Research*. New York: Aldine de Gruyer.

Oliver, Daniel G., Serovich, Julianne M., and Mason, Tina M. (2005) 'Constraints and Opportunities with Interview Transcription: Towards Reflection in Qualitative Research', *Social Forces*, 84(2): 1273–89.

Polkinghorme, D. (1988) *Narrative Knowing and the Human Sciences*. Albany, NY: SUNY Press.

Presser, L. (2004) 'Violent Offenders, Moral Selves: Constructing Identities and Accounts in the Research Interview', *Social Problems*, 51(1): 82–101.

Richards, Helen Mary and Schwartz, Lisa Jennifer (2002) 'Ethics of Qualitative Research: Are There Special Issues for Health Services?' *Family Practice*, 19: 135–9.

Ricoeur, Paul (1984) *Time and Narrative*. Chicago: The University of Chicago Press.

Riessman ,Catherine Kohler (1990) 'Strategic Uses of Narrative in the Presentation of Self and Illness: a Research Note', *Social Science and Medicine*, 30: 1195–200.

Riessman, Catherine Kohler (1993) *Narrative Analysis*. London: Sage.

Riessman, Catherine Kohler (1994) 'Narrative Analysis'. In Lewis-Beck, M.S., Bryman, A., and Futing Liao, T. (eds) *Encyclopedia of Social Science Research Methods*. London, UK, and Newbury Park, CA: Sage.

Riessman, Catherine Kohler (2002) 'Illness Narratives: Positioned Identities'. Invited Annual Lecture, Health Communication Research Centre, Cardiff University.

Sandelowski, Margaret (1995) 'Sample Size in Qualitative Research', *Research in Nursing and Health*, 18(2): 179–83.

Smith, J.K. (1984) 'The Problem of Criteria for Judging Interpretive Inquiry', *Educational Evaluation and Policy Analysis*, 6: 379–91.

Ten Have, Paul (1999) *Doing Conversation Analysis: A Practical Guide*. London: Sage.

Thomas, W.I. (1923) *The Unadjusted Girl*. Boston: Little Brown.

Van den Hoonaard, W. (ed.) (2002) *Walking the Tightrope: Ethical Issues for Qualitative Researchers*. Toronto: University of Toronto Press.

Waitzkin, Howard (1991) *The Politics of Medical Encounters: How Patients and Doctors Deal with Social Problems*. New Haven: Yale University Press.

Wales, U.K., May 2002. Available at http://www.cardiff.ac.uk/encap/hcrc/comet/prog/narratives.pdf [accessed on August 11, 2008].

West, C. (1984) *Routine Complications: Trouble with Talk between Doctors and Patients*. Bloomington: Indiana University Press.

Whittemore, Robin, Chase, Susan K., and Mandle, Carol Lynn (2001) 'Validity in Qualitative Research', *Qualitative Health Research*, 11(4): 533–7.

17

Focus Groups

Rosaline S. Barbour

INTRODUCTION

It is no surprise that focus groups are widely used in health research: this method of collecting data is both efficient and amenable to a broad range of topics. However, the attractiveness of the method masks some of its subtleties and can lead to its lazy and uncritical use. Although most novice focus group researchers possess life skills that can be transferred to this research method – including dinner party conversations, committee work, teaching through seminars, or use of group-work methods in a therapeutic context – these experiences alone are insufficient preparation for doing focus group research. Different skills are needed when group discussions are used to generate research data. Focus group discussions may resemble informal conversations, but they serve a different purpose and demand additional competencies.

Moderators' skills are sometimes presented as involving little more than a set of techniques which can be imported to address a range of research questions. However, good focus group moderating is an art, requiring the researcher to use pre-existing abilities whilst learning from experience (throughout a research career and during the life of a single research project), always reflecting on the purpose and scope of the particular research project involved.

Strict adherence to prescriptive texts can give rise to difficult problems that will send the focus group researcher back to the text looking in vain for solutions. The key to successful use of focus groups is to use them appropriately and imaginatively. The researcher must be prepared to accept the fact that other methods may be more suitable for addressing the topic in hand and must be willing to use rigorous piloting of topic guides and exercises to ensure the generation of quality data. Careful planning is essential for eliciting relevant and rich data that transcend the purely descriptive and allow ample scope for comparative analysis. Attention to research design enables researchers to move beyond the descriptive to furnishing potential explanations.

It is noteworthy that there is considerable confusion as to what constitutes a focus group, with the terms 'group discussion', 'group interview' or even 'focus group interview' being used interchangeably. The definition used in this chapter is a broad one, which argues that, 'any group discussion may be called a "focus group" as long as the researcher is actively encouraging of, and attentive to, the group interaction' (Kitzinger and Barbour, 1999, p. 20). This definition emphasizes the importance of interaction *between* participants and avoids the mistaken notion that participants will always address their remarks via the moderator. Instead, a focus group discussion is likely to involve participants talking 'across' the moderator, who may literally take a back seat during the discussion (provided that the topic guide is successful in focusing discussion around desired topics).

This definition demands quite a lot of the moderator, who is required to 'keep several balls in the air' at any one time. Running a focus group requires the researcher to generate data (by stimulating discussion through active questioning and active listening) *and* anticipate analysis (by remaining alert to the content of discussion, variations in opinion and nuanced differences). Notice how this definition of a focus group underscores the dual imperative of planning ahead whilst continuously revising and refining our ideas, reflecting the iterative process that characterizes the qualitative research endeavour.

In this chapter, I provide advice on how to effectively design focus group studies, run focus group discussions, and interpret focus group data. I begin by locating focus groups with reference to key research traditions, highlighting the special benefits and resources afforded by placing focus groups firmly within the qualitative tradition.

LOCATING FOCUS GROUPS WITHIN QUALITATIVE RESEARCH TRADITIONS

Focus groups have been used in a variety of research traditions, including marketing research, organizational research and development, community development, and social science research. Each tradition has its own particular 'take' on the method, reflecting the different end points desired. While marketing researchers are charged with determining the likely reception of a new product or advertising campaign, community development workers or action researchers are concerned with effecting social – even political – change, and those employing focus groups within a professional context tend to be seeking to develop protocols for practice. Consequently, the advice dispensed with regard to carrying out focus group discussions in these varying contexts tends to emphasize particular aspects of the process at the expense of others. Marketing researchers are concerned with extrapolating from focus group members' views to those of the wider target group and use sampling strategies to this end. Action researchers (who aim to effect change – either in professional practice, service delivery, organizational procedures, or even political structures) are less concerned with canvassing opinions with regard to 'representativeness' and are more likely to seek to engage with key stakeholders or those with the capacity to instigate shifts in perspectives, professional practice, policies, or even social structure. Their goal is to understand and facilitate the process of change.

What counts as 'data' also varies, depending on the purpose of focus group research. While some focus group researchers stress the need to produce verbatim transcripts to afford the opportunity for detailed analysis, others are more concerned with providing a summary or focusing on the outcome of the discussion, which may simply involve deciding whether or not to pursue a particular advertising or political campaign or furnishing a professional protocol. With action research, the success of the research project may simply be judged with regard to what it has achieved (Hilsen, 2006) or what has been learnt through the exercise (Meyer, 2000).

APPROPRIATE AND INAPPROPRIATE USE OF FOCUS GROUPS

Many studies have used focus groups opportunistically, not capitalizing on their strengths, but using them, instead, to overcome perceived problems of arranging individual interviews with busy or potentially reluctant respondents. This may encourage them to treat the data generated as 'second best', limiting themselves to using focus groups to access respondents' perspectives through providing a window onto individual experience. However, the extra effort required to extricate individual stories and sequences of events from focus group data should disabuse those who hope that focus groups can provide a short cut to the sort of data usually generated via one-to-one interviews (Barbour, 2008).

Many of the problems experienced by new converts to focus group research can be understood in terms of unrealistic expectations, which reflect a lingering adherence to quantitative approaches. This can lead some focus group researchers to perceive as problematic features that are part and parcel – indeed, often particular strengths – of qualitative research. Once data have been generated, perceived difficulties in interpreting apparently 'slippery' views reflect a view of opinions as fixed and measurable. It is misguided to attempt to extrapolate from focus group discussions in order to attempt to identify individuals' attitudes: focus groups should *not* be used as a 'back door' survey technique (Barbour, 2008).

Similarly, concerns that surface during analysis about the differences between focus groups may reflect an over-simplistic expectation that the same questions will give rise to similar discussion, regardless of context, group composition, and dynamics. The more wily or experienced focus group researcher is likely to be aware that thoughtful sampling can help to highlight differences between groups and afford potential for comparison. Importantly, some approaches to using focus groups also fail to acknowledge the impact of the researcher on the data generated. While it is not always possible to match the researcher and focus group participants, it is certainly important to bear in mind the effect that researcher characteristics may have on the direction and content of discussion (Kitzinger and Barbour, 1999). Differences between focus groups are, in fact, a potential resource for analysis, as responses to different moderators may give important clues as to how people construct and modify their perceptions. Qualitative methods excel at accessing context, using it to make sense of data.

Although this emphasis on process and context locates focus groups within a broadly conceived qualitative paradigm, their provenance is not clear. As Kidd and Parshall observe, 'focus groups developed and (have been) maintained outside of the major methodological traditions of qualitative research, and they are thus relatively agnostic in terms of the methodologies attending them' (Kidd and Parshall, 2000, p. 296). Focus groups are frequently used in a rather loose or casual way without giving due attention to their positioning – and hence, their full potential. There has been some discussion and debate about the fit between focus groups and the various qualitative traditions, which, although similar in some respects, nevertheless have differing and potentially contradictory ideas as to what constitutes appropriate research questions and what counts as data (Barbour, 1998).

Focus groups have usefully been described by Powney (1988) as 'structured eavesdropping' and there has been spirited debate as to where exactly focus groups fit on the continuum between structure and spontaneity. Located midway between structured interviewing and observational fieldwork, as Powney's description suggests, focus groups are often viewed as a poor relation of anthropology and ethnography, the hallmark of such approaches being that they afford insights into naturally occurring human behaviour. In fact, focus groups may have some advantages over the more laborious and opportunistic aspects of observational fieldwork. Bloor et al. argue that focus groups can provide, 'concentrated and detailed information on an area of group life which is only occasionally, briefly, and allusively available to the ethnographer over months and years of fieldwork' (Bloor et al., 2001, p. 6).

WHEN TO USE FOCUS GROUPS

Focus groups really come into their own when the topic of the research relates to group processes, such as establishing group norms, developing a consensus statement, resolving differences of opinion, or interrogating new developments, procedures, or advice dispensed. Since they do not require individual participants to talk at length about the topic involved, focus groups are extremely useful in eliciting responses to issues that may not be of prime importance to respondents. The group situation allows them to step back from their taken-for-granted behaviours and assumptions and provides space to 'problematize' concepts and ideas to which they may previously have paid scant attention. It is for this reason that focus groups excel at answering what I would term 'Why not?' questions. Although individuals might find it hard to explain their reasons for neglecting to follow professional advice (such as taking up screening opportunities), group discussion gives them permission to formulate and articulate their responses – perhaps for the first time. This is one of the most significant advantages of focus groups as compared to other methods.

A recent study provides an illustration. The goal of the research was to establish women's reasons for not taking folic acid during and in the lead-up to pregnancy. Our concerns were sparked by the high rate of neural tube defects recorded in a particular area of Scotland. In situations such as this, focus groups are useful in allowing researchers to establish the level of knowledge of group members without putting them 'on the spot' in the way that a one-to-one interview might. The focus groups we organized brought together women with similar histories of folic acid use and provided valuable insights into the reasoning behind women's choices. We found considerable ambivalence about folic acid, even amongst the three women in the excerpt below who *did* take folic acid once they knew they were pregnant (a discovery that highlights the value of including some individuals who did comply with health promotion advice, rather than concentrating exclusively on those who did not):

Excerpts from Folic Acid Focus Group (Group F)

In the early part of the focus group discussion, the women were asked to comment on the role of folic acid. Although one recalled having read about spina bifida this was not mentioned straight away:

Frances: It's for the baby eh? I knew it was to do with the bones and ... to aid that ... more as a preventative.
Sarah: That's right.
Frances: Spina bifida and that...?
Sarah: Yeah ... I saw something about that.

The moderator sought later in this same focus group discussion to find out more about the women's knowledge about prevention of neural tube defects. In the following excerpt, the three women involved can be seen co-constructing an explanation:

Sarah: There's no proven fact that it's good for you or not good for you. But, as Frances (who'd talked about having had a miscarriage and wondering if taking folic acid might have prevented this) said, you want to cover every track. But ...
Linda: Or how much is staying in your system. Like me, I was sick all the time.
Moderator: Why do you think there's an emphasis on the first 12 weeks of pregnancy?
Frances: Is that no(t) to do with your risk of miscarriage – in the first twelve weeks?
Sarah: I'd think its .... it's maybe that after that the baby's stopped forming ...
Moderator: Is that something you read in a leaflet?
Sarah: Just something I made up in my own head.
Linda: After 12 weeks, it's already starting to develop.

Sarah:	I'd assumed that whatever the folic acid prevents or helps to prevent has already done its job by the twelve weeks.

At several points through the discussion, these women alluded to the need for proof with regard to the impact of folic acid on pregnancy outcome:

Frances:	It's hard to say, because there's, like, two people on either side of me and one took and one didn't. They could end up exactly the same healthwise. It's one of the things, It's an unknown. You can't say
Sarah:	You can't say 'Did you take folic acid? Well, your baby'll turn out like mine or if you didn't it won't'.
Frances:	Every pregnancy's different. I'd a great one. I sailed right through it, so did that have something to do with it?
Linda:	That's right.
Frances:	If you're getting it all through food anyway, I don't know that taking the tablet does any good.
Moderator:	What do you think might encourage women to take folic acid supplements?
Sarah:	It's so hard because you're obviously thinking 'I want to start a family', It's just supposed to be one of those natural things you do …
Frances:	I don't know if you'd need proof. If they could maybe come up with 4 or 5 mums who – I don't meant it nastily – who didn't take folic acid and did have problems with their children. We're all sitting here with healthy babies, but is it the folic acid? We're all in the same boat …
Linda:	Yes.
Frances:	Would it make a difference if somebody came in and said I took it every day and I still had problems? You just don't know …
Sarah:	Is a lot of this not hereditary too? Maybe a family gene or at risk with age. That's one of the reasons I took it because I was older.

Many focus group researchers have used the method opportunistically, either indulging in 'brain-storming' sessions (expending minimum effort with regard to formulating topic guides or stimulus materials) or capitalizing on social situations with no attempt to select participants. The art of successful design for focus group studies, however, requires careful attention to sampling, the development of topic guides, and the selection of stimulus materials. Although discussion appears to emerge in a relatively spontaneous fashion, it must be skilfully cultivated through putting markers in place from the outset in order to guide discussion. If you put in the necessary effort 'up front', you can sit back to a degree – albeit remaining alert to distinctions and nuances – as discussion flows in the desired direction.

SUCCESSFUL USE OF FOCUS GROUPS

Recruitment and ethical issues

Focus groups are frequently recommended when researchers wish to engage with groups that are notoriously hard-to-reach, since the informal nature of group discussions is generally considered to be less threatening to those who may have an antipathy towards authority, for example. For this reason focus groups have been used extensively with children (Mauthner, 1997), minority ethnic groups (Chiu and Knight, 1999), those out of contact with services, or who have chosen not to take up opportunities such as screening or immunization (Barbour, 2007).

It is important not to alienate potential participants through insensitive approaches. An obvious example is the use of ethnic, religious, or ageist labels which may be offensive; care must also be taken with labels such as 'obese' which are frequently used by health researchers but will likely provoke an unfavourable response in our target group. Even where the research design relies on 'stand-alone' focus groups (without employing any other methods), the researcher would be well-advised to carry out some observational groundwork – or to carry out some background reading or to seek advice from knowledgeable individuals – in order to ensure that unfortunate mistakes are avoided (Baker and Hinton, 1999). Culley, Hudson and Rapport (2007), for example, drew on their knowledge of South Asian communities in deciding not to hold intergenerational focus groups, due to the practice of deferring to older people. Another problem is that of 'sampling by deficit' (MacDougall and Fudge, 2001), where researchers may highlight 'deviant' behaviour, such as failure to turn up for screening. Our folic acid study had the original title of 'Reasons for Sub-optimal Intake of Folic Acid Pre-pregnancy and in Early Pregnancy' but we decided to amend this title for the information sheets to be used in recruiting focus group participants, opting to use the more user-friendly and less censorious title of 'Folic Acid and Pregnancy'.

Although some researchers believe that one-to-one interviews are most suitable for sensitive topics, focus groups can afford 'safety in numbers'. Focus groups do not force each participant to answer each question and may, therefore, cede a greater degree of control to participants in terms of what they choose to share or withhold from discussions. Recent developments afforded by the Internet (in the shape of online discussion fora), can be harnessed – either as a means of generating fresh data or allowing the researcher to 'harvest' as data contributions posted in naturally occurring settings. Using the Internet in this way can afford enhanced anonymity and may be a particularly attractive option for younger people who are more likely to be comfortable with this medium. This was the case with young people with potentially stigmatizing skin conditions who took part in synchronous (i.e., real-time) online discussion in one study (Fox et al., 2007).

The issue of confidentiality – no longer a matter to be resolved merely between researcher and 'researched' – has to be addressed at the outset of focus group discussions, as there is, obviously, the potential for subjects to leak information after the event. This applies to all participants and flagging up this issue at the beginning also alerts participants to the potential for tempering their contribution accordingly. Researchers who are keen to share transcripts with research respondents should give careful consideration to the implications of providing focus group members with concrete accounts of each other's contributions to the discussion.

The other constituency that needs to be taken into account with respect to recruitment is gatekeepers – key individuals who can facilitate access to our sample and provide advice as to how best to approach them, or where to hold groups. Such people include managers or professionals in contact with clients, and, depending on the study involved, they may sometimes undertake to present our research on our behalf to potential participants. This can be useful in situations where participants are likely to be especially wary of overtures from researchers but gatekeepers' input can significantly shape our resulting sample – and, hence, the potential of our dataset. It pays to be mindful of the ways in which gatekeepers can block access – either intentionally or inadvertently. They may screen out potential participants through employing their own judgment as to who is or is not a suitable group member and may be selective with regard to how they receive or present our research message. Keep in mind that gatekeepers may not always be the senior people we envisage – Umaña Taylor and Bámaca (2004), for example, talk of the key role played by bilingual children who frequently answered the telephone to researchers attempting to recruit Latina women for a research project.

Sampling and group composition

Although qualitative researchers are seldom called upon to formulate the precise inclusion and exclusion criteria that are a standard feature of sampling decisions for randomized control trials, it is still crucial that we give some thought as to the ethical issues involved. In the context of the folic acid study, for example, we were careful not to recruit any women whose babies have experienced health problems following delivery. Whilst it might be illuminating, as a researcher, to discover whether having a sick baby might make women more likely to follow health care professionals' advice in subsequent pregnancies, we considered that it would be unethical to explore or, potentially, to create such doubts. Ensuring that focus group participants had healthy babies also avoided the danger of women whose babies have experienced health problems comparing themselves unfavourably with those who have followed advice about folic acid supplements. This is something that focus group researchers need to consider carefully before convening groups comprising individuals who may, for example, be at different stages of an illness, or who may have differing prognoses, where comparison with others might be upsetting for those involved.

Although some focus group projects rely on selecting fresh samples, we are sometimes in the fortunate position of being able to use a larger dataset (replies to a questionnaire, for example) as a sampling pool from which to select focus group participants on a more systematic basis – provided that agreement has been obtained to recontact respondents. This has the added advantage that preliminary analysis can help identify important relationships between quantitative variables and, therefore, characteristics of focus group discussants that are likely to reflect differing perceptions or experiences, making for richer discussion and debate. For our study of low uptake of folic acid supplements, we opted to employ a short researcher-administered screening questionnaire at mother and baby clinics in order to recruit women who had recently given birth. A research midwife administered the questionnaire and recruited a total of 202 women who were willing to take part in focus groups. The information that we collected related to women's parity (number of births), age, marital status, education, employment, area of residence (measured by reference to deprivation categories developed for studying Scottish populations) and, crucially, their experience of taking folic acid supplements prior to and during their most recent pregnancy.

As with all qualitative research, sampling holds the key to the systematic comparisons which our data allow us to make and, hence, determines the analytic potential of our studies. Whether described as 'purposive' (Kuzel, 1992) or 'theoretical' sampling (Mays and Pope, 1995) the intention is the same: to use what is already known about the variety encompassed by the group or population we are studying to make informed guesses as to how these differences may affect experiences and perceptions and to select our sample in order to explore these more fully.

Rather than taking up valuable discussion – and transcribing time – by asking focus group participants to provide detailed information, it can be useful to collect standard data by employing a pro forma. If this is done in preparation for the group session, this can have the added advantage of aiding recall and ensuring the accuracy of information obtained. When conducting a study about decision making in relation to redeeming prescriptions and taking medication, we asked participants to complete a short pro forma at home which recorded details and dosages of the medication they were currently taking. Filling in these forms at home allowed individuals to record the relevant information with reference to the labels on their pill bottles – and also prevented focus group discussions being hijacked by stories about who was taking which medication, which, although possibly compelling for participants, was not, in this instance, the topic of the research.

In the context of the folic acid study, we used the information collected from women attending clinics in order to draw up a sampling grid to provide a total of six focus groups, and to include all the women who indicated that they had not taken folic acid during their most recent pregnancy. We identified six potential focus groups:

GROUP A

Seven primiparous women (with first babies) who had NOT taken folic acid
Age range 22–37 years
Deprivation categories 2–5 (where one is least deprived and seven most deprived)
All with standard grades (exams taken at 16 years of age)
Five single; two cohabiting

GROUP B

Eight primiparous women (with first babies) who had taken folic acid, but not as recommended (Some had taken it throughout their pregnancies; others had taken it only very briefly; and some had taken it only during the later stages of pregnancy)

Age range 20–33 years
Deprivation categories 1–5
Range of educational qualifications
Three single; three cohabiting; two married

GROUP C

Five multiparous women (with one or more previous births) who had taken folic acid during this pregnancy, but not as recommended

Age range 19–40 years
Deprivation categories 4–6
Range of educational qualifications
Two single; three married

GROUP D

Six multiparous women (with one or more previous births) who had NOT taken folic acid during this pregnancy or during a previous pregnancy/ies

Age range 19–36 years
Deprivation categories 4 and 5
Range of educational qualifications
All cohabiting

GROUP E

Six multiparous women (with one or more previous births) who had NOT taken folic acid during this pregnancy but who had a different experience of folic acid in a previous pregnancy/ies

Age range 22–37 years
Deprivation categories 2–5
Standard grades (exams taken at 16 years of age) or vocational qualifications
Three cohabiting; three married

GROUP F

Selected from the remaining pool of 170 women who had taken folic acid as recommended during their most recent pregnancy

6–8 women who HAD taken folic acid during this pregnancy

Mix to be determined depending on outcome of the other five groups and the comparisons we wished to explore

It is easy, as a researcher, however, to fall into the trap of thinking that we are in control of sampling decisions when, in the event, focus group participants may turn up accompanied by friends or partners and can, of course, always elect not to turn up at all. Nevertheless, it pays to give due consideration to the rationale for bringing certain individuals together. The usual advice to convene focus groups on the basis of some shared characteristic or experience is sound and should help to ensure that people feel comfortable with each other – especially where they may share some stigmatizing condition (Bloor et al., 2001).

In the foregoing example, we decided, for similar reasons, not to mix women who had taken folic acid as recommended with those who had not. However, it is also important not to end up with a group that is so similar that there is little room for discussion or debate (Morgan, 1988). Fortunately, our potential focus group participants are invariably less one-dimensional than our desk-based sampling plans might suggest, and it is likely that further differences will emerge in the course of discussions – participants selected because of their role as health care professionals may, for example, also have acted as carer and patients are also likely to be fathers or mothers, brothers or sisters and will, in all likelihood, draw on these multiple identities in mulling over our research questions. In the folic acid study, we initially assigned women of similar parity to groups, but women selected for our primiparous groups might reveal that they had experienced previous still births or terminations. In addition, practical issues, such as women's availability and their need for a crèche meant that we had to be flexible. Although we still wished to avoid mixing those who had taken folic acid as recommended with those who had not taken it at all, we took a more relaxed attitude to mixing women of differing parity and to assigning to the same group those had taken folic acid (but not as recommended) and women who had not taken it at all.

Focus group researchers engaged in studies of professionals frequently ask whether it is better to hold multidisciplinary or single-discipline focus group sessions. As is often the case, the answer ultimately depends on the purpose and topic of the research – whether the main research interest is in how teams function as entities or how the individual professional groups involved construct the issue in question. Holding some of each type of group, however, can yield useful comparative data. If the researcher is tasked, for example, with evaluating a series of group therapy sessions, it may make more sense to convene separate groups with all the fathers, all the mothers, and all the children involved, rather than holding focus group discussions with family units, which might begin to look and sound remarkably like the sessions they were set up to study.

Although it is tempting to use pre-existing management meetings or tutorial groups, or the like, for generating data, this may not be appropriate for the specific research question being addressed and may yield data which tells us more about these specific contexts than it does about the more general processes in which we are interested (Kevern and Webb, 2001). The decision about the use of pre-existing meetings should be made after considering whether the access afforded (both in terms of the nature of discussion and group membership) fits with the research aims, rather than merely offering a solution to logistical problems – whether these be saving time or allowing a recalcitrant researcher to sidestep considerations about sampling and group composition.

This is not to say that pre-existing groups should be avoided as potential sources of data. Peer groups, friendship groups and family units, in particular, provide the context for many of the health-related discussions that shape our attitudes, routines, and behaviours. In the context of the study on decisions about medication, several participants did turn up with their spouses, which afforded valuable insights into the way in which joint decision-making provided the backdrop for and ultimately engineered individuals' responses. Focus groups can provide a window onto the intimacies of family life, as Crossley (2002) discovered when analyzing some rather acrimonious exchanges between two sisters in a focus group concerned with responses to health promotion advice.

However, when more formal pre-existing groups with their own clear agendas – such as work groups or committees – are used, it is paramount that attention be paid to the ordering and content of the topic guide and stimulus material. This ensures that some 'structure' is provided to give direction and focus to the discussion. This is the only way to ensure that the researcher is not merely 'eavesdropping' on a conversation or discussion which, although of consuming interest for participants, will not, in all likelihood, touch on issues salient to the research project.

Obtaining permission from a group is seldom a straightforward business, as membership is likely to fluctuate and those who turn up on the day may not, in fact, be the same individuals who agreed to providing access for the focus group. This means that it is important to ensure that participants are provided with relevant information in sufficient time to enable them to make an informed decision regarding attendance. A further issue in relation to capitalizing on pre-existing groups relates to the implications for the future of the group and its members of taking part in the research. On balance, though, focus group discussions are unlikely to stimulate particularly heated discussions between individuals who are not already prone to interacting in this way and, in such instances, they probably have a repertoire of ways of accommodating and moving on from such disagreements. Nevertheless, it is wise to try to end a focus group discussion on a conciliatory or positive note – a topic I explore in the next session.

RUNNING FOCUS GROUPS, DEVELOPING TOPIC GUIDES AND SELECTING STIMULUS MATERIAL

Running focus groups

Before the group takes place the researcher must make important decisions. The choice of venue is important, as this may determine the emphasis given to particular issues. A focus group held in a hospital seminar room complete with posters of surgical interventions is likely to give rise to more discussion around medical treatment than is a session held in a community centre or University office. This does not mean, of course, that there is such a thing as an 'ideal location' for a focus group – rather that the researcher should give thought as to the likely impact of the setting on the nature of the discussion and that s/he should take care to structure the topic guide to ensure that the whole range of potential topics is covered. Access can be important, particularly where the research aims to be inclusive of those with physical disabilities. Travelling distance may also affect turnout (and expenses if the project undertakes to provide compensation to participants).

Another decision relates to whether to audiotape (or videotape) discussions. Many focus group researchers do audiotape discussions and produce verbatim transcripts, but do not subject these to detailed analysis. It is not the existence of a transcript that guarantees rigour – it is the attention to detail and degree to which the researcher engages systematically with the data (Barbour, 2007; 2008). In my view, this can be achieved either by means of audio-recording and verbatim transcripts, or via meticulous analysis of notes or repeated re-listening to recordings. If a recording is to be made, good quality equipment is essential. It pays to practice so that the researcher is confident in using the equipment and does not become distracted from the task in hand – which is to facilitate and focus discussion. Notes on nonverbal cues may be especially valuable, when it comes to interpreting data, as can information on individual speakers. For these reasons, it is useful to enlist the help of an assistant moderator, who can manage the recording equipment and take notes on expressions, gestures, tone of voice, and note the sequence of talk (in order to help identify individual speakers).

As discussed earlier, many of the skills that researchers are likely to have developed in other group contexts will serve them well when they turn to moderating focus groups. However, the purpose of the research focus group is rather different to these other groups. Owen (2001) provides an insightful discussion about the difference between running groups for therapeutic purposes and using them in order to generate research data. When using groups in a research context it is more important to encourage contributions from everyone and to explore the reasons behind differing perspectives or qualifications that people may make – this is because the focus is on *process* rather than the outcome of the group discussion. It is also worth giving some thought to the match – or potential mismatch – between moderator and group members. Although participants may be more likely to talk openly with someone they identify as belonging to their group or community, it is easy to slip into making unwarranted assumptions about shared meanings and the 'seduction of sameness' (Hurd and McIntyre, 1996) may prevent moderators from asking the penetrating questions necessary in order to process discussions as research data. Rather than attempting the impossible in terms of matching moderator and group, it is probably better to remain alert to the impact of the researcher's persona on the data generated and to use this as a resource in the analysis – alongside consideration of participants' characteristics, for example.

When conducting focus groups with members of ethnic minorities whose first language may not be that of the researchers, it is also easy to make unwarranted assumptions about 'sameness' based on shared language skills. Dialects are important here, as are shared cultural and religious referents. Language skills alone do not necessarily qualify an individual to moderate a focus group. Training in the conduct of focus groups is important. Translation can be a potential minefield and it is important to enlist the help of bilingual moderators in carrying out back translation to ensure that offensive and insensitive vocabulary is avoided (Culley et al., 2007).

Despite observations about the potential of focus groups to create consensus (see, for example, Sim, 1998) not all focus group discussions arrive at a consensus (as pointed out by Waterton and Wynne, 1999). Moreover, careful development of topic guides and facilitation of discussion by an attentive moderator can help interrogate apparent consensus. The central focus is, thus, on providing a window on whatever is being achieved during the discussion, whether this is the airing of conflicting views, developing a shared understanding, refining individual perceptions, or making decisions. By now, it is clear that there is much more to carrying out focus group research than simply 'sitting back and seeing what transpires'.

Focus group moderators should attempt throughout to anticipate analysis, and this ultimate aim should guide their requests for clarification or encourage them to follow up on potentially interesting distinctions employed by, or alluded to, by participants. Moderators (as well as assistant moderators) need to look out for nonverbal cues which may provide an opportunity to engage otherwise quiet members and must also remain alert to the tenor of the discussion and potential impact on participants. Even with online focus groups, this can be achieved by paying attention to emoticons (Fox et al., 2007), which may actually leave less room for misinterpretation by the researcher. As Bloor et al. (2001) acknowledge, focus group participants can sometimes 'under-react' to our questions and one of the most important skills for the novice moderator to master is that of learning to tolerate silences, in order to allow participants time to formulate responses – whether this is verbally or in terms of typing as in the online discussions moderated by Fox et al. (2007).

Developing topic guides

Novice focus group researchers may be unnerved by the rather short and somewhat broadly focused topic guides which are recommended in order to encourage discussion throughout their research encounters. The apparent brevity of focus group topic guides can be particularly frightening for researchers used to administering tightly structured survey instruments. Although topic guides may list what look like rather vague areas for discussion 'the devil is in the detail' in the form of prompts which ensure that more specific issues are covered, but which allow the moderator to judge when to wait and when to raise these subtopics. For example, in the case of our folic acid project, we were keen to explore some of the misconceptions that women had about folic acid and its role in preventing neural tube defects, such as spina bifida. These specific issues are included in the topic guide reproduced in the following section as prompts (*in italics*) to be employed only if discussion about this does not spontaneously occur:

1   Can I start by asking you what your thoughts are about taking supplements during pregnancy?
   • *What other supplements, if any, did you take?*
   • *Were any of you involved in Healthy Start? (A scheme directed at mothers of young children living in economically deprived areas)*

- *Fears?*
- *Perceived benefits?*

2   What other changes did you make either in the run up to or during your pregnancy?
- *Diet*
- *Smoking*
- *Exercise*
- *Alcohol*
- *What was the main reason for making any of these changes?*
- *Where did you get advice about this? Was any of it confusing?*

3   What about folic acid specifically?
- *How important is it to take folic acid?(Maternal OR foetal health?)*
- *Where did you get information – clinics/friends/family/mother/mother-in-law/antenatal classes?*
- *Were any of your friends pregnant at the same time?*
- *Prevention – knowledge of spina bifida*
- *Do any of you know anyone with a child with spina bifida?*
- *Benefits?*
- *How often did you take it?/What is the recommended dose?*
- *What about your friends – did they take folic acid?*

4   Current recommendations:
- *Women who could become pregnant? – Aware of this advice?/How practical?/Where would you get folic acid while you were trying to conceive?/Planned pregnancies?/How easy did you find it to get pregnant?*
- *Taking until 12th week of pregnancy? – Aware of this advice?/Why do you think there's an emphasis on this early part of pregnancy?/How practical?/Did you take folic acid on its own or with other vitamins?/Are there any benefits to taking folic acid beyond 12 weeks?*

5   For those of you for whom this was not a first pregnancy (Not Group A) – how did your experiences compare with previous pregnancies in terms of taking folic acid?
- *Did you take folic acid supplements prior to conception?*
- *Did you take folic acid from conception to 12th week?*

6   Why do you think women might decide not to take folic acid supplements or to stop taking them?
- *Have you discussed this with other women?*
- *Possibility of increasing folic acid intake through changes to diet?*
- *Knowledge about foods high in folic acid/foods with added folic acid?*
- *Do you think that most women know about the advice on folic acid?*
- *What sort of barriers are there to taking folic acid as recommended?*

7   Can you please have a look at this leaflet (an excerpt from 'Ready, Steady Baby' – a book routinely given to pregnant women at booking):
- *Do you remember seeing this – or something similar before you got pregnant/early pregnancy/during pregnancy?*
- *Do you think it should target – women who are planning pregnancy/trying to conceive? OR all women who might become pregnant? OR women not using contraception? OR all women of childbearing age?*
- *Is this information helpful/how could it be changed?*

8   Do you think other mothers share your own views?

9   If you were to have another baby would you change anything regarding taking folic acid/other supplements?
- *What do you think might encourage other people to take folic acid supplements?*
- *What about women who are at greater risk than you? Who might these be and how might they be encouraged to take folic acid supplements?*

An especially valuable skill for moderators is knowing when to let discussion develop. Although, at times, it might appear that participants are going 'off piste' such speculation can ultimately lead to unanticipated insights. In one of the focus groups where people were discussing their decision making with regard to medication, participants initially appeared to be trading horror stories about inconsistencies in the system. However, they then went on to collaboratively attempt to find an elusive logic for an arbitrary and inconsistent system, revealing an underlying faith in the National Health Service that was at variance with the antagonism that some of these comments, if taken at face value, suggested.

Selecting stimulus material

Although some focus group researchers like to use stimulus material at the beginning of groups in order to 'break the ice', this approach should be employed with caution, as individuals may bring a lot of unforeseen 'baggage' to groups. One person's delightful parlour game can be another's worst nightmare, due to associations of which the unwary focus-group moderator may be completely unaware. Colucci (2007) provides a useful catalogue of exercises suitable for use in focus group research, including some tasks which can be performed prior to the group sessions. It is not always necessary to use exercises and a warm and unthreatening introduction from the moderator; coupled with the opportunity to introduce oneself to the group will often be sufficient to set the scene for an informal and productive discussion. Stimulus materials can, however, be of much greater value if used at a later stage in the discussion, where they can be used in order to tease out similarities and differences in participants' perspectives.

There is no definitive guidance regarding the superiority of pre-existing over specially developed stimulus materials: the test is always whether these give rise to the sort of discussion you require. Colucci (2007) adds: 'However, exercises are meant to be the input for further discussion, and they accomplish their role best if the moderator goes further than the fulfilment of the task and invites participants to describe their answers more in depth, provide more detail, apply them to a real situation, and express agreement or disagreement with other participants' answers' (p. 1430). For this reason, piloting of stimulus material is necessary. Television soaps, for instance, offer a wealth of possible material and are readily accessible to participants. However, these sometimes have particularly compelling storylines and the focus of the research may become lost as participants engage in animated discussion about fictional characters and plot lines of little relevance to the research topic.

For our folic acid research, we opted to use an excerpt relating to taking folic acid supplements drawn from a pamphlet routinely given to pregnant women at booking. We hoped that the familiarity of the layout would put women at their ease and would reassure them that we were not seeking to put their knowledge to the test in a threatening way. Although all of the women taking part in the focus groups could recall being given this book and having read the text, they sometimes commented that they had skipped over this section quite quickly and that, in any case, the information was often redundant by the time they read it, since they might be more than 12 weeks pregnant by then.

When carrying out another research project looking at how health visitors identified and responded to problems in mother-infant relationships we decided to show a short video, selected precisely because it was unlikely to give rise to straightforward assessments, since it depicted a grey area of practice. On other occasions, you might want to develop your own vignettes, taking care to incorporate problematic or uncertain areas. The brevity of such materials belies the significant amount of work that is likely to be involved in selecting or constructing such examples. The ultimate test of what to include is always the focus of the research in question and whether the vignettes are likely to encourage discussion around desired areas. The attentive focus group moderator should always be anticipating analysis, teasing out similarities and differences – whether these are stark oppositions or delicately nuanced variations. S/he should be engaged in exploring with participants the ideas behind these comments, inviting them to join her/him in speculating as to how to explain these. The use of stimulus materials aids systematic comparison between groups, as the researcher can, for once, be certain that participants are referring to the same items, which have been presented to them in the same way by the moderator.

However, initial focus groups are quite likely to furnish material that can be employed in later groups as stimulus material – as was the case in a study of GPs' views and experiences of sickness certification (Hussey et al., 2004). Both in this project and in the study of health visitors' practice (Wilson et al., 2007), the researchers elected to show participants in later focus groups some quotes from earlier focus group discussions (sometimes altered slightly to clarify our questions or concerns).[1]

CHALLENGES IN ANALYZING FOCUS GROUP DATA

Coding

Coding is, quite simply, an attempt to categorize excerpts of data with reference to a set of key themes and related subcategories developed by the researcher. The principles involved are much the same, whether you are coding field notes, interview or focus group transcripts. However, it is important not to slip into routinely coding individual comments in focus group discussions, but, rather to look out for collaborative efforts and what is being achieved in sections of consecutive talk. In focus group research, group dynamics sometimes *are* the data – particularly where we are interested in accessing how peer groups make decisions or formulate collective understandings. At the very least, group dynamics are a valuable resource for interpreting our data. Wilkinson, Rees and Knight (2007) offer a helpful discussion on the ways in which humour can be employed in focus groups in order to accomplish a range of tasks – including the creation and expression of solidarity, negotiating conflict, reflecting or challenging power relationships.

What is *not* said can be as important as what *is* articulated during group discussions, but this can present a challenge for analysis. Hopefully, sensitive moderating will already have ensured that any apparent silences have been probed, using gambits such as 'Other groups have mentioned X – is that a concern/issue for you at all?' Differences in emphasis – and even de-emphasis – initiated in response to the same stimulus material, however, can be particularly revealing, provided that groups have been given equal opportunity to reflect on materials.

Sometimes novice qualitative data analysts agonize over allocating multiple codes to a piece of text. However, this is not only permissible – it is highly likely that even a small piece of interaction will encompass several related – or even disparate – issues. This richness is one of the key strengths of qualitative methods in general and focus groups in particular.[2] Most researchers use one of several coding programs to analyze their data. While these programs differ in their use of labelling language, the underlying coding strategies are remarkably similar. However, you should not be deceived: use of coding software is not a substitute for becoming conversant with the principles of qualitative data analysis. Novices who do not understand the process of qualitative analysis run the risk of their analysis being driven by the properties of a given package, rather than the more important aims of the specific research project. For example, these packages afford the opportunity of isolating and retrieving all segments of talk produced by one focus group participant. It is important to weigh up carefully the disadvantages involved and not just to carry out a procedure simply because it is possible to do so.

'In-Vivo' codes and grounded theory

Grounded theory emphasizes the importance of developing '*in-vivo*' codes, which Kelle (1997) helpfully defines as 'theories of members of the investigated culture'. These are key analytical tools and provide evidence of thoughtful and thorough engagement with the data. However, '*a-priori*' or researcher-generated codes also have their place – especially at the outset of the process of analysis. It is important, though, to ensure that you do not rely overly on such largely descriptive codes.

Many focus group texts give advice to focus group moderators to remain alert to the possibilities of exploring further comments or distinctions made by participants, but researchers may not always be the ones who make the initial steps towards such theorizing. Focus group participants frequently engage in the development of 'grounded theory' that characterizes the social science research enterprise, providing '*in vivo*' coding categories that can help us to make sense of our data. In the course of discussions, participants can draw each other's and the moderator's attention to underlying assumptions or contradictions and may provide thoughtful commentaries.

For example, researchers who studied health visitors' practice in relation to problematic mother-infant relationships (Wilson et al., 2007) developed several '*in-vivo*' codes, including 'Are they holding the baby lovingly?' This code called on a combination of observational skills and health visitors' initial reactions to mothers and concerns that were hard to articulate. One of the most experienced (and respected) health visitors described situations where the 'hairs on the back of her neck stood up', illustrating dramatically both the immediacy with which problems were recognized *and* the way in which an 'automatic response' draws on many years' of painstaking experience and familiarity with the research literature. A further code used in this project was that of 'this is all these women know' which referred to the cycle of disadvantage as a backdrop to health visitors' work and the balancing of realism, sympathy, and potential for discouragement that was a feature of their engagement with such families. A useful way of describing '*in-vivo*' codes likens them to the 'soundbites' so beloved of journalists. These short and colourful phrases often sum up complex ideas.

Identifying patterns and being analytical

Although many qualitative data analysts are content to identify and provide illustrations of themes that arise in discussions, this is only half of the story. In order to develop more analytically sophisticated accounts, it is essential to explore patterning in our data and to seek to provide explanations for these patterns – including seeking to explain contradictions and exceptions. This is what is meant by the term 'analytic induction' (see, for example, Frankland and Bloor, 1999).

Systematic and thorough comparison lies at the root of the 'constant comparative method' (Green, 1998) and provides the means through which we begin to articulate and test out our emergent theoretical explanations, paying particular attention to exceptions (Barbour, 2001). Although most of the comparisons that focus group researchers are likely to make will probably be at the level of groups, supplementary information also allows us as researchers to pay attention to individual voices within groups. This can be a useful feature to incorporate in framework grids (Ritchie and Spencer, 1994) that provide a means of depicting – and ultimately the basis for interrogating – patterning in data. This can be especially valuable as it may provide suggestions for further sampling (see discussion in the following section).

In seeking to account for patterns and exceptions we identify during analysis, it is often necessary to retrospectively collect more information about specific groups, whether this relates to individuals, their relationships to each other, or other features of the setting. Although the moderator, will, hopefully, have provided a good deal of such contextual information it is impossible to anticipate all of the details that might be helpful. Traulsen et al. (2004) recommend 'interviewing the moderator after each focus group session', but, in my experience, it is infinitely preferable to have the original moderator on hand and even actively participating in analysis in order that such questions can be raised and answered.

Provided that the researcher engages systematically in such comparisons, the small scale of qualitative research and its iterative nature allow room to manoeuvre in the form of the potential to convene further groups. As with the example provided by the folic acid project earlier, it is not necessary to stipulate in advance what the selection criteria for such additional 'wild card' (Kitzinger and Barbour, 1999) groups will be, but to await preliminary analysis in order to further investigate tentative hypotheses. The original formulation of 'grounded theory' (Glaser and Strauss, 1967) advocated returning to the field to test out the hypotheses developed as data is analyzed. This is rarely done in today's climate of shorter timescales and pressure to publish (Barbour, 2003) but focus group research is particularly well placed to fulfil this requirement, allowing the researcher to follow up 'hunches' developed through paying attention, for example, to individual voices within focus group discussions. Moreover, relatively little additional work may be involved in convening a small number of additional groups. Notably, this involves bringing individuals from the same original sampling pool together (i.e., people who have agreed to take part in focus groups) in different constellations rather than recruiting additional people. Thus, this approach is unlikely to require further permission from ethics committees.

In the context of the health visitor study referred to in the preceding section, the researchers elected to run focus groups with health visitors working in affluent areas, deprived areas, and mixed areas, and recruited health visitors with a range of levels of experience. Because the researchers were particularly interested in the acquisition of skills they also convened one group of recently qualified health visitors. In the course of the study, the researchers were struck by discussions about the importance of learning from the experience of being a parent oneself. For this reason, and in order to, hopefully, elaborate the distinctions and claims being made they decided to hold a focus group with male health visitors. This, as it turned out, threw several issues into particularly sharp focus and alerted the researchers to some issues which, although present in other discussions, had not been so evident to the research team. These included, importantly, the establishment of rapport with mothers and working relationships with other health visitors – an issue that was implicit in much of the discussion in other focus groups, but only thrown into sharp focus in this one group. For the male health visitors claims to professional competence around breast feeding were a particularly fraught area, but once researchers were alerted to this as an issue, they became aware of its relevance for female health visitors who were not, themselves, mothers.

THE CONTRIBUTION OF FOCUS GROUP RESEARCH

The contribution that focus groups can make depends on why the research is being carried out: is the goal to produce a theorized account that addresses disciplinary concerns, or is the aim affect social, organizational, or political change?

FOCUS GROUPS**347**

Of course, these different end points may not be mutually exclusive. Even where focus group researchers do not explicitly set out to work within an action research context, it is possible that merely taking part in such discussions can have a beneficial effect for participants, as did the focus groups held by Jones and Neil-Urban (2003) for fathers of children with cancer. Focus groups certainly have the potential to provide insights for participants as well as for researchers. As Crabtree et al. argue: 'People can recognize previously hidden parts of themselves in others. They can also reconstruct their own life narrative from others' stories' (Crabtree et al., 1992, p. 146). Whether or not this is used overtly in a therapeutic fashion depends, ultimately, on the purpose of the research and the predisposition and skills of the researcher.

Nor does working in an overtly interventionist manner preclude the development of a theoretically sensitized account. Johnson (1996) argues that focus groups can access uncodified knowledge and can stimulate the sociological imagination in both researchers and participants. We can, and sometimes do, enlist the help of interviewees in making sense of and contextualizing their experiences and perspectives. Focus groups, as a complex piece of social interaction, have added potential for harnessing the insights of participants. It is essential, however, that in acknowledging the importance of representing the views of our respondents, we, as researchers, do not sidestep the important responsibility of providing an overview. Only the researcher can do this – whether this involves furnishing broadly descriptive findings or, indeed, more analytically sophisticated explanations.

Although the question as to whether respondents are telling us the truth does surface in relation to other types of qualitative research, focus groups have probably attracted more than their fair share of such comments. Again, this question derives from the practice of viewing focus groups through the unforgiving and inappropriate lens of quantitative research.

Where focus groups are used in conjunction with one-to-one interviews, the latter are often viewed as the 'gold standard', with focus group findings, should they contradict the accounts produced by interviews, seen as lacking. Agonizing over which method produces the most 'authentic' data is a futile exercise. This misses the fundamental point that complementary methods generate parallel data, with focus groups eliciting 'public' rather than 'private' accounts. However, focus groups can provide insights that interviews cannot. As Wilson reminds us: 'We will never know what respondents might have revealed in the 'privacy' of an in-depth interview but we do know what they are prepared to elaborate and defend in the company of their peers' (Wilson, 1997, p. 218). We are usefully reminded by Brannen and Pattman (2005, p. 53) that the qualitative research context is a 'site of performance'. Focus groups afford perhaps unrivalled access to such performances and this constitutes valuable data.

Rather than using focus groups and interviews to cross-check or 'triangulate' findings, the two methods should be seen as a fertile resource for exploring the limits of and subtleties involved in managing or making sense of both the 'public' and the 'private' and the tensions between the two. Morgan (1993) reminds us, '...if research finds differences between the results from individual and group interviews, then the methodological goal should be to understand the *sources* of these differences' (Morgan, 1993, p. 232; my emphasis).

Only by paying attention to contradictions and exceptions – not 'cherry-picking' those comments that support our emergent frameworks – can we engage in systematic and thorough interrogation of our data. This, together with subjecting theoretical frameworks to interrogation using our own data, is what allows us to claim theoretical transferability. Reassurance with regard to rigour can be provided only by documenting the steps we have followed and tracing our analytical journey.

Good qualitative research – and focus groups, in particular – have the potential to furnish explanations in the form of developing theoretical frameworks, whether these relate to disciplinary or professional preoccupations. This is because focus groups are located at the intersection between the 'micro' and the 'macro'. Studies focusing on the 'micro' – or minutiae of consultations, conversations, or other verbal exchanges – have traditionally paid close attention to detail, as, for example, is advocated by conversation or discourse analysts. In contrast, studies focusing on 'macro' elements have concentrated on taking into account the social, economic, political, and policy context. One of the main strengths of focus groups as a method is their capacity to engage with both dimensions. However, this potential will only be realized if focus group researchers pay due attention to research design. Again, thoughtful sampling provides the key to allowing such factors to be taken into consideration. This paves the way for systematic interrogation of data and tentative explanations in order to produce an analytical account.

In order to illustrate both the scope and flexibility of focus group methods in health research, I have selected a few exemplary studies that use this approach to data collection and analysis. These articles also highlight the wide variety of journals which now publish findings from focus group studies:

Some Examples of the Use of Focus Groups in Health Research

Example 1:

Edwards, A., Matthews, e., Pill, R., and Bloor, M. (1998) 'Communication About Risk: Diversity Among Primary Care Professionals', *Family Practice,* 15(4): 296–300 plus appendices.

   Focus groups were selected for this study of approaches to conveying risk to patients, due to their capacity to access group norms and to elicit experiential data through peer group interaction. Separate discipline-specific focus groups were held with primary care staff. Both inter- and intra-group comparisons were employed. Differences between professional groups as well as overlaps in concerns and approaches were identified. Exceptions were also highlighted – such as the finding that the general practitioner groups were the only ones to highlight medico-legal issues in risk communication. The study illuminated the complexities involved and the diversity of influences on professional practice. Charts were used as stimulus material and these are provided in the appendices accompanying this paper. These helped to focus discussion and facilitated comparison between groups.

Example 2:

McEwan, M.J., Espie, C.A., Metcalfe, J., Brodie, M., and Wilson, M.T. (2003) 'Quality of Life and Psychological Development in Adolescents with Epilepsy: a Qualitative Investigation using Focus Group Methods', *Seizure*, 13: 15–31.

This study used existing databases from two Scottish epilepsy centres to furnish a sampling pool for focus groups with adolescents. This paper also provides a helpful account of the development and refinement of coding frames which were used to inform development of a Quality of Life measure for adolescents with epilepsy.

Example 3:

Green, J.M., Draper, A.K., Dowler, E.A., Fele, G., Hagenhoff, V., Rusanen, M., and Rusanen, T. (2005) 'Public Understanding of Food Risks in Four European Countries: A Qualitative Study', *European Journal of Public Health*, 15(5): 523–527.

Strategic sampling (in terms of including individuals at different life stages in Finland, Germany, Italy and the United Kingdom) here allowed the researchers to study public understanding of food risks in these contrasting international cultural contexts.

Example 4:

Waller, J., Marlow, L.A.V., and Wardle, J. (2006) Mothers' Attitudes Towards Preventing Cervical Cancer through Human Papillomavirus Vaccination: A Qualitative study, *Cancer Epidiol. Biomarkers Prev.*, 15(7): 1257–1261.

Focus groups were used to elicit the views of mothers of girls aged between 8 and 14 years with regard to a new vaccination program under discussion at the time the research was carried out. The researchers emphasize the importance of 'naturally occurring' groups for investigating sensitive issues, and explain that they utilized their own personal networks for recruitment, as well as approaching the parents of girls attending a school in a deprived area. Reflecting on differences in emphasis of groups held at different time points within the study, the authors make an interesting point about the shift in views observed in groups held after exposure to media coverage and comment that this appeared to give rise to a more positive response. This highlights the capacity of focus groups to reflect rapid and incremental change in perspectives – one of the reasons why the method is favoured by marketing researchers.

Example 5:

Vincent, D., Clark, Zimmer, L.M., and Sanchez, J. (2006) 'Using Focus Groups to Develop a Culturally Competent Diabetes Self-Management Program for Mexican Americans', *The Diabetes Educator*, 32: 89–97.

This paper highlights the potential for focus groups in informing the design of culturally competent interventions. The focus groups conducted for this study highlighted the challenge of modifying the typical (and culturally highly valued) Latino diet to conform to American Diabetes Association recommendations. Groups were convened to take account of both gender and age and the researchers sought to over-recruit men in anticipation of difficulties in persuading them to attend focus group sessions.

Example 6:

Evans, M., Stoddard, H., Condon, L., Freeman, E., Grizell, M., and Mullen, R. (2001) 'Parents' Perspectives on the MMR Immunization: A Focus Group Study', *British Journal of General Practice*, 51: 904–910.

This study provides an example of the usefulness of focus groups for exploring 'why not?' questions. One of the strengths of this study is that the researchers chose to compare the views of parents who had accepted MMR immunization with those who had refused, allowing for a greater understanding of the reasoning behind 'non-compliance' and showing that such parents did not differ markedly in terms of their concerns from those who reached a different decision.

Example 7:

Angus, J., Rukholm, E., St. Onge, R., Michel, I., Nolan, R.P., Lapum, J., and Evans, S. (2007) 'Habitus, Stress and the Body: the Everyday Production of Health and Cardiovascular Risk', *Qualitative Health Research*, 17: 1088–1102.

   This paper engages in an overtly theoretical discussion in order to illuminate the complex conditions in which health and patterns of cardiovascular risk are produced, allowing the researchers to explore 'the deeply sedimented, often pre-reflexive relationship between person and place within the numerous social and material locations of everyday life' (page 1100).

CONCLUSION

Rather than using focus groups in a descriptive manner in order to simply bear witness to our respondents' experiences (Atkinson, 1997), we should seek to draw on the full potential inherent in this method to produce analytical insights. Attention to structure is paramount in getting the most out of focus groups. This means paying attention to sampling, which is the key to the comparisons that can be made and that provide comparative – and hence – analytical potential. Honing topic guides and employing moderators' skills also have an important part to play in the thoughtful application of focus group research, as has the use of the constant comparative method from conception of the project to completion of analysis.

   A critical appreciation of the use of focus groups throws into sharp focus some of the perennial dilemmas and challenges involved in doing qualitative research. Debates about the use of focus groups illuminate fundamental issues concerning appropriate research topics, framing of research questions, matters of epistemology, ontology, methodology, politics, ethics, reflexivity, and representation. Focus groups are an inherently flexible method and can allow for testing and refining of theoretical propositions in an especially economical way (provided that due attention is paid to judicious research design). If employed thoughtfully, focus groups can produce qualitative research at its very sharpest.

NOTES

   1 The probes used in the second round of focus groups held for the sickness certification study are reproduced in full as part of the supplementary material deposited on the *British Medical Journal* website.

   2 For an example of a coded focus group transcript and discussion of coding strategies see Frankland and Bloor (1999) who employed 'Ethnograph' – one of the older software packages available.

REFERENCES

Atkinson, P. (1997) 'Narrative Turn or Blind Alley?' *Qualitative Health Research*, 7: 325–44.
Baker, R. and Hinton, R. (1999) 'Do Focus Groups Facilitate Meaningful Participation in Social Research?'. In R.S. Barbour and J. Kitzinger (eds) *Developing Focus Group Research: Politics, Theory and Practice* (pp. 79–98). London: Sage.

Barbour, R.S. (1998) 'Mixing Qualitative Methods: Quality Assurance or Qualitative Quagmire?' *Qualitative Health Research,* 8: 352–61.

Barbour, R.S. (2001) 'Checklists for Improving the Rigour of Qualitative Research: A Case of the Tail Wagging the Dog?' *British Medical Journal*, 322: 1115–7.

Barbour, R.S. (2003) 'The Newfound Credibility of Qualitative Research? Tales of Technical Essentialism and Co-Option', *Qualitative Health Research*, 13(7): 1019–27.

Barbour, R.S. (2007) *Doing Focus Groups.* London: Sage.

Barbour, R.S. (2008*) Introducing Qualitative Research: A Student Guide to the Craft of Doing Qualitative Research.* London: Sage.

Bloor, M. (1997) 'Techniques of Validation in Qualitative Research: A Critical Commentary'. In G. Miller and R. Dingwall (eds) *Context and Method in Qualitative Research.* London: Sage.

Bloor, M., Frankland, J., Thomas, M., and Robson, K. (2001) *Focus Groups in Social Research.* London: Sage.

Brannen, J. and Pattman, R. (2005) 'Work–Family Matters in the Workplace: The Use of Focus Groups in a Study of a UK Social Services Department', *Qualitative Research*, 5(4): 523–42.

Brink, P.J. and Edegecombe, N. (2003) 'What is Becoming of Ethnography?', *Qualitative Health Research*, 13(7): 1028–30.

Chiu L.F. and Knight, D. (1999) 'How Useful are Focus Groups for Obtaining the Views of Minority Groups?'. In R.S. Barbour and J. Kitzinger (eds) *Developing Focus Group Research: Politics, Theory and Practice* (pp. 99–112). London: Sage.

Coffey, A. and Atkinson, P. (1996) *Making Sense of Qualitative Data: Complementary Research Strategies.* London: Sage.

Colucci, E. (2007) '"Focus Groups Can Be Fun": The Use of Activity-Oriented Questions in Focus Group Discussions', *Qualitative Health Research*, 17: 1422–33.

Crabtree, B.F. et al. (1992) In B.F. Crabtree and W.I. Miller (eds) *Doing Qualitative Research.* Newbury Park, CA: Sage.

Crossley, M.L. (2002) '"Could You Please Pass One of Those Health Leaflets Along?": Exploring Health, Morality and Resistance Through Focus Groups', *Social Science and Medicine*, 55(8): 1471–83.

Culley, L., Hudson, N., and Rapport, F. (2007) 'Using Focus Groups with Minority Ethnic Communities: Researching Infertility in British South Asian Communities', *Qualitative Health Research*, 17: 102–12.

Fox, F.E., Morris, M., and Rumsey, N. (2007) 'Doing Synchronous Online Focus Groups with Young People: Methodological Reflections', *Qualitative Health Research,* 17: 539–47.

Frankland, J. and Bloor, M. (1999) 'Some Issues Arising in the Systematic Analysis of Focus Group Materials'. In R.S. Barbour and J. Kitzinger (eds) *Developing Focus Group Research: Politics, Theory and Practice* (pp. 144–55). London: Sage.

Glaser, B. and Strauss, A. (1967) *The Discovery of Grounded Theory.* Chicago: Aldine.

Green, J. (1998) 'Commentary: grounded theory and the constant comparative method', *British Medical Journal*, 316: 1064–65.

Hilsen, A.I. (2006) 'And They Shall be Known by Their Deeds: Ethics and Politics in Action Research', *Action Research*, 4(1): 23–36.

Hurd, T.L. and McIntyre, A. (1996) 'The Seduction of Sameness: Similarity and Representing the Other'. In S. Wilkinson and C. Kitzinger (eds) *Representing the Other* (pp. 78–82). London: Sage.

Hussey, S., Hoddinott, P., Dowell, J., Wilson, P., and Barbour, R.S. (2004) 'The Sickness Certification System in the UK: A Qualitative Study of the Views of General Practitioners in Scotland', *BMJ*, 328: 88–92.

Johnson, A. (1996) '"It's Good to Talk": The Focus Group and the Sociological Imagination', *The Sociological Review*, 44(3): 517–38.

Jones, J.B. and Neil-Urban, S. (2003) 'Father to Father: Focus Groups of Fathers of Children with Cancer', *Social Work in Health Care*, 37(1): 41–61.

Kelle, U. (1997) 'Theory Building in Qualitative Research and Computer Programs for the Management of Textual Data', *Sociological Research Online*, 2(1) . Available at: http:www.socresonline.org.uk/2/2/1.html

Kevern, J. and Webb, C. (2001) 'Focus Groups as a Tool for Critical Social Research in Nurse Education', *Nurse Education Today*, 21: 323–33.

Kidd, P.S. and Parshall, M.B. (2000) 'Getting the Focus and the Group: Enhancing Analytical Rigour in Focus Group Research', *Qualitative Health Research*, 19(3): 293–308.

Kitzinger, J. and Barbour, R.S. (1999) 'Introduction: The Challenge and Promise of Focus Groups'. In R.S. Barbour and J. Kitzinger (eds) *Developing Focus Group Research: Politics, Theory and Practice* (pp. 1–20). London: Sage.

Kuzel, A.J. (1992) 'Sampling in Qualitative Enquiry'. In B.F. Crabtree and W.I. Miller (eds) *Doing Qualitative Research* (pp. 31–44). Newbury Park, CA: Sage.

MacDougall, C. and Fudge, E. (2001) 'Planning and Recruiting the Sample for Focus Groups and In-Depth Interviews', *Qualitative Health Research*, 11(1): 117–25.

Mauthner, M. (1997) 'Methodological Aspects of Collecting Data from Children: Lessons from Three Research Projects', *Children and Society*, 11: 16–28.

Mays, N. and Pope, C. (1995) 'Rigour and Qualitative Research', *British Medical Journal*, 311: 109–12.

Meyer, J. (2000) 'Using Qualitative Methods in Health Related Action Research', *British Medical Journal*, 320: 178–81.

Morgan, D.A. (1988) *Focus Groups as Qualitative Research*. London: Sage.

Morgan, D.L. (1993) 'Future Directions in Focus Group Research'. In D.L. Morgan (ed.) *Successful Focus Groups: Advancing the State of the Art* (pp. 225–44). London: Sage

Owen, S. (2001) 'The practical, methodological and ethical dilemmas of conducting focus groups with vulnerable clients', *Journal of Advanced Nursing*, 36(6): 652–8.

Powney, J. (1988) 'Structured Eavesdropping', *Research Intelligence (Journal of the British Educational Research Foundation)*, 28: 10–2.

Ritchie, J. and Spencer, L. (1994) 'Qualitative Data Analysis for Policy Research'. In A. Bryman and R.G. Burgess (eds) *Analyzing Qualitative Data* (pp. 173–94). London: Routledge.

Seale, C. (1999) *The Quality of Qualitative Research*. London: Sage.

Sim, J. (1998) 'Collecting and Analyzing Qualitative Data: Issues Raised by the Focus Group', *Journal of Advanced Nursing*, 28(2): 345–52.

Traulsen, J.M., Almarsdóttir, A.B., and Björnsdóttir, I. (2004) 'Interviewing the Moderator: An Ancillary Method to Focus Groups', *Qualitative Health Research*, 14(5): 714–25.

Umaña-Taylor, A.J. and Bámaca, M.Y. (2004) 'Conducting Focus Groups with Latino Populations: Lessons from the Field', *Family Relations*, 53(3): 261–72.

Waterton, C. and Wynne, B. (1999) 'Can focus groups access community views?' In R.S. Barbour and J. Kitzinger (eds) *Developing Focus Group Research: Politics, Theory and Practice* (pp. 127–43). London: Sage.

Wilkinson, C.E., Rees, C.E., and Knight, L.V. (2007) '"From the Heart of My Bottom": Negotiating Humor in Focus Group Discussions', *Qualitative Health Research*, 17: 411–22.

Wilson, P., Barbour, R.S., Graham, C., Currie, M., Puckering, C., and Minnis, H. (2008) 'Health Visitors' Assessment of Parent-Child Relationships: A Focus Group Study', *International Journal of Nursing Studies*, 45: 1137–47.

Wilson, V. (1997) 'Focus Groups: A Useful Qualitative Method for Educational Research?' *British Educational Research Journal*, 23(2): 209–24.

18

Fieldwork and
Participant Observation

Davina Allen

INTRODUCTION

Fieldwork is growing in popularity as a method for researching health care. It entails generating data by observing and participating in the daily life of a group or social setting and is particularly effective for studying everyday activities in context. The origins of field research lie in social anthropology and the tradition of discovering unfamiliar non-Western societies. The method has been adopted by social scientists to study developed societies and is increasingly being used by the 'natives' themselves to examine their own cultures. Health professionals, for example, have employed participant observation to understand their practice and evaluate technologies and policies.

Field study can take a variety of forms. The method is strongly associated with the 'lone ranger model' of research in a single site but team approaches in multiple locales are becoming increasingly common (Risk, 2001). Similarly, whilst the fieldwork tradition is to avoid fixing research questions too rigidly at the outset, many fieldworkers now specify lines of inquiry in advance and focus their studies around a limited set of concerns. What it means to be a participant observer can differ markedly in practice and a variety of roles may be adopted in the field. A recent review of a decade of observational literature on nursing work (Allen, 2004a) identified field roles which ranged from the 'detached observer', where the aim was to develop a dispassionate description of nurses' work in an Emergency Call Centre (Tjora, 2000), through to full participation with the objective of achieving an embodied understanding by 'standing in someone else's shoes' (Savage, 1995). Field researchers also employ a diversity of reporting genres. Some maintain a clear separation of the field data and analysis in order to allow the reader to exercise 'joint responsibility' (Murphy et al., 1998) for assessing the fidelity of the report (see, for example, Purkis, 1996, 2001); others adopt a richly descriptive style designed to evoke a particular gestalt (see, for example, Latimer, 2000). Thus, while the essence of observational research is easy to describe, the term encapsulates a complex field. Although subtle, such differences can be highly significant for key elements of the research process and as a consequence, fieldwork defies the application of standard cookbook formulae.

In this chapter, I draw on five of my own studies in order to examine the methodological choices involved in designing field research. Although united by a focus on the social organization of health care work and informed by a similar theoretical orientation,[1] the projects differ in ways consequential for data generation and analysis. I first provide a brief introduction to the salient features of each study. Subsequent sections consider each example in more detail illustrating the issues field researchers must consider and the balances that need to be struck when doing this type of research.

CASE STUDIES

The changing shape of nursing practice

This doctoral study was supported by the UK Department of Health Nursing and Allied Health Professions Research Training Studentship. It examined the practical accomplishment of nursing jurisdiction at a time when policy changes were reshaping the roles of nurses, doctors and health care assistants. The fieldwork was undertaken on two wards (medical and surgical) in a large District General Hospital over 10 months. Participant observation, audio-recorded interviews and documentary analysis were used to produce data. The study followed the traditional lone researcher model; I was responsible for all aspects of the project's execution under the guidance of academic supervisors.[2] The work was carried out over three years.

Negotiating care

This project was supported by the Nursing, Health and Social Care Research Centre, University of Wales College of Medicine, Cardiff where I was employed as a research fellow. It focused on an issue of interest arising from my doctoral study, namely: how nurses, patients and their friends and family negotiated care work (James, 1992). These broadly defined study aims allowed for a progressive narrowing of focus around key issues and lines of inquiry as these were identified in the field. The observational work was undertaken on two wards in the acute sector (medical and surgical) in a large university teaching hospital over four months. Fieldwork, audio-recorded interviews and documentary analysis were the data generation methods. Like my doctoral study, this project followed the lone researcher model. The study timeframe was flexible so as to fit around other work commitments.

Delivering health and social care

This policy-oriented project was funded by the Wales Office of Research and Development in Health and Social Care. It used multiple case studies to examine how health and social care providers managed their respective roles and responsibilities in the care of adults who had suffered a first acute stroke. The research team comprised three grant holders and two research assistants appointed to undertake the fieldwork. I was not the formal Principal Investigator for the project, but I assumed responsibility for project management as part of my postdoctoral professional development. The research was based on two sites and a research assistant allocated to each. Data generation methods included: field observations, audio-recorded interviews and documentary analysis. The study was funded for 18 months.

Transitions

This on-going study is funded by the UK National Institute for Health Research. I am leading a multidisciplinary team comprising a clinical psychologist, academic psychologist, health economist, statistician and medical and nursing representatives from child and adult diabetes services. The project is a realistic evaluation (Pawson and Tilley, 1997) of transitional services for young people with diabetes and is designed to establish which elements of practice work best to promote a 'smooth transition' for whom and in what circumstances. Observation is a major data generation method combined with audio-recorded interviews, user diaries and a survey. Two research assistants are undertaking data generation. Fieldwork is scheduled over a two-year period in five health care locales.

The social organization of integrated care pathway development

This internally funded project is an observational study of the development and implementation of integrated care pathways (ICPs).[3] I am sharing the fieldwork with a research assistant, appointed for three years to support several related projects. The primary data generation methods are audio-recordings of team meetings, documentary analysis and interviews with key stakeholders.

THE RESEARCH PROCESS: DECISIONS, DECISIONS, DECISIONS

The hallmarks of high-quality qualitative research are the hallmarks of all good science: a commitment to rigour, clarity and systematicity (Murphy et al., 1998). In field studies, this entails adopting a fieldwork role and data generation strategy compatible with project goals and providing a clear description of the processes through which data were generated and the steps taken in reaching the final analysis.

Settling upon a fieldwork role?[4]

In field studies, data are generated through the researcher's participation in a social setting.[5] In quantitative research, questionnaire surveys are the preferred methodological tool, whereas in observational studies, the field worker becomes the research instrument. Just as survey researchers devote considerable effort to the development of their questionnaires, field researchers give careful consideration to their participation in the field. Settling upon and negotiating a field role entails consideration of a range of factors.

Of the many methodological discussions that have shaped fieldwork practice, few have generated as much heat as the insider-outsider debate. Centred on the relative merits of familiarity and detachment in observational research, the 'insider' position is founded on the case for developing an affiliation with research subjects in order to ensure an authentic account; the 'outsider' position is built on the claim that a detached stance can ensure a freedom from bias arising from too deep an immersion in the field. These considerations have been a particular preoccupation for health professionals researching their own culture and practice (see, for example, Bonner and Tolhurst, 2002; Gerrish, 1995; Reed, 1995). On the one hand, an 'insider' status confers certain advantages. A sensitivity to the preoccupations of health care providers is valuable when negotiating access to a setting and helps to reassure participants that the researcher has sufficient native wit not to disrupt activity in the field; familiarity with medical jargon brings advantages of understanding and can be particularly valuable in deciphering official documentation; and knowledge of the places and events likely to yield rich data relevant to the research focus can facilitate efficiency in data generation. On the other hand, an insider participant observer can sometimes be desensitized to those features of the setting that would be interesting to others with no-prior association. For example, Reed (1995) describes how, following two hours of fieldwork on a ward for older people, her 'sheets of paper were as blank as they had been at the beginning of the session'. Recounting her experiences later during supervision her claim that 'nothing interesting had happened', was challenged: her observation that '[i]n the space of 2 hours, the nurses had got 24 patients out of bed, toileted, washed and dressed them and given them their medications and breakfasts' was of immediate interest (Reed, 1995: 48).

In real life, it is rarely the case that settings are completely familiar or completely strange and the researcher's insider-outsider status varies over the lifetime of a project, with different social groups and for different data generation processes. Furthermore, the arguments underpinning both positions assume a pre-existing social reality which can be objectively represented using methods analogous to those deployed in the natural sciences, a stance that is increasingly recognized as naïve. It is an inescapable existential fact that we are part of the world that we study and our 'findings' are inevitably a product of our location and relationships in the field. As Emerson et al. have argued, '*[w]hat* the ethnographer finds out is inherently connected with *how* she finds it out' (Emerson et al., 1995: 11). This insight is encapsulated in the notion of researcher reflexivity which recognizes that rather than devising strategies to limit 'bias' it is more productive to work towards a better understanding of the fieldwork role and its impact on the research findings. Reflexivity includes:

- Attention to how the phenomena of interest is filtered through the singular interpretative lens of the researcher
- Recognizing that the field will have an impact on the researcher
- Acknowledging that the researcher will affect the study setting

The practice of reflexivity requires that these processes are made transparent. Evidence of careful attention to the fieldwork role and analytic sensitivity to how study data were generated is an important quality indicator in observational research. Nevertheless, there is a delicate balance to be struck between the inclusion of sufficient autobiographical information to enable the reader to locate the fieldworker and accounts which seem to suggest that the researcher is a more interesting topic than the study participants (Spencer, 2001). In some hands, the call for reflexivity has generated a tendency towards naval-gazing, producing fieldwork reports which say rather more about the effects of the research on the researcher and very little about how the researcher managed their fieldwork role and the consequences of this for the study findings.

Because some aspects of identity are fixed – age, ethnicity and gender – consideration must be given to how these will affect research relationships and the possibilities for participation in the field. If the aim of the study is to understand the occupational socialization of nursing students into evidence-based practice, a middle-aged university professor would negotiate different field relationships with research participants than would a postgraduate researcher, and the latter would have a different relationship with the traditional undergraduates than that they would have with the mature entrants within the cohort. The fieldworker's biography also shapes the assumptions with which they approach a field study and such 'foreunderstandings' (Ashworth, 1995) are typically made explicit before fieldwork commences. This can be particularly important for health professionals using observational research to understand their own practices and is a helpful device in making explicit taken-for-granted assumptions. It is also essential in team studies, where data generation and analysis is shared and members need to agree upon a common theoretical orientation.

Participant observation is a form of social encounter and should be treated as such. However, unlike other social relationships, the role is played for a particular purpose and is not designed to satisfy the personal needs of the researcher (Gans, 1968, cited by Ashworth, 1995). At the heart of the participant observer role is 'identity work' (Snow and Anderson, 1987). This term is used by eth-nomethodologists to refer to the methods we employ in presenting 'self' and include our choice of clothing, the language and discourse we use and the stories we tell. Clearly, such 'impression management' (Goffman, 1959) is not wholly within our control, but is shaped through our interactions with others, who act as a mirror to our self-presentation. Ordinarily, we may be barely conscious of this activity. However, for research purposes, a more explicit awareness of these microlevel processes enables the fieldworker to plan the fieldwork role and to analyze its effects on the research findings. In the first of my five examples, 'The Changing Shape of Nursing Practice', I wished to develop even-handed relation-ships with nurses, health care assistants and doctors in order to understand nursing work in relation to those with whom they interacted (Allen, 2001a). My own background is in nursing and therefore, relationships in the field required careful management in order to avoid the perception that I was more closely aligned with this particular group than others were. Managing such 'closeness' or 'detachment' was consciously attended to and accomplished by talk and actions (Hunt and Bedford, 1994). I was open about my nursing background but used this selectively in negotiating my relationships with different groups. For exam-ple, because health care assistants are subordinate to nurses in hospital hierarchies, I tried to downplay my nursing identity in my interactions with them in order to equalize these relationships. In developing my contacts with doctors, I drew on my clinical experience, but also emphasized my research student status as the world of academia was one to which they could readily relate. In my relation-ships with nursing staff, I brought my nursing identity into play by telling self-effacing stories from my own practice so as to position myself as someone who knew how things really were. Such disclosures were managed in order to develop trust and discourage subjects from relying on careful public accounts of their work. At the same time, I was at pains to emphasize my 'rustiness' as a clinician in order to reassure participants that I was not in a position to be evalu-ating their practice, which was clearly how some people perceived me.

Another issue that warrants attention in planning the fieldwork role is the extent of participation in the setting. This is linked to decisions about one's insider-outsider orientation, in as much as different degrees of participation may be one strategy adopted in accomplishing closeness to a given social group and distance from another. It is more helpful, however, to keep the two issues ana-lytically distinct. Methods texts books often describe different modes of participation in terms of Gold's (1958) continuum which extends from complete observer to complete participant. In actual practice, however, within any one study, a researcher may adopt a number of positions along this spectrum depend-ing on the aims of the research and circumstances in the field. For example, in 'The Changing Shape of Nursing Practice' study, I sometimes participated in the work, but on other occasions I adopted more of an observer role, positioning myself in a strategic spot to observe the ebb-and-flow of ward life, shadowing staff in their everyday work or observing discrete activities – such as medical administration or patient processing. The fieldworker's level of participation in a setting or social group has important implications for the type of field data it is possible to generate and consequently the analytic possibilities for the research. In this particular example, it was my intention to undertake a fine-grained analysis of occupational boundary construction at work. To achieve this, it was necessary to generate detailed fieldnotes of naturally occurring interaction. Direct participation in the work had to be limited, therefore, because it would have prohibited construction of a contemporaneous research record.

In the second of my case study examples – 'Negotiating Care' – my aim was to observe care delivery in the private spaces of the ward in order to understand how patients and their families contributed to care work. I concluded that the only way in which this would be possible was by participating in care delivery. Therefore, although my general preference is for low-inference, near verbatim, fieldnotes, I recognized that it would be necessary to sacrifice this aspiration if I was to observe activity 'behind the screens' (Lawler, 1991). Accordingly, I dressed in a style that was similar to that of ward-based staff and adopted a support worker role on the ward. This entailed undertaking mundane activities – bed making, attending to patient comfort, emptying urinals and bedpans and replenishing water jugs – and assisting core staff with patient hygiene and minor clinical procedures – such as wound care. In practice, this aspect of my fieldwork role was of limited value, partly because family carers had little involvement in caregiving of this kind (itself an interesting finding) and partly because so much of my energy was taken up with the activities in which I was participating that my recapture of the detail of the scene was poor.

Fieldwork is labour intensive, demanding of resources and requires a degree of flexibility and responsiveness on the part of the researcher. As my career has progressed, it has become difficult to manage the demands of participant observation alongside other academic responsibilities. Moreover, external funding bodies can be reluctant to support the salaries of senior academics to the level that would be required by field study. As a consequence, in all the other projects in which I have been involved – the third, fourth and fifth of my examples – research fellows have been employed to undertake the majority of the participant observation. Doing fieldwork 'at a distance' presents some interesting personal and intellectual challenges that are rarely discussed in the methodological literature and which, as I shall describe in subsequent sections, need to be built into all aspects of the research design.

MAKING OBSERVATIONS AND GENERATING DATA

All research, be it qualitative or quantitative, bench science or social science, requires flexibility and the ability to adapt in the light of changing circumstances, in the field, laboratory or test tube. Field researchers, however, are often especially reluctant to impose prior assumptions on the people or settings being studied, particularly when researching issues or social groups which are poorly understood and/or relatively unexplored, preferring instead to allow phenomena of interest to be uncovered. Accordingly, the aims of observational studies are often described in broad terms, whilst the flexibility of the method, allows subtle changes in tactics and direction in response to developing understanding through immersion in the field. For example, I began 'The Changing Nursing Practice' study with what I thought were well-founded reasons for anticipating an increased need for negotiation and inter-occupational tension between doctors and nurses about their respective work roles. My data generation strategy was designed to capture examples of this occupational boundary 'at work'. Once I had entered the field, however, I realized that the situation in the study site was rather different. There was some evidence of inter-occupational negotiation in management arena, but the division of labour between doctors and nurses was being redrawn in the clinical areas with minimal negotiation and little evidence of explicit conflict. I initially interpreted these findings as the death knell for my carefully crafted study, but was encouraged by my supervisors to consider how a research 'problem' might be considered an interesting intellectual puzzle. Accordingly, the study was reframed in order to develop an understanding of why such shifts in occupational boundaries were taking place so smoothly (Allen, 1997, 2001).

Flexibility of research design should not be taken to imply a lack of rigour. In field research, data generation and analysis are undertaken concurrently in an iterative process. At the beginning of a study, data are collected on a wide range of issues, the focus of the work subsequently narrowing as strategic decisions are made about what to observe, who to speak to and what questions to ask. These are in effect within-case sampling decisions. In a theoretical sampling strategy, decisions are driven by the requirement to develop categories, concepts and theories. Data generation ceases when no new cases can be identified which modify the emerging analysis. This is referred to as 'theoretical saturation' and in practice is reflected in a growing feeling of boredom on the part of the fieldworker. When the desire is to make empirical generalizations, decisions about data generation are driven by the need to establish that the cases being studied are sufficiently similar to other cases of the same type to permit case-to-case transfer. Both kinds of sampling can be present within a single project, and field researchers maintain a careful record of these decisions so that the processes through which they reached their final analyses are rendered transparent.

In the 'Negotiating Care' project, undertaken in the immediate postdoctoral period, I began with a general interest in how nurses, patients and their families accomplished care work. As the study evolved the focus narrowed to concentrate on two main concerns: different categories of family carer and their relationships with nursing staff (Allen, 2000) and the contextual factors supporting patient and family participation in care activity (Allen, 2002). Theoretical sampling was used to develop these main lines of inquiry. For illustrative purposes, I will say a little more about the second of these themes. I began fieldwork on a surgical ward and was immediately struck by its 'participatory caring environment'.

This was not easy to describe, rather it was something that one became aware of by being there. Data generation was progressively driven by the aim of establishing those features of the field setting which contributed to this overall effect. Over the course of the research, these were identified as: 'a culture of openness', a 'people-orientation', 'a focus on individuals' and 'care plans'. The study design also included a period of participant observation on a medical ward for comparative purposes. Although sharing similar philosophies of care with the surgical setting, medical staff had only been partly successful in creating an environment supportive of participative caring relationships and the culture and practices on the ward were quite different. Data generation in the second site was driven *inter alia* by the need to identify those factors which made the aspirations of the staff on the medical ward more difficult to attain. Resource constraints – skill mix, patient turnover and unpredictable ward 'shape' (Strauss et al., 1985) – which were highly consequential for work organization, emerged as key factors restricting staff's ability to put their caring philosophies into practice. This progressive narrowing of focus led to a conceptualization of patient/family-nurse relationships which took into account the effects of context on participation rather than exclusively focusing on the quality of caring relationships, as was typical of orthodox discussions of this issue at the time. Such a reframing shifted the spotlight away from the personal attributes and skills of individual nurses and directed attention to features of the work setting. Hospital skill mixes are based on models of care which render much of nursing work invisible. Because patients on the medical ward often require high levels of assistance with activities of daily living but low levels of technological intervention,[6] the calculation of staffing levels is driven by the physically intensive nature of the work, and tends to overlook the work associated with communicating with patients and their families and the skills that this involves. Three years after completion of the fieldwork, a review of the nursing establishment figures was undertaken in the Medical Directorate in response to growing concerns about care standards. The report recommended a 3-year plan to improve the staffing levels and increase the ratio of qualified to unqualified staff.

While flexibility clearly confers certain benefits in field studies, a growing number of researchers are prepared to specify questions at the beginning of the research. In one respect, this reflects the pragmatic and political necessity to address the requirements of certain external funding bodies, which understandably wish to have some indication of the likely outcomes of the work they are supporting. In another, as scientific knowledge of a given field accumulates, it is becoming more common to build on previous research rather than attempting to discover everything de novo.

In two of my five study examples, research questions were specified at an early stage. The 'Delivering Health and Social Care' and 'Transitions' projects both received external funding and the research questions were delineated in the original funding applications. 'Delivering Health and Social Care' involved case studies of the care of eight adults who had suffered a first acute stroke to address a policy priority in Wales: the provision of integrated health and social services to people with complex care needs. It drew on previous research on the social organization of hospital work and was informed by interactionist theories of the division of labour. The research grant-holders included myself, an experienced research professor with no prior experience of ethnography and another social scientist experienced in field study methods. We were all known to each other but had not previously collaborated on a research project. As we intended to apply for responsive mode funding, there was an extended process in which we developed the funding application that enabled us to reach a shared understanding about the study aims and overall approach. This was not without its challenges, revealing another dimension of the fieldwork career, the need to develop skills in working out a partnership with experienced colleagues. This kind of collaboration is becoming increasingly common as the trend for large-scale multidisciplinary research projects accelerates. We eventually agreed upon a focus and research design and had clearly defined objectives that we specified in the application for research funding. These were to:

• Map the network of health and social care providers delivering services to the case study subjects over a three month period.
• Undertake detailed study of how health and social care providers manage their respective roles and responsibilities.
• Identify factors related to interagency collaboration which contribute to or detract from the effectiveness and quality of service provision in the study settings.

The study was carried out in two contrasting health economies and two researchers were appointed to carry out the fieldwork. Undertaking observational research through others can be challenging because, despite their many talents, research assistants are by definition relatively junior team members and do not normally have extensive knowledge of the substantive field. In this particular case, neither research assistant had prior experience of health care settings. Given that the project was funded for a limited period and had clearly defined aims, it was necessary for the fieldwork to be precisely directed through regular team meetings during which the three grant holders and research assistants pooled our collective expertise in order to progress the study objectives. This data generation strategy was documented, providing a record of the decisions taken at different points during the research process and the underlying reason for these decisions.

Drawing on my experience in the above example, in the ongoing 'Transitions' study I have developed a framework to guide data generation. This aim of this large-scale study is to evaluate different service models' success in ensuring a 'smooth transition' from child to adult diabetes services. Data is being generated in five sites by two research assistants with limited prior experience of fieldwork in health care settings. The sites are some distance from our base of operation, and so field visits must be used to maximum effect. The study is informed by a realistic evaluation framework (Pawson and Tilley, 1997) that

---

Box 18.1   CONTEXT: Clinic milieu/culture (from user/carer perspective)

(a) *Rich description of physical environment, décor, facilities*

(b) *Rich description of atmosphere in the clinic waiting areas: what would a young person and their carer waiting to be seen be observing?*

(c) *Culture – is it formal/informal? Do staff use first names with young people, each other? Is there evidence of familiarity and established relationships?*

(d) *Do young people mix in the clinic setting?*

(e) *Do parents mix in the clinic setting?*

(f) *Do staff endeavour to encourage interaction between service users?*

(g) *How does the service represent itself in official documents, information sheets, posters on walls in clinics?*

(h) *Are there picture boards identifying staff and roles etc?*

---

directs attention to the contexts, mechanisms and outcomes (CMO) in relation to the phenomena of interest.[7] Participant observation is being used as a method for generating data on context and mechanisms with interview and survey data used to assess outcomes. Previous studies that used a realistic evaluation approach have noted some of the difficulties of using the CMO framework to classify features relevant to the investigation (Byng, 2005; Pedersen et al., 2005). Nevertheless, I have found it to be a valuable guide for field activity in a context where data generation is being shared, has to be accomplished efficiently and must allow cross-site comparisons. The example here illustrates the suggestions offered for generating data to build up a picture of the children's and adult diabetes clinic milieu from the perspective of the young person and their carer. Similar guidance has been developed for all the context and mechanisms on which we wish to generate data in order to address the study aims.

This framework is not intended to be exhaustive, but to act as a resource for the researchers to sensitize them to possible sources of material and ensure that the same information is obtained in each of the participating sites. Therefore, although in this case the study design is more prescriptive in its aims than the traditional field study, a degree of flexibility is still necessary in order to respond to exigencies in the field. As the lead for the qualitative element of this study, I plan to meet together with the research fellows regularly in order to review the emerging findings and consider their implications for data generation.

MAINTAINING A RECORD

Data generated through participant observation is typically recorded in the form of fieldnotes. Writing fieldnotes is the process through which scenes, actions, dialogues and experiences are turned into written text. In general, researchers make notes, jottings and/or audio-recordings of their observations and experiences in the field, which are later transcribed and expanded upon in order to preserve as much as possible of what was noticed. Given the centrality of fieldnotes to the craft of participation observation, there has been relatively little explicit instruction available to guide their production (*pace* Emerson et al., 1995). Novice researchers have tended to learn under the direction of supervisors and more experienced researchers; one element of my own practice is to share examples of fieldnotes with students

Fieldwork is demanding. It requires the fieldworker to attend to presentation of self, whilst simultaneously observing and participating in the study setting to gain understanding. It is necessary to achieve a balanced approach to participation in the field and the writing of fieldnotes. Tempting as it is to remain in the research setting for prolonged periods in case something of interest is missed, it is advisable to limit field observations to a maximum of four hours unless there are good strategic reasons for extending this[8] as thereafter the quality of fieldnotes tends to deteriorate. Some fieldworkers develop their own private systems of shorthand in order to quickly record observations in flight. Care should be taken to use transcription conventions which identify the status of the material so, for example, directly recorded verbatim exchanges can be distinguished from indirect quotation and reported speech. The interval between making an observation and creating a record of it will vary depending on one's fieldwork strategy. In some instances, it is possible to record almost verbatim examples of interaction as they occur. In others, it will be necessary to make a record after an event has occurred. This should happen at the earliest opportunity in order to ensure all pertinent details are captured. If the demands of the field make detailed written records difficult, an alternative strategy is to dictate observations into an audiotape recorder and transcribe these later. This is a tactic we have used in the 'Transitions' study, as the field visits are particularly intensive owing to the fact that the study sites are some distance from the university and so each visit is costly and must be used to maximal effect.

Notes made in the field are typically written up in a more polished form and usually transcribed using word processing software. As with the recording of observations in the research setting, the writing up of fieldnotes should be done as soon as possible after each observational episode, because with the passage of time, it becomes increasingly difficult to recall details of an event for even the most astute observer. This process is time consuming moreover, and, as a general rule of thumb, fieldworkers allow two hours of transcription for every hour spent in the field.

When planning fieldwork, consideration must be given to the data to be generated, the anticipated style of report and its likely audiences. Reports of early observational studies contained very few examples of the original field materials on which they were based and the relationship between data and analysis was opaque. Validity was established by published accounts of the fieldwork which were seen as establishing the authority of the work by demonstrating the human qualities and skills of the fieldworker in having immersed themselves in the field of study. Whilst the fieldwork role is still a central preoccupation of researchers in this tradition, it is no longer acceptable for the validity of a study to rest on the authority and reliability of the researcher through their sustained immersion in the study setting. There is now an expectation that accounts of observational research should make the relationship between data and analysis clear by providing supporting text for claims made.

Despite the more exacting requirements on fieldworkers to make the relationship between the data and their analyses transparent, there is still a tendency in lone ranger studies for researchers to write fieldnotes for themselves. This partly reflects the very real demands that fieldwork imposes. When it is fast approaching midnight and fieldwork is scheduled to start at 7 am, it is very tempting to truncate the field account. However, self-discipline is essential. Fieldnotes need to contain sufficient contextual information to enable it to be analyzed by another researcher with no involvement in the initial study.[9] Writing fieldnotes for a team audience is actually very useful in encouraging good practice in this regard, as the process directs more explicit attention to the contextual features that inform the emergent analysis and the respective insider-outsider positions of the fieldworkers and other team members can be used to good effect. In the 'Transitions' study, we are reviewing the researchers' fieldnotes regularly to identify any areas which need to be amplified before transcripts are finalized as the official record of a fieldwork episode.

Field researchers use a variety of fieldnote styles determined by the aims of the study, theoretical orientation and research questions. For those concerned with identifying broad patterns of activity and evoking a setting holistically, fieldnotes tend to have an overarching style and little distinction is drawn between data generation and the personal responses of the researcher to the field. In my own work, I have adopted low-inference style field notes that focus on concrete details which show rather than tell about behaviour and in which 'data' is clearly separated from the researcher reactions to the field. This is partly a methodological preference for the study of that which is directly observable. However, in team research where the activities of data generation and analysis are shared, if one behaviourizes activities in this way, it provides a means of analyzing a situation without adding anything to it which is not directly perceptible (Maso, 2001). In the 'Delivering Health and Social Care' study, having data of this kind was essential, as the research associates moved on to new positions when the project funding ended, and data analysis was refined after the report had been produced for the funding body.

With developments in technology, 'observations' may also be made through other means such as audio and video recording devices. Such strategies have the advantage of capturing naturally occurring interactions and are particularly effective for recording meetings and other such organized events. In some cases, it may even be possible for events to be recorded without the researcher having to set foot in the field, and indeed research participants may consider this to be a less intrusive observational strategy than participant observation. For example, in the 'Transitions' study, we wish to audio-record consultations in the diabetes clinics in order to generate data on the culture and ethos of paediatric, interim and adult services. In the course of our access negotiations, several of the doctors have indicated that although they are happy for the event to be audio-recorded, they do not wish for there to be another 'body' in the, already cramped, consulting room. Another advantage of audio-recoded observations is that it is possible for the material to be transcribed by a professional typist, if resources are available. This is less likely to be feasible in those situations involving multiple participants because of the challenges of identifying the contributors to the interaction. In these circumstances, it is preferable for the person processing the data to have observed the event in person in order to facilitate transcription of the audio recording. This also enables the audio-transcript to be enriched with observational materials on nonverbal behaviour. The transcription of complex meetings is very time-consuming, and so it is important to be strategic about the volume of data that is recorded. It may be possible to transcribe instances of observation selectively. Analysis in these circumstances is undertaken by listening and re-listening to the transcripts and a summary made of the main discussion points, with detailed transcription of only the salient sections.

In the context of fieldwork at a distance, the use of audio-recorded materials can be particularly attractive. In the last of my five examples, 'The Social Organization of Integrated Care Pathway Development' study, the primary sources of data are audio-recordings of meetings, documentary analysis and interview transcripts. In this study, the majority of data generation was undertaken by a research assistant, but I had responsibility for the analysis. It was therefore, essential that the data was in a form which enabled me to understand and interpret it. Despite efforts to improve research career pathways, short-term researcher contracts remain an unfortunate fact of life and fieldworkers often move on to new projects before all the data has been analyzed. Deploying behaviourist style fieldnotes and strategically employing audio recordings is not only good fieldwork practice, but also it is a means of future proofing projects so that they can be progressed by another not intimately involved in data generation.

SENSE-MAKING

In field studies, even those in which research questions have been defined in advance, data generation and analysis are undertaken concurrently. 'Analysis' in this context can take a number of forms. For example, the process of writing fieldnotes may stimulate ideas about the significance of observations and these are typically added to fieldnotes as embedded researcher reflections and asides. In addition to these 'in-flight' analyses, periodically, the researcher will take time away from the field to review a series of fieldnote entries or audio transcripts and consider in a more systematic way issues and themes of interest. Field researchers will write up these deliberations as analytic memos which will inform decisions about future data generation and stimulate exploration of related literature. At this stage, the analysis remains tentative and open to alternative interpretations and possibilities. In lone-ranger research studies, the fieldworker can be flexible about when these processes take place. In team projects, it is necessary to schedule regular meetings for this purpose. In the 'Delivering Health and Social Care' study, regular data sessions were held. Prior to the meeting, team members reviewed the data independently and created individual memos. Individual's memos were shared prior to the meeting, discussed and the strategic focus agreed. The meetings served as a useful reminder of the research focus, ensuring that the data generation strategy was directed at producing an in-depth understanding of the phenomena of interest, and that our efforts were not diluted by interesting but unrelated events and/or issues.

Whilst data analysis is an ongoing feature of field research, at some point, a decision is taken to end data generation and undertake a systematic analysis of the data as a whole. At this stage, the corpus of fieldnotes is reviewed and earlier hunches and tentative interpretations are refined. My preference is to read fieldnotes in chronological order as this preserves the progressive narrowing of focus and the developing analysis. Emerson et al.'s (1995) recommendation of approaching fieldnotes as if one were a stranger reading them for the first time is also a very helpful strategy.

Field research generates large volumes of data, and there are now several computer-assisted qualitative data analysis packages (CAQDAS) available to support data management. Such software permits electronic codes to be attached to segments of data in order to facilitate retrieval. Some fieldworkers maintain that CAQDAS makes them feel too removed from their materials, but this has not been my experience. All of the projects in which I have been involved have generated a large data corpus and the software made analysis more manageable. Nevertheless, CAQDAS functionality has become increasingly sophisticated, and it is important not to get too seduced by the technology. It can be tempting to use facilities, simply because they are available, irrespective of their value in progressing the analysis, and much time can be wasted in learning the relevant skills and manipulating the data. Moreover, it is important to be clear that such software is only another tool to *support* analysis, it does not obviate the need for careful and clear thinking. Indeed, in smaller projects, the investment of time to learn a new technology may not be justified and in other studies, there may be elements of the analysis which can be handled without the use of CAQDAS. Modest volumes of data can be managed quite satisfactorily by word processing packages or using highlighter pens on hard copies of fieldnotes.

Whatever 'technology' the fieldworker employs, the approach to analysis is the same and usually entails a process of coding and categorization. Fieldworkers typically begin with an initial reading of the data and adopt an open coding strategy covering a range of analytic possibilities. The codes are a means through which to think about the data and explore interesting lines of inquiry and relationships between different elements of the phenomena of interest. As the analysis is refined, coding becomes more focused around key themes and issues, in which subcodes are developed and consideration given to the linkages between them. For example, in 'The Changing Shape of Nursing Practice' study, the first stage coding included a combination of descriptive and conceptual codes. I had descriptive codes for each category of health care professional and key events (such as nursing handovers and ward rounds) and several conceptual codes (for example 'boundary work', 'temporal–spatial organization of the work' and 'atrocity story'). In the second stage of coding, 'boundary blurring' and 'boundary maintaining' were added as subcategories of 'boundary work', and 'atrocity stories' were identified as one mechanism through which the latter was accomplished (Allen, 2001b). In 'The Social Organization of Integrated Care Pathway Development' study, 'evidence' was an initial code which was later refined to include the subcodes: 'evidence as challenge', 'evidence as legitimation', 'evidence as problem', 'evidence in pathways' and 'evidence to inform standards'. One of the advantages of utilizing CAQDAS is that it is relatively easy to refine and reassign codes as the analysis develops. With the growing popularity of CAQDAS and fieldworker awareness of the need for transparency of research process, there seems to be a trend to include copies of the study coding frame as evidence of the analytic process. My own view is that this is insufficient and that in writing a fieldwork report, it is important to describe the processes through which the findings were derived from the data. This involves clarifying concepts and categories and tracing the interplay between theory and data.

The processes of analysis are rather more complex in team projects. In some team studies, a division of labour is agreed through which different members take responsibility for analyzing different lines of inquiry (Erickson and Stull, 1997). In others, the processes of coding and analysis are divided. This was the case in the 'Delivering Health and Social Care' study in which the fieldworkers took responsibility for coding the data generated in their respective sites using a common coding frame based on descriptive codes and agreed by the team. We piloted this to ensure inter-rater reliability with the two researchers liaising by telephone to reach a common understanding. The decision to limit the coding frame to descriptive codes reflected a number of pragmatic considerations. The project was time-limited and there was a requirement to produce a report for the funding body for which descriptive codes were quite adequate. We knew that both researchers would be leaving before the detailed analysis could be undertaken and that somebody else from the team would be required to develop the analysis for the final report. In this case, the coding frame applied by the researchers provided a means for negotiating the data corpus and developing the analysis for other purposes.[10]

CONCLUDING REMARKS

High-quality field studies can make an important contribution to health research. They are a means for developing holistic understanding of a setting in all its complexity and for exploring human activity in the contexts in which it happens. Field methods are powerful tools for rendering visible hidden practices. In a given social setting, there will always be things that are not evident to the subjects themselves and which interviews and focus groups struggle to reveal. The only way to see these things is to get out into the field. Such insights can inform human service innovations and facilitate judgments about the likely effects of change and how undesirable unintended consequences might be minimized. Field studies are also a valuable means of evaluating policies and service interventions. Because they reveal how policies are put into action, they can facilitate understanding of the relationships between processes and outcomes and organizations in action (Griffiths, 2003). For this reason, they are also a useful addition to randomized controlled trials (Bradley et al., 1999; Campbell et al., 2000), particularly when the intervention in question is complex and its generative mechanisms poorly understood. A further value of fieldwork methods is that they circumvent some of the methodological limitations associated with interview data when one attempts to treat participant responses as proxies for actual behaviour. Indeed, observational methods frequently highlight differences between what people do and what they say they do and get behind public accounts to what actually happens in practice, not in some ironic way, but in order to further illuminate an issue of concern.

Field study is gaining credibility in health policy circles, but as its value is increasingly acknowledged, the opportunities created by the growing willingness of research councils to fund observational research have created new challenges for the community. The primary narrative of this chapter is the methodological choices made in a range of subtly different field studies undertaken over a 15-year period. The secondary narrative is the story of an evolving fieldwork career, beginning with doctoral research (The Changing Shape of Nursing Practice) and moving through postdoctoral study (Negotiating Care) to Principal Investigator of large scale externally funded multisite projects (Delivering Health and Social Care, Transitions). The vast majority of methodological guidance in the extant literature, assumes a lone research model (*pace*, Erickson and Stull, 1997) in which the field worker and analyst functions are assumed by one person. However, for experienced researchers, it can become increasingly challenging for these two activities to be combined partly because of the restrictions of funding bodies and partly because of the challenges of combining field work with a senior academic role. To date little has been written about the practical and personal implications of these trends for senior and junior colleagues alike. If field studies are to achieve their very real potential to illuminate health care, the next methodological challenge is to identify systems that enable senior researchers to avoid becoming trapped in a research manager role and bring their knowledge and experience to the fieldwork process whilst ensuring opportunities for new researchers to hone their skills and progress their own research careers.

NOTES

1 All studies draw selectively on symbolic interactionism and ethnomethodology and synthesize certain elements.

2 Thanks are due to Robert Dingwall and Veronica James, who supervised the study.

3 Integrated Care Pathways (ICPs) are workflow technologies believed to address the many factors which contribute to service integration. They are a means of formalizing multidisciplinary working, a mechanism for embedding guidelines and protocols into local practice and a system of clinical audit.

4 While there is no reason why participant observation cannot be used exclusively as a method of data generation, it is more typical for researchers to combine fieldwork with other qualitative techniques, such as audiotape-recorded interviews and analysis of documents, in order to develop understanding of social phenomena.

5 The arguments in this section draw on those developed in Allen (2004b).

6 Surgical staffs tend to be skill rich because of the presumed technical complexity of caring for post-operative patients.

7 The underlying rationale for this approach is that if we know and understand how different interventions produce varying impacts in different circumstances, we are better able to decide what policies/services to implement in what conditions. Pawson and Tilley express this in the simple formula: mechanism + context = outcomes (CMO).

8 For example, in my doctoral study, several of my fieldwork visits lasted 14 hours, as I was shadowing the on-call junior doctors and wanted to understand their perspective.

9 In the United Kingdom, researchers funded by the Economic and Social Research Council are required to make their data available for archiving for use by the wider social scientific community and guidance is available for the appropriate standards required.

10 Outputs from this work include: Allen et al. (2001; 2002; 2004a; 2004b).

REFERENCES

Allen, D. (1997) 'The Nursing–Medical Boundary: A Negotiated Order', *Sociology of Health and Illness*, 19(4): 498–520.

Allen, D. (2000) 'Negotiating the Role of Expert Carers on an Adult Hospital Ward', *Sociology of Health & Illness*, 22(2): 149–71.

Allen, D. (2001a) *The Changing Shape of Nursing Practice: The Role of Nurses in the Hospital Division of Labour*. London: Routledge.

Allen, D. (2001b) 'Narrating Nursing Jurisdiction: Atrocity Stories and Boundary Work', *Symbolic Interaction*, 24(1): 75–103.

Allen, D. (2002) 'Creating a "Participatory Caring Context" on Hospital Wards'. In D. Allen and D. Hughes (eds) *Nursing and the Division of Labour in Healthcare* (pp. 151–81). Basingstoke: Palgrave Macmillan.

Allen, D. (2004a) 'Re-Reading Nursing and Re-Writing Practice: Towards an Empirically Based Reformulation of the Nursing Mandate', *Nursing Inquiry*, 11(4): 271–83.

Allen, D. (2004b) 'Ethnomethodological Insights into Insider–Outsider Relationships in Nursing Ethnographies of Healthcare Settings', *Nursing Inquiry*, 11(1): 14–24.

Allen, D., Griffiths, L., and Lyne, P. (2004) Understanding Complex Trajectories in Health and Social Care Provision, *Sociology of Health and Illness*, 26(7): 1008–30.

Allen, D., Griffiths, L., and Lyne, P. (2004) 'Accommodating Health and Social Care Need: Routine Resource Allocation Processes in Stroke Rehabilitation', *Sociology of Health and Illness*, 26(4): 411–32.

Allen, D., Lyne, P., and Griffiths, L. (2002) 'Studying Complex Caring Interfaces', *Journal of Clinical Nursing*, 11: 297–305.

Allen, D., Griffiths, L., Lyne, P., Monaghan, L., and Murphy, D. (2001) 'Delivering Health and Social Care: Changing Roles, Responsibilities and Relationships', *Journal of Interprofessional Care*, 16(1): 79–80.

Allen, D., Griffiths, L., Lyne, P., Monaghan, L., and Murphy, D. (2001) 'Delivering Health and Social Care: Changing Roles, Responsibilities and Relationships', Spotlight Wales Office of Research and Development for Health and Social Care.

Ashworth, P.D. (1995) 'The Meaning of "Participation" in Participant Observation', *Qualitative Health Research*, 5: 366–87.

Baszanger, I. and Dodier, N. (1997) 'Ethnography: Relating the Part to the Whole'. In Silveman, D. (ed) *Qualitative Research: Theory, Method and Practice* (pp. 8–23). London: Sage.

Bonner, A. and Tolhurst G. (2002) 'Insider-Outsider Perspectives of Participant Observation', *Nurse Researcher*, 9: 7–19.

Bradley, F., Wiles, R., Kinmouth, A-L., Mant, D., and Gantley, M. for the SHIP Collborative Group (1999) 'Development and Evaluation of Complex Interventions in Health Services Research: Case Study of the Southampton Heart Integrated Care Project (SHIP)', *British Medical Journal*, 318: 711–5.

Byng, R. (2005) 'Using Realistic Evaluation to Evaluate a Practice-Level Intervention to Improve Primary Healthcare for Patients with Long-Term Mental Illness', *Evaluation*, 11(1): 69–93.

Campbell, M., Fizpatrick, R., Haines, A., Kinmouth, L., Sandercock, P., Spiegelhalter, D., and Tyrer, P. (2000) 'Framework for Design and Evaluation of Complex Interventions to Improve Health', *British Medical Journal*, 321: 694–6.

Emerson, R.M., Fretz, R.I., and Shaw, L.L. (1995) *Writing Ethnographic Fieldnotes*. Chicago: The University of Chicago Press.

Erickson, K.C. and Stull, D.D. (1997) *Doing Team Ethnography: Warnings and Advice*. Beverly Hills: Sage.

Gans, H.J. (1968) 'The Participant Observer as a Human Being: Observations on the Personal Aspects of Fieldwork'. In R.G. Burgess (ed.) *Field Research: A Sourcebook and Field Manual* (pp. 53–61). London: Allen and Unwin.

Gerrish, K. (1995) 'Being a "Marginal Native": Dilemmas of the Participant Observer', *Nurse Researcher*, 5: 25–34.

Gold, R.L. (1958) 'Roles in Sociological Fieldwork', *Social Forces*, 36: 217–23.

Goffman, E. (1959) *The Presentation of Self in Everyday Life*. New York: Doubleday.

Griffiths, L. (2003) 'Making Connections: Studies of the Social Organization of Healthcare', *Sociology of Health and Illness*, 25(Silver Anniversary Issues): 155–71.

Hunt, S.A. and Benford, R.D. (1994) 'Identity Talk in the Peace and Justice Movement', *Journal of Contemporary Ethnography*, 22: 488–517.

James, N. (1992) 'Care, Work and Carework: A Synthesis?'. In J. Robinson, A. Gray, and R. Elkan (eds) *Policy Issues in Nursing*. Milton Keyenes, UK: Open University Press.

Latimer, J. (2000) *The Conduct of Care: Understanding Nursing Practice*. Oxford: Blackwells.

Lawler, J. (1991) *Behind the Screens: Nursing, Somology and the Problem of the Body*. London: Churchill Livingstone.

Maso, I. (2001) 'Phenomenology and Ethnography'. In P. Atkinson, P.A. Coffey, S. Delamont, J. Loftland, and L. Loftland (eds) *Handbook of Ethnography* (pp. 136–44). London: Sage.

Murphy, E., Dingwall, R., Greatbatch, D., Parker, S., and Watson, P. (1998) 'Qualitative Research Methods in Health Technology Assessment: A Review of the Literature', *Health Technology Assessment*, 2(16).

Pawson, R. and Tilley, N. (1997) *Realistic Evaluation*. London: Sage.

Pedersen, L., Rieper, O., and Sørensen E.M. (2005) 'Is Realistic Evaluation a Realistic Approach for Complex Reforms?'. Paper presented at the Nopsa conference in Reykavik, Iceland 11–3 August.

Purkis, M.E. (1996) 'Nursing in Quality Space: Technologies Governing Experiences of Care', *Nursing Inquiry*, 3: 101–11.

Purkis, M.E. (2001) 'Managing Home Nursing Care: Visibility, Accountability and Exclusion', *Nursing Inquiry*, 8: 141–50.

Reed, J. (1995) 'Practitioner Knowledge in Practitioner Research'. In J. Reed, and S. Procter (eds) *Practitioner Research in Healthcare* (pp. 46–61). London: Chapman & Hall.

Risk, R.C. (2001) 'Bliztkrieg Ethnography: Of the Transformation of a Method into a Movement'. In A. Bryman (ed.) *Ethnography Vol III* (pp. 197–201). London: Sage.

Savage, J. (1995) *Nursing Intimacy: An Ethnographic Approach to Nurse-Patient Interaction*. London: Scutari Press.

Snow, D.A. and Anderson, L. (1987) 'Identity Work Among the Homeless: The Verbal Construction and Avowal of Personal Identities', *American Journal of Sociology*, 92: 1336–71.

Spencer, J. (2001) 'Ethnography After Postmodernism'. In P. Atkinson, A. Coffey, S. Delamont, J. Loftland, and L. Loftland (eds) *Handbook of Ethnography* (pp. 443–52). London, Sage.

Strauss, A., Fagerhaugh, S., Suczet, B., and Weiner, C. (1985) *The Social Organization of Medical Work*. Chicago: University of Chicago Press.

Tjora, A. (2000) 'The Technological Mediation of the Nursing–Medical Boundary', *Sociology of Health and Illness*, 22: 721–41.

19

Video-based Conversation Analysis

Ruth Parry

INTRODUCTION

It is often said that 90 percent of our communication is nonverbal. While perhaps not literally true, this adage draws our attention to a matter easy to overlook: gaze, gesture, facial expressions, touch, manipulation of objects, and arrangements and shifts of body position are very important in how we build meaning and understanding. These complex activities typically go unnoticed as we get on with the business of life and interaction, but for those with analytic interests in understanding what people do and why, alertness to these matters is vital.

For quite some time, video data have been used by those doing both quantitative and qualitative studies in health care (e.g., Bottorff, 1991; Caldwell and Atwal, 2005; Coleman, 2000; Stewart, 1992). In this chapter, I focus on ethnomethodological and conversation analytic (EMCA) approaches to handling these data. Within these approaches, developments in both recording and analysing video data are providing increasingly sophisticated ways to identify, describe, and understand what people do and why, in ways that carefully attend to the contribution of nonvocal and vocal conduct.

Video-based EMCA studies in health care are not confined to investigating and identifying 'communication skills'; rather they provide information about many core aspects of health care. For instance, this type of research has been used to examine how people secure one another's participation and cooperation (Heath, 1986); accomplish technical tasks such as physical examination and movement re-education (Martin, 2004); formulate and understand questions, instructions, diagnoses, and explanations (Maynard and Heritage, 2005); and coordinate teamwork (Hindmarsh and Pilnick, 2005). Other investigators have looked at how practitioners balance the work of eliciting and listening to patients' contributions with other requirements of their jobs (Robinson and Stivers, 2001) including their computer-based note-taking and prescribing (Greatbatch, 2005), and how people manage to avoid some of the potential difficulties associated with health care, such as embarrassment (Heath, 1988).

Because a large proportion of health care is delivered through face-to-face interaction and because it involves bodily topics and activities, the value of research that can systematically handle both vocal and nonvocal (bodily) elements of interactions is obvious. It should also be noted that health care communication regularly concerns topics and activities that are somewhat 'delicate', and nonvocal activities are a pervasive resource for communicating about such matters (Kendon, 1985). Finally, vocal and nonvocal conducts are central to many domains of health care policies, users' views and experiences, and practitioners' skills and expertise. These domains include, for instance, recognizing and protecting patients' dignity (Picker Institute Europe, 2003), conveying and inspiring trust (Burkitt Wright et al., 2004), and conveying professional and technical expertise (Jensen et al., 1992). However, there is very little empirical evidence about what these matters look like in practice, that is, about how people actually accomplish and recognize them. Producing empirically grounded evidence means facing the daunting challenges of analysing these complex phenomena in ways that are rigorous and focused, and confronting the almost overwhelming level of detail contained in video data (Heath et al., 2007).

Although challenging, video-recordings offer significant advantages for health research. Multiple and complex elements of behaviour can be analyzed and there is access to a level of detail unavailable in other data. The availability of recordings for analysis and presentations allows repeated, systematic, detailed scrutiny not only by the primary researcher but also by others (for instance academic researchers, practitioners, and service users) who can enrich analysis through their own insights and knowledge, thus improving levels of validity and reliability (Heath and Luff, 1993; Jordan and Henderson, 1995; Peräkylä, 1997; Heath et al., 2007). The comprehensive nature of video-data also makes it possible to pursue a variety of questions and interests (although this raises considerations for research design and ethics that I will discuss later).

Overview: use of video in EMCA studies

The earliest developments in CA utilized audio-recordings, especially of telephone conversations (Sacks and Jefferson, 1992), but it was not long before analysts began to make and use film and then videos. Some studies use videos as a way of adding to the understanding of *talk* and its organization. Others emphasize that social action and interaction are assembled from multiple components and use video as a means of conducting analyses that emphasize this perspective. Goodwin's trailblazing work used video materials to closely analyze the practices[1] and functioning of nonvocal aspects of communication in workplaces (Goodwin, 1994) and more informal settings (Goodwin, 1979), and to anatomize the intimate and systematic interrelations of talk and nonvocal actions. He developed a transcription system for gaze (Goodwin, 1979) which has been widely employed (e.g., Heath, 1986) as have his practices for illustrating and representing analyses (Curley, 1998; Martin, 2004). Another key figure in developing methods and findings that use the full potential of video is Christian Heath. Like Goodwin, he takes inspiration from the substantial body of prior work relating to the nonvocal by scholars such as Kendon (1977), Birdwistell (1970) and Goffman (1983). Heath's work has particular relevance for this chapter because much of it has examined data from health care settings. The most recent developments in the field of video-based EMCA have prioritized, explored and illuminated the inherently 'multi-modal' nature of social interaction in medical settings (e.g., Mondada, 2003; Koschmann et al., 2007) and elsewhere (e.g., Jones and LeBaron, 2002; Stivers and Sidnell, 2005).

Existing video-based EMCA studies in health care

There are several ways video-based EMCA can be used to understand the sociological and behavioural features of health care.

Some researchers use health care-related video-recordings to focus on the individual components of behaviour from which people assemble their activities. These include investigations of the forms and functions of gesture (Heath, 1992; Koschmann et al., 2007) and gaze (Frankel, 1993). In some of these studies, the fact that the data are health care-related is incidental: they are used as a way of gaining access to foundational aspects of how nonvocal communication works in any context. Some researchers who have conducted this sort of analysis have used the same data to conduct other investigations of issues specific to health care – Heath's work, referred to in the following section, is a key example.

It is not unusual for 'component level' investigations to examine the interrelations of components, that is, how different elements of social interaction are organized with respect to one another, and how they function together. Researchers interested in multimodality are developing understandings of the coordination, similarities and differences between the structures and functions of various nonvocal practices and those of vocal practices (Stivers and Sidnell, 2005). These studies elucidate how nonvocal practices function in concert with vocal activity, pursuing the same lines of action (for instance where pointing draws the interlocutor's attention and helps establish precisely what is being referred to). The nonvocal can also work to pursue distinct, or even contrary trajectories of action (Stivers and Sidnell, 2005), as seen for instance when patients grimace whilst verbally aligning with 'good news' about cancer prognosis (Beach, 2005). These studies show how the resources made available through combinations of vocal and nonvocal practices are drawn on and used during health care interactions.

Other EMCA video-based studies focus on health care functioning, activities, tasks or problems. Many of these studies examine the vocal aspects of interaction and use the visual data available within videos in a supplementary manner. Unsurprisingly then, these studies have tended to consider matters and activities which are to a considerable extent conducted through talk – for instance, asking and answering questions (Boyd and Heritage, 2006), providing explanations (Collins, 2005), medical history taking (Boyd and Heritage, 2006) and reporting (Halkowski, 2006), making recommendations (Stivers, 2005), and treatment goal-setting (Parry, 2004).

Other studies use video to produce what might be termed 'integrated analyses' of vocal and visual conduct in health care relevant activities. Some of these focus on fairly broad-scale phenomena. For instance, one of Heath's studies (1988) investigated embarrassment, particularly how it is precipitated and how it is avoided during physical examinations in primary care consultations. In this same vein, Heath (1989; 2002) also studied the constitution of pain and suffering, describing how patients express pain and convey their experiences within consultations and how doctors respond. Hindmarsh and Pilnick's (2005) study in anaesthetics settings used video to address questions about the objectification of patients by health care practitioners. These empirical, observational studies challenge theoretically based or anecdotally informed considerations of their topics. Heath, for example, demonstrates that it is a misconception to understand pain or embarrassment as simply the outpourings of some internal state or emotion. Rather, displays of embarrassment and expressions of pain are shaped in interaction: intimately coordinated with and responsive to the actions and attention of the recipient (e.g., the doctor) and functioning to manage the particular requirements of the consultation. This can be seen in how patients vigorously convey the sensation of pain whilst also acquiescing to and cooperating with the physical examination (Heath, 1988).

Integrated analyses may also focus on how specific health care activities, tasks, and events are achieved and performed. For example, Robinson and Stivers' work (2001) on primary care interviews examines how people manage shifts between phases and tasks within consultations. Their study emphasizes the important role of nonvocal actions and of objects such as patients' notes and doctors' pens in the process. In his paper on cancer fears, Beach (2005) analyzes the various and often subtle ways that patients express fears in relation to cancer in oncology clinics, and how doctors' respond to these expressions. Nishizaka (2007) examines how midwives physically examine women's abdomens, and how they teach students what and how to palpate. Martin (2004) describes and elucidates therapists' physical and linguistic practices for teaching and demonstrating particular movement activities and patients' practices for demonstrating understanding and learning; Hindmarsh and Pilnick (2005) elucidate practices by which co-workers in operating theatres coordinate their work, and how senior staff advise and correct trainees on their actions.

Some studies of this type focus on how material objects are used and incorporated within interactions. Greatbatch (2005) and colleagues (1995a; 1995b) examined how computers that are used for maintaining records and writing prescriptions affect doctor-patient communication. They show how patients time their contributions to occur when the doctor is less intensively engaged with the keyboard and screen, and they make observations about how doctors' talk can be disrupted by the requirements of the software's data input interface.

APPLICABILITY OF FINDINGS AND IMPACT ON PRACTICE AND POLICY

There is at present scant empirical evidence on whether and how studies *can* and *do* impact upon policy and practice (a topic I revisit at the end of this chapter). Some researchers propose that their analyses will enable health care providers and recipients to better understand one another's activities and orientations and that this will influence practice (Beach, 2005; Halkowski, 2006). Others go further, making fairly specific recommendations about the sorts of actions practitioners should perform. For instance, Gill and Maynard (2006) propose that when patients offer their own explanations for their conditions, doctors should verbally acknowledge them then and there, even if they do not pursue these explanations until later in the consultation. Other researchers choose to offer specific information and illustrations of practices that seem to cause or prevent trouble, and draw attention to possible implications without making direct recommendations. In his study of embarrassment, Heath (1988) demonstrates the 'interpersonal' troubles that can arise when doctors attempt to maintain or establish close rapport during intimate physical examinations of patients, and he illustrates the way that regularly, people work to establish distance rather than rapport during such activities (particularly through use of gaze). He notes that the real world conventions of how people communicate with one another in such situations are worth taking into account in professional policy and guidance. Peräkyla and Vehviläinen (2003) offer a discussion (illustrated with numerous research examples) of how conversation-analytic investigations might engage with practitioners, policy makers and educators (see also ten Have, 1999, Chapter 8; Pilnick and Dingwall, 2007). Growing debate about the policy implications of this video-based research can be expected as researchers dialogue with those who commission, assess, and use their work.

COLLECTING DATA

Effects of recording on the phenomena under investigation and how these are dealt with

Before addressing practical matters of accessing and collecting data, we must consider overarching concerns about the validity of video-based studies. These concerns revolve around the ways that the process of recording might undermine the integrity of the research. This objection to the use of video in research is worth addressing 'head on', because it is frequently raised as a concern by potential participants and those with oversight of review and ethics processes.

Doubtless, the presence of recording equipment influences participants' conduct. Unfortunately, there is no way to precisely verify this: one cannot observe the consequences of presence or absence of observation without some sort of observation process – this is the Observer's Paradox (Labov, 1972).

At the outset, it is worth pointing out that this problem is innate to all research endeavours, because collecting data inevitably requires use of one tool or another. Therefore, data will always and inevitably be affected by its means of collection. Integrity of the research thus depends upon explicit consideration of the nature of these effects and the use of these considerations to guide appropriate study design, analysis, and claims.

What do we know about the effects of video recording on people's behaviour? First, we can suggest by logical argument that recording processes will influence different aspects of conduct differentially: those activities that go on at an unnoticed level and at a rapid pace are unlikely to be changed and changeable by video recording (Jordan and Henderson, 1995; Clayman and Gill, 2004). Therefore, physical actions, particularly at the 'micro' level, such as gaze and postural adjustments, are unlikely to be much affected. On the other hand, some verbal actions, for instance choice and frequency of particular topics are more likely to be more affected. By the same logic, it seems less likely that the basic structural organizations of talk will be altered. Second, people seem to habituate to the presence of a camera quite rapidly, especially if certain procedures are followed (Heath and Luff, 1993; Jordan and Henderson, 1995; Peräkylä, 1997). Third, if the health care activity – e.g., making a diagnosis or instructing and participating in balance exercises – is accomplished whilst recording is ongoing, it seems likely that people will be doing much of whatever they regularly do in order to accomplish their activities.

How can the potential effects of recording on conduct be ameliorated? Because habituation to the equipment and researcher lessens effects (Heath and Luff, 1993; Jordan and Henderson, 1995), a prolonged presence of both in the field is ideal. In addition, the less the equipment and data collector are involved in the interaction, the less likely are reactive effects. In some settings, the researcher can avoid being present in the room or even at the site during recording. Remotely controlling the camera is useful here as is the use of a camera that allows recording of several hours of data without changing storage media; fixing the camera high in a corner of the area; and use of a fish-eye lens to capture a wide visual field. It is not always possible for the researcher to avoid being present: in the physical therapy settings where I have worked, participants moved between positions and locations so much that even a fish-eye lens would not allow continuous capture, so I sat close to the treatment area, out of sight if possible, and made adjustments to the camera angle as necessary. Even more intrusive operator-presence may be required, as in the case of Martin's (2004) study of the fine detail of touch and gaze in physical therapy, which led her to handhold the camera. In dealing with the problem of reactivity, the researcher should consider two further issues: their demeanour, and the participants' perceptions of their role and conduct. Researchers should strive to maintain a neutral demeanour and promote expectations of fair and constructive analysis.

Effects of recording can also be ameliorated at the analysis stage. Researchers should take into account possible effects of recording and draw on information from participants. The latter may come from explicit feedback about perceived effects of recording or from implicit orientations observable within the video data themselves. Awareness of potential recording effects will make the researcher wary about making claims about the wider relevance of matters more likely to be influenced by recording, such as frequency of occurrence of topics participants know are of interest to the researcher. In this situation, the researcher can more legitimately make claims relating to *how* something is regularly done than they can about *when* and *how often* it is done. Finally, observable and/or audible behaviours with respect to the recording and related equipment can provide analytic insights (see Lomax and Casey, 1998; Speer and Hutchby, 2003).

Amount and form of data

Decisions about how much data to collect are subject to similar considerations to those in other qualitative methods. However, an additional consideration with video is that it takes little time to collect large volumes of data (preparation for data collection is likely to take far more time than actual data collection). Since it is not imperative to analyze all of the data in depth, it is worth collecting sufficient volume to allow subsequent sampling from within the dataset depending on emerging questions and issues.

In terms of the video data, it is becoming increasingly common to use more than one camera in order to allow maximal access to conduct from a variety of angles. Greatbatch and colleagues (1995b), mentioned earlier, describe use of multiple cameras in their work on doctor–patient–computer interactions.

Video studies can also entail collection of other forms of data. Quite commonly, systematic ethnographic observations are made both before and alongside video-recordings. As Heath and Hindmarsh (2002) point out, these are often required in order for the researcher(s) to understand the complex and specialized settings and activities studied and thus to ensure optimal data collection and analysis. Video researchers may also collect interview data. Collins and colleagues (2003) describe a study of consultations with patients which used both video-recording consultations and interviewing the participants. Using interview data alongside EMCA-based video analysis can be challenging, because the concepts and assumptions upon which EMCA is founded lead to scepticism about the status and value of interview data (for accessible discussions of this matter, see ten Have, 2004, and Murphy and Dingwall, 2003). However, some researchers (Collins, 2005; Pomerantz, 2005) have gathered data through a specialized form of interviewing: 'video stimulated comments'; Pomerantz (2005) usefully discusses the status and use of such comments from an EMCA perspective.

Preparations

As in all research, the researcher must consider the issue of coercion when negotiating access. It is worth spending several hours or even days, familiarizing yourself with the research setting and participants. This allows for learning about the routines and organization of the setting, collaborating with participants with regards optimal placement of equipment, and discerning when the best opportunities for observation are likely to arise. Equipment should be tested by making some pilot recordings to check that microphones pick up sound adequately and that different items of electrical equipment do not interfere with one another. An equipment bag should be stocked with adequate supplies including spare batteries, electrical tape and bulldog clips for securing wires, curtains and so on, paper or electronic forms for demographic and/or other supplementary data collection, and scissors for opening packaging around recording tapes or disks.

Equipment

It is a challenge to give advice in a technological field that is rapidly changing. Bountiful information is available in archives and through current Internet-based networks of active researchers such as: the Languse and Ethno online discussion forums; the support section of the Transana site (Fassnacht and Woods, 2009); the technical advice site Mediacollege.com; and the websites of specialist research centres (e.g., http://www.ucl.ac.uk/cair/). Expertise within one's local institution and in the commercial sector should also be consulted. Aspects of camera choice include: how many to use, whether to use additional lenses, battery life, remote control facility, data storage medium, availability of microphone input and headphone output jacks (the latter for unobtrusively monitoring and checking sound recording), and of a lens cap (useful if some participants consent to audio but not video-recording); and equipment for camera positioning. A clamp that attaches the camera to stable structures in the setting or to a pole means a far smaller 'footprint' than a tripod, and so can be more functional and safe in a busy environment. Adequate sound capture is very important and can be challenging in health care environments. Integral microphones on cameras are almost always inadequate, and a variety of external microphones is available. Many researchers find 'boom' microphones work well in multiparty environments. Those who wish to restrict sound capture to the environment near the camera (as I have done in busy physical therapy gyms where patient–therapist pairs are separated from each other only by curtains) may want to opt for lapel microphones and transmitters worn by one of the participants, transmitting to a receiver connected to the camera. Some researchers opt to record an additional digital voice recorded sound track.

Actual recording

It is quite common in audio data-based studies to arrange for participants to make their own recordings. With video, practicalities mean it is usually useful to have a researcher or equipment operator do this work. The researcher will need to collaborate with participants to schedule recording so it minimally disrupts what would normally go on in the setting. To help habituation, it is ideal to have the equipment sited, but not running, for as much time as possible. In an effort to minimize recording effects (and provided consent has been explicitly discussed and granted beforehand and will be rechecked afterwards), it is ideal to avoid pointed references to the equipment or related activity at the actual time of recording. Nevertheless, some means for participants to stop the recording at any point should be available – whether via a remote control device or by communicating with the researcher.

Background data should be recorded in a manner that can be easily linked to the recording. This includes time of recording and various details not captured on the video, for instance nonvisible but co-present others, preceding events which may be of significance, any problems that arose during recording (for instance equipment failure). I have used customized forms to record this information, with additional space to record reflective notes. It is essential to adequately label the recording with information such as participants, date, time and place. It can be useful to take still images and to sketch the layout of the setting and placement of recording equipment.

Contact information is needed to allow subsequent communication with participants, for instance for consultation and feedback on analysis and for distribution of final reports. Personal email addresses are useful in this regard, particularly for clinicians who move often. A 'debriefing' including feedback from participants on the experience of being recorded can provide useful supplementary data. As implied in the foregoing section, more and less formal consultation with participants can augment analysis.

ETHICAL MATTERS IN COLLECTING AND USING VIDEO DATA

Video data is personal data; it reveals a considerable amount of detail about individuals. Analysis and presentation of findings rely upon those details (e.g., facial expression, body movements, and tone of voice) making it impossible to delete them from the research materials (Arafeh and McLaughlin, 2002). This makes it imperative that researchers using video data have a high degree of ethical sensitivity.

What are the ethical risks and dangers of video-based research? Before recording begins, there is a risk of coercing people into participating. Recording procedures, if not carefully designed, can significantly influence the treatment people receive, or may cause people to experience additional anxiety or distress. There is also the ethical dilemma created when the researcher records recognizably bad practice. Finally, there is the issue of confidentiality. During analysis, reporting, and subsequent application of findings (e.g., in teaching), it is possible that individuals accessing the data may personally recognize participants. It is however, worth noting that some level of recognition is inevitable if only by the researcher who recorded and will do the analysis of the data. It is also worth noting that recognition itself may or may not actually be harmful. Harms include negative communications by others about the participants and distress to observers, for instance on recognizing a relative who is now deceased.

Various procedures can minimize these risks and give potential participants adequate opportunity to consider whether they are willing to accept the possibility of these events. Unfortunately, there is no standard consensus guidance on good practices in this area (see Arafeh and McLaughlin, 2002 for a related discussion). This makes it difficult for ethical review bodies to justify their decisions and often leads to lengthy processes and massive variations in permissions granted with regards collection and use of video data. In my own practice, I have sought to minimize such problems by highlighting related guidance, for instance that designed to guide collection of clinical data and videos for teaching (e.g., General Medical Council, 2002; Royal College of General Practitioners, 2008), by noting prior decisions by other review bodies, and by pointing out applied benefits that have accrued from this sort of research.

Procedures for avoiding coercion are the same as those for other research. Information and consent procedures carried out before recording should normally include provision of adequate information (given the particular circumstances) about what sorts of audiences will see the recordings, in what circumstances, and for what purposes. Given the emergent nature of qualitative analysis, and the potential to conduct multiple investigations using the same video data, it may be appropriate to ask participants if they will permit a relatively wide remit of academic analysis of communication and activities rather than restricting consent to a small preselected element. Participants can be given the option to consent to a variety of levels of use of data, and to different levels of access (undisguised video, sound only, transcript only, etc.) by different audiences. At the recording stage, it is usual to give participants the option to halt recording or require subsequent deletion of all or parts of it without having to give reasons. Ideally, the researcher should seek advice about the legal and ethical issues that arise in the unlikely event that problematic or even illegal practice is recorded. After recording, anonymized codes should be used for labelling recordings, and pseudonyms used in transcripts. If consent has been given to show undisguised data to certain audiences, good practice includes explicitly instructing audience members not to refer to participants by name if they recognize them, and not to talk about them in personal or negative terms within or outside the arena. The researcher should remind audiences to treat with respect those who have allowed their conduct to be scrutinized.

DATA ANALYSIS PROCEDURES

Organizing and storing data

All recordings should be comprehensively labelled and catalogued. A spreadsheet for compiling (anonymized) details about participants and recordings can be constructed. Video data need to be moved from the camera's storage media to a form that can be easily accessed via computer. The way this is done will depend on the type of recording technology and computer operating system being used. There are numerous formats for digital video including Mpegs, AVI, and Quicktime files (www.MediaCollege.com and www.transana.org/support provide useful overviews). In order to make good decisions about format, one needs to know which software one will use for playback, analysis and editing. At the time of writing, some software only runs on one form of computer operating system. It is worth extensive investigation and advice seeking in making these choices, as it can be time-consuming and inefficient to have to convert one's whole dataset between different formats.

Given the size of digitized video, researchers regularly store and back up data on external hard drives. Some opt to keep a separate folder or even hard-drive for each recording, and store within the folder the digital video file, and all associated transcripts, still images, notes and recordings from group data sessions, reflective notes and so on. Others keep all recordings in one folder, all notes in another, and so on.

The next step involves watching all, or some selection of the data, and making some form of index or log of the contents of each recording. This will inevitably be selective and partial, and recordings will need to be scrutinized again during subsequent analysis. Nevertheless, this initial stage provides an early grasp on the whole dataset, allowing work towards identifying analytic themes and episodes of interest. Software programs such as ELAN (Max Planck Institute for

Psycholinguistics, 2009) and Transana (Fassnacht and Woods, 2009) can support this process and the subsequent stages of analysis.

At this stage, researchers often commence picking out and collecting together sets of episodes. A balance has to be struck between gaining an initial and broad grasp of the data as a whole, and identifying specific themes and episodes on which to focus.

Analysis software

There are various forms of software that support analysis and presentation of data and findings. Some form of soft- or hardware is needed for transfer of data from camera to computer. In addition, software packages have been designed to support CA analysis, including Transana (Fassnacht and Woods, 2009) and CLAN (MacWhinney), and ELAN (Max Planck Institute, 2009) which is particularly useful for detailed and multimodal analysis of video. Whilst some people prefer to use separate software for playback and transcription, these programs offer the advantage of automatically establishing links between specific locations in the transcript and specific time points in the video. They allow collection of multiple episodes through creating links that 'point' to specific sections of a particular video recording and collecting those links together. This allows one to view some or all of the episodes in a collection in series and repeatedly. Some programmes, including ELAN, offer a systematic structure for complex transcription; some, including Transana include shortcut keys for CA transcription symbols which somewhat ease the task of transcribing. Most analysis packages have no or limited video editing capacity, so editing software is needed in order to take frame grabs (still images) from the video, and to splice small sections of the large video files so they are more easily portable to workshops or presentations. These editing tasks are very easy and can be accomplished with simple software programmes. Blurring video images requires more complex software such as Pinnacle or Adobe Premiere (further information is widely available on the web, including at www.MediaCollege.com).

Choosing initial foci and starting to build collections of episodes

The process of choosing specific foci is perhaps even more difficult than in other qualitative investigations, because the video data is so comprehensive. Foci will be influenced by the researcher's own interests and knowledge and that of others consulted, by the research commissioner's interests, and by the researcher's ability to be alert to unanticipated but relevant elements.

Initial collections often comprise episodes, sometimes called 'noticings' (ten Have, 1999), that strike the researcher as relevant almost immediately. It is common at this stage for the researcher's eye to be caught by unusual, problematic instances or deviant cases (Clayman and Maynard, 1994), and thus for initial collections to mainly comprise of episodes that feature the activities of interest in a problematic or prevalent way. It is very important to follow initial collecting with more systematic searches for all instances – not just problematic ones. Even at the initial collection stage, it is important to ensure that one has a sizeable collection of clear, straightforward cases to focus upon. Another form of initial collection comprises episodes that 'catch the researcher's eye' even though they are not clearly relevant to the key research topic. Gathering these episodes into a separate additional collection helps the researcher avoid becoming distracted, while allowing easy retrieval for later work. Collections at this stage will tend to be unsystematic, but allow the researcher to develop initial analytic descriptions and proposals by analysing a small set of examples in depth. This entails repeated viewing, transcription and consultation with other researchers and with other interested parties. Transcription, considered in the next section, is key for both the analyst's own analysis and for sharing data and analyses with others.

Transcription

Whilst the video forms the actual data, transcripts form a very important tool (Heath and Luff, 1993). Much of the nonvocal conduct will be missed or misconstrued even on repeated watching and will only become apparent and clear through the laborious work of producing a transcript (Heath and Hindmarsh, 2002).

Whilst conversation analysts (except some of those who focus primarily on prosody and phonetics) generally share a single set of conventions for transcribing vocal activity – the Jeffersonian system (Jefferson, 2004) – a broader range of practices exists for transcribing non-vocal elements. Nonvocal conduct presents particular problems because any attempt to describe it in words will make prejudgements about actions before they are actually analyzed (Schegloff, 1984). Therefore many analysts rely heavily upon use of stills from recordings to accompany transcripts and on various devices that can map out directions and timings of actions (Goodwin, 2000), also on multilayered or 'tiered' annotation systems such as that allowed within ELAN (Max Planck Institute, 2008). Figure 19.1 includes a transcript adapted from one created using ELAN.

There are different ways of organizing and structuring transcripts to meet the needs of the particular investigation. Jordan and Henderson's overview (1995) considers various practices for laying out vocal and nonvocal conduct. Heath and Hindmarsh's more recent piece (2002) includes detailed examples of transcripts created and used by analysts for picking apart the vocal, gaze, gestural, and other bodily conduct of participants.

A transcript can never be complete; it will always be selective depending on the analyst's interests and abilities. The level of detail will depend on what is being analyzed and will also differ across episodes, so that those upon which the analyst is relying particularly heavily for building and presenting descriptions and claims will need transcribing in (even) more detail than other episodes. Accurately transcribing activities can take repeated, slow motion, and even

Image from within sequence:

Transcript of vocal activity:

```
Therapist:          Just gonna bring this ba- this t^op leg back with me: Dave.
```

Mutli-tiered transcript of segment from which this image is taken
(exported from ELAN as 'traditional transcript text', opened in MSWord and then adjusted for
presentation here)

```
P position:        Left side lying both legs extended
T position:        Behind patient, near leg kneel on treatment bed, far leg stand on floor

Therapist:         [Just gonna bring this ba- this [t^op leg back with me: [Dave.
T R hand contact:  [P's lower anterior thigh        [off P thigh           [on P thigh
T R hand shape:    [fingers extended flat palm      [abduct fingers        [↓abduction fingers
T L hand contact:  [behind P uppermost iliac crest                         [uppermost P iliac crest
T L hand shape:    [flat                            [extend fingers        [flex fingers round crest
```

Italicised text has been used for all nonvocal actions

Labels for the different annotation 'tiers' are as follows:
Therapist: vocal conduct of therapist
P position: patient's overall position
T position: therapist's overall position
T R hand shape: shape of therapist's right hand
T R hand contact: part of patient's body with which therapist's right hand is in contact
T L hand shape: shape of therapist's left hand
T L hand contact: part of patient's body with which therapist's left hand is in contact

Figure 19.1   Image and ELAN transcript from a collection of episodes where body part is referred to using determiners 'this' or 'that'

frame-by-frame viewing. In terms of actually doing detailed transcribing, my rule of thumb is that one second of transcript takes one minute to transcribe. Finally, when transcripts are used for presenting and reporting the research, most researchers opt to modify them so as to increase their accessibility or clarity.

In-depth analysis of individual cases

Analysis relies on the principles spelled out in the chapter on EMCA (Gill and Halkowski, this volume). Every unique interaction is understood as built from recurrent methodical practices and conventions which people use to produce their own behaviour and understand that of others. Key is the recognition that actions are designed and operate in sequences; specifically that each action systematically takes the one before into account (Maynard and Heritage, 2005) and that the timing of actions is vital for how they are understood. This sequential nature of communication means that analysts can use people's responses to what came before in order to 'ascertain whether and how they were understood' (Clayman and Gill, 2004, p. 598). This is one of the ways by which claims can be derived from the data, rather than from the analyst's interpretations. However, people's responses do not always 'reveal a wholly transparent understanding' (Clayman and Gill, 2004, p. 599) of what came before. Furthermore, some actions, including many nonvocal ones, do not always elicit a response. Analysis can handle this by examining in detail how people *recurrently* deploy a given practice (Clayman and Gill, 2004). This means examining precisely when and where something is done across multiple episodes. In addition, analysis is advanced by searching for and analysing cases where participants observably emphasize, amend, correct, comment on or otherwise overtly deal with the practice or action under investigation. Such occasions can allow the analyst to notice more clearly the regular patterns (Clayman and Maynard, 1994; Heath, 1988) and to augment evidence beyond that which merely relies on the researcher's understanding of a particular gesture or facial expression. Conducting joint data analysis sessions with other analysts or with participants has similar benefits.

The resources the analyst uses can be further unpacked. One key resource is the researcher's own knowledge. For example, a researcher uses her/his social and cultural knowledge of the meaning of particular facial expressions or gestures. Further resources include the specialist forms of knowledge the researcher builds from their observations of the environment under investigation. For example, Greatbatch and colleagues' (1995a and 1995b) knowledge about the organizational functions and the technical elements of the computer systems that the doctors were using enabled them to recognize the significance and functioning of particular key strokes.

In summary, analysis includes identifying episodes of interest in sufficient numbers to identify recurrent features, and the range of types of cases. Analysis then involves watching and rewatching these episodes, transcribing with a focus on the particular features likely to be important to the topic of analysis – entailing further close dissection of the timing, shape (for instance of a gesture), speed or intensity (for instance of a head nod), and so on. It entails careful attention to recurrent patterns across an accumulation of cases, including what happens just before and just after a particular practice. Analysis of the video data entails detailed examination of the temporal features of actions, particularly their juxtapositions with other actions including vocal actions and identifying recurrent and unusual circumstances in which practices and actions are deployed and the consequences of their use. This allows building of claims about the functioning and utility of practices.

Developing collections of cases through systematic searching procedures

In-depth analysis of individual episodes reveals much about what the practices actually are and how they are being used. However, in order to develop claims about practices in terms of what they consist of (and the range and variations in their characteristics) and what their locations and functions are, the researcher must balance in-depth analysis of individual cases with collecting and closely analysing multiple instances. This requires development of substantial collections, produced on the basis of systematic searching through data. Making these substantial collections depends on carefully considering what counts as a 'case'. Collections should include both 'clear' and unusual or 'boundary' cases. It is rather easy to get caught up in struggling to analyze the latter form, and worth remembering that analysis usually progresses better if analysis focuses primarily on straightforward cases.

The appropriate strategy for systematically searching for cases across data sets will vary with the nature of the research question and the volume of data. Although the full corpus may be searched, some form of sampling strategy is needed if the dataset is too large to permit comprehensive analysis of every recording, or if the phenomenon is being examined in such detail that analysis of every instance would not be feasible (often the case if non-vocal activity is being examined in detail). Examples from my work illustrate the sorts of considerations that come into play in terms of selecting which data will be focused upon and searched comprehensively.

An ongoing study of how patients and clinicians talk about the body (Parry, 2007) includes examining how people refer to body parts by using touch and talk at the same time. Amongst other matters, I am interested in how these practices are used in ways that help clinician and patient achieve congruent understandings – or not – about what part of the body is being referred to. An initial collection of instances was made during the course of another study; therefore, although it contained some noticeable and apparently interesting cases, it was not a systematic collection. The full video data collection comprised 46 complete treatment sessions, approximately 35 hours of data. Searching through the whole collection for every instance of touching alongside body part reference would have been too time-consuming within the constraints of the project. Therefore, so as to ensure analysis across a spread of the full data and so as to avoid certain biases in my selection (for instance towards sessions I prejudged as interesting or special in some way), a random sampling strategy was adopted. The research primarily focused upon clinicians' practices; therefore, the sample was stratified so as to ensure that one session with each of the 19 therapist participants was included. (Figures 19.1 and 19.2 show images and transcripts from this study.) Other sampling strategies are possible. For instance, I used purposive sampling within a study of how clinicians made their clinical reasoning available to patients. Prior research findings, field observations, initial viewing of the complete dataset, and

T: Just gonna bring this ba- this t^op leg back with me: Dave.

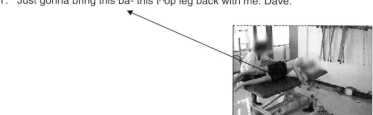

Figure 19.2   Example of a still image placed close to a transcript of the vocal action as might be used in a published report

analysis of the initial collection of episodes all suggested that clinicians' and patients' communication about clinical reasons was likely to have some relations to level of experience of both patient and therapist and to the sorts of impairment the patient was experiencing. In addition, initial watching and analysis had shown that the phenomenon under investigation was not neatly confined to one part of each consultation/treatment session, and that it sometimes formed a recurrent and developing topic over the course of sessions which lasted between 30 minutes and an hour. Therefore, because of the features and questions emerging from initial analysis, I selected for detailed analysis a number of full sessions that included clinician participants at a variety of levels of vocational experience and patient participants with different forms of impairments at different stages of rehabilitation.

Searches of other datasets (including extracts available in academic publications) can also augment analysis and allow claims making about the pervasiveness of identified practices, and about whether and how they seem to be adapted for the particular context under study.

Presenting data and analysis

It can be laborious for both writer and reader to deal with detailed textual descriptions of the many dimensions and actions examined in analysis. As in all qualitative research, the writer faces challenging choices in deciding how much detail to provide. Textual descriptions can be enlivened and their volume reduced by including visual illustrations.

Making data available in as 'raw' a state as possible allows for clear tying of analytic claims to evidence and allows others to scrutinize and assess the validity of analyses. In keeping with this, some authors have made extracts of video data available online. For example, see http://www.york.ac.uk/depts/soci/about/Merran_hm_data.mpg which makes available the video data analyzed in Toerien and Kitzinger (2007). Because of the ethical complications of providing open access to video data that involve people providing and undergoing health care, authors of published reports usually use still video-images disguised to varying degrees (depending on the level of consent permitted by participants) alongside transcripts which may or may not include an attempt to depict nonvocal communication. Software programmes can be used to disguise images, e.g., Pixia which is freeware, and Adobe Photoshop, which has additional capabilities. There are various ways of laying out transcripts and images in published research reports. Perhaps the simplest way is to place a still image from the video close to a transcript of the vocal action, and to use an arrow to indicate the point in the talk at which the still was taken. Figure 19.2 is one example, many others can be seen in: Heath, 1986, 2002; Goodwin, 2000; Robinson and Stivers, 2001; Heath and Hindmarsh, 2002; and Beach, 2005.

CURRENT AND FUTURE CHALLENGES AND DEVELOPMENTS VIDEO-BASED EMCA IN HEALTHCARE

Challenges discussed below include: (1) the laborious nature of this form of work, including the process of transcribing and in particular the long periods of concentrated observation of the video data required to find and transcribe both vocal and nonvocal phenomena, (2) the need to make appropriate selections of data on which to focus analysis, and (3) the ethical problems associated with this form of research and the presentation of findings.

Another challenge, perhaps the most important one, concerns the evidence for the utility of this kind of research in health-related practice and policy. Why should practitioners, policy makers, and funding bodies support this form of work? Much existing work has focussed on fundamental sociological concerns rather than directly health-related concerns, raising problems in terms of the accessibility of this work to those with more applied health interests. Even when a more overt focus on health-related matters has been taken, products of the research are not always accessible to health-related users of research. The knowledge and understandings yielded by video-based analyses are incremental and fine-grained – they elucidate properties, patterns, and characteristics of human conduct one small step at a time. Despite the attention many researchers pay to *potential* applications, there is currently very little *empirical evidence* of effects upon practice and policy. All this can make the work rather 'unappetizing' to funders and users with applied health interests. In practical terms, these matters make for challenges in justifying the case for expenditure upon this sort of research by funders whose interests lie in practical applications and impacts of research upon practice and policy.

However, there are ways to make this case. The most obvious application of research on communication entails designing and evaluating communication training interventions based upon findings of the research. Importantly, the effectiveness of communication training is greatest where it is underpinned by high-quality research evidence about the form and functioning of specific practices (Hulsman et al., 1999; Parry, 2008), and as I have argued in this chapter, video-based EMCA can produce such high-quality evidence. Basic communication research can also underpin design of valid measurement tools and scales. Conversation analysis is increasingly being used to underpin health care-relevant training interventions and quantitative studies of health care communication behaviours. These applied studies have focused by and large on verbal practices. This may reflect the earlier stage of development of research on nonvocal practices, although it may also relate to the potential difficulties of influencing nonvocal elements of conduct, given how tacit and context-fitted these are.

Studies that have applied conversation analytic findings about *vocal* practices raise issues and methodological challenges that are equally relevant to potential applications developed from findings about *nonvocal* and *multimodal* practices. For this reason, I briefly describe some of these existing applied studies, then discuss some pertinent methodological issues.

One important study used a quantitative evaluation of a communication training intervention for primary care physicians that was derived from conversation analytic findings (Heritage et al., 2007). Doctors underwent brief training to use a particular question format when asking patients about their concerns. The intervention proved effective in increasing patients' expression of their concerns within the consultation. Training interventions for various health care professionals and recipients have also been described and evaluated in qualitative case studies (Booth and Perkins, 1999; Tapsell, 2000; Kitzinger and Kitzinger, 2007). Other applied studies have involved examining statistical associations of particular communication practices identified via CA with other variables: Robinson and Heritage (2006) examined association between doctors' opening questions and patient-reported satisfaction; Stivers and Majid (2007) examined consultations between doctors and child patients attending with their parents and found that parents' ethnic origins and education were associated with how and whether doctors addressed questions to the children.

Several of these studies have relied on quantitative measurements. Such quantification is underpinned by the view amongst some proponents of CA that CA allows interactional phenomena to be described in ways that can form a rigorous basis for well-defined categories. These categories can then be used to quantify aspects of conduct (see Heritage, 2005, p. 137 and also Clayman and Gill, 2004, p. 592). Mainstream funders and consumers of health-related research are likely to be more familiar with quantitative than qualitative studies and to place them higher up the 'evidence hierarchy'. The potential for conversation analytic work to inform subsequent quantitative studies can thus form one argument for conducting and funding conversation analytic examinations of vocal and non vocal aspects of health care,

However, one should be aware that other proponents of CA have expressed major concerns about quantification of communication conduct, a debate initially laid out by Schegloff some years ago (1993). This side of the debate sees quantification as a dangerous direction for analysis to pursue; arguing that it ignores fundamental tenets of the approach, and is inconsistent with empirically demonstrated properties of people's conduct and communication. These properties include the way that our communicative actions and the sense we make of them are very much tied up with local sequential and individual contextual matters. The 'strong' version of this argument holds that quantification efforts are meaningless. There are also concerns that quantification can lead to conflation of quantity with quality, which would be to oversimplify the way communication works. Those conducting video-based EMCA or applying its findings should engage with these concerns so as to be able to adequately design and defend analytic strategies that entail quantification.

Clearly, much work remains for those who wish to examine whether and how conversation analytic investigations and findings can influence practice and policy. The task is even larger for those who use video and hence include nonvocal elements of conduct. Fortunately, the field is developing in terms of shared and systematic procedures for data collection and analysis, fascinating research outputs, and its potential for producing interventions and tools with obvious applications to health-related research, practice and policy.

NOTE

1 In referring to studies in this field, I describe how they identify and examine the functioning of 'interactional practices', rather than 'communication skills' for instance. The term 'practices' emphasizes the way that these are *practical methodical procedures* that people recurrently use and employ in particular circumstances in the course of achieving particular things. The term 'interactional' emphasizes the collaborative nature of our communication with one another, and the way that it entails not merely passing on and receiving information, but rather involves *jointly* doing and achieving things – such as building trust, coming to a diagnosis, or teaching and learning a correct movement pattern.

REFERENCES

Arafeh, S. and McLaughlin, M. (2002) *Legal and Ethical Issues in the Use of Video in Education Research.* Working Paper Series National Center for Education Statistics (ed.). Washington DC: Educational Statistics Services Institute.

Beach, W. (2005) 'Disclosing and Responding to Cancer "Fears" During Oncology Interviews', *Social Science and Medicine*, 60: 893–910.

Birdwhistell, R. (1970) *Kinesics in Context: Essays on Body Motion Communication.* Philadelphia: University of Pennsylvania Press.

Booth, S. and Perkins, L. (1999) 'The Use of Conversation Analysis to Guide Individualized Advice to Carers and Evaluate Change in Aphasia: A Case Study'. *Aphasiology*, 13(4): 283–303.

Bottorff, J.L. (1991) 'Using Videotaped Recordings in Qualitative Research'. In J.M. Morse (ed.) *Critical Issues in Qualitative Research Methods.* Thousand Oaks, CA: Sage.

Boyd, E., and Heritage, J. (2006) 'Taking the Patient's Medical History: Questioning During Comprehensive History Taking'. In J. Heritage and D. Maynard (eds.) *Communication in Medical Care: Interactions Between Primary Care Physicians and Patients* (pp. 151–84). Cambridge: Cambridge University Press.

Burkitt Wright, E., Holcombe, C., and Salmon, P. (2004) 'Doctors' Communication of Trust, Care, and Respect in Breast Cancer: Qualitative Study', *BMJ,* 328: 864–9.

CAIR, Centre for Applied Interaction Research, http://www.ucl.ac.uk/cair

Caldwell, A. and Atwal, A. (2005) 'Non-Participant Observation: Using Video Tapes to Collect Data in Nursing Research', *Nurse Researcher*, 2: 42–52.

Clayman, S. and Maynard, D. (1994) 'Ethnomethodology and Conversation Analysis'. In P. ten Have and G. Psathas (eds.) *Situated Order: Studies in the Social Organization of Talk and Embodied Activities* (pp. 1–30). Washington DC: University Press of America.

Clayman, S.E. and Gill, V.T. (2004) 'Conversation Analysis'. In M. Hardy and A. Bryman (eds) *Handbook of Data Analysis*. Beverly Hills, CA: Sage.

Coleman, T. (2000) 'Using Video-Recorded Consultations for Research in Primary Care: Advantages and Limitations', *Family Practice*, 17: 422–7.

Collins, S. (2005) 'Communicating for a Clinical Purpose: Strategy in Interaction in Healthcare Consultations', *Communication and Medicine*, 2(2): 111–22.

Collins, S. (2005) 'Explanations in Consultations: The Combined Effectiveness of Doctors' and Nurses' Communication with Patients', *Medical Education,* 39: 785–96.

Collins, S., Watt, I., Drew, P., Local, J., and Cullum, N. (2003) 'Effective Consultations with Patients: A Comparative Multidisciplinary Study. Full Report of Research Activities and Results'. Report to the Economic and Social Research Council UK. Available via search of repository at: http://www.esrcsocietytoday.ac.uk/ESRCInfoCentre

Curley, C.A. (1998) 'Teaching the Body to Make Tea within Social Interaction', *Issues in Applied Linguistics,* 9(2): 151–78.

ETHNO discussion list, CIOS, Communication Institute of Online Scholarship, http://www.cios.org/www/forums.htm

Fassnacht, C. and Woods, D. (2009) Transana 2.12 [Computer software]. Madison WI: The Board of Regents of the University of Wisconsin System. http://www.transana.org

Frankel, R.M. (1993) 'The Laying on of Hands: Aspects of the Organization of Gaze, Touch, and Talk in a Medical Encounter'. In A.D. Todd and S. Fisher (eds) *The Social Organization of Doctor–Patient Communication* (2nd Edition) (pp. 71–105). New Jersey: Ablex Publishing Corporation.

The General Medical Council (2002) 'Making and Using Visual and Audio Recordings of Patients', http://www.gmc-uk.org/guidance/current/library/making_audiovisual.asp

Gill, V.T. and Maynard, D. (2006) 'Patients' Explanations for Health Problems and Physicians' Responsiveness in the Medical Interview'. In J. Heritage and D. Maynard (eds) *Practising Medicine: Talk and Action in Primary Care Encounters* (pp. 115–50). Cambridge: Cambridge University Press.

Goffman, E. (1983) 'The Interaction Order', *American Sociological Review*, 48: 1–17.

Goodwin, C. (1979) 'The Interactive Construction of a Sentence in Natural Conversation'. In G. Psathas (ed.) *Everyday Language: Studies in Ethnomethodology* (pp. 97–121). New York: Irvington.

Goodwin, C. (1994) 'Professional Vision', *American Anthropologist*, 96(3): 606–33.

Goodwin, C. (2000) 'Action and Embodiment Within Situated Human Interaction', *Journal of Pragmatics*, 32: 1489–522.

Greatbatch, D. (2005) 'Prescriptions and Prescribing: Coordinating Talk and Text-Based Activities'. In J. Heritage and D. Maynard (eds) *Communication in Medical Care: Interaction Between Primary Care Physicians and Patients* (pp. 313–39). Cambridge: Cambridge University Press.

Greatbatch, D., Heath, C., Campion, P., and Luff, P. (1995a) 'How Do Desk-Top Computers Affect the Doctor–Patient Interaction?' *Family Practice*, 12(1): 32–6.

Greatbatch, D., Heath, C., Luff, P., and Campion, P. (1995b) 'Conversation Analysis: Human-Computer Interaction and the General Practice Consultation'. In Monk, A.F. and Gilbert, G.N. (eds) *Perspectives on HCI, Diverse Approaches*. London: Academic Press.

Halkowski, T. (2006) 'Realizing the Illness: Patients' Narratives of Symptom Discovery'. In J. Heritage and D. Maynard (eds) *Communication in Medical Care: Interaction Between Primary Care Physicians and Patients*. Cambridge: Cambridge University Press.

ten Have, P. (1999) *Doing Conversation Analysis: A Practical Guide.* London: Sage.

ten Have, P. (2004) *Understanding Qualitative Research and Ethnomethodology.* London: Sage.

Heath, C. (1986) *Body Movement and Speech in Medical Interaction.* Cambridge: Cambridge University Press.

Heath, C. (1988) 'Embarrassment and Interactional Organization'. In P. Drew and A. Wootton (eds) *Erving Goffman – Exploring the Interaction Order* (pp. 136–60). Cambridge: Polity Press.

Heath, C. (1989) 'Pain Talk: The Expression of Suffering in the Medical Consultation', *Social Psychology Quarterly,* 52(2): 113–25.

Heath, C. (1992) 'Gesture's Discrete Tasks: Multiple Relevancies in Visual Conduct and in the Contextualization of Language'. In P. Auer and A. DiLuzio (eds) *The Contextualization of Language* (pp. 101–27). Amsterdam: John Benjamins.

Heath, C. (2002) 'Demonstrative Suffering: The Gestural (re)Embodiment of Symptoms', *Journal of Communication,* 52(3): 597–616.

Heath, C. and Hindmarsh, J. (2002) 'Analysing Interaction: Video, Ethnography and Situated Conduct'. In T. May (ed.) *Qualitative Research in Action* (pp. 99–121). London: Sage.

Heath, C., and Luff, P. (1993) 'Explicating Face-To-Face Interaction'. In N. Gilbert (ed.) *Researching Social Life* (pp. 306–26). London: Sage.

Heath, C., Luff, P., and Svensson, M. (2007) 'Video and Qualitative Research: Analysing Medical Practice and Interaction', *Medical Education,* 41: 109–16.

Heritage, J. (2005) 'Conversation Analysis and Institutional Talk'. In K. Fitch and R. Sanders (eds), *Handbook of Language and Social Interaction.* Mahwah, NJ: Lawrence Erlbaum.

Heritage, J., Robinson, J., Elliott, M., Beckett, M., and Wilkes, M. (2007) 'Reducing Patients' Unmet Concerns in Primary Care: The Difference One Word Can Make', *Journal of General Internal Medicine,* 22(10): 1429–33.

Hindmarsh, J. and Pilnick, A. (2005) 'Knowing Bodies: Embodiment, Teamwork and Anaesthetic Practice', *Organization Studies,* 28(9): 1395–416.

Hulsman, R.I., Ros, W., Winnubst, J., and Bensing, J.M. (1999) 'Teaching Clinical Experienced Physicians Communication Skills. A Review of Evaluation Studies', *Medical Education,* 33: 655–68.

Jefferson, G. (2004) 'Glossary of Transcript Symbols with an Introduction'. In G.H. Lerner (ed.) *Conversation Analysis: Studies from the First Generation* (pp. 13–31). Amsterdam: John Benjamins Publishing Company.

Jensen, G.M., Shepard, K.F., Gwyer, J., and Hack, L.H. (1992) 'Attribute Dimensions that Distinguish Master and Novice Physical Therapy Clinicians in Orthopedic Settings', *Physical Therapy,* 72(10): 711–22.

Jones, S. and LeBaron, C. (2002) 'Research on the Relationship Between Verbal and Nonverbal Communication: Emerging Integrations', *Journal of Communication,* 52(3): 499–521.

Jordan, B. and Henderson, A. (1995) 'Interaction Analysis: Foundations and Practice', *The Journal of the Learning Sciences,* 4(1): 39–103.

Kendon, A. (1977) *Studies in the Behavior of Face-to-Face Interaction.* Lisse: Peter De Ridder Press.

Kendon, A. (1985) 'Some Uses of Gesture'. In D. Tannen and M. Saville-Troike (eds), *Perspectives on Silence* (pp. 215–234). Norwood, New Jersey: Ablex.

Kitzinger, C. and Kitzinger, S. (2007) 'Birth Trauma: Talking with Women and the Value of Conversation Analysis', *British Journal of Midwifery,* 15(5): 256–64.

Koschmann, T., LeBaron, C., Goodwin, C., Zemel, A., and Dunnington, G. (2007) 'Formulating the Triangle of Doom' *Gesture,* 7(1): 97–122.

Labov, W. (1972) *Language in the Inner City: Studies in the Black English Vernacular.* Philadelphia: University of Pennsylvania Press.

Languse Internet Forum, http://www.list.hum.aau.dk/mailman/listinfo/languse

Lomax, H. and Casey, N. (1998) 'Recording Social Life: Reflexivity and Video Methodology'. *Sociological Research Online,* 3(2). Available at: http://www.socresonline.org.uk/3/2/1.html

MacWhinney, B. The CHILDES Project: Software programmes, http://childes.psy.cmu.edu/clan/

Martin, C. (2004) *From Other to Self. Learning as Interactional Change.* PhD dissertation. Uppsala Universitet, Uppsala.

Max Planck Institute for Psycholinguistics T.G. (2009) *ELAN, Extended Linguistic Annotator.* Available at: http://www.lat-mpi.eu/tools/elan

Maynard, D., and Heritage, J. (2005) Conversation Analysis, Doctor–Patient Communication and Medical Communication, *Medical Education,* 39, 428–35.

MediaCollege.com, http://www.mediacollege.com

Mondada, L. (2003) 'Working with Video: How Surgeons Produce Video Records of Their Actions' *Visual Studies,* 18(1): 58–73.

Murphy, E. and Dingwall, R. (2003) *Qualitative Methods and Health Policy Research* Chapter 5. New York: Aldine dr Gruyter.

Nishizaka, A. (2007) 'Hand Touching Hand: Referential Practice at a Japanese Midwife House', *Human Studies,* 30: 199–217.

Parry, R.H. (2004) 'Communication During Goal Setting in Physiotherapy Treatment Sessions', *Clinical Rehabilitation,* 18(9): 668–82.

Parry, R.H. (2007) 'Indexing Embodiment: When is 'Your' Arm 'the' Arm?'. Paper Presented at the International Pragmatics Association 10th Conference, Goteborg (abstract incorrectly printed in the abstracts book, an extended abstract available from the author).

Parry R.H. (2008) 'Are Interventions to Enhance Communication Performance in Allied Health Professionals Effective, and How Should They be Delivered? Direct and Indirect Evidence', *Patient Education and Counseling,* 73(2): 186–95.

Peräkylä, A. (1997) 'Reliability and Validity in Research Based on Tapes and Transcripts'. In D. Silverman (ed.) *Qualitative Research: Theory, Methods and Practices* (pp. 201–19). London: Sage.

Peräkylä, A. and Vehviläinen, S. (2003) 'Conversation Analysis and the Professional Stocks of Interactional Knowledge', *Discourse Studies,* 14(6): 727–50.

Picker Institute Europe (2003) Improving Patients' Experience: Sharing Good Practice: Respect, Privacy and Dignity. Newsletter, http://www.pickereurope.org/Filestore/News/resp_priv_dign_newsletter_feb03.pdf

Pilnick, A. and Dingwall, R. (2007) 'On the Remarkable Persistence of Asymmetry in Doctor/Patient Interaction', Paper given at the *American Sociological Association Conference.* New York.

Pomerantz, A. (2005) 'Using Participants' Video Stimulated Comments to Complement Analyses of Interactional Practices'. In H. te Molder and J. Potter (eds) *Conversation and Cognition* (pp. 93–113). Cambridge: Cambridge University Press.

Robinson, J. and Heritage, J. (2006) 'Physicians' Opening Questions and Patients' Satisfaction', *Patient Education and Counseling,* 60(3): 279–85.

Robinson, J. and Stivers, T. (2001) 'Achieving Activity Transitions in Physician-Patient Encounters from History Taking to Physical Examination', *Human Communication Research,* 27(2): 253–98.

Royal College of General Practitioners (2008) 'Video Assessment of Consulting Skills in 2008: Workbook and Instructions'. http://www.rcgp.org.uk/gp_training/mrcgp/video_workbook.aspx

Sacks, H. and Jefferson, G. (1992) *Lectures on Conversation.* Oxford: Blackwell.

Schegloff, E. (1984) 'On Some Gestures' Relation to Talk'. In J. Atkinson and J. Heritage (eds) *Structures of Social Action: Studies in Conversational Analysis* (pp. 266–96). Cambridge: Cambridge University Press.

Schegloff, E.A. (1993) 'Reflections on Quantification in the Study of Conversation', *Research on Language and Social Interaction,* 26(1): 99–128.

Schegloff, E.A. (1997) 'Whose Text? Whose Context?', *Discourse and Society,* 8(2): 165–87.

Speer, S. and Hutchby, I. (2003) 'From Ethics to Analytics: Aspects of Participants' Orientations to the Presence and Relevance of Recording Technologies', *Sociology,* 37(2): 315–37.

Stewart, M. (1992) 'Approaches to Audiotape and Videotape Analysis: Interpreting the Interactions Between Patients and Physicians'. In B. Crabtree and W. Miller (eds) *Doing Qualitative Research.* Newbury Park: Sage.

Stivers, T. (2005) 'Non-Antibiotic Treatment Recommendations: Delivery Formats and Implications for Patient Resistance', *Social Science and Medicine*, 60: 949–64.

Stivers, T. and Majid, A. (2007) 'Questioning Children: Interactional Evidence of Implicit Bias in Medical Interviews', *Social Psychology Quarterly,* 70(4): 424–41.

Stivers, T. and Sidnell, J. (2005) 'Introduction: Multimodal Interaction', *Semiotica,*156(1) (Special Issue on Multimodal Interaction): 1–21.

Tapsell, L. (2000) 'Using Applied Conversation Analysis to Teach Novice Dieticians History Taking Skills', *Human Studies*, 23: 281–307.

Toerien, M. and Kitzinger, C. (2007) 'Emotional Labour in Action: Navigating Multiple Involvements in the Beauty Salon', *Sociology*, 41: 645–62.

20

Practising Discourse Analysis in Healthcare Settings

Srikant Sarangi

INTRODUCTION

This chapter offers a practically relevant – albeit critical and reflexive – introduction to the methodological tradition generally known as discourse analysis. After a brief overview of the notion of discourse and the three constituent steps – data collection, data transcription and data categorization – I introduce and illustrate theme-oriented discourse analysis, which regards discourse as activity and as account. I conclude by calling attention to the many ways the findings of discourse analysis have been, and can be, used.

THE CIRCUMFERENCE OF DISCOURSE

What we understand by the term 'discourse' has immediate implications for what is collected as 'discourse data' and for the analytical framework adopted for interpreting these data. As a concept, 'discourse' crosses different disciplinary boundaries – e.g., history, literature, philosophy, sociology, psychology, anthropology – although linguistics is commonly regarded as its home turf. As early as 1935, J.R. Firth anticipated how conversation, in the sense of discourse, would become central to linguistic inquiry:

> Conversation is much more of a roughly prescribed ritual than most people think. Once someone speaks to you, you are in a relatively determined context and you are not

> free just to say what you please. We are born individuals. But to satisfy our needs we have to become social persons ... it is [in] the study of conversation ... that we shall find the key to a better understanding of what language really is and how it works (cited in Stubbs, 1993:19).

Firth's formulation suggests that there are interactional and activity-specific constraints to language use, e.g., an answer follows a question. No communicative activity, however, is entirely formulaic and predictable. In an early attempt, Mitchell (1957) studied the activity of buying and selling and identified five distinctive stages: (i) salutation; (ii) enquiry as to the object of sale; (iii) investigation of the object of sale; (iv) bargaining; and (v) conclusion. He was, however, quick to acknowledge that these stages were flexible in terms of sequential ordering and that none of the stages was obligatory in a given encounter.

From within a linguistic perspective, 'discourse' is simply defined as anything beyond the sentence/utterance, emphasizing coherence and patterned alignment. The following is a more inclusive definition:

> Discourse is a level or component of language use, related to but distinct from grammar. It can be oral or written and can be approached in textual or sociocultural or sociointeractional terms. And it can be brief like a greeting and thus smaller than a single sentence or lengthy like a novel or narration of personal experience (Sherzer, 1987:296).

In a nutshell, human actions and practices are constituted in discourse. In healthcare encounters, for instance, activities such as symptoms presentation, history taking, delivery of diagnosis, negotiation of treatment and referral are accomplished through language, although they are not reducible to language use or interaction as such. The notion of discourse can be extended to include the semiotic modes of representation – the visual, the gestural, the spatial and so on – with distinctive 'grammars' that lend themselves to differently oriented traditions of discourse analysis.

COLLECTION OF DISCOURSE DATA: MINIMIZING OBSERVER'S AND PARTICIPANT'S PARADOXES

The first stage in discourse analysis is the collection of data with one's analytic priority in mind. In the healthcare setting, textual material (e.g., medicine labels, patient leaflets, patient records, referral letters, newspaper reports on health scare and health information websites) are all worthwhile data sources that can be collected as a corpus following designated sampling procedures (e.g., across timelines, across cultures and across conditions). Two other types of data are: (i) recordings of naturally occurring professional–client or interprofessional encounters, and (ii) dyadic or focus group research interviews. Invariably research ethics committees raise concerns about audio/video recording of clinic encounters on the grounds that this would constitute intervention and can affect the process and outcome of the encounter. It is, however, conceivable that given the high stakes involved in a clinic setting, participants are very likely to overcome the presence of a recorder or observer and continue to perform naturally. Likewise, in research interviews, the role-identity of the researcher can introduce participation bias but this may not last for the entire course of the encounter. The illness account a patient produces in an interview will be influenced by many other factors, including their personal biographies, current health status and treatment/care provision. From the perspective of research ethics, if a patient is undergoing treatment, the timing of the interview may influence, positively or negatively, the trajectory of service delivery.

Whether spoken data is collected in audio/video format or via participant observation, the mediating role of the researcher and/or the recording equipment is an issue. What is called 'observer's paradox' (Labov, 1972) refers to how the act of observation itself can influence the data being gathered – the so-called Hawthorne effect. The practical question then concerns how the recording equipment and/or the human observer are positioned/introduced in the research setting to minimize bias.

The notion of 'participant's paradox' (Sarangi, 2002; 2007) refers to the activity of participants observing the observer against routine expectations. The researcher–observer adopting a 'fly-on-the-wall' stance may occasion discomfort for co-present participants. In clinics, professionals and patients are used to having third-party observers, so the presence of the researcher–observer is less of an issue if the latter can blend within the setting. In order to minimize the observer's participant effect, one option is to record the clinic activity without the observer being present. This may amount to the researcher missing the context-specific details, but there is always the opportunity for the researcher to socialize into the clinic activity prior to the recording, given the ritualized character of clinical encounters.[1]

Some discourse analysts believe that video data is more authentic and robust than audio data. This is also echoed by professional practitioners who expect discourse analysis to include paralinguistic and nonverbal aspects of communication. It is, however, worth noting that if our aim is to capture participants' mutual orientations to each other, the video camera introduces an inevitable bias. Video data, more than audio data, raise issues about anonymity and confidentiality. Routinely, the faces of participants can be protected from the camera or are consequently blocked, which rules out the possibility of undertaking any micro-analysis of facial expressions, gaze etc. It is no doubt helpful to interpret the interaction with the aid of video data where possible. When it comes to data sharing and dissemination, both video and audio data need to be anonymized suitably with names of individuals and locations suppressed. Sometimes it may be necessary to withhold the disease condition for purposes of confidentiality, although this may distort data interpretation.

REPRESENTING RECORDED DATA: THE PRAGMATICS OF TRANSCRIPTION

The second stage is the preparation of recorded data for analysis. This is known as transcription, which is based on multiple listenings/viewings and remains a time-costly activity. An hour of recording could take up to 6–12 hours or longer to transcribe, depending on the level of detail, which needs to align with the research questions. Transcription has to be fit for purpose rather than just an application of a standard set of conventions. It is necessary to balance issues of authenticity with issues of intelligibility and representation. The problems become compounded when transcribing video data. The level of transcription – which ultimately means the level of context to be accounted for – can lead to differential interpretation of the data. It is an inescapable fact that transcription is theoretically motivated interpretation (Ochs, 1979; Mishler, 1986). Cicourel (1992) provides a paradigm case of staging different levels of information in data presentation and how this practice interpenetrates data interpretation.

Researchers who work with data recorded in a language other than their own and/or wish to reach an audience beyond their linguistic community need to address the issue of translation alongside transcription. Where differences between source and target languages are marked, analytic points need to be made via the source data. Similarly, there are risks and benefits associated with conducting research interviews in a source language and then translating into the target language as opposed to using the target language as the medium of interaction which may constrain the participants.

When presenting transcripts for analysis, researchers choose to number the lines or turns for ease of cross-referencing vis-à-vis analytic commentaries. Speaking turn is usually taken as the unit of transcription, but what constitutes a turn can be variable. A turn can be constituted in silence or in a lengthy monologue. This is why it is useful to make a distinction between turn frequency and turn duration, as I shall illustrate later.

PRACTISING CATEGORIZATION: BEYOND CODING

The core activity in discourse analysis is categorization of actions, intentions, characters, events, etc. The first blind spot concerns equating categorization with coding. Coding-based interaction analysis dates back to Bales (1950), which has been adapted for analysing medical consultations (Byrne and Long, 1976; see also Davis, 1968; Korsch and Negrete, 1972). The Roter Interaction Analysis System (RIAS), which offers a taxonomy of speech action in healthcare provider-patient encounters, is a relatively recent case in point (Roter and Hall, 1992; Roter, 2001). The coding of data is motivated by a desire to quantify the interaction process in a systematic, rigorous way in order to provide outcome measures. This analytic activity, however, overlooks the fact that coding is inevitably interpretive; that interaction is a dynamic, cumulative activity which defies any one-to-one correspondence between linguistic/semiotic form and function. For instance, the coding of questions in interactional settings is problematic: repetitions, statements with rising intonation and backchannels can all function as questions in a given interaction. If we consider rhetorical questions, these take the interrogative form but function as assertions. Meaning in interaction is always negotiated sequentially and simultaneously in an ongoing basis (see Mishler [1986] on implicit assumptions made about the relationship between language and meaning). Many of the RIAS codes, in this respect, are quasi-social action labels, reducing the meaning of conversational data to simplistic, preset categories.

Beyond the coding-based healthcare studies, very broadly, one can identify two further strands of empirically grounded qualitative studies: one strand informed by conversation analysis with its focus on sequential organization of talk (e.g., Heath, 1986, Drew and Heritage, 1992, Heritage and Maynard, 2006, Stivers, 2007); the other strand is informed by discourse analysis which draws insights from a number of analytical frameworks such as pragmatics, sociolinguistics, and microsociology (e.g., Wadsworth and Robinson, 1976; Fisher and Todd, 1983; Atkinson, 1995; Ainsworth-Vaughn, 1998; Sarangi and Roberts, 1999; Gwyn, 2002; Gotti and Salagar-Meyer, 2006; Iedema, 2007). Because of space constraints, it is not possible to list the many studies that have contributed to our understanding of healthcare encounters (for an overview, see Candlin and Candlin, 2003; Sarangi, 2004). The following are selected book-length publications that use qualitative discourse analysis in healthcare settings:

1   Mishler (1984) characterizes clinical encounters as a tension between the voice of medicine and the voice of the lifeworld. This tension is manifested at the interactional level and can influence health outcomes.
2   Silverman (1987) and Atkinson (1995), working in settings such as paediatric cardiology and haematology respectively, have shown that the tension between the two voices is quite nuanced and the different voices are strategically drawn upon by healthcare professionals and patients for specific purposes.
3   Waitzkin (1991) demonstrates convincingly that the medical and the social are inextricably linked, requiring a more social contextual approach to interpreting medical encounters both by healthcare practitioners and analysts.
4   West (1984) examines the uneven distribution of questions across doctors and patients, which is suggestive of a power imbalance with important consequences for the clinical encounter.

There are also studies that go beyond mainstream doctor-patient consultation (e.g., Morris and Chenail, 1995). Fisher (1995) examines the different communicative styles of doctors and nurses and the extent to which their different styles may foreground or background psychosocial dimensions of patients' lives and thus influence the consultation process and outcome. Ribeiro (1994) investigates the psychiatric setting by focusing on frames and topic coherence vis-à-vis joint construction of meaning. Studies in psychotherapy, especially those by Labov and Fanshel (1977) and Ferrara (1994), are very rich in interactional detail, exploring, respectively, the role of specific interactional features such as cueing of shared knowledge and patterns of repetition following interpretive summaries. Another domain is counselling where information-giving and advice-giving are delicately managed (Peräkylä, 1995; Silverman, 1997).

TOWARDS A THEME-ORIENTED DISCOURSE ANALYSIS

In what follows, I focus on two discourse data settings: encounters between healthcare professionals and clients, and research interviews. Both these communicative settings operate with context-specific constraints and we can generally conceptualize these in terms of 'discourse as activity' and 'discourse as account'.

DISCOURSE AS ACTIVITY AND AS ACCOUNT

Inspired by Wittgenstein's notion of 'language games', Levinson (1979 [1992:69]) proposes the notion of 'activity type' to characterize the goal-defined nature of speech events such as teaching and job interviews where participants are faced with constraints created by the setting and by definitions of 'allowable contributions'. Such activity-specific constraints, while being flexible, 'help to determine how what one says will be "taken" – that is, what kinds of inferences will be made from what is said'. Levinson offers an explanatory framework that takes into account speaker intentionality (see Gumperz, 1982 on contextualization cues and conversational inferencing) as well as participant framework, frames and footing (Goffman, 1981).

Healthcare encounters, with encompassing variations across sites, certainly count as activity types where constraints on contributions imply a corresponding set of *inferential schemata*. For instance, the doctor's opening question 'How are you?' is routinely understood by patients as a request for a statement about their current health status rather than as a ritual greeting. This does not mean that in some circumstances the doctor's 'How are you?' cannot be interpreted otherwise, i.e., as a formulaic greeting, depending on participants' role-relationships and locally available social norms.

In professional-client encounters and research interviews, social actions and social selves are interactionally accomplished. The notion of account, i.e., how we become 'accountable' to others for our actions/behaviours (Garfinkel, 1956), is central here. Accounts are 'descriptions', 'ordinary explanations' or 'self-reports' about everyday activities (Antaki, 1988). Accounts can also be viewed as 'the use of language to interactionally construct preferred meanings for problematic events' (Buttny, 1993:21). Drawing upon Goffman's (1959) notion of self-presentation, Scott and Lyman (1968:46) see an account as 'a linguistic device employed whenever an action is subjected to evaluative inquiry' – 'a statement made by a social actor to explain unanticipated or untoward behaviour'.

They (1968:47) suggest a distinction between *excuses* ('one admits that the act in question is bad, wrong, or inappropriate but denies full responsibility') and *justifications* ('one accepts responsibility for the act in question, but denies the pejorative quality associated with it'). Beyond individual actions, accounts reflect culturally embedded normative explanations. Thus, accounts are always oriented towards the other and have a moral underpinning. Such a perspective is particularly relevant in healthcare encounters where patients describe their symptoms, and outside the clinical setting where people make sense of their illness experience and cope with their patienthood (Kleinman, 1988; Charmaz, 1991; Frank, 1995).

In what follows, I illustrate the framework of theme-oriented discourse analysis (Roberts and Sarangi, 2005; see also Sarangi (2005a) on 'activity analysis') focusing on two selective procedures:

- Focal Themes: e.g., normality, responsibility, autonomy, choice, decision making, patient-centredness, professional neutrality, symptoms presentation, delivery of diagnosis, voice of medicine, voice of lifeworld, quality of life, coping, risk, reassurance, trust, etc.
- Analytic Themes: e.g., frames and footing; contextualization cues and inferences; face and facework; other devices (contrast, constructed dialogue, repetition, lists, metaphor, analogy, extreme case formulation, character, event work etc.).

ILLUSTRATIVE EXAMPLES

Let us first consider structural, interactional and thematic maps of healthcare encounters as an activity type. In primary care consultations, Byrne and Long (1976) suggest the following structural components:

I   Relating to the patient
II   Discovering the reason for the patient's attendance
III Conducting a verbal or physical examination or both
IV   Considering the patient's condition
V   Detailing treatment or further investigation
VI   Terminating

When mapping these categories on to naturally occurring consultations, we should not regard them as rigid units (see Mitchell, 1957). Consider the structural mapping, using slightly modified categories, for examining the use of antibiotics at two different paediatric clinics.

Clinic A

Turns	Phase
1–4	Opening
5–9	Symptoms
10–14	Treatment
14–16	Symptoms
16–20	Examination
20	Diagnosis

20–28	Treatment
28–31	Symptoms
32–36	Treatment
37–39	Closing

Clinic B

Turns	*Phase*
1–4	Opening
2–26	Symptoms
27–31	Treatment
31–40	Symptoms
41–43	Examination
44–51	Symptoms
52	Treatment
53–54	Examination
55	Causal explanation
56–58	Symptoms
59–63	Examination
64–65	Non-medical
66–72	Symptoms
73–83	Causal explanation
83–85	Treatment
86–92	Symptoms
93	Treatment
94–98	Symptoms
99–101	Miscellaneous
101–115	Treatment
116–121	Closing

From a cursory glance, we can see that the structural components Byrne and Long (1976) have identified are present in these two clinic encounters, but not in a neat sequential order. Byrne and Long's model, it should be said, privileges the professional agenda. A situated consultation, especially in a paediatric setting, unfolds in a much more nuanced manner. As can be seen, the structural variations across the two clinics are striking. It is interesting to note that Clinic A concludes with a prescription of antibiotics, whereas Clinic B ends with a nonprescription. Unlike in Clinic A, no diagnosis is offered in Clinic B. The systematic structural mapping of the two encounters suggests that (i) consultations where antibiotics is prescribed are comparatively shorter in duration, with physical examination routines occurring earlier on in the consultation process; (ii) consultations where antibiotics is not prescribed are longer in duration, with elaborate and complex explanation and assessment of symptoms, interspersed with physical examination(s). If we were to look closely at the corresponding transcripts (not shown here), it is possible to identify how the clinician in Clinic B is delaying a prescription, getting the parent involved in symptoms description, in assessment of various treatment and nontreatment options, and in eliciting the parent's potential aversion to antibiotics. Symptoms description can be variable and dispersed across clinics. Roughly, 54 percent turns are used for symptoms discussion in Clinic B as opposed to 31 percent in the case of Clinic A. These differences are dynamically embedded in the interaction/content flow. However, from a structural map, we cannot ascertain the exact details of participant structure in relation to content of talk. To make sense of the dispersed nature of participant and content structure, it is desirable to map the encounters interactionally and thematically (see the following section).

For the rest of this chapter I will use examples from genetic counselling which constitutes a hybrid activity type with elements of medical, counselling and service encounter protocols (Sarangi, 2000). Unlike many other counselling/ therapeutic settings where clients take centre stage in troubles-telling, in genetic counselling, the counsellors spend considerable time explaining the causes and consequences of a genetic condition, the risks associated with knowing one's genetic status, the psychological and sociomoral issues concerning decisions to undergo predictive tests and decisions about disclosing (or not disclosing) one's test results.

Let us begin with a broad structural map of a typical genetic counselling session:

- Purpose of visit and agenda setting
- Counsellors enquiring about what clients already know
- Clients seeking information/explanation on inheritance; diagnosis; prognosis
- History taking (medical history and family history)
- Counsellors' explanations for diagnosis, nondiagnosis (including inheritance, future risk, uncertainty and disclaiming expertise)
- Counsellors' handling of scientific evidence, clinical evidence and family pedigree
- Clients' accounts of decisions about testing, decisions about disclosure of testing process and test results, psychosocial coping etc.
- Additional themes and concerns
- Outlining future procedure and clinic appointments.

As with the antibiotics clinics earlier, these phases are bound to be dispersed and variable in a given encounter.

Now consider the interactional maps of three different sessions where each client is at risk of having inherited the Huntington's Disease.[2]

We find in Figure 20.1 that there is a noticeable difference in the interactional patterns between Session HD01 and Session HD08 on the one hand,

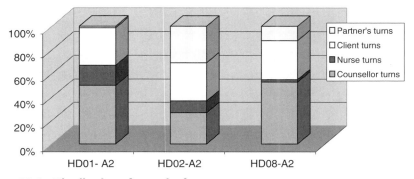

Figure 20.1   Distribution of turns by frequency

and Session HD02, on the other. With regard to HD01 and HD08, the genetic counselling professionals (i.e., the counsellor and the nurse) occupy most of the turns as far as frequency is concerned. By comparison, in the case of HD02, the client and her partner dominate the turn taking. If we were to get a feel of the interactional environment in genetic counselling, we need to look at turn distribution, given that these are multiparty encounters unlike mainstream doctor-patient consultations where turns are at least equally distributed, although turn duration may vary considerably.

Let us consider the same sessions, this time mapping the encounters in terms of turn duration/volume.

In Figure 20.2, where I measure the distribution of the amount of speech, we notice parallel interactional patterns. It emerges that the genetic professionals, in HD01 and HD08, are taking up between 70 and 80 percent of speaking time. A closer look at the data transcripts reveals, rather unsurprisingly, that the genetic professionals foreground their expertise and responsibility to explain various aspects of a genetic condition such as HD and the risks associated with testing and dealing with test results. In other words, a considerable part of the interaction is framed as information giving.

It still remains for us to see why the session involving HD02 is so characteristically different. We notice, both in Figure 20.1 and Figure 20.2, that the client and his/her partner maintain a high level of involvement in their interactional participation. Let us map the turn contents as far as the client (HD02) is concerned.

In Figure 20.3, out of the 186 turns, 51 are quasi-turns (i.e., backchannelling cues, minimal confirmations) and 41 are direct answers to the counsellor's and the nurse's questions and directives. What is striking is that 93 turns are taken up by the client to introduce and elaborate topics that are of a major concern. As it happens, this client has had other medical problems to deal with, in addition to genetic testing. Therefore, it turns out to be more of a troubles-telling activity, which is patiently tolerated by the genetic professionals. However, only in one instance the client gets to ask a self-initiated question.

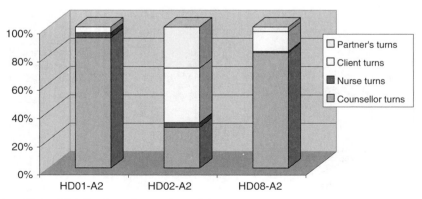

Figure 20.2   Distribution of turns by volume

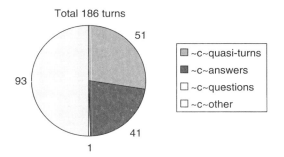

Total 186 turns

Figure 20.3   A client's turn types (HD02-A2)

The mapping at structural and interactional levels gives us an indication of the broad thematic content and the division of participation/involvement within a given encounter. Comparisons across encounters, as we have seen, can provide useful insights. Nevertheless, we need a more sophisticated level of thematic mapping to grasp what is going on in a single encounter. For instance, how do the counsellor and the client come to determine the reasons for undergoing a genetic test and how do they discuss future decisions about disclosure of genetic status, as the latter will have implications for current thinking? We can then look for patterns of similarities and differences because of individual, family circumstances. A comparative framework allows for deviant case analysis (as HD02 earlier). Another option would be to pursue a specific focal theme as a part of a case study.

Let us isolate a focal theme – risk explanation – which can be mapped interactionally. In the context of breast cancer, notions of population risk and individual genetic risk – in relation to first and second order relatives – on the one hand, and test risk and screening risk, on the other, become important.[3]

As can be seen, the topic of individual genetic risk assumes utmost significance in both clinics, CA01 and CA04, although the distribution is not quite the same. Discussion of test risk and screening risk is uneven across the two clinics.

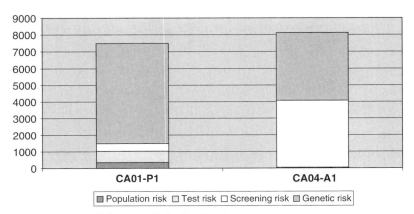

Figure 20.4   Types of risk and their distribution

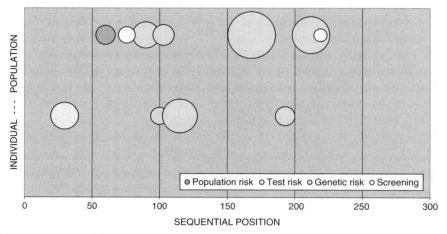

Figure 20.5   At-risk talk in CA01-PI

It is noteworthy that population risk is not even mentioned in CA04. Whereas screening risk is thematized considerably in CA04, it is less salient in CA01. It is possible to locate this difference sequentially, as in figures 20.5 and 20.6.

In the case of CA01, population risk and test risk are discussed early on in the session – which is a typical feature of breast cancer clinics. In CA04, unlike in CA01, the screening risk is discussed much more in length in the middle of the session.

In what follows I have chosen an extended data extract from a genetic counselling session for Familial Breast Cancer.[4] The client, a woman in her mid-forties, has had several relatives dying of breast cancer at a young age. Because of this family history, the client has been receiving regular mammograms for the last

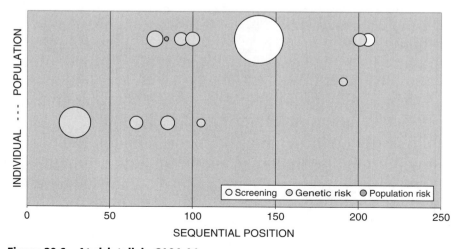

Figure 20.6   At-risk talk in CA04-A1

few years. Just before the extract begins, the genetic counsellor (GC) has explained to the client (CL) that the faulty gene is unlikely to have been passed down through her side of the family, as her mother has reached the age of seventy without having developed any cancers. The focal theme here is the interface of risk and responsibility, and the main analytic theme is the shifting use of professional-medical, institutional, psychological and sociomoral frames.[5]

```
01   GC: women who have the faulty gene, by her age we'd say at least two thirds of them would have had
          cancer by now
02   CL: yes
03   GC: yeah. (pause) I'm not sure whether you're going to be pleased about this or not, but I, I think you're
          in the group of women that we'd think are low risk
          ((pause))
04   CL: oh right
05   GC: mm (.) and therefore I think you're in the group of women for whom we'd say- probably additional
          screening is not necessary
06   CL: ri::::::ght
07   GC: now- (.) you've just had a mammogram
08   CL: mm
09   GC: and when you're fifty you qualify for the ((region)) breast screening programme anyway
10   CL: =oh right
11   GC: =in which case you would start having them three-yearly from that point anyway
12   CL: oh right
```

The extract opens with a statement about general population risk centred around the current age of CL's mother. In turn 03, which is designed as delivery of good news, GC categorizes CL as 'low risk', i.e., belonging to the general population risk of breast cancer, on the basis of available medical evidence (here, family pedigree). The category 'low risk' is not defined in precise terms, but is intended as reassurance, although formulated with several hedges ('I think', 'we'd think', 'we'd say'). CL's formulaic responses in turns 04, 06, 10, 12 are markers of newsworthiness. Her perception of at-risk status does not instantly go away in light of expert, evidence-based explanations. GC is aware of this, as can be seen from the prefacing of the 'psychological' orientation: 'I'm not sure whether you are going to be pleased about this or not' (turn 03). In subsequent turns, GC outlines the course of institutional action, including eligibility for screening: 'additional screening is not necessary' (turn 05); three-yearly screening when CL is fifty (turns 9 and 11).

The interaction continues as follows:

```
13   GC: em (.) I mean having (.) said that, what's going through your mind now (.) is it sort of like-
          ((pause))
14   CL: ehm ((pause)) ((exhales, sighs)) *pf:::::::* (.) I- I (don't feel) very comfortable with it, I almost felt like
          >>uh I wish I hadn't come then<<
15   GC: mm
16   CL: because I had my mammogram every year
17   GC: yeah
18   CL: but ehm
          ((pause))
```

19 CL: obviously I do appreciate what you've said about- about the risk and that (.) ehm but I still got- (.) ehm
    an irrational emotional sort of thing because of ((cousin who died from breast cancer at 30))
20 GC: I understand that (.) and-
21 CL: =and
22 GC: =and the experience you go through in your family is more powerful than anything I can say to you
23 CL: ((emphatically agreeing)) mm what you're saying to me makes sense (.) em
    ((pause))
24 CL: ((tats)) but I can understand what you're saying and I also understand about ehm resources and one
    figure or another (.) I mean in the ideal world every woman would have one (.) ehm every year (.) and
    obviously I do appreciate that. (.) but ehm
25 GC: I mean it's not only resources in terms of pure cost-cutting, but it is ehm little bits of additional x-ray
    you're getting, and also the fact that you're- you know (.) before the menopause- (.) you know, it's not
    as reliable- you know (.) mammograms aren't as reliable as after the menopause and
26 CL: no
27 GC: ehm
28 CL: so what you're actually sort of suggesting perhaps is that I wouldn't need any screening now until I'm
    fifty, that's what you're sort of putting to me (.) isn't it?
29 GC: yea::::h (.) but I'm not- I don't think that we ever should <u>discount</u> the emotional <u>side</u> of things

In turn 13, GC returns to the psychological aspects already introduced in turn 03, this time inviting a response from CL. There is noticeable hesitation in how CL responds as she makes it clear that to her the loss of reassurance in the form of regular (annual) breast screening outweighs any relief regarding her new-found low-risk status (turn 14). She even holds herself responsible for having decided to come to the clinic to receive this reassessment of her risk status, which amounts to foregoing the annual mammogram check-up. Later CL formulates her psychological concern as 'an irrational emotional sort of thing' (turn 19), while acknowledging the medical assessment of her 'low risk' status. She implicitly challenges the credibility of GC's assessment by introducing the cousin's death from breast cancer at the young age of 30. CL uses this alternative evidence as a way of upgrading her at-risk status, but this does not quite fit into the genetic frame of evidence since a cousin does not count as a first-order relative.

Interestingly, rather than challenging CL's perception and emotional state with a reiteration of medical facts, GC in fact goes on to empathize with CL by explicitly undermining the medical voice (turn 22). This statement has a moral undertone as can be seen from what follows. In turn 24, CL presents a moral stance in saying that 'in the ideal world every woman would have (a mammogram) every year'. She implies that her newly affirmed low risk status places her outside the most deserving group to have access to a scarce resource (i.e., regular breast screening before the age of fifty).

GC responds to CL's moral challenge of the healthcare system by switching back to the medical voice (turn 25). The rationing of resources is reframed as a medical, rather than financial, cost–benefit calculation: 'bits of additional x-ray'; 'not as reliable before the menopause' (turn 25). When CL reiterates the unwanted consequences associated with her low-risk status in turn 28 (as in turn 05), the counsellor mitigates her gate-keeping role by re-establishing the psychological implications: 'I don't think we ever should discount the emotional side of things' (turn 29).

In turns 30–41 (not shown) GC offers further reassurance, as well as pointing to the need for collegial consultation for exploring the possibility of negotiating at least some extra screening for the client prior to her reaching the age of fifty despite her low risk status.

Consider the next sequence where CL returns to her psychological, emotional concerns:

42 CL: and I know– I mean it is an emotional thing (.) it's not – but then a lot of these things are (.) or <u>even</u> psychological some of these eh-
43 GC: mm. (.) and know I completely understand that when you've lost a cousin of similar age at such a young age (.) that is very powerful and scary (.) really?
44 CL: and I had to fight quite hard to get any breast screening <u>at all</u>
45 GC: yeah
46 CL: eh a lot of people thought I was just being sort of paranoid or-
47 GC: yeah
48 CL: but it wasn't actually just paranoia. there- >>I suppose there is a certain amount<< when you've got somebody close in the family like that (.) and also at the time my children were small and I thought oh- fancy having to leave them without a mother
49 GC: yeah, yeah
50 CL: and also, <u>now that I'm on my own</u>, so I'm a <u>single</u> mother, even though my children are older, ((daughter)) is only fifteen, she's coming up to fifteen, so she's ((whispering) *she-s still my baby*
51 GC: mm
52 CL: so there's that sort of additional uh what would happen if (...)
53 GC: yeah, [yeah I understand]

Following CL's reiteration, in turn 42, of the 'emotional' and 'psychological' concerns associated with her risk status, GC returns, in turn 43, to the client's traumatic experience of her cousin's death to build a case on the psychological level for such an exception (which amounts to disregarding CL's mother's current health status). CL's account is formulated as a series of further moral claims: she had to 'fight quite hard' to get screening in the first place (turn 44); she was branded unfairly as 'paranoid' (turn 46); and she had to be careful about her health for the sake of her children which is realized as self-reported thought to achieve significance: 'oh- fancy having to leave them without a mother' (turns 48). These formulations work as warrants to distance herself from the 'worried well' and to establish herself, in turn 50, as a responsible mother ('she's still my baby'), presumably seeking expression of solidarity from the female counsellor.

Let us, finally, consider a data extract from a research interview setting, which should also be regarded as a jointly constructed activity type (Briggs, 1986, Mishler, 1986). The interviewer is a genetics professional and the interviewee is the parent who has a son in his early 20s with Ectodermal Dysplasia[6] (PM: Parent; Int: Interviewer; D = Patient). The interview takes place at PM's home:

01 PM: And he's had these same friends – he's still got the friends now – but when he went to college … he went to college completely on his own without any of his friends and he was looking forward to meeting new people, just like anyone would. And … he's got some really nice friends there now that he's made. And he has since found out … he thinks they're (unclear) and they enjoy his company, they think he is good fun. But he has found out that when they first met him they thought 'Woah! Scary! Won't talk to that one!'. D thought 'well I am going to have to make friends with people' so he walked over to them, smiled,

and said 'Hello, I'm (his name)' and shook their hands and they were all friends ever since! So it's how you do things. [Int: Yes] If you sit in the corner being afraid of what life's going to be like you'll find it harder, I think. [Int: Yeah] Someone on the train the other day asked D (name) if he'd got cancer. [Int: Yes.] And he was a bit upset about that

02 Int: Just with the hair … looking as if he's had hair loss with radiation

03 PM: and because, kind of, he's got pretty bad eczema on his neck and stuff at the moment. He was a bit upset because he said 'do I look …' you know … 'I know I look …' He knows he looks a bit different but he's Ok with it and we never point out any failings that he might have because we don't want his confidence to be knocked. So sometimes when someone says that…it did upset him. So I just had to say 'you can't change the way you look. You are who you are'. And we've always made sure he's been dressed in a trendy way like everybody else. But he was upset about that. But he soon bounced back. Lots of times it's only people. … people don't mean to be unkind – sometimes they do – that person didn't mean to be unkind, perhaps he'd had a sister, a granny or an uncle or someone and he was trying to make sense of something.

04 Int: Yeah, seeing a child – adolescent – with very little hair it does make you think of leukaemia.

05 PM: It does. Especially because people survive those things these days, whereas they never did and you never saw them.

[15 turns omitted – discussion of hair options]

06 PM: Yeah. He came home and said that and was a bit quiet in the evening and then we had a chat about it… and he actually did have a little tear about it,'cause he said 'do I look so awful', this was only a couple of months ago. Well I said 'no you don't – well you don't!'. We always start with 'you've got two arms, two legs, a good brain. I know he's hurt you but if you let it get to you' that's what I always say 'if you let it get to you it will just affect all your life all the time. So you've just got to pick yourself up and think that was unfortunate that chap said that but he didn't really mean any harm by it – he was just being insensitive'. And the next morning he was as alright – it was my influence – he was on the train again. He's very good like that. I think he's lucky that he's such a sunny personality, he can bring himself to pick himself up. It's a very sensitive age.

This is an open-ended interview, with the interviewee doing most of the talking, as is typical of research interviews. The level of transcription is rather basic, unlike the counselling encounter, and this is partly justified in light of the analytic focus here on the relationship between stigma perception and coping mechanisms. We notice a prevalence of reported speech (marked between single quotes) in PM's talk as a way of reconstructing the events as they unfolded in the past. Reported speech affords PM an activity-specific role in the interview setting, especially as she talks as the carer for her son, D.

Throughout we have normalization (D has friends, he likes meeting new people just like anyone would, he is dressed in a trendy way like everybody else). D's character is also portrayed as being proactive by invoking relevant event scenarios where he embarks on making friends, but gets hurt when he becomes the target of undue attention, although he usually bounces back. The mother comes to accept D's 'differentness' (Goffman, 1968) despite the earlier parallel drawn between D and everyone else: she reinforces the idea that 'you can't change the way you look', while acknowledging the extent to which visible differentness of the kind D embodies can attract public response, which may seem unjustified but not meant as unkindness or meanness (turn 03). Following Goffman, stigma is embarrassing – not just for the stigmatized person but also for those who are confronted with it and have to react to it. In turn 06, we notice the foregrounding of normality once again, with PM's scaffolding role in sustaining D's coping mechanism. In general, the mother offers accounts, comprising excuses and justifications, including character work. It emerges that stigma is as much a matter of attribution as it is perception – the latter is referred to as 'felt stigma' (Green, 1995) leading to various coping mechanisms as seen earlier.

To summarize, within a framework of theme-oriented discourse analysis (comprising activity analysis and accounts analysis), interactions (in clinic and research interview settings) are seen as a narrative unfolding of events and characters, organized temporally and spatially. In addition to the sequential order, rhetorical moves are also central to how actions, events and characters are portrayed and managed in interaction.

CONCLUSION: ANALYTIC ECLECTICISM AND THE USES OF DISCOURSE RESEARCH

Discourse analysis can be applied to both talk and text data, to clinical encounters as well as research interviews. Rather than simply provide a recipe-style hands-on checklist of how to do discourse analysis, I have demonstrated possible ways of engaging with discourse data, while keeping an eye on the value of discourse analytic findings and claims. A discourse analytic undertaking in the healthcare setting inevitably needs to be linked to evidence-based professional practice, which implies that discourse analysts must acquire adequate knowledge and experience via 'thick participation' in the specific site being investigated as a condition for practising discourse analysis (Sarangi, 2007).

Discourse analysis is a composite activity. Because any interpretation of a slice of data is incomplete both in itself and with regard to the overall context of illness and healthcare, a combination of clinic data, interview data, ethnographic fieldwork and other documentary data must be used to approximate 'ecological validity' (Cicourel, 2007).

This kind of eclecticism is a foregone conclusion at all stages of discourse analysis, but the researcher needs to be aware of potential criticism that awaits a butterfly collection approach. A robust discourse analysis requires a systematic selection of focal and analytic themes which align with the research design. Depending on what becomes one's chosen focus, different interpretive outcomes are unavoidable.

Finally, I want to raise some practical issues concerning the relevance of discourse analytic research in healthcare settings. Our analytic discoveries are not intended to be professionally and practically relevant (Sarangi, 2005b). Healthcare professionals and patients whose talk and text we analyze are the ultimate arbiters of the relevance or otherwise of our analytic findings. Minimally, discourse analysis can offer a metalanguage which can facilitate communication in institutional and professional settings (Roberts and Sarangi, 1999; 2003). In other words, discourse analytic findings can potentially provide a sound platform to base assessment of professional practice, with the possibility of raising awareness, planning training activities and fostering change in communicative practices. However, raw discourse analytic findings can rarely be applied directly, a fact that means – like all good researchers – we must be reflective about our discourse analytical practice.

NOTES

1 For a detailed discussion of the three paradoxes in discourse analysis – observer's paradox, participant's paradox and analyst's paradox – see Sarangi (2002, 2007).

2 Huntigton's Disease is a degenerative neuropsychiatric disorder. There is a 50 percent chance that the child of an affected parent will have inherited the disease-associated mutation. While predictive tests are available, there are uncertainties about the exact age of onset and the way in which the disease will manifest. The data are taken from The Wellcome Trust funded project titled 'Communicative Frames in Counselling for Predictive Genetic Testing'. I am grateful to Lucy Brookes-Howell and Kristina Bennert for preparing the transcripts and maps.

3 A further distinction can be made about risk of occurrence vs. risk of knowing (Sarangi et al., 2003), which is not mapped here.

4 For an extended analysis, see Sarangi (2005a).

5 The following transcription conventions are used: (.) (..): micropause up to one second; *words*: decreased volume; underlining: increased emphasis as in stress; >> words<<: increased volume; question mark [?]: rising intonation; :::::: lengthening of a sound; -: cut-off of prior word or sound; ((text in double round brackets)): description or anonymized information; (text in round brackets): transcriber's guess; =: a continuous utterance.

6 This condition is characterized by reduced mucus production in respiratory and gastrointestinal tract, reduced sweating and overheating as well as dental malformation, sparse hair, which can be stigmatized and can have consequences for relationships. I am grateful to Angus Clarke for making this data extract available.

REFERENCES

Ainsworth-Vaughn, N. (1998) *Claiming Power in Doctor-Patient Talk.* Oxford: Oxford University Press.
Antaki, C. (1988) *Analysing Everyday Explanation.* London: Sage.
Atkinson, P. (1995) *Medical Talk and Medical Work.* London: Sage.
Bales, R.F. (1950) *Interaction Process Analysis.* Mass: Addison-Wesley.
Briggs, C.L. (1986) *Learning How to Ask: A Sociolinguistic Appraisal of the Role of the Interview in Social Science Research.* Cambridge: Cambridge University Press.
Buttny, R. (1993) *Social Accountability in Communication.* London: Sage.
Byrne, P.S. and Long, B.E.L. (1976) *Doctors Talking to Patients.* Exeter: RCGP.
Candlin, C.N. and Candlin, S. (2003) 'Healthcare Communication: A Problematic Site for Applied Linguistics Research', *Annual Review of Applied Linguistics*, 23: 134–54.
Charmaz, K. (1991) *Good Days, Bad Days: The Self in Chronic Illness and Time.* New Brunswick, NJ: Rutgers University Press.
Cicourel, A.V. (1992) 'The Interpretation of Communicative Contexts: Examples from Medical Encounters'. In A. Duranti and C. Goodwin (eds.) *Rethinking Context: Language as an Interactive Phenomenon* (pp. 291–310). Cambridge: Cambridge University Press.
Cicourel, A.V. (2007) 'A Personal, Retrospective View of Ecological Validity', *Text and Talk,* 27(5): 735–52.

Davis, M. (1968) 'Variations in Patients' Compliance with Doctors' Advice: An Empirical Analysis of Patterns of Communication', *American Journal of Public Health,* 58: 274–88.

Drew, P. and Heritage, J. (eds.) (1992) *Talk at Work: Interaction in Institutional Settings.* Cambridge: Cambridge University Press.

Ferrara, K.W. (1994) *Therapeutic Ways with Words.* New York: Oxford University Press.

Firth J.R. (1935 [1957]) 'The Technique of Semantics'. In *Papers in Linguistics 1934–51* (pp. 7–33). London: Oxford University Press.

Fisher, S. (1995) *Nursing Wounds: Nurse Practitioners/Doctors/Women Patients/ and the Negotiation of Meaning.* New Brunswick, NJ: Rutgers University Press.

Fisher, S. and Todd, A.D. (eds.) (1983) *The Social Organization of Doctor-Patient Communication.* Washington DC: Centre for Applied Linguistics.

Frank, A.W. (1995) *The Wounded Storyteller: Body, Illness and Ethics.* Chicago: University of Chicago Press.

Garfinkel, H. (1956) 'Conditions of Successful Degradation Ceremonies', *American Journal of Sociology,* 61: 240–244.

Garfinkel, H. (1967) *Studies in Ethnomethodology.* Englewood Cliffs, NJ: Prentice Hall.

Goffman, E. (1959) *The Presentation of Self in Everyday Life.* New York: Doubleday.

Goffman, E. (1968) *Stigma: Notes on the Management of Spoiled Identity.* Harmondsworth: Penguin.

Goffman, E. (1981) *Forms of Talk.* Oxford: Blackwell.

Gotti, M. and Salagar-Meyer, F. (eds.) (2006) *Advances in Medical Discourse Analysis: Oral and Written Contexts.* Bern: Peter Lang.

Green, G. (1995) 'Attitudes Towards People with HIV: Are They as Stigmatising as People with HIV Perceive Them to Be', *Social Science & Medicine,* 41(4): 557–68.

Gumperz, J. (1982) *Discourse Strategies.* Cambridge: Cambridge University Press.

Gwyn, R. (2002) *Communicating Health and Illness.* London: Sage.

Heath, C. (1986) *Body Movement and Speech in Medical Interaction.* Cambridge: Cambridge University Press.

Heritage, J. and Maynard, D. (eds.) (2006) *Communication in Medical Care: Interaction between Primary Care Physicians and Patients.* Cambridge: Cambridge University Press.

Iedema, R. (ed.) (2007) *Discourses of Hospital Communication: Tracing Complexities in Contemporary Health Organizations.* Basingstoke: Palgrave-Macmillan.

Kleinman, A. (1988) *The Illness Narratives: Suffering, Healing and the Human Condition.* New York: Basic Books.

Korsch, B.M. and Negrete, V.F. (1972) 'Doctor-Patient Communication', *Scientific American,* 227: 66–74.

Labov, W. (1972). *Sociolinguistic Patterns.* Philadelphia: Pennsylvania University Press.

Labov, W. and Fanshel, D. (1977) *Therapeutic Discourse: Psychotherapy as Conversation.* New York: Academic Press.

Levinson, S. (1979) 'Activity Types and Language', *Linguistics,* 17: 365–399 (also reprinted in Drew and Heritage (ed.) *Talk at Work: Interaction in Institutional Settings.* Cambridge: Cambridge University Press.

Mishler, E.G. (1984) *The Discourse of Medicine: Dialectics of Medical Interviews.* Norwood, N.J.: Ablex.

Mishler, E.G. (1986) *Research Interviewing: Context and Narrative.* Cambridge, Mass: Harvard University Press.

Mitchell, T.F. (1957) 'The Language of Buying and Selling in Cyrenaica', *Hesperis* 44: 31–71. Also, published in T.F. Mitchell (1975) *Principles of Firthian Linguistics* (pp. 167–200). London: Longman.

Morris, G.H. and Chenail, R.J. (eds.) (1995) *The Talk of the Clinic: Explorations in the Analysis of Medical and Therapeutic Discourse.* Hillsdale, NJ: Lawrence Erlbaum.

Ochs, E. (1979) 'Transcription as Theory'. In E. Ochs and B. Schieffelin (eds.) *Developmental Pragmatics.* New York: Academic Press.

Peräkylä, A. (1995) *AIDS Counselling: Institutional Interaction and Clinical Practice.* Cambridge: Cambridge University Press.

Ribeiro, B. (1994) *Coherence in Psychotic Discourse.* Oxford: Oxford University Press.

Roberts, C. and Sarangi, S. (1999) 'Hybridity in Gatekeeping Discourse: Issues of Practical Relevance for the Researcher'. In S. Sarangi and C. Roberts (eds.) *Talk, Work and Institutional Order: Discourse in Medical, Mediation and Management Settings*. Berlin: Mouton de Gruyter. (pp. 473–503).

Roberts, C. and Sarangi, S. (2003) 'Uptake of Discourse Research in Interprofessional Settings: Reporting from Medical Consultancy', *Applied Linguistics,* 24(3): 338–59.

Roberts, C. and Sarangi, S. (2005) 'Theme-Oriented Discourse Analysis of Medical Encounters', *Medical Education,* 39: 632–40.

Roter, D. (2001) *The Roter Method of Interaction Process Analysis*. Baltimore: The Johns Hopkins University.

Roter, D. and Hall, J. (1992) *Doctors Talking to Patients/Patients Talking to Doctors: Improving Communication in Medical Visits*. Westport, CT: Auburn House.

Sarangi, S. (2000) 'Activity Types, Discourse Types And interactional Hybridity: The Case of Genetic Counselling'. In S. Sarangi and M. Coulthard (eds.) *Discourse and Social Life* (pp. 1–27). London: Pearson.

Sarangi, S. (2002) 'Discourse Practitioners as a Community of Interprofessional Practice: Some Insights from Health Communication Research'. In C. N. Candlin (ed.) *Research and Practice in Professional Discourse* (pp. 95–135). Hong Kong: City University of Hong Kong Press.

Sarangi, S. (2004) 'Towards a Communicative Mentality in Medical and Healthcare Practice', *Communication & Medicine*, 1(1): 1–11.

Sarangi, S. (2005a) 'Activity Analysis in Professional Discourse Settings: The Framing of Risk and Responsibility in Genetic Counselling', *Hermès*, 41: 111–20.

Sarangi, S. (2005b) 'The Conditions and Consequences of Professional Discourse Studies', *Journal of Applied Linguistics,* 2(3): 371–94.

Sarangi, S. (2007) 'The Anatomy of Interpretation: Coming to Terms with the Analyst's Paradox in Professional Discourse Studies', *Text & Talk,* 27(5): 567–84.

Sarangi, S. and Roberts, C. (eds) (1999) *Talk, Work and the Institutional Order: Discourse in Medical, Mediation and Management Settings*. Berlin: Mouton de Gruyter.

Sarangi, S., Bennert, K., Howell, L., and Clarke A. (2003) 'Relatively Speaking': Relativisation of Genetic Risk in Counselling for Predictive Testing', *Health, Risk and Society,* 5(2): 155–69.

Scott, M.B. and Lyman, S. (1968) 'Accounts', *American Sociological Review,* 33(1): 46–62.

Sherzer, J. (1987) 'A Discourse-Centred Approach to Language and Culture', *American Anthropologist,* 89: 295–309.

Silverman, D. (1987) *Communication and Medical Practice: Social Relations in the Clinic*. London: Sage.

Silverman, D. (1997) *Discourses of Counselling: HIV Counselling as Social Interaction*. London: Sage.

Stivers, T. (2007) *Prescribing Under Pressure: Patient-Physician Conversations and Antibiotics*. Oxford: Oxford University Press.

Stubbs, M. (1993) 'British traditions in text analysis: from Firth to Sinclair'. In M. Baker, G. Francis and E. Tognini-Bonelli (eds.), Text and Technology: In Honour of John Sinclair. Amsterdam: John Benjamins; 1–33.

Wadsworth, M. and Robinson, D. (eds.) (1976) *Studies in Everyday Medical Life*. London: Martin Robertson.

Waitzkin, H. (1991) *The Politics of Medical Encounters: How Doctors and Patients Deal with Social Problems*. New Haven, Conn: Yale University Press.

West, C. (1984) *Routine Complications: Troubles in Talk between Doctors and Patients*. Bloomington: Indiana University Press.

21

Documents in Health Research

Lindsay Prior

'A verbal contract isn't worth the paper it is written on'.
Attributed to Sam Goldwyn (film producer)

INTRODUCTION: THE ROLE OF DOCUMENTS IN HEALTH RESEARCH

In the realm of health and almost all other areas of research, documents tend to enter and to leave the 'field' in relative silence. Indeed, their role in empirical research is more often than not linked to the use of 'unobtrusive' techniques. This is mainly because documents are most commonly viewed as containers and carriers of content – divorced and detached from the circumstances in which they are produced and in which they are used. Put bluntly, documents contain data, and the task of the social or health researcher is assumed to involve the extraction of data – as evidence – from the relevant container or receptacle into which it has been placed. One of my aims in this chapter is to disabuse the reader of that rather comfortable and convenient presupposition, and to emphasize how documents always enter the field in at least two roles. The first is, indeed, as a container for content. The second, however, is as an active agent involved in the configuration of the very settings in which it is found. Indeed, the somewhat tormented logic of the opening quotation is in many ways testament to the fact that written documents have potency as well as capacity, in a way that ephemeral, verbal communications do not.

In that vein I demonstrate how documents should not be regarded merely as containers for words, images, information, instructions and so forth, but how they can influence episodes of social interaction and schemes of social organization.

I will provide a range of examples – many of which draw upon my own data, and virtually all of which relate in one way or another to research problems associated with the field of medical sociology. My examples, however, are not offered so much for any substantive interest they might hold, but are intended to be illustrative of a wider argument – namely, that in matters of social research, documents should be considered as being capable of *doing* things as well as of *saying* things.

Throughout the chapter, I shall talk of documentation as if it is equivalent to text – though that is clearly not so. Indeed, architectural drawings, books, paintings, X-ray images, film, World Wide Web pages, bus tickets, shopping lists, tapestries, and sequences of DNA can all be considered as 'documents' – depending on the use that is made of such artefacts in specific circumstances (Prior, 2003). For heuristic purposes, however, I will ignore nontextual forms of data and proceed as if the terms text and documentation were synonymous.

FOUR APPROACHES TO THE STUDY OF DOCUMENTS IN HEALTH RESEARCH

In one of the most influential texts on qualitative research methods produced during the second half of the twentieth century, Glaser and Strauss (1967:163) argued that, in matters of sociological investigation, documents ought to be regarded as akin 'to the anthropologist's informant or a sociologist's interviewee'. The authors subsequently devote an entire chapter to how the principles of grounded theory could and should be deployed on inert text. Nowadays, of course, grounded theory is commonly viewed as a method to be deployed solely on interview (speech) data, and the prominence that was given to text by the two 'discoverers' is routinely overlooked. Nevertheless, the work of Glaser and Strauss represents a typical way in which documents have come to be positioned as data. In fact, a focus on documents primarily as containers of evidence was well established in social science research texts from the work of Goode and Hatt (1952) onward. As a key source of data, it is commonly recommended that document content be screened, counted, and coded for appropriate evidence in support or refutation of relevant hypotheses (Weber, 1990; Krippendorf, 2004). In this frame, reports, letters, texts, photographs, and other images, as well as biographies and autobiographies (Angrosino, 1989; Plummer, 2001) – not to mention documents containing statistical data – are most commonly regarded as a 'resource' for the researcher.

Such an understanding of documents as inert carriers of content is, unsurprisingly, well reflected in standard textbook statements on the place and position of documents in social research and is often associated with the idea that documents and humans exist in entirely separate realms (May 1997; Hodder, 2000; Bowling, 2002; Bryman, 2004). Indeed the most common claim is that documents exist as a mute, inert, nonreactive and isolated source of evidence particularly well suited to unobtrusive research (see Scott, 1990; Lee, 2000).

While the most-used techniques for dealing with documents as a research resource are drawn from varieties of content or thematic analysis – of various degrees of complexity – data analysis strategies can shift from content into discourse analysis (Wood, 2000) with relative ease. Whenever that occurs there is at least a nod to the notion that documents might actually enter into the stream of interaction rather than remaining external to such interaction. For example, there is a notable tendency within social studies of science and technology for examining the role of scientific rhetoric in structuring our notions of 'nature' and the place of human beings (especially scientists) within nature (see, for example, Gilbert and Mulkay, 1984; Bazerman, 1988; Gross, 1996, Prior, 2007).

Following in the traditions of ethnomethodology and discourse analysis, however, it can be argued that documents might be more fruitfully approached as 'topic' (Zimmerman and Pollner, 1971) rather than as 'resource'. This shift moves the focus to the ways in which documents come to assume their content and structure. This approach, which, following Foucault, might be called an 'archaeology of documentation', is well represented in studies of such things as how mortality, morbidity, suicide, and other forms of health data are routinely generated (for detailed examples see Prior, 2003).

Naturally, the distinction between topic and resource is not always easy to hold to – especially in the hurly-burly of doing empirical research. Putting an emphasis on 'topic', however, can open up a further dimension of research, concerning the ways in which documents function in the everyday world. For, when we focus on function, it becomes apparent that documents serve not merely as containers of content, but as active agents in episodes of interaction, and schemes of social organization. There are many examples of studies that emphasize function rather than content in the realm of health research, and I shall shortly refer to a few of them. Before I do that, however, I offer a typology (Table 21.1) of the ways in which documents can be used in social research.

While no form of categorical classification can capture the inherent fluidity of the world, its actors, and its objects, Table 21.1 offers a useful typology of the various ways in which documents have been dealt with by social and health researchers. Thus, approaches that fit into Cell 1 have been dominant in the history of sociology, in social science, and in health research generally. In this approach, documents (especially as text) are scoured and coded for what they

Table 21.1 Approaches to the study of documents in health research

Focus of research approach	Document as resource	Document as topic
Content	(1) Approaches that focus almost entirely on what is 'in' the documents.	(2) 'Archaeological approaches that focus on how document content comes into being.
Use & Function	(3) Approaches that focus on how documents are used as a resource by human actors for purposeful ends.	(4) Approaches that focus on how documents function independently of their producers.

Source: Prior, L. (2008)

contain in the way of descriptions, reports, images, representations, and accounts. In short, they are scoured for evidence. Data analysis strategies concentrate almost entirely on what is in the 'text' (via various forms of content analysis, thematic analysis, or even grounded theory).

This emphasis on content is carried over into the approaches described in Cell 2 with the key difference being a focus on how document content comes into being. The attention here is on the origin and social production of written reports, descriptions, statistical data and so forth. Many kinds of discourse analysis reflect such concerns, and so too does the work of ethnomethodologists insofar as they elaborate on how clinical, police, and other reports and records get constructed.

In contrast, the focus in Cell 3 is on how documents are used as a resource by different kinds of 'readers'. Here, concern with document content or how a document has come into being are marginal, and the analysis concentrates on the relationship between specific documents and their use or recruitment by identifiable human actors for purposeful ends – such as the use of clinical records in ward settings.

The approaches that fit into Cell 4 regard content as secondary. The focus here is on how documents, as 'things', function in schemes of social activity, and with how such things can drive, rather than be driven by, human activity. In the following sections, I provide more detail on what these various approaches look like.

1. A focus on content: researching health policy

Clinics, hospitals, health centres and their respective bureaucracies are awash with documentation. Forms, cards, reports, procedure manuals, patient charts and records, as well as policy statements are just a few examples of the documentation that can be drawn upon and used as data by a wide range of health researchers. I shall make reference to clinical records in the next section. Here, however, I am going to focus on some ways in which the content of policy documents can be used as research material.

In the United Kingdom, as in many other countries, governments and NGOs produce new policy documents in abundance. For example, I estimate that the UK government published some 228 health policy and guidance documents on its website during 2007 alone. The content of such documents can often be dealt with in a relatively straightforward manner – beginning with a simple concordance – executed via one of the freely available concordance programmes available on line. Such a programme provides an identification and count of all of the words used in the document, and the resulting listings provide key insights into the concerns and points of emphasis of the document (as well as highlighting issues that are absent). It may also be possible to develop a semantic map from such data – by focusing on, say, the co-occurrence rather than the single occurrence of words. Inevitably as any analysis moves from words to sentences, and on to paragraphs and sections, more sophisticated forms of data analysis need to be considered – these might include thematic analysis, analysis of rhetorical form, or they may be structured in terms of grounded theory. Naturally, the method to be adopted has to mesh with the aims of the research project. In this section, I will outline just one of many ways of approaching document content as a research resource.

Health policy documents can relate to vastly different areas of activity, but they often contain a similar storyline. Roughly speaking, this storyline argues that what has gone on until now is insufficient or not good enough ('for too long...' this that or the other has been the case); that the existing state of affairs is bolstered only by people with narrow and sectional interests at heart; that there is a consequent need to transform, modernize, change, and improve services; that the current government is going to achieve that by listening to; by empowering; by working in partnership with; and by enabling the voter – as a consumer, an individual, or whatever, to create things afresh. As an example, consider the following; it is drawn from a speech made in 1961 by the then British Minister of Health. It was a speech that served as a prelude to the closure of virtually every large psychiatric hospital ('asylum') in the United Kingdom between the 1960s and the 1990s. Despite the substantial time lapse between then and now, the speech contains some structural features worthy of study:

> Now look and see what are the implications of [my] bold words. They imply nothing less than the elimination ·of by far the greater part of this country's mental hospitals as they exist today. This is a colossal undertaking, not so much in the new physical provision which it involves, as in the sheer inertia of mind and matter which it requires to be overcome. There they stand, isolated, majestic, imperious, brooded over by the gigantic water-tower and chimney combined, rising unmistakable and daunting out of the countryside – the asylums which our forefathers built with such immense solidity to express the notions of their day. Do not for a moment underestimate their powers of resistance to our assault. Let me describe some of the defences which we have to storm... (Enoch Powell, Minister of Health (GB), speech 1961, heralding the closure of the psychiatric hospitals in the United Kingdom; available variously on the Internet).

Powell offers a narrative that points to a past, a present, and a future. This excerpt contains virtually all of the elements of narrative form, including reference to an impending drama. Indeed, it is possible to analyze this and many other such speeches and associated policy documents in a narrative frame precisely because they tend to have this distinctive chronology based format (Roe, 1994; Van Eeten, 2007). Let us consider another example.

In the United Kingdom, contemporary health and other policy documents usually carry a foreword by the Prime Minister of the day, plus another foreword by the appropriate Secretary of State. These prefaces and forewords are important, because they normally highlight key elements of a government's policy narrative. Thus, in almost all health policy documents produced in the United Kingdom since the 1980s, the main narrative has been about empowering individuals, expanding their scope for choice, emphasizing how people need to take responsibility for their own health, and how people can mollify the health risks to which they are subject. Inevitably, each government adds its own points of emphasis. Thus, UK Labour governments since 1997 have talked about 'tailoring' a system of universal health care to individual need, about 'personalizing' health care, and most recently, about extending choice of where and by whom to be treated. Consider the following extract from a document entitled 'Choice Matters 2007–08. Putting Patients in Control':

> People's willingness and capacity to take part in decisions about health and social care have increased, and choice should be offered to everyone, not just those who are best able to demand it. We can promote social inclusion by ensuring choice for groups who tell us it is important to them but have sometimes been denied it... (DH, 2007:4).

Statements of this kind point to the construction of the patient as a consumer who wants tailor-made and personalized health services. This consumerist creature stands in sharp contrast to the inert 'patient' of the original UK National Health Service, and is made and remade in many documents. Interestingly, this recasting of the patient role is justified in terms of an appeal to social inclusion – an objective that it would be difficult for any social democrat to argue against. More importantly, from the standpoint of a researcher, the documents, together with the political speeches to which they are related, and the actions of the politicians who make these speeches and presentations, add up to an analyzable narrative. In the words of Newman and Vidler (2006:195): '[Health policy documents] are presented as part of a story that situates new initiatives, drives or targets into a history, and draws on images of societal change and/or institutional problems to legitimate their proposals. Such an approach views policies – and the political speeches that surround their presentation – as providing a linguistic repertoire on which managers, professionals, user groups and other stakeholders can draw'.

The issue with these narratives is not, of course, to judge them as right or wrong – as in accord with the truth (or otherwise) of the historical events to which they invariably refer, or the principles to which they appeal – but to enquire about what is recruited into the policy story and what is being generated as a result of the storytelling. Thus, we can view the water-tower speech not simply as fine words from a politician, but as a signal of what was to happen in the coming decades; how what was to happen could be justified; and how opposition to any plans might be rhetorically countered. In fact, with the advantage of hindsight, the example serves to highlight something rather important about policy narratives, namely that they are represented not just by words on a page, or sentiments expressed in a speech, but are tied into action. The task of the health (policy) researcher in that respect is not to be beguiled by content, but to examine content as a component of a wider network of action.

2. A focus on document content: approaching content as 'topic'

It is something of paradox that the death rate – or, more accurately, the mortality rate – has become one of the most useful quantitative measures for assessing the 'health' of populations. The rate (per thousand born) of babies of who die in the first year of life (the infant mortality rate) has long been used as a key measure of both the health and quality of life of a population. Health agencies are, of course, also interested in what people die from. Thus, the World Health Organization (WHO) publishes, on an annual basis, an array of mortality and morbidity statistics (http://www.who.int/research/en/). The latter provides data on both the numbers of people who die in any one country during a given year, along with the causes of death. In that respect, the manual exists as a resource for social scientific or epidemiological study. One can take statistics from the online sources and scour them for facts about mortality, or health, or, if one wishes, transpose and integrate the data into a measure of the 'quality of life'. Of course, to approach the statistics in that spirit would be to approach them as a resource, and whilst that is a perfectly legitimate thing to do in many frames of health research (especially quantitative styles of research), it is always useful to step back from such readily available facts and to ask some questions as to how the facts were generated. Statistics themselves must be treated as a topic.

The foundation of statistical reports – such as the WHO report – are often designed and set at some distance from the final product. In the WHO case, this is so in both a bureaucratic and a geographical sense. For example, one rather important 'foundation stone' for the production of the report is the death certificate (Prior, 2000). The latter has many functions – and, as with all documents, those functions tend to alter according to the occasion of use. In most Western societies, a medical practitioner completes the certificate on the death of an individual, and it forms an occasion to explain why a person died. (It lists a medical and legally acceptable form of a 'cause of death'.) Such certificates are then processed through a series of local, regional, and national agencies in order to compile a picture of mortality in any given country. It is from the national pictures that the international (WHO) picture is derived. Indeed, at all stages in the production of the statistical picture, detailed documentation is involved.

In the style of 'secondary analysis', most researchers would use such data as a resource – to describe or account for variations and trends in cause specific mortality patterns across the globe. However, it always serves us well to ask detailed questions about *how* any such data set has been put together and processed. To that end, in some of my work I have concentrated on the medical certificate of cause of death as a feature of medical decision making – looking at how causes are selected and at the ways in which decision making feeds into the manufacture of routine health data (Prior and Bloor, 1993). There is no need to summarize that work here, but suffice it to say that the manipulation of routine data on mortality and morbidity involves various actors drawing upon both (a) conceptual structures and (b) technical rules of data selection and manipulation. Modifications of either the conceptual structures or the technical rules can result in different pictures of 'what is going on in the world'.

For example, when people die they commonly die of many things at one and the same time, and it is not always easy to disentangle one cause from another (see, for example, the sequence in Box 21.1). It is not simply a question of differentiating one physiological cause from another, but also of interpreting the social contexts in which the death has occurred (as might be indicated by the deceased's biography). Timmermans (2006) describes the problems involved in decision making about cause of death and shows how pathologists and other professionals have to 'make a case' for concluding that a person died of, say, heart disease rather than some alternative cause. More directly, in so far as any of the things that have contributed to a specific death are recorded (and not all relevant items are), they generate a further decision-making problem for the person who has to code the death (for statistical purposes). This is essentially because the latter must, in most cases, select principal, underlying, as well as secondary causes of death. Such decision making is commonly undertaken by consulting with rule books, precedent, organizational culture and so forth. However, key changes in any of the latter can produce changes in the data set that researchers will later draw upon as an 'objective' resource.

One of the most important 'rule-books' for the selection of underlying causes of death is The International Classification of Diseases and related Health Problems, currently known as ICD-10.1[1] ICD-10 provides a list of all of the accepted causes of death, and these are classified in terms of 'chapters'. Thus, there are chapters relating to diseases and disorders of the respiratory system, the circulatory system, the nervous system and so on. In different decades, different diseases and causes of death are added and deleted from the manual. HIV/AIDS is an obvious example of an addition, and it appears as a cause of death only in ICD-10, while 'old age' as a cause of death was eliminated in ICD-6. Clearly, these basic decisions affect the possibility of analyzing the ways in which such things as 'starvation' (not included in the ICD for many decades), poverty, old age, and isolation – as well as, say, various forms of trauma relate to patterns of human mortality.

Box 21.1   Documents as Actors

Typical sequences to be found in a medical cause of death certificate

Cause of Death:
I(a) Bronchopneumonia
 (b) Brain haemorrhage (subdural & Intracerebral mid-brain & brain stem)
 (c) Trauma

The sequence as presented is indicative of a death narrative, and a medical professional has written the sequence in such a way that the underlying cause of death is listed as I(c). However, when the certificate eventually arrives for coding at a data processing office these judgements are open to revision. In this Instance I(b) might be more likely to be coded as the underlying cause, since I(c) is vague and covers a wide range of possibilities. I(c) might nevertheless be coded as a supplementary and external cause of death. All of these judgements are being made in the light of other data that is contained on this and associated certificates that refer to the age, sex, occupation and other biographical details of the deceased.

The ICD also contains rules about which causes of death should take precedence over other causes. So that when a person dies of many conditions, the people responsible for coding the data on which the health statistics depend, 'know' which cause to select as the underlying cause of death. Thus, diseases of the heart, for example, commonly take precedence over diseases of any other organ, and cancers take precedence over infections and so on. These rules also change from decade to decade. Thus, during the early part of the twentieth century, diseases of the liver and lung took precedence over disease of the heart (see Prior, 1989).

In the context in which it is here considered, the ICD-10 is an excellent example of what we might call a 'generative document'. It contains both the conceptual structure used to explain human mortality and the rules for building those explanations. Generative documents come in various forms. The ICD is, perhaps, one of the most important for coming to grips with professional, 'expert', understandings of physical health and illness and serves, in many ways, as a window into Western medical culture (Bowker and Star, 1999). A related publication – *The Diagnostic and Statistical Manual of Mental Disorders* (American Psychiatric Association, 2000) or DSM IV – is available for the classification of psychiatric (mental) conditions. One might say that the DSM provides the conceptual architecture that organizes Western ideas about disorders of the mind. As with the ICD, the DSM also variously includes, excludes, and renames disorders. Tracking the biography of multiple personality disorder (MPD) would, for example, provide an excellent case study of the cultural and organizational processes involved in defining mental illness.

The essential point here is that examining documents (or data sets) as topic is not simply an arcane and trivial exercise, but one that reveals the basis on which many of the generalizations about such things as patterns and trends in cardiovascular disease, suicide, drug and alcohol abuse, psychiatric disorder, and so forth are commonly made. Treating documents (reports, case-notes, death certificates, etc.) as a topic reveals an entire universe of decision making that is often taken for granted. The task of the researcher in this case is to render the unremarkable, remarkable.

3. A focus on use and function: medical documents as resource

Text, documentation, and images are commonly deployed in the exercise of medical expertise. Yet, for any given setting, if we were to ask, 'where is the medical expertise?' it is unlikely that we would point to document content as its sole repository. Rather, we would gesture towards the ways in which images, text, and tools were being used by an individual or a group in a clinical environment. In other words, it would be the ways in which human agents called up and manipulated things (including documents) rather than the things themselves that would constitute the focal point of the demonstration. For example, in a study of a Norwegian thoracic clinic Måseide (2007) investigated how X-rays are used and drawn upon in everyday clinical discussions – commenting on how the presentation of X-ray images to members of a medical team can form the occasion for a joint and agreed interpretation of what can be 'seen', rather than an occasion for presenting the self-evident 'facts' of the case. In this sense, the medical images function not simply as containers of data and information, but as focal points for the routine work and display of expertise among medical professionals.

Similarly, Hak (1992) provides an illustration of how a psychiatrist routinely transforms items of patient talk and observed behaviour into a written record. He demonstrates how the psychiatrist – as note taker – highlights essential details of a patient's conversation, translates the conversation into professional language (of delusions, hallucinations, or other diagnostic terms) and makes suggestions for future action (e.g., entry into a psychiatric unit). In short, Hak demonstrates how the psychiatric notes display the expertise of the psychiatrist and serve to confer identities and qualities to the patient that the hospital or medical service will draw upon to justify the 'appropriate' management of the patient's case.

Medical files and notes are of special interest here, because they commonly serve to define the human beings and pathologies in specific and particular ways. In so far as they do so, they usually call upon and activate a whole series of 'membership categorization devices' or MCDs (Silverman, 1998). How a particular device (such as an 'at-risk', 'obese', or 'schizophrenic' patient) comes to be associated with any individual and how that categorization might be used and called upon to account for and explain an individual's behaviour in specific circumstances can form the occasion for important and fundamental research projects in their own right. In my own study of a psychiatric hospital (Prior, 1993), for example, I was interested, among other things, in how patients came to be classified in different ways through routine procedures. It became clear that the use of notes and records formed only one support for the categorization system that surrounded patients; everyday conversation and casual interchanges formed another, and as in any organization, there was a constant interchange between talk and text. Thus, I provided in my 1993 study a short extract of an exchange between nurses in the ward office concerning 'what was wrong with X':

Nurse 1: Does anyone know what's supposed to be wrong with X?
          [Blank looks and silence meet the question]
Nurse 2: Schizophrenia, I suppose.
Nurse 1: Hmm. I've never seen any sign of it.
Nurse 3: Well, he's on chlorpromazine, so he must be schizophrenic.

The MCD of 'schizophrenic' that is recorded in the (nursing if not the psychiatric) notes is thereby sustained and underlined by means of a casual conversation – and especially with reference to 'X's' medication. (The use of medication to define a specific psychiatric disorder, rather than the other way around is not uncommon in psychiatry.) If, however, there were any real doubt about 'what was wrong with X', it would be the notes that would carry the day. Therefore, the researcher who wishes to concentrate on the use of documents in action has to be constantly aware as to how the written record is tied into and anchored within other aspects of organizational life such as conversations at the nursing station. Nevertheless, it is only when assessments are written down and can be pointed to, that they are used to form a foundation on which routine social actions are built. Thus, medical professionals can and do use 'the files' as a license for action – showing how what they do to patients is warranted by the information in the files and on the records. Indeed, in the context of psychiatry, Barrett (1996:107) has underlined how 'clinical writing' not merely describes the treatment of patients, it also constitutes the treatment.

In a wider context, Bowker and Star (1999) and Young (1995) have pointed out how (documented) nomenclatures of disease are routinely tied into the financial accounting mechanisms of hospital life. So, psychiatrists, say, routinely take a diagnostic category from the aforementioned ICD, or DSM, 'fit' it to a given patient, and then justify what was done for and to the patient/client in the light of the category. This is done in the full knowledge that categories and patients rarely make a 1:1 fit. Indeed, the naming of diseases and disorders in modern medical systems is often used more for purposes of financial reimbursement (to and from insurance companies, especially in the market-based health system found in the United States), and other accounting and monitoring purposes, than they are for forming accurate descriptions of a given patient's condition.

Arguing along a similar path, Zerubavel (1979:45) observed how notes written up by medical and nursing professionals were 'among the main criteria used by their supervisors to evaluate their clinical competence', as well as forming the primary mechanism through which continuous supervision of patients was maintained. In fact, Zerubavel's study highlights the centrality of charts, graphs, and records of all kinds in underpinning the routine social organization of hospital life. Printed schedules are used to organize the patient/staff day; printouts of various kinds are routinely used to monitor patients, and notes are written in order to indicate how the 'hospital' cares for its clients. (In US hospitals, of course, patient records are, as we have already indicated, also used as a hook on which to hang financial costs and transactions.)

This capacity of medical records to mediate social relationships of all kinds has been further studied by Berg (1996; 1997) who points out how hospital patients are both structured and accessed through records. One important feature of patient existence emphasized by Berg is the manner in which medical records are used to keep the case (and the patient) 'on track'. Such structuring of patient trajectories through records is achieved in numerous ways – planning and monitoring being two of them.

Patient trajectories are not, of course, the only things that are kept 'on track' by the use of records. As I have suggested in the preceding section, patient identities are also constructed and sustained through documentation, and it is usually the case that identities and trajectories bear a close relationship one with the other. For example, in a recent study (Scott et al., 2005) we examined how genetic risk assessments of clients attending a cancer genetics clinic led to the ascription of an identity (low, moderate, and high risk), and a trajectory through the medical services that reflected the relevant assessment. Thus, those identified at 'high' risk were channelled through a screening programme that was considered inappropriate for low risk individuals. Interestingly, many of the patients identified as being at low risk felt short-changed by such assessments and would have preferred to have been deemed high risk. In the following interview, extract a patient who has been deemed by the genetics clinic to be at moderate risk of inheriting a mutation related to the onset of colorectal cancer displays obvious pleasure at his new at-moderate-risk identity. Note how it is the letter that he received from the clinic, and the notes lodged within, that underpins his new sense of security:

Patient 41: This [holds risk assessment letter from the clinic] is in the background.
   Am I going to get to 60? Let's worry about it when I get to it. You say what do I think about it? Yeah I am glad. I know that I can say 'Hey, I want some screening now'. And they have to do it too. Whereas if I go along and say – 'my dad and grand-dad died of cancer can I have some screening?' – unless I had a genetic risk they would have said 'on your bike, back of the queue'. And at least now this is in my notes and when my time comes at least I know.

In the section that follows, I shall use an extract from a clinical genetics meeting to illustrate how documents enter into such risk assessments. The emphasis there, however, will be on the role of documents as actors, rather than as resources, that can be used by medical professionals or their clients in their everyday activities.

4. A focus on use and function: documents as actors

The idea of conceptualizing nonhuman agents as actors was first proposed by adherents of what is often referred to as actor–network theory or ANT (see, Law and Hassard, 1999; Callon and Law, 1997). One key plank of the ANT argument is that the traditional distinction – indeed, the asymmetry – between material and human objects be overturned. In the same way, it is argued that the traditional distinction between subject and object be discarded. Therefore, when studying schemes of social interaction, material objects are not to be regarded as mere (passive) resources that are important only when activated by human actors, but are seen to play a part in social configurations in their own right. That is to say, material objects can be seen to instigate and direct as well as be directed (Callon and Law, 1997:101).

In what follows, I provide an example of the ways in which documents enter into an episode of clinic based interaction. The episode involves exchanges between a clinical geneticist (designated as CG), and some specialist genetic nurse–counsellors (designated as NC). The aim of their discussion is to assess the degree to which a client of the genetics service might be at risk of expressing an inherited proclivity to breast cancer. The details are contained in Box 21.2.

Note how the session opens with (and is structured by) a statement of the relevant issues as conveyed in a letter from the patient's primary care physician (lines 2 to 9). Such letters serve as triggers for consideration by the service, and 'frame' the relevant clinical problems. In addition to giving the client's clinical and biographical details, the letters usually contain a justification as to why the patient has been referred to the service. In this case, it is suggested that the patient is 'naturally concerned' about her family history.

Between lines 11 and lines 18, the clinical geneticist is examining the patient's genetic pedigree or family tree. The 'black lines' referred to indicate deaths from cancer, and the pedigree will normally be inscribed with the names, ages, and current states of health of people in the patient's family over as many generations as is possible. (For an example of a genetic pedigree, see Prior, 2003.) Here, the pedigree is brought into the discussion via pointing and looking. It provides a field in terms of which the discussion can proceed. Note how it is recruited as evidence by both NC and CG for variable interpretations of 'what is important' (lines 14 and 15).

A crucial point is arrived at in line 19, and there is evident disappointment expressed in the talk contained in lines 19–22. The disappointment arises, because an expert computer-based decision-aid has generated a much lower risk assessment for the client than was expected. CG states, 'I suspect that puts her into a high – oh! – 24.6 percent. (1.0) Mm'.

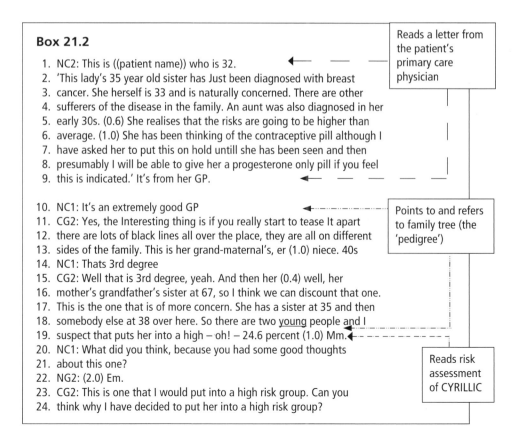

Box 21.2

1. NC2: This is ((patient name)) who is 32.
2. 'This lady's 35 year old sister has Just been diagnosed with breast
3. cancer. She herself is 33 and is naturally concerned. There are other
4. sufferers of the disease in the family. An aunt was also diagnosed in her
5. early 30s. (0.6) She realises that the risks are going to be higher than
6. average. (1.0) She has been thinking of the contraceptive pill although I
7. have asked her to put this on hold untill she has been seen and then
8. presumably I will be able to give her a progesterone only pill if you feel
9. this is indicated.' It's from her GP.

10. NC1: It's an extremely good GP
11. CG2: Yes, the Interesting thing is if you really start to tease It apart
12. there are lots of black lines all over the place, they are all on different
13. sides of the family. This is her grand-maternal's, er (1.0) niece. 40s
14. NC1: Thats 3rd degree
15. CG2: Well that is 3rd degree, yeah. And then her (0.4) well, her
16. mother's grandfather's sister at 67, so I think we can discount that one.
17. This is the one that is of more concern. She has a sister at 35 and then
18. somebody else at 38 over here. So there are two young people and I
19. suspect that puts her into a high – oh! – 24.6 percent (1.0) Mm.
20. NC1: What did you think, because you had some good thoughts
21. about this one?
22. NG2: (2.0) Em.
23. CG2: This is one that I would put into a high risk group. Can you
24. think why I have decided to put her into a high risk group?

Reads a letter from the patient's primary care physician

Points to and refers to family tree (the 'pedigree')

Reads risk assessment of CYRILLIC

The decision-aid is known as Cyrillic. Cyrillic draws a pedigree for any given family member and – on the basis of quite complicated processes that involve data bases and statistical calculations – produces a lifetime risk estimate of the onset of breast cancer. Very roughly stated, a low risk would be below 12 percent, a moderate risk between 12 and 24 percent, and a high risk above 25 percent. The difference here is marginal, but sufficient to generate doubt (lines 19–22). Such doubts are overturned in lines 23–24, and in the subsequent discussion – beyond line 24 – a justification for ignoring the results of the decision-aid is provided.

We can see then that there are various actors inscribed in this setting. These include not merely the human actors, but also the nonhuman referral letter, the pedigree and the Cyrillic print out. Of these the latter probably serves our purpose best. It does so, because it advances an assessment of a problem and as such it must be noted and then countered. In this instance, the countering is easily achieved, but were things to 'go wrong' for the patient at some future stage (say as a result of a screening procedure), we might guess that the status of Cyrillic and of the risk-assessment produced by Cyrillic could be elevated to entirely different heights. In short, the Cyrillic print out would be cast in the role of an independent expert that was wilfully ignored.

All in all, then, it is clear that instead of a focus on talk and human agents, it is the entire complex of events that deserve study. In that complex, documents function as props, allies, rule-makers, calculators, decision-makers, experts and illustrators. In short, they appear as what might justifiably called 'hybrids' (Callon and Rip, 1992), and as such they deserve attention. How documents – especially in the form of decision-aids – can drive medical decision-making procedures is, at present, a poorly researched field.

CONCLUSIONS

The emphasis that social scientists commonly place on human actors manifests itself most clearly in the attention that they give to what such actors say and do. Moreover, should we wish to study human actors in a rigorous social scientific manner, there are many manuals and textbooks to instruct us as to how we might capture and analyze speech and behaviour. However, few social science research manuals concentrate on the written word and, more specifically, on documents that contain words. Indeed, when documents are put forward for consideration they are usually approached in terms of their content rather than their status as 'things'. That is, the focus is usually on the language contained in the document as a window into the thoughts and actions of human beings. Yet, as I emphasized in the introduction, it is quite clear that each and every document stands in a dual relation to fields of action. Namely, as a receptacle (of instructions, commands, wishes, reports, descriptions, etc.), and as an agent that is open to manipulation and/or use as an ally to be mobilised for further action.

As a receptacle of content, one set of questions that a social scientific researcher may ask concern the processes and circumstances that led to the creation of document 'X'. That is, the document becomes a topic of investigation rather than a resource. Of course, as I have indicated, documents are not just manufactured, they are also consumed (used), and as with all tools, they are manipulated in organized settings for many different ends.

Indeed, documents emerge in organizational settings in many different ways – irrespective of human manipulations – and documents have important effects. Therefore, a further route of analysis for the researcher is to ask questions about how documents function in specific circumstances. Naturally, the way in which a document functions is often affected by its content, but the latter is rarely a determinant of the former. In fact, we need to keep in mind that the content of a document is never fixed and static – it is 'situated', and therefore, sensitive to context. In fact, the analysis of content, production, and function form the three points around which we can think about how to develop a suitable research strategy for dealing with documents in both their inert and their active/dynamic states.

NOTE

1 Current update available at, http://www.who.int/classifications/apps/icd/icd10online/

REFERENCES

American Psychiatric Association (2000) *Diagnostic and Statistical Manual of Mental Disorders. DSM-IV-TR*. Washington, DC: American Psychiatric Association.

Angrosino, M.V. (1989) *Documents of Interaction. Biography, Autobiography, and Life History in Social Science Perspective.* Gainsville FLA: University of Florida Press.

Barrett, R. (1996) *The Psychiatric Team and the Social Definition of Schizophrenia. An Anthropological Study of Person and Illness.* Cambridge: Cambridge University Press.

Bazerman, C. (1988) *Shaping Written Knowledge. The Genre and Activity of the Experimental Article in Science.* Madison, Wisconsin: University of Wisconsin Press.

Berg, M. (1996) 'Practices of Reading and Writing: The Constitutive Role of the Patient Record in Medical Work'. *Sociology of Health and Illness*, 18(4): 499–524.

Berg, M. (1997) *Rationalizing Medical Work. Decision-Support Techniques and Medical Practices.* Cambridge, MA: The MIT Press.

Bowker, G.C. and Star, S.L. (1999) *Sorting Things Out. Classification and its Consequences.* Cambridge: MA. MIT Press.

Bowling, A. (2002) *Research Methods in Health.* Buckingham: Open University Press.

Bryman, A. (2004) *Social Research Methods.* Oxford: Oxford University Press.

Callon, M. and Law, J. (1997) 'L'irruption des non-humains dans les sciences humains: quelques lecons tirées de la sociologie des sciences et des techniques'. In, B.Reynaud (ed.) *Les limites de la rationalité* (pp. 99–118). Paris: La Découverte.

Callon, M. and Rip, A. (1992) 'Humains et non-humains: morale d'une coexistence'. In J. Theys and B. Kalaora (eds.) *La Terre outrage Les experts sont formels!* (pp. 140–56). Paris: Autrement.

Department of Health (2007) *Choice Matters 2007–08. Putting Patients in Control* (p. 4). London: DH.

Gilbert, G.N. and Mulkay, M. (1984) *Opening Pandora's Box. A Sociological Analysis of Scientists' Discourse.* Cambridge: Cambridge University Press.

Glaser, B.G. and Strauss, A.L. (1967*) The Discovery of Grounded Theory. Strategies for Qualitative Research.* New York: Aldine De Gruyter.

Goode, W.J. and Hatt, P.K. (1952) *Methods in Social Research.* NY: McGraw-Hill.

Gross, A. G. (1996) *The Rhetoric of Science.* Cambridge. MA: Harvard University Press.

Hak, T. (1992) 'Psychiatric Records as Transformations of Other Texts'. In G. Watson and R.M. Seiler (eds.) (1992) *Text in Context. Contributions to Ethnomethodology* (pp.138–55). London: Sage.

Hodder, I. (2000) 'The Interpretation of Document sand Material Culture'. In, N.K. Denzin and Y.S. Lincoln (eds.) *Handbook of Qualitative Research* (2nd Edition) (pp. 703–16). London: Sage.

Krippendorf, K. (2004) *Content Analysis. An Introduction to its Methodology* (2nd Edition). London: Sage.

Law, J. and Hassard, J. (eds.) (1999) *Actor–Network Theory and After.* Oxford: Blackwell.

Lee, R.M. (2000) *Unobtrusive Methods in Social Research* (p. 16). Buckingham: Open University Press.

Måseide, P. (2007) 'The Role of Signs and Representations in the Organization of Medical Work: X-rays in Medical Problem Solving'. In, R. Iedema (ed.) *The Discourse of Hospital* (pp. 201–21) *Communication.* Basingstoke: Macmillan.

May. T. (1997) *Social Research. Issues, Methods and Process.* Buckingham: Open University Press.

Newman, J. and Vidler, E. (2006) 'Discriminating Customers, Responsible Patients, Empowered Users. Consumerism and the Modernisation of Health Care', *Journal of Social Policy,* 35(2): 193–210.

Plummer, K. (2001) *Documents of Life, 2. An Invitation to Critical Humanism.* London: Sage.

Prior, L. (1989) *The Social Organization of Death.* Basingstoke: Macmillan.

Prior, L. (1993) *The Social Organization of Mental Illness.* London: Sage.

Prior, L. (2000) 'Reflections on the Mortal Body in Late Modernity'. In Gabe, J., Williams, S., and Calnan, M. (eds.) *Health, Medicine and Society* (pp. 186–202). London: Routledge.

Prior, L. (2003) *Using Documents in Social Research.* London: Sage.

Prior, L. (2007) 'Talking about the Gene for Cancer. A Study of Lay and Professional Knowledge of Cancer Genetics', *Sociology,* 41(6): 985–1001.

Prior, L. (2008) 'Repositioning Documents in Social Research', *Sociology,* 42: 5821–36.

Prior, L. and Bloor, M. (1993) 'Why People Die: Social Representations of Death and Its Causes', *Science as Culture,* 3(16): 346–74.

Roe, E. (1994) *Narrative Policy Analysis.* Durham, NC: Duke University Press.

Scott, J. (1990) *A Matter of Record. Documentary Sources in Social Research.* Cambridge: Polity Press.

Scott, S., Prior, L., Wood, F., and Gray, J. (2005) 'Re-Positioning the Patient. The Implications of Being-at-Risk', *Social Science and Medicine,* 60: 1869–79.

Silverman, D. (1998) *Harvey Sacks. Social Science and Conversation Analysis.* Cambridge: Polity Press.

Timmermans, S. (2006) *Postmortem: How Medical Examiners Explain Suspicious Deaths.* Chicago: Chicago University Press.

Van Eeten, M.J.G. (2007) 'Narrative Policy Analysis'. In, Fischer, F., J. G. Miller, and M.S. Sidney (eds.) *Handbook of Public Policy Analysis* (pp. 251–69). Boca Raton: Fl. CRC Press.

Weber, R.P. (1990) *Basic Content Analysis.* London: Sage.

Wood, L.A. (2000) *Doing Discourse Analysis. Methods for Studying Action in Talk and Text.* London: Sage.

Young, A. (1995) *The Harmony of Illusions. Inventing Post-traumatic Stress Disorder.* Princeton NJ: Princeton University Press.

Zerubavel, E. (1979) *Patterns of Time in Hospital Life: A Sociological Perspective.* London: University of Chicago Press.

Zimmerman, D.H. and Pollner, M. (1971) 'The Everyday World as a Phenomenon'. In J.D. Douglas (ed.) *Understanding Everyday Life* (pp. 80–103). London: Routledge and Kegan Paul.

22

Participatory Action Research: Theoretical Perspectives on the Challenges of Researching Action

Louise Potvin, Sherri L. Bisset and Leah Walz

INTRODUCTION

Participatory action research (PAR) was first developed in the 1940s by the social psychologist Kurt Lewin as a practice characterized by the continuous interplay between research and intervention activities. Traditionally in PAR, there is no real distinction between interveners and researchers; these two roles are highly integrated in their contribution to social betterment. However, over the past 30 years, PAR has become increasingly associated with applied research and program evaluation and less as a means of intervention. Thus, the roles of the researcher and intervener have also become increasingly distinct (for a more complete discussion of the various versions of PAR, see Reason, 1994). Participatory Evaluation Research (PER), in which evaluators and various program stakeholders develop collaborative evaluation activities (Springett, 2001a; 2001b), is now recognized as a legitimate type of inquiry that enhances the use of evaluation results (Patton, 1997). Today, the distinction between PAR and PER is mainly semantic. Both describe a research endeavour in which researchers, interveners and various program stakeholders collaborate in order to produce knowledge that supports the improvement of interventions. The main difference between PER and PAR is that PAR is mainly concerned with producing knowledge about a program or intervention (how it works and produces effects), rather than assigning it a value (see Springett, 2001a for review of the distinctions between PAR and PER).

Our objective in this chapter is to argue that PAR is the preferred research practice for studying systems of action. There exist many excellent discussions of the principles and various definitions of PAR and other participatory inquiry methods in the literature (Reason and Bradbury, 2006) and their applications to health intervention (Cargo and Mercer, 2008; Green et al., 1995; Israel et al., 1998; Minkler, 1999). Our aim is not to add another such review. Instead, we argue for the necessity to incorporate a corpus of relevant theoretical propositions into PAR research activities, in order to produce knowledge that is more generally relevant for population health interventions defined as organized actions that aim to modify the determinants and conditions that shape health in a population (Hawe and Potvin, 2009).

A practical definition of PAR

Each of the three elements that compose PAR, participation, action and research refers to a huge literature and theoretical discussion. The term 'research' refers to the scientific activity of producing empirical knowledge, the term 'action' identifies the object of that research, and 'participatory' refers to the type of practices implemented in conducting the research. As will be clear in the rest of the chapter, and following Latour (1999), our conception of research is one that emphasizes the work of researchers in 'knowledge in the making'. Our particular focus in this chapter is on the action dimension of PAR and how it conditions the participatory nature of the research, a topic rarely discussed in the PAR literature. We do so because the current focus on the participatory and research elements of PAR has led to an emphasis on the local nature of the knowledge produced, related to an almost exclusive reliance on constructivist frameworks in PAR. In its place, we propose an alternate epistemology, critical realism. We believe that producing knowledge about action necessarily calls for some form of participatory interaction between the action under study and the researcher.

We understand interventions to be dynamic and made up of interacting and interrelated activities, processes, and practices performed by interdependent actors working in coordination to accomplish a set of predetermined objectives (Potvin et al., 2001; Potvin and McQueen, 2008). As you will see, we do not view interventions as purely objective and static, uniquely composed of ordered lists of instructions, rules, and procedures to be followed and resources to be mobilised, nor do we see them as ephemeral and fluid representations or imaginings which cannot be translated beyond their immediate context. Theories of social action, seen as conceptual frameworks, can produce transferable knowledge from participatory studies of population health intervention. Ultimately, the role of PAR is to contribute knowledge about the functioning of population health interventions, showing how they contribute to the social transformations that lead to improved health.

With this in mind, we use our experience of doing research on the implementation of a health promotion program in a school setting to explore the practical challenges of studying the dynamic processes of interventions to promote health. Our aim is to demonstrate that PAR requires researchers to enter the field equipped with epistemological and methodological strategies that provide the conceptual tools necessary to account for the processes and mechanisms at play. Further, we develop the argument that a research practice that acknowledges the participation of both researchers and research subjects into a common project is the only means by which one can derive knowledge from – and about – the actions taking place within interventions. Finally, we propose that this type of research requires that the relationships between researchers and other actors be structured by formal agreements keeping in mind the need for researchers to be reflexive about the impact of their research on the program they are studying.

When interventions are conceptualized as systems of action or characterized by collaboration and reflexivity, we must consider the local conditions and contexts that surround the implementation of interventions and that shape their processes and effects (Poland et al., 2008). This reorientation of PAR is highly relevant in light of recent calls for more 'practice-based evidence' (Green, 2006: 406) in the field of public health. We interpret this call as pointing to the need to complement and balance the current knowledge base, wherein local conditions are conceived as confounding factors which have to be 'controlled for', with a broader understanding of what context is and how it interacts with a program to produce intended (and unintended) program effects (Poland et al., 2008).

CASE IN POINT: THE NUTRITION INTERVENTION PETITS CUISTOTS-PARENTS EN RÉSEAU

In order to illustrate our approach we draw on an evaluative research program we did in collaboration with several organizations: a Montreal community organization called 'Les ateliers cinq epices' the operators of Petits Cuistots-Parents en Réseau (translated as Little Cooks – Parental Networks and referred to as LC-PN), the Montreal School Board, and a private foundation that funded the project (Fondation Lucie et André Chagnon (www.fondationchagnon.org). The nutrition education intervention LC-PN is a school-based initiative promoting nutritional and culinary education for primary school children and their families. The program was initiated in 1989 by mothers who were active in their children's school through lunch-time supervision roles. Based upon their active involvement with their community and their recognition of the poor quality of lunches for school children, this small group of women initiated a nutrition intervention which became increasingly professionalized over time (Bisset and Potvin, 2007). As a community initiative, the program is not based exclusively upon research knowledge of how health behaviour can be changed, but rather incorporates the knowledge of laypeople, health practitioners, and education specialists.

In effect, the program which is now known as Little Cooks – Parental Networks was originally designed not with public health goals in mind, but for social reasons: mothers who volunteered decided to start a collective kitchen in order to break the monotony and solitude of preparing family meals alone. Through the involvement of a community nutritionist and with the help of funding from a government food security initiative, these mothers expanded the mandate of the program to include free hot lunches for disadvantaged children and later added nutrition education and food preparation components. Additional partnerships and the addition of other types of stakeholders, including food security activists, led to the standardization and expansion of the program into several new schools both within and outside of the original community (see Bisset and Potvin, 2007 for more details on the evolution of LC-PN). However, despite several iterations, the program retains two of its original characteristics: students' active involvement in food preparation (i.e., Little Cooks) and continued parental participation (i.e., Parental Networks).

Briefly, LC-PN is targeted at elementary school children and their families living in Montreal's most disadvantaged neighbourhoods. It was incrementally implemented in a total of eight schools for students in kindergarten through grade six classes during the period from 2000 to 2009. The Little Cooks component of the program consists of eight annual teacher- and parent-assisted monthly nutrition workshops, created and facilitated by community nutritionists offering concrete experiences with food, via food preparation and tasting activities. Each workshop includes: (1) didactic knowledge transmission on topics such as food transformation, food types, nutrition and health; (2) hands-on recipe completion using a cooperative learning approach; and (3) tasting of the finished recipe with samples to be taken home. The main objective of this component was to promote the development of nutritional knowledge and culinary abilities of elementary school children to improve their health and development. Parents are invited to participate with their child during the nutrition workshops and to attend collective dinners and family outings. The parental component is organized by community development workers and aims to support social integration and the development of mutual support networks through parents' active involvement in the school, in an effort to highlight their economic and parental responsibilities.

Throughout the evolution of the program, its objectives and priorities shifted and new goals developed. Although the program began as a simple way to make cooking more enjoyable for a few women, it developed into formalized interventions based on the tenets of public health and social welfare: (1) to improve child health and development through food provision, nutrition education, and behaviour change, based on the premises that disadvantaged children did not have access to nutritious meals, and that they lacked knowledge about food and nutrition and the ability to prepare a variety of healthy meals, and (2) to improve parental (and by extension child) well-being by encouraging the involvement of parents in school activities, based on the premise that many parents in disadvantaged neighbourhoods were isolated and lacked social support networks. (Parents may also have benefited from free meals and/or exposure – via their child, or their direct involvement in the program – to information about nutrition and food preparation.)

The program positively influenced family participation in school activities as well as students' knowledge of the nutrient content of food, food produce and cooking, attitude and experience with tasting of new or less common foods, and perceived cooking capacity (Bisset et al., 2008). However, it is also important to think about why or how a program works, in order to be able to generalize research findings, to correct existing problems, and to implement the program in other locations.

A CRITICAL REALIST EPISTEMOLOGY FOR PARTICIPATORY ACTION RESEARCH

Before a researcher can attempt to explain how and why a population health intervention works, she/he must clarify her/his epistemological position. In order to produce the desired knowledge about the intervention, she/he must be clear about the kind of relationship that must take place between her/him as a knowing subject and the intervention to be studied. One epistemological position, often referred to as positivism, is generally thought to be incompatible with PAR. Positivism is based on the premise that a researcher or observer can remain 'objective' and can observe and produce knowledge about a distant object, the intervention, without interfering with its natural trajectory. The positivist position *is* compatible with representations of interventions as logic models, which describe interventions according to four components: (1) inputs, including staff and financial resources, (2) activities or processes that lead to the desired effect, (3) outputs, which describe the services and goods provided to clients, and (4) outcomes, the short- or long-term results or impacts of the intervention. In their usual form, logic models do not take into account the agency of intervention actors, paying no attention to their capacity to exercise causal power on the situation, outside of that engineered by the program (Potvin and McQueen, 2008). From this perspective, the LC-PN nutrition program could be analyzed by examining the explicit mandates of the program (e.g., to provide information on the nutritional content of foods), the fidelity of the nutritionists and teachers' actions with regards to program's instructions, the content of the workshops and lessons delivered to the participating students, and the extent to which students were able to learn the information presented and acquired and maintained the skills the program was intended to transfer.

Another epistemological position, known as constructivism, holds that all knowledge is 'subjective' and so-called truths are 'constructed' rather than discovered; therefore, each individual will have a different understanding of a program. This paradigm holds that law-like regularities which are part of the physical world do not exist in the social world. In this light, the social world lacks an 'objective' truth or one 'true' reality, and instead knowledge is the result of specific perspectives. Here, interventions are uniquely described based upon the representations that actors offer of the situation and their interactions with other actors. With regards to the LC-PN nutrition program, a constructivist analysis might focus on specific contextual factors which may have been important to the implementation or success of LC-PN in different school environments. For example, parents might see the nutrition program:

- As a way to gain access to nutritious foods
- As a site for the creation of enduring social relationships with other parents facing similar social and economic challenges or
- As a location where their knowledge about food and their personal culinary practices and traditions were challenged or delegitimized

In some instances, qualitative research is assumed to be constructivist in orientation, and similarly, because it challenges the subject-object divide through its emphasis on participatory approaches, PAR has been overwhelmingly associated with constructivist epistemology. In addition, in contrast to logic models, PAR recognizes program actors as having causal powers whereby they may influence program operations in unexpected ways. Rejecting a view of programs as logic models and of participants as passive subjects, Guba and Lincoln (1989) argue for a complete departure from an objectivist approach and the exclusive use of constructivist models. However, this epistemological position is not without its weaknesses. For example, while this approach may prove useful for the purposes of facilitating local collaboration, it does not guide research towards the identification of generalizable knowledge regarding the social processes that underlie the operations of a program (Greene, 2007). In other words, a constructivist approach restricts accounts of intervention events and operations to a particular situation and context, and in so doing, offers little in terms of knowledge which can be generalized beyond the study context (Connell and Kubisch, 1998; et al., 2005).

In our minds, this lack of generalizability limits the extent to which research based on this epistemology can contribute to the creation and/or improvement of population health interventions, and as such we are reluctant to subscribe entirely to this position. However, more importantly, while recognizing the importance of constructivist approaches to qualitative research and PAR, we reject a hidden assumption behind the heated debates between those who defend positivist or constructivist approaches – that these are the only two tenable epistemological positions. Instead, we suggest the use of a critical realist perspective (Bhaskar, 1978; Sayer, 2000). Critical realism can resolve the epistemological dilemma posed by the objectivist/constructivist divide by providing a way to account for, and explain, the dynamism and changing nature of the systems (or interventions) under study, while producing knowledge that can be generalized and used to guide action in other situations. Critical realism can do so, because it shifts the focus of attention to the mechanisms that generate health problems (such as a lack of knowledge about nutrition) and the mechanisms that improve population health and well-being (including providing children with the practical skills required to prepare nutritious meals). Because it is not as well known as objectivism or constructivism, we offer a brief explanation of the tenets of critical realism.

Critical realism: the search of context–mechanism–outcome connections

In contrast to constructivism, which emphasizes the need to 'understand people's constructions of meanings in the context being studied, because it is these constructions that constitute social realities and underlie all human action' (Greene, 2007: 986), critical realism holds that a reality exists beyond our perceptions and control. In short, 'the (social) world should not be conflated with our experience of it' (Pawson and Tilley, 1997: 11), and human experience does not account for all possible underlying social processes that lead to particular occurrences or events. Thus, while acknowledging the role of perception and the existence of individual social realities, a critical realist epistemology holds that there is an objectively knowable reality and argues that the social world can be understood by examining patterns and regularities (and thus, it is possible to acquire knowledge from the social world that can be generalized beyond a particular situation, a point we revisit in the following section).

According to critical realism, patterns and regularities within the social world are best explained not through the logic of cause and effect, but by thinking in terms of generative mechanisms, which produce particular outcomes if these mechanisms are triggered (or 'activated') in the right conditions. Thus, critical realism argues that 'the world is characterized by emergence' where the causal powers that lie within the social processes are either 'activated or remain dormant' (Pawson and Tilley, 1997: 12), depending on whether or not these mechanisms are triggered or counteracted by other processes. Particularly within open systems, such mechanisms are numerous and are continuously interacting with one another, creating an ever-changing landscape of events; therefore, it is challenging to map out all of the processes and predict future events. Importantly, according to Bhaskar (1978), while social processes have causal law-like properties, they are not directly visible; rather, they are perceptible through the influence they exert upon social episodes, patterns or events which are observable and can be inscribed (Latour, 1999a) and recorded through measurement devices. Making these inscriptions into some form of material and objective reality (answers to items in a questionnaire, t-cells count in a blood sample, density and shades of grey on an x-ray image, check mark on an observation grid, verbatim transcript from an interview, and so on) is the vehicle by which the empirical experience they capture can be taken out of its context and linked to other sets of inscriptions.

The challenges of applied research

It is only possible to account for these generative mechanisms if they are activated (and not counteracted by other mechanisms), and it is only possible to record and measure the influence of these mechanisms if we possess the necessary technical and conceptual tools to observe events generated by the mechanisms in question. To clarify what we mean by tools and mechanisms, it is useful to think about the difference between laboratory research and applied research, such as research on the LC-PN nutrition program. Generative or causal mechanisms exist in both types of research, but they are much easier to isolate and identify in the laboratory, because laboratory experiments are characterized by the scientist's capacity to create a situation in which he can study the effects (or causal power) of one thing (e.g., a virus) while holding everything else constant (e.g., all subjects are male mice, of a certain breed and age, etc.). Thus, all potential causal mechanisms (such as the potential effects of being male) exercise their causal power in a constant and/or known manner except for the one element under study. The scientific research process in the laboratory essentially aims at linking observable outcomes (e.g., the presence or absence of infection) with specific mechanisms (the causal power of the virus), while taking into account, or 'controlling for', other contextual conditions (e.g., sex, age, etc.). The simple cause and effect relationship (e.g., introduction of the virus results in infection 100 percent of the time) is a special case where relevant and known contextual conditions are held constant (Bhaskar, 1978). However, even this simple relationship is only observable if the scientist possesses the necessary tools, such as the laboratory equipment, the training, and the disciplinary knowledge to identify the presence of the virus and the infection in the mice under study. Furthermore (and this will become more important to our discussion of reflexivity in the following section), from a critical realist perspective, it is *not* assumed that the laboratory scientist lacks causal power in this situation, as implied by objectivist descriptions of researchers as neutral observers whose actions do not interfere with what is observed. Instead, as Bhaskar (1978) points out, and as Latour (1999a) describes, the laboratory scientist has a great deal of causal power, but it is exerted in a controlled and predictable manner, and it is accounted for through detailed recording of the scientist's activities in diaries and logs.

Applied research rarely functions in this manner. More than 30 years ago, in his presidential address to the American Psychological Association, Lee J. Cronbach discussed the chasm that exists between laboratory and applied sciences. For him, in experimental situations involving human subjects, the potential for an 'aptitude by treatment interaction' can never be completely eliminated – in lay terms, people respond to changes in their social world (such as treatments or the implementation of a nutrition program such as LC-PN) in decidedly human ways. The psychological characteristics of human subjects, with their infinite potential for variation, always have the possibility of interacting with the treatment under study, and this can create what statisticians call higher-order interactions (Cronbach, 1975), interactions which involve more than three variables and the effects of which are very difficult to interpret. Cronbach was working in the quantitative domain, but the same argument can be made for qualitative analyses: namely, that in the (social) world outside of the laboratory, it is impossible to keep all contextual factors constant, or to exclude them from your study, and examine only the effects of one element at a time – such as the impact of a nutrition program on the health and development of children. That is, events are created by the interactions among causal mechanisms, none of which can be truly isolated from other contextual mechanisms.

For Callon and Rabeharisoa (2003), this is the main difference between conducting research in the wild as compared with conducting research in the controlled environment of a laboratory. Nevertheless, a researcher conducting research in the wild has many powerful conceptual tools at her/his disposal, including theories, accumulated empirical knowledge, and established disciplinary conventions in the form of observation and measurement techniques and instruments. Armed with these tools, the researcher's task is to link her/his observations (made possible by the theories and methods she employs) with what is known of the potential contextual and program-generated mechanisms at play (based, in part, on a survey of the academic literature) and to develop plausible explanation(s) to link events and outcomes with their generative mechanisms and the contextual conditions in which they were triggered. Like the laboratory context, the researcher must attempt to account for the effects of her own research activities; however, with research in the wild, the exact reproduction of her/his activities (in a controlled and predictable manner, like in the laboratory) is both impossible and inappropriate, in part because of the continuously changing conditions. As such, she/he must aim to record her/his own practices as well as the causal mechanisms that may be triggered by her/his research activities, and include these elements as part of her overall analysis – a point we discuss in the last section of this chapter.

In the following two sections, we explain in more detail the kinds of tools that qualitative researchers can employ to fully account for the mechanisms at play within social worlds or programs. These tools allow the findings of PAR to be generalized beyond the context in which they are generated. We outline the tenets of the actor–network theory (ANT) in order to show how it helped us to better understand and represent the mechanisms at play in the implementation and evolution of the PC-PR nutrition program and how it helped us engage in better and more collaborative research. In the final section, we explain how distinct features of PAR make it necessary for researchers to account for the effects of their presence and activities.

A RELEVANT THEORY OF ACTION FOR PARTICIPATORY ACTION RESEARCH

A population health intervention consists of organized collective action aiming to resolve a population health problem (Dab, 2005). The legitimacy of such interventions and their capacity to contribute to the resolution of health problems is frequently attributed to their use of up-to-date scientific knowledge and state-of-the-art know-how. Seen in this light, as innovative solutions to public health problems, public health interventions are health technologies (or innovations) (Lehoux, 2006). Conceptualizing health interventions as technologies (or innovations) expands our frame of reference into the Social Studies of Technology (SST). SST explores the constitution of technologies, responding to questions such as why some technologies succeed while others fail or why a technology takes on one form but not another. Explanations of these questions focus upon the duality between 'the social' and 'the technical' components of an innovation, where the actions and formation of one realm are understood in terms of the other.

More precisely, as a conceptual apparatus, SST permit interventions, as systems of action, to be understood in terms of the people and the things that make a system, as well as their complex interactions. Here, interventions are not uniquely understood in terms of tangible (e.g., services, resources, and logic planning models) and intangible (e.g., up-to-date scientific knowledge and state-of-the-art know-how) things (i.e., technical components), but also in terms of the uptake of roles and the development of new relationships (i.e., social components). From within this large field of SST, we select one theoretical framework, the Actor-Network Theory (ANT) an approach that regards social and technical components as being mutually constitutive, that is, in a continuous process of co-formation. In other words, instead of being separate and distinct, the actions of people in a system are understood to develop in response to available technologies, and likewise, technologies are the product of the actions of people. As its name implies, the network is used to capture the constitution of innovation or technology where the network is a set of coordinated movements or negotiations (i.e., 'work') forming connections between social and technical entities (Akrich et al., 2002; Callon, 1986; Latour, 1987).

Interventions as sociotechnical networks

The sociotechnical network thus consists of social and technical entities (or actors) that become connected through their actions or 'work'. The theory uses the term 'actor' or 'actant' in reference to, respectively, a human or a nonhuman entity. While we do not dwell upon this here, put simply, the description of people and technologies as actors comes from the principle of symmetry where both human and nonhuman actors are considered to exercise causal power and to take form from the influence of the other. The ANT asserts that the identities or the defining qualities of the social and technical entities in a network are shaped through the 'work' of interpreting, translating, negotiating, or compromising goals, capacities or interests when forming connections. According to ANT, an open system is one where the roles and identity of the entities are still being 'worked out' or negotiated. Here, connections are not yet stable. In contrast, a closed system is characterized by entities with a role or identity that is stable and predictable. In essence, intervention as a sociotechnical network captures the process whereby the social and technical entities negotiate how to organize together and achieve a set of collective goals. The goals that define an intervention become aligned during its implementation. Once again, when we recall that each entity belongs to multiple networks, we appreciate the inherent challenge of this process.

ANT helps us reflect upon population health intervention as a set of constantly unfolding actions, which occur in a sociotechnical network. The emerging network is not stable; connections may become broken and new connections are always forming. In contrast to seeing the intervention as 'floating' in a particular context or seeing context as something to be 'controlled' so that confounding factors do not interfere with the validity of attributing interventions effects to the intervention (Poland et al., 2008), ANT makes no a priori distinction between 'contextual' and 'intervention' entities. A sociotechnical network (i.e., a program) simply becomes the connection between human and nonhuman entities, between intervention and contextual entities.

With regard to the subject of our work, it is important to note that at any one time network entities are involved with a multitude of networks, not all of which have an association with a population health intervention. This point is important, because it reminds us that intervention entities have defining qualities or interests which may not necessarily 'align' with those of the intervention itself. Further, to become aligned, these entities must view their connection as being of interest for achieving their goals, which may also lie outside of the intervention.

Aligning interests and connecting entities; implementing a health program in an educational setting

According to this theoretical framework, the success of an intervention depends *not* upon the strictness or fidelity with which plans are implemented but rather on how well intervention entities 'align' or come together to form stable connections and thus work as 'allies'. When an intervention entity (i.e., an 'actant') becomes enrolled as an ally, he, she, or it has an interest in taking on the attributed role, which consequently stabilizes the network. Entities have properties determining, to a certain extent, what they can or cannot, will or will not, do. By conforming to the interests of the network, an entity's own interests correspond with the interests of the network, which is working to resolve a particular issue. In ANT terminology, when human or nonhuman entities play their anticipated roles, they act as 'intermediaries' and when they do not behave in a way that is expected or anticipated, they act as 'mediators'. When an entity does not (or ceases to) take on a role which coordinates with network goals, a 'controversy' occurs, and an entity that emerges as a 'controversy' behaves like a 'mediator'.

Networks are thus defined by the establishment of connections that serve to stabilize a network, although, as explained in the foregoing section, a stable connection can become unstable when a controversy occurs (i.e., an entity no longer plays an anticipated role or behaves in expected ways). We now go on to discuss this process of forming connections in more detail, using our study of the implementation of the PC-PR school-based nutrition intervention.

Tracing the genealogy of this school-based nutrition intervention tells an interesting story of how a program takes form in response to the interests of a range of social and technical entities that come together and move apart over time (Bisset and Potvin, 2007). On the other hand, looking more precisely at the program operations during one particular time-frame provides an opportunity to analyze the microprocesses which underlie these kinds of shifts in the intervention's form. According to ANT, the formation of a connection occurs when actors use negotiation, compromise, or persuasion, to align their identities, goals, and interests with one another, thereby reinforcing each other (Callon, 1986; 1999).

Generally speaking, the interests and concerns of education actors (e.g., teachers, students, parents, and school direction) are not centred upon health and health education. The focal actor group (i.e., nutritionists) that was responsible for implementing the program in the school was, therefore, in a precarious position whereby, according to ANT, the success of their innovation lies in the alignment of their interests with those of actors whose need for the innovation is uncertain. Analysis of data from interviews and observations revealed that nutritionists deployed translation strategies to interest these actors, either by compromising their aims (those of the nutritionists) or by convincing the other actors that participating or collaborating with the nutrition education program was necessary for the achievement of their own goals (Bisset et al., 2009).

Nutritionists often referred to education actors in terms of what they needed or aimed to achieve (i.e., goals). Interestingly, nutritionists' accounts further situated these goals alongside what the program was offering. For example, according to several of the nutritionists, teachers were preoccupied with implementing and evaluating newer components of the education program but they found themselves lacking resources such as time and tools. According to the nutritionists, the method employed for the cooking workshop was a time-saving device and a necessary tool for the successful implementation and evaluation of these educational components. Students were also identified by the nutritionists as needing the workshop. For example, beyond interests of long-term health (which is often of little interest to students) nutritionists situated the program as a response to the students needs for the following: having applied activities at school, showing off their practical knowledge and know-how with family members, and engaging in cooperative, teamwork activities with classmates.

In our interviews with nutritionists, we were able to develop an overview of common strategies employed by nearly all nutritionists across the various school settings; however, we also noted school-specific tactics employed by individual nutritionists as a result of their individual areas of interest or expertise and/or in response to the needs and conditions specific to of their school context. As a consequence, the nutrition workshop was not implemented uniformly in all school environments. For example, several nutritionists noted that their schools were particularly interested in health education. This was described variously in terms of the leadership role of the school administration, a young, sportive teaching staff, or simply as a value which had been transmitted during the nutritionists' interactions with teachers. When this occurred, the operation of the workshop was distinguished by an accent placed upon passing health messages and completing the 'sit and listen' lesson plan. Where this interest was not strong, nutritionists made compromises and employed various techniques to run the workshop in a way that teachers and students could recognize it as responding to their needs.

In addition, our observations of the nutrition workshops provided us with an opportunity to see how the various entities may or may not have behaved as 'mediators' or 'intermediaries'. For example, parent volunteers (particularly for older students) were asked to provide 'hands-off' assistance to students so that students would work with, and rely upon, their classmates. Some nutritionists also wanted students to have enough freedom to make mistakes. When parents assumed a 'motherly role' they were more likely to take control of a task which challenged a student. Similarly, several parents took on a 'friendly role' whereby they focused upon developing social affiliations with the teacher or other parents, often abandoning their 'assistant role' and at times disrupting the lesson by chatting amongst themselves. When a parent revealed their interest for a 'motherly role' they acted as mediators and introduced controversy into the network. Similarly, the food sample had possibilities for actions that did not align with the program aims, putting it into the role of mediator. A portion of the food prepared by the class was given to student to take home and in some cases, the take-home food sample became an object of trade amongst students, was eaten before arriving home, was forgotten, or was accidentally (or purposefully) thrown away.

When nutritionists modified their descriptions of the workshop and adjusted its operation based upon their perceived need to build new connections or to stabilize others, they were negotiating with program entities in order to build a network of stable connections. In other words, nutritionists developed strategies to convince program entities to behave more like 'intermediaries' and less like 'mediators'. In our foregoing example, this was attempted by revisiting parental roles and reinforcing the purposes of those roles, and by distributing food samples at the end of the day, instead of at the conclusion of the workshop. Our aim with these examples was to demonstrate that it is risky to base intervention connections upon anticipated or predefined roles, because identities and internal qualities often reveal themselves through interactions with contextual conditions when the intervention is in operation (Poland et al., 2008).

A PLACE FOR REFLEXIVITY IN PARTICIPATORY ACTION RESEARCH

Although we have focused most of our attention on the 'action' dimension of PAR, we do not mean to downplay the importance of participation. In fact, as implied by our emphasis on establishing explicit partnerships, we would argue that participatory research is the only means by which one can derive knowledge from others' actions and make sense of the way local conditions and contexts shape intervention actions and their effects. However, the closer a researcher is to the action, the greater the effect the researcher will have on the system. Speaking in terms of ANT, the researcher and her necessary connections with some of the intervention components must be considered as a part of the system of action. In this instance, she can be best understood as a mediator, whose role and identity in the system must be negotiated and whose primary interest (to produce knowledge about the system of action) must be aligned with those of other actors. Whether she is conscious of this or not, in order to undertake her research she must interest other actors by convincing them that her objectives are relevant to them or can assist them in the accomplishment of their goals. This, in turn, can have a ripple effect on the actions and priorities of others in the network. As a result – if she wishes to account for, and differentiate between, all mechanisms at play (in keeping with critical realist approach) – the researcher must acknowledge her/his own impact on the system, her/his own role as an actor within the network she/he is studying, and the ways in which her/his presence and activities can trigger other causal mechanisms. That is, adopting a critical realist position requires that we make an effort to account for all relevant mechanisms at play, in order to assess the impact of each and to differentiate between those mechanisms which are integral to the problem (or intervention), those which counteract or contribute to the whole, and those which are superfluous and merely complicate the picture. In order to do this, the researcher must turn her/his analysis back upon the research apparatus and be reflexive.

Defining reflexivity

Increasingly, within the social sciences, it is taken for granted that reflexivity is desirable, but the meaning of the term varies, and the reasons why it is considered important – if not imperative – are also diverse. On the most basic definition of reflexivity, there is a degree of consensus: it entails some form of recursive, turning-back upon, or mirroring of the self (Foley, 2002; Lynch, 2000; Robertson, 2002; Salzman, 2002). However, from there, things can get complicated. For example, Lynch's (2000) inventory of reflexivities includes six overlapping forms (mechanical, substantive, methodological, meta-theoretical, interpretive, and ethnomethodological) and fourteen subcategories. There is not space here to outline every formulation of reflexivity or to weigh the pros and cons of each one. Our intention is to outline the ways in which participatory action research can employ reflexive practices, while touching on some of the common critiques of reflexivity, by providing concrete examples of what reflexivity-in-action might have looked like for researchers involved with the LC-PN nutrition program. Because the aim of this volume is to guide qualitative research, we have focused on researcher reflexivity; however, we would also like to note that reflexivity is not the exclusive domain of researchers, because many other actors, including intervention practitioners can and do reflect on their own practices and beliefs.

We focus on two forms of reflexivity: meta-theoretical reflexivity and methodological reflexivity (Lynch, 2000). These two forms of reflexivity are not mutually exclusive. They both suggest ways to manage the (systemic-)reflexivity which is inherent to modernity, by calling for critical self-awareness or self-consciousness about one's own assumptions, research methods, analyses, interpretations, writing practices, and participation in systems of knowledge-production. Meta-theoretical reflexivity is a general orientation, perspective or attitude whereby one steps back from full engagement in a cultural activity in order to gain a heightened awareness of taken-for-granted assumptions (Lynch, 2000). Reflexive objectification, or what Marcus (1998) refers to as theoretical reflexivity, falls under this rubric. This is reflexivity where the researcher seeks to produce a reasonably objective, authoritative account while simultaneously critically evaluating what a fully situated member would take for granted as objective, and paying attention to the ways in which 'the practices and discourses of his/her own discipline affect what and how he/she thinks and writes' (Foley, 2002: 476). Standpoint reflexivity is also included within this category, which encourages existential identification with the lives and positions of those who are neglected or oppressed by established conceptual frameworks because of their gendered, racial, or cultural standpoints (Lynch, 2000: 31).

Methodological reflexivity, while closely allied to meta-theoretical reflexivity, is perhaps the most commonly employed and most widely understood form of reflexivity. Within the social sciences, methodological self-consciousness and self-criticism are the most common forms of methodological reflexivity. Methodological self-consciousness has become a key feature of participant-observation; researchers are expected to take into account their own relations to the group(s) they study, to be conscious of their own prejudices and assumptions, and to be attentive to sources of bias (Lynch, 2000). What Marcus (1994) terms null or basic reflexivity fits here – the self-critique or personal quest narrative which emphasizes the subjective, experiential, and empathetic elements of research; that is, the researcher includes reflection on her own actions, feelings, activities, and interactions (Salzman, 2002). However, this also emerges via confessional reflexivity (Marcus, 1998), particularly within American ethnography, whereby the researcher includes openly subjective reflections within their formal academic work as a means to undermine 'grandiose authorial claims of speaking in a rational, value-free, objective, universalizing voice' (Foley, 2002: 474). In some instances, methodological self-criticism follows from self-consciousness as outlined in the foregoing section, but this subcategory also refers to the traditional practices of empirical science whereby ideas are subjected to rigorous testing according to the standards of the discipline.

With regards to the LC-PN nutrition program, the incorporation of meta-theoretical reflexivity within the research endeavour encourages the researcher to think about her own biases and assumptions or try to take on the perspective of one of the participants. For example, if the researcher was trained as a nutritionist, she/he might view the educational components of the program as the most valuable or important elements; therefore, she/he might overemphasize their importance in evaluations of the success of failure of the program. Alternately, if she/he took the standpoint of a child involved in the program, she/he might acknowledge that this type of teaching can be dry and repetitive, that if it takes up too much time, student drop-out increases, and that the most important element for students was learning how to prepare different kinds of foods (which only happen to be nutritious).

Incorporating methodological reflexivity into her/his practices might lead the researcher to write about or simply reflect on the ways in which her/his research methods and questions shaped the conclusions she/he was able to draw, affected the ways students and other participants thought about the LC-PN program or responded to her/his inquiries, or even how her/his engagement with the program caused her/him to question the value of population health interventions which she/he had previously accepted as beneficial. Depending on the home discipline of any researcher, the sites where she/he chooses to disseminate her findings, and her/his personal aptitudes, these types of reflexive practices may be appropriate and informative. In addition, these could help her/him to better understand the mechanisms which led to successes, durability and positive outcomes as well as challenges, program-dissolution, and limited effects. These insights can help her/him differentiate between those aspects of the program which were contextually specific and not exportable from those elements of the program which could be instituted in other environments. Nevertheless, this does not mean that all forms of reflexivity are equally valid.

Critical perspectives on reflexivity

The deployment of (purportedly) reflexive practices has been critiqued on a number of fronts. For example, if reflexivity is supposed to deflate or at least call into question claims regarding absolute truth and objectivity (Foley, 2002), in practice it can be employed by researchers to assert authority. This is a relatively common critique of reflexive writing by those who are more postmodern or constructivist in orientation. They argue that meta-theoretical and methodological reflexivity do not break sufficiently with modernist epistemological assumptions and scientific ideals and therefore, do little to undermine the positivist and objectivist foundations of social science (Foley, 2002). For example, when researchers describe their practices in a reflexive manner and write about how their activities and assumptions may have shaped their findings, they are implying that they are dealing with the problem of reflexivity; and, in so doing, they are reasserting their authority and the validity of their claims to be able to understand and represent reality (Clifford and Marcus, 1986; Watson, 1987). With regards to the LC-PN program, critics might argue that the researcher's discussion of her/his disciplinary affiliations and their influence on her/his work masks the underlying assumptions which she/he is not addressing, and encourages her/his audience to 'believe' her/his accounts.

In a slightly different vein, authors who attempt to incorporate reflexive practices into their research and writing can be criticized for not being reflexive enough as a result of self-essentializing and/or misleading accounts. In particular, the inclusion of positionality, in which the author explicitly states that they are writing as a woman, black, Jew, lesbian, American, middle-class, or any other category, has become commonplace within academic works (Robertson, 2002, p. 788). This type of self-stereotyping implies that the researcher – and anyone else, for that matter – is reducible to a ready-to-wear identity, and that one's general characteristics of gender, religion, nationality, race, and class, among others, tell the reader something substantial about the perspective of the individual (Robertson, 2002; Salzman, 2002). A formulaic incantation in which one comes clean about one's positioned identity – such as a researcher of LC-PN explaining that she is an Anglophone, a non-mother, or a tenured professor, thereby implying that these identities were paramount to her experience and analyses – thus serves both as a sterile form of identity politics and as an empty gesture in the interests of political correctness (Marcus, 1994). Moreover, wearing these categories as self-evident can recapitulate the problem that reflexivity aims to solve, actually obscuring one's unique personal history while imparting an illusion of self-consciousness, intellectual engagement, and theoretical rigour (Robertson, 2002). Thus, positioning oneself can be misleading. In fact, according to Salzman (2002) the reliability of any supposedly reflexive account should be questioned, as 'one of the main psychological and social purposes of declarations about the self' is to mislead (Salzman, 2002: 809). Purportedly reflexive accounts can be deliberately deceptive, manipulative, and dishonest at worst, or simply fallible and untrustworthy for reason of self-deluding, a lack of self-awareness, and the subjective inclusion of certain contingencies in the place of others.

The most common critique of reflexivity is that it is self-indulgent, narcissistic, navel-gazing that allows researchers to evade the hard work of understanding and engaging with the real world (Clifford, 1999). In its more radical, interpretive, textualist forms (which we are not specifically addressing here), reflexivity is described by some as excessively subjective and shallow (Bourdieu and Wacquant, 1992), preoccupied with rhetoric, writing, and 'playful aestheticism' (Clifford, 1999: 643). On the other hand, more confessional, methodological forms of reflexivity are derided for their solipsism and egocentricity (Robertson, 2002).

In effect, most supporters of reflexive writing will admit that self-consciousness can become an end in itself such that the writer can become preoccupied with self-representation (Robertson, 2002), and that 'in the hands of an unskilled or egocentric practitioner, [it] can degenerate into self-serving, narcissistic, heroic portrayals' of the individual (Foley, 2002: 475). Whether in its more rhetorical or confessional forms, reflexivity can retain a 'self-absorbed, elitist, or apolitical quality removed from the nitty-gritty of social life' (Myers, 1988). Some fear that displays of one's reflexivity will crowd out other things (Watson, 1987) and that the trend towards reflexivity is leading the social sciences in unproductive directions (Marcus, 1994). For example, an account of the LC-PN program which focuses exclusively on the researcher's experiences navigating the complex relationships between nutritionists, teachers, parents, and children, in light of her/his past work experience in a school environment, or which champions her/his contribution to the success of the program, is not be the best or most useful kind of scholarship.

Finally, some have argued that, rather than serving a more substantive purpose, accounts reflecting reflexivity act as a shibboleth, marking the author as having a postmodern inclination, 'dedicated theoretically to epistemological relativism, perspectivism and positionality, subjectivity, and moral and political commitment' (Salzman, 2002: 807), in contrast to those of more objectivist, empiricist, and positivist inclinations. Just as the rhetoric surrounding participation is normative and serves as a means to judge the worth of a given process, performing reflexivity can serve to position the author, in contrast to others who write unreflexively, as possessing superior insight, perspicacity or awareness (Lynch, 2000). Consequently, a degree of epistemological hubris can accompany self-consciously reflexive claims (Lynch, 2000: 47). This, in turn, can spark competitive 'more reflexive than thou' critiques and counter-critiques, wherein those who attempt to write reflexively are derided not being sufficiently self-critical (Marcus, 1994: 392). While this may, in fact, be occurring, we are not encouraging reflexivity for its own sake – or as a marker of our own legitimacy and superiority as thinkers – rather we argue that reflexivity is good for something: its ability to help us better understand the objects or systems of action which we study.

Research, context and intervention mechanisms

Salzman proposes that 'we have accepted and adopted reflexivity rather too cavalierly and uncritically' (Salzman, 2002: 812) and have overlooked the basic assumption of the scientific method too readily. That is, in place of self-interrogation, auto-correction, self-analysis, and solitary research, he argues for a return to the collective, intersubjective processes of old, wherein debate among individuals, testing and replication of results, and collaborative, team research contribute to the advancement of knowledge through the creation of a 'vital and vigorous marketplace of ideas' (Salzman, 2002: 811). While we agree with Lynch that 'there is no particular advantage to being reflexive, or doing reflexive analysis, unless something provocative, interesting, or revealing comes from it' (Lynch, 2000: 42), we see an important place for reflexivity in participatory action research. Notably, it is our contention that one should not have to choose between collaboration/participation and self-consciousness/reflexivity; rather, if employed in a critical manner, the two can contribute to a more in-depth understanding of the complex, dynamic processes which shape population health interventions. This type of understanding is only possible if the researcher is willing and able to step back and examine the practices, discourses, and constraints of her discipline, the assumptions and biases that will influence her perceptions and interpretations, and the ways in which her research activities – questionnaires, observations, formulation of research question – affect the system that she is trying to understand. Only in this manner will the researcher have a chance of knowing and portraying the system of action – even if only in a partial, provisionally accurate, and situated manner (Foley, 2002; Mauthner and Doucet, 2003). While we agree that 'reflexivity in general offers no guarantee of insight or revelation' (Lynch 2000: 47), failing to think about what one is doing and the effects of one's actions and research does automatically restrict one's ability to account for, and explain, a dynamic system of action as well as the generalizability of one's findings beyond the local.

CONCLUSION

In this chapter, we have discussed the components of PAR (research, action, and participation) from relevant theoretical perspectives, in an attempt to show how theory can assist overcome the local nature of the knowledge produced through PAR. Rather than simply describing PAR, we showed how exploration of an alternate epistemology, the use of social theory, and the relevance of reflexivity, can help you to do better participatory action research, research which is more attentive to all of the mechanisms and processes inherent to program planning and implementation. This will, in turn, result in the production of more complete – and more broadly applicable – explanations of how programs work; explanations that will contribute to policy-development and decision making in the domain of public health.

REFERENCES

Akrish, M., Callon, M., and Latour, B. (2002) 'The Key to Success in Innovation Part 1: The Art of Interessment', *International Journal of Innovation Management*, 6: 187–206.
Bhaskar, R. (1978) *A Realist Theory of Science* (2nd Edition). London: Harvester Wheatsheaf.
Bisset, S., Daniel, M., and Potvin, L. (2009) 'Exploring the Intervention-Context Interface. A Case from a School-Based Nutrition Intervention', *American Journal of Evaluation*, 30(4): 554–71.

Bisset, S. and Potvin, L. (2007) 'Reconceptualising Implementation Evaluation: The Genealogy of a Nutrition-Based School Program', *Health Education Research*, 22: 737–46.

Bisset, S.L., Potvin, L., Daniel, M., and Paquette, M. (2008) 'Assessing the Impact of the Primary School-Based Nutrition Intervention Petits Cuistots – Parents En Réseaux', *Canadian Journal of Public Health*, 99: 107–13.

Bourdieu, P. and Wacquant, L.J.D. (1992) *An Invitation to Reflexive Sociology*. Chicago: University of Chicago Press.

Callon, M. (1986) 'Some Elements of a Sociology of Translation: Domestication of the Scallops and the Fishermen of St. Brieuc Bay'. In J. Law (ed.) *Power, Action and Belief. A New Sociology of Knowledge?* (pp. 196–233). London: Routledge and Kegan Paul.

Callon, M. (1999) 'Le réseau comme forme émergente et comme modalité de coordination: le cas des interactions stratégiques entre firmes industrielles et laboratoires académiques'. In M. Callon, P. Cohendet, N. Curien, J-M. Dalle, F. Eymard-Duvernay, D. Foray, and E. Schenk (eds.) *Réseau et coordination* (pp. 13–64). Paris: Economica.

Callon, M. and Rabeharisoa, V. (2003) 'Research in the Wild and the Shaping of New Social Identities', *Technology in Society*, 25: 193–204.

Cargo, M. and Mercer, S.L. (2008) 'The Value and Challenges of Participatory Research: Strengthening its Practice', *Annual Review of Public Health*, 29: 325–50.

Clifford, J. (1999) 'After Writing Culture', *American Anthropologist*, 101: 643–51.

Clifford, J. and Marcus, G.E. (eds.) (1986) *Writing Culture: The Poetics and Politics of Ethnography*. Berkeley, CA: University of California Press.

Connell, J. and Kubisch, A. (1998) 'Applying a Theory of Change Approach to the Evaluation of Comprehensive Community Initiative: Progress, Prospects and Problems'. In K. Fulbright-Anderson, A. Kubisch and J. Connell (eds.) *New Approaches to Evaluating Community Initiatives: Theory Measurement, and Analysis*. Washington, DC: Aspen Institute.

Cronbach, L.J. (1975) 'Beyond the Two Disciplines of Scientific Psychology', *American Psychologist*, 30: 116–27.

Dab, W. (2005) 'Reflections on the Challenges of Health Programming', *Promotion and Education*, Supplement, 3: 77–9.

Foley, D.E. (2002) 'Critical ethnography: The reflexive turn', *Qualitative Studies in Education*, 15: 469–90.

Green L.W. (2006) 'Public Health Asks of Systems Science: To Advance Our Evidence-Based Practice, Can You Help Us Get More Practice-Based Evidence?', *American Journal of Public Health*, 96: 406–9.

Green, L.W., George, A., Daniel, M., Frankish, J.C., Herbert, C.J., Bowie, W.R., and O'Neill, M. (1995) *Study of Participatory Research in Health Promotion: Review and Recommendations for the Development of Participatory Research in Health Promotion in Canada*. Ottawa: The Royal Society of Canada.

Greene, J.C. (2007) 'Understanding Social Programs Through Evaluation'. In N.K. Denzin and Y.S. Lincoln (eds). *Collecting and Interpreting Qualitative Materials* (pp. 981–99). San Francisco, CA: Sage.

Guba, Y. and Lincoln, E. (1989) *Fourth Generation Evaluation*. Thousand Oaks, CA: Sage.

Hawe, P. and Potvin, L. (2009) 'What is Population Health Intervention Research?', *Canadian Journal of Public Health*, 100(1 insert): I8–I14.

Israel, B.A., Schultz, A.J., Parker, E.A., and Becker, A.B. (1998) 'Review of Community-Based Research: Assessing Partnership Approaches to Improve Public Health', *Annual Review of Public Health*, 19: 173–202.

Latour, B. (1987) *Science in Action*. Cambridge, MA: Harvard University Press.

Latour, B. (1999) *Pandora's Hope. Essays on the Reality of Science Studies*. Cambridge MA: Harvard University Press.

Lehoux, P. (2006) *The Problem of Health Technology. Policy Implications for Modern Health Care Systems*. New York: Routledge.

Lynch, M. (2000) 'Against Reflexivity as an Academic Virtue and Source of Privileged Knowledge', *Theory, Culture and Society*, 17: 26–54.

Marcus, G.E. (1994) 'On Ideologies of Reflexivity in Contemporary Efforts to Remake the Human Sciences', *Poetics Today*, 15: 383–404.

Marcus, G.E. (1998) *Ethnography Through Thick and Thin*. Princeton, NJ: Princeton University Press.

Mauthner, N.S. and Doucet, A. (2003) 'Reflexive Accounts and Accounts of Reflexivity in Qualitative Data Analysis', *Sociology*, 37: 413–31.

Minkler, M. (1999) 'Using Participatory Action Research to Build Healthy Communities', *Public Health Report*, 115: 191–9.

Myers, F. (1988) 'Locating Ethnographic Practice: Romance, Reality, and Politics in the Outback', *American Ethnologist*, 15: 609–24.

Patton, M. (1997) *Utilization-Focused Evaluation: The New Century Text* (3rd Edition). California: Sage.

Pawson, R. and Tilley, N. (1997) *Realistic Evaluation*. London: Sage.

Poland, B., Frohlich, K.L., and Cargo, M. (2008) 'Context as a Fundamental Dimension of Health Promotion Program Evaluation'. In L. Potvin, D.V. McQueen, M. Hall, L. Di Salazar, L. Anderson, and Z.M. A. Hartz (eds.) *Health Promotion Evaluation Practices in the Americas: Values and Research* (pp. 299–317). New York: Springer.

Potvin, L., Gendron, S., Bilodeau, A., and Chabot, P. (2005) 'Integrating Social Theory into Public Health Practice', *American Journal of Public Health*, 95: 591–5.

Potvin, L., Haddad, S., and Frohlich, K. L. (2001) 'Beyond Process and Outcome Evaluation: A Comprehensive Approach for Evaluating Health Promotion Programmes'. In I. Rootman, M. Goodstatd, B. Hyndman, D.V. McQueen, L. Potvin, J. Springett, and E. Ziglio (eds.) *Evaluation in Health Promotion. Principles and Perspectives* (pp. 45–62). Copenhagen: WHO Regional Publications, European Series, No. 92.

Potvin, L., and McQueen, D. V. (2008) 'Practical Dilemmas for Health Promotion Evaluation'. In L. Potvin, D. V. McQueen, M. Hall, L. Di Salazar, L. Anderson, and Z. M. A. Hartz (eds.) *Health Promotion Evaluation Practices in the AMERICAS: Values and Research* (pp. 25–45). New York: Springer.

Reason, P. (1994) *Participation in Human Inquiry*. London: Sage.

Reason, P. and Bradbury, H. (2006) *Handbook of Action Research*. London: Sage.

Robertson, J. (2002) 'Reflexivity Redux: A Pithy Polemic on "Positionality"', *Anthropological Quarterly*, 75: 785–92.

Salzman, P.C. (2002) 'On Reflexivity', *American Anthropologist*, 104: 805–13.

Sayer, A. (2000) *Realism and Social Science*. London: Sage.

Springett, J. (2001a) 'Participatory Approaches to Evaluation in Health Promotion'. In I. Rootman, M. Goodstatd, B. Hyndman, D.V. McQueen, L. Potvin, J. Springett, and E. Ziglio (eds.) *Evaluation in Health Promotion. Principles and Perspectives* (pp. 83–105). Copenhagen: WHO Regional Publications, European Series, No. 92.

Springett, J. (2001b) 'Appropriate Approaches to the Evaluation of Health Promotion', *Critical Public Health*, 11: 139–51.

Watson, G. (1987) 'Make me Reflexive, But Not Yet: Strategies for Managing Essential Reflexivity in Ethnographic Discourse', *Journal of Anthropological Research*, 43: 29–41.

ACKNOWLEDGEMENTS

L. Potvin is the holder of a Canadian Health Services Research Foundation Chair award. S. Bisset is supported by a Canadian Institute of Health Research post doctoral fellowship award and L. Walz by a Canadian Health Services Research Foundation post doctoral fellowship award. This research was funded in part by the Canadian Institute of Health Research.

23

Qualitative Research in Programme Evaluation

Isobel MacPherson and Linda McKie

In this chapter, we focus on the collection and analysis of qualitative data for the purposes of conducting a programme evaluation within health services. In so doing, we draw upon an example from our own work to provide a practical example. We anchor data collection and analysis in the broader commissioning and design process and the need to understand the rationales behind the commissioning of a programme evaluation that affects both the design method used and the subsequent data collection and analysis. The chapter is presented across eight sections: the evaluation exemplar of Managed Clinical Networks; understanding motivations and expectations through evaluation briefs; general evaluation approaches; negotiating an evaluation; the role of previous evaluations; data collection methods; data analysis and validation; and reporting on evaluation findings.

THE EVALUATION EXEMPLAR: MANAGED CLINICAL NETWORKS

Managed Clinical Networks (MCNs) are multiprofessional, multilevel initiatives developed by the National Health Service (NHS) in Scotland as a direct response to the variations in the availability and quality of acute services (Scottish Office Dept of Health, 1998; Scottish Office Dept of Health Mel, 1999). (An MEL is a Management Executive Letter) a particular form of government communication.) MCNs are designed to bring together groups of health professionals and organizations from the primary, secondary and tertiary health care sectors around a specific clinical topic; for example, the treatment of cancer, diabetes and vascular conditions. The central aim of MCNs is to enhance coordination, encourage flexible and imaginative work, and move beyond existing professional and health board boundaries.

THE EVALUATION BRIEF: UNDERSTANDING MOTIVATIONS AND EXPECTATIONS

Evaluations can be commissioned for many reasons, but principally they fall into three categories (though they can contain all three elements):

- Self-preservation: funds have become available to develop a new service and the evaluation becomes the evidential means to turn the 'experimental' into the 'established'.
- Justification: evaluation as a compulsory component of the funding contract; the evaluation is seen as an administrative aside, endured but rarely enjoyed.
- Trail blazers: groups who want to be seen to be 'out-there' leading the line with new developments and the evaluation is their publicity vehicle.

Knowing which is crucial to understanding why an evaluation is undertaken and how it might be ultimately viewed and valued by commissioners, participants and funders. The MCN example was a combination of trail blazing and self-preservation.

OVERVIEW OF EVALUATION APPROACHES

There are four basic recognized approaches of evaluation summarized in Table 23.1. In complex programme evaluations done over time, it is highly likely that a combination of approaches would be used. The use of qualitative methods within evaluation has been most closely associated with process evaluation but they can also inform the other approaches. For example in:

- Formative evaluation: both interview and observation data gathering can illuminate the day to day operation of services.
- Impact/Outcome evaluation: qualitative methods can help define, refine and prioritize what is meant by 'outcomes' by exploring these issues through interviews and/or focus groups (more of these methods later) with evaluation participants.

The MCN example combined a process and impact/outcome evaluation using a specific qualitative approach namely, pluralistic evaluation which we shall briefly elaborate in the next section.

NEGOTIATING AN EVALUATION

The evaluation commissioning process generally means responding to either a detailed specification or an open specification. In this section, we also include a

Table 23.1   Approaches to evaluation

Style of evaluation	Looks at	Ultimate focus
Formative	Development, operation, outcomes	Provides information to make changes in the programme
Summative	Resources going in and the outputs achieved	Did the programme achieve what it set to?
Process	Operational processes	Understanding of how the programme worked and why
Impact/Outcome	Wider impact of the programme	Measuring the outcomes of the programme

brief word on the use of logic models as a variant of negotiating and pre-planning evaluations.

Detailed specification

Generally, do not accept any evaluation tender on face value. If a specific evaluation approach is mentioned, then ask yourself 'is what they are asking for the best way of tackling this?' In the MCN example, the commissioners requested a qualitative approach '...*because we need to get at the depth of feeling about the MCN and a survey would not have done that*'. Moreover, they wanted a pluralistic approach (Smith and Cantley, 1985; Gerrish, 2001; Hall, 2004; Moss et al., 2008) that accepted and worked with multiple agendas for measuring 'success'. As Walker (1985) put it: '*Traditional evaluation studies frequently overlook that services may mean different things to different people. In part, this is because the criteria for success employed in evaluation are generally restricted to those held by the sponsors*'. A pluralistic approach teases out participants' agendas and enables you to establish a core of commonly agreed 'success' criteria and criteria specific to each group of participants. The data gathering evidence can then be used to assess the extent to which these agendas had been met.

Having read the background papers to the development of the particular clinical MCN and heard the explanations underlying the commissioning of the evaluation, the evaluator agreed that a pluralistic framework would be necessary given the complex professional and political agendas. As a result of this exploration, the original aims and objectives were re-worked into an *Expectation versus the Reality of the MCN* to better reflect the circumstances of the evaluation and the qualitative methodology. The reworking is outlined as follows.

SUMMARY OF EVALUATION AIM AND ISSUES

Overall Aim

To determine the impact of the MCN on the operation of the service.

KEY ISSUES

Baseline: description of the 'service' at work

- Who does what, where and how?
- Service issues; priorities, delivery
- Strengths/weaknesses of joint working and service

Managed clinical network: the expectation

- Pros and cons
- Stated and perceived role/s
- Criteria for 'success'

Managed clinical network: the practice

- What is the network in reality?
- How is it considered with reference to aim and expectations?
- Methods and levels of participation/commitment
- Effects of methods and levels of participation/commitment
- What agendas emerge and why?
- Key elements for a 'successful' network
- On-going monitoring and evaluation plans

Open specification

If there is no evaluation specification as such; the commissioners expect you to adopt the approach and design. In this case:

- Talk to the commissioners of the evaluation and find out:
  1 Why they want the evaluation done?
  2 What issues they wish to concentrate on and why?
  3 What timescale they have set and why?
  4 What resources (help with organizing data collections, actually gathering data, preparing data for analysis) they might contribute?
- Check any background papers on the programme related to aims, objectives, expectations, outputs and outcomes.
- Consult any previous relevant evaluations on the programme for insights to the programme that might inform the design of the current evaluation (*see following section for caveats on this element*).
- Check the relevant literature (*academic, policy and practice*) to see if similar programmes have been evaluated and what they focused on and what insights.

From these, adopt an evaluation approach and, draft aims and objectives, and feed this back. Once you have agreed these, you can then work on the potential data gathering methods and discuss these to ensure feasibility.

Logic models

It is worth noting that, in the United States and Canada, more formal, structured approaches to negotiating evaluations are now the norm. These are not new

Table 23.2   The AMT logic model approach

Process	Focus
Step 1: Identifying Antecedent Conditions	Defining the problem of interest
Step 2: Targeting antecedent conditions and programme strategies	Establishing the conditions and outcomes that are important to focus on
Step 3: Measurement	Deciding the components of the Impact/Outcome evaluation

techniques per se, but have been re-incarnated as federal agencies seek to improve accountability. Millar et al. (2001) defines logic models as: '...*word or pictorial depictions of real-life events/processes that depict graphically the underlying assumptions or bases upon which the undertaking of one activity is expected to lead to the occurrence of another activity or event'*. The focus of any evaluation developed in the logic model mode becomes the key issues that are agreed to affect outcomes. Table 23.2 shows one of the more straightforward expositions of the steps necessary to creating a logic model (Renger and Hurley, 2006).

What logic models try to do is to provide a visual and rationally based game plan to lay bare the components and linkages within the programme and target the evaluation on agreed issues and pathways. These are not evaluations in and of themselves; they are the preparatory stage, and you will still have to decide the appropriate evaluative approach having gone through the logic model. And Rogers, quoted in Gugui et al. (2007) makes the important point that, '*while evaluators can use logic models to develop evaluation plans, these plans must retain enough flexibility to search for other potentially important outcomes'*.

THE RELATIONSHIP OF PREVIOUS EVALUATIONS TO THE CURRENT EVALUATION

Policy/programmes may well have been subject to a previous evaluation. This can impinge on what you are allowed to or decide to do in terms of the evaluation design, data gathering and analysis. The reasons for having a repeat evaluation may be many but broadly fall into three camps:

- Review Cycle: the programme has been running for a number of years since the last evaluation, and it is felt timely to review the running of the programme.
- Development: there have been new developments in the programme's operation since the last evaluation, and there is a need or desire to know their specific impact.
- Funder: there has been a change of funder and funding criteria, and a new evaluation becomes necessary.

In the MCN example, the first and second rationales prevailed: the network had been going for a number of years and had previously been evaluated, but it was felt timely to revisit its progress. A new post of network manager had been created to improve coordination and communication among the various parties and the commissioners wanted to record the potential effect on the functioning of the MCN of that change.

In terms of repeat evaluations, one needs to think about:

- How useful or necessary is it to have direct or indirect 'comparability' of findings over time?
- Were there issues flagged up previously for future investigation that are useful to take on board?
- What might earlier evaluations reveal about the ease or otherwise of data collection in that setting?

In our MCN example, a decision was made not to read the previous organizational evaluation report or utilize the findings. This reflected the evaluator's knowledge of the politics underlying the development of the MCN and that the previous qualitative evaluation had not been universally welcomed. In this way, if the current evaluation brought up the same themes and issues then no one could point the finger and argue 'influenced-by' and use that to dismiss uncomfortable findings a second time.

DATA COLLECTION METHODS

As a general point, in choosing your data collection methods you should think about what the individual technique can provide that other data gathering methods would not. And in so doing, you should be thinking about how the methods complement each other, that is, how the strengths of one counteract the weaknesses of the other.

The use of interviews as data gathering

If you are going to use interviewing techniques then you need to ask yourself:

- What does this technique give me that I cannot get from other data gathering techniques? For example, do you need to explore or understand individual perspectives on the evaluation issues?
- Who should I interview? That will be determined by the focus of the evaluation, so in our example we needed to interview all those who were part of the formal MCN group and we added staff on the front line via the observation work. Think about whether your evaluation focus means concentrating on one particular group (e.g., diabetic patients); or all those working within a specific work setting (e.g., cardiology ward); or key people (e.g., all those involved in planning a new clinic, etc.). If you are unsure you will capture the right 'people' for your evaluative purpose ask some of those you propose to interview if there are any obvious gaps in your list of people.
- How will I construct my interview schedule? You can use your aims and objectives as a guide; 'background' papers related to the issues or similar evaluations and see what topics they used. You can ask the funders and potential participants what they consider the key questions and issues to be? If relevant, you can undertake a period of observation to help focus the interviews. Nevertheless, at all points remember this is an evaluation, not research as such and you have a specific remit, so be sure your schedule delivers. In programme evaluation, as in most qualitative research, you may have different groups of people (e.g., clinicians, nurses, paramedics, pharmacists, managers, patients and relatives) to interview, and this has implications for the content of the interview schedule. For example, there may be topics you want to ask

everyone about: that is the 'common core' of the schedule but you also need to ask yourself if there are 'specific' issues you should add to your schedule germane to each group.

- How many people should I interview? Again, this depends on the evaluation, the potential range of participants and whether you need to conduct more than one run of interviews with the same participants: there is no right or wrong answer. Discuss this with the evaluation commissioners and relevant research colleagues. Most qualitative interviewing falls into either: purposive, convenience or opportunistic sampling. In our MCN example, approximately 30–40 people were interviewed, comprising those who sat on the MCN, plus new members joining the MCN over the evaluation period plus those staff met during the observation phase. This was largely a purposive sample with an edge of opportunism. Thirty people were reinterviewed after nine months to re-assess the issues and progress of the MCN.
- Where and when will I interview people? Ask the potential interviewee the best time and place to meet; for example just before people start work or just after they finish, before or after ward rounds or in between clinics. Think about how practical it might be to interview people at their place of work: front line health services work can be very fluid and you could be left hanging around waiting or find people called away before you have finished the interview. The alternative is to do the interviews over the phone again at a time suitable to the interviewees. It may lack the face to face 'signals', but there are still 'signals' to be found in the tone of voice that will help you to interpret the data. Be mindful that people are busy and some may consider the evaluation irrelevant so you may have to prioritize questions. Consider core questions/issues in advance. That said, it is notable how many people relax into an interview and once they start, give much more time that they said was available.
- How will I 'record' data? You can use a digital recorder with the interviewee's permission: this will give you a full account; you can make notes that will give you a partial account or you can use a combination of both. Using the digital recorder means less distraction for you and the interviewee. Using notes means devising a game plan as to what you will note and how, for example, write down key words, key phrases; create headings under which to write as the interview proceeds/use the topics as the headings. Regardless of method, make a note once you leave the interview setting that sums the interview from your point of view and notes any points of interest about the venue, environment, atmosphere and the effects of any interruptions on the interview.

TWO DIFFERENT APPLICATIONS OF 'INTERVIEWING' AS DATA GATHERING IN EVALUATION

Here we offer insights and reflection from our evaluation:

A. *Monthly Reviews with the MCN Manager:* these were semi-structured interviews which took place after the first round of baseline interviews and continued until the final assessment interviews. The monthly review was designed to get a handle on the network manager role in practice, thus the evaluator and the MCN manager would have a chat over the phone in the last week of every month. This would address 'how's the month been'; a working through of all the issues currently on the MCN table; any new developments to add since the last month and what's on the agenda for the next month; lastly, anything else either party wished to add. The data gathered provided the everyday detail of the workings of the MCN and:

- Illuminated the politics and tactics of people's reactions to and participation in the MCN.
- Put the role of the MCN manager in perspective and the uphill battles that had to be fought not just to move agendas forward but to garner respect and support to the role itself.
- Demonstrated in a very clear way the crucial role the manager was playing in keeping the show on the road by sheer perseverance and force of character.

It should be noted that the MCN manager felt this technique created a real sense of involvement and sharing: *'because we had our monthly catch-ups, I felt very involved. It (the evaluation) was responsive as far as I'm concerned'*. Here we note that evaluation research can overlap with participatory action research, that is, research that involves those using and working in a service and feeds back from the ongoing analysis to inform regular reviews (see Shaw, 1999).

B. *'Chats'*: These were the semi-structured interviews undertaken at baseline and follow-up with all members of the MCN formal group but also included the interviews undertaken during the observation phase. These were very much discursive conversations and the use of the word 'chat' is deliberate to indicate a more informal style designed to put people at their ease and facilitate difficult issues. These were in the main phone interviews, but a few were conducted at places of work (clinics) and on two, the hospital coffee shop and a restaurant. This was the aspect of the MCN data gathering that opened up positions and enabled the comparative theory versus practice work to be reviewed. One particular benefit of these 'open handed' conversations was to pre-empt claims that the evaluation findings were biased to one group or individual. Further, the value of the 'chats' was noted by one of the commissioners of the evaluation:

'You could go back, you could amass knowledge and probe connections, things that felt odd or helpful. … I was aware people were sharing with you. … It persuaded people to think more deeply about what was going on'.

Observation

In a strict sense, observation is about watching people and is a particularly useful method in situations too complex to record in other ways (Payne and Payne, 2004). It allows for the recording of:

- Realities: It allows you to gain first-hand knowledge of a process in action, you see the day-to-day realities.
- Interactions: It can illuminate the interactions across an operation/process so that you gain insight into communication issues, negotiation issues, resourcing issues and delivery issues as they occur as well as the tactical/political issues that might permeate these.
- Components: It allows the 'informal' components of decision making to be illuminated, that is, it gets behind the official version.

While these summarize the broad rational, it should be noted that in some situations you may also have to use this technique for tactical or political reasons. For example, the evaluator needs to be seen to be experiencing something of the issues or contexts under evaluation for the evaluation to have any kudos and value with the parties involved. This would rarely be a sole consideration, but it might be an underlying pressure. For example, one of the authors was evaluating an acute medical patient receiving system and was challenged by junior doctors to stay over night. The author had already decided that time was important to observe but the challenge from the junior doctors was about the street-level credibility of the evaluation, what really experiencing their world meant and this was their priority data gathering event.

If you are going to use this technique, you need to ask yourself:

- What insights will this give me that I cannot get any other way? Think about what other data gathering techniques you are using, how does the data gathered from observation complement these? Are you filling data gaps? Are you triangulating/strengthening data?
- How am I going to focus the observation? Think about whether you need to undertake some interviews to gain insight into the perceived issues that you might then use as your observation loci. If other similar evaluation studies have used observation, how did they locate that and why? What can you realistically get access to? What is imperative to observe and what is not?
- What should I observe? There are five basic components that should be considered: (a) the setting, that is, the physical boundaries both facilitate and constrain actions and interactions; (b) the people and their relationships, that is, the regular and intermittent relationships, the groupings, the power differences; (c) the behaviours, actions and activities, that is, the routinized, the clandestine, the coping mechanisms; and (d) the verbal behaviours, that is, who speaks to whom, why, what is imparted, what are the consequences. In all likelihood, a mix of these will be chosen depending on the focus and rational for the observation. For example, in the MCN meetings, it was the people and their relationships and the verbal behaviours that were the key observation components.
- How much time can I devote to this? The timing of, and time given, to the observation depends on the nature of the evaluation. Are you going to be looking at sequential events (for example, the daily functioning of a family doctor practice over a period) or non-sequential events (for example, mental health service planning which may take place in a variety of settings/time frames). This is crucial, especially if you are operating alone. You have to be realistic about your time use, and take into account that you will still have to analyze the data you collect. Take advice from people in the field setting on how long they think you should spend and how you could best target your time.
- How will I relate to those in the setting that I want to observe? Our advice is to be up front about who you are, what you are doing and why. Put people at ease by answering their questions openly and honestly. There is an argument that it could distort their behaviour, but reality suggests any distortion does not last long.
- How will I gather data in the setting? This has three components: (a) in practical terms you will be making notes and these will relate to the purpose of the observation; (b) relatedly, you need to decide the balance between only focusing on the things of interest to the evaluation and the wider context. Sometimes a seemingly obscure moment turns out later to have great significance and it is impossible to second-guess such things. The advice is to keep the detail of the data gathering on the observation remit but keep a contextual note of the observation period, that is, note the little things that strike you as interesting about that period; (c) it is not always practical to make a full note at the time, so create your own system of noting words, phrases, sentences and writing these up more fully when you have time, either in the setting or when you leave the setting.

Observation Example – the MCN Meetings: the evaluator attended almost all such meetings during an 18-month period in the guise of reporting on the progress of the evaluation. The observation provided a multi-layered perspective on the meetings and their various internal and external dynamics.

- Who turned up shed light on the status of the MCN meeting among other diary commitments and highlighted those sectors for who the MCN seemed at best an ambivalent development and those that did not see tactical advantage in going along with the MCN development.

- Who spoke gave a good insight into the power structures but over time gave an insight into the positively changing confidence levels of people who might initially have felt on the margins of the development some of whom really started to 'get stuck in' to making the MCN work at their level.
- Cross-chat provided a broader perspective on how developments or otherwise in one area could bounce through to impact on current and future functioning of the MCN itself giving a context to the perceived 'disappointments' and 'successes' of the MCN.
- The handling of the agenda issues gave insight into who was keen on what as well as insight into the reasons behind the progress or otherwise of each item.
- The value of the meeting as a broader information-sharing forum as the various levels represented round the table did not necessarily cross regular paths (the exception being those with co-sectoral management responsibilities).
- Participants and evaluator could reference issues in their 'chats' that might otherwise have been delicate to introduce, that is, the evaluator already had prior knowledge of the point of contention via the meetings.

The data gathered from these MCN meetings was central to shaping conversations, themes, and ideas of what might work and what might not and to maintaining an underlying running conversation with the MCN participants: in effect the qualitative 'interviews' with the participants were more than just two 'chats'; there was an element of a running conversation, through attendance at the meetings. The general point is that observation and interviewing can be used as complementary data gathering techniques and feed off each other. For example, and as indicated earlier, you can do a round of interviews to gain an insight into the general issues and use the results of that to help focus the observation. After having done the observation, you can interview people in the field to look in more depth at the observation findings. As Donaldson (in Fitzpatrick, 2004) states, *'I can't emphasize how important it is to pull away from the conceptual jargon and go and see what is happening'*.

Focus groups

These person-to-group discussions and interviews are considered in-depth in Chapter 17 in this Handbook. Here are a few things to keep in mind when using focus groups to do evaluation research:

- What will the research gain from focus groups? They offer the chance to explore ideas and issues across a group of people who may contradict or agree with each other. It may be, however, that concerns about role and hierarchy stifle comments. So you do have to consider what you would gain from a group-based discussion and how are the groups best put together to promote debate.
- How can I get a venue and what do I need in it? Do not assume a venue will just appear, especially in primary and community care where rooms are being 'hot-bedded' with, for example, clinics, not just during the day but at night.
- How long will a session be? We find that for the purpose of evaluation research 45 minutes to an hour is long enough, as after that people start to get tired and attention wanders. If you must go beyond that, then a break for 10/15 minutes is in order during the session. Tell people the length of the session at the time you invite them. Sessions can and do overrun which is fine if no one else needs the room so know if that's the case before you begin and then you can react accordingly.

Sessions can end before the allotted time: the discussion may have exhausted itself for whatever reason.

- How many sessions do I need to hold? That depends on a number of factors, for example, the complexity of the issue being explored, the range of potential sampling frames, the potential complexity of the analysis you wish to undertake, the time and resources you have to conduct the work and analyze the data.
- How will you structure the session? You need to decide what the focus of each session is to be and whether you wish to use one issue and let the group run with it or whether to split that issue into sub-issues/questions (no more than four questions per session or you risk spending too little time on each) to provide some structure and guidance.
- What is my role? The evaluator can either lead the session or sit back and observe the session having appointed someone from within the group to lead it. There are advantages and disadvantages (see Barbour, 2008) both ways but if you decide to lead then be careful, you don't end up 'driving' the group instead of facilitating the group discussion.
- How will I actually gather the data? The most common physical methods are: a Flip Chart, a notebook, a digital recorder. It is better to have two forms of data collection such as a digital recorder and either a flip chart or a note-book. Use a Flip Chart not a white board, because you will want to take the data away with you for analysis. If you are using a digital recorder, you need to ask the groups' permission and if anyone says no, then leave it. At all points, you are trying to capture some of the: ideas, explanations, rationalizations, commonality, and divergence, within the group, as it relates to your evaluation issue/issues.

Focus groups have a value in themselves and can act as a valuable partner in a multi-method design. They are not cheap and not necessarily easy to set up and they certainly demand good organizational and facilitation skills but if you want to understand aspects of a 'collective' mentality such as values, norms, meanings, decision-making processes then focus groups provide that opportunity.

Documentation

Another form of qualitative data gathering is to use existing documentation such as patient case notes, care plans, discharge summaries, specific internal reports, minutes of meetings, health guidance briefs and statistical accounts. Do not discount the latter just because you are doing a qualitative evaluation; remember the statistics can provide a context for interview, observation, focus group topics. For example, knowing the flows (amount and timings) of patients into and out of medical wards over the previous month can facilitate and illuminate discussion around the perceptions of workloads, the perceptions of responsibilities re-discharging, the balance re-direct/indirect patient care within wards.

The principal advantages of using 'documentation' are to provide:

- A time line/context for the 'development'/operation working of the topic
- A formal account and baseline for comparative purposes
- A way to refine the focus of other data gathering.

You do, however, need to be aware of some inherent pitfalls:

- Access to patient case notes will be subject to data protection and ethical permissions and that can take time to get.

- Some documentation has routine categories (for example, admission/discharge summaries) that keep the data more or less consistent but other documentation may not (for example, mental health case notes, beyond the proscribed areas such as medication).
- Minutes of meetings may simply be abbreviated versions of the event and not a full record.
- Contents may not be representative of the possible range of views/interests (keep an eye on who attends meetings; if it is not obvious, ask who contributed to the report or guidelines). What is left out might tell you as much as what is written about.
- The wording used may be deliberate in content and tone to convey a particular sense such as 'consensus' but gives no insight into the process or how far it was achieved.
- As 'policy' keeps moving/evolving so does the content of the 'documentation' with seemingly new concepts/ideas arising. These may not be new and through other data collection methods, you may find these are old ideas in a new format.

If you wish to access 'documentary' evidence, you need ask yourself:

- Why am I doing this? To provide an overview of the topic? To illuminate formal positions on the topic? To provide historical context for the topic and its development?
- How does this fit in with my other data gathering methods? Is this the best way of getting what I want? Tracking documentation, reading and picking out the salient key points takes time.
- How will I decide what to read about? One way is to go back to your evaluation aims and questions and use these to guide you. Another way is to ask advice from insiders as to what might be useful; compare that with what you thought and make a decision accordingly. Lastly, you could just take a random selection across the sources especially if time is tight and you simply want an overview.
- If there have been previous evaluations, do I want to read them at all, before I start, or at the end? This will depend on the extent to which the evaluations overlap with yours and whether you are being asked to repeat, follow-on, bring a fresh perspective to something. Think tactically; what might you gain, what might you loose?

In terms of our evaluation example, the background papers utilized:

- Illuminated the rational behind the development of the MCN within the particular specialty, that is, to address service fragmentation and provide a more coordinated, coherent service.
- Highlighted the locus of sustained support (managerial) and indifferent support (clinical).
- Outlined the original intention of the organizational design with a core group and a range of subgroups and allowed us to chart the subsequent adjustments.
- Indicated the development issues that arose over the years and their impact.
- Presented the formal rational for the changes made to the MCN structures and the hoped for outcomes of the functioning of the MCN.

Documentation can be very illuminating in various ways including practical, tactical and political. They can give you a quick start in an area, alert you to issues you might not have thought of, give a basis for discussion and assist in making decisions on locations and foci for observation. A quick look is fine; a detailed usage needs a clear purpose.

In summary, each of these main qualitative data gathering techniques can stand on its own or work in combination, and it is likely you will use more than one especially in complex evaluations. The data gathering is led by the evaluation aims and issues and not the other way around. There should be no evaluation aim or objective without an identifiable data gathering method. You should be clear in your mind why you chose what you did and how they each contribute to the whole. In terms of our MCN example then:

- The set-up documents were central in highlighting why the MCN had been established.
- The monthly reviews were crucial to keep a handle on a complex and sometimes fast moving situation.
- The interviews opened the door to the underlying specific issues: they also made the evaluator and respondents lift their eyes to the bigger picture and take a more reflective stance than a simple indulgent moan-feast.
- The observation at the MCN meetings illuminated the real core of support and gave insights into the MCN role (and its solidity or otherwise) in the wider Health Board plans.
- The observation at service level threw new light on the practicalities of delivering the specialty services and provided other views that would not have been covered necessarily by the organizational evaluation as commissioned.
- The secondary statistical sources brought a seeming side issue (audit) into the spotlight not just for its own sake but what it illuminated about people's priorities and commitment in having a cohesive well-evidenced specialty.

As a general point, always remember it matters that you use the best techniques to generate the best data appropriate to your evaluation. However, the realities of fieldwork can challenge the theory-practice nexus: Fitzpatrick quotes House (2002), '*Practices are highly constrained by contextual and structural factors. That is, time, costs and necessary interactions with clients push evaluators in similar directions whatever their orientation.*'

DATA MANAGEMENT AND ANALYSIS

Before setting out the practicalities of this section, it is important to briefly reflect on the nature of qualitative analysis, which is a way of making sense of data by giving meaning and significance to the ideas and words of participants (Walker, 1985). Bulmer (1982) reminds us 'the very process of deciding what is, and what is relevant and significant in what is, involves selective interpretation and conceptualization'.

This applies as much to the quantitative as to the qualitative tradition. Someone has to decide what clinical data to collect, what analysis to apply, what statistical tests are appropriate, what results are reported and how that will be done. In everything, there is selection, interpretation and presentation. In essence, qualitative data analysis is about data reduction, data display and conclusion drawing or verification (Miles and Huberman, 1994).

A general strategy for analysing data for the programme evaluation

Strategies for analyzing data are covered elsewhere in this Handbook. In this section, we look at how those strategies can be effectively employed in evaluation research. Data collection and analysis should interact, as you collect ideas and thoughts will be stimulated and these should feed back into the data collection. The key to qualitative analysis is illuminating the range of what is there and then by means of data reduction making sense of that range. You need to prepare the data to make an evaluative judgement. In presenting your analysis, you want to achieve a balance between the description and analysis; a balance between interpretation of data and analysis; and appropriately elaborated analysis.

Working within data sets

Qualitative data analysis is predicated on structuring the data through some type of categorising system and setting this out in such a way that you can create meaning for yourself and others. There is a wide range of ways in which you can work with the data but these tend to fall into three broad approaches.

1   Mapping: this is about creating 'pictorial' accounts with a method for example, arrows and plus or minus signs to indicate relationships and linkages in the data (see Jones, 1985). Here you are literally 'exploding' a piece of data and creating visual patterns that have connective meanings in terms of your analysis. The following interview extract and its treatment gives a very basic flavour of this approach

  'In terms of the cons, it's more difficult to organize a network because of their resources spread around the place and because you don't necessarily have a convenient meeting place or focus for what happens so it is more difficult to achieve. It does I think need significantly more financial input than if you had a single small self-contained service which could be managed by people like clinicians who know little about financial issues whereas the network has more people who have managerial skills. And that's where I think a project manager is actually quite important to drive the project and to achieve what somebody on a part time basis could not achieve'.

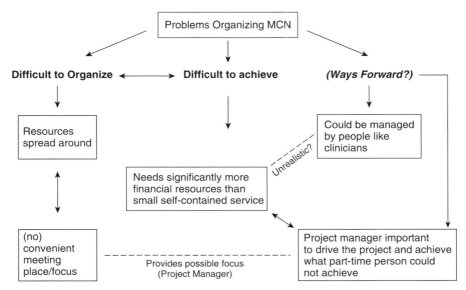

Figure 23.1   Mapping Example

Table 23.3   Analytic grid example: questions

	Why is it a problem	What does it affect	Who does it affect	What can be done about it
Unit of Analysis				
Structures				
Organization				
Rational				
Agendas				
Roles				
Relationships				
Resources				
Location				

2   Analytic Grids: using questions along one axis and units of data along the other axis (Lofland and Lofland, 1984). Using the same interview extract you could set up units of analysis you are interested in related to your evaluation and then questions you wished to address (see Table 23.3). It is likely you would keep the same units across your various data selection structures, resources and so on, and adjust the questions accordingly, for example, 'why is it a problem' becomes 'why is it a benefit'.

Ordered Lists: for example, interview topic, inducted theme, profession, setting and relevant combinations (Tesch, 1990). Here, you are bringing together respondents, data under specific topics (deductively or inductively) gleaned from your coding of the interviews and using this to determine the key components and underlying themes at a common and specific level.

Coding Data
In simple terms, these may be defined as 'labels' that allow you to assign units of meaning to the text data you have gathered. A code can be added to a phrase, sentence, and paragraph to give meaning. It is quite possible to have more than one set of meanings attributable to a sentence, paragraph. As illustrated earlier, data may be managed in various ways. It is important to:

- Consider and note the advantages and disadvantages of approaches to data handling and coding. This is important as the analysis and recommendations may be challenged on the grounds of what others may consider inappropriate methods and analysis.
- Code each data collection whether that be interviews, observation notes and relevant documentation.
- Use code words or labels to help you bring together chunks of data in a coherent manner to, address an aim in the evaluation, discover a new theme running through the data, to illuminate a professional view on an issue. These 'chunks' are the evidential basis of your analysis from which conclusions are drawn from the data.

In qualitative analysis, three broad types of codes are recognized: *descriptive* (for example, the functioning of the MCN); *interpretative* (for example the problems) and *thematic* (for example, fragmentation as a theme running through the organization and functioning of the MCN). In an evaluation, that basic range would be expanded to take into account *evaluative* components of the work.

For example in the MCN evaluation impact codes were developed to highlight the relationships between factors or events critical to assessing the workings of the network.

Create a coding system

There are two broad ways you can approach this:

- A deductive approach: e.g., using your evaluation aims and objectives and/or the interview topics as a coding scheme. In terms of the MCN interview topic basic code words were developed: Mrole (role of MCN); Mpros/Mcons (pros and cons of the MCN); Mimpact (impact of MCN) and so on.
- An inductive approach: whereby you create a coding scheme through your reading of the data and noting what seems important, interesting. For example, in the MCN evaluation, a topic that seemed to run through much of what was said by interviewees was 'responsibility' in terms of making the MCN a success and this was represented using the terms Mrespon.

To an extent, an evaluation tends to draw coding towards a more deductively focused format as you have an agenda to address for the commissioners. They want to know how processes work, whether outcomes have been achieved, how learning has been transferred, does the theory match up with the practice. However, we would argue it is possible to combine elements of both in such a way as to keep the evaluative delivery focus but open up the analysis. If you are fully transcribing the interview then you can apply the inductive method, followed by a deductive coding as outlined in Table 23.4 next.

In Table 23.4, the contextual code is Mprobl (Problems with the MCN), and it is a deductive code and a topic of the interview schedule. The data extracts are

Table 23.4   Example of combined deductive and inductive coding

Deductive Code: Mprobl	Inductive Codes
MCNA1 In terms of the cons, it's more difficult to organize a network because of their resources spread around the place and because you don't necessarily have a convenient meeting place or focus for what happens so it is more difficult to achieve	resprobl; focprobl = illustrative codes orgprobl; achvprobl= impact codes fragm= thematic codes
MCNC1 There needs to be clearer understanding of what groups are out there, accountability in terms of who to report to who for work that is being progressed so that you don't end up with fragmentation, or sub groups going off at a tangent from what the core group believes is the preferred direction of travel.	clarprobl=illustrative code acctbprobl=impact code tangprobl=impact code fragm=thematic code

Key to the Codes
Resprobl= resource problem
Focprobl= focus problem.
Orgprobl= organizational problem
Achievprobl=achievement problem
Clarprobl =clarity problem
Acctbprobl=accountability problem
Tangprobl = tangent problem
Fragmen = fragmentation

ordered by professional catalogues. The reading of the data shows the Mprobl has a number of dimensions: there are illustrations of problems; impact areas; and suggestions of wider themes regarding the functioning of the MCN.

Getting started

Drawing upon the example of the MCN evaluation that follows, we offer a method for analysis applicable to observation notes, focus groups and documentation as it is to interviews but for illustrative purposes, we focus on interviews.

- Preparation: Transcribe your interviews either fully or partially. Read each transcript at least twice to get a real sense of the data.
- Basic Coding: Take the first five transcripts, read each and create a coding schema. If you are working with a team, each member does likewise and you come together to discuss and rationalize the schema. Apply that coding schema to the next tranche of interviews and note any new topics/themes that come up. Adjust your coding scheme accordingly and recheck your first tranche of interviews. Repeat the coding process until your have coded all your interviews.
- Layering a Coding Scheme to Create Analytic Themes: Review your codes to see their connections. Sort out overarching themes (the big picture), then disentangle each one into its component parts and their relationships. For example, an overarching theme in the MCN interview data was 'pushing the service agenda' and the component parts making up the theme were: content of the service, promotional strategies, cultural contexts, responsibilities, policy agendas.
- Creating Analytic Catalogues: This begins the process of comparing and contrasting your findings across professions, communities, and work settings with regard to your analytic themes. The easiest way to do this is to place the code you are interested in looking at the top of a sheet of paper and its data source (interview, observation and document), then order (for example, by profession, by setting, etc.) the contributions from the interviewees under that heading. In most qualitative computer programmes, you can do the exact same thing by setting up data catalogues. You can then search by code word across the data sets; for example, all clinician's views on the role of the network manager. It will then be possible to 'read' the data not just within a group but also across groups. By doing this for the MCN theme 'pushing the agenda', it became noticeable that the hospital clinicians were very much focused on their own narrow resource agenda, whereas most of the other groups were focused on creating more partnership working; thus what was meant by 'the agenda' and how could this be addressed became a crucial issue to emerge from the analysis.

Working across the data sets

As stated earlier, it is likely you will have more than one data gathering method and you now need to bring findings together within an evaluative context. There are many ways to do this and the following gives a flavour of three main approaches using the MCN example:

- Use the aims and objectives and start to piece the evidence across the data sets: One of the aims of the MCN evaluation was to address 'what would happen if the specialty MCN was not there?' The interview and observation data sets provide data not just on the range of views from positive to negative but also anchored those to the rationale given. The extract that follows gives a flavour of this. *How would key agendas have been coordinated and addressed?* '... .The second point made by respondents was that the quality agenda would have been much more difficult to organize and address as it was not clear to respondents what other forum could have coordinated that effort. The fact the network has taken on this work ensured that the quality agenda (upon which the inspection would be based) would be adjusted to more closely reflect the reality of the specific service rather than the usual trying to fit the service into a generic quality template. As one respondent noted *'We now have more of a focus on the quality aspects...'*. Further, and as another respondent remarked, it ensured that *'...it is the key issues being addressed and not just someone's hobby horses'*.

- Apply an 'emergent' themes approach: 'Raising the Profile of the MCN' emerged as a key concern across all data sets. Using the baseline and follow-up data, we were able to assess progress by the end of the evaluation period. The analysis revealed the:
  - specialty service now appears in the same section of the *Health Plan* as stroke services and CHD and in turn helps to raise the profile at a strategic level and cements the specialty clinical relationship to two of the key national health target arenas.
  - specialty MCN was now part of the Regional *MCN Managers Group* and linked in to *Pan MCN groups* for example, on health improvement and on information technology. This type of participation has opened up opportunities to spread the word on the specialty, for example, specific health information has gone into a regional health improvement initiative specifically targeted on ethnic minority communities.
- Your evaluative 'theory' may require you to incorporate a specific analytic approach: for example, in pluralistic approaches of evaluation you will want to set up the criteria for success and assess these against the evidence in and across the data sets. The interviews with MCN members were used to elicit their criteria for success and these were then analyzed and formatted as the Core Criteria (those commonly cited) and the Specific Criteria (those germane to particular professions). The observation data sets (reports/discussion of progress on agenda items), the second wave of respondent interviews (progress since the first interview), and the MCN network manager's monthly review interviews (what's happened under each development heading) were then analyzed with a view to assessing the extent to which the criteria were met (yes, no, or partial). Table 23.5 next gives examples from the assessment of the Core Criteria.

Table 23.5   Assessment of the criteria for success

Core criteria	Assessment			Comment
	Yes	No	Partial	
Increased awareness public re importance of the speciality to health in general			P	For those patients who get the targeted lifestyle leaflet re speciality; Speciality included in Black & Minorities HP Leaflet going out region wide
Improved referral pathways between primary and secondary care	Y			The ECCI (electronic referral) protocols for use by GPs are now live
Reductions in morbidity e.g., fewer amputations		N		This is a long-term goal and predicated on the development of an active prevention strategy and a freeing up of acute resources to tackle the relevant cases asap; although there is data on amputees within the region, identifying the speciality is difficult; there is no robust baseline.

The foregoing tabular technique can be used in different types of evaluations from process to outcome to knowledge generation.

Regardless of the analytic technique used, qualitative analysis in evaluation has to function at two broad and connected levels: addressing the specific aims and objectives of the evaluation while staying open to the potential for new avenues of influence and explanation.

In summary, qualitative analysis is similar in its broad principles and practices regardless of whether the focus is evaluative or research. Data still has to be physically and conceptually organized. This is a dynamic process: analysis evolves and through that process reveals the subtle layers of meaning in data and opens up the range of interpretations and explanations.

VALIDATION OF THE EVALUATION FINDINGS

There has been a growing debate over the past decade as to how one can validate qualitative findings (research or evaluation), which has resulted in a variety of approaches being championed and criticized from grounded theorising, to member checking (respondent validation), to data triangulation, to reflexivity, to peer review of data coding, and the use of constant comparative techniques (e.g., Hamberg et al., 1994, Hamersley, 1995, Angen, 2000, Barbour, 2003). Indeed, some have argued that validity should be reconfigured so that the focus is on 'ethical validation' and 'substantive validation' (Angen, 2000). In the United Kingdom, as part of a general move towards developing good research governance, a framework for judging qualitative evaluation has been published by the UK Cabinet Office (Spencer et al., 2003) that outlines no less than 88 quality indicators upon which to judge the conception, design, data collection, reporting and utilization of evaluation. In effect validation 'lists' are appearing and as Barbour (2003) puts it, a 'technical essentialism' is taking hold in which the more you can tick-off, the more valid the evaluation and its results are assumed to be (Barbour, 2001, 2003). The key to the validation of qualitative work is not fulfilling the 'lists' per se, its how the components are applied and for what purpose: for example we would argue that data triangulation should not primarily be about validity, it should be about getting the necessary range of data to address the evaluation questions.

Validation should be integral to the evaluation rather than something that appears at the end like an afterthought. All the way through you will be reflecting on, and ensuring understanding of the design, process and outcome of the evaluation. You need to ask:

- Why am I trying to validate the findings? For example, as a requirement of the evaluation grant; to try to make people take the qualitative findings seriously; to enhance the chances of the findings being implemented. If there is a 'requirement' then you need to either follow the funder's own criteria if they have such/or use validation techniques or negotiate an agreed package of measures. If there is no guidance, then you must decide what the validation foundations will be (get advice from experienced colleagues; look at how similar studies have approached this issue).

- How will I conduct the validation? That depends on the component parts. If you are using data triangulation in this way then you will have to make sure you have a common core of questions or you will have no comparability of data sets and therefore, of findings. If you are using reflexive techniques, this will have to be done on an ongoing basis and you need to keep a diary. If you are using constant comparison technique, this needs to be ongoing through the evaluation. If you are using other studies to contextualize your findings, then you will probably do this at the end of your analysis if only because you may wish to consider your findings for themselves, in the first instance, so you do not unduly narrow the analysis. If you are using respondent validation techniques, you need to be clear about what is subject to comment and the extent to which such comments can be incorporated in any reporting mechanism.
- How do I incorporate the validation into the evaluation report? The most common method is to write a separate section in the methods chapter of the report both outlining and reporting on the validation. Nevertheless, it is open to you to write a section in the methods chapter explaining your approach and then write a section at the end of the findings reporting on the validation in practice. You can also get a colleague to write the validation section on the basis of the validation evidence.

In terms of our MCN example, respondent validation was used as part of the wider pluralistic strategy of recognizing that the various participants would also have different reactions to and thoughts about the evaluation findings. There had been a strong element of feeding back as the evaluation proceeded and in effect, the respondent validation acted more as a 'round-up' mechanism of an ongoing process. In this case, the draft interim report and the final report were the subject of the formal respondent validation. Respondents were given a copy and asked to comment at three levels:

- The extent to which the evaluation findings were a fair and accurate representation of the workings of the MCN.
- The extent to which suggestions/recommendations arising from the evaluation were practical and implementable.
- The accessibility of the reports in terms of layout and terminology.

Respondent validation has been criticized as being a potentially cosy admiration society with no real critique of the findings or a feeding-frenzy in which the findings are torn and revamped beyond recognition (Barbour, 2003). Whose truth should prevail: the evaluator, the respondents and which respondents? (Angen, 2000). One way round these criticizms is to be clear on the salience of the contributions and the relationship of those to the original analysis. The golden rule running through the MCN process was 'The respondent can add to the report but cannot subtract unless it is a clear error of fact' (MacPherson and Williamson, 1990, p. 23). In this way, the original analysis is retained, but any new interpretations respondents may produce having reflected on the draft findings, can be added without compromising the original evaluation findings.

The MCN validation exercise was new to many of the respondents (especially the clinicians), in the sense of its structure and golden rule. The main comments received centred on:

- Surprise from the clinicians (positive) at the degree of accessibility of the presentation and content and the 'plain-speaking' style for a 'qualitative' report.
- Agreement from all that the evaluation (interim and final) had captured the workings of the MCN and had not shied away from the political undertones and their consequences.
- The reality check on the responsibilities of those involved to make the MCN work.
- Some surprise (positive) at the practical nature of the suggestions for the way forward.
- The fact that it made the respondents think hard about what they were doing with the MCN and their own involvement.

Validation is not about right and wrong answers per se, it is about interpretations and understandings; it is not an end point as it can (and often does) function as additional reflexive data gathering; it is about confidence not certainties (Hammersley, 1995); there is no one right or wrong way to do this: techniques change and flow in and out of fashion therefore, it is the 'why are we doing validation' that should determine the 'how we do validation'.

REPORTING EVALUATION FINDINGS

The mode of reporting and dissemination should be negotiated at the outset of the evaluation. Do not assume that what was acceptable in a previous evaluation will be acceptable in any new evaluation. There are three broad areas you need to think about:

- Time Period for Reporting: you will have a time period for doing the evaluation but you should also check whether there are any salient dates within the contract period, when 'feedback' (formal or informal) would be helpful to the commissioners. In particular, if you asked for an interim report, is that linked to any forthcoming decision-marker and if so what would be helpful to focus on? Make sure the reporting time period/s are realistic vis-à-vis data gathering and analysis.
- Reporting Formats: most evaluation commissioners ask for an interim and a final report. Here you need to think about the balance between the two so that both remain useful. Get agreement on this and make sure all respondents know what is happening so that no one has any erroneous expectations. For example, in the MCN project, the evaluator elected to do a full report for the notional 'interim' and an updated report for the notional 'final' as this suited the nature of the evaluation and the ongoing needs of the commissioners. You may be asked to do presentations for the commissioners as you go along and again you need to negotiate this or it can become a dangerous distraction. If you are asked for presentations, make sure you understand why: are they showing-off their department and its work to others? Are they trying to influence a wider audience: is it a simple information giving exercise? One useful reporting technique especially with large complex programme evaluations is to use a briefing paper or develop a system of briefing papers. These are particularly useful for busy operational managers and policy makers and give them the key points quickly and effectively. You can either have one summary briefing paper for the evaluation or you can split the evaluation findings into a series

of briefing papers (e.g., by thematic topic) thus letting your audiences access the information germane to their agenda. You also need to be clear if they wish you to supply hard copies of any reports or simply an electronic copy and the same goes for any presentation materials. Regardless of the reporting formats, get this sorted out at the outset of the evaluation so you have in effect a 'publications plan' that will be responsive to the needs of the evaluation commissioners.

- *Publication of Evaluation Findings*: it is crucial you agree this with the commissioners at the outset of the evaluation. Remember that many evaluations will have a 'political' dimension that might make them sensitive in relation to external publication and you must decide how far to stand your ground republication. For example, one of the authors was involved with a colleague in an evaluation of a local health board's handling of a major sea-based disaster and had to battle hard to get the evaluation findings made public as the commissioner felt the evaluation did not reflect well on the local disaster plan. In fact, the nature of the disaster was such, that large parts of the local plan were redundant. The local hospital had risen to the occasion, but the occasion was not what had been anticipated and as a result, the local disaster plan was re-written to take into account this particular type of situation. Funders may wish to have pre-publication sight of potential publications and a right of comment/adjustment and here the golden rule of respondent validation can be most useful.
- *Information Additionals*: If you have developed any information databases through the evaluation that the customer will continue to use, then make sure you and your institution are included in any copyright arrangements. Also, make sure that no adjustments are undertaken without you having a right of comment and agreement. With the advent of freedom of information legislation in many counties participants can ask to review data you have collected that concerns them. Therefore, keep data archived for an agreed number of years and in an accessible format and make sure such data is anonymised. Copies of consent forms and reports of any ethical issues must also be kept.

CONCLUDING REMARKS

There is no one evaluation game-plan for health services to be applied across the board, the evaluation game-plan chosen and its subsequent data collection and analysis should be meaningful, manageable and measurable within the relevant health service context. Good data collection and sound analysis are predicated on a coherent and justified design in negotiation with the key people in all aspects of the project. Researchers must strike between:

- *Proximity* to gain access and collect data and *distance* to offer feedback sometimes with difficult points to make.
- The *independence* of the evaluator who must feedback to the commissioner while ensuring all parties can *trust* enough to be happy to offer data and views.

Ultimately, data collection and analysis continue through combinations of subjectivity and objectivity; neither state can be fully achieved, rather the researcher provides an honest context to the evaluation design, the everyday realities of data and analysis and the need to come to final conclusions for a report. As Henry, 2000 (in Fitzpatrick, 2004) reflects:

'We are trying to give solid information to people. ... so that they can make judgements about whether they are achieving the results they feel are important. If I can provide a good description based on outcome information which can be digested in very little time with very little effort. ... I've succeeded ... my highest order goal was to provide a clear, low-cost description. Methods instructors who said that the highest-order goal is always a causal analysis were just wrong'.

The greater the attention to evaluation design and the justification for the choice of methods and analysis the more quality can be identified. In this way, those who challenge the value of qualitative evaluation may have their concerns allayed. Identifying and exploring the processes of policy and service development and delivery is best explored through qualitative research in programme evaluation (Grbich, 1999; Shaw, 1999).

REFERENCES

Angen Maureen, J. (2000) 'Evaluating Interpretative Inquiry: Reviewing the Validity Debate and Opening the Dialogue', *Qualitative Health Research*, 10: 378–95.

Barbour, R.S. and Kitzinger, J. (1999) *Developing Focus Group Research: Politics, Theory and Practice*. London: Sage.

Barbour Rose (2001) 'Checklists for Improving Rigour in Qualitative Research: A Case of the Tail Wagging the Dog?', *British Medical Journal*, 322: 1115–7.

Barbour Rose (2003) 'The New Found Credibility of Qualitative Research? Tales of Technical Essentialism and Co-Option', *Qualitative Research*, 13: 1019–27.

Barbour R.S. (2008) *Doing Focus Groups. Book 5. Qualitative Research Kit*. London: Sage.

Bulmer, M. (1982) *The Uses of Social Research: Social Investigation in Public Policy Making*. London: George Allen & Unwin.

Fitzpatrick Jody, L. (2004) 'Exemplars as Case Studies: Reflections on the Links Between the Theory, Practice and Context', *American Journal of Evaluation*, 25: 541–59.

Gerrish Kate (2001) 'A Pluralistic Evaluation of Nursing/Practice Development Units', *Journal of Clinical Nursing*, 10(1): 109–18.

Grbich, C. (1999) *Qualitative Research in Health*. London: Sage.

Gugui P. Cristian and Rodriguez-Campos Liliana (2007) 'Semi-Structured Interview Protocol for Constructing Logic Models', *Evaluation and Programme Planning*, 30: 339–50.

Hall, J.E. (2004) 'Pluralistic Evaluation: A Situational Approach to Service Evaluations', *Journal of Nursing Management*, 12(1): 22–7.

Hamberg Katarina, Johansson Eva, Lingren Gerd, and Westman Goran (1994) 'Scientific Rigour in Qualitative Research: Examples from a Study of Women's Health in Family Practice', *Family Practice*, 11(2): 176–81.

Hammersley, M. (1995) 'Theory and Evidence in Qualitative Research', *Quality and Quantity*, 29: 55–66.

Hart Elizabeth (2002) 'The Use of Pluralistic Evaluation to Explore People's Experiences of Stroke Services in the Community', *Health and Social Care*, 7(4): 248–56.

Jones Sue (1985) 'The Analysis of Depth Interviews'. In Walker, R. (ed.) *Applied Qualitative Research*. London: Gower.

House E.R. (2003) 'Stakeholder bias.' In C.A. Christie (ed.) *New Directions for Evaluation*. No. 97. The practice-theory relationship in evaluation (pp. 57–67) San Francisco.: Jossey Bass.

Kaplan Sue, A. and Garrett Katherine, E. (2005) 'The Use of Logic Models by Community-Based Initiatives', *Evaluation and Program Planning*, 28: 167–72.

Lofland, J. and Lofland, L. (1984) *Analysing Social Settings: A Guide to Qualitative Observation and Analysis*. CA: Wadsworth.

Managed Clinical Network (2002) *Specialty MCN Newsletter*, August.

Mark, M.M., Henry, G.T., and Julnes, G. (2000) 'Evaluation: An Integrated Framework for Understanding, Guiding and Improving Policy Programmes'. San Francisco: Josey Bass.

Marshall, C. and Rossman, G.B. (1989) *Designing Qualitative Research*. London: Sage.

Miller Annie, Simoene Ronald, S., and Carnavale John, T. (2001) 'Logic Models: A Systems Tool for Performance Management', *Evaluation and Programme Planning*, 24: 73–81.

Miles, M. and Huberman, M. (1994) *Qualitative Data Analysis*. California: Sage.

Morse Janice, M. (1989) *Qualitative Nursing Research: A Contemporary Dialogue*. Maryland: Aspen.

Moss Cheryle, Walsh Kenneth, Jordan Zoe, and MacDonald Lindsay (2008) 'The Impact of Practice Development in an Emergency Department: A Pluralistic Evaluation', *Practice Development in Health Care*, 7(2): 93–107.

MacPherson, I.A. and Williams, P. (1990) '"Not Quite What I Meant!" The Use of Respondent Validation', *Research Policy and Planning*, 10(1): 10–3.

McKeganey, N.P. and Bloor, M. (1984) 'On the Retrieval of Sociological Descriptions: Respondent Validation and the Case of Ethnomethodology', *International Journal of Sociology and Social Policy*, 1(3): 58–69.

McKie, L. (2003) 'Rhetorical Spaces: Participation and Pragmatism in the Evaluation of Community Health Work', *Evaluation*, 9(3): 307–24.

New Directions in Evaluation Spring (2003) *Special Issue: The Theory/Practice Relationship in Evaluation*: 1–93.

New Directions in Evaluation Summer (2005) *Special Issue: Theorists Models in Action:* 1–128.

Patton, M. (2002) *Qualitative Research & Evaluation Methods*. London: Sage.

Payne, G. and Payne, J. (2004) *Key Concepts in Social Research*. London: Sage.

Renger Ralph and Hurley Caroline (2006) 'From Theory to Practice: Lessons in the Application of the ATM Approach to Developing Logic Models', *Evaluation and Programme Planning*, 29: 106–19.

Rog, D.J. and Fitzpatrick, J.L. (1999) 'The Evaluation of the Homeless Families Programme. Dialogue with Debra J. Rog', *American Journal of Evaluation*, 20: 558–75.

Scottish Office Department of Health (1998): *The Acute Services Review Report*. Stationary Office.

Scottish Office Department of Health Mel (1999) 10: Introduction of Managed Clinical Networks within the NHS in Scotland.

Shaw, I. (1999) *Qualitative Evaluation*. London: Sage.

Silverman, D. (1993) *Interpretation of Qualitative Data: Methods for Analysing Talk, Text, and Interaction*. London: Sage.

Smith, G. and Cantley, C. (1985) *Assessing Health Care: A Study in Organizational Evaluation*. Open University Press.

Spencer, L.J., Ritchie, J., Lewis, J., and Dillon, L. (2003) *Quality in Qualitative Evaluation: A Framework for Assessing Research Evidence*. London: Cabinet Office.

Tesch, R. (1990) *Qualitative Research: Analysis Types and Software Tools*. The Falmer Press.

Walker, R. (ed.) (1985) *Applied Qualitative Research*. England: Gower.

24

Autoethnography: Making Sense of Personal Illness Journeys

Elizabeth Ettorre

'The first fruit of the sociological imagination – and the first lesson of the social sciences that embodies it – is the idea that the individual can understand his[1] own experience and gauge his own fate only by locating himself within his period, that he can know his own chances in life only by becoming aware of those individuals in his circumstances' (*The Sociological Imagination* by C. Wright Mills, 1971: 12).

MID-FEBRUARY 2001

I sit in my study asking myself, 'Why am I so floppy? I fall on the stairs. I've had terrible diarrhoea. Maybe it's food poisoning but, I never had diarrhoea like this. It's probably because I am working too hard. ... Maybe it's menopause. I get palpitations and hot flashes. ... I am frightened of what is happening to my body. I am becoming not well and resisting this change' (Ettorre, 2005: 537–8).[2]

BEGINNING ON A PERSONAL NOTE

On the third of October 2007, I received an email asking me to contribute a chapter on 'Autoethnography' for the *Handbook of Qualitative Methods in Health Research*. After reading the email, I was excited. Over the past five years, I had become an advocate for the inclusion of autoethnography as a proper, recognized method in health research. However, my excitement was quickly followed by a sense of dread. I remembered my frustration and feelings of rejection when my paper, 'Autoethnography: Making sociological sense of an illness journey from thryrotoxicosis to health' was rejected for publication by two major social science journals specializing in health. I recalled the reviewers' comments. 'This piece is self-indulgent'. 'On what basis does the author make these ludicrous claims? Perhaps, she was hysterical'. 'No one can be cured from hyperthyroidism. I've never heard of such a thing'. 'Tell the author to call it a day'. I was also told by one editor that 'our chief editor does not like this kind of work'. 'Reject', 'Reject', 'Reject', 'Reject', 'Reject' was the tone of these comments and the rejection and hurt returned when I recollected them four years later. I also remember that it took me a while to recover from these rejections.

Nevertheless, I persevered. Even though I believed my paper had an important contribution to make in the field of health research, I was aware that 'observational studies' (in which autoethnography can be included) may be the most controversial element of qualitative research in health studies (Dingwall, 1992). In addition, I was aware that using 'an emotional narrative mode of autoethnographic writing' appeared to go against established canons in health research (Ellis and Bochner, 1999).[3] I would have to publish in non-health-related journals. 'What a pity', I thought because it would be good for health researchers to use this valuable method. At that time, I devised a plan to publish my paper and split the paper into two. I submitted the first part to *Auto/biography* and the second to *Women's Studies International Forum*. After my initial submissions, editors of both journals gave a clear indication that they were interested in publishing my work. The referees at these journals offered very helpful comments and suggestions. Some asked me to be more critical of the medical profession, which surprised me. I had toned down my criticisms when I submitted to health-related journals, because I assumed it would make my papers more publishable.

After my papers were published (see Ettorre, 2005; 2006) I received encouraging comments. A week after publication in *WSIF*, one well-known health researcher emailed me to say that she found my paper 'inspiring'. Later, another health sociologist said she 'loved the paper'. I sent my paper to a key theorist in autoethnography who responded that she really enjoyed reading my paper and thanked me for sending it. In addition, at that time, some of my students told me they had also enjoyed reading the paper.[4] I remember feeling that my paper could not be as bad as the initial reviewers had suggested.

This is where I begin my current paper: with a sense of relief, joy and expectation, knowing that I now have an ideal opportunity to demonstrate why authoethnography – a relatively new method for health researchers – is a useful way of studying health, illness, and medicine. Contemporary autoethnographies (See for example Ellis, 1995; 2004; Frank, 1991; 1995) do a good job of making connections between bodies, gender, illness, health and healing (Clarke and Olesen, 1999), but, with a few exceptions, they are not yet considered to be part of the academic debates within medical sociology and health research.

Both of these fields will benefit from innovative methods of data collection (Foster et al., 2006; Lawton, 2003) and data interpretation (Slaughter et. al., 2007).

EARLY MARCH 2001

> I lose weight even though I am eating like a pig. I should be relaxed ... but I am not. I am nervous all of the time. My partner is beginning to notice. 'It feels as if a river is running through my body', I tell her ... (Ettorre, 2005: 538).

LAYING THE GROUNDWORK FOR AUTOETHNOGRAPHY

In health sociology, there exists a long tradition of sociologists reflecting on their illness experiences and using these experiences as data for sociological analysis (Adamson, 1997; Davis and Horobin, 1977; Frank; 1991; 1995; Rier, 2000; Roth, 1963; Sparkes, 1996; 2003a; 2003b; Zola, 1982). Within this work, two related but disparate genres appear: 'modernist observers' and 'postmodernist witnesses'. Notably, these genres are not a strict binary and a few 'modernist' accounts (see Jobling, 1977; Macintyre and Oldman, 1977) hint at 'postmodern' autobiographies to come.

Modernist observers (Roth, 1963; authors included in Davis and Horobin, 1977; Zola, 1982) scrutinize the multiplicity of processes involved in performing the sick role. I cannot fault these authors for lack of detail or complex analyses. Nevertheless, when observing their health problems, they treat their illness accounts as alien – an abnormal state of being – revealing an essentialist frame of mind. Their propensity towards fixity in analysing consultation behaviour (Jobling, 1977), hospitalization (Fairhurst, 1977), medical routines (Strong, 1977) and marking time (Roth, 1963) creates the image of omniscient onlooker, satiated with rational, scientific explanations, but somewhat devoid of emotions. The body is mostly invisible. There are exceptions: on occasion, the pregnant body becomes visible, lying in examination rooms, resplendent in clinical functionality (Camaroff, 1977). However, for the most part, the virile, masculinist voice dominates as privileged male patients bond with their doctors when 'the old school tie is delicately indicated' (Strong, 1977: 48); an ideal patient adopts 'the role of man on the street' (Atkinson, 1977: 27) and the abstract patient is referred to as 'he' (Mapes, 1977).

Taking an autocritical stance to work in this genre, Irving Zola, a modernist observer, contends that:

> We were locked into a view of ourselves as patients in the sick role'. 'Our protest was silent and individual' ... 'personal not social', and 'nobody but us learned anything (Zola, 1991:3).

Interestingly, Zola points to 'the sexist bias' (p. 7) that influenced certain diagnoses as well as sociological work in the area. Most importantly, Zola contends that 'medicine's view of [the patient's] reality was essentially unchanged and unchallenged (p. 4)'. Zola's lucid account calls for a new paradigm that brings the body into medical sociology and takes up the challenge of feminism as a way of leading to a new praxis in medical sociology and health research. In his appeal, Zola makes a distinction between the illness narrations of modernist observers and postmodernist witnesses.

While both genres link autobiographical narratives with the experience of illness, the postmodernists are receptive to the vagaries of patienthood and the instability of ill bodies. They move towards a 'plurality of truths' (Bell, 2000: 132) that embraces different kinds of healthy and ill bodies, full of uncertainties and away from universalistic conceptions of doctors, patients and health and illness experiences.

This postmodern turn (or perhaps 'twist') goes beyond the fixed notion that a single cultural perspective – one that reveals an irrefutable set of truths – exists. That any health researcher is able to achieve an understanding of illness experiences outside of specific historical contexts or without recognition of shifting relations of power and inequalities becomes questionable for postmodernists (Bell, 2000: 132). This cannot be said of modernists.

Postmodern witnesses (Admanson, 1997; Frank, 1991; 1995; Rier, 2000; Sparkes, 1996; 2003a; 2003b) bring the body, emotions, participation and existential uncertainty into health research and medical sociology. They do this in such a powerful way that our understanding of the many-layered texture of illnesses is shaped by actively engaging with anxiety, despair, disgust, and pain as well as triumph, hope, desire, and pleasure. Their narratives generate useful ways of creating knowledge about suffering and of grappling not only with the intricate, interior language of wounding, despair, and moral pain but also the victory of living with an illness (Bell, 2000: 139). They deploy a type of 'anti-narrative' that frustrates closure (Scholes, 1980), brings performative codes to our critical attention (Denzin, 2003; 2006), and sees these codes as cultural rather than fixed aspects of human nature. Emotional and vulnerable, these witnesses give voice to the structured silence of embodied illness experiences. They also offer cultural shape to the diverse, complementary and conflicting awareness that the experience of the self and the body bring to health and illness. What do we learn from these postmodern accounts?

Rier's (2000) experience of critical illness in an Intensive Care Unit shows how the current discourse on patient participation and negotiation is not relevant to the critically ill. Sparkes (2003a; 2003b) chronicles the devastating sense of loss that occurs when injury shapes a performing athletic body into 'a failed' disabled one. One of the unsuspected rewards of being ill is to tell a story that can transform struggle, survival, and revulsion into a significant embodied, social and moral life that is self-authenticating and productive of desire (Frank, 1995).

By giving testimony to what has been traditionally abject in illness accounts, these 'postmodernists' made way for the current interest in health autoethnographies and new, more reflexive, gender sensitive, (White et al., 2001), feminist communitarian

(Denzin, 1997: 274–6) ways of doing patienthood. Atkinson (1997), one of the major critics of this genre, argues that physicians are demonized while patients emerge as heroes. Denying this claim, Bochner (2001: 148), a major proponent of autoethnography, shows that Atkinson[5] overlooks the power dynamics to which many illness stories respond and the level of control and power between those who are ill and those who represent them in narrative. We tell illness narratives not only because telling gives us the therapeutic benefits of redemptive understanding, but also because the 'political consequences of connecting the body to the self reveals embodiment and emotionality as legitimate mediums of lived experience, inscribing bodily dysfunction with value' (Bochner, 2001:148). Successful illness narratives offer the reader multiple places to stand in the story (Berger, 2001) and require an active and reflexive reader who wants to enter into dialogue with the writer and story (Bochner, 2001). Autoethnography is, in practice, more akin to the work of postmodernist witnesses than modernist observers' works.

Both modernist observers and postmodern witnesses have opened the way for health researchers to use autoethnography as a viable research tool. Certainly, in the last ten years, the area of health autoethnography has grown considerably, particularly in the field of nursing research (Foster et al., 2006). Recent work in this area has included autoethnographies on those who work with mothers of schizophrenic children (Schneider, 2005), those with aphasia (Hinckley, 2005) and elderly women in care (Evans, 2007). Work has included stories of personal experiences of arthritis (Felstiner, 2005); mental breakdown (Short et al., 2007); seeing a psychiatrist (Burnard, 2007); anorgasmia (Neville-Jan, 2004); academic depression (Jago, 2002); trauma (McClay Borawski, 2007); and an unpleasant eight-day hospital stay (Feder-Alford, 2006). Cassell (2005) tells the story of a friend's experience of open-heart surgery.

JUNE 2001

> [I go to my doctor's (Dr. Walsh's) nurse] 'I have come to get a blood test. My diarrhoea has not stopped', I say as I come into her room. 'So how long has this been going on for?' she asks. 'A few months now. I came here about five weeks ago. Then, Dr. Walsh said that I didn't need a blood test. Don't you remember?', I ask, feeling frustrated. The nurse opens the cabinet door above the sink. 'OK I'll get the syringe', she says.

ONE DAY LATER

> ... I receive a phone call from the receptionist telling me to see Dr. Walsh. I sit in front of Dr. Walsh whose manner seems rather upbeat when she comes smiling to fetch me from the waiting room. I say, 'You wanted to see me about ...' Before I am able to finish my sentence, she says, 'Yes, your thyroid has packed in'. 'What does that mean?' I say feeling immediately confused. She continues in a reassuring voice, 'Your thyroid is overactive. Your antibodies are attacking and destroying it. You are the second person today that has been diagnosed with this condition. The other is my father-in-law'. Sensing that she is in her element, I see

her as the knowledgeable doctor. I think, 'She is trying to be friendly but at this moment I don't want to share my consultation with her father-in-law'. She continues, 'There are three options. We can cut the thyroid out. You can swallow radioactive iodine which kills it. Or you can take anti thyroid tablets. I usually recommend the latter, carbimazole, which is perfectly harmless. What do you want?' I am confused and angry; I don't want to become chronically ill. I say, ''Well, I don't want surgery. The radioactive iodine doesn't sound too good. My mother has had cancer and I'd be afraid of taking any thing if I am susceptible'. 'Oh there is no connection with cancer. Radioactive iodine is perfectly safe', she retorts. A nervous laugh comes out of me and I say, 'I am not sure. I'll take the pills'. The prescription is handed to me as she moves her swivel chair towards me. 'I wonder when she wrote this', I think. She takes my wrist, 'Your pulse is 126, a little high but this is to be expected. Just take the pills. Come in a month's time for a blood test and we'll review your dosage' (Ettorre, 2005: 538–9).

AUTOETHNOGRAPHY IN THE FIELD OF HEALTH RESEARCH

Although autoethnography is related to the aforementioned social scientific tradition, it has no allegiance to any one discipline (Wolcott, 2004). Autoethnography, a term which has been in circulation for approximately three decades, is defined as 'an autobiographical genre of writing and research that displays multiple layers of consciousness, connecting the personal to the cultural' (Ellis and Bochner, 2000: 739). As a relatively new method, autoethnography is a reformulation of the traditional binary emic and etic positions and lies firmly within the realm of postmodern (critical theory) ethnography (O'Byrne, 2007). In general terms, autoethnography is a study of culture that involves the self.

Autoethnographers vary in their emphasis on the research process (graphy), on culture (ethnos) and on self (auto) (Reed-Danahay, 1997 quoted in Ellis and Bouchner, 2000: 740). Furthermore, there are various ways that researchers are able to study culture that involves themselves: reflexive autoethnography (looking at self-other interactions in one's own culture); native autoethnography (those from marginalized cultures interpreting their cultures for others), complete-member autoethnography (exploring groups that the authors are already members of, or have become members of during research) and literary autoethnography (identification as an autobiographer rather than a social scientist) (Ellis and Bochner, 2000: 740).

Writing in the first-person voice, autoethnographers look back and forth 'first through an ethnographic wide-angle lens, focusing outward on social and cultural aspects of their personal experience [and then] they look inward, exposing a vulnerable self that is moved by and may move through, refract, and resist cultural interpretations' (Ellis and Bochner 2000: 739). The leading proponents of autoethnography, Carolyn Ellis (1991; 1995; 1999; 2000), Laurel Richardson (2000a; 2000b; 2000c; 2003) and Arthur Bochner (2000; 2001; 2003) ask, 'What is good autoethnography?' They answer by identifying a clear set of criteria for evaluating this genre.

Ellis, Richardson and Bochner share a consensus here: autoethnography needs to be evaluated through two lenses, science and art, and must bridge the gap between scientific and literary writing. For Richardson (2000a), autoethnography is consistently situated in human activity bearing both the strength and limitation of human perceptions and feelings (p. 254). It needs to make a substantive contribution to an understanding of social life, have aesthetic merit, demonstrate an author's reflexivity and accountability, have an impact on the reader, and express a reality (p. 254).

Privileging evocation over cognitive contemplation, Ellis' (2000: 274) criteria of quality are based on whether or not conversations 'feel' real to life and the ability of the story to promote dialogue and stimulate social action. Bochner (2000) contends that autoethnographies signal a change in form as well as in purpose. As narratives of the self, autoethnoraphers extract meaning from experience rather than depict experience as it was lived (p. 270). Bochner asks for copious and solid detail, a temporal structure that revolves between past and present, emotional integrity of the author that reflects deeply on her/his own actions, a plausible journey of transition from 'who I was' to 'who I am', ethical awareness of other people, and a story that is capable of moving a reader (pp. 270–1). In sum, when autoethnography is done well, the intention, shape and rapport of the artistic piece should emulate the emotional and scientific commitment of the author, story and reader.

In translating these criteria to health research, I as a health autoethnographer[6] use the insights of theses authors, in particular, Ellis and Bochner (1999). I assume that there are many types of authors, stories and readers. No orthodox canon or single standard of value determines how illness stories should be conceived or constructed. I seek to be thoughtful, reflexive and ethically self-aware in portraying others and to give evidence of emotional reliability. My portrayals should at the very least depict the contours of the patient's sphere and the status of illness and health within that sphere. My autoethnographic story should be flexible, believable, told in enough detail to express the realities of everyday life and have an aesthetic appeal. I need to ensure explication of what is going on with others, even if their actions and perceptions of events, risk, health, well-being, etc. differ dramatically from mine. I want my reader to be inspired and stimulated into social action by the depiction of my story. One way of ensuring this sort of connection with my reader is to be clear about the type and scope of influence of the medical authority to which my illness narrative responds.

In a context of health and illness, autoethnographers present events that are embodied and situated in time, making clear how these events were shaped and emblematic of wider cultural meanings and social trends (See in particular Feder-Alford, 2006; Hinckley, 2005; Muncey and Robinson, 2007; Neville-Jan, 2004; Sparkes, 2003a; 2003b; Sparkes and Smith, 2002). Because of its empathic form, health autoethnographies have the potential to provide a tool to fashion a needed 'non-dualistic ontology of the mindful body in which emotions play a central role in the human experience and cultural scripts of health, sickness, disability and death' (Williams and Bendelow, 1996: 47). Autoethnography is one way of doing what Seymour (2007: 1191) calls 'exhuming the body' in ethnographic research.

Indeed, for me autoethnography has been a valuable way of writing 'my body' into my research, as Ellingson (2006) suggests.

In health research, autoethnographies allow both the reader and author to enter into various narratives of illness. As an autoethnographer, I gain an understanding of what illness is and does to me or those I observe. In my health autoethnography, do I dare contemplate risk, stigma and suffering alongside control, acceptance and victory? In my own life with sickness, do I interrogate myself as 'witness and doer' (Chawla, 2003). Do I consider how the various people I encounter come to treat me in the way they do? What constrains them? What allows them to feel empowered as patients, physicians, nurses, etc.? As Berger (2001: 514) suggests, 'Am I willing to include details that might reflect badly on me' that might show me as an intransigent, nasty patient or an unattractive or stubborn person? Ellis's (2000: 273) optimal concern is, 'I want to think and feel with my story'.

JUNE 2001

> ... I phone my partner. I tell her about my encounter with Dr. Walsh, the diagnosis and prescription. I am worried and remember that my mother had the same condition. I decide to ring an alternative physician, Dr. Fish, who my osteopath recommended once when I had hot flashes. My partner says reassuringly, 'That sounds like a good idea if you are afraid'. And I was (Ettorre, 2005: 539).

AUTOETHNOGRAPHIC 'DATA' AND WHAT TO DO WITH IT

Whether we are reflexive autoethnographers, native autoethnographers, complete-member autoethnographers or literary autoethnographers, we who do autoethnography construct a 'research text' or 'stories' that connect the personal to the cultural. In a general research context or health-related one, the stories we construct become the data for interpretation and analysis. As Ellis and Bochner (2000: 745) note, 'The research text is the story, complete (but open) in itself, largely free of academic jargon and theory'. Our stories are privileged over analysis, and this allows alternative readings and multiple interpretations. When I write an autoethnography, I use diaries or personal notes[7]; my main focus is on writing 'my story or 'research text'. In the following section, I describe my experience of constructing my 'research text' drawing on the two-year period when I was suffering from hyperthyroidism or thyrotoxicosis (i.e., overactive thyroid).

Creating a research text: thinking and feeling with my illness story

My autoethnography drew on data and analysis from diaries that I kept over a two-year period. In my diaries, I recorded key events with times, places, and people as well as my feelings, emotions and bodily states such as pulse rates, blood pressure and weight. Attached to my diaries were relevant articles, letters from families and friends and blood test results collected during that time. Before writing my research text, I did an intensive two-month study of my diaries. I read them in their entirety at least three times. On the fourth reading and before I began any interpretation, I wrote down a list of all key events in chronological order. This proved difficult, because remembering was painful. At times, I felt desperate, frustrated, disappointed and lost. Similar to Ellis and Bochner (2000), I wanted 'to write from the heart, bring the first person in my work and merge art and science'. 'Can I do it?' I kept asking myself.

As I read, wrote and sat before my computer, I found myself stroking my neck. I remembered the intense thyroid pain. I remembered my fear of dying. I sat back in my swivel chair and looked out the window. I stopped stroking my neck. As I remembered key events, I was processing them – these data moved through me as the now 'healthy', but once 'sick subject'. While reading, remembering, writing and processing these data brought me emotional and almost physical pain. I revisited my past by moving in and out of these sorrowful experiences. I was moved to work harder. I began to recall conversations and interactions that I had with 'significant others' such as my partner, friends, colleagues and doctors. I was excited, because I felt strong and for the first time I was able to think clearly and write, even though I felt vulnerable and alone. I became acutely aware that I was interpreting past events from my current position and that I would not get it entirely right nor would I be able to represent my 'significant others' completely (Pyett, 2003). Ley and Spelman's (1968) classic work, demonstrating that the amount of information patients recall in communications with their doctors is limited, loomed in my memory. I was afraid, but I reassured myself, 'There is no such thing as getting it totally right, Betsy. Seek verisimilitude. Remember Ellis (1999: 674): 'Evoke in your readers a feeling that your experience is described as lifelike, believable and possible'. I felt relieved. My narrative of my acute illness was my story about the past, constructed in the present. I described it from my specific viewpoint at that point in time, exploring my movement from being a 'sick' to a 'healthy body'. I was confronted with specific biographical events, placing me in shifting relations of power, with myself on the healing trajectory, and with others who provided different levels and types of care. After all, health and providing health care is power in our world. Gradually, I became aware that I was using the method of autoethnography to make sense of my personal journey from thyrotoxicosis to health.

As I wrote my list of key events, I used the process of emotional recall in which I imagined being back in key events emotionally and physically (Ellis, 1999: 675). Emotional recall is embedded in sociological introspection, a process which can be accomplished in dialogue with the self and represented in the form of narratives (Ellis, 1991). It felt good to do this – somehow healing. My sociological introspection allowed me as the researcher to study my lived experiences not 'as an internal state but as an emotional process which I recognize internally and construct externally' (Ellis, 1991: 32). This type of introspection was intrinsically bound up with my emotions and visceral reactions to significant others in specific sites and social exchanges. While emotional work can be a way of reaffirming one's identity and managing the disruption of illness to one's daily life and biography (Exley and Letherby, 2001), I began to construct scenes and dialogue from the partial descriptions in my diaries. I analyzed them according to what each story said, and I placed them in a time line. I knew my story was not totally accurate and that certain events were out of place. But I pressed on. I knew this work would take weeks to complete, but I felt satisfied and was curious about what I would find and more importantly how I would feel. I wanted to do this. I wrote and wrote and wrote. It felt like a year had gone by. I felt exhausted. I had not only events before me but also situated settings, sites, and conversations. I finished. I noticed in my writing and analyzing process a sense of triumph prevailed. I had survived death. I beat this severe, sharp punishing illness. Nevertheless, I felt overwhelmed with tenderness. I had suffered. I wanted to learn from my knowledge of illness and explore my multiple subject positions experienced through my destabilized, now stabilized, and transformed healthy identity. Yes, I was healthy but a different 'healthy Betsy' than before I had become ill. The cartography of acute illness had brought me back to health via a circuitous route, one that involved many choices.

Perhaps, in my being focused on what my story was telling us, I misunderstand, or worse, misrepresented what was going on for the significant others involved in my story. Yes, I found some of their behaviour difficult. My narrative was no less true than theirs was. However, my narrative provided comfort in the midst of suffering in a way that differed from their biomedical way of expressing it (Ahlberg and Gibson, 2003). The narrative gave me access to my experience of an unwelcome and painful process, while allowing me to look more critically at biomedical conventions and norms.

As an autoethnographer, I needed to be accountable to methodological principles of how I portray others and my personal, embodied integrity. With regards the former, the source of data was personal diaries or memoirs. There were no research participants as defined by the remit of Research Ethics Committees (Beyleveld et al., 2002: 114) nor was anyone identified as a conventional respondent from whom I was required to gain informed consent (Crow et al., 2004). Ethical approval was not necessary. Nevertheless, I informed all significant others with one exception[8] of this account either in writing or verbally. I was conscious of protecting the anonymity of all involved. I had done this by changing the names of people and places. With three significant others, I discussed in detail what I planned to do. I felt relieved when I received their support and encouragement. One of them agreed to read the first draft and found it 'realistic' and 'riveting'. To me talking to others who were involved in my story was important. I gained self-assurance, while they gained important information along with the opportunity to consider that understanding an older female patient's experience of an acute illness could enrich their own practice. I was encouraged and gained a sense of confidence.

JUNE 2001

... I ring Dr. Fish. I say that I received a diagnosis of overactive thyroid. I am afraid to take the pills my NHS doctor prescribed. I mention that I would like to explore the possibility of taking alternative medicine and to discuss this with her as soon as possible. Luckily, she has a time later in the day (Ettorre, 2005: 539).

THE VALUE OF AUTOETHNOGRAPHY

As implied in the foregoing, autoethnography is a 'reflexive methodology' which emphasizes the need for critical reflection on behalf of a researcher with respect to the production of narrative, to acknowledge how my social, cultural, and disciplinary positioning has shaped the narrative (Heapy, 2007: 44). With regards this sort of reflexive methodology, Alvesson and Sköldberg (2000: 7–8) contend that there are four elements in reflective research in which social science researchers should be engaged, regardless of the specific methods he or she prefers. These four reflective areas include: (1) techniques in research procedures with well-reasoned logic in interacting with one's data; (2) an understanding of the primacy of interpretation; (3) awareness of the political–ideological character of one's research and (4) recognition of the problem of representation of 'the text' and authority of the 'researcher'.

Autoethnography contributes to our understanding of the kinds of problems faced when doing reflective research and more specifically, reflection *per se*. Reflection is the interpretation of interpretation and the launching of critical self-exploration (Alvesson and Sköldberg, 2000: 6). We, autoethnographers, are involved deeply with reflection.

For example, in constructing research texts, autoethnographers do not follow a coherent and clearly prescribed methodology, but they do use a well-reasoned logic in analyzing these research texts. Autoethnographers do not fixate on data or claim that their stories represent reality. Rather, the focus is on how best to study culture/s that involve/s ourselves. In all types of autoethnography, there is explicit recognition of the significance of interpretation. As an author, I commit myself to insuring a level of authenticity in the research text and more importantly, it is my responsibility to give the reader a sense of emotional reliability in the story (Ellis and Bochner, 2000: 749).

The political–ideological character of autoethnographic research is explicit in the need for autoethnographers to appraise their own weaknesses, bewilderment and uncertainty and to demonstrate why different cultural interests are preferred (or not). Cultural assumptions and interpretations are not neutral: they construct the political and ideological conditions within which the story will be interpreted by others (See Alvesson and Sköldberg, 2000: 8).

I do not regard the problem of representation of 'the text' and authority of the 'researcher' as an overwhelming problem for autoethnography. The research text lives its own life, separate from me as the author. I am able to move in and out of the text as writer, observed, observer and participant, and never as 'truth-sayer'. I am merely 'a storied subject' among others. While there may be a sense of wholeness to a story, there will always be evidence of fragmentation and chaos. For an autoethnographer, there is a profound risk involved in projecting my private troubles onto a larger cultural scene. In this sense, the quandary of vulnerability replaces the problem of representation.

The question of the truth of my data, or the truth claims of researchers, brings us to the delicate issues of reliability and validity. Do autoethnogrpahies accurately represent the social phenomenon presented? Autoethnographers view reliability as linked with self-consciousness and the integrity of one's stories; validity emerges from the emotional integrity of the author. As an author, I must acknowledge how what I know, my position in the world and my experience combine to shape my analysis (Cho and Trent, 2006: 331; Pyett, 2003: 1171). I must monitor the emotional reliability of the story, its aesthetic appeal, and most important, its usefulness in promoting empathy (see Sandelowski, 2004: 1373).

JANUARY 2003

> I am feeling much better. The palpitations stop. My pulse is down .... I go for a blood test. By this time, I agree that I ring the phlebotomist directly for my results. In mid February, I am abroad at a meeting and during a short break; I ring the phlebotomist. After I hear her voice I say, 'Hi it's me Elizabeth. Do you have my results?' She responds quickly saying, 'Yes, let me find them'. There is a long pause and shuffling of paper. 'OK Elizabeth, here they are – 15.2 your free thyroxine and 0.46 your TSH. They are normal'. 'That is great', I say with joy. 'Do you know this is the first time my TSH is normal since I started having my blood tests almost 18 months ago?' 'No, Elizabeth I didn't. That is very nice to hear', she responds excitedly. 'Congratulations', she adds. I feel full of delight. 'OK, I'll see you at my next blood test and thanks', I say before I hang up (Ettorre, 2005: 541).

DOING AUTOETHNOGRAPHY: THEORIZING 'A RESEARCH TEXT'

In order to explain the place of an autoethnographic illness story in the context of health and illness and how to theorize 'the research text', I return to my personal experience of autoethnography (Ettorre 2005; 2006). In my autoethnographies, I used the idea of 'sentimental work' (Strauss et al., 1982) to explore how my body works when I am ill. I also examined how notions of embodied (i.e., bodily) adjustments, nomadic flexibility, and most importantly, identification/s served to challenge constructions of acute illness – constructions that rely on notions of a fixed, unitary illness identity, mastered, if not tyrannized, by health.

Theorizing the social: sentimental work

With the backdrop of sorrow, my autoethnography detailed certain physiological changes that occurred in my ill body, the choices I made, and the participatory framework in which these were set. When I was ill, there was work to be done by me and by others. The amount of work organized over the course of an illness was incalculable. Making embodied judgements was hard work for me as the patient, because my judgements were being shaped by the doctor, a technician of practical and technical knowledge. In this context, Strauss et al. (1982: 254), define instrumental work or more accurately, ' "sentimental work" as any work where the object being worked on is alive and sentient'. While they translate this work into the treatment of the chronically ill in 'technologized hospitals', their ideas are useful in a wider cultural context and specifically, for providing a context for understanding my illness story. Their analyses allowed me to move across and beyond established medical categories, corporeal boundaries, organized exchanges within the clinic, and various intensities of experience, all of which shaped, as well as resisted, categorization. Most important, the idea of sentimental work suggested to me the problematization of illness and desire for health as powerful forces that needed to be morally regulated.

For Strauss and his colleagues (1982), the sources of sentimental work are found in both the expressive (i.e., based on feelings) and instrumental (i.e., based on reason) work of medical personnel. Sentimental work includes the ever present possibility of clinical danger, it is commonly done by people who are strangers to the patient, it takes priority over other considerations including getting to know a patient, and, from the viewpoint of time, it can last for days or even weeks.[9] This identification of different types of sentimental work describes a wide range of procedures and work routines that guide the behaviour of individuals in the clinic. In their research, Strauss and his colleagues demonstrated the clinical significance of: interactional and moral rules, trust work, composure work, biographical work, identity work, awareness context work and rectification work. These theoretically compelling ideas allowed me to make a step-by-step analysis of how different types of sentimental work emerged in my research text. For example, I recorded who did what type of sentimental work, when and where. By using the idea of sentimental work, I was able to theorize my own and others, bodily work routines in a variety of illness encounters.

Theorizing the cultural: moving from identity to identifications

In my illness story, my body broke down and the tiny butterfly shaped gland in the front of my neck drew my body silently into organic degeneration and tissue death. The process of losing myself (Charmaz, 1983) – becoming less than me – the consciousness that I was ill, and most importantly, the overpowering awareness of medical images of myself as ill became increasingly clear over time. I was in the process of losing the body I had always known.

Turner (1992: 256) contends that to change one's body is to change one's identity. I felt insecure. I was unsure. The difficulty I had with this and other 'identity notions' in medical sociology was that there was little, if any, room for any interpretations of technologies of the self (Foucault, 1984). Technologies of the self refer to the ways in which we as subjects create and monitor our 'identities' in society. These also refer to the specific practices by which we constitute ourselves within and through systems of power (Best and Kellner, 1991: 61), such as medicine.

At this stage of my autoethnography, I remembered thinking that if I was turning out to be unhealthy, my identity was an identity of a sick person, an identity variously described as 'threatened' (Coyle, 1999), a 'disrupted biography' (Bury, 1982) a 'narrative reconstituted' (Williams, 1984), in need of 'identity work' (Strauss et al., 1982) and a 'restricted life' (Charmaz, 1983). I felt as if my identity was judged by what was considered a 'normal body', leading to feelings of exclusion. I knew healthy bodies are given priority over ill ones. I felt as if medicine was in control of my existence.

In my autoethnography, I highlighted a number of bodily practices that I engaged in as a sick person. I remembered how Kathy Charmaz (1983) was able to transform a restricted, medicalized view of the chronically ill person's pain into a broader view of suffering. Why can't health researchers, in their quest for a greater understanding of health and illness, create wider, more 'stylized' illness identities that are open rather than fixed? How might we be able to resist medical discourses which authorize and legitimize *a morality of health*? If I keep to narrow conceptions of myself as 'ill', how am I able to embrace new ways of being in my body? How am I able to nurture pleasure, pain and desire in my illness experience? In asking these questions, I challenged health researchers to take up the feminist philosopher Rosi Braidotti's (1994: 22) idea of 'nomadic flexibility'. Nomadic flexibility embeds us in a critical consciousness that resists culturally coded modes of thought and behaviour. Using nomadic flexibility allows us to relinquish all ideas, desires or nostalgia for fixity (Braidottoi, 1994: 22). For me, as an ill person doing autoethnography, this position emphasized *identifications* more than *identity*.

Braidotti (1994: 166) says that 'Identity is a play of multiplicity, fractured aspects of the self; it is relational, in that it requires a bond to the other; it is retrospective, in that it is fixed through memories and recollections, in a genealogical process'. Identity is related to the unconscious and differs from conscious choice. How conceptions of me (and my identifications) were produced was important (Scott, 1991). As unconscious, internalized images, they were outside of my rational control. I remember thinking, 'If my body, ill or healthy, cannot be fully understood, how can I fully understand my identity?'

One way I answered this question, and survived my illness, was to use various 'technologies of self' to adjust my own ill body to the internalized images of the whole body that I was. In my autoethnography, I paid attention to identity as complexity and multiplicity, speaking of my internal contradictions, confusions, and uncertainties (Braidotti 1994: 166). I soon found that holding on to *identifications of myself* was strategic for me. I learned how to really think about my body – where 'she' was and where 'she' came from. My wounded body became a reflexive body. I was 'capable of ruminating, deliberating, cogitating, studying and thinking carefully' (Martin, 2003: 356). The dominant identity, 'healthy body', was no longer as important to me. This identity receded in my consciousness. As a result, my identifications were deeply embodied and became those of 'in-betweenness'. They were flawlessly cultural, because they were created through the regulation and monitoring of myself in a society that upholds health.

FEBRUARY 2003

> [Dr. Fish] looks up, 'When you first came to see me, you had all the symptoms of acute thyrotoxicosis. I was very worried about you. You could have easily gone into what we call "thyroid storm",[10] had a cardiac arrest or even died. I just kept my fingers crossed that you would pace yourself so you would go slower. I am very pleased for you ...' I smile and feel deep joy ... (Ettorre, 2005: 541–2).

WHERE DO WE GO FROM HERE?

This paper has been based on the premise that autoethnography is a helpful method of telling illness stories as well as creating social and cultural insights into patienthood. Autoethnographers who study illness, health and health care are able to clarify and authenticate their self-images and feelings through writing illness stories. As one practitioner of the method notes, autoethnographers become 'the epistemological and ontological nexus upon which the research process turns' (Spry, 2001: 711). In my own autoethographic work, I desired to become a communicative body (Frank, 1995), offering generous greetings to other ill bodies with similar experiences. Whether or not I have achieved this level of generosity, I have used autoethnography to 'give voice to my body' (Sparkes, 2003b: 64), to experience a connectedness to others (Richardson, 2001) and to bear witness to how embodied identifications with others are able to induce dialogical exchanges. The invitation to autoethnography is an invitation to story-telling which differs from other research genres. Autoethnography offers researchers the opportunity to give voice to their experience, to bring 'reflexive authenticity' to their work, and to use the tools of sociology to analyze their experience in the world in a way that enlightens the experiences of others.

ACKNOWLEDGEMENTS

I am very appreciative to the Editors for the helpful comments on my earlier draft. Also, a very special thank you to Kathryn Church for her excellent review.

NOTES

1 Mills was not gender-sensitive and used 'his' and 'he' throughout his work.
2 I will insert excerpts from my previously published autoethnography before each new section of this paper.

3 Indeed, in their article, Ellis and Bochner refer to Rose Weitz's (1999) article published in *Health* in which they contend that there was a blatant absence of emotion. For Ellis and Bochner, emotions are a key factor in writing illness stories in autoethnographies.

4 Nowadays, students refer regularly to these articles in their essays for my *Health, Culture and Society* course.

5 Atkinson obviously changed his somewhat negative views on autoethnography, as he and his colleagues welcomed the exploration of autoethnographic texts in the Editorial of the first issue of *Qualitative Research* (see Atkinson et al., 2001: 7).

6 Stone (2004) prefers to use the word, autopathography to describe an autobiographical story of illness.

7 Other autoethnographers do memory work rather than diaries (See Ellis, 1991).

8 I could not find a current address.

9 These ideas are perhaps a bit outdated, as evidenced by the work of Zussman (1992), Chambliss (1996), Timmermans and Berg (2003) and Foucault (1973), but they remain theoretically useful.

10 This is over-activity of the thyroid that has run out of control. With it, one becomes critically ill.

REFERENCES

Adamson, C. (1997) 'Existential and Clinical Uncertainty in the Medical Encounter: An Idographic Account of an Illness Trajectory Defined by Inflammatory Bowel Disease and Avascular Necrosis', *Sociology of Health and Illness*, 19(2): 133–59.

Ahlberg, K. and Gibson, F. (2003) Editorial: 'What is the Story Telling Us?: Using Patient Experiences to Improve Practice', *European Journal of Oncology*, 7(3): 149–50.

Alvesson, M. and Sköldberg, K. (2000) *Reflexive Methodology. New Vistas for Qualitative Research*. London: Sage.

Atkinson, P. (1977) 'Becoming a Hypochondriac'. In Davis, A. and Horobin, G. (eds) *Medical Encounters: The Experience of Illness and its Treatment* (pp. 17–31). London: Croom Helm.

Atkinson, P. (1997) 'Narrative Turn or Blind Alley', *Qualitative Health Research*, 7(3): 325–44.

Atkinson, P., Coffey, A. and Delamont, S. (2001) 'A Debate About Our Canon', *Qualitative Research*, 1: 5–21.

Bell, S.E. (2000) 'Experiences of Illness and Narrative Understandings'. In Brown, P. (ed.) *Perspectives in Medical Sociology* (pp. 130–145). Prospect Heights, Illinois: Waveland Press, Inc.

Berger, L. (2001) 'Inside Out: Narrative Autoethnography as a Path Toward Rapport', *Qualitative Inquiry*, 7(4): 504–18.

Best, S. and Kellner, D. (1991) *Postmodern Theory: Critical Interrogations*. New York: The Guilford Press.

Beyleveld, D., Brownsword, R., and Wallace, S. (2002) 'Independent Ethics Committees in the United Kingdom'. In Guy Lebeer (ed.) *Ethical Function in Hospital Ethics Committees* (pp. 111–23). Amsterdam: IOS Press.

Bochner, A. (2000) 'Criteria Against Ourselves', *Qualitative Inquiry*, 6(2): 266–72.

Bochner, A. (2001) 'Narratives' Virtues', *Qualitative Inquiry*, 7(2): 131–57.

Bochner, A. (2003) 'An Introduction to the Arts and Narrative Research: Art as Inquiry', *Qualitative Inquiry*, 9(4): 506–14.

Braidotti, R. (1994) *Nomadic Subjects: Embodiment and Sexual Difference in Contemporary Feminist Theory*. New York: Columbia University Press.

Burnard, P. (2007) 'Seeing the Psychiatrist: An Autoethnographic Account', *Journal of Psychiatric and Mental Health Nursing*, 14: 808–13.

Bury, M. (1982) 'Chronic Illness as Biographical Disruption', *Sociology of Health And Illness*, 4(2): 167–82.

Camaroff, J. (1977) 'Conflicting Paradigms of Pregnancy: Managing Ambiguity in Ante-natal Encounters'. In Davis, A. and Horobin, G. (eds) *Medical Encounters: The Experience of Illness and its Treatment* (pp. 115–34). London: Croom Helm.

Cassell, J. (2005) 'Miracles or Modern Medicine/Casualties of Modern Medicine', *Qualitative Health Research*, 15(4): 555–63.

Chambliss, D. (1996) *Beyond Caring*. Chicago: University of Chicago Press.

Charmaz, K. (1983) 'Loss of Self: A Fundamental Form of Suffering in the Chronically Ill', *Sociology of Health and Illness*, 5(2): 168–95.

Chawla, D. (2003) 'Two Journeys', *Qualitative Inquiry*, 9(5): 785–804.

Cho, J. and Trent, A. (2006) 'Validity in Qualitative Research Revisited', *Qualitative Research*, 6: 319–40.

Clarke, A.E. and Olesen, V.L. (1999) 'Revising, Diffracting and Acting', In A. E. Clarke and V.L. Olesen (eds) *Revisioning Women, Health and Healing* (pp. 3–48). New York: Routledge.

Coyle, J. (1999) 'Exploring the Meaning of 'Dissatisfaction' with Health care: The Importance of 'Personal Identity Threat', *Sociology of Health and Illness*, 21(1): 95–124.

Crow, G., Charles, V., Heath, S., and Wiles, R. (2004) 'Informed Consent and the Research Process: Following Rules or Striking Balances'. Paper presented at the Annual Conference of the British Sociological Association, York, England, 22–24 March.

Davis, A. and Horobin, G. (eds) (1977) *Medical Encounters: The Experience of Illness and its Treatment*. London: Croom Helm.

Denzin, N.K. (1997) *Interpretive Ethnography. Ethnographic Practices in the 21st Century*. London: Sage.

Denzin, N.K. (2003) *Performance Ethnography. Critical Pedagogy and The Politics of Culture*. London: Sage.

Denzin, N.K. (2006) 'Pedagogy, Performance and Autoethnography', *Text and Performance Quarterly*, 26(4): 333–58.

Dingwall, R. (1992) '"Don't Mind Him – He's From Barcelona" Qualitative Methods in Health Research'. In J. Daly, I. McDonald and E. Willis (eds) (1992) *Researching Health Care: Designs, Dilemmas, Disciplines* (pp. 161–175). London: Routledge.

Ellingson, L. (2006) 'Embodied Knowledge: Writing Researchers' Bodies into Qualitative Research', *Qualitative Health Research*, 16: 298–310.

Ellis, C. (1991) 'Sociological Introspection and Emotional Experience', *Symbolic Interaction*, 14(1): 23–50.

Ellis, C. (1995) *Final Negotiations: A Story of Love, Loss and Chronic Illness*. Philadelphia: Temple University.

Ellis, C. (1999) 'Heartful Ethnography', *Qualitative Health Research*, 9(5): 669–83.

Ellis, C. (2000) 'Creating Criteria: An Ethnographic Short Story', *Qualitative Inquiry*, 6, 2: 273–7.

Ellis, C. (2004) *'The Ethnographic I: A Methodological Novel About Autoethnography*. Walnut Creek: Rowman Altimira.

Ellis, C. and Bochner, A. (1999) 'Bringing Emotion and Personal Narrative into Medical Social Science', *Health*, 3: 229–37.

Ellis, C. and Bochner, A. (2000) 'Autoethnography, Personal Narrative, Reflexivity: Researcher as Subject'. In Norman K. Denzin and Yvonna S. Lincoln (eds.) *Handbook of Qualitative Research* (pp. 733–68). Thousand Oaks, CA: Sage.

Ettorre, E. (2005) 'Gender, Older Female Bodies and Autoethnography: Finding my Feminist Voice by Telling My Illness Story' *Women's Studies International Forum*, 28: 535–46.

Ettorre, E. (2006) 'Autoethnography: Making Sense of My Illness Journey From Thyrotoxicosis to Health', *Auto/Biography*, 14: 1–23.

Evans, K.D. (2007) 'Welcome to Ruths' World: An Autoethnography Concerning the Interview of an Elderly Woman', *Qualitative Inquiry*, 13(2): 282–91.

Exley, C. and Letherby, G. (2001) 'Managing a Disrupted Lifecourse: Issues of Identity and Emotion Work', *Health*, 5(1): 112–32.

Fairhurst, E. (1977) 'On Being a Patient in an Orthopaedic Ward: Some Thoughts on the Definition of the Situation'. In Davis, A. and Horobin, G. (eds) *Medical Encounters: The Experience of Illness and its Treatment* (pp. 159–74). London: Croom Helm.

Feder-Alford, E. (2006) 'Only a Piece of Meat: One Patient's Reflections on her Eight Day Hospital Experience', *Qualitative Inquiry*, 12(3): 596–630.

Felstiner, M. (2005) *Out of Joint: A Private and Public Story of Arthritis*. Lincoln, NB: University of Nebraska Press.

Foster, K., McAllister, M., and O'Brien, L. (2006) 'Extending the Boundaries: Autoethnography as an Emergent Method in Mental Health Nursing', *International Journal of Mental Health Nursing*, 15: 44–53.

Foucault, M. (1973) *The Birth of Clinic*. London: Tavistock Publications.

Foucault, M. (1984) *The Care of the Self (The History of Sexuality*, Volume 3) London: Penguin Books.

Frank, A. (1991) *At the Will of the Body: Reflections on Illness*. Boston: Houghton Mifflin.

Frank, A. (1995) *The Wounded Storyteller: Body, Illness and Ethics*. Chicago: University of Chicago Press.

Frank, R. (2002) 'Integrating Homeopathy and Biomedicine: Medical Practice and Knowledge Production among German Homeopathic Physicians', *Sociology of Health and Illness*, 24(6): 796–819.

Heapy, B. (2007) *Late Modernity and Social Change: Reconstructing Social And personal Life*. London: Routledge.

Hinckley, J.J. (2005) 'The Piano Lesson: An Autoethnography about Changing Clinical Paradigms in Aphasia Practice', *Aphasiology*, 19(8): 765–79.

Jago, B.J. (2002) 'Chronicling an Academic Depression', *Journal of Contemporary Ethnography*, 31(6): 720–57.

Jobling, R. (1977) 'Learning to Live with it: An Account of a Career of Chronic Dermatological Illness and Patienthood'. In Davis, A. and Horobin, G. (eds) *Medical Encounters: The Experience of Illness and its Treatment* (pp. 72–86). London: Croom Helm.

Lawton, J. (2003) 'Lay Experiences of Health and Illness: Past Research and Future Agendas', *Sociology of Health and Illness*, 25(Silver Anniversary Issue): 3–40.

Ley, P. and Spellman, M.S. (1968) *Communicating with the Patient*. London: Staples Press.

Macintyre, S. and D. Oldman (1977) 'Coping with Migraine'. In Davis, A. and Horobin, G. (eds) *Medical Encounters: The Experience of Illness and its Treatment* (pp. 55–71). London: Croom Helm.

Mapes, R. (1977) 'Patient Manipulation of the System: An Ethno-Biographic Account'. In Davis, A. and Horobin, G. (eds) *Medical Encounters: The Experience of Illness and its Treatment* (pp. 32–7). London: Croom Helm.

Martin, P.Y. (2003) '"Said and Done" versus "Saying and Doing": Gendering Practices, Practicing Gender at Work', *Gender and Society*, 17(3): 342–66.

McClay Borawski, B. (2007) 'Reflecting on Adversarial Growth and Trauma Through Autoethnography', *Journal of Loss and Trauma*, 12: 101–10.

Muncey, T. and Robinson, R. (2007) 'Extinguishing the Voices: Living with the Ghost of the Disenfranchised', *Journal of Psychiatric and Mental Health Nursing*, 14: 79–84.

Neville-Jan, A. (2004) 'Selling Your Soul to the Devil: An Autoethnography of Pain, Pleasure and the Quest for a Child', *Disability and Society*, 19(2): 113–27.

O'Byrne, P. (2007) 'The Advantages and Disadvantages of Mixing Methods: an Analysis Combining Traditional and Autoethnographic Approaches', *Qualitative Health Research*, 17: 1381–91.

Pyett, Priscilla M. (2003) 'Validation of Qualitative Research in the "Real World"', *Qualitative Health Research*, 13(8): 1170–79.

Richardson, L. (2000a) 'Evaluating Ethnography', *Qualitative Inquiry*, 6(2): 253–5.

Richardson, L. (2000b) 'Introduction – Assessing Alternative Modes of Qualitative and Ethnographic Research: How Do We Judge? Who Judges?', *Qualitative Inquiry*, 6(2): 251–2.

Richardson, L. (2000c) 'Writing: A Method of Inquiry'. In Norman K. Denzin and Yvonna S. Lincoln (eds) *Handbook of Qualitative Research* (pp. 923–49). Thousand Oaks, CA: Sage.

Richardson, L. (2001) 'Getting Personal: Writing Stories', *Qualitative Studies in Education*, 14(1): 33–8.

Richardson, L. (2003) 'Looking Jewish', *Qualitative Inquiry*, 9(5): 815–821.

Rier, D. (2000) 'The Missing Voice of the Critically Ill: A Medical Sociologist's First-Person Account', *Sociology of Health and Illness*, 22(1): 68–93.

Roth, J.A. (1963) *Timetables: Structuring the Passage of Time in Hospital Treatment and Other Careers*. Indianapolis: The Bobbs Merrill Company Inc.

Sandelowski, M. (2004) 'Using Qualitative Research', *Qualitative Health Research*, 14: 1366–86.

Scholes, R. (1980) 'Afterthoughts on Narrative: Language, Narrative and Anti-Narrative'. *Critical Inquiry*, 17(1): 204–12.

Schneider, B. (2005) 'Mothers Talk about Their Children with Schizophrenia: A Performance Autoethnography', *Journal of Psychiatric and Mental Health Nursing*, 12: 333–40.

Scott, J. (1991) 'The Evidence of Experience', *Critical Inquiry*, 17: 773–97.

Seymour, W. (2007) 'Exhuming the Body: Revisiting the Role of the Visible Body in Ethnographic Research', *Qualitative Health Research*, 17: 1188–97.

Short, N.P., Grant, A., and Clarke, L. (2007) 'Living in the Borderlands; Writing in the Margins: An Autoethnographic Tale', *Journal of Psychiatric and Mental Health Nursing*, 14: 771–82.

Slaughter, S., Dean, Y., Knight, H., Kreig, B., Mor, P., Polegato, E., Shenfield, D.G., and Sherwood, E. (2007) 'The Inevitable Pull of the River's Current: Interpretations Derived from a Single Text Using Multiple Research Traditions', *Qualitative Health Research*, 17(4): 548–61.

Sparkes, A. (1996) 'The Fatal Flaw: A Narrative of the Fragile Body-Self', *Qualitative Inquiry*, 2(4), 463–494.

Sparkes, A. (2003a) 'From Performance to Impairment: A Patchwork of Embodied Memories'. In Evans, J. Davies, B., and Wright, J. (eds) *Body Knowledge and Control* (pp. 157–72). London: Routledge.

Sparkes, A. (2003b) 'Bodied, Identities, Selves: Autoethnographic Fragments and Reflections'. In Denison, J. and Markula, P. (eds) *Moving writing: Crafting Writing in Sport Research* (pp. 51–76). New York: Peter Lang.

Sparkes, A. and Smith, B. (2002) 'Sport, Spinal Cord Injury, Embodied Masculinities, and the Dilemmas of Narrative Identity'. *Men and Masculinities* 4(3), 258–85.

Spry, Tami (2001) 'Performing Autoethnography: An Embodied Methodological Praxis', *Qualitative Inquiry*, 7(6): 706–732.

Stone, B. (2004) 'Towards a Writing Without Power: Notes on the Narration of Madness', *Auto/Biography*, 12: 16–33.

Strauss, A., Fagerhaugh, S., Suczek, B., and Weiner, C. (1982) 'Sentimental Work in the Technologized Hospital', *Sociology of Health and Illness*, 4(3): 54–78.

Strong, P. (1977) 'Medical Errands: A Discussion of Routine Patient Work'. In Davis, A. and Horobin, G. (eds) *Medical Encounters: The Experience of Illness and its Treatment* (pp. 38–54). London: Croom Helm.

Timmerman, S. and Berg, M. (2003) *The Gold Standard: The Challenge of Evidence Based Medicine and Standardization in Health Care*. Philadelphia: Temple University Press.

Turner, B. (1992) *Regulating Bodies: Essays in Medical Sociology*. London: Routledge.

Weitz, R. (1999) 'Watching Brian Die: The Rhetoric and Reality of Informed Consent', *Health*, 3(2): 209–27.

White, M.T., Lemkau, J.P., and Clasen, M.E. (2001) 'Fibromyalgia: A Feminist Biopsychosocial Perspective', *Women and Therapy*, 23(1): 45–58.

Williams, G. (1984) 'The Genesis of Chronic Illness', *Sociology of Health and Illness*, 6(2): 175–200.

Williams, S. and Bendelow, G. (1996) 'Emotions, Health and Illness: The Missing Link in Medical Sociology'. In Veronica James and Jon Gabe (eds) *Health and the Sociology of Emotions* (pp. 25–53). Oxford: Blackwell Publishers.

Wolcott, H.F. (2004) 'The Ethnographic Autobiography', *Auto/Biography*, 12(2): 93–106.

Wright Mills, C. (1971) *The Sociological Imagination*. Harmondsworth: Penguin Books.

Zola, I. (1982) *Missing Pieces: A Chronicle of Living with a Disability*. Philadelphia: Temple University Press.

Zola, I. (1991) 'Bringing Our Bodies and Ourselves Back in: Reflections on a Past, Present and Future Medical Sociology', *Journal of Health and Social Behaviour*, 32(1): 1–16.

Zussman, R. (1992) *Intensive Care: Medical Ethics and the Medical Profession*. Chicago: University of Chicago Press.

25

Institutional Ethnography

Marie L. Campbell

There is nothing special about the *methods* used for collecting data for an institutional ethnography (IE) – nothing that any well-trained ethnographer would not know how to do. Institutional ethnographers observe, conduct interviews, and collect documents for text analysis. However, institutional ethnographers look and listen for somewhat different features of a health care setting than do anthropologist-ethnographers. Consequently, the analysis of data, and indeed, the character of the knowledge produced in an institutional ethnography differ significantly from other ethnographies. Dorothy Smith,[1] the originator of institutional ethnography and its leading spokesperson, says that 'the aim of the sociology we call 'institutional ethnography' is to reorganize *the social relations of knowledge of the social...*' (2005: 29, emphasis in original). What might it mean to reorganize the social relations of knowledge of the social in health care? What kind of contribution can be made to health research by doing so? Before getting to these questions I begin by discussing how to 'think' in the way that institutional ethnographers do.[2] Most basic is the importance that institutional ethnographers attach to understanding the social world that is enacted in institutions. In IE, as in other post-positivist approaches, things – including the objects of social research – are both created and interpreted in actions. In the IE approach, meanings are never fixed and the definition of terms, while possible, is not the best way to understand IE.[3] That being said, an introduction to IE requires that we understand how institutional ethnography's terms 'work' in the contexts of their use.

  Smith's comment about reorganizing the relations of knowing highlights institutional ethnography's feminist critique of the objectivity that is claimed for most social science and health research. Because they insist that all knowledge is socially organized, institutional ethnographers cannot stand outside the social relations of any setting in some 'neutral space'. For institutional ethnographers, the standpoint of the researcher and of the research is always an issue for what is being learned and made known. This concern with standpoint comes out of 'the discoveries of the feminist movement ... when women explored the ruptures between their everyday experience and the dominant forms of knowledge which, although seemingly neutral and general, concealed a standpoint in particular experiences of gender, race and class' (McCoy 2007: 702). Smith developed institutional ethnography as an alternative sociology, one that avoids mainstream sociology's use of theory in research that, she says, establishes 'the knower's discursive position as transcending the everyday worlds of people's experience' (2005: 50). This gets at an essential claim made for institutional ethnography – that its inquiry addresses a problematic or puzzle discoverable in people's own experiences in their everyday worlds, and does so from their own perspectives. As McCoy (2007) explains, institutional ethnographers try as much as possible to begin their research 'outside of academic theories, professional discourses and administrative categories ... because all of these may become objects of analysis' (704). Adopting them to frame one's research interest, she continues, 'renders them invisible as distinct practices of knowledge' (704).

IE makes an analytic advantage out of the understanding that the knowledge it generates is never neutral. Because institutional ethnographers position themselves and their inquiries explicitly to establish and work from a particular standpoint, it can be said that an inquiry in institutional ethnography is embedded in and expresses a particular politics of knowing. Smith says: '... institutional ethnographies produce a kind of knowledge that makes visible to (those) directly involved the order they both participate in and confront. Because the research is ethnographic, it describes and analyzes just how that order is put together. Knowing how things work ... is invaluable for those who often have to struggle in the dark. For example, knowing the implications for practice of changing the concepts and categories that operate in coordinating institutional processes can be very useful at the point where changes have not yet been settled and where there is room for maneuver' (2005: 32). Not everybody in a health care setting needs this kind of knowledge, but Smith's words help us identify who can be expected to benefit from it, about which I will say more later.

The contemporary organization of health care creates many kinds of problems that institutional ethnography can help us understand. In the Canadian context, where most of my own research[4] has been done, public policy mandates the exercise of certain kinds of authority over health care, which gives a high profile and definite political sensitivity to the public administration and professional regulation of health care. Always a complex and difficult field to manage, an array of new challenges in health care arose by the turn of the twenty-first century in Canada, as in other health systems around the industrialized world. Health care researchers play a variety of roles in relation to the new organizational solutions being put in place, and institutional ethnography enters debates about problems in health care on somewhat different grounds than other analyses and critiques of health care do. Studying the health care institution[5] as it is enacted by people means being able to see it 'in motion' and to explore its operation as a social organization. A health care system's constitutional and regulatory specificities – including policy and financing, monitoring and reporting practices, scientific, therapeutic, and professional discourses, and the design and implementation of management and accountability measures, create its particular shape. It is that range of institutional effort that establishes how any participant in the system, whether policy-maker, administrator, health care professional, health care recipient, or other, is expected to and does orient their respective health-related actions. Management of such a system is information-based and text-mediated. It is no exaggeration to say that various forms of knowledge and discourse occupy a place just as important to the satisfactory operation of the contemporary health care institution as do professional personnel.

Institutional ethnographers are cognizant that creating the knowledge that is an increasingly significant element of the coordination and control of all aspects of work in health care settings is now a major institutional task. Understanding how texts mediate the actions of health care personnel is crucial to analyzing health care problems. Both on the therapeutic and the management side of operations, the operational health and sustainability of the institution is almost entirely accomplished in text-based activities that absorb more and more resources. That new 'solutions' also create new problems may not be self-evident. As different institutional priorities and methods replace previously unquestioned ways of delivering and administering health care, values also shift. Emerging within this dynamic institutional regime are new philosophical and practical dilemmas. Claims and counterclaims are made by politicians, product and service promoters, and variously located health experts, including scientists, administrators, and professional practitioners, while the truth about the institutional regime is hidden in (or behind) a proliferating mass of information. Institutional ethnographers are beginning to bring their 'social organization of knowledge' approach into these institutional environments, helping to redefine the problems, rethink the questions, and design and conduct studies that illuminate how things *actually* work.[6]

Because institutional ethnography explores a problematic that arises *in the everyday world*, the attention of the researcher is directed in a particular way. Whether studying health care or any other topic, institutional ethnographers must learn about the social world of actual settings from the people who are conducting their lives and work there. Smith points out that institutional ethnographers do not study people or their problems – the notion of problematic 'refers to the translation of … people's ordinary doings into a topic for ethnographic research. It locates the step that is taken from the ordinary doings and ordinary language that are the stuff of people's lives onto the terrain of a sociological discourse, the business of which is to examine how that stuff is hooked into a larger fabric not directly observable from within the everyday' (2005: 39).

The larger fabric referred to by Smith is the work of institutions. Institutional ethnographers study health care as a complex of institutional relations, making analytic use of how people, in enacting the institution, coordinate their own doings. Discovering how people's activities are coordinated is central to IE's analysis of any institution. People in institutions have to know what to do and that means learning how to work in institutionally correct ways, to take appropriate action even as policy changes and as situations shift. IE extends inquiry into what we call 'institutional regimes' where the research focus remains on 'what people do' as coordination, and does not rely on concepts – say, of managerial ideology, professional dominance, or organizational power. Smith clarifies how coordination is understood in IE: 'Coordination isn't isolated as a phenomenon that can be differentiated from people's activities; it is not reified as 'social structure', nor as rules; it is not conceived to be a specialized form of action itself. For institutional ethnography, the social as a focus of sociological inquiry is specified as *people's activities* as they are coordinated with others. ... The focus of research is never the individual, but the individual does not disappear. His or her doings ... are to be taken up *relationally*' (2005: 59).

To illustrate, I have selected some excerpts of institutional ethnographies conducted in health care settings as exhibits of data collection and their analytic use. These exhibits show researchers making use of some of institutional ethnography's central ideas, and I use them to extend readers' understanding of IE in a manner that definitions cannot do.[7] The analytic goal here, as always in IE, is discovery and description of the specific organizational practices that make a setting 'work' as people know it, do it, and talk about it. Nevertheless, here I also have pedagogical goals. Transformations in health care settings that the following ethnographic studies address are being displayed not as 'organizational change', or as 'strategic plans implemented successfully', or as 'improvements in policy', but as knowledge-based activities. Huge investments are made in building the schema, purchasing the technologies and putting personnel in place to support all such transformative efforts. Ethnography in health care settings finds people using the ideas that have come to hand as 'information' or 'research communication' or 'knowledge transfer/translation', but little is known about how things *actually* work. In what follows, you will see how the notion of social relations guides the researcher's efforts to track several instances of how ruling relations of knowledge operate across the ordinary boundaries of people's work experience. Notice how ethnographic data offer clues to guide the exploration of aspects of a site's informational coordination – to discover what would otherwise escape notice.

DOING IE

Research published by Mykhalovskiy (2001) and Rankin[8] (Rankin and Campbell, 2006) exhibit some important features of doing IE, and show, as well, the particular kind of insights that an IE offers.[9] In his research, Mykhalovskiy introduces a health care professional whom I call PCD (she is the Patient Care Director of a hospital's Acute Myocardial Infarction unit). She tells Mykhalovskiy about a text that she has found useful in understanding the efficient management of her unit. The analysis shows her understanding being transformed into a technological and comparative calculation whereby efficiency becomes, authoritatively, a matter of reduced length of patient stay in hospital. Mykholovskiy discovers how reading the health services research text (re)organizes PCD's thinking and acting, in line with the standpoint of the health care institution. He concludes that through her reading of this particular science-based report, she was coached to adopt a managerial standpoint, and to participate knowledgeably in new and institutionally authorized ways.

The second example is taken from Rankin's ethnography of hospital nurses. Rankin learned how nurse managers' concerns about efficiency came to be expressed in new expectations of the nurses, including the use of care pathways to standardize length of patients' stay and to guide nurses towards consensual views about caregiving. Rankin was interested in the specific institutional efforts undertaken to transform nurses' judgement and persuade them to recognize that discharging patients 'on time' (according to care pathways) is not just an institutional priority but also a nursing responsibility. Both of these studies show the textually mediated features of actual transformations in professional practice. More interestingly for our purposes, the excerpts make visible the actual efforts being made to reorganize health care professionals' understandings in line with institutional texts, to persuade them to transform certain of their actions.

The two examples share conceptual and analytic features of institutional ethnography that are important for newcomers to IE to grasp. In my discussion of Mykhalovskiy's and Rankin's research, I focused on 'ruling relations'. Both attend precisely to how ruling relations enter a local health care setting in the processes of actual people doing their work. Both researchers find in their ethnographic data accounts of practices ruling their informants' actions. Both trace (through texts) the social relations of this ruling back from the local sites of action to their origins external to the setting.

In the next sections, you will notice that the idea of ruling relations is brought to the study by the researcher *not* as a theoretical concept, but as a strategy for looking. The researcher keeps his or her attention on what is actually happening. During data collection, the researcher is on the lookout for what institutional ethnographers call the 'trans-local coordination' of a setting: what informants do and what comes of it. They look for answers to such questions as 'What are the people in this setting doing? How do they know what to do? What coordinates their work? What texts do they consult? Where did that text originate and from whose hands did it travel?'

The researcher's choice of a problematic for inquiry occurs from getting to know the setting. Central to the choice of problematic is IE's commitment to being a research approach 'for people' (Smith, 2005). This claim places demands on how the research is conducted. For instance, the researcher establishes his or her research topic in relation to the people in the setting and to their experiences. Research topics and questions are not imported from the literature or elsewhere, because, among other reasons, the analysis begins where actual people are, with what they know and how they know it. Mykhalovskiy and Rankin identified what issue, as it was understood and communicated by their informants, needed to be accounted for. In what follows, I am returning, as promised, to show more specifically, what is meant in IE by relations of knowledge. From what I show of Mykhalovskiy's and Rankin's research, I discuss how they analyze the relations of knowledge to make explicit the ruling practices that organize the experiences of informants. These relations are not treated as necessarily malign, but they are recognized to be purposeful and authoritative. In their identification and mapping of social relations, researchers aim to make visible as practices the social organization of institutional power that are otherwise accepted as neutral, or more often, unquestioningly beneficial.

EXHIBIT ONE: A MANAGERIAL PERSPECTIVE CONSTRUCTED

Mykhalovskiy's research goal is to discover if health services research works differently from self-characterizations made by its practitioners and proponents in hospital management. The literature, Mykhalovskiy writes, 'puts forward a cybernetic model of the active character of knowledge, wherein research as information 'input' guides or should be made to guide individuals' decision-making 'outputs'. Such accounts position health services research as a benevolent tool that improves the delivery of health care services' (2001: 272). Focusing on a high profile research report on hospital length-of-stay by Chen and Naylor (1993), Mykhalovskiy uses interviews to get at the text-in-action that is the object of his research; he describes using his interview data as 'an empirical window onto the textual mechanics of hospital reform that the Chen/Naylor report helps to organize' (280). His ethnographic data collection includes attention to how this text enters the setting, how it is taken up by the patient care director (PCD) and how she uses it – what he calls her adoption of a new interpretive strategy. His analysis shows how he learns from talking to PCD how the Chen/Naylor text has contributed to her recognition of the problem of inefficiency of patient care in her own unit. As she reads the report she learns how to coordinate her perceptions and actions with it. In Mykhalovskiy's analysis, the perceptual standardization of 'inefficiency' is crucial to a course of restructuring action that PCD undertakes following her 'recognition'.

But what has actually happened? Mykhalovskiy discovers that 'the report acts not simply by entering a set of discrete findings into the local setting, but by contributing a text-mediated way of knowing hospital care' (280). The report shows PCD that the correct interpretation of a workplace's efficiency is comparative and necessarily textual, and it coordinates her recognition of her 'problem of inefficiency' with a similar recognition of 'the solution'. It coordinates her use of a range of texts and a discourse of efficiency already available in the setting with some specific new managerial efforts and technologies. As Mykhalovskiy discovers, PCD reads, she learns (interprets in the terms given in the text), and then she acts – to get physicians' agreement to reorganize their professional care on the unit.

Here is how Mykhalovskiy reports his own finding that a health services research text *coordinates action* and does not simply inform: he reports that PCD took up the baseline data made available in the report to make a comparative reading – 'comparing "herself" to "others"' (279) – a generally accepted managerial task. The report also supplies the terms in which inefficiency is to be calculated, making patient 'length of stay' the textual criterion. In this case, encouraged by the coaching voice of the Chen/Naylor report, and using figures it supplied, the director learns to compare her hospital's length of stay for patients in her unit to 'peer' institutions and to recognize her unit as lagging behind the leaders, thus to see it as inefficient.

Mykhalovskiy notes that 'local inefficiency emerges through practices of textual engagement that *accord a preference* or take for granted the superiority of lower lengths of stay' (281, my emphasis). The Chen/Naylor report contributes that preference, as an authoritative voice, expressing the standpoint and interests of the Canadian health care institutional regime. At that time in Ontario, reducing hospital costs was part of an 'efficiency' discourse that was circulating widely and was available for PCD to key into. Yet, it took the Chen/Naylor report to help her draw the particular conclusions that she did about her own unit, and its inefficiency. The crucial point to which Mykhalovskiy draws our attention is that inefficiency is not objectively observable until it is *made* observable through definite interpretive strategies. The report helped PCD make the connections between ideas about efficient use of resources and her own unit: the report proffered an authoritative way of reading managerial success or lack thereof (as efficiency or inefficiency *in relation to her unit's bed utilization*), and thus it rationalized the need for PCD to develop a pathway for care. The research shows how the act of reading a health services research text coordinates the actions of a reader/knower with the standpoint of the text. Adopting its standpoint creates PCD as an institutional subject who can participate knowledgeably in courses of action that are of concern from a ruling standpoint. (And for whom competing standpoints are subjugated.)

EXHIBIT TWO: LANGUAGE AND PERSUASION

My second example of IE focuses on a managerial use of language in efforts to reorganize the standpoint of hospital nurses, encouraging their willing contribution to what Rankin calls the health care institution's 'accounting logic'. Nurses, like physicians, must often determine for themselves, and on the spot, what to do, what to do next, what is most important to do now, and so on. While crucial to their nursing practice, the level of discretion they retain can disrupt new forms of organizational efficiency. In this case, nurses are the objects of persuasion to adopt new practices supporting more efficient bed utilization. Rankin contrasts a ruling standpoint, associated with institutional priorities, to nurses' experience-based professional standpoint, showing how the ruling standpoint enters and dominates nurses' practice.

Rankin observed as she supervised nursing students on hospital wards and she also interviewed front line staff and managerial nurses. Nurses employed to provide direct care to patients know their work from a variety of knowledge sources. Practical experience offers a different and competing form of knowledge from that offered through various professional discourses, including the discourses of health care reform. Experience-based knowledge and judgement is conjoined, however uneasily, with the application of nursing theory and its abstract concepts in nurses' education.[10] Yet, nurses' trained competence in working with discourse and abstract language offers a particularly fertile ground for coordinating their responses with the institutional project, or as Smith says, of 'sustaining the dominance of a particular standpoint as universal' (1999: 145).

Rankin heard her informants speaking the language of ruling that was circulating in their work settings, and as an institutional ethnographer, she knew that language use changes as the settings of its use change. 'Efficiency', as nurses come to know it under health care reform is one example: it means something different now than it did to previous generations of nurses.[11] Now, in addition to nurses knowing to not waste time and hospital supplies, 'efficiency' expresses the accounting logic associated with speeding up the movement of patients into and through hospital beds and out the door.

Clinical care paths contribute to efficiency by coordinating the care given for standard procedures and patient conditions. Where care paths are in use, they hold nurses and other caregivers to pre-established discharge dates. To support this efficiency goal, Rankin's nurse informants were asked to take on certain new discharge planning work, including the completion of a special section of a routine hospital admission form. To fill its categories usefully, nurses were expected to engage with patients in ways that identified potential discharge-related problems and where it seemed necessary to make referrals. An example would be engaging in conversation to discover that a patient's family members live at a distance and are thus unavailable to nurse a newly discharged relative. Because this would present a potential discharge problem, nurses would be expected to make a referral to a social worker or hospital liaison nurse. Rankin learned that the nurses resisted filling out the discharge-related forms, seeing this as inappropriate use of their very scarce nursing time. This was a big problem for nurse managers for whom bed utilization represented a major responsibility. Nurse managers explained (in interviews) that their work included 'getting the referral process moving quickly' and 'really trying to work on [those discharge-related activities] with nurses' (Rankin and Campbell, 2006: 108).

The utilization of beds (along with bed mapping and the computerized admissions process in which the efficient discharge was embedded) was of interest to

Rankin's nurse informants only when it intruded into their daily nursing work. Rankin's inquiry attempted to discover how such 'intrusion' was organized. She learned, for instance, that in order for their nurse managers to exercise their responsibility to 'clear beds' to facilitate the computer-assisted flow of new admissions, they needed the staff nurses' active cooperation. Rankin's interviews with nurse managers reported on how they monitored nurses' involvement in treating new admissions as the 'discharges' they must soon become. Rankin heard from staff nurse informants about being caught in a real-time dilemma – they were faced with actual patients whose bodily needs after surgery are the nurses' primary responsibility and whose recovery trajectories might or might not match the discharge dates set by the care pathways. Nurses had to manage the disjunctures created by the dominance of the abstract or virtual order when it conflicted with clinical actualities. Nurse managers had the task of making the efficiency agenda rule what would happen.

Notes of the meetings of the hospital's discharge planning committee helped Rankin see the perspective about nurses' work being organized at the nursing managerial level. The notes reported that:

> (s)ome nurses do not feel ... [completing the discharge planning fields on the admission form] is relevant to their work with patients .... We need education to help nurses see the significance of the social history in provision of holistic care (Minutes, Discharge Planning Committee meeting).

Rankin took up the specific language, 'holistic care' in the notes of the meeting, to inquire into what was significant about it for nurses to see.

With language, as with any other social act, institutional ethnography looks for the workings of its coordinative function. Rankin's analysis of this particular use of language relies on Mikhail Bakhtin's (1986) notion of speech genres – and his theory of 'how words mean' in a particular setting. Attention to language matters analytically because language use arises in and can be traced back to social organization and to what Bakhtin calls particular 'spheres of activity' (1986: 60). Drawing from Bakhtin's notion of speech genres, Rankin discovered how 'holism' was being used persuasively to disrupt nurses' knowing and to substitute a ruling perspective. She examined instances where 'it becomes apparent that (people) were speaking from different locations within the health care setting and using the respective speech genres of each, where different knowledge and skills are required and exercised' (Rankin and Campbell, 2006: 142). Rankin, herself a nursing instructor familiar with nursing's 'sphere of activity', recognized 'holism' as a speech genre within a specific *nursing* discourse. There, its characteristic usage instructs nurses how to respond to patients and their needs. Holism applied to nursing means, according to nurses Potter and Perry (1997), attending to 'the physical, emotional, social, economic and spiritual needs of the person' (1485).

Rankin saw the same word, 'holism', being used by members of different groups, each referring to something rather different, as in the case of 'efficiency'. Appearing in the situation of nurses and expedited discharges, nurses and managers work in different 'spheres of activity' and the words they use 'bear the imprint' of their different responsibilities. For nurses, holism and holistic nursing care are abstract concepts, empty of actual tasks, but nurses know how to fill in the appropriate activities. Rankin's data suggest that nurses in her research setting were being expected (and, indeed, 'educated' as the discharge planning text recommends) to treat discharge planning work as a member of this nursing speech genre. They are expected to fill the empty category 'holistic nursing care' with tasks arising in another sphere of activity – the managerial responsibility for bed utilization. Rankin argues that nurse managers are using a language ploy to overcome resistance that nurses base in their professional discourse. Through blending of the two speech genres, nurse managers are attempting to draw nurses seamlessly into the accounting logic of health care management.

THE RELATIONS OF KNOWLEDGE REORGANIZED

The ethnographic data analyzed in these examples of IE were chosen by the researchers not because they expressed or elaborated a framework originating in a theoretical discourse or a prior research question. Rather, the data offer an entry into the actual workings of an institutional regime. The research objective is discovery, making possible what is often referred to in IE as a mapping of the social relations that connect local experiences to the extra- or trans-local terrain of ruling. In the second example, we see Rankin taking the standpoint of the nurses, and discovering how their actions are being ruled. It is a knowledge relation although not a determinate one. The expected outcome is that nurses will accept that their newly required contribution to more efficient bed utilization is 'holistic nursing practice'. To the extent that this language ploy persuades or can be enforced, nurses' own professional knowledge will be altered.[12]

Rankin's findings support a serious critique of health care. Having nurses prepared and properly supported to intervene at the interface between the various forms of institutional knowledge and the actualities of patients' bodies is crucial to maintaining good health care. Rankin argues that to the extent that the experiential part of nurses' knowledge is downgraded and replaced by a managerially authorized perspective, patients' safety is endangered. Rankin's analysis is part of a challenge to a misplaced trust of objective knowledge in health care management, as it supersedes other forms of knowing. Institutional ethnography's positioning of the inquiry in a standpoint outside the ruling order makes this critique possible and credible.

Like Rankin's, Mykhalovskiy's research offers a glimpse into the textual coordination of the institutional regime that governs the local settings of health care. Analysing the relations of knowledge is of paramount importance in both situations. Mykhalovskiy's analysis shows how a new form of expertise becomes central to the then emerging and now dominant text-based form of hospital governance. Such reorganization of the relations of knowledge is of great importance for all the next steps of implementation and committed use of pathway technology (and other technologies, more or less similarly organized) emerging in hospitals. As Mykhalovskiy's paper shows, PCD's new kind of knowing informs her immediate managerial actions and she uses it to good effect to gain the cooperation of physicians who were sceptical about the pathways project she was advocating. Seeing how texts are drawn on by Mykhalovskiy's informant to coordinate her local setting with extended processes of institutional rule elaborates *what a ruling relation is and how it works*. Evidential relations and cost-cutting merge in her activation of the pathways technology, drawing physicians' practice closer to managerial priorities.

In today's world, the use of care pathways has become naturalized[13] and accepted as a best practice in Canadian hospitals, but at the time Mykhalovskiy was collecting his data, it was a new and untested idea in the research hospital. What happens is usually glossed as organizational change, and theoretical or speculative accounts stand in for how it comes about.[14] Mykhalovskiy's version of events, on the other hand, shows a unitary standpoint being constituted through specific textual coordination of the institutional regime. Lessons such as these about orienting to preferences arising in text-mediated knowledge have had to be learned wherever health care reform and restructuring are undertaken. Absent analysis of the kind offered here, the institutionalization of new text-based forms of ruling can be accepted as an improvement in governance, and misrepresented as health care management's own neutral, even beneficial, responsibility.

FROM DATA TO KNOWLEDGE THAT IS TRUSTWORTHY AND USEFUL

These examples illustrate we can use institutional ethnography to 'reach beyond the local particularities of people's everyday lives and into the regions of the relations that organize them' (Smith, 2005: 57–8). Explicating ruling relations and ruling practices is institutional ethnography's approach to generalization. In contrast to how generalization is conceptualized and practiced in other research, institutional ethnography looks for and describes the practices that actually generalize social settings themselves. The research is not generalizable as such, but it displays the relations that generalize, that can be found operating similarly across similar sites. This point is important to doing IE: the institutionally coordinated activities that IE shows people undertaking organize *generalized local responses* in line with the ruling ideas of the discourses that circulate,[15] and this discursive coordination accounts for how the ideas are taken up similarly in multiple settings around the globe. The trustworthiness of an institutional ethnographic account is an empirical matter. Institutional ethnographers encourage other researchers to go and see how things work in the original or similar sites and then to offer extensions, corrections, and updates to the original analysis. Since any site is 'in motion', an account of it can always be revised and improved.

An analyst can take up any piece of the puzzle that appears in a setting. For Mykhalovskiy, from his own location as a health services researcher at the University of Toronto,[16] questions emerged about how research plays out in local settings of health care. He already had an institutional account of the workings and importance of health services research, and in using his institutional ethnographic framework, he queried the institutional standpoint. He tells us that he is interested in the relation between discourse and action, specifically in how health services research coordinates 'medical and managerial practices and rationalities' and the practical outcomes in health care settings. Rankin's research interests arose in her intensive involvement with hospital nurses in her work of supervising the hospital placements of undergraduate students. Learning about nurses' worries and frustrations motivated her attempt to discover what was happening. Both researchers started their inquiries in the actualities they encountered where they were located; they moved from there to research sites, identifying informants similarly engaged there. They then followed clues arising from their ethnographic data into the trans-local sites of coordination of informants' activities. The design of an institutional ethnography is emergent, with the scope of the inquiry not planned in advance. Besides not knowing who will become an informant until 'in the field', for institutional ethnographers, the secondary level of data gathering to open up trans-local sites of ruling must emerge from the primary ethnography.[17] In my two examples, as is typical, the inquiries took shape from what the researchers found that they needed to learn next in order to explicate the problematic that emerged. Here texts are crucial, showing the direction to be followed to discover a setting's social organization.

The kind of inquiry I have been describing generates knowledge that *extends what the actor/informants already know* from being there. Among other things, Rankin sees the potential of her study for nursing education, to extend what is taught nursing students, while Mykhalovskiy's work extends health care critique itself. Such findings help to extend knowledge beyond the nominalizations we all use to name what we see – for instance, 'managerialism', 'neoliberalism', or 'the new public management'. Each of these studies expresses a politics of knowing that disrupts institutional accounts. They enable participants in health care settings to make sense of the mysteries they encounter in their everyday work life and to provide nonideological accounts of the drift in health care away from its grounding in clinical actualities. Learning how things actually work can return confidence to the subjugated knower – however he or she is located – about the basis of his or her own expertise. Or it may open a door for deconstruction and critique of expertise that appears otherwise unassailable. When differences of expert opinion occur, institutional ethnography can allow knowers to better sustain an argument about which account best represents a local situation, and why. Knowing more accurately what is actually happening, people may not be so vulnerable to manipulation supported by authoritative explanations, rationalizations, and professional shibboleths.

Interests within any organization are never unitary. This view underpins institutional ethnography's attention to the standpoint of the research and of the knowledge being produced. Expressing how the health care setting is in motion creates an inevitable lack of stability in institutional ethnographic accounts. While this makes institutional ethnography unfit for ruling purposes, its insights are useful for anyone attempting to understand how things actually work. Knowing that institutional knowledge gains its stability precisely through its ideological grounding (Clarke and Newman, 1997) may be helpful in the contemporary institutional environment where a good deal of managerial effort goes into promoting ideological (ruling) versions of organizational practice.

Because of IE's interest in how things work, the research often produces insights into what is not working well. It can be extremely useful to see how strategies organized for definite purposes have unexpected outcomes. IE can be used to guide revisions to policies and practices to address unforeseen problems that may have arisen. On the other hand, because its inquiries take the standpoint of institutional participants who are subject to ruling relations, the findings from institutional ethnographies do not fit smoothly into discussions in which ruling concepts and assumptions are privileged. This is not a 'weakness' of IE.[18] Rather it is a political problem that has somehow to be addressed. But beyond all this, it must be said that doing IE is difficult – not least because it demands a commitment to seeing the world differently from how the major research approaches are taught and practised. Like all ethnographic work, it is time-consuming and thus costly. These are real limitations in its usefulness. Yet, in exploring what works for whom, IE enables the expression of differently located voices. It offers new knowledge resources to everybody with a stake in health care. Without such an analytic grounding, people are at the mercy of ruling explanations about what is best for health care. IE can show us how the health care institution coordinates its ruling agenda and how its participants at all levels are engaged in making possible that capacity to rule.

NOTES

1 Smith's first book *The Everyday World as Problmatic*, 1987, introduces the thinking that led to institutional ethnography, while her comprehensive overview of the approach, *Institutional Ethnography*, was published in 2005. Campbell and Gregor (2002) *Mapping Social Relations: A Primer in Doing Institutional Ethnography*, offers a more basic introduction.

2 It is important to grasp 'how words work' in one's use of them – the way that institutional ethnographers attend to the use of words by participants in research sites.

3 Dorothy Smith's (2005) glossary (pp. 223–229) in *Institutional Ethnography: A Sociology for People* is helpful.

4 My own experience of doing institutional ethnography in health care settings has been in Canada between 1980 and 2006, and more recently in the United States, where I am currently a consulting member of an interdisciplinary research team conducting an institutional ethnography of off-peak nursing experiences in several Texas hospitals (Hamilton and Gemeinhardt, 2008).

5 Institutional ethnography's notion of institution is not synonymous with an organization or system of organizations, but is a complex of activities organized around any distinctive function such as the law, or government, or in this case, health care.

6 This kind of inquiry has been conducted on health-related experiences of HIV/AIDS patients (Mykhalovskiy et al., 2004, and Mykhalovskiy, 2008), of people with disabilities (Campbell et al., 1999); of health professionals (Campbell and Jackson, 1992; Gregor, 1994 and 2001; Townsend, 1998; Rankin, 2000; Campbell, 2000; 2001; McGibbon, 2004; Webster 2005), of nonprofessional health care workers (Diamond, 1992; Campbell, 2008). Various aspects of the institutional coordination of Canadian health care are the focus of institutional ethnographies by G.W. Smith, 1995; Mykhalovskiy, 2001 and 2003, Rankin and Campbell, 2006, and Webster,2009. In addition, other institutional ethnographic inquiries illuminate the health-related aspects of problems such as poverty and violence (e.g., Manicom, 1995; Pence, 2001).

7 Definition of terms used in IE may seem to offer a secure grasp of how to understand the approach, or, at least, to understand what I am saying about it. This is somewhat misleading. The important idea of IE is that because the social world, institutions, everything, is in motion and is happening now, the research must be able to make that activity visible. To attempt to pin down the meaning of words used suggests that they are static when it is their use by people that is crucial to grasp if one hopes to understand how a setting works. Both examples illustrate this.

8 This analysis appeared first in Rankin's unpublished (2004) dissertation. When I quote it here, I cite its later appearance in Rankin and Campbell (2006).

9 Using material from the two studies in such a fragmented way may be disappointing to readers who may hope to see a more comprehensive coverage of the research. The purpose and the scope of this chapter do not allow me to include sufficient details to bring either of these analyses to life here. For those who wish to read more and to talk back to the researchers, please read the original publications. Dr. Mykhalovskiy can be reached at ericm@yorku.ca; Dr. Rankin at jmrankin@ucalgary.ca and I am at mariecam@uvic.ca

10 For IE analysis of nursing education that explores their management of this conjunction, see Campbell and Jackson, 1992, and Campbell, 1995.

11 See Rankin and Campbell, 2006, for an account of Janet Rankin's experience of the shifting meanings of efficiency in her own nursing career, first as taught in her basic nursing education in the 1970s and then as the concept appeared in a nursing management course in her baccalaureate nursing preparation in the 1980s. In the first instance, nurses were being trained to work efficiently – to be thoughtfully organized as they went about their work; in the second instance, the language of 'inputs' and 'outputs' put in place an economic view of 'doing more with less'.

12 See Rankin and Campbell (2006) for examples of how the profession is adopting and teaching a ruling perspective and some instances of its negative impact on nurses' practice.

13 Bowker and Star (1999) problematize the notion of what can be called natural or naturalized, in their writing about the effects of information and what they call built information landscapes where the experienced world has been transliterated mysteriously through classification and categorization.

14 The 'reinventing government' movement (e.g., Osborne and Plastrik, 2000 and the private consultants engaged in it, offer prescriptions for making such change. A fully ideological undertaking, this kind of account takes for granted the otherwise controversial value of the enterprise, rather than querying it.

15 Academic, professional and trade journals, policy think-tanks, research conferences and health management consultancies are everyday vectors of such discourses.

16 At the time he wrote the 2001 article that I am relying on here, Mykhalovskiy was a postdoctoral fellow in the Department of Public Health Sciences at the University of Toronto.

17 If, on reading to this point in the chapter, you think that you cannot yet see how to do an IE, this assertion about 'not being planned in advance' may suggest why. No one set of instructions works. The main thing is to put yourself into a setting and learn from the people there what is happening *as they know and do it*. A problematic for inquiry emerges when some aspect of the local setting appears sufficiently interesting and puzzling to absorb research attention.

18 Or rather, its 'weakness' appears only from a ruling perspective.

REFERENCES

Bakhtin, Mikhail (1986) *Speech Genres and Other Late Essays* (trans., V. W. McGee). Austin: University of Texas Press.

Bowker, G. and Star, S. (1999) *Sorting Things Out: Classification and its Consequences*. Cambridge: MIT Press.

Campbell, M.L. (1995) 'Teaching Accountability: What Counts as Nursing Education'. In M. Campbell and A. Manicom (eds) *Knowledge, Experience and Ruling Relations: Studies in the Social Organization of Knowledge* (pp. 221–33). Toronto: University of Toronto Press.

Campbell, M.L. (2000) 'Knowledge, Gendered Subjectivity and Re-Structuring of Health Care: The Case of the Disappearing Nurse'. In S. Neysmith (ed.) *Restructuring Caring Labour: Discourse, State Practice and Everyday Life* (pp. 187–208). Oxford: Don Mills.

Campbell, M.L. (2001) 'Textual Accounts, Ruling Action: The Intersection of Knowledge and Power in the Routine Conduct of Community Nursing Work', *Studies in Cultures, Organizations and Societies*, 7(2): 231–50.

Campbell, M.L. (2008) '(Dis)continuity of Care: Discovering the Ruling Relations of Home Support'. In M. Devault (ed.) *People At Work: Life, Power, and Social Inclusion in the New Economy*. New York: New York University Press.

Campbell, M.L., Copeland, B., and Tate, B. (1999) Project Inter-Seed: Learning From the Health Care Experiences of People with Disabilities, Final Research Report to BC Health Research Foundation, December.

Campbell, M. and Gregor, F. (2004) *Mapping Social Relations: A Primer in Doing Institutional Ethnography*. Lanham, MD: AltaMira Press.

Campbell, M.L. and Jackson, N.S. (1992) 'Learning to Nurse: Plans, Accounts and Action', *Qualitative Health Research*, 2(4): 475–96.

Campbell, M. and Manicom, A. (eds) (1995) *Knowledge, Experience and Ruling Relations: Studies in the Social Organization of Knowledge*. Toronto: University of Toronto Press.

Chen, E. and Naylor, C. (1993) *Hospital Specific Data on Length of Stay for Patients with Acute Myocardial Infarction in Ontario in Fiscal 1991*. Toronto: Institute for Clinical Evaluative Sciences, Working Paper 21.

Clarke, J. and Newman, J. (1997) *The Managerial State: Power, Politics and Ideology in the Remaking of Social Welfare*. London: Sage.

Diamond, Timothy (1992) *Making Gray Gold: Narratives of Nursing Home Care*. Chicago: University of Chicago Press.

Gregor, Frances (1994) *The Social Organization of Nurses' Educative Work*. Unpublished PhD dissertation, Dalhousie University, Halifax.

Gregor Frances (2001) 'Nurses Informal Teaching Practices: Their Nature and Impact on the Production of Patient Care', *International Journal of Nursing Studies*, 38: 461–70.

Manicom, Ann (1995) 'What's Health Got To Do With it? Class, Gender and Teachers' Work'. In M. Campbell and A. Manicom (eds) *Knowledge Experience and Ruling Relations: Studies in the Social Organization of Knowledge* (pp. 135–48). Toronto: University of Toronto Press.

McCoy, Liza (2007) 'Institutional Ethnography and Constructionism'. In J. Holstein and J. Gubrium (eds) *Handbook of Constructionist Research*. New York: The Guildford Press.

McGibbon, E. (2004) *Reformulating the Nature of Stress in Nurses' Work in Pediatric Intensive Care: An Institutional Ethnography*. Unpublished PhD, University of Toronto.

Mykhalovskiy, E. (2001) 'Troubled Hearts, Care Pathways and Hospital Restructuring: Exploring Health Services Research as Active Knowledge', *Studies in Cultures, Organizations and Societies*, 7(2): 269–96.

Mykhalovskiy, E. (2003) 'Evidence-Based Medicine: Ambivalent Reading and the Clinical Recontextualization of Science', *Health: An Interdisciplinary Journal for the Social Study of Health, Illness and Medicine*, 7(3): 331–52.

Mykhalovskiy, E. (2008) 'Beyond Decision Making: Class, Community Organizations and the Healthwork of People Living With HIV/AIDS. Contributions from Institutional Ethnographic Research', *Medical Anthropology: Cross Cultural Studies in Health and Illness*, 27(2): 136–63.

Mykhalovskiy, E., McCoy, L., and Besalier, M. (2004) 'Compliance/Adherence, HIV/AIDS and the Critique of Medical Power', *Social Theory and Health*, 2(4): 315–40.

Osborne, D. and Plastrik, P. (2000) *The Reinventor's Fieldbook: Tools for Transforming your Government*. San Francisco, CA: Jossey-Bass.

Pence, E. (2001) 'Safety for Battered Women in a Textually Mediated Legal System', *Studies in Cultures, Organizations and Societies*, 7(2): 199–230.

Potter, P.A. and Perry, G. (1997) 'Glossary'. In J.R. Kerr and M. Sirotnik (eds) *Canadian Fundamentals of Nursing*. Toronto: Mosby Year Book.

Rankin, Janet (2001) 'Texts in Action: How Nurses are Doing the Fiscal Work of Health Care Reform', *Studies in Cultures, Organizations and Societies*, 7(2): 251–68.

Rankin, Janet (2004) *How Nurses Practise Health Care Reform: An Institutional Ethnography*. Unpublished PhD dissertation, University of Victoria, Victoria.

Rankin, J.M. and Campbell, M.L. (2006) *Managing to Nurse: Inside Canada's Health Care Reform*. Toronto: University of Toronto Press.

Smith, D.E. (1987) *The Everyday World as Problematic: A Feminist Sociology*. Toronto: University of Toronto Press.

Smith, D.E. (1999) *Writing the Social: Critique, Theory and Investigations*. Toronto: University of Toronto Press.

Smith, D.E. (2005) *Institutional Ethnography: A Sociology for People*. Lanham, MD: AltaMira Press.

Smith, G.W. (1995) 'Accessing Treatments: Managing the AIDS Epidemic in Ontario'. In M. Campbell and A. Manicom (eds) *Knowledge, Experience and Ruling Relations: Studies in the Social Organization of Knowledge* (pp. 18–34). Toronto: University of Toronto Press.

Townsend, Elizabeth (1998) *Good Intentions Overruled: A Critique of Empowerment in the Routine Organization of Mental Health Services*. Toronto: University of Toronto Press.

Webster, Fiona (2005) 'Physician Use of Evidence in Decision-Making Related to Acute Stroke Therapies', Paper Presented at the Annual Meeting of the Society for the Study of Social Problems, Philadelphia, August, 2005.

Webster, Fiona (2009) *Investigating Physician Use of t-PA for Acute Stroke in Ontario: An Institutional Ethnography*, PhD thesis, University of Toronto/OISE, Toronto.

26

Visual Methods for Collecting and Analysing Data

Susan E. Bell

INTRODUCTION

Images are familiar in medicine, from anatomical drawings in *Gray's Anatomy* and medical textbooks, to x-rays, ultrasound, CT (Computed Tomography) scans, and MRIs (Magnetic Resonance Imaging) in diagnosis and treatment, and the use of the Visible Human Project in medical education (Petchesky, 1987; Lawrence and Bendixen, 1992; Cartwright, 1995; Kevles, 1997; Kapsalis, 1997; Petersen, 1998; Burri and Dumit, 2008). Nevertheless, for the most part, images such as these have been produced and used conventionally in clinical or experimental research and practice.[1] In this chapter, I respond to the growing interest within the health community in the use of qualitative methods to answer questions about policy or practice that cannot easily be addressed with the conventional quantitative approaches of most research. I demonstrate how visual methods can become more firmly embedded in health research, practice, and policy by drawing from qualitative approaches in social science, particularly the field of visual sociology.

I begin with a definition of visual sociology, reviewing main issues in the field and looking at how visual sociologists collect data and what they do with it. Next, I consider what qualitative visual methods can contribute to the study of health care institutions, practices, and experiences with illness.[2] Throughout, I give attention to two ways health community researchers and practitioners can incorporate visual materials into their work: by *making* images to study specific questions and issues and by asking questions *about* images as a way of under-standing and improving the practice and experience of health care.

WHAT IS VISUAL SOCIOLOGY?

Visual sociology is a way of doing research that generates and employs 'visual material as an integral part of the research process, whether as a form of data, a means of generating data, or a means of representing "results"' (Knowles and Sweetman, 2004: 5). In an effort to understand social life, this way of 'seeing' employs many kinds of visual evidence including maps, drawings, diagrams, plans, tables and charts, films, paintings, and photographs (Harrison, 2002a). As with all qualitative research, the interpretation and analysis of visual materials requires systematic selection of images, coding, identifying patterns, or themes (and noting absences) in the images, and being attentive to references to dis-courses beyond the images themselves (Bell, 2002). To do visual sociology successfully, researchers must convince others that 'their visual work furthers the enterprise of sociology, however the mission of the discipline is defined … At a minimum, it should help to answer questions raised in the discipline in a way acceptable to one or more disciplinary factions' (Becker, 1995: 8). That is, visual sociology is a theoretical as well as an empirical project, 'a process of seeing guided by theory' (Harper, 2000: 717).

Howard Becker, who has been a long-term advocate for the use of visual meth-ods in sociological research, argues that visual images are so thoroughly embedded in our worlds that not to take them seriously – to ignore them in soci-ological analysis – is to reduce our understandings of subjects' worlds (Becker, 2000). Beyond their ubiquity, visual sociologists argue that people employ images to make statements that would be impossible to make with words alone. Thus, to understand our subjects we need to take seriously the visual images they make (Harper, 1998; Knowles and Sweetman, 2004).

In the early twentieth century when sociology was allied with social reform, visual images were included in the analysis and presentation of sociological research, but 'as sociology became more scientific and less openly political' the use of photographs, along with other visual approaches to understanding social life, was marginalized (Becker, 1974: 230). The circulation of key texts (Becker [1974], Goffman [1979], Wagner [1979], Harper [1982]), the creation of the International Visual Sociological Association in 1981 and its professional journal in 1986, and the development of new technologies have facilitated the incorpora-tion of visual methods into recording, organizing, analyzing and presenting sociological research (Prosser, 1998; Knowles and Sweetman, 2004). For exam-ple, until the introduction of portable video recorders in the early 1980s film was an expensive and clumsy research tool – costing upwards of $1000 per minute of documentary film, and requiring a sound recorder working along with the filmmaker (Harper, 2000). Today those interested in visual culture have easy access to portable video recorders, digital cameras, hypertext, CD-ROM, the Internet, and easy-to-use software programs for editing images and video. These technologies, as well as new visually oriented journals, have prompted some advocates to claim that 'the technology to both see and produce pictures has literally gone around the world' (Ruby, 2005: 162; see also Harper, 2005).

HOW DO SOCIOLOGISTS 'DO' VISUAL SOCIOLOGY?

There are two basic approaches to employing visual methods. The first is what Douglas Harper (2005: 474) calls 'the empirical wing of visual sociology', studying social life *with* images, for example making images to study specific questions and issues and cataloguing life visually with a camera or drawings. Making still or moving images with a 'sociological consciousness' and gathering information with these images enables sociologists to build, confirm, and/or develop existing theory (Harper, 2000: 729). Visual documentation allows 'the tacit, "seen but unnoticed" character of human activity and social organization' to become noticed and taken into account in understanding the production of social life. Recording a series of still photographs or moving film provides a resource for repeated scrutiny and attention to 'details of conduct, both talk and bodily comportment' (Heath and Hindmarsh, 2002: 103).[3]

Once the visual images are made – whether by researchers or informants – they can be coded and interpreted or they can become the basis for further information gathering. Systematic scrutiny of film/video recordings requires the division of the recording into fragments that are then transcribed and then analyzed (Heath and Hindmarsh, 2002; Rich and Patashnick, 2002). These practices are similar to 'the well-established research practice of using text transcriptions as records of verbal data collected in qualitative interviews or focus groups' (Rich and Patashnick, 2002: 251).

As with qualitative research more generally, the collection of visual data is guided by research questions. Sometimes these are operationalized in the form of 'shooting scripts', lists of research topics or questions that a documentary photographer, photojournalist, or social scientist generates and then uses to guide the collection of still or moving images (Suchar, 1997).[4] In his study of an urban community in the United States, undergoing gentrification, for example, Charles Suchar (1997) shot several rolls of film to answer each question in his shooting script and complemented these with daily field notes. Suchar developed each roll and printed it on a contact sheet. He logged each frame that responded to the shooting script question by writing a description and entering it into a logging book. He then assigned a summary label to each logged photograph. This categorizing process enabled him to compare images within and between categories. He integrated photographic data, associated word narratives, and open coded categories to generate new conceptual understandings of the changes in material cultural that accompany gentrification.[5]

Whereas 'shooting scripts' are made and followed by researchers, 'photovoice' is a strategy that relies on informants to produce images. Photovoice 'embraces the basic principles [sic] that images carry a message – images can influence policy – and citizens ought to participate in creating and defining the images that make healthful public policy' (Wang, 2000: Introduction). It was developed as a form of participatory action research methodology based on the assumption that people are experts on their lives. Photovoice consists of providing people (who are usually the subjects of others' photos) with cameras, showing them how to use the cameras, meeting with them regularly and using the pictures they take to promote critical group discussion about personal and community issues (Strack et al., 2004; Wang et al., 2004). In an iterative process of data collection and analysis, photovoice makes elements of community life visible to community members. This visibility can enable them to promote social change by communicating issues of concern and pride to policy makers and society at large.

According to the model created by Carolyn Wang and her colleagues, participants in photovoice projects typically meet to write and talk in facilitated groups about the photographs they have made using the 'SHOWeD' rubric (What do you See here? What is really Happening? How does this relate to Our lives? Why does this problem or strength exist? What can we Do about it?) (Wang et al., 2004). The groups meet monthly over a period of 4 – 6 months. Each month, each person making photographs chooses one or two images to write about and to talk about in the group. The groups codify the photographs into themes which are exhibited publicly at the end of the project. Public officials are invited to the exhibitions, where they see the images and talk with the photographers.[6]

In a photovoice project inspired by this approach, Brinton Lykes collaborated in a participatory action research project with a group of women in Chajul, Guatemala after almost four decades of civil war. The photovoice project was an outgrowth of earlier work Lykes had done with the women in the community to facilitate workshops and collaborate in the formation of a woman's organization – the Association of Maya Ixil Women-New Dawn in Chajul. These earlier collaborations provided psychosocial and educational activities for women and children as well as an economic development project.

In the Chajul photovoice project, the women used photography and interviews to document the effects of civil war and massacres on their community as well as the traditional and contemporary resources they were deploying to survive and change. Each of 20 women took one roll of photographs a month for ten months, generating between 3,500 and 4,000 usable photographs. Their photographs captured images of the community that the women interpreted and used along with interviews, analysis, and storytelling to reframe the history of the war and their engagement and survival in words and images, represented in their coauthored book *Voces e imágenes*: *Las mujeres Maya Ixiles de Chajul/Voices and Images*: *Mayan Ixil women of Chajul* (Women of ADMI and Lykes, 2000). According to Lykes (2008: 12), 'this iterative analytic process was a site for developing and documenting varying understandings of war, rural poverty, and the effects of globalization on a local economy and a context for creatively responding to some aspects of this extreme poverty through several economic development projects as well as human rights activist truth-telling'. In other words, this photovoice project promoted justice and social change within the community by making visible the effects of civil war and providing a vehicle for economic development.

Visual images can also be used as alternatives to the standard question-answer format of interviews. 'Photo-elicitation', for example, consists of 'using photographs to guide interviews and ask questions about social, cultural, and behavioural realities' (Suchar, 1997: 35).[7] Photo-elicitation can bring to the surface and make explicit ideas that are not easily articulated, such as community ideas about social class or the invisibility of whiteness to whites during their daily lives (Johnson and Weller, 2002; Farough, 2006). In addition, when the subject matter or domain defies the use of strictly verbal or written approaches – in the case of young children or people with traumatic brain injury for example – photo-elicitation may be more effective than the use of interview questions and answers (Johnson and Weller, 2002; Lorenz, 2008).

The second approach, or the 'cultural studies' wing of visual sociology, consists of *studying* images, or 'visual culture writ large' as a way of understanding social life (Harper, 2005: 748). According to this approach, 'the visual itself is the subject of investigation'; sociologists ask what visual images such as paintings, drawings, film, photography, postcards, posters, religious iconography, and advertising 'do' (Harrison, 2002b: 858). Visual materials are of interest to sociologists, because they reflect and help to construct 'the lifeworlds and social relations of their makers and users' and may contain 'documentary information about their subjects' (Caulfield, 1996: 57). Analysts in the cultural studies wing consider the practices of production, interpretation and use; they take into account 'the social and historical contexts of both the production of the images and the social and historical contexts of spectatorship – expectations of viewing' (Clarke, 2005: 217). Their research considers who is involved in image production, how the images are produced, how they are used and by whom, how they travel and enter into different social milieus and how they interact with different forms of knowledge.[8] A consistent refrain in the cultural studies wing is that visual materials – especially photography and documentary film – are important, precisely because they claim to represent reality and because viewers both expect and support these claims (Clarke, 2005: 209). Unpacking how images persuade and what the consequences of this persuasion are is a key task of this type of visual sociology: 'doing visual analysis requires us to stop and stare trebly hard in order to rupture the taken-for-grantedness of "good looking"', to learn how to decode the images (Clarke, 2005: 223).

A good example of studying images is provided by Dowdall and Golden (1989) who analyzed the organizational environment and interactions of individuals living and working in a large state mental hospital in the United States during the early twentieth century. Documents from the hospital's archive, including data on more than 4,000 individual patients were subjected to statistical analysis. The quantitative data generated did not provide a 'sense of everyday life' in this complex organization, so Dowdall and Golden turned to photographs. From more than 800 photographs – the majority collected by the hospital's director of public information – Dowdall and Golden selected a purposive sample of 343 photographs. They used these photographs to conduct a multilayered analysis:

- First, they compared all 343 with images of 'peer institutions' and on the basis of this comparison identified a genre 'that might be labelled mental hospital photography' characterized by a picture of daily life that neither exposed abuses (as did the documentary photographs at the time) nor celebrated bureaucratic efficiency (Dowdall and Golden, 1989: 186).
- Next, they coded the photographs and sorted them into thirteen subject categories (Dowdall and Golden, 1989: 186).[9]
- The third layer of analysis consisted of a 'thick description' in which they compared the images with the hospital's textual record and closely interpreted individual images in terms of the specific historical context in which they were created.[10]

This last layer of visual analysis enhanced their statistical data on overcrowding. The photos depicted 'men crowded onto a porch, women parked in their chairs, nurses warily guarding an overcrowded dayroom' (Dowdall and Golden, 1989: 207). Crowding not only diminished the quality of patient life but it also placed extra burdens on staff. In addition to enhancing the statistical analysis, the incorporation of photographs made visible the hospital workers' highly stressful, low-paying custodial positions. This dimension of hospital work had been invisible in previous scholarship, which had provided only 'brief and dramatic exposes of abuse and neglect' (Dowdall and Golden, 1989: 194). The 20 black and white photographs reprinted in their article immerse viewers in the past alongside the textual account, and give evidence to support the authors' conclusion that 'the state hospital was a world of patients and attendants, of idleness punctuated by brief and often coerced activity, and of custody rather than treatment' (Dowdall and Golden, 1989: 206).

VISUAL METHODS IN QUALITATIVE HEALTH RESEARCH

Social scientists have explored an enormous and rich array of visual materials, from well-researched documentary films and photo-essays (see the following section) to posters (Sharf, 1995), tattoos and piercings (Langellier, 2001, Pitts-Taylor, 2003), medical illustrations (Moore and Clarke, 1995; Clarke, 2005), book covers (Davis, 2007), advertisements (Mamo and Foskett, 2008), artists' books (Bell, 2006), and graphic memoirs (Brabner and Pekar, 1994; B, 2005). These materials have yet to be taken up and explored within the health community for what they can contribute to policy and practice.

Studying health *with* images as well as studying images *of* health and medical care can answer questions about policy and practice: it enables others to *see and experience* hospitals and other institutional settings *as* patients do (Radley and Taylor, 2003a, b) and to follow patients home to see how they negotiate the incorporation of medical interventions for chronic illness and disability (Berland, 2004; Chalfen and Rich, 2004). The study of illness experiences considers 'people's everyday lives living with and in spite of illness' (Conrad, 1987: 4). Findings from these sorts of investigations can improve the effectiveness of medical practice by enabling clinicians to develop plans of treatment that fit with patients' daily environments and more generally, 'provide medical care that is more responsive, sensitive and effective' (Rich and Patashnick, 2002: 246).

Qualitative and visual approaches have been used by those in clinical settings to understand illness experiences and transform medical practice. In late twentieth century medicine, the long-standing tradition in the humanities, arts, film, and photography of exploring ways to make sense of and learn from pain and suffering gained attention as a strategy for addressing the consequences of 'an excessively reductionistic, scientific approach to illness and disease' (Callahan, 1998: 85).[11] Although the scientific approach to health led to technological progress, it also compromised the quality and effectiveness of medical care by focusing medicine's gaze narrowly on the bodies of patients, ignoring the interpersonal aspects of care. To remedy these problems, medical participants and critics have turned to the humanities – and to qualitative approaches to understanding patients' experiences – for ways of reconnecting the world of lived experience with medical science. Social scientists have added rich ethnographic material to the study of why and how qualitative approaches to understanding illness experiences can improve medical care (Frank, 1995; Farmer, 1999; Mishler, 1999).

Another driving force in introducing visual materials into qualitative health research is patients who have written and performed plays, made documentary films, and created paintings, sculpture, and photographs to make visible and to give voice to silenced or stigmatized illnesses (Hevey, 1992; Spence, 1995; Eikenberry, 1998). In addition to making meaning for the people producing them, these visual media educate a wider public and promote relationships with other patients, families, and caregivers. Visual media can connect personal experiences with place, time, and circumstances, help create support networks and improve social life.

The turn to studying health institutions and practices and the experiences of illness *with* images intersects with the work of documentary filmmakers, photographers, and photojournalists, whose work continues to inform visual sociology as it has since the turn of the twentieth century. Relevant examples in this vast corpus of materials include the hundreds of well-researched documentary films distributed by Fanlight Productions, Zipporah Films, and Women Make Movies.[12] A particularly influential documentary filmmaker is Frederick Wiseman, whose 'Hospital' (1969), records daily activities in a large urban hospital in the emergency ward and outpatient clinics. Wiseman's strategy is to shoot continuously, as unobtrusively as possible. 'Near Death' (Wiseman, 1989) was filmed in a medical intensive care unit of a Harvard-affiliated hospital in Boston, Massachusetts and records intimate moments of deliberation and discussion between families and physicians. Without voiceovers, interviews, clear protagonists, or simplistic storylines, Wiseman's films draw viewers into the image to *see* the world through the eyes of patients and caregivers. A recent example of the potential in documentary film for understanding the experience and organization of health and illness is 'Unnatural Causes: Is Inequality Making Us Sick' (Herbes-Sommers and Smith, 2008), a six-part documentary produced by California Newsreel (the oldest nonprofit documentary production and distribution centre in the United States) that tracks between individual experiences and larger social circumstances in its exploration of the connection between socioeconomic and racial inequalities and patterns of disease and illness.[13]

Photography projects are another treasure trove of visual materials that can contribute to better understandings of medicine and health care. These include studies of living with illness that combine photographs and texts from the 'outside' and 'inside'. Examples of the outside perspective include *Minamata* (Smith and Smith, 1975), a look at the effects of mercury poisoning in Japan, and Nicholas Nixon's *People with AIDS* (Nixon and Nixon 1991) a documentation of living with AIDS during the early years of the AIDS epidemic.[14] Insider accounts of living with illness are also powerful resources; examples include *Putting Myself in the Picture* (1988), an autobiographical study of living with breast cancer by Jo Spence, and *Exploding into Life*, a collaboration between photographer Eugene Richards and his wife Dorothea Lynch to represent her experience of breast cancer in photographs and extracts from Lynch's diary (Lynch and Richards, 1986). These examples from outside the disciplines of social science attest to the larger field in which visual studies of health policy and practice are located.[15]

VISUAL ILLNESS NARRATIVES AND OTHER WAYS OF MAKING SENSE WITH IMAGES

The visual turn in qualitative studies of illness intersects with the field of narrative (Frank, 1995; Bell, 2000; Riessman, 2008). Narrative is a strategy for reconnecting lived experience with medical science. When a person's life is interrupted by an illness, narrative offers 'an opportunity to knit together the split ends of time, to construct a new context', and to fit the disruption caused by illness 'into a temporal framework' (Hydén, 1997: 53). According to Arthur Frank, when people are ill, their bodies are affected by external inscriptions (diagnoses, surgery, and social attitudes), as well as by interior realities such as 'the pain of tumours creating pressure on organs' (Frank, 1996: 56). Narrative gives a person a vehicle for reflecting on, making sense of, and organizing these experiences.[16] Physician Rita Charon has been one of the most vocal proponents of employing narrative in medicine. She argues that narratives can extend 'empathy and effective care towards the patients we serve and build community with colleagues with whom we do our work' (Charon, 2006: 131; see also Kleinman, 1988 and Hurwitz et al., 2004).[17]

One visual narrative approach to understanding the experience of illness uses moving pictures (made with film, video, or digital cameras). Physician and documentary filmmaker Gretchen Berland gave video cameras to three people who use wheelchairs – all adults living in Southern California – so they could look at their lives through a camera lens and record processes related to activities of daily life.[18] She asked what a video camera could show about the experience of disability that had not already been documented in the medical literature or in memoirs and films. Each of the participants 'used the camera as a confidant' and recorded 'nuances' of experiences, details that are 'often overlooked, or missed, in clinical research conducted in more traditional ways' (Berland, 2007: 2533). Over a two-year period, the three participants recorded more than 200 hours of material. Berland met regularly with each of them to review footage. She then logged and transcribed the footage and edited the material into a one-hour film, 'Rolling', in which the three narratives are interwoven.

'Rolling' shows and tells people who do not use wheelchairs how to see the world from a wheelchair – sidewalks, stairs, medical consultations – from the perspective of a user. It also reveals previously unseen details to the people using wheelchairs who are wielding cameras. One of the three participants 'cringes' each time he watches one of the scenes in the film, not because he waited 40 minutes in an examination room before seeing his physician, but because of how he subsequently collaborated with his examining physician in his avoidance of the real reasons for his visit (Buckwalter, 2007: 2534). Beyond the experiences of these three individuals, 'Rolling' graphically reveals dysfunctions in US health care institutions, such as the length of time patients routinely wait in examination rooms before being 'seen' and problems with insurance coverage.

In her work, Berland drew from participant action research, narrative medicine, and ethnography. Although the project was generated and directed by the researcher, footage was made by the informants/subjects, and decisions about what to include and exclude, as well as the meaning of different scenes were made jointly. Berland's project gave the participants – the researcher and the subjects – a vehicle for reflecting on and seeing themselves differently.

Another narrative approach is that of pediatrician Michael Rich and anthropologist Richard Chalfen in a Video Intervention/Prevention Assessment (VIA) program seeking to improve medical care. Their multidisciplinary, labor-intensive research strategy supplies video cameras to 'children and adolescents with chronic medical conditions … [thus giving them] the opportunity to create videotaped diaries of their everyday experiences with illness' (Chalfen and Rich, 2004: 18).[19] A primary goal of VIA is to 'increase the flow of information and understanding between representatives of the illness community and representatives of the medical community' (Chalfen and Rich, 2004: 21). Giving cameras to patients relocates the base of power between children and the clinicians caring for them because 'clinicians look and listen [and] patients' perspectives and statements are given authority' (Chalfen and Rich, 2004: 24).

Participants in VIA are taught the mechanics of using camcorders, given unlimited videotapes, and encouraged 'to carry their camcorders at all times and document their day-to-day lives for four to eight weeks' (Rich and Patashnick, 2002: 248). A Field Coordinator meets with each participant each week to exchange tapes and discuss what has been recorded and provides (optional) 'video assignments' to guide filmmaking. Recording ends when, by mutual agreement, the VIA Field Coordinator and participant determine a 'full narrative' has been produced (Rich and Patashnick, 2002: 248).

The pilot program on asthma included 21 participants who filmed four to seventy-eight hours of audio-visual data (489 hours total), 'much of it dense with information on a diverse variety of health-related topics' (Rich and Patashnick, 2002: 249). The videotapes are transcribed into text logs using 'direct word processing of logs' and managed and coded using a software program for qualitative analysis. Through multiple 'passes', multiple loggers record objective descriptions – emotionally neutral data elements such as where the participants are, what they say and do – and subjective accounts – 'the spontaneous thoughts and feelings elicited in loggers by the visual narratives' they see (Rich and Patashnick, 2002: 252). Medical, public health, and social work researchers evaluate the visual narratives, using the coded logs as maps (Rich and Patashnick, 2002: 257).

The VIA study of asthma patient-generated videotapes revealed 'that information about patients' known asthma triggers that was derived from the comprehensive "standard of care" medical history missed as much as 95 percent of the participants' actual exposure to asthma triggers' (Chalfen and Rich, 2004: 23). Making and then looking at videotapes also made visible 'taken-for-granted aspects' of daily life to patients; VIA became a 'therapeutic intervention'. Strikingly, 'the process of self-examination … resulted in quantifiable improvements in patients' asthma status' (Chalfen and Rich, 2004: 23). Not only does VIA interrupt standard relations of power but it also makes visible aspects of illness experiences to patients and clinicians. As a consequence, 'revisions are being made in what to look for, what to ask for, and what needs to be changed' in caring for children with asthma. VIA reveals 'obstacles to effective management' and 'strengths that a particular patient and his family bring to the healing process' (Chalfen and Rich, 2004: 5). VIA enables clinicians to see as do their patients; making the visual diaries provides opportunities for patients to reflect on their illness experiences and to see aspects of their daily lives that have been 'too close' for them to notice; and to connect the world of lived experience with medical science; and to improve medical practice.

Visual images also shed light on and can be incorporated into the process of recovery from serious illness (Radley and Taylor, 2003; Prosser, 2007). For example, in a recent autobiographical account, visual sociologist Jon Prosser (2007: 185) reflects on the way a range of visual imagery 'mediated' his experience of 'heart attack and stroke and their physical, social and psychological consequences' and became part of his healing strategy. This imagery included drawings by his daughters, images from popular culture, memories of family photographs, and ECG readouts.

STUDYING IMAGES TO MAKE SENSE OF LIVING WITH ILLNESS

In the following example, I draw on my research to consider how studying images can contribute to understanding illness experiences and improving health care practices. My study of breast cancer images examines artists' books made by a woman who had breast cancer in order to understand how she lived with and made sense of living with breast cancer, and how making art was part of her strategy. Artists' books are books created as original works of art, not just retrospective collections or catalogues of an artist's work. Some artists' books are produced as unique copies while others are produced in limited editions. Artists' books emerged particularly in the context of the antiestablishment, democratic social movements of the 1960s (Drucker 1995). Women have been highly influential in the growing field of artists' books, attracted to the gendered possibilities in the field, including 'the power of books to confer authority upon their makers' and the ability of making and reading books to bridge public and private spaces (Drucker, 2007: 16).[20] My study of these objects as images takes into account the social and historical contexts of practices of production, interpretation and use.

Martha Hall made artists' books as a healing strategy. For her, it was a way of connecting with (and talking back to) her physicians, family and friends, and a tool for organizing with other women with breast cancer. Hall was a professional white woman who lived in Maine on the northeastern coast of the United States in the late twentieth century. She was diagnosed with breast cancer in 1989 (when she was 39 years old) and died in 2003.[21] She began to make artists' books four years after she was first diagnosed with breast cancer. Although Hall had written poetry and taught weaving for many years, it was not until her breast cancer recurred that she began to make artists' books, ultimately completing more than 100 (Hall, 2003). Making the books brought to light emotions Hall had not previously acknowledged and became a powerful part of the healing strategy she developed. The healing strategy included incorporating the books in negotiations of power/knowledge with clinicians. One of her books was written in response to and collaboration with one of her physicians; she addressed others to physicians and took them with her to 'talk back' and 'talk with' her caregivers. I identified themes in books from a retrospective exhibit of her work and closely analyzed the books that represented turning points in Hall's breast cancer experience and/or illustrated themes in breast cancer discourse.

The production of Hall's artists' books took place in the context of a large and diverse field of breast cancer discourse. This field includes plays, films, photographs, drawings, sculpture, personal websites, books and collections containing 'true' and 'fictional' stories by and about women with breast cancer, and breast cancer art exhibitions (Lerner, 2001). One common theme in breast cancer discourse is the need to increase public awareness and knowledge about breast cancer, or, as Martha Hall put it, 'to educate others about cancer' (Hall, 2003). Another running theme in this field is the importance of creating support networks with others. By 'sharing stories, women with breast cancer offer mutual support, a forum for exploring the body, psyche, relationships and community that are relevant to them as well as a sense that their knowledge and experience are resources for others' (Pitts, 2004: 47). Making the private agony of suffering into something social and sharable also makes possible a 'collective outcome' (Radley, 2002: 12). A third common theme in breast cancer discourse is the portrayal of suffering and the world of the sick person, using the artwork to exemplify something about life and how it can be lived. The pictures are both ways of seeing women's bodies and ways of *seeing as* the sick person sees (Radley, 2002: 19). The negotiation of medical relationships – demystifying medicine and contesting hierarchical relationships between doctors and patients – is also common in breast cancer discourse. This entails the depiction of complicated relationships with physicians and medicine – and different relationships with different individuals at different stages of illness (Spence, 1988, 1995; Lerner, 2001; Klawiter, 2008). Hall's books reflected and contributed to these practices.

Hall wanted to place her 'work in public collections, particularly college libraries' so that her books could be held as well as seen, calling on readers' tactile as well as intellectual and emotional engagement with her body (Hall, 2003: 12). As Hall (2003: 14) wrote, 'People may not want to "touch" the topics I explore in my books; yet the books invite handling, touching, interaction'. Hall's artists' books engage audiences through sight and touch, word and image, feeling and thinking – encouraging us to attend to our own embodiment just as she made meaning of hers. At the same time that placing books in college libraries makes them more widely accessible than they would be in museums or galleries, the genre by definition limits the number of books in circulation. Understanding the genre of artists' books as well as the world of breast cancer in which Hall lived are both important contexts for the visual analysis of living with breast cancer. These contexts shape the interpretation of the artists' books made by Martha Hall.

As an example of the use of visual media, I offer a close reading of one of Martha Hall's artists' books, *The Rest of My Life* (2000), made during the year she was diagnosed and treated (with chemotherapy) for metastatic breast cancer in her ribs, spine, skull and liver. I begin with a description of the book itself, because in the case of artists' books, the physical object itself is key to understanding its meaning.

The Rest of My Life, by Martha A. Hall, 2000. (Photography by Stephen Petegorsky. Courtesy of Alan Hall. From the collections of the Mortimer Rare Book Room, Smith College.)

The Rest of My Life (2000) is a small artists' book by Martha Hall, made of medical appointment cards that were issued to her, most of them filled in by the same hand, for chemotherapy for a year (October 1999 to October 2000) in her life. The book is the same size as the appointment cards, 2 ¼" × 4 ½" × 3". The cards are put together, with surgical tape and bandages, and at intervals, a yellow manila pill package of the same size is substituted for an appointment card. Some of the prescribed medications are still in the packages.

The book opens like a long two-sided accordion, to 64". On one side, the appointment cards are pink, printed with the words, 'Maine Center for Cancer Medicine & Blood Disorder'. On the other side of the card is a white background, printed with the Cancer Center's address and telephone number, and spaces to be filled in with a patient's (given) name, day of the week, date, and time of the appointment. These appointment cards document Hall's repeated treatments and themselves signify what the words say. All of them have been 'used'. The book is contained in a small box covered with Hall's appointment calendar for October 1999.

On the back of the cards are several layers of handwritten text by Hall in different colours of ink and different styles of handwriting. In brown ink, there is a timeline covering the period from 1989, when Hall discovered a lump in her left breast, to the time of writing, in 2000. This layer of text is neatly printed. Another layer of text, cursive and written in black ink, records an internal dialogue, beginning, 'It has been more than a year since I was diagnosed with a recurrence' as well as questions and answers between Hall and other patients and friends.

In one of the internal dialogues, Hall sets out a range of alternative answers to a question posed by another patient:

> 'When will you be through?' 'Never'. 'Until I die'. Or 'as long as I live' 'until there is a new treatment' or 'until this treatment stops working' There is no answer. I don't have an answer. The doctors don't have an answer. Yes I do. 'I am living with cancer'. 'I am buying time'. 'I have a chronic disease. I'll be back for more treatment on Monday'.

A third layer of text, in pencil, haphazardly records episodes of pain, life events such as 'Chemo vacation for Haystack' and other cryptic notations. Haystack is an international crafts school located on the Maine coast offering residential studio-based workshops for as long as two-weeks. The three layers of text show how Hall continually renegotiates the disruptions to her biography brought by the trajectory of her breast cancer (Charmaz, 1991; Williams, 1984).

The sequence of appointments in the book conveys Hall's decision to stick with allopathic medical tests and treatments (CT scan, x-ray, mammogram, mastectomy, chemotherapy, radiation therapy, and bone marrow transplant) rather than turn to acupuncture, macrobiotics, or other therapies. The appointment cards and the pill packages with the name of the drug stamped on each cover document this.[22]

The strung-together appointment cards and pill packets overlaid with the other texts make it possible for readers to witness Hall's suffering and see it *as she sees* it. The repeated medical events dominate but do not efface her lifeworld and her coming to terms with living with cancer, and cancer treatments, for the rest of her life. She has transformed her daily life, inside and outside of medicine, into an artists' book, taking her readers along with her. Over and over again, they see the same loopy handwriting filling in the cards, each time for 'Martha' and each time for a different date. They can hold the same cards and the same pill packages that Martha held, first as a breast cancer patient and then as an artist.

In *The Rest of My Life* Hall uses appointment cards, pill packages, pen and pencil, and surgical tape, to fashion a metaphoric world of breast cancer out of the mundane world occupied by a cancer patient undergoing chemotherapy. The details invite reflection (Radley, 2002). To this artists' book, I bring my own experiences of having appointments, sitting in waiting rooms, taking medications, navigating between the worlds of home and medicine, but not of having breast cancer.

I wonder why some of the pills are still in their packages, and what they signal to Hall about the meaning of medications (Conrad, 1985). *The Rest of My Life* sheds light on when and under what circumstances Hall took her medications, and when and under what circumstances she did not. For example, when she travelled for an artist's workshop she stopped taking her medications, electing to make books instead. After the workshop, she resumed taking her medications. The record of pill taking in the book can become the basis of a conversation between Hall and her physicians, making visible to her caregivers the ways in which she incorporates her medical treatment into her lifeworld and increasing the flow of information between them.

Martha Hall uses elements of her daily life to fabricate a metaphoric life after a year of chemotherapy. These fabrications – works of art – produce meanings about suffering, questioning, resisting, and becoming a woman with breast cancer for the rest of her life. These meanings are worked out in the course of her daily life as she struggles to make art, preserve health, seek medical care, and make connections with other women with breast cancer. As 'data' for interpretation, they do more than show, or tell about, the life of Martha Hall. They also produce sensuous experiences for viewers. Just as they represent embodied subjects, so do they produce embodied knowers who *see* the world as Hall sees it. At the same time, they shed light on how this breast cancer patient lives with the routines of living with cancer, its recurrences, and its treatments.

The example from my research demonstrates how visual qualitative health research can contribute to the study of health care practices and experiences with illness. Studying artists' books made by and for a woman who had breast cancer, and locating their production within the field of breast cancer discourse at the end of the twentieth century provides a way of understanding illness experience, of bridging biomedical science and lifeworlds, and of opening up dialogues between patients and caregivers in the interests of more effective and humane health care.

COMPLICATIONS AND ISSUES IN VISUAL METHODS

As with qualitative health research in general, there are ethical and methodological issues in visual research. Some issues are especially pressing in visual studies. Ironically, images are typically 'transformed into words in order to communicate about them' (Cross et al., 2006: 192). Because it is relatively new, visual researchers have not yet developed a standard system of visual sampling (Prosser and Loxley, 2008), notation for transcribing visual and tactile conduct (Heath and Hindmarsh, 2002), or ethical guidelines for what constitutes 'good practice in different contexts and different socio-political environments' (Prosser and Loxley, 2008: 48).

Informed consent and the protection of privacy and confidentiality take on added complexities when visual media are employed, especially when images are generated by respondents in projects that employ photo–voice (Wang and Redwood-Jones, 2001). Ensuring anonymity and confidentiality are hallmarks of social science and medical research. Whether researchers make images or interpret (found) images made by others, anonymity and confidentiality are 'highly problematic in visual research' especially in the digital age. As it becomes simpler to copy, transform, and post images in cyberspace, anonymity and confidentiality become less and less possible to guarantee (Prosser and Loxley, 2008: 51). Members of the International Visual Sociology Association have been in dialogue about visual research practice and ethics in visual research, including publication of a special issue of its journal, *Visual Studies* (Papademas, 2004).

Qualitative social scientists are cautious about the use of visual evidence, 'often asking how to interrogate images without background in the visual arts, media studies, or art criticism' (Riessman, 2008: 142). For example, even though photographs may appear to be neutral and transparent images, they draw upon 'a heterogeneous complex of codes' (Burgin, 1982: 143). Each photograph signifies on the basis of multiple codes. That is, 'images contain theories based upon imagemakers' understanding about what they are looking at' (Riessman, 2008: 143). To engage in visual research successfully entails developing sufficient background to make, select, and interpret images knowledgeably.

A related reason for caution in the use of visual evidence is the persuasiveness of images. Photographs, film, and videorecordings may give the illusion of being simple transcriptions of the real, 'traces touched directly the events they record' (Hirsch, 1997: 7). However, they are 'places of work' and, like other visual materials, 'they are structured and structuring spaces' produced in particular contexts for particular purposes (Bell, 2002: 9; see also Clarke, 2005: Chapter 6). Scientific imaging and visualizations 'are exceptionally persuasive because they partake in the objective authority of science and technology, and they rely on what is regarded as immediate form of visual apprehension and engagement' (Burri and Dumit, 2008: 299). Researchers' use of captions, which reflect their preferred reading, add to this persuasiveness and simultaneously mask the multiple possible readings that different audiences might bring to images (Prosser and Loxley, 2008: 44–45). Viewers project wholeness, coherence, and identity onto a depicted scene, refusing an 'impoverished reality in favour of an imaginary plenitude' (Burgin, 1982: 147). Usually, this work takes place instantaneously, unselfconsciously, and apparently naturally.

In addition, all visual methods in qualitative health research must come to terms with how best to circulate findings. The introduction of academic journals specializing in visual research as well as more receptive editors of other journals facilitates communication with other scholars. Yet, as Harper (2005: 750) points out, even more impressive are 'emerging technologies [that] have revolutionized the use of imagery in social science' leading to radically transformed ways of communicating findings and the possibility for engaged and reflective international scholarship. This includes websites organized around 'modules' and CD-ROMs packaged 'with different kinds of information (still photographs, graphs, tables, and extensive texts)' (Harper, 2005: 751).

CONCLUSION

Visual images can be usefully incorporated in clinical research to answer questions about policy and practice that cannot be easily addressed with conventional quantitative approaches. Making images or studying images can make visible dimensions of health care – particularly in patients' experiences – that are not possible to represent with words alone or are not otherwise visible to participants.

The incorporation of visual methods in qualitative health research can also shift the balance of power in medical settings by giving authority to patients' perspectives and statements. Qualitative research *with* images and *of* images offers an important tool for making empirically grounded health policies and – by enabling more responsive, sensitive and effective plans of treatment – visual sociology can improve clinical practice.

NOTES

1 Ironically, although visual images are key to biomedicine, and 'learning to see with the help of diagrams and models has been documented throughout science and medicine', visual methods were marginalized in sociology from the 1920s till the 1970s, because they were considered too unscientific (Burri and Dumit 2008: 304). Now that the meaning of 'doing science' has opened up and moved into post-enlightenment research, there's room for visual approaches again so they're moving further into the centre of social science. Exploring this irony is beyond the scope of this chapter. See Prosser (1998) and Clarke (2005).

2 Although my focus is on sociological perspectives in visual studies, the field is vast and multidisciplinary. There is extensive work in anthropology and this work overlaps with sociology in many respects. For more on their twin histories see Prosser (1998), Pink (2001), Clarke (2005), Ruby (2005).

3 The documentary tradition of photography and film began in the nineteenth century. 'Documentary' is typically distinguished from 'fiction' in its goal of 'reporting, not inventing, whatever is in the world', Ball and Smith (2001: 304). However, documentary seeks to persuade as well as to describe and thus, 'the realism of documentary is ... a professional ideology' that rests on the assumption that cameras never lie and that they faithfully record the world as it appears (Ball and Smith 2001: 304–305). Sekula (1982: 86) writes that this 'myth of photographic truth' consists of the belief that 'the photograph is seen as a re-presentation of nature itself, as an unmediated copy of the real world. The medium itself is considered transparent. The propositions carried through the medium are unbiased and therefore, true'. For more on the realist assumption, see Sekula (1982), Ball and Smith (2001), Bell (2002), and Burri and Dumit (2008).

4 Shooting scripts, initiated in consultation with sociologists Robert and Helen Lynd, were first used by US Farm Security Administration photographic staff during the 1930s and 1940s to document rural poverty (Wagner, 2002; Finnegan, 2003).

5 Specifically, Suchar (1997: 41) identified particular value sets in the presentation of material culture – expressed in exterior artwork, and the design of walls, gates and fences – which he deemed 'urban romanticism'.

6 People living in the community document their worlds with cameras and critically discuss the images they produce with Holga cameras (inexpensive 35-mm film cameras). On the basis of these group discussions, themes are developed. A criterion for identifying a theme is the presence 'of at least four compelling photographs and stories'. In Flint, Michigan, during a period of economic transition, participants identified six themes – public health, quality of neighbourhoods, economic development, religion, racism, and youth opportunities – to use as the basis for community change (Wang, 2000).

7 Elicitation using photographs that are 'found' or made by researchers or subjects, or using drawings, diagrams, objects, 'or virtually anything that can be visualized' has been used in social science research since the 1950s (Johnson and Weller, 2002: 510). In a recent introduction to visual methods, Jon Prosser and Andrew Loxley write that photo-elicitation 'is a complex and multi-layered process' in which 'the context of viewing, the importance of a meaningful link between the image content and respondents, the degree of preferred reading or level of abstraction determined by the researchers, the influence of triggered memories, the range of emergent discussion and the insightfulness of informant's understanding' are all implicated (Prosser and Loxley, 2008: 21).

8 Because visual materials do many different kinds of work, analysts need to be alert to this. Sociologist Adele Clarke lists the different sorts of work visual materials do. They can be 'colonizing,

racializing, gendering, sexing, classifying, stratifying, fetishizing, deceiving, authenticating, mesmer-izing, transgressing, clarifying, stunning, muting, distracting, subjecting, cherishing, preserving, cluttering, and so on'. Moreover, they can do multiple and contradictory things simultaneously (Clarke, 2005: 218).

9 More than half of the photographs were in three of the categories: 'employees and volun-teers', 'male patients at work', and 'architectural and interior views'.

10 'Thick description' is a standard ethnographic tool that interprets events and scenes by building up a detailed picture in the context of the culture and setting in which they live (Geertz, 1973).

11 A vast corpus of literary, film, and artistic resources is catalogued in the online Literature, Arts and Medicine Database sponsored by New York University:http://litmed.med.nyu.edu/Main?action=new

By the turn of the twenty-first century, there were literature and medicine programs in a rapidly growing number of US medical schools, hospitals, colleges, and universities emphasizing the study of literature and ethics, the development of the skills of listening and understanding, and a respect for alternative cultures (Calman, 1997; Charon, 2000, 2006).

12 Fanlight productions: http://www.fanlight.com/
Women Make Movies:http://www.wmm.com/
Zipporah Productions: http://www.zipporah.com/

13 Unnatural Causes results from a collaboration among documentary filmmakers, social epide-miologists, public health physicians and nurses, and health activists. In the first year of circulation, 'more than 12,000 community dialogues, policy forums, trainings, and town hall meetings' took place in the United States that were built around 'Unnatural Causes' (California Newsreel, 2009).

14 For a recent collection, see *The Body at Risk*: *Photography of Disorder, Illness, and Healing*, edited by Carol Squiers (2005).

15 In a variety of ways these documentations grapple with the same issues as do visual sociolo-gists: 'truth', 'power', and the ethics and possibilities of representing the other (Sontag, 2003). For example, when an early part of the AIDS project was displayed at the Museum of Modern Art (MOMA), activists from ActUp mounted a protest, charging Nixon with exploiting and dehumaniz-ing the people he photographed (Ogdon, 2001).

16 The field of narrative is vast and multidisciplinary. For a recent review of narrative work in the social sciences, see Riessman (2008). For social science introductions to illness and narrative see Frank (1995), Bell (2000), and Mattingly and Garro (2000).

17 Narrative medicine draws from narratology and other literary theories to explain why and how doing medicine is like doing reading, interpreting, and writing, and thus how these practices can be more knowledgeably used in medicine to help make better doctors. A narrative approach to clinical medicine consists of three stages, attention (bearing witness), representation (conferring form on what has been witnessed), and affiliation (acting on the basis of what has been witnessed and represented) (Charon, 2006). Medicine is a practical enterprise, and so affiliation is the outcome of narrative work, defined by Charon as healing affiliations with patients and collegial affiliations with our fellow nurses, doctors, and social workers (Charon, 2006: 150). The journal, *Literature and Medicine*, is a rich resource for exploring connections between literary and medical understandings, including narrative. http://www.press.jhu.edu/journals/literature_and_medicine/index.html

18 Each of the three participants volunteered for the project after learning about it 'through the UCLA medical community': Galen Buckwalter used a wheelchair as a result of a cervical spinal cord injury during his teens; Vicki Elman had had multiple sclerosis for 20 years at the start of the study, and Ernie Wallgreen had amyotrophic lateral sclerosis (Berland, 2007: 2533).

19 Specifically, VIA has been used for the study of visual narratives from children and adoles-cents with asthma, sickle cell, spina bifida, and obesity (Rich and Patashnick, 2002). See the Video Intervention/Prevention Assessment website: http://www.cmch.tv/via/home/

20 In her contribution to the catalogue accompanying an international exhibition of artists' books by women organized by The National Museum of Women in the Arts, *The Book as Art*, Johanna Drucker (2007: 16, 17) further explores the gendered power of artists' books: how the 'activities associated with bookmaking [sewing pages, detailed drawings, carefully cut figures and openings] are socially coded in a positive way as feminine' and how these books 'are spaces in which to make community as well as to be left alone'. See also Wasserman, 2007.

21 The breast lump Hall discovered in 1989 was early invasive breast cancer – stage 1. She had a mastectomy followed by six months of chemotherapy. In 1993, she was diagnosed with a recurrence of breast cancer, which by this time had spread to lymph nodes in her neck – stage 4 – and she was hospitalized for three months and treated with high-dose chemotherapy, followed by a bone marrow transplant and radiation. In 1998, a recurrence of cancer in her neck was treated with radiation; in 1999 she was diagnosed with metastatic breast cancer and treated with chemotherapy.

22 But at the same time, Hall relied on prayer, visualization, special clothing, and holding smooth round stones for good luck, documented in other artists' books that she made.

REFERENCES

B. David. (2005) *Epileptic*. NY: Pantheon.

Ball, Mike and Smith, Greg (2001). 'Technologies of Realism? Ethnographic Uses of Photography and Film'. In P. Atkinson, A. Coffey, S. Delamont, J. Lofland, and L. Lofland (eds) *Handbook of Ethnography* (pp. 302–19). London: Sage.

Banks, Marcus (1998) 'Visual Anthropology: Image, Object and Interpretation'. In Jon Prosser (ed.) *Image-Based Research: A Sourcebook for Qualitative Researchers* (pp. 9–23). London and Philadelphia: Routledge Falmer.

Becker, Howard, S. ([1974]1986) 'Photography and Sociology'. In H.S. Becker, *Doing Things Together: Selected Papers* (pp. 225–69). Evanston, ILL: Northwestern University Press.

Becker, Howard, S. (1995) 'Visual Sociology, Documentary Photography, and Photojournalism: It's (almost) all a Matter of Context'. *Visual Sociology* 10(1–2): 5–14. Reprinted in J. Prosser (ed.) (1998) *Image-Based Research: A Sourcebook for Qualitative Researchers* (pp. 84–96). London: Routledge Falmer.

Becker, Howard, S. (2000) 'What Should Sociology Look Like in the (Near) Future?' *Contemporary Sociology*, 29(2): 333–6.

Bell, Susan, E. (1999) 'Narratives and Lives: Women's Health Politics and the Diagnosis of Cancer for DES Daughters', *Narrative Inquiry*, 9(2): 1–43.

Bell, Susan, E. (2000) 'Experiencing Illness in/and Narrative'. In C.E. Bird, Peter Conrad, and Allan M. Fremont (eds) *Handbook of Medical Sociology* (5th Edition) (pp. 184–99). Upper Saddle River, NJ: Prentice Hall.

Bell, Susan, E. (2002) 'Photo Images: Jo Spence's Narratives of Living with Illness', *Health*, 6(1): 5–30.

Bell, Susan, E. (2004) 'Intensive Performances of Mothering: a Sociological Perspective', *Qualitative Research*, 4(1): 45–75.

Bell, Susan E. (2006) 'Living with Breast Cancer in Text and Image: Making Art to Make Sense', *Qualitative Research in Psychology*, 3(1): 31–44.

Berland, Gretchen (2004) 'Rolling'. Produced and co-directed by Gretchen Berland, co-directed by Mike Majoros. Fourwheeldrive Productions.

Berland, Gretchen (2007) 'The View from the Other Side – Patients, Doctors, and the Power of a Camera', *New England Journal of Medicine*, 357(25): 2533, 2535–6.

Brabner, Joyce and Pekar, Harvey (1994) *Our Cancer Year*. NY: Four Walls Eight Windows.

Buckwalter, J. Galen (2007) 'The Good Patient', *New England Journal of Medicine*, 357(25): 2534–5.

Burgin, Victor (1982) 'Looking at Photographs'. In V. Burgin (ed.) *Thinking Photography* (pp. 142–53). London: Macmillan.

Burri, Regula Valérie and Dumit, Joseph (2008). 'Social Studies of Scientific Imaging and Visualization'. In E.J. Hackett, D. Amsterdamska, M. Lynch, and J. Wajcman (eds) *The Handbook of Science and Technology Studies* (3rd Edition) (pp. 297–317). MIT Press.

California Newsreel (2009). 'Top Broadcast Journalism Honor Goes to Documentary on Health Inequalities'. Press release. January 12. Retrieved January 16 2009. http://www.newsreel.org/

Callahan, D. (1998). 'Medical Education and the Goals of Medicine', *Medical Teacher*, 20: 85–7.

Calman, K.C. (1997). 'Literature in the Education of a Doctor', *Lancet*, 350: 1622–5.

Cartwright, Lisa (1995) *Screening the Body: Tracing Medicine's Visual Culture*. Minneapolis: University of Minnesota.

Caulfield, Jon (1996). 'Visual Sociology and Sociological Vision, Revisited', *The American Sociologist*, 27(3): 56–68.

Chalfen, Richard and Rich, Michael (2004) 'Applying Visual Research: Patients Teaching Physicians Through Visual Illness Narratives', *Visual Anthropology Review*, 20(1): 17–30.

Charmaz, Kathy (1991) *Good Days, Bad Days: The Self in Chronic Illness and Time*. New Brunswick, NJ: Rutgers.

Charon, Rita (2000). 'Literature and Medicine: Origins and Destinies', *Academic Medicine*, 75: 23–7.

Charon, Rita (2006). *Narrative Medicine: Honoring the Stories of Illness*. Oxford, New York: Oxford University Press.

Clarke, Adele (2005) *Situational Analysis: Grounded Theory after the Postmodern Turn*. Thousand Oaks, CA: Sage.

Conrad, Peter ([1985] 2005) 'The Meaning of Medications: Another Look at Compliance'. In P. Conrad (ed.) *The Sociology of Health and Illness Critical Perspectives* (7th Edition) (pp. 150–62). NY: Worth Publishers.

Conrad, Peter (1987) 'The Experience of Illness: Recent and New Directions', *Research in the Sociology of Health Care*, 6: 1–21.

Cross, Katherine, Kabel, Allison, and Lysack, Cathy (2006) 'Images of Self and Spinal Cord Injury: Exploring Drawing as a Visual Method in Disability Research', *Visual Studies*, 21(2): 183–93.

Davis, Kathy (2007) *The Making of Our Bodies, Ourselves: How Feminism Travels Across Borders*. Durham, NC: Duke University Press.

Dowdall, George W. and Golden, Janet (1989) 'Photographs as Data: An Analysis of Images from a Mental Hospital', *Qualitative Sociology*, 12(2): 183–212.

Drucker, Johanna (1995) 'Chapter 1: The Artist's Book as Idea and Form'. In J. Drucker, *The Century of Artist's Books. Granary Books*. Retrieved November 2004, from http://www.granarybooks.com/books/drucker2/drucker2.html

Drucker, Johanna (2007) 'Intimate Authority'. In Krystyna Wasserman (ed.) *The Book as Art: Artists' Books from the National Museum of Women in the Arts* (pp. 14–17). New York: Princeton Architectural Press.

Eikenberry, Jill (1998) *Art, Rage, Us: Art and Writing by Women with Breast Cancer*. San Francisco, CA: Chronicle Books.

Farmer, Paul. (1999) *Infections and Inequalities*. Berkeley: University of California.

Farough, Steven D. (2006) 'Believing is Seeing: The Matrix of Vision and White Masculinities', *Journal of Contemporary Ethnography*, 35(1): 51–83.

Finnegan, Cara (2003) *Picturing Poverty: Print Culture and FSA Photographs*. Smithsonian Books.

Frank, Arthur W. (1995) *The Wounded Storyteller*. Chicago: University of Chicago.

Frank, Arthur W. (1996) 'Reconciliatory Alchemy: Bodies, Narratives and Power', *Body & Society*, 2(3): 53–71.

Geertz, Clifford (1973) *The Interpretation of Cultures*. New York: Basic Books.

Goffman, Erving (1979) *Gender Advertisements*. New York: Harper and Row.

Gray, Ross and Sinding, Christina (2000). *Handle with Care? No Big Deal?* Videorecording. Toronto: Toronto-Sunnybrook Regional Cancer Centre.

Gray, Ross and Sinding, Christina (2002) *Standing Ovation: Performing Social Science Research about Cancer*. Walnut Creek, CA: AltaMira Press.

Hall, Martha, A. (2000) *The Rest of My Life*. Northampton, MA: Smith College, Mortimer Rare Book Room. Photograph by Stephen Petegorsky.

Hall, Martha, A. (2002) *I Make Books*. Videorecording. A production of the Maine Women Writers Collection. Biddeford, ME: University of New England's Media Services.

Hall, Martha, A. (2003) *Holding In, Holding On: Artist's Books* by Martha A. Hall. Northampton, MA: Smith College, Mortimer Rare Book Room.

Haraway, Donna J. (1988) 'Situated Knowledges: The Science Question in Feminism as a Site of Discourse on the Privilege of Partial Perspective', *Feminist Studies*, 14: 575–99.

Harper, Douglas (1982) *Good Company*. Chicago: University of Chicago Press.

Harper, Douglas (1998) 'An Argument for Visual Sociology'. In J. Prosser (ed.) *Image-Based Research: A Sourcebook for Qualitative Researchers* (pp. 9–23). London and Bristol, PA: Falmer Press.

Harper, Douglas (2000) 'Reimagining Visual Methods'. In Norman K. Denzin and Yvonne S. Lincoln (eds) *Handbook of Qualitative Research* (2nd Edition) (pp. 717–32). London: Sage.

Harper, Douglas (2005) 'What's New Visually?'. In Norman K. Denzin and Yvonne S. Lincoln (eds) *Handbook of Qualitative Research* (3rd Edition) (pp. 747–762). London: Sage.

Harrison, Barbara (2002) 'Photographic Visions and Narrative Inquiry', *Narrative Inquiry*, 12(1): 87–111.

Harrison, Barbara (2002) 'Seeing Health and Illness Worlds – Using Visual Methodologies in a Sociology of Health and Illness: A Methodological Review', *Sociology of Health & Illness*, 24(6): 856–72.

Heath, Christian and Hindmarsh, Jon (2002). 'Analysing Interaction: Video, Ethnography and Situated Conduct'. In T. May (ed.) *Qualitative Research in Action* (pp. 99–121). London: Sage.

Herbes-Sommers, Christine and Smith, Llewellyn M. (2008) 'Unnatural Causes: Is Inequality Making Us Sick?' produced by California Newsreel in association with Vital Pictures. San Francisco, CA: California Newsreel. http://www.newsreel.org/

Hevey, David (1992) *The Creatures Time Forgot: Photography and Disability Imagery*. London, NY: Routledge.

Hirsch, Marianne (1997) *Family Frames: Photography, Narrative, and Postmemory*. Cambridge, MA: Harvard University Press.

Hurwitz, Brian, Greenhalgh, Trisha, and Skultans, Vieda (eds) (2004) *Narrative Research in Health and Illness*. Malden, MA; Oxford: BMJ Books/Blackwell.

Hydén, Lars-Christer (1997) 'Illness and Narrative', *Sociology of Health & Illness*, 19(1): 48–69.

Johnson, Jeffrey C. and Weller, Susan C. (2002) 'Elicitation Techniques for Interviewing'. In J.F. Gubrium and J.A. Holstein (eds) *Handbook of Interview Research: Context & Method* (pp. 491–514). Thousand Oaks, CA: Sage.

Kapsalis, Terri (1997) *Public Privates: Performing Gynecology from Both Ends of the Speculum*. Durham, NC: Duke University Press.

Kevles, Bettyann (1997) *Naked to the Bone: Medical Imaging in the Twentieth Century*. New Brunswick, NJ: Rutgers.

Klawiter, Maren (2008) *The Biopolitics of Breast Cancer: Changing Cultures of Disease and Activism*. Minneapolis, MN: University of Minnesota Press.

Kleinman, Arthur (1988) *The Illness Narratives: Suffering, Healing and the Human Condition*. NY: Basic.

Knowles, Caroline and Sweetman, Paul (eds) (2004) *Picturing the Social Landscape: Visual Methods and the Sociological Imagination*. New York: Routledge.

Langellier, Kristin M. (2001) '"You're Marked": Breast Cancer, Tattoo, and the Narrative Performance of Identity'. In J. Brockmeier and D. Carbaugh (eds) *Narrative and Identity* (pp. 145–84). John Benjamins Publishing,.

Lawrence, Susan, C. and Bendixen, Kae (1992) 'His and Hers: Male and Female Anatomy in Anatomy Texts for U.S. Medical Students, 1890–1989', *Social Science and Medicine*, 35(7): 925–34.

Lerner, Barron (2001) *The Breast Cancer Wars: Hope, Fear, and the Pursuit of a Cure in Twentieth Century America*. NY: Oxford University Press.

Lorenz, Laura S. (2008) 'Using Photovoice to Explore Lived Experience: Eliciting the Perspective of Brain Injury Survivors Through Visual Methods'. Paper Presented during the Symposium, Emergent Seeing and Knowing: Mapping Practices of Participatory Visual Methods, Radcliffe Institute, Cambridge, MA, Nov. 13–5.

Lykes, M. Brinton (2008) 'Activist Scholarship, the Visual, and Gross Violations of Human Rights: Documentation, Critical Analysis, and Social Change'. Paper Presented during the Symposium, Emergent Seeing and Knowing: Mapping Practices of Participatory Visual Methods, Radcliffe Institute, Cambridge, MA, Nov. 13–5.

Lynch, Dorothea and Richards, Eugene (1986) *Exploding into Life*. NY: Aperture in association with Many Voices Press.

Mamo, Laura and Foskett, Jennifer Ruth (2008). 'Scripting the Body: Pharmaceuticals and the (re) Making of Menstruation', *Signs*, 34(4): 925–49.

Mattingly, Cheryl and Garro, Linda C. (1994) 'Introduction', *Social Science and Medicine*, 38(6): 811–22.

Mattingly, Cheryl and Garro, Linda C. (eds) (2000) *Narrative and the Cultural Construction of Illness and Healing*. Berkeley, CA: University of California.

Mishler, Elliot G. (1999) *Storylines*. Cambridge, MA: Harvard University Press.

Moore, Lisa Jean and Clarke, Adele E. (1995) 'Genital Conventions and Transgressions: Graphic Representations in Anatomy Texts, c. 1900–1991', *Feminist Studies*, 22(1): 255–301.

Nixon, Nicholas and Nixon, Bebe (1991) *People with AIDS*. Boston, MA: D.R. Godine.

Ogdon, Bethany (2001) 'Through the Image: Nicholas Nixon's "People with AIDS"', *Discourses*, 23(3): 75–105.

Papademas, Diana (2004) 'Editor's Introduction: Ethics in Visual Research', *Visual Studies*, 19(2): 122–5.

Petchesky, Rosalind Pollack (1987). 'Fetal Images: The Power of Visual Culture in the Politics of Reproduction', *Feminist Studies*, 13(2): 263–92.

Petersen, Alan (1998) 'Sexing the Body: Representations of Sex Differences in *Gray's Anatomy*, 1858 to the present', *Body & Society*, 4(1): 1–15.

Pink, Sarah (2004) 'Applied Visual Anthropology Social Intervention, Visual Methodologies and Anthropology Theory', *Visual Anthropology Review*, 20(1): 3–16.

Pitts, Victoria (2004) 'Illness and Internet Empowerment: Writing and Reading Breast Cancer in Cyberspace', *Health*, 8: 33–59.

Pitts-Taylor, Victoria (2003) *In the Flesh: The Cultural Politics of Body Modification*. New York: Palgrave Macmillan.

Prosser, Jon (ed.) (1998) *Image-Based Research: A Sourcebook for Qualitative Researchers*. London and Philadelphia: Routledge Falmer.

Prosser, Jon. (2007) 'Visual Mediation of Critical Illness: An Autobiographical Account of Nearly Dying and Nearly Living', *Visual Studies*, 22(2): 185–99.

Prosser, Jon and Loxley, Andrew (2008) Introducing Visual Methods. ESRC National Centre for Research Methods Review Paper, October. National Centre for Research Methods, NCRM/010. Unpublished. http://eprints.ncrm.ac.uk/420

Radley, Alan (2002) 'Portrayals of Suffering: On Looking Away, Looking At, and the Comprehension of Illness Experience', *Body & Society*, 8(3): 1–23.

Radley, Alan and Bell, Susan E. (2007) 'Artworks, Collective Experience, and Claims for Social Justice: The Case of Women Living with Breast Cancer', *Sociology of Health & Illness*, 29(3): 366–90.

Radley, Alan and Taylor, Diane (2003a) 'Remembering One's Stay in Hospital: A Study in Photography, Recovery, and Forgetting', *Health*, 7(2): 129–59.

Radley, Alan and Taylor, Diane (2003b) 'Images of Recovery: A Photo-Elicitation Study on the Hospital Ward', *Qualitative Health Research*, 13(1): 77–99.

Rapold, Nicolas (2008) 'Reflections in a Golden Eye', *Sight & Sound*, 18(9): 42–5.

Renov, Michael (1999) 'Domestic Ethnography and the Construction of the "Other" Self'. In Jane M. Gaines and Michael Renov (eds) *Collecting Visible Evidence* (pp. 140–155). Minneapolis and London: University of Minnesota Press.

Rich, Michael and Patashnick, Jennifer (2002) 'Narrative Research with Audiovisual Data: Video-intervention/Prevention Assessment (VIA) and NVivo', *International Journal of Social Research Methodology*, 5(3): 245–61.

Rich, Michael, Patashnick, Jennifer, and Chalfen, Richard (2002) 'Visual Illness Narratives of Asthma: Explanatory Models and Health-Related Behavior', *American Journal of Health Behavior*, 26(6): 442–53.

Richards, Eugene (1989) *The Knife and Gun Club: Scenes from an Emergency Room*. NY: Atlantic Monthly Press.

Riessman, Catherine Kohler (2008) *Narrative Methods for the Human Sciences*. Los Angeles, CA: Sage.

Ruby, Jay (2005) 'The Last 20 Years of Visual Anthropology – A Critical Review', *Visual Studies*, 20(2): 159–70.

Sekula, Allan (1982) 'On the Invention of Photographic Meaning'. In V. Burgin (ed.) *Thinking Photography* (pp. 84–109). London: Macmillan.

Seidman, Steven (1992) 'Postmodern Social Theory as Narrative with a Moral Intent'. In S. Seidman and D. Wagner (eds) *Postmodernism and Social Theory* (pp. 47–81). Oxford, U.K. and Cambridge, MA: Blackwell.

Sharf, Barbara F. (1995) 'Poster Art as Women's Rhetoric: Raising Awareness about Breast Cancer', *Literature and Medicine*, 14(1): 72–86.

Smith, Brian K., Frost, Jeana, Albayrak, Meltem, and Sudhakar, Rajneesh (2006) 'Facilitating Narrative Medical Discussions of Type 1 Diabetes with Computer Visualizations and Photography', *Patient Education and Counseling*, 64: 313–21.

Smith, W. Eugene and Smith, Aileen Mioko (1975) *Minamata*. NY: Holt, Rinehart and Winston.

Sontag, Susan (2003) *Regarding the Pain of Others*. NY: Farrar, Straus & Giroux.

Spence, Jo (1988) *Putting Myself in the Picture*. Seattle, WA: The Real Comet Press.

Spence, Jo (1995) *Cultural Sniping: The Art of Transgression*. London, NY: Routledge.

Squiers, Carol (2005) *The Body at Risk: Photography of Disorder, Illness and Healing*. NY: International Center of Photography; Milbank Memorial Fund; Berkeley, CA: University of California.

Strack, Robert W., Magill, Cathleen, and McDonagh, Kara (2004) 'Engaging Youth Through Photovoice', *Health Promotion Practice*, 5(1): 49–58.

Suchar, Charles S. (1997) 'Grounding Visual Sociology Research in Shooting Scripts', *Qualitative Sociology*, 20(1): 33–55.

Swidler, Ann (2001) 'What Anchors Cultural Practices'. In T.R. Schatzki, K. Knorr Cetina and Evon Savigny (eds) *The Practice Turn in Contemporary Theory* (pp. 74–92). London: Routledge.

Wagner, Jon (ed.) (1979) *Images of Information: Still Photography in the Social Sciences*. Beverly Hills, CA: Sage.

Wagner, Jon (2002) 'Contrasting Images, Complementary Trajectories: Sociology, Visual Sociology and Visual Research', *Visual Studies*, 17(2): 160–71.

Wang, Caroline C. (ed.) [coeditors Morrel-Samuels, Susan, Bell, Lee, Hutchison, Peter, and Powers, Lisa S.] (2000) *Strength to Be: Community Visions & Voices*. Ann Arbor MI: University of Michigan.

Wang, Caroline C. and Redwood-Jones, Yanique A. (2001) 'Photovoice Ethics: Perspectives from Flint Photovoice', *Health Education & Behavior*, 28(5): 560–72.

Wang, Caroline C., Morrel-Samuels, Susan, Hutchison, Peter M., Bell, Lee, and Pestronk, Robert M. (2004) 'Flint Photovoice: Community Building Among Youths, Adults, and Policymakers', *American Journal of Public Health*, 94(6): 911–13.

Wasserman, Krystyna (2007) *The Book as Art: Artists' Books from the National Museum of Women in the Arts*. New York: Princeton Architectural Press.

Williams, Gareth (1984) 'The Genesis of Chronic Illness: Narrative Re-Construction', *Sociology of Health & Illness*, 6(2): 175–200.

Wiseman, Frederick (1969) *Hospital*. Zipporah Films, Inc. Cambridge, MA.

Wiseman, Frederick (1989) *Near Death*. Zipporah Films, Inc. Cambridge, MA.

Wiseman, Frederick (2001) 'Privacy and Documentary Filmmaking', *Social Research*, 68(1): 41–7.

Women of PhotoVoice/ADMI and Lykes, M.B. (2000) *Voces e Imágenes: Mujeres Mayas Ixiles de Chajul/ Voices and Iimages: Mayan Ixil Women of Chajul*. Guatemala: Magna Terra. Texts in Spanish and English, with a methodology chapter by Lykes.

27

Keyword Analysis: A New Tool for Qualitative Research

Clive Seale and
Jonathan Charteris-Black

In this chapter, we show how keyword analysis can be applied in qualitative health research, drawing on our experience of the method over the past few years on a variety of projects. This is a new method for qualitative health researchers. It exploits interdisciplinarity (between linguistics and social research) and integrates quantitative and qualitative approaches. It is made possible by contemporary technological conditions, chiefly the increasing availability of electronic text material concerning health experiences, and the power of modern personal computers. It builds on the computing expertise gained by qualitative researchers through the use of 'qualitative data analysis' software such as *NVivo* or *ATLASti*. It is adapted from approaches developed by people working in the 'corpus linguistics' tradition, whose access to large university computers meant they could pioneer software and analytic methods for analysing very large collections of language (known as 'corpora').

To illustrate the potential of keyword analysis in health research, consider the opportunity (and problem) we faced when we collected the texts used in a study of the experience of breast and prostate cancer (Seale, 2006; Seale et al., 2006). This involved the analysis of an archive of 97 qualitative interviews with people who had experienced these diseases (collected by the DIPEx organization – see www.healthtalkonline.org) and another archive of postings to Internet-based discussion and support groups visited by people with these illnesses, their family members and others. The interviews contained

727,100 words of text, and the web forums contained 2,145,337 words posted by 1,534 people. This volume of material is very large by the standards of conventional qualitative research, meaning that our collection had the potential to overcome a common criticism made of qualitative research: that the emphasis on analytic depth is only possible where small and possibly unrepresentative samples are analyzed. Yet, reading all of the material we had collected to produce a fine-grained discourse or narrative analysis, or to develop and apply a conventional qualitative thematic coding scheme, would take many months.

Keyword analysis helped us identify, very rapidly, segments of text to focus on for more detailed analysis. In this sense, keyword analysis is like an aerial view of a landscape, whose undulations and patterns of vegetation growth reflect the outline of ancient buildings, only possible to see from the air. At this point, the 'aerial archaeologist' descends to ground level and starts to dig. Once key passages are identified by keyword analysis, the researcher 'descends' to do more detailed analytic work, using procedures with which qualitative researchers are more familiar (such as discourse analysis or thematic coding). Alternatively, some of the procedures developed by corpus linguists can be used to provide an interpretive and, essentially, qualitative understanding of key passages. However, before returning to our example of the cancer experience study and outlining the procedures of keyword analysis for qualitative health research, a short summary of the foundational principles of corpus linguistics will be helpful.

CORPUS LINGUISTICS

A corpus is a large, electronically stored collection of texts that arise from actual language use; this is in contrast to language that has been invented specifically for illustrating a point about language. The history of corpus linguistics is summarized in Stubbs (1996) where he outlines the contributions of Firth, Halliday and Sinclair in orienting the discipline away from a theoretically driven approach associated with Chomsky and towards the empirical study of language as it is actually used.

To illustrate the power of this empirical approach to the study of language, consider the difference between spoken and written language. As Carter (2004) observes, written language has often been assumed to be the model for accounts of English grammar. At school, we may have been taught about the basic structure (subject, verb and object) of a sentence, and learned the names of parts of speech such as noun, pronoun, adjective, adverb and so on. Yet, empirically oriented linguistics, exploiting the technology of the audio-recorder, has established that speech possesses, to an extent, its own grammar. For example, it is much more likely than written language will contain 'heads', occurring at the front of clauses and helping listeners orient to a topic. Carter provides examples of such topic-fronting (heads shown in bold):

> **The white house on the corner,** is that where she lives?
>
> **A friend of mine, his** uncle had the taxi firm when we had the wedding.

In addition, speech also contains 'tails', occurring at the end of clauses, often reiterative echoing of an earlier pronoun which both highlights and reinforces the topic:

> **She**'s a very good swimmer **Jenny is**
>
> **I**'m going to have steak and fries, **I am**

Speech also contains a lot of words and phrases indicating vagueness, such as 'sort of', 'stuff like that', 'whatever' or 'kind of thing', frequently found tacked onto the end of statements. These are often used to soften expressions that would otherwise appear too direct or assertive, so are part of a strategy of managing the needs of speakers to preserve a polite and cooperative relationship, perhaps more important in the face-to-face context of spoken language.

These things, if they appeared in written texts, are things of which a traditional grammar teacher might disapprove. Nevertheless, in speech situations, they might be precisely what is needed, and their absence marked as a sign of stylistic incompetence.

Now, it may seem odd to a qualitative social researcher that linguists have only recently been catching up with the idea that the empirical study of language-in-use is important. Discourse and conversation analysts have known that for a long time. Yet, the tools which corpus linguists have developed to fulfil this project within linguistics possess a degree of rigour and objectivity from which many qualitative health and social researchers might benefit. Until recently, though, these tools have been used largely within the linguistics discipline, albeit by linguists who are sometimes interested in discourse analysis (see particularly Baker, 2006; Adolphs, 2006, Chapter 6).

KEYWORD ANALYSIS IN SOCIAL RESEARCH: THE BASICS

The ease with which researchers can now obtain large amounts of health-related electronic material is a valuable opportunity. The archiving of qualitative data for secondary analysis is increasing, although it is perhaps not as developed as quantitative data archiving (Akerstrom et al., 2007; Corti and Thompson, 2007). The availability of electronic texts produced for nonresearch purposes has also increased. The text on Internet discussion forums, personal websites, blogs, and other Internet-based sources constitute a rich source of data about health-related experiences and issues (Robinson, 2001; Seale et al., 2009). Until recently, computer-assisted text analysis of large amounts of material for social research purposes was the province of quantitatively oriented content analysts (e.g., Popping, 2000). Software designed for qualitative data analysis (such as *ATLASti* or *NVIVO*) prioritizes coding and retrieval approaches that assumes a conventional reading of texts, with quite limited facilities for individual word searching when compared with concordance and other software developed for corpus linguistics (such as *Wordsmith Tools*).

Keyword analysis on the breast and prostate cancer project enabled us to identify areas of text worth analysing further, using more conventional qualitative approaches. In this respect, we were in a similar position to conversation analysts who, having collected a large number of audio-recordings, then have to choose segments to apply the time-consuming full transcription technology of CA (Conversation Analysis) (Jefferson, 2004). Very frequently, a preliminary transcript is prepared by a typist so that it can be scanned for segments likely to be of interest if investigated further, so that analysis can proceed with economy of effort. Like CA, then, keyword analysis proceeds with an initial 'quick' overview before digging deeper in particular locations where mining is likely to be successful.

Corpus linguists when describing the particular characteristics of a text will often compare this text with a 'reference corpus'. This is normally a multimillion word collection of language examples, often chosen to represent typical usage of a language across a variety of genres (e.g., written, spoken, speeches, conversations, published writing, emails and letters). An example of a reference corpus designed to be representative of British English usage is the British National Corpus (BNC). If a word, or a group of words, or a part of speech occurs more frequently in the text being analyzed in comparison with the reference corpus, this is often an indicator of some interesting aspect of the style or content of the text being analyzed, so that this is then a signal for further qualitative investigation of these features.

Nevertheless, on our breast and prostate cancer project, we were initially interested in differences between men and women, so we carried out a comparative keyword analysis in which the relative frequencies of words contained in men's text were compared with those in women's text. Table 27.1 displays output from Wordsmith Tools, containing 17 of the top 25 words more common in postings by men with prostate cancer to web forums than in postings by women with breast cancer to web forums. The first column lists the word and the second lists its frequency on the prostate cancer text. Thus, 'PSA' occurs 1,164 times in the prostate cancer text. This constitutes 0.42 percent of all of the words in the prostate cancer text. The word only occurred one time in the breast cancer text (shown in the 'RC.Freq' column). This is too low to be worth calculating a percentage for, so the 'RC.%' column is blank. The final column is a statistical indicator of 'keyness' based on a significance test. You can see that 'keyness' reduces somewhat for the word 'Prostate' even though it occurs with a similar frequency as 'PSA' in the prostate cancer corpus. This is because 'prostate' occurs 28 times in the breast cancer text, meaning the two texts are not as different on this item as they are on 'PSA'.

Table 27.1   Top prostate cancer keywords: comparison of people with prostate and breast cancer in web forums

Key word	Freq.	%	RC.Freq.**	RC. %	Keyness
Positive					
PSA*	1,164	0.42	1		4,141.74
PROSTATE	1,080	0.39	28		3,606.20
RP*	339	0.12	2		1,186.17
PC*	377	0.14	30		1,142.48
GLEASON	285	0.10	0		1,017.19
PCA*	299	0.11	6		1,010.35
REGARDS	393	0.14	111		912.12
RT*	290	0.10	44		790.90
BRACHYTHERAPY	151	0.05	0		538.87
MEN	286	0.10	180	0.01	465.20
SCORE	154	0.06	31		393.73
CATHETER	128	0.05	14		370.49
UROLOGIST	89	0.03	0		317.60
BLADDER	110	0.04	15		306.32
PROSTATECTOMY	83	0.03	0		296.18
HORMONE	214	0.08	193	0.01	271.52
DAD	177	0.06	125		267.95

* PSA=Prostate specific antigen, RP=Radical prostatectomy, PC and PCA=Prostate cancer, RT=Radiotherapy
** RC.Freq=Reference corpus frequency (ie: frequency in the breast cancer text, in this case)
Excluded words: 'the' and 7 names of other forum participants.

Comparative keyword analysis proceeds by then doing the same for the breast cancer text, to see which words occur more frequently in that text than in the prostate cancer text. Table 27.2 shows the relevant output. It is immediately evident that personal pronouns ('I', 'she', 'her', 'I'm' and 'me') and words

Table 27.2   Top breast cancer keywords: comparison of people with prostate and breast cancer in web forums

Key word	Freq.	%	RC.Freq.**	RC. %	Keyness
CHEMO*	3578	0.26	16		1169.09
BREAST	3653	0.27	40	0.01	1045.87
I	53671	3.91	8174	2.95	624.75
BC*	1702	0.12	2		602.35
MASTECTOMY	1594	0.12	0		586.45
SHE	3330	0.24	167	0.06	479.34
HER	2797	0.20	113	0.04	476.60
TAMOXIFEN	1270	0.09	0		467.20
LOVE	1681	0.12	55	0.02	326.67
IT	20472	1.49	2988	1.08	300.87
LUMP	1008	0.07	9		299.87
DCIS*	792	0.06	0		291.31
HAIR	834	0.06	6		256.91
I'M	3508	0.26	303	0.11	256.03
WOMEN	1060	0.08	22		253.44
MOLE	662	0.05	0		243.48
RECONSTRUCTION	648	0.05	0		238.33
ME	8757	0.64	1127	0.41	228.16
X*	1085	0.08	34	0.01	215.86
MUM	706	0.05	7		205.98
THINK	3800	0.28	386	0.14	199.65

* Chemo=Chemotherapy, BC=Breast Cancer, DCIS=Ductal carcinoma in situ, X= Mostly kiss
** RC.Freq=Reference corpus frequency (ie: frequency in the prostate cancer text, in this case)
Excluded words: 'it', 'really', 'don't', 1 name of another forum participant.

referring to people ('women', 'mum') or indicating relationships between people ('love' and 'X' for kiss, both usually used by women to 'sign off' their messages to each other) are prominent in the breast cancer text. In the prostate cancer text, there are no personal pronouns. 'Regards' rather than 'love' or 'X' for kiss is more commonly used to sign off messages, and the 'people' words ('men', 'urologist' and 'dad') includes one referring to a medical specialist.

Wordsmith Tools produces lists of keywords to a specified level of significance, and this list can become very lengthy in a study involving quite large bodies of text. The next step in our comparative keyword analysis was therefore to group keywords taken from the top 200 appearing on each side of the comparison into words that seemed to share some characteristic, usually a semantic one (e.g., all words referring to people) but also sometimes a grammatical category (e.g., all personal pronouns, all superlative adjectives). This is the point at which keyword analysis is reminiscent of conventional qualitative thematic coding, in which analysts allocate labels to segments of text according to whether that text has a particular characteristic relevant to the research question (e.g., segments of text in which pain is discussed, in a study of pain control; segments of text demonstrating 'alienation', 'despair' or 'hope' by interviewees). However, in comparative keyword analysis the 'codes' are used to label groups of words, rather than segments of text. Extracts from our 'coding scheme' for keywords in the breast and prostate cancer project are given in Table 27.3.

The assignation of words to categories requires investigation of the predominant way in which they are being used in the text concerned. For example, perhaps the word 'support' refers to a device used to 'support' a part of the body, such as a 'support stocking' rather than a supportive relationship between people. Perhaps 'XXX' has nothing to do with kisses, but has been used to delete references to the names of individuals whose anonymity must be preserved. 'Best' could refer to a positive evaluation of a medical treatment rather than forming part of a formulaic closing sequence. At this point a qualitative data analyst might feel

Table 27.3   Coding scheme identifying meaningful categories of keywords (extract)

Keyword category	Examples of keywords
Greetings	Regards, thanks, hello, welcome, [all the] best, regs (=regards)
Support	Support, love, care, XXX, hugs
Feelings	Feel, scared, coping, hate, bloody, cry, hoping, trying, worrying, nightmare, grateful, fun, upset, tough
Health care staff	Nurse, doctor, oncologist, urologist, consultant, specialist, Dr, Mr
Clothing and appearance	Nightie, bra, wear, clothes, wearing
Internet and web forum	www, website, forums, [message] board, scroll
Knowledge and communication	Question, information, chat, talk, finding, choice, decision, guessing, wondering
Research	Study, data, trial, funding, research
Lifestyle	Organic, chocolate, wine, golf, exercise, fitness, cranberry [juice]
Superlatives	Lovely, amazing, definitely, brilliant, huge, wonderful

[ ] – square brackets are used to give commonly associated word showing a word's predominant meaning
(=) – rounded brackets and = sign used to explain a term's (predominant) meaning

that this is a method that does not respect a basic tenet of qualitative research; that understanding the meaning of a phenomenon (such as a word) requires knowledge of the context in which it occurs, normally acquired through a close reading of the (small amount of) text being analyzed.

Fortunately, it is not difficult in keyword analysis to discover the context in which words are being used in order to understand the meanings of keywords. To appreciate this, it is necessary to understand keyword-in-context (KWIC) displays, and the idea of collocation. Both of these help the researcher get involved with the text at the more 'interpretive' level with which qualitative researchers will be familiar.

KEYWORDS-IN-CONTEXT (KWIC) AND COLLOCATION

The English linguist John Firth is famous for his saying 'You shall know a word by the company it keeps' (Firth, 1957: 11). *Collocation* is the term that has developed to refer to the company a word keeps, that is, the other words with which it is typically found. In statistical terms, collocates are therefore words that occur together with a higher frequency that would be expected by chance alone.

A concordance shows the linguistic contexts of a given word, or 'keyword', and concordance software allows us to explore the 'company that words keep'. Keyword-in-context displays are a standard type of output in most concordance software. They allow a specified number of words, or concordances, occurring on either side of a particular word to be displayed. The following are the first five KWIC displays of 24 instances of the word 'xxxxx' in the breast cancer web postings:

> for kind replies, was sad to read of Jean's passing, she wrote so well lurve Anne **xxxxx** Where do you live? I'm going to Skye tomorrow for AGES, hurrah!

> breast cancer, I hope we can as much as possible, enjoy Christmas. Annette. **xxxxx** I have been diagnosed with invasive ductal carcinoma, grade 3,

> can. As the saying goes: Life is for living! Good health to you all Love Sarah **xxxxx** Hi It was the vodka that kept me going! I was on the tango trial

> up, not that I think that is going to happen. Good health to you all. Love Sarah **xxxxx** thanks to both of you. Seen the liver specialist on the 21st sep

> fed in the Breast Unit. My operations have been cancelled. much love to you all **xxxxx** Hi Yes the boxes and ingredients do differ on the tamoxifen.

It is clear from this (and from the other 19 instances not shown) that 'xxxxx' is being exclusively used to indicate kisses at the end of messages, with new messages generally beginning straight after the xxxxx. The KWIC display thus allows for no other interpretation.

However, in the case of 'x', where there are 1,085 instances in the breast cancer web postings things are more complicated. Firstly, reading through this many KWIC displays would take quite a bit of time. To estimate the predominant meanings of 'x', we can therefore take a look at its most common collocates – words frequently located near 'x'. This is displayed in Table 27.4

Table 27.4   Top 10 words adjacent to 'x'; left hand side (L1), right hand side (R1)

Descending order of L1			
Word	*L1*	*Centre*	*R1*
BELINDA	48	0	0
JOY	45	0	0
JEAN	40	0	0
PEARLY	38	0	3
4	32	0	1
6	32	0	10
JANE	28	0	2
CLAIRE	26	0	0
MELANIE	26	0	0
WENDY	23	0	2
Descending order of R1			
HI	0	0	192
I	0	0	122
RAY	1	0	56
RAYS	0	0	47
FEC	5	0	26
THANKS	4	0	26
X	23	1,085	22
HELLO	0	0	20
I'M	0	0	19
JUST	1	0	14

The 'Descending order of L1' display shows that women's names were very commonly placed just before 'x', consistent with the interpretation of 'x' as a farewell kiss. Nevertheless, the occurrence of the numerals '4' and '6' on further inspection turned out to be instances where 'x' was being used as a multiplication sign. The 'Descending order of R1' display shows with the words 'Hi', 'I', 'thanks', 'hello', 'I'm' and 'just' that 'x' occurred at the end of a message, these being words with which next messages typically begin. The occurrence of 'x' as a collocate of itself is also consistent with the 'kiss' interpretation, as this occurs where 'x x x' is written rather than 'xxx'. But the occurrence of 'ray' and 'rays' indicates the term 'x ray' and the occurrence of 'FEC' indicates the use of 'x' as a multiplication sign, as in the phrase '4 x FEC' used by women to describe the frequency of their chemotherapy treatments.

Thus, the sign 'x' is predominantly a kiss, but not exclusively so. As linguists would say, we have 'disambiguated' the meaning of this term and discovered that it has various subsidiary meanings, as well as its predominant one as a kiss. Even when employed as a kiss, there may be variation and significance in the number of times it occurs in sequence: more kisses convey the meaning of more affection. A similar analysis of 'x' in the postings of men with prostate cancer reveals that only four of the 34 instances of 'x' in the men's text were used to denote a kiss, finally confirming the view that women are much more likely to end their messages with a kiss.

KWIC and collocation are therefore important ways in which words can be investigated in their contexts so that valid inferences are drawn about how they are being used. The raw collocation display shown in Figure 27.1 is usually sufficient to provide disambiguation evidence, but more sophisticated ways of displaying collocation statistics are also sometimes used. For example, extremely common words like 'the' or 'and' often appear as collocates of words, simply because they are common. A 'mutual information' (MI) score is designed to adjust for this phenomenon, indicating which collocates co-occur more often than might be expected by chance alone. This is helpful where fairly uncommon words are involved, such as those used in medical jargon (although other statistics, such as a t-test, are more appropriate where words are extremely rare).

An MI score can also take account of words occurring within a specified distance of the keyword being analyzed (not just the immediately adjacent ones). This can be very useful in establishing common connotations, or *semantic prosodies* for words. The semantic prosody of a given word is determined by the frequency that it occurs in the context of other words that have positive or negative evaluations (Louw, 1993). A type of 'leakage' occurs whereby the positive or, more usually, negative senses of these other words 'overflows' onto the given word with which they co-occur. This is a way of communicating covert evaluations that are often not merely idiosyncratic, but highly constitutive of cultural stereotypes with ideological implications (Stubbs, 2001; Charteris-Black, 2004, 2005). Thus, Baker (2006) in an investigation of the British National Corpus uses a procedure similar to the MI score to show that the word 'bachelor' is disproportionately found within three words of 'eligible', 'confirmed', 'flat', 'days' and 'party', indicating fairly positive connotations of youth or freedom. But the word 'spinster' is collocated with 'elderly', 'widows', 'sisters' and 'three', this last being reminiscent of the three witches in Macbeth. This last example demonstrates the use of collocation to expose and reveal aspects the persuasive and ideological character of texts and provides a link between keyword and discourse analysis.

COMPARATIVE KEYWORD ANALYSIS (CKA)

Equipped with a coding scheme to categorize keywords that characterize a text, it becomes possible to compare texts to identify key areas of difference. In our study of breast and prostate cancer texts we showed that men with prostate cancer were more likely to use words that referred to research and the Internet; whereas women were more likely to use words referring to feelings, people, clothing and appearance, as well as use 'superlatives' (shown in Table 27.5).

Now these findings fit in with a very large literature on 'gender differences' in both linguistics (for example, Coates, 2004) and health behaviour (for example, Kiss and Meryn, 2001; Gray et al., 1996). In this sense, they are not surprising. Nor is it uncontroversial to focus on gender 'difference'. Gender is one of the easiest dimensions on which human beings can be divided and many social researchers have succumbed to the temptation to compare men with women. Some now feel that this tends to reinforce ideas about difference rather than recognize similarity and overlap (Cameron, 2007). It also tends to essentialize the

Table 27.5   Keywords by gender in web forums: selected categories*

Research

Prostate	*Breast*
study, data, funding, median	NO KEYWORDS

The internet

Prostate	*Breast*
www, justgiving, http, prostate cancerwatchfulwaiting, .com, cancerwww, [message] board, htm, co, topic, .org, .asp	Forums, Bacup

Feelings

Prostate	*Breast*
beat	feel, feeling, scared, hard, cope, coping, feels, brave, hate, felt, wanted, glad, nice, upset, tough, scary, bad, loved, lost, fear, losing, [better] safe [than sorry], luckily, cry, bloody, liked, fun, nightmare, living [with], try, deal [with], grateful, nasty, crying, bear, funny, blame, hoping, trying, worrying

People

Prostate	*Breast*
men, dad, wife, his, dads, he, man, patients, dad's	I, she, her, I'm, women, me, mum, they, my children, I've, them, people, ladies, women, family, mother, you, sister, friends, baby, husband, kids, daughter, I'm, myself, girls, friend, partner, someone, you've, person, yourself, married, I'd, hubby, you've, son, lady, boys, he's, mine, she's, everyone

Clothing and appearance

Prostate	*Breast*
NO KEYWORDS	wear, clothes, wearing

Superlatives

Prostate	*Breast*
NO KEYWORDS	lovely, amazing, definitely, brilliant, huge, wonderful

* Keywords are words appearing proportionately more frequently in one text than the other. Each section lists keywords in descending order of 'keyness'; words with two or more predominant meanings are excluded.

idea of gender difference as a universal and context-free phenomenon, missing the fact that in many social contexts gender is 'performed' differently. As well as being influenced by upbringing and social expectations, individuals can often resist these influences and increasingly do so in relation to gendered identities in (for example) urban, secular and more wealthy environments. The desire to recognize this has become particularly acute amongst gender scholars influenced by feminist post structuralism (Butler, 1990; Speer, 2005; Kiesling, 2005).

This leads us to recognize two main methodological issues relevant for comparative keyword analysis (CKA) of the type we have described here: the need to discover more than what is already known or obvious, and the tendency of the method to emphasize difference at the expense of similarities. Additionally, we might ask, when is this chapter going to become more 'qualitative'? (Or: 'when are we going to see some quotes?')

CHOOSING INTERESTING COMPARISON GROUPS AND (FINALLY) READING THE TEXT

We have said that the initial analysis of crude gender differences between men and women with these two types of cancer told us, broadly speaking, what we might have expected. This is not entirely fair, as we provided what we believe is the first empirical confirmation about women's higher usage of superlative adjectives, something long ago predicted by Lakoff (1975) (she called them 'empty adjectives' and gave 'divine' and 'charming' as examples from her own experience). However, our experience with the method has shown us that much of the art of producing unusual and unexpected findings with CKA lies in choosing interesting comparison groups. The success of this strategy can be illustrated by further work done on the web forum postings (Seale, 2006) in which the postings of men on the breast cancer forum and women on the prostate cancer forum were examined.

Regarding women on the prostate cancer forum, it was striking that they constituted almost half the people posting to this forum and that they posted more words, overall, than did men. These were, on the whole, people who identified themselves as the wives, daughters, other relatives and friends of men with prostate cancer. There were some men on the breast cancer forum too, and for the most part, these were also relatives and friends of people with the disease, although men constituted only a small proportion of the participants on the breast cancer forum. We decided to use CKA to investigate these people and, first of all, compared them with their 'own' gender on the other forum. Thus, male relatives and friends on the breast cancer forum were compared with men with prostate cancer on the prostate cancer forum; female relatives and friends on the prostate cancer forum were compared with women with breast cancer on the breast cancer forum.

The women relatives and friends on the prostate cancer forum showed very little difference from women elsewhere (apart from referring to prostate cancer a lot more, of course). However, we noticed one interesting feature of their keywords, in that these contained the words 'welcome', 'thank you' and 'hello'. A KWIC display and associated collocational analysis revealed that these words were being used as part of the following phrases:

'welcome to this [board / forum / message board]'

'thank you for your [words / kind words / message / replies]'

'hello [all / everyone / again / (name of person)]'

Thus, these women were more frequently fulfilling a 'hostess' function, oiling the wheels of sociability so that interaction could proceed smoothly. In Fishman's (1977) graphic terms, women turned out to be doing a lot of the 'interactional shitwork' on this forum, pacifying quarrels and making newcomers feel welcome. Particular women, usually people who had been participating in the groups over a long period, tended to contribute more of these phrases.

Examining the men on the breast cancer forum provided more of a surprise, as they demonstrated many points of difference with men elsewhere. These men, according to the CKA results, were more likely to refer to feelings, a wide range of other people including children, friends and family, to use words indicating an interest in interpersonal communication and to talk about 'love', 'care', 'support' and 'help'. Thus, they appeared to be less like conventional 'men' and more like conventional 'women' in their choice of words and topics. Yet, CKA showed that these men were also different in key respects from women relatives and friends on the prostate forum, using the following keywords more often:

> want, wanted, feel, feels, wants, scared, lost, strong, angry, upset, feelings, cope, emotional, hard, feeling

Faced with this keyword evidence, it became relevant to investigate the stories of these men further through a conventional reading of their stories. They turned out to be people who were often facing, or responding to loss of a partner, or in some case loss of a mother. They responded by becoming particularly communicative about their feelings (which often involved anger) and concerned about other people, these frequently being the children that they had to look after now that their partner was unable to do so. Interestingly, many of these men reflected on their 'new man' identity, and the final research report contained several quotes illustrating this, of which the following are two examples:

> I suppose it is a fact that some men find it hard to get it across as well as they should! Me after all we went through it has left me with some sort of feeling of opening up more and just saying whatever I feel. This thing has some strange side effects on emotions that I don't think you can read or learn about other than experience them personally.

> I gave up work to look after [our children] and am now a full time carer. I found it very difficult to come to term with my wife's original diagnosis (about 2 and a half years ago). I concentrated purely on being practical (very male!) and denied not only my wife's emotional needs but mine too. Matters came to a bit of head and I had to seek counselling which I think was the bravest thing I've ever done!!! … I'm in touch with my feminine side which I think is important too!

Thus, CKA enabled a very large quantity of text to be scanned for promising features that could be investigated further, identifying interesting and somewhat unusual phenomena located in small parts of the larger corpus that could then be read and analyzed conventionally. Contrary to expectations that an emphasis on 'difference' would result in a stereotyped and 'essentialized' picture of gender, it in fact led to a discovery of people 'doing gender' in nonconventional ways in response to biographical circumstances and social context. Additionally, because the method is backed up by counts of keywords, the classic problem of anecdotalism that affects much qualitative research (only showing quotations that support

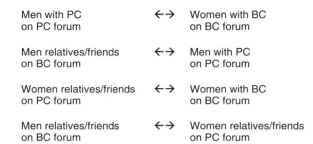

Men with PC   ←→   Women with BC
on PC forum   on BC forum

Men relatives/friends   ←→   Men with PC
on BC forum   on PC forum

Women relatives/friends ←→ Women with BC
on PC forum   on BC forum

Men relatives/friends   ←→   Women relatives/friends
on BC forum   on PC forum

Figure 27.1   Multiple comparisons made in CKA study of breast and prostate cancer (BC and PC) web forums

the writer's argument at the expense of negative or deviant cases) is avoided. In this respect, CKA fulfils the promised benefits of counting in qualitative research perceived by Silverman (1993) and one of the several advantages of mixed method research outlined by Bryman (1988).

Figure 27.1 shows in diagrammatic form the different comparisons made in the course of this project.

MORE CONTROLLED AND EVEN MORE INTERESTING COMPARISONS

While the comparisons made on the BC/PC project led to some unexpected results, in one respect the initial comparison between PC and BC was flawed in so far as the study was a study of gender difference. This was so because, to use the language of quasi-experimental design (Campbell and Stanley, 1966), in the initial comparison gender was confounded with type of illness. This means that any differences we found could have been the result of differences between breast and prostate cancer rather than differences between men and women. For example, we found that men spoke about choice between treatment options a great deal, whereas women did less of this. Does this mean that men are more interested in choice as an expression of some masculine norm, or that there are simply more difficult treatment choices to be made in prostate cancer?

This consideration, of course, reflects a causal logic that some 'qualitative' researchers may find difficult to swallow on the grounds that qualitative researchers do not investigate causality. We, on the other hand, believe in a mixed method approach to research and CKA, in particular, is a method that does not identify as either quantitative or qualitative, but draws on the advantages and rationales of both traditions. Sometimes social researchers – even 'qualitative' ones – become involved in drawing conclusions that contain causal assumptions, and it is important that underlying procedures are adequate to sustain these.

Taking this further, it is relevant to consider techniques for controlling the comparison groups selected for CKA so that valid inferences can be drawn from any comparisons made.

MATCHING COMPARISON GROUPS

It became possible to make more controlled comparisons when an archive of 1,035 transcribed qualitative interviews was made available for our secondary analysis by the DIPEx project (www.healthtalkonline.org and www.youthhealthtalk.org), this being a collection of narrative interviews about illness and health experiences collected for display on an associated educational web site. This collection ranged across 26 different illness conditions or health-related experiences, from which 96 interviews were selected to enable matched comparisons across gender and social socioeconomic category (SEC). The 96 interview transcripts (containing nearly one million words of text) were divided into four subgroups of 24, the first of these containing women of higher SEC, the next containing women of lower SEC, and then the third and fourth group containing men of high and then low SEC. Each person in each group of 24 was matched, or 'twinned', with another one in each of the groups according to age, type of health/illness condition and gender of interviewer.

This selection resulted in four groups with similar mean ages, falling between 50 and 52 years, with a range between 16 and 81. Each group of 24 contained interviews with people speaking about their chronic pain (two interviewees in each group), colorectal cancer (2), depression (4), termination of pregnancy (1), epilepsy (2), heart attack (1), heart failure (3), receiving intensive care (2), lung cancer (4), terminal illness (2), teenage cancer (1). Thus, when we compared the groups using CKA, we knew that we were comparing like with like – any differences would not be due to the fact that we were comparing people talking about different illnesses, or being different in age or social class. The CKA comparisons then carried out are summarized in Figure 27.2.

This multiple comparison showed that the stereotyped gender differences so often reported in small scale 'gender difference' studies of the sort summarized by Coates (2004) needed to be modified by a consideration of social position. High SEC men were more likely to engage in self-revelation than low SEC men and in this respect were more like women. Yet, they were also more likely that any other group to produce a 'command and control' discourse that represented themselves as active choice-makers and planners in relation to the 'problem' of their illness. These high SEC men were particularly likely to

Women high SEC   ←→   Men high SEC
Women low SEC   ←→   Men low SEC

Women high SEC   ←→   Women low SEC
Men low SEC   ←→   Men high SEC

Figure 27.2   Multiple comparisons made in CKA study of the interaction of social class and gender in illness narratives (Seale and Charteris-Black 2008a)

reflect on gendered norms, and were often critical of stereotyped performances of masculinity. For example:

> They say in the macho thing big men don't cry and things but it was six foot six friends coming to see me after the hospital and one of them gave me a huge hug and started crying you know (*High SEC man reflecting on his experience of intensive care*).

Low SEC women, on the other hand, were particularly likely to refer to an informal 'support group' culture, a key symbol of which was having a 'cup of tea' and designating supportive people in their social networks as 'lovely' people.

These claims depend on having matched groups so that like is being compared with like, a fundamental principle of quasi-experimental design. If, for example, the high SEC men had all been elderly men speaking about prostate cancer and the low SEC women had all been younger women speaking about, say, breast cancer, these claims would not have been convincing. Perhaps older men with prostate cancer 'command and control' more because this is how older men in general tend to behave in adversity; perhaps younger people with breast cancer are particularly good at generating informal support networks because of the highly successful breast cancer awareness social movement which attracts younger women in particular. All of these, Campbell and Stanley (1966) would say, are threats to the 'internal validity' of the study, which matching (or 'twinning') is designed to defend against.

Applying this approach to analyses that matched genders both for social class (Seale and Charteris-Black, 2008a) and age (Seale and Charteris-Black, 2008b) resulted in a number of findings that modified the account of gender difference in qualitative research literature that drew on small, undifferentiated samples. Thus, comparative keyword analysis depends on finding interesting comparison groups and on controlling confounding variables, so is a 'quantitative' method. However, it also involves exploring the context-dependent meanings of words and using knowledge of relevant literature and intuition to conduct an exploratory 'qualitative' analysis that uses emergent findings to follow up promising leads and discover phenomena not previously known to exist. It is therefore a method in which the logics of both quantitative and qualitative research are thoroughly integrated.

FINDING AND PREPARING TEXTS

Many qualitative health researchers will have spent a great deal of time carrying out their own qualitative interviews or using one of the other standard methods for generating qualitative data: focus groups, participant observation and so on. Occasionally qualitative researchers analyze documents or visual images too, but interviews remain the most common method, as these appear to offer the opportunity of exploring subjective perceptions and experiences. This is something which many (though not all) researchers who identify as 'qualitative' think is the essence of the qualitative approach. It is also an economical method for studying things which are hard to observe, perhaps because of access issues, or because they are infrequent, or because they happened in the past, or because they are 'inner' experiences of the psyche. An interview means that you can get reports of these things, packed into a short amount of research time, together with an account of the meaning which these things had for the speaker.

Nevertheless, interviews are second hand reports constructed in an artificial 'research' setting and a significant strand of methodological thinking from Becker and Geer (1957) onwards has involved the argument that direct observation of phenomena is somehow better or more 'natural' data. Additionally, modern technological conditions now make available vast electronic collections of text of all sorts, many of which are useful in health social research. As we have seen, people write messages to each other in Internet discussion groups devoted to illness experience, thus 'doing' illness experience directly rather than reporting it in a research interview. They produce personal blogs about experiences which can be used for research purposes, as can the content of websites produced by organizations. People post transcripts of speeches, policy and historical documents on the Internet. Health scientists produce research articles which, in searchable and downloadable form, constitute suitable archives of data for use in studying biomedical and scientific discourse. Newspaper articles are stored in huge searchable archives such as NEXIS (www.lexisnexis.co.uk). Qualitative data archives such as Qualidata (www.esds.ac.uk/qualidata) or the Murray Research Archive (www.murray.harvard.edu) makes available increasingly large collections of qualitative materials.

With this wealth of material already available for research purposes, it behoves health researchers to consider carefully before embarking on time-consuming data-gathering exercises. The decision to do this is generally driven by the existence of research questions that appear, to the researcher, to require original data collection. Nevertheless, the exploratory nature of a qualitative research project means that research questions often change during the course of a project. Extending this logic, it may often be wise to construct research questions that suit an available data set, rather than pluck them out of the imagination and then spend many months labouring to collect a small amount of material. If, then, an existing data source is considered suitable for a particular set of research questions and all ethical issues pertaining to its use have been addressed, one then confronts the issue of preparing it for computer-assisted analysis.

At this point, some computing skills are useful. *Wordsmith Tools*, for example, likes to analyze files that have been saved as 'text only' files, so that no hidden codes are contained. If a file is in *Word* format then it must be saved in this mode before being imported into the program. If a file has been downloaded from a web page in html format, it will need to be converted to text format. If you type 'html to text converter' into Google, you will find many freeware programs that will do this for groups of html files.

Word has a number of useful features that enable files to be prepared. For example, an interview transcript is likely to contain both interviewer and interviewee speech. Frequently, a typist will have put something like 'Int:' when interviewer speech begins and 'Resp:' when respondent speech begins. *Wordsmith Tools* can be set to ignore text occurring between the following two marks: < >. For a keyword analysis of respondents' speech only, the interviewer's speech would need to be enclosed in these marks or alternatively, deleted from the transcript. To do this, the 'search and replace' and the 'macro' facilities of *Word* are helpful. Take for example the following sequence of text:

```
Int:    How was it for you?
Resp:   Fine, thanks
```

The 'search and replace' facility of Microsoft Word can be used to replace every occurrence of 'Int:' with '<Int:'. With a macro, a sequence of keystrokes can be recorded, so that first this can be done for one instance of 'Int:' and then Microsoft Word can be set to search for the next hidden paragraph break at the end of the first line, and replace it with another (hidden) paragraph break and '>'. This macro, which is assigned to a particular keystroke combination (Ctrl and # for example) can then be repeated ad infinitum through a document so that the conversions are all done in one go. Alternatively a similar logic can be applied to a macro that will delete the respondent's speech.

Of course, the preparation of files for analysis is never quite as simple as this. Typists are inconsistent and features of text that appear repetitive can sometimes change, or have exceptions. The process of file preparation can require considerable application of time and effort, but programming routines of the sort described mean that the time taken to do this is relatively short when compared with the effort of original data collection. With very large quantities of text, where only suggestive statistical patterns are sought for in the initial overview keyword analysis, it is acceptable to have a few errors in the original files. Once interesting features have been identified, the detailed examination of words in context will weed out the occasional example that has been left behind in error. For example, at one point we found that 'id' occurred quite often in a large body of text. At the time we were experimenting with software that automatically tags and groups words into semantic categories (*WMatrix*) and 'id' was identified by this software as a word pertaining to the psyche (as in 'id', 'superego' etc.). Inspection of the word in context revealed that the typist had omitted an apostrophe in a small proportion of attempts to type the very common words 'I'd'.

CONCLUSION

Keyword analysis has several strengths: it enables much larger amounts of material to be analyzed than in conventional qualitative analysis, while retaining a commitment to in-depth, interpretive analysis of key aspects of these larger texts. It exploits the ready availability of electronic text archives concerning health issues, something which is particularly attractive at a time when ethical committee and IRB procedures add to the difficulties of collecting qualitative data from scratch. It is a conjoint qualitative and quantitative method that draws on many of the advantages of both traditions, being particular good at helping to respond to criticism of selective anecdotalism and to ensure representativeness and empirical generalizability (noting, of course, that theoretical rather than empirical generalization is sometimes the preferred goal of qualitative work (Seale, 1999)). The procedures also often show things that are hard to see in a conventional reading of text, and the analyst's pre-existing ideas are sometimes disturbed or extended in surprising ways. We have used it on a number of studies now, moving on from studies of cancer experience to studies of newspaper reporting of health issues (Seale et al., 2007) and a comparative analysis of academic cultures as shown in a large collection of journal abstracts (Seale, 2008). Like any method, there are things to guard against, chief amongst which is the need to be aware that differences rather than similarities between texts are identified, and the need to investigate the variable meanings of words in their original contexts before drawing conclusions.

Interest in keyword and comparative keyword analysis is growing outside linguistics and, currently, the book most likely to help social researchers using the method – particularly if they want to use it to pursue discourse analytic projects – is by Paul Baker (2006) who has shown what the approach can do in a study of the public discourses of gay men (Baker, 2005). Other books – for example Adolphs (2006), McEnery et al. (2006) – are more geared towards linguists, but nevertheless make useful reading for social researchers interested in health issues. Nevertheless, any research method is learned by a combination of general education in the method, derived from courses and reading chapters or books of this sort, and through practical experience of trying to use the method. Therefore, we end on a note of encouragement: try it and see!

WEB SITES

a. Software

Wordsmith Tools
www.lexically.net/wordsmith
The software most corpus linguists use,
and the one we have used most.

Wmatrix
http://ucrel.lancs.ac.uk/wmatrix

Web-based software that automatically categorizes ('tags') words into semantic and grammatical categories before enabling wordlists and comparative keyword lists to be produced. Warning: can be useful to think with, but always check out the meanings of individual words thus categorized

Concordance
www.concordancesoftware.co.uk
Produces wordlists and KWIC displays

b. Archives useful for qualitative researchers

Qualidata
www.esds.ac.uk/qualidata
Important UK source of archived qualitative data

Murray Research Archive
www.murray.harvard.edu
Important US source of archived qualitative data

Nexis
www.lexisnexis.co.uk

Source of world newspaper texts, fully searchable and downloadable to those with a subscription

c. Corpus linguistics links

Bookmarks for corpus-based linguists
http://devoted.to/corpora/
'Links to anything and everything to do with language corpora' are on this site

British National Corpus (BNC)
www.natcorp.ox.ac.uk
The classic 'reference corpus' of British English

REFERENCES

Adolphs, S. (2006) *Introducing Electronic Text Analysis: A Practical Guide for Language and Literary Studies.* London: Routledge.

Akerstrom, M., Jacobsson, K., and Wasterfors, D. (2007) 'Reanalysis of Previously Collected Material'. In Seale C., Gobo, G., Gubrium, J.F., and Silverman, D. (eds) *Qualitative Research Practice* (pp. 314–27). London: Sage.

Baker, P. (2005) *Public Discourses of Gay Men.* London: Routledge.

Baker, P. (2006) *Using Corpora in Discourse Analysis.* London: Continuum.

Becker, H.S. and Geer, B. (first published 1957) 'Participant Observation and Interviewing: A Comparison'. In McCall, G. and Simmons, J.L. (eds) (1969) *Issues in Participant Observation* (pp. 322–31). New York: Addison-Wesley.

Bryman, A. (1988) *Quantity and Quality in Social Research.* London: Unwin Hyman.

Butler, J. (1990) *Gender Trouble: Feminism and the Subversion of Identity.* New York: Routledge.

Cameron, D. (2007) *The Myth of Mars and Venus.* Oxford: Oxford University Press

Campbell, D.T. and Stanley, J.C. (1966) *Experimental and Quasi-Experimental Design for Research.* Chicago: Rand McNally.

Carter, R. (2004) *Language and Creativity: the Art of Common Talk*. London: Routledge

Charteris-Black, J. (2004) *Corpus Approaches to Critical Metaphor Analysis*. Basingstoke and New York: Palgrave-MacMillan.

Charteris-Black, J. (2005) *Politicians and Rhetoric: The Persuasive Power of Metaphor*. Basingstoke and New York: Palgrave-MacMillan.

Coates, J. (2004). *Women, Men and Language: A Sociolinguistic Account of Gender Differences in Language*. London: Pearson Education.

Corti, L. and Thompson, P. (2007) 'Secondary Analysis of Archived Data'. In Seale C., Gobo, G., Gubrium, J.F. and Silverman, D. (eds) *Qualitative Research Practice* (pp. 297–313). London: Sage.

Firth, J.R. (1957) *Papers in Linguistics 1934–1951*. London: Oxford University Press.

Fishman, P.M. (1977) 'Interactional Shitwork'. *Heresies* 2: 99–101.

Gray, R., Fitch, M., Davis, C., and Phillips, C. (1996). 'Breast Cancer and Prostate Cancer Self Help Groups: Reflections on Differences', *Psycho-oncology*, 5: 137–42.

Jefferson, G. (2004) 'Glossary of Transcript Symbols with an Introduction'. In Lerner, G.H. (ed.) *Conversation Analysis: Studies from the First Generation* (pp. 13–31). Amsterdam/Philadelphia: John Benjamins.

Kiesling, S.F. (2005) 'Homosocial Desire in Men's Talk: Balancing and Re-creating Cultural Discourses of Masculinity', *Language in Society*, 34: 695–726.

Kiss, A. and Meryn, S. (2001) 'Effect of Sex and Gender on Psychosocial Aspects of Prostate and Breast Cancer', *British Medical Journal*, 323: 1055–8.

Lakoff, R. (1975) *Language and Women's Place*. New York: Harper and Row.

Louw, B. (1993) 'Irony in the Text or Insincerity in the Writer? The Diagnostic Potential of Semantic Prosodies'. In Baker, M., Francis, G., and Tognini-Bonelli, E. (eds) *Text and Technology: In Honour of John Sinclair*. Philadelphia/Amsterdam: John Benjamins.

McEnery, T., Xiao, R., and Tono, Y. (2006) *Corpus-based Language Studies: An Advanced Resource Book*. London: Routledge.

Popping, R. (2000) *Computer-Assisted Text Analysis*. London: Sage.

Robinson, K.M. (2001) 'Unsolicited Narratives from the Internet: A Rich Source of Qualitative Data', *Qualitative Health Research*, 11(5): 706–14.

Seale, C. (1999) *The Quality of Qualitative Research*. London: Sage.

Seale, C. (2006) 'Gender Accommodation in Online Cancer Support Groups', *Health*, 10(3): 345–60.

Seale, C. (2008) 'Mapping the Field of Medical Sociology: A Comparative Analysis of Journals', *Sociology of Health and Illness*, 30(5): 677–95.

Seale, C., Charteris-Black, J., and Ziebland, S. (2006) 'Gender, Cancer Experience and Internet Use: A Comparative Keyword Analysis of Interviews and Online Cancer Support Groups', *Social Science and Medicine*, 62(10): 2577–90.

Seale, C. and Charteris-Black, J. (2008a) 'The Interaction of Class and Gender in Illness Narratives', *Sociology*, 42(3): 453–469.

Seale, C. and Charteris-Black, J. (2008b) 'The Interaction of Age and Gender in Illness Narratives', *Ageing and Society*, 28(7): 1025–43.

Seale, C., Boden, S., Lowe, P., Steinberg, D., and Williams, S. (2007) 'Media Constructions of Sleep and Sleep Disorders: A Study of UK National Newspapers', *Social Science and Medicine*, 65(3): 418–30.

Seale, C., Charteris-Black, J., MacFarlane, A., and McPherson, A. (2009) 'Interviews and Internet Forums: A Comparison of Two Sources of Data for Qualitative Research', *Qualitative Health Research* (forthcoming).

Silverman, D. (1993) *Interpreting Qualitative Data: Methods for Analysing Talk, Text and Interaction*. London: Sage.

Speer, S. (2005) *Gender Talk: Feminism, Discourse and Conversation Analysis*. London: Routledge.

Stubbs, M. (1996) *Text and Corpus Analysis: Computer-Assisted Studies of Language and Culture*. Oxford: Blackwell.

Stubbs, M. (2001) *Words and Phrases: Corpus Studies of Lexical Semantics*. Oxford and Malden, MA: Blackwell.

Issues in Qualitative Health Research

28

Recognizing Quality in Qualitative Research

Kath M. Melia

'If that's not true, it ought to be'

My family's aphorism could also be applied to the products of qualitative research, in the sense that some arguments and items of data are very compelling and seem to exude veracity. The question is, however: how do we demonstrate this?

Quality is one of those baggage-laden words which bears the burden of everyone's meanings and is, as a result, rather hard to nail down. There is often an implicit assumption that, if research is qualitative, this is sufficient to assure its quality. Qualitative methods are sold on the rather vague notion that they can take us to places that quantitative methods cannot. They come to be perceived as good simply because they are qualitative. Qualitative research cannot, however, be regarded indulgently as if it has a charm all of its own. How do we know that qualitative research is quality research? Its charm, or qualitativeness, is part of the problem. Quantitative methods can be assessed by reference to apparently objective criteria of sample design and use of appropriate statistics. How can we demonstrate that less obviously rigorous qualitative methods are in fact worth their keep? Are these methods robust? Can they be shown to produce valid data capable of replication? Are the findings transferable? Or is this not the point?

Richardson (1994: 517) states that:

> Unlike quantitative work, which can carry its meaning in its tables and summaries, qualitative work depends upon people's reading it. Just as a piece of literature is not equivalent to its 'plot summary', qualitative research is not contained in its abstracts. Qualitative research has to be read, not scanned; its meaning is in the reading.

On first reading, I found this appealing and a possible route to take. However, as it was written in the context of a piece which welcomed postmodernism and its tendency to doubt all methods equally, I have revised my view. Postmodernism rejects the idea of grand theory or grand narrative and does not entertain generalized explanations. For the postmodernist, understanding comes through individual interpretation of the empirical world. Taken to extremes, postmodernism would lead one to ask of a research design, 'if it is really postmodern, how would we know?' In other words, if we can make no assumptions about the status of knowledge and interpretation of data, how can we have a view on research methods and findings? In a previous paper (Melia, 1997), I argued that postmodernism has become an excuse for taking what would otherwise be thought of as a somewhat loose approach to methods. There has to be some connection between the epistemological starting point and the explanation of the data in the final write up. While I am not suggesting that Richardson has loose methodological practice in mind, I am not convinced that her suggestion takes us far in the search for quality in qualitative research beyond arguing that one has to work at getting meaning from the final product. Richardson does, however, point up the fact that there is a range of views on what we mean by qualitative methods. This complicates the business of making useful comment on the quality in qualitative research!

GENERALIZABILITY AND TRANSFERABILITY

Prior to the recent proliferation of texts, qualitative sociologists and anthropologists rarely wrote explicitly about their methods or methodology. It was almost implied that the relationship between fieldworker and data was so fragile that any exposure to inspection would constitute some kind of breach of faith which would make the project untenable. With notable exceptions, such as WF Whyte's appendix to his famous *Street Corner Society*, very little was published on qualitative method. Even Whyte notes in the preface to his second edition, for which he wrote the account of his methods, 'I have placed [it] in an appendix because I feel it will mean more to the reader if he goes through the body of the study first' (Whyte, 1955: viii).

   If qualitative research took us no further than the specific study and its associated data, it would probably not be worth undertaking. Therefore, our question is really about the nature of the generalizability. Several matters come together here. Quantitative methods appear to have cornered the market for generalization, although there have been attempts to emulate this for qualitative research, with links, if only by association, to statistics as a means towards generalization. One example would be the comparison made by Glaser and Strauss (1967) between statistical and theoretical sampling. In quantitative research, sampling is part and parcel of statistical analysis. When sampling follows the rules of probability, conclusions can be drawn which are capable of being generalized beyond the immediate data. Theoretical sampling involves pursuing leads which come from the data. Glaser and Strauss emphasize that it is the search for emergent ideas and concepts that leads to theoretical explanation of the phenomenon under study by guiding the collection of data – hence *theoretical* sampling. One might wonder whether the description of this process as *sampling* was designed to create a subliminal link with already acknowledged methods of producing generalizable data.

QUANTITATIVE WAYS SPILL OVER INTO QUALITATIVE METHODS

Murphy and Dingwall (2003: 169) note that:

> The relative absence of probability sampling generates concerns that qualitative work is merely anecdotal and therefore of no practical use to policy makers or practitioners.

They also point out, in common with others, that there are no fundamental reasons for qualitative researchers not to adopt probability-sampling methods. However, I prefer not to play up the purported similarities so much as to note that the differences are less problematic than they are sometimes made out to be.

Qualitative methods appear to have to defend themselves in the face of quantitative methods, a strange position given their longer history. Once qualitative methods had been separated from their heritage in anthropology and sociology, and re-emerged as a style of research, it took a long time for them to escape from the idea that they are only useful in small precursors to the real work of the quantitative social sciences. Survey research developed between the two World Wars with the application of statistical techniques from agricultural research to studies of human populations and received a substantial boost from its contributions to population studies during the Second World War. More recently, the introduction of increasingly powerful computers has increased the power and sophistication of the work that can be done. However, qualitative methods have never entirely gone out of favour, although they went through some thin times in the 1950s before their revival in the 1960s in research on crime and deviance, which later extended into studies of health and medicine. Within the latter setting, the search for defences against criticism from quantitative researchers has led to a particular concern for rigour, through devices like triangulation and data verification.

In my view, this search is misdirected and more likely to undermine than strengthen qualitative methods. While these have their, important, place in social research, we also need to remember their limitations when used to produce near law-like statements. The randomized controlled trial (RCT), the so-called gold standard of medical research, has difficulties too. When findings based on clearly specified rule-following samples are taken back to the original population, without all the niceties of an RCT, there are questions to be raised.[1] Lewsey et al. (2001: 149), for example, say that

> Routine data present problems regarding their adequacy and precision for the two studies (timing of surgery following cerebral bleed and comparing angioplasty and bypass grafting

in coronary artery disease) but can still be used to complement trials in the intended manner. However, they also provide valuable information concerning the context of trials: in terms of the epidemiology of sub-arachnoid haemorrhage and, in the case of coronary revascularization, providing detail as to the treatment and subsequent outcomes of those patients who would not meet eligibility criteria for trials.

We do not often remind ourselves that seemingly more clear-cut statistical or experimental research has still made decisions about inclusion and exclusion at an earlier stage.

Even where health research uses the 'gold standard' RCT, it is often an anecdote that clinches an argument rather than the power of a statistical claim. I recall being part of a heated debate at a consensus conference on colorectal cancer about the ethics of aggressive palliative surgery. The patients in question were young mothers and the photographic evidence of an improved quality of life, albeit measured in months rather than years, made the case for surgery far more compellingly than did the familiar presentation of blue slides displaying the statistical evidence. When arguing their claims for a new treatment, clinicians produce data from RCTs, yet often drive their point home with real cases and photographs – with qualitative data.

Our evidence base may have more success in changing policy and practice if it is based on trials and experimentation. It is, however, often case histories that communicate this evidence. The uses to which qualitative data can be put are demonstrated in a paper by Smith (2008). She was interested in the data that never made it into the dataset when ordinary people were asked to complete postal questionnaires. She began from an observation that 'respondents frequently write unsolicited comments on their questionnaires'. Smith treats this as 'as an attempt at dialogue' with a figure she calls 'the imagined researcher'. For some researchers, both qualitative and quantitative, these additional comments are an indication of trouble. Smith raises two questions about these addenda: can they be treated as data and, do they indicate poor questionnaire design? She goes on to explore 'the nature of a communicative event that takes the form of a task requiring the attenuation of personal experience into a limited range of questions and answers'. Marginalia serve to nuance, or even offer quite other insights into, interpretations of questionnaire data. The uses to which marginalia can be put mean that they, in effect, become data.

The merits of qualitative research are often portrayed through the idea that qualitative research methods offer something that quantitative approaches cannot. However, it is not really a very satisfactory argument to say qualitative research is good, just because it delivers something different, particularly when this claim rests on taking quantitative methods as a gold standard and using qualitative methods to fill the residual gaps. Vidich and Lyman (1994: 24) observe that

In [a] fundamental sense all research methods are at bottom qualitative and are, for that matter, equally objective; the use of quantitative data or mathematical procedures does not eliminate the inter-subjective element that underlies social research. Objectivity resides not in method, per se, but in the framing of the research problem and the willingness of the researchers to pursue that problem wherever the data and their hunches may lead.

Similarly, Murphy and Dingwall (2001: 32) also note that claims made for the distinctiveness of qualitative and quantitative research 'often exaggerate the differences between the two traditions and downplay their common ground'.

Murphy and Dingwall (2001: 28) identify three myths of qualitative research – one of which is that qualitative methods reach parts that other methods cannot, or, as they put it, 'qualitative research allows us to capture the understandings and meanings that make people behave as they do'. They go on to remark that:

> The problem of 'other people's minds' is one of the oldest conundrums in the human sciences. How can we know what is going on in another person's head when we are not a telepathic species? ... We simply cannot argue that the explanations that people offer to us as researchers or to others in the settings under study allow us to grasp what was going on inside an individual's head as he or she decided to act in one way rather than another.

This is a useful insight, particularly when evaluating the phenomenologists' contribution to qualitative research, given their general neglect of the problem of gaining access to whatever is going on in other people's minds when proposing their interpretive understandings of action.

QUALITATIVE METHODS – HEALTH CARE RESEARCH

What are the attractions of qualitative methods for research in the health field? Their flexibility can be more responsive to the individual dimensions of health care. It is not difficult to see why health care researchers are drawn to qualitative methods if they offer the possibility of understanding the experience of health, illness and the delivery of care from the perspective of the patient or service user. Health work is concerned with individuals, albeit in their own social contexts and often in the context of institutions where the needs of individuals have to be balanced with those of groups or populations. Qualitative methods can make a particular contribution to exploring the tensions between these concerns. The 'soft' nature of much of the data concerned with the interface between individual humans and the scientific foundations of medical practice, reflecting the unique intersection of genetic, material and social environments that shapes the course of any particular disease, requires qualitative analysis. A good example was the 1980s HIV/AIDS public health media campaign in the United Kingdom. The television element involved crashing waves, volcanoes and tombstones, with cinematography more reminiscent of horror films than a public health production and a strap line 'don't die of ignorance'. The public reaction was in many ways a moral rather than a medical panic. Even health care professionals seemed to forget that they had successfully handled plague, infection, contagion, and other catastrophes in the past, with strategies that could be adapted to this new challenge.

They totally missed the everyday context within which the AIDS 'catastrophe' was playing out (Shilts, 1987).

Part of the difficulty is the challenge of data management and presentation. As Becker et al. (1961) noted, in reference to their celebrated study of Kansas medical students in the late 1950s:

> Observational research produces an immense amount of detailed description; our files contain approximately five thousand single-spaced pages of such material. Faced with such a quantity of 'rich' but varied data, the researcher faces the problem of how to analyze it systematically and then to present his conclusions so as to convince other scientists of their validity.

He goes on to note – bear in mind this comment is now nearly half a century old:

> Participant observation (indeed, qualitative analysis generally) has not done well with this problem, and the full weight of evidence for conclusions and the processes by which they were reached are usually not presented, so that the reader finds it difficult to make his own assessment of them and must rely on his faith in the researcher.

Although the technological possibilities for data handling have expanded since that time, the problem of presentation remains unresolved – but, of course, we also have to trust quantitative researchers and experimenters to report their data scrupulously and responsibly.

In their introduction to *Qualitative Research Practice*, Seale et al. (2004) note that those who argue for qualitative research beyond the limits of methodological logic are broadly associated with postmodernism:

> … those positions broadly associated with post modernism (Denzin and Lincoln, 2000). … appear to be driven by an anti-methodological tenor that prefers the substance (research topics) to the form (methodology). Such a perspective, born partly in reaction to positivism, waved a flag of the superiority of qualitative research to surveys and experiments and considered methodological principles incapable of achieving a deeper understanding of a fragmented and dislocated culture. However, this research style has not always maintained its promise of achieving a deeper kind of research. The consequences are too often exposed to view: low quality qualitative research and research results that are quite stereotypical and close to common sense.

Similarly, Murphy and Dingwall (2003: 7) attack those who undertake qualitative research to bring 'romance back into a world that has been dulled by number crunching', criticizing the more precious defences that have been put forward to legitimate dismissing the need for rigour. Their opening chapters offer (2003: 7) an explanation of:

> … why many qualitative researchers have been reasserting the virtues of precision, rigour and science against the recent fashion for subjectivity, empathy and emotional politics'.

In the process, they argue that, 'qualitative research can be done in a scientific fashion with rigour and precision'.

The pressure to respond to issues such as verification, rigour, transferability and generalization, sampling and replication in ways that reflect the procedures of quantitative methods has evoked a nihilistic reaction rather than the creative development of method-appropriate strategies. Grounded theory has been a particular casualty. As Green and Thorogood (2004: 183) observe:

> ... 'grounded theory' is perhaps one of the most abused phrases in the qualitative health literature. Increasingly, researchers are making claims to have used a 'grounded theory' approach in what emerges as rather superficial thematic content analysis.

They go on to detail what can be thought of as essential to qualitative research:

> An analysis that has used grounded theory should provide a detailed, saturated account of the data rather than a list of key themes. It should be possible to read the account to see how variation within the data set has been used comparatively to develop the analysis, and how deviant cases have contributed to a credible and thorough account of the data (p. 183).

This is not only one of the best descriptions of the essentials of grounded theory, but identifies what we need to be looking for to establish whether there is quality in qualitative research.

Even then, there are differences as to what grounded theory should look like in practice. Its founders, Barney Glaser and Anselm Strauss famously came to disagree, a quarrel that came into the public domain when in 1992 Glaser published *Emergence vs. Forcing* in which he claimed that Strauss never understood what they were doing in 1967 when they published the *Discovery of Grounded Theory*. Nevertheless, they probably share more common ground than their robust defences of their positions suggest (Melia, 1996). Glaser is critical of the over-formulaic approach to analysis allegedly adopted by Strauss, which he says results in data being forced into categories, this contravening the emphasis on emergence that is so central to grounded theory. In Glaser's words, 'if you torture the data enough it will give up!' (Glaser, 1992: 123). According to Glaser, the central tenet of grounded theory, constant comparative method, is a breeze:

> ... using the constant comparison method gets the analyst to the desired 'conceptual power' quickly, with ease and joy. Categories emerge upon comparison and properties emerge upon more comparison. And that is all there is to it (Glaser, 1992: 43).

Strauss's indirect response to this tirade came in the *Handbook of Qualitative Research*. Buried in a section overviewing grounded theory, Strauss and Corbin (1994:283) note that its central features are:

> ... the grounding of theory upon data through data-theory interplay, the making of constant comparisons, the asking of theoretically-oriented questions, theoretical coding and the development of theory.

Denzin (1970: 5) draws attention to the way 'order is given to theory, methodology and research activity through the use of what Mills termed the *sociological imagination*'. Denzin is referring to C Wright Mills (1959, Pelican edition 1970: 232) who defines the sociological imagination as:

> ... the capacity to shift from one perspective to another, and in the process to build up an adequate view of a total society and its components. It is this imagination, of course, that sets off the social scientist from the mere technician.

TRIANGULATION

There have been efforts to validate and replicate qualitative research as if the assurance of its validity rests on the same principles that hold for quantitative research. Increasingly the research enterprise in health care, especially when associated with evidence-based practice and Health Technology Assessment [HTA][2] has to be shown to be adding value, and have demonstrable utility, so claims that qualitative research is somehow too special to be evaluated will not work. Triangulation and respondent validation figure largely in this enterprise. Triangulation is a simple idea which has become both complicated and confusing. It has become complicated, in that it is often used synonymously with multiple methods, and confusing because it has been championed as a means of validation. As Murphy and Dingwall (2001: 172) put it, there are 'significant problems if triangulation is elevated to the status of a validity test'.

Denzin's (1970) original idea of between method triangulation involved combining dissimilar methods to measure the same unit or concept, based on the assumption that, '… the flaws of one method are often the strengths of another, and by combining methods, observers can achieve the best of each, while overcoming their unique deficiencies'. It is worth noting that Denzin was arguing for what he calls 'multiple triangulation' which exists when, 'researchers combine in one investigation multiple observers, theoretical perspectives, sources of data and methodologies'. Denzin identifies triangulation with multiple methods:

> … because each method reveals different aspects of empirical reality, multiple methods of observation must be employed … since no method is ever free of rival causal factors, (and thus seldom leads to completely sound causal propositions), can ever completely satisfy the demands of interaction theory, or can ever completely reveal all of the relevant features of empirical reality necessary for a theory's test or development (Denzin, 1970: 26–7).

Agreeing with Webb et al. (1966), Denzin asserts that:

> … 'the combination of multiple methods – each with their own biases, true – into a single investigation will better enable the sociologist to forge valid propositions that carefully consider relevant rival causal factors'.

On re-reading this forty-year-old enthusiasm for multimethods, I find myself wondering why this is being treated as a new idea. Is it the Harley Davidson of qualitative research?

The whole argument seems to display a lack of faith in the chosen method. One should never expect a single method to answer every question: however, one should also expect that method to achieve what it is capable of achieving. There is an analogy with theories in moral philosophy, which rarely seek to cover all possible moral choices, but leave obvious gaps to be filled by other theories as with, for example utilitarianism and deontology. However acknowledging the gap seems preferable to appearing to lack confidence in the method and adopting another to patch it up. Silverman (1985: 21) notes that:

> ... we have to be careful about inferring a master 'reality' in terms of which all accounts and actions are to be judged. ... [this] casts great doubt on the argument that multiple research methods should be employed in a variety of settings in order to gain a 'total' picture of some phenomenon.

In one of the clearest critiques of triangulation, Silverman, referring to Denzin's 1970 position, goes on to say:

> Putting the picture together is more problematic than such proponents of 'triangulation' would imply. What goes on in one setting is not a simple corrective to what happens elsewhere – each must be understood in its own terms.

Silverman sustains this view throughout his writings on method noting, in a third (2006) edition of *Interpreting Qualitative Data*, triangulation and respondent validation are 'usually inappropriate to qualitative research'. In support of this view, Silverman refers to Fielding and Fielding (1986: 35) who suggest that it is worth using multiple methods and multiple theories for reasons other than Denzin's. They state that:

> ... the accuracy of a method comes from its systematic application, but rarely does the inaccuracy of one approach to the data complement the accuracies of another.

Hammersley and Atkinson (1983: 199) sum up the position:

> One should not, therefore, adopt a naively 'optimistic' view that the aggregation of data from different sources will unproblematically add up to produce a more complete picture.

Similarly, Blaikie (2000: 266) notes that:

> ... there is a danger in adopting a simple-minded view of triangulation, i.e., that a combination of different methods and data will provide a more complete picture of some phenomenon, like taking photographs of an object from different points of view.

In demonstrating one of the problems with triangulation, Murphy and Dingwall (2001) draw on Stimson and Webb's (1975) study of UK general practice. This study drew on both participant observation and patient interviews. There were, as Murphy and Dingwall put it, 'striking inconsistencies between patients' reports of their interactions with doctors and the researchers' own observations of such interaction'. Given that triangulation involves a focus on identifying a single reality, Murphy and Dingwall point out that, had triangulation been employed by Stimson and Webb as a check for validity, 'they would have been forced to adjudicate between their observations and the accounts given by patients in interviews, presumably judging the latter to be invalid'. Stimson and Webb actually treated the interview data as the patients' accounts of interactions with general practitioners, portraying their role in those encounters in ways which presented their character in particular ways to the interviewer, or to other patients, in group interviews. Murphy and Dingwall note that, while Stimson and Webb's analysis has since been the subject of methodological debate, its implications for triangulation remain vitally important.

In his discussion of triangulation, Blaikie (2000: 262) notes that, although Denzin's (1970) account has been particularly influential, the idea actually came into the social sciences through the work of Webb et al. (1966), building on arguments by Campbell and Fiske (1959). Webb et al.'s (1966) interest was in triangulation of 'measurement processes in the search for the validity of theoretical propositions'. Blaikie suggests that the 'triangulation metaphor in social science grossly misrepresents its use in surveying'. He continues:

> The triangulation metaphor makes some sense if it is applied to the common procedure used in questionnaires where a number of questions designed to elicit the same information are scattered throughout. Similarly, in attitude scaling, a number of items are used to measure an attitude, or a dimension of an attitude. In both cases, the multiple measures can improve validity, but, more particularly, precision. This was part of the original conception of triangulation and what Denzin (1970) has referred to as *within-method* triangulation (Blaikie, 2000: 265).

He concludes that:

> Triangulation has become an icon towards which researchers are supposed to genuflect. However, as we have seen, closer examination reveals some serious difficulties in its implementation. The distortion in its adaptation from surveying and navigation, the vagueness in the manner in which it has been formulated, the naivety with respect to differences in ontological assumptions, the tendency to impose a single, absolutist ontology on multiple socially constructed realities, and the problems of interpreting convergent and divergent results, make the triangulation of methods and data a very doubtful activity (Blaikie, 2000: 270).

Can the findings of qualitative research be generalized in the same way as those of quantitative research? The answer is 'probably not', but what can be 'generalized', to use the quantitative terminology, are the theoretical insights. These can have a life beyond the data and be developed in further studies that are not necessarily straightforward replications. It is in the attempts to validate and justify qualitative research that triangulation and respondent verification come in for misuse and even abuse. Methods texts must carry some responsibility for this confused thinking, if only because of the amount of print devoted to discussing how one might generalize from qualitative data, when the strict view is that we probably cannot do any such thing. It is the ideas and shifts in thinking that can be taken forward.

GENERALIZABILITY AND RESPONDENT VALIDATION

In a discussion of judging the quality of qualitative research Murphy and Dingwall (2003: 171) adopt the position that:

> All HTA research, whether qualitative or quantitative should be evaluated in terms of the robustness of its truth claims, on the one hand, and its usefulness in informing policy making and practice, on the other.

The checklist approach to establishing the validity of qualitative research has become popular. However, even if it could be useful, it is not clear what should be included in such a list, 'frequent candidates to get onto this check list are respondent validation and triangulation' We have seen that objections to the triangulation or respondent validation approaches to the validation of qualitative research findings centre on what Silverman (2006: 292) has described as the 'context boundedness' of data and the epistemological basis upon which methods rest.

Triangulation carries the problem of appearing to be looking for a single reality. Bloor (1997) argues that a fundamental problem with triangulation is the asymmetry of the conclusions drawn. He points out that triangulation can only *corroborate* findings. Since it cannot *refute* them, it cannot be some form of validity test. I have thought much the same thing in relation to the practice of returning to research participants with a view to verifying, and thereby supposedly validating, data. I think of it as the 'Wednesday effect'. Suppose, for instance, when I return to the participants they agree with my analysis, would they still give the same response if I went back on the following Wednesday and asked them again. Participants are just that, participants, and it is not their role to produce the analysis or validate the data. Validity cannot be totally assured: it is like the light in a refrigerator – how can you really know it has gone out when the door is closed? All you can do is settle for the most rigorous approach that a researcher can adopt within the available time and finances.

In contrast to the replication approach of establishing validity, which is common in the natural sciences, Bloor (1983) states that, 'In the social sciences validation is conventionally equated with a different sort of replication [sometimes called triangulation see Denzin 1970], the use by the investigator of different methods to produce the same findings'. Bloor goes on to identify the validity problems inherent in this approach:

> … it is difficult to see the warrant for rejecting findings that are the product of a seemingly appropriate method simply because they are not 'triangulated' by additional findings generated by seemingly less appropriate methods' Bloor (1983: 156).

In my own work on ethics and intensive care (Melia, 2004) interviews with intensive care clinicians in the Netherlands first appeared to suggest that the doctors and nurses saw each other's viewpoint on the withdrawal of treatment. One nurse put it rather starkly when she said, 'the doctors think nurses want to do euthanasia and the nurses think that the doctors want to do science'. When I examined all such comments in the context of the strong emerging theme of the importance of teamwork to the intensive care unit, I was able to propose a different, and less alarming, explanation Melia, 2001).

Bloor's (1997: 39) discussion, *Triangulation: replicating chalk with cheese*, clearly sets out the logical objections to triangulation as a validation tool. Given general agreement that there particular methods are best suited to particular projects, then:

> … triangulation may be said to involve juxtaposing findings gathered by the best available method with findings generated by an inferior method.

There is no difficulty when the findings agree, but real trouble when they do not. This is similar to Campbell's (1975: 41) objections to individual ethical conscience being a basis for settling matters of right and wrong, because it is based on the assumption that:

> ... the plain man's [sic] feeling that his conscience knows best ... such a view seems sensible enough until we meet two plain men who disagree. Then we have to think more carefully about what we mean by conscience.

Lapsley and Melia (2001) examined the provision of intensive care in the context of excess demand and explored the limits to the managerial option of rationing provision. Their analysis was based on interview transcripts and various accounting data, spreadsheets, and reports as evidence of budget profiles, staffing levels and other policies. The study included an examination of reports and statistics concerning the costs of intensive care provision and an analysis of clinical outcomes using TISS (Therapeutic Intervention Scoring System) and APACHE[3] (Acute Physiology And Chronic Health Evaluation) scoring systems.

Although on the face of it these scoring systems appear to provide very precise measures of patients' morbidity, they are of no use to clinicians with respect to managing individual cases. One problem for the management of the ICU budget is that accounting is about quantification. There are no sophisticated workload models readily available to assist in this and the only means of clinical quantification that exist to date are the scoring systems (TISS and APACHE), neither of which is sufficiently precise or refined for use in budget construction. As a consequence, the professional judgement of the clinicians provides a 'precision' which available budgetary numbers cannot, and so their views prevail (Lapsley and Melia, 2001: 735).

The activity of the clinicians and the strength of professional clinical judgement have to be understood along with the idea of rationing being thought of as a constraint, which does or does not exist.

Even the APACHE score – used to evaluate various treatments or care facilities – is not sufficiently honed to allow individual case decisions to be made on its basis. If these measures were used, a lot of unnecessary admissions to ICU (Intensive Care Unit) would be prevented, but one patient in twenty would die where the scoring dictated refusal of admission. This is clinically, and indeed morally, unacceptable. Qualitative research does not provide the whole answer but identifies the limitations of the quantitative data available to the clinicians and managers and explains how they produce practical and justifiable solutions to the problems thus created for them.

If we were to abandon triangulation we could do a lot worse than replace it with Miller and Fox's (1997) idea of 'bridging'. This metaphor is intended to convey the idea of linking analytic formations just as land formations are linked by bridges. They suggest that 'two or more analytic formations may be linked and made mutually informative, while also respecting the distinctive contributions and integrity of each perspective'.

WHAT ARE WE TO MAKE OF ALL THIS?

Discussions of method have a tendency to become overly formulaic and bogged down in detail or to move in epistemological and philosophical directions where it is possible to sustain any argument provided that it is not troubled by data. An attraction of grounded theory is the way it seeks to steer a course between these extremes. If qualitative research is to take ideas and interpretations – theoretical insights – forward, we must be able to produce them. Silverman (2006: 386) notes that 'there is a danger of reducing analytic questions to technical issues to be resolved by cookbook means, e.g., good interviewing techniques, simplistic versions of grounded theory, or the appropriate computer-aided qualitative data analysis system'. He goes on to say that, while not wanting to criticize these methods, he seeks to 'underline that, as most of their proponents recognize, they are no substitute for theoretically inspired reasoning.

The virtues of qualitative methods should not be over or undersold. They do what they do and at their most useful, they generate theoretical insights and ideas to be applied elsewhere. If qualitative methods cannot deliver this, its 'findings' deserve no more than a 'well, there's interesting' kind of response. Silverman recalls an insight into Everett Hughes's approach to theory. Hughes apparently 'responded grumpily when students asked what he thought about theory. 'Theory of what?' he would reply (Becker, 1998). Silverman endorses the view, if less grumpily, by saying:

> For Hughes, as for me, theory without some observation to work upon, is like a tractor without a field … Without theory, research is impossibly narrow. Without research, theory is mere armchair contemplation' (Silverman, 2006: 388).

CONCLUSION

When Becker and Geer (1957) opened their paper, *Participant observation and interviewing – a comparison*, with the words 'The most complete form of the sociological datum after all is the form in which the participant observer gathers it'., they gave birth to the idea that participant observation should be the yardstick against which to measure qualitative methods. They may have had tongues firmly in cheeks, but they triggered a response from Martin Trow (1957: 35) which was memorable and more wide-ranging than their focus invited. Trow said:

> Every cobbler thinks leather is the only thing. Most social scientists, including the present writer, have their favourite research methods with which they are familiar and have some skill in using. And I suspect that we mostly choose to investigate problems that seem vulnerable to attack through these methods. But we should at least try to be less parochial than cobblers.

I was moved by these words at the start of my graduate studies. Although much of the dispute hinged on the definition of participant observation, I still have much sympathy with Trow's view and sometimes wonder if we have not become overly methodologically squeamish (Melia, 1997). There are many real methodological doubts which should cause us to pause and think, but if every epistemological and ontological quibble results in us abandoning research on the grounds that it is impossible to determine the status of the data, we do the research enterprise no favours.

If qualitative research produces analysis capable of explaining the data, and offers some theoretical insights, it is doing its job. It may be less easily validated by quantitative standards, but it should show its true colours if it tells a story and adds theoretical insights. Silverman (2006: 237) sums up the central matter of quality in qualitative research when he says:

> If there is a gold standard for qualitative research, it should only be the standard for any good research, qualitative or quantitative, social or natural science. Namely, have the researchers demonstrated successfully why we should believe them? And does the research problem tackled have theoretical and/or practical significance?[4]

In all of this, we need to remember that all research methods are subject to phases and fads. As Denzin and Lincoln (1994: 575) remind us:

> Just as the post-modern, for example, reacts to the modern, some day there may well be a neo-modern phase that extols Malinowski and the Chicago school and finds the current post-structural, post-modern movement abhorrent.

NOTES

1 O'Connel, D., Glasziou, P., Hill, S., Sarunac, J., Lowe, J., and Henry, D. (2001) 'Results of Clinical; Trials and Systematic Reviews: To Whom Do They Apply?'. In Stevens et al. (ed.) *The Advanced Handbook of Methods in Evidence Based Healthcare* (pp. 56–72). London: Sage.

2 Health Technology Assessment refers to scientifically based means of evaluating health care technologies and organizational systems

3 APACHE and TISS quantitative systems for measuring effectiveness of care and clinical interventions using various key physiological measures as a means of estimating the severity of the illness. A means of measuring clinical workload and is employed as a management tool to cost the process of care.

Knaus, W.A., Wagner, J., and Zimerman, S. (1981) 'APACHE Acute Physiological and Chronic Health Evaluation: A Physiologically Based Classification System', *Critical Care Medicine*, 9: 581–97.

Cullen, D., Keene, R., and Waternoux, C. (1974) 'Therapeutic Intervention Scoring System: A Method for Quantitative Comparison of Patient Care', *Critical Care Medicine*, 2: 57–62.

4 Silverman (2006: 294–295) discusses where to turn to if we 'are not fully convinced' by either triangulation or members' validation in order to claim validity for data. He says that 'more appropriate methods include analytic induction; the constant comparative method; deviant-case analysis; comprehensive data treatment'.

REFERENCES

Becker, H.S. and Geer, B. (1957) 'Participant Observation and Interviewing: a Comparison', *Human Organization*, 16(3): pp. 28–32.

Becker, H.S. (1998) *Tricks of the Trade How to Think About Your Research While Doing It*. Chicago: University of Chicago Press.

Becker, H.S., Geer, B., Hughes, E.C., and Strauss, A.L. (1961) *Boys in White*. Chicago: University of Chicago Press.

Blaikie, N. (2000) *Designing Social Research*. Cambridge: Polity Press.

Bloor, M. (1983) 'Notes on Member Validation'. In Emerson, R. (ed.) *Contemporary Field Research: A Collection of Readings* (pp. 156–72). Prospect Heights, IL: Waveland Press.

Bloor, M. (1997) 'Techniques of Validation in Qualitative Research: A Critical Commentary'. In Miller, G. and Dingwall, R. (eds) (1997) *Context and Method in Qualitative Research* (pp. 37–50). London: Sage.

Campbell, A.V. (1975) *Moral Dilemmas in Medicine* (2nd Edition). Edinburgh: Churchill Livingstone.

Campbell, D.T. and Fiske, D.W. (1959) 'Convergent and Discriminant Validation by the Multi-Trait-Multi-Method Matrix', *Psychological Bulletin*, 56: 81–105.

Denzin, N. K. (1970) *The Research Act in Sociology*. London: Butterworths.

Denzin, N.K. and Lincoln, Y.S. (1994) 'The Fifth Moment'. In Denzin, N.K. and Lincoln, Y.S. (eds) *Handbook of Qualitative Research*. London: Sage.

Denzin, N.K. and Lincoln, Y.S. (2000) *Handbook of Qualitative Research* (2nd Edition). Thousand Oaks, CA: Sage.

Fielding, N.G. and Fielding, J.L. (1986) *Linking Data*. London: Sage.

Glaser, B.G. (1992) *Emergence vs. Forcing Basics of Grounded Theory Analysis*. Mill Valley, CA: The Sociology Press.

Glaser, B.G. and Strauss, A.L. (1967) *The Discovery of Grounded Theory*. Chicago: Aldine.

Green, J. and Thorogood, N. (2004) *Qualitative Methods for Health Research*. London: Sage.

Hammersley and Atkinson (1983) *Ethnography Principles in Practice* (p. 199). London: Tavistock.

Lapsley, I. and Melia, K. (2001) 'Clinical Actions and Financial Constraints: The Limits to Rationing Intensive Care', *Sociology of Health and Illness*, 23(5): 729–46.

Lewsey, J., Murray, G.D., Leyland, A.H., and Boddy, F.A. (2001) 'Using Routine Data to Complement and Enhance the Results of Randomized Controlled Trials'. In Stevens, A., Abrams, K., Brazier, J., Fitzpatrick, R., and Lilford, R.(eds) *The Advanced Handbook of Methods in Evidence Based Healthcare* (pp.149–165). London: Sage.

Melia, K.M. (1996) 'Rediscovering Glaser', *Qualitative Health Research*, 6: 368–78.

Melia, K.M. (1997) 'Producing Plausible Stories'. In Miller, G. and Dingwall, R. (eds) *Context and Method in Qualitative Research* (pp. 26–36). London: Sage.

Melia, K.M. (2001) 'Ethical Issues and the Importance of Consensus for the Intensive Care Team', *Social Science and Medicine*, 53: 707–19.

Melia, K.M. (2004) *Health Care Ethics: Lessons from Intensive Care*. London: Sage.

Miller, G. and Fox, K.J. (1997) 'Building Bridges: The Possibility of Analytic Dialogue Between Ethnography, Conversation Analysis and Foucault'. In Silverman, D. (ed.) *Qualitative Research Theory, Method and Practice* (pp. 35–55). London: Sage.

Mills, C. Wright (1959, Pelican edition 1970) *The Sociological Imagination*. London: Pelican.

Murphy, E. and Dingwall, R. (2001) 'Qualitative Methods in Health Technology Assessment'. In Stevens, A., Abrams, K., Brazier, J., Fitzpatrick, R., and Lilford, R. (eds) *The Advanced Handbook of Evidence Based Healthcare*. London: Sage.

Murphy, E. and Dingwall, R. (2003) *Qualitative Methods and Health Policy Research*. New York: Aldine De Gruyter.

Richardson (1994) 'Writing – A Method of Inquiry'. In Denzin, N.K. and Lincoln, Y.S. (eds) *Handbook of Qualitative Research*. Sage: London.

Seale, C., Gobo, G., Gubrium, J., and Silverman, D. (2004) *Qualitative Research Practice*. London: Sage.

Shilts, R. (1987) *And the Band Played On*. London: Penguin.

Silverman, D. (1985) *Qualitative Method and Sociology*. London: Gower.

Silverman, D. (2006) *Interpreting Qualitative Data – Methods for Analysing Talk Text and Interaction* (3rd Edition). London: Sage.

Smith, M.V. (2008) 'Pain Experience and the Imagined Researcher', *Sociology of Health and Illness*, 30(7): 992–1006.

Stimson, G. and Webb, B. (1975) *Going to See the Doctor*. London: Routledge.

Strauss, A.L. and Corbin, J. (1994) 'Grounded Theory: an Overview'. In Denzin, N.K. and Lincoln, Y.S. (eds) *Handbook of Qualitative Research* (pp. 273–85). London: Sage.

Trow, M. (1957) 'Comment on Participant Observation and Interviewing a Comparison', *Human Organization*, 16(3): 33–5.

Vidich, A.J. and Lyman, S.M. (1994) 'Qualitative Methods Their History in Sociology and Anthropology'. In Denzin, N.K. and Lincoln, Y.S. (eds) *Handbook of Qualitative Research*. London: Sage.

Webb, E.J., Campbell, D.T., Schwartz, R.D., and Sechrest, L. (1966) *Unobtrusive Measures*: *Nonreactive Research in the Social Sciences*. Chicago, IL: Rand McNally.

Whyte, W.F. (1955) *Street Corner Society: The Social Structure of an Italian Slum* (2nd Edition). Chicago: University of Chicago Press.

29

Mixed Methods Involving Qualitative Research

Alicia O'Cathain

INTRODUCTION

Mixed methods research has been discussed in social research for many years (Brannen, 1992b; Bryman, 1988; Sieber, 1973), but there has recently been renewed interest (Bryman, 2006a; Creswell and Plano-Clark, 2007; Tashakkori and Teddlie, 2003). Health researchers have contributed to these methodological discussions with input from a range of specialisms, including qualitative research (Morgan, 1998; Morse, 1991; 2005), nursing research (Sandelowski, 2000; Wendler, 2001), public health (Baum, 1995), health promotion and education (Milburn et al., 1995; Steckler et al., 1992) and health services research (Adamson, 2005; Barbour, 1999; Johnstone, 2004; O'Cathain and Thomas, 2006).

Mixed methods research is defined as 'integrating quantitative and qualitative data collection and analysis in a single study or a program of inquiry' (Creswell et al., 2004). Bryman (1992) distinguishes between integrating research, where two methods produce two sets of data, and integrating data, where a single method produces both quantitative and qualitative data. For example, Bryman would not consider a survey with closed and open-ended questions to be a genuine combination of quantitative and qualitative research, because it does not reflect the strengths of the different methods (Bryman, 1992).

In this chapter, the first issue considered is the debate about whether researchers can combine qualitative and quantitative methods. I then examine why health researchers undertake mixed methods research, the ways in which methods can be combined, how such studies can be written up, and how their quality can be assessed. Finally, I consider future directions for mixed methods research in health, picking up on some issues which can have a significant effect on research but that tend not to receive much attention in the literature. The chapter is shaped by my background as a health services researcher in the United Kingdom where quantitative research has historically been dominant.

CAN QUALITATIVE AND QUANTITATIVE RESEARCH BE COMBINED?

There is a well-established argument concerning the incommensurability of qualitative and quantitative research – that quantitative methods are associated with positivism and qualitative methods with interpretivism, so that it is not possible to combine paradigms and, by association, methods (Smith and Heshusius, 1986). Bryman (1988) took issue with this position, objecting that qualitative and quantitative methods are not exclusively associated with different philosophical paradigms. It is, then, possible to combine them. Researchers associated with the incommensurability position have come to agree: they have recently claimed that their view that *philosophical* paradigms are incommensurable has been misinterpreted as implying that *methods* are incommensurable. They claim that mixed methods research *within* paradigms has always been acceptable, and are now even willing to accept that some of the range of current paradigms may be commensurable (Guba and Lincoln, 2005).

Concerns about paradigm incommensurability can result in researchers struggling to find a philosophical stance when undertaking mixed methods research. One solution is simply to ignore the problem and adopt a pragmatic approach, using whatever seems to work in relation to any particular research question (Bryman, 2006b; O'Cathain et al., 2007b). This should not be confused with adopting a pragmatist approach, based on traditions in American philosophy that have provided a basis for a number of social constructionist paradigms in social science (Morgan, 2007). Pragmatic health researchers tend to be relatively indifferent to questions of ontology and epistemology. However, these cannot ultimately be avoided if researchers are to develop plausible arguments to justify how they can claim to know what they claim to know. In recent years, a variant on classic pragmatism – 'subtle realism' – has become increasingly influential. Subtle realism acknowledges that there is an external reality but that we can only ever know this through human observations that are unavoidably partial and uncertain. This means that any knowledge claims are also necessarily uncertain and that there is a possibility of multiple noncompeting views of any aspect of the social world that is being studied (Hammersley, 1992). Subtle realism can accommodate both qualitative and quantitative methods, requiring a reflexive approach to both components in a study. Alternatively, researchers can choose to adopt different paradigms for different components within a study and use the resulting tensions as an opportunity to better understand the phenomenon being researched (Greene and Caracelli, 2003). This may be challenging for the individual mixed methods researcher as they shift between different value sets, and for researchers working in teams who may find that their colleagues have different beliefs and values about the meaning of research and how best to undertake it.

WHY DO HEALTH RESEARCHERS UNDERTAKE MIXED METHODS RESEARCH?

Researchers who believe that it is possible to combine qualitative and quantitative methods offer a range of justifications for using mixed methods research (O'Cathain and Thomas, 2006). A key justification is that of *comprehensiveness*, where using both qualitative and quantitative methods allows an issue to be addressed more widely and more completely because of the strengths of different methods (Morse, 2003). Comprehensiveness is a common justification for using mixed methods within health research, because researchers consider that the complexity of health, health care, and the environment in which health research is undertaken, requires the use of both qualitative and quantitative methods (O'Cathain et al., 2007b). An example might be an ethnographic study undertaken alongside a randomized controlled trial when investigating the use of evidence-based leaflets for promoting informed choice in maternity care – the randomized controlled trial was undertaken to measure the effectiveness of the intervention in delivering informed choice (O'Cathain et al., 2002) and the ethnographic study was undertaken to gain a better understanding of the practice of informed choice and the way in which the intervention was delivered in the real world (Stapleton et al., 2002). Another example is an interview survey of 400 adults who were asked to keep diaries of their health problems and health care seeking behaviour, followed by in-depth interviews with deviant cases from the survey analysis to explore patterns of use of primary care (Rogers and Nicolaas, 1998). The authors discuss how the mixed methods approach gave a broader understanding of the dynamics of health care use, with the survey showing the extent to which people used self care in relation to primary care services, while the qualitative component illuminated the ways in which past experience and domestic context affected decision making (Rogers and Nicolaas, 1998).

A second justification is that mixed methods research can increase *confidence* in findings when the results from two different methods agree, thereby increasing validity (Glik et al., 1986). The term 'triangulation' is often applied in this context but researchers have expressed concerns about the confusion that can result because this term can also be used to describe the process of comparing findings from different methods in order to explore different perspectives of a phenomenon, that is, with a meaning of *comprehensiveness* (Sandelowski, 1995). For this reason, I will avoid the use of the term altogether within this chapter. Returning to the combination of qualitative and quantitative methods to seek convergence of findings, this justification has been much discussed in the literature on mixed methods research, but has also been heavily criticized. Barbour (1999) and Murphy et al. (1998) discuss these criticisms in the context of health research, including concerns that convergence may be present due to shared bias between methods, and the difficulty of determining which method has given the 'right answer' if they disagree. There is little evidence that this justification is used for combining methods in health services research (O'Cathain et al., 2007b).

A third justification is *development* or *facilitation*, where one method guides the sampling, data collection or analysis of the other (Sandelowski, 2000). An example of this is a postal survey of 800 women with heavy periods followed by in-depth interviews with 32 of the survey respondents to explore women's management of menstrual symptoms, where the survey was used to facilitate sampling for the qualitative component of the study (Santer et al., 2008).

Finally, mixed methods research may be used for the purpose of *emancipation*, where the use of a variety of methods ensures that marginalized voices are heard (Mertens, 2003). This justification may be particularly pertinent to researchers in health promotion, or to those undertaking action research. Health services researchers who tend not to use mixed methods research with this intent have nonetheless noted the power of qualitative research to bring the voice of the patient and health professional into a research study (O'Cathain et al., 2007b).

When mixed methods research is used for comprehensiveness, one could argue that the qualitative and quantitative components could be undertaken independently by different research teams rather than within the same study. In the example of the leaflets in maternity care, the randomized controlled trial could have been undertaken in different maternity units at a different time by different researchers than the ethnographic study. Researchers may undertake the qualitative and quantitative components together, because it seems more convenient or efficient to do so, or because they believe that mixed methods studies can produce more knowledge than two independent qualitative and quantitative studies, that is, 'a whole greater than the sum of the parts' (Barbour, 1999; Teddlie and Tashakkori, 2003). This extra knowledge or insight has been termed 'yield', and researchers have been challenged to show what mixed methods research contributes over and above the knowledge that might be gained from undertaking a qualitative study and a quantitative study independently (O'Cathain et al., 2007a).

The motivations for adopting a mixed methods approach may not always be based on the intrinsic value of mixed methods research for addressing a research question: they may also be strategic (Bryman, 2007; O'Cathain et al., 2007b). Researchers may combine methods to increase their chances of funding, or to facilitate dissemination of their research. They may also be driven by a belief that this approach is inherently A Good Thing. Researchers may, however, find themselves floundering if they have not thought through exactly why this approach is appropriate to their research question.

TYPES OF MIXED METHODS STUDIES

Having considered why health researchers might combine qualitative and quantitative methods within a study, I now turn to the different types of mixed methods studies that can be undertaken. Much attention has been paid to developing typologies of mixed methods designs (Creswell et al., 2003; Tashakkori and Teddlie, 1998), including their use in health research (Morgan, 1998). Morgan describes four designs based on the dominance of either the qualitative or quantitative component, with the assumption that methods will be undertaken in sequence, for example 'quantitative preliminary' and 'qualitative follow-up'. Such typologies are useful for introducing researchers to the range of designs available for use, and have been summarized and discussed elsewhere (Creswell and Plano-Clark, 2007). There is, however, no dominant model, and a typology's relevance may depend on the research objective – for example, a number of typologies exist for evaluation. Rather than discussing any one typology in detail, it seems more useful to consider key aspects of mixed method study design, including the purpose of combining methods (Greene et al., 1989), the priority and sequence of mixing (Morgan, 1998), and the integration between methods (Sandelowski, 2000).

Purpose of combining methods

Greene et al. (1989) describe a number of reasons why methods might be combined. These resemble the justifications for undertaking mixed methods research outlined earlier: *complementarity* where two methods are used to assess different aspects of a research question and the findings from one method used to elaborate or explain the findings of the other method; *confirmation* where the findings from two different methods are compared and agreement is sought; and *development* where one method is used explicitly to assist another. Two methods may be combined with more than one purpose in mind, particularly to achieve both complementarity and development.

Priority and sequence of methods

The priority and sequence of methods can be used to distinguish different mixed methods designs (Morgan, 1998). Priority denotes whether one method is dominant, in terms of being the main focus of the study. An example of a 'quantitative dominant' approach is where qualitative interviews or focus groups are undertaken prior to a survey to generate items and language for the structured questionnaire; the qualitative component is considered to be a means of ensuring that the questionnaire is both relevant and comprehensible to potential respondents. An example of a 'qualitative dominant' approach is a survey undertaken prior to in-depth case studies or interviews to identify context and a sampling frame for the qualitative component. These 'dominant' designs can be undertaken in such a way that they really fall outside the definition of mixed methods research, which requires recognition of both qualitative and quantitative methods. A subordinate qualitative component may not be formally analyzed and reported but used merely to offer a few illustrative quotes to a survey, or a subordinate survey used to support sampling for a qualitative component may pay little attention to strict probability criteria. We also find equal partnerships, where each method contributes to knowledge development in its own right rather than one method simply facilitating the other. The examples of 'survey and interview' combinations introduced earlier in the chapter represent this latter type (Rogers and Nicolaas, 1998; Santer et al., 2008). Even though the quantitative component produced a sampling frame for the qualitative component, a sophisticated analysis of both components was reported (Rogers and Nicolaas, 1998).

Methods can be undertaken sequentially, concurrently, or iteratively. Morgan's typology is limited to sequential designs. The strength of this approach is that researchers build into their design the impact of one method on another: for example, interviews with survey respondents might help to explain surprising survey results. Concurrent designs are frequently used in health research (O'Cathain et al., 2007b). These can be more problematic when it comes to integration between methods, because this is not explicitly built into the design. In iterative designs, a qualitative method might be undertaken first to generate hypotheses, which are then tested using a quantitative method, with any unusual findings from the quantitative method followed up in further qualitative investigation.

Integration

Finally, researchers need to consider when and how links will be made between methods within a study (Sandelowski, 2000). As discussed in the foregoing section, this may be built in to some designs more than others, particularly sequential designs. A common approach to integration is to bring the findings from both methods together, comparing and contrasting them to see if further understanding can be gained. Not *a priori* assumption of convergence is needed when doing this, and apparent contradictions between findings – called 'inter-method discrepancy' – may lead to further valuable insights about the issue under study (Fielding and Fielding, 1986). Alternatively, integration can happen earlier in a study, where the findings of one method affect how the other method is analyzed. For example, a typology might be identified in the qualitative component which can then be used within the analysis of the quantitative data. There is also scope for the raw data from the qualitative and quantitative components to be brought together during analysis. For example, the questionnaire and interview transcript for an individual can be compared to identify patterns that can then be traced through other cases included in both the qualitative and quantitative components of a study. This may involve 'quantitizing' qualitative data, that is, assigning codes to the presence and absence of themes within individual cases

(Sandelowski, 2000). Matrices have been promoted as a way of displaying qualitative and quantitative data on the same cases in mixed methods studies (Creswell and Plano-Clark, 2007; Wendler, 2001). Integration can also take place at the sampling stage of a study, where key variables in a survey, or the findings of the survey analysis, are used to identify people for qualitative interviews or case studies.

While integration is a key aspect of mixed methods research (Creswell et al., 2004), its absence has been noted in mixed methods studies within UK health services research (O'Cathain et al., 2007a). Bryman (2007) considered the barriers to integration in mixed methods studies in UK social research, noting the differing timelines of methods, and the skills and preferences of researchers. Although there are barriers to integration, researchers need to address these if the potential of mixed methods is to be fully exploited.

Contexts

Some design types are more likely to be used in some contexts than others are. Three contexts are relevant to health research. First, the exploration of health issues using a combination of survey and fieldwork. This combination is commonly used in social research (Bryman, 2006a) and will often involve a sequential design. Second, the development of standardized instruments to measure health status and patient satisfaction. Researchers tend to use focus groups or interviews with patients to generate items for inclusion in a new measure, using a sequential quantitative dominant design. However, some researchers exploit the strength of the qualitative component by undertaking a full and sophisticated qualitative analysis to understand the underlying concepts of the health issue under study. When developing an instrument to measure patients' views of the interface between primary and secondary care, the qualitative research identified the sense of being 'left in limbo' underlying this experience of health care use (Preston et al., 1999). Third, mixed methods research has been used extensively in the context of evaluation (Greene et al., 1989; McConney et al., 2002), including evaluation of health technologies (Murphy et al., 1998) and complex interventions. Quantitative dominant designs have been promoted, with randomized controlled trials as the priority component, and qualitative research employed to better understand how the intervention might work, improve how the intervention is delivered in practice during the early phases of research, and explore how it is used in the real world (Campbell et al., 2007). Concurrent designs are common in evaluation, with qualitative methods used within a process evaluation undertaken alongside an experimental design such as a randomized controlled trial, or controlled before and after study, to study how an intervention works in the real world (Oakley et al., 2006). An excellent example of this is a qualitative study undertaken concurrently with a pilot trial which helped to optimize an intervention to support people with a diagnosis of myocardial infarction or angina (Bradley et al., 1999).

REPORTING MIXED METHODS RESEARCH

Once researchers have designed and implemented their mixed methods research, they need to consider how to report it. This can be a challenging aspect of mixed methods research (Bryman, 2006a; Johnstone, 2004; Sandelowski, 2003) in the context of writing final reports for funding bodies, books, dissertations, theses, and peer-reviewed journal articles. Researchers can struggle with the order of presentation of different methods, the voice to use throughout the report, and the format of presentation (O'Cathain, 2009).

The order of presentation, in terms of whether researchers report the qualitative or quantitative research first, may be dictated by the order in which methods are undertaken in sequential mixed methods designs. Methods undertaken concurrently present more of a challenge. In this case, the order may depend on the story the researchers wish to present, and, indeed, this may also be the case for sequential studies because of the nonsequential interplay between sampling, data collection, analysis, and write up of different study components.

Qualitative research can be reported using the first person whereas it is usual to report quantitative research in the third person. Therefore, researchers may face a quandary about the voice to use in a mixed methods study (Johnstone, 2004; Sandelowski, 2003). They might choose a single voice associated with the dominant component of their study, their philosophical stance, or the voice most accepted within their research community. An alternative approach is to use two voices – the first person for the qualitative and the third person for the quantitative method. This will still leave the researcher with a decision to be made about the voice of the joint or integrated parts, such as the introduction and discussion of a report.

Finally, researchers can choose to take either a segregated or integrated approach to reporting their study (O'Cathain, 2009). The former approach is where the methods, results, and sometimes the discussion, are reported separately for each component. The latter is where the qualitative and quantitative methods are reported in the same chapter; results are reported in chapters based on themes from the research and each theme draws on the findings of both the qualitative and quantitative research; and the study findings are discussed as a whole in the final discussion chapter. Santer et al. (2008) take an integrated approach to reporting their mixed methods study in a journal article. A segregated approach to reporting studies may be easier for the researcher but an integrated approach allows for explicit attention to the overall design of a study as well as the individual methods, and may encourage integration between data and findings from different methods.

Peer reviewed journal articles

It is worth paying special attention to peer-reviewed journal articles because of the added challenge of word limits. Journal editors have recently considered how researchers can publish mixed methods studies in peer reviewed journals (Creswell and Tashakkori, 2007a; Stange et al., 2006). Researchers can attempt to publish all or some part of their study in a mixed methods article which reports the methods and results of both the qualitative and quantitative research. Bryman (2006a) found over 200 mixed methods articles in social research, a number in health journals. Creswell and Tashakkori (2007a) offer advice on how best to construct such articles if researchers wish to contribute to the development of mixed methodology as well as report the substantive findings of their study.

Not all mixed methods studies are published as mixed methods articles. Stange et al. (2006) detail the range of approaches available to researchers. One approach is to publish the qualitative component of a study in one article and the quantitative component in another (Stange et al., 2006). These can be reported side by side in the same journal (O'Cathain et al., 2002; Stapleton et al., 2002) offering the reader of the hard copy of the journal the chance to consider two pieces of a jigsaw together. Studies can also be broken up into methodological pieces and each piece can be published in different journals at different times. If these sets of papers make no reference to each other then they appear to have emerged from a number of mono-method studies (O'Cathain et al., 2007a). Separate publications of different study components can be used to great effect if the study component addressed in one paper explicitly considers the influence on context, analysis, or interpretation of the component described in another paper. Unfortunately, it may also be the case that some components of a study are never published (O'Cathain et al., 2007a), leaving mixed methods studies less than the sum of their parts.

ASSESSING QUALITY

Once a study has been reported, commissioners, users of research and researchers themselves, need to judge whether a mixed methods study has been undertaken well or poorly. The quality of mixed methods research has been given some consideration (Caracelli and Riggin, 1994; Dellinger and Leech, 2007; O'Cathain et al., 2008a; Sale and Brazil, 2004), but there are no agreed assessment criteria (Creswell and Plano-Clark, 2007).

Researchers have attempted to develop quality criteria for mixed methods studies by devising separate lists for the quantitative and the qualitative elements (Sale and Brazil, 2004). Their assumption is that methods are linked to paradigms so that the criteria used to assess different methods should also be linked to paradigms. Criteria for qualitative research address the goals of credibility, transferability, and dependability; those for quantitative research address internal validity, external validity, and reliability. However, not everyone agrees that different criteria are needed for qualitative and quantitative research. The same criteria of validity and relevance are appropriate for both, although the means for judging against these criteria may differ because of the research practices employed in different methodological approaches (Murphy et al., 1998).

This 'individual methods' approach is very useful, but it ignores the fact that within a mixed methods study, consideration need also be given to the design, integration between methods, and overall inferences. A mixed methods design may not be appropriate for the research question in hand, or may be undertaken in a way which invalidates a key aspect of the design. Attempts have been made to develop quality criteria which address the whole mixed methods study rather than simply the individual methods. Caracelli and Riggin (1994) consider a range of issues relevant to combining methods, for example whether data transformations are defensible, contradictory findings are explained, and convergent findings are not related to shared bias between methods (Caracelli and Riggin, 1994). Teddlie and Tashakkori (2009) introduce new terms to help researchers consider the 'inference quality' of the whole study: 'data quality' for the degree to which the most appropriate procedures have been used to address the research question and 'interpretive rigour' for the degree to which credible interpretations have been made of the study results. Dellinger and Leech (2007) focus on the validity of a mixed methods study by presenting the 'validation framework' which includes the quality of the overall design, the validity of different aspects of the design such as how 'sampling integration' was undertaken, and the rigour of interpretation of the findings.

Discussions on how to assess the quality of mixed methods studies are continuing. Quality criteria may depend on researchers' philosophical and political paradigms, and on the type of mixed methods study (Bryman, 2006b). It is unlikely that any one set of criteria will suit all researchers or studies. An attempt has been made to devise a set of 'quality questions' about mixed methods research in one specialism of health research and apply them to the proposals and reports of 75 studies (O'Cathain et al., 2008a). The quality questions addressed whether a study had been completed successfully, and the quality of the individual components, the design, the integration and the inferences. The conclusions were that this particular health research community could improve their mixed methods studies by giving more consideration to describing and justifying the design, being transparent about the qualitative component, and attempting more integration between data and findings from the individual components.

FUTURE DIRECTIONS

It is likely that there will be increasing use of mixed methods research over coming years, and that more attention will be paid to the methodology of this approach. There is scope for further development of techniques to facilitate integration between methods, and exploration of the meaning of the quality of mixed methods research. There are also issues which tend to receive little attention in the literature on mixed methods research and which deserve consideration in the future.

Training in mixed methods research

Working between qualitative and quantitative data sets requires particular skills, an understanding of the techniques which can facilitate this process, and the epistemological considerations involved (Mason, 1994). Yet, how many researchers have learnt about how to combine methods in either their undergraduate or postgraduate training? If mixed methods research is to be undertaken well, then training early career researchers must be a priority. It is essential that postgraduate courses in research methods explicitly address mixed methodology, and consider innovative ways of doing so (Onwuegbuzie and Leech, 2005).

Interdisciplinary team working

A single researcher may undertake both the qualitative and quantitative methods in a study. In larger studies, it will more likely be a team effort. Teams may be made up of qualitative researchers only, who conduct the quantitative as well as the qualitative component (Brannen, 1992a). Alternatively, there may be researchers from different disciplines, each providing a component of the study. Qualitative researchers may find themselves working on teams where they are the only qualitative researcher, or they are part of a group of qualitative researchers on a larger team. The way in which qualitative and quantitative researchers work together within a team can affect the level of integration which occurs within a study (O'Cathain et al., 2008b). In future, more consideration needs to be given to developing researchers' understanding of team dynamics and their respect for different methodologies, and to training principal investigators to be willing and able to promote integration within a mixed methods study.

SUMMARY AND CONCLUSION

Mixed methods research is commonly used in health research to offer a more comprehensive understanding of a health issue. A range of mixed methods designs are useful within health research and progress is being made on understanding how these types of studies can be reported and their quality assessed. Future challenges require more attention to be paid to training health researchers in mixed methods research, acknowledging the importance of team dynamics on research outputs, and keeping up with the rapidly expanding methodological developments in this area.

REFERENCES

Adamson, J. (2005) 'Combined Qualitative and Quantitative Designs'. In Bowling, A. and Ebrahim, S. (eds) *Handbook of Health Research Methods: Investigation, Measurement and Analysis.* Berkshire: Open University Press.

Barbour, R.S. (1999) 'The Case for Combining Qualitative and Quantitative Approaches in Health Services Research', *Journal of Health Services Research and Policy*, 4(1): 39–43.

Baum, F. (1995) 'Researching Public Health: Behind the Qualitative–Quantitative Methodological Debate', *Social Science and Medicine*, 40(4): 459–68.

Bradley, F., Wiles, R., Kinmonth, A.-L., Mant, D., and Gantley, M. (1999) 'Development and Evaluation of Complex Interventions in Health Services Research: Case Study of the Southampton Heart Integrated Care Project (SHIP)', *British Medical Journal*, 318: 711–5.

Brannen, J. (1992a) 'Combining Qualitative and Quantitative Approaches: An Overview'. In Brannen, J. (ed.) *Mixing Methods: Qualitative and Quantitative Research*. Aldershot: Ashgate.

Brannen, J. (ed.) (1992b) *Mixing Methods: Qualitative and Quantitative Research*. Aldershot: Ashgate.

Bryman, A. (1988) *Quantity and Quality in Social Research*. London: Routledge.

Bryman, A. (1992) 'Quantitative and Qualitative Research: Further Reflections on Their Integration'. In Brannen, J. (ed.) *Mixing Methods: Qualitative and Quantitative Research*. Aldershot: Ashgate.

Bryman, A. (2006a) 'Integrating Quantitative and Qualitative Research: How Is It Done?' *Qualitative Research*, 6: 97–113.

Bryman, A. (2006b) 'Paradigm Peace and the Implications for Quality', *International Journal of Social Research Methodology*, 9: 111–26.

Bryman, A. (2007) 'Barriers to Integrating Quantitative and Qualitative Research', *Journal of Mixed Methods Research*, 1(1): 8–22.

Campbell, N., Murray, E., Darbyshire, J., Emery, J., Farmer, A., Griffiths, F., Guthrie, B., Lester, H., Wilson, P., and Kinmonth, A.L. (2007) 'Designing and Evaluating Complex Interventions to Improve Health Care', *BMJ*, 334: 455–9.

Caracelli, V.J. and Riggin, L.J.C. (1994) 'Mixed-Method Evaluation: Developing Quality Criteria Through Concept Mapping', *Evaluation Practice*, 15(2): 139–52.

Creswell, J.W. and Plano-Clark, V. (2007) *Designing and Conducting Mixed Methods Research*. Thousand Oaks, CA: Sage.

Creswell, J.W. and Tashakkori, A. (2007a) 'Developing Publishable Mixed Methods Manuscripts', *Journal of Mixed Methods Research*, 1(2): 107–11.

Creswell, J.W., Fetters, M.D., and Ivankova, N.V. (2004) 'Designing a Mixed Methods Study in Primary Care', *Annals of Family Medicine*, 2(1): 7–12.

Creswell, J.W., Clark, V.L.P., Gutmann, M.L., and Hanson, W.E. (2003) 'Advanced Mixed Methods Research Designs'. In Tashakkori, A. and Teddlie, C. (eds) *Handbook of Mixed Methods in Social and Behavioural Research*. London: Sage.

Dellinger, A.B. and Leech, N.L. (2007), 'Toward a Unified Validation Framework in Mixed Methods Research', *Journal of Mixed Methods Research*, 1(4): 309–32.

Fielding, N.G. and Fielding, J.L. (1986) *Linking Data*. London: Sage.

Glik, D.C., Parker, K., Muligande, G., and Hategikamana, B. (1986) 'Integrating Qualitative and Quantitative Survey Techniques', *International Quarterly of Community Health Education*, 7(3): 181–200.

Greene, J.C. and Caracelli, V.J. (2003) 'Making Paradigmatic Sense of Mixed Methods Practice'. In Tashakkori, A. and Teddlie, C. (eds) *Handbook of Mixed Methods in Social and Behavioural Research*. London: Sage.

Greene, J.C., Caracelli, V.J., and Graham, W.F. (1989) 'Toward a Conceptual Framework for Mixed-Method Evaluation Designs', *Educational Evaluation and Policy Analysis*, 11(3): 255–74.

Guba, E.G. and Lincoln, Y.S. (2005) 'Paradigmatic Controversies, Contradictions, and Emerging Confluences'. In Denzin, N.K. and Lincoln, Y.S. (eds) *The SAGE Handbook of Qualitative Research* (3rd Edition). London: Sage.

Hammersley, M. (1992) *What's Wrong with Ethnography?* London: Routledge.

Johnstone, P.L. (2004) 'Mixed Methods, Mixed Methodology Health Services Research in Practice', *Qualitative Health Research*, 14(2): 259–71.

Mason, J. (1994) 'Linking Qualitative and Quantitative Data Analysis'. In Bryman, A. and Burgess, R.G. (eds) *Analysing Qualitative Data*. London: Routledge.

McConney, A., Rudd, A., and Ayres, R. (2002) 'Getting to the Bottom Line: A Method for Synthesizing Findings within Mixed-Method Program Evaluations', *American Journal of Evaluation*, 23(2): 121–40.

Mertens, D.M. (2003) 'Mixed Methods and the Politics of Human Research: The Transformative–Emancipatory Perspective'. In Tashakkori, A. and Teddlie, C. (eds) *Handbook of Mixed Methods in Social and Behavioural Research*. London: Sage.

Milburn, K., Fraser, E., Secker, J., and Pavis, S. (1995) 'Combining Methods in Health Promotion Research: Some Considerations About Appropriate Use', *Health Education Quarterly*, 54: 347–56.

Morgan, D.L. (1998) 'Practical Strategies for Combining Qualitative and Quantitative Methods: Applications to Health Research', *Qualitative Health Research*, 8(3): 362–76.

Morgan, D.L. (2007) 'Paradigms Lost and Pragmatism Regained: Methodological Implications of Combining Qualitative and Quantitative Methods', *Journal of Mixed Methods Research*, 1(1): 48–76.

Morse, J. (1991) 'Approaches to Qualitative–Quantitative Methodological Triangulation', *Nursing Research*, 40(2): 120–3.

Morse, J. (2005) 'Evolving Trends in Qualitative Research: Advances in Mixed-Method Design', *Qualitative Health Research*, 15(5): 583–5.

Morse, J.M. (2003) 'Principles of Mixed Methods and Multimethod Research Design'. In Tashakkori, A. and Teddlie, C. (eds) *Handbook of Mixed Methods in Social and Behavioural Research*. London: Sage.

Murphy, E., Dingwall, R., Greatbatch, D., Parker, S., and Watson, P. (1998) 'Qualitative Research Methods in Health Technology Assessment: A Review of the Literature', *Health Technology Assessment*, 2(16).

O'Cathain, A. (2009) 'Reporting Results'. In Andrew, S. and Halcomb, E. (eds) *Mixed Methods Research for Nursing and the Health Sciences*. Oxford: Blackwell Publishing.

O'Cathain, A., Murphy, E., and Nicholl, J. (2007a) 'Integration and Publications as Indicators of "Yield" from Mixed Methods Studies', *Journal of Mixed Methods Research*, 1(2): 147–63.

O'Cathain, A., Murphy, E., and Nicholl, J. (2007b) 'Why, and How, Mixed Methods Research Is Undertaken in Health Services Research: A Mixed Methods Study', *BMC Health Services Research*, 7: 85.

O'Cathain, A., Murphy, E., and Nicholl, J. (2008a) 'The Quality of Mixed Methods Studies in Health Services Research', *Journal of Health Services Research and Policy*, 13(2): 92–8.

O'Cathain, A., Murphy, E., and Nicholl, J. (2008b) 'Multidisciplinary, Interdisciplinary or Dysfunctional? Team Working in Mixed Methods Research', *Qualitative Health Research*, 18(11): 1574–85.

O'Cathain, A. and Thomas, K. (2006) 'Combining Qualitative and Quantitative Methods'. In Pope, C. and Mays, N. (eds) *Qualitative Research in Health Care* (3rd Edition). Oxford: Blackwell Publishing.

O'Cathain, A., Walters, S.J., Nicholl, J.P., Thomas, K.J., and Kirkham, M. (2002) 'Use of Evidence Based Leaflets to Promote Informed Choice in Maternity Care: Randomized Controlled Trial in Everyday Practice', *BMJ*, 324: 643–6.

Oakley, A., Strange, V., Bonell, C., Allen, E., Stephenson, J., and Team, R.S. (2006) 'Process Evaluation in Randomized Controlled Trials of Complex Interventions', *BMJ*, 332: 413–6.

Onwuegbuzie, A.J. and Leech, N.L. (2005) 'Taking the "Q" Out of Research: Teaching Research Methodology Courses Without the Divide Between Quantitative and Qualitative Paradigms', *Quality and Quantity*, 39: 267–96.

Preston, C., Cheater, F., Baker, R., and Hearnshaw, H. (1999) 'Left in Limbo: Patients' Views on Care Across the Primary/Secondary Interface', *Quality in Health Care*, 8(1): 16–21.

Rogers, A. and Nicolaas, G. (1998) 'Understanding the Patterns and Processes of Primary Care Use: A Combined Quantitative and Qualitative Approach', *Sociological Research Online*, 3(4), http://www.socresonline.org.uk/3/4/5.html

Sale, J.E.M. and Brazil, K. (2004) 'A Strategy to Identify Critical Appraisal Criteria for Primary Mixed Method Studies', *Quality and Quantity*, 38(4): 351–65.

Sandelowski, M. (1995) 'Triangles and Crystals: On the Geometry of Qualitative Research', *Research in Nursing and Health*, 18: 569–74.

Sandelowski, M. (2000) 'Combining Qualitative and Quantitative Sampling, Data Collection, and Analysis Techniques in Mixed-Method Studies', *Research in Nursing and Health*, 23: 246–55.

Sandelowski, M. (2003) 'Tables or Tableaux? The Challenges of Writing and Reading Mixed Methods Studies'. In Tashakkori, A. and Teddlie, C. (eds) *Handbook of Mixed Methods in Social and Behavioural Research*. London: Sage.

Santer, M., Wyke, S., and Warner, P. (2008) 'Women's Management of Menstrual Symptoms: Findings from a Postal Survey and Qualitative Interviews', *Social Science and Medicine*, 66: 276–88.

Sieber, S.D. (1973) 'The Integration of Fieldwork and Survey Methods', *The American Journal of Sociology*, 78(6): 1335–59.

Smith, J.K. and Heshusius, L. (1986) 'Closing Down the Conversation: The End of the Quantitative-Qualitative Debate Among Educational Researchers', *Educational Researcher*, 15(4): 4–12.

Stange, K.C., Crabtree, B.F., and Miller, W.L. (2006) 'Publishing Multimethod Research', *Annals of Family Medicine*, 4(4): 292–4.

Stapleton, H., Kirkham, M., and Thomas, G. (2002) 'Qualitative Study of Evidence Based Leaflets in Maternity Care', *BMJ*, 324: 639–43.

Steckler, A., Mcleroy, K.R., Goodman, R.M., Bird, S.T., and McCormick, L. (1992) 'Toward Integrating Qualitative and Quantitative Methods: An Introduction', *Health Education Quarterly*, 19(1): 1–8.

Tashakkori, A. and Teddlie, C. (1998) *Mixed Methodology: Combining Qualitative and Quantitative Approaches*. London: Sage.

Tashakkori, A. and Teddlie, C. (eds) (2003) *Handbook of Mixed Methods in Social and Behavioural Research*. London: Sage.

Teddlie, C. and Tashakkori, A. (2003) 'Major Issues and Controversies in the Use of Mixed Methods in the Social and Behavioural Sciences'. In Tashakkori, A. and Teddlie, C. (eds) *Handbook of Mixed Methods in Social and Behavioural Research*. London: Sage.

Teddlie, C. and Tashakkori, A. (2009) *Foundations of Mixed Methods Research*. London: Sage.

Wendler, M.C. (2001) 'Triangulation Using a Meta-Matrix', *Journal of Advanced Nursing*, 35(4): 521–5.

30

A Practical Guide to Research Ethics

Laura Stark and Adam Hedgecoe

INTRODUCTION

How should researchers treat their study participants? This chapter is intended for qualitative health researchers trying to answer this question as they head into the field. We start the chapter (Section I) by naming and explaining key practical problems that qualitative health researchers have faced in the past, in order to attune researchers to potential trouble spots for their own studies, and to point to models for managing them. Today, the issue of research ethics demands dedicated readings like this one, because most qualitative studies are now required by state regulation to be formally approved in advance. Consequently, we describe in Section II ways to accommodate researchers' personal sensibilities about the distinctive needs of their study participants, while at the same time satisfying 'human subjects' regulations efficiently. Our focus is on how successfully to fulfil two particular regulatory demands: getting people's 'informed consent' to participate in a study, and getting prior approval from an ethics review committee. In this section, we draw on our own research to provide a brief background on ethics committees in the United States (commonly called Institutional Review Boards, or IRBs) and in the United Kingdom (commonly called Research Ethics Committees, or RECs). We explain *what* ethics review boards do in practice, and *why* qualitative researchers are bound by them. In so doing, our goal is to clarify the underlying logic of our advice for working with them – which we hope not only justifies our specific suggestions, but also provides useful guidance when researchers find themselves improvising in new regulatory situations.

In the spirit of a practical guide, we have made a few organizational choices that merit note: we address specific problems and strategies for the majority of the chapter, and bring in broader reflections in final Concluding Remarks; we highlight the distinctive troubles facing *health* researchers, in particular, who use qualitative methods; and finally, we do not engage the normative debates over whether qualitative researchers ought to be regulated. We expect that some researchers will feel agitated or indignant reading the strategy section, because human subjects regulations, some have argued, embed unfair assumptions about the hierarchical nature of research relationships (e.g., that researchers impose their will on participants; that the state legitimately dominates professions. For a primer on these issues, see Jacobson et al., 2007). We take as our starting point the observation that much of our research is now bound by government regulation, and the belief that learning from other researchers can ease the way into the field.

COMMON PROBLEMS, PRACTICAL SOLUTIONS

In this section, we survey key ethics problems for qualitative health researchers. We focus first on issues generated by the *place* of qualitative health research including health care settings, cross-cultural field sites, and cyberspace. For qualitative health studies in particular, the place of research is especially salient, because we often work in settings where ethics standards for other research methods (e.g., randomized controlled trials) are well established and used by default. Whereas state-mandated regulations tend to bind physical locations (such as hospitals, universities, or geographic areas), professional ethics are generally thought to adhere to individuals as they move in and out of different places.

From the place of research, we turn to issues generated by the *timing* of research. Specifically, we overview the problems that qualitative health researchers can face before they head to the field, and the problems that commonly emerge after their data are collected.

ETHICS AND THE PLACE OF RESEARCH

Health care settings

The concept of 'therapeutic misconception' in clinical research refers to the finding that sick people often believe that their conditions will improve through their participation in studies (Applebaum et al., 1987). In the two decades since the phrase was coined, scholars and clinicians have developed a more respectful view of participants' clinical ideas than the term may connote (Kimmelman, 2007). Nonetheless, studies still show that some participants continue to believe that enrolling in research will aid their personal health even after researchers have tried to disabuse them of the idea.

The quandary surrounding participants' **therapeutic perceptions** of research is distinctively relevant for qualitative *health* researchers, because our studies often involve places, like clinics, in which participants can assume 'research' means clinical research, and practices, like asking questions, serve their health assessments and treatments. Ironically, there are excellent qualitative studies on the therapeutic misconception in clinical research, but few reflections on how the problem might infuse qualitative health research itself (Bosk, 2000, is a refreshing exception). Given that health researchers of all methodological persuasions want to be sensitive to how research can easily be conflated with medical care, qualitative health researchers might draw from the literature on clinical ethics when considering how best to communicate with their own research participants in health care settings (e.g., Molyneux et al., 2005). As a starting point, Sankar (2004) urges researchers to aspire not only to convey important content-based information, but also to ensure they are satisfied with the answer their participants might give to the classic 'framing' question: 'What is going on here?'

The concern with participants' **'institutional vulnerability'** (Andrews, 2006) refers to people's tendency to feel compelled to participate in research because of the settings in which they have been approached to enroll. This concept does not address participants' sense of hope, in other words, but their sense of obligation.

Originally used to refer to ethical tensions in US military research in Nepal (Andrews, 2006), institutional vulnerability may come into play whenever potential participants depend on the institution that is sponsoring or hosting the study for their income, protection, or well-being. Most research regulations include components designed to reduce the overt appearance of institution-based coercion for clearly demarcated groups (or 'vulnerable populations'): to research incarcerated people, for example, US regulations require that a prisoners' advocate approve the study. Qualitative health researchers, in particular, might be sensitive to the more subtle dynamics of institutional persuasion in their research when studying, for example, health care professionals (especially workers with relatively low institutional authority), or bounded groups that require consensus before research can go forward (such as patient support groups).

Although the concern that people may enrol in studies out of institutional obligation, rather than personal choice, itself raises questions of paternalism, researchers have developed useful practices to mitigate potential place-based coercion. Andrews, for example, urges both review boards and researchers to involve 'consultants' earlier and more deeply in research planning. On the model of the prisoner advocate, consultants would offer a third-party perspective on the host institution, the envisioned group of participants, and their sensibilities about the organizational setting in which they will be involved (whether a political jurisdiction, a corporate facility, or a charity group).

At the same time, qualitative research in paediatrics has shown that the physical design of buildings affects whether people are quite literally included or excluded from decision making (Alderson and Morrow, 2004; Heimer and Staffen, 1998). Alderson urges researchers to stay attentive to the 'ethics of space' in clinics (2007: 85).

Cross-cultural sites

The effects of globalization are apparent in the new sites of health research, as well as in the debates over research ethics in a global context. Three tensions in particular have been brought to the fore, which are relevant for studies that cross both distant political borders and more proximate community boundaries.

First, health researchers contend that **linguistic translation** is difficult in cross-cultural research sites, because the meanings of words and concepts – whether the vocabularies of regulatory ethics or of biomedicine – are distinctively Western ideas that tend to get treated as universals. In previous decades, some commentators claimed that Western ethics could not meaningfully be articulated to non-Western participants, and that forcing researchers to do so was ethnocentric. This argument, however, has been more-or-less discarded as paternalistic and, more to the point, empirically wrong (Lykes). Carolyn Fluehr-Lobban (2000) writes that her fellow anthropologists on the whole report 'that people, illiterate and well educated alike, are at least curious, if not seriously interested, in what they [researchers] are doing in their community and nation', and furthermore that social scientists have had no dearth of participants even after 'the research procedures and goals have been clearly articulated to possible participants in the local language' (174).

Researchers have, nonetheless, identified legitimate problems with translating research ethics. To begin with, qualitative health researchers are beginning to document their struggles with the *literal translation* of materials across language communities, especially given limited financial or human resources (namely, lean budgets to compensate translators and few people fluent in both bureaucratic language and the local idiom of participants: for an example, see Molyneux et al., 2004). In addition, the problem of *conceptual translation* remains an enduring trouble for cross-cultural researchers – not when translating regulatory concepts to participants, but when moving participants' ideas into regulatory language. What counts as a 'risk' or a 'benefit' (to use the parlance of regulation) differs profoundly across settings (Slovic, 1999). The social 'risks' that researchers aim to mitigate, moreover, cannot be specified in the same way as physical risks, and are thus difficult to debate (Hamilton, 2004). A growing literature, however, suggests that it would be misguided (and quite easy) to make false assumptions about how people will feel about participating in health research (especially on seemingly 'sensitive' topics) and the implications for participants of local power disparities (especially the gendered nature of research risks in studies of kinship, reproduction, and sexuality; see Fairhead et al., 2005).

Second, the **meaning of practices** involved in 'doing ethics' can be complicated in cross-cultural settings. The practice of signing consent forms serves as the classic example. Today, regulations allow many alternatives to signed consent documents (a topic that we take up in Section II). Yet, participants who prefer to use an alternative method may have an unusually 'sophisticated' engagement, as Fluehr-Lobban argues, with the consent process (2003: 170). Researchers have found particularly among traditionally exploited groups that participants' *refusal* to sign consent forms offers a way for them to assert their authority and thus shape consent practices in the way they see fit (Shannon, 2007).

It is only appropriate that regulations offer multiple ways to develop and document consent. Yet, these alternatives are often taken to be just that: deviations from default procedures that require special justification. Researchers report having anticipated and satisfied demands of both participants and regulators in several ways. Engaging community groups is one option commonly used in public health research and in biomedical fields, like emergency medicine, where it is impossible to get prior consent as traditionally defined. In these instances, people who are similar to (or who are in fact) potential study participants offer feedback on the research design and ethics procedures (Ragin et al., 2008). Another option taps into the stratified nature of most field settings by getting feedback from select individuals who most easily traverse community boundaries. Many researchers turn to community leaders for counsel (Dawson and Kass, 2005). Sociologist Janet Billson (1991) advocates getting feedback on ethics procedures from people who participate earliest in the study. Ethics practices can be refined, or researchers can develop multiple standards as the traits of the participants change.

A third problem, also affecting studies that cross political boundaries, is that of **overlapping jurisdictions** in ethics regulation. At times, the requirements for research in sponsoring countries (or researchers' home institutions) conflict with the demands of the site hosting the study (e.g., Bledsoe et al., 2007). An added layer of complication in the United States is that many universities and hospitals have multiple review boards: the implication for qualitative health researchers is that it can be unclear which board – or how many boards – can claim oversight of a social science project located in a biomedical site.

Ad hoc solutions can work. In some countries, ethics committees will have reciprocal agreements, either formally or informally (National Conference on Alternative IRB Models, 2006). While there have been calls for international human subjects regulation and more cross-national agreements, there is no immediate, easy, or binding solution on the horizon (Fluehr-Lobban, 2000). Instead, researchers have come to anticipate serving as mediators between multiple regulatory systems. It is clear, however, that as global health research continues apace, qualitative researchers will want to ensure that international efforts do not splinter along disciplinary or methodological lines.

Cyberspace

Health researchers and health care users alike have noted that the Internet, despite its limitations, has shifted the balance of power in patient treatment and medical research (Collins and Evans, 2007; Dumit, 2006). Appropriately, qualitative health researchers have relocated their field sites in response to this trend (Fox and Ward, 2008; Rier, 2007). In many ways, researchers studying blogs, online support groups, and new health social movements face the same constraints as other qualitative health researchers. Yet, studies in cyberspace challenge conventional ethics grounded on assumptions about the physical place of research. Here, we overview emerging concerns regarding the ethics of research in cyberspace, by which we mean the virtual locations of 'new, technology-induced social formation[s]' enabled through the Internet and the personal computer (Hakken, 2000: 192).

Some problems are procedural. First, the question of how to document informed consent among research participants becomes troublesome when spoken words are rarely exchanged, and when it is not possible to verify that a participant can legally consent (based on age or cognitive ability, for example). In addition, researchers in health fields often aim to restrict who can access research sites. Researchers are still exploring how best to secure sites, from whom to restrict them, and how to manage breaches (Kelly and McKenzie, 2002; Whitehead, 2007).

Such logistical issues take for granted a shared understanding of what constitutes research in 'public'. In many cases, however, there is no clear consensus among researchers, regulators, and participants on what information and actions should be considered public or private. The simple fact that people choose to post seemingly intimate health information and experiences online has encouraged some IRBs in the United States to treat it as analogous to 'public behaviour', and thus exempt from ethics review. Matters become more complicated – and the outcome may turn on how researchers collect and retain data – when health information is available online along with other identifying information, as is often the case on social networking sites. Finally, it remains to be seen how the court of public opinion will rule on strictly observational research in cyberspace (Bakardjieva and Feenberg, 2001). Observational studies raise the question of whether researchers are simply 'lurking' on sites, or engaging in covert observation of people who might not expect to be objects of study.

Like the medium itself, the ethics of research in cyberspace is emerging at a fast pace. Stories and standards to guide health research are in progress, and many advocate looking across both institutional and disciplinary boundaries as we confront this new terrain. As a case in point, Hakken reports that while ' "Failure to gain IRB approval" has been used as an excuse for forcing at least one ethnographer to abandon his fieldwork on medical informatics. ... At other schools, IRBs have been "captured" by ethnographers, resulting in thicker, more nuanced approaches to informed consent'. As more ethnography is done in cyberspace, Hakken portends, 'our ability to monitor the ethics of ethnographic practice will depend upon dense dialogues with other professionals' (2000: 182).

ETHICS AND THE TIMING OF RESEARCH

Before research begins

Getting participants' **prior consent** to be involved in research has long been the desideratum of ethical research. Yet, describing research to potential participants before the study takes place creates two problems for researchers – one logistical, the other methodological. Telling people about the nature of the research in advance may change how they behave, and thus bias study results. Even if it were advisable, however, it is not always possible to reach participants in advance (Katz, 2006).

Two solutions – waiver of consent and blanket consent – have eased both of these problems. First, many regulatory systems (e.g., the United States) now allow ethics committees to waive consent if the research cannot otherwise be conducted. (More on this regulatory option in Section II.) Another possibility, more palatable than a waiver to some researchers and ethics committees, is to get consent for the study using a broad-scale, blanket method. Audit studies offer models of how this can be done. These research designs are commonly used to analyze how physicians interact with patients in clinical settings. By training 'standard patients' to behave in the same way, audit studies create replicable, seemingly natural social situations through which researchers can compare the actual choices physicians make. Researchers have resolved the problem of biasing their findings by working through the consent process with physicians, who are told as a part of the process that a standard patient will be among their 'clients' within a given period, such as the upcoming year. This allows participants both to consent to the study in advance and, the theory goes, behave naturally in the study.

A distinctive set of issues surround the issue of when researchers should **re-contact** former study participants. Instead of enrolling new people, following up with participants in an earlier study can yield rich longitudinal data. Often, researchers plan for this contingency years in advance and avoid the charge that they are exploiting the goodwill (or misusing the personal data) of former participants. When researchers have not anticipated doing follow-up work, nonetheless, options are available. US IRBs have approved, for example, sending 'opt-in' or 'opt-out' requests to former participants. By replying to (or ignoring) researchers' requests, participants are given some agency, and can signal whether they would be willing to learn more about a new study. Essentially, opt-in and opt-out letters ask permission to contact people, and do not stand in for consent. This cuts the size of the participant pool, to be sure, but it does appear to work.

Researchers can also pre-empt the problem of re-contacting altogether. Some ethics boards have encouraged researchers to include with consent documents a supplemental page (or question) about whether participants can be contacted again for future studies, even if researchers do not have any plans. Although this practice is not immediately relevant, the technique can avoid the problem for future studies yet unimagined.

After data are collected

Sociologist Charles Bosk described the problem of **local confidentiality** in the aftermath of his ethnographies of surgeons, genetic counsellors, and workers in a paediatrics intensive care unit (Bosk, 2000). Researchers usually promise participants that their identities will be concealed in published accounts. Although masked from general readers, participants can nonetheless identify their fellow participants. Ethnographers have described participants' sense of betrayal and their hurt feelings when learning what was said behind closed doors by other participants – whether colleagues, family members, or friends. This problem is endemic, Bosk argues, to studies with 'highly literate subjects within one's own culture' (2000: 199).

Formal ethics rules do little to prepare researchers for the effect that interview quotes and analyses of field notes will have on their relationships with participants and on participants' relationships with each other. One consequence of local confidentiality (and its discontents) is that researchers' analyses can change the social climate of the site with effects that endure long after they have left the field. This feature of ethnographic research suggests that group-level acknowledgement of such issues may be in order (e.g., at a staff meeting), in addition to individual-level consent. The fallout from an inevitable loss of local confidentiality can also be addressed through one-on-one discussions. Seasoned ethnographers have recommended being radically clear with participants from the outset that they will most likely disagree with the researchers' account when they read it. Such efforts serve to minimize participants' rage, tears, and legal threats (Bosk, 2000), but also to discourage researchers from self-censoring their writing out of fear of repercussions (Fox, 1999).

Qualitative researchers might describe themselves as taking an 'ironic' position towards the field – to explore how people's belief, claims, and practices are other than what they seem. At a point, however, researchers have felt compelled to step outside of their anticipated roles when they have unexpectedly been witness to actions that they regard not as different, but wrong. Our focus here is on **whistle-blowing** – researchers' sense of responsibility to report illegal or dangerous behaviour witnessed unexpectedly.

To be sure, researchers often do anticipate dangerous and illegal behaviors, especially in research that is expressly on drug use, sexuality, abuse, or violence, and researchers in the United States and United Kingdom have reported problems getting approval from ethics committees that aim to protect their institutions as much as research participants (Roberts et al., 2007; Jaschik, 2007). In these cases, researchers can consider applying for federal assurances that protect their data from the court system. Not all data can be protected, however, and (despite the effect on enrolment and trust) researchers are obligated to tell participants that they must report specific worrisome behaviour, such as suspicion of child abuse or plans to hurt someone. In other instances, researchers intend from the outset to use their studies as vehicles for social commentary and to expose corruption in powerful institutions: whistle blowing is the point of research (Murphy and Dingwall, 2007).

In practice, qualitative health researchers decided whether to blow the proverbial whistle depending on, first, whether they observed behaviour (or had knowledge of potential or suspected action) and, second, whether appropriate authorities also knew (or whether the researcher possessed sequestered or rare knowledge). Anthropologist Gill Barber (2003) reflected on her experience as witness to a midwife's botched delivery in rural Malawi. Having previously recorded in field notes that the midwife seemed reckless, naïve, and possibly incompetent compared with others, Barber struggled over the question of whether she should take steps to prevent the woman from working as a midwife again. Three issues shaped her thinking: Barber knew that local women were aware of the midwife's virtues and vices; Barber herself believed that, in general, midwives benefited women in rural Africa despite politicians' desires to ban their practice; and Barber, admirably, acknowledged that she was loath to compromise her access to the field. In the end, Barber decided not to take action, because the midwife's superiors knew about the dangerous episode and seriously reprimanded her, which helped Barber to feel satisfied that authorities are aware of the situation, shared her views, and had control over the problem. If a women's life had been in immediate danger, however, Barber writes that she would have 'blown the whistle' even though this would have hurt her access to the field site.

STRATEGIES FOR MANAGING REGULATION

Many of the tensions outlined in the previous section have become logistical conundrums for researchers, because, paradoxically, there are so many sources of guidance. Chief among them are state human subjects regulations, which often appear to conflict with professional ethics codes and the methodological demands of good research. In this section, we emphasize the limits of when and how human subjects regulations apply, and encourage researchers to use these underappreciated features of regulation. We start by looking at the inner workings of two particularly influential regulatory systems – those of the United States and the United Kingdom – to point out where and why flexibility emerges. Then, we detail the bureaucratic meanings (as opposed to the colloquial meanings) of two regulatory phrases: prior approval and informed consent.

TWO CASES: THE UNITED STATES AND UNITED KINGDOM

Regulation in the United States

In the United States, the introduction of human subjects regulations were part of a broader move by the federal government during the late 1960s and early 1970s to research institutional legally responsible for what researchers (including social scientists) did with public money (Stark, forthcoming). The history of this period has been well documented. Suffice it to say that the origins of the federal regulations reveal several important points about how IRBs work today. First, IRBs are declarative groups. That is to say, what board members and administrators say is acceptable. Of course, boards are broadly constrained by written rules. Health research on prisoners, minors, or other specially protected populations, for example, will always go to full-board review regardless of the research methods used. Nonetheless, applying abstract rules to concrete cases requires interpretation. Human subjects regulation, in the words of commentator Jeremy Wood, 'is not intended to paint for individuals a bright line that distinguishes acceptable and unacceptable conduct, [but] is intended to structure the wide discretion afforded IRBs' (2003: 4).

Second, and related to this, it is reviewers' case-to-case decisions that make research practices acceptable. IRBs tend to judge new studies against regulations, and, just as importantly, against the studies that have come before them. In other words, boards tend to use 'local precedents' when making decisions (Stark, forthcoming). This decision making heuristic allows board members to make decisions more speedily than if they worked through the regulations point-by-point with each new protocol. It also allows board members to feel they are making consistent decisions over time. The implication, however, is that these decisions are only consistent with the prior decisions of a given board, because different boards develop different local precedents. Thus, US human subjects regulations are in one sense set in stone; and yet, they are always translated through the flesh and blood of IRB members and administrators. To get qualitative health studies approved as efficiently as possible, remember what bind every policy is a person enacting it.

Regulation in the United Kingdom

Research ethics review for social science in the United Kingdom differs from that in the United States in a number of ways. While bodies for the ethical review of research, called research ethics committees (RECs), started in the late 1960s these organizations were not located within the University system but rather the United Kingdom's National Health Service, and only applied to research carried out on NHS patients and, later, NHS staff and property. University based RECs are, by and large, a far more recent development (since 2004).

The origin of RECs in the United Kingdom lies in the same 1966 memo from the US Surgeon General that started the development of IRBs in the United States. The result was a 1967 report by the Royal College of Physicians (endorsed by the

Ministry of Health in 1968) recommending that hospitals set up committees of doctors to review research (Royal College of Physicians of London, 1967).

This pattern of recommendations from the RCP followed by clear, if nonbinding, support from the government of the day characterized the development of RECs for the next two decades; the RCP produced a series of reports, steadily increasing in detail the duties, composition and methods of RECs (1973; 1984; 1990) while the Ministry of Health, or its successor the Department of Health and Social Security (1975) supported the College's efforts but stopped short of becoming formally involved in the oversight of RECs. Thus, in the United Kingdom, Research Ethics Committees originated as a form of professional self-regulation on the part of doctors, rather than a legally required, centrally mandated system of governance, as in the United States.

This situation continued until 1991 when, after complaints from researchers about the apparent inconsistency of ethics review across the country, the Department of Health (DH) stepped in to publish its 'Red Book' which formally brought Research Ethics Committees under the control of central government (Department of Health, 1991). The resulting guidelines were relatively light-touch, focusing on issues around the membership of committees, now known as local research ethics committees (or LRECs), the bodies to which they were responsible (regional health authorities) and other general structural issues (rather than the specifics of the issues they needed to take into account).

The Red Book explicitly introduced oversight of social scientific research, by making clear that the range of studies that needed REC approval covered not just clinical studies but any research involving, not just the obvious topics (such as NHS patients, or foetal material) but also 'the use of, or potential access to, NHS premises or facilities' (p. 7). Thus, ethnographic studies of NHS staff, even if they did not involve patients, would now require REC approval. Complaints on the part of those wishing to carry out social science research in the NHS about RECs predate the Red Book (Cartwright, 1990; Robinson, 1990) and indeed can be traced back as far as 1973, when Archie Cochrane complained about ethics review stifling a survey of colleagues he wished to carry out,[1] but 1991 was the first explicit attempt to regulate social scientific research on the grounds of ethics, in the United Kingdom.

Almost as soon as the Red Book had been published, complaints began about the intrusiveness of the REC system, including significant contributions from researchers using social science methods (Benster and Pollock, 1992; Middle et al., 1995; Moodie and Marshall, 1992; White, 1995). In the biomedical sciences, problems centred on multicentre research (such as drug trials and epidemiological studies) which required repeated applications to a large number of different LRECs. By 1997, calls for greater standardization had lead to the development of Multicentre Research Ethics Committees (MRECs), set up to review and give nationwide approval for studies that took place in more than four sites. Social scientists researching in a number of areas, perhaps with a nationwide survey of professionals, were obvious beneficiaries.

Following on from the setting up of MRECs, research ethics review in the United Kingdom has continued on a path of centralization and standardization, mainly driven by COREC, the Central Office for Research Ethics Committees, which was set up in 2000 to coordinate RECs and run training courses. In addition to publishing clear governance documents for all RECs (GAfREC, published in 2001) and a set of standard operating procedures (SOPs) for RECs in 2004, COREC managed to negotiate centralized funding for all RECs (not just MRECs), putting local committees on the same firm footing in terms of administrative support and training (COREC, 2004).

One of COREC's roles was to prepare the UK ethics review system for the implementation of the EU 'Clinical trials Directive' which, after five years in development, was signed in 2001, and came into force in May 2004. The Directive was only focused on clinical trials of pharmaceutical products, but had a far wider impact on the UK REC system, most obviously by expanding the number of committees with MREC-like powers (over 50 LRECs were upgraded to so called Type-3 status) and expanding the nature of these powers, so that multi-centre research was now defined as taking place at more than two sites (as opposed to four or more under the old MREC system). This expanded the number of studies, including social science research, which could qualify, with a single application, for ethics approval for anywhere in the United Kingdom.

Further changes to the REC system are currently being implemented, in response to the so-called Warner Report (Ad Hoc Advisory Group, 2005), a review sparked by concerns in Parliament over implementation of the clinical trials directive, including a form of expedited review for studies with 'no material ethical issues'. Of course, what does and does not count as a 'material ethical issue' is a contentious point, but it seems likely that much social science research may fall under this rubric and thus be spared a full REC review. In addition, a number of RECs are now being 'flagged' as having specific expertise in qualitative research. While COREC has resisted the idea of specialist committees (who only review one kind of study, paediatrics for example), a flagging system has been used to direct particular kinds of study (most obviously those involving prisoners) to particular RECs. The development of expedited review, and the extension of the flagging system suggests that, contra the claims of pessimists among the social science community, the UK research ethics review system (in the NHS at least) is not unresponsive to their claims and concerns (Hedgecoe, 2008).

The NHS REC system is now complemented by the growing number of University-based ethics committees. In autumn 2002, the Economic and Social Research Council (ESRC), the United Kingdom's main funding body for social scientific research, commissioned a review of the status of the ethics of social science research. The result was the Council's Research Ethics Framework (REF), which came into effect at the beginning of 2006, requiring institutions that receive research funding from the ESRC to have in place a set of 'minimum requirements', such as the need to address ethical issues of research proposals, the need for ethics committee approval, and procedures for institutional monitoring.

Superficially, the developing University-based system of research ethics review seems more suited to social science research than the biomedically focused NHS REC system. The ESRC guidance was deliberately kept quite broad in its requirements, allowing Universities to set up specialist subcommittees to review specific kinds of research. Thus committees can be formed with majority social science membership, reducing the likelihood of the perennial complaints against NHS RECs, that the committee members did not understand qualitative research properly, and thus could not deal with the ethical issues raised by, for example, ethnography.

Yet, anecdotal evidence has begun to accumulate which suggests that the University-based system, while it avoids the drawbacks of NHS RECs, introduces new problems which are centred on the institutional basis of these committees. As a number of US authors have suggested, review bodies based in specific research institutions can, on occasion, make decisions which appear to be aimed at protecting the institution concerned, rather than potential research participants. In the United Kingdom, cases where research into paedophilia or student sex-workers has been delayed or redesigned as a result of being submitted to a University REC suggest that such problems may also occur here (Goode, 2007; Roberts et al., 2007).

GETTING 'APPROVAL' FROM ETHICS COMMITTEES

As we have described it, ethics review is broadly constrained by regulations, but decisions also require a good deal of interpretation from reviewers. Thus, 'approval' is the outcome of a declarative process: what reviewers say is acceptable according to their interpretation of the regulations makes it so. To interpret the regulations, reviewers tend to use case-based reasoning – thinking through proposed projects in terms of previous studies. The following suggestions are designed to aid researchers in working with these features of ethics review:

- **Talk with administrators before submitting a study for review:** Ask points of clarification, offer to speak with primary reviewers if the study goes to full board, or ask for suggestions on how to meet your research needs within the framework of the regulations. More than anything else, talking (or emailing) with committee representatives in advance allows researchers to: tailor study applications to the particular demands of their specific committee; establish a line of communication that reviewers can reactivate if there are problems with the application; and unmask the human beings behind the paperwork for both researchers and reviewers. Especially for field sites that are distant (physically or technologically) from the ethics committee, talking before going to the field can forestall bureaucratic problems that are often more difficult to manage from afar.
- **In the proposal, cite or give examples of similar studies:** Demonstrate that it is not unprecedented to base studies on the proposed (1) research population and (2) research method. Prior studies can serve not only as scholarly evidence, but also as ethics evidence. Whereas funding and editorial applications may emphasize novel features of research findings, ethics review applications can accentuate the commonplace aspects of the research methods and population. (See section on case sharing in Concluding Remarks.)

- **In the proposal, give evidence of research participants' experiences in similar studies:** Justify the level and type of risks and benefits participants can expect. The first goal is to remove the issue of risks and benefits from the realm of first-hand experience – of both the reviewer and the researchers. Do this by providing previous participants' accounts of their experiences, especially in research on unfamiliar people or 'sensitive' topics. The second goal is to set the limits of what counts as a 'risk' in qualitative health research, since risks in observational and interview-based studies are notoriously difficult to define and quantify. Consider using published studies (epilogues can be treasure troves). If there are no prior studies, propose to conduct a brief pilot study, or volunteer a follow-up deadline set for the early stages of the full study, by which the reviewers will get a report on how participants are feeling about the study.
- **Attend review meetings:** Many ethics committee meetings are, by regulation, open to the public, even if the meetings are closed by custom. In the United Kingdom, researchers are regularly invited to attend meetings. In the United States, where roughly one in ten IRBs invite researchers (Taylor et al., 2008), the researchers themselves can nonetheless ask to attend the session in which the study will be discussed (if it goes to full-board review). Discussing a protocol in person streamlines the review process, because it removes a layer of bureaucracy. Symbolically, attending meetings is taken to indicate researchers' commitment to the ethics review process and it allows researchers to acknowledge and quickly move past the inevitable typographical errors in an application. Although visitors cannot observe the formal vote, meetings can fruitfully be used to assuage reviewers' concerns, to speed the review process, and to teach students how to prepare studies. Attending meetings from distant field sites is of course difficult, but researchers can be available remotely or ask a proxy to attend the meeting.
- **Read the regulations, then err on the side of caution:** Familiarity with the regulations can be taken to be a good-faith effort to engage the ethics review process (Bosk and De Vries, 2004). In addition, the regulations mark the specific language and concepts that are open for debate, many of which also have colloquial meanings. (e.g., in US regulation, it is not an option to state a study has 'no risk', but instead 'no more than minimal risk;' the level and type of risk and benefit in part determines which of the three tiers of review the study falls under.) Importantly, opting for a conservative interpretation of the regulations will allow researchers to propose ethics practices they find workable, rather than to have reviewers impose practices that the research will then be obliged to use or to negotiate.

GETTING 'INFORMED CONSENT' FROM PARTICIPANTS

In the idiom of human subjects regulation, 'informed consent' has a technical meaning that refers to specific practices. In the next section, we spell out what those specific technical practices are in the parlance of most regulations; we do not delve into the epistemological debate over whether participants (or researchers for that matter) can ever really truly be informed.

Researchers need *informed consent when:*

- Their project meets the regulatory definition of 'research'. Often, program evaluations and assessments and pedagogical exercises are excluded.
- They intend (at least) to talk with people. Most observational research does not require informed consent.
- They collect information that will make someone identifiable. This includes all private information recorded (such as car license plate numbers) even if words are not exchanged. Qualitative health researchers are particularly bound by restrictions on private health information.

Researchers have *informed consent after participants*

- Are told that interviews, questions, observations, and other interactions with the participant will be for the purpose of completing a research project.
- Are told what the study will involve for them – what researchers might think of as research method, like asking questions, or filling out a survey.
- Are told whether the information they provide will be associated with them personally. Some researchers choose not to conceal participants' identities or not to conceal the identities of some participants, such as prominent figures in a community. The first layer of information and identity concealment is **confidentiality**: this means that the information participants provide in the study will not be revealed as belonging to them, personally. Confidentiality is not to be confused with **anonymity**: this is a more restrictive layer of concealment in which participants' identifying information is never recorded. Instead, participants can be kept track of through other identifiers, like numbers.
- Are told what 'risks' are involved. For qualitative health research, these are rarely physical risks. Nonetheless, any potentially negative emotional, legal, or interpersonal consequences of participating may be included.
- Are told what 'benefits' they will receive. Whereas 'risks' tend to be interpreted in more imaginative ways by regulators, 'benefits' tend to be thought of exclusively in tangible terms, such as material compensation or information about themselves or their group (such as a copy of the results of the study).
- Are told that they can drop out of the study at any time with no repercussions.
- Are told that they can ask questions now – and are given a chance to ask.
- Are told who they can contact with any questions that they might have in the future. This includes contact information for the researcher, an ethics committee with jurisdiction, and a local host or resource person.
- Are provided with relevant information that they can keep.

Stylistically, this information has to be offered using the appropriate languages and vocabulary levels. Because participants' education and experience varies, preparing more than one way to convey material may be useful, such as a long signed form and a short research summary to accompany verbal consent.

Researchers substantiate *informed consent through*

- **Written consent**: This is the most traditional method of documenting consent for qualitative health researchers, and most ethics committees have developed templates that researchers can follow. Researchers may consider standard language distasteful, but technical informed consent is not exhaustive (and researchers can do more themselves) (Wendler and Rackoff, 2001).
- **Non-written consent**: In many cases, written consent is impractical for qualitative health researchers, and researchers are even encouraged to waive documented consent when this is the only information that will link participants to the research. Thus, most regulations leave room for alternative methods of getting informed consent, including verbal consent, consent-by-proxy (for example community leaders on behalf of members), and documentation in formal transcripts (such as notation of a vote in meeting minutes of a group). In these cases, researchers nonetheless produce and maintain their own documentation, but they are not forced to get participants' signatures on standard consent forms. In the United Kingdom, for example, guidance was written with explicit reference to social science professional standards, and as a result non-written consent is explicitly allowed. In sum, researchers can explore the possibilities for waiving not only informed consent (see the foregoing) and *documentation* of informed consent within their regulatory systems, given that many explicitly enable ethics reviewers to use these practices.

CONCLUDING REMARKS

Where can we go from here? Beyond the strategies, we presented for individuals to manage ethics regulations, researchers have also proposed forward-thinking (if labour-intensive) efforts that could aid the broader health-research community. To begin with, researchers might develop ways to exchange details about study reviews within and across committees. Although informal learning between researchers may flow within institutions or regions, the aim of **case sharing** is to create forums through which researchers can compare notes across committees and jurisdictions. Advocates see this as a way to counteract the idiosyncratic decision making habits of individual review boards (or what we refer to earlier as local precedents). Through case sharing, researchers learn both what might be expected of them from a given committee and how other researchers and committees have managed similar studies, especially of potentially uncommon practices, which researchers can use to advocate for approval of their own studies. Proponents of case sharing see the Internet as an untapped resource through which researchers exchange cases and strategies (Miller and Boulton, 2007; Harper, 2007), much like the American-based online IRB Forum.

A second option is for researchers and reviewers to invest in teaching each other about the tacit assumptions behind research methods and review procedures. Although advocates of **mutual education** often place the burden more heavily with either researchers or reviewers, learning how appropriately to protect participants without undermining research does appear to be a shared obligation. Advocates of mutual education suggest that people in the dual role of researcher-and-reviewer are best positioned to educate other reviewers about method and other researchers about regulation (Bledsoe et al., 2007; Bosk and De Vries, 2004; Miller and Boulton, 2007). As we agitate for change, however, there is research to be done.

NOTE

1   UK National Archives: FD 9/896 – Ethical Committee: ethical principles and their application on experiments in Wales, Letter from A.L. Cochrane to Dr. M. Ashley-Miller of the Medical Research Council, 17 January 1973.

REFERENCES

Ad Hoc Advisory Group on the Operation of NHS Research Ethics Committees (2005) Report of the Ad Hoc Advisory Group on the Operation of NHS Research Ethics Committees (London, Department of Health).
Alderson, P. (2007) 'The Ethics of Space in Clinical Practice', *Clinical Ethics*, 2(2): 85–91.
Alderson, P. and Morrow, V. (2004) *Ethics, Social Research and Consulting with Children and Young People*. Ilford: Barnardo's.
Andrews, J. (2006) 'Research in the Ranks: Vulnerable Subjects, Coercible Collaboration, and the Hepatitis E Vaccine Trial in Nepal', *Perspectives in Biology and Medicine*, 49(1): 35–51.

Applebaum, P., Roth, L., Lidz, C., Benson, P., and Winslade W. (1987) 'False Hopes and Best Data: Consent to Research and the Therapeutic Misconception', *The Hastings Center Report*, 17(2): 20–4.

Bakardjieva, M. and Feenberg, A. (2001) 'Involving the Virtual Subject: Conceptual, Methodological and Ethical Dimensions', *Journal of Ethics and Information Technology*, 2(4): 233–40.

Barber, G. (2003) 'To Tell or Not to Tell? Ethics and Secrecy in Anthropology and Childbearing in Rural Malawi'. In P. Caplan (ed.) *The Ethics of Anthropology: Debates and Dilemmas*. New York: Routledge.

Benster, R. and Pollock, A. (1992) 'Letter: Ethics and Multicentre Research Projects', *British Medical Journal*, 27 June, 304: 1696.

Billson, J.M. (1991) 'The Progressive Verification Method: Toward a Feminist Methodology for Studying Women Cross-Culturally'. *Women's Studies International Forum*, 14(3): 201–15.

Bledsoe, C. et al. (2007) 'Regulating Creativity: Research and Survival in the Irb Iron Cage.' *Northwestern University Law Review*, 101(2): 593.

Bledsoe, C. et al. (2007) 'Regulating Creativity: Research and Survival in the Irb Iron Cage.' *Northwestern University Law Review*, 101(2): 593.

Bledsoe, C., Galinsky, A., Headley, N., Heimer, C., Kjeldgaard, E., Lindgren, J., and Miller, M. (2007). Available at: http://www.aamc.org/research/irbreview/irbconf06rpt.pdf

Bosk, C. (2000) 'Irony, Ethnography, and Informed Consent'. In B. Hoffmaster (ed.) *Bioethics in Social Context*. Philadelphia: Temple University Press.

Bosk, C. and De Vries, R. (2004) 'Bureaucracies of Mass Deception: Institutional Review Boards and the Ethics of Ethnographic Research', *The Annals of the American Academy of Political and Social Sciences*, 595: 249–63.

Cartwright, A. (1990) 'Letter: Research Ethics Committees', *British Medical Journal*, 3 March, 300: 607.

Collins, H. and Evans, R. (2007) *Rethinking Expertise*. Chicago University of Chicago Press.

COREC (2004) *Standard Operating Procedures for Research Ethics Committees in the United Kingdom*. London: COREC.

Dawson, L. and Kass, N.E. (2005) 'Views of US Researchers About Informed Consent in International Collaborative Research', *Social Science and Medicine*, 61(6): 1211–22.

Department of Health and Social Security (UK) (1975) Supervision of the Ethics of Clinical Research Investigations and Fetal Material Circular June, HSC(IS)153.

Department of Health (1991) Local Research Ethics Committees HSG(91)5. London: HMSO.

Dumit, J. (2006) 'Illnesses You Have to Fight to Get: Facts as Forces in Uncertain, Emergent Illnesses', *Social Science and Medicine*, 62(3): 577–90.

Epstein, S. (1996) *Impure Science: AIDS, Activism, and the Politics of Knowledge*. Berkeley: University of California Press.

ESRC (2005) *Research Ethics Framework*. Swindon: ESRC.

Fairhead, J., Leach, M., and Small, M. (2005) 'Public Engagement with Science? Local Understandings of a Vaccine Trial in the Gambia', *Cambridge Journals Online*, 38: 103–16.

Final Report of the National Conference on Alternative IRB Models (2006) November 19–21. Washington D.C. Available at: http://www.aamc.org/research/irbreview/irbconf06rpt.pdf

Fluehr-Lobban, C. (2000) 'Globalization of Research and International Standards of Ethics in Anthropology', *Ethics and Anthropology: Facing Future Issues in Human Biology, Globalism, and Cultural Property*. E. F. Anne-Marie Cantwell and M. Tramm. New York, New York Academy of Sciences 925.

Fluehr-Lobban, C. (2003) 'Informed Consent in Anthropological Research: We Are Not Exempt', In C. Fluehr-Lobban (ed.) *Ethics and the Profession of Anthropology: Dialogue for Ethically Conscious Practice*. Walnut Creek, CA: AltaMira Press.

Fox, N. and Ward, K.J. (2008) 'You Are What You Eat? Vegetarianism, Health and Identity', *Social Science and Medicine*.

Fox, R. (1999) 'Contract and Covenant in Ethnographic Research'. In N. King, G. Henderson, and J. Stein (eds) *Beyond Regulations: Ethics in Human Subjects Research*. Chapel Hill, NC: The University of North Carolina Press.

Gilbert, C., Fulford, K. and Parker, C. (1989) 'Diversity in the Practice of District Ethics Committees', *BMJ*, 9 December, 299: 1437–39.

Goode S. (2007) 'My Career Has Been Damaged', *Times Higher Educational Supplement*, April 20: 7.

Hakken, D. (2000) 'Ethical Issues in the Ethnography of Cyberspace'. In E. F. Anne-Marie Cantwell and Tramm M. (eds) *Ethics and Anthropology: Facing Future Issues in Human Biology, Globalism, and Cultural Property*. New York: New York Academy of Sciences, 925: 170–86.

Hakken, D. (2003) 'An Ethics for an Anthropology in and of Cyberspace'. in C. Fluehr-Lobban (ed.) *Ethics and the Profession of Anthropology: Dialogue for an Ethically Conscious Practice*. Walnut Creek, CA: AltaMira Press.

Hamilton, M. (2004) 'Some Precision Would Be Helpful', *IRB: A Review of Human Subjects Research*, 26(5): 19.

Haney, W.H. and Lykes, M.B. (2000) 'Practices, Participatory Research and Creative Research Designs: The Continuing Evolution of Ethical Guidelines for Researcher'. In F. Sherman and B. Tolbert (eds) *Transforming Social Inquiry, Transforming Social Action: New Paradigms for Crossing the Theory/Practice Divide in Universities and Communities*. Boston: Kluwer Academic Publishers.

Harper, I. (2007) 'Translating Ethics: Researching Public Health and Medical Practices in Nepal', *Social Science and Medicine*, 65(11): 2235–47.

Hedgecoe, A. (2008) 'Research Ethics Review and the Sociological Research Relationship', *Sociology*, 42(5): 857–70.

Heimer, C. and Staffen, L. (1998) *For the Sake of the Children: The Social Organization of Responsibility in the Hospital and the Home*. Chicago: University of Chicago Press.

Hirshon, J.M., Krugman, J.D., Witting, M.D., Furuno, J.P., Limcangco, M.R., Perisse, A.R., and Rasch, E.K. (2002) 'Variability in Institutional Review Board Assessment of Minimal-Risk Research', *Academic Emergency Medicine*, 9(12): 1417–20.

Jacobson, N., Gewurtz, R., and Haydon, E. (2007) 'Ethical Review of Interpretive Research: Problems and Solutions', *IRB: Ethics and Human Research*, 29(5): 1–8.

Jaschik S. (2007) 'Who's Afraid of Incestuous Gay Monkey Sex?' *Inside Higher Education*, August 14. Available at: www.insidehighered.com

Katz, J. (2006) 'Ethical Escape Routes for Underground Ethnographers', *American Ethnologist*, 33(4): 499–506.

Kelly, G. and McKenzie, B. (2002) 'Security, Privacy, and Confidentiality Issues on the Internet', *Journal of Medical Internet Research*, 4(2): e12.

Kimmelman, J. (2007) 'The Therapeutic Misconception at 25: Treatment, Research, and Confusion', *The Hastings Center Report*, Nov–Dec: 36–42.

Larcombe, I. and M. Mott (1999) 'Multicentre Research Ethics Committees: Have They Helped?', *Journal of the Royal Society of Medicine*, 92: 500–01.

Lock, S. (1990) 'Editorial: Monitoring Research Ethical Committees', *BMJ*, 13 January, 300: 61–2.

Mark Risjord, J.G. (2001) 'When IRBs Disagree: Waiving Parental Consent for Sexual Health Research on Adolescents', *IRB: A Review of Human Subjects Research*, 24(2): 8–14.

Middle, C., Johnson, A., Petty, T., Sims, L., and Macfarlane, A. (1995) 'Ethics Approval for a National Postal Survey: Recent Experience', *BMJ*, 311: 659–60.

Miller, T. and Boulton, M. (2007) 'Changing Constructions of Informed Consent: Qualitative Research and Complex Social Worlds', *Social Science and Medicine*, 65(11): 2199–211.

Molyneux, C.S., Peshu, N., and Marsh, K. (2004) 'Understanding of Informed Consent in a Low-Income Setting: Three Case Studies from the Kenyan Coast', *Social Science and Medicine*, 59(12): 2547–59.

Molyneux, C.S., Peshu, N., and Marsh, K. (2005) 'Trust and Informed Consent: Insights from Community Members on the Kenyan Coast', *Social Science and Medicine*, 61(7): 1463–73.

Moodie, P. and Marshall, T. (1992) 'Guidelines for Local Research Ethics Committees', *British Medical Journal*, 16 May, 304: 1293–95.

Murphy, E. and Dingwall, R. (2007) 'Informed Consent, Anticipatory Regulation and Ethnographic Practice', *Social Science and Medicine*, 65(11): 2223–34.

Ragin, D., Ricci, E., Rhodes, R., Holohan, J., Smirnoff, M., and Richardson, L. (2008). 'Defining the "Community" in Community Consultation for Emergency Research: Findings from the Community VOICES Study', *Social Science and Medicine*, 66(6): 1379–92.

Rier, David (2007) 'The Impact of Moral Suasion on Internet HIV/AIDS Support Groups: Evidence from a Discussion of Seropositivity Disclosure Ethics', *Health Sociology Review*, 16(3–4): 237–47.

Roberts, R., Bergström, S., and La Rooy, D. (2007) 'UK Students and Sex Work: Current Knowledge and Research Issues', *Journal of Community and Applied Social Psychology*, 17: 141–6.

Robinson, J. (1990) Letter Research Ethics Committees, *BMJ*, 7 April, 300: 943.

Roloff, and Uttal, D. (2007) 'Regulating Creativity: Research and Survival in the IRB Iron Cage', *Northwestern University School of Law*, 101(2): 593–641.

Royal College of Physicians of London (1967) Report of the Committee on the Supervision of the Ethics of Clinical Investigations in Institutions. London: Royal College of Physicians of London.

Royal College of Physicians of London (1973) Supervision of the Ethics of Clinical Research Investigations in Institutions. London: Royal College of Physicians of London.

Royal College of Physicians of London (1984/1990) Guidelines on the Practice of Ethics Committees in Medical Research Involving Human Subjects. London: Royal College of Physicians of London.

Sankar, P. (2004) 'Communication and Miscommunication in Informed Consent to Research', *Medical Anthropology Quarterly*, 18(4): 429–46.

Shannon, J. (2007) 'Informed Consent: Documenting the Intersection of Bureaucratic Regulation and Ethnographic Practice', *PoLAR*, 30: 229–48.

Shore, N. (2004) *Human Subjects Regulations and the Ethical Review Process: Conventional Social Science and Community-Based Participatory Researchers' Perceptions and Recommendations for Change*. University of Washington.

Slovic, P. (1999) 'Trust, Emotion, Sex, Politics, and Science: Surveying the Risk-Assessment Battlefield', *Risk Analysis*, 19.

Stark, L. (2006) *Morality in Science: How Research is Evaluated in the Age of Human Subjects Regulation*, Department of Sociology. Princeton, NJ: Princeton University, PhD: 280.

Stark, L. (2007) 'Victims in Our Own Minds? IRBs in Myth and Practice', *Law and Society Review*, 41(4): 777–86.

Stark, L. (forthcoming) 'Behind Closed Doors', Chicago: University of Chicago Press.

Taylor, H., Currie, P., and Kass, N. (2008) 'A Study to Evaluate the Effect of Investigator Attendance on the Efficiency of IRB Review', *IRB: Ethics and Human Research*, 30(1): 1–5.

Wendler, D. and Rackoff, J. (2001) 'Informed Consent and Respecting Autonomy: What's a Signature Got To Do With It?' *IRB: A Review of Human Subjects Research*, 23(3): 1–4.

White, A. (1995) 'Impediment to Research or Guardian of Ethical Standards', *BMJ*, 311: 661.

Whitehead, L.C. (2007) 'Methodological and Ethical Issues in Internet-Mediated Research in the Field of Health: An Integrated Review of the Literature', *Social Science and Medicine*, 65(4): 782–91.

Wood, J. (2003) 'Guiding IRBs and Educating Researchers', *American Journal of Bioethics Routledge*, 3: 4–4.

31

Using Qualitative Research Methods to Inform Health Policy: the Case of Public Deliberation

Julia Abelson

Qualitative research methods are essential tools for health policy researchers who are tackling a multitude of research questions that involve describing, explaining and informing policy. Case studies, participatory action research, key informant interviews, focus groups, documentary analysis and historiography are just a few of the traditions and methods that fall into this category. Each may be used independently, or in combination with each other, or as part of mixed method designs that also include quantitative studies (Creswell, 1998; Devine, 2002; Fulop et al., 2002; Ritchie and Spencer, 2002).

As with any research that is designed to describe, explain and inform policy, qualitative researchers working in the health field must ensure the integrity of their research through the rigorous application of methods while adapting to the 'real-world' requirements of the policy makers and processes they are seeking to inform. Pursuing the latter objective can pose considerable challenges to achieving the former. Researchers engaged in policy-relevant research often rely on the cooperation of government and organizational decision makers to carry out their work, including the granting of interviews and access to staff and programme users to obtain important perspectives on the topic under study. Moreover, research-funding agencies encourage the formation of collaborative teams of researchers and decision maker partners to promote end-user involvement in the research process and the uptake of research results (CIHR, 2009). These types of collaborative research models challenge qualitative health researchers striving to conduct methodologically rigorous research that produces relevant results.

A particularly thorny rigour-relevance problem faced by qualitative health policy researchers is the duality of the research method as policy input. The incorporation of patient and public views into health care policymaking using qualitative techniques is a prime example of this duality, and will be used as an illustrative case study throughout the chapter.

PATIENT AND PUBLIC INVOLVEMENT IN HEALTH CARE POLICY: METHODS AS POLICY INPUTS

The way to incorporate the views of those affected by health care programmes and policies has preoccupied health system managers and policy makers for decades. Traditional techniques involved patient surveys, to elicit preferences for certain types of services and delivery arrangements, and opinion polls, to gauge the public's mood and confidence in health systems as a whole or in specific policy initiatives (Jacobs, 1993; Mullen, 2000; Burstein, 2003). The technical complexity and value-laden nature of health care presents methodological challenges for quantitative researchers seeking to provide useful input to policy makers. As a result, qualitative data collection methods, such as focus groups, have become helpful complementary or alternative sources of patient and public preferences and values. Similarly, participatory action research (PAR) is increasingly being used to improve the responsiveness of programmes and policies to the needs and preferences of end users (Meyer, 2000; Reason and Bradbury, 2007).

Within the qualitative paradigm, a new method has emerged that resembles, but is distinguishable from, focus group and PAR methods in a number of ways. This method's defining feature is the element of deliberation, which has its roots in democratic deliberative theory (Manin, 1987; Cohen, 1989; Fishkin, 1991; Gutmann and Thompson, 1996, Dryzek, 2000) and refers to 'a particular sort of discussion – one that involves the careful and serious weighing of reasons for and against some proposition' (Fearon, 1998). The act of considering different points of view and coming to a reasoned decision is what distinguishes deliberation from other group methods.

The deliberative turn represents a 'problem-solving' discussion … [which]:

> allows individuals with different backgrounds, interests and values to listen, understand, potentially persuade and ultimately come to more reasoned, informed and public-spirited decisions (Abelson et al., 2003).

Deliberative methods, as they will be referred to in this chapter, have become popular methods for eliciting patient and public values and priorities to inform health services programme and policy decisions, and to promote social change in the health and health-care policy arena. Despite their origins in deliberative democratic theory, deliberative methods are emerging as practical aids to decision makers tackling challenging public policy issues that require consideration of a range of evidentiary inputs. Experimentation with deliberative methods has occurred over decades in a variety of public policy fields but is a relatively recent addition to the health care arena (Abelson et al., 2003). In the following sections, the evolution of the deliberative method within the health policy and health services research fields is traced and situated in the qualitative research methods paradigm. The challenges associated with its use as a method for contributing to policy-informing research are then examined, followed by reflections on its strengths and weaknesses and on what it might offer to the qualitative research paradigm as it evolves.

EXPERIENCE WITH DELIBERATIVE METHODS IN HEALTH CARE POLICY

In the 1990s, health policy makers and public policy scholars began to identify the need for more informed, effective and legitimate methods for involving patients and publics in the decisions affecting them (Donovan and Coast, 1996; Lenaghan et al., 1996; Graham and Phillips, 1998; Simrell King, 1998; Lenaghan, 1999; Pratchett, 1999). This convergence of activity arose from different underlying motivations – some ideological (i.e., the desire to pursue democratic ideals of legitimacy, transparency and accountability) and others more pragmatic (i.e., the desire to achieve popular support for potentially unpopular decisions) (Rowe and Frewer, 2000; Abelson et al., 2002). Much of the emphasis on the design of new participation methods also arose from political concerns that methods used in the past were no longer adequate or appropriate for current decision making processes or for a more educated, sophisticated and less deferential public seeking more meaningful ways to contribute to policy processes (Inglehart, 1995; Inglehart et al., 1996).

A common thread weaving through the public participation discourse has been the need for approaches that emphasize *two-way interaction between decision makers and the public as well as deliberation among participants* (Graham and Phillips, 1998). Increasingly complex decision making processes require a more informed citizenry that has weighed the evidence on the issue, discussed and debated potential decision options and arrived at a mutually agreed decision, or at least one by which all parties can abide. The creation of an appropriate 'public sphere' (Habermas, 1984) for dialogue in the health system was seen as a necessary response to mounting pressures for governments to clarify the relative roles of the private and public sectors in funding and delivering what have historically been largely 'public goods'. As a result, the deliberative democratic paradigm has become a vehicle for governments and research organizations to engage the public in values-based discussions about various aspects of their health care systems (Commission on the Future of Health Care in Canada, 2002; O'Donnell and

Entwistle, 2004; Pivik et al., 2004; Royle and Oliver, 2004) and for planning, priority setting and resource allocation processes to inform local health authority decision making (Mitton and Donaldson, 2002; Abelson et al., 2003; Wiseman et al., 2003).

The use of deliberative methods has had a much longer history in other sectors such as environmental, food and biotechnology policy which are characterized by tensions between technocratic and democratic approaches to developing policy (Beierle and Konisky, 2000; Collins and Evans, 2002; Campbell and Townsend, 2003; Einsiedel, 2006). Experimentation with the use of deliberative methods in health care began in the 1990s in the UK's National Health Service (NHS) (Bowling et al., 1993; Bowie et al., 1995; Lenaghan et al., 1996; Coote and Lenaghan, 1997; Cookson and Dolan et al., 1999; Dolan et al., 1999; Lenaghan, 1999). These methods have been used elsewhere to involve citizens in a variety of national and local public involvement initiatives (Abelson et al., 1995; Stronks et al., 1997; Smith and Wales, 1999; Bostwick, 1999; Beierle and Cayford, 2002; Einsiedel, 2002; Abelson et al., 2003). In the 2000s, the appeal of deliberative methods as either a stand-alone method for eliciting public values or as a complement to traditional quantitative survey techniques led to numerous ad-hoc and institutionalized forums. Some examples include the establishment of a high-profile *Citizens Council* to guide decisions about new technology coverage decisions in the United Kingdom (*BMJ*, 2001); the use of *citizens dialogues* to incorporate citizens values about options for health care transformation into the recommendations of the Romanow Commission (2002) (Maxwell et al., 2003); the establishment of a *population forum* to advise the Quebec Commissioner of Health and Well-Being on the performance of the Quebec health system (2007) and many one-off deliberative 'experiments' led by researchers on different topics (e.g., genetics and genomics, xenotransplantation, health care planning and resource allocation) (Einsiedel, 2002; Litva et al. 2002; Abelson et al., 2003; Forest et al., 2004; Abelson et al., 2007). Common to all of these is the implementation of a methodology that includes a core set of reproducible elements including a particular approach to participant recruitment, information sharing and knowledge acquisition, followed by a critical discussion and exchange component for the purposes of eliciting participants' values.

SITUATING THE DELIBERATIVE METHOD WITHIN THE QUALITATIVE HEALTH RESEARCH PARADIGM

Clarifying the purpose of the method

Of the policy goals most often cited for employing deliberative methods, that of soliciting service user and public opinions to inform the design of programmes and policies resonates most closely with its use as a research method. Both qualitative and quantitative research methods are commonly used to gather information for the purposes of designing, evaluating and improving policies and programmes that are responsive to the needs and preferences of intended users or recipients. Surveys are commonly used quantitative tools; focus groups tend to be the qualitative equivalent. Deliberative methods can be a hybrid of the two but tend to be categorized within the qualitative research paradigm.

Researchers working with end users to inform the design of health care programmes and policies need to ensure that the purpose and intended use for the output obtained from the deliberation is carefully specified at the outset of the project so that appropriate data collection and analysis processes can be designed and executed. A key decision point is whether deliberation is to be used for the purposes of eliciting *individual* opinions, preferences or values or whether there is a desire to observe, analyze and report on the deliberation in a more holistic way. If the sole purpose is to collect and aggregate individual data, which is the basis of the deliberative polling method (Fishkin et al., 2000), then the methods and principles of survey design would apply and the method would fall into the quantitative research paradigm. Much of the recent experimentation with deliberative methods has treated the data collection and analysis process as a qualitative endeavour, focusing on group discussion for the purposes of generating and identifying themes, more akin to focus group methodology. For example, in a recent article in the *American Journal of Bioethics*, the authors describe a public deliberation study about the use of social distancing measures in the event of a pandemic in which they convened four 90-minute focus groups of 8–10 adults to discuss the topic (Baum et al., 2009). Although the authors carefully describe the generic features of deliberative methods, they do not go on explicitly to describe the key features of *their* own 'deliberative' process and how it differs, if at all, from focus group methods.

Other challenges arise when the objective is to observe and analyze the deliberation as a sociopolitical process, for example, through the examination of power relations between deliberative participants, or the forms of evidence that are used to support arguments for and against a particular policy. This type of approach requires the selection of appropriate data collection methods that will allow for the rigorous application of content, process and discourse analysis methods. Whether the purpose of the deliberation is to collect individual or collective views, or to examine interactions among participants, these are key decisions that are likely to be negotiated with the end user of the deliberation output and should be made explicit in the description of the methodology.

CODIFYING THE METHOD

The need for a clearly articulated description of a research method is essential for its reproducibility. As the use of deliberation expands, a key question for health policy researchers to resolve is what constitutes 'the deliberative method' and how it is distinguishable from other methodologies such as PAR, interviews and focus groups.

As an emerging research method, and because of its popularity among public participation practitioners and policy makers, it has been plagued by ambiguity over its core elements.

As described earlier, deliberative methods have been categorized as a broad grouping of public involvement approaches that include citizens' juries, planning cells, deliberative polling, consensus conferences and citizens' panels (Rowe and Frewer, 2005), all of which involve the following design features: (i) a clearly articulated purpose; (ii) the selection and recruitment of participants; (iii) the selection and design of information materials to be shared before and during the deliberative session; (iv) the facilitation of structured, problem-based group discussion; and (v) an explicit process for eliciting and synthesizing individual and/or collective input. Each of these features is discussed in the following section.

Participant selection and recruitment

The identification and recruitment of participants for deliberative public involvement processes is a key aspect of the research method. Since deliberation commonly involves the convening of groups, based on voluntary participation, their assembly can easily introduce bias and must be carefully considered in the selection and recruitment process. Due to its close links to public opinion polling, some sampling strategies involve stratified or proportional random sampling to achieve representativeness across desired characteristics (e.g., age, gender, geography, culture, etc.). For example, the formation of the 30-member Citizens Council of the National Institute of Clinical and Health Excellence in the United Kingdom in 2001–02 involved an initial solicitation of expressions of interest followed by the selection of 15 men and 15 women who were, once they met certain selection criteria (e.g., not employed in the NHS), selected to 'reflect the make-up of the population in England and Wales' (NICE, 2002).

Substantive representation is also used to guide participant selection and recruitment that is linked to the policy or programme that the deliberation is intended to guide. This resembles the practice of 'stakeholder involvement'. For example, in a comparative study of five deliberative experiments across Canadian regional health authorities, the participant recruitment process involved the selection of 20–25 leaders of community organizations with a general interest in the programme or policy under deliberation. In one region, this was a group of family members and community service organizations providing services for autistic children who came together to discuss and plan for the allocation of resources for children with autism. In another region, the communities of interest were service organizations and families living in a rapidly expanding city suburb who were convened to inform the planning of health promotion programmes for young children in the newly established community (Abelson et al., 2007).

Greater clarity in the description of the sampling and recruitment methods used and their underlying rationales is required.

Data collection

The collection of qualitative data from deliberative exchanges generally takes one of the following forms: audio recording, video recording or note taking through direct observation. The choice of recording technique is normally driven by the objectives of the research study and the desire to minimize the obtrusiveness of the research team members. For example, a study of the deliberative engagement process itself for the purposes of assessing the fairness of exchange or the interactions among participants would call for visual data collection through video recording and/or direct observation. In contrast, standard audio recording followed by the preparation of a transcript for content and thematic analysis would be more appropriate for studies guided by content-related research questions.

The adoption of the most appropriate or desirable data collection technique can be constrained by several factors. Decision maker sponsors of deliberative processes are sometimes reluctant to allow video recording of the proceedings due to resource constraints or concerns about the intrusiveness of the equipment and its effect on the participants. Second, the presence of multiple members of the research team as note takers to ensure high-quality observations (especially important when video recording is not available) may also be met with opposition from decision maker sponsors due to concerns about intrusiveness. These issues should be negotiated early in the research process between the research team and the decision makers to ensure that the quality of the data collected is not compromised.

Data analysis

Among the most significant challenges of conducting collaborative policy-informing research is that of meeting the dual, and often competing, objectives of carrying out rigorous analysis while providing end users with a product that can be incorporated into their decision making process in a timely way. These challenges are particularly acute for qualitative researchers involved in the analysis of data generated from deliberative fora as they are frequently very long, sometimes lasting for a day or more, producing hours of recordings to be transcribed, cleaned and entered into a qualitative data analysis program before any analyses can be performed. Researchers in this field would benefit from developing distinct, but potentially overlapping, analytic plans to meet the needs of decision maker partners who may require a more narrative or summative analysis in a short period and to address the questions posed by the research team, which will likely call for a combination of interpretive and content analysis methods for analyzing text, talk and group interaction (Silverman, 2006). In particular, rigorous approaches to the analysis of video recordings of deliberative processes are needed. These should draw much more comprehensively on the range of available qualitative analytic techniques to ensure appropriate and reproducible analyses (Miles and Huberman, 2002). To date, only a few exemplary studies of this kind exist (Mendelberg, 2002; Delli Carpini et al., 2004; Davies et al., 2005).

Rigorous analysis of transcripts of audio recordings could also be improved. The current body of work in the qualitative analysis of verbatim transcripts of deliberative processes is a mix of thematic content and process analysis, with greater emphasis on the content. The focus on content analysis is often driven by the end user's desire for usable output to inform a decision making process. This priority often steers the analytic process away from a more thorough analysis of themes or the deliberation process itself. Lack of attention to these aspects of the analysis limits researchers' abilities to properly assess the merits of deliberation as a method for complementing traditional public opinion surveys, which should be in the interest of end users given the resources involved in initiating and sustaining these deliberative mechanisms.

RESEARCH METHOD AS POLICY INPUT: CAN A RIGOUR–RELEVANCE BALANCE BE STRUCK?

In its current state, the deliberative method has not been sufficiently codified to justify its place in the qualitative health policy researcher's toolbox. A number of elements need to be addressed in order to elevate it to a credible, traceable method within this toolbox. First, the tensions between the political and instrumental goals of deliberative processes need to be adequately reconciled to ensure its robustness as a legitimate research method. Pandering to the political goals of deliberation often results in greater attention being paid to 'process' (i.e., ensuring that participants are satisfied) over 'substance' (i.e., the output that is produced from the deliberative process) (Abelson and Gauvin, 2006). Small-scale successes and the use of opinion leaders can be effective champions for the pursuit of multiple goals simultaneously. For example, the commitment of United Kingdom's National Institute for Clinical and Health Excellence (NICE) to the rigorous evaluation of its citizens' council, including a focus on both process and content, represents one of the most comprehensive qualitative analyses of a deliberative process undertaken to date (Davies et al., 2005).

Involvement of the end user or 'deliberation sponsor' is essential for deliberative methods to develop and mature as a qualitative research method. These collaborations can be highly rewarding for both decision makers and researchers. Decision makers have the opportunity to work with researchers skilled in the design and implementation of the deliberative method and researchers are provided with an exciting real-world laboratory in which to generate and test hypotheses and advance their field of knowledge. In highly politicised contexts, however, where members of the public may be concerned about sponsors using a poorly defined method to reach predetermined conclusions (Campbell and Townsend, 2003), close relationships between researcher and sponsor subject the researchers to vulnerabilities that can constrain the rigorous implementation of the method and raise challenges about the validity of the scientific process.

First and foremost, the *resource, time and political constraints* of the end user can pose challenges to ensuring rigorous design and implementation. Sponsors of deliberation are often working within tight timelines to host and produce results from a deliberation in order to inform a decision making process. They are keen to have immediate results. This poses challenges to the standard convention of producing a transcript of the deliberation prior to analysis. There are several ways to address this. First, ongoing interaction between researchers and end users throughout the design of the deliberative project can often mitigate these problems, or at least raise awareness between the parties of the conflicts between their timelines. Up-front negotiations to produce preliminary or partial findings can often satisfy end users while maintaining the integrity of the research process. Efficiencies in transcription can be achieved through the use of experienced transcribers and targeted transcription, guided by the research team, to focus on the richest sections of the deliberation that are likely to yield important content data for the end user.

Due to their novelty as a method for obtaining public views, as compared with public opinion surveys, deliberations also tend to be subjected to *modest budgets* implying modest implementation, analysis and evaluation components. If working under modest budgets, researchers may need to scale back the scope of the research (e.g., collect and analyze only a portion of the deliberation) to ensure that the integrity of the research process is preserved. Increased comparative studies of the costs and outputs of these types of studies as compared with other methods is recommended to improve decision maker awareness of the trade-offs from committing adequate resources to these studies.

As discussed earlier, end user concerns about *participant burden and researcher intrusiveness* can threaten the quality and comprehensiveness of the data collection process. These concerns are typically manifested through limits to the number of researchers who can observe a deliberative process and requirements for researcher–observers to minimize their obtrusiveness by taking notes rather than having the proceedings audio- or video-recorded. Often, these concerns rest with the end users of the deliberation and not the participants themselves. Through clear explanation of the purpose of the research and role of the research team, in the context of a comprehensive informed consent process, these concerns are often easily addressed. Careful attention to the location of researchers in the room and guidance regarding appropriate researcher body language can also reduce their obtrusiveness and mitigate any possible negative influence on participants. Clear articulation of the rationale and complementary roles for the research observers (e.g., one to observe visual cues and the process of deliberation and one to record content) can also reduce end user concerns.

Respectful and cooperative relationships between the research team and organizational staff are essential to the successful implementation of the method. Often the collaborative project is negotiated between the executive of the organization and the principal investigator of the research team, but the project is implemented by organizational and research team staff who may not understand each others' respective roles. Encouraging organizations to recognize the value of research has become a major focus of attention within the organizational studies literature (Pettigrew and Fenton, 2000; Hinings et al., 2004; Denis and Langley, 2005; Abelson et al. 2007; Casebeer, 2007).

Finally, in order for the deliberative method to mature as an applied qualitative research method, a clear *distinction between analysts and advocates of deliberative methods* must be made. The growing popularity of deliberative methods has been driven in part by advocates of participatory democracy and their ideological commitment to these forms of public involvement. While this motivation is likely to continue to drive experimentation with these methods, effort should be made to ensure that this experimentation provides an opportunity for the development of a rigorous set of methods that guide this work.

In this chapter, we have explored the rigour–relevance challenges facing qualitative researchers working in the field of health policy, with a specific focus on the duality that often exists between the research method and the production of policy inputs. Using the newly emerging deliberative method as a case study, we traced the evolution of the deliberative method within the health policy and health services research fields and situated in the qualitative research methods paradigm. The challenges associated with its use as a method for contributing to policy-informing research were discussed with recommendations for increasing its robustness as a qualitative research method as it develops and matures in the future while ensuring that it continues to meet the needs of its end users.

REFERENCES

Abelson, J. and Gauvin, F.-P. (2006) *Assessing the Impacts of Public Participation: Concepts, Evidence and Policy Implications*. Research report of the Public Involvement Network, Canadian Policy Research Networks, January 2006.

Abelson, J., Forest, P-G., Eyles, J., Smith, P., Martin, E., and Gauvin, F.-P. (2002) 'Obtaining Public Input for Health Systems Decisionmaking: Past Experiences and Future Prospects', *Canadian Public Administration*, 45(1): 70–97.

Abelson, J., Eyles, J., McLeod, C., Collins, P., and Forest, P.-G. (2003) 'Does Deliberation Make a Difference? A Citizen's Panel Study of Health Goals Priority Setting', *Health Policy*, 66(1): 95–106.

Abelson, J., Lomas, J., Eyles, J., Birch, S., and Veenstra, G. (1995). 'Does the Community Want Devolved Authority?' *Canadian Medical Association Journal*, 153: 3–12.

Abelson, J., Forest, P.-G., Eyles, J., Smith, P., Martin, E., and Gauvin, F.-P. (2003) 'Deliberations About Deliberative Methods: Issues in the Design and Evaluation of Public Consultation Processes', *Social Science and Medicine*, 57: 239–51.

Abelson, J., Forest, P.-G., Eyles, J., Casebeer, A., Martin, E., Mackean, G., and the Effective Public Consultation Project Team (2007) 'Exploring the Role of Context in the Implementation of a Deliberative Public Participation Experiment: Results from a Canadian Comparative Study', *Social Science and Medicine*, 64: 2115–28.

Baum, N., Goold, S., and Jacobson, P. (2009) ' "Listen to the People": Public Deliberation About Social Distancing Measures in a Pandemic', *American Journal of Bioethics*.

Beierle, T.C. and Cayford, J. (2002) *Democracy in Practice*: *Public Participation in Environmental Decisions*. Washington, DC: Resources for the Future.

Beierle, T. and Konisky, P. (2000) 'Values, Conflict and Trust in Participatory Environmental Planning', *Journal of Policy Analysis and Management*, 19(4): 587–602.

Bostwick, M. (1999) 'Twelve Angry Citizens: Can Citizens' Juries Improve Local Democracy in New Zealand?', *Political Science*, 50(2): 236–46.

Bowie, C., Richardson, A. and Sykes, W. (1995) 'Consulting the Public About Health Service Priorities', *British Medical Journal*, 311: 1155–8.

Bowling, A., Jacobson, B., and Southgate, L. (1993) 'Explorations in Consultation of the Public and Health Professionals on Priority Setting in an Inner London Health District', *Social Science and Medicine*, 37(7): 851–7.

Burstein, P. (2003) 'The Impact of Public Opinion on Public Policy: A Review and an Agenda', *Political Research Quarterly*, 56(1): 29–40.

Campbell, S. and Townsend, E. (2003) 'Flaws Undermine Results of UK Biotech Debate', *Nature* (Letter), 425(6958): 559.

Canadian Institutes of Health Research. The Partnership in Health System Improvement (PHSI) Program (2009). http://www.cihr-irsc.gc.ca/e/34347.html (accessed July 14, 2009).

Canadian Policy Research Networks (2000) 'Canadians Speak Out on Health Care', *The Society We Want Newsletter*, 5: 1–7.

Casebeer A.L. (2007) In Wallace, M., Fertig, M., and Scheller, E. (eds) *Learning to Navigate the Noise of Change: Lessons from Complex Health System Contexts*, *Managing Change in the Public Sector*. Oxford: Blackwell.

Coast, J. (1996) 'Core Services: Pluralistic Bargaining in New Zealand'. In J. Coast, J. Donovank, and S. Frankel (eds) *Priority Setting: The Health Care Debate* (pp. 65–82). Chichester: Wiley.

Cohen, J. (1989) 'Deliberation and Democratic Legitimacy'. In A. Hamlin and P. Pettit (eds) *The Good Polity: Normative Analysis of the State* (pp. 17–34). Oxford: Basil Blackwell.

Collins, H. and Evans, R. (2002) 'The Third Wave of Science Studies', *Social Studies of Science*, 32(2): 235–96.

Cookson, R. and Dolan, P. (1999) 'Public Views on Health Care Rationing: A Group Discussion Study', *Health Policy*, 49(1–2): 63–74.

Coote, A. and Lenaghan, J. (1997) *Citizens' Juries*: *Theory into Practice*. London: Institute for Public Policy Research.

Creswell, J.W. (1998) *Qualitative Inquiry and Research Design*: *Choosing Among Five Traditions*. Thousand Oaks, CA: Sage.

Davies, C., Wetherell, M., Barnett, E., and Seymour-Smith, S. (2005) *Opening the Box*: *Evaluating the Citizens Council of NICE*. Milton Keynes, UK: The Open University.

Delli Carpini, M.X., Cook, F.L., and Jacobs, L. (2004) 'Public Deliberation, Discursive Participation and Citizen Engagement: A Review of the Empirical Literature', *Annual Review of Political Science*, 7: 315–44.

Denis, J.L. and Langley, A. (2005) 'Rethinking Leadership in Public Organizations'. In E. Ferlies, L.E. Lynn and C. Pollitt (eds) *The Oxford Handbook of Public Management* (pp. 446–67). Oxford University Press.

Devine, F. (2002) 'Qualitative Methods'. In Marsh, D. and Stoker, G. (eds.) *Theory and Methods in Political Science* (pp. 197–215). New York, NY: Palgrave Macmillan.

Dolan, P., Cookson, R., and Ferguson, B. (1999) 'Effect of Discussion and Deliberation on the Public's Views of Priority Setting in Health Care: Focus Group Study', *British Medical Journal*, 318: 916–9.

Donovan, J. and Coast, J. (1996) 'Public Participation in Priority Setting: Commitment or Illusion?'. In J. Coast, J. Donovan, and S. Frankel (eds) *Priority Setting: The Health Care Debate* (pp. 203–24). Chichester: Wiley & Sons.

Dunkerley, D. and Glasner, P. (1998) 'Empowering the Public? Citizens' Juries and the New Genetic Technologies', *Critical Public Health*, 8(3): 181–92.

Dryzek, J.S. (2000) *Deliberative Democracy and Beyond*. Oxford: Oxford University Press.

Editorial team (2001) 'In Brief: NICE to Get Advice from a Citizens Council', *BMJ*, 323(7324): 1268.

Einsiedel, E. (2002) 'Assessing a Controversial Medical Technology: Canadian Public Consultations on Xenotransplantation', *Public Understanding of Science*, 11: 315–31.

Einsiedel, E.F. (2006) 'TransAtlantic Perspectives on Public Engagement with Science'. In J. Turney (ed.) *Engaging Science: Thoughts, Deeds, Analysis, and Action*. London: Wellcome Trust.

EKOS Research Associates, Inc. (2000) Rethinking Citizen Engagement: Citizen Engagement and Social Cohesion—Moving from Theory to Practice.

Fearon, J.D. (1998) 'Deliberation as Discussion'. In J. Elster (ed.) *Deliberative Democracy* (pp. 44–68). Cambridge: Cambridge University Press.

Fishkin, J.S. (1991) *Democracy and Deliberation*. New Haven: Yale University Press.

Fishkin, J.S., Luskin, R.C., and Jowell, R. (2000) 'Deliberative Polling and Public Consultation', *Parliamentary Affairs*, 53(4): 657–66.

Forest, P.-G., Gauvin, F.-P., Martin, E., Perrault, C., Abelson J., and Eyles, J. (2004) 'Une expérience de consultation publique délibérative dans Charlevoix', *Recherches Sociographiques*, 2004, XLV(1): 77–104.

Fulop, N., Allen, P., Clarke, A., and Black, N. (2002) *Studying the Organization and Delivery of Health Services: Research Methods*. New York: Routledge.

Government of Quebec. 2005. An Act Respecting the Health and Welfare Commissioner. L.R.Q. Bill 38 (chapter 18).

Graham, K.A. and Phillips, S.D. (1998) 'Making Public Participation More Effective: Issues for Local Government'. In K.A. Graham and S. D. Phillips (eds) *Citizen Engagement: Lessons in Participation from Local Government* (pp. 1–24). Monographs on Canadian Public Administration, No. 22. Institute of Public Administration of Canada: Toronto.

Gutmann, A., and Thompson, D. (1996). *Democracy and Disagreement*. Cambridge: Harvard University Press.

Habermas, J. (1984) *The Theory of Communicative Action I: Reason and the Rationalization of Society*. Boston: Beacon Press.

Hinings, C.R., Greenwood, R., Reay, T., and Suddaby, R. (2004) 'Dynamics of Change in Organizational Fields'. In Poole, M.S. and Van de Ven, A.H. (eds) *Handbook of Organizational Change and Innovation* (pp. 304–23). New York: Oxford University Press.

Inglehart, R. (1995) 'Changing Values, Economic Development and Political Change', *International Social Science Journal*, 47(3): 379–403.

Inglehart, R., Nevitte, N., and Basanez, M. (1996) *The North American Trajectory: Social Institutions and Social Change*. New York/Berlin: Aldine de Gruyter.

Jacobs, L.R. (1993) *The Health of Nations: Public Opinion and the Making of American and British Health Policy*. Ithaca: Cornell University Press.

Lenaghan, J. (1999) 'Involving the Public in Rationing Decisions. The Experience of Citizens' Juries', *Health Policy*, 49(1–2): 45–61.

Lenaghan, J., New, B., and Mitchell, E. (1996) 'Setting Priorities: Is There a Role for Citizens' Juries?' *British Medical Journal*, 312: 1591–3.

Leroux, T., Hirtle, M., and Fortin, L.-N. (1998). 'An Overview of Public Consultation Mechanisms Developed to Address the Ethical and Social Issues Raised by Biotechnology', *Journal of Consumer Policy*, 21(4): 445–81.

Litva, A., Coast, J., Donovan, J., Eyles, J., Shepherd, M., Tacchi, J., Abelson, J., and Morgan, K. (2002) "The Public Is Too Subjective": Public Involvement at Different Levels of Health-Care Decision Making', *Social Science and Medicine*, 54(12): 1825–37.

Manin, B. (1987) '*On Legitimacy and Political Deliberation'*, Political Theory, 15(3): 338–68.

Maxwell, J.S., Rosell, S., and Forest, P.-G. (2003) 'Giving Citizens a Voice in Health Care Policy in Canada', *British Medical Journal*, May, 326: 1031–3.

McIver, S. (1998) *Healthy Debate? An Independent Evaluation of Citizens' Juries in Health Settings*. London: King's Fund Publishing.

Mendelberg T. (2002) 'The Deliberative Citizen: Theory and Evidence'. In Delli Carpini, M.X., Huddy, L., and Shapiro, R. (eds) *Research in Micropolitics: Political Decisionmaking, Deliberation and Participation*. Greenwich, CT: JAI Press, 6: 151–93.

Meyer, J. (2000) 'Using Qualitative Methods in Health Related Action Research', *BMJ*, 320: 178–91.

Mitton, C., and Donaldson, C. (2002) 'Setting Priorities in Canadian Regional Health Authorities: A Survey of Key Decision Makers', *Health Policy*, 60(1): 39–58.

Mullen, P. (2000) 'Public Involvement in Health Care Priority Setting: Are the Methods Appropriate and Valid?' In C. Ham and A. Coulter (eds) *The Global Challenge of Health Care Rationing* (pp. 163–74). Buckingham, UK: Open University Press.

National Institute of Clinical and Health Excellence (2002) Available at: www.nice.org.uk

Nevitte, N. (1996) *The Decline of Deference: Canadian Value Change in Cross-National Perspective*. Peterborough, ON: Broadview Press.

O'Donnell, M. and Entwistle, V. (2004) 'Consumer Involvement in Decisions About What Health-Related Research Is Funded', *Health Policy*, 70(3): 281–90.

Pettigrew, A.M. and Fenton, E.M. (2000) *The Innovating Organization*. Thousand Oaks, CA: Sage.

Pivik, J., Rode, E., and Ward, C. (2004) 'A Consumer Involvement Model for Health Technology Assessment in Canada', *Health Policy*, 69(2): 253–68.

Pratchett, L. (1999) 'New Fashions in Public Participation: Towards Greater Democracy?', *Parliamentary Affairs*, 52(4): 617–33.

Reason, P. and Bradbury, H. (2007) *The SAGE Handbook of Action Research: Participative Inquiry and Practice*. Thousand Oaks, CA: Sage.

Richardson, A., Charny, M., and Hanmer-Lloyd, S. (1992) 'Public Opinion and Purchasing', *British Medical Journal*, 304: 680–4.

Ritchie, J. and Spencer, L. (2002) 'Qualitative Data Analysis for Applied Policy Research'. In Huberman, A.M. and Miles, M.B. (eds) *The Qualitative Researcher's Companion* (pp. 305–30). Thousand Oaks, CA: Sage.

Romanow (2002) *Building on Values: The Future of Health Care in Canada – Final Report*. Ottawa, ON: Commission on the Future of Health Care in Canada.

Rowe, G. and Frewer, L.J. (2000) 'Public Participation Methods: A Framework for Evaluation', *Science, Technology and Human Values*, 25(1): 3–29.

Rowe, G. and Frewer, L. (2004) 'Evaluating Public Participation Exercises: A Research Agenda', *Science, Technology and Human Values*, 29(4): 512–56.

Rowe, G. and Frewer, L.J. (2005) 'A Typology of Public Engagement Mechanisms', *Science, Technology and Human Values*, 30(2): 251–90.

Royle, J. and Oliver, J. (2004) 'Consumer Involvement in the Health Technology Assessment Program', *International Journal of Health Technology Assessment in Health Care*, 20(4), 493–7.

Silverman, D. (2006) *Interpreting Qualitative Data: Methods for Analyzing Talk, Text and Interaction*. Thousand Oaks, CA: Sage.

Simrell King, C. (1998) 'The Question of Participation: Toward Authentic Public Participation in Public Administration', *Public Administration Review*, 58: 317–26.

Smith, G. and Wales, C. (1999) 'The Theory and Practice of Citizens' Juries', *Policy and Politics*, 27(3): 295–308.

Stronks, K., Strijbis, A., Wendte, J.F., and Gunning-Schepers, L.J.G. (1997) 'Who Should Decide? Qualitative Analysis of Panel Data from Public, Patients, Health Care Professionals, and Insurers on Priorities in Health Care', *British Medical Journal*, 315: 92–6.

Wiseman, V., Mooney, G., Berry, G., and Tang, K.C. (2003) 'Involving the General Public in Priority Setting: Experiences from Australia', *Social Science and Medicine*, 56(5): 1001–12.

32

Cross National Qualitative Health Research

Carine Vassy and Richard Keller

What do researchers mean when they say they are undertaking international comparison in social science research? Typically, they mean the comparison of a phenomenon in a given national setting with another, similar, phenomenon in a different national setting. This geographical comparison, which tends to privilege national borders as key parameters, is sometimes compounded by a historical perspective designed to capture the dynamic nature of the phenomena being investigated. In this chapter, we shall apply a rigorous definition of cross national comparative research that distinguishes it from other forms of comparative research and from other implicitly comparative references to foreign countries. We call 'an international comparison' a work that is explicitly and systematically comparative, in which, from the outset, researchers plan to examine similarities and differences among the phenomena they study in different countries. This allows them to produce, to modify, or confirm a generalization, or even a theory (Maurice, 1989).

Since the late nineteenth century, research in the social sciences has shown the influence of national characteristics on health. Emile Durkheim, the founder of French sociology, revealed that the incidence of suicide was higher in some countries than in others through a quantitative analysis of suicide rates in different European countries (Durkheim, 1986). For much of the second half of the twentieth century, researchers have continued to privilege quantitative methods in comparative studies of health. Some, for example, have drawn on a battery of statistical indicators to compare health systems in North America and Europe (Whiteford and Nixon, 2000). However, international comparisons based on qualitative methods also began to appear: early examples include the work of the American sociologist William A. Glaser on the organization of hospitals, and the professions that work in them, in both industrialized and developing countries (Glaser, 1963; 1970), or the work of Eliot Freidson (1970) on the political organization of the medical profession.

Such comparisons remain fashionable in Europe and the United States in a range of domains, including health. Yet, effective comparative research can be costly and time-consuming. What does international comparison entail in the health social sciences? Why might studying different occurrences of a similar phenomenon in a single country not prove as interesting as undertaking an international comparison? Does the current vogue for international comparisons actually limit the range of questions asked in a given project, instead of broadening them, by focussing the researcher's attention on certain phenomena?

To reflect on these questions, we propose to study first the motives that lead researchers to study health in an international and comparative context. Then we explore how researchers organize their study on the practical and intellectual levels, what methods they use, the difficulties they encounter, and the potential limits to this exercise.

WHY THIS FASCINATION WITH INTERNATIONAL COMPARISONS IN HEALTH SOCIAL SCIENCES?

Acceleration of international exchanges

Social science researchers have adapted to the globalization of their objects of study, which, where health is concerned, dates to antiquity. The Hippocratic texts, with their emphasis on the necessity of striking an equilibrium between body and environment, necessarily dwelt on the meaning of health in diverse geographical contexts, and physicians have travelled for their education since the beginnings of Western medicine: to the universities of large European metropolises in the medieval period, for example. International exchanges of knowledge have at times consisted of international scientific comparisons: physicians and epidemiologists have compared the causes of mortality in the United States, Britain, and France since the mid-nineteenth century, for example. And certainly European and American encroachment on the tropics in the age of high imperialism both depended upon and facilitated the development of medical geography and tropical medicine as professional subfields in their own right, as well as the deployment of medical power in colonial settings (Arnold, 1993; Keller, 2007). These exchanges have assisted the diffusion of Western biomedical knowledge and amplified its pretensions towards universal applicability. These exchanges concern both medicine itself, and other professions linked to health and health care, whether in the clinical, scientific, political, administrative, or industrial realms.

The development of communications and transportation in the twentieth century saw a parallel development in the exchange of ideas in public policy, research, biomedical technology, and organizational innovation. Actors in health care have increasingly borrowed and adapted foreign formulae, particularly in Europe. Similar public debates, institutions, and legislation have appeared at the same time in different countries, driving towards the creation of public welfare systems in the aftermath of the Second World War, for example, or towards the legalization of abortion. If those observed by social scientists are aware of what their 'homologues' in other countries are doing, and are influenced by their example, how can research be limited to a national setting?

This internationalization of exchange also affects social scientists. Ideas circulate beyond borders, particularly in international English-language journals. Reading the work of authors from a different nationality, even if they only speak of their own countries, allows for the discovery of foreign examples and can arouse interest in international comparisons.

Finally, many calls for research proposals have prioritized the funding of international comparative research. This is particularly the case for studies financed by the European Union, which typically requires that research must apply to a certain minimum number of countries or include researchers from different countries or regions. Also in Europe, certain national research funders prefer to support projects that have a comparative dimension, intending to use the results for improving governance practices by drawing on foreign examples. These agencies see comparative study as a source of helpful lessons for the improvement of administrative effectiveness.

Intellectual appeal of comparison

Researchers' interest in the intrinsic intellectual value of comparative and international research has matched that of funding agencies, especially in the study of the implications of macro-level policy choices for downstream organization and practice. Globally, health care systems are organized with often dramatically different emphases on social solidarity and collective or private provision. For example, many researchers who look at the United States and Canada want to know whether it makes a difference that the United States has a pluralistic system based on extensive use of managed care and that Canada has social insurance. To what extent do these factors affect issues such as the organization of hospitals, the coordination of community health services and matters such as resource allocation and rationing (e.g., Bourgeault et al., 2001)? Micro-level studies can shed light on the question of whether political or ideological differences at the macro level result in continued system differences at the organizational level or whether there are more powerful forces pushing towards convergence between different types of systems (Field, 1999; Wessen, 1999). In the EU, this is also a critical issue because of the requirement for all members to comply with certain general principles represented in EC

(European Community) Directives, while being free to develop detailed policies in different ways under the principle of subsidiarity, that member states should be able to implement common policies in ways that are sensitive to their particular traditions (Hauray, 2006).

Much of the intellectual impetus that has pushed social scientists towards international comparisons is not exclusive to the study of health. International comparison allows social scientists to broaden their scope and to escape certain prejudices. It introduces surprises to researchers, contributes to their awareness of the constructed nature of certain facts, and allows for the rediscovery of relations they may have ignored in their own countries. As with most new arrivals to a foreign country, researchers are often confronted with their prejudices and forced to modify their preconceptions (Schütz, 1964). This is of course an eternal problem for the social sciences: researchers often have *a priori* perspective on a given phenomenon before beginning to study it, by virtue of the socialization that has accustomed them to the particular representations and social categories that are necessary for daily life in a given society (Durkheim, 1987). In the health social sciences, these *a priori* representations are extremely significant. Everyone has had health problems, and has an idea of what the ideal health system should be. The challenge for scientific work is to pass from such social categories and representations to rigorously founded concepts. International comparison, among other research methods, can help reduce the weight of these preconceptions by revealing the fluid nature of certain categories as they vary from one country to another.

International comparison also helps researchers to become aware of the socially situated nature of knowledge. They are influenced by intellectual traditions and by contemporary public debates. Doing research in foreign countries can increase their awareness of the limits of their scientific knowledge. Collaboration with researchers trained in other countries can help reveal this ethnocentrism: that is, a tendency to draw on one's own social group as the only model of reference (De Vries et al., 2001a; Wrede et al., 2006).

Another interesting aspect of international comparison is that it is not a method, but a strategy (Lallement and Spurk, 2003; Oyen, 1990). It is therefore compatible with a wide range of qualitative and quantitative research methods and can be applied to the study of a broad array of objects and phenomena, such as public policy, social interactions, cultural representations, social mobilisations, scientific and technological innovations, professions, and organizations. It is also compatible with a number of theoretical perspectives. Hantrais (1999: 99) emphasizes that the amount of material collected in an international comparison is 'capable of sustaining the diverse interests of universalists, culturalists and societalists'. Take, for example, the study of hospitals as the emblematic institutions of modern medicine. In a functionalist perspective, an international comparison can reveal that certain aspects of hospitals appear to be present regardless of the national milieu, because hospitals perform the same social function from one country to another. However, it also reveals the microcosm that the hospital represents, which reflects the environment in which it is set, as defined by social and economic structures, cultural values, or other factors (Fox, 1988; Glaser, 1970). These opposing theoretical perspectives are both relevant. As with other social facts, national similarities and differences are constructed, not self-evident. In this work, researchers can direct their attention towards either similarities or differences. It is not a matter of saying that scientific objectivity does not apply to social science, but rather that its practitioners recognize the role of theoretical perspectives and the researcher's subjectivity when faced with the empirical richness of qualitative studies (Vassy, 2003). When the studies are international, the materials collected can be vast and vastly difficult to interpret: we return to this point below.

HOW DOES INTERNATIONAL COMPARISON CHANGE THE WORK OF THE SOCIAL SCIENTIST?

International comparative research forces scholars to modify their work in several ways. It first necessitates the choice of one or several foreign countries and the resolution of sampling problems and access to the field.

The choice of countries included in the comparison can follow from a range of scientific criteria (Hantrais, 1999). In contrast to those colleagues who work essentially with quantitative indicators, researchers who use qualitative methods tend to select a small number of sites. The extent to which the countries studied are representative of the rest of the world is secondary to the goal of conducting a deep analysis and collecting extensive material in each. In general, sociologists and political scientists compare industrialized countries at the same level of economic, scientific, and technological development, which are also the countries in which their discipline and their concepts have been developed (Oyen, 1990: 16). Other factors also influence the selection of research sites: for example, as a function of the constraints imposed by funding agencies, or by practical considerations such as the researcher's language skills or the material and temporal constraints of the research.

In any case, Hantrais (1999) recommends that researchers justify the scientific pertinence of their choice and its consequences for the study's results. Appropriate problem-choice is critical to such research: do the settings placed in comparison have sufficient shared factors to make for a useful and illustrative study? A study of health care delivery in Ouagadougou and Paris will clearly reveal dramatic contrasts, but to what extent are such contrasts useful? Contrasting approaches to health and healing in Ouagadougou and Dakar, or in Paris and Berlin, would likely prove more informative to readers and researchers.

Cross national multisited ethnography

Effective comparative research requires researchers to become familiar in detail with the research settings. Multisite ethnography, a research strategy that has become increasingly common among American anthropologists, reveals some of the inherent promise and challenge of comparative research. Anthropologists have traditionally trained through intensive fieldwork in one setting, often spending years learning a language and culture. Comparative anthropology therefore requires extensive retraining: learning a new language and new cultural dimensions inherent to a new locale. Anthropologists have tried to avoid these problems through constructing comparative studies which set their own field-work alongside the published accounts of others. However, this may be problematic in its reliance on secondary sources and the filtration of original data through the analyses and interpretations of other scholars.

Multi site ethnography tries to get round this difficulty by immersing the researcher in diverse settings in one or more countries. The practice is not new and several scholars have defined its methodology (Mintz, 1986; Marcus, 1995; Bestor, 2001). However, its implementation is far from simple, and researchers must strike a balance between the number of countries studied and the depth of the analysis of each. For example, the North American anthropologist Nancy Scheper-Hughes (2000) has studied the traffic in human organs destined for transplantation by conducting fieldwork in three countries – India, South Africa, and Brazil – and by drawing on information about other countries, notably in South America and Eastern Europe. Nevertheless, critics have also charged that such work resembles journalism rather than scholarly research, as its financial and temporal constraints require shortcuts if the project is to be feasible for a single researcher (e.g., Marshall, 2000).

In studies that require fieldwork, country selection can also be influenced by ease of access to different sites. Certain sites can be difficult or even closed to access for researchers because of their personal characteristics (age, sex, or social origins). When they conduct an international comparison, their nationality can be a handicap for working in certain countries. The researchers Prue Chamberlayne and Annette King (1996), who both speak English and German, confronted this problem by working as a team. They studied how in East and West Germany, before and after reunification, families managed the care of disabled persons by mobilising resources in their environment. The researchers conducted interviews to obtain the biographies of caregivers. Because of the antagonism between certain citizens of the two countries, King, the West German researcher, conducted fieldwork only in her own country. The East German fieldwork was conducted either by Chamberlayne, the English researcher, or by local interviewers, and was presented to subjects as a study being conducted for a 'lady in London' (p. 102).

Even when the researcher's nationality does not produce difficulties, unfamiliarity with a foreign country could obstruct access to certain areas and compromise the selection of a proper sample. As in one's own country, one may require a network of contacts to gain access to key persons, who can, in turn, arrange introductions to others in a snowball effect. The selection of key persons is thus extremely important, because they can act as gatekeepers, and thus effectively play a decisive role in identifying the most appropriate field sites. Certain researchers rely, then, on international contacts through those with whom they have already conducted studies in their own country, for example, health professionals.

Methodological difficulties

Once researchers have gained access to foreign field sites, they try to adapt their usage of qualitative research methods. Several examples centred on the most frequently used methods follow.

Researchers often face linguistic difficulties while interviewing subjects in the course of conducting a comparative study.[1] As the British political scientist Steen Mangen has noted (1999), language difficulties and linguistic competence are often 'downgraded' in the presentation of qualitative research in the social sciences, which is all the more curious in that it is difficult to translate a great number of figures of speech: metaphors, understatements, euphemisms, irony, proverbs, and so forth. Researchers who conduct interviews in a foreign language generally understand the language well, without being completely bilingual. They can thus make errors in their interpretation of data. One of the major errors consists in making linguistic and conceptual equivalences too quickly in their translations. A clear example exists in the simple denomination of employment categories: the terms 'nurse' in England, 'infirmière' in France and 'Krankenschwester' in Germany are often considered synonymous in dictionaries. These words signify those persons who have had similar training for similar durations, whose work consists of caring for the sick, and who benefit from policies of reciprocity in their diplomas, which facilitates their professional mobility in Europe. Moreover, in hospitals in the three countries, the profession is largely feminine, and always exists in a subordinate position to the medical profession that in part directs its activity. Yet, when one studies the organization of health care services, 'nurses', 'infirmières', and 'Krankenschwester' do not perform the same tasks, do not offer the same care to patients and are not situated in the same divisions of labour with regard to other caregivers and the medical profession (Vassy, 2003).[2] Seemingly equivalent linguistic categories do not signify the same phenomena in the three countries, and translation thus becomes a particularly acute problem in establishing a rigorous comparison. Many terms pose similar problems: 'care' is a particular example (Ungerson, 1990).

To confront these problems, researchers are often tempted to conduct their interviews in English, as this language has become international. This solution is effective for studying certain subjects; for example, a comparative analysis of public policy, in which researchers can collect satisfactory data from 'experts' in each country who are competent in English, and can complete their work by reading official documents that have been translated into English. However, such work is dependent upon the compliance of specific experts, who in some cases drive data-collection in the direction that can be most advantageous to them. English-language interviewing can also lead to the oversimplification of data and ideas, because in some cases these actors are expressing themselves in a foreign language that they may not have entirely mastered. Moreover, there is the ethical argument that linguistic obstacles should be surmounted by the researcher who stands to benefit from the research rather than by the interviewees (Mangen, 1999). The use of English is in any event impossible when one is conducting research among so-called 'ordinary' subjects who are not part of a socioeconomic elite with English-language skills.

Interviewing in a foreign language

Interviewing people in their native language does not require researchers to completely master that language. But it is preferable that researchers do not hesitate to interrupt the interviewee to request clarification when they have not understood the subject perfectly. Moreover, one can play on the effects of learning a language when one conducts a significant number of interviews. For example, one can leave interviews with the most important informants – those where not a word can be missed – to the end of the study, at which point the investigator will have achieved a higher level of competence in the language. Recording interviews can also be useful, so as to allow for subsequent analysis and identification of specific nuances in vocabulary. One could also potentially listen to the recordings with the assistance of a native speaker of the interviewee's language.

Steen Mangen (1999: 117) argues that, in general, the researcher who conducts an interview in a foreign language is in a 'much more non-directive, passive position' and is, therefore, less likely to get specific responses to his questions. He finds that 'requesting clarification of colloquialisms, and so forth, can prove tedious and can antagonize respondents by interrupting the flow of their discourse' (Mangen, 1999: 117). This is possible, but we must also not lose sight of the fact that there are also many advantages to conducting interviews in a foreign language. The fact of being a foreigner can work in a researcher's favour because, in most cases, foreigners are a temporary presence. Interviewees may thus confide in them – under normal conditions of anonymity – with reduced fears that the information will be locally released and that the persons concerned will become aware of it. Moreover, certain interviewees are truly interested in a dialogue with the researcher to know if the problems that they describe for their situation also exist elsewhere. Finally, having an imperfect mastery of a language, demonstrating that imperfection, and apologizing for it with the interviewee can allow the researcher to pose certain awkward, yet direct, questions on sensitive subjects. Researchers can also repeat their questions – while citing poor language skills as the reason – in the search for a more precise answer to a given question.

Another means of confronting language problems is the use of interpreters. Several researchers have revealed this method's advantages and difficulties when they have conducted interviews on sensitive subjects, such as women's experiences with obstetric health services (Pitchford and Van Teijlingen, 2005). These difficulties are similar to those encountered by researchers who study linguistic minorities in their own countries through interpreters (Bowler, 1997; Bradby, 2002).

Interpreters can transform questions – either consciously or unconsciously – reducing researchers' control over their projects. Similar problems can arise in the process of transcription and translation.

Observation and document analysis

Observation is another method that one can use in international comparative social science research. It occasionally allows the researcher to discover information or interactions about which actors are reluctant to speak. However, when one observes, one listens as well. A lack of language skills can therefore upset the practice of observation in a foreign terrain. In certain cases, interviews can appear easier to accomplish than observations, because they require less time and the researcher can stop the interviewee to request an explanation for something that has not been understood. However, in many cases, researchers have a strong motivation for observing subjects, even if they do not understand everything that is said: actors then know that the researchers have attended certain events and can make reference to them during informal discussions or interviews. Researchers can also take the initiative to speak with actors about these events and request explanations.

Finally, in qualitative studies, researchers often analyze documents, such as archives, professional or administrative documents, judicial texts, or press articles. Working on documents presents researchers conducting a foreign study with an enormous advantage: they can complete this work with a certain temporal flexibility, and can often seek help from others with the text's translation. As a function of the way in which they have learned foreign languages, it may be easier for some researchers to understand the written language than the spoken word. Nevertheless, the difficulties that researchers encounter with the analysis of written documents in their own languages persist and are even amplified with the study of foreign texts: these documents have been prepared for specific purposes. Researchers must necessarily decode the purposes of these documents' authors. The same problem exists for the comparison of statistics collected in different countries, because they are not homogeneous from one country to the next, having been constructed according to neither the same categories nor the same concerns (Desrosières, 1996; Smelser, 2002).

Organizing research

The results of comparative research can vary as a function of the way in which researchers organize their work. Many comparative researchers in the health social sciences work alone. One advantage of solitary work is consistency: the questions the scholar poses in different countries can be completely identical, perhaps with minor variations that result from the development of knowledge over the course of the project. The researcher avoids problems of coordination and the elaboration of protocols for coherent research in the context of a team dynamic. The disadvantage of solitary research is that certain questions and hypotheses that guide the research can remain implicit. However, as Monika Steffen (2004), a German-born political scientist who works in France, has emphasized, exposition of the problem can be done later, for example, at the final stage of analyzing the collected materials.

Other researchers choose to conduct comparative research by working in teams. This allows the group to benefit from the group's analytical strength and collective imagination. It is particularly useful to work with an international group of researchers who are citizens of a given project's relevant countries, as each brings a familiarity with his or her site. Each researcher is thus an 'insider' as an expert specialist in his or her country, and an outsider concerning the other nations. This model demands that the researcher who initiates the project have a solid network of foreign colleagues before the project begins. It is also significantly more costly than solitary work. It increases coordination costs, for example, the organization of meetings among the group, and it requires time for intellectual exchange. Even if electronic communications greatly facilitate these exchanges, not everything can be handled through the written word, and there is significant potential for misinterpretation (De Vries et al., 2001a: xvi). Yet, the quality of the results depends on that of the exchanges among researchers and their mutual comprehension. If the coordination is weak, they wind up with the publication of books that dedicate each chapter to the description of the problem studied in each country, without approaching the problem in the same way, thus reducing the comparison's potential interest. Yet, attaining effective coordination is not easy when the researchers speak different languages and belong to different intellectual traditions. Some directors of international projects are satisfied with the quality of cooperation among their team members (De Vries et al., 2001a; Wrede, 2006). Nevertheless, there are also researchers who remain centred on their own preoccupations, and whose work thereby suffers from 'parochialism' (Smelser, 2002).

These international teams often choose English as their working language, because it allows for communication with the greatest number of researchers in industrialized countries. This is of course problematic for researchers for whom this is not their native language. The risk that they will simplify their thought and lose their nuances as a result of their linguistic handicap is significant. Moreover, at the final writing stage, translating everything into one language presents the basic problem of imposing a cultural and linguistic mould onto the project's questions, data, and results. The same problem exists for the solitary researcher. Clare Ungerson (1996: 64) emphasizes that the language problem, which she calls the 'corruption of data by translation', is major where qualitative research is concerned, and is particularly difficult in research conducted from the perspective of 'grounded theory'. She suggests the solution of working with an international team through the writing stage, which assumes lengthy and generous funding.

Research teams can also be distinguished by the degree of disciplinary diversity of their members. Smelser (2002) issued a plea for the development of interdisciplinary teams in the social sciences, noting that social phenomena are too complex to be interpreted by a single discipline. The interdisciplinary gaze is particularly useful at certain stages of research, for example, when one passes from the description of national similarities or differences to their explanation. At the same time, we must not underestimate the difficulties of working as an interdisciplinary team: when the differences among researchers are too significant, due to their nationalities, their intellectual traditions, or their disciplinary orientations, some may abandon their projects (Wrede et al., 2006). Single-discipline teams and solitary researchers can of course also incorporate a degree of interdisciplinarity by reading the works of relevant complementary disciplines.

The normative positioning of the researcher

The goal of qualitative social science research is only rarely the evaluation of the object of research and the measurement of its performance according to pre-established criteria, towards the end of recommending improved practices. In general, researchers avoid the adoption of an evaluative perspective, because it can diminish the academic quality of their work. The British political scientist Robert Walker (1996) argues that certain scholars who have undertaken international comparisons with an explicitly evaluative end – for example, because they have been financed by the European Commission to evaluate social policies in Europe – have obtained poor quality results. One of the main difficulties of such projects is the choice of 'whether the performance of policies should be matched against the national (or local) objectives that spawned them or against some standardized checklist that may ignore local imperatives and conditions' (Walker, 1996: 148). Sheila Jasanoff (2005), a North American specialist in science and technology studies, also considers it difficult to evaluate policies objectively and to define best practices for an administrative elite because of the embedded character of both policy and knowledge.

This does not prevent international qualitative social science research from being useful to those who want to implement change: policymakers, health professionals, legislators, and users of health systems. Indeed, comparative research allows the better comprehension of the factors that shape the systems that actors seek to transform. The American sociologist Raymond De Vries and his colleagues (2001a: xvii) give an example of this normative positioning in their study of maternity care systems in Europe and in the United States.

But it is impossible to maintain the idea of absolute neutrality in the social sciences, and in certain works, researchers express what we can call a 'preference for the foreign', that is, they indicate that the problems they study are better resolved in countries other than their own. This is more common when researchers have free choice over their subjects, as opposed to responding to an assignment on a subject with which they are less familiar. They have already intellectually constructed a 'problem' in their country and an international comparison provides one or more foreign examples useful for critiquing the situation, in the hope of reinforcing their observations and perhaps transforming the situation. This is the same literary device that Montesquieu used in his *Persian Letters* in the eighteenth century, in which he describes his country, France, through the eyes of two visiting foreigners. This strategy provides him with the basis for a bitter critique of French society. In the social sciences, using a foreign example as a model is not a fatal flaw affecting the quality of the research, as long as the study is conducted rigorously. However, researchers must indicate in their description of their methodology that this perspective, guiding the research from the outset, has not oriented their data collection in a direction that is systematically unfavourable to their own country. The American sociologists Renée Fox and Judith Swazey (1984) do this in a convincing manner in their study of bioethics in China and the United States. As long-time specialists in the study of American bioethics, they conducted a study in a Chinese hospital and outlined the characteristics of what the Chinese call 'medical morality'. They juxtapose these traits with those of American bioethics and seek the intellectual frameworks and social structures that have influenced their development in the two countries. This allows them to show the ways in which some principles of American bioethics reflect the values of a highly conservative and individualist sector of American society. By contrast, Chinese 'medical morality' encourages the expression of individuals' moral obligations based on their position in social networks. In this study, the comparison reinforces the critical strength of the sociological examination.

The use of theories and 'context'

We mentioned earlier the empirical richness of qualitative social science research. International comparison can further add to the quantity and complexity of collected data. The theoretical perspectives that orient research towards certain questions thus play a critical role. At the same time, researchers insist on the inappropriate and limiting nature of certain theoretical perspectives, such as functionalism or culturalism (Maurice, 1989; Hantrais, 1999). Some theoretical frameworks are favourable to the integration of certain, originally unanticipated elements as explanatory variables of the differences observed, while others are oriented principally towards endogenous explanations, that is, explanations internal to the phenomenon studied, which can implicitly bring the researcher to limit the collection of data.[3]

To avoid these limitations, some recommend taking the 'context' of the phenomenon into account. The British sociologist Linda Hantrais (1999: 93) notes that the 'theory and practice of contextualization (is) at the nexus of cross-national comparative studies'. The American political scientist Neil Smelser (2002) instructs researchers to 'systematiz[e] the context'. The Finnish sociologist Sirpa Wrede and her colleagues (2006) argue for a 'context sensitive analysis'. And Steen Mangen (1999) recommends that researchers 'contextualize the research material' and 'complete the contextual research in advance'. This omnipresent idea is only rarely the object of a critical analysis.[4] How is it used?

Comparative social science researchers choose an object or question at the beginning of their research, and they consider everything that they do not place in the field of detailed examination, but which they think could potentially have a relationship to the phenomenon that they are studying, the 'context'. They label this context 'national', 'social', 'cultural', 'economic', or 'political', to name but a few. The 'context' is therefore an intuitive construction of the researcher for designating political regimes, judicial regulations, systems of social welfare, education systems, representations, events, and many other things as well. What the authors cited in the foregoing recommend is that researchers include as many contextual elements as possible among the variables that can potentially explain their results. Context is a metaphor, whose interest resides in its vague and shifting character. Researchers can add elements of the context in the course of the research, and can also remove or abandon them. The concept of a context is therefore useful, but if two precautions are taken. First, it is preferable to consider the boundaries of the context in a flexible way, to retain the possibility of including elements that emerge in the course of the research. This is what the French social scientists Marc Maurice, Francois Sellier, and Jean-Jacques Silvestre (1982), the founders of societal analysis, did in their study of business organization.[5] Second, the use of this metaphor can drive the researcher to think that the context influences the object of study, and not the reverse. Yet, this is not always the case. Monika Steffen (2004) showed that AIDS control policies in France in the 1990s, in contrast with English, German, and Italian policies, transformed what she calls the context, meaning national political institutions: the scandal of haemophiliacs infected with HIV brought the government to reform state public health institutions.

In order to specify the context of a cross-national comparison, social scientists can draw on noncomparative works, or studies situated at a different analytical level. For example, in studying organizations, one could use the works of Richard Scott (1995), who has studied the diversity of institutionalist approaches in various organizations. He presents several institutions that could support or constrain a given organization. This analytic framework can be used for international comparisons. In studying microsocial phenomena, one can also draw on works that have attempted to identify macrosocial contexts. Some authors have tried to move beyond the umbrella term of 'context' to specify some of the factors that differentiate and shape health care systems (Wessen, 1999). This can provide an analytical frame for microlevel studies.

The overvaluation of the national dimension

International comparative studies often assign critical importance to the role of the nation-state. Most political scientists assume that differences in social representations and norms are reflected in systems of law and institutions that do in many cases stop at national boundaries. In many cases, this is appropriate: nation-states clearly influence the form and direction of health care systems, and the systems' structural characteristics influence in turn the practices of both professionals and lay people.

However, the influence of the nation-state should not be overvalued. Some researchers produce unconvincing generalizations, for example, by overemphasizing the national dimension. When researchers note differences between two phenomena in two countries, they tend to attribute the explanation to national factors. In certain cases, it is essential to relativize their importance. Awareness of national differences is moreover a historically contingent phenomenon, appearing in Europe only at the end of the eighteenth century (Espagne, 1994). For the vast majority of its history, humanity has existed with little or no national consciousness. Nation-states have acquired such legitimacy in the course of the past two centuries that, in certain cases, we overvalue their influence. It is easy to overstate the sociolinguistic, cultural, and institutional homogeneity within national boundaries (Hantrais, 1999).

It is perhaps because they are conscious of the overvaluation of the national framework that medical anthropologists claim to do international comparisons less frequently than other social scientists. One of the key concepts of anthropology is that of 'culture'. There are many different definitions of this concept,[6] but, regardless of the definition, anthropologists often consider that many cultures can coexist in the same country or across national boundaries.

Other scholars use the concept of culture by associating it with a country or countries. This can be the case with sociologists, such as Raymond De Vries and his colleagues, who argue in their study of maternal health in Europe and the United States that 'each of the countries represented here has distinctive cultural values that play an important role in the design of maternity care. The Nordic countries are marked by a thoroughgoing pragmatism that seeks to combine cost-effectiveness with best results. This same attitude is found in the United Kingdom' (De Vries et al., 2001a: xiii). In certain cases, anthropologists can associate cultural particularities with a given country or group of countries. This is the case in one text on the medicalization of pregnancy and birth, in which the authors argue that a 'belief in the 'technological imperative' – that any available technological intervention should be used – does not have the same cultural support in Europe that it has in the United States' (Cartwright and Thomas, 2001: 226). However, it would be more prudent to note that a culture belongs to a specific social group rather than a nationality: a group that can play an essential role in the elaboration of the representations and dominant practices in a given country. Other groups may well exist, with alternative representations and perspectives, without being influential. When we speak of belief or value systems, or systems of ideas, it is intellectually risky to assume national homogeneity.

In the domain of access to health care, the overemphasis on the boundaries of the nation-state is extremely problematic. Given the critical importance of economic inequality to health care provision and outcomes, the nation-state is often less important than social divisions within its borders. As the American anthropologist Paul Farmer (1999) has argued, wealthy Zairois were at roughly the same risk of contracting the Ebola virus during its 1995 outbreak in Kikwit as were wealthy Bostonians, given the central role played by an impoverished clinic in the propagation of the disease. Likewise, poor Americans, and African-Americans in particular, share the bleak health profile of those living in developing countries, despite being surrounded by prosperity.

The generalization of results

Another means of overvaluing the national dimension is attributing to it certain facts that relate in reality to local factors. This problem exists particularly for research that includes a fieldwork component. Because the time investment is so high, international qualitative research is often based on the study of just a few sites. This research is productive to the extent that it allows for the generation of new hypotheses, but the problem of the interpretation of results is significant when it finds important differences in a small number of sites in each country.

Michaela Schunk (1996), for example, a German specialist in social policy, has compared the custodial care of the dependent elderly in Germany and England. She produced two monographs, one on Nuremberg and the other on Manchester, cities of comparable size, as a means of studying the services at the disposal of the elderly and their families. She noted specificities in each site, but how should they be interpreted? To what extent do these sites reflect national policies, and to what extent do they reflect local variations in the implementation of national policies?

In an ideal configuration, one could expand the number of field sites in each country in order to neutralize local differences and to determine what is nationally specific, belonging to all the sites in a given country but not to those in another. One way to reduce the significance of this problem is to study at least two sites in each country, or to expand the inquiry, even slightly, by conducting at least a few interviews at other sites in the same country. A better solution consists in working with a team of researchers of different nationalities, each expert in their own country (De Vries et al., 2001b; Wrede, 2006).

CONCLUSION

This paper has discussed several works that feature international comparisons in the domain of health. Nevertheless, in the end, there is little that is specific to the study of health as opposed to other fields in the social sciences, such as the family, work, gender, business, or education, because what social scientists consider under the rubric of health is vast. In this field, they study representations and practices, professionals and lay users, techno-scientific developments and everyday activities, public policy and the private sphere, among other examples.

We seek to join other scholars, in the health social sciences and elsewhere, to emphasize that international comparison is a productive research strategy, and to call for its further development (De Vries et al., 2001b; Smelser, 2002; Wrede, 2006). Research that is based on international comparisons, and the study and critical discussion of this research by a wide range of scholars of different nationalities, allows for the development of an internationalization of social scientific knowledge. This research allows for a better comprehension of the problems marked by multiple influences in an era of accelerating international transformation. It also allows for a critical approach to categories such as medicalization, or human rights to health, which some use as if they are universally applicable.

Neil Smelser (2002) goes so far as to propose the development of a form of knowledge that would be widely applicable across borders (p. 654) and that would be consensual (p. 645). It seems as if we are seeing here a tendency of Western science, which seeks a universal knowledge and which is based on the assumption of its superiority to other forms of knowledge. The health social sciences appear for the moment to have more modest ambitions: to document the limits of the explanatory weight of social categories used by actors, as well as the concepts developed by researchers. International comparisons are a useful tool for attaining these modest, but useful goals, above all when the public debate is supported by intuitive comparisons.

NOTES

1 One can always contend with this difficulty by conducting an international comparison in two countries that belong to the same linguistic sphere.

2 In her own research, Vassy nevertheless translated all these terms as 'infirmière' in order to avoid overburdening the text, but even though this translation immediately makes sense to the reader, it is also misleading. Not translating the terms would have required multiplying the untranslated terms in the text, because the same problem exists for all categories of assistants, auxiliary personnel, caregivers, and so forth, where the diversity of duties, statuses, and perspectives on professional development is strong in the three countries considered.

3 Take for example a type of sociological analysis, the strategic analysis of organizations, developed by Michel Crozier and Erhard Friedberg in France beginning in the 1960s (Crozier, 1963; Crozier and Friedberg, 1977). To explain organizational characteristics, such as the division of labour or power relations, this analysis privileges elements that are endogenous to the systems of action studied, such as for example choices and decisions made by actors. With this theoretical perspective, researchers have studied the organization of wards in European and American hospitals (Kuty, 1973; Binst 1988). They have directed the focus of their studies towards actors whose strategies are similar from one country to the next, and have clouded aspects that might have indicated national differences (Vassy, 2003).

4 The French historian Jacques Revel (1996), however, has criticized the notion of context as used by historians. He denounces the 'lazy' use of the concept, which consists for the researcher in presenting in publications the general historical conditions that surround the scholar's particular concern, without going beyond presenting these two levels of observation in parallel.

5 They were initially interested in the salary inequity in industrial businesses in Germany and France. They ultimately widened their study to the organizational modes of businesses, their types of union representation for employees, and training systems.

6 Because of the multiple meanings of the term 'culture', we have avoided using the term 'transcultural research'.

REFERENCES

Arnold, D. (1993) *Colonizing the Body: State Medicine and Epidemic Disease in 19th-Century India*. Berkeley: University of California Press.

Bestor, T. (2001) 'Supply-Side Sushi: Commodity, Market, and the Global City', *American Anthropologist*, 103(1): 76–95.

Binst, M. (1988) *Modernité de l'organisation patriarcale en milieu hospitalier. étude comparative du fonctionnement de services de chirurgie cardiaque en France, Suisse et aux Etats-Unis*, Thèse de sociologie sous la direction de M. Crozier, Institut d'Etudes Politiques de Paris.

Bourgeault, I.L., Armstrong, P., Armstrong, H., Choiniere, J., Lexchin, J., Mykhalovskiy, E., Peters, S., and White, J. (2001) 'The Everyday Experiences of Implicit Rationing: Comparing the Voices of Nurses in California and British Columbia', *Sociology of Health and Illness*, 23(5): 633–53.

Bowler, I. (1997) 'Problems with Interviewing Experiences with Service Providers'. In G. Miller and R. Dingwall (eds) *Context and Method in Qualitative Research* (pp. 66–76). London: Sage.

Bradby, H. (2002) 'Translating Culture and Language: A Research Note on Multilingual Settings', *Sociology of Health and Illness*, 24(6): 842–55.

Cartwright and Thomas (2001) 'Constructing Risk: Maternity Care, Law and Malpractice'. In De Vries R., Benoit, C., Van Teijlingen, E.R., and Wrede, S. (eds) *Birth by Design*. (pp. 218–28). London: Routledge.

Chamberlayne, P. and King, A. (1996) 'Biographical Approaches in Comparative Work: The "Cultures of Care" Project'. In Hantrais, L. and S. Mangen (eds) *Cross National Research Methods*. London: Pinter.

Crozier, M. (1963) *Le phénomène bureaucratique*. Paris: Seuil.

Crozier, M. and Friedberg, E. (1977) *L'acteur et le système*. Paris: Seuil.

Desrosières, A. (1996) 'Statistical Traditions: An Obstacle to International Comparisons'. In Hantrais, L. and Mangen, S. (eds) (1996) *Cross National Research Methods* (pp. 17–27). London: Pinter.

De Vries R., Benoit, C., Van Teijlingen, E.R., and Wrede, S. (2001a) 'Introduction: Why Maternity Care Is Not Medical Care'. In De Vries R., Benoit, C., Van Teijlingen, E.R., and Wrede, S. (eds) (2001b) *Birth by Design: Pregnancy, Maternity Care and Midwifery in North America and Europe* (pp. xi–xviii). London: Routledge.

De Vries, R., Benoit, C., Van Teijlingen, E.R., and Wrede, S. (2001b) *Birth by Design: Pregnancy, Maternity Care and Midwifery in North America and Europe*. London: Routledge.

Durkheim (1986) (1st Edition 1897) *Le suicide. Etude de sociologie*. Paris: PUF.

Durkheim (1987) (1st Edition 1894) *Les règles de la méthode sociologique*. Paris: PUF.

Espagne, M. (1994) 'Sur les limites du comparatisme en histoire culturelle', *Genèses*, 17: 112–21.

Farmer, P. (1999) *Infections and Inequalities: The Modern Plagues*. Berkeley: University of California Press.

Field, M.G. (1999) 'Comparative Health Systems and the Convergence Hypothesis: The Dialectics of Universalism and Particularism'. In F.D. Powell and A.F. Wessen (eds) *Health Care Systems in Transition: An International Perspective* (pp. 35–46). Thousand Oaks, CA: Sage.

Fox, R. (1988) 'The Hospital: A Social and Cultural Microcosm'. In Fox, R. (ed.) *The Sociology of Medicine*. NJ: Prentice Hall.

Fox, R.C. and Swazey, J.P. (1984) 'Medical Morality Is Not Bioethics: Medical Ethics in China and the United States', *Perspectives in Biology and Medicine*, 27(3): 336–60.

Freidson, E. (1970) *Profession of Medicine: A Study of Sociology of Applied Knowledge*. New York: Harper & Row.

Glaser, W.A. (1963) 'American and Foreign Hospitals: Some Sociological Comparisons'. In E. Freidson (ed.) *The Hospital in Modern Society*. New York: The Free Press.

Glaser, W.A. (1970) *Social Settings and Medical Organization: A Cross-National Study of the Hospitals*. New York: Atherton Press.

Hantrais, L. (1999) 'Contextualization in Cross-National Comparative Research', *International Journal of Social Research Methodology*, 2(2): 93–108.

Hantrais, L. and Mangen, S. (1996) *Cross National Research Methods*. London: Pinter.

Hauray, B. (2006) *L'Europe du médicament. Politique – Expertise – Intérêts privés*. Paris: Presses de Sciences Po.

Jasanoff, S. (2005) *Designs on Nature: Science and Democracy in Europe and the United States*. Princeton: Princeton University Press.

Keller, R. (2007) *Colonial Madness: Psychiatry in French North Africa*. Chicago: University of Chicago Press.

Kuty, O. (1973) *Le pouvoir du malade, analyze sociologique des unités de rein artificiel*, Thèse de sociologie sous la direction de M. Crozier, Université Paris V.

Lallement, M. and Spurk, J. (eds) (2003) *Stratégies des comparaisons internationals*. Paris: Editions du CNRS.

Mangen, S. (1999) 'Qualitative Research Methods in Cross-National Settings', *International Journal of Social Research Methodology*, 2(2): 109–24.

Marcus, G. (1995) 'Ethnography in/of the World System: The Emergence of Multi-Sited Ethnography', *Annual Review of Anthropology*, 24: 95–117.

Marshall, M. (2000) Comment on N. Scheper-Hughes, 'The Global Traffic in Human Organs, *Current Anthropology*', 41(2): 215–6.

Maurice M. (1989) 'Méthode comparative et analyze sociétale: Les implications théoriques des comparaisons internationales', *Sociologie du travail*, 21(2): 175–91.

Maurice, M., Sellier, F., and Silvestre, J.J. (1982) *Politique d'éducation et organization industrielle en France et en Allemagne*, Paris: Presses Universitaires de France.

Mintz, S. (1986) *Sweetness and Power: The Place of Sugar in Modern History*. New York: Penguin.

Montesquieu, Ch. (2003) *Lettres Persanes*. Paris: Gallimard.

Oyen, E. (1990) 'The Imperfection of Comparisons'. In Oyen E. *Comparative Methodology: Theory and Practice in International Social Research* (pp. 1–18). London: Sage.

Pitchford, E. and Van Teijlingen, E., (2005) 'International Public Health Research Involving Interpreters: A Case Study from Bangladesh', *BMC Public health*, 5: 71, Available on line: http://www.biomed central.com/1471-2458/5/71

Revel, J. (ed) (1996) *Jeux d'échelles: La micro-analyse à l'expérience*. Paris: Seuil-Gallimard.

Scheper-Hughes, N. (2000) 'The Global Traffic in Human Organs', *Current Anthropology*, 41(2): 191–225.

Schunk, M. (1996) 'Constructing Models of the Welfare Mix: Care Options of Frail Elders'. In Hantrais, L. and Mangen, S. (eds) *Cross National Research Methods* (pp. 84–94). London: Pinter.

Schütz, A. (1964) 'The Stranger: An Essay in Social Psychology'. In *Collected papers. Vol. II: Studies in Social Theory*. The Hague: Martinus Nijhoff.

Smelser, N.J. (2002) 'On Comparative Analysis, Interdisciplinarity and Internationalization in Sociology', *International Sociology*, 18(4): 643–57.

Scott, R.W. (1995) *Institutions and Organizations*, Thousand Oaks, CA: Sage. (Chapter 3 'Contemporary Institutional Theory', pp. 33–62).

Steffen, M. (2004) 'La comparaison internationale comme révélateur des apprentissages institutionnels: L'exemple de la lutte contre le Sida', *Revue Internationale de Politique Comparée*, 11 (3): 389–411.

Ungerson, C.l. (1990) 'The Language of Care: Crossing the Boundaries'. In Cl. Ungerson (ed) *Gender and Caring: Work and Welfare in Britain and Scandinavia*. Hemel Hempstead: Harvester Wheatsheaf.

Ungerson, C.l. (1996) 'Qualitative Methods'. In L. Hantrais and S. Mangen (eds) *Cross National Research Methods* (pp. 63–5). London: Pinter.

Vassy, C. (1999) 'Travailler à l'hôpital en Europe: Apport des comparaisons internationales à la sociologie des organizations', *Revue Française de Sociologie*, 40(2): 325–56.

Vassy, C. (2003) 'Données qualitatives et comparaison internationale: L'exemple d'un travail de terrain dans des hôpitaux européens'. In M. Lallement and J. Spurk (eds) *Stratégies des comparaisons internationales* (pp. 215–27). Paris: Editions du CNRS.

Walker, R. (1996) 'Evaluation'. In Hantrais, L. and Mangen, S. (eds) *Cross National Research Methods* (pp. 148–51). London: Pinter.

Wessen, A.F. (1999) 'The Comparative Study of Health Care Reform'. In F.D. Powell and A.F. Wessen (eds) *Health Care Systems in Transition: An International Perspective* (pp. 3–24). Thousand Oaks, CA: Sage.

Whiteford, L. and Nixon, L.L. (2000) 'Comparative Health Systems: Emerging Convergences and Globalization'. In G. Albrecht et al. (eds) *Handbook of Medical Studies in Health and Medicine* (pp. 440–53). London: Thousand Oaks, CA: Sage.

Wrede, S., Benoit, C., Bourgeault, I.L., van Teijlingen, E., Sandall, J., and De Vries R. (2006) 'Decentred Comparative Research: Context Sensitive Analysis of Maternal Health Care', *Social Science and Medicine*, 63: 2986–97.

Applying Qualitative
Methods

33

Researching Reproduction Qualitatively: Intersections of Personal and Political

Kerreen Reiger and
Pranee Liamputtong

The emergence of qualitative inquiry into reproduction has gone hand in hand with broader methodological debates in the social and health sciences on the one hand, and with the ups and downs of feminism as a social, political and intellectual movement on the other. Although men's health has also emerged as an important field (Pease, 2000a, b; Annandale, 2008), this chapter focuses on women's distinctive life experiences with regard to fertility and childbearing. A wide range of qualitative studies has now explored the social and personal significance of practices associated with menstruation, conception, infertility, abortion, pregnancy and birth, motherhood and menopause. Most importantly, qualitative evidence has been central to the politics of making health services more gender-sensitive and equitable. In debates on the management of childbirth and menopause for example, qualitative research has been drawn on to challenge the hegemony of the biomedical paradigm institutionalized in health policies and institutions (e.g., Oakley, 1979; Davis-Floyd, 1992; Liamputtong Rice, 1995; Liamputtong, 2005, 2007a, b; Reiger, 2001, 2006). At the same time, interpretative research remains contested, both at the intellectual level by debates around modernist/postmodernist approaches and politically, by differences of opinion concerning how to interpret and manage women's reproductive rights. Reproductive health is likely to remain controversial, simply because of its considerable political, economic and social importance. It involves a major social investment in both the present and future generations, and reproductive experiences are deeply felt at the personal level. Policy-makers, researchers, health professionals and research participants thus bring quite disparate interests, experiences and viewpoints to undertaking and using qualitative research.

Instead of structuring this chapter around the reproductive life course, we will situate qualitative women's health research in its social and intellectual context, and then consider some epistemological and methodological issues associated with different research strategies. Interviews and fieldwork, textual analyses and forms of action research have all been used to study women's diverse experiences of reproductive embodiment; the discursive and institutional settings in which they are located; and cultural constructions of meaning by women, the media and professional care providers. The widely discussed dilemmas of qualitative research – questions of how reliable or trustworthy, diverse and useful is the evidence it provides (Liamputtong, 2009) – take on particular intensity in the reproductive arena, because they are further complicated by the politics of what counts in health care as 'authoritative knowledge' (Jordan, 1993). Medical research and clinical practice generally rely on biological factors to explain many women's health problems, such as hormonal influences on postnatal depression, and tend to take for granted the value of modern systems of medicalized reproduction. By contrast, critical health researchers, including historians, anthropologists and sociologists, have contested this dominant construction of what counts as 'knowledge' (Davis-Floyd, 1992; Murphy-Lawless, 1998; Reiger, 2001). They point instead to the social, structural, political and cultural factors that shape reproduction and to their consequences for women. Rather than seeing women's reproductive functioning as a passive response to biological exigencies, feminist writers have stressed women's agency as 'reproducers' (Oakley, 1980; Edwards, 2005). In view of renewed interest in the material reality of human embodiment in recent years, simplistic dichotomies between biological and social factors are breaking down. More complex theoretical analyses of the intersection between cultural discourses, institutionalized power relations and physiological processes (e.g., Reiger and Dempsey, 2006) have gone hand in hand with increasingly diverse approaches to empirical research.

PLACING REPRODUCTIVE HEALTH ON THE KNOWLEDGE AND POLICY AGENDA

Since the 1970s and 1980s, feminist activism in Western countries has established new institutional contexts for research into women's lives, including their health and well-being (Olesen, 2000; Jaggar, 2008). With the Boston Women's Health Collective's influential *Our Bodies Ourselves* (1973) leading the way, women's health activists brought a distinctive array of topics to public attention, from sexual, mental and occupational health to all aspects of women's reproductive lives – menstruation, fertility control, and pregnancy, birth and lactation. By the 1980s, the introduction of contentious new reproductive technologies (NRTs) and the management of menopause through hormone replacement therapies (HRTs) raised new questions. As the field expanded, research projects were undertaken not only in university and non-government organizations, but also in voluntary community settings. Community-based research was encouraged by women's health policy units which were auspiced, most notably in Australia and Canada, by state and federal governments (Broom, 1991; Ruzek, 1978). At the grassroots level, questions of the gendered politics of research were triggered in some locations by scandals, such as that around deeply unethical cervical cancer research in New Zealand (Coney, 1988). Research agendas have often been shaped, therefore, by the *politics* of reproduction – from controversy over the harm done by artificial infant feeding formula, especially in the developing world, to struggles around access to safe contraception and abortion, conflicts over the medical management of birth and the implications of NRTs (Ehrenreich and English, 1973; Rapp and Ginsburg, 1995; Blum, 1999).

As a consequence, a primary task of feminist health researchers has been to reform the treatment of women by some health professionals and to make the research process itself more women-centred. Critical analysis of the social construction of knowledge was central to this project. At first, the critique was directed at how traditional biomedicine obscured gendered power structures of society (Annandale and Clark, 1996; Oakley, 1998; Olesen, 2000, Hesse-Biber and Leckenby, 2004). Feminist critics questioned how knowledge was traditionally produced and used. They argued that traditional 'malestream' methods of research, especially clinical trials, not only largely ignored or dismissed women's experiences (Hesse-Biber and Leckenby, 2004), but inappropriately applied generalizations to women which were derived from research exclusively by and on men (Du Bois, 1983). As diverse interest groups generated new dimensions of inquiry by the 1980s–1990s, quantitative paradigms were increasingly deemed inadequate to the task of bringing the views and experiences of women themselves – the 'patient patients' in Helen Roberts' (1985) classic phrase – into health planning. The goal of articulating the 'voices of women' produced a strong preference instead for qualitative methods – indeed, as Ann Oakley (1998) has commented, in-depth interviews came to be seen as the feminist research strategy *par excellence.* Feminist researchers have commonly rejected traditional epistemological claims to 'knowing' a quantifiable, calculable universe and methodological stress on the objectivity of the researcher as being inimical to articulating the voices of women as an oppressed or marginalized group (Hesse-Biber and Leckenby, 2004; Liamputtong, 2007b). Qualitative methods and data were judged less oppressive, less concerned with finding the 'truth' and more likely to create closeness to and emotional bonds with the people being studied (Hesse-Biber and Leavy, 2005; Liamputtong, 2007b, 2009). By revealing women's own interpretations of their lives and their personal, everyday experiences (e.g., Bowles and Duelli-Klein, 1983; Stanley and Wise, 1983; Roberts, 1985), qualitative studies appeared more aligned to the project of emancipation of the socially marginalized (Reinharz, 1992; Naples, 2003).

Qualitative research in reproduction, as into other aspects of women's health, focused at first mainly on middle-class white women's experiences (Reid, 1983). Yet, as women's studies and health services became institutionalized, theoretical and political positions became more complex than tensions between liberal, radical and socialist strands of feminist thought (see Weedon, 1999; Ch.1). The emerging body of research studies and methodological analysis (e.g., Stanley and Wise, 1983, 1990; Reinharz 1992) increasingly had to contend with the question of women's 'differences'. Challenges came from two sources – a stinging critique of ethnocentrism from African-American band postcolonial scholars (e.g., Collins, 1990; Mohanty et al., 1991), and an assault on the idea of a unitary category of 'women' from postmodernist researchers, with important implications for fields such as childbirth in which women's views vary (Annandale and Clark, 1996). Influenced by debates over how to 'speak' for 'women', or the 'crisis of representation' (Pillow, 2003), feminist researchers encouraged greater reflexivity, especially about their own social positions and the difficulties of representing participants' diverse views (Liamputtong, 2007b). The emergence of distinctive research traditions within indigenous and other culturally specific groups has thus broadened and enriched the field of qualitative inquiry by paying greater attention to racialized constructions of knowledge and researchers' ethical responsibilities to communities not just individuals.

Acceptance of women's diversity also has implications for research practice. Not only did earlier feminist dichotomies between medical study of the biological, and feminist stress on investigating social factors, become less tenable, but the preference for qualitative, and rejection of quantitative methods, also became questioned. The study of disadvantaged populations for example, often requires large-scale aggregate data as well as evidence of women's experiences. Ann Oakley (1998), for example, later moved away from her initial emphasis on interviews, asserting the continued importance of 'measurable facts' in formulating evidence-based policy. The relationship between qualitative and quantitative inquiry as legitimate forms of knowledge has nonetheless remained contentious, especially in view of the institutionalized dominance of medical science. Yet, changes have been under way here too. In public health, qualitative approaches from medical anthropology and sociology have become widely recognized as central to responding to the needs of those affected by contemporary lifestyle-related and other chronic illnesses. In the mainstream medical sector, qualitative 'process' evaluations are being advocated within studies of complex interventions, including randomized controlled trials (May, 2006). Accordingly, contemporary researchers often draw upon both approaches (see Oakley, 1998; Campbell and Wasco, 2000). While clearly there is now no *one* 'feminist methodology' as such, as Reinharz (1992) has argued, feminist research generally shares core values and some common emphases. These include attention to the particular and everyday, to the significance of the researcher herself, and to collaborative research that is oriented to gender justice and social change (Olesen, 2000; Ramazanaglu and Holland, 2002; Naples, 2003; Hesse-Biber and Leckenby, 2004; Jaggar, 2008). While feminist methodology continues to promote use of in-depth interviews and focus groups, multiple methodologies are seen as allowing pragmatic responses to the 'situation at hand' (Fonow and Cook, 1991; Liamputtong, 2007b). More action-oriented, innovative and flexible techniques are also being adopted as collaborative strategies in a research environment that is caring and non-hierarchical (Liamputtong and Rumbold, 2008).

RESEARCHING THE SOCIAL PROCESSES OF REPRODUCTION

In any society, human reproduction involves a series of biological processes and events. As these always occur within a sociocultural context, they are shaped by the perceptions and practices of that society and culture (Jordan, 1993; Liamputtong, 2007a, c). Research based only upon experimental science such as randomized controlled trials (RCTs) or investigations using quantitative measurements alone cannot explore the complex meanings involved in reproduction, including the experiences of women. Using qualitative or interpretive inquiry allows researchers to examine the discourses that women draw on and allows understanding of how knowledge and power operate within health care institutions and professions. By situating our interpretations within diverse social, cultural and political contexts, qualitative researchers are able to offer new understandings of women's and their caregivers' perceptions and practices. Coming from a different vantage point at least than that of the dominant injustice, they are often better placed to make sense of the intersections of physiological and social processes, such as those involved in childbirth (see Jordan, 1993; Miller, 1998; Standing, 1998; Edwards, 2005; Reiger and Dempsey, 2006).

The intellectual and political context shaping feminist and related women's health research has given rise to distinct themes in the literature on reproduction. First, the *political* significance of reproduction has meant the frequent positioning of social researchers as activists, if not at the outset of their projects, then later in response to justice and the mistreatment of women as 'patient patients'. Second, as reproductive decisions are highly personal as well as politically contentious, researchers tend to report findings that indicate a heightened *emotionality* in this field. As research topics concern distinctively female experiences and raise sometimes strongly held views and values, the researcher and participants often have shared experiences. Researchers, like their women participants, also face possible defensiveness about personal and often emotionally-fraught reproductive 'choices', such as terminating a pregnancy after prenatal testing, natural or medically managed birth or breast versus bottle feeding. Finally, this suggests that the *identities* as well as the experiences of women and other participants, researchers and health care practitioners can come to the fore in this area of research.

MANAGING CONCEPTUAL, PERSONAL AND PRACTICAL CHALLENGES

In the following sections on applying qualitative inquiry, the themes already outlined are evident in studies of women's reproductive health provision, practices and experience, including those we have undertaken ourselves. While we are not aiming at a comprehensive overview here and our analysis is restricted to English-language studies, we will draw on research from both sides of the Atlantic along with examples from South East Asia and Australia. In view of the interdisciplinary approach of feminist research, several methodologies used in the health and social sciences are discussed to indicate some of the challenges that qualitative researchers face.

CONCEIVING WOMEN AS REPRODUCERS: THE VALUE OF INTERVIEWS

Since the reflections of British sociologist, Ann Oakley on 'interviewing women' based on her pioneering research into both housework and mothering (Oakley, 1974, 1979, 1981), a staple theme in feminist research has been that a special relationship emerges when women interview other women. In her foundational study, published as *Women Confined* and *Becoming a Mother*, Oakley undertook both a substantial observational component in a maternity hospital and a subsequent series of four in-depth interviews with 66 mothers having first babies in 1975–6. In her reports, Oakley paid close attention to the interactions between health professionals and the women, articulated the mothers' voices at length, and discussed her own role in the women's lives and the significance of the research project in her own life, including having her third child during the project. Commenting that not only do 'academic research projects bear an intimate relationship to the researcher's life' she reports that, at times 'I began to confuse my roles – researcher, pregnant woman, mother, feminist, participant observer and so on. I found such confusion disturbing but healthy' as human boundaries and experience are often not 'neat and tidy' (Oakley, 1980: 4).

In this research, Oakley tackled the problems presented for women by medical control of birth and the denial of their agency in reproduction. Having asked her interviewees their opinions of the research process, Oakley reflected on the research as itself a strategy the women used to facilitate their adjustment to the difficulties of becoming a mother. As the trust relationship became established during the series of interviews, they asked her many questions, including some about health issues and childrearing to which she found it morally impossible not to respond (Oakley, 1981). Indeed, some of the friendship-like bonds continued well after completion of the project. Yet, as Janet Finch (1984) has also discussed, this close intimacy involves the ethical dilemma of possibly exploiting the relationship if the exchange is treated as merely 'data-gathering' rather than genuine reciprocity. Finch also asks if feminist researchers might fall into the trap of convincing themselves that power relations are absent when they are not. Similarly, in a critical review of Oakley's early work, Reid (1983) pointed out that her class position gave her a shared frame of reference to that of the primarily middle-class women in her study. Research on childbirth with other groups of women involves different social relationships, and Reid and others had found different attitudes and issues, including a more instrumental approach to childbirth itself (Reid, 1983).

More recently, Nadine Pilley Edwards (2005) also developed a close relationship with thirty middle-class women she, like Oakley, interviewed on four occasions about their process of decision making around birth practices. As a Scottish childbirth educator as well as a mother, Edwards already had a potentially strong connection to her interviewees, and had used her community midwifery networks to recruit them. Writing in the context of the 2000s, Edwards provides a thoughtful account of the relationships between her intellectual and ethical dilemmas in the research process. It is not possible, she argues, to treat qualitative inquiry into birth experiences and women's voices as though this is a straightforward process. 'Experience' is always mediated by culture and situation, our social relations are embodied in complex ways and power relations are ever-present in interactions. As Edwards' closely documented analysis of home-birthing women's search for birthing autonomy demonstrates, a critical feminist research perspective encourages careful and reflexive attention to both coherence and diversity in narratives and to acknowledging 'the tensions, complexities and contradictions that ultimately enrich our understandings of our worlds' (Edwards, 2005: 62).

Questions of how women exercise agency within social structural contexts have arisen in interviews about breastfeeding too. Interviews by Pam Carter (1995) in Britain and Linda Blum (1999) in the United States raise the issue of the cultural specificity of mothering norms and of how these are responded to according to class and race/ethnic differences. Set overtly within debates on the politics of breastfeeding promotion, Carter's research sought to illuminate breastfeeding through the eyes of mothers rather than through those of the health professionals who dominated public discourses. She reports the stories of women who had babies between 1920 and 1980 in Northern England, situating them in their local and historical context and especially in common discourses and practices. Her conclusion is that for many women, the 'working conditions' surrounding breastfeeding are more important than health judgements, a finding that reflects the experiences of working class and ethnic women in particular.

Similarly, Blum's interviews also led her to argue strongly that decisions on infant feeding were usually a pragmatic response to women's material circumstances. In a thoughtful methodological appendix, Blum (1999) discusses the challenges of using an interdisciplinary approach influenced by feminist and postmodernist cultural studies as well as by her home discipline of sociology. Her research had initially focused on analysis of pro-breastfeeding mothers in the La Leche League (LLL), a mothers' support organization, but she then extended the sample to gain greater insight into the breastfeeding experiences of African-American and working class women. Blum discusses in some detail the complexities of her research journey over several years. She had to negotiate LLL women's expectations that she shared their philosophy of intensive mothering, coming to recognize that her own status as a white middle-class working mother contributed to gaining the trust of women more like herself, but not that of those from different backgrounds. The interviews with 26 African-American women in particular, threw important light on the overall data on these women's negotiation of racialized cultural constructions of breastfeeding. Blum says that her encounters with social and racial 'difference' did not always make for a comfortable process, but her comment that 'I learned most from those facets of African-American women's stories which I had the most trouble hearing' (Blum, 1999: 213) points to the value of qualitative research.

Even taking into account the class and 'race' differences identified by Blum and others, reproduction research has still tended to reflect a culturally privileged image of the white, Western nuclear family, thus socially constructing those lying outside this image as 'other'. By contrast, one of the authors, Pranee Liamputtong (2007a) carried out an in-depth interviewing study of the journey of becoming a mother among women in Northern Thailand. As in other parts of the developing world, in recent decades, rapid social, cultural and economic transformations have changed Thai women's lives, including their reproductive roles. Pranee interviewed 30 women about pregnancy, childbirth, postpartum practice and infant feeding practices. Half the women were from middle class and urban backgrounds in Chiang Mai City and the other half were women with rural peasant backgrounds and from the Mae Chantra (a fictitious name) subdistrict. Coming from a Thai background herself, Pranee conducted all interviews in the Thai language to maintain the subtlety and meaning of the women's voices as accurately as possible. The narratives of these Thai women, like those in Carter's and Blum's research, pointed to significant contestation around breastfeeding and showed how their own practices were socially constrained by social and economic considerations. Research such as these interviews in which women were able to put forward their own interpretations, which differed significantly from those of the often moralizing discourses of health professionals, have significant implications for breastfeeding promotion.

SOCIAL RELATIONSHIPS AND PRACTICES OF ETHNOGRAPHY

The methodological implications of interviewing women about reproductive experiences become still more complex for those whose interviews form part of an ongoing ethnographic project. In the examples selected for discussion here, questions of ongoing social relationships, trust, negotiation of values and degree of responsibility towards participants are writ large. In particular, Brigitte Jordan's reflections on her work in *Birth in Four Cultures,* which is one of the most respected and influential texts in this field, draws attention to the personal and professional challenges of fieldwork not only in an 'exotic' culture but also in one's own. In the later edition of her work, Jordan looks back over how she came to the study of childbirth as a novice ethnographer, so imbued with obstetric dominance of birth that she had little idea of what a midwife even was (Jordan, 1993). In recounting stories of her work with midwife Doña Juana in Yucatan, Jordan provides a vivid account of the demands of early days of carrying equipment for video-ethnography and the importance of capturing as much rich detail as possible (Jordan, 1993: 106). Her relationships with Doña Juana and with other women in the community eventually required her to become more than a 'participant observer' but to take on the responsibility of being an active and increasingly knowledgeable birth helper. As she points out, 'birth is an event of a different order than those which anthropologists routinely investigate' and her 'female experiential expertise' became part of the research process (Jordan, 1993: 119).

In her discussions of subsequent investigations of the cultural assumptions embedded in Dutch, Swedish and American ways of birth, Jordan also points to how inappropriate it became to appear merely a traditional 'disinterested' academic observer. Indeed, her story of one of her 'failures' is instructive. In the face of the medical establishment she felt powerless to speak up and support a frightened and very young woman whose wrists were strapped down to give birth in a lithotomy position in a typical American labour ward (Jordan, 1993: 113). Jordan gives a harrowing account of this systemic violation of a birthing woman's right to movement, reflecting on how her knowledge of, and experience with, alternative birthing practices failed to prevent her from being intimidated by medical authority. Feeling paralysed, she was unable to respond humanely to the woman's need for direct support, clearly illustrating the ethical researcher's stark moral dilemma of 'whose side are you on'?

The challenges of another highly contentious reproductive arena, that of prenatal diagnosis, have been discussed by American anthropologist, Rayna Rapp (1999). In *Testing Women, Testing the Fetus*, Rapp reports on ethnographic work that extended over several years and across different sites in New York. She provides a nuanced account of the negotiations women and professionals were making, and of her increasing understanding of the politics of the field. As with other feminist researchers, her personal experience was her starting point and remained crucially important. Having terminated an earlier pregnancy for foetal abnormality before having a child, her status as a mother laid the basis for relating to the women and couples who were making difficult decisions in the course of genetic counselling. Rapp slowly became more accepted by the professionals in the field, studying laboratory techniques to understand their clinical work and the implications of reproductive technologies. She also became closely involved in lives and practices of women who had children with disabilities, a process that challenged her to develop a more complex understanding of 'reproductive rights'. Rapp discusses the ways in which 'methodology bleeds into daily life' through the personal networks she established and the ways in which participants and others came to treat her knowledge as a resource to tap into. Her own learning about how to handle her complicated data included dealing with the open and porous boundaries of a project conducted 'at home' in her own environment rather than in an 'exotic' society – here, she found that research and personal life constantly intersected (Rapp, 1999: 14). Several ethical issues arose including how to manage confidentiality in such a sensitive field, and when to use technical or lay language. Most importantly, she grappled with the question of how to negotiate 'contaminating' her own data if she intervened to support women by offering information or resources to women less powerful than those like herself – a role to which as a feminist activist, she was strongly committed. In Rapp's research, the diversity of women's reproductive experiences, especially as shaped by class and 'race'/ethnicity, the social provision of services, feminist advocacy of reproductive rights and her personal life story were interwoven.

Pranee Liamputtong's ethnographic study of Hmong women living in Melbourne, Australia also meant she became involved in the lives of individual women and in the community (Liamputtong Rice, 2000). Undertaking not only thirty in-depth interviews but also extensive participant observation became more than a mere attempt to collect data. It was a process in which, as the researcher, she formed close and reciprocal relationships with the women, some of which continued after she left the 'field' (Liamputtong, 2007b). What came after the initial fieldwork was an extended contact with the Hmong community in which Pranee's role was now seen not so much as a researcher wanting to discover their lives, but rather as a friend, invited to family functions and asked for advice, including about health-related and family matters. She was also *given* advice on health issues such as when her daughter was accidentally burned with hot coffee and was referred to local healer. That the bonds forged reflected identification with Pranee as not merely a researcher but also as a migrant mother was evident from other women's comments. As she had only two daughters, some would tell her to have more children, particularly boys. They also promised that if she had another child they would make her a baby carrier so that she could carry her baby like them. In spite of these familiarities, there remained certain aspects of the Hmong that she was told not to write about, for to do so could harm the community. Moreover, her research role as an academic and not a social worker was clearly understood. Many times the Hmong would comment that they were happy to tell her about Hmong culture and customs, but that they did not expect her to help them to improve their lives in their new homeland.

PUTTING MEMORIES TO WORK AS A RESEARCH STRATEGY

The use of 'memory work' as a distinctive feminist technique was pioneered by Frigga Haug (1987) and a group of women in Germany as an extension of the feminist 'consciousness-raising' process. As a research method, memory work is based on the assumption that if something is remembered, it must be in some way problematic. Memories, written in the third person and shared with a group, therefore, become the 'raw data for analysis' (Liamputtong, 2009: 130).

Australian sociologist, Glenda Koutroulis (1990, 1996, 2001) used the technique to examine the embodied experience and social construction of menstruation. The group discussed the meanings given to menstruation, the taken-for-granted rules and social practices about its management and how they had negotiated them. In keeping with the collegial principles of the feminist health movement, Koutroulis herself was not a mere observer or researcher but, like the others, wrote a memory narrative about significant menstruation experiences. These written and shared memories formed 'the catalyst, the prompt, the inspirer of other stories' as a means to tap into wider social issues. Koutroulis argues that the meanings of concepts ('clean' and 'dirty') were socially constructed and transcended class, ethnicity, gender and age. Koutroulis's study challenges homogeneous conceptualizations of the menstrual experience and, like that of Mitchell (1991, 2000) on menopause, contributes to developing memory work further as a collaborative research technique.

TEXT-BASED RESEARCH STRATEGIES

Other researchers have sought to use various forms of text to allow new ways of understanding women's reproductive experiences outside the medical frame of reference or to critically assess their own assumptions. Even historical materials such as government inquiries can, as feminist social historians have shown, be used to articulate women's voices by 'reading against the grain' to reveal experiences subordinated by the dominant narrative (Reiger, 1985). For example, obstetric texts from the eighteenth to the twentieth century have been carefully interrogated to allow understanding of the medicalization of reproduction as constructed by the obstetric worldview (Martin, 1987; Reiger, 1985, 2001; Murphy-Lawless, 1998). As anthropologists exploring the study of cultural meanings about birth in their own society, both Brigitte Jordan and Emily Martin found that it took some time to notice assumptions they had largely taken for granted. American systems of birth seemed 'normal' compared with the 'exotic' of other fieldwork locations. Both in reading medical texts and in interviewing women, Martin at first regarded discussions of contractions as 'distinct and separate from the self', as 'something [a woman] goes through rather than what one does' (10) as self-evident. Indeed, she was at first disappointed that women's stories seemed just to be commonsense and 'scientific fact' – until she suddenly recognized her own cultural location. Rather, she concluded, 'statements about uterine contractions being involuntary are not brute, final, unquestionable facts but rather cultural organizations of experience' grounded in the medical interpretations of birth.

As a consequence, Martin closely interrogated some widely used Western obstetric texts more critically than, examining their portrayal of women's reproductive processes, not only birth but menstruation and menopause. Paying close attention to the diagrams as well as to the words and metaphors used in professional literature, Martin unpacked the complex sets of meanings she found embedded there. Underlying medical practice were deep-seated assumptions based in industrial society's stress on order, hierarchy and production. Using the texts in concert with ethnographic interviews meant that Martin came to 'see' quite different realities. She reflects that doing such work in her own society had deep and personal impact – leaving her either 'exhilarated or cast down' and noting that 'the emotional effects [of many interviews] lingered, as if we had had the most profound events of someone else's life shoehorned into our own' (1987: 9). Martin found her life became personally more complicated as she shared stories and books with other women, and went with birth activists to meetings. She was also professionally challenged by doing work so critical of medicine from an organizational base at John Hopkins University which had a prestigious medical school: 'I often felt like a mouse in the den of a lion, and a disrespectful mouse at that' (Martin, 1987: 13).

Similarly Kerreen Reiger (1985, 2001) found that doing qualitative research on childbirth had both professional and personal implications. She examined Australian medical texts from the late nineteenth century to the development of the 'natural childbirth' movement in the 1970s. Earlier texts showed widespread concerns about the impact of 'civilized' urban life on women's reproductive functioning and the emergence of the idea that modern medical management was essential. Reading detailed accounts of early twentieth century gynaecological surgery, often on weekends in the depths of an old library, was experienced as deeply depressing, as was evidence of the later triumphalism of modern obstetrics. In *Our Bodies, Our Babies: the Forgotten Women's Movement* (2001) she also examined the Australian obstetric journal literature to trace the impact of critics of over-medicalization who advocated a return to 'natural' birth and breastfeeding. The systematic use of texts sampled from medical curricula and journals allowed identification of influential individuals and of a diverse range of interpretations. These were then further explored in interviews with obstetricians, both those who saw modern medicine as 'saving' women from dying in childbirth and those working to lessen professional control and treat women more respectfully. As with Martin's American research, this data was closely connected to that emerging in interviews. As with many other reproduction researchers, the research process resulted in a greater degree of political activism around birth issues, especially as, like Ann Oakley, she had another baby while the research was under way.

BECOMING INNOVATIVE: NEW TECHNOLOGIES, NEW KNOWLEDGES

In recent years, new technologies are opening up new possibilities not only for interaction amongst childbearing women and professional care providers, but also for qualitative researchers as well. Some innovative strategies entail textual analysis of visual and print media, others allow new ways of connecting participants, and yet others bring them together in new forms of collaborative research (Liamputtong, 2007b; Liamputtong and Rumbold, 2008). There are some situations particularly where conventional qualitative methods may not work and can be alienating for some women. Adopting unconventional approaches such as visual imagery, drawing, drama, poetry, diary, dance and the Internet in their research, feminist researchers have been able to recognize and tap into alternative forms of knowledge to that of the mainstream (Cook and Fonow, 1991; Reinharz, 1992; Olesen, 2000; Liamputtong, 2006, 2007b; Liamputtong and Rumbold, 2008; Morgan et al., 2009). For example, traditional research methods such as focus groups have been transformed by new technologies. Strickland and colleagues, for instance, used 'virtual' focus groups in their study of premenopausal women. The success of the research strategy lay, Strickland et al. (2003: 254) tell us, in making it possible 'to have an ongoing discussion board/focus group with women from diverse geographical locations and in different time zones.

Similarly, the photovoice method is now being employed as an 'innovative participatory action research (PAR) method' to 'promote dialogue, encourage action, and inform polity' (Wang, 1999: 185) by allowing people to record and reflect the concerns and needs of their community via taking photographs. By promoting critical discussion of important issues based on displaying the photographs in public forums, marginalized groups' concerns may reach policy makers whom they would otherwise not have impacted. Such a photovoice research strategy was employed to develop reproductive and sexual health initiatives by working with young Indigenous people in rural Victoria, Australia (Marie Stopes Foundation, 2005). The project, aimed in part, to develop, motivate and empower young Indigenous people to have more control over their reproductive and sexual health. After a six-day workshop taking photos, the young people's discussions were documented, photos were enlarged and then exhibited in the local Art Gallery. This project provided powerful insights into the reproductive and sexual health issues important to young Indigenous people in rural Victorian communities and thus enhanced development of culturally appropriate health initiatives (Marie Stopes Foundation, 2005).

IN CONCLUSION

It should be clear from this chapter that the methodological dilemmas associated with research into reproduction – clearly a very 'fertile' and lively field of inquiry – are distinctive. Whilst in these postmodern times, there are no neat and tidy conclusions to be drawn, the intersections of personal, political and scholarly interests make this an especially challenging and emotionally complex area of qualitative research. It remains one that is both contested and socially important. We argue here that it is essential to understand the social and political context in which qualitative research into women's health care developed, as this shaped practice. We have also pointed out that qualitative research offers the means for us to understand better the shifting contexts shaping health and illness. In recent decades many important qualitative projects have been undertaken with the explicit goal of bringing the voices of women as reproducers – their agency – to bear on health policy and clinical practice in diverse national and international contexts. Investigations into women's experience of the embodied, emotional and practical demands associated with childbearing have also posed a challenge to biomedical viewpoints and to the institutions in which they are embedded. In terms of childbirth especially, qualitative research has reflected and also contributed to concerns that excessive medical intervention impinges on women's autonomy and negatively affects their well-being and that of their babies (e.g., Reiger, 2001; Edwards, 2005; Liamputtong, 2005, 2007a). Since the foundational work of Ann Oakley in the early 1970s, hospital and other practices have changed considerably, reflecting both the efforts of groups of reformers to 'demedicalize' maternity care, and the increased professional authority of midwifery.

Other developments have also influenced qualitative research into reproduction, notably the growth on the one hand of an international network of women's health activists and researchers, and on the other, the rapid expansion of new forms of reproductive technology. Since the 1990s, a neoliberal political climate, along with a cultural mood of 'postfeminism', has generated further challenges. Funding of women's reproductive health services became politically contentious, and it can be difficult to gain acceptance of seemingly 'soft' qualitative methods in a 'bean-counting' era. Yet, findings from qualitative studies continue to be central to improving reproductive health care, and are increasingly used both to study men's health issues and to problematize simplistic analyses of gender in health care (e.g., Pease, 2000a, b; Annandale, 2008).

The research potential of this health care field thus continues to expand. As we have argued here, however, feminist researchers in particular have provided a rich legacy of reflection on what it means to be women doing qualitative research into women's reproductive decision making and processes. Their example makes it abundantly clear that, while much has been accomplished, many more aspects of reproduction remain to be studied. Emotional, ethical and political issues are central to the process as well as conventionally methodological ones. Emerging research strategies – from use of online data to adoption of visual techniques in working with marginalized groups – offer new means of achieving the goal that remains central to this field of inquiry, that of seeing women as reproductive agents not as passive patients, and bringing their diverse voices into the formulation of health policy and the conduct of professional practice.

ACKNOWLEDGEMENTS

We thank the anonymous reviewer for helpful critical comment and especially Monica Campo, not only for her editorial assistance with this paper, but also for discussion of ideas and sources. Monica's current doctoral research combines strategies discussed here, linking interviews with birthing women with medical and popular texts and online discussions.

REFERENCES

Annandale, E. (2008) *Women's Health and Social Change*. London: Routledge.

Annandale, E.C. and Clark, J. (1996) 'What is Gender? Feminist Theory and the Sociology of Human Reproduction', *Sociology of Health and Illness*, 18(1): 17–44.

Blum, L. (1999) *At the Breast: Ideologies of Breastfeeding and Motherhood in the Contemporary United States*. Boston: Beacon Press.

Boston Women's Health Book Collective (1973) *Our Bodies, Ourselves*. New York: Simon and Schuster.

Bowles, G. and Klein, R. (eds) (1983) *Theories of Women's Studies*. London: Routledge.

Broom, D. (1991) *Damned if We Do: Contradictions in Women's Health Care*. Sydney: Allen and Unwin.

Campbell, R. and Wasco, S.M. (2000) 'Feminist Approaches to Social Sciences: Epistemological and Methodological Tenets', *American Journal of Community Psychology*, 28(6): 773–791.

Carter, P. (1995) *Feminism, Breasts, and Breast-feeding.* Houndmills: Macmillan.

Collins, P. Hill (1990) *Black Feminist Thought: Knowledge, Consciousness, and the Politics of Empowerment*. Boston: Unwin Hyman.

Cook, J. and Fonow, M. (1991) *Beyond Methodology: Feminist Scholarship as Lived Research*. Bloomington: Indiana University Press.

Coney, S. (1988) *The Unfortunate Experiment*. Auckland, N.Z: Ringwood [Vic.]: Penguin.

Davis-Floyd, R. (1992) *Birth as an American Rite of Passage*. Berkeley: University of California Press.

Du Bois, B. (1983) 'Passionate Scholarship: Notes on Values, Knowing and Method in Feminist Social Science'. In G. Bowles and R. Klein (eds) *Theories of Women's Studies* (pp. 105–116). London: Routledge.

Edwards, N.P. (2005) *Birthing Autonomy*. London: Routledge.

Ehrenreich, B. and English, D. (1973) *Witches, Midwives and Nurses: A History of Women Healers*. New York: Feminist Press.

Finch, J. (1984) '"It's Great to Have Someone to Talk To". The Ethics and politics of Interviewing Women'. In C. Bell and H. Roberts (eds) *Social Researching: Politics, Problem, Practice* (pp. 70–87). London: Routledge.

Fonow, M. and Cook, J. (eds) (1991) *Beyond Methodology: Feminist Scholarship as Lived Research*. Bloomington: Indiana University Press.

Haug, F. (ed.) (1987) *Female Sexualisation: A Collective Work of Memory*. London: Verso.

Hesse-Biber, S.N. and Leavy, L.P. (2005) *The Practice of Qualitative Research*. Thousand Oaks, CA: Sage.

Hesse-Biber, S.N. and Leckenby, D. (2004) 'How Feminists Practice Social Research'. In S.N. Hesse-Biber and M.L. Yaiser (eds) *Feminist Perspectives on Social Research* (pp. 209–226). New York: Oxford University Press.

Jaggar, A. (ed.) (2008) *Just Methods: an Interdisciplinary feminist Reader*. Boulder, CO: Paradigm Publishers.

Jordan, B. (1993) *Birth in Four Cultures: A Cross-Cultural Investigation of Childbirth in Yucatan, Holland, Sweden, and the United States*. Prospect Heights: Waveland Press.

Koutroulis, G. (1990) 'The Orifice Revisited: Women in Gynaecological Texts', *Community Health Studies,* XIV(1): 73–84.

Koutroulis, G. (1996) 'Memory-Work and Menstruation'. PhD dissertation, La Trobe University. Melbourne.

Koutroulis, G. (2001) 'Soiled Identity: Memory-Work Narratives of Menstruation', *Health,* 5(2): 187–205.

Liamputtong, P. (2005) 'Birth and Social Class: Northern Thai Women's Lived Experiences of Caesarean and Vaginal Birth', *Sociology of Health & Illness,* 27(1): 243–70.

Liamputtong, P. (ed.) (2006) *Health Research in Cyberspace: Methodological, Practical and Personal Issues.* New York: Nova Science Publishers.

Liamputtong, P. (2007a) *The Journey of Becoming a Mother amongst Women in Northern Thailand.* Lanham, MD: Lexington Books.

Liamputtong, P. (2007b) *Researching the Vulnerable: A Guide to Sensitive Research Methods.* London: Sage.

Liamputtong, P. (2007c) *Reproduction, Childbearing and Motherhood: A Cross-Cultural Perspective.* New York: Nova Science Publishers.

Liamputtong, P. (2009) *Qualitative Research Methods* (3rd Edition). Melbourne: Oxford University Press.

Liamputtong, P. and Rumbold, J. (eds) (2008) *Knowing Differently: Arts-Based and Collaborative Research Methods.* New York: Nova Sciences Publishers.

Liamputtong Rice, P. (1995) 'Pog Laus, Tsis Coj Khaub Ncaws Lawm: The Meaning of Menopause in Hmong Women', *Journal of Reproductive and Infant Psychology, Special Issue on The Menopause,* 13: 79–92.

Liamputtong Rice, P. (2000) *Hmong Women and Reproduction.* Westport: CT, Bergin & Garvey.

Marie Stopes International Australia (2005) *Photovoice: Sexual Health through the Eyes of Indigenous Youth.* Melbourne: Marie Stopes International Australia.

Martin, E. (1987) *The Woman in the Body: A Cultural Analysis of Reproduction.* Milton Keynes: Open University Press.

May, C. (2006) 'A Rational Model for Assessing and Evaluating Complex Interventions in Health Care', BMC Health Serv Res. 2006; 6: 86. Published online July 7. doi: 10.1186/1472-6963-6-86.

McMahon, M. (1995) *Engendering Motherhood: Identity and Self-Transformation in Women's Lives.* New York: The Guilford Press.

Miller, T. (1998) 'Shifting Layers of Professional, Lay and Personal Narratives in Longitudinal Research on Childbirth'. In J. Ribbens and R. Edwards (eds) *Feminist Dilemmas in Qualitative Research* (pp. 58–71). London: Sage.

Mitchell, P. (1991) 'Memory-Work: A Primary Health Care Strategy for Nurses Working with Older Women'. In *Proceedings of National Nursing Conference on Science, Reflectivity and Nursing Care: Exploring the Dialectic,* Melbourne, pp. 43–48.

Mitchell, P. (2000) 'Letting Your(Self) Go: Older Women Use Memory-Work to Explore the Impact of Relationships on Experiences of Health'. PhD dissertation, Flinders University.

Mohanty, C., Russo, A., and Torres, L. (eds) (1991) *Third World Women and the Politics of Feminism.* Bloomington: Indiana University Press.

Morgan, M., Rumbold, J., McInerney, F., and Liamputtong, P. (2009) 'Drawing the Experience of Chronic Vaginal Thrush and Complementary and Alternative Medicine: Methodological Issues', *International Journal of Social Research Methodology,* special issue on 'Innovative research methods in the 21st century', 12(2): 127–146.

Murphy-Lawless, J. (1998) *Reading Birth and Death: A History of Obstetric Thinking.* Indianapolis: Indiana University Press.

Naples, N. (2003) *Feminism and Method: Ethnography, Discourse Analysis and Activist Research.* New York: Routledge.

Oakley, A. (1974) *Housewife.* London: Allen Lane.

Oakley, A. (1979) *From Here to Maternity: Becoming a Mother.* Harmondsworth: Penguin.

Oakley, A. (1980) *Women Confined: Toward a Sociology of Childbirth.* Oxford: Martin Robertson.

Oakley, A. (1981) 'Interviewing Women'. In H. Roberts (ed.) *Doing Feminist Research* (pp. 30–61). London: Routledge.

Oakley, A. (1998) 'Gender, Methodology and People's Ways of Knowing: Some Problems with Feminism and the Paradigm Debate in Social Science', *Sociology*, 32(4): 707–731.

Olesen, V.L. (2000) 'Feminisms and Qualitative Research at and into the Millennium'. In N.K. Denzin and Y.S. Lincoln (eds) *Handbook of Qualitative Research* (2nd Edition) (pp. 215–256). Thousand Oaks, CA: Sage.

Pease, B. (2000a) 'Beyond the Father Wound: Memory-Work and the Deconstruction of the Father-Son Relationship', *Australian & New Zealand Journal of Family Therapy*, 21(1): 9–15.

Pease, B. (2000b) 'Reconstructing Heterosexual Subjectivities and Practices with White Middle-class Men', *Race, Gender & Class,* 7(1): 133–145.

Pillow, W. (2003) 'Confession, Catharsis, or Cure? Rethinking the Uses of Reflexivity as Methodological Power in Qualitative Research', *International Journal of Qualitative Studies in Education*, 16: 175–196.

Ramazanaglu, C. and Holland, J. (eds) (2002) *Feminist Methodology: Challenges and Choices.* London: Sage.

Rapp, R. (1999) *Testing Women, Testing the Fetus: The Social Impact of Amniocentesis in America.* New York: Routledge.

Rapp, R. and Ginsburg, F.D. (eds) (1995) *Conceiving the New World Order: the Global Politics of Reproduction.* Berkeley: University of California Press.

Reid, M. (1983) 'Review Article, A Feminist Sociological Imagination? Reading Ann Oakley', *Sociology of Health and Illness*, 5(1): 83–94.

Reiger, K. (1985) *The Disenchantment of the Home: Modernizing the Australian Family, 1880–1940.* Melbourne: Oxford University Press.

Reiger, K. (2001) *Our Bodies, Our Babies: The Forgotten Women's Movement.* Melbourne: Melbourne University Press.

Reiger, K. (2006) 'The Neoliberal Quickstep: Contradictions in Australian Maternity Care Policy', *Health Sociology Review*, Special Issue, *Childbirth, Politics and the Culture of Risk,* 15(4): 330–340.

Reiger, K. and Dempsey, R. (2006) 'Performing Birth in a Culture of Fear: an Embodied Crisis of Late Modernity', *Health Sociology Review*, 15(4): 364–73.

Reinharz, S. (1992) *Feminist Methods in Social Research.* New York: Oxford University Press.

Roberts, H. (1985) *The Patient Patients: Women and their Doctors.* London: Pandora Press.

Ruzek, S.B. (1978) *The Women's Health Movement: Feminist Alternatives to Medical Control.* New York: Praeger.

Standing, K. (1998) 'Writing the Voices of the Less Powerful: Research on Lone Mothers'. In J. Ribbens and R. Edwards (eds) *Feminist Dilemmas in Qualitative Research: Public Knowledge and Private Lives* (pp. 186–202). London: Sage.

Stanley, L. and Wise, S. (1983) *Breaking Out Again: Feminist Ontology and Epistemology.* London: Routledge.

Stanley, L. and Wise, S. (1990). 'Method, Methodology and Epistemology in Feminist Research'. In L. Stanley (ed.) *Feminist Praxis: Research: Theory and Epistemology in Feminist Sociology* (pp. 20–64). London: Routledge.

Strickland, O.L., Moloney, M.F. et al. (2003) 'Measurement Issues Related to Data Collection on the World Wide Web', *Advances in Nursing Science,* 26(4): 246–56.

Wang, C.C. (1999) 'Photovoice: A Participatory Action Research Strategy Applied to Women's Health', *Journal of Women's Health,* 8(2): 185–192.

Weedon, C. (1999) *Feminism, Theory and the Politics of Difference.* Oxford: Blackwell.

34

Understanding the Shaping, Incorporation and Coordination of Health Technologies through Qualitative Research

Tiago Moreira and Tim Rapley

INTRODUCTION

In the past two decades or so, health technologies have increasingly become a topic for qualitative social and health researchers. An intensification in the development, evaluation and use of technology in health care (Clarke et al., 2003) has drawn qualitative researchers into the problem of technology, often supported by the needs of policy makers to understand the 'human factors' leading to its implementation and uses. Within the social and health sciences, understanding the role of technology in health care also became an integral part of the work of analysing the social and cultural organization of health and illness in the later part of the twentieth century (Strauss et al., 1985). Yet, by the beginning of the twenty-first century, Heath et al. (2003), could still complain that many researchers have 'been a little reticent in exploring the ways in which … technologies feature in everyday practice in work and organizations' (76). In this chapter, we take this reticence as a challenge. Our aim is not to review qualitative research on health technologies (see Lehoux, 2006; Webster, 2007) but to provide a set of problematics, contexts and exemplars for the use of qualitative research to understand health technologies.

The first difficulty in achieving this aim is the very definition of health technology. Most of us would agree that medical imaging apparatuses such as Positron Electron Tomography or diagnostic tests such as genetic screening are examples of health technologies. How many would, however, see paper-based patient records as another example (Berg, 1996)? When in the beginning of the twentieth century, a variety of instruments and diagnostic tools were introduced in (mostly American) hospitals, some clinical commentators voiced concerns about the diminishing role of clinical judgment in health care (Howell, 1995), forgetting that those cherished skills had themselves only recently come into being, supported by other 'clinical' technologies such as the patient-centred record (Berg and Harterink, 2004). Rather than showing us the shortsightedness of practitioners, this example alludes to the methodological problems involved in identifying and studying health technologies. The definition of what counts as a medical or health technology is often entangled with the degree of *novelty* ascribed to the object/technique in question (Brown and Webster, 2004), and this is frequently embedded in scenarios of change proposed by groups of actors. In this chapter, we focus on a range of technologies, from ultrasound to pharmacological therapies to paper-based clinical guidelines.

Realizing the negotiated and contested character of health technologies is a point of departure to understand their role in health care. This means that not only their definition but also their uses and their very design are prone to change in interaction with the social relations around them. This perspective, which Timmermans and Berg (2003) have called 'technology-in-practice' and Heath et al. (2003) have called 'technology in action', allows qualitative researchers to focus on technology, without either reifying its power ('technological determinism') or seeing it simply as the product of 'social construction'. Our suggestion is that qualitative research methods are ideally suited to understand these interactive processes between technology and society: they can capture how practices, discourses and identities enter in dynamic relationships with the shape, design, requirements and effects of technologies.

In what follows, we focus on three domains where these dynamic relationships are particularly important. In the first section, we explore how such technologies come into being: how socioeconomic, professional and cultural contexts shape the design of health technologies and how such devices come to embody versions of patient and professional identities and desires and the social organization of health care. In the second section, we investigate how technologies – and their embedded social contexts – arrive in clinical practice or patient's homes, how they are incorporated, challenged, modified or rejected in these contexts. In the final section of the chapter, we delve into technologies as coordinating devices, bringing together different practical, professional or moral worlds.

SHAPING TECHNOLOGIES

Where do health technologies come from? One remarkably prolific perspective is that of economics, which provides us with two general answers. One emphasizes the role of advances in science or technology in proposing new drugs, devices or procedures – this is known as the 'science push theory'. Another answer emphasizes the role of market demand in pulling the development of innovation – thus known as 'demand pull' theory. In fact, a growing number of researchers agree that the knowledge and engineering base interact with the complex social processes of identification of 'need' (Mowery and Rosenberg, 1989).

Rather than seeking general answers to this question, social and health scientists in the field of medical anthropology, medical sociology and science and technology studies, have mostly written case studies, based on archival, documentary or more rarely ethnographic research (May and Ellis, 2001), to understand the interaction between technology and society. There are two methodological reasons for this. If one is to engage with and understand the 'contents' of science or technology as well as their 'context' (Callon and Law, 1989), it is appropriate to limit oneself to one particular domain of innovation. This is not only a pragmatic consideration, it also attends to the demands put on qualitative researchers when entering and trying to understand social contexts that are at once intuitively familiar – after all we live in highly technological societies – and remarkably strange – most social and health scientists are not trained in the specific fields of science or engineering that they are studying (Hirschauer, 1994; Lynch, 1994). The second consideration is linked with the kind of knowledge that is derived from a case-oriented approach. As 'meaningful but complex configurations of events and structures' (Ragin, 2004: 125), cases provide detailed insight into the processes that shape health technologies.

One particularly useful example of this is Yoxen's (1987) study of the development of ultrasound as a diagnostic technology. Initially developed for marine navigation and naval warfare purposes, sonar later became a useful technology in manufacturing and was first tested in medicine for its potential curative properties before it moved into neurology and obstetrics. Yoxen's question concerns the processes by which the ultrasound was seen to 'work' in the clinical context and argues that this question cannot be answered without considering the views of the different professions involved in developing and evaluating this technology. Yoxen shows how the development of the technology as a 'health technology' was only possible, because it became entangled with the consolidation of radiology as a profession and as a distinct form of expertise. Images gained meaning insofar as they related to the development of the specific role of radiologists as 'interpreters' of ultrasound in health care organizations.

What the case of ultrasound brings to light is how the delineation of a technology is underpinned by a mutual adjustment between the understanding of disease, the technological means used to depict or cure it and the actors that are deemed to carry out such actions. In this, the 'success' of a technology is often equivalent to the validation of specific professional perspectives on illness and the human body and on the organization of health care. In the case of cerebral angiography, a widely used technique of visualizing blood vessels through the injection of contrast dye, the usefulness of the technology only became fully available in tandem with neurosurgeons' newly found clinical leadership in defining and treating pathologies of the central nervous system around the middle of the twentieth century (Moreira, 2000). This entailed abandoning surgeons' reliance on neurologists' diagnosing skills and, concurrently, neurosurgeons' developing their own means of correlating structure and function so as to achieve precise localization of lesions. It is also from this perspective that professional resistance to medical innovation should be interpreted. When in the 1910s–1920s the sphygmomanometer, formerly a physiological instrument used to measure blood pressure in laboratory experiments, was championed by some American clinicians in order to make medicine more scientific and 'precise', critics emphasized that such innovation would move doctors away from embodying diagnostic skills which they saw as crucial to the trade (Evans, 1993). In this, critics were also proposing a version of clinical medicine where doctors were more concerned with the 'stories' and bodies of patients than with instrumental measurements, and a version of health care where doctors were less reliant on 'science' and 'technology' to make decisions.

This example, leads us to our next topic: the way in which health technologies embody particular version of patients, their role and identities. In her study of the emergence of foetal surgery, Casper (1998) suggests that the consolidation of the knowledge, techniques and technologies that support such approach was only possible through the construction of a new identity, a new patient, that of the 'the unborn child', in detriment of the concerns and interests of pregnant women. This, she argues, was in turn only possible because of how proponents of foetal surgery related the possibility of knowing and treating the foetus to wider concerns about the politics of reproduction and abortion in the 1960s–1970s.

Indeed, the embodiment of patient's roles in technology appears often linked to wider social, contested understandings of health and illness and life-course expectations (Brown and Webster, 2004). The development of new pharmaceutical technologies, like drug therapies for Alzheimer's disease since the 1970s, is a good illustration of this. Behaviours formerly seen as characteristic of 'old age' became framed within a coherent etiological model, and this shift contributed to the establishment of a broader societal understanding of 'normal ageing' (Holstein, 2000) that excluded cognitive decline ('memory loss'). The development of Alzheimer's therapies became linked to a version of 'abnormal ageing' that focuses attention on cognitive abilities and particularly memory (Moreira, 2009). Access to such therapies in mainstream systems of health care is mediated by an assessment where patients' insight into their illness is contrasted and 'checked against' cognitive tests and 'informants' interviews' (normally the main carer). In this way, patient's reduced cognitive agency is both presupposed and enacted by the drug that is deemed to alleviate it. From this perspective, the drug embodied a categorization of disease and correlated illness identities that focused on 'memory' rather than on the, arguably more important, behaviour and emotional features of dementia.

Does this mean that patients are excluded from participating in the negotiations that lead to the development of health technologies? Although there are now policies to involve 'consumers' in health research programmes, little is know about the roles and contribution they offer (Boote et al., 2002). One problem might be the way in which consumer involvement is 'framed' within public institutions. Harrison and Mort (1998), for example, have argued that these practices of involvement could be seen as 'technologies of legitimation' of previously taken managerial decisions. Patients are brought in as 'consumers' to exercise 'choice' about already predefined or delineated technologies or services (Mol, 1999). There are trends in the opposite direction, however, that move beyond individuals simply acting as the obligatory 'voice of the patient' on public decision-making committees and groups (Caron-Flinterman et al., 2005). In this context, Callon and Rabeharisoa (2008) show how, instead of relying on 'experts' to define technological expectations, some patient groups are able to harness the knowledge and uncertainty that surround their illness to forge new collaborative networks across traditional expertise lines and move technological development into unpredictable avenues. In this way, different forms of articulation between research, development and political identities are emerging.

INCORPORATING TECHNOLOGIES

How do technologies come to be integrated in the organization of health care? How do they affect and interact with health care work? Answering this question has been the focus of concern for many policy makers and researchers for a number of years, particularly as there are increasing demands to make health care more effective and efficient (Banta, 2003). Research has focused on assessing whether cost and effectiveness justify such use rather than understanding the social, political and cultural dimensions that are deployed by these technologies (Lehoux and Blume, 2000). Only recently, a consistent body of work became interested in how technologies interact with health care work.

One consistent feature of qualitative studies of these processes is that, instead of assuming that technologies will 'naturally' diffuse into ever expanding contexts – unless impeded by external factors (Coleman et al., 1966) – they sought to explore the conditions and practices through which implementation actually happens (May et al., 2003). In this area of work, researchers are aware of the issues we discussed in the last section: that technologies have social and organizational forms embodied or 'written into' them. Once a technology acquires a distinctive and more or less stable shape, it can be said to have a 'script' delineating the relationship between social and technological actors that will make it 'work' (Akrich, 1992). When a technology is put in place, it is rarely the case that its specifications will match the reality of the working environment it encounters. What follows can best be described as a mutual adjustment between the newly arrived technology and the contexts of practice, leading often to rearticulations of both technologies and social relations. For example, in an ethnographic study of cardiopulmonary resuscitation (CPR), Timmermans (1999) suggests that this technique's 'script' implies that staff's reaction to sudden death should follow procedures that exclude emotional concerns for the person. In practice, however, staff and family members are able not only to include such concerns within CPR situations but also to produce through it 'new' meanings to the process of sudden death. The very technology that was supposed to prevent death is used as a resource in explaining and describing the process of dying and so helps family members come to terms with their unexpected loss.

One should, however, avoid thinking that this mutual adjustment leads to an increasing 'convergence' and 'tight fitting' between technology and implementation setting. As Berg (1998) has argued, technologies 'persist because of the existence of loose ends and different logics' (168). The mutual adjustment is a continuous, fluid, ongoing process. For example, research on protocol-driven tasks – be they working with computerized 'expert' systems (Whalen and Zimmerman, 1987; Whalen, 1995) or completing quality of life questionnaires (Antaki and Rapley, 1996) – shows how such technologies shape and are intimately shaped by and adapted to their moment-by-moment enactment. Greatbatch et al.'s (2005) study of audiotapes of calls to a telephone triage system, NHS Direct, highlights how a technology aimed at standardizing medical advice is actually used in practice.

In the United Kingdom, patients or their representatives can call NHS Direct for health advice and information. With the nurse-led aspect of the service, once the nurses have established the patient's symptoms and past medical history, they select a symptom-based algorithm from the computerized clinical assessment system (CAS), and ask a series of questions prompted by CAS. They input the information from patient's answers and CAS offers expert clinical judgement: an on-screen 'disposition' (e.g., 'Contact GP within 4 hours [as soon as possible]') and advice (e.g., 'Drink a warm drink with lemon and honey to soothe a cough'). In some cases, nurses work through CAS and then simply tailor advice that the system provides. At other times, they override CAS:

Nurse: So what I sugge – I mean what it's advising me is for you – for you to go to Accident & Emergency but (...) you know I think you'd better go to see your GP today. You ring them up.
Caller: Yeah.
Nurse: You tell them that you've been in touch with NHS Direct.
Caller: Yeah.
Nurse: And that we've advised you that you be seen. Because (...) uhm maybe – I'm just looking at your age may be your blood pressure's gone up for some reason.

(Simplified Transcript; Greatbatch et al., 2005: 817)

When nurses shift from a CAS-based recommendation, they have to account for their reasoning, by typing this into the system. Moreover, this requirement nicely illustrates the ideals embedded in CAS: acts of individual expertise or judgement are inherently secondary.

In all cases, whether the CAS disposition and advice is simply reported, underridden or overridden, the nurses 'adapt, tailor, qualify and supplement' (ibid: 425) CAS recommendations drawing on their individual experience and expertise.

Greatbatch and colleagues argue that any ideal of the standardization of the delivery of care through the CAS is a practical impossibility. Not only does it go against the professional discourse of nursing, in that they work with patients as 'individuals', but also that all rule-based systems are based on ideals and abstractions, yet any rule-following relies on adaptation to the case-at-hand (Garfinkel, 1967). In addition, such protocol-driven systems can deny the phonetic judgements (Flyvbjerg, 2001), the practical wisdom that people employ in interaction with others. For example, is this person just phoning for reassurance? Technologies like telephone triage transform the process of care delivery and in so doing, shift the rights and responsibilities of the parties involved. Notably, it redistributes trajectories of care increasingly towards the space of the home and community, extending the regime of self-care.

Linked to these shifts in the responsibility of care and a perceived increased burden of chronic illness, policy makers have recently advocated an emphasis on community care supported by new arrangements between health and social care, ambulatory services and the domestic use of monitoring and maintenance technologies. Information and communication technologies are seen as key in this development, as they can potentially improve current methods and facilitate new ways of delivering health care (Royal Society, 2006). Therefore, it is important to be able to understand how technologies' specifications interact with the domestic environment and the social practices within it. This is the task that qualitative researchers are uniquely equipped to do as they are able to describe how households deploy complex relationships between patterns of consumption, illness identities and social networks that cannot be fully compatible with the intentions of technology designers and the recommendations of researchers and professionals (Lehoux et al., 2004; Mort et al., 2008). Indeed, a consistent finding of qualitative studies of telecare is that the incorporation of these devices requires a variety of forms of work from the patient and household members (see similar discussion in Chapter 2).

In a case study of the ambulatory Electro Cardiogram recorder in the Netherlands, Oudshoorn (2008) found that, while procedural tasks where written as instructions to patients, these instructions assumed an expertise of patients as diagnostic agents: they are expected to catch the right moment to register an ECG that shows their heart rate dysfunction. This is a very difficult task, because patients not only have to learn to master the new technology but also learn how to 'read' their bodies in view of the requirements of the technology. This, in turn, entails shifts in the temporal routine of households and adjusting illness identities accordingly. In effect, such practices and identities are not fully malleable, and users who cannot or will not meet the requirements scripted in technologies are at risk of being excluded from these new digital health care services. A useful case to understand this process concerns Continuous Positive Airway Pressure (CPAP), an airflow generator used to prevent the onset of apnoeas during sleep. In a study of a Web-based discussion group about sleep disorders and sleep apnoea, Moreira (2006) found that the 'successful' incorporation of CPAP at home was linked to the deployment of a 'collective expertise' amongst patients. With little help from clinicians or sleep researchers, patients assembled specific and practical knowledge on how to use and adapt the technology. This enabled them to physically alter their sleeping environments and to extend their use of CPAP at home.

It appears that users' role in the successful incorporation of technologies requires much more than following 'doctor's orders'. Incorporation also implies that users try out – at different times in their illness trajectory – different arrangements between their routines and the requirements of the technology. Through such continuous and dynamic adaptation, these devices can become *tools of care* (Willems, 1995) in that they enable users to construct a form of embodied expertise that is specific to their individual situation and so supports them in the day-to-day management of their illness.

COORDINATING TECHNOLOGIES

How do health technologies contribute to the organization of social life? In a variety of ways, this question has been answered already in the preceding sections. From another point of view, we have mostly explored how technologies shape, and are shaped by, health care – from interactions between health professionals and patients to health expectation of the wider population. It has been argued that, in advanced capitalist societies, we are observing a shift from the problem of disease to the problem of health (Crawford, 1980). According to this approach, the focus is not on how to 'restore' health – the main focus of health care – but in how to *maintain* or *not lose it*. This entails changes in the way health is researched and managed, in the way authorities govern populations through epidemiological surveillance, screening programmes and health promotion initiatives and in the technologies used to deploy such policies.

One of the important consequences of this shift is at the subject level, as individuals are expected to draw on ideas about the future in the organization of their present conduct (Armstrong, 1995). Social scientists have emphasized that a new conception of the self emerges as risk is individualized. Drawing on Foucault's (1991) concept of *governmentality*[1] – social studies of health risk have suggested that these changes are themselves linked to a shift in the responsibility of care from professionals to collaborations between patients and clinicians and an emphasis on individual monitoring of lifestyle choices. The prominence given in contemporary societies on 'choice' is underpinned by a particular conceptualization of individuals as rational calculative subjects. In the past decade, studies have focused on how technologies such as the Internet (Nettleton and Burrows, 2003) give body to this type of citizen and enable the forms of subjectivity that underpin such political order. New technologies of risk that enable policy actors, clinicians or patients to develop, collect, discuss and act on risk-based information, have become increasingly significant. In recent years, we have seen the expansion of paper, audio, video and web-based decision support tools to be used in clinics and at home, with the aim to assist patients and their family in making treatment and lifestyle decisions (May et al., 2005).

The issue of accountability is particularly important to understand changes in health in contemporary society. Attention has focused on a new range of 'technologies of accountability', focusing on how clinical practice is coordinated through technologies like guidelines, care pathways and other such local and national policy statements. These initiatives attempt to align everyday managerial and clinical working practices, increasingly demanding that the worlds of practice are informed by 'the judicious use of evidence' about what is clinically and cost-effective. Research has focused on how these technologies are developed (Moreira, 2005; Will, 2005) as well as how they interact with clinical work (Tanenbaum, 1994; Gabbay and le May, 2004). They are evidence that systems of regulation and the establishment of standards are becoming internal requirements for biomedical knowledge production and clinical work, rather than simply forms of external control by the State, employers or the 'public' (Cambrosio et al., 2006) (see similar discussion in Chapter 3).

Another perspective on the coordinating power of health technologies is concerned with how technologies can bring together or break apart the different pragmatic worlds we as social actors navigate in our everyday lives. Drawing on Boltanski and Thevenot's (2006) explorations of the multiple forms of justification through which people legitimize their actions, there has been increased interest in understanding the role of technologies in such processes (Berg and Mol, 1998). In an ethnographic study of asthma therapies, Willems (1998) demonstrates how different regimes – inhaler vs. oral medication – give rise to different practical worlds underpinned by differently enacted 'lung geographies'. For inhaler users, therapy is dependent upon their 'technique' of deployment of the device so that the drug is effectively delivered through the lung as 'a tree with ever finer branches'. This makes it important for users to learn how and when to use the inhalator. Oral medication users are less burdened with these issues as they can rely on the heart to deliver the therapeutic agent to the lungs. This means that they are less able to control and understand the relationship between activities in their lives and the onset of breathing difficulties.

Health technologies can also enable the coming together of worlds that illness has set apart. Willems, again drawing on the case of asthma therapies, argues that one important way of looking at the effectiveness of technologies focuses on how 'norms' are connected through them (Vos et al., 2004). This reveals an innovative and crucial way in which qualitative health research can contribute to the debates around effectiveness of technologies and 'evidence-based medicine'. For example, it is argued that currently available dementia drugs are only modestly effective in terms of outcomes on cognition and clinical impression (Loveman et al., 2005). In an ethnography of clinical management of 'cognitive impairment' in an

English memory clinic, it was observed that, more than cognitive loss, an important problem for patients with early dementia was that the illness eroded the practical arrangements that people have constructed during their lives; their ability to maintain workable balances between different aspects of their life deteriorates as forgetfulness starts setting in. This can be exemplified by the case of Mrs Moffat:[2]

> Mrs. Moffat, a 60 something year old woman, was an independent and active member of her local community (church, clubs, etc.). Until recently, this engagement in the community had been supported by her use of the motorized car, which she could drive independently to meetings and events in the community. She had however lost her orientation a couple of times, which had been distressing for her and her relatives as her panic had led her to make hasty decisions in busy roads. This presented Mrs. Moffat and her family with a predicament: her autonomy was coming into conflict with her safety. On the one hand, her autonomy, and involvement in the community was obviously an important component in her – subjectively defined – quality of life. On the other hand, there were threats to her and others' safety and body integrity coming from the disorientation episodes. Having been prescribed with dementia drugs, Mrs. Moffat was able to continue to balance these two demands for another few months, and as such, cholinesterase inhibitors served as a temporary link between one normative world – autonomy for the person – and another – safety for self and others (Moreira, unpublished data).

In bringing together two worlds, health technologies – such as dementia drugs – articulate between different 'moral goods' (or forms of 'good life') rather than producing effects in singular measurements of quality of life. This represents a potential challenge to how health technologies are evaluated (Murphy et al., 1998; Lehoux, 2006). Instead of focusing on changes in single or aggregate measures of health induced by a technology, qualitative research can provide data on how technologies sustain the mobility of persons across 'lived worlds'. This entails understanding how different illnesses affect different links between established pragmatic worlds for different groups of people. From a purely social science perspective, illnesses provide us with the 'breaching experiments' (Garfinkel, 1967; Bury, 1982) that are necessary to explore the taken-for-granted aspects of our lives. From a wider perspective, this potentially comes to redefine 'illness identities' in sociological rather than biomedical terms, which could be of assistance for patient participation in technological development and assessment.

CONCLUSION

In this chapter, we have demonstrated how qualitative researchers are ideally equipped to understand the processes of generation, mediation and use of health technologies. In being able to capture the meanings attributed to and the social processes around the shaping and use of health technologies, qualitative researchers can provide unique accounts of the dynamic relationships between identities, practices, discourses and technologies. These are accounts that seek to describe and understand how these relationships are enacted in the real world rather than assuming overarching pathways of causation. These accounts are also, for this reason, neither optimistic nor pessimistic about the role of technology in medicine. They provide means of critical, reflexive assessment of technologies-in-action, to be used by practitioners, policymakers and other citizens in their deliberations about the worth of specific technologies. Attributing such a key role for qualitative research in health technology assessment does, however, raise a series of concerns that should be attended to in further research.

First, how to design and develop research on emerging, not fully stabilized health technologies? Due to the configuration of factors identified in the introduction, social and health scientists are increasingly called upon to investigate the social and ethical consequences and/or context of technologies that are still being developed (stem cells, pharmacogenetics, etc.). In this context, Brown and Michael have argued that the construction of expectations is key to the mobilisation of resources and groups around a particular technology but that this process is underpinned by an uneven awareness of the uncertainty of technological 'promises' between experts and lay public (Brown and Michael, 2003). An important stream of research has been focused on detailing how such processes affect different emerging technologies. Less is understood about the effect social and health science research has on the technology – and the promises – it intends to study. In this respect, Law has called our attention to the ambivalent relationship social analysts of technology sustain with the objects of their enquiries (Law, 2002). If, on the one hand, they are invested in pursuing a critical analysis of the uncertainties and contingencies that surround technological projects, there is also an inherent fascination with the beauty and power embedded in those devices. Understanding the methodological, rhetorical and social processes through which qualitative research frames and publicly presents its objects cannot be separated from design and process of conducting research in this area. This does, however, entail developing much further social studies of research-in-action (Maynard and Schaeffer, 2000) with particular attention to qualitative research.

Second, how should qualitative researchers conceive of and investigate the 'contexts' in which health technologies are used and transformed? Most of the research we looked at in the second section of this chapter was conducted through explorations of how technologies entered in particular types of interaction or local forms of health care work. While this provided the background for conceptualizing the relationship between technology and 'practice' as dynamic and fluid, there has been no consistent programme of work to date that investigates in detail how technologies relate to extended, distributed organizational processes (Rapley, 2008). Such an investigation presents considerable challenges, because, as we argued in the foregoing section, the shape and scope of a particular technology can change radically from one site to the next. More creative, methodologies need to be drafted to enable one to follow one technology through its different incarnations without having to assume an inherent stability to the technology itself. Ideally, investigations need to shift beyond interview-based, single-site, or snapshot studies and towards more longitudinal and multisite studies, with a focus on how technologies shape (and are shaped by) practice over time, courses of action, lay and professional identities and contexts.

Third, and finally, to what extent should qualitative researchers be committed to particular theories or conceptualizations of the relationships between technology and 'society'? In this chapter, we have drawn on studies framed by different traditions within social science – actor-network theory, ethnomethodology, feminism, symbolic interactionism, etc. – without emphasizing their diversity and potential incommensurability. We could have specified the way in which different theories structure research questions and data analysis and perhaps argued for one perspective as opposed to another. It was our intention to draw on a range of frameworks to offer different ways of understanding research problems. Favouring one tradition over another runs risk of hindering the theoretical innovation that comes from debates and controversies within and between disciplines. This is particularly acute in the context of health research where methodological robustness is preferred to theoretical development.

NOTES

1 Whereas traditional formulations of power would emphasize sovereignty and authority, a governmentality perspective directs analysis towards the productive, fostering powers of the knowledges (savoirs) and techniques that frame economic and social life. Governmentality focuses on the practices that frame individuals' behaviour, their relations to others and to themselves, that enable ways of acting 'at a distance' upon the conduct of individuals.

2 This case is composed from fieldnotes and does not correspond to a living person.

REFERENCES

Akrich, M. (1992) 'The De-Scription of Technical Objects'. In W. Bijker and J. Law (eds) *Shaping Technology/Building Society: Studies in Sociotechnical Change* (pp. 206–24). Cambridge, MA: MIT Press.

Antaki, C. and Rapley, M. (1996) '"Quality of Life" Talk: The Liberal Paradox of Psychological Testing', *Discourse and Society*, 7: 293–316.

Armstrong, D. (1995) 'The Rise of Surveillance Medicine', *Sociology of Health and Illness*, 17(3): 393–404.

Banta, D. (2003) 'The Development of Health Technology Assessment'. *Health Policy*, 63(2): 121–32.

Berg, M. (1996) 'Practices of Reading and Writing: the Constitutive Role of the Patient Record in Medical Work', *Sociology of Health and Illness*, 18(4): 499–524.

Berg, M. (1998) *Rationalizing Medical Work: Decision-Support Techniques and Medical Practices*. Cambridge, MA: MIT Press.

Berg, M. and Harterink, P. (2004) 'Embodying the Patient: Records and Bodies in Early 20th-century US Medical Practice'. *Body and Society*, 10(2–3): 13–41.

Berg, M. and Mol, A. (eds) (1998) *Differences in Medicine. Unraveling Practices, Techniques and Bodies*. Durham,NC and London: Duke University Press.

Boltanski, L. and Thevenot, L. (2006) *On Justification:Economies of Worth*. Princeton, NJ: Princeton University Press.

Boote, J., Telford, R., and Cooper, C. (2002) 'Consumer Involvement in Health Research: A Review and Research Agenda', *Health Policy*, 61(2): 213–36.

Brown, N. and Michael, M. (2003) 'A Sociology of Expectations: Retrospecting Prospects and Prospecting Retrospects', *Technology Analysis & Strategic Management*, 15(1): 3–18.

Brown, N. and Webster, A. (2004) *New Medical Technologies and Society: Reordering Life.* Cambridge: Polity Press.

Bury, M. (1982) 'Chronic Illness as Biographical Disruption', *Sociology of Health and Illness*, 4: 167–82.

Callon, M. and Law, J. (1989) 'On the Construction of Sociotechnical Networks: Content and Context Revisited', *Knowledge and Society*, 8: 57–83.

Callon, M. and Rabeharisoa, V. (2008) 'The Growing Engagement of Emergent Concerned Groups in Political and Economic Life: Lessons from the French Association of Neuromuscular Disease Patients', *Science, Technology and Human Values*, 33(2): 230–61.

Cambrosio, A., Keating, P., Schlich, T., and Weisz, G. (2006) 'Regulatory Objectivity and the Generation and Management of Evidence in Medicine', *Social Science & Medicine*, 63(1): 189–99.

Caron-Flinterman, J.F., Broerse, J.E.W., and Bunders, J. (2005) 'The Experiential Knowledge of Patients: A New Resource for Biomedical Research?', *Social Science & Medicine*, 60(11): 2575–84.

Casper, M. (1998) *The Making of the Unborn Patient: A Social Anatomy of Fetal Surgery.* New Brunswick: Rutgers University Press.

Clarke, A.E., Mamo, L., Fishman, J.R., Shim, J.K., and Fosket, J.R. (2003) 'Biomedicalization: Technoscientific Transformations of Health, Illness, and U.S. Biomedicine', *American Sociological Review*, 68(April): 161–94.

Coleman, J.S., Katz, E., and Menzel, H. (1966) *Medical Innovation: A Diffusion Study.* Indianapolis, IN: Bobbs-Merrill.

Crawford, R. (1980) 'Healthism and the Medicalization of Everyday Life'. *International Journal of Health Services*, 10: 663–80.

Evans, H. (1993) 'Losing Touch: The Controversy over the Introduction of Blood Pressure Instruments into Medicine', *Technology and Culture*, 34(4): 784–807.

Flyvbjerg, B. (2001) *Making Social Science Matter: Why Social Inquiry Fails and How It Can Succeed Again.* Cambridge: Cambridge University Press.

Foucault, M. (1991) *Governmentality. The Foucault Effect: Studies in Governmentality*, G. Burchell, C. Gordon and P. Miller (eds). Chicago: University of Chicago Press.

Gabbay, J. and le May, A. (2004) 'Evidence Based Guidelines or Collectively Constructed "Mindlines?" Ethnographic Study of Knowledge Management in Primary Care'. *BMJ*, 329(7473): 1013.

Garfinkel, H. (1967) *Studies in Ethnomethodology.* Cambridge: Polity Press.

Greatbatch, D., Hanlon, G., Goode, J., O'Cathain, A., Strangleman, T., and Luff, D. (2005) 'Telephone Triage, Expert Systems and Clinical Expertise', *Sociology of Health and Illness*, 27(6): 802–30.

Harrison, S. and Mort, M.M. (1998) 'Which Champions, Which People? Public and User Involvement in Health Care as a Technology of Legitimation', *Social Policy and Administration*, 32(1): 60–70.

Heath, C., Luff, P., and Svensson, M.S. (2003) 'Technology and Medical Practice', *Sociology of Health & Illness*, 25: 75–96.

Hirschauer, S. (1994) 'Towards a Methodology of Investigations into the Strangeness of One's Own Culture: A Reply to Collins', *Social Studies of Science*, 24: 335–46.

Holstein, M. (2000) 'Aging, Culture and the Framing of Alzheimer's Disease'. In P.J. Whitehouse, K. Maurer and J. Ballenger (eds) *Concepts of Alzheimer's Disease* (pp. 158–80). Baltimore: Johns Hopkins University Press.

Howell, J.D. (1995) *Technology in The Hospital. Transforming Patient Care in the Early Twentieth Century.* Baltimore: John Hopkins University Press.

Law, J. (2002) *Aircraft Stories. Decentering the Object in Technoscience.* Durham, NC: Duke University Press.

Lehoux, P. (2006) *The Problem of Health Technology: Policy Implications for Modern Healthy Care Systems.* London: Routledge.

Lehoux, P. and Blume, S. (2000) 'Technology Assessment and the Sociopolitics of Health Technologies', *Journal of Health Politics Policy and Law*, 25(6): 1083–20.

Lehoux, P., Saint-Arnaud, J. and Richard, L. (2004) 'The Use of Technology at Home: What Patient Manuals Say and Sell vs. What Patients Face and Fear', *Sociology of Health & Illness*, 26(5): 617–44.

Loveman, E., Green, C., Kirby, J., Takeda, A., Picot, J., Bradbury, J., Payne, E., and Clegg, A. (2005) *The Clinical and Cost-Effectiveness of Donepezil, Rivastigmine, Galantamine, and Memantine for Alzheimer's Disease*. Southampton: Southampton Health Technology Assessment Centre.

Lynch, M. (1994) 'Collins, Hirschauer and Winch: Ethnography, Exoticism, Surgery, Antisepsis and Dehorsification', *Social Studies of Science*, 24: 354–69.

May, C. and Ellis, N.T. (2001) 'When Protocols Fail: Technical Evaluation, Biomedical Knowledge, and the Social Production of 'Facts' About a Telemedicine Clinic', *Social Science and Medicine*, 53: 989–1002.

May, C., Mort, M., Williams, T., Mair, F.S., and Gask, L. (2003) 'Health Technology Assessment in its Local Contexts: Studies of Telehealthcare', *Social Science and Medicine*, 57: 697–710.

May, C., Rapley, T., Moreira, T. Finch, T., and Heaven, B. (2005) 'Technogovernance: Evidence, Subjectivity, and the Clinical Encounter in Primary Care Medicine', *Social Science and Medicine*, 62(4): 1022–30.

Maynard, D.W. and Schaeffer, N.C. (2000) 'Toward a Sociology of Social Scientific Knowledge: Survey Research and Ethnomethodology's Asymmetric Alternates', *Social Studies of Science*, 30(3): 323–70.

Mol, A. (1999) 'Ontological Politics'. In J. Law and J. Hassard (eds) *A Word and Some Questions. Actor-Network Theory and After* (pp. 74–89). Oxford: Blackwell.

Moreira, T. (2000) 'Translation, Difference and Ontological Fluidity: Cerebral Angiography and Neurosurgical Practice (1926–45)', *Social Studies of Science*, 30: 421–46

Moreira, T. (2005) 'Diversity in Clinical Guidelines: The Role of Repertoires of Evaluation', *Social Science and Medicine*, 60: 1975–85.

Moreira, T. (2006) 'Sleep, Health and the Dynamics of Biomedicine', *Social Science & Medicine*, 63: 54–63.

Moreira, T. (2009) 'Testing Promises: Truth and Hope in Drug Development and Evaluation in Alzheimer's Disease. Do We Have a Pill for That?'. In J.F. Ballenger, P.J. Whitehouse, C. Lyketsos, P. Rabins and J.H.T. Karlawish (eds) *Interdisciplinary Perspectives on the Development, Use and Evaluation of Drugs in the Treatment of Dementia*. Baltimore: Johns Hopkins University Press.

Mort, M., Finch, T., and May, C. (2008) 'Making and Unmaking Telepatients: Identity and Governance in New Health Technologies', *Science, Technology and Human Values* (published in OnlineFirst on 4 March 2004).

Mowery, D. and Rosenberg, N. (1989) *Technology and the Pursuit of Economic Growth*. Cambridge: Cambridge University Press.

Murphy, E., Dingwall, R., Greatbach, D., Parker, S., and Watson, P. (1998) 'Qualitative Research Methods in Health Technology Assessment: A Review of the Literature', *Health Technology Assessment*, 2(16): 1–276.

Nettleton, S. and Burrows, R. (2003) 'E-scaped Medicine? Information, Reflexivity and Health', *Critical Social Policy*, 23(2): 165–85.

Oudshoorn, N. (2008) 'Diagnosis at a Distance: The Invisible Work of Patients and Healthcare Professionals in Cardiac Telemonitoring Technology', *Sociology of Health and Illness*, 30(2): 272–88.

Ragin, C. (2004) 'Turning the Tables: How Case Oriented Research Challenges Variable Oriented Research'. In H. Brady and D. Collier (eds) *Rethinking Social Inquiry: Diverse Tools, Shared Standards*. Lanham: Rowman & Littlefield.

Rapley, T. (2008) 'Distributed Decision Making: The Anatomy of Decisions-in-Action', *Sociology of Health and Illness*, 30(3): 429–44.

Rose, N. and Miller, P. (1992) 'Political Power Beyond the State: Problematics of Government', *British Journal of Sociology*, 43: 173–205.

Royal Society (2006) *Digital Healthcare: The Impact of Information and Communication Technologies on Health and Healthcare.* London: Royal Society.

Strauss, A., Fagerhaugh, S., Suczek, B., and Wiener, C. (1985) *The Social Organization of Medical Work.* New Brunswick: Transaction.

Tanenbaum, S.J. (1994) 'Knowing and Acting in Medical Research: The Epistemological Politics of Outcomes Research', *Journal of Health Politics, Policy and Law,* 19: 27–44.

Timmermans, S. (1999) *Sudden Death and the Myth of CPR.* Philadelphia: Temple University Press.

Timmermans, S. and Berg, M. (2003) 'The Practice of Medical Technology'. *Sociology of Health & Illness,* 25: 97–114.

Vos, R., Willems, D., and Houtepen, R. (2004) 'Coordinating the Norms and Values of Medical Research, Medical Practice and Patient Worlds – The Ethics of Evidence Based Medicine in Orphaned Fields of Medicine', *Journal of Medical Ethics,* 30(2): 166–70.

Webster, A. (2007) *Health, Technology and Society.* Houndmills: Palgrave.

Whalen, J. (1995) 'A Technology of Order Production: Computer-Aided Dispatch in Public Safety Communications'. In P. Ten Have and G. Psathas (eds) *Situated Order: Studies in the Social Organization of Talk and Embodied Activities* (pp. 187–230). Washington DC: University Press of America.

Whalen, M. and Zimmerman, D.H. (1987) 'Sequential and Institutional Contexts in Call for Help', *Social Psychology Quarterly,* 50(2): 172–85.

Will, C. (2005) 'Arguing About the Evidence: Readers, Writers and Inscription Devices in Coronary Heart Disease Risk Assessment', *Sociology of Health and Illness.* 27: 780–801.

Willems, D. (1998) 'Inhaling Drugs and Making Worlds: The Proliferation of Lungs and Asthmas'. In M. Berg and A. Mol (eds) *Differences in Medicine. Unraveling Practices, Techniques and Bodies* (pp. 105–18). Durham, NC and London: Duke University Press.

Willems, D.L. (1995) *Tools of Care: Explorations into the Semiotics of Medical Technology.* Maastricht, NL: Maastricht University.

Yoxen, E. (1987) 'Seeing with Sound: A Study of the Development of Medical Images'. In W.E. Bijker, T.P. Hughes and T.J. Pinch (eds) *The Social Construction of Technological Systems* (pp. 281–306). Cambridge, MA: MIT Press.

35

Transgressive Pleasures: Undertaking Qualitative Research in the *Radsex* Domain

Dave Holmes, Patrick O'Byrne
and Denise Gastaldo

INTRODUCTION

If one follows Foucault (1978), it is possible to suggest that since classical antiquity, Western cultures have been preoccupied with controlling both the meaning and the experience of pleasure. As part of this, MacKendrick (1999) suggests that pleasure has been compartmentalized as arising from either normal or abnormal sources, with those emerging from the latter often being deemed either unacceptable or deviant. However, despite numerous historical attempts to contain pleasure through medical, legal, and social mechanisms, pleasure has never been successfully controlled. It has instead proven itself to be a force that resists confinement and which impels action (Bataille, 1962). Within this chapter, these nonmainstream or so-called 'deviant' pleasures, particularly in relation to human sexuality, are described as *radsex*. This term, which arises from the combination of the words '*rad*ical' and '*sex*uality', applies the destabilizing undertones present within the word 'radical', but does so in relation to 'sexuality', thus making *radsex* a fluid and subjective concept that encompasses all sexual expressions that are seen to be unaccepted within any jurisdiction, at any time. As a direct result of the disruptive nature of *radsex*, much research has been dedicated to this topic, but usually only with the focus of understanding these practices in order to create interventions that will abolish them; for example, the exploration of *bareback sex* in an effort to design counselling strategies that will effectively stop individuals from having unprotected anal sex (see Halkitis et al., 2005; O'Leary et al., 2005; Gerbert et al., 2006). Consequently, almost no attention has been given to understanding the basic foundations of pleasure, or to addressing *radsex* as a set of perfectly acceptable sexual expressions.

In reaction to the foregoing, the aim of this chapter is to discuss both the importance of using, and the means by which to employ, qualitative research methods when undertaking exploratory research on marginal or radical sexualities. In this context, such a discussion will occur by means of a three-part process, which will commence with a brief analysis of *radsex* (part one) and its two related concepts of 'pleasure' and 'counter-pleasure' (part two). While some could argue that any description of the foregoing concepts (i.e., *radsex*, pleasure, and counter-pleasure) is irrelevant within a book on research methods, it is important to heed the guidance of Guba and Lincoln (2008) when they state (1) that methodology often emerges from theory, and (2) that as a result of this, qualitative researchers' theoretical framework must permit an accurate reporting of the phenomena being studied from the participants' internal perspective. However, without an adequate understanding of one's theoretical position, or alternatively, without any understanding of the theoretical concepts that underpin one's study, this process of acquiring the research participants' internal perspective becomes much less rigorous. As Emmons (2001) states, in her discussion of Koepsell et al. (1992), a thorough and forthcoming understanding of one's guiding theoretical principles is required 'to clarify the … "black boxes" of [one's] work' (p. 250). The exposure of one's 'black boxes' enhances a project's transparency, because it permits a clear and honest overview of the researcher's pre-existent belief systems. As such, it is important that theoretical discussions about some concepts which are central to understanding *radsex* are delineated as part of this methodological discussion.

Once this background explanation has occurred, we will then address some of the challenges that may arise when conducting qualitative health research in this domain (part three). In this third part, the discussion will begin to confront more of the technical aspects of *radsex* research, including, for example, the associated personal exasperations (such as, the interference of one's personal beliefs and feelings about sexuality), theoretical and methodological complexities (such as, tension between the paradigm of inquiry and the politics of the research context), and ethical difficulties (such as, requirements to maintain the research participants' personal privacy). This section of the chapter will constitute the more traditional aspect of a methodological discussion.

EXPLORING *RADSEX*: SITUATING THE PRESENT

While the exploration of *rad*ical *sex*ual practices (*radsex*) might at first glance appear to be an unusual enterprise, further investigation reveals that this topic became a research topic of central importance within the eighteenth century. With what could be considered its official debut approximately a century-and-a-half ago, health-based investigations of nonmainstream (or radical) sexualities began to occur, most notably, with the independent but interrelated works of Richard von Krafft-Ebing and Sigmund Freud (see, for example, Krafft-Ebing, 1965; Freud, 1961, 2006). During this time, the previously aesthetic depictions, of authors such as Leopold von Sacher-Masoch (1989) and Marquis de Sade (1965), began to transform into a scientifically discussed topic. Indeed, both Krafft-Ebing and Freud built their theories of human sexuality from the findings of their systematic assessments: in-depth analyses of their patients' dialogue and direct observation of their patients' daily interactions. By today's standards, the approaches employed by these two men could be considered a mixture of case study, narrative analysis, and ethnography: in-depth data collection through discussion and direct observation, and then subsequent analysis of the information presented by individual cases to create theories about both the individual specifically (e.g., Freud's well-known Wolfman) and the human condition generally (e.g., Krafft-Ebing's sadomasochism). This generalization of their results constitutes a major problem for these authors, however. Indeed, regardless of one's paradigmatic perspective (e.g., positivism, postpositivism, critical theory, and constructivism), proclaiming that one's findings from such a small sample represent the entire population is problematic. This, obviously, resulted in severe criticisms of the methods and the findings of Krafft-Ebing and Freud.

While many other significant and influential writers continued/refined Krafft-Ebing's and Freud's work after their deaths, the next individual to be discussed is one of the first formally trained researchers who turned his attention to the field of human sexuality. This man is Alfred Kinsey. Although originally an entomologist who employed quantitative methods in his studies of sex, Kinsey is worth mentioning here for two main reasons. First, his work initiated a massive reshaping of the puritanical perceptions of human sexuality that pervade North America. While this may seem unlikely because much of what Kinsey and his team wrote seems less than radical by today's standards, that is only because this group of researchers persevered in the face of intense abuse and negative reaction in their attempts to *normalize* the diversity of human sexual expression. In fact, their original demonstration of the widespread practice of masturbation, anal sex, and homosexuality was enough to provoke such international outrage that they lost most of their sources of research funding (Pomeroy, 1982). Ultimately, however, Kinsey and his colleagues succeeded in broadening the acceptance of behaviours such as female masturbation, which, thankful to these researchers, is no longer seen as immoral or pathological. In addition, as a result of this work, the discourse surrounding homosexuality also lost much of its contention (but unfortunately, only in some jurisdictions).

The second reason why Kinsey and his colleagues' work is important within this context is due to the data collection methods that this team of researchers employed. Namely, they ultimately utilized statistical analyses; however, the relevance here is that they did so based on case histories that were developed from in-depth interviews (see Kinsey et al., 1948, *Sexual Behaviour in the Human Male*, Part I, Chapter 2, and Kinsey et al., 1953, *Sexual Behaviour in the Human Female*, Part I, Chapter 3 for a review of these methods). As an introduction to the foregoing chapter on methods in their first book, Kinsey et al. (1948) explain in great detail that no matter how 'satisfactory the standard deviations may be, no statistical treatment can put validity into generalizations which are based on data that were not reasonably accurate and complete to begin with' (p. 35). Immediately after stating this, these authors then explain the precise means by which they gathered their data: in-depth, personal, case-history interviews. Careful review of their methods reveals, one, that much of what these authors wrote in 1948 still remains valid today, and, two, that novice researchers in the *radsex* domain should review Kinsey and colleagues' approach, particularly in relation to participant recruitment, establishing rapport, assuring privacy/confidentiality, and contemporaneous data collection.

After Kinsey and his team had left their mark, a large number of other researchers began exploring the taboo topic of human sexuality. This list includes Masters and Johnson, and their laboratory-based explorations of human arousal. While interesting, (both personally and professionally perhaps), these authors will be omitted in this discussion of qualitative *radsex* research. As Humphreys (1970) so clearly articulates, although 'Masters and Johnson might gather clinical data in a clinical setting without distortion, [ ] a stage is a suitable research site only for those who wish to study the 'onstage' behaviour or actors' (p. 26). As such, these two authors will be skipped, thus leaving the next author to be discussed as Laud Humphreys – the controversial sociologist who expanded scientific knowledge in the domain of *radsex* in his acclaimed and scorned exploration of anonymous male sexual encounters in public washrooms. To explain the mixed reactions to Humphreys' work, one must be aware of what he studied and how he did so. Humphreys (1970) investigated the sexual practices of men who engage in fellatio in 'tearooms', which is a term used to describe the usage of spaces/places which have an intended nonsexual function, but which are used nonetheless for the purpose of sexual relations between men. In his study, Humphreys (1970) focused most specifically on the public-washroom tearoom.

To gather his data, Humphreys undertook direct observation, interviewed participants, and statistically analyzed their responses. The first of these two methods were actualized by (1) observing men having sex in public washrooms, (2) engaging in discussions with these men on-site whenever possible, (3) noting the car license plates of the men with whom he did not dialogue, (4) tracking these license plates to a fixed address, and then (5) interviewing these same men a full calendar year later, but under the guise of a different research project. In addition, Humphreys (1970) also altered his appearance for the second, year-later encounter, to ensure that he would not be recognized by the men he interviewed. While indubitably full of ethical concerns, this study revealed that men who were socially considered *normal*, because they are well-employed family men, were surreptitiously having sex with other men (Humphreys, 1970).

The principal importance of this study was twofold: first, an intense ethical debate about social science research methods ensued, and second, the empirical findings illustrated that 'homosexuals' are normal people.

Shortly after the release of Humphreys' work, another now well-known author began to investigate human sexuality. This was Michel Foucault. In his three-volume classic, *The History of Sexuality* (Vol. 1, 1978; Vol. 2, 1985; Vol. 3, 1986), Foucault presented the results of his historical analysis of human sexuality, during which he carefully identified aspects of sexuality that are central to current social existence, but which are often effaced by one's (i.e., *our*) being in and of the current period. This historical analysis thus helped, to use a well-known phrase, discern the forest from the trees. Moreover, by investigating the historical developments of sex and sexuality which started in ancient Greece, which subsequently developed through the Christian period, and which then flowered during the Victorian era into its modern state, Foucault (1978; 1985; 1986) identified how sexuality is a prime component of an individual's subjectivity – with the integral nature of sexuality sculpting an individual both in relation to how the individual sees him/herself and how others view him/her. For example, Foucault (1985) argued in *Volume Two* of *The History of Sexuality* that a young boy's sexual conduct often determined whether or not he could ever hold a position of social authority; excessive indulgence in sexual pleasures diminished one's future social status because one's sexual conduct was considered to reflect the calibre of one's inner-essence or self (Foucault, 1985).

The reception of *The History of Sexuality*, in its totality, however, has been mixed. Some use it as a theoretical framework for guiding further study, while others criticize its historical accuracy. The latter criticisms range from suggestions that Foucault oversimplified historical events to accusations that he outright ignored empirical evidence about the past. In many cases, these accusations are not without merit, and in part, illustrate the need for qualitative researchers to be rigorous in their methods. Thus, notwithstanding the benefits that can be achieved by an open reading of Foucault's work, his methodological shortcomings have rendered his work susceptible to easy dismissal by many of his critics. In an inherently politically charged and fundamentally disruptive field of inquiry, *radsex* researchers must be vigilant not to allow their results to be easily discarded due to methodological errors or oversights. This includes having a clear theoretical understanding of the topic under study in order to follow Emmons' (2001) suggestion that it is absolutely necessary to comprehend the 'black boxes' of one's work. In the *radsex* domain, Foucault's *History of Sexuality* illustrated that pleasure is one such black box.

EXPLAINING TWO 'BLACK BOXES' OF *RADSEX* RESEARCH: PLEASURE AND COUNTER-PLEASURE

Studies of human sexuality are more than just investigations about a specific human practice; they are explorations that either support or refute some fundamental beliefs about humanity and human nature. For example, the acts of either stating that *radsex* is normal, or alternatively, of positioning it as a deviant practice, both (1) firmly position the sexual activities being explored on the spectrum of normalcy, and (2) simultaneously reveal the researcher's beliefs about the topic that s/he is investigating. In his book, *Death and Sensuality – A Study of Eroticism and Taboo*, Georges Bataille (1962) makes an interesting comment on this process when he states that the practice of identifying sexual practices as inherently dysfunctional, deviant, or abnormal is a sign that one has only understood them from an external position. In other words, it is to negate the internal experiences of joy, satisfaction, and pleasure that individuals experience during these so-called deviant acts (Dean, 2009). To gather the internal perspective of sexuality, Bataille (1962) posits that one must move beyond the label of abnormality, and instead consider how and why a specific sexual practice, or form of sexuality, is desirable for and desired by its participants. For Denzin and Lincoln (2008), the quest to acquire such an internal understanding, and thus to accurately represent the participants' voice, is of central importance during qualitative research, especially when it involves already marginalized populations. Qualitative researchers must, therefore, actively work to overcome the fact that 'from the very beginning, qualitative research was implicated in a racist [and otherwise Eurocentric] project' of representing non-Europeans as less than equal (Denzin and Lincoln, 2008: 2). This 'racist project' that Denzin and Lincoln (2008) describe is Bataille's (1962) external representation. From our perspective, as it relates to *radsex* research, moving away from such an external representation involves following the suggestions of Foucault and subsequent Foucauldian scholars by reconceptualizing two of the fundamental pillars of sexuality: pleasure, and its corresponding experience of counter-pleasure.

Pleasure: understanding the external perspective

To ground our understanding of pleasure so that qualitative researchers can acquire the internal experience of an activity, we will begin with the following definition of pleasure from the New Oxford American Dictionary [Computer software]: it is 'a feeling of happy satisfaction or enjoyment'. To expand on this dictionary definition, pleasure can be understood as an enjoyable feeling, or, put otherwise, as a collection of sensations that are liked/likeable throughout both their duration and postoccurrence period. For example, sex and eating produce pleasure both because of the physical and psychological feelings that occur while they are occurring and because of the sense of satiation/satisfaction that materializes upon their completion. What is essential to note in this basic definition of pleasure is that it can include anything (whether action, thought, or emotion) that brings gratification to an individual (MacKendrick, 1999).

However, as all-inclusive and nonjudgemental as this starting definition may seem, covertly embedded within its broader social definition are elements of the biological/evolutionary model (MacKendrick, 1999). The result of this hidden biological undertone is that the traditional definition of pleasure limits this concept to being little more than a strictly physiological outcome of hormones that induces constant reactions within all individuals; it is an idea stripped of its subjective and cultural aspects. All that remains is a comprehension of pleasure that positions it as a physiologically induced release of catecholamines and endorphins that dictates unalterable physical feelings (Dean, 2000). In approaching the concept of pleasure from such a perspective, it becomes a purposively sought feeling; that is, it becomes the goal towards which all individuals should naturally migrate (MacKendrick, 1999). For Freud (1961), this would include what he believes is an individual's natural desire to eat, sleep, eliminate, and have sex. While this Freudian perspective seems intuitively sound, this may not be the case; his interpretation quickly falls apart when used to explain situations wherein individuals experience pleasure during activities that damage them, or conversely, when they do not experience pleasure during activities that supposedly should be pleasurable. Examples of this would be when pain is pleasurable (e.g., masochism), or when eating/having sex is unpleasant (e.g., anorexia nervosa/ vaginismus). In such cases, the traditional definition of pleasure, with its biological undertones, offers only one explanation: individuals who experience pleasure from self-damaging or so-called unnatural practices, or alternatively, individuals who do not experience pleasure when they are expected to, are deviant; they are inherently abnormal and are classified with their corresponding diagnostic labels.

However, while it is possible to say that aforementioned descriptions of pleasure are archaic and no longer in use, such Freudian thought continues to underpin many, if not most, contemporary perspectives on pleasure (MacKendrick, 1999). This means that, despite his thinking being regularly critiqued, ridiculed, and/or outright rejected, Freud's work still underlines much of the current research on *radsex*. As such, it is important to shed light on this theoretical black box by explaining how Freud (1961) conceptualizes pleasure: it is the release of tension for the sole reason that tension is understood as being inherently unpleasant (Freud, 1961). His is thus a hydraulic conceptualization of pleasure: either a discharge of tension or an escape from an unpleasant status, whether sexual, emotional, or psychological (e.g., anxiety) (Freud, 1961; MacKendrick, 1999). The result of limiting pleasure in this way is its containment within the dichotomy of what is deemed normal or pathological, often with these extremes being put forth as the only two available options. Unfortunately, the psychoanalytic conceptualization of pleasure fails to capture this concept from what Bataille (1962) describes as the internal perspective – most notably because Freud's work retains underlying assumptions about normality and abnormality. The outcome is that we are left with an external understanding of pleasure that, because it excludes many forms of legitimately experienced pleasure, renders the traditional definition of this concept theoretically inadequate for guiding in-depth qualitative research. Indeed, to use traditional conceptualizations of pleasure is to undertake top-down qualitative research that categorically fails to understand how enjoyment could ensue from activities that are considered *counter* to *pleasure*.

Counter-pleasure: moving toward an internal perspective

As a result of the abovementioned inadequacies of the traditional, psychoanalytically driven understanding of pleasure, other authors such as Karmen MacKendrick (1999) developed the term *counter-pleasure*. This new concept, while far from perfect, is an excellent theoretical starting point for a qualitative research approach that is sufficiently sensitive to Bataille's (1962) internal perspective – one that Denzin and Lincoln (2008) suggest is needed to overcome the longstanding tradition of colonialism and *other-ing* that has pervaded qualitative research. Within the realm of health-based qualitative research, particularly in relation to *radsex* research, this new concept can be used as an alternative framework for scientific investigations which aim to garner a qualitative understanding of sexual practices in which the transgression of societal rules produces pleasure (Bataille, 1989).

To explain this concept further, counter-pleasure is the attainment of pleasure by means that are seen as being in opposition to the traditional sources of pleasure; that is, it is pleasure that occurs as an outcome of *radsex* practises (MacKendrick, 1999). By recognizing that pleasure can arise from the act of challenging social taboos, the field of pleasure shows more of its limitless potential: a pleasure within one culture, or for one individual, can be a counter-pleasure within another culture or for a different individual (MacKendrick, 1999). Using pain as an example, Yost (2007), in her interview-based study of 'sexual fantasies of s/m [sadomasochism] practitioners', describes how counter-pleasure is not so much a negative sensation as it is a pleasurable experience that is achieved from direct negative stimulation (p. 135). Chaline (2007) illustrates a similar point in her discourse analysis of how some men become gay sadomasochists when she reports that the act of becoming a *bona fide* sadomasochist involves a rigorous indoctrination process during which one must learn the appropriate responses to, and desires for, group-accepted counter-pleasures. A review of Chaline's (2007) work reveals that her use of a counter-pleasure theoretical basis produces an interesting résumé of how the participants have embodied their counter-pleasures to the point that they not just understand it, but also experience its meaning on a profoundly physical level. Put differently, this study can be described as an internal-perspective depiction of the desires of individuals who indulge in a process that is similar to Kafka's (1996) writing machine in his story *The Penal Colony*. In combination, the outcome of these two studies, and many others (such as, Bronski, 1998; Gagnon, 2004; Dean, 2009), is the realization that counter-pleasure can also be achieved in both moral and erotogenic ways: for example, the deconstruction of a social code of conduct, such as heterosexuality, through the practice of homosexuality, or the desire for nongender specific anal sex because it is a cultural taboo. In this way, pleasure is not limited to action alone; rather, it can be experienced as a result of ideas, thoughts, and/or emotions (MacKendrick, 1999). It, thus, is as much the cognitive/emotional aspects of a desired activity or person as it is his/her/its physical components. All of this is to say that there is more to sexuality than genitalia (Halperin, 1995).

By broadening the understanding of pleasure to include not necessarily genital-based counter-pleasures, one can begin to appreciate a more fluid and less constrained sexuality that flows out from the mainstream and into a multiplicity of possible directions (Bronski, 1998). It is an experience of satisfaction, joy, and happiness that is not constrained to socio-political conceptualizations of normality. From a methodological standpoint, it is likely that qualitative research is better suited to such a style of exploration (Creswell, 1998) – but this can only be said if *radsex* researchers are dedicated to acquiring and presenting the internal experience of their participants' nontraditional sexualities and sexual experiences. Qualitative researchers must thus remain mindful of pleasure and counter-pleasure as fluid and dynamic processes that vary across populations, as well as between and within individuals. This also requires that researchers remain sensitive to the fact that pleasure and counter-pleasure may arise from a variety of sources: for example, the experience of pain or the reversal of gender roles (i.e., gender bending) – put simply, the breaking of boundaries as the means to actualize the ultimate orgiastic state (Airaksinen, 1995; Holmes et al., 2006). Such practices, which may seem radical when compared to those of the 'mainstream', are the specific activities that may result in ecstasy (Tobias, 2005). This change in perspective permits a reduction in researchers' inherently judgemental task of filtering/sorting phenomena by allowing the description to be done from an internal perspective. To explore this statement, and to more fully provide insight in relation to qualitative *radsex* research, we will now discuss the specific personal, methodological, and ethical concerns related to engaging in qualitative research of human sexuality, particularly of radical human sexuality (i.e., *radsex*).

RESEARCHING *RADSEX*: EXPLORING BAREBACK SEX, SADOMASOCHISM, SWINGING AND GROUP-SEX

With the foregoing description of how one can alternatively conceptualize pleasure in order to better garner an internal understanding of nonmainstream or radical sexualities, we will now ground our discussion of *radsex* research methods in *radsex* research projects that we have either already explored (*bareback sex* and sadomasochism), or are presently exploring (swinging and group-sex). The goal of such a description is to, first, illustrate examples of the aforementioned theoretical work in practice, and, second, to provide substance for the in-depth methodological discussion that will ensue shortly.

Bareback sex

If one compares the 1970s with the 1990s, it is evident that a significant reversal has occurred: only 30 years ago, unprotected sex probably would have been considered natural, whereas today, in the post-AIDS (Acquired Immunodeficiency Syndrome) era, the idea of having sex without a condom with an anonymous partner is socially denounced for its potential to transmit HIV (Human Immunodeficiency Virus) and other sexually transmitted infections (STIs) (Dean, 2009; Sammoun, 2004). As a result of these infections, unprotected sex has not only become viewed as dangerous, but also has become the focus of intense investigation (Dean, 2009; Halkitis et al., 2001; 2003; 2005a; 2005b; Holmes and Warner, 2005; Holmes and O'Byrne, 2006). Labelled 'bareback sex' – a slogan that implies the ruggedness and masculinity of the American cowboy: 'real men ride horses without saddles' – this practice is seen today as a major risk factor in the transmission of STIs and HIV among men who have sex with other men (MSM). In spite of this, barebacking (unprotected anal sex) seems to be regaining popularity, as is suggested by increases in HIV infection rates (Public Health Agency of Canada, 2006 and other research (Dean, 2009). What this means is that the aspect of barebacking that makes it radical, which is/was its social denouncement and infrequent occurrence, is partially dissolving.

The hypothesis that ensues from a pleasure/counter-pleasure theoretical position is that once a practice becomes accepted, or seen as normal within a specific group, it moves to the centre (Fiske, 1989). This is the transition of bareback sex from counter-pleasure to pleasure. The outcome is the drive to construct and/or discover new barriers to transgress (Bataille, 1962). In other words, when a boundary is eliminated, new ones must be found. In the case of bareback sex, such a process can be seen when HIV-negative individuals (i.e., those who do not have HIV) intentionally seek HIV infected-partner(s) with whom to have unprotected anal sex in an effort either to flirt with the possibility of becoming infected, or to purposively acquire HIV (Gauthier and Forsyth, 1999). While engaging in bug-chasing, as this phenomenon is called, may seem to indicate a gross impairment of judgement, or a lack of sanity, it can also be seen as an example of one of the next levels of radicalism (Holmes and Warner, 2005; Dean, 2009). It is a means by which individuals can re-capture the excitement that transgression produces.

This latter explanation, while nontraditional, arose from qualitative research wherein the goal was to develop an internal-perspective understanding of bareback sex, and some of it corollary practices. To accomplish this, the authors of this chapter undertook 147 hours of direct observation in gay bathhouses, administered self-directed surveys to 414 men within these bathhouses, and then engaged an additional 28 men in in-depth, semi-structured interviews. The outcome was the development of a contra-mainstream understanding of bareback sex (Holmes et al., 2008). Rather than it being the behavioural manifestation of poor adaptation, internalized homophobia, or desires to overcome an increasingly individualistic society, these men explained how their sexual practices occur as a result of a desire to indulge in the resultant sensations, a longing for the excitement that transgressing boundaries produces, and a wish to resist traditional understandings of normal sexuality. While their sexual practices involved a chance of disease/death, the drive was the fulfilment and maximization of life. A counter-pleasure underpinning within this project permitted the creation of an internal, and thus nonpathological, perspective of the research participants. An unintended outcome that must be noted, however, is how our and others' (qualitative) research that was undertaken on this *radsex* practice resulted in the destruction of the specific attribute of this practice that made it pleasurable: transgression of taboo. Nonpathological understandings of barebacking may reduce the pleasure associated with this practice because it reduces its transgressive nature by making this practice better known and more socially accepted. This type of research may, in part, thereby functionally remove the transgressive and resistance components of *bareback sex* that make it pleasurable.

Sadomasochism (S&M)

In addition to exploring *bareback sex* as part of our bathhouse research project, (Holmes et al., 2007) we also investigated S&M practices. This occurred through purposive recruitment, during which individuals were specifically sought-out to discuss these practices, and an S&M bathhouse was visited/observed. This signifies, most notably, that *radsex* encompasses activities other than those which increase the likelihood of STI transmission. First, it is important to describe S&M practices briefly as *radsex* acts which require either the giving, or the accepting, of pain in order to produce a sensation of pleasure. Before continuing, however, it is essential to recognize the similarities and distinctions between sadism and the 'sado-' component of sadomasochism. For clarity, henceforth, these two different forms of behaviour will be textually differentiated as 'sadism/ sadistic' and 'S&M'. From both the sadistic and the S&M perspectives, pleasure is derived from the achievement of power over another human being through the inscription of pain on another's body up to the point where there is no more room to inscribe (Langdridge and Barker, 2007). MacKendrick (1999) describes this in metaphorical terms: When the white space on the page is completely obliterated, i.e., the body destroyed, or all social limits surpassed, it is discarded and a new page must then be defaced. The purpose therein is to take restrictions (social, physical, and emotional) and to systematically exceed them – to simultaneously transgress both the limits of practices and the limits of the victim or the masochist (Airaksinen, 1991). It is a violence that is driven by the knowledge that, ultimately, there will be an eventual limit to the limitless that is desired. The limitless power and control over another is strictly an ephemeral sensation that culminates and ends in climax (Bataille, 1962). For both the sadist and S&M, this power ends as quickly as it starts, with the exact limit of limitlessness being precisely the point where the sadist and the S&M perspectives differ.

The difference between the two resides in the fact that, for the sadist, it is that infinitesimal fleeting point between life and death that is the climax: the point of ultimate destruction that results in the death of the sadist's victim (Bataille, 1962). For S&M, the pinnacle is the actual sexual climax of the masochist, an orgiastic state of sexual ecstasy (Moser and Kleinplatz, 2007). At this point, however, both sadism and S&M again merge in their logic, because once the climax (whether death/destruction or sexual release) occurs, the process is complete, and must subsequently be initiated with either a new individual, or a new experience. Although in the S&M relationship, the ultimate goal is not the death of the masochist, but the pushing of his/her body to the point just before it breaks (Airaksinen, 1995), both of these practices are ultimately edgeworks of the body's limits (Lyng, 2005). This is true for both the sadist who wishes to absolutely destroy his/her victim, in which case murder is the eventual outcome (after having inflicted a maximum amount of pain in the process) and, for S&M, where it is the maximization of sensation without irreparable damage to the masochist that is desired (Airaksinen, 1995).

In relation to qualitative research methods, S&M and sadism both contain unique methodological hurdles. More specifically, S&M and sadism are difficult to research, and ultimately to comprehend, if an external position is maintained. As such, these practices necessitate the usage of an alternative theoretical underpinning for one's methods. This could, quite readily, be the use of counter-pleasure rather than pleasure. By modifying one's perspective towards the outcome of these sexual practices, the likelihood of *other-ing* can be relatively diminished. Again, however, a simple change in theoretical perspective does not necessarily mean that more inclusive research will ensue. The adoption of a counter-pleasure process is exclusively one step among many. Thereafter, researchers must employ explorative data collection methods, such as semi or unstructured interviews. Using the predetermined Kinseyian case history approach will most likely not provide a sufficiently open approach to gather S&M practitioners' internal perspective on the experience.

Swinging and group-sex

After completing the above gay bathhouse study, with its two corresponding areas of investigation of *bareback sex* and S&M, we turned our attention to the sexual practices of *swinging* and group-sex. For the practitioners of these two practices, being 'straight' does not encompass all heterosexual social assumptions, because it aims to dispense with monogamy, a morally laden principle that mandates sex must only occur in the context of a single, continuous relationship (Gould, 1999). For swingers and group-sex participants, however, the radical component of their sexuality revolves around the idea that one can have sex with someone other than one's partner without anger and without jealousy (Gould, 1999). It is a culture in which pleasure is obtained from knowing that one's primary partner is experiencing ecstasy, and involves celebrating with one's partner as s/he experiences pleasure from many sources (Jenks, 1998; Bergstrand and Williams, 2008). This overcomes, or at least tries to reject, the sexually constraining possessiveness regarding source(s) of pleasure that group-oriented sexual beings believe is inherent within contemporary relationship standards – that is, the enforced restriction of sexual variety that exists within monogamy. These forms of sexual indulgence thus challenge the Western ideology that combines sex and love. Swinging and group-sex could be described as sexual experiences in which the rigid line of exclusive sexual expression in monogamy is openly – not deceitfully – transgressed (Gould, 1999).

The qualitative issues that are particularly problematic in relation to swinging and group-sex include, first and foremost, the need to overcome personal judgements about promiscuity. It requires a fundamental reposition of outlook – as occurs in the theoretical transition from pleasure to counter-pleasure. In this case, the counter-pleasure arises from a transgression of normative sexual mores. It is about indulging in the many varieties, options, flavours, et cetera that life offers. Simultaneously, promiscuity means exploration, and a rejection of the conservatism which makes life stagnant and repetitive. As Crimp (1988) argues, promiscuity permits exploration, innovation, and development. It is the exploration of the other on a truly physical and intimate level. Returning to the effects that this counter-pleasure perspective of promiscuity has on qualitative health research, we must all be mindful to study different sexualities, sexual practices, and sexual cultures without the underlying goal of ranking these groups and activities (Rubin, 1992). This means forgoing, as much as is possible, one's cultural position in an effort to explore the meaning, significance, and (counter)pleasure of another's sexuality. As noted in the foregoing, if one's goal is to openly explore another's sexual existence and experience, appropriate data collection methods must be used. As the authors of this chapter are currently doing, critical ethnography (as defined by Thomas, 1993, and informed by Hammersley and Atkinson, 1995) is one means by which to accomplish this task. In assuming this theoretical and methodological perspective of counter-pleasure and ethnography, we approach these two unique forms of *radsex* with a rejection of objectivity, a genuine interest in the sexual experiences of our participants, and a wish to obtain their internal perspective. All of this is said, however, with the caveat that the internal perspective that we hope to produce will be, at best, our internal perspective of our research participants' internal perspective. As discouraging as this may seem, it nevertheless should not stop qualitative research from occurring in this domain.

Summary of radsex

While barebacking, S&M, swinging, and group-sex are all seemingly different to one another, these practices are related within the field of *radsex* because they are all sexual preferences that transgress Western health, moral or religious conventions. At a very basic level, they achieve this boundary infringement, in part, because they are practices that result in nonreproductive orgasm. Such a basic and unrefined explanation is unsatisfactory because, if the lack of reproductive function were the criterion for defining a practice as radical, then onanism should also be included. While historically this has been the case, in our current sociopolitical context, much of the fervour and focus has dissipated surrounding masturbation (Laqueur, 2003). Consequently, the religiously reprehensible nature of sexual actions is not the exclusive factor that places them within the domain of the radical. From the qualitative researcher's point of view, these practices become seen as radical based on their seemingly low self-reported frequencies and due to the fact that many individuals who do engage in these practices do so without others knowing. Fearing social, and in some cases legal, repercussions, or simply not wanting their *radsex* practice to be discovered, and thus removed from the margin, practitioners of alternative forms of sexuality may conceal their practices from mainstream society, which in many cases is presumed to include researchers. Thus, their outward rejection by mainstream society is a more precise commonality between these varied sexual practices, and, as such, places unique constraints on researchers who attempt to study these groups/practices.

RESEARCHING *RADSEX*: PERSONAL REFLECTIONS

One of the central components of *radsex* research is the personal reaction or interpretation of the individual who is undertaking this research. The myth of scientific neutrality has not allowed for an exploration of the role of personal experience within research. Due to the influence of postpositivism and its assumed incompatibility with emotions, Guba and Lincoln (2008) argue that some qualitative health researchers continue to push for personal experiences to be erased from all final scientific reports. We, in conjunction with Guba and Lincoln (2008), believe that it is vital that these emotional experiences be part of the cognitive process of knowledge generation in all scientific analyses. At present, only those working within the interpretative and critical traditions (regardless of their respective disciplines) acknowledge the beliefs, attitudes, and opinions of researchers through different approaches to reflexivity (Finlay, 2002). Many qualitative health researchers, however, still attempt to camouflage the researcher's impact and effect on his or her research results. As a result, one can often read research reports in which the researcher is presented as a superficially impartial third person, producing his/her findings while denying the fact that s/he is a feeling, thinking, living, human being with personal motivations for observing, documenting, surveying, analysing, measuring, and/or recording fellow human beings. An interesting case of the exact opposite of this is Tim Dean's (2009) latest book, *Unlimited Intimacy: Reflections on the Subculture of Barebacking*, wherein he not only confesses his personal practices of barebacking and how his personal desires for this practice interacted with his analysis and data collection, he also opens the book by relaying his HIV serostatus. While such a degree of openness may not be politically strategic for everyone, Dean's approach exemplifies the openness, the honesty, and the forthcoming-ness that is often sought in qualitative research.

Furthermore, Dean's (2009) work illustrates that in the field of sexual health research (especially in the *radsex* domain), the feelings and beliefs of researchers may be much more intense than in other fields. In undertaking research in sex clubs, bathhouses, and swingers' clubs (please see: Holmes and Warner, 2005; Holmes and O'Byrne, 2006; Holmes et al., 2006; Holmes et al., 2007; Holmes et al., 2008; O'Byrne and Holmes et al., 2008), it would be naive to pretend that each of the authors of this paper has never been told, or has never witnessed something that caused personal discomfort, such as, when an individual showed us (Holmes and O'Byrne) what resembled a primary syphilitic chancre and then proceeded to engage in unprotected sex. This situation, in particular, put us in a precarious situation. As both registered nurses and university-employed researchers, and due to our knowledge of infectious disease disclosure laws (see Holmes and O'Byrne, 2006), we suggested to the participant that he follow-up with appropriate sexual health services as soon as possible, and to refrain from sex in the meantime. The latter recommendation, as noted, did not occur, and thus created a situation of personal conflict between the need to maintain confidentiality and the desire to prevent suspected infectious disease transmission. As Humphreys (1970) noted in his tearoom research, 'no amount of intellectual exercise alone can enable the ethnographer to make such emotional adjustments, and ethical concerns serve to complicate this task' (p. 17). This, we experienced first hand.

Moreover, in the gay sex clubs and bathhouses, where our research was conducted, other examples of personal influence occurred, including the two male authors (Holmes and O'Byrne) initially experiencing feelings of excitement induced by the darkness, the loud music, and the maze-like layout of the venues. After a short period, these reactions were replaced by sensations of uncleanliness, discomfort and disgust. The incessant pornography alone was enough to induce feelings of being in Burgess's *A Clockwork Orange* (1972) experiments, in which individuals were forced to watch incessant pornography to the point that it became a painful experience. It is important, however, not to judge these reactions simply as negative – either personally or scientifically – because they are emotional reactions to situations that may be unfamiliar. In contrast, qualitative researchers need sufficient knowledge and self-awareness to accept these feelings as indications to engage in self-reflection and introspection to allow for an acceptance and awareness of when and why they are experiencing feelings of discomfort, disgust, or arousal. Our reaction was to record detailed field-notes about how we were feeling, including a description of the space and time when the feeling(s) started. Contemporaneous analysis was added in these notes whenever possible. By considering the influence of these emotive responses during the research process, researchers can account for how emotions have influenced data collection, and perhaps, have lead to avoidance of certain issues, or a superficial analysis of a theme which causes discomfort.

In *radsex* research, reflexivity, as Bourdieu (2004) defines it, should function as one mechanism which can be used to diminish the sheer reproduction of social stereotypes, and thus, this method can serve as an instrument to promote greater research quality. In total, the combination of a critical or interpretative theoretical framework with a reflexive approach could promote greater understanding of the researchers' own belief systems and how they shape relationships with the participants, and conduct the subsequent data analysis. The goal of this intro-spection should be to create a mechanism that allows researchers to concomitantly identify the traditional or morally dominant discourses influencing the research-ers' thinking (revealing the broader social context where the practices take place), and create emotional and cognitive space to understand participants' radical social positions on sexuality. This means that we propose that reflexivity be used as a compass by researchers navigating sexually charged environments.

RESEARCHING *RADSEX*: METHODOLOGICAL AND ETHICAL REFLECTIONS

Once a sound understanding of the theoretical and personal aspects of qualitative research in the domain of *radsex* and health have been obtained, it is important to appreciate the methodological and ethical issues related to such undertakings. The importance of such an analysis is to recognize the interconnectedness of the entire research process as it relates to *radsex*. Despite our presentation of the subject as two separate sections, the methodological and ethical issues presented here are, in reality, closely intertwined in practice.

Methodological issues

In the field of *radsex* research, sensitivity and awareness are very important methodological issues. When recruiting individuals who engage in particular marginalized sexual behaviours or practices, one must be sensitive to the con-cerns that surround the population under study. Thus, when studying individuals who self-define as *barebackers*, one must be sensitive to the legal, political, and psychosocial aspects of such a practice (Holmes and Warner, 2005; Holmes et al., 2006). In addition, one must be conscious of the locations where one might recruit individuals who engage in the targeted behaviour (Hammersley and Atkinson, 2005; Humphreys, 1970). In fact, in our experience, identifying the location of a marginalized group, and then gaining access to that milieu, has proven to be one of the most challenging aspects of the research process. It is crucial that the researchers acquire and maintain the trust and respect of the mar-ginalized group under study in order to be granted access (Platzer and James, 1997). In the case of our project (Holmes et al., 2007), this process involved find-ing bathhouses that were large enough to not be inconvenienced, or have their atmosphere altered excessively by our presence. It required that we be sensitive to the fact that bathhouses have historically been sites of contention between government, the police, and the public, that these establishments are for-profit, and that there is virtually no incentive for bathhouse owners to allow research to be done on their premises. In fact, such research could be seen as the reopening of a sensitive political issue (Bérubé, 1996), which has only recently begun to lose its controversy in Canada.

Thus, the marginal nature of bathhouses has shaped our research process in many ways. While the owners were supportive of our research, they nonetheless had concerns about the nature of the data gathered, how it would be used, and ultimately, how it might affect their businesses. As a result, we provided an overview of the entire research process to the three bathhouse owners, and discussed the utilization of a room/cubicle to recruit individuals for self-administered surveys. All measures for ensuring confidentiality and anonymity were discussed, and feedback was requested. This negotiation process resulted in the owners being highly accommodating and helpful, and granting us full access to their facilities. As a personal note, public health authorities in one of the cities wherein this project took place asked the research team during a conference thereafter how we had obtained such cooperation from the bathhouse owners and patrons. In retrospect, our suspicion is that these individuals understood that our goal was not to obtain an epidemiological or public health-based external understanding of their sexualities and sex practices, but rather, to gather as best we could a glimpse of their internal perspective. In other words, we sought to explore and understand a sexual culture, not a mechanical sexual activity as health professionals often do (Dean, 2009).

In stating this, however, *radsex* researchers must be cognisant of the fact that they also must face the delicate balancing act of fully disclosing their research objectives while attempting to obtain in-depth and candid accounts of the targeted practice. A lack of privacy and feelings of exposure brought about by the divulgence of highly personal information may prove to be a barrier to the study of *radsex* practices: individuals may feel embarrassed or judged by the researcher. As Humphreys (1970) noted: 'To wear a button that says "I Am a Watchbird, Watching You" into a tearoom, would instantly eliminate all action except the flushing of toilets and the exiting of all present' (p. 25). Consequently, the successful researcher must adapt strategies for data collection to minimize this effect as much as possible. Self-administered questionnaires are an example of a potentially less intrusive and more ethical way to collect data, and portraying the research goals within a political and social context and presenting a justification for the study may help to facilitate a greater degree of acceptance towards it. Nevertheless, these methods are not without limitation. Both of these methods are also subject to the problems of self-report (such as, an inability to recall a past situation or the tendency to describe oneself in a particular fashion as a result of one's positive or negative self-esteem). In addition, these research methods are also limited by the ability of the researcher to elicit certain information (for the questionnaires), and to comprehend and synthesize the interviewee's statements both during the interview and then during the formal analysis phase.

Above and beyond the methodological problems described in the foregoing section, the central concern of *radsex* research is, and should remain, the influential effect of the *researcher's internal perspective* – although within the context of this paper, the negative connotation generally associated with bias is not applicable because, in this context, it is accepted as an irrevocable aspect of all research designs (see Denzin and Lincoln, 2003). Therefore, the goal of the researcher should be to recognize, accept, and include their perspective into the total research process, rather than to attempt to artificially reduce it (Angrosino and Mays de Perez, 2003). Rather than trying to acquire an objective internal perspective understanding of another's sexual practices (because this process ultimately equate to an external perspective understanding), one should simply accept from the outset that any comprehension of another's internal perspective is always one's internal perspective of another's internal perspective. As previously stated, by acknowledging discomfort, the researcher may be recognizing the power of internalized social norms. In other words, it is the recognition of our biases, manifested in our beliefs and attitudes towards a particular sexual practice or group under study, which can help us to understand the phenomenon in its relations to the mainstream social and political contexts in which it takes place. In the research we conducted in bathhouses (Holmes et al., 2007), examples of our own influences might be manifested through questions such as: As a gay man in a long-term relationship, what is my initial reaction towards gay men who have multiple anonymous partners during an eight-hour period? As a heterosexual man in a monogamous relationship, what are my beliefs about and reactions to male homosexuality? As a coupled, heterosexual woman, what is my attitude towards married men who go to bathhouses, and engage in unprotected anal sex? These questions (and a legion of others) might all be pertinent in disclosing our social locations as individuals collecting and analysing the data and, therefore, should be taken into account at all stages of the research process. Thus, it is not sufficient that, once these questions have been addressed, the subsequent answers should be disregarded. Instead, researchers must incorporate their reflective questions and answers into the data collection and analysis process (Denzin and Lincoln, 2003), because by doing so, they might then develop a heightened awareness of their personal reactions, their purpose for undertaking a specific project, their reasons for doing it in a specific fashion, and their reasons for proposing particular hypotheses (Bourdieu, 2004). Thus, from a methodological perspective, reflexivity remains at the centre of the research enterprise, and is an imperative in the realm of *radsex* research.

Ethical considerations

It cannot be overemphasized that, although, due to the constraints of written communication, the methodological and ethical analyses are presented separately here, they are, in fact, highly interconnected. The majority of the ethical issues surrounding *radsex* involve methodological concerns (Buchanan et al., 2002). Approaching a field of marginalized practices may involve contacting people without disclosing, upfront, the complete purpose of the study that the researcher has in mind. Although covert data collection may facilitate the acquisition of information that would not otherwise be obtained, it is critical that the researcher weigh the risks and harms of subterfuge and lack of informed consent against the potential benefits of the research results (O'Byrne and Holmes, 2008). Again, reflect on Laud Humphreys (1970) covert research in tearooms. Therefore, the issue of informed consent can be an important challenge for *radsex* research, given that the principle of informed consent is a foundational component of modern social and health sciences research, and must not be discarded recklessly. Hence, researchers are forced to analyze whether the reasons for the project are so critically compelling that they warrant this form of research, and even if the latter is so, we stress the importance of exercising caution. When gaining access and obtaining informed consent, it is crucial that the issues surrounding the publication of findings be discussed openly with participants (Tri-Council, 2002). Researchers must warn that there is never any guarantee that results will favourably represent the group (Madden et al., 1997). Optimally, researchers should engage in this conversation at the outset of the project, thus allowing the opportunity for an open relationship to develop, and to mitigate any future problems, which may arise if the target group is expecting positive outcomes, but the research findings are actually perceived as negative by the community under study.

In addition, confidentiality is of the utmost concern regarding practices that are deemed to be radical by mainstream society (Clarke, 1996). Researchers must take any and all precautions necessary to protect the identity of the research participants because individuals who might superficially appear to be in the mainstream may not be when it comes to their sexual practices. The exposure of the intimate details of a participant's private life to public scrutiny could result in severe social reprisal for this individual. This, in turn, could have important repercussions beyond the individual and the researcher level by restricting further access to marginalized populations for the entire scientific community (Pepler and Craig, 1995). In our bathhouse study, we strove to ensure absolute confidentiality at all phases of the research project. When participants were completing questionnaires within the bathhouses, they did so in the privacy of a room that had been provided by the owners; this limited their identification as individuals who were engaging in research on *risky* sexual practices. Our intention was to provide a secure environment, not shared by the researcher, within which surveys could be completed without other individuals attempting to ascertain why a particular individual was participating, or what answers the individual had provided on the survey. Furthermore, questionnaires were completely anonymous and individuals were instructed not to put any identifying information on the questionnaires. During the interview process, these same principles were applied and participants were instructed not to mention names or locations. In addition, information about participants (occupation, age, etc.) was presented in clusters to avoid singling out any individual. This process, while labour-intensive for the researchers, helped to foster rapport with the research participants.

Field research in the *radsex* domain is influenced by the researchers' perceptions of the elements within the field at a given point in time – a perception that is shaped both by personal values and by the nature of the researched phenomena.

According to Punch (1998), qualitative researchers must be sensitive to the interplay of these elements as they are their own 'research instruments' (p. 158). This having been said, it is important to recognize that in this field of research, science is also a political process, which may encounter censorship, as exemplified by the public reaction to Laud Humphreys' *Tea Room Trade* (1970), for which he won a research prize from the Society for the Study of Social Problems, but subsequently received a virulent reaction. In our own case, unforeseen barriers were created by certain Research Ethics Board members who reacted to our project for reasons that are not within the scope of an ethics review. In our experience, such research ethics board members may enforce personal feelings of morality, and attempt to block research projects by mandating a surfeit of nearly irrelevant corrections. While extreme in our case, the difficulties that were constructed in attempts to block research in the realm of *radsex* illustrate the direct link between ethics and politics. Personal objections to alternative or radical sexual practices are never a valid reason to create additional difficulties for researchers.

FINAL REMARKS

Historically, the power of science has increased in direct correlation to the power of its microscopic lens, but only as long as its gaze is pointed outward.It is now important that qualitative researchers turn this same power inward in an effort to achieve at least some degree of reflexivity. We have attempted to do so here by indicating a potential path leading to a less repressive science of sexuality. The seeming paradox of counter-pleasure forces the margins of how and why some sexual practices are seen as counter to pleasure (MacKendrick, 1999). We must ask ourselves if these activities are, in fact, counter to the psychological and physiological experience of pleasure, or are these activities only contrary to the current social constructions of pleasure that limit the scope of the sexual practices which individuals are socially sanctioned to enjoy? Another issue that remains to be explored is the role of sexual health research in *normalizing* sexual behaviours and the potential consequences to counter-pleasure for making *radsex* practices more acceptable. Science, as a dominant discourse, can produce social effects of inclusion or exclusion that should be examined. Finally, methodological considerations of *radsex* research reveal power relations in science and in the whole research process, from securing funds, ethics review, and accessing the field to publishing on the subject of human sexuality. Perhaps, qualitatively studying transgressive sexual behaviours produces transgressive methodologies, which expose, at times, the political nature of any scientific enterprise.

REFERENCES

Airaksinen, T. (1991) *The Philosophy of the Marquis de Sade.* London: Routledge.

Angrosino, M.V. and Mays de Perez, K.A. (2003) 'Rethinking Observation: from Method to Context'. In N. Denzin and Y. Lincoln (eds) *Collecting and Interpreting Qualitative Materials,* (2nd Edition). (pp. 107–54). Thousand Oaks, CA: Sage.

Bataille, G. (1962) *Death and Sensuality.* Salem, New Hampshire: Ayer.

Bataille, G. (1989) *The Tears of Eros.* (trans. P. Connor). San Francisco: City Lights Books (original work published 1961).

Bergstrand, C. and Williams, J.B. (2008) 'Today's Alternative Marriage Styles: The Case of Swingers', *Electronic Journal of Human Sexuality,* 3. Retrieved from http://www.ejhs.org/volume3/swing/body.htm

Berube, A. (1996) 'The History of Gay Bathhouses'. In Dangerous Bedfellows (Ephen Glenn Colter, Wayne Hoffmann, Eva Pendleton, Aliison Redick and David Serlin, eds) *Policing Public Sex* (pp. 187–220). Boston, MA: Southend Press.

Bronski, M. (1998) *The Pleasure Principle: Sex, Backlash, and the Struggle for Gay Freedom.* New York: St. Martin's Press.

Bourdieu, P. (2004) *Science of Science and Reflexivity.* Chicago: University of Chicago Press.

Buchanan, D., Khoshnood, K., Stopka,T., Shaw, S., Santelices, C., and Singer, M. (2002) 'Ethical Dilemmas Created by the Criminalization of Status Behaviours: Case Examples from Ethnographic Field Research with Injection Drug Users'. *Health Education and Behaviour,* 29(1): 30–42.

Burgess, A. (1972) *A Clockwork Orange.* Toronto: Penguin Classics (original work published 1962).

Clarke, L. (1996) 'Participant Observation in a Secure Unit: Care, Conflict, and Control'. *NT Research,* 1: 431–40.

Chaline, E. (2007) 'On Becoming a Gay SMer: A Sexual Scripting Perspective'. In D. Langdridge and M. Barker (eds) *Safe, Sane, and Consensual: Contemporary Perspectives on Sadomasochism* (pp. 155–76). New York: Palgrave MacMillian.

Creswell, J.W. (1998) *Qualitative Inquiry and Research Design: Choosing Among Five Traditions.* Thousand Oaks, CA: Sage.

Crimp, D. (1988) 'How to Have Promiscuity in an Epidemic'. In D. Crimp (ed.), *AIDS: Cultural Analysis / Cultural Activism* (pp. 237–71). Cambridge: MIT Press.

Dean, T. (2000) *Beyond Sexuality: Desire.* Chicago: The University of Chicago Press.

Dean, T. (2009) *Unlimited Intimacy: Reflections on the Subculture of Barebacking.* Chicago: The University of Chicago Press.

Denzin, N.K. and Lincoln, Y.S. (2003) 'Introduction: The Discipline and Practice of Qualitative Research'. In N. Denzin and Y. Lincoln (eds) *Collecting and Interpreting Qualitative Materials,* (2nd Edition) (pp. 1–46). Thousand Oaks, CA: Sage.

Denzin, N.K. and Lincoln, Y.S. (2008) 'Introduction: The Discipline and Practice of Qualitative Research'. In N. Denzin and Y. Lincoln (eds) *The Landscape of Qualitative Research,* (3rd Edition) (pp. 1–43). Thousand Oaks, CA: Sage.

de Sade, M. (1965) *Justine, Philosophy in the Bedroom, & Other Writings* (trans. R. Seaver and A. Wainhouse). New York: Groe Press (original work published 1740–814).

Emmons, K.M. (2001). 'Health Behaviors in a Social Context'. In L.F. Berkman and I Kawachi (eds) *Social Epidemiology* (pp. 242–66). New York: Oxford University Press.

Finlay, L. (2002) 'Negotiating the Swamp: The Opportunity and Challenge of Reflexivity in Research Practice', *Qualitative Research,* 2(2): 209–30.

Fiske, J. (1989) *Understanding Popular Culture.* Boston, MA: Unwin Hyman.

Foucault, M. (1978) *The History of Sexuality: An Introduction, Volume 1.* (trans. R. Hurley). New York: Vintage (original work published 1976).

Foucault, M. (1985) *The History of Sexuality: The Use of Pleasure, Volume 2.* (trans. R. Hurley). New York: Vintage (original work published 1984).

Foucault, M. (1986) *The History of Sexuality: The Care of the Self, Volume 3.* (trans. R. Hurley). New York: Vintage (original work published 1984).

Freud, S. (1961) *Beyond the Pleasure Principle: The Standard Edition.* (trans. J. Strachey). New York: Norton.

Freud, S. (2006) *The Psychology of Love.* (trans. S. Whiteside). Toronto: Penguin Classics (original work published 1905–18).

Gagnon, J.H. (2004) 'Theorizing Risky Sex'. In J.H. Gagnon (ed.), *An Interpretation of Desire: Essays in the Study of Sexuality* (pp. 201–27). Chicago: The University of Chicago Press.

Gauthier, D.K. and Forsyth, C.J. (1999) 'Bareback Sex, Bug Chasing, and the Gift of Death', *Deviant Behaviour,* 20: 85–100.

Gerbert, B., Danley, D.W., Herzig, K., Clanon, K., Ciccarone, D., Gilbert, P., and Allerton, M. (2006) 'Reframing "Prevention with Positives": Incorporating Counselling Techniques that Improve the Health of HIV-Positive Patients', *AIDS Patient Care and STDs,* 20(1): 19–29.

Gould, T. (1999) *The Lifestyle: A Look at the Erotic Rites of Swingers.* Toronto: Vintage Canada.

Guba, E.G. and Lincoln, Y.S. (2008) 'Paradigmatic Controversies, Contradictions, and Emerging Confluences'. In N.K. Densin and Y.S. Lincoln (eds) *The Landscape of Qualitative Research* (3rd Edition) (pp. 255–86). Thousand Oaks, CA: Sage.

Halperin, D. (1995) *Saint = Foucault.* New York: Oxford University Press.

Halkitis, P.N., Wilton, L., Wolitski, R.J., Parsons, J.T., Hoff, C.C., and Bimbi, D. (2005c) 'Barebacking Identity among HIV-Positive Gay and Bisexual Men: Demographic, Psychological, and Behavioural Correlates', *AIDS,* 19 (suppl 1): S27–S35.

Halkitis, P.N. and Parsons, J.T. (2003) 'Intentional Unsafe Sex (Barebacking) Among HIV-Positive Gay Men Who Seek Sexual Partners on the Internet', *AIDS Care,* 15(3): 367–78.

Halkitis, P.N., Parsons, J.T., and Bimbi, D.S. (2001) 'Intentional Unsafe Sex (Barebacking) Among Gay Men Who Seek Sexual Partners on the Internet', Personal Communication – unpublished manuscript.

Halkitis, P.N., Wilton, L., and Drescher, J. (2005a) 'Introduction: Why Barebacking?', *Journal of Gay & Lesbian Psychotherapy,* 9(3/4): 1–8.

Halkitis, P.N., Wilton, L., and Galatowitsch, P. (2005b) 'What's in a Term? How Gay and Bisexual Men Understand Barebacking', *Journal of Gay & Lesbian Psychotherapy,* 9(3/4): 35–48.

Hammersley, M. and Atkinson, P. (1995) *Ethnography: Principles in Practice* (2nd Edition). New York: Sage.

Hammersley, M. and Atkinson, P. (2005) *Ethnography: Principles in Practice,* (2nd Edition). New York: Routledge.

Holmes, D. and Warner, D. (2005) 'The Anatomy of a Forbidden Desire: Men, Penetration and Semen Exchange'. *Nursing Inquiry,* 12(1): 10–20.

Holmes, D. and O'Byrne, P. (2006) '*Bareback Sex* and the Law: the Difficult Issue of HIV Status Disclosure', *Journal of Psychosocial Nursing,* 44(7): 26–33.

Holmes, D., O'Byrne, P., and Gastaldo, D. (2006) 'Raw Pleasure as Limit Experience, A Foucauldian Analysis of Unsafe Anal Sex between Men', *Social Theory and Health,* 4: 319–33.

Holmes, D., O'Byrne, P., and Gastaldo, D. (2007) 'Setting the Space for Sex: Architecture, Desire and Health Issues in Gay Bathhouses', *International Journal of Nursing Studies,* 44: 273–84.

Holmes, D., Gastaldo, D., O'Byrne, P., and Lombardo, A. (2008) 'Bareback Sex: A Conflation of Risk and Masculinity'. *International Journal of Men's Health,* 7(2): 171–91.

Humphreys, L. (1970) *Tearoom Trade: Impersonal Sex in Public Places.* New Jersey: Aldine Transaction.

Jenks, R.J. (1998) 'Swinging: A Review of the Literature', *Archives of Sexual Behaviour,* 27: 507–21.

Kafka, F. (1996) 'In the Penal Colony'. In S. Appelbaum (ed.), *The Metamorphosis and Other Stories* (pp. 11–52). Mineola: Dover Publications, Inc (Original work published 1919).

Kinsey, A.C., Pomeroy, W.B., and Martin, C.E. (1948) *Sexual Behaviour in the Human Male.* Philadelphia: W.B. Saunders.

Kinsey, A.C., Pomeroy, W.B., Martin, C.E., and Gebhard, P.H. (1953) *Sexual Behaviour in the Human Female.* Philadelphia: W.B. Saunders.

Koepsell, T.D., Wagner, E.H., Cheadle, A.C., Patrick, D.L., and Martin, D.C. et al. (1992) 'Selected Methodological Issues in Evaluating Community-Based Health Promotion and Disease Prevention Programs', *Annual Review of Public Health,* 31: 31–57.

Krafft-Ebing, R.V. (1965) *Psychopathia Sexualis*. (trans. F.S. Klaf). New York: Arcade Publishing.

Langdridge, D. and Barker, M. (2007) 'Situation Sadomasochism'. In D. Langdridge and M. Barker (eds) *Safe, Sane, and Consentual: Contemporary Perspectives on Sadomasochism* (pp. 3–9). New York: Palgrave MacMillan.

Laqueur, T.W. (2003). *Solitary Sex: A Cultural History of Masturbation*. New York: Zone Books.

Lyng, S. (2005) 'Edgework and the Risk Taking Experience'. In S. Lyng (ed.), *Edgework: The Sociology of Risk-Taking* (pp. 3–16). New York: Routledge.

MacKendrick, K. (1999) *CounterPleasures*. Albany: Southern University of New York Press.

Madden, J., Quick, J., Ross-Degnan, D., and Kafle, K. (1997) 'Undercover Careseekers: Simulated Clients in the Study of Health Provider Behaviour in Developing Countries', *Social Science and Medicine*, 45(10): 1465–82.

Moser, C. and Kleinplatz, P.J. (2007) 'Themes of SM Expression'. In D. Langdridge and M. Barker (eds) *Safe, Sane, and Consentual: Contemporary Perspectives on Sadomasochism* (pp. 35–54). New York: Palgrave MacMillan.

O'Byrne, P. and Holmes, D. (2008) 'Researching Marginalized Populations: Ethical Concerns about Ethnography'. *Canadian Journal of Nursing Research*, 40(3): 144–59.

O'Leary, A., Wolitski, R.J., Remien, R.H., Woods, W.J., Parson, J.T., Moss, S., and Lyles, C.M. (2005) 'Psychosocial Correlates of Transmission Risk Behaviour among HIV-Seropositive Gay and Bisexual Men', *AIDS*, 19(suppl. 1): S67–S75.

Pepler, D. and Craig, W. (1995) 'A Peek Behind the Fence: Naturalistic Observation of Aggressive Children with Remote Audiovisual Recording', *Developmental Psychology*, 31(4): 548–53.

Platzer, H. and James, T. (1997) 'Methodological Issues Conducting Sensitive Research on Lesbian and Gay Men's Experience of Nursing Care', *Journal of Advanced Nursing*, 25: 625–33.

Pomeroy, W.B. (1982) *Dr. Kinsey and the Institute for Sex Research*. Yale: Yale University Press.

Public Health Agency of Canada (PHAC) (2006) *HIV/AIDS – Epi Updates, November 2007*. Retrieved on August 7, 2009 from: http://www.phac-aspc.gc.ca/aids-sida/publication/epi/epi2007-eng.php

Punch, M. (1998) 'Politics and Ethics in Qualitative Research'. In N. Denzin and Y. Lincoln (eds) *The Landscape of Qualitative Research: Theories and Issues* (pp. 157–84). Thousand Oaks, CA: Sage.

Rubin, G. (1992) 'Thinking Sex: Notes for a Radical Theory of the Politics of Sexuality'. In Carole S. Vance (ed.). *Pleasure and Danger: Exploring Female Sexuality* (pp. 267–93). London: Pandora.

Sacher-Masoch, L.V. (1989) 'Venus in Furs'. In *Masochism* (pp. 143–76). New York: Zone Books.

Sammoun, M. (2004) *Tendance SM: essai sur la representation sadomasochiste*. Paris: La Musardine.

Silverman, H.J. (2000) 'Twentieth-Century Desire and the Histories of Philosophy'. In H.J. Silverman (ed.), *Continental Philosophy VII: Philosophy & Desire* (pp. 1–13). New York: Routledge.

Thomas, J. (1993) *Doing Critical Ethnography*. Newbury Park, CA: Sage.

Tobias, S. (2005). 'Foucault on Freedom and Capabilities', *Theory, Culture, & Society*, 22(4): 65–85.

Tri-Council. Canadian Institutes of Health Research, Natural Sciences and Engineering Research Council of Canada, Social Sciences and Humanities Research Council of Canada, (1998 with 2000, 2002, 2005 amendments) *Tri-Council Policy Statement: Ethical Conduct for Research Involving Humans*. (Ottawa: Tri-Council).

Yost, M.R. (2007) 'Sexual Fantasies of S/M Practitioners: the Impact of Gender and S/M Role on Fantasy Content'. In D. Langdridge and M Barker (eds) *Safe, Sane, and Consensual: Contemporary Perspectives on Sadomasochism* (pp. 135–54). New York: Palgrave MacMillian.

36

The Challenges and Opportunities of Qualitative Health Research with Children

Ilina Singh and Sinéad Keenan

INTRODUCTION

While it may be true that we simply 'do not have a culture of listening to children' (Lansdown, 1994: 38), it is nonetheless remarkable how little qualitative health research has been conducted with children. The use of qualitative methods with children has been recognized as a valuable route to a better understanding of children's perspectives of their illness experiences (e.g., Woodgate, 2000). These methods tend to yield information that reflects the perspectives of the child participants, rather than those of the adult researchers (Woodgate, 2000). Indeed, the absence of qualitative research on children's experiences in medical settings can be said to reflect a distorted orientation of care towards the *parent* as client rather than the *child* (Bernheimer, 1986).

This chapter will discuss the challenges and opportunities of qualitative health research with children, focusing in particular on questions of potential ethical risks around children's competence, capacity and consent. We begin with a brief review of children's voices in qualitative health research. This is followed by a discussion of some of the ethical cornerstones in research with children before we go on to consider, more generally, the concept of children's agency and competence. We will then outline some of the practical considerations in doing qualitative research with children as well as the methods and techniques available and the methodological concerns these give rise to such as reliability and validity. Finally, we will consider the policy relevance of qualitative health research with children.

Throughout the chapter, we stress our belief that children's vulnerabilities in research have often been over- or mis-stated. Increased participation in qualitative health research by children is critical to expanding our understanding of the risks and benefits of children's participation in health-related research of all kinds, including clinical trials, experimental therapies, and psychosocial interventions. In addition, such research will fill a gap in our understanding of the impact of child health-related services and interventions on children themselves and on the experiences of childhood.

CHILDREN'S VOICES IN QUALITATIVE HEALTH RESEARCH

Darbyshire et al. (2005) note the 'paradox of the 'missing child' in child health research:

> The predominant approach to researching children's experiences is grounded in 'research on' rather than 'research with' or 'research for' children (Darbyshire, 2000; Oakley, 1994), ignoring the views of children as active agents and 'key informants' in matters pertaining to their health and wellbeing (p. 419).

It is hardly surprising, therefore, that there is relatively little literature available on methods for conducting qualitative research with children. A number of useful texts have begun to emerge from varying disciplines such as psychology (e.g., Greene and Hogan, 2005), social work and social policy (e.g., Greig and Taylor, 1999; Hill et al., 1996), education (e.g., Lewis and Lindsay, 2000), nursing (e.g., Kortesluoma et al., 2003; Woodgate, 2000) and occupational therapy (e.g., Curtin, 2001). Much of the qualitative research conducted has focused on preschoolers and adolescents, note Greig and Taylor (1999), because these stages are thought to be critical phases in child development.

The existing qualitative health research literature has tended to focus on children's experiences of their illness and/or children's experiences of treatment. Studies about children's experiences of their illness have shown that this experience shapes not only what children know but also more significantly, how they use that knowledge (Bluebond-Langner et al., 1990; Hockenberry-Eaton and Minicke, 1994). Ireland and Holloway (1996) argue that qualitative research on children's experiences of illness provides a complementary view to any existing quantitative research, offering a sense of children's beliefs and expectations about their condition and how they adapt to it.

Qualitative research with children has not only contributed valuable information about children's experiences of illness, it has also contributed to our understanding of their experiences of treatment, thus informing parents and professionals about issues such as noncompliance with medication (e.g., Buston and Wood, 2000; Singh et al., 2008) and follow-up care after intensive treatments such as cancer therapy (e.g., Haase and Rostad, 1994).

A limited amount of qualitative health research has been conducted by social policy institutes. The Joseph Rowntree Foundation in the United Kingdom, for instance, has funded qualitative studies on a variety of health issues such as the experiences of children living with a hidden disability (Cavet, 1998), the experiences of children with complex needs of various health care settings (Stalker et al., 2003) and the experiences of disabled children in the school playground (Wooley et al., 2006). Social policy institutes and federal funding initiatives have also supported qualitative research on social issues that impact on children's well-being, e.g., children's views and experiences of parenting (Madge and Willmott, 2007), divorce and separating (Hawthorne et al., 2003), studies about the views of adolescent drug users (Perri et al., 1997), and adolescent boys' experiences of masculinity norms (Frosh et al., 2002).

As these rich examples suggest, qualitative health research with children includes studies of children's well-being as well as studies of children's experiences with a variety of illnesses, treatments and health care delivery systems. The importance of involving children as active participants in health-related research is increasingly acknowledged. Alongside this development, researchers are becoming increasingly aware of the relevant ethical issues in research with children. In what follows, we outline several of the most significant areas of ethical concern.

CHILDREN AS A VULNERABLE POPULATION: ETHICAL IMPLICATIONS FOR RESEARCH

Within research ethics, children are, not surprisingly, one of the populations to have been most readily designated as 'vulnerable'. Regulations and policy documents concerning the ethical dimensions of research have defined vulnerability in terms of a diminished ability to protect one's own interests, typically evident in a reduced capacity to provide informed consent (Levine et al., 2004). To the extent that children may be regarded as similar to, or different from adults, Morrow and Richards (1996) conclude that from an adult perspective children are generally perceived as vulnerable and incompetent. This protective stance towards children may reduce children's potential to participate in research. As Grodin and Glantz (1994) suggest, the protective impulse towards children is in tension with the need to increase knowledge about children in order to develop relevant and constructive interventions. Indeed, Morrow and Richards (1996) argue that children are conceived to be the *objects* rather than the *subjects* of research, and are not seen as social actors in their own right.

We now consider several fundamental ethical issues in doing qualitative research with children: consent, competence, agency and confidentiality.

Consent

Consent is both an interaction between researcher and participant and a bureaucratic procedure intended to minimize harm and legal liability. It is an increasingly complex process in health research, especially in US medical contexts, where institutional review boards (IRBs) require standardized consent procedures with patients. The paradox of the consent process is that with bureaucratization it becomes increasingly difficult to amend consent forms for research with non-standard populations. Moreover, standards for consent documents can vary considerably across national ethical committees and between institutions, both intra- and internationally. This can make ensuring access to diverse populations within one study very time-consuming.

It could be argued that the lack of flexibility is warranted, because children under 18 are not considered able to give informed consent in a research process in any case. This means that children are not considered able to fully understand the information on the consent form, nor are they able to make independent decisions as to whether or not to participate, or comprehend the risks and benefits of participation in the research project. Therefore all such persons must have an adult carer co-sign the forms (if written consent is being obtained) consenting to research participation. Technically, participants are giving their assent to participate, but someone else is giving capacitated consent. This is also the case if a researcher is obtaining verbal consent from participants as for example, in telephone interviews. It is still important to obtain assent from a child participant, however, even if the assent is, for the moment, still largely symbolic. In undertaking procedures to obtain a child's assent, the researcher signals to the child that his/her agency is fully respected in the research process and invites the child to consider his/her decision to participate.

Children are probably far more able to consider this decision, and other aspects of informed consent, than has previously been thought. Evidence from child research participants in health-related studies suggests that the assumption that children are not competent to understand aspects of consent may be an overly protective intuition that is not necessarily supported empirically (Alderson, 1995; Bluebond-Langner et al., 1990). In our studies with children who have a diagnosis of ADHD (Attention Deficit Hyperactivity Disorder), for example, young children, aged 9–12, spontaneously raised aspects of anonymity and confidentiality during the interview, in ways that suggested they had a good understanding of these elements of informed consent and could use them to make decisions about disclosures during interviews (Singh, 2007). Children asked relevant questions about confidentiality while filling out the consent form with their parents (e.g., 'would you have to tell my parents if I tell you I'm selling my Ritalin at school?'), suggesting that they had understood this aspect of the ethics information outlined in the information leaflet on the study.

Children's agency and competence

In our research with children around issues related to health and illness, we have repeatedly found that when the approach resonates with a child, he or she has the potential to astonish us with insights, understanding, and explanations. We believe that children's capacity to exhibit their active understanding of the research process, as well as to engage fully and even to challenge aspects of the process, is related to the extent to which children feel empowered by and in that process.

It is important to consider the concept of children's agency, and to encourage the researcher to examine any presuppositions about what children are capable of contributing as research participants. As we have discussed, the protectionist impulse that governs the ethical orientation towards research with children and vulnerable populations tends to assume that these populations lack capacity as research participants, but this orientation is not necessarily empirically founded. A related issue is the research orientation towards participants' agency. Research with vulnerable populations runs the risk of equating relative innocence with victim status. We believe this is not an empowering orientation for research participants. Researchers might consider whether participants are being constructed as passive in the research process; or are they considered capable of being agents with impact in their own lives, as well as in the research process.

We have found that when given the opportunity, children readily adopt the role of 'expert' on their medical condition and, defend their right to that role when an interviewer slips back into an authoritative voice. Children's agency also shaped the research process; their desire to draw in response to a complicated set of questions changed our methods in one study. It was sometimes difficult to coax children out of rote explanations, however, and it is increasingly clear to us as child health and illness researchers that children are far too rarely engaged by family members, teachers, or physicians, in conversations about the physical, social and emotional implications of their condition and treatments. In our work, children's incomplete or incorrect explanations of their condition, or their treatments (e.g., 'my [ADHD] tablet is like what children with diabetes take'), are frequently linked to partial parental and/or expert explanations. In clinical settings, little value is attributed to giving full explanations to children about their illness and treatments; similarly, little value is attributed to children's ongoing reports of the social and emotional impacts of illness and treatments. Follow-up visits rarely involve conversations with children beyond a check on known physical side effects of treatments. We hope our discussion will encourage researchers undertaking health-related research with children and other vulnerable populations to consider both the research-based and structural barriers to empowering participants to be active agents in the process of research and their own illnesses.

Breaking confidentiality

The researcher's obligation to break confidentiality must be emphasized here alongside the discussion of children's capacity to understand aspects of the consent process. Ethical guidelines for research with patients in most Western countries require that the patient information leaflet contain language about the need for the researcher to break the contract of confidentiality if a participant reveals that he/she has, or intends to, harm him/herself or others; or if the participant reveals that someone is harming him/her. As we related earlier, in our experience, many children understand this aspect of confidentiality and refer to it in the interviews. (We told the child who asked about selling his stimulants that we would have to tell an adult about it, because he would be engaging in illegal activity that was potentially harmful to someone else.) It is also the case that children are more likely than adults to impulsively disclose private aspects of their lives, or the life of the family, and often they establish trust with a stranger more easily than adults do. Researchers engaged in in-depth interviews with children are likely to hear disclosures that raise questions about the need to break confidentiality. There should be a plan in place for this eventuality, one which addresses the need to minimize harm for all parties involved in the research study.

METHODS FOR DOING QUALITATIVE RESEARCH WITH CHILDREN

Framing the research questions

Empowering children as qualitative research participants is greatly dependent on research methods – and a researcher's experience with those methods. This section on methods begins with a discussion of research questions, because research methods should always be organically linked to research questions. We then proceed to a discussion of access and recruitment.

A qualitative study offers the opportunity to ask research questions that are relevant not only to research and clinical communities, but also to participants themselves. Relevance is particularly important in health research with marginal and/or vulnerable populations, because these groups are rarely given a voice in their experiences of services and treatments, nor do they normally contribute to the formulation of relevant questions, either directly or indirectly. No matter the research approach used, the process of framing research questions with these populations should be embedded in an in-depth understanding of, and (ideally) engagement with, these populations. Researchers can use various techniques to 'get to know' the population of interest; in the case of children, either educational or clinical environments offer ways to gain access and familiarity. What a researcher learns in such settings is often an important comparative to what is learned from the literature; and if direct access is impossible for structural or institutional reasons, informational interviews with teachers, clinicians, parents and other caregivers, or others close to the target population, can be very helpful to a process of trying to achieve an on-the-ground understanding as part of the process of formulating relevant research questions.

Once research questions have been decided upon, they should be tested in a small pilot study. Even if a researcher is relatively sure that questions have relevance to the target population, it is still important to test whether the questions are comprehensible to participants during interviews. Without a pilot study, it is very difficult to know how children will react to the research process and inquiry. Are they competent to respond to the questions asked; and is lack of competence a problem located with the participants, or a problem with the way in which questions are framed by the researcher? A small pilot study offers an opportunity to work these issues out.

Access and recruitment

The problem of access is, unfortunately, a major barrier to research with vulnerable or marginal populations, and it requires planning and effort to overcome. Most research ethics committees require extra caution when approaching vulnerable populations for participation in research, and for qualitative health researchers this can cause a significant problem if the researcher or member of the research team is not a member of the community that surrounds the target population. In addition to providing access, insiders can provide important information about the relevance of research questions to clinical and/or policy issues. On the other hand, insider researchers need to be careful that their easier access to the target population does not cause confusion or conflict with their other roles, such as when a clinician researcher is providing care as well as conducting interviews with patients for a research project. In such situations, the potential for unintended coercion must be carefully attended to.

Recruitment of children and vulnerable populations can be sufficiently difficult to invite a lack of rigour in case selection. It may be easier to gather a 'convenience sample' than to properly think through issues of case selection, and to identify a sample that fits the research aims well. This can result in samples of children of mixed ages, ethnicity, social class, gender, and health status in studies where examination of this variation is not part of the research questions, nor is the variation properly attended to in the analysis of data. When qualitative health research of this type finds its way into publication, it can undermine the strengths of a qualitative approach by encouraging negative questions about the methodological rigour of the research, as well as reliability and validity of results (discussed later in this chapter).

Methods and techniques

A growing range of techniques have been developed to access children's perspectives. Possible methods include observation, individual interviews, focus groups, creative methods, self-reports and spontaneous narratives, projective techniques as well as ethnographic methods (Greene and Hill, 2005). Within qualitative health research specifically, individual interviews (e.g., Baxley et al., 1978; Enskar et al., 1997; Haase and Rostad., 1994; Kendall et al., 2003; Kortesluoma and Nikkonen, 2006) and focus groups (e.g., Kreuger and Kendall, 2001; Singh et al., 2008) appear to have been the most commonly used methods for researching children's perspectives. This may be because the individual interview gives a researcher maximum control over the research process. The researcher is able to focus exclusively on one child, rather than having to manage a group of children, as with a focus group; or having to simply observe children, as with an ethnography. Ethnography and focus groups, however, will also be addressed in this chapter.

The following discussion describes various methods used to access children's experiences and perspectives. We do not outline in a comprehensive way the research aims of particular studies. We emphasize that methods chosen for a given research project should have a close fit with the primary research aims of the project.

Interviews

There are several overlapping elements to successful interviews with children (by 'successful' we mean that the child feels empowered by the interview, and the researcher feels the interview will add knowledge and value in the study). Some of these elements obviously generalize to other methods we discuss later, but all are critical in interviews.

The interview should be *age appropriate*. This means that the language, concepts, and any games or standardized tasks given during the interview should be sensitive to the participant's developmental stage. If children of various ages are being interviewed, it may be necessary to adapt the interview for various age groups. For example, middle-childhood (ages 8–12) is a frequent target for research with children; however, a child aged 8 is at a different cognitive level than a child aged 12.

The interview should take into account the participant's *health status*. This incorporates both structural and substantive dimensions of the interview. Structural dimensions include sensitivity to a child's mobility and location (e.g., if the child is on a hospital ward, is it appropriate to move the child to a private room to ensure confidentiality during the interview, and if so, how will that be done?). Medication status is another important structural dimension of the interview: how will the interview be organized around required medication doses, and do medications affect a child's ability to focus on and engage in the interview? This issue is relevant to children with a range of medical issues, from asthma and diabetes, to ADHD and cancer. In our research with children who take behaviour-modifying medication, for example, we need to decide ahead of time whether a child should be medicated for the interview, or unmedicated, and this decision then affects the time of day during which the interview can be held.

The interview also needs to take into account the participant's health status by ensuring that interviews require an appropriate length of time and concentration. Most child participants should be offered at least one break in an interview of an hour; children with mental disorders, or children who suffer physical discomfort or pain may require more than one break. A break can be organized with sensitivity to a participant's particular needs; for example, with children with ADHD, we encourage children to get rid of excess energy; we do star jumps and press ups and shadow boxing. Anxious children can be given time to cuddle a favourite toy; and children with social-communication difficulties can be given time to play without the stress of questions. It is sometimes helpful to set a timer, or to remind children of the time left in a break, to ensure a smooth transition back into the interview.

Setting of the interview

It is probably clear from the foregoing discussion that we believe in creating casual, relaxed settings for interviews with participants. We believe that such settings encourage participants to engage in the interview process, and they help to defuse some of the power inequalities that are inherent both in the interview process and in the relationship between an adult authority and the research participants. Children can be influenced by the perceived power and status of adults in interview situations and by their own beliefs about what answers are expected (Garbarino et al., 1992).

The reality of research with children around health-related issues is that interviews will often take place in hospital or clinical settings. Even when interviews must take place in institutional settings, there are ways to make the interview less formal, and the interviewer appear less authoritative. In interviews with children, we bring food and drinks for participants (this should only be done if medically appropriate); we encourage children to think of themselves as experts in their condition, and we translate this encouragement physically by trying as best we can to arrange the room and our bodies so that the child and the researcher are sitting informally. This can mean sitting on the floor, or sitting next to the child, dressing informally, and encouraging curiosity about recording devices and other things in the room before the interview begins.

Interviews in homes are naturally less formal, and more on the participants' terms, so to speak. In fact, in home interviews, an opposite set of concerns can pertain, in that the researcher must ensure that the setting maintains boundaries appropriate to a structured or semistructured interview. For example, interviews should take place in a quiet room, with no interruptions. Participants cannot wander off to play with their toys and electronic devices, or visit other members of the family or friends.

Topic guide

The topic guide is the list of questions or themes that will guide the researcher through the interview. It is an essential piece of equipment for a successful interview with children. It is extremely difficult even for experienced researchers to keep children on track whilst also keeping track of where the interview has been, where it is going, and whether research questions have been covered. It is important to provide sufficient structure in interviews with children, because children are more likely to respond to specific concrete prompts especially if the subject matter is quite abstract (Hill et al., 1996). Flexibility is equally important, in no small part, because varied and imaginative research methods help to overcome problems of perceived expert authority (Mahon et al., 1996). A good topic guide, therefore, provides a healthy combination of boundaries, flexibility and security.

The most difficult part of interviewing any child is maintaining their interest and focus on the interview. We have found children respond well to interviews when there is a mixture of talk and tasks. We intersperse discussions around various themes with drawing, standardized pictures, vignettes, sentence completions, and ordering tasks. Others have used brainstorming tasks, role-plays, and 'eco-maps' (a map of relationships in a child's life, with different relationships characterized in terms of strength, importance, time, and so forth) (Hill et al., 1996). Depending on the research aims, standardized elements within an interview can be useful both qualitatively and quantitatively.

Focus groups

Focus groups with children provide access to children's own language and concepts, and encourage elaboration of their concerns and agendas. The collective nature of focus group discussion is often said to provide 'more than the sum of its parts' (Wilkinson, 1998). Interactive data result in enhanced disclosure, better understanding of participants' own agendas, the production of more elaborated accounts and the opportunity to observe the co-construction of meaning in action.

Hill et al. (1996) recommend individual and focus group interviews for engaging children's views and set out a useful framework for conducting this type of research. Their study also sheds light on some of the differences between the two methods. Contrary to some observations that groups can be inhibiting, the researchers found that there was a great openness shown by most of the children; indeed the situation seemed to give confidence to certain members of the group to voice their opinions and to develop their points in response to the stimulation and challenge of other opinions. In fact, focus groups may be particularly suitable for use with children, because as Mauthner (1997) points out, they create a comfortable peer environment and reproduce the type of small group settings that children are familiar with. The peer support that children may feel in this small group setting may somewhat level out the power imbalance that exists between researcher and child in individual interviews (Hennessy and Heary, 2005).

On the other hand, it was found that in the individual interviews conducted by Hill et al. (1996), children provided more measured responses than in the groups, where conversation tended to be more spontaneous. In some cases, some feelings came out in more depth and complexity in individual interviews. The individual format also appeared to encourage some more reticent children who might not have felt comfortable contributing to a group whereas for other children the individual interview was quite intimidating. Interestingly, boys appeared more comfortable confiding particular fears in a one-to-one interview. Another notable difference was observed across the age groups: younger children generally directed their comments at the researcher, whereas older children were more likely to interact with each other.

Finally, there are the ethical issues which arise in focus group discussions that do not arise when using other methods. Two of the key issues identified by Hennessy and Heary (2005) are: '(a) the fact that disclosures by participants are shared with all group members and not just the researcher; and (b) intense group discussion may give rise to stress or distress in individual participants' (p. 239). Confidentiality may also be at risk when children leave a focus group. It is important that children are reminded of the need to maintain confidentiality as the group is ending. This is especially the case if the children attend the same schools, church, or other community centres. As focus groups should be more engaged with group discussion than with individual disclosures, however, it is less likely that an individual child will reveal something highly confidential in the focus group setting. We should also note that the ethical issues we raise here are all as relevant to focus group research with adults as they are to children.

Ethnography

Classic ethnography means participant observation in a naturalistic setting – often a culturally 'other' setting, combined with interviews. Crucial to the ethnographic approach is the need to stand back from the usual adult/child roles (e.g., Leonard, 1990), although it has been debated whether an adult researcher can ever become fully participant in the social world of children (James et al., 1998). There is a rich and valuable ethnographic literature on the life-worlds and well-being of children, which grew up initially around what some have called the field of psychological anthropology (see Monroe et al., 1981). The original intention to explore and extend psychoanalytic concepts in nontraditional societies has been modernized in more recent work by scholars such as Robert LeVine (e.g., LeVine et al., 1994) and Sara Harkness and Charlie Super (e.g., Harkness and Super, 1996), who combine ethnographic observations of children and families with interview and quantitative measures to achieve a multifaceted and multilayered view of comparative child development processes in different cultural settings. Such studies suggest that ethnography is most likely to produce outcomes that have translational value (that is, the outcomes have theoretical or policy implications) when used in combination with other research methods.

Ethnography is also a key method in a 'new sociology of childhood' movement that has been developing for over a decade. This movement is responsible for shifting longstanding assumptions and biases about children in social and by extension health science research. Children are conceptualized as active social agents, who have impact on their life-worlds in ways that create meaning and change. These ideas have been applied to ethnographic studies of children in health-related settings, and there is a growing literature in this area (e.g., Emond, 2005; Geissler et al., 2000).

Existing child health-related ethnographies frequently engage with socio-logical or anthropological concerns about the impact of macro-structural processes and institutions. For example, there are ethnographic investigations of access to or provision of health care (e.g., Ensign and Gittelsohn, 1998; Peterson et al., 1999); and the relationship of poverty and child health (e.g., Howard and Millard, 1997). Potential ethnographic researchers should be aware that there is some tendency in the literature to claim the use of 'ethnographic methods' when in fact the research method is at-home or within-neighbourhood interviews without accompanying participant observation (e.g., Clark, 2002; Mull et al., 2001).

As in our discussion of individual and group interviews in the preceding sec-tion, ethnographic research with children also gives rise to ethical issues such as informed consent and the informant–researcher relationship. Jokinen et al. (2002) provide a useful overview of these issues in ethnographic nursing research with children and elderly adults. Their paper highlights the parallels that may be drawn between research with children and research with other vulnerable groups, because, as they note, such groups may have limited authority in this context and limited capacity to act independently. Therefore, if assent from children is sought in an ethnographic setting, it will probably be necessary to also seek informed consent from a parent or guardian.

The informant–researcher relationship and the inherent power relations involved have received considerable attention within ethnographic research (Alderson, 1995; James, 2001). The complexity of children's practices, accord-ing to Christensen (2004), shows that the issue of power is multifaceted and cannot be addressed through simply viewing power as a matter of social position. Rather, in the research process, Christensen says, 'power moves between differ-ent actors and different social positions, it is produced and negotiated in the social interactions of child to adult, child to child and adult to adult in the local settings of the research' (p.175).

To overcome the position of authoritative adult in a child's social world, some researchers such as Mandell (1991) have chosen to become immersed as much as possible in the child's world through participating with the child in their play activities. Others, however, have argued that the unavoidable differences between adults and children ought to be accepted (e.g., Mayall, 2000) and that only when it is recognized that adult researchers can ever partially partici-pate in children's lives, can the power differentials be effectively managed (James, 2001).

RELIABILITY AND VALIDITY IN QUALITATIVE HEALTH RESEARCH WITH CHILDREN

Reliability

Reliability is perhaps one of the biggest concerns in qualitative research with children. Lewis (2002) defines reliability in this context as the notion that a child's response is representative of what he or she actually believes. Children's responses to questions, observes Lewis, may be inadvertently altered by the researcher's questioning style or by their way of prompting. For example, children are often inclined to confirm what is said to them, highlighting the importance of asking about both sides of an issue.

Reliability also refers to the question of whether an interview with the same child but with another researcher using the same topic guide would result in the same, or strongly similar data. One answer to this concern is that it is not relevant to qualitative research, because of the assumption of the uniqueness – the non-replicability – of each encounter between researcher and participant. If qualitative health research is going to make an impact in the clinical world, where quantitative standards of evidence largely inform health practices and policies, then this response is insufficient, and only serves to marginalize qualitative approaches. It is possible to address concerns about reliability through rigorous research design and analysis methods. A pilot study to develop age-appropriate questions that elicit relevant responses is a first step in ensuring reliable data. A second step is the development of a coding frame for data analysis. We encourage qualitative health researchers to develop a coding frame in a coding team, so that the person doing interviews is not the same person doing the coding, at least not initially. Codes can be developed using any number of qualitative data analysis methods, including those found in grounded theory, discourse analysis, narrative analysis, and interpretative phenomenological analysis. Here we wish to emphasize strongly the special importance of rigorous coding and analysis in qualitative health research with children, given the political and intellectual concerns that can arise when children's voices enter public and theoretical discourses about health and wellbeing.

Validity

According to Lewis (2002), validity concerns the fairness of the process leading to a child's response, while validation refers to ways of confirming that responses are being interpreted in a fair manner. There has been increasing debate about the validation of responses in interviews with children which has prompted researchers at organizations in the United Kingdom such as the Children's Society and the Joseph Rowntree Foundation to use peers as interviewers (Lewis, 2002). In Kendall et al.'s (2003) grounded theory study of children's accounts of ADHD, the credibility of the data was maintained through consulting other expert qualitative researchers about the analyses and conceptual abstractions. This process highlighted any researcher biases and clarified the basis on which interpretations had been made. Another way of ensuring valid interpretation of responses is the use of a coding team, as mentioned earlier; when the interviewer is always the same person doing the coding, interpretations inevitably become somewhat subjective.

POLICY RELEVANCE OF QUALITATIVE HEALTH RESEARCH WITH CHILDREN

From the preceding discussion, it should be increasingly clear that qualitative research with children around health and wellbeing has an active political dimension that grows out of the longstanding absence of children's contributions to discussion and debates around health care policies and practices. Therefore, we encourage researchers to consider the ways in which their research could be policy or clinically relevant. Governmental organizations as well as children's charities have been actively promoting child participatory research that has policy relevant outcomes. For example, the Early Childhood Unit (ECU) at the National Children's Bureau in the United Kingdom was recently funded to support a number of local authorities to establish 'Young Children's Voices Networks'. The stated aims of these networks are: 'to be a place where practitioners can share ideas and tools as to how to listen to young children' and 'to provide a platform to share young children's views and feed them into service policy, planning and design'.[1] The Early Childhood Unit has published a report providing evidence of the importance of listening to young children and how their views can change service planning and delivery (McAuliffe, 2003). In the United States, the RAND Corporation, a nonprofit think tank has an ongoing research programme that covers child policy, education, health and wellbeing; RAND projects involving children often include mixed-method research approaches (e.g., http://www.rand.org/pubs/research_briefs/2009/RAND_RB9482.pdf).

CONCLUSION

It is an exciting time for qualitative health researchers who want to work with children. The epistemological approach to children as active agents has encouraged the development of interactive, age-appropriate, rigorous methods, as well as a substantive intellectual engagement around questions of research design and policy relevance. Qualitative researchers have the opportunity and indeed the responsibility to work at the interface of the clinic, regulatory agencies, and the world of children; facilitating understanding and communication amongst these bodies, as well as helping to ensure safe and effective child health care policies and practices.

NOTE

1 See http://www.ncb.org.uk/Page.asp?originx_617gn_2644695187566s87f_200711163040u

REFERENCES

Alderson, P. (1995) *Researching with Children: Children, Ethics and Social Research.* London: Save the Children.

Baxley, G.B., Turner, P.F., and Greenwold, W.E. (1978) 'Hyperactive Children's Knowledge and Attitudes Concerning Drug Treatment', *Journal of Pediatric Psychology,* 3(4): 172–76.

Bernheimer, L. (1986) 'The Use of Qualitative Methodology in Child Health Research', *Children's Health Care,* 14(4): 224–31.

Bluebond-Langner, M., Perkel, D., Goertzel, T., Nelson, K., and McGeary, J. (1990) 'Children's Knowledge of Cancer and Its Treatment: Impact of an Oncology Camp Experience', *Journal of Pediatrics,* 116: 207–13.

Buston, M. and Wood, S.F. (2000) 'Non-Compliance Among Adolescents with Asthma: Listening to What They Tell Us about Self-Management', *Family Practice,* 17(2): 134–8.

Cavet, J. (1998) *People Don't Understand': Children, Young People and Their Families Living with a Hidden Disability.* London: National Children's Bureau in association with the Joseph Rowntree Foundation.

Christensen, P.H. (2004) 'Children's Participation in Ethnographic Research: Issues of Power and Representation', *Children & Society,* 18: 165–76.

Clark, L. (2002) 'Mexican-Origin Mothers' Experiences Using Children's Health Care Services', *Western Journal of Nursing Research,* 24: 159–79.

Clark, A. and Moss, P. (2001) *Listening to Young Children: The Mosaic Approach.* London: National Children's Bureau.

Curtin, C. (2001) 'Eliciting Children's Voices in Qualitative Research', *American Journal of Occupational Therapy,* 55(3): 295–302.

Darbyshire, P. (2000) 'Guest Editorial: From Research on Children to Research with Children', *Neonatal, Paediatric and Child Health Nursing,* 3(1): 2–3.

Darbyshire, P., MacDougall, C., and Schiller, W. (2005) 'Multiple Methods in Qualitative Research with Children: More Insight or Just More?', *Qualitative Research,* 5(4): 417–36.

Dean J.P. and Whyte, W.F. (1990) 'How Do You Know When the Informant is Telling the Truth?'. In J. Brynner and K.M. Stribley (eds) *Social Research: Principles and Procedures* (pp. 179–88). Essex: Longman.

Emond, R. (2005) 'Ethnographic Research Methods with Children and Young People'. In S. Greene and D. Hogan (eds), *Researching Children's Experiences* (pp. 123–40). London: Sage.

Ensign, J. and Gittelsohn, J. (1998) 'Health and Access to Care: Perspectives of Homeless Youth in Baltimore City, U.S.A.', *Social Science Medicine,* 47(12): 2087–99.

Enskar, K., Carlsson, M., Golsater, M., Hamrin, E., and Kreuger, A. (1997) 'Life Situation and Problems as Reported by Children with Cancer and Their Parents', *Journal of Pediatric Oncological Nursing,* 14(1): 18–26.

Frosh, S., Phoenix, A., and Pattman, R. (2002) *Young Masculinities: Understanding Boys in Contemporary Society.* London: Palgrave.

Garbarino, J., Stott, F.M., and Erikson Institute (1992) *What Children Can Tell Us.* San Francisco, CA: Jossey-Bass.

Gates, B. and Waight, M. (2007) 'Reflections on Conducting Focus Groups with People with Learning Disabilities. Theoretical and Practical Issues', *Journal of Research in Nursing,* 12(2): 111–26.

Geissler, P.W., Nokes, K., Prince, R.J., Achieng' Odhiambo, R., Ochieng' Maende, J., and Aagaard-Hansen, J. (2000) 'Children and Medicines: Self-Treatment of Common Illnesses Among Luo School Children in Western Kenya', *Social Science and Medicine,* 5: 1771–83.

Gray-Vickrey, P. (1993) 'Gerontological Research: Use and Application of Focus Groups', *Journal of Gerontological Nursing*, 19: 21–7.

Greene, S. and Hill, M. (2005) 'Researching Children's Experience: Methods and Methodological Issues'. In S. Greene and D. Hogan (eds) *Researching Children's Experiences* (pp. 1–21). London: Sage.

Greene, S. and Hogan, D. (2005) *Researching Children's Experience: Approaches and Methods*. London: Sage.

Greig, A. and Taylor, J. (1999) *Doing Research with Children*. London: Sage.

Grodin, M.A. and Glantz, L.H. (1994) *Children as Research Subjects: Science, Ethics, and Law*. Oxford: Oxford University Press.

Haase, J.E. and Rostad, M. (1994) 'Experiences of Completing Cancer Therapy: Children's Perspectives', *Oncological Nursing Forum*, 21(9): 1483–92.

Harkness, S. and Super, C. (eds) (1996) *Parents' Cultural Belief Systems*. New York: Guilford Press.

Hawthorne, J., Jessop, J. Pryor, J. and Richards, M. (2003) *Supporting Children Through Family Change: A Review of Interventions and Services for Children of Divorcing and Separating Parents*. York: YPS in association with the Joseph Rowntree Foundation.

Hennessy, E. and Heary, C. (2005) 'Exploring Children's Views Through Focus Groups'. In S. Greene and D. Hogan (eds) *Researching Children's Experiences* (pp. 236–52). London: Sage.

Hill, M., Laybourn, A., and Borland, M. (1996) 'Engaging with Primary-Aged Children About Their Emotions and Well-Being: Methodological Considerations', *Children and Society*. 10: 129–44.

Hockenberry-Eaton, M. and Minicke, P. (1994) 'Living with Cancer Children with Extraordinary Courage', *Oncology Nursing Foundation*, 21(6): 1025–31.

Howard, M. and Millard, A.V. (1997) *Hunger and Shame: Poverty and Child Malnutrition on Mount Kilimanjaro*. London: Routledge.

Ireland, L.M. (1997) 'Children's Perceptions of Asthma: Establishing Normality', *British Journal of Nursing*, 6(18): 1059–64.

Ireland, L.M. and Holloway, I. (1996) 'Qualitative Health Research with Children', *Children and Society*, 10(2): 155–164.

James, A. (2001) 'Ethnography in the Study of Children and Childhood'. In P. Atkinson, A. Coffey, S. Delamont, J. Lofland and L. Lofland (eds) *Handbook of Ethnography* (pp. 246–57). London: Sage.

James, A., Jenks, C., and Prout, A. (1998) *Theorising Childhood*. Cambridge: Polity Press.

Jokinen, P., Lappalainen, M., Meriläinen, P., and Pelkonen, M. (2002) 'Ethical Issues in Ethnographic Nursing Research with Children and Elderly People', *Scandinavian Journal of Caring Sciences*, 16(2): 165–70.

Joseph Rowntree Foundation (2001) *Consulting with Disabled Children and Young People*. York: Joseph Rowntree Foundation.

Kendall, J., Hatton, D., Beckett, A., and Leo, M. (2003) 'Children's Accounts of Attention-Deficit/Hyperactivity Disorder', *Advanced Nursing Science*, 26(2): 114–30.

Kipnis, K. (2001) 'Vulnerability in Research Subjects: A Bioethical Taxonomy'. *Ethical and Policy Issues in Research Involving Human Research Participants* (pp. G-1–G-13). Bethesda, MD: National Bioethics Advisory Commission.

Kortesluoma, R.L. and Nikkonen, M. (2006) '"The Most Disgusting Ever": Children's Pain Descriptions and Views of the Purpose of Pain', *Journal of Child Health Care*, 10(3): 213–27.

Kortesluoma, R.L., Hentinen, M., and Nikkonen, M. (2003) 'Conducting a Qualitative Child Interview: Methodological Considerations', *Journal of Advanced Nursing*, 42(5): 434–41.

Krueger, M. and Kendall, J. (2001) 'Descriptions of Self: An Exploratory Study of Adolescents with ADHD', *Journal of Child and Adolescent Psychiatric Nursing*, 14(2): 61–72.

Lansdown, G. (1994) 'Children's Rights'. In B. Mayall (ed.), *Children's Childhoods. Observed and Experienced* (pp. 33–44). London: Falmer Press.

Leonard, D, (1990) 'Persons in their Own Right: Children and Sociology in the UK'. In L. Chisholm, P. Buchner, H.-H. Kruger and P. Brown (eds) *Childhood, Youth and Social Change* (pp. 58–70). London: Falmer Press.

Levine, C., Faden, R., Grady, C., Hammerschmidt, D., Eckenwiler, L., and Sugarman, J. (2004) 'The Limitations of "Vulnerability" as a Protection for Human Research Participants', *American Journal of Bioethics*, 4(3): 44–9.

LeVine, R.A., LeVine, S., Leiderman, P.H., Brazelton, T.B., Dixon, S., Richman, A., and Keefer, C.H. (1994). *Child Care and Culture: Lessons from Africa.* Cambridge: Cambridge University Press.

Lewis, A. (2002) 'Accessing, Through Research Interviews, the Views of Children with Difficulties in Learning', *Support for Learning*, 17(3): 110–16.

Lewis, A. and Lindsay, G. (2000) *Researching Children's Perspectives.* Buckingham: Open University Press.

Madge, N. and Willmott, N. (2007) *Children's Views and Experiences of Parenting.* London: National Children's Bureau in association with the Joseph Rowntree Foundation.

Mahon, A., Glendinning, C., Clarke, K., and Craig, G. (1996) 'Researching Children: Methods and Ethics', *Children and Society*, 10(2): 145–54.

Mandell, N. (1991) 'The Least Adult Role in Studying Children'. In F. Waksler (ed.), *Studying the Social Worlds of Children: Sociological Readings* (pp. 38–59). London: Falmer Press.

Mauthner, M. (1997) 'Methodological Aspects of Collecting Data from Children: Lessons from Three Research Projects', *Children and Society*, 11(1): 16–28.

Mayall, B. (2000) 'Conversations with Children'. In P. Christensen and A. James (eds) *Research with Children: Perspectives and Practices* (pp. 120–35). London: Falmer Press.

McAuliffe, A-M. (2003) *When Are We Having Candyfloss? Early Childhood Unit Report.* London: National Children's Bureau.

Monroe, R.H., Monroe, R.L, and Whiting, B.B. (eds) (1981) *Handbook of Cross-Cultural Human Development.* New York: Garland Press.

Morrow, V. and Richards, M. (1996) 'The Ethics of Social Research with Children: An Overview', *Children and Society*, 10(2): 90–105.

Mull, D.S., Agran, P., Winn, D.G., and Anderson, C.L. (2001) 'Injury in Children of Low-Income Mexican, Mexican American, and Non-Hispanic White Mothers in the USA: A Focused Ethnography', *Social Science & Medicine*, 52: 1081–91.

Oakley, A. (1994). 'Women and Children First and Last: Parallels and Differences Between Children's and Women's Studies'. In B. Mayall (ed.), *Children's Childhoods Observed and Experienced* (pp. 13–32). London: The Falmer Press.

Owen, S. (2001) 'The Practical, Methodological and Ethical Dilemmas of Conducting Focus Group Research with Vulnerable Clients', *Journal of Advanced Nursing*, 36: 652–8.

Peterson, J.W., Sterling, Y.M., and Weekes, D. (1999) 'Access to Health Care: Perspectives of African American Families with Chronically Ill Children'. In J.G. Sebastian and A. Bushy (eds) *Special Populations in the Community: Advances in Reducing Health Disparities* (pp. 135–48). Gaithersburg, MD: Aspen.

Perri, C., Jupp, B., Perry, H., and Lasky, K. (1997) *The Substance of Youth: The Role of Drugs in Young People's Lives Today.* York: Joseph Rowntree Foundation.

Singh, I. (2007) 'Capacity and Competence in Children as Research Participants', *EMBO Reports*, 8: 35–9.

Singh, I., Keenan, S., and Mears, A. (2008) 'The Experiences of Children and Young People of Stimulant Medication for ADHD', *Attention Deficit Hyperactivity Disorder: Full Guideline for Consultation* (pp. 94–8). London: National Institute for Health and Clinical Excellence.

Stalker, K., Carpenter, J., Phillips, R., Connors, C., MacDonald, C., Eyre, J., Noyes, J., Chaplin, S., and Place, M. (2003) *Care and Treatment? Supporting Children with Complex Needs in Healthcare Settings.* Sussex: Pavilion Publishing in association with the Joseph Rowntree Foundation.

Vygotsky, L.S. (1978) *Mind in Society: The Development of Higher Psychological Processes.* Cambridge, MA: Harvard University Press.

Wilkinson, S. (1998) 'Focus Group Methodology: A Review', *International Journal of Social Research Methodology Theory and Practice*, 1(3): 181–203.

Wood, D., Bruner, J., and Ross, G. (1976) 'The Role of Tutoring in Problem Solving', *Journal of Child Psychology and Psychiatry*, 17: 89–100.

Woodgate, R. (2000) 'Part I: An Introduction to Conducting Qualitative Research in Children with Cancer', *Journal of Pediatric Oncological Nursing*, 17(4): 192–206.

Woolley, H., Armitage, M., Bishop, J., Curtis, M., and Ginsborg, J. (2006) *Inclusion of Disabled Children in Primary School Playgrounds*. London: National Children's Bureau in association with the Joseph Rowntree Foundation.

37

The Dilemmas of Advocacy: the Paradox of Giving in Disability Research

Ruth Pinder

'Not I, not I, but the wind that blows through me' (Lawrence, 1972)

Recent decades have seen a flowering of interest in disability studies, adding depth, if not a welcome touch of modesty, to attempts to develop an emancipatory research project. Therefore, in revisiting the debate on advocacy research that I had not addressed for some years, it was reassuring to find some familiar names and arguments. Nevertheless, ethnographic research and teaching, if not life itself, have taken me elsewhere. Living with a partner who resolutely refuses to do his disability in line with any model, social or otherwise, is the stuff of tragicomedy, given the uncertainties of independence in later life. Any easements in daily living that have come our way from disability campaigns have been welcome. Yet, change, deep change, does not come to order either. It has a habit of slipping in by the back door when you are busy doing something else.

The point of such reflections for this chapter found me weaving between personal experience, theories of reciprocity, and attempts to find ethnographies of disability that spoke to what the Disability Movement was after. Theorizing about exchange has been well established academically since Marcel Mauss (1954) showed how a gift is not fully a gift until it is given away again. Exchange is always ambiguous, capable of generosity and violence, altruism and self-interest, calculation and freedom (Hyde, 1979; Laidlaw, 2000; Komter, 2005). Nor can it be separated from the moral taint of commerce. Analysts have therefore changed tack. Rather than reciprocity, researchers have begun to explore what cannot be given away (Wiener, 1992). In what is closely guarded can often be found what is most meaningful to people. Therefore, the paradox of keeping-while-giving may cast fresh light on the research criteria developed by disabled people that are now regarded as foundational to good practice. Such a project forms the first part of this chapter.

However, the ethnographer in me was restless. Ethnography scores by working outwards from the fine grindings of everyday life, rather than simply illustrating predetermined theoretical positions – *'the hallmark of pointless field-work'* as Willis, (2005) has it. Locating a study that spoke to the carnival of social action, not just its determinants was harder to come by than I anticipated. Then I remembered Gelya Frank's cultural biography of Diane de Vries (2000) that had left its mark on me earlier. This study of a woman born, Frank writes, *'with all the physical and mental equipment she would need to live in our society – except arms and legs'* takes us to the heart of the matter in the second part of the chapter: namely how the tensions between openly ideological research and disinterested enquiry have worked out in practice. The dilemma is always the same: it is not enough for research to interpret and understand the world. It must also change it to empower disadvantaged groups. As Wolcott notes: *'Critical theorists insist that ethnography stops one step short. While* their *critics wonder instead whether they overstep bounds in creating their own "regime of truth"'* (1999).

Using the metaphor of gift exchange, the following questions for qualitative researchers across the human and social sciences who wish to follow an emancipatory logic will be addressed:

- Does theory help or hinder understanding disabled people's experience?
- Who owns disability research, and how far can ownership be made accountable?
- How objective can or should disability research be?
- What kind of a gift is possible between researchers and disabled people?

My quest is simple enough: if qualitative – particularly ethnographic – research is not to lose its power to unsettle, then we need to explore how far we should learn to leave a gift alone, and how far it must be disciplined if research is both to enhance the moral imagination and be mutually sustaining. After all, the point of exchange is not to resolve that tension, but to keep it circulating.

THE EMERGENCE OF EMANCIPATORY RESEARCH AND THE SOCIAL MODEL

No discussion of disabled people's attempts to make the terms in which research can be put to work their own without understanding the social model of disability – the 'Big Idea' particularly in the United Kingdom (Shakespeare, 2008).

Rooted in the Enlightenment, the move towards openly ideological enquiry has been fuelled by the retreat from positivism typical of the 1960s. A heightened concern with the moral responsibilities of research has 'given voice' to women, indigenous peoples, or those suffering racism (Paine, 1995): for example the 'militant anthropology' of Scheper-Hughes (2006), or Farmer's impassioned ethnographies on poverty, inequality and AIDS in Haiti and Peru (1999; 2005). In this, the newly formed Disability Movement caught the spirit of the times as the older orthodoxies unstiffened, and more liberating ways of conducting research gained momentum. At the same time, qualitative research has been caught up in the demands of the new knowledge economy, with its stress on techniques rather than epistemological and ontological concerns (Law, 2004). Audit and contract enter the soul. In particular, ethnography has become dominated by high speed, 'drive-by' studies conducted in large multidisciplinary teams with tight predefined schedules that reach for answers quicker than questions can be posed. Asking disabled people for their stories may be to ask in bad faith when it is problem solving not problem seeking that people are after (Small, 1998).

For disability theorists, this mix threw into relief the threadbare nature of reciprocity within disability research, provoking sharp criticism of academics with clean hands – if they had hands at all. A defining moment came with a series of articles in Disability and Society (Oliver, 1992), (the term 'Handicap' was jettisoned later), where the political nature of research was made explicit. In critiquing both positivist and interpretivist research as *'disablist'*, the Movement formally embraced emancipatory research and the social model became the key symbol for *'a fully formed materialist account of the social creation of disability within Western society'* (Oliver, 1990). In rejecting a view of disability as pathology-to-be-corrected, it promised to highlight both the dark underbelly of academia that disenfranchised disabled people, and directly translate research findings into practical outcomes: for example, the user-centred research seminars commissioned by the Rowntree Trust inspired lobbying for Direct Payments, now seen as key to independent living in the West (Zarb and Nadash, 1994). Its style of communication was direct, emotional and dramatic; witness the references to *'rape'*, *'parasite research'*, or simple oppositions between *'oppressors and oppressed'* that still find their way into academic texts (Mercer, 2002 op cit). In offering hope of redress, such exuberance was redemptive for that first wave of disabled researchers, bringing in its train a profound sense of cohesion – a vital strategy in sustaining the human need for disabled people to be more than bystanders in the stories of their own lives (Jackson, 2005). There is dignity in sharing.

So in a world that's forever flying apart, drawing lines around what can and cannot be given away is, as Wiener (op cit) notes, *'a skilful accomplishment'*. For the social model to circulate is one thing: to prevent it from wandering requires careful husbandry. Like all deeply cherished symbols, it is dangerous for outside researchers to meddle with, yet equally imprudent to ignore. Yet, the demand for practical benefits as *the* condition for research highlighted its transactional rather than its transformational possibilities, and anomalies soon appeared, nervously articulated at first. For example, the darker side of disability that had Parker puzzling why '... *adaptation to impairment was essentially a form of false consciousness'* (1993) in her qualitative study of caring within marriage, could not be wished away. The Movement has been slow to acknowledge that great leveller, dementia in later life; slower still to recognize the paranoia behind the democratizing ideals of transparency in research (Strathern, 2000). Some gifts have to be refused, at least for the time being. Their transformative potential may only be realized later.

Living in the light of ideals is always more complex than merely conforming to them. In recognizing the real difficulties in sustaining and making visible an internal democracy, Stone and Priestley's (1996) observations galvanized, because they came from within. Practicalities, such as recruiting and retaining researchers, particularly those with fluctuating impairments, were often stumbling blocks. Vernon's study of black disabled women points to other difficulties. Despite efforts to develop a research agenda with participants, and return interview transcripts for amendment, participation was still compromised by *'deference to the experts'* (1997). More worrying still, Dewsbury et al. (2004) found the social model hindered rather than helped their attempts to design assistive technologies with disabled study participants. In a rare disclaimer, even Oliver, one of the key architects of the UK Movement, remarks on *'the time and energy'* necessary to put genuinely collaborative research to work. In a world continually on the boil, some have retreated from stronger versions of the Model (Shakespeare op cit, 2008), even as its message is currently being rekindled by action researchers in mental health (Beresford, 2006). Doing research has brought with it the obligation to preserve *its* vitality too, enabling experiences with the wider research community to be shared. Something deeper than the representational veneer of the successful research project is at stake.

THEORIZING EXPERIENCE, EXPERIENCING THEORY IN QUALITATIVE RESEARCH

If the reach of emancipatory research is forever expanding and contracting, so is the place of disabled people's experience within it. Several strands are apparent.

The difficulties of accounting for disabled women's experience have since blossomed into a sophisticated feminist scholarship that has added depth and perspective to research (see Fine and Asch, 1988; Morris, 1992; Thomas, 1999). In nurturing her intellectually disabled daughter – an eloquent use of auto-ethnography – Hillyer found herself handicapped, *'socially, because of stigma, but also physically because of stress, and emotionally because of grief'*. Better able to accept help over time, she writes *'I no longer expect reciprocity'* (1993).

Predictably, though, stealing the limelight brought in its wake intense irritation with the internal rumblings of the self that characterized 'the experience of illness' scholarship of the 1980s, then the preserve of medical sociologists. Many qualitative studies were ahistorical and impairment specific, for example Kelly on ulcerative colitis (1992), Pinder on Parkinson's Disease (1992), Scambler on epilepsy (1989). At their best, the emphasis on medical regimes, coping styles, and stigma was important in challenging medical hubris and paternalism, a goal shared with disability theorists. With hindsight, the genre tended to drown in its own limitations, the intricacies of levodopa management – a distraction from those in search of March of History explanations. For studies not to foreground the political economy of disability not only lacked authority, but also a sense of reality, disability theorists argued, and risked descending into irrationalism. The turf has since been ceded to health psychologists, now busy with their own transformative projects.

Nevertheless, this is too cavalier. Other qualitative research that stressed the creative, if not anarchic possibilities of ageing or sickness were making their mark: for example Myerhoff on preserving identity in later life (1978), (See Box 37.1). Robert Murphy's profound meditation on his own deteriorating impairment (1987) addressed those meaning-of-life questions that give courage for living. However, his blend of intimate scholarship and disciplined fieldwork skills were initially rejected by disability theorists, his depiction of disability as '*liminal*' too reminiscent of the tragedy mould in which their lives had often been cast. Nonetheless, gifts ripple outwards in unexpected ways: the intense reflexivity that characterizes the genre has inspired a broader range of studies, for instance Kleinman et al.'s (1997) work on social suffering amongst refugees and victims of genocide; or Lock's powerful comparative ethnography of brain stem death and organ transplantation in Japan and North America that weaves personal testaments into a wide-ranging historical analysis (2002).

Box 37.1   Myerhoff on Preserving Identity in Later Life

Barbara Myerhoff's affectionate yet probing study of elders and Holocaust survivors at a Jewish Centre is ethnography at its best (1978). Through intimate acquaintance with key Centre members we learn how meaning, identity and continuity were woven together through storytelling. Myerhoff's approach was improvisatory. A broad set of topics – being old, being a Jew, memories of the Old World, and life in the United States today, was crystallized from that acquaintance, and specific methods evolved rather than being designed in advance. She met and talked with over 100 Centre members, visited their homes, went out on trips, attended funerals, but spent most of her time with a small group, developing a close relationship with one key participant Shmuel, who became her foil and mentor. The weekly Living History classes she eventually held over ten months provided extensive biographical material, which was tape-recorded and transcribed – a testament to suffering and resilience that is never idealized. Placing herself fully in the text, Myerhoff describes her attempts to enter the Centre world imaginatively whilst preserving her own separateness and 'a measure of objectivity'. The result is a beautifully etched portrayal of character and plot in action, which shows how self-knowledge is intimately linked to the possibilities of understanding others in ethnographic fieldwork.

Using qualitative research as a form of cultural brokerage, then, seems to be an attractive proposition. Following Irving Zola's mistrust of cultural fences (1989), Williams, for example, has sought to unite the twin poles of idealism and materialism, illness and disability (1996; 2001) Such a move brought disability theorists and medical sociologists together to 'Explore the Divide' in London (Barnes and Mercer (1996). Yet, mediating may foment as well as nourish. In giving to others what we most like to give is closure; such is the fear of depletion (Keitzer, 2004). A partial connection perhaps, that did more to unsettle respective satisfactions with their own evidence than ask how they came to be polarized in the first place.

Nevertheless, even modest engagements can surprise and delight. Attempts to theorize the field and avoid being classed as a victim discipline, along with lesbian and gay studies (Garber, 2001), have brought geographers, historians and educationalists into the fold in a succession of edited handbooks on disability. Each has vied to outdo the other in the Research Assessment stakes – Leonard Davis's fine collection on toleration (1997), Armstrong and Barton's study of inclusive education (1999), and recently Albrecht et al.'s 800-page state of the art compendium (2001). Indeed, it is precisely the emergence of critical social theory that has given credence to emancipatory research and created a niche amongst more traditional methodologies.

Yet, theory cannot be everywhere at once. In turning once more towards abstraction, research seems to have lost sight of the obligation to reflect the everyday world of people's lives – a point consistently made by Morris (1996), who has argued against all models as being part of the objectification that disabled people were contesting in the first place.

A third strand to the picture concerns the privileging of Euro-American experience in disability studies. Problems of translation are sharper now that definitions of 'what belongs' and 'what does not belong' have become more elastic, and the discourses on human rights and the environment more complex. As Ingstad and Reynolds-Whyte note (2007), anthropologists working in different cultural communities have been reluctant to entrust their ethnographic experience with the dispossessed to disabled theorists lest it lose its shape. The discipline's strong tradition of relativism and the difficulties of addressing social transformation conceptually have always made too facile claims to the universal language of rights suspect. Yet, there have been some surprising alliances: Stoller, for example, has drawn richly on his West African fieldwork with the Songhay, finding that their notions of enfolding and unfolding have better equipped him to face his own cancer than 'Western' idioms of mastery and control (2004). Similarly, simple divisions of the world into perpetrators and victims can be unravelled in the hands of a sensitive ethnographer in ways that go beyond the pseudo-concrete: for example, Staples' more nuanced understanding of the leprosy experience that had been masked under such blanket terms as stigma, social exclusion and rehabilitation (2007). Political change can come about via people's moral transformation as much as through the dictates of historical materialism.

Such a patchwork is a chastening reminder of the thin line between improving the conditions of people's lives and improving people, and the value of intensive ethnographic fieldwork over time in minimizing the worst excesses of mistranslation. In 'developing' countries, the struggle may be as much about survival as political emancipation, and the risks of proselytizing that find their way into otherwise exemplary texts intense. Ingstad (2007) found that poor villagers in the Kalahari had little interest either in the definitional issues that have preoccupied Western scholars, or in an independence that underplays kinship relations. A poor woman's agenda *'would more realistically be summarized as access to food and firewood, and care from her children tomorrow'* she writes. For rights to remain on the right side of righteousness requires a modest touch.

ACCOUNTABILITY IN QUALITATIVE RESEARCH: CALCULATION OR FREEDOM?

Determined efforts to bring giver and receiver closer together in planning and implementing research is one way of ensuring that the gift is received in the spirit in which it is given.

Initially such moves led to a tightening of disability research with disabled people being seen as the best (if not the only) people able to conduct it. The optimism that it was in their power to effect change and that progress could be cumulative heightened self-confidence. In reversing the traditional researcher/ researched hierarchy to ensure that outcomes were meaningful to disabled participants, Barnes' seminal work on antidiscrimination legislation (1991), for example, has paved the way for subsequent research, with themes echoing and complementing each other: witness Davis' (2000) feedback to policy makers and educators countering attributions of passivity in disabled children. Extending that process, Rodgers (1999) and Owens (2007) have developed more imaginative life history interviewing techniques in their work with intellectually disabled people. To share moral agency is to emancipate in its broadest sense.

In other ways, though, such a strategy brought into sharp relief the seeds of its own limitations. Kitchin's conclusion that disabled people prefer an *'inclusive, action-based strategy, where /they/ are involved as consultants and partners, not just as subjects'* gives a sense of déjà vu, of empiricism confirming its own assumptions (2000). Nor does everyone want to become a skilled researcher. Emancipation might be a mixed blessing. Accordingly, able-bodied researchers have cautiously been invited back into the fold. Sensible of the privilege, for example, Moore et al.'s review identifies critical points at which *'well-intentioned research switched to being potentially abusive'* (1998), their ideas *'at odds with the criteria for projects adopted by conventional research sponsors'* in their commitment to disabled people. The lessons of the past were not to fall by the wayside.

However, this is not simply levelling in the name of equivalence. For activists the claim is stronger: research can only be properly emancipatory when disabled

---

Box 37.2 Shakespeare et al's study of sexuality

Shakespeare et al.'s (1996) collaborative study of sex, love and intimacy raises issues that have largely been ignored alike by academics and campaigners. Flatter and less introspective than Myerhoff's ethnography, their narrative style still gives depth as well as breadth to the enquiry. Drawing on first-hand accounts of disabled people, a multimethod approach was used, including interviews, questionnaires, letters and tape-recordings of participants' experiences. The problems of generalizability are dealt with at some length: many of their 46 participants were more 'vocal' members of the gay and lesbian community than may be the case elsewhere, but attempts to represent other minorities, particularly older disabled people and those in residential accommodation, were only partly successful. In treading a delicate balance between optimism and pessimism, the study nonetheless ends with a resounding credo that reflects the politically active nature of the authors' shared commitment: any lack of emotional fulfilment resides less in the defects of the body than in social restrictions and crude stereotyping by others. In contesting such images, they conclude, sexual citizenship is simultaneously vigil and gift, an entitlement, not a hand-out.

---

people are free to set their own agenda. A new distinctiveness has become apparent, with Leeds University now a centre of excellence for disability studies, with its own publishing house. At the same time, some disabled people now run research projects that speak to more elastic goals of personal and emotional development, for example Shakespeare et al.'s study of sexuality (1996) (Box 37.2). Nevertheless, such is the ambivalence towards expertise that some theorists worry it has become an ally of the very tendencies activism set out to resist. Like all gift relationships, the search for active involvement and accountability is profoundly ambivalent. There is no simple way to resolve the conflict between individual advancement (the books, the academic prestige), funding pressures, and the disability community.

OBJECTIVITY AND THE SEARCH FOR CREDIBILITY

Standing at the furthest pole from the gift that makes no call on giver or receiver is the noisy problem of objectivity. As Hyde notes (op cit), it is precisely because dilemmas of bias are forever being squabbled over that they can never achieve the equivalence of the pure gift, the gift that is given in silence.

Agreed, the world is not out there like pebbles on a beach waiting to be collected, and that ultimately the act of looking changes the nature of what is being looked at. Agreed further, with too great an openness, there is a risk of featurelessness. Some definition is required. However, it does not follow that just because interpretation is always part of knowledge creation that disability researchers can wash their hands of the difficulties altogether. If as Stone and Priestley (op cit) argue *'the problem of relevance'* for the disabled community has to be confronted, so also does the inherently unpopular nature of the intellectual's task, especially in a climate where scholarship is expected to be easily accessible. To ask how researchers select this fact but not that from all the material that clamours for attention is part of a cherished tradition of respect for accuracy and fairness in argument. Indeed for research to publicly influence policy in the way disability theorists demand relies for its credibility on just this seemingly old-fashioned commitment to 'go looking for trouble' in the best Popperian fashion. In a climate where research is becoming so de-mystified that it is in danger of losing its shape, research needs its teeth too, if it is not just to reproduce truths that are already well known.

So for researchers to become cultural 'agents provocateurs', not only reporting on society but promoting attitudes within it, is to worry whether they are not getting above themselves. To argue with Farmer that neutrality masks the structural violence surrounding poverty and AIDS in Latin America, for example, certainly dramatizes the tension. *'Openly on the side of the destitute sick'*, Farmer finds himself unable to *'serve as a compassionate reporter or chronicler of misery'* (2005 op cit). Like all powerful writers, his rhetorical skills keep alive the moral blindness of an objectivity that is careless of values and feelings. But for a doctor who works publicly for changes in public health whilst still setting bones in his Haiti clinic, his labours cannot all be accomplished with equal intensity, and may fuel feelings of inadequacy as much as gratitude. If researchers are to be explicit about their assumptions as disability theorists insist, then advocates themselves form part of the topic at hand. This is the sticking point: the longed for unity in the face of loss and change has to be wary about engaging in a free-for-all. The challenge to surrender is simultaneously the challenge to remain aloof from the fray.

Objectivity, therefore, is not an absolute, a quality that either exists or not, but an ideal that is forever being pulled and pushed at, taking its shape according to the research tasks at hand. Any result, therefore, may be more tentative, the impulse to moral indignation tempered with the realization that passion can best aid our understanding if well leavened. If, as Phillips (2002) has it, *'We can be at our most ferociously political by being mild mannered'* keeping a proper distance may paradoxically be an act of engagement.

COMMENT

So far, I have followed the paradox of keeping-whilst-giving into the everyday relations of disability research. I have argued that it is no longer sufficient to assume that gifts given are just about gifts returned: some aspects of research, such as objectivity are publicly argued about and fought over, whilst others, such as the appearance of subtle new hierarchies of belonging, are more elusive. These are not fixed distinctions; they are ones which are continually being fashioned as disability research gains strength and gradually transforms itself in the process. The criteria, then, are processes not things: movements one can discern rather than be dogmatic about. The sense that can be made of them is always particularistic.

Therefore, it is to the detailed exploration of Gelya Frank's cultural biography of Diane de Vries that I now turn to for more illumination.

I cannot cover all the features that for me make this work a remarkable achievement. Three are central to the dilemmas of emancipatory research already discussed: namely, its scholarship, its sustained reflexivity, and its ethics of intimacy. They will bring into sharper relief the way that things given are always also about things kept.

A LABOUR OF LOVE

A scene in the opening chapter takes us to the heart of the matter. Professor Frank describes her first sight of De Vries, when as a graduate student in anthropology, she allowed her gaze to *'fall upon (and penetrate) Diane from a seat high up in a lecture hall'*. More aware than most of the freedoms taken at others' expense, turning anthropology's potential for exploitation around prompted some awkward questions. If she was to 'give voice' to De Vries, she writes, *'Didn't she have a voice already? Did she need my help to be heard? … Has she been merely an informant, passive and compliant, recounting her experiences to me? Or an agent who has actively constructed her life in the telling?'* Whatever the desire for symmetry in our relationships with others, this was to be no ordinary research encounter between two people.

THE REACH OF SCHOLARSHIP: 'ONCE I HAD MET MY OWN STANDARDS …'

The image grips, the questions are tenacious. Yet, the ease, if not elegance of expression is deceptive. This is unashamedly a work of scholarship. Frank's methodology draws eclectically on observations, interviews, extracts from De Vries' unpublished autobiography, interviews with others close to her, letters and other secondary data, to place De Vries' life in the context of American culture at the time. There are lengthy extracts about her earlier exposure to rehabilitation and her eventual rejection of a prosthesis; her quest to carve out a career and gain a degree; and the fault lines in independent living that taxed the resources of those around her. A whole chapter is devoted to the vexed question of typicality, with de Vries emerging, apparently, as a *'perfect example'* of a disabled woman in a Western 'can-do' society, though the emotional resilience demanded for research such as this might suggest more unusual qualities. The picture that emerges is of a woman with presence who deals with the world on her own terms.

The book is full of lovely detours. Here the reader can explore Levinas' ethics of substitution, a practice that threads through Frank's analysis, mirroring but not replicating a self-standing world of objects; or the paradoxes of reflexivity understood so well by Gadamer whose 'fusion of horizons' spoke eloquently to

724 THE SAGE HANDBOOK OF QUALITATIVE METHODS IN HEALTH RESEARCH

the prospect of reaching over into others' worlds. These issues (and many others) are richly elaborated in footnotes. Once the exacting standards of scholarship had been secured, the '*sharing, borrowing and cross-fertilisation*' that took place between them served the book's strong educational purpose: provoking readers to '*clarify their empathy, projections and transference related to images in the text*'. When de Vries and Frank are taking each other's words and making them their own, some form of appropriation is always involved in writing about another's life.

However, the gift that pleases everyone pleases no one. The fullness of mind, reflective of an intellectual journey over the years is irritating for those who like to get straight to the point (Taub, 2001); or the strict disciplinarian who laments the book's absence of sociological theory as the only candidate in town (Peyrot, 2001). It is a scholarship that has to be earned as well as given. The conclusions are the richer by the distance the reader has had to travel to attain them.

THINKING FROM THE INSIDE OUT: 'WHOLEHEARTEDLY TRYING TO HEAR IT AS YOU HEAR IT'

Such an exercise does not proceed in straight lines. As Frank delved deeply into herself to uncover her own 'invisible disabilities', she found that 'A radical practice of self-examination is needed by anyone who hopes to transform the cultural legacy of disability oppression'. The language has a familiar ring even if no mention of the social model appears in her index. If the paradoxes at the heart of all intense fieldwork relationships are to be explored, the task of introspection and clarification is a question-asking process rather than an answer-producing thing, and the book details some of the problems and possibilities of putting such self-conscious reflexivity to work.

In trying to work out their respective responsibilities for each other, Frank reconsidered her own childhood speech defects, the anxiety and depression that both she and De Vries were sometimes heir to, and the links with her own Jewish background. Bodies were forever getting in the way of things. Other attempts were less happy. Frank compared what it would be like to live without arms with flippers on a pinball machine. The result on the page is chilling; deliberately so. Assured at first that '*this was the best thing you've done'*, De Vries only conveyed her discomfort later. It is not simply that transparency has its limits. The sting lay in the tail – the unseen demand that De Vries should take Frank's standpoint and see the world through *her* eyes. A transformative moment came when, understanding better how De Vries thought of herself as lovely rather than lacking, reciprocity was given concrete form: they arrived at the title of the book through a shared metaphor, that of the Venus de Milo. We learn ethnographically via faint clues and indirections, rather than straight question and answer. Moreover, we learn through the skin as much as by logical argument.

AN INTIMATE ETHICS: 'IT WAS SHE WHOM I HAD TO PLEASE ...'

The ethical foundations for their relationship were cemented early on – namely that both would share in the royalties, and De Vries would see everything that Frank wrote. At what point (or points) in their encounter De Vries declined the offer of joint authorship is decently veiled such is the fugitive nature of trade-offs between propriety and property. Had she accepted, it would have been a different book.

The bare bones of informed consent give little hint of the flux of need that exists in any encounter lasting longer than the survey-and-single-interview format that passes for much qualitative research these days. Slowing down allows one better to hear the tension between normative ideals of reciprocity and the ethnographer's need always to hold something back from the encounter. Small, seemingly insignificant incidents provided the stuff of reflection: Frank's help with De Vries' job applications, decisions whether to give or refuse a loan, or the souvenir pair of Lapp reindeer boots that turned sour: *'Little boots, how cute'* was De Vries' response. *'I have tried to give only what I would not resent'* Frank writes. Never symmetrical, power dynamics were constantly shifting, as cruder discriminations gave way to more nuanced ones. For example, De Vries introduced Frank as *'my biographer'* to a group of friends (rather than the reverse); it was, Frank writes, De Vries who had the real authority to terminate the agreement. However, when dependence and independence are continuously in and out of each other's pockets, matters were unlikely to be so transparent.

When candour is often stifled in the name of objectivity, bringing scholarship and intimacy into close proximity always invites charges of exhibitionism, if not prurience. The charge of *'too much Frank and not enough Diane'* (Rosenthal, 2001) is familiar. Yet, the scholarly emphasis of the book provides a clue to its reticence. What de Vries and Frank have chosen to declare and in what detail, both reveals and conceals. In foregrounding de Vries' public message, *'to use my disability to encourage people to live their lives as best they can',* something is always held back from the pressures of give and take: a fugitive sensibility perhaps, the better for not being pinned down too tightly.

Two contrasting incidents express that sensibility. At one stage, Frank presented a paper using psychoanalytic concepts to discuss De Vries' autobiography at a conference on childhood which De Vries was only able to read afterwards. *'Diane was furious'* Frank writes, and her letter of protest reveals the struggle for control over whose interpretations were to carry the day. Frank withdrew the paper. Such were the feelings of betrayal that little contact between them occurred for a year – a largesse over which funding committees might well hesitate. If qualitative research writes with a sharper sense of responsibility than before, it is knowing when scholarship has to yield too.

Different in tone were the carefully structured workshops with Barbara Myerhoff (1978). Sailing into the room *'as if on a palanquin'*, De Vries talked about her experiences, then Frank the research. Generous extracts from students' responses attest to the way the fruits of gifts can themselves be gifts, the mantel of power passing from hand to hand when we need each other to survive. When researchers never know how their studies will be used, how far afield they travel is always a mystery.

COMMENT

The relationship between de Vries and Frank is not one of applying precoded schema to analysis, recognizable though the criteria outlined earlier are. Like life itself, their encounters twist and turn, embodying a commitment that goes beyond any mechanical adherence to the social model. If there is emancipation here, and I believe there is, it is not of the 'input "x" leads to output "y" kind that directly yields practical solutions, or that sees itself animating an inert object. Rather, the spirit of the book lies in a subtle education of attention, in which two people come together to understand themselves – and almost always to understand others – better. The result is life-affirming in its ability to sustain warmth and affection in the face of disagreement and rejection. The demands of scholarship are paramount but hardly inflexible; an intimate ethics teaches us how to over-hear ourselves when we talk to ourselves, and a sustained reflexivity shows how much can be learnt from an 'n' of one. This was a giving-to, not a giving-up: a model to be contemplated rather than a blueprint to be put into effect.

CONCLUSIONS

I return to the key question that animated this chapter: namely, what kind of a gift is possible if advocacy research is both to enrich the moral imagination and be mutually sustaining. As I have tried to show, the Disability Movement's gaze has been trained on gaining control over resources and the political process. As such, its research agenda has been tied to the stricter calculation of determinate values, even as several studies in the first part of this chapter have creatively engaged with these. Frank does not neglect them. Nevertheless, her work highlights the play of feelings about disability that involve more elusive moral values, such as fair play, presence and dignity. These show just how hard it is to breathe life into such 'must-do' terms as advocacy or empowerment, how tenacious the little contempts with which we routinely judge others.

   I am wary of prescriptions. Outcomes are in a sense in the mind's eye. However, if understanding the central paradox of exchange, namely when to leave a gift alone, and when to discipline it may help novice ethnographers avoid the brash-ness or pedestrianism that is so often the lot of social science, not simply disability research, then some generalizations are in order. First, ethnographic research is an embodied practice. Profound lessons are, quite literally, learnt through the skin: the chill of rejection that is felt in terms of sleepless nights or periods of depression alert ethnographer (and reader) to the invisible thresholds of tolerance that matter most to people. Therefore, the ability to open oneself to others and absorb their worlds without being annihilated is an analytical strength not a methodological weakness. It is not for the faint-hearted. At the same time, thorough fieldwork can bring the world's trouble spots intensely alive, potentially widening the field of human discourse, solidarity and self-understanding (Willis op cit, 2005). There is much to be said for the lost art of indirection when research may be powerless to directly redress the injustices of deprivation or indifference. Secondly, ethnography is improvisatory. As Frank shows, people have to work it out as they go along, and the design rarely follows the compositional format of research bids (Cerwonka and Malkki, 2007). To argue against any preparatory design in today's bureaucratized funding climate would be absurd. However, it needs to be sufficiently loose to allow ethnography to 'follow the brush' if it is not simply to reproduce findings that are already known. Becoming more at ease with the vertigo of doing without ready answers, or settling for more fragmentary ones, suggests settling for a more modest research agenda that is wary of the drift towards authoritarianism (see Law, 2004, for example). Thirdly, ethnography is humanitarian and relational: humanitarian in that it calls for an attentive engagement to the rhythms of others, much like the continuing adjustments of trapeze artist to wire, wire to artist (Ingold, 2007); relational in the sense that such dynamics always draw in history and circumstance. Just how much context to embrace for research to be meaningful is a matter of careful judgement. Finally, this iterative process is a temporal activity that reaches forward in order to understand backwards. Unlike the closed circle of disinterested reflection, the coming and going between information, understanding and inspiration that is integral to ethnographic fieldwork is not evenly paced – a salutary lesson in just how long things take to say what they mean to us. Like life itself, ethnographic research is not for those in a hurry.

If ethnography's special project is to count in the volatile mix of give and take, then it means nourishing what the psychoanalyst D.W. Winnicott referred to as the 'professional attitude': that 'activity of the mind' that puts itself at risk in the bid to extend the conversations we have with others, the amount of conflict we can bear (1949). In this sense ethnography is more a medium for whatever happens to happen within it, than an instrument delivering predetermined goals. Neither disabled people's bid for practice, nor its deferral can stand up on their own. The energizing potential of each lies in their respective capacities to enrich, complement, yet go beyond each other. In ethnographic research's ability to pass through us and leave us altered lies its continued relevance.

REFERENCES

Albrecht, G., Seelman K., and Bury, M. (2001) *Handbook of Disability Studies.* London: Sage.

Armstrong, F. and Barton, L. (1999) *Disability, Human Rights and Education: Cross-Cultural Perspsectives.* Buckingham: Open University Press.

Barnes, C. (1991) 'Disabled People in Britain and Discrimination: a Case for Discrimination Legislation'. London: Hurst and Co/BCODP.

Barnes, C. and Mercer, G. (eds) (1996) *In Exploring the Divide: Illness and Disability*. Leeds: The Disability Press.

Beresford, P. (2006) 'Identity Crisis'. Available at: http:www.guardian.co.uk/society/2006/nov/29

Cerwonka, A. and Malkki, L. (2007) *Improvising Theory: Process and Temporality in Ethnographic Fieldwork*. Chicago: University of Chicago Press.

Davis, J. (2000) 'Disability Studies as Ethnographic Research and Text: Research Strategies and Roles for Promoting Social Change?' *Disability and Society*, 15(2): 191–206.

Davis, L. (1997) (ed.) *The Disability Studies Reader*. London: Routledge.

Dewsbury, G., Clarke, K., Randall, D., Rouncefield, M., and Somerville, I. (2004) 'The Anti-Social Model of Disability', *Disability and Society*, 19(2): 145–58.

Farmer, P. (1999) *Infections and Inequalities: The Modern Plagues*. Berkeley and Los Angeles: University of California Press.

Farmer, P. (2005) *Pathologies of Power: Health, Human Rights and the New War on the Poor*. Berkeley and Los Angeles: University of California Press.

Fine, M. and Asch (1988) (eds) *Women with Disabilities: Essays in Psychology, Culture and Politics*. Philadelphia: Temple University Press.

Frank Gelya (2000) *Venus on Wheels: Two Decades of Dialogue on Disability, Biography and Being Female in America*. Berkeley and Los Angeles: University of California Press.

Garber, M. (2001) *Academic Instincts*. NJ: Princeton University Press.

Hillyer, B. (1993) *Feminism and Disability*. Oklahoma: University of Oklahoma Press.

Hyde, L. (1979) *The Gift: How the Creative Spirit Transforms the World* (3rd Edition). NY: Random House.

Ingold, T. (2007) *Lines: A Brief History*. London: Routledge.

Ingstad, B. (2007) 'Seeing Disability and Human Rights in Local Context: Botswana Revisited'. In Ingstad, B. and Reynolds-Whyte (eds) *Disability in Local and Global Worlds*. Berkeley and Los Angeles: University of California Press.

Jackson, M. (2005) *Existential Anthropology: Events, Exigencies and Effects*. Oxford: Berghan Books.

Keitzer, G. (2004*) Help: The Original Human Dilemma*. NY: Harper Collins.

Kelly, M. (1992) *Colitis*. London: Routledge.

Kitchin, R. (2000) 'The Researched Opinions on Research: Disabled People and Disability Research', *Disability and Society*, 15(1): 25.

Kleinman, A., Vas, D., and Lock, M. (eds) (1997) *Social Suffering*. Berkeley and Los Angeles: University of California Press.

Komter, A. (2005) *Social Solidarity and the Gift*. Cambridge: Cambridge University Press.

Laidlaw, J. (2000) 'A Free Gift Makes No Friends', *J. Roy. Anthropol. Instit.*, 6: 617–34.

Law, J. (2004) *After Method: Mess in Social Science Research*. Abingdon: Routledge.

Lawrence, D.H. (1972) *The Complete Poems*. 2 vols. London: Heinemann.

Lock, M. (2002) *Twice Dead: Organ Transplants and the Reinvention of Death*. Berkeley and Los Angeles: University of California Press.

Mauss, M. (1954) *The Gift*. Cohen and West: London.

Mercer, G. (2002) 'Emancipatory Disability Research'. In Barnes, C., Oliver, M., and Barton, L. (eds) *Disability Studies Today*. Polity Press.

Moore, M., Beazley, S., and Malzer, J. (1998) *Researching Disability Issues*. Buckingham: Open University Press.

Morris, J. (1992) 'Personal and Political: A Feminist Perspective on Researching Physical Disability', *Disability, Handicap and Society*, 7(2): 157–66.

Morris, J. (ed.) (1996) *Encounters with Strangers: Feminism and Disability*. London: The Women's Press.

Murphy, R. (1987) *The Body Silent*. London: J.M. Dent.

Myerhoff, B. (1978) *Number Our Days*. NY: Simon and Schuster.

Oliver, M. (1990) *The Politics of Disablement.* Tavistock: Macmillans.

Oliver, M. (1992) 'Changing the Social Relations of Research Production?', *Disability, Handicap and Society*, 7(2):101–14.

Owens, J. (2007) 'Liberating Voices through Narrative Methods: the Case for an Interpretive Research Approach', *Disability and Society*, 22(3): 299–313.

Paine, R. (1995) (ed.) *Advocacy and Anthropology: First Encounters* (3rd Edition). St. John's, Newfoundland: Institute of Social and Economic Research, Memorial University.

Parker, G. (1993) *With this Body: Caring and Disability in Marriage.* Buckingham: Open University Press.

Peyrot, M. (2001) 'Method and Substance in Sociological Studies of Disability', *Qualitative Sociology*, 24(3): 409–12.

Phillips, A. (2002) *Equals.* London: Faber.

Pinder, R. (1992) 'Coherence and Incoherence: Doctors' and Patients' Perspectives on the Diagnosis of Parkinson's Disease', *Sociology of Health and Illness,* 14: 1–22.

Rodgers, J. (1999) 'Trying to Get it Right: Undertaking Research Involving People with Learning Difficulties', *Disability and Society,* 14(4): 421–33.

Rosenthal, S. (2001) *A Matter of Perspective.* Available at: http://www.ragged-edge-mag.com/0900/0900bkrev.htm

Scambler, G. (1989) *Epilepsy.* London: Tavistock.

Scheper-Hughes, N. (2006) 'The Primacy of the Ethical: Propositions for a Militant Anthropology'. In Moore, H. and Sanders, T. (eds) *Anthropology in Theory: Issues in Epistemology.* Oxford: Blackwell.

Shakespeare, T. (2008*) Disability Rights and Wrongs.* London: Routledge.

Shakespeare, T., Gillespie-Sells, K., and Davies, D. (1996) *The Sexual Politics of Disability: Untold Desires* London: Cassell.

Small, N. (1998) 'The Story as Gift: Researching AIDS in the Welfare Marketplace'. In Barbour, R. and Huby (eds) *Meddling with Mythology: AIDS and the Social Construction of Knowledge.* London: Routledge.

Staples, J. (2007) *Peculiar People, Amazing Lives: Leprosy, Social Exclusion and Community Making in South India.* Hyderabad: Orient Longman.

Stoller, P. (2004*) Stranger in the Valley of the Sick: A Memoir of Cancer, Sorcery and Healing.* Boston, MA: Beacon Press.

Stone, E. and Priestley, M. (1996) 'Parasites, Pawns and Partners: Disability Research and the Role of Non-Disabled Researchers', *British Journal of Sociology*, 47(4): 699–716.

Strathern, M. (2000) 'The Tyranny of Transparency', *British Educational Research Journal,* 26(3): 309–21.

Taub, D. (2001) 'Review of Venus on Wheels', *American Journal of Sociology,* 106: 1794–6.

Thomas, C. (1999) *Female Forms: Experiencing and Understanding Disability.* Buckingham: Open University Press.

Vernon, A. (1997) 'Reflexivity: The Dilemmas of Researching from the Inside'. In Barnes, C. and Mercer, G. (eds) *Doing Disability Research.* Leeds: The Disability Press.

Wiener, A. (1992) *Inalienable Possessions: The Paradox of Keeping-While-Giving.* Los Angeles, CA: University of California Press.

Williams, G. (1996) 'Representing Disability: Some Questions of Phenomenology and Politics'. In Barnes, C. and Mercer, G. (eds) *Exploring the Divide: Illness and Disability.* Leeds: The Disability Press.

Williams, G. (2001) 'Theorising Disability'. In Albrecht, Seelman K. and Bury, M. (eds) *Handbook of Disability Studies.* London: Sage.

Willis, P. (2005) *The Ethnographic Imagination.* Cambridge: Polity.

Winnicott, D. (1949) 'Hate in the Counter-transference'. *International Journal of Psychoanalysis*, 30: 69–74.

Wolcott, H. (1999) *Ethnography: A Way of Seeing.* Lanham, MD: AltaMira Press.

Zarb, G. and Nadash, P. (1994) *Cashing In on Independence*, British Council of Disabled People.

Zola, I. (1989) *Socio-Medical Inquiries: Recollections, Reflections and Reconsiderations.* Philadelphia: Temple University Press.

38

Qualitative Approaches for Studying Environmental Health

Phil Brown

INTRODUCTION: WHY WE NEED QUALITATIVE METHODS

Health researchers increasingly turn to qualitative methods either on their own, or in combination with quantitative methods. Qualitative methods are especially important to community environmental health research, since they give voice to individuals and community organizations, as well as describe the community in a full and complex fashion. By giving such voice, qualitative researchers often support lay discovery of, and action on, hazards and diseases. Even when quantitative data is needed to determine the existence of environmental health effects, qualitative data is necessary to understand how people and communities experience and act on these problems, since quantitative data can only render an imperfect or partial picture of health effects and their causes.

My focus is on health effects caused by chemicals, air pollution, and radiation, because they have generated much conflict, policymaking, legislation, public awareness, media attention, and social movement activity. Further, community-based qualitative studies of these concerns have been very prevalent, often spurring other qualitative health research. Increasingly, much of this epidemiological research involves community-based participatory research (Quigley et al., 2000). Despite my specific focus, many of the lessons are widely applicable to many arenas of health research. Indeed, one interesting thread of work from environmental health has become widely useful for health – emphasis on the built environment and its health effects. Current and past program officers at the National Institute of Environmental Health Sciences and the Centers for

Disease Control have pursued an extension of environmental health research into an array of diseases and conditions, including obesity and diabetes, which stem from a combined environmental assault of fast food and high-fructose corn syrup, lack of safe and healthy walking areas, dangerous housing conditions, and lack of green space (Srinivasan et al., 2003; Jackson, 2007). Those approaches are now being used by National Institute of Environmental Health Sciences to develop an entirely new multiprogram initiative, the Partnerships for Environmental Public Health. This is the sort of approach sought by Andrews' (2006), who urges that environmental health pay more attention to clinical and service applications.

In-depth qualitative studies of contaminated communities are undertaken mainly by sociologists, but also by geographers, psychologists, public health scholars, and political scientists. Researchers typically come in to study how laypeople have discovered environmental problems and how they have acted on this knowledge. Such ethnographic research is usually done following a health study, because at that point the 'contaminated community' (Edelstein, 1988) is in the public eye. Sometimes social scientists enter the research setting as part of a team that is doing the epidemiological research. These hybrid qualitative-quantitative forms are increasingly prevalent, and current interest makes it possible that methods will evolve to a point where there is no distinction between health effects research and community ethnography, where any project seeking to examine environmental health would combine epidemiological approaches with social science analysis rooted in community collaboration.

This chapter focuses on in-depth ethnographic studies of contaminated communities. There are, of course, other forms of qualitative methods used in environmental health research. For researchers less engaged in reflexive ethnographic work, techniques include structured interviewing (O'Connell, 2003), focus groups (Scammell et al., 2009), policy analysis (Raffensperger and Tickner, 1999; Weissman, 2000), media analysis (Anderson, 1997; Foskett et al., 2000; Brown et al., 2001), content analysis of documents (Markowitz and Rosner, 2002), and cultural critique (Miller, 2000; O'Neal, 2000). Apart from my focus on contaminated communities, qualitative methods can play important roles in environmental epidemiology and environmental justice research. For example, qualitative approaches to community mapping, often a part of environmental justice organizations' work, are now frequently being integrated with quantitative GIS techniques (Corburn, 2005).

Environmental justice research often involves quantification of racial and class disparities in exposure to environmental hazards and in diseases, though some research examines the community discovery of, and action on, environmental problems. For example, Robert Bullard (1990) based his earliest work on the environmental justice movement on his participation in local activism. Bullard's (1993) *Confronting Environmental Racism: Voices from the Grassroots*, a collection of accounts of the environmental justice movement, demonstrates how environmental racism leads to health inequalities by excluding certain segments of the population based on race and class from environmental decision making.

Most of these accounts are voices from the grassroots, as many of the contributors are narrating the struggles of these environmental justice groups from a participant's perspective. Others have provided analyses of environmental justice organizing efforts, using community voices extensively, though written by the scholars rather than the activists (e.g., Timmons and Toffolon-Weiss, 2001).

Virtually all cases of contaminated communities are detected by lay discovery, largely because affected populations tend to notice environmental problems. As well, scientists and government agencies are not usually carrying out routine surveillance that would detect such problems. Even routine surveillance is insufficient; for example, a state cancer registry may be mandated to publish annual reports of cancer excesses by town and city, but will not be required to notify places that have the excess. Even when asked by communities, the agencies do not do enough. Many health departments discouraged informants, sometimes requesting extensive data before they would investigate. Health departments typically offered a routine response emphasizing the lifestyle causes of cancer, the fact that one of three Americans will develop some form of cancer, and that clusters occur at random (Greenberg and Wartenberg, 1991).

Laypeople's role as the typical discoverers of crises creates a special dynamic that makes qualitative research important. Neighbourhood residents are trying to figure out what is happening to them, and once they believe they know what is happening, they have a long and complicated route to get something done. They have a multitude of stories of learning about hazards, sharing their problems, organizing politically, challenging scientific and governmental authority, dealing with resistance by fellow townspeople, and becoming scientifically capable. These stories, woven into various narratives, can only be understood through the in-depth study provided by ethnographic research. To convey this, I begin with a look at the history and legacy of ethnographic studies of contaminated communities. Next, I discuss personal and scholarly insights on qualitative research from my study of the Woburn childhood leukemia cluster, other community studies, and from my more recent work on contested environmental illnesses. Last, I look at giving voice and meeting community needs through 'advocacy science' and 'citizen–science alliances'.

HISTORY AND LEGACY OF QUALITATIVE RESEARCH IN ENVIRONMENTAL HEALTH

The study of qualitative methods in environmental health research takes us to the very origins of the field of environmental sociology. When the 1972 Buffalo Creek flood occurred, Kai Erikson was called by the plaintiff's lawyers to write a report on the damage done to the residents of the poor Appalachian community that was so thoroughly destroyed by corporate malfeasance. A lake of coal mining sludge, held back by a poorly constructed and inadequately maintained dam, swept down the hollow. It destroyed whole villages with hundreds of homes, uprooted miles of railroad tracks, killed 125 people, wounded many others, and left immense psychological scars on the residents of the coal mining hamlets (Erikson, 1976).

While not a toxic crisis, Buffalo Creek nevertheless served as the first book-length community study of human-caused environmental disaster. Erikson used the eloquent descriptions of the residents to fashion an emotionally powerful, sociologically astute account, tying together the shock of individual trauma and the collective loss of communality. He excelled in showing the centrality of community effects, and in highlighting both mental health and physical health outcomes. Further, it situated the human-made disaster in the cultural, social, and historical context of the community, while serving to improve the conditions of the affected people.

The rich legacy continued with Adeline Levine's (1982) *Love Canal: Science, Politics, and People*, which recounted the story of a buried waste site in a small suburb of Niagara Falls and the environmental disaster it produced. The story began with routine dumping of hazardous chemicals in the 1940s and ends with the insidious poisoning of children and families, some of whom were forced into a fight with local and national authorities. For several years, Levine and her students conducted interviews with residents and local organizations and attended public meetings and events, maintaining a constant presence in the community.

Other ethnographies of toxic-assaulted communities followed: Michael Edelstein's (1988) *Contaminated Communities: The Social and Psychological Impacts of Residential Toxic Exposure* examined a water contamination episode in Legler, NJ; Steve Kroll-Smith and Stephen R. Couch's (1990) *The Real Disaster is Above Ground: A Mine Fire and Social Conflict* studied an underground mine fire in Centralia, PA; Michael Reich's (1991) *Toxic Politics: Responding to Chemical Disasters* compared the Seveso, Italy dioxin explosion, the Michigan PBB cattle-feed contamination, and the PCB contamination of cooking oil in Japan; Lee Clarke's (1989) *Acceptable Risk: Making Decisions in a Toxic Environment* detailed the Binghamton, NY state office building fire; Martha Balshem's (1993) *Cancer in the Community: Class and Medical Authority* looked at the hazard perception of people in a Philadelphia working class neighbourhood; and Steven Picou (1990) examined *Social Disruption and Psychological Stress in an Alaskan Fishing Community: The Impact of the Exxon Valdez Oil Spill*. These studies recounted stories not told in the routine scientific literature, offering a rich texture of personal experiences and community effects. They emphasized the democratic rights of individuals and communities to learn about the hazards and disasters befalling them, and to achieve remediation, compensation, and justice. The researchers were largely allied with the concerns of the affected populations, and this was the body of literature that influenced me, some of it predating my Woburn research, and some of it coming later, affecting my subsequent research.

In *No Safe Place: Toxic Waste, Leukemia, and Community Action* (Brown and Mikkelsen, 1990; revised 1997), I developed the concept of 'popular epidemiology' to describe lay involvement in community health studies, and to demonstrate an approach for using ethnographic data alongside clinical, epidemiological, and natural science findings. As well, the approach emphasizes concerns of access, trust, confidentiality, sharing of data, researcher reflexivity, and benefits to the people and community being studied. Woburn families pressured state and federal agencies to investigate the cluster, and sued W.R. Grace and Beatrice Foods for contaminating municipal water wells with organic compounds known to be animal carcinogens, especially trichloroethylene (TCE) and tetrachloroethylene (PCE – perchloroethylene), leading to a large number of leukemia cases, mostly in children. The Woburn residents, without prior activist histories or health knowledge, had educated and organized themselves in an incredibly effective way. They worked with biostatisticians to conduct 5,010 interviews, covering 57 percent of Woburn residences with telephones, and results showed clear connections between contaminated water and leukemia and other health outcomes. Their efforts made national attention, putting the Woburn case alongside Love Canal as a key example of toxic waste organizing and of community-initiated research. Lessons learned from Woburn and the other cases noted in this section lead to some general features of qualitative environmental health research.

IMPORTANT COMPONENTS OF QUALITATIVE RESEARCH METHODS IN ENVIRONMENTAL HEALTH RESEARCH

Access and trust

Access is more important in qualitative methods than in quantitative methods, since qualitative methods involve intensive interviewing and create the space for more personal and emotional contact. The very nature of the kinds of questions and answers makes for a more charged situation; hence, access is a negotiated interaction. Access often results from connections – Kai Erikson was brought in by lawyers to assess the impact of the Buffalo Creek Flood, and his idea to write a book was a later decision. My coauthor, Ed Mikkelsen, had interviewed the Woburn families to prepare psychiatric data for the suit, and they trusted him further as a confidant who had helped them examine their emotional reactions to illness, suffering, and death. Ed Mikkelsen and I went together to the interviews that I conducted, to help cement the connection; later I continued interviews and observations alone. I further had access through attorney Jan Schlictmann, who the families trusted as the person who was bringing their story to public light and helping them focus blame on W.R. Grace and Beatrice. Jan called each family personally to encourage them to cooperate with me. In this sense, access and trust are thoroughly intertwined.

What happens when people do not have 'automatic' access as I did? They have to build access from scratch. Adeline Levine did not have a prior connection. Rather, she presented herself as a trustworthy scholar who could help tell the Love Canal story to the world. Access was a question of how she presented herself.

Often a single key organizer opens the way to major community access, as Lee Clarke found with his study of the toxic contamination from the Binghamton, NY state office building fire. Community groups can tell who is sincere or not, having already been through many tests of sincerity involving public health and environmental officials. Sincerity, however, is not enough; researchers have to be educated enough about the background of the situation. That is both a sign of the researcher's interest and their capabilities, as well as an indication that the residents will not have to spend needless effort in bringing the researcher up to a basic level of knowledge about the situation.

Connections do not guarantee that residents will share their experiences. The researcher still has to generate personal trust and confidence, as well as a belief that the research will be helpful to people and the community. Sufficient trust is a level in which you are convinced that the people you are researching have faith in your rationale for doing the study, and feel you are trying to tell their story in a supportive fashion. This means that they will, therefore, include you in notification of meetings, go out of their way to connect you to other people, and give you broad access to themselves and to relevant materials.

Flexible study design

The qualitative researcher must decide how to frame the study, and thus how to tell the story. In truth, we do not always know until we're well into the project where we are placing our emphasis. Often we change directions and take new tacks in the midst of the work, due to our own realizations about the material, and in part from the ongoing interaction with people.

Part of framing the study is also deciding how much historical and cultural context should be included. Kai Erikson's Buffalo Creek research was saturated with social history of the Appalachian region, going back to the last century, in order to show the isolation, but also the resiliency, of the people. Steven Kroll-Smith and Stephen Couch's (1990) research on an underground mine fire, and Steven Picou's (1990) work on the Exxon Valdez oil spill are other notable examples of intense local background. Louise Kaplan's (1997) work on lay efforts to uncover the Hanford Historical Documents, that showed accidental and deliberate radiation releases at the Hanford, WA nuclear weapons facility, required a historical overview of the local salience of a pronuclear culture in a community that primarily wanted to avoid conflict. Not all researchers go into such depth. In my Woburn book, I provided a very small amount of such background, primarily the town's history of tanning and chemical production, preferring to focus on the contamination crisis.

Furthermore, how much attention should be placed on conflicts within the community on how to organize and carry out research? Again, the unique constellation of community, industry, and government actors helps shape the focus. Steven Kroll-Smith and Stephen Couch's *The Real Disaster is Above Ground* (1990) details the events in the Pennsylvania community of Centralia following the discovery of a rapidly spreading coal fire underneath the town. They later expanded this concern to a generalized idea of 'corrosive communities', since there were other such areas with internal conflict among residents. Levine's Love Canal research mentioned such conflicts but did not make them central. My choice in Woburn was to mention, but not dwell on internal conflicts, largely because it did not seem a major part of the situation, nor did it affect the outcomes.

How closely grained will the research process be? Steven Kroll-Smith and Stephen Couch decided that one of them would actually move into the community in order to ensure good access relations and to be present at all possible meetings. After two years of collecting field data from various public events conducting interviews, Steven Kroll-Smith moved into the affected area, where for eight months he became part of the contaminated community and was able to 'observe and experience daily life in a hazardous area' (Kroll-Smith and Couch, 1990). Participation in the daily life of the community also made Kroll-Smith subject to the internal ideological divisions within the community. Various town factions sought validation of their positions regarding the fire. This close working relationship with the community forced Kroll-Smith and Couch to face a 'complex moral and methodological quandary' (175). Caught between competing interests, the line between research and advocacy was blurred. In this instance, the tandem efforts of the authors provided enough objectivity to produce a critical interpretation of the events in Centralia. Kai Erikson lived and breathed the aftermath of the Buffalo Creek flood during prolonged stays in the area. I had come to the Woburn situation too late to be present at the many meetings that fashioned that struggle, but I tried to attend any ongoing meetings to observe the continuing organizing.

In part, framing also requires thinking about rich data sources. Most scholars working in this area use open-ended interviewing as their primary data source, in addition to observation and documentary materials. Documentary material for Woburn included activist newsletters and leaflets, newspaper articles, legal documents, government reports and documents, and medical and scientific reports (neurology, cardiology, hydrology, and immunology). Interviews are the main tool to bring alive the lived experience of people and communities. For my Woburn work, I focused on the families who were parties to the lawsuit, and who were by extension the main activists, but I also interviewed other activists who were not health-affected and thus not part of the lawsuit. I interviewed relevant state and federal officials who had been involved in the case, as well as health professionals who had conducted health studies with and for the residents.

Deciding on the nature of the study also includes the decision on what theoretical frameworks to employ, and what themes, concepts, and issues to analyze. It is important to have this pretty well in mind before beginning, since it shapes the way the research project is framed and conducted. I drew on several frameworks – Edelstein's (1988) notion of threats to the assumed safety of the home ('inversion of the home'), Krimsky and Plough's (1988) work on lay-professional disputes in environmental hazards, scholarship on citizen participation by Nelkin (1984), and a variety of inputs concerning the critique of value-neutral science and the political economy of environmental hazards – and working on weaving them together into my new popular epidemiology approach.

Themes, concepts and issues for analysis are decided in several ways, and need not be all in hand before starting. First, they may be known from prior research by other scholars in similar work. This is especially useful, since you want to contribute to a standard body of knowledge, and hence sharing concepts is the key. Without some starting point, it will be impossible to develop good questionnaires and coding schemes. Second, themes, concepts, and issues may be detected in pilot interviews and in initial examination of observations and interviews. Third, themes, concepts, and issues may be observed during the expanded analysis of the observations and interviews. This can be determined by word counts, concept counts, and by skilled multiple readings of transcribed material. All three approaches are typically used together, since you never know ahead of time the full range of material you are dealing with.

The foregoing elements of flexible study design are congruent with Marcus' (1995) notion of 'multi-sited ethnography'. Individual research sites, while amenable to rich description and analysis, are insufficient to convey larger trends in an increasingly complex and interdependent world. Hence, the ethnographer must trace a cultural formation across diverse sites, while simultaneously developing the interaction of the macro-social context with those specific sites. For Marcus, what knowledge the researcher gains of the micro-level affects their understanding of the macro-level, and vice versa. Further, this 'mobile ethnography' enables the researcher to have a more emergent and complex view of the local site than would be possible by merely studying that single site (Marcus, 1995). As Burawoy (2000) remarks, in a postmodern world where there are many local connections to the world system, it is necessary to engage in 'welding ethnohistory to ethnography, combining dwelling with movement'. For the multisited ethnographer to do their job, Burawoy argues, he or she must have 'delved into external forces', 'explored connections between sites', and 'uncovered and distilled imaginations from daily life'. Rapp (1999, 12) speaks of this multi-sited ethnography as an 'endeavor to break the connection of space, place, and culture', because there are no clear boundaries to the research sites, the people who populate them, and the places from which those people came.

Indeed, this multisited approach describes my current research on disputes over environmental factors in asthma, breast cancer, and Gulf War illnesses. In this project, I began with four main research sites: Silent Spring Institute in Newton, MA on breast cancer, the Boston Environmental Hazard Center in Boston on Gulf War illnesses, Alternatives for Community and Environment in Boston on asthma, and the Toxic Use Reduction Institute in Lowell, MA on toxics reduction. From those, I expanded to a variety of other environmental breast cancer activist groups, another environmental justice group working on asthma, and an environmental activist group that developed out of the toxics reduction approach. Observations and interviews at these sites were supplemented by interviews with scientists and government officials, formal media analysis, document analysis, review of scientific literature, and historical/political–economic analysis of the issues under study. Throughout, I am tracing interconnected locales that make up environmental and health social movements without being tied together in a formal organizational form, and whose boundaries are continually in flux. I further theorize this in terms of 'boundary movements' that traverse a wide range of actors and institutions, with continual boundary crossings (Brown et al., 2004; Brown, 2007).

Stemming from work on a broad range of health social movements, I developed two tools: *field analysis* and *policy ethnography*, which can be utilized in many areas of health, since health social movements are increasingly prevalent. Field analysis situates social movements in their lineage from other movements, and in their interaction with multiple scientific, political, academic, and public arenas. Policy ethnography studies social movements by including organizational and policy analysis alongside ethnographic observations and interviews, and operates with a policy goal in mind (Brown et al., 2009). Policy ethnography combines (1) ethnographic interview and observation material, (2) background history on the organizations under study, (3) current and historical policy analysis, (4) evaluation of the scientific basis for policy making and regulation, and in some cases, (5) researchers' engagement in policy advocacy through ongoing collaborations. Using these multiple categories of data, we shifted our analytic focus between the three tracks of analysis. We moved between analysis at the micro- (personal experiences and interactions), meso- (organizational and institutional factors), and macro-level (government structures and political–economic forces). Throughout, we focused on the 'interstitial spaces' and boundaries between science, policy, and civil society, because health problems and solutions are defined and debated through interactions and exchanges among these sectors rather than any one sector in particular.

EMPATHY, BIAS, AND PERSONAL SHIFTS IN THE RESEARCHER'S WORLDVIEW

When ethnography frequently shifts to policy ethnography, researchers often have a reflexive and sympathetic relation to the people and settings they study. My empathy for the Woburn families' plight was visible to them, and I think that hastened their trust in me. I worked hard to come across as genuinely interested and concerned, not like the voyeurism of the many journalists who had sought catchy quotes, and some of whom had even asked parents to stage reenactments of their children getting in and out of the car to go to the hospital. I felt very sad in talking to people who had lost a child, and the weight of this clearly coloured how I approached the book – I wanted to convey to readers the sense of these families' loss, and how that was amplified by the corporations' mean-spirited approach to the situation and by the problems in state and federal agencies' research processes. Deep empathy is necessary in order to adequately study contaminated communities. All the other scholars I have seen engage in such work have had that spirit, giving honor and respect to the community. The result is better access to participants, as well as deeper, more complex responses.

Martha Balshem (1993) not only obtained much trust through her interaction, but also experienced a major shift in her professional role. Hired as a medical anthropologist by a Philadelphia cancer prevention project, she soon found that cancer centre's risk-factor approach to individual responsibility clashed with the White, working-class neighbourhood's belief system. The project identified excess cancer in this area, a fact already widely known by the residents and the media. The medicalized approach of the health educators focused on individual habits, especially smoking, drinking, and diet. Tannerstown residents countered this worldview with their belief that the local chemical plant and other sources of contamination are responsible. The professionals approached the working-class as a monolithic mass of people with many unhealthy behaviours and nonscientific attitudes that they considered working-class 'fatalism', which they actually termed a 'disease'. For Balshem, residents' health behaviours appeared more sensible when viewed as a response to economic insecurity in the face of Philadelphia's declining industrial workforce. The health educators focused on people's failure to comply with cancer prevention experts' prescriptions. Yet, from a community standpoint, mainstream lifestyle change approaches to prevention amount to what Balshem notes as 'to adapt to life in the "cancer zone"' (p. 57). Balshem shifted away from thinking individual-level explanations were important, to believing that there were broader, structural explanations for elevated cancer rates. Hence, she could no longer tolerate her job, and left it.

Whether access comes from connections, or is built from scratch, the emotional and political context of such endeavours puts the researcher into close contact, often involving friendships, with the people s/he is studying. Critics of such reflexive research argue that this closeness of access colours the nature of the research and introduces bias. I would argue that there is some bias – if that is really the appropriate term – in that we study these situations because we sympathize with the affected citizens. Indeed, all research has some implicit values, despite claims to the contrary. By virtue of conducting a research project with Edwin Mikkelsen, the plaintiffs' psychiatric expert, I had to recognize the potential for siding with the residents. Nevertheless, our underlying sympathy does not mean that we accept uncritically all the beliefs and perspectives of the citizens. Our goal is to understand the scientific nature of community discovery and action, both to make our society healthier and to increase our knowledge of how people, organizations, and communities perceive and act on important matters. Many researchers have had to deal with the fact that there was no confirmation of community claims of environmental health effects. These scholars may have hoped for such positive findings, as did the communities, but the scholars had to adjust their conclusions as a result.

There is a second bias to consider. Are environmental health researchers already biased towards community groups? The origin of the whole field of environmental sociology, for example, is tinged with a procommunity ethos that is very supportive of community concerns, and takes seriously the community's need to control their destiny. Social scientists often perceive community contamination episodes as insults brought about by corporate malfeasance and amplified by government inattention or failure to act. They believe that residents groups and other environmentally affected populations lack the resources to adequately learn about and act on environmental crises, and hence social scientists feel a responsibility to balance the resource inequity by allying with affected people. Such alliances bring higher-quality data, since residents have a strong motivation to carry out observations and other data collection which they know will be accepted and useful.

The matter of bias can be examined by the researcher throughout the research process. Becker (1967) argues that research uninfluenced by personal and political sympathies is an impossible goal for social scientists. He proposes instead the question of whose side are we on? By confronting that directly, we are able to examine possible sources of bias. Only by not allowing sympathy to guide our work and by recognizing and reporting the limitations of our studies will we move in the direction of eliminating bias from our work (Becker, 1967). Yet, many researchers contend that it is not possible to completely remove such bias, even though they would argue that we gain much by the open presentation of potential for bias. Scott et al. (1990) argue that a 'symmetrical analysis', purporting to equally explain competing sides, is an illusion, and researchers who fail to acknowledge this are involved in perpetuating the illusion of symmetry.

More generally, the initial choice of topics, research sites, and specific organizations on which to focus is itself full of value commitments. Qualitative researchers, typically well versed in a critique of positivism, usually believe that all research is based on some sort of commitment, implicit or explicit. Some fieldworkers face the challenge of bias and wind up actually intervening in the process they are studying. Such scholars argue that this is justified, because not to intervene is a value choice, just as is the choice to intervene, since research cannot be value-neutral despite claims to be so (Scott et al., 1990; Martin, 1996). Opposing such an interventionist stance, Collins (1996) holds that rather than choosing one side in a debate, it is the role of researchers to demonstrate the asymmetrical nature of scientific controversies.

Roles, reflexivity and member validation

Positivism seeks to use natural science as a model for all science, attempting to apply universal laws and to employ neutral language. Positivist approaches try to quantify as much as possible, to have measures that appear to be universally valid. In opposition to positivism, many researchers seek to take a 'naturalist' approach that claims to study the world in its 'natural' state, undisturbed by researcher.

In such an approach, the researcher would try to describe more phenomenologically the community or group they are studying, without being involved in it. However, in truth, this is similar to positivism in that the researcher assumes that there is a 'natural' world that all observers would view similarly. It is thus similar to positivism in seeking to identify a positive fact or phenomenon. The seemingly opposite poles of positivism and naturalism in epistemology and research methodology share something in common: they both maintain a sharp distinction between social scientists and the group or community being studied.

Qualitative researchers seek to repair that distinction, by realizing that the people we study also shape the data. Our conversations and observations with people in our research sites lead them to make their own analyses, which then provide an iteration of their initial perceptions and experiences. By entering the field, we have changed it; quite literally, people know what we are interested in and they may change their thoughts, conversations, and actions to reflect our interests.

This leads us to be concerned about the role we are taking in our research site; do we seek as neutral as possible a stance, hoping that it will avoid such coconstruction of data, or do we move towards that level of coconstruction of data while simultaneously making all efforts to identify and grapple with that coconstruction? What is the appropriate role to take? It is not always possible to decide ahead of time what role to take, since roles change along with other features of the project. As I mentioned earlier, my collaboration with Ed Mikkelsen put me into the role of an interested party who was attached to the case. Nevertheless, I also sought to have my independent role as a scholar who knew about other environmental struggles, and an activist who had been involved in many political efforts. Both these roles made me into someone who understood the Woburn situation beyond the bounds of just the legal case. It is not wise, or even possible, to take a markedly detached and disinterested stance. Such a stance would mean a loss of residents' trust, and would yield less comprehensive data about personal and collective illness experience. Even if one wanted to take a disinterested stance, the community might not let you in if they perceived you to be detached, since it is a lot of effort for them to cooperate with you. In addition, if they did let you in, despite feeling you were detached, they would not likely open up that much, and, therefore, might only provide you with a very small part of their story.

Reflexivity helps avoid the problems associated with how both positivism and naturalism try to remove the effects of the researcher on the data. As Hammersley and Atkinson (1995) point out, 'we are part of the social world we study'. Reflexivity tells us that we actually change the social field by studying and interacting with it. Reflexivity also forces us to realize that another sociologist, even sharing similar sympathies to the situation, would likely experience and analyze the case differently, and hence we must analyze why we do it a particular way.

For example, my published work on the Woburn case presented a public face of the Woburn situation that will in some sense appear as representative of the residents and their organized efforts. Therefore, I felt it incumbent on me to 'get it right', using 'member validation' techniques. This involves sharing parts of the research process and its products with the members, the people you are studying. Member validation can correct factual errors, but more importantly, it can point to additional areas for current and future research. As participants hear and/or read what you have said about them, they can reassess their initial interview responses or come up with new material, thus enriching the whole dataset. This process changes the field and alters subsequent narrative content. Member validation and data sharing communicate narratives that may otherwise have been kept private. Scientists draw from a different perspective that participants inside the phenomena do not have, precisely because they are embedded and their purpose is direct action rather than research and publication. Member validation may provide new concepts or language from which community members may draw when constructing subsequent narratives.

At the same time, member validation fulfils an ethical responsibility to involve community members in the research. I shared the completed book manuscript with three leaders of the citizens' group For a Cleaner Environment (FACE), one epidemiologist involved in the case, and the lead attorney. I was glad that these people were able to detect some factual inaccuracies that I would not have wanted to see in print, but more so that they felt I had successfully told the Woburn story in a useful and interesting fashion.

Michael Bloor (1988) notes: 'While my accounts were recognizable to members, they were not isomorphic with their common-sense knowledge of their work practices'. Indeed, they should not be isomorphic. Woburn residents did not have the concept of popular epidemiology; they were simply doing what they and other contaminated communities had to do: investigating the environmental health crisis in which they were enmeshed. Qualitative researchers are feeding back not just facts, but also analytic concepts, thus helping residents shape the social scientist research literature on their community and similar places. They might later come to accept such an analytic concept, but it is not their initial framework.

Kai Erikson's member validation from his study of an underground petroleum leak in East Swallow, CO is unique. He asked twenty-one residents to read copies of his report to the court while sitting with a tape recorder, and to dictate comments when they were struck by anything in the report. Erikson describes several purposes for such an effort. He wanted 'to bring the people I was writing about into the composing of their own story'. Moreover, he also wanted them to help provide material that could be useful in cross-examination by the defendant's lawyers. Erikson published the entire report in *A New Species of Trouble* (Erikson, 1994), with almost half the space devoted to footnotes on each page where he provided residents' responses from sitting with their tape recorders. Lather and Smithies (1997: 215–236) did a similar thing in their *Troubling the Angels: Women Living With HIV/AIDS*, in which they self-published a draft version of the book to send to all women they had observed and interviewed. They met with the women in the support groups that were the focus for the study, engaging in detailed discussions that led them to change the book title, rearrange chapters, and shorten 'intertext' chapters that dealt with historical and literary material. Lather and Smithies provide process notes and large segments of dialog resulting from their member validation work. As with Erikson, the idea is to give a rich voice to the people being studied, and to do it through interaction rather than in a merely formal method.

GIVING VOICE AND MEETING COMMUNITY NEEDS THROUGH ADVOCACY SCIENCE AND CITIZEN–SCIENCE ALLIANCES

Lay participation in science forces the professional scientist to step outside of their traditional training, to consider the importance of first-hand knowledge possessed by the community. Furthermore, for laypeople, traditional methods may not be suitable to capture concerns related to environmental hazards. Researchers interested in academic–community partnerships may need to develop innovative techniques to incorporate lay knowledge. Qualitative research methods can do just this. For example, researchers studying potential environmental causes of breast cancer in collaboration with community groups have used innovative methods such as creating life histories of possible exposures and conducting 'shopping trips' to determine chemical exposures from common household and commercial products. The 'shopping trip' model was actually used by Silent Spring Institute to develop quantitative measures, but it represents the type of innovative techniques that community-based research often employs.

'Advocacy scientists' (Krimsky, 2000) are those individuals who extend their personal responsibility and commitment to their professional work. In his narrative of the emergence of the environmental endocrine disruptor hypothesis, Krimsky witnessed several scientists become visible activists for the hypothesis despite gaps in their knowledge and the subsequent risks for their image and professional careers. Advocacy scientists, Krimsky tells us, 'view their role as bifurcated between advancing the scientific knowledge base and communicating to the public, the media, and policymakers'.

'Citizen–science alliance' (CSA) – my term for a lay-professional collaboration in which citizens and scientists work together on issues identified by laypeople – is one way in which advocacy science is practiced. Collaboration between community groups and scientists serves to educate both parties. While researchers clearly benefit from the input of community members, the collaboration also educates the community about strengths and limitations of the scientific process. Citizen groups often have expectations about science that may not be achievable within the scope of the proposed research. Collaboration between citizens and scientists also eases apprehensions either party may feel towards each other; community members may feel exploited by outside researchers while the researcher can feel intimidated by activist groups. Overall, the CSA benefits both parties by introducing laypeople's concerns into the research project and by allowing the researcher an insider's glimpse into the community.

By doing community ethnographies of contaminated communities, researchers are helping to uncover data that might not otherwise surface. This is a notable contribution, but to what extent does the community directly benefit? In addition to reflexivity and member validation, another way to ensure community control is to freely share data. Researchers who study contaminated communities have often presented their work at activist conferences. This is one way to make the information public so that community groups can use it as they see fit. It provides an ethically based approach by researchers to the communities they are studying and collaborating with. This is clearly an important area, given the history of problems with many forms of research on communities. It also taps a growing scientific interest in open-access to research and publications.

CONCLUSION

Qualitative methods are an important instrument enabling community narratives to be constructed and shared. Furthermore, they also provide social scientists with an opportunity to contribute to community activism and advocacy. Research efforts over the past two decades have laid a foundation for continued use of, and funding for qualitative methods as either a solo methodology, or in tandem with quantitative epidemiological studies.

Not all environmental sociologists that draw on qualitative methods will act in such advocacy fashion, but in practice, many do. They are acting to help create, modify, and present to the world the community narratives of grassroots and grassroots-related environmental health research and advocacy. Often, these narratives are untapped; qualitative researchers help the community to develop narratives. Gareth Williams (1984) writes about 'narrative reconstruction', the ways that people reconstruct how they believe they 'got' diseases. People often employ broader viewpoints than the biomedical model, some imputing a political and economic causality, others locating aetiology in a nest of social relationships and in their own psychological makeup, others using a mystical explanation. Their goal is to produce a coherent self-analysis for their own narrative, thus providing a way to repair the rupture which disease causes in their relationship with the world.

The valuable legacy we have created in this field is possible because of acceptance by significant sectors of social science and life science professional organizations, but mostly because of acceptance from, and collaboration with, affected communities. Researchers need to find ways of building even further support from sympathetic government agencies and programs, from private foundations, and from scientists and their organizations. Scholars need to cement stronger alliances with community groups with whom they collaborate, since they can exert important influence on the funders. Moreover, researchers need to carefully document their methods, especially those that improve academic–community partnerships.

ACKNOWLEDGEMENTS

This research is supported by a grant from the National Institute of Allergies and Infectious Diseases (T15 A149650–01), the Robert Wood Johnson Foundation Investigator Awards in Health Policy Research Program (Grant #036273) and the National Science Foundation Program in Social Dimensions of Engineering, Science, and Technology (SES-9975518). Brian Mayer provided research assistance. Rebecca Gasior Altman, Ann Grodzins Gold, Sheldon Krimsky, and Dianne Quigley read an earlier version of the manuscript and provided valuable comments.

REFERENCES

Anderson, Alison (1997) *Media and the Environment*. New Brunswick, NJ: Rutgers University Press.

Andrews, Gavin (2006) 'Guest Editorial: Health and Social Care for Environmental Health – Realigning Geographic Traditions', *Health and Social Care in the Community*, 14: 281–83.

Balshem, Martha (1993) *Cancer in the Community: Class and Medical Authority*. Washington, DC: Smithsonian Institution Press.

Becker, Howard (1967) 'Whose Side Are We On?', *Social Problems*, 14: 239–47.

Bloor, Michael (1988) 'Notes on Member Validation'. In Robert Emerson (ed.) *Contemporary Field Methods* (pp. 156–72). Prospect Heights, IL: Waveland Press.

Brown, Phil (2007) *Toxic Exposures: Contested Illnesses and the Environmental Health Movement*. New York: Columbia University Press.

Brown, Phil and Edwin Mikkelsen (1990) revised edition (1997) *No Safe Place: Toxic Waste, Leukemia, and Community Action*. Berkeley: University of California Press.

Brown, Phil, Steven Zavestoski, Sabrina McCormick, Joshua Mandelbaum, and Theo Luebke (2001) 'Print Media Coverage of Environmental Causation of Breast Cancer', *Sociology of Health and Illness*, 23: 747–75.

Brown, Phil, Stephen Zavestoski, Sabrina McCormick, Brian Mayer, Rachel Morello-Frosch, and Rebecca Gasior (2004) 'Embodied Health Movements: Uncharted Territory in Social Movement Research', *Sociology of Health and Illness*, 26: 1–31.

Brown, Phil, Rachel Morello-Frosch, Stephen Zavestoski, Laura Senier, Rebecca Altman, Elizabeth Hoover, Sabrina McCormick, Brian Mayer, and Crystal Adams (2009) 'Field Analysis and Policy Ethnography: New Directions for Studying Health Social Movements'. In Mayer Zald, Jane Banaszak-Holl, and Sandra Levitsky (eds) *Social Movements and the Development of Health Institutions*. Oxford University Press.

Bullard, Robert (1990) *Dumping in Dixie: Race, Class and Environmental Quality*. Boulder: Westview Press.

Bullard, Robert (ed.) (1993) *Confronting Environmental Racism: Voices from the Grassroots*. Boston: South End Press.

Burawoy, Michael (2000) 'Introduction: Reaching for the Global'. In Michael Burawoy (ed.) *Global Ethnography: Forces, Connections and Imaginations in a Postmodern World* (pp. 1–59). Berkeley, CA: University of California Press.

Clarke, Lee (1989) *Acceptable Risk: Making Decisions in a Toxic Environment*. Berkeley, CA: University of California Press.

Collins, Harry (1996) 'In Praise of Futile Gestures: How Scientific is the Sociology of Scientific Knowledge', *Social Studies of Science*, 26: 229–44.

Corburn, Jason (2005) *Street Science: Community Knowledge and Environmental Health Justice*. Cambridge, MA: MIT Press.

Edelstein, Michael (1988) *Contaminated Communities: The Social and Psychological Impacts of Residential Toxic Exposure.* Boulder, CO: Westview.

Erikson, Kai (1976) *Everything in its Path: Destruction of Community in the Buffalo Creek Flood.* New York: Simon and Schuster.

Erikson, Kai (1994) *A New Species of Trouble: Explorations in Disaster, Trauma, and Community.* New York: Norton.

Fishman, Jennifer (2000) 'Assessing Breast Cancer: Risk, Science and Environmental Activism'. In Laura Potts (ed.) *Ideologies of Breast Cancer: Feminist Perspectives* (pp. 181–204). Basingstoke, UK: Palgrave Macmillan.

Foskett, Jennifer, Angela Karran, and Christine LaFia (2000) 'Breast Cancer in Popular Women's Magazines from 1913 to 1996'. In Anne Kasper and Susan Ferguson (eds) *Breast Cancer: Society Shapes an Epidemic* (pp. 302–24). New York: Palgrave.

Greenberg, Michael and Daniel Wartenberg (1991) 'Communicating To an Alarmed Community About Cancer Clusters: A Fifty State Study', *Journal of Community Health,* 16: 71–82.

Hammersley, Michael and Paul Atkinson (1995) *Ethnography: Principles in Practice.* New York: Routledge.

Harr, Jonathan (1995) *A Civil Action.* New York: Random House.

Jackson, Richard (2007) 'Environment Meets Health, Again'. *Science,* Mar 9, 315:1337.

Kaplan, Louise (1997) 'The Hanford Education Action League: An Informed Citizenry and Radiation Health Effects', *International Journal of Contemporary Sociology,* 34: 255–66.

Krimsky, Sheldon (2000) *Hormonal Chaos: The Scientific and Social Origins of the Environmental Endocrine Hypothesis.* Baltimore: John Hopkins University Press.

Krimsky, Sheldon and Alonzo Plough (1988) *Environmental Hazards: Communicating Risks as a Social Process.* Dover, MA: Auburn House.

Kroll-Smith, Steven, J. and Stephen Couch (1990) *The Real Disaster is Above Ground: A Mine Fire and Social Conflict.* Lexington, KY: University Press of Kentucky.

Lather, Patricia and Christine Smithies (1997) *Troubling the Angels: Women Living With HIV/AIDS.* Boulder, CO: Westview Press.

Levine, Adeline (1982) *Love Canal: Science, Politics, and People.* Lexington, MA: Lexington Books.

Marcus, George (1995) 'Ethnography In/Of The World System: The Emergence of Multi-Sited Ethnography', *Annual Review of Anthropology,* 24: 95–117.

Markowitz, Gerald and David Rosner (2002) *Denial and Deceit: The Deadly Politics of Industrial Pollution.* Berkeley: University of California Press.

Martin, Brian (1996) 'Sticking a Needle into Science: The Case of Polio Vaccines and the Origin of AIDS', *Social Studies of Science,* 26: 245–76.

McCormick, Sabrina, Julia G. Brody, and Phil Brown (2004) 'Public Involvement in Breast Cancer Research: An Analysis and Model for Future Research', *International Journal of Health Services,* 34: 625–46.

Miller, Branda (2000) 'Media Art and Activism'. In Richard Hofrichter (ed.) *Reclaiming the Politics of Health: Environmental Debate in a Toxic Culture* (pp. 313–25). Cambridge, MA: MIT Press.

Nelkin, Dorothy (1984) 'Science and Technology Policy and The Democratic Process'. In J. Peterson (ed.) *Citizen Participation in Science and Policy* (pp. 18–39). Amherst: University of Massachusetts Press.

O'Connell, Virginia (2003) 'When a Child Has Cancer: Protecting Children from a Toxic World'. In Monica Casper (ed.) *Synthetic Planet: Chemical Hazards and the Politics of Modern Life* (pp. 111–29). New York: Routledge.

O'Neal, John (2000) 'For Generations Yet to Come: Junebug Productions' Environmental Justice Project'. In Richard Hofrichter (ed.) *Reclaiming the Politics of Health: Environmental Debate in a Toxic Culture* (pp. 301–11). Cambridge, MA: MIT Press.

Office of Behavioral and Social Sciences Research, NIH (1999) 'Qualitative Methods in Health Research: Opportunities and Considerations in Application and Review', report from workshop held September 30–October 1, Bethesda, MD.

Picou, Steven (1990) *Social Disruption and Psychological Stress in an Alaskan Fishing Community: The Impact of the Exxon Valdez Oil Spill*, Boulder, CO: University of Colorado Natural Hazards Center.

Quigley, Diane, Dan Handy, Robert Goble, Virginia Sanchez, and Patricia George (2000) 'Participatory Research Strategies in Nuclear Risk Management for Native Communities', *Journal of Health Communication*, 5: 305–31.

Raffensperger, Carolyn and Joel Tickner (1999) (eds) *Protecting Public Health and the Environment: Implementing the Precautionary Principle*. Washington D.C.: Island Press.

Rapp, Rayna (1999) *Testing Women, Testing the Fetus: The Social Impact of Amniocentesis in America*. New York: Routledge.

Reich, Michael (1991) *Toxic Politics: Responding to Chemical Disasters*. Ithaca, NY: Cornell University Press.

Srinivasan, Shobha, Liam O'Fallon, and Allan Dearry (2003) 'Creating Healthy Communities, Healthy Homes, Healthy People: Initiating a Research Agenda on the Built Environment and Public Health'. *American Journal of Public Health,* 93: 1446–50.

Scammell, Madeleine Kangsen, David Ozonoff, Laura Senier, Jennifer Darrah, Phil Brown, and Susan Santos (2009) 'Tangible Evidence and Common Sense: Finding Meaning in a Community Health Study', *Social Science and Medicine*, 68:143–53.

Scott, Pam, Evelleen Richards and Martin Brian (1990) 'Captives of Controversy: The Myth of the Neutral Social Researcher in Contemporary Scientific Controversies', *Science, Technology, and Human Values*, 15: 474–94.

Timmons, Roberts J. and Melissa Toffolon-Weiss (2001) *Chronicles from the Environmental Justice Frontline*. Cambridge, New York: Cambridge University Press.

Weissman, Carol (2000) 'Breast Cancer Policymaking'. In Anne Kasper and Susan Ferguson (eds) *Breast Cancer: Society Shapes an Epidemic* (pp. 213–34). New York: Palgrave.

Williams, Gareth (1984) 'The Genesis of Chronic Illness: Narrative Reconstruction', *Sociology of Health and Illness*, 6: 175–200.

Index

NOTE: The page numbers set in bold denote tables and the page numbers set in italics denote figures.